NORMS OF WORD ASSOCIATION

Norms of Word Association

EDITED BY   **LEO POSTMAN** AND   **GEOFFREY KEPPEL**

University of California,
Berkeley, California

ACADEMIC PRESS   1970   NEW YORK AND LONDON

ACADEMIC PRESS, INC.
111 Fifth Avenue, New York, New York 10003

United Kingdom Edition published by
ACADEMIC PRESS, INC. (LONDON) LTD.
Berkeley Square House, London W1X 6BA

LIBRARY OF CONGRESS CATALOG CARD NUMBER: 72-117109

PRINTED IN THE UNITED STATES OF AMERICA

PREFACE

This book consists of a heterogeneous collection of word association norms that will be of interest to the historian as well as to researchers in the field of verbal learning and verbal behavior. A large number of association norms have been referred to in the literature, but only a few of these are readily available in published form. Cramer (1968, pp. 258-260) has listed over 60 relatively current norms, but only a few of these have been published. This book represents a partial remedy to this situation by bringing together nine sets of association norms that were collected independently at different times during a 15-year period. No particular plan was followed in bringing together this collection. Rather, there were simply a number of researchers who knew about each other's norms and found this method of joint publication both a convenient and an economical way of making these data available to potential users of the norms.

Each chapter is a self-contained unit. Preceding each set of norms is a brief description of the procedures by which the norms were collected, the methods of analysis, and a summary of the data. These introductory comments differ with respect to the degree of analysis that is reported. We left it up to the authors to include summary analyses that they felt might be useful to researchers in their fields. It should also be noted that the manuscripts were prepared and submitted to the editors at different times over the last few years. As a consequence, some of the "older" manuscripts do not include recent and relevant citations. In our opinion, the introductory comments are still applicable to the sets of norms in question and so revisions designed to update the discussions and references were not specifically requested.

The order in which the norms are presented is arbitrary, although we did group norms that seemed to belong together. We will conclude these comments with a brief description of the different sets of norms included in this book. The 1952 Minnesota norms appear first, both for reasons of "age" and in recognition of the fact that a number of the norms that follow are direct outgrowths of this work. Jenkins recounts the thinking that led to the collection of the 1952 norms. For years these norms, commonly referred to as the Russell-Jenkins norms, provided estimates of the associative hierarchies of college students for the Kent-Rosanoff stimuli. Although these data have been replaced by the recent and more extensive Palermo-Jenkins (1964) norms, they have been employed widely in research for 10-15 years. In view of their extensive use, it was felt that a need would still be served by making these norms available at this time. The next three norms in this collection are responses to the Russell-Jenkins stimuli obtained from subjects representing different linguistic communities. Miller reports a summary of association norms he collected from British and Australian subjects. Russell presents the complete set of associations produced by German college students. Rosenzweig offers norms he collected from French college students and French workmen. In addition, he provides comparisons among these different sets of association norms that point up consistent differences among subjects residing on the European continent and English-speaking subjects in the United States, Australia, England, and Canada.

The next four sets of norms are also word association norms, but are not directly related to the 1952 Minnesota collection. Keppel and Strand report free-association responses to the primary and other associates of the Palermo-Jenkins norms. As indicated in the introduction to their norms, these data provide an assessment of the directionality of a large number of Palermo-Jenkins associates as well as a large pool of three-step chain associations, i.e., the first two steps estimated from the Palermo-Jenkins norms and the next step from the Keppel-Strand collection. Postman reports the California norms in the next chapter. The stimuli in these norms are two-syllable nouns sampled from four ranges of Thorndike-Lorge (1944) word frequency. Also presented is a comparison of individual and group association hierarchies and independent estimates of meaningfulness for the stimuli included in the association norms. Cramer reports association responses to homographs, i.e., stimuli having two distinct meanings. As she indicates, homographs have served an analytical function in studies of semantic generalization. The complete association norms for these stimuli are presented as well as an evaluation of the degree to which the association responses represent one or the other meaning. Finally, Marshall and Cofer present association norms obtained for stimuli that were the strongest category responses from a sample of 21 categories selected from the Connecticut norms (Cohen, Bousfield, & Whitmarsh, 1957).

In the last section, Ervin-Tripp reports a combination of free-association norms and linguistically defined determinations. Specifically, following the collection of free associations to content words or to words from a variety of grammatical classes, subjects were asked to construct sentences containing each stimulus word and also to produce words that could substitute for the stimulus words. In her discussion of these data, Ervin-Tripp describes relations among these qualitatively different determinations of the ways in which words are combined in sentences and given as free associates to discrete stimulus words.

REFERENCES

Cohen, B. H., Bousfield, W. A., & Whitmarsh, G. A. (1957), Cultural norms for items in 43 categories. Technical Report No. 22, University of Connecticut, ONR Contract Nonr-631(00).

Cramer, P. (1968). *Word association.* New York: Academic Press.

Palermo, D. S., & Jenkins, J. J. (1964). *Word association norms.* Minneapolis: University of Minnesota Press.

Thorndike, E. L., & Lorge, I. (1944). *The teacher's word book of 30,000 words.* New York: Teachers College.

CONTENTS

CHAPTER 1

THE 1952 MINNESOTA WORD ASSOCIATION NORMS

James J. Jenkins
University of Minnesota, Minneapolis, Minnesota

The norms which follow are those usually referred to as the Minnesota norms for the Kent-Rosanoff word association test. Their previous publication was as a technical report (Russell & Jenkins, 1954) in a series concerned with the role of language in behavior. The research was sponsored by the Office of Naval Research. The norms have been widely used and have earned a modest place in the history of research in verbal learning and verbal behavior. Over 3000 copies have been distributed to interested research workers and students. Dr. Russell and I welcome the opportunity to include them in this collection.

The history of the collection of the norms is of some interest and will help to explain some of the defects which may be found in them. In 1951, Dr. Russell and I heard Professor Bousfield deliver a paper on categorical clustering in the organization of recall (Bousfield, 1953). During the discussion, it occurred to us that one might avoid some of the limitations involved in Bousfield's use of logical categories if one used words whose relationship could be inferred from some behavioral measure rather than category membership. We believed some behavioral index would offer at least the possibility of relating the measure to a construct of habit and habit strength. This, in turn, would tend to keep verbal-behavior research related to learning and behavioral theory rather than setting it apart as a separate domain of study. The stimulus-response relation of word association immediately suggested itself.

Fortunately, we had available at Minnesota part of the word association norms collected by Schellenberg (1930) for university freshmen. We used these norms as a means of putting our notion to empirical test. We discovered that the phenomenon of associative clustering in recall could readily be observed (Jenkins & Russell, 1952a) and proceeded to attempt a quantification of clustering as a function of normative associative strength. Our first effort involved the evaluation of clustering in the recall of three lists. The lists were made up of the association test stimuli and their primary responses, the same stimuli and their secondary responses, and the same stimuli and tertiary responses. The hypothesis was, of course, that the amount of associative clustering in recall would decrease from the first list to the third list. The first list did, indeed, produce more clustering than the second and third, but clustering produced by the last two was not appreciably different (Russell & Jenkins, 1952).

We hypothesized that the frequency of a response was likely to be a better index of its strength than its rank in the response hierarchy and we therefore set up an experiment using associates of differing normative strength in an attempt to establish a simple functional relationship. Four lists of widely differing mean associative strength were employed in recall tasks. Clustering in recall was measured. To our great surprise, this study yielded very systematic but puzzling data. Clustering increased nicely as a function of associative strength over three lists and then decreased somewhat in the list in which it should have been most pronounced.

Having more faith in our hypothesis than in the old norms, we decided not to postulate some ceiling effect on clustering but rather to reevaluate the normative frequencies we needed in our analysis. We then, more or less casually, gave the Kent-Rosanoff word association test to two large introductory psychology classes at the University of Minnesota in October and November of 1952. It was not our intention at that time to establish a set of norms but rather to obtain specific information necessary for the functional study. We hurriedly tabulated the word pairs we needed and discovered that rather major changes had taken place in the frequency of popular associates since Schellenberg's norms had been collected. This increased our interest in the norms themselves and led us to conduct more complete tabulations than we had originally contemplated.

Our study of associative clustering as a function of the normative strength of the associates turned out rather successfully with these new materials (Jenkins, Mink, & Russell, 1958), and we became even more convinced that the norms furnished a powerful tool for the investigation of verbal behaviors. As our work with word associations increased, we completed the tabulation of the norms and, in 1954, prepared a technical report giving the results of those tabulations (Russell & Jenkins, 1954).

As a result of this more or less haphazard approach, the norms have a number of shortcomings of which the user should be aware. In the first place, the data on the subject population leave much to be desired. We had not collected and, after a year's lapse of time, could not ascertain the exact population of the group from which the norms had been obtained. All subjects were students in introductory psychology. They were largely sophomores but, since college class data had not been obtained, we could not specify the variation in the population, although certainly a small percentage of juniors and seniors were also in the course. We assigned Ss to sex groups on the basis of their first names where this was possible and determined that the sample had been approximately 60% male and 40% female, but precision in this respect is lacking. Similarly, we cannot specify the age of the population, except as the normative sophomore age may be assumed.

A second major deficiency is that the screening of the sample with respect to incomplete data forms, omissions, illegible responses, etc., was never uniformly accomplished. In the course of the early tabulations, when we were interested in only a small number of pairs, test forms were rejected in which large numbers of blanks had appeared and forms may have been discarded where Ss appeared not to take the directions seriously. No record was kept of these and it is not known what the initial sample size was. When we decided to tabulate for the technical report, we no longer had the complete pool of initial forms available, some words had been tabulated, some had not, and on studying the norms, there appears to have been some "slippage" with respect to the number of forms tabulated for any given word. The "official" number in the sample is given as 1008 (certainly an awkward number to work with and one that no one would ever ordinarily choose). It seems, however, that larger samples than this were tabulated in the early stages for some of the words and, thus, the effective N on the norms appears to have varied between 1008 and possibly as much as 1031. In the long run, such a small variation in a large population makes little difference but, of course, it should never have been permitted to occur. All of this information is given here to explain the irregularities in the norms and to serve as a caution to norm builders in the future in the hope that they will obtain more accurate information than we obtained in 1952.

METHOD

The norms were collected in a classroom setting. The Ss wrote responses in a blank provided beside each stimulus word. The test consisted of two pages, 50 stimulus words to a page. The order in which the words were presented (the classic Kent-Rosanoff order) is given in Table 1.

The instructions were as follows:

This is one of the studies in verbal behavior being done at Minnesota. This particular experiment is on free association. Please write your name on the outside of the paper passed to you. (You can ignore the place for your name on the other side.) When you open these sheets, you will see a list of 100 stimulus words. After each word write the first word that it makes you think of. Start with the first word; look at it; write the word it makes you think of; then go on to the next word.

Use only a single word for each response.

Do not skip any words.

Work rapidly until you have finished all 100 words.

When you are through, turn your paper over and write on the back the letter that appears on the board at that time.

Are there any questions?

Ready. Go.

TABLE 1 *Word Association Test*

Name _____ Class_____ Date_____

No.	Stimulus	Response	No.	Stimulus	Response
1.	Table	_____	51.	Stem	_____
2.	Dark	_____	52.	Lamp	_____
3.	Music	_____	53.	Dream	_____
4.	Sickness	_____	54.	Yellow	_____
5.	Man	_____	55.	Bread	_____
6.	Deep	_____	56.	Justice	_____
7.	Soft	_____	57.	Boy	_____
8.	Eating	_____	58.	Light	_____
9.	Mountain	_____	59.	Health	_____
10.	House	_____	60.	Bible	_____
11.	Black	_____	61.	Memory	_____
12.	Mutton	_____	62.	Sheep	_____
13.	Comfort	_____	63.	Bath	_____
14.	Hand	_____	64.	Cottage	_____
15.	Short	_____	65.	Swift	_____
16.	Fruit	_____	66.	Blue	_____
17.	Butterfly	_____	67.	Hungry	_____
18.	Smooth	_____	68.	Priest	_____
19.	Command	_____	69.	Ocean	_____
20.	Chair	_____	70.	Head	_____
21.	Sweet	_____	71.	Stove	_____
22.	Whistle	_____	72.	Long	_____
23.	Woman	_____	73.	Religion	_____
24.	Cold	_____	74.	Whiskey	_____
25.	Slow	_____	75.	Child	_____
26.	Wish	_____	76.	Bitter	_____
27.	River	_____	77.	Hammer	_____
28.	White	_____	78.	Thirsty	_____
29.	Beautiful	_____	79.	City	_____
30.	Window	_____	80.	Square	_____
31.	Rough	_____	81.	Butter	_____
32.	Citizen	_____	82.	Doctor	_____
33.	Foot	_____	83.	Loud	_____
34.	Spider	_____	84.	Thief	_____
35.	Needle	_____	85.	Lion	_____
36.	Red	_____	86.	Joy	_____
37.	Sleep	_____	87.	Bed	_____
38.	Anger	_____	88.	Heavy	_____
39.	Carpet	_____	89.	Tobacco	_____
40.	Girl	_____	90.	Baby	_____
41.	High	_____	91.	Moon	_____
42.	Working	_____	92.	Scissors	_____
43.	Sour	_____	93.	Quiet	_____
44.	Earth	_____	94.	Green	_____
45.	Trouble	_____	95.	Salt	_____
46.	Soldier	_____	96.	Street	_____
47.	Cabbage	_____	97.	King	_____
48.	Hard	_____	98.	Cheese	_____
49.	Eagle	_____	99.	Blossom	_____
50.	Stomach	_____	100.	Afraid	_____

Following the instructions and the ready signal, the *S*s began to work at the association test. After 4 min, the experimenter wrote a letter on the board which was changed at 30-sec intervals until virtually all of the class had completed the test form. The forms for a few *S*s were lost at this point since the test was terminated at 13 min.

SOME CHARACTERISTICS OF THE NORMS

If the frequency of occurrence of responses to the particular stimulus word is tabulated and then arranged in order of descending frequency, it is customary to speak of this series as the associative hierarchy or the associative response hierarchy for the particular stimulus word. One may then, depending on one's assumptions, deal with the absolute frequency given in the normative tables or, if one prefers, use the rank of the response in the hierarchy, with the most popular response being given rank 1 (the primary response), the next highest response, rank 2 (the secondary response), and so on. Past research has shown that, over several sets of stimulus words, the form of the rank-frequency function of the response hierarchies is relatively stable. Skinner (1937) demonstrated that if one grouped the various response hierarchies obtained by Kent and Rosanoff (1910) and averaged the frequencies found at each response rank, the general plot of the averages conformed to a Zipf-type curve (Zipf, 1949) with a slope of −1.3. Skinner concluded that whatever was being tapped by the word association test was very similar to whatever governed continuous discourse (where rank-frequency counts of words often yield Zipf-type curves with a slope of about −1). In a later study, Cook and Skinner (1939) showed that the general relationship also held for a set of 250 other stimulus words used as free association stimuli by Schellenberg (1930). The Skinner studies suggest that the response hierarchies, taken in general, are lawfully constituted, with a systematic relationship between rank and frequency. In addition, Cook and Skinner concluded that the frequency of usage of the stimulus had little bearing on the form of the hierarchy observed (although only a small range of frequencies of usage of stimuli were involved in those studies).

In our norms, a tabulation of response frequencies for the various ranks yields the familiar Zipf-type curve but with a slightly more severe slope (−1.4) than Skinner found in his study of the earlier norms. This may be interpreted by pointing out that the most popular responses in our norms are given with considerably higher frequencies than were the popular responses in the Kent-Rosanoff and Schellenberg norms, while our rare responses are given at somewhat lower frequencies.

In the Minnesota norms, the most popular response was given by 37.5% of the Ss on the average. The second most popular response was given by 16.3%, and the third most popular by 8.1%. Popularity of the primary responses ranged from 83.25% for *table-chair* to 8.83% for *trouble-bad*, indicating the enormous variety found even to this relatively homogeneous list of stimulus words. The average number of different response words given to a stimulus was 104.8, ranging from a low of 41 words for the stimulus *dark* to a high of 260 words to the stimulus word *trouble*.

It is reasonable to suppose that there is a general negative relationship between the frequency of popular responses to stimuli and the number of different responses made to the stimuli. At one limit, one might imagine that the frequency of the popular response reaches 100%; the response hierarchy, therefore, is limited to one word. At the other limit, one might imagine that no S agreed with another as to the response word. In this case, the popularity of responses is minimal and the number of different responses is the same as the sample size. In the Minnesota norms, the frequency of the primary response correlates −.59 with the number of different response words. The combined frequency of the primary and secondary responses taken together correlates −.71 with the number of different responses. Over a population of more heterogeneous stimuli, one would suppose that these correlations would be even more substantial.

One should not confuse the correlations just reported with the correlation between the strength of the primary response and the number of different responses Ss could give to a stimulus in a continuous-association situation. This correlation, it could be argued, should be positive, since words which evoke a strong popular response tend to be high-frequency words with which Ss should have many associates, even though they agree in their choice of a particular associate when the response is limited to a single word. While we have not systematically tested the Kent-Rosanoff stimuli in continuous association, a small study using 38 words from Noble's list (Noble, 1952) has demonstrated that the strength of the primary response in the usual free-association situation correlates significantly positively with the number of different responses given in a 60-sec period. Conversely, the number of different response words given in free association correlates significantly negatively with the number of different response words given in continuous association. It should be noted that this study involved stimuli varying from nonsense material through very high-frequency words. The relationships within the Kent-Rosanoff list would presumably be slight. Overall, however, the data suggest that meaningfulness tends to vary inversely with the number of different responses obtained in the free-association situation and positively with the strength of the primary response.

Johnson (1956) and Howes (1957) have shown that response hierarchies are stratified by frequency of usage.

Highly popular responses are customarily highly frequent words. Less frequent words make their appearance farther down in the response hierarchies or not at all. Howes has gone on to argue that the pooling of response hierarchies to a variety of stimuli shows the responses to represent the frequency of usage tables to a close degree of approximation. While we have had neither the resources nor the dedication necessary to repeat Howes' extensive work, our data appear to conform to his expectations. As a very crude test of his hypothesis, we correlated the number of responses in the complete norms beginning with each letter of the alphabet with the number of pages given to each letter in the *Thorndike-Barnhard 1952 High School Dictionary*. Our working assumption was that frequency of usage was independent of initial letter and, hence, availability of responses was roughly indexed by the total number of words in each alphabetical category in the dictionary. We further assumed that the number of words in a given section of the dictionary was proportional to the number of pages. The correlation between frequency of occurrence of words beginning with a given letter and number of pages given to the letter in the dictionary was .80, a result congruent with Howes' finding.

USES OF THE NORMS IN RESEARCH

The norms have found a wide variety of uses in the experimental laboratory and have also provided a measure (of somewhat limited value) of individual differences. Overall, it seems fair to say that the norms provide an index of powerful verbal habits likely to be shared by members of the college student community. In any situation in which such inferred habits may be presumed to be operative, the norms provide materials which readily lend themselves to experiments. Examples of the uses we have made of them at Minnesota are given below.

Recall

As indicated above, our work with word associations began with the demonstration of associative clustering in recall and proceeded to a quantification of the clustering effect as a function of the strength of the normative associations involved. In addition, it was shown that associative clustering was modified by a subject variable which we called *commonality*. This was defined as "the tendency to give popular responses on the word association test" and was measured by simply counting the number of primary responses given by each subject. In three experiments, the correlations between commonality score and the number of associative clusters produced by the subjects were .22, .32, and .38 (Jenkins & Russell, 1952b).

Perceptual Facilitation

Professor William O'Neil, working in our laboratories, investigated the tachistoscopic threshold for a word when it was presented in the context of an associated word (O'Neil, 1953). In this and several subsequent experiments, it was demonstrated that perception could be markedly facilitated by the presence of the associate. The phenomenon appeared to be "all or none," with virtually any degree of associative strength producing the facilitative effect.

Learning

Studies involving paired-associate learning have been concerned with three problems: the learning of pairs observed to be associatively linked in the norms; transfer and interference effects between paired-associate lists when the stimuli or responses were observed to be related in the norms; and transfer effects when an inferred chain of associates mediates between two learning lists.

With college students as Ss and lists ranging in length from nine to 35 pairs, it has not been possible to show differential facilitation in the learning of a paired-associate list when the pairs are taken from the norms. All degrees of associative strength from 80% to .2% facilitate learning very markedly. Two studies with children by Wicklund, Palermo, and Jenkins (1964), using appropriate children's norms, indicate that, for that population, a functional relationship can be found (see also Palermo, 1963).

With regard to transfer, Bastian (1961) showed that when responses in a second list are associatively related to responses in the first list, with stimuli held constant, facilitation in second-list learning results. Ryan (1960) demonstrated that facilitation in second-list learning may be observed when the stimuli of the two lists are associatively related and responses held constant. Carlin (1958) tested the effects of varying degrees of associative strength in the associates employed in studies such as those of Bastian and Ryan but found maximal facilitation at all degrees of strength employed.

When chains of associates are used to mediate the learning of a second list, facilitation of learning may also be detected. Russell and Storms (1955) selected associative chains of the form: A elicits B in free association, B elicits C in free association, but A does not elicit C in free association. Their Ss first learned a paired-associate list of the form X-A and then transferred to a list of the form X-C. The X-C pairs were found to be more readily learned than X-controls (unassociated words).

Generalization

An extensive series of studies has been carried out on the transfer of a simple instrumental response from one set of words to another set that is associatively linked to the words in the first set. Mink (1963) showed that the direction of the association was important in such associatively mediated generalization. Martin (1961) confirmed this work and extended the investigation to test other parameters in the experimental situation. These studies have been discussed in relation to other studies of semantic generalization by Jenkins (1963). Current data suggest that the amount of generalization observed is a monotonic function of associative strength, but the function has not as yet been adequately described.

Individual Associative Behavior

To provide a convenient reference scale for commonality scores, centile norms were developed on a sample of 400 students. Table 2 gives centile ranks for the frequency of primary responses. Thus, a scoring key which simply lists the primary response for each stimulus may be used. The number of primary responses given by S is counted and entered as his score. His centile rank may then be read directly from the table. This method of commonality scoring correlates highly (in the neighborhood of .96) with the more elaborate and time-consuming methods which involve weighting of frequencies and scoring of all responses.

TABLE 2   Percentiles for Commonality Scores[a]

Score	Centile	Score	Centile
57 or more	100	32	38
56	99	31	36
55	98	30	33
54	97	29	31
53	96	28	29
52	96	27	26
51	95	26	24
50	92	25	22
49	89	24	20
48	85	23	19
47	82	22	17
46	79	21	15
45	74	20	12
44	72	19	10
43	69	18	8
42	67	17	7
41	64	16	6
40	62	15	5
39	59	14	3
38	54	13	3
37	51	12	2
36	49	11	2
35	46	10	2
34	44	9	2
33	41	8 or less	1

[a]Score = frequency of primary responses; N = 400 university sophomores.

Many studies have focussed on the individual S's associative behavior. Rosen and Russell (1957) discovered that in successive association, Ss tend to give more and more remote associations to the stimulus word (as judged by the free-association norms) regardless of whether or not their first association was the most popular. Other, unpublished, research of the project strongly suggests that the norms provide reasonable estimates of the response hierarchies of individuals. In repeated testings, Ss are more likely to persist in a response if the response is of high popularity. Similarly, repetition is more likely for high strength primaries than for lower strength primaries and high commonality Ss are more likely to persist in a response than low commonality Ss.

A case study of two Ss (one scoring high in commonality and one scoring low) by Peterson and Jenkins (1957) demonstrated that all of the phenomena which had been obtained with groups could be reproduced at the individual level, using the Ss own associates obtained on another occasion. This study also suggested that the behavior of the low commonality S could be predicted more accurately from normative data than from his own previous associative behavior since he changed so markedly from test to test.

A series of detailed studies of many verbal and nonverbal behaviors of high and low commonality subjects has been summarized elsewhere (Jenkins, 1960). In general, the findings suggest that commonality is a variable of some importance in tasks involving intraverbal behaviors with minimal outside criteria, but that it is of little import in behaviors involving abilities and aptitudes which may be directed toward specific goals. Examples of the first group of behaviors are other association tests and certain sentence completion tests. Examples of the latter are color naming and intelligence tests. Test-retest stability on personality and interest tests seems also to be related to commonality, with the high commonality Ss showing greater stability (see Volsky, 1958).

Two studies were conducted on the effect on free association behavior of the set to produce popular responses (Jenkins, 1959). It was found that commonality scores increased on the average by about one standard deviation under "popular" set. Scores under "normal" and "popular" instructions correlated .67 in one study and .48 in the other.

Normative Comparisons

The comparison of the Schellenberg norms with our own led to a general study of the major normative word-association studies in the United States (Jenkins & Russell, 1960). The data suggest that general changes in the norms have taken place during this century. Popular responses are, for the most part, stronger than they were in the early part of the century. Words used as responses in each rank change slowly but systematically over time, with the highest ranking responses being the most stable. Superordinate responses and synonyms seem to be decreasing steadily in popularity, while coordinates and contrasts are increasing. It was felt that changes in test taking attitudes, increasing linguistic sophistication, and changes in the meaning of stimuli over time play some part in the changes observed.

It must be obvious at this point that we have found the Minnesota norms to be extremely valuable adjuncts to our research endeavors in verbal behavior. Our colleagues at other schools, whose work regrettably cannot be summarized here, have extended these studies in a variety of ways and have pioneered new and more sophisticated applications of the data in these and other norms. We think that their work, as well as ours, justifies our hope that the free-association technique may well be instrumental in unlocking the secrets of verbal behavior and, indeed, perhaps of language itself.

REFERENCES

Bastian, J. R. (1961). Associative factors in verbal transfer. *Journal of Experimental Psychology* 62, 70-79.

Bousfield, W. A. (1953). The occurrence of clustering in the recall of randomly arranged associates. *Journal of General Psychology* 49, 229-240.

Carlin, J. E. (1958). Word-association strength as a variable in verbal paired-associate learning. Unpublished doctoral dissertation, University of Minnesota.

Cook, S. W., & Skinner, B. F. (1939). Some factors influencing the distribution of associated words. *Psychological Record* 3, 178-184.

Howes, D. H. (1957). On the relation between the probability of a word as an association and in general linguistic usage. *Journal of Abnormal and Social Psychology* 54, 75-85.

Jenkins, J. J. (1959). Effects on word-association of the set to give popular responses. *Psychological Reports* 5, 94.

Jenkins, J. J. (1960). Commonality of association as an indicator of more general patterns of verbal behavior. In T. A. Sebeok (Ed.), *Style in Language*. New York: Wiley, pp. 307-329.

Jenkins, J. J. (1963). Mediated associations: paradigms and situations. In C. N. Cofer & B. S. Musgrave (Eds.) *Verbal behavior and learning.* New York: McGraw-Hill, pp. 210-245.

Jenkins, J. J., Mink, W. D., & Russell, W. A. (1958). Associative clustering as a function of verbal association strength. *Psychological Reports* **4**, 127-136.

Jenkins, J. J., & Russell, W. A. (1952a). Associative clustering during recall. *Journal of Abnormal and Social Psychology* **47**, 818-821.

Jenkins, J. J., & Russell, W. A. (1952b). Associative clustering and commonality of response on the Kent-Rosanoff test. Technical Report No. 3, University of Minnesota, Contract N8-ONR-66216, Minneapolis, Minn.

Jenkins, J. J., & Russell, W. A. (1960). Systematic changes in word association norms: 1910-1952. *Journal of Abnormal and Social Psychology* **60**, 293-304.

Johnson, D. M. (1956). Word-association and word-frequency. *American Journal of Psychology* **69**, 125-127.

Kent, G. H., & Rosanoff, A. J. (1910). A study of association in insanity. *American Journal of Insanity* **67**, 37-96, 317-390.

Martin, J. G. (1961). Mediated transfer in two verbal learning paradigms. *Studies in verbal behavior,* Report No. 5, University of Minnesota, NSF Grant G 18690.

Mink, W. D. (1963). Semantic generalization as related to word association. *Psychological Reports* **12**, 59-67.

Noble, C. E. (1952). An analysis of meaning. *Psychological Review* **59**, 421-430.

O'Neil, W. M. (1953). The effect of verbal association on tachistoscopic recognition. *Australian Journal of Psychology* **5**, 42-45.

Palermo, D. S. (1963). Word associations and children's verbal behavior. In L. P. Lipsitt & C. C. Spiker (Eds.), *Advances in child development and behavior.* Vol. 1. New York: Academic Press, pp. 31-68.

Peterson, M. S., & Jenkins, J. J. (1957). Word association phenomena at the individual level: a pair of case studies. Technical Report No. 16, University of Minnesota, Contract N8-ONR-66216, Minneapolis, Minn.

Rosen, E., & Russell, W. A. (1957). Frequency-characteristics of successive word association. *American Journal of Psychology* **70**, 120-122.

Russell, W. A., & Jenkins, J. J. (1952). Associative clustering and response rank in the Kent-Rosanoff test. Technical Report, No. 2, University of Minnesota, Contract N8-ONR-66216, Minneapolis, Minn.

Russell, W. A., & Jenkins, J. J. (1954). The complete Minnesota norms for responses to 100 words from the Kent-Rosanoff word association test. Technical Report No. 11, University of Minnesota, Contract N8-ONR-66216, Minneapolis, Minn.

Russell, W. A., & Storms, L. H. (1955). Implicit verbal chaining in paired-associate learning. *Journal of Experimental Psychology* **49**, 267-293.

Ryan, J. J. (1960). Comparison of verbal response transfer mediated by meaningfully similar and associated stimuli. *Journal of Experimental Psychology* **60**, 408-415.

Schellenberg, P. E. (1930). A group free-association test for college students. Unpublished doctoral dissertation, University of Minnesota.

Skinner, B. F. (1937). The distribution of associated words. *Psychological Record* **1**, 71-76.

Volsky, T. C., Jr. (1958). Modality of word-association test responses as a factor in improving counselor predictions. Unpublished doctoral dissertation, University of Minnesota.

Wicklund, D. A., Palermo, D. S., & Jenkins, J. J. (1964). The effects of associative strength and response hierarchy on paired-associate learning. *Journal of Verbal Learning and Verbal Behavior* **3**, 413-420.

Zipf, G. K. (1949). *Human behavior and the principle of least effort.* Cambridge, Mass: Addison-Wesley.

Afraid

No.	Response	Total
1.	fear	261
2.	scared	240
3.	dark	98
4.	brave	63
5.	frightened	23
6.	run	12
7.	scare	12
8.	happy	11
9.	unafraid	10
10.	courage	9
11.	fearless	8
12.	no	8
13.	fright	7
14.	never	7
15.	terror	7
16.	coward	6
17.	cry	6
18.	danger	6
19.	fight	6
20.	night	6
21.	not	6
22.	bad	5
23.	quiet	5
24.	war	5
25.	bold	4
26.	child	4
27.	fearful	4
28.	hurt	4
29.	accident	3
30.	(not) afraid	3
31.	anger	3
32.	confident	3
33.	dog	3
34.	horror	3
35.	snakes	3
36.	worried	3
37.	animal	2
38.	army	2
39.	content	2
40.	courageous	2
41.	darkness	2
42.	death	2
43.	finals	2
44.	mad	2
45.	scream	2
46.	secure	2
47.	shrink	2
48.	shy	2
49.	sick	2
50.	spider(s)	2
51.	tense	2
52.	terrified	2
53.	trouble	2
54.	worry	2

55-158. (f = 1)
alarm, alone, anxiety, anxious, awake, bark, bell, bomb, calm, can't, carry, cats, certain, cold, conflicts, cringe, crouch, crying, defiant, despair, drop, eager, enemy, eyes, fire, flunk-out, friendly, frighten, ghost, girl, glad, gun, hate, hatred, heart, help, hide, high, hot, jungle, kind, laugh, light, lion, lonely, loud, mean, men, mice, morrow, murder, mystery, nah, nervous, Negroes, of, of what?, passive, people, pest, physics, queer, quiver, reaction, recall, running, sad, scar, senses, shake, shaky,

Afraid (contd)

No.	Response	Total

shirk, silly, sissy, sleep, smear, soldier, something, sound, stop, strong, sun, sure, sweat, tests, tiger, timid, tired, to dream, tremble, troubled, trust, uneasy, unhappiness, unhappy, unknown, unprepared, west, why, window, wolf, yellow, yes, you

Anger

No.	Response	Total
1.	mad	353
2.	fear	83
3.	hate	61
4.	rage	49
5.	temper	35
6.	red	28
7.	ire	21
8.	wrath	21
9.	happy	20
10.	fight	19
11.	hatred	13
12.	man	12
13.	fright	11
14.	calm	10
15.	hit	8
16.	love	8
17.	disgust	7
18.	hurt	7
19.	frustration	6
20.	fury	6
21.	joy	6
22.	mean	6
23.	friendly	5
24.	bad	4
25.	boy	4
26.	emotion	4
27.	hot	4
28.	person	4
29.	sad	4
30.	shout	4
31.	sorrow	4
32.	calmness	3
33.	dislike	3
34.	eyes	3
35.	hat	3
36.	kind	3
37.	laugh	3
38.	madness	3
39.	tears	3
40.	yell	3
41.	afraid	2
42.	cross	2
43.	fire	2
44.	frown	2
45.	frustrated	2
46.	hard	2
47.	harsh	2
48.	hope	2
49.	hunger	2
50.	jealousy	2
51.	loud	2
52.	me	2
53.	noise	2
54.	pain	2
55.	peace	2
56.	pleasure	2
57.	soft	2

Anger (contd)

No.	Response	Total
58.	strike	2
59.	swear	2
60.	teeth	2

61-168. (f = 1)
adrenalin, anger, annoyed, baby, bitter, black, blocked, blush, burn, charity, clamor, confusion, contempt, cool, crazy, cruel, cry, danger, deep, delight, desire, disturb, disturbance, divorce, dog, excitement, face, fearful, fierce, fist, fit, fool, foolish, friend, furious, gentle, get, grief, growl, gutburst, happiness, headache, heat, Helen, high blood pressure, insult, irate, irritability, joyful, jump, kids, knife, laughter, life, like, malice, mildness, mood, mother, nasty, parents, patience, placid, pleasant, pleasing, pout, pride, psychology, rashness, regret, resentment, rest, rouse, sadness, scorn, scream, set, severe, smile, solitude, soothe, sore, sound, still, stomach, stubborn, sullen, surprise, sweetness, sweat, teacher, tense, terror, thirst, threat, tired, torment, tranquility, uncomfort, unpleasant, upset, violence, voice, want, will, women, worry, yell

Baby

No.	Response	Total
1.	boy	162
2.	child	142
3.	cry	113
4.	mother	71
5.	girl	51
6.	small	43
7.	infant	27
8.	cute	21
9.	little	18
10.	blue	17
11.	diapers	14
12.	crib	13
13.	crying	13
14.	bed	11
15.	sitter	11
16.	soft	11
17.	born	10
18.	bottle	10
19.	brother	10
20.	doll	9
21.	pink	9
22.	sleep	9
23.	toy(s)	9
24.	adult	8
25.	blanket	8
26.	spoon	8
27.	sweet	8
28.	young	8
29.	rattle	7

Baby (contd)

No.	Response	Total
30.	coo	6
31.	love	6
32.	food	5
33.	kid	5
34.	tiny	5
35.	birth	4
36.	cuddle(y)	4
37.	dog	4
38.	noise	4
39.	woman(e)	4
40.	buggy	3
41.	carriage	3
42.	helpless	3
43.	laugh	3
44.	man	3
45.	milk	3
46.	parents	3
47.	smile	3
48.	wet	3
49.	ball	2
50.	bunting	2
51.	care	2
52.	happy	2
53.	humor	2
54.	joy	2
55.	playpen	2
56.	sister	2
57.	sit	2
58.	six	2
59.	son	2

60-119. (f = 1)
babboon, bath, bedroom, big, boone, caps, Carol, clean, clothes, cow, coy, cried, daughter, delicate, dependence, doctor, dress, face, fat, fondness, fun, grownup, hands, high chair, innocent, hospital, Jerry, learn, lotion, marriage, maybe, Nancy, neonate, nephew, new, nice, no, nursemaid, on the way, pair, pleasant, pregnancy, pretty, rattles, rocker, shoes, small child smooth, snooks, softness, spill, stupid, talk, thumb, tot, twins, ugly, wear, whimper, yell

Bath

No.	Response	Total
1.	clean	314
2.	water	220
3.	soap	102
4.	tub	98
5.	wash	42
6.	shower	38
7.	dirty	23
8.	cleanliness	14
9.	dirt	14
10.	warm	14
11.	house	13
12.	hot	10
13.	room	9
14.	towel	9
15.	cold	5
16.	salts	5
17.	bathe	4
18.	bathtub	4
19.	bubble	4
20.	wet	4
21.	England	3
22.	relax	3
23.	Saturday	3

Bath (contd)

No.	Response	Total
24.	swim	3
25.	oil	2
26.	sleep	2
27.	take	2

28-70. (f = 1)
basketball, batholith, bed, bird, boy, cleanness, cleanse, comfort, dart, draw, dress, drink, Feb, filth, girl, hah, health, home, hygiene, ish, knight, lake, Maine, mat, naked, nice, powder, refresh, scrub, scum, Shakespeare, smell, soft, soothing, spa, sponge, steam, suds, todays, toilet, town, use, washing

Beautiful

No.	Response	Total
1.	ugly	209
2.	pretty	144
3.	girls	142
4.	woman	106
5.	homely	67
6.	lovely	45
7.	nice	23
8.	picture	18
9.	lady	15
10.	flowers	12
11.	mountain	10
12.	snow	10
13.	Ohio	7
14.	good	6
15.	music	6
16.	scene	6
17.	soft	6
18.	day	5
19.	lake(s)	5
20.	scenery	5
21.	dreamer	4
22.	gorgeous	4
23.	landscape	4
24.	nature	4
25.	queen	4
26.	color	3
27.	hair	3
28.	painting	3
29.	sky	3
30.	sweet	3
31.	tree	3
32.	wonderful	3
33.	beauty	2
34.	blonde	2
35.	butterfly	2
36.	cute	2
37.	dumb	2
38.	exquisite	2
39.	horrible	2
40.	house	2
41.	Marilyn	2
42.	song	2
43.	sunset	2
44.	tall	2
45.	view	2

46-135. (f = 1)
actress, adore, America, angelic, appearance, art, attractive, awful, bird, black, blue, brown, bountiful, car, church, Cinderella, colorful, country, countryside, dark, deep, deer, delicate, desirable, dog, doll, door, dress, dull,

Beautiful (contd)

enchanting, Ester, exciting, eyes, face, fair, fine, forests, for spacious, garden, gay, girlfriend, glass, good-looking, handsome, happy, heavens, hills, icicle, intelligent, joy, knockout, lack, light, like, line, looks, man, Mary Ann, mirror, moonlight, morning, neat, night, object, orderly, person, pink, plain, pleasing, red, religion, ring, river, sad, scenic, schön, see, sex, Shirl, skin, slick, spring, star, summer, terrific, water, white, window, wish, ♀ body

Bed

No.	Response	Total
1.	sleep	584
2.	soft	73
3.	sheet	36
4.	pillow	29
5.	rest	25
6.	covers	18
7.	blankets	16
8.	night	16
9.	room	16
10.	comfort	9
11.	chair	8
12.	girl(s)	8
13.	mattress	8
14.	table	8
15.	tired	8
16.	board	6
17.	wet	6
18.	sleepy	5
19.	warm	5
20.	wetting	5
21.	bug(s)	4
22.	post	4
23.	ridden	4
24.	spread	4
25.	stead	4
26.	time	4
27.	cot	3
28.	heavy	3
29.	house	3
30.	lamp	3
31.	quilt	3
32.	springs	3
33.	white	3
34.	woman(e)	3
35.	big	2
36.	blue	2
37.	clothes	2
38.	dream	2
39.	dresser	2
40.	furniture	2
41.	go	2
42.	good	2
43.	hard	2
44.	home	2
45.	lie	2
46.	light	2
47.	made	2
48.	make	2
49.	sex	2
50.	sick	2

51-88. (f = 1)
asleep, bath, black, comfortable, down, enjoyment, flag,

Bed (contd)

No.	Response	Total

floor, fornication, fuck, gown,
happiness, head, honeymoon, hot,
hug, in, jacket, large, lay,
lead, led, linen, passion,
parlor, pink, pleasure, read,
rice, river, salt, slept, son,
twin, warmth, window, yes, you

Bible

No.	Response	Total
1.	God	236
2.	book	205
3.	church	125
4.	religion	100
5.	story(ies)	56
6.	holy	50
7.	read	39
8.	Jesus	22
9.	good	14
10.	Christ	11
11.	truth	10
12.	study	8
13.	black	7
14.	Moses	7
15.	faith	6
16.	prayer	6
17.	reading	5
18.	history	4
19.	home	4
20.	life	4
21.	school	4
22.	testament	4
23.	verse(s)	4
24.	Lord	3
25.	word	3
26.	Joseph	2
27.	Korean	2
28.	love	2
29.	pray	2
30.	Psalms	2
31.	right	2
32.	"salm"	2
33.	salvation	2
34.	true	2

35-86. (f = 1)
ancient, bad, bah!, Christ
Good, Christian, Christianity,
class, cross, English, ethic,
false, fantasy, fiction, fool,
girl, God's word, goodness,
gospel, great, heaven, heavy,
Jesus Christ, journey, joy,
law, leather, lessons, Luke,
me, memory, minister, necessary,
newspaper, pages, passage,
peace, preacher, pulpit, pure,
reap, red, religious, revised,
saints, scripture, sermon,
shmible, stible, table, tale,
teach, why

Bitter

No.	Response	Total
1.	sweet	652
2.	sour	125
3.	taste	43
4.	chocolate	15
5.	rice	13

Bitter (contd)

No.	Response	Total
6.	cold	9
7.	lemon	9
8.	angry	8
9.	bad	8
10.	hard	6
11.	mad	6
12.	acid	5
13.	almonds	5
14.	herbs	5
15.	grape	4
16.	anger	3
17.	food	3
18.	fruit	3
19.	grapefruit	3
20.	hate	3
21.	vinegar	3
22.	angostura	2
23.	drink	2
24.	icky	2
25.	not good	2
26.	quinine	2
27.	strong	2
28.	tongue	2
29.	unhappy	2

30-90. (f = 1)
acrid, against, agony, anacasta,
apple, argument, awful, base,
beer, berries, bitters, butter,
chills, coffee, cranberries,
dandelion, disappointment, distasteful, dose, drug, duerer,
eat, fat, flower, grimace,
happy, harsh, horseradish, hot,
ish, me, medicine, mellow, mild,
misery, olive, oranges, pickle,
poison, red, resent, resentment,
retch, rid, saccharin, salt,
shame, sharp, stem, story, tast-
ing, tea, tears, terrible,
tough, Truman, truth, unpleasant,
weed, whiskey, worse

Black

No.	Response	Total
1.	white	751
2.	dark	54
3.	cat	26
4.	light	22
5.	night	20
6.	sheep	11
7.	color	10
8.	red	9
9.	blue	6
10.	dog	6
11.	cloth	5
12.	bottom	3
13.	car	3
14.	coal	3
15.	paper	3
16.	shoe	3
17.	blackboard	2
18.	board	2
19.	brown	2
20.	button	2
21.	coat	2
22.	cold	2
23.	dress	2
24.	gray	2
25.	horse	2
26.	wool	2

27-77. (f = 1)
afraid, big, blouse, body, book,
cap, casket, cave, chair,

Black (contd)

No.	Response	Total

darkness, dead, death, depth,
dirt, dirty, dismal, eat,
ebony, eye, good, green, hair,
hole, ink, jack, kitten,
magic, marble, midnight, moon,
murder, Negro, nice, pants,
pit, pitch, rake, Sam, satin,
shiny, singe, spade, stocking,
stove, suit, telephone, velvet,
wagon, whiten, whittle, witch

Blossom

No.	Response	Total
1.	flower	672
2.	apple	78
3.	bloom	35
4.	time	28
5.	spring	20
6.	smell	19
7.	rose	18
8.	bud	13
9.	plant	11
10.	pretty	11
11.	tree(s)	11
12.	pink	9
13.	orange	5
14.	Seeley	5
15.	sweet	5
16.	cherry	4
17.	out	4
18.	beauty	3
19.	red	3
20.	stem	3
21.	apple blossom	2
22.	apple tree	2
23.	bird	2
24.	blue	2
25.	bough	2
26.	breast	2
27.	fruit	2
28.	leaf	2

29-62. (f = 1)
bean, beautiful, blood, bush,
carnation, child, clover, cow,
day, field, flowed, fool,
forth, fragrance, fragrant,
gal, girl, lily, magnolia,
man, name, Negroes, nice,
petals, petunia, root, skunk,
spread, sun, top, wedding,
white, wilt, yellow

Blue

No.	Response	Total
1.	sky	175
2.	red	160
3.	green	125
4.	color	66
5.	yellow	56
6.	black	49
7.	white	44
8.	water	36
9.	grey	28
10.	boy	20
11.	bird	14
12.	dress	14
13.	pink	9
14.	gold	8

Blue (contd)

No.	Response	Total
15.	moon	7
16.	night	7
17.	cold	6
18.	dark	6
19.	earth	6
20.	flag	6
21.	heaven	6
22.	car	5
23.	coat	5
24.	Danube	5
25.	orange	5
26.	baby	4
27.	cool	4
28.	eyes	4
29.	light	4
30.	navy	4
31.	ocean	4
32.	pretty	4
33.	river	4
34.	sad	4
35.	sea	4
36.	berries	3
37.	book	3
38.	cloth	3
39.	lake	3
40.	mood	3
41.	purple	3
42.	sweater	3
43.	Air Force	2
44.	azure	2
45.	cheese	2
46.	day	2
47.	eagle	2
48.	ribbon	2
49.	room	2
50.	soft	2
51.	song	2
52.	true	2
53.	uniform	2

54-108. (f = 1)
angel, bad, bank, beauty, beetle, best, blood, blue, boat, bonnet, brown, bull, bunny, clothes, clouds, emotion, fish, flower, gown, haze, hope, horizon, horn, house, Hungarian, ink, light blue, lightning, limpid, lonely, low, mold, Monday, music, nice, pie, prelude, (red, white &), ski, soldier, sore, south, sport coat, stone, strip, suit, tan, tango, tin roof, tri, truth, ugly, virgin, washing, wide

Boy

No.	Response	Total
1.	girl	768
2.	man	41
3.	scout	37
4.	dog	10
5.	friend	8
6.	play	8
7.	small	8
8.	young	8
9.	brother	7
10.	child	7
11.	little	7
12.	school	6
13.	lad	5
14.	fish(ing)	4
15.	male	4
16.	blue	3

Boy (contd)

No.	Response	Total
17.	rough	3
18.	son	3
19.	bad	2
20.	barefoot	2
21.	boy	2
22.	gal	2
23.	sex	2
24.	toys	2
25.	wagon	2
26.	youth	2

27-82. (f = 1)
bail, ball, bat, blonde, brat, Brian, brown, cap, carving, clothes, corduroy, cott, crewcut, curly, date, dirt, dirty, eager, father, fight, football, fun, gargon, hair, happy, he, hit, hunt, Jr., love, kite, mischief, naughty, nephew, oh boy, outside, pal, pants, pep, person, playing, Roger, ship, short pants, sign, sir, 6, soldier, son, sports, stone, stop, trouble, trousers, Winslow, young man

Bread

No.	Response	Total
1.	butter	610
2.	food	94
3.	eat	76
4.	water	29
5.	white	15
6.	jam	14
7.	milk	14
8.	flour	11
9.	jelly	9
10.	dough	7
11.	crust	6
12.	knife	6
13.	rolls	6
14.	slice	6
15.	wine	6
16.	loaf	5
17.	cake	4
18.	sandwich	4
19.	toast	4
20.	wheat	4
21.	basket	3
22.	board	3
23.	box	3
24.	brown	3
25.	good	3
26.	hunger	3
27.	rye	3
28.	soft	3
29.	starch	3
30.	yeast	3
31.	dark	2
32.	fresh	2
33.	fruit	2
34.	hard	2
35.	hungry	2
36.	line	2
37.	meat	2
38.	rise	2
39.	stale	2

40-68. (f = 1)
bun, carbohydrate, course, crumb, cut, cutter, dry, gray, Greek, home, homemade, juice, lunch, Master, moist, muffin, pan, penicillin, plate, pork,

Bread (contd)

No.	Response	Total

raisin, rice, salami, staff, staff of life, stomach, sunflower, tasty, texture, wrappers

Butter

No.	Response	Total
1.	bread	637
2.	yellow	81
3.	soft	30
4.	fat	24
5.	food	22
6.	knife	20
7.	eggs	16
8.	cream	14
9.	milk	13
10.	cheese	9
11.	cow	9
12.	oleo	9
13.	fly	7
14.	eat	6
15.	spread	6
16.	cup	5
17.	grease	5
18.	salt	5
19.	scotch	5
20.	toast	5
21.	good	4
22.	nut	4
23.	ball	3
24.	expensive	3
25.	lard	3
26.	melt	3
27.	pat	3
28.	rum	3
29.	smooth	3
30.	square	3
31.	sweet	3
32.	taste	3
33.	margarine	2
34.	salty	2

35-72. (f = 1)
better, bitter, brain, brickle, broad, brown nose, bull, bum, butter, carrots, carton, churn, creamy, dish, doctor, drink, finger, greasy, health, jam, lawyer, lemon, loaf, man, meat, oar, oil, potato, popcorn, pound, printing, red, sandwich, smear, sugar, sweet, tub, up

Butterfly

No.	Response	Total
1.	moth	144
2.	insect	117
3.	wing(s)	104
4.	bird	84
5.	fly	78
6.	yellow	62
7.	net	42
8.	pretty	34
9.	flower(s)	33
10.	bug	27
11.	cocoon	23
12.	summer	22
13.	color(s)	21
14.	bee(s)	20

Butterfly (contd)

No.	Response	Total
15.	monarch	20
16.	stomach	14
17.	beauty	9
18.	worm	9
19.	flying	7
20.	animal	6
21.	beautiful	6
22.	blue	5
23.	caterpillar	4
24.	flight	4
25.	Madam	4
26.	opera	4
27.	ant	3
28.	butter	3
29.	catch	3
30.	dance	3
31.	flutter	3
32.	spring	3
33.	colorful	2
34.	dog	2
35.	dragonfly	2
36.	jet plane	2
37.	lagoon	2
38.	lepidoptera	2
39.	light	2
40.	mouse	2
41.	orange	2
42.	sky	2
43.	soft	2
44.	song	2
45.	spots	2
46.	sunshine	2
47.	warm	2
48.	wasp	2

49-103. ($f = 1$)
air, blind, buttercup, butterfly's, California, canary, car, Cecropia, chase, collection, cow, crazy, curtain, dainty, dandelion, delicate, dust, feather, felt, field, flap, flea, fragile, freedom, game, garden, girl, grace, grass, hobby, hornet, Japan, look, louse, maggot, morn, mosquito, nature, nothing, Orthoptera, outside, roach, robin, silk, smooth, Spanish fly, sun, swim, thing, tiger, tree, watch, wheat, woods, zoology

Cabbage

No.	Response	Total
1.	head	165
2.	lettuce	149
3.	vegetable	139
4.	food	80
5.	salad	54
6.	eat	51
7.	green	47
8.	garden	34
9.	leaf	27
10.	sauerkraut	22
11.	smell	19
12.	slaw	16
13.	patch	15
14.	plant	14
15.	carrots	11
16.	corned beef	10
17.	soup	10
18.	ham	9
19.	fruit	7

Cabbage (contd)

No.	Response	Total
20.	king	7
21.	rabbit	6
22.	cook(ed)	5
23.	field	5
24.	can	4
25.	cole slaw	4
26.	eating	4
27.	round	4
28.	sour	4
29.	garbage	3
30.	kraut	3
31.	odor	3
32.	stew	3
33.	vinegar	3
34.	worm	3
35.	bett	2
36.	boil	2
37.	good	2
38.	meat	2
39.	raw	2
40.	spinach	2
41.	waste	2

42-90. ($f = 1$)
apple, bad, bag, beans, boiled, broccoli, bundle, burn, butterfly, cauliflower, celery, cheese, chew, corn, cream, crisp, dinner, distaste, dorm, dressing, grape, hard, hay, heat, horrible, insect, ish, jiggs, kitchen, lousy, man, money, nasty, pail, pigs feet, red, rhubarb, root, rutabega, sauce, skunk, spareribs, steps, stink, taste, terrible, ugh, vegetable soup, weiners

Carpet

No.	Response	Total
1.	rug	460
2.	floor	165
3.	soft	82
4.	red	27
5.	sweeper	21
6.	tack	20
7.	walk	17
8.	bag	16
9.	room	11
10.	house	10
11.	bagger	10
12.	green	9
13.	chair	8
14.	sweep	8
15.	thick	8
16.	home	6
17.	blue	5
18.	deep	5
19.	magic	5
20.	wool	5
21.	beetle	4
22.	color	4
23.	living room	4
24.	plush	4
25.	comfort	3
26.	mat	3
27.	smooth	3
28.	black	2
29.	clean	2
30.	cloth	2
31.	feet(foot)	2
32.	grey	2
33.	hall	2
34.	Mohawk	2

Carpet (contd)

No.	Response	Total
35.	Persian	2
36.	rough	2
37.	slipper	2
38.	table	2
39.	vacuum	2
40.	warm	2
41.	weave	2

42-94. ($f = 1$)
army, Bagdad, beater, blanket, brad, broom, brought, called, caps, cleaner, cover, covering, dad, dean, depth, design, dirt, door, flat, flow, flowers, flying, furniture, knee, lay, lecture, long, lounge, maroon, mop, nail, nap, new, nice, none, pillow, pretty, ray, rich, role, scold, shoe, sit, slip, spring, topaz, use, velvet, washer, weaving, wet, white, wine

Chair

No.	Response	Total
1.	table	493
2.	sit	205
3.	leg(s)	45
4.	seat	38
5.	soft	26
6.	desk	19
7.	arm	15
8.	sofa	12
9.	wood	9
10.	cushion	8
11.	rest	8
12.	stool	7
13.	hard	6
14.	bed	5
15.	comfort	5
16.	high	5
17.	sitting	5
18.	brown	4
19.	couch	4
20.	floor	4
21.	house	4
22.	pillow	4
23.	back	3
24.	cloth	3
25.	relax	3
26.	window	3
27.	bench	2
28.	blue	2
29.	car	2
30.	davenport	2
31.	easy	2
32.	electric	2
33.	home	2
34.	lamp	2
35.	man	2
36.	rocker	2
37.	room	2
38.	rung	2
39.	sleep	2
40.	swivel	2
41.	top	2
42.	woman	2

43-75. ($f = 1$)
armchair, black, bottom, cover, cozy, embroidered, execution, fall, foot, glue, green, hat, height, lazy, leather, living room, magazine, me, modern, office, overstuffed, paint,

Chair (contd)

No.	Response	Total

piano, president, red, round,
rug, small, straight, study,
upholstery, wheel, wicker

Cheese

No.	Response	Total
1.	crackers	108
2.	mouse(ice)	94
3.	bread	82
4.	eat	70
5.	food	68
6.	milk	47
7.	yellow	47
8.	cake	42
9.	butter	37
10.	cottage	32
11.	blue	25
12.	holes	24
13.	sandwich	23
14.	smell	21
15.	rat	20
16.	moon	19
17.	green	18
18.	swiss	15
19.	wise	15
20.	cream	11
21.	American	8
22.	bacon	7
23.	cheddar	7
24.	cow	7
25.	beer	6
26.	cut	6
27.	good	6
28.	roquefort	6
29.	sour	6
30.	dairy	5
31.	kraft	5
32.	limburger	5
33.	pie	5
34.	spread	5
35.	orange	4
36.	smile	4
37.	big	3
38.	burger	3
39.	macaroni	3
40.	taste	3
41.	tasty	3
42.	apple pie	2
43.	bitter	2
44.	cave	2
45.	cutter	2
46.	dry	2
47.	edam	2
48.	factory	2
49.	Friday	2
50.	Holland	2
51.	ish	2
52.	picture	2
53.	soft	2
54.	tangy	2
55.	velveeta	2

56-107. (f = 1)
age, and, apple, beans, brick,
camemburt, cards, carton, cat,
Christmas, cloth, corn, curd,
dislike, eating, home, icebox,
king, knife, longhorn, meat,
mild, mite, mold, no, parmesan,
photography, please, popcorn,
porus, pumpernickle bread,
read, roll, rotten, rye, salad,
salt, sausage, sharp, shorm,
slices, stinky, strong, sweet,

Cheese (contd)

No.	Response	Total

swift, Switzerland, toast,
waffles, wedge, whey, white,
wrapper

Child

No.	Response	Total
1.	baby(ies)	159
2.	mother	117
3.	adult	74
4.	boy	69
5.	small	62
6.	young	39
7.	kid(s)	33
8.	little	30
9.	man	28
10.	infant	21
11.	parent(s)	21
12.	girls	20
13.	play(s)	20
14.	children	19
15.	woman	18
16.	good	14
17.	love	12
18.	care	10
19.	cute	10
20.	welfare	9
21.	school	8
22.	birth	7
23.	cry	7
24.	brother	6
25.	son	6
26.	sweet	6
27.	toy(s)	6
28.	innocence(nt)	5
29.	nice	5
30.	niece	5
31.	tot	5
32.	bear(ing)	4
33.	father	4
34.	grown-up	4
35.	happy	4
36.	psychology	4
37.	youth	4
38.	bad	3
39.	brat	3
40.	crying	3
41.	dog	3
42.	doll	3
43.	labor	3
44.	sister	3
45.	sleep	3
46.	adolescent	2
47.	ball	2
48.	born	2
49.	Christ	2
50.	clothes	2
51.	crib	2
52.	diapers	2
53.	friend	2
54.	fun	2
55.	grow	2
56.	health	2
57.	home	2
58.	learn	2
59.	nurse	2
60.	pregnant(cy)	2
61.	trouble	2

62-131. (f = 1)
bed, bottle, breast, bright,
Charles, childish, cold, creep,
Dave, development, Dick, dis-
obedience, family, feed, future,
Galen, grass, hand, happiness,

Child (contd)

No.	Response	Total

have one, human, John, joy,
kind, lad, laugh, mess, mischief, monster, nephew,
nursery, pain, pediatrics, person, pest, playful, playing,
pleasant, pleasing, pretty,
prodigy, room, sad, scold,
scrawny, see, service, sex,
simple, 6, sleepy, smile,
snowball, soft, Sonia, spoiled,
Stephen, sweet, too, try, twin,
two, type, walk, well, wept,
white, yes, you, youngster

Citizen

No.	Response	Total
1.	U.S.(A.)	114
2.	man	112
3.	person	105
4.	American	92
5.	country	87
6.	alien	79
7.	people	39
8.	state	35
9.	vote(s)	22
10.	me	15
11.	patriot	15
12.	flag	13
13.	voter	12
14.	foreigner	11
15.	government	11
16.	America	10
17.	France	9
18.	Paine	9
19.	foreign	7
20.	good	7
21.	immigrant	6
22.	Kane	6
23.	Genet	5
24.	member	5
25.	soldier	5
26.	aid	4
27.	city	4
28.	comrade	4
29.	John Doe	4
30.	nation	4
31.	patriotic	4
32.	public	4
33.	ship	4
34.	town	4
35.	community	3
36.	democracy	3
37.	duty	3
38.	friend	3
39.	individual	3
40.	loyal	3
41.	native	3
42.	president	3
43.	rights	3
44.	Russia	3
45.	upstanding	3
46.	world	3
47.	yes	3
48.	army	2
49.	bad	2
50.	building	2
51.	committee	2
52.	convict	2
53.	criminal	2
54.	enemy	2
55.	fellow	2
56.	free	2
57.	French	2

Citizen (contd)

No.	Response	Total
58.	Ike	2
59.	mayor	2
60.	myself	2
61.	non-citizen	2
62.	not	2
63.	paper	2
64.	plebian	2
65.	pol. sci.	2
66.	Roman	2
67.	slave	2
68.	solid	2
69.	traitor	2
70.	voting	2

71-129. (f = 1)
back, bank, belong, big wheel, bold, bourgeois, boy, citizen, club, communist, constitution, council, court, courthouse, displaced person, exile, flea, freedom, Greece, guilt, heel, history, human, inhabitants, Jones, judge, king, leg, mean, mercenary, Minneapolis, mister, natural, naturalization, navy, neighbor, number, official, panic, partiant, patrician, patriotism, peasant, police, politics, privilege, proud, red, resident, revolution, social contract, spy, staunch, sucker, take, taxpayer, teacher, tired, united

City

No.	Response	Total
1.	town	353
2.	Minneapolis	121
3.	state	74
4.	country	69
5.	square	64
6.	people	32
7.	street	32
8.	St. Paul	24
9.	building(s)	22
10.	block(s)	20
11.	big	15
12.	New York	12
13.	house(s)	11
14.	large	10
15.	light(s)	9
16.	noise	8
17.	farm	7
18.	village	7
19.	block	5
20.	Chicago	5
21.	dirty	5
22.	busy	4
23.	hall	4
24.	traffic	4
25.	dirt	3
26.	dump	3
27.	home	3
28.	round	3
29.	water	3
30.	car(s)	2
31.	day	2
32.	here	2
33.	live	2
34.	man	2
35.	parks	2
36.	place	2
37.	smoke	2
38.	streetcar	2

City (contd)

No.	Response	Total
39.	towers	2

40-92. (f = 1)
Ames, bustle, club, concrete, cop, county, court, crowds, dark, Des Moines, downtown, Duluth, dust, Excelsior, excitement, factory, Faribault, fun, gas, hard, high, hinge, life, map, Memphis, metropolis, Milwaukee, Montevideo, New Orleans, ocean, pig, pipe, plant, population, Preston, Rochester, RR, rural, school, Seattle, sidewalk, sin, site, skyscrapers, snow, stand, suburb, subway, triangle, urban, vast, wells, window

Cold

No.	Response	Total
1.	hot	348
2.	snow	218
3.	warm	168
4.	winter	66
5.	ice	29
6.	Minnesota	13
7.	wet	13
8.	dark	10
9.	sick	9
10.	heat	8
11.	weather	8
12.	outside	7
13.	freeze	6
14.	hard	6
15.	nose	6
16.	sneeze	5
17.	air	3
18.	coat	3
19.	cough	3
20.	day	3
21.	freezing	3
22.	temperature	3
23.	wind	3
24.	brrr	2
25.	chilly	2
26.	head	2
27.	icy	2
28.	ill	2
29.	night	2
30.	room	2
31.	shiver	2
32.	shower	2
33.	sweat	2
34.	white	2

35-79. (f = 1)
Al, angry, artic, ball, bitter, blue, brisk, coal, clothes, clouds, clover, degree, discomfort, drinks, drip, dry, frost, had, hand, hoarse, icicle, jacket, old, out, pain, radiator, school, sharp, shelter, shoulder, side, slaw, slow, sniff, sore, steel, sun, today, uncomfortable, war, warming, water, woman, yes, zero

Comfort

No.	Response	Total
1.	chair	117
2.	bed	99
3.	ease	76
4.	home	71
5.	soft	69
6.	discomfort	55
7.	sleep	40
8.	rest	23
9.	health	21
10.	warm	20
11.	hard	19
12.	hardship	19
13.	easy	18
14.	warmth	15
15.	uncomfortable	13
16.	lazy	12
17.	nice	11
18.	blanket	10
19.	pillow	10
20.	relax	10
21.	pain	9
22.	happy	8
23.	help	8
24.	couch	7
25.	good	7
26.	house	7
27.	luxury	7
28.	sickness	7
29.	sick	6
30.	sofa	6
31.	southern	6
32.	easy chair	5
33.	enjoyment	5
34.	pleasure	5
35.	sorrow	5
36.	uneasy	5
37.	console	4
38.	cozy	4
39.	davenport	4
40.	happiness	4
41.	mother	4
42.	peace	4
43.	Tom	4
44.	content	3
45.	fire	3
46.	girl(s)	3
47.	hardness	3
48.	hurt	3
49.	illness	3
50.	joy	3
51.	misery	3
52.	money	3
53.	safe	3
54.	smooth	3
55.	aid	2
56.	car	2
57.	comfortable	2
58.	comforter	2
59.	cold	2
60.	fireplace	2
61.	food	2
62.	ill	2
63.	leisure	2
64.	love	2
65.	quiet	2
66.	relaxation	2
67.	sad	2
68.	satisfaction	2
69.	solid	2
70.	station	2
71.	uncomfort	2
72.	wife	2
73.	yes	2

15

Comfort (contd)

No.	Response	Total

74-151. (f = 1)
age, armchair, baby, bath, bell,
Bill, bliss, boat, book, care,
cart, child, clean, convenience,
convenient, cove, crap, cushion,
despair, distress, don't,
dreary, fatigue, feeling, fine,
foot, fort, friendly, friends,
full, grief, harsh, heart, heat,
heaven, hot, kind, laziness,
living, lounge, me, monk, music,
night, people, person, Peter,
pity, quilt, relaxed, restful,
rocks, room, round, sadness,
sea, security, sit, sitting,
sleeping, smell, snuggle, soft-
en, suffering, swing, television, tired, unease, unrest,
wealth, weary, well, whiskey,
wine, women, ye, you, yum

Command

No.	Response	Total
1.	order	196
2.	army	102
3.	obey	78
4.	officer	65
5.	performance	33
6.	do	27
7.	tell	27
8.	general	26
9.	shout	26
10.	halt	23
11.	voice	20
12.	soldier	18
13.	harsh	16
14.	attention	15
15.	sharp	13
16.	stop	12
17.	navy	11
18.	go	10
19.	demand	9
20.	yell	9
21.	ask	8
22.	sargeant	8
23.	air	7
24.	Air Force	7
25.	talk	7
26.	bark	6
27.	decision	6
28.	give	6
29.	march	6
30.	ROTC	6
31.	word	6
32.	man	5
33.	leader	5
34.	military	5
35.	action	4
36.	answer	4
37.	discipline	4
38.	force	4
39.	lead	4
40.	loud	4
41.	act	3
42.	captain	3
43.	dog	3
44.	hard	3
45.	law	3
46.	request	3
47.	respond	3
48.	response	3
49.	sir	3
50.	speak	3

Command (contd)

No.	Response	Total
51.	call	2
52.	car	2
53.	chief	2
54.	colonel	2
55.	control	2
56.	execution	2
57.	follow	2
58.	hear	2
59.	jump	2
60.	mean	2
61.	post	2
62.	power	2
63.	respect	2
64.	rule(s)	2
65.	service	2
66.	signal	2
67.	Spanish	2
68.	strong	2
69.	task	2
70.	teacher	2
71.	wish	2
72.	yes	2

73-158. (f = 1)
agreement, anarchy, attack,
bellow, big, book, boss, Caesar,
change, charm, choose, commander,
correct, crisp, deep, demanding,
direct, direction, disobey,
displeasure, disregard, dominat-
ing, don't, drill, duty, erect,
execute, father, firm, forward,
fulfill, gun, hat, head,
headqtrs, heard, hell, help,
high, hike, Hitler, holler, Ike,
instruction, learn, lecture,
Le Roy, load, lord, Lt., major,
make, marine, me, no, noise,
obedience, overseer, pass,
perform, Pfc., pilot, planes,
play, plea, polite, regiment,
relax, repeat, report, reprimand,
retrieve, salute, shant, sit,
situation, start, stern,
sterness, stupid, sword, take,
tough, war, wave, whistle

Cottage

No.	Response	Total
1.	house	298
2.	lake	138
3.	cheese	111
4.	home	87
5.	white	33
6.	cabin	32
7.	small	27
8.	door	18
9.	fence	16
10.	vines	14
11.	country	12
12.	woods	11
13.	ivy	10
14.	summer	9
15.	roses	7
16.	cozy	6
17.	flowers	6
18.	hut	6
19.	vacation	5
20.	fun	4
21.	grove	4
22.	marriage	4
23.	roof	4
24.	stones	4
25.	trees	4

Cottage (contd)

No.	Response	Total
26.	window	4
27.	yard	4
28.	boat	3
29.	cute	3
30.	honeymoon	3
31.	nice	3
32.	peace	3
33.	room	3
34.	sea	3
35.	seashore	3
36.	shore	3
37.	shutters	3
38.	swim	3
39.	abode	2
40.	Cape Cod	2
41.	cot	2
42.	farm	2
43.	fishing	2
44.	for two	2
45.	garden	2
46.	green	2
47.	green shutters	2
48.	hill	2
49.	inn	2
50.	live	2
51.	log	2
52.	love	2
53.	rest	2
54.	two	2

55-117. (f = 1)
beach, bed, beer, book, building, camp, chimney, clean,
comfort, comfortable, contentment, convenient, cottage for
sale, cream, dog, dwelling,
field, fireplace, forest,
grill, happy, Hasslen's,
hearth, hillside, homey, hoses,
house-lake, housing, lamp,
landscape, lane, lea, line,
little, mansion, mountain,
neat, path, peacefulness,
place, porch, pretty, rail,
river, salad, sale, scene,
secluded, serenity, shingle,
sleep, spa, stream, summer
home, take, thatched, village,
warm, waterfall, white fence,
Winchell, woman

Dark

No.	Response	Total
1.	light	829
2.	night	55
3.	room	33
4.	black	31
5.	white	9
6.	closet	5
7.	bright	4
8.	ink	3
9.	alley	2
10.	dark	2
11.	girl	2
12.	house	2
13.	love	2
14.	movie	2

15-41. (f = 1)
bark, brown, camera, coat,
cold, color, Katy, lonely,
mood, moon, murder, music,
Negro, noise, noon, obscure,
owl, photo, photography,
picture, red, sleep, stanky,

Dark (contd)

No.	Response	Total

tight, window, women, wood

Deep

No.	Response	Total
1.	shallow	318
2.	dark	131
3.	water	101
4.	sea	76
5.	high	52
6.	ocean	48
7.	soft	38
8.	hole	24
9.	low	23
10.	well	19
11.	sleep	17
12.	blue	13
13.	down	12
14.	pit	11
15.	purple	9
16.	river	9
17.	narrow	8
18.	wide	8
19.	far	7
20.	black	5
21.	light	5
22.	lake	4
23.	long	4
24.	south	4
25.	voice	4
26.	complex	3
27.	depth	3
28.	hollow	3
29.	steep	3
30.	cave	2
31.	mine	2
32.	night	2
33.	snow	2

34-71. ($\underline{f}$ = 1)
afraid, base, bed, bottom, cavern, chair, clear, crevace, cushion, deeper, dirty, drop, falling, fathom, gold, ground, height, little, loft, music, open, pool, raft, red, roots, seat, sea, slow, slumber, song, thick, tide, Tom, trouble, valley, very, under, wave

Doctor

No.	Response	Total
1.	nurse	238
2.	sick	146
3.	lawyer	133
4.	medicine	50
5.	health	45
6.	sickness	38
7.	hospital	24
8.	man(e)	23
9.	dentist	22
10.	help(s)	20
11.	ill(s)	20
12.	illness	17
13.	white	15
14.	heal	11
15.	patient	11
16.	physician	11
17.	bag	8
18.	good	8

Doctor (contd)

No.	Response	Total
19.	M.D.	8
20.	office	8
21.	stethoscope	7
22.	cure	6
23.	aid	4
24.	dad(dy)	4
25.	healing	4
26.	pill(s)	4
27.	school	4
28.	surgeon	4
29.	bill	3
30.	hurt	3
31.	kind	3
32.	bed	2
33.	Berens	2
34.	boy	2
35.	call	2
36.	death	2
37.	fix	2
38.	friend	2
39.	healer	2
40.	life	2
41.	Lund	2
42.	medical school	2
43.	operation	2
44.	pain	2
45.	study	2
46.	well	2
47.	work	2

48-119. ($\underline{f}$ = 1)
ambition, aunt, baby, Baker, chief, child, church, clean, clinic, coat, cold, college, cost, cuts, door, ether, explore, father, fee, feel, Gass, gentle, getting well, gilder, grey, grief, hat, health center, healthy, herr, home, house, husband, I, Jordan, Kildare, kit, knowledge, law, Livingstone, look, man-white coat, me, medic, medical, mend, metabolism, mom, Morsey, mother, needle, no, old, ouch, people, Ph.D., rest, Richardson, rich man, said, sawbones, scalpel, stitch, teacher, them, throat, till, visit, wall, white robe, woman, wound

Dream

No.	Response	Total
1.	sleep	453
2.	night	89
3.	nightmare	50
4.	wish	35
5.	girl	31
6.	day	25
7.	bed	22
8.	boat	17
9.	good	15
10.	think	14
11.	awake	13
12.	vision	10
13.	clouds	9
14.	daydream	8
15.	nice	8
16.	sweet	8
17.	bad	7
18.	fantasy	7
19.	thought	7
20.	wet	7
21.	Freud	6

Dream (contd)

No.	Response	Total
22.	wake	6
23.	conscious (unconscious)	5
24.	soft	5
25.	pillow	4
26.	pleasant	4
27.	story	4
28.	world	4
29.	daze	3
30.	funny	3
31.	house	3
32.	man	3
33.	NR	3
34.	picture	3
35.	rest	3
36.	time	3
37.	true	3
38.	boy	2
39.	color	2
40.	comfort	2
41.	dark	2
42.	delight	2
43.	desire	2
44.	dreamer	2
45.	happy	2
46.	hazy	2
47.	morning	2
48.	now	2
49.	real	2
50.	reality	2
51.	see	2
52.	sex	2
53.	sleeping	2
54.	wander	2

55-128. ($\underline{f}$ = 1)
about, adventure, always, analyze, asleep, auto, avid, beauty, best, Bill, Bing Crosby, blue, boy, car, child, come, concerts, confession, content, Darlene, Dick, dream, drifting, ecstasy, expression, fear, float, figure, forget, gaze, have, idea, illusia, image, imagine, intense, land, last nite, lazy, light, love, Marilyn Monroe, mediate, memory, mind, nest, night time, nope, of, peace, people, pit, plan, playing, pleasure, psych., queer, read, Roger, scream, scene, slept, slow, snakes, subconscious, symbol, tired, trip, ugly, walking, when, white, yellow, you

Eagle

No.	Response	Total
1.	bird	550
2.	fly	72
3.	scout	34
4.	wings	28
5.	nest	23
6.	America	16
7.	bald	16
8.	U.S.	14
9.	symbol	13
10.	beak	12
11.	flag	12
12.	hawk	11
13.	sky	11
14.	high	10
15.	feathers	9

Eagle (contd)

No.	Response	Total
16.	flight	9
17.	soar	9
18.	emblem	8
19.	flying	8
20.	eye	7
21.	claw	6
22.	coin	6
23.	money	6
24.	mountain	5
25.	air	4
26.	dollar	4
27.	gold	4
28.	army	3
29.	colonel	3
30.	lion	3
31.	sparrow	3
32.	animal	2
33.	birch	2
34.	country	2
35.	double	2
36.	free	2
37.	large	2
38.	liberty	2
39.	majestic	2
40.	power	2
41.	robin	2
42.	rock	2
43.	spread	2
44.	vulture	2
45.	wren	2

46-103. (f = 1)
a, banner, beaver, bend, Bernie Bierman, big, brush, bugle, buzzard, chicken, cliff, colored, craig, dive, duke, egg, erne, eyrie, falcon, field, fish, football, freedom, globe, golden, gray, head, indian, keen, might, mighty, monarch, neat, noble, north woods, owl, parrot, patriotism, pencil, point, polka, quarter, screech, sharp, sharpness, soaring, stop, strength, squadron, summit, switch, talon, tear, temple, trees, uniform, victory, $10

Earth

No.	Response	Total
1.	round	130
2.	dirt	118
3.	ground	108
4.	moon	79
5.	sky	62
6.	world	60
7.	land	36
8.	planet	35
9.	soil	33
10.	sun	28
11.	globe	26
12.	heaven	26
13.	worm	22
14.	Mars	16
15.	universe	14
16.	black	7
17.	hard	7
18.	man	7
19.	star	6
20.	air	5
21.	mud	5
22.	quake	5
23.	sphere	5

Earth (contd)

No.	Response	Total
24.	tremble	5
25.	water	5
26.	big	4
27.	good	4
28.	life	4
29.	people	4
30.	brown	3
31.	clay	3
32.	crust	3
33.	geology	3
34.	red	3
35.	sand	3
36.	sod	3
37.	stone	3
38.	tremor	3
39.	ball	2
40.	blue	2
41.	cold	2
42.	grass	2
43.	green	2
44.	hill	2
45.	hole	2
46.	home	2
47.	mover	2
48.	pearl	2
49.	plants	2
50.	plow	2
51.	sail	2
52.	salt	2
53.	sea	2
54.	space	2
55.	terra	2
56.	trouble	2
57.	tumble	2
58.	U. S.	2
59.	Venus	2
60.	war	2
61.	warm	2

62-131. (f = 1)
astronomy, atmosphere, below, body, bound, Columbus, countries, crops, crusher, dark, deep, depth, diety, dry, earth, equator, farm, field, fire, food, foundation, garden, geography, germs, God, grain, gravel, gravity, hand, hemisphere, immense, Jupiter, live, loam, low, mass, metals, mine, misery, molten, mother, mountainous, move, nice, north, ocean, Pearl Buck, physics, revolving, rich, rock, rocket, rotate, rotation, sad, science, shake, smell, soiled, solar, solar system, sound, spin, steam shovel, store, strength, wander, wet, white, work

Eating

No.	Response	Total
1.	food	390
2.	drinking	138
3.	sleeping	122
4.	hungry	45
5.	full	22
6.	starving	22
7.	fat	16
8.	good	12
9.	steak	12
10.	hunger	11
11.	mouth	11
12.	drink	10

Eating (contd)

No.	Response	Total
13.	table	10
14.	chewing	9
15.	dinner	9
16.	sleep	9
17.	fork	8
18.	fasting	7
19.	lunch	7
20.	apple	6
21.	habit(s)	6
22.	biting	5
23.	meat	5
24.	sick	5
25.	stomach	5
26.	candy	4
27.	spoon	4
28.	bite	3
29.	digesting	3
30.	eat	3
31.	fast	3
32.	meal(s)	3
33.	bread	2
34.	burp	2
35.	carrot(s)	2
36.	chew	2
37.	dishes	2
38.	fun	2
39.	gorging	2
40.	place	2
41.	smoking	2
42.	starve	2
43.	supper	2
44.	taste	2
45.	writing	2

46-103. (f = 1)
appetite, ate, banana, breathing, brook, cheese, chicken, consuming, dessert, dieting, dining, eated, egg, enjoy, fill, fish, giants, gourmand, grapes, gulping, ham, hand, happy, head, heartily, hearty, horse, ice cream, in, inn, Le Roy, lettuce, life, lion, living, looking, malt, man, masticating, mouthful, much, noon, not, people, pig, plate, potato, restaurant, resting, satisfy, sitting, soup, swallow, swallowing, teeth, through, turkey, vomit

Foot

No.	Response	Total
1.	shoe(s)	232
2.	hand	198
3.	toe(s)	191
4.	leg	118
5.	soldier	26
6.	ball	23
7.	feet	23
8.	walk	14
9.	ankle	13
10.	arm	10
11.	sore	9
12.	inch(es)	8
13.	boot	7
14.	yard	6
15.	mouth	5
16.	sock(s)	5
17.	head	4
18.	hurt	4
19.	12 inches	4

Foot (contd)

No.	Response	Total
20.	body	3
21.	finger(s)	3
22.	kick	3
23.	sleep	3
24.	slipper	3
25.	step	3
26.	ache	2
27.	bed	2
28.	big	2
29.	note	2
30.	pad	2
31.	ped	2
32.	pound	2
33.	ruler	2
34.	small	2
35.	stool	2
36.	walking	2
37.	wear	2

38-100. (f = 1)
afoot, appendage, asleep,
athlete, band, bath, below,
bone, break, broke, cement,
club, cold, distance, doctor,
dog, end, essential, football,
fly, frozen, galosh, ground,
hander, hang, hat, horseback,
knee, large, length, limb,
lye soap, mark, measure,
movement, mule, nail, operation,
pedal, person, physics, powder,
print, rabbit, rat, rest,
shoulder, sidewalk, ski boots,
skin, slow, smell, snow, sole,
spider, stand, stocking, stub,
traveler, ungainly, wall,
wash, web

Fruit

No.	Response	Total
1.	apple	378
2.	vegetable	114
3.	orange	94
4.	fly	62
5.	berry	46
6.	eat	43
7.	pear	31
8.	banana	27
9.	cake	23
10.	cherry	15
11.	food	15
12.	juice	14
13.	tree	13
14.	salad	11
15.	sweet	8
16.	candy	6
17.	good	6
18.	bowl	5
19.	flower	5
20.	grapefruit	5
21.	grapes	5
22.	peach	5
23.	seed	5
24.	nut	4
25.	basket	3
26.	fairy	3
27.	queer	3
28.	stand	3
29.	strawberry	3
30.	bitter	2
31.	boot	2
32.	citrus	2
33.	cup	2
34.	eating	2

Fruit (contd)

No.	Response	Total
35.	jello	2
36.	lemon	2
37.	summer	2
38.	taste	2
39.	yellow	2

40-70. (f = 1)
animal, beverage, blossom, boy,
child, cocktail, dark, Harry,
healthful, healthy, house, meat,
monkey, pickle, pleasant, Ralph,
raspberry, ripe, roast, route,
slurp, smell, sour, squishy,
strange, tail, tangerine,
tomato, vine, walnut, weed

Girl

No.	Response	Total
1.	boy	704
2.	woman	49
3.	friend	18
4.	young	17
5.	dress	14
6.	pretty	13
7.	hair	11
8.	nice	11
9.	man	10
10.	beautiful	7
11.	cute	6
12.	date	6
13.	school	6
14.	scout	6
15.	female	5
16.	good	4
17.	lady	4
18.	love	4
19.	sex	4
20.	girl	3
21.	hat	3
22.	student	3
23.	bed	2
24.	car	2
25.	child	2
26.	curls	2
27.	dance	2
28.	fine	2
29.	guide	2
30.	high school	2
31.	house	2
32.	Joan	2
33.	laugh	2
34.	Mary	2
35.	me	2
36.	party	2
37.	pigtails	2
38.	she	2
39.	Shirley	2

40-103. (f = 1)
age, Ardis, baby, Barb, beauty,
Beverly, blonde, bobby sox,
body, braids, broad, Christmas,
clothes, college, companion,
cousin, daughter, dog, doll,
fat, fellow, gay, girlfriend,
glamor, horse, kid, large,
legs, lipstick, little, look,
lovely, Marilyn, mother, my
girl, myself, Nancy, niece,
piano, play, player, question
mark, red, scarf, Sharon,
sharp, sister, skirt, smile,
soft, spy, Sue, Susie, sweater,
sweet, sweetheart, sweetness,

Girl (contd)

No.	Response	Total

tall, touch, virgin, wife,
wow, yeah, youth

Green

No.	Response	Total
1.	grass	262
2.	red	216
3.	blue	122
4.	yellow	66
5.	color	53
6.	go	23
7.	light	21
8.	white	20
9.	sea	16
10.	black	14
11.	tree(s)	12
12.	plant(s)	10
13.	eyes	6
14.	grey	6
15.	water	6
16.	Irish	5
17.	leaf(ves)	5
18.	brown	4
19.	dark	4
20.	giant	4
21.	Ireland	4
22.	purple	4
23.	shirt	4
24.	valley	4
25.	cloth	3
26.	cool	3
27.	emerald(s)	3
28.	envy	3
29.	forest	3
30.	orange	3
31.	peas	3
32.	pepper	3
33.	salad	3
34.	cabbage	2
35.	dress	2
36.	felt	2
37.	field	2
38.	gold	2
39.	ground	2
40.	lake	2
41.	lawn	2
42.	ocean	2
43.	pastures	2
44.	shoe(s)	2
45.	sick	2
46.	sleeve(s)	2
47.	sweater	2

48-105. (f = 1)
A.F.L., bag, beans, book,
bright, chair, chartreuse,
cheese, clay, cost, comfort
death, earth, flower, food,
fresh, golf, green, habits,
hair, hay, house, jade,
jealousy, jelly, kelly, land,
lettuce, lynne, man, meadow,
milk, money, moss, peace,
pink, plush, quiet, read,
(red-yellow), restful, river,
robe, shimmer, signal, sky,
snake, soft, spinach, spring,
stoplight, stuff, suit, ten,
traffic, vegetable, wave,
wear

Hammer

No.	Response	Total
1.	nail(s)	537
2.	saw	83
3.	hit	57
4.	pound	52
5.	head	50
6.	tongs	38
7.	tool(s)	27
8.	hard	21
9.	sickle	14
10.	anvil	11
11.	hurt	8
12.	carpenter	6
13.	noise	6
14.	work	6
15.	thumb	5
16.	iron	4
17.	Russia	4
18.	thong	4
19.	wood	4
20.	chisel	3
21.	pliers	3
22.	arm	2
23.	axe	2
24.	build	2
25.	building	2
26.	claw	2
27.	forge	2
28.	handle	2
29.	heavy	2
30.	loud	2
31.	ouch	2
32.	tack	2

33-75. (f = 1)
able, axle, barb, beat, bench,
blow, blunt, board, boy,
break, can, cycle, Don, dough,
father, finger, friend, hawk,
house, housework, implement,
knock, melt, metal, Mike,
packing, pain, prong, repair,
shovel, sledge, sock, sound,
steel, strike, strong, struck,
sword, tackle, toe, thread,
throw, whistle

Hand

No.	Response	Total
1.	foot(ee)	255
2.	finger(s)	237
3.	arm	131
4.	glove	53
5.	shake	38
6.	ring	36
7.	mouth	27
8.	soft	23
9.	face	15
10.	nail	12
11.	leg	10
12.	hold	8
13.	wrist	7
14.	ball	6
15.	hard	6
16.	heart	6
17.	palm	6
18.	touch	6
19.	food	5
20.	lotion	5
21.	skin	5
22.	white	5
23.	write	5
24.	body	4
25.	head	4
26.	cold	3

Hand (contd)

No.	Response	Total
27.	grasp	3
28.	shoe	3
29.	short	3
30.	woman	3
31.	book	2
32.	chapped	2
33.	eye	2
34.	man	2
35.	right	2
36.	smooth	2
37.	strong	2
38.	toe	2
39.	work	2

40-99. (f = 1)
action, appearance, art, back,
bed, big, Bill, callous, chin,
cream, cuff, dexterity, digit,
dirt, down, feel, find, finger-
nail, fist, form, friend, girl,
give, hand, handcream, heel,
house, human, hurt, ink, job,
large, left, limb, Lois, long,
made, maiden, make, mark, me,
mitten, money, nice, paw, piano,
reach, revealing, shaking, some,
stool, table, teeth, thumb,
towel, warm, watch, welcome, wet,
writing

Hard

No.	Response	Total
1.	soft	674
2.	rock	48
3.	easy	24
4.	egg	23
5.	boiled	19
6.	work	16
7.	head	13
8.	smooth	12
9.	stone	12
10.	steel	11
11.	wood	10
12.	nail	9
13.	ice	7
14.	table	7
15.	tough	7
16.	floor	6
17.	ground	6
18.	difficult	5
19.	metal	5
20.	bed	3
21.	brittle	3
22.	candy	3
23.	diamond	3
24.	light	3
25.	man	3
26.	rough	3
27.	solid	3
28.	surface	3
29.	tack	3
30.	ball	2
31.	board	2
32.	hand	2
33.	iron	2
34.	knock	2
35.	luck	2
36.	pencil	2
37.	shell	2
38.	top	2

39-84. (f = 1)
adamant, angry, apple, auto,
block, box, bread, breaks,
brick, cash, cement, cold,

Hard (contd)

compact, desk, econ., effort,
feel, firm, get, glass, hammer,
headed, hit, hunt, hurt, knife,
lard, lead, leather, liquor,
lumpy, money, peanuts, point,
pool ball, rubber, salt,
sauce, secure, set, school,
shiny, sidewalk, stiff, touch,
way

Head

No.	Response	Total
1.	hair	129
2.	foot	126
3.	shoulders	68
4.	neck	58
5.	body	56
6.	hat	34
7.	eyes	33
8.	face	31
9.	top	29
10.	hands	28
11.	ache	23
12.	brain	23
13.	heart	22
14.	toe	20
15.	arms	19
16.	tail	17
17.	cabbage	16
18.	think	16
19.	man	15
20.	cap	14
21.	hard	12
22.	lettuce	11
23.	toilet	11
24.	person	10
25.	high	8
26.	mind	7
27.	round	7
28.	strong	7
29.	cold	5
30.	nose	5
31.	beer	4
32.	can	4
33.	cheese	4
34.	scarf	4
35.	start	4
36.	big	3
37.	ear	3
38.	hot	3
39.	leader	3
40.	mouth	3
41.	soft	3
42.	stone	3
43.	waiter	3
44.	above	2
45	anatomy	2
46.	bald	2
47.	bed	2
48.	bolt	2
49.	brown	2
50	chief	2
51.	class	2
52	first	2
53.	food	2
54.	haircut	2
55.	heels	2
56	John	2
57.	leader	2
58.	over	2
59.	people	2
60.	red	2
61.	table	2

Head (contd)

No.	Response	Total
62.	thought	2

63-125. (f = 1)
back, band, bathroom, before,
behind, bottom, Chinese, coach,
cover, cranium, curly, dark,
dean, dirty, dome, dress, falit,
fall, fat, father, features,
fore, forehead, glasses, globe,
glove, guillotine, halt,
handsome, horse, house, hunter,
hurts, hydraulics, intelligence,
John the Baptist, lavatory,
less, long, looks, monument,
memory, move, navy, on, organ,
pate, pointed, Ruth, Sally,
scripture, shirt, shoe, sick,
skull, small, storm, tall,
thick, thinker, torso, upper,
water

Health

No.	Response	Total
1.	sickness	250
2.	sick	160
3.	good	80
4.	happiness	75
5.	wealth	42
6.	happy	36
7.	well	34
8.	ill	33
9.	illness	29
10.	doctor	27
11.	service	19
12.	strong	14
13.	food	12
14.	hospital	11
15.	disease	10
16.	body	7
17.	vigor	5
18.	center	4
19.	pain	4
20.	robust	4
21.	athlete	3
22.	boy	3
23.	clinic	3
24.	comfort	3
25.	energy	3
26.	fine	3
27.	fun	3
28.	life	3
29.	red	3
30.	book	2
31.	building	2
32.	class	2
33.	clean	2
34.	condition	2
35.	department	2
36.	eat	2
37.	healthy	2
38.	insurance	2
39.	light	2
40.	medicine	2
41.	milk	2
42.	physical	2
43.	pills	2
44.	play	2
45.	public	2
46.	safety	2
47.	school	2
48.	sports	2
49.	strength	2
50.	teeth	2
51.	unhealthy	2

Health (contd)

No.	Response	Total
52.	vitamins	2
53.	well being	2

54-126. (f = 1)
able, accidental, active,
anxious, apples, aspirin, blood,
Boy Scout, bureau, can I walk,
certificate, death, drink,
eager, enjoyment, exercise, feel,
feel good, feeling, first aid,
fit, form, 4-H, gift, girl,
good care, good food, good
natured, green, harmony, heart,
home, hope, humor, hygiene, joy,
lively, love, man, me, mother,
myself, nurse, nutrition, I-A,
people, person, personal, poor,
public health, PH-3, purity,
radiance, resort, rosy, ruddy,
salud, smallpox, smile, son,
standard, state, swim,
thermometer, trouble, us, warn,
weight lifting, welfare, window,
Y.M.C.A., young, youth

Heavy

No.	Response	Total
1.	light	583
2.	load	65
3.	hard	47
4.	weight	35
5.	lead	19
6.	soft	17
7.	big	12
8.	lift	10
9.	work	10
10.	fat	9
11.	iron	9
12.	sleep	9
13.	burden	7
14.	tired	7
15.	books	6
16.	coat	6
17.	large	6
18.	man	6
19.	stone	5
20.	carry	4
21.	water	4
22.	bag	3
23.	dark	3
24.	foot	3
25.	girl	3
26.	hang(s)	3
27.	hearted	3
28.	slow	3
29.	boot	2
30.	box(es)	2
31.	brick(s)	2
32.	difficult	2
33.	eyelids	2
34.	hand	2
35.	loud	2
36.	object	2
37.	sack	2
38.	sins	2
39.	smoke	2
40.	snow	2
41.	ton	2
42.	trunk	2

43-121. (f = 1)
ache, air, awkward, back, back-
ache, bad, blanket, Bob Slater,
bread, breath, cardboard,
carrying, casting, cement, chair,

Heavy (contd)

cloth, clothes, cloud, cow,
cumbersome, deep, dense, drink,
drinker, drop, eater, effort,
elephant, fatigue, food, foot-
steps, gravey, gut, hurt, lid,
liquor, logs, long, lot, low,
lug, mass, mg, night, obese,
odor, on, oppressive, package,
pen, piano, plump, ponderous,
push, rock, round, rule, set,
sharp, ship, shoes, shotput,
sleep, smell, sound, square,
start, stout, strain, strength,
sugar, sunlight, thick, thug,
tog, truck, ugh, wood, wrestler

High

No.	Response	Total
1.	low	675
2.	school	49
3.	mountain	32
4.	up	18
5.	chair	17
6.	tall	17
7.	tower	13
8.	jump	11
9.	ladder	10
10.	building	8
11.	noon	8
12.	above	7
13.	cliff	7
14.	sky	6
15.	drunk	5
16.	heels	5
17.	hill	5
18.	top	4
19.	wide	4
20.	bridge	3
21.	clouds	3
22.	down	3
23.	fence	3
24.	height	3
25.	horse	3
26.	long	3
27.	moon	3
28.	place	3
29.	shoes	3
30.	steep	3
31.	wire	3
32.	airplane	2
33.	ceiling	2
34.	dizzy	2
35.	dry	2
36.	fall	2
37.	liquor	2
38.	perch	2
39.	plane	2
40.	short	2
41.	wall	2
42.	way	2
43.	wind	2

44-90. (f = 1)
ambitious, ball, bar, beer,
beyond, big, board, broad,
climb, deep, dive, diving,
diving board, fly, Foshay
Tower, fun, giant, high chair,
huge, kite, lights, lofty,
mark, mighty, music, note,
peak, ride, river, room, round,
scaffold, score, Scotland,
sick, sight, small, space,
steeple, stepladder, strong,

High (contd)

No.	Response	Total

table, tall building, toll, water, white, window washer

House

No.	Response	Total
1.	home	247
2.	door	93
3.	garage	47
4.	barn	40
5.	roof	33
6.	white	33
7.	windows	23
8.	yard	23
9.	wood	20
10.	room	19
11.	car	17
12.	live	16
13.	brick	15
14.	chair(s)	14
15.	mouse	14
16.	big	13
17.	building	13
18.	family	13
19.	shack	13
20.	top	12
21.	people	11
22.	chimney	10
23.	red	10
24.	build	9
25.	dark	9
26.	warm	8
27.	lawn	7
28.	light	7
29.	black	6
30.	boat	6
31.	cottage	6
32.	dog	6
33.	hut	6
34.	man	6
35.	cabin	5
36.	farm	5
37.	furniture	5
38.	street	5
39.	comfort	4
40.	garden	4
41.	paint	4
42.	porch	4
43.	table	4
44.	children	3
45.	dwelling	3
46.	hotel	3
47.	life	3
48.	lot	3
49.	mother	3
50.	square	3
51.	tree	3
52.	apartment	2
53.	bed	2
54.	castle	2
55.	clean	2
56.	coat	2
57.	fence	2
58.	gable	2
59.	grass	2
60.	green	2
61.	hold	2
62.	key	2
63.	kitchen	2
64.	living	2
65.	mansion	2
66.	me	2
67.	rent	2
68.	road	2

House (contd)

No.	Response	Total
69.	shed	2
70.	sleep	2
71.	small	2
72.	tent	2
73.	warmth	2
74.	wife	2
75.	work	2

76-142. (f = 1)
abode, alley, antenna, back, baker, birch, blinding, block, blue, breaker, bungalow, burned, cat, cleaner, color, Comstock, construction, cord, cozy, den, detective, Don, doctor, fly, furnace, habitat, hamburgers, haunted, haven, heaven, hell, horse, jack, lake, land, large, louse, maid, manor, money, moving, new, out, park, party, payments, pillars, pink, prostitution, ranch, representative, rest, shade, shelter, shutter, sidewalk, still, stone, swift, tall, tiling, trailer, well, wide, women, worm, yellow

Hungry

No.	Response	Total
1.	food	362
2.	eat	174
3.	thirsty	69
4.	full	57
5.	starved	29
6.	stomach	29
7.	tired	25
8.	dog	21
9.	pain	11
10.	man	10
11.	eating	8
12.	me	8
13.	beast	6
14.	boy	6
15.	cold	6
16.	people	6
17.	starving	6
18.	appetite	5
19.	dinner	5
20.	horse	5
21.	lunch	5
22.	animal	4
23.	bread	4
24.	empty	4
25.	feed	4
26.	now	4
27.	pangs	4
28.	person	4
29.	sleepy	4
30.	steak	4
31.	yes	4
32.	cat	3
33.	country	3
34.	famished	3
35.	fast	3
36.	hungry	3
37.	mouth	3
38.	sad	3
39.	satisfied	3
40.	starve	3
41.	ache	2
42.	angry	2
43.	bear	2
44.	Europe	2
45.	fed	2

Hungry (contd)

No.	Response	Total
46.	foot	2
47.	Greece	2
48.	satiated	2
49.	sick	2
50.	turkey	2

51-116. (f = 1)
all, ate, avid, baby, bad, bed, beef, bird, child, China, content, court, desire, discomfort, DP, exile, eyes, feast, feeling, 5,000, frustration, goat, graveling, ingot, green, ham, hamburger, hash, heart, hurt, Jack, knowing, Koreans, like, lips, mad, meal time, meat, misery, need, never, not now, old, orphan, pigs, peasants, pie, priest, rat, ravenous, real, sails, searching, sister, state, stimulus, strictly, swallow, table, taste, thin, tramps, unhappiness, unpleasant, want, well-fed, wolf

Joy

No.	Response	Total
1.	happy	209
2.	sorrow	202
3.	happiness	135
4.	grief	33
5.	sad	33
6.	sadness	33
7.	Christmas	25
8.	glad	23
9.	soap	21
10.	love	14
11.	fun	13
12.	world	13
13.	girl	12
14.	hate	11
15.	gladness	10
16.	anger	9
17.	good	9
18.	smile	9
19.	laugh	8
20.	elation	7
21.	hope	7
22.	laughter	7
23.	boy	6
24.	fear	5
25.	delight	4
26.	health	4
27.	peace	4
28.	tears	4
29.	to	4
30.	bliss	3
31.	gay	3
32.	mirth	3
33.	relief	3
34.	bells	2
35.	child(ren)	2
36.	cry	2
37.	despair	2
38.	dishes	2
39.	dog	2
40.	enjoy	2
41.	excitement	2
42.	exuberance	2
43.	gaiety	2
44.	help	2
45.	pleasure	2
46.	shout	2

Joy (contd)

No.	Response	Total
47.	wash	2
48.	wonderful	2

49-131. (f = 1)
alacrity, Arnold, bad, bed, behold, benefit, birth, bless, bread, bright, Buggsy, canon, cheer, Christ, crying, dance, depression, divine, dream, eating, emotion, fight, freedom, fright, gal, glee, great, hardship, hat, heaven, holiday, home, hurt, hymn, Joyce, jump, know, leap, life, light, made, man, Marlys, Mary, money, mourn, music, nature, navy, news, New Year's, nice, night, noel, none, packard, pain, party, perfume, pride, Proctor & Gamble, radiance, rage, rapture, rejoice, reminisce, restraint, ride, Roger, room, Schiller, school, sister, sour, sweet, swell, thrill, tullock, unhappy, vacation, washing, whoopee, woman

Justice

No.	Response	Total
1.	peace	250
2.	law	182
3.	courts	163
4.	judge(s)	102
5.	injustice	38
6.	right	33
7.	good	12
8.	liberty	12
9.	government	9
10.	jury	9
11.	truth	9
12.	blind	8
13.	fair	8
14.	man	7
15.	supreme	7
16.	crime	5
17.	department	5
18.	of-the-peace	5
19.	trial	5
20.	equality	4
21.	evil	4
22.	freedom	4
23.	police	4
24.	scale(s)	4
25.	black	3
26.	cops	3
27.	duty	3
28.	Holmes	3
29.	honor	3
30.	mercy	3
31.	none	3
32.	statue	3
33.	America	2
34.	balance	2
35.	democracy	2
36.	equal	2
37.	fairness	2
38.	honesty	2
39.	lack	2
40.	Plato	2
41.	power	2
42.	punishment	2
43.	righteous	2
44.	robe(s)	2
45.	Supreme Court	2

Justice (contd)

No.	Response	Total
46.	triumphs	2
47.	unfair	2

48-112. (f = 1)
Aristotle, boy, chief, choo choo, city, clear, command, criminal, cruelty, day, deceit, desire, die, done, due, essential, F.B.I., fear, football, fruit, Galsworthy, goodness, grace, graft, grape, guilty, hope, illegal, impartial, irony, jail, Jean Valjean, judiciary, just, land, legislation, legislative, light, love, maljustice, marriage, marshall, now, of, office, order, peach, person, preacher, prevails, prison, rule, slow, stern, suspect, to be done, true, uncle, unjust, unknown, U.S., war, woman, word, worthy

King

No.	Response	Total
1.	queen	751
2.	England	20
3.	crown	18
4.	pin	13
5.	George	11
6.	ruler	10
7.	Kong	9
8.	man	9
9.	throne	9
10.	cards	6
11.	Tut	6
12.	chess	5
13.	rule	5
14.	subjects	5
15.	county	4
16.	Edward	4
17.	Henry(IV, VIII)	4
18.	monarch	4
19.	power	4
20.	royal	4
21.	Solomon	4
22.	John	3
23.	kingdom	3
24.	leader	3
25.	prince	3
26.	Siam	3
27.	Cole	2
28.	Farouk	2
29.	Jack	2
30.	James	2
31.	lion	2
32.	reign	2
33.	royalty	2
34.	story	2
35.	top	2
36.	I	2

37-101. (f = 1)
Ace, Anna, Anthony, Arabia, Arthur, beast, blue, checkers, checkmate, cheese, chief, clubs, cock, cotton, court, crab, dead, despotism, dog, duke, emperor, empire, feudal, fish, friend, gold, gout, head, hearts, Herod, high, highway, jewels, Julius, king, kingly, knight, land, lard, large, Lear, Leo, lord, Louis, Louis XIV, men, Midas, money, mountain king, no-good, peasant, pomp, president,

King (contd)

No.	Response	Total

purple, regal, rex, rich, ring, robe, sceptre, serve, shit, size, sovereign, street

Lamp

No.	Response	Total
1.	light	633
2.	shade	125
3.	table	62
4.	bulb	35
5.	post	25
6.	black	12
7.	floor	8
8.	cord	7
9.	desk	7
10.	bright	5
11.	chair	5
12.	lighter	5
13.	read	5
14.	on	4
15.	bed	3
16.	burn	3
17.	dark	3
18.	stand	3
19.	Aladdin	2
20.	base	2
21.	chimney	2
22.	glow	2
23.	lamp	2
24.	oil	2
25.	see	2
26.	stem	2
27.	study	2

28-66. (f = 1)
animal, boy, broken, card, chop, cottage, door, electric, electricity, filiment, glame, globe, house, kerosene, lathe, limp, living, room, metal, modern, odd, port, poster, power, pretty, pump, rug, sheep, shelf, stool, stove, sun, tight, ugly, vase, warm, white, wick, window, worm

Light

No.	Response	Total
1.	dark	647
2.	lamp	78
3.	bright	30
4.	sun	25
5.	bulb	23
6.	day	16
7.	heavy	16
8.	house	12
9.	see	11
10.	window	10
11.	black	5
12.	candle	5
13.	darkness	5
14.	heat	5
15.	soft	5
16.	switch	5
17.	white	5
18.	night	4
19.	brightness	3
20.	color	3
21.	heaven	3

Light (contd)

No.	Response	Total
22.	red	3
23.	shade(s)	3
24.	weight	3
25.	yellow	3
26.	blue	2
27.	clear	2
28.	electric	2
29.	green	2
30.	hair	2
31.	health	2
32.	match	2
33.	morning	2
34.	shadow	2
35.	street	2

36-91. ($f = 1$)
air, apple, awaken, beach, beam,
boat, brown, ceiling, cheery,
club, creamy, dark or heavy,
daytime, desert, dirt, earth,
easy, Edison, electric bulb,
electricity, eyes, fair,
feather, flame, glass, glow,
hand, hard, head, high, hurts
eyes, lamb, lift, lightning,
look, love, luminous, object,
out, path, post, read, shine,
sky, snow, sound, spot, star,
study, sunshine, time, truth,
warm, waves, world, year

Lion

No.	Response	Total
1.	tiger	261
2.	animal	148
3.	roar	69
4.	cat	31
5.	cub	30
6.	den	28
7.	jungle	27
8.	zoo	27
9.	cage	19
10.	tamer	19
11.	mouse	16
12.	bear	15
13.	lamb	15
14.	hearted	12
15.	mane	11
16.	Africa	9
17.	dog	9
18.	Leo	9
19.	fear	8
20.	growl	8
21.	head	8
22.	strong	8
23.	circus	7
24.	hunter	7
25.	king	7
26.	lioness	7
27.	teeth	7
28.	big	6
29.	Daniel	6
30.	fierce	6
31.	beast	5
32.	eat	5
33.	fur	5
34.	hunt	5
35.	man	5
36.	Androcles	4
37.	ferocious	4
38.	hair	4
39.	jaw	4
40.	MGM	4
41.	mouth	4

Lion (contd)

No.	Response	Total
42.	yellow	4
43.	horse	3
44.	kill	3
45.	leopard	3
46.	movies	3
47.	paw	3
48.	Richard	3
49.	claws	2
50.	cruel	2
51.	dangerous	2
52.	England	2
53.	furious	2
54.	hear	2
55.	kitten	2
56.	lady	2
57.	land	2
58.	mountain	2
59.	sea	2
60.	share	2
61.	street	2
62.	strength	2
63.	tail	2

64-126. ($f = 1$)
agile, angry, ate, bad, brave,
Britain, brown, chain, chase,
creep, cries, cut, desert,
devour, down, eating, Fagen,
fight, fox, giraffe, girl, gold,
Goliath, Greek, growling, heart,
house, huge, hunger, hungry, is
busy, joy, lair, mad, meat,
monkey, noise, of, pen, point,
powerful, pretty, rabbit, rock,
run, Sampson, scared, shepherd,
shield, show, stalk, story,
tawny, tender, terrible, throne,
trainer, tree, wild, wolf,
woods, ZAE, zebra

Long

No.	Response	Total
1.	short	758
2.	fellow	11
3.	narrow	10
4.	John	9
5.	time	9
6.	far	8
7.	hair	8
8.	island	7
9.	road	7
10.	thin	7
11.	underwear	6
12.	distance	5
13.	leg(s)	5
14.	line	5
15.	low	5
16.	rope	5
17.	ruler	5
18.	tall	5
19.	beach	4
20.	run	4
21.	arm	3
22.	knife	3
23.	lake	3
24.	length	3
25.	want	3
26.	wide	3
27.	big	2
28.	board	2
29.	endless	2
30.	hard	2
31.	horizontal	2
32.	lean	2

Long (contd)

No.	Response	Total
33.	life	2
34.	pants	2
35.	river	2
36.	sleeve	2
37.	slim	2
38.	stick	2
39.	stockings	2
40.	story	2
41.	string	2

42-113. ($f = 1$)
angleworm, around, awaited,
barrel, bon, class, day, dog,
don, down, dress, feet,
fingers, for, gone, gun,
height, hands, head, hollow,
hood, horn, Huey, jeole, large,
legged, lengthy, Louie, many,
meter, much, nose, painful,
past, path, pencil, pier, pole,
post, psych., ribbon, rifle,
rod, rog, school, shot,
silence, snake, song, spaghetti, stand, steel, stilt,
straight, straws, stream,
stretch, tail, tedious, train,
trip, true, vacation, wall,
wait, walk, walking, way, winding, winter, wire, yard-stick

Loud

No.	Response	Total
1.	soft	541
2.	noise	210
3.	quiet	68
4.	noisy	27
5.	sound	19
6.	mouth(ed)	15
7.	bang	9
8.	silent	6
9.	sharp	5
10.	shout	5
11.	blast	3
12.	crash	3
13.	long	3
14.	music	3
15.	clear	2
16.	cry	2
17.	deafening	2
18.	drum	2
19.	gun	2
20.	harsh	2
21.	horn	2
22.	hurt	2
23.	low	2
24.	speaker	2
25.	strong	2
26.	thunder	2
27.	voice	2
28.	yell	2

29-90. ($f = 1$)
annoying, bag, band, base,
bear, bell, big, boisterous,
boob, boone, bothersome, call,
car, cheerleading, child,
clang, clap, coarse, crazy,
deafen, decibel, din, disturbance, door, ear, faint, fair,
fear, fight, hammering, hard,
heard, heavy, horrid, kids,
louder, machinery, math, me,
no, nuisance, Phyliss, rachet,
radio, recoil, report, salt,
sox, scream, short, shot,

Loud (contd)

No.	Response	Total

shrill, song, still, talk,
talking, thief, tie, train,
waves, whistle, woman

Man

No.	Response	Total
1.	woman(e)	767
2.	boy	65
3.	girl	31
4.	dog	18
5.	lady	17
6.	mouse	10
7.	animal	5
8.	male	5
9.	men	5
10.	father	4
11.	strong	4
12.	friend	3
13.	human	3
14.	pants	3
15.	tall	3
16.	wife	3
17.	beard	2
18.	child	2
19.	leg(s)	2
20.	me	2
21.	person	2
22.	sex	2
23.	sports	2
24.	suit	2

25-70. (f = 1)
anthropology, bad, beast,
being, big, body, boxer, Bruce,
build, cow, dark, date, earth,
Ed, farm, fellow, figure, God,
hair, hand, handsome, hat, hit,
home, Joe, large, lean, life,
made, money, moon, muscle,
normal, older, panes, Pat,
poor, race, Rodney, Roger,
Roosevelt, sheep, shirt,
strength, superman, tough

Memory

No.	Response	Total
1.	mind	119
2.	remember	99
3.	forget	80
4.	think	58
5.	thought(s)	41
6.	psychology	35
7.	recall	32
8.	good	25
9.	dream	22
10.	school	20
11.	learn(ed)	19
12.	learning	18
13.	test	18
14.	image	16
15.	past	16
16.	poor	16
17.	bad	15
18.	brain	15
19.	retention	15
20.	sleep	14
21.	lane	13
22.	thinking	13
23.	forgetting	11

Memory (contd)

No.	Response	Total
24.	study	10
25.	book(s)	9
26.	forgetfulness	9
27.	work	8
28.	loss	7
29.	blank	6
30.	short	6
31.	intelligence	5
32.	lost	5
33.	verse	5
34.	word(s)	5
35.	happy	4
36.	know	4
37.	long	4
38.	pleasant	4
39.	read	4
40.	retain	4
41.	youth	4
42.	amnesia	3
43.	forget	3
44.	idea	3
45.	lapse	3
46.	love	3
47.	memorize	3
48.	none	3
49.	pleasure	3
50.	poem	3
51.	quiz	3
52.	remind	3
53.	reminiscing	3
54.	sad	3
55.	span	3
56.	wish	3
57.	yesterday	3
58.	childhood	2
59.	elephant	2
60.	gone	2
61.	imagination	2
62.	language	2
63.	life	2
64.	memory	2
65.	nothing	2
66.	objects	2
67.	poetry	2
68.	remembering	2
69.	sharp	2
70.	stimulus	2
71.	time	2
72.	vision	2

73-160. (f = 1)
absent minded, age, alert,
armory, behind, black, car,
church, class, dates, daydream,
deep, drudgery, east, education,
events, experience, fair, false,
father, fly paper, forgotten,
friends, girl, grandmother,
hard, head, hear, heart, help,
home, hotel, hunger, I.Q., Joe,
joke, knowledge, lacking, lake,
land, lasting, learning, lesson,
listen, man, mist, mom, no good,
nostalgia, numbers, of, O.K.,
paper, photographic, plan,
problems, recalling, recognition,
recognize, recollect, remem-
brance, response, retaining,
retentive, see, seem, serve,
ship, sins, songs, story, strong,
sweet, system, temporal lobe,
tester, text, things, traces,
train, try, understanding, urge,
use, verbal, vivid, wow, yes

Moon

No.	Response	Total
1.	stars	205
2.	sun	168
3.	night	87
4.	light	64
5.	shine(s)	50
6.	sky	43
7.	earth	33
8.	yellow	26
9.	beam(s)	18
10.	bright	18
11.	June	18
12.	round	17
13.	blue	15
14.	white	13
15.	glow	12
16.	love	12
17.	planet	10
18.	spoon	9
19.	cheese	8
20.	full	6
21.	high	6
22.	rocket	6
23.	romance	6
24.	big	5
25.	crescent	5
26.	dark	5
27.	face	5
28.	man(e)	5
29.	satellite	5
30.	beautiful	4
31.	cold	4
32.	maid	4
33.	pretty	4
34.	rise	4
35.	silver	4
36.	Mars	3
37.	noon	3
38.	universe	3
39.	astronomy	2
40.	crater	2
41.	distance	2
42.	goon	2
43.	half	2
44.	heaven	2
45.	lake	2
46.	lunatic	2
47.	nice	2
48.	Over Miami	2
49.	Saturn	2
50.	shape	2
51.	soft	2
52.	water	2

53-114. (f = 1)
away, beauty, body, box, Buck
Rogers, car, circle, clear,
clouds, cool, date, down,
dream, eat, environment, evening, exciting, face, far,
fascinating, flight, fly, girl,
glass, God, gold, green, green
cheese, honey, kiss, large,
look, loon, luna, moon, morning, necking, new, niad, nigh,
night, pale, parking, pole,
reflection, saucer, science,
sixpence, smooch, solar system,
solunar, space, stroke, study,
summer, swoon, telescope, tide,
travel, trip, tune, 12

Mountain

No.	Response	Total
1.	hill(s)	266
2.	high	127
3.	snow	65
4.	valley	64
5.	climb	46
6.	top	43
7.	molehill	24
8.	peak(s)	24
9.	climbing	22
10.	man	22
11.	plain	20
12.	goat	18
13.	stream	13
14.	rock(s)	11
15.	lake	10
16.	big	9
17.	climber	9
18.	range	9
19.	tree(s)	9
20.	height	8
21.	horse	7
22.	river	7
23.	steep	7
24.	Everest	6
25.	Rocky(ies)	6
26.	ski	6
27.	lion	5
28.	plateau	5
29.	Alps	4
30.	Colorado	4
31.	west	4
32.	Yellowstone	4
33.	air	3
34.	cave	3
35.	cliff	3
36.	glacier	3
37.	green	3
38.	large	3
39.	magic	3
40.	road	3
41.	sky	3
42.	trip	3
43.	blue	2
44.	cloud(s)	2
45.	crag(s)	2
46.	crevice	2
47.	Denver	2
48.	fall	2
49.	home	2
50.	Kilimanjaro	2
51.	land	2
52.	male	2
53.	mound	2
54.	point	2
55.	prairie	2
56.	scenery	2
57.	sheep	2
58.	stone	2
59.	tall	2
60.	water	2

61-116. (f = 1)
barrier, base, basement, Berge, bluff, canyon, chain, cold, desert, dirt, face, faith, flat, foot, glory, Grand Teton, grass, ground, grown, heap, Himalayas, hole, house, huge, hunt, ice, Idaho, incline, jump, Jungfrau, king, knoll, large hill, Montana, moon, Moses, Mt. Ranier, mule, path, Penna., picture, Pike's Peak, rain, scene, Seattle, shallow, slope, snow-capped, squirrel, table, thru air, Tohans, whip-poor-will, white, women, village

Music

No.	Response	Total
1.	song(s)	183
2.	note(s)	168
3.	sound	124
4.	piano	51
5.	sing	28
6.	noise	26
7.	band	23
8.	horn	16
9.	art	15
10.	instrument	14
11.	soft	14
12.	sweet	14
13.	symphony	13
14.	play	12
15.	jazz	11
16.	tone	11
17.	orchestra	10
18.	dance	9
19.	Bach	8
20.	Beethoven	8
21.	bar(s)	7
22.	radio	7
23.	harmony	6
24.	melody	6
25.	score	6
26.	beauty	5
27.	chair	5
28.	concert	5
29.	dancing	5
30.	hall	5
31.	laughter	5
32.	nice	5
33.	sheet	5
34.	words	5
35.	chord	4
36.	drum	4
37.	opera	4
38.	stand	4
39.	trumpet	4
40.	tune	4
41.	voice	4
42.	beautiful	3
43.	clef	3
44.	composer	3
45.	hear	3
46.	key(s)	3
47.	listen	3
48.	maestro	3
49.	music	3
50.	record	3
51.	rhythm	3
52.	scale	3
53.	singing	3
54.	time	3
55.	trombone	3
56.	aria	2
57.	box	2
58.	chair	2
59.	Chopin	2
60.	clarinet	2
61.	flute	2
62.	good	2
63.	pleasant	2
64.	pleasure	2
65.	poetry	2
66.	popular	2
67.	pretty	2
68.	room	2
69.	singer	2
70.	staff	2
71.	theory	2
72.	violin	2

73-145. (f - 1)
A, accordian, appreciation, ballet, Bartok, Basie, baton, beat, blue, bow, Brahms, camera, chamber, charm, chimes, choral,

Music (contd)

chorus, class, classical, cold, color, composition, conductor, cornet, daughter, deaf, death, Dick, discord, dissonance, ear, emotion, enjoyment, fast, fine, fond, 4 Aces, fun, Grieg, happiness, harmonica, ingenue, Jan, jangle, joy, lessons, light, literature, lyrics, me, mother, musician, old time, organ, page, peace, phonograph, pianissimo, quiet, rat, rhapsody, rice, sax, Sebastian, silence, sinister, soothing, Stravinsky, string, therapy, tuba, Wayne, wind

Mutton

No.	Response	Total
1.	lamb	365
2.	sheep	295
3.	meat	96
4.	chops	56
5.	beef	32
6.	food	25
7.	veal	12
8.	collar	10
9.	leg	9
10.	Jeff	7
11.	eat	6
12.	fat	6
13.	coat	5
14.	stew	5
15.	dog	4
16.	fur	4
17.	pork	4
18.	steak	4
19.	animal	3
20.	cotten	3
21.	wool	3
22.	bread	2
23.	deer	2
24.	ish	2
25.	goat	2
26.	ham	2
27.	rabbit	2
28.	sleve	2

29-64. (f = 1)
bake, baseball, biscuit, bone, breakfast, button, cake, calf, cat, Christmas, cloth, cold, crown, dislike, fleecy, ghetto, G.I. stew, glove, good, grease, hole, hook, horse, lousy, role, scarf, scrap, shoulder, sit, song, soup, steam, suffolk, sutton, ugh, white

Needle

No.	Response	Total
1.	thread	464
2.	pin(s)	140
3.	eye	72
4.	sew	64
5.	sharp	55
6.	haystack	44
7.	point	27

Needle (contd)

No.	Response	Total
8.	prick	22
9.	sewing	18
10.	pain	5
11.	cloth	4
12.	doctor	4
13.	hole	4
14.	steel	4
15.	thimble	4
16.	hay	3
17.	hurt	3
18.	injection	3
19.	long	3
20.	shot(s)	3
21.	stick	3
22.	string	3
23.	yarn	3
24.	art	2
25.	embroidery	2
26.	knitting	2
27.	pine	2
28.	spool	2
29.	stack	2
30.	tailor	2
31.	tree	2

32-68. (f = 1)
addict, barb, blood, button, craft, dragonfly, finger, foot, head, hot, hypo, instrument, jab, knit, machines, magnet, me, metal, narrow, needle, nose, phonograph, pierce, pine tree, plasma, pricked, record, sewing machine, shall, sliver, soap, spin, stab, thin, threat, use, valve

Ocean

No.	Response	Total
1.	water	314
2.	sea	233
3.	blue	111
4.	deep	48
5.	waves	48
6.	Atlantic	28
7.	ship	20
8.	lake	15
9.	Pacific	15
10.	wide	15
11.	big	11
12.	river	9
13.	boat	8
14.	salt	7
15.	wet	7
16.	floor	6
17.	green	6
18.	liner	5
19.	depth	4
20.	fish	4
21.	land	4
22.	large	4
23.	rough	4
24.	spray	4
25.	vast	4
26.	voyage	3
27.	cold	2
28.	distance	2
29.	foam	2
30.	H_2O	2
31.	huge	2
32.	Indian	2
33.	roar	2
34.	sail	2
35.	salty	2

Ocean (contd)

No.	Response	Total
36.	sky	2
37.	swim	2
38.	tide	2
39.	travel	2
40.	wind	2

41-83. (f = 1)
baby, beach, beauty, bed, Black Sea, breeze, Calif., cape, coast, dark, deeds, drown, earth, fear, fog, France, going, gulls, living, low, motion, navy, perch, pond, red, roll, salt water, seasick, shell, shore, sick, side, steamer, stormy, swimming, top, trip, tub, vessel, west, whiskey, white, white caps

Priest

No.	Response	Total
1.	church	328
2.	Catholic	189
3.	religion	80
4.	minister	66
5.	man	43
6.	father	41
7.	black	25
8.	God	23
9.	robe	17
10.	pastor	14
11.	nun	12
12.	holy	11
13.	good	10
14.	rabbi	10
15.	Bible	8
16.	collar	5
17.	pray	5
18.	bishop	4
19.	preacher	4
20.	priestess	4
21.	altar	3
22.	clergy	3
23.	hood	3
24.	mass	3
25.	prayer	3
26.	preach	3
27.	white	3
28.	cassock	2
29.	Catholicism	2
30.	Christ	2
31.	doctor	2
32.	high	2
33.	peace	2
34.	pope	2
35.	pulpit	2
36.	queer	2
37.	religions	2
38.	Roman	2
39.	saint	2
40.	teacher	2

41-98. (f = 1)
another, beads, book, byde, Catholic church, celibacy, child, cloak, confession, confessor, convent, damn, deacon, devil, faith, fish, flock, fool, fraud, friar, garb, gather, helper, honor, house, Inca, jerk, love, marry, no good, official, oxygen, pagan, parish, parson, person, pious, potentate, prelate, prophet, pure, rest, Rev., sacraments, scientist, serve, single, sir, sleep, solemn, song,

Priest (contd)

No.	Response	Total

St. Thomas, Sunday, surplice, temple, think, understanding, Vatican

Quiet

No.	Response	Total
1.	loud	348
2.	noisy	113
3.	noise	98
4.	soft	63
5.	sleep	53
6.	man	38
7.	still	34
8.	hospital	27
9.	peace	26
10.	night	23
11.	library	10
12.	peaceful	10
13.	silent	10
14.	rest	8
15.	room	8
16.	sound	8
17.	dark	7
18.	calm	6
19.	nice	6
20.	silence	6
21.	study	5
22.	please	4
23.	shhh	4
24.	zone	4
25.	sleepy	3
26.	church	2
27.	cool	2
28.	front	2
29.	girl	2
30.	home	2
31.	light	2
32.	mouse	2
33.	noiseless	2
34.	serene	2
35.	solitude	2
36.	soundless	2
37.	time	2

38-98. (f = 1)
alone, awake, be, bed, boy, candle, class, classroom, country, day, dignified, down, Dr., easy, evening, eyes, fast, fear, gentle, golden, hear, hours, house, impact, ish, jump, lake, lost, loudness, mice, moody, multitude, now, nursery, ocean, person, psychology, radio, relaxation, restless, rock, rustle, scream, sea, sign, sleeping, small, softly, something, spring, step softly, stillness, stop, summer, sun, sweet, test, think, thinking, warm, yet

Red

No.	Response	Total
1.	white	221
2.	blue	196
3.	black	124
4.	green	93
5.	color	46

Red (contd)

No.	Response	Total
6.	blood	29
7.	communist	23
8.	yellow	19
9.	flag	17
10.	bright	15
11.	light	10
12.	hot	9
13.	hair	8
14.	shoes	8
15.	stop	8
16.	cloth	7
17.	river	7
18.	Russian	7
19.	coat	6
20.	fire	6
21.	Russia	6
22.	apple	5
23.	bull	5
24.	dress	5
25.	Commie	4
26.	dark	4
27.	head	4
28.	warm	4
29.	cap	3
30.	China	3
31.	danger	3
32.	hat	3
33.	house	3
34.	paint	3
35.	sea	3
36.	spy	3
37.	sweater	3
38.	anger	2
39.	ball	2
40.	cape	2
41.	crayon	2
42.	dog	2
43.	eye(s)	2
44.	mad	2
45.	paper	2
46.	pink	2
47.	sails	2
48.	shirt	2
49.	star	2
50.	sunset	2
51.	tape	2
52.	underwear	2

53-107. (f = 1)
alive, barn, beard, bee, blanket, beautiful, brilliant,
carpet, Christmas, clothes,
communism, cow, deep, dept.,
exciting, face, feather, flame,
flier, girl, handkerchief,
heart, heat, heifer, hood, hut,
hurt, incorrect, jacket,
Indians, ink, left, lips, lipsticks, nose, orange, painting,
pen, purple, rage, rose, school,
sharp, sheep, shy, sign, skirt,
stop light, string, sun, USSR,
velvet, vibrant, wagon, wine

Religion

No.	Response	Total
1.	church	285
2.	God	196
3.	Bible	70
4.	Catholic	37
5.	faith	37
6.	belief	27
7.	good	23
8.	priest	22

Religion (contd)

No.	Response	Total
9.	Lutheran	19
10.	life	16
11.	minister	11
12.	Protestant	10
13.	Christ	9
14.	book	8
15.	Methodist	8
16.	atheism	7
17.	Christian	7
18.	holy	7
19.	Episcopal	6
20.	Baptist	5
21.	Christianity	5
22.	Jewish	5
23.	people	5
24.	worship	5
25.	love	4
26.	man(e)	4
27.	peace	4
28.	pray	4
29.	prayer	4
30.	Presbyterian	4
31.	sect	4
32.	atheist	3
33.	Jesus	3
34.	law	3
35.	no	3
36.	none	3
37.	philosophy	3
38.	right	3
39.	think	3
40.	agnostic	2
41.	Congregational	2
42.	heathen	2
43.	learning	2
44.	necessary	2
45.	opium	2
46.	orthodox	2
47.	pious	2
48.	sacred	2
49.	soul	2
50.	study	2
51.	thought	2

52-125. (f = 1)
argument, bad, believe, bishop,
Buddhist, bull, bunk, camp,
ceremony, chill, cloudy, Communist, confusion, creed, creek,
cross, demagoguery, denomination,
die, distaste, doctor, drab,
dream, drug, escape, ethics,
fake, fanatic, fervor, fooey,
form, goofy, guidance, hate,
hell, holiness, hypocrite, ideas,
important, Jack, Jew, live,
Luther, mad, mass, me, meaning,
mind, mine, mission, moral,
Moses, my own, mystery, mysticism, nature, Newman, non,
non-religion, now, nun, one,
orders, person, pew, piety, poor,
practice, preach, preacher,
question, race, reverence,
reverend, rite, ritual, rosary,
salvation, school, science, see,
service, St. Olaf, St. Thomas,
Sunday, talk, theme, theology,
tolerance, trouble, truth,
way, way of life, weak, week,
Wesley, word, yes

River

No.	Response	Total
1.	water	246
2.	stream	211
3.	lake	105
4.	Mississippi	86
5.	boat	38
6.	deep	29
7.	wide	16
8.	flow	14
9.	run	14
10.	bed	12
11.	creek	12
12.	blue	11
13.	wet	8
14.	fast	7
15.	fish	7
16.	Red	7
17.	bank	6
18.	bend	6
19.	ice	6
20.	bridge	5
21.	brook	5
22.	long	5
23.	mountain	5
24.	ocean	5
25.	swift	5
26.	winding	5
27.	rapid	4
28.	sea	4
29.	swim	4
30.	tree(s)	4
31.	white	4
32.	cold	3
33.	dirty	3
34.	falls	3
35.	flowing	3
36.	road	3
37.	Styx	3
38.	wind	3
39.	black	2
40.	drown	2
41.	flood	2
42.	Ganges	2
43.	green	2
44.	hill	2
45.	H₂O	2
46.	Jordan	2
47.	large	2
48.	Minnesota	2
49.	Nile	2
50.	pond	2
51.	St. Marie	2
52.	slow	2
53.	wash	2

54-111. (f = 1)
abyss, bad, boating, cross,
dam, dark, Des Moines, drive,
fare, flying, garden, gorge,
grass, ground, India, interesting, jump, land, lazy, life,
liver, man, marsh, mouth, mud,
muddy, narrow, old, old man,
Po, Rio, rock, row, scenery,
side, skate, skating, sleep,
song, Souix St. Marie, summer,
swamp, swan, swimming, Thames,
tight, tile, torrent, town,
trail, transportation, trout,
twist, Valley, Volga, was,
Weser, woods

Rough

No.	Response	Total
1.	smooth	439
2.	hard	69
3.	road	44
4.	tough	42
5.	sandpaper	38
6.	soft	38
7.	hand(s)	26
8.	ready	18
9.	coarse	15
10.	wood	11
11.	riders	10
12.	rugged	10
13.	sand	10
14.	board(s)	7
15.	man	7
16.	ground	6
17.	sea	6
18.	gravel	5
19.	sharp	5
20.	water	5
21.	dark	4
22.	harsh	4
23.	jagged	4
24.	mountain	4
25.	weather	4
26.	brown	3
27.	edge	3
28.	emery	3
29.	even	3
30.	field	3
31.	golf	3
32.	hewn	3
33.	skin	3
34.	stone(s)	3
35.	street(s)	3
36.	surface	3
37.	bad	2
38.	bark	2
39.	beard	2
40.	bump	2
41.	calm	2
42.	cement	2
43.	citizen	2
44.	course	2
45.	cowboy	2
46.	easy	2
47.	feel	2
48.	football	2
49.	gentle	2
50.	guy	2
51.	heavy	2
52.	house	2
53.	ice	2
54.	land	2
55.	life	2
56.	light	2
57.	nut(s)	2
58.	paper	2
59.	pebbles	2
60.	time	2
61.	stucco	2
62.	uneven	2
63.	weak	2
64.	wool	2

65-151. (f = 1)
bay, brush, bumpy, callous, CE 142, chair, chapped, character, cold, corduroy, criminal, cough, cut, difficult, dirt, dog, enoot, estranged, fast, file, finish, fought, frog, game, gang, going, grass, handle, hazy, headache, heart, hilly, hills, icy, iron, it, log, long, lumber, math, morning, nail, noise, north woods, painful, physics, picture, plow, plowing, post, red, ride,

Rough (contd)

riding, rocky, row, sailing, sandy, saw, scratch, sewage, shallow, shod, sled, sides, sport, steep, stick, stiff, strong, stuff, Superior Wisconsin, table, tangle, tender, terrain, test, texture, touch, tumble, tweed, unsmooth, wall, waves, west, whiskers, wind, women, zoology

Salt

No.	Response	Total
1.	pepper	430
2.	sugar	83
3.	water	76
4.	taste	50
5.	sea	33
6.	bitter	31
7.	shaker	30
8.	food	29
9.	ocean	23
10.	lake	19
11.	sweet	19
12.	eat	15
13.	meat	12
14.	Peter	11
15.	seasoning	9
16.	sour	9
17.	NaCl	7
18.	white	6
19.	spice	5
20.	table	5
21.	earth	4
22.	flavor	4
23.	free	4
24.	good	4
25.	lick	4
26.	bread	3
27.	celery	3
28.	grains	3
29.	mines	3
30.	popcorn	3
31.	salty	3
32.	savour	3
33.	season	3
34.	thirsty	3
35.	butter	2
36.	cellar	2
37.	dry	2
38.	flat(s)	2
39.	french fries	2
40.	Morton's	2
41.	soup	2
42.	tomato(es)	2

43-85. (f = 1)
apple, baby, base, black, blue, body, carrots, cheese, chemistry, coffee, compound, cow, crackers, cuts, desert, diet, drink, eating, eggs, fish, flour, grimace, halite, iodine, iodized, lemons, mineral, pork, port, potato, pour, sharp, sodium, song, sore throat, spray, sprinkle, sting, strongs, tart, tasty, use, water taffy

Scissors

No.	Response	Total
1.	cut	671
2.	sharp	90
3.	paper	43
4.	cloth	38
5.	knife(ves)	33
6.	shears	15
7.	cutting	13
8.	thread	13
9.	needle	9
10.	snip	9
11.	material	8
12.	sew	8
13.	sewing	8
14.	clip	3
15.	razor	2

16-51. (f = 1)
barber, black, clippers, clothes, cross, fabric, forceps, fork, game, grinders, grip, hair, hard, hold, instrument, iron, machine, metal, mother, nails, nostril, pair, pins, pliers, pointed, rabbi, saw, shear, silver, spool, string, strip, table, tongs, wrestle, wrestling

Sheep

No.	Response	Total
1.	wool	201
2.	lamb	198
3.	animal	75
4.	mutton	66
5.	goats	64
6.	dog	41
7.	herd	39
8.	black	25
9.	pasture	18
10.	cows	17
11.	shepherd	17
12.	baa	15
13.	cattle	15
14.	count(ing)	14
15.	farm	14
16.	sleep	14
17.	flock	10
18.	white	9
19.	fence	7
20.	ewe	6
21.	herder	6
22.	dip	5
23.	field	5
24.	meat	5
25.	grass	4
26.	lamp	4
27.	shear	4
28.	eat	3
29.	fleece	3
30.	fold	3
31.	follow	3
32.	food	3
33.	fur	3
34.	horse	3
35.	meadow	3
36.	ranch	3
37.	shorn	3
38.	soft	3
39.	wooly	3
40.	boy	2
41.	bulls	2
42.	calves	2
43.	graze	2
44.	hair	2

Sheep (contd)

No.	Response	Total
45.	lanolin	2
46.	people	2
47.	skin	2
48.	staff	2
49.	stray	2
50.	wolf	2

51-151. (f = 1)
beard, bed, bells, Bible, bleat, block, call, Christmas, cloth, clothes, country, countryside, creep, deep, farmer, fat, foot, fuzzy, glass, good, God's people, grazing, group, hand cream, hoof, house, hungry, jump, jumping, legs, meek, money, Montana, mouse, mouton, oxen, pasture, peace, peep, poems, prairie, ram, red, run, sacrifice, shearing, sow, style, wake, wander, wood

Short

No.	Response	Total
1.	tall	397
2.	long	336
3.	fat	76
4.	small	21
5.	man	18
6.	hair	11
7.	dark	9
8.	stout	9
9.	girl	7
10.	pants	6
11.	stocky	6
12.	hand	5
13.	light	5
14.	shirt	4
15.	stubby	4
16.	high	3
17.	little	3
18.	stop	3
19.	wide	3
20.	cake	2
21.	day	2
22.	dwarf	2
23.	good	2
24.	length	2
25.	line	2
26.	low	2
27.	pencil	2
28.	person	2
29.	quick	2
30.	snort	2
31.	stature	2
32.	story	2
33.	tail	2
34.	time	2
35.	wave	2

36-82. (f = 1)
baby, bald, basketball, beer, black, blonde, box, brief, Carol, child, curt, cut, digit, distance, dog, Filipino, fingers, funny, general, gun, heavy, height, inch, lady, less, limited, lion, lived, loud, me, midget, name, ness, nose, plump, ruler, shorter, side, skinny, square, step, stick, stuff, sweet, thick, tiny, trousers

Sickness

No.	Response	Total
1.	health	376
2.	ill	159
3.	death	153
4.	bed	64
5.	well	58
6.	illness	26
7.	doctor	21
8.	hospital	13
9.	disease	12
10.	bad	7
11.	cold	6
12.	dead	6
13.	flu	6
14.	healthy	5
15.	sea	5
16.	sick	5
17.	man	4
18.	pain	4
19.	me	3
20.	medicine	3
21.	cancer	2
22.	fever	2
23.	hurt	2
24.	measles	2
25.	nausea	2
26.	pills	2
27.	room	2
28.	stomach	2
29.	vomit	2
30.	weak	2

31-76. (f = 1)
aches, beer, boat, dad, darkness, die, discomfort, dislike, dog, dying, ear, famine, gah, goodness, grandmother, grief, headache, heal, heart, ish, live, misery, mom, mother, no, nurse, pale, pleuresy, recovery, sad, sheets, ship, Sister Kenny, sore, sour, TB, tests, tooth, threat, trouble, ugh, uncomfortable, unhappy, weakness, wellness, you

Sleep

No.	Response	Total
1.	bed	238
2.	rest	110
3.	awake	100
4.	tired	90
5.	dream	81
6.	wake	48
7.	night	44
8.	comfort	22
9.	eat	22
10.	sound	21
11.	slumber	19
12.	snore	17
13.	deep	11
14.	pillow	11
15.	good	8
16.	soft	8
17.	awaken	6
18.	walk	6
19.	nice	5
20.	peace	5
21.	well	5
22.	doze	4
23.	drink	4
24.	tight	4
25.	dark	3
26.	drowse	3
27.	eyes	3

Sleep (contd)

No.	Response	Total
28.	insomnia	3
29.	lay	3
30.	long	3
31.	quiet	3
32.	relax	3
33.	anger	2
34.	baby	2
35.	classes	2
36.	die	2
37.	down	2
38.	girl	2
39.	health	2
40.	more	2
41.	morning	2
42.	mutton	2
43.	peaceful	2
44.	sick	2
45.	slept	2
46.	study	2
47.	walker	2

48-108. (f = 1)
beer, best, black, blanket, bliss, block, child, closed, covers, dead, dog, don't, drowsy, ease, enjoy, eyelids, grass, happy, hard, haven't, home, hours, hunger, in, late, light, little, lots, lounge, mattress, me, more off, nap, need, nod, No-Doz, nothing, now, out, pill, pills, pleasure, recline, resting, rise, satisfy, sheets, silent, sleepy, soundly, stand, stop, talk, till noon, tire, wakefullness, wake up, window, wool, work, yawn

Slow

No.	Response	Total
1.	fast	752
2.	car(s)	23
3.	stop	22
4.	down	17
5.	snail	12
6.	sign	10
7.	train	9
8.	poke	8
9.	traffic	8
10.	turtle	8
11.	walk	7
12.	go	6
13.	speed	6
14.	lazy	4
15.	quick	4
16.	streetcars	4
17.	ant	3
18.	boat	3
19.	drive	3
20.	driver	3
21.	movement	3
22.	pokey	3
23.	sluggish	3
24.	bus	2
25.	dog	2
26.	easy	2
27.	impatient	2
28.	light	2
29.	move	2
30.	moving	2
31.	run	2
32.	skid	2
33.	sleet	2
34.	stop sign	2

Slow (contd)

No.	Response	Total
35.	street	2

36-94. (f = 1)
accident, bear, brain, caution, clock, cold, country, cow, crawl, curve, dance, dark, drag, driving, dull, Ford, glow, good, halt, hard, heavy, highway, horse, Jean, laborious, lag, late, long, molasses, mother, motion, Mpls., music, nervous, now, plane, plow, policeman, roomate, round, slide, slug, soft, speedy, steady, sticky, stream, streetcars, stupid, tortoise, wagon, walking, white, woman driver, women, work

Smooth

No.	Response	Total
1.	rough	328
2.	soft	206
3.	hard	135
4.	silk	40
5.	hands	29
6.	skin	18
7.	glass	13
8.	ice	12
9.	surface	11
10.	velvet	11
11.	even	10
12.	flat	8
13.	level	7
14.	sharp	7
15.	shiny	7
16.	table	7
17.	sandpaper	6
18.	satin	6
19.	cloth	4
20.	coarse	4
21.	creamy	4
22.	harsh	4
23.	silky	4
24.	slick	4
25.	bumpy	3
26.	clean	3
27.	clear	3
28.	round	3
29.	rugged	3
30.	wood	3
31.	feel	2
32.	felt	2
33.	floor	2
34.	ice cream	2
35.	light	2
36.	marble	2
37.	mellow	2
38.	metal	2
39.	nice	2
40.	plane	2
41.	road	2
42.	sailing	2
43.	sand	2
44.	slippery	2
45.	stone	2
46.	top	2

47-117. (f = 1)
aluminum, beard, blackboard, block, board, bore, brittle, chalk, cool, cut, cylinder, dark, desk, drink, easy,

Smooth (contd)

No.	Response	Total

exciting, face, fine, finish, flowing, frictionless, frosting, glass, good, grass, irregular, iron, ivory, jerky, lines, long, lumpy, man, mohogany, muscle, music, narrow, neat, ocean, oil, pavement, person, pillow, porcelain, ride, rigid, river, rocky, sandy, satiny, scratch, sea, shave, share, sheet, simple, skater, slide, slossy, steel, stout, svelte, taste, touch, uneven, warm, water, whiskey, white, woman, wrinkled

Soft

No.	Response	Total
1.	hard	445
2.	light	87
3.	pillow	81
4.	bed	42
5.	smooth	28
6.	loud	22
7.	cotton	18
8.	music	18
9.	fur	16
10.	touch	13
11.	chair	12
12.	fluffy	12
13.	feather(s)	11
14.	drink	10
15.	warm	10
16.	heavy	9
17.	velvet	9
18.	cushion	8
19.	silk	7
20.	dark	6
21.	downy	6
22.	easy	6
23.	kitten	5
24.	nice	4
25.	skin	4
26.	deep	3
27.	furry	3
28.	girl	3
29.	hair	3
30.	rug	3
31.	sweet	3
32.	tender	3
33.	water	3
34.	wool	3
35.	cloud	2
36.	cuddly	2
37.	down	2
38.	head	2
39.	high	2
40.	mattress	2
41.	mellow	2
42.	mushy	2
43.	pretty	2
44.	quiet	2
45.	rough	2
46.	satin	2
47.	shoe	2
48.	snow	2
49.	spongy	2
50.	sweater	2
51.	tissue	2

52-104. (f = 1)
airy, blanket, blue, body, breath, butter, candy, cat, cloth, cloy, comfort, cold, cool, couch,

Soft (contd)

No.	Response	Total

custard, dim, doll, egg, fat, feathery, feel, felt, fish, flesh, fluff, fuzzy, harsh, heart, hollow, Ivory Snow, Lee, long, material, near, pad, paper, quilt, rough, seat, sheet, sink, sleep, smooth, soap, soothing, sound, sponge, spot, tooth, weak, white, woman

Soldier

No.	Response	Total
1.	army	187
2.	sailor	182
3.	man(e)	101
4.	war	87
5.	gun	86
6.	uniform	56
7.	fight	40
8.	boy	23
9.	Korea	17
10.	march	12
11.	civilian	9
12.	foot	9
13.	G.I.	8
14.	draft	5
15.	fighter	5
16.	navy	5
17.	brother	4
18.	captain	4
19.	field	4
20.	infantry	4
21.	military	4
22.	rifle	4
23.	R.O.T.C.	4
24.	service	4
25.	friend	3
26.	Ike	3
27.	khaki	3
28.	marching	3
29.	marine	3
30.	me	3
31.	officer	3
32.	private	3
33.	shoot	3
34.	warrior	3
35.	Air Force	2
36.	airman	2
37.	brave	2
38.	carbine	2
39.	citizen	2
40.	command	2
41.	cross	2
42.	death	2
43.	(h)gah	2
44.	good	2
45.	helmet	2
46.	straight	2
47.	tin	2
48.	wac	2
49.	weapon	2

50-130. (f = 1)
airdale, armed, arms, away, battle, brass, care, chocolate, combat, country, courage, cute, discharge, discipline, doggie, dummy, enemy, enlistment, excitement, fighting, fire, fool, fortune, future, gay, general, German, grey, guard, guy, halt, Hank, head, hero, hurt, jed, jerk, John, leave, "looie", major, medal,

Soldier (contd)

No.	Response	Total

murderer, Napoleon, nurse,
nuts, O.K., olive drab, open,
orders, patrol, peace, peon,
person, pirty, policeman, pony,
put, rank, salute, sargeant,
scar, shoe, sing, slave, states-
man, steel, strong, sucker,
suit, tan, three, trap, two
years, U.S.A., walk, walking,
where, wife, woody, woman

Sour

No.	Response	Total
1.	sweet	568
2.	grapes	91
3.	lemon	63
4.	bitter	60
5.	milk	40
6.	taste	24
7.	cream	22
8.	dough	21
9.	apples	18
10.	pickle	14
11.	vinegar	12
12.	bad	6
13.	fruit	5
14.	grapefruit	5
15.	mash	5
16.	puss	4
17.	whisky	4
18.	buttermilk	3
19.	acid	2
20.	pucker	2
21.	sauerkraut	2
22.	soup	2
23.	tart	2

24-57. (f = 1)
alum, awry, bad taste, bread,
can, cheese, chocolate milk,
disagreeable, dish, distaste,
dry, earth, food, gin, good,
green apple, high, hurt, juice,
lunch, mix, neighbor, orange,
pie, plum, pop, sleep, soured,
spit, spoiled, stable, sugar,
tongue, wine

Spider

No.	Response	Total
1.	web	454
2.	insect	152
3.	bug(s)	97
4.	leg(s)	50
5.	fly	37
6.	black	34
7.	crawl	18
8.	animal	16
9.	ant	12
10.	Black Widow	9
11.	fear	6
12.	poison	6
13.	afraid	5
14.	worm	5
15.	bite	4
16.	spin	4
17.	ugly	4
18.	arachnoid	3
19.	dog	3

Spider (contd)

No.	Response	Total
20.	eight	3
21.	fright	3
22.	ish	3
23.	net	3
24.	widow	3
25.	bird	2
26.	cobwebs	2
27.	crawling	2
28.	creepy	2
29.	dark	2
30.	horrid	2
31.	icky	2
32.	(Miss) Muffet	2
33.	poisonous	2
34.	run	2
35.	scared	2
36.	snake	2
37.	Tarantula	2
38.	wall	2
39.	zoology	2

40-83. (f = 1)
alarm, arm, avoid, awful,
beetle, boy, cat, chills, claw,
cockroach, corner, distaste,
evil, feelers, fur, furry,
gray, horrible, insect,
interesting, jump, Lady Bug,
life science, man, mites,
morbid, mouse, orthoptera, pan,
rat, room, scream, shape,
shiver, sit, small, spider web,
spinning, squirm, thin, turn,
ugh, unbeneficial, unpleasant

Square

No.	Response	Total
1.	round	372
2.	circle	211
3.	block	65
4.	dance	26
5.	root	22
6.	city	20
7.	triangle	19
8.	head	17
9.	box	13
10.	cube	12
11.	rectangle	12
12.	time(s)	11
13.	geometry	7
14.	town	7
15.	chocolate	5
16.	corner	5
17.	oblong	5
18.	park	5
19.	butter	4
20.	figure	4
21.	foot	4
22.	math	4
23.	mile	4
24.	person	4
25.	table	4
26.	village	4
27.	wood	4
28.	angles	3
29.	carpenter	3
30.	house	3
31.	London	3
32.	lumber	3
33.	Madison	3
34.	meal	3
35.	sharp	3
36.	small	3
37.	Boston	2

Square (contd)

No.	Response	Total
38.	buildings	2
39.	city square	2
40.	deal	2
41.	diamond	2
42.	dice	2
43.	dumb	2
44.	green	2
45.	hard	2
46.	peg	2
47.	ring	2
48.	shape	2
49.	solid	2
50.	statue	2
51.	street	2
52.	tool	2
53.	trees	2
54.	Washington	2

55-125. (f = 1)
bill, board, bond, bop, Cadillac,
candy, centimeter, church,
circular, country, courthouse,
dark, dope, dot, easy, even,
fence, floor, formula, four,
flowers, frame, France, fudge,
garden, geometric figure, grass,
hep, hexagon, hillbilly, hole,
inch, jerk, John, knot, lines,
love, man, market, mouse, not
round, nut, N.Y., pack, pencil,
πr^2, plaza, policemen,
psychology, public, red, rhombus,
right, right angle, rule, ruler,
same, 7 corners, shaft, shops,
shoulders, sides, St. Paul, sum,
ta, tee, three, tie, Times Square,
writing, yard

Stem

No.	Response	Total
1.	flower	402
2.	plant	224
3.	leaf(ves)	125
4.	root	47
5.	tree	27
6.	branch	16
7.	pipe	12
8.	stern	12
9.	lamp	11
10.	rose	11
11.	apple	8
12.	bud	7
13.	glass	7
14.	trunk	7
15.	green	6
16.	bulb	4
17.	fruit	4
18.	stalk	4
19.	from	3
20.	petal	3
21.	stem	3
22.	twig	3
23.	bird	2
24.	brain	2
25.	core	2
26.	leg	2
27.	limb	2
28.	long	2
29.	responses	2
30.	tide	2
31.	tulip	2
32.	watch	2
33.	water	2
34.	words	2

Stem (contd)

No.	Response	Total
35-73.	(f = 1)	

asparagus, base, blade, blossom, botany, bottom, bowl, cherry, come, flat, flow, grass, ground, handle, hay, lem, line, locum, mushroom, ocean, pear, pistol, psych, pumpkin, reed, rhubarb, NR, start, stipules, string, thread, tip, vapor, vascular, verb, vine, weed, wind, worm

Stomach

No.	Response	Total
1.	food	211
2.	ache	210
3.	eat	86
4.	intestine	69
5.	ulcer	47
6.	hungry	42
7.	body	28
8.	organ	23
9.	pains	20
10.	hunger	18
11.	belly	13
12.	full	13
13.	pump	13
14.	digestion	11
15.	gut	10
16.	sick	10
17.	trouble	10
18.	eating	8
19.	hurt	8
20.	abdomen	7
21.	empty	7
22.	flu	7
23.	heart	7
24.	upset	7
25.	head	5
26.	liver	5
27.	mouth	5
28.	muscle	5
29.	sour	4
30.	gastric	3
31.	inside	3
32.	juices	3
33.	person	3
34.	soft	3
35.	sore	3
36.	zoology	3
37.	anatomy	2
38.	appendix	2
39.	digest	2
40.	gas	2
41.	growls	2
42.	health	2
43.	hit	2
44.	ill	2
45.	indigestion	2
46.	kidney	2
47.	man	2
48.	round	2
49.	sack	2
50.	sickness	2
51.	viscera	2
52-99.	(f = 1)	

bear, burp, butterflies, cancer, cast iron, cavity, churning, cramp, diaphragm, disorder, duodenum, ear, esophagus, fat, feed, fill, film, gastric juice, gastro-vascular, green and white, grind, hand, HCl, large,

Stomach (contd)

No.	Response	Total

leg, low, lunch, lung, me, middle, nerves, orange, part, peptic, physiology, pot, pylorus, saliva, satisfied, science, smooth, throat, throw-up, turn, ulster, vomit, want, worm

Stove

No.	Response	Total
1.	hot	235
2.	heat	184
3.	pipe	109
4.	cook	72
5.	warm	61
6.	fire	54
7.	black	36
8.	oven	35
9.	food	23
10.	warmth	20
11.	wood	17
12.	kitchen	16
13.	lid	12
14.	coal(s)	9
15.	cooking	8
16.	gas	8
17.	iron	8
18.	light	7
19.	range	7
20.	burn	6
21.	furnace	5
22.	leg	5
23.	pot	5
24.	bolt	4
25.	pan(s)	4
26.	burner	3
27.	chimney	3
28.	lamp	3
29.	pot belly	3
30.	electric	2
31.	fuel	2
32.	house	2
33.	icebox	2
34.	old	2
35.	red	2
36.	smoke	2
37.	top	2
38-67.	(f = 1)	

bake, bellow, big, boil, bulky, cabin, camping, chair, coffee, cook stove, eat, fireplace, flame, glow, grate, handle, heater, in, kettle, lead, league, length, lining, lit, poker, post, room, smell, tube, white

Street

No.	Response	Total
1.	avenue	190
2.	road	128
3.	cars	112
4.	light(s)	51
5.	city	46
6.	alley	38
7.	walk	33
8.	sign	30
9.	house(s)	24
10.	corner	20

Street (contd)

No.	Response	Total
11.	sidewalk	20
12.	town	16
13.	number	14
14.	scene	13
15.	drive	9
16.	lamp(s)	9
17.	name	9
18.	lane	8
19.	long	8
20.	pavement	8
21.	cleaner	7
22.	narrow	7
23.	address	6
24.	cross	6
25.	dark	6
26.	live	5
27.	traffic	5
28.	curb	4
29.	dirt	4
30.	home(s)	4
31.	main	4
32.	straight	4
33.	dance	3
34.	4th	3
35.	noise	3
36.	path	3
37.	rue	3
38.	6th	3
39.	Walker	3
40.	Washington	3
41.	Basin	2
42.	black	2
43.	clothes	2
44.	crossing	2
45.	dreams	2
46.	5th	2
47.	fight	2
48.	gutter	2
49.	highway	2
50.	icy	2
51.	people	2
52.	sour	2
53.	St. Clair	2
54.	tar	2
55.	trees	2
56.	University	2
57.	way	2
58.	wide	2
59.	winding	2
60-151.	(f = 1)	

across, Ashland, asphalt, automobiles, beach, beat, Blair, block, boulevard, brick, Burr, call, cement, chowen, Church, clean, Cleveland, cobblestone, Columbia, concrete, coordinate, corridor, country, crowded, destination, direction, dirty, down, 15th, First, fountain, 14th, Emerson, go, green, Halifax, Hennepin, Holley, ice, in, King, Knox, lamppost, land, Larue, Lawson, line, Logan, Lyndale, major, meet, Melbourne, Minnesota, Morgan, name, New York, Nicollet, nob, oil, Osceola, paved, Payne Ave., picture, Plymouth, pole, post, puddle, Queen Ave., railroad, Raymond, repair, ruts, shade, side, sitter, slush, snow, song, square, stores, streetcar, 3rd, 312 W. Walnut, ton, units, village, walking, wall, Walnut, wet, white, #

Sweet

No.	Response	Total
1.	sour	434
2.	candy	162
3.	sugar	80
4.	bitter	76
5.	music	33
6.	soft	22
7.	girl	17
8.	good	15
9.	taste	13
10.	tooth	13
11.	nice	11
12.	low	8
13.	honey	7
14.	smell	6
15.	chocolate	5
16.	Sue	4
17.	heart	3
18.	lovely	3
19.	pickle	3
20.	sound	3
21.	cake	2
22.	cream	2
23.	cute	2
24.	eat	2
25.	gentle	2
26.	hard	2
27.	harsh	2
28.	lemon	2
29.	light	2
30.	loud	2
31.	love	2
32.	mellow	2
33.	milk	2
34.	pie	2
35.	pretty	2
36.	sick	2
37.	smile	2
38.	strong	2
39.	talk	2
40.	woman	2

41-87. (f = 1)
acid, Barb, bird, breath, cookie, dark, delicious, Dixie, dream, food, good looking, grass, innocent, joy, La Vonne, lips, little, me, melody, nausea, notes, nothings, nut, potato, sacharine, safe, scent, sentimental, sharp, simple, sing, sixteen, smooth, song, spice, sticky, sweater, sweetheart, tangy, tart, tender, thick, thing, Virginia, whistle, wife, young

Swift

No.	Response	Total
1.	fast	369
2:	slow	238
3.	river	33
4.	meat	32
5.	Jonathan	27
6.	current	21
7.	bird	19
8.	bacon	13
9.	rapid(s)	13
10.	stream	12
11.	water	12
12.	quick	11
13.	Gulliver	10
14.	ham	8
15.	run	8
16.	sure	8

Swift (contd)

No.	Response	Total
17.	deer	7
18.	car	6
19.	lard	6
20.	author	5
21.	company	5
22.	flight	5
23.	Gulliver's Travels	5
24.	horse(s)	5
25.	running	5
26.	wind	5
27.	Armour	4
28.	arrow	4
29.	book	4
30.	shortning	4
31.	Tom	4
32.	airplane	3
33.	cheese	3
34.	chimney	3
35.	eagle	3
36.	runner	3
37.	rush	3
38.	speed	3
39.	swallow	3
40.	blue	2
41.	county	2
42.	creek	2
43.	dog	2
44.	food	2
45.	kick	2
46.	mercury	2
47.	Oliver	2
48.	packing co.	2
49.	poet	2
50.	race	2
51.	silent	2
52.	speedy	2
53.	streaks	2
54.	sudden	2

55-100. (f = 1)
block, blow, butter, calm, cattle, Charles, clear, cold, cream, Crusoe, David, family, feet, fire, flowing, food company, go, greyhound, hawk, hurry, indian, John, lightning, meat packing, mighty, north, novel, pleasant, premium, products, quickly, rifle, sad, slick, smooth, strong, thrust, tide, track, trade, train, travel, true, work, wren, writing

Table

No.	Response	Total
1.	chair	840
2.	food	41
3.	desk	21
4.	top	15
5.	leg(s)	11
6.	eat	9
7.	cloth	8
8.	dish(es)	7
9.	wood	6
10.	dinner	3
11.	Mable	3
12.	tennis	3
13.	cup	2
14.	door	2
15.	floor	2
16.	fork	2
17.	room	2
18.	round	2

Table (contd)

No.	Response	Total
19.	silver	2

20-47. (f = 1)
bed, black, board, book, card, company, door, drink, flat, four, hard, house, huge, kitchen, lamp, leaf, maple, meat, mesa, plate, pool, sable, set, sink, spoon, stable, study, tablecloth

Thief

No.	Response	Total
1.	steal	286
2.	robber	138
3.	crook	69
4.	burglar	54
5.	money	37
6.	cop	25
7.	bad	23
8.	stole	23
9.	rob	21
10.	stolen	19
11.	jail	14
12.	man	14
13.	night	14
14.	police	14
15.	run	14
16.	beggar	13
17.	criminal	13
18.	gun	12
19.	law	8
20.	river	7
21.	dark	6
22.	jewels	6
23.	take	6
24.	movie	5
25.	robbery	5
26.	villain	5
27.	bandit	4
28.	crime	4
29.	sneak	4
30.	theft	4
31.	bicycle	3
32.	honest	3
33.	murderer	3
34.	stealing	3
35.	stop	3
36.	accomplice	2
37.	bag	2
38.	Bagdad	2
39.	catch	2
40.	Dillinger	2
41.	good	2
42.	jewelry	2
43.	mask	2
44.	merchant	2
45.	person	2
46.	poor	2
47.	rat	2
48.	silver(ware)	2
49.	sly	2
50.	stealer	2
51.	window	2
52.	wrong	2
53.	vandal	2

54-137. (f = 1)
alarm, angel, arrest, bank, bedroom, (beggar (man)), block, boy, break, brother, bum, chair, chase, chickens, chief, city, clever, clothes, coward, crafty, culprit, Damascus, danger, diamond, dishonest, doctor, dog, don't, evil, fail,

Thief (contd)

No.	Response	Total

fast, fiend, fire, flee, flight, gam, gamble, giver, gold, goods, guilt, harm, help, house, in, Indian, in the night, jerk, judge, lawyer, leaf, London, loot, lose, loss, lout, murder, no dialogue, noise, nut, petty, pocket, pocketbook, policeman, prison, property, purse, red, River Falls, roar, show, sole, sorrow, spoil, stealth, stoled, stolen goods, the, took, unlawful, victim, voleur, wit, woman

Thirsty

No.	Response	Total
1.	water	348
2.	drink	296
3.	dry	121
4.	hungry	99
5.	beer	16
6.	cold	9
7.	wet	8
8.	whiskey	8
9.	H$_2$O	7
10.	glass	6
11.	hot	6
12.	tired	6
13.	pop	5
14.	quench	5
15.	desert	4
16.	coke	3
17.	milk	3
18.	boy	2
19.	cup	2
20.	drunk	2
21.	eat	2
22.	parched	2
23.	satiated	2
24.	thirst	2

25-67. (f = 1)
avid, bar, content, cool, crave, craving, drank, drown, drought, eat, fast, filled, food, full, gin, glue, horse, hunger, just whistle, liquid, liquor, man, mouth, nail, no, rasp, rats, salt, satisfied, shy, soda, Squirt, stimulus, sugar, summer, sweet, tasty, throat, uncomfortable, wake, warm, well, wish

Tobacco

No.	Response	Total
1.	smoke	515
2.	cigarette	191
3.	pipe	49
4.	cigar	31
5.	road	27
6.	juice	23
7.	chew	20
8.	smoking	18
9.	smell	14
10.	leaf(ves)	11
11.	nicotine	8
12.	bad	6
13.	brown	5

Tobacco (contd)

No.	Response	Total
14.	stain	5
15.	Luckies	4
16.	plant	4
17.	cough	3
18.	good	3
19.	match	3
20.	pouch	3
21.	spit	3
22.	stink(y)	3
23.	taste	3
24.	Camels	2
25.	enjoyment	2
26.	no	2
27.	odor	2
28.	user	2
29.	weed	2

30-69. (f = 1)
acrid, add, bitter, boubon, breath, can, Chesterfield, chromosome, Copenhagen, distasteful, field, food, fun, growers, habit, heavy, ish, Kools, land, Lucky Strike, man, money, no good, noise, nuts, on the wagon, paper, patch, puff, quit, satisfying, small, south, spitoon, stimulus, terrible, ugh, wheeze, whiskey, white

Trouble

No.	Response	Total
1.	bad	89
2.	shooter	49
3.	worry(ies)	45
4.	danger	41
5.	sorrow	32
6.	fear	26
7.	school	24
8.	problem	23
9.	police	20
10.	fight	19
11.	sad	19
12.	happy	18
13.	difficulty(ies)	17
14.	peace	16
15.	hard	15
16.	help	14
17.	maker	14
18.	anger	12
19.	jail	12
20.	man(e)	10
21.	pain	10
22.	bubble	9
23.	cop(s)	9
24.	double	9
25.	ease	9
26.	war	9
27.	anxiety	8
28.	easy	8
29.	fun	8
30.	woman(e)	8
31.	grief	7
32.	sadness	7
33.	accident	6
34.	boy	6
35.	car	6
36.	happiness	6
37.	misery	6
38.	sickness	6
39.	disaster	5
40.	mess	5
41.	money	5

Trouble (contd)

No.	Response	Total
42.	bother	4
43.	comfort	4
44.	error	4
45.	hate	4
46.	ill	4
47.	law	4
48.	people	4
49.	smooth	4
50.	some	4
51.	unhappiness	4
52.	unhappy	4
53.	work	4
54.	world	4
55.	wrong	4
56.	ail	3
57.	bothered	3
58.	care	3
59.	confusion	3
60.	court	3
61.	girl(s)	3
62.	hardship	3
63.	mad	3
64.	me	3
65.	misfortune	3
66.	pleasant	3
67.	scared	3
68.	sick	3
69.	sin	3
70.	solution	3
71.	time	3
72.	toil	3
73.	unpleasant	3
74.	woe	3
75.	angry	2
76.	black	2
77.	brewing	2
78.	cause	2
79.	children	2
80.	concern	2
81.	crying	2
82.	enemies	2
83.	good	2
84.	gun	2
85.	illness	2
86.	joy	2
87.	mischief	2
88.	mistake	2
89.	nerves	2
90.	now	2
91.	O.K.	2
92.	peaceful	2
93.	pleasure	2
94.	psychology	2
95.	punishment	2
96.	rough	2
97.	safe	2
98.	tail	2
99.	tough	2
100.	trial	2
101.	turmoil	2
102.	water	2
103.	with	2

104-260. (f = 1)
aggravation, ahead, aid, air, alley, annoy, argue, arrest, avoid, basketball, beef, blues, Bob, brig, brother, business, calm, class, come, comfort, complex, conflicts, conscience, content, counsel, crash, crook, crime, criminal, cry, dark, death, delinquent, despair, dick, discomfort, discontent, discouragement, disease, disgust, dislike, distant, distress, disturb, disturbed, do, dutch, ear, eat, econ., evil, exams, excited, face,

Trouble (contd)

family, father, flunk, fine,
fix, food, forget, free, freedom, frown, frustrate, gasp,
God, gripe, guest, hard times,
harmony, headache, helpless,
home, hope, horror, hurt, in,
innocent, involved, irk, jam,
Janet, Jerry, kids, kill, kind,
Korea, land, luck, Madame
Butterfly, many, marry, me,
mine, Mr. Bengston, more, much,
muddle, murder, neat, necessary,
need, negro, night, no, non-
trouble, nothing, party, punish,
quarrel, quiet, relatives, rest,
run, Russia, S.A.B., safety,
scold, scrap, seen, shoot,
sinister, sleep, slow, soft,
soldier, some, sorry, sound,
spinster, spot, starter,
streetcars, strife, study,
sweat, teacher, teeth, terror,
test, theft, ticket, travail,
trick, trouble, trying, uneasy,
uneasyness, U. of M., weak,
web, witch, worried, word,
worth, yes

Whiskey

No.	Response	Total
1.	drink(s)	284
2.	drunk	123
3.	sour(s)	78
4.	beer	52
5.	liquor	44
6.	gin	41
7.	bottles	39
8.	bad	32
9.	alcohol	18
10.	good	18
11.	rye	15
12.	glass	11
13.	women	11
14.	wine	10
15.	drinking	9
16.	rum	9
17.	bourbon	8
18.	evil	8
19.	bar	7
20.	scotch	7
21.	Four Roses	6
22.	soda	6
23.	brandy	5
24.	drunkard	5
25.	sick	5
26.	ad	4
27.	bitter	4
28.	booze	4
29.	hot	4
30.	no	4
31.	party	4
32.	water	4
33.	hangover	3
34.	liquid	3
35.	rebellion	3
36.	Seagram's	3
37.	taste	3
38.	ugh	3
39.	alcoholic	2
40.	beverage	2
41.	brown	2
42.	cold	2
43.	drunkenness	2

Whiskey (contd)

No.	Response	Total
44.	fool	2
45.	headache	2
46.	intoxicated(ion)	2
47.	Irish	2
48.	jug	2
49.	mix	2
50.	Old Granddad	2
51.	Saturday(night)	2
52.	7 & 7	2
53.	stimulant	2
54.	warm	2

55-131. (f = 1)
adian, aged, ahhh, barred, bill,
binge, bonded, bum, bunk, burn,
burp, (clear, club), coke,
color, contempt, Corky's,
cuttysarp, dad, delicious, dirt,
dislike, distrust, drug, dry,
dull nerves, enjoyment, fail,
foul, fun, ginger ale, Haig &
Haig, happy, heave, history,
horrible, ice, immoral, ish,
joviality, middle class, morals,
never touch it, New Year's, nice,
no good, nose, nuts, O.K., Old
Crow, old man, pain, pleasure,
poison, powerful, prohibition,
sea, 7 Crown, sickening, sin,
social, spirits, squelch,
Stevens, still, stimulus,
strong, stupid, tavern, thirsty,
vile, vodka, white, wild woman,
woolly, wrong, yes

Whistle

No.	Response	Total
1.	stop	131
2.	train	89
3.	noise	73
4.	sing	62
5.	blow	56
6.	tune	49
7.	girls	39
8.	sound	39
9.	dog	37
10.	song	33
11.	shrill	31
12.	boy	26
13.	man	24
14.	lips	21
15.	wolf	18
16.	call	17
17.	loud	17
18.	mouth	15
19.	cop	11
20.	police	10
21.	woman	10
22.	horn	8
23.	music	8
24.	sharp	8
25.	work	8
26.	policeman	7
27.	yell	7
28.	high	6
29.	pop	6
30.	shout	6
31.	teeth	6
32.	tone	6
33.	bell	5
34.	happy	5
35.	toot	5
36.	bird	4
37.	note(s)	4

Whistle (contd)

No.	Response	Total
38.	pucker	4
39.	talk	4
40.	siren	3
41.	tin	3
42.	tweet	3
43.	wood	3
44.	bait	2
45.	dark	2
46.	drink	2
47.	flirt	2
48.	hard	2
49.	hear	2
50.	holler	2
51.	hum	2
52.	mother	2
53.	pipe	2
54.	purse	2
55.	scream	2
56.	shriek	2
57.	signal	2
58.	sweet	2
59.	thistle	2

60-108. (f = 1)
at, bark, basketball, blew,
circle, come, cord, ear, Elita,
face, fellow, find, French, game,
gym, harsh, jay, Joe, kettle,
locomotive, long, low, melody,
nice, orange, pierce, pretty,
pursed lips, reed, referee, ring,
run, screech, screen, short,
silver, small, smile, speech,
sport, start, station, stopped,
tongue, wait, watch, wind,
wolf-call, wooden

White

No.	Response	Total
1.	black	617
2.	snow	136
3.	dark	39
4.	light	24
5.	house	23
6.	blue	12
7.	red	11
8.	clean	10
9.	color	8
10.	Christmas	7
11.	bear	6
12.	cloud	6
13.	pure	6
14.	rat	6
15.	beautiful	4
16.	sheet	4
17.	cat	3
18.	cloth	3
19.	dress	3
20.	nurse	3
21.	sky	3
22.	wash	3
23.	wedding	3
24.	bright	2
25.	cotton	2
26.	gown	2
27.	horse	2
28.	rain	2
29.	rose	2
30.	shirt	2

31-83. (f = 1)
ambulance, angel, ball, bells,
bird, blank, blanket, boy,
bride, bright, brilliant, brown,
castle, chalk, cliff, colt,

White (contd)

No.	Response	Total

cool, crayon, dog, dove, earth, face, glare, gold, green, grey, hack, hair, hospital, lace, linen, marble, milk, no, paper, rabbit, river, sacred, sands, scarf, show, skin, slow, spotless, straight, tie, uniform, Virgin Mary, wall, warm, water, white, yellow

Window

No.	Response	Total
1.	door	191
2.	glass	171
3.	pane	126
4.	shade	66
5.	light	59
6.	sill	49
7.	house	33
8.	see	33
9.	open	28
10.	look	23
11.	curtain	20
12.	frame	12
13.	view	12
14.	ledge	11
15.	scene	10
16.	chair	8
17.	outside	8
18.	clear	7
19.	frost	7
20.	sash	7
21.	bay	6
22.	snow	6
23.	air	5
24.	high	5
25.	box	4
26.	picture	4
27.	room	4
28.	wash	4
29.	opening	3
30.	screen	3
31.	sight	3
32.	sun	3
33.	transparent	3
34.	tree(s)	3
35.	wall	3
36.	washer	3
37.	woman	3
38.	dirty	2
39.	dressing	2
40.	fenetre	2
41.	flower	2
42.	hole	2
43.	home	2
44.	porthole	2
45.	seat	2
46.	shutter	2
47.	space	2
48.	street	2

49-90. (f = 1)
bars, bench, break, bright, broken, buildings, cleaner, cloud, cold, cord, curtail, dream, ear, floor, husband, landscape, large, man, million, mirror, nice, old, orphan, outdoors, peek, peeper, people, rain, rock, scenery, shelf, shape, shop, shopping, sky, storm, vision, wide, wind, wiper, wood, world

Wish

No.	Response	Total
1.	want	124
2.	dream	118
3.	desire	112
4.	hope	99
5.	well	70
6.	think	60
7.	star(s)	48
8.	bone	35
9.	ring(s)	33
10.	wash	14
11.	thought	12
12.	money	10
13.	true	10
14.	command	9
15.	get	9
16.	for	8
17.	Christmas	7
18.	birthday	6
19.	fairy	6
20.	thinking	6
21.	car	5
22.	gift	5
23.	make	5
24.	will	5
25.	wishbone	5
26.	you	5
27.	could	4
28.	happy	4
29.	have	4
30.	request	4
31.	chicken	3
32.	do	3
33.	fulfill	3
34.	good	3
35.	happen	3
36.	luck	3
37.	magic	3
38.	not	3
39.	receive	3
40.	ask	2
41.	child	2
42.	day dreaming	2
43.	demand	2
44.	die	2
45.	fish	2
46.	grant	2
47.	had	2
48.	here	2
49.	horse	2
50.	I	2
51.	idea	2
52.	like	2
53.	penny	2
54.	prayer	2
55.	rainbow	2
56.	reward	2
57.	song	2
58.	were	2
59.	wishful	2

60-157. (f = 1)
aim, always, anything, bath, beggar, behave, believe, boy, call, can, candle, cat, Cinderella, clear, comfort, dish, dreaming, drumstick, fairy tale, false, finger, forever, forget, fulfillment, game, given, gotten, granted, gratification, happiness, hawks, health, help, house, howl, ideal, idealist, Joan, keep, know, life, longing, love, man, marriage, materials, may, me, movie, must, myself, need, nice, object, obtain, okay, order, part, poet, pond, pray, present, promise, quirer, regret, repeat, reply, resourceful, response, say, school, secret, sex, sing,

Wish (contd)

No.	Response	Total

sleep, something, subjunctive, surprise, take, tale, three, thumb, time, to, travel, try, turkey, useless, vague, war, was, water, wealth, what, win, women, would, you were there

Woman

No.	Response	Total
1.	man(e)	646
2.	girl	88
3.	child	75
4.	mother	16
5.	lady	15
6.	dress	12
7.	sex	11
8.	female	8
9.	clothes	7
10.	hair	7
11.	hat	7
12.	nice	7
13.	baby	5
14.	cold	5
15.	figure	4
16.	old	4
17.	whistle	4
18.	beauty	3
19.	love	3
20.	pretty	3
21.	skirt	3
22.	wife	3
23.	boy	2
24.	friend	2
25.	furs	2
26.	Mom	2
27.	purse	2
28.	set	2
29.	soft	2

30-87. (f = 1)
adult, Ann, apron, Ardis, bad, bag, Barb, beautiful, Betty, birth, blind, block, blonde, blouse, breast, call, crown, date, dog, Erlys, face, fat, feminine, femininistic, femininity, flirt, frau, furcoat, gentle, goal, ha, head, her, hourglass, ill, kind, little, looks, lovely, Marilyn, Nancy, pregnate, prostitute, read, shape, shawl, shop, short, stocking, talk, tall, teacher, tender, whow, women, work, world

Working

No.	Response	Total
1.	hard	132
2.	loafing	99
3.	sleeping	79
4.	playing	65
5.	man	48
6.	money	45
7.	labor	42
8.	resting	42
9.	lazy	40
10.	job	29
11.	tired	28
12.	hours	18

Working (contd)

No.	Response	Total
13.	rest	13
14.	fast	11
15.	busy	9
16.	school	9
17.	pay	8
18.	play	8
19.	doing	7
20.	loaf	7
21.	sleep	7
22.	studying	7
23.	sweat	6
24.	fun	5
25.	idle	5
26.	store	5
27.	time	5
28.	work	5
29.	eating	4
30.	girl	4
31.	hospital	4
32.	hours	4
33.	laboring	4
34.	late	4
35.	people	4
36.	relaxing	4
37.	slaving	4
38.	slow	4
39.	sweating	4
40.	wages	4
41.	class	3
42.	earning	3
43.	fatigue	3
44.	leisure	3
45.	no	3
46.	office	3
47.	out	3
48.	shovel	3
49.	sitting	3
50.	summer	3
51.	toil	3
52.	tools	3
53.	typing	3
54.	bad	2
55.	book	2
56.	boredom	2
57.	conditions	2
58.	day	2
59.	Dayton's	2
60.	effort	2
61.	haul	2
62.	helping	2
63.	railroad	2
64.	relax	2
65.	rough	2
66.	shop	2
67.	stopping	2
68.	studies	2
69.	vacation	2

70-174. (f = 1)
action, axe, bank, baracade, bench, boss, brand, bricklayer, cafeteria, carpenter, clerk, cold, college, crew, desk, digging, diligently, dislike, do, dogs, dough, drawing, drudgery, drugstore, east, exercise, factory, father, flower, good, gravel, had, hand, hay, help, house, hurry, if, ish, Jim, La Belle, laborers, law, lax, lend, living, machines, making, mine, monotonous, mop, move, moving, music, nights, nix, non-employed, not, occupation, parking lot, part-time, payday, perspiration, plugging, powers, problem, production, progress, quiet, reactor, roof, run, saw, Sears,

Working (contd)

sewer, shift, shoes, shorthand, shoveling, sick, singing, sit, skilled, slave, sledge hammer, soft, steady, stop, straining, streetcar, table, tail, talking, task, telephone, thinking, too much, tough, trouble, truck, unemployed, walking, waste, with, women

Yellow

No.	Response	Total
1.	blue	156
2.	red	115
3.	color	106
4.	green	89
5.	black	73
6.	brown	29
7.	flower	29
8.	white	29
9.	bright	24
10.	orange	24
11.	butter	21
12.	coward	17
13.	sun	17
14.	birds	15
15.	gold	12
16.	cab	11
17.	light	11
18.	canary	10
19.	fever	9
20.	hair	9
21.	ribbon	8
22.	dress	7
23.	banana	6
24.	butterfly	6
25.	corn	6
26.	dog	6
27.	lemon	6
28.	car	5
29.	chicken	5
30.	river	5
31.	sea	5
32.	caution	4
33.	jacket	4
34.	pretty	4
35.	bed	3
36.	Chinese	3
37.	Jap	3
38.	jaundice	3
39.	pink	3
40.	room	3
41.	rose	3
42.	sweater	3
43.	afraid	2
44.	bee	2
45.	bellied	2
46.	belly	2
47.	convertible	2
48.	daffodil	2
49.	daisy	2
50.	fellow	2
51.	kitchen	2
52.	man	2
53.	picture	2
54.	purple	2
55.	shirt	2
56.	sky	2
57.	soft	2
58.	spread	2
59.	sunflower	2
60.	wall	2

61-125. (f = 1)

Yellow (contd)

No.	Response	Total

back, badge, band, bead, board, bug, bulb, carrot, circle, cloth, cloud, coin, cold, crayon, dandelion, doll, dye, egg, eyes, flag, flat, fly, fruit, guts, hazlenut, head, hornet, jack, leave, maid, mine, mountain, narcissus, orchid, paint, pear, pencil, pus, race, rod, run, sap, scared, scarf, seeds, shade, sick, sign, slow, spider, stars, stone, stoplights, straw, streak, stripe, taxi, top, tulip, ugly, violet, wallpaper, warm, wheat, yarn

CHAPTER 2

FREE-ASSOCIATION RESPONSES OF ENGLISH AND AUSTRALIAN STUDENTS TO 100 WORDS FROM THE KENT-ROSANOFF WORD ASSOCIATION TEST

Kenneth M. Miller

Independent Assessment and Research Center, Ltd., London, England

Free-association responses to words from the original Kent-Rosanoff word association test (Kent & Rosanoff, 1910) were obtained from students residing in England and in Australia. Professor Rosenzweig, in his chapter, compares certain characteristics of these data with the responses to the same stimuli by Ss in France, Germany, Italy, and the United States. Readers who are interested in such comparisons are referred to this discussion (see pp. 95-176). We will now describe the subject populations represented in the present norms and indicate critical aspects of the procedure that was followed.

THE ENGLISH SAMPLE

The English sample consisted of 200 men and 200 women who were drawn from seven universities located throughout England.[1] Approximately 60% were enrolled in first-year courses in one of the social sciences (psychology, sociology, economics, social administration, or social science), while the remainder were studying arts, science, or education. The median age of the subjects was 18 years, 5 months. The test was administered by a lecturer in each department, using the instructions and procedures reported by Russell and Jenkins (1954). The data were collected during 1961 and 1962.

THE AUSTRALIAN SAMPLE

The Australian Ss were drawn from the universities of Sydney and Tasmania.[2] They were first-year students of psychology of whom less than half would continue with further courses in the subject. The others would complete their studies in law, science, arts, or education. There were 100 Ss from Sydney, evenly divided by sex, and 72 females and 28 males in the Tasmanian group. The test was administered individually, using the conventional Kent-Rosanoff procedure. Response latencies were recorded. The Sydney norms were collected in 1958 and the Tasmanian norms equally in 1957 and 1958.

[1]The assistance of Dr. S. Chown, Dr. H. Himmelweit, Dr. P. McKellar, Dr. J. Newson, Professor F. V. Smith, Dr. F. Warburton, and Mr. A. Yates who arranged the testing in the various universities is gratefully acknowledged.

[2]The Sydney data were collected and made available by M. Nicol, while the Tasmanian data were collected for the author by Mrs. P. Waters.

RESULTS

The results of these tests are presented in abbreviated form in the Appendix to this chapter. For both the English and Australian samples, the five most frequent responses to each stimulus word are listed, together with their respective frequencies of occurrence. (Note: the total number of Ss in the English sample is 400 and in the Australian sample is 200.) Also provided is the number of different responses given to each stimulus. In compiling the results, the Russell-Jenkins procedure was followed, i.e., singular and plural forms of nouns were combined. For the English sample, all other responses were treated separately. For the Australian sample, certain other responses were combined: verbs and participles, nouns and adverbs, and variances of nouns, e.g., *sit* and *sitting, peace* and *peaceful, worm* and *earthworm.* In all, 50 words had one or more of this type of response, but as the frequency of the minor response was always very low, it is unlikely that the order of dominant responses was affected. The actual number of different responses for these words is fewer by one for 34 words and by two for 16 words.

REFERENCES

Kent, G. H., & Rosanoff, A. J. (1910). A study of association in insanity. *American Journal of Insanity,* **67**, 37-96, 317-390.

Russell, W. A., & Jenkins, J. J. (1954). The complete Minnesota norms for responses to 100 words from the Kent-Rosanoff word association test. Technical Report No. 11, University of Minnesota, Contract N8-ONR-66216, Minneapolis, Minn.

1. Table

No.	Response	Frequency
1.	chair	311
2.	cloth	12
3.	talk	12
4.	desk	10
5.	food	5

No. diff. resp. 39

2. Dark

No.	Response	Frequency
1.	light	271
2.	night	56
3.	room	17
4.	black	15
5.	bright	3

No. diff. resp. 39

3. Music

No.	Response	Frequency
1.	sound	59
2.	note(s)	39
3.	piano	35
4.	song(s)	22
5.	Beethoven	17

No. diff. resp. 100

4. Sickness

No.	Response	Frequency
1.	health	203
2.	bed	33
3.	ill	32
4.	death	18
5.	illness	18

No. diff. resp. 66

5. Man

No.	Response	Frequency
1.	woman	311
2.	dog	20
3.	boy	10
4.	child	8
5.	hat	5

No. diff. resp. 45

6. Deep

No.	Response	Frequency
1.	shallow	92
2.	sea	79
3.	water	39

6. Deep (contd)

No.	Response	Frequency
4.	dark	26
5.	soft	17

No. diff. resp. 59

7. Soft

No.	Response	Frequency
1.	hard	130
2.	cushion	22
3.	light	21
4.	bed	18
5.	pillow	13

No. diff. resp. 93

8. Eating

No.	Response	Frequency
1.	drinking	118
2.	food	98
3.	sleeping	28
4.	apple	11
5.	mouth	10

No. diff. resp. 91

9. Mountain

No.	Response	Frequency
1.	hill	73
2.	valley	37
3.	snow	24
4.	high	23
5.	molehill	20

No. diff. resp. 99

10. House

No.	Response	Frequency
1.	home	54
2.	garden	40
3.	door	29
4.	bricks	23
5.	chimney, roof	17

No. diff. resp. 112

11. Black

No.	Response	Frequency
1.	white	281
2.	night	18
3.	cat	9
4.	dark	8
5.	sheep	6

No. diff. resp. 63

12. Mutton

No.	Response	Frequency
1.	chop	111
2.	lamb	109
3.	sheep	71
4.	beef	21
5.	meat	19

No. diff. resp. 38

13. Comfort

No.	Response	Frequency
1.	ease	62
2.	chair	56
3.	bed	29
4.	warmth	22
5.	home	20

No. diff. resp. 94

14. Hand

No.	Response	Frequency
1.	foot (ee)	88
2.	finger(s)	66
3.	glove	54
4.	arm	36
5.	mouth	26

No. diff. resp. 72

15. Short

No.	Response	Frequency
1.	long	167
2.	tall	102
3.	fat	26
4.	small	10
5.	man	6

No. diff. resp. 66

16. Fruit

No.	Response	Frequency
1.	apple(s)	122
2.	orange	41
3.	vegatable	18
4.	tree(s)	17
5.	juice, fly, flies	12

No. diff. resp. 81

17. Butterfly

No.	Response	Frequency
1.	moth	110
2.	wing(s)	43

17. Butterfly (contd)

No.	Response	Frequency
3.	net	25
4.	insect	15
5.	color	15
No. diff. resp. 84		

18. Smooth

No.	Response	Frequency
1.	rough	126
2.	soft	62
3.	hard	32
4.	silk	17
5.	hands	11
No. diff. resp. 88		

19. Command

No.	Response	Frequency
1.	order	127
2.	obey	78
3.	army	21
4.	officer	13
5.	soldier	10
No. diff. resp. 98		

20. Chair

No.	Response	Frequency
1.	table	163
2.	leg	43
3.	seat	30
4.	sit	26
5.	cushion	20
No. diff. resp. 60		

21. Sweet

No.	Response	Frequency
1.	sour	138
2.	sugar	44
3.	bitter	37
4.	tooth	19
5.	chocolate(s)	18
No. diff. resp.		

22. Whistle

No.	Response	Frequency
1.	stop	56
2.	train	46
3.	blow	23
4.	dog	23
5.	sing	18
No. diff. resp. 90		

23. Woman

No.	Response	Frequency
1.	man	205
2.	child	58
3.	girl	19
4.	mother	7
5.	clothes	7
No. diff. resp. 79		

24. Cold

No.	Response	Frequency
1.	hot	138
2.	snow	75
3.	ice	40
4.	warm	30
5.	water	11
No. diff. resp. 60		

25. Slow

No.	Response	Frequency
1.	fast	159
2.	quick	63
3.	train	12
4.	snail	11
5.	tortoise	7
No. diff. resp. 100		

26. Wish

No.	Response	Frequency
1.	desire	69
2.	well	34
3.	want	32
4.	bone	28
5.	hope	26
No. diff. resp. 100		

27. River

No.	Response	Frequency
1.	water	80
2.	streem	62
3.	flow	19
4.	thames	16
5.	boat, bank	14
No. diff. resp. 111		

28. White

No.	Response	Frequency
1.	black	189
2.	snow	57
3.	pure	16
4.	sheet	6
5.	white wash, blue	6
No. diff. resp. 98		

29. Beautiful

No.	Response	Frequency
1.	ugly	109
2.	woman(en)	32
3.	lovely	29
4.	girl	28
5.	pretty	16
No. diff. resp. 115		

30. Window

No.	Response	Frequency
1.	glass	54
2.	pane	51
3.	door	36
4.	light	35
5.	view	32
No. diff. resp. 74		

31. Rough

No.	Response	Frequency
1.	smooth	246
2.	hard	14
3.	sea	10
4.	hands	9
5.	ready	7
No. diff. resp. 79		

32. Citizen

No.	Response	Frequency
1.	city	34
2.	man(e)	34
3.	state	32
4.	town	29
5.	kane	27
No. diff. resp. 128		

33. Foot

No.	Response	Frequency
1.	shoe(s)	86
2.	hand	50
3.	toe(s)	50
4.	leg(s)	45
5.	mouth	34
No. diff. resp. 70		

34. Spider

No.	Response	Frequency
1.	web	195
2.	fly(ies)	58
3.	legs	25
4.	insect	25
5.	black	10
No. diff. resp. 64		

35. Needle

No.	Response	Frequency
1.	thread	140
2.	cotton	58
3.	pin	41
4.	eye	40
5.	sharp	37

No. diff. resp. 42

36. Red

No.	Response	Frequency
1.	white	62
2.	blue	54
3.	blood	33
4.	black	28
5.	green	21

No. diff. resp. 98

37. Sleep

No.	Response	Frequency
1.	bed	94
2.	dream(s)	43
3.	awake	27
4.	rest	27
5.	deep	16

No. diff. resp. 87

38. Anger

No.	Response	Frequency
1.	temper	36
2.	red	35
3.	race	32
4.	fear	26
5.	hate	16

No. diff. resp. 128

39. Carpet

No.	Response	Frequency
1.	floor	95
2.	soft	37
3.	rug	37
4.	pile	22
5.	slipper(s)	15

No. diff. resp. 84

40. Girl

No.	Response	Frequency
1.	boy	277
2.	school	13
3.	hair	8
4.	woman	6
5.	Young, youth	5

No. diff. resp. 65

41. High

No.	Response	Frequency
1.	low	249
2.	mountain	22
3.	wall	11
4.	jump	7
5.	tall, heel	5

No. diff. resp. 73

42. Working

No.	Response	Frequency
1.	hard	53
2.	man(e)	46
3.	sleeping	37
4.	class(es)	20
5.	playing	20

No. diff. resp. 115

43. Sour

No.	Response	Frequency
1.	sweet	172
2.	grape(s)	51
3.	lemon(s)	34
4.	milk	33
5.	bitter	23

No. diff. resp. 45

44. Earth

No.	Response	Frequency
1.	soil	47
2.	sky	43
3.	ground	23
4.	round	22
5.	heavens, glove	18

No. diff. resp. 98

45. Trouble

No.	Response	Frequency
1.	worry	25
2.	maker	18
3.	sorrow	15
4.	fear	15
5.	anger	12

No. diff. resp. 168

46. Soldier

No.	Response	Frequency
1.	sailor	125
2.	army	43
3.	uniform	36
4.	war	27
5.	gun, man	18

No. diff. resp. 91

47. Cabbage

No.	Response	Frequency
1.	green	59
2.	vegetable	45
3.	cauliflower	25
4.	patch	20
5.	garden	16

No. diff. resp. 97

48. Hard

No.	Response	Frequency
1.	soft	234
2.	nail(s)	11
3.	egg(s)	9
4.	stone	7
5.	iron, steel	7

No. diff. resp. 82

49. Eagle

No.	Response	Frequency
1.	bird(s)	90
2.	nest	28
3.	mountain	20
4.	wings	19
5.	eyrie	17

No. diff. resp. 98

50. Stomach

No.	Response	Frequency
1.	food	81
2.	ache	59
3.	pain	35
4.	ulcer(s)	17
5.	intestines	14

No. diff. resp. 98

51. Stem

No.	Response	Frequency
1.	flower	151
2.	plant	52
3.	leaf	36
4.	stalk	33
5.	root	18

No. diff. resp. 64

52. Lamp

No.	Response	Frequency
1.	light	244
2.	shade	42
3.	bulb	15
4.	standard	9
5.	lighter	8

No. diff. resp. 54

53. Dream

No.	Response	Frequency
1.	sleep	134
2.	nightmare	25
3.	bed	19
4.	night	15
5.	Freud	15

No. diff. resp. 110

54. Yellow

No.	Response	Frequency
1.	blue	33
2.	red	32
3.	green	29
4.	sun	23
5.	black	22

No. diff. resp. 105

55. Bread

No.	Response	Frequency
1.	butter	222
2.	jam	15
3.	cheese	14
4.	food	14
5.	water	14

No. diff. resp. 63

56. Justice

No.	Response	Frequency
1.	law	72
2.	peace	60
3.	judge	59
4.	court	39
5.	injustice	11

No. diff. resp. 93

57. Boy

No.	Response	Frequency
1.	girl	291
2.	scout	9
3.	blue	7
4.	friend	5
5.	man, school	4

No. diff. resp. 70

58. Light

No.	Response	Frequency
1.	dark	181
2.	lamp	23
3.	darkness	17
4.	heavy	14
5.	sun	11

No. diff. resp. 88

59. Health

No.	Response	Frequency
1.	sickness	106
2.	wealth	34
3.	happiness	29
4.	doctor(s)	18
5.	illness	17

No. diff. resp. 93

60. Bible

No.	Response	Frequency
1.	God	63
2.	book	61
3.	story	48
4.	religion	27
5.	black	24

No. diff. resp. 83

61. Memory

No.	Response	Frequency
1.	mind	24
2.	thought	21
3.	forgetfulness	17
4.	remember	16
5.	forgetting	14

No. diff. resp. 140

62. Sheep

No.	Response	Frequency
1.	lamb	70
2.	goat(s)	44
3.	wool	36
4.	field(s)	20
5.	Sleep, shepherd	17

No. diff. resp. 78

63. Bath

No.	Response	Frequency
1.	water	149
2.	clean	24
3.	soap	20
4.	tub	17
5.	wash	13

No. diff. resp. 84

64. Cottage

No.	Response	Frequency
1.	house	63
2.	country	44
3.	pie	34
4.	thatch	34
5.	rose(s)	19

No. diff. resp. 86

65. Swift

No.	Response	Frequency
1.	slow	72
2.	birds	62
3.	swallow	57
4.	fast	41
5.	sure	22

No. diff. resp. 84

66. Blue

No.	Response	Frequency
1.	sky(ies)	99
2.	green	32
3.	sea	28
4.	black	24
5.	red	21

No. diff. resp. 81

67. Hungry

No.	Response	Frequency
1.	food	99
2.	thirsty	77
3.	eat	17
4.	empty	11
5.	cold	11

No. diff. resp. 104

68. Priest

No.	Response	Frequency
1.	church	107
2.	collar	14
3.	Catholic	13
4.	vicar	12
5.	parson	12

No. diff. resp. 115

69. Ocean

No.	Response	Frequency
1.	sea(s)	117
2.	water	41
3.	deep	35
4.	wave(s)	28
5.	bed	24

No. diff. resp.

70. Head

No.	Response	Frequency
1.	hair	53
2.	shoulders	46
3.	foot(ee)	36
4.	hat	25
5.	master	25

No. diff. resp. 79

71. Stove

No.	Response	Frequency
1.	fire	47
2.	pipe	47
3.	heat	39
4.	cooking	37
5.	oven	37

No. diff. resp. 67

77. Hammer

No.	Response	Frequency
1.	nail	145
2.	tong(s)	61
3.	sickle	38
4.	chisel	17
5.	herd	15

No. diff. resp. 67

83. Loud

No.	Response	Frequency
1.	soft	178
2.	noise	73
3.	quiet	21
4.	clear	14
5.	speaker, bang	11

No. diff. resp. 59

72. Long

No.	Response	Frequency
1.	short	261
2.	road	13
3.	tall	11
4.	thin	9
5.	ruler	5

No. diff. resp. 78

78. Thirsty

No.	Response	Frequency
1.	drink	116
2.	water	76
3.	dry	55
4.	hungry	44
5.	beer	18

No. diff. resp. 55

84. Thief

No.	Response	Frequency
1.	burglar	37
2.	robber	36
3.	steal	36
4.	night	30
5.	policeman(e)	24

No. diff. resp. 129

73. Religion

No.	Response	Frequency
1.	church(es)	73
2.	God	60
3.	faith	24
4.	Christianity	21
5.	Roman Catholic	17

No. diff. resp. 129

79. City

No.	Response	Frequency
1.	town	89
2.	square	48
3.	London	35
4.	street	15
5.	people	10

No. diff. resp. 110

85. Lion

No.	Response	Frequency
1.	tiger	93
2.	mane	27
3.	roar	21
4.	lioness	19
5.	unicorn	17

No. diff. resp. 100

74. Whisky

No.	Response	Frequency
1.	drink	76
2.	soda	59
3.	gin	31
4.	bottle	21
5.	scotch	16

No. diff. resp. 86

80. Square

No.	Response	Frequency
1.	round	113
2.	circle	42
3.	peg	12
4.	oblong	11
5.	box, trees	10

No. diff. resp. 120

86. Joy

No.	Response	Frequency
1.	happiness	80
2.	sorrow	66
3.	sadness	25
4.	happy	15
5.	grief	12

No. diff. resp. 110

75. Child

No.	Response	Frequency
1.	mother	88
2.	baby	30
3.	parent(s)	24
4.	man	21
5.	adult	18

No. diff. resp. 105

81. Butter

No.	Response	Frequency
1.	bread	155
2.	margarine	33
3.	yellow	21
4.	cheese	18
5.	milk	18

No. diff. resp. 62

87. Bed

No.	Response	Frequency
1.	sleep	133
2.	breakfast	39
3.	sheets	18
4.	rest	16
5.	comfort	13

No. diff. resp. 89

76. Bitter

No.	Response	Frequency
1.	sweet	225
2.	lemon	60
3.	beer	37
4.	sour	15
5.	mild	6

No. diff. resp. 44

82. Doctor

No.	Response	Frequency
1.	nurse	59
2.	illness	38
3.	patient	36
4.	medicine	31
5.	stethoscope	18

No. diff. resp. 112

88. Heavy

No.	Response	Frequency
1.	light	187
2.	weight(s)	40
3.	load	23
4.	lead	18
5.	hard, soft	6

No. diff. resp. 86

89. Tobacco

No.	Response	Frequency
1.	smoke	145
2.	pipe	70
3.	cigarette	54
4.	pouch	16
5.	smoking	15
No. diff. resp. 65		

95. Salt

No.	Response	Frequency
1.	pepper	107
2.	sea	37
3.	water	28
4.	sugar	20
5.	earth	20
No. diff. resp. 82		

90. Baby

No.	Response	Frequency
1.	boy	47
2.	mother	46
3.	child	23
4.	cry	22
5.	cot	22
No. diff. resp. 106		

96. Street

No.	Response	Frequency
1.	road	78
2.	lamp	36
3.	house(s)	34
4.	town	20
5.	cars	14
No. diff. resp. 101		

91. Moon

No.	Response	Frequency
1.	stars	87
2.	sun	56
3.	sky	24
4.	shine	24
5.	night	23
No. diff. resp. 76		

97. King

No.	Response	Frequency
1.	queen	265
2.	crown	18
3.	kong	15
4.	George	8
5.	cole, throne	7
No. diff. resp. 60		

92. Scissors

No.	Response	Frequency
1.	cut	162
2.	sharp	33
3.	cutting	27
4.	knife	17
5.	material	16
No. diff. resp. 69		

98. Cheese

No.	Response	Frequency
1.	bread	67
2.	biscuits	
3.	mouse (mice)	24
4.	milk	22
5.	butter	18
No. diff. resp. 95		

93. Quiet

No.	Response	Frequency
1.	loud	65
2.	peace	53
3.	noisy	32
4.	noise	26
5.	soft	23
No. diff. resp. 85		

99. Blossom

No.	Response	Frequency
1.	apple	106
2.	flower	90
3.	tree(s)	47
4.	spring	22
5.	pink	15
No. diff. resp. 67		

94. Green

No.	Response	Frequency
1.	grass	134
2.	yellow	30
3.	blue	29
4.	field	20
5.	belt	20
No. diff. resp. 88		

100. Afraid

No.	Response	Frequency
1.	fear	133
2.	dark	38
3.	frightened	16
4.	scared	12
5.	terror	9
No. diff. resp. 107		

1. Table

No.	Response	Frequency
1.	chair	174
2.	cloth	4
3.	top	3
4.	mat	3
5.	leg, wall, wood, food, desk	2

No. diff. resp. 15

2. Dark

No.	Response	Frequency
1.	light	140
2.	night	20
3.	room	11
4.	black	11
5.	cat, bright, white	2

No. diff. resp. 18

3. Music

No.	Response	Frequency
1.	piano	47
2.	notes	22
3.	sound	17
4.	songs	16
5.	orchestra	7

No. diff. resp. 60

4. Sickness

No.	Response	Frequency
1.	health	73
2.	bed	45
3.	ill(ness)	21
4.	doctor	18
5.	hospital	8

No. diff. resp. 26

5. Man

No.	Response	Frequency
1.	woman	154
2.	boy	6
3.	hat	4
4.	child	4
5.	clothes, car, wife, horse	2

No. diff. resp. 28

6. Deep

No.	Response	Frequency
1.	shallow	55
2.	water	38
3.	sea	29
4.	dark	17
5.	blue, ocean	6

No. diff. resp. 34

7. Soft

No.	Response	Frequency
1.	hard	64
2.	light	16
3.	loud	13
4.	bed	13
5.	pillow	8

No. diff. resp. 54

8. Eating

No.	Response	Frequency
1.	food	79
2.	drinking	33
3.	apple	14
4.	sleeping	13
5.	hungry(er)	10

No. diff. resp. 33

9. Mountain

No.	Response	Frequency
1.	hill	63
2.	climb	25
3.	valley	18
4.	high	14
5.	snow	11

No. diff. resp. 44

10. House

No.	Response	Frequency
1.	chimney	22
2.	door	21
3.	roof	21
4.	home	18
5.	garden	13

No. diff. resp. 57

11. Black

No.	Response	Frequency
1.	white	133
2.	dark	17
3.	darkness	11

11. Black (contd)

No.	Response	Frequency
4.	night	8
5.	colour	5

No. diff. resp. 31

12. Mutton

No.	Response	Frequency
1.	lamb	58
2.	sheep	40
3.	beef	26
4.	meat	21
5.	bird	14

No. diff. resp. 23

13. Comfort

No.	Response	Frequency
1.	chair	68
2.	bed	19
3.	ease	18
4.	discomfort	12
5.	home	9

No. diff. resp. 49

14. Hand

No.	Response	Frequency
1.	fingers	72
2.	foot(ee)	58
3.	arm	21
4.	mouth	7
5.	fingernail	6

No. diff. resp. 26

15. Short

No.	Response	Frequency
1.	tall	75
2.	long	55
3.	fat	18
4.	man	6
5.	person	4

No. diff. resp. 37

16. Fruit

No.	Response	Frequency
1.	apple	69
2.	tree(s)	34
3.	pear(s)	25
4.	vegetable	15
5.	bananna(s)	8

No. diff. resp. 31

17. Butterfly

No.	Response	Frequency
1.	moth	57
2.	wing(s)	21
3.	insect	20
4.	bird	16
5.	caterpillar, net	9

No. diff. resp. 43

18. Smooth

No.	Response	Frequency
1.	rough	75
2.	soft	23
3.	table	10
4.	flat	9
5.	hard	8

No. diff. resp. 57

19. Command

No.	Response	Frequency
1.	order	74
2.	obey	33
3.	soldier	11
4.	army	9
5.	teacher	6

No. diff. resp. 48

20. Chair

No.	Response	Frequency
1.	table	119
2.	sit	17
3.	legs	16
4.	seat	10
5.	desk	4

No. diff. resp. 27

21. Sweet

No.	Response	Frequency
1.	sour	78
2.	sugar	29
3.	lolly(s)	20
4.	bitter	9
5.	chocolate(s)	7

No. diff. resp. 44

22. Whistle

No.	Response	Frequency
1.	sing	30
2.	tune	16
3.	blow	14
4.	dog	12
5.	train	12

No. diff. resp. 56

23. Woman

No.	Response	Frequency
1.	man	118
2.	child	13
3.	girl(little)	13
4.	dress	10
5.	female	5

No. diff. resp. 32

24. Cold

No.	Response	Frequency
1.	hot	77
2.	warm	17
3.	ice	13
4.	winter	11
5.	snow	9

No. diff. resp. 54

25. Slow

No.	Response	Frequency
1.	fast	88
2.	quick	15
3.	train	13
4.	tortoise	9
5.	snail	9

No. diff. resp. 52

26. Wish

No.	Response	Frequency
1.	want(ing)	32
2.	hope	20
3.	think(ing)	19
4.	desire	18
5.	well	13

No. diff. resp. 41

27. River

No.	Response	Frequency
1.	stream	48
2.	water(running)	38
3.	flow(ing)	11
4.	deep	8
5.	lake, creek	7

No. diff. resp. 53

28. White

No.	Response	Frequency
1.	black	109
2.	snow	23
3.	wall	8
4.	sheet	7
5.	dark, clean	4

No. diff. resp. 39

29. Beautiful

No.	Response	Frequency
1.	ugly	53
2.	pretty	25
3.	woman(en)	20
4.	lovely	18
5.	girl	16

No. diff. resp. 51

30. Window

No.	Response	Frequency
1.	door	28
2.	pane	28
3.	glass	24
4.	view	21
5.	light	17

No. diff. resp. 45

31. Rough

No.	Response	Frequency
1.	smooth	108
2.	sea	9
3.	road	8
4.	hard	7
5.	surface	5

No. diff. resp. 50

32. Citizen

No.	Response	Frequency
1.	person	38
2.	man(en)	32
3.	people	14
4.	town	14
5.	city	11

No. diff. resp. 63

33. Foot

No.	Response	Frequency
1.	toe(s)	41
2.	shoe	41
3.	leg(s)	38
4.	hand	36
5.	walking	4

No. diff. resp. 34

34. Spider

No.	Response	Frequency
1.	web(cob)	86
2.	insect	19
3.	fly(ies)	19
4.	leg(s)	8
5.	black	6

No. diff. resp. 43

35. Needle

No.	Response	Frequency
1.	thread	75
2.	cotton	29
3.	pin	27
4.	sharp	15
5.	eye	12
No. diff. resp. 27		

36. Red

No.	Response	Frequency
1.	white	40
2.	black	27
3.	blue	25
4.	blood	12
5.	colour	8
No. diff. resp. 51		

37. Sleep

No.	Response	Frequency
1.	bed	62
2.	wake	31
3.	rest	14
4.	pillow	12
5.	dream(s)	10
No. diff. resp. 42		

38. Anger

No.	Response	Frequency
1.	temper	23
2.	red	13
3.	fury(ious)	13
4.	hate(red)	11
5.	wrath	7
No. diff. resp. 79		

39. Carpet

No.	Response	Frequency
1.	floor	72
2.	soft(ness)	30
3.	rug	11
4.	mat	10
5.	chair	7
No. diff. resp. 48		

40. Girl

No.	Response	Frequency
1.	boy	121
2.	dress	13
3.	clothes	7
4.	woman	7
5.	hair	5
No. diff. resp. 37		

41. High

No.	Response	Frequency
1.	low	108
2.	mountain	25
3.	tall	11
4.	sky	5
5.	short, ceiling	3
No. diff. resp. 43		

42. Working

No.	Response	Frequency
1.	hard	27
2.	sleeping	18
3.	man	16
4.	lazy(ing)	11
5.	busy	9
No. diff. resp. 67		

43. Sour

No.	Response	Frequency
1.	sweet	100
2.	lemon(s)	33
3.	bitter	14
4.	grape(s)	10
5.	milk	9
No. diff. resp. 26		

44. Earth

No.	Response	Frequency
1.	ground	29
2.	dirt(y)	14
3.	soil	14
4.	sky	12
5.	brown	10
No. diff. resp. 67		

45. Trouble

No.	Response	Frequency
1.	worry	33
2.	sorrow	12
3.	work	6
4.	punishment	5
5.	care, anger(y) pain, harm, anxiety	4
No. diff. resp. 86		

46. Soldier

No.	Response	Frequency
1.	army	41
2.	sailor	28
3.	war	24
4.	uniform	19
5.	man	14
No. diff. resp. 46		

47. Cabbage

No.	Response	Frequency
1.	vegetable	38
2.	cauliflower	37
3.	leaf(ves)	14
4.	garden	11
5.	food, lettuce	9
No. diff. resp. 52		

48. Hard

No.	Response	Frequency
1.	soft	112
2.	wood	9
3.	easy	5
4.	work	5
5.	rock, stone	4
No. diff. resp. 53		

49. Eagle

No.	Response	Frequency
1.	bird(big)	80
2.	hawk	18
3.	nest	15
4.	high	7
5.	beak, wings, mountain	6
No. diff. resp. 46		

50. Stomach

No.	Response	Frequency
1.	food	71
2.	body	18
3.	pain	14
4.	hunger	10
5.	intestines	8
No. diff. resp. 48		

51. Stem

No.	Response	Frequency
1.	flower	112
2.	plant	23
3.	stalk	14
4.	leaf	8
5.	tree	7
No. diff. resp. 35		

52. Lamp

No.	Response	Frequency
1.	light	143
2.	shade	19
3.	reading	5
4.	bulb	4
5.	globe	3
No. diff. resp. 25		

53. Dream

No.	Response	Frequency
1.	sleep	77
2.	nightmare	34
3.	night	11
4.	bed	9
5.	awake, wish(es) sleeping	4

No. diff. resp. 54

54. Yellow

No.	Response	Frequency
1.	black	24
2.	colour	18
3.	flower(s)	18
4.	blue	15
5.	red	9

No. diff. resp. 55

55. Bread

No.	Response	Frequency
1.	butter	84
2.	food	25
3.	water	13
4.	knife	12
5.	eat(ing)	11

No. diff. resp. 38

56. Justice

No.	Response	Frequency
1.	peace	56
2.	law	30
3.	judge	23
4.	court	14
5.	injustice	10

No. diff. resp. 41

57. Boy

No.	Response	Frequency
1.	girl	137
2.	man	8
3.	football	3
4.	dog	3
5.	brother	3

No. diff. resp. 40

58. Light

No.	Response	Frequency
1.	darkness	61
2.	dark	41
3.	lamp	10
4.	sun	9
5.	window	8

No. diff. resp. 41

59. Health

No.	Response	Frequency
1.	sickness	57
2.	happiness	33
3.	illness	14
4.	strength	13
5.	wealth	13

No. diff. resp. 40

60. Bible

No.	Response	Frequency
1.	book	38
2.	religion	27
3.	God	24
4.	church	17
5.	prayer	13

No. diff. resp. 43

61. Memory

No.	Response	Frequency
1.	mind	23
2.	thinking	15
3.	thought	14
4.	remember	13
5.	forget(ing) forgetfulness	9

No. diff. resp. 60

62. Sheep

No.	Response	Frequency
1.	lamb	42
2.	wool	36
3.	goats	18
4.	cattle	16
5.	cows	8

No. diff. resp. 41

63. Bath

No.	Response	Frequency
1.	water	102
2.	wash	18
3.	clean	12
4.	cleanliness	11
5.	tub	9

No. diff. resp. 25

64. Cottage

No.	Response	Frequency
1.	house	94
2.	home(s)	10
3.	garden	9
4.	thatch	6
5.	chimney --small	5

No. diff. resp. 48

65. Swift

No.	Response	Frequency
1.	slow	43
2.	fast	40
3.	quick(ly)	15
4.	bird(s)	14
5.	river	14

No. diff. resp. 46

66. Blue

No.	Response	Frequency
1.	sky(ies)	55
2.	red	21
3.	green	19
4.	water	15
5.	black sea	13

No. diff. resp. 33

67. Hungry

No.	Response	Frequency
1.	food	71
2.	thirsty	32
3.	bread	12
4.	eat(ing)	8
5.	stomach	7

No. diff. resp. 47

68. Priest

No.	Response	Frequency
1.	church	55
2.	religion	17
3.	black	11
4.	minister	9
5.	nun	7

No. diff. resp. 61

69. Ocean

No.	Response	Frequency
1.	sea(s)	49
2.	water	47
3.	ship(s)	20
4.	blue(ness)	19
5.	wave(s)	17

No. diff. resp. 27

70. Head

No.	Response	Frequency
1.	hair	77
2.	body	14
3.	shoulders	14
4.	foot(ee)	12
5.	hand(s)	8

No. diff. resp. 45

71. Stove

No.	Response	Frequency
1.	cooking	40
2.	heat	26
3.	fire	18
4.	hot	16
5.	oven	11
No. diff. resp. 41		

72. Long

No.	Response	Frequency
1.	short	122
2.	road	11
3.	tall	5
4.	thin	4
5.	hair	4
No. diff. resp. 54		

73. Religion

No.	Response	Frequency
1.	church	58
2.	God	25
3.	bible	16
4.	priest	12
5.	faith	11
No. diff. resp. 59		

74. Whiskey

No.	Response	Frequency
1.	drink(ing)	59
2.	soda	18
3.	beer	12
4.	rum	10
5.	bottle, gin, alcohol	10
No. diff. resp. 36		

75. Child

No.	Response	Frequency
1.	mother	38
2.	baby	19
3.	boy	13
4.	man	11
5.	parent(s) adult	10
No. diff. resp. 55		

76. Bitter

No.	Response	Frequency
1.	sweet	102
2.	sour	27
3.	lemon	13
4.	taste	6
5.	drink, angry	4
No. diff. resp. 41		

77. Hammer

No.	Response	Frequency
1.	nail	121
2.	tongs	20
3.	sickle	7
4.	anvil	5
5.	hit	5
No. diff. resp. 37		

78. Thirsty

No.	Response	Frequency
1.	water	68
2.	drinking	57
3.	hungry	33
4.	dry	7
5.	hunger, lemon, glass	3
No. diff. resp. 29		

79. City

No.	Response	Frequency
1.	town	78
2.	people	21
3.	country	10
4.	citizen	7
5.	standing	7
No. diff. resp. 40		

80. Square

No.	Response	Frequency
1.	round	87
2.	circle	16
3.	franklin	7
4.	rectangle	5
5.	box, garden, park	4
No. diff. resp. 60		

81. Butter

No.	Response	Frequency
1.	bread	97
2.	yellow	11
3.	melting	9
4.	knife	8
5.	cow, sugar	6
No. diff resp. 39		

82. Doctor

No.	Response	Frequency
1.	nurse	63
2.	sick(ness)	27
3.	lawyer	14
4.	medicine	12
5.	hospital	12
No. diff. resp. 43		

83. Loud

No.	Response	Frequency
1.	soft	97
2.	noisy	27
3.	noise	21
4.	quiet	6
5.	clear, voice	5
No. diff. resp. 35		

84. Thief

No.	Response	Frequency
1.	steal(ing)	38
2.	robber	38
3.	burglar	14
4.	jewelry	10
5.	money	10
No. diff. resp. 58		

85. Lion

No.	Response	Frequency
1.	tiger	82
2.	animal(s)	12
3.	roar(ing)	12
4.	cage	9
5.	cub	7
No. diff. resp 62		

86. Joy

No.	Response	Frequency
1.	happiness	78
2.	sorrow	36
3.	sadness	8
4.	peace	8
5.	gladness	8
No. diff. resp. 46		

87. Bed

No.	Response	Frequency
1.	sleep	88
2.	blanket(s)	14
3.	sheets	8
4.	breakfast	8
5.	pillow	8
No. diff. resp. 46		

88. Heavy

No.	Response	Frequency
1.	light	70
2.	load	16
3.	weighty	11
4.	weight(s)	8
5.	soft, lead	7
No. diff. resp. 52		

89. Tobacco

No.	Response	Frequency
1.	smoke(ing)	114
2.	pipe	35
3.	cigarette	29
4.	smell	6
5.	pouch, cigar	2

No. diff. resp. 18

90. Baby

No.	Response	Frequency
1.	mother	33
2.	child(ren)	33
3.	cry(ing)	21
4.	boy	9
5.	girl, cradle	7

No. diff. resp. 60

91. Moon

No.	Response	Frequency
1.	stars	44
2.	sun	33
3.	sky	24
4.	light	20
5.	night	18

No. diff. resp. 43

92. Scissors

No.	Response	Frequency
1.	cut(ting)	95
2.	material	17
3.	sharp	15
4.	paper	14
5.	sharp(ness)	9

No. diff. resp. 27

93. Quiet

No.	Response	Frequency
1.	peace(ful)	31
2.	soft	28
3.	noise(y)	26
4.	loud	24
5.	room	9

No. diff. resp. 48

94. Green

No.	Response	Frequency
1.	grass	48
2.	blue	25
3.	yellow	23
4.	red	12
5.	tree, field	7

No. diff. resp. 48

95. Salt

No.	Response	Frequency
1.	pepper	107
2.	water	14
3.	sugar	9
4.	taste	8
5.	sea	7

No. diff. resp. 39

96. Street

No.	Response	Frequency
1.	road	38
2.	people	22
3.	cars	21
4.	lamp	17
5.	city	11

No. diff. resp. 44

97. King

No.	Response	Frequency
1.	queen	146
2.	crown	14
3.	throne	5
4.	royal	4
5.	country, royalty	3

No. diff. resp. 29

98. Cheese

No.	Response	Frequency
1.	mouse	38
2.	bread	29
3.	butter	25
4.	milk	12
5.	rat	10

No. diff. resp. 50

99. Blossom

No.	Response	Frequency
1.	tree	60
2.	flower	53
3.	spring	16
4.	cherry	12
5.	pink	10

No. diff. resp. 33

100. Afraid

No.	Response	Frequency
1.	fear(ful)	63
2.	scared	26
3.	dark(ness)	20
4.	frightened	16
5.	night	6

No. diff. resp. 51

CHAPTER 3

THE COMPLETE GERMAN LANGUAGE NORMS FOR RESPONSES TO 100 WORDS FROM THE KENT-ROSANOFF WORD ASSOCIATION TEST[1]

Wallace A. Russell
University of Minnesota, Minneapolis, Minnesota

The collection of German language norms for the Kent-Rosanoff word association test was undertaken as one phase of a larger project (Jenkins & Russell, 1952; Russell & Jenkins, 1954; Russell & Storms, 1955) dealing with the manner in which linguistic habits may modify such aspects of behavior as perception, learning, recall, and generalization. The generality of the experimental results obtained from English language groups was in doubt as long as comparable effects had not been observed in other language communities. In order to make such observations possible, it was necessary to obtain word association norms in languages other than English as a basis for experiments to be conducted in those languages.

These norms were compiled during the academic year of 1957-1958 in and around Wuerzburg, Germany, using native German-speaking students as Ss. They have been briefly described in an article by Russell and Meseck (1959) which also reports some of the research which has utilized these norms. Comparisons of responses of these German Ss to the free association responses of French and American Ss have been made by Russell and Meseck (1959) and by Rosenzweig (1961). None of these sources, however, has dealt systematically with responses beyond the primaries, and no publication until now has undertaken to publish all of the responses made by the German Ss.

METHOD

The normative project was carried out in the following manner: first, a translation from English to German was made of the Kent-Rosanoff word association test (Kent & Rosanoff, 1910); second, the translated test was administered to a normative group of German students; third, the results were analyzed to determine the frequency of each response to each stimulus word.

Translation of the Kent-Rosanoff Word Association Test

The 100 stimulus words of the Kent-Rosanoff word association test occur quite frequently in the English

[1]The work reported here was carried out during the writer's tenure as a Senior Research Scholar at the University of Wuerzburg under a United States Government Grant (Fulbright Act). Appreciation must be expressed for the cooperation given by Dr. W. Arnold, head of the Psychological Institute at Wuerzburg. The assistance of Oskar R. Meseck at all stages of data collection is also acknowledged, as is the invaluable aid of Drs. Erwin Roth, Klaus Foppa, and Ferdinand Merz, particularly pertaining to translation of English into German.

language and have been considered, as a whole, to be emotionally neutral. The effort to translate single words into equivalent single German words and to maintain these characteristics met with inevitable difficulties. The stimulus words finally chosen were worked out in consultation with Dr. Erwin Roth of the Psychological Institute at Wuerzburg. Problematic cases were submitted to other members of the staff of the Institute for resolution. Obviously, there were instances where it was not possible to find German words which were judged to be completely equivalent to English words of the test, but in each case an effort was made to select the German word which seemed to approximate this goal most closely.

The Normative Group

The *S*s were drawn from psychology classes at the University of Wuerzburg and from advanced classes in *Hochschulen* and *Gymnasiums* in the cities of Wuerzburg, Aschaffenburg, and Schweinfurt (Table 1). These latter schools were at the level of advanced secondary education and, with respect to the age of the students involved, were roughly equivalent to the freshman and sophomore groups in American colleges. The age range of *S*s was from 16 to 30 years, with a heavy concentration between the ages of 17 and 21 years. The exact composition of the total group by age and sex is given in Table 1. There were 331 *S*s included in the final analysis. Of these, 300 were male and 31 were female. There were 26 *S*s to whom the test was administered but who were not included in the final analysis. The reasons for rejection and the numbers in each category were: non-German native language, 9; *S* over 30 years old, 10; test sheet contained 20 or more omissions of response, 6; *S* responded in English, 1.

TABLE 1 *The Composition of the Normative Group*

Subgroups	Age range	No. of males	No. of females	Total subjects
A. Psychology Seminar (Univ. of Wuerzburg)	19-30	8	7	15
B. Wuerzburg Oberealschule				
Section 1	18-21	30	–	30
Section 2	16-22	28	1	29
C. Humanistisches Gymnasium Aschaffenberg				
Section 1	16-18	23	–	23
Section 2	17-20	15	4	19
Section 3	18-20	16	1	17
Section 4	18-22	19	–	19
Section 5	17-20	22	–	22
Section 6	16-19	11	6	17
D. Humanistisches Gymnasium Schweinfurt				
Section 1	16-20	50	4	54
Section 2	18-20	21	4	25
E. Psychology Lecture (Univ. of Wuerzburg)	17-30	57	4	61
Totals	16-30	300	31	331

Administration of the Test

The test forms were prepared on two mimeographed sheets, with numbered stimulus words arranged in columns of 25 words each, two columns to a sheet. After each stimulus word was a line on which *S* could write his response. The two mimeographed sheets were stapled together so that only the blank sides of the test sheets were immediately observable when the tests were distributed. On one of these the *S*s were instructed to write their name, the date, their sex, and their native language. In the University groups the exception was made that the *S* could, if he wished, omit his name.

The test was administered to the 12 separate subgroups and sections listed in Table 1. The number in each administration group varied from 15 to 61. The test sessions were conducted by Oskar R. Meseck, a graduate student in psychology at the University of Wuerzburg and a native German speaker. The writer was present as an observer and nonspeaking assistant. The German language instructions were modeled after those used in gathering the Russell-Jenkins norms (Russell & Jenkins, 1954). The German form has been reported by Russell and Meseck (1959) and the following is a direct retranslation into English:

At the University of Wuerzburg, a series of investigations of verbal behavior is being carried out. The following experiment is one of this series. It is on free association.

You have received two test sheets. Please write your name on the outside of the first sheet and answer the questions listed before you. Open the sheets only after I have read you the instructions.

On the inside of these sheets you will find a list of 100 stimulus words. Your task is to write after each word the first word that it makes you think of. Write only one word for each response. Begin with word number 1, read it and write beside it the first word that occurs to you; then read the second word, and so on, until the list is finished. Work as fast as you can and do not leave any words out.

When you have finished, close the sheets and write on the back the letter which you see written on the board at that time. (Demonstration) Are there any questions? Are you ready? Please begin!

All Ss worked according to these instructions for 4 min. After 4 min, the letter A was written on the blackboard. Every 30 sec thereafter, a new letter was substituted in alphabetical sequence. This procedure was adopted to serve as a motivator for rapid work and to make possible a rough index of the time taken by each S.

ANALYSIS OF THE RESULTS

The major analysis of the results appears in the normative lists in the Appendix. The stimulus words of the German language test appear at the top of each list, numbered in the same sequence in which they appeared in the test. This sequence corresponds to the order of the equivalent English words in the Russell-Jenkins norms (1954). Below each stimulus word appear the responses which were made to that word. The responses are listed in order of their frequency of occurrence in the normative group. These frequencies are shown after each response word. The number preceding each response word indicates its rank in terms of frequency, except that within tied ranks the words are listed alphabetically with the tied ranks assigned sequentially to them. Tables 2 and 3 provide alphabetical keys to the numbering of the stimulus words in the normative lists for both the German words and their English equivalents.

TABLE 2 *Alphabetical Listing of German Stimulus Words with Their English Equivalents and Their Numbering within the Norms and the Kent-Rosanoff Test*

Adler, eagle, 49	Freude, joy, 86	Krankheit, sickness, 4
aengstlich, afraid, 100	Fuss, foot, 33	kurz, short, 15
Arbeiten, working, 42	Gedaechtnis, memory, 61	Lampe, lamp, 52
Arzt, doctor, 82	gelb, yellow, 54	lang, long, 72
Baby, baby, 90	Gerechtigkeit, justice, 56	langsam, slow, 25
Bad, bath, 63	Gesundheit, health, 59	Laut, loud, 83
Bequemlichkeit, comfort, 13	glatt, smooth, 18	Licht, light, 58
Berg, mountain, 9	gruen, green, 94	Loewe, lion, 85
Bett, bed, 87	Hammelfleisch, mutton, 12	Maedchen, girl, 40
Bibel, Bible, 60	Hammer, hammer, 77	Magen, stomach, 50
bitter, bitter, 76	Hand, hand, 14	Mann, man, 5
blau, blue, 66	hart, hard, 48	Mond, moon, 91
Bluete, blossom, 99	Haus, house, 10	Musik, Music, 3
Brot, bread, 55	Haeuschen, cottage, 64	Nadel, needle, 35
Buerger, citizen, 32	hoch, high, 41	Obst, fruit, 16
Butter, butter, 81	hungrig, hungry, 67	Ofen, stove, 71
Dieb, thief, 84	Junge, boy, 57	Ozean, ocean, 69
dunkel, dark, 2	kalt, cold, 24	Pfeifen, whistle, 22
durstig, thirsty, 78	Kaese, cheese, 98	Priester, priest, 68
Erde, earth, 44	Kind, child, 75	Quadrat, square, 80
Essen, eating, 8	Kohl, cabbage, 47	rauh, rough, 31
Fenster, window, 30	kommandieren, command, 19	Religion, religion, 73
Fluss, river, 27	Koenig, king, 97	rot, red, 36
Frau, woman, 23	Kopf, head, 70	ruhig, quiet, 93

TABLE 2 *(Continued)*

Salz, salt, 95	Soldat, soldier, 46	tief, deep, 6
sauer, sour, 43	Sorge, trouble, 45	Tisch, table, 1
Schaf, sheep, 62	Spinne, spider, 34	traeumen, dream, 53
Schere, scissors, 92	Stadt, city, 79	weiss, white, 28
Schlafen, sleep, 37	Stiel, stem, 51	weich, soft, 7
Schmetterling, butterfly, 17	Strasse, street, 96	Whisky, whisky, 74
schnell, swift, 65	Stuhl, chair, 20	wuenschen, wish, 26
schoen, beautiful, 29	Suess, sweet, 21	Zorn, anger, 38
schwarz, black, 11	Tabak, tobacco, 89	
schwer, heavy, 88	Teppich, carpet, 39	

TABLE 3 *Alphabetical Listing of English Stimulus Words with Their German Equivalents and Their Numbering within the Norms and the Kent-Rosanoff Test*

afraid, aengstlich, 100	fruit, Obst, 16	salt, Salz, 95
anger, Zorn, 38	girl, Maedchen, 40	scissors, Schere, 92
baby, Baby, 90	green, gruen, 94	sheep, Schaf, 62
bath, Bad, 63	hammer, Hammer, 77	short, kurz, 15
beautiful, schoen, 29	hand, Hand, 14	sickness, Krankheit, 4
bed, Bett, 87	hard, hart, 48	sleep, Schlafen, 37
Bible, Bibel, 60	head, Kopf, 70	slow, langsam, 25
bitter, bitter, 76	health, Gesundheit, 59	smooth, glatt, 18
black, schwarz, 11	heavy, schwer, 88	soft, weich, 7
blossom, Bluete, 99	high, hoch, 41	soldier, Soldat, 46
blue, blau, 66	house, Haus, 10	sour, sauer, 43
boy, Junge, 57	hungry, hungrig, 67	spider, Spinne, 34
bread, Brot, 55	joy, Freude, 86	square, Quadrat, 80
butter, Butter, 81	justice, Gerechtigkeit, 56	stem, Stiel, 51
butterfly, Schmetterling, 17	king, Koenig, 97	stomach, Magen, 50
cabbage, Kohl, 47	lamp, Lampe, 52	stove, Ofen, 71
carpet, Teppich, 39	light, Licht, 58	street, Strasse, 96
chair, Stuhl, 20	lion, Loewe, 85	sweet, suess, 21
cheese, Kaese, 98	long, lang, 72	swift, schnell, 65
child, Kind, 75	loud, Laut, 83	table, Tisch, 1
citizen, Buerger, 32	man, Mann, 5	thief, Dieb, 84
city, Stadt, 79	memory, Gedaechtnis, 61	thirsty, durstig, 78
cold, Kalt, 24	moon, Mond, 91	tobacco, Tabak, 89
comfort, Bequemlichkeit, 13	mountain, Berg, 9	trouble, Sorge, 45
command, kommandieren, 19	music, Musik, 3	whisky, Whisky, 74
cottage, Haeuschen, 64	mutton, Hammelfleisch, 12	whistle, Pfeifen, 22
dark, dunkel, 2	needle, Nadel, 35	white, weiss, 28
deep, tief, 6	ocean, Ozean, 69	window, Fenster, 30
doctor, Arzt, 82	priest, Priester, 68	wish, wuenschen, 26
dream, traeumen, 53	quiet, ruhig, 93	woman, Frau, 23
eagle, Adler, 49	red, rot, 36	working, Arbeiten, 42
earth, Erde, 44	religion, Religion, 73	yellow, gelb, 54
eating, Essen, 8	river, Fluss, 27	
foot, Fuss, 33	rough, rauh, 31	

REFERENCES

Jenkins, J. J., & Russell, W. A. (1952). Associative clustering during recall. *Journal of Abnormal and Social Psychology* 47, 818-821.

Kent, G. H., & Rosanoff, A. J. (1910). A study of association in insanity. *American Journal of Insanity* 67, 37-96, 317-390.

Rosenzweig, M. R. (1961). Comparisons among word-association responses in English, French, German and Italian. *American Journal of Psychology* 74, 347-360.

Russell, W. A., & Jenkins, J. J. (1954). The complete Minnesota norms for responses to 100 words from the Kent-Rosanoff word association test. Technical Report No. 11, University of Minnesota, ONR, Contract No. N8 onr-66216, Minneapolis, Minn.

Russell, W. A., & Meseck, O. R. (1959). Der Einfluss der Assoziation auf das Erinnern von Worten in der Deutschen, Franzoesischen und Englischen Sprache. *Zeitschrift fuer Experimentelle und Angewandte Psychologie* 6, 191-211.

Russell, W. A., & Storms, L. H. (1955). Implicit verbal chaining in paired associate learning. *Journal of Experimental Psychology* 49, 287-293.

1. Tisch

No.	Response	Total
1.	Stuhl	97
2.	Bein(e)	49
3.	Tuch	23
4.	essen	22
5.	Decke	20
6.	Bank	8
7.	Holz	8
8.	Platte	8
9.	Tischtuch	8
10.	Moebel	5
11.	Tischbein	5
12.	Fisch	4
13.	Bett	3
14.	Haus	3
15.	rund	3
16.	Tafel	3
17.	eben	2
18.	gedeckt	2
19.	Herrentisch	2
20.	Kuechentisch	2
21.	Schreibtisch	2
22.	Schreiner	2
23.	Speisetisch	2
24.	Teller	2
25.	Tischdecke	2
26.	Vase	2
27.	Wohnung	2
28.	Zimmer	2

29-66. (f = 1)
am, Biertisch, Billartisch, Brett, daheim, Dish, Eck, eckig, Esstisch, flach, Gegenstand, glatt, grob, gruen, hart, Hund, Katheder, Klavier, Mahl, Mahlzeit, Mensa, Moebelstueck, Mutter, Pult, Rauch, Rauchtisch, Schuessel, Sessel, Stamm-, steht, Suppe, Tasche, Tischle, Tischleindeckdich, Tischplatte, Trapez, viereckige Flaeche, Zimmertisch

2. Dunkel

No.	Response	Total
1.	Hell(e)	145
2.	Nacht	38
3.	Dunkelheit	30
4.	Kammer	21
5.	Licht	19
6.	schwarz	8
7.	Mond	4
8.	Finsternis	3
9.	Helligkeit	3
10.	munkeln	3
11.	tief	3
12.	Abend	2
13.	duester	2
14.	Fenster	2
15.	finster	2
16.	Mann	2
17.	Raum	2
18.	stockdunkel	2
19.	unheimlich	2
20.	Zimmer	2

21-56. (f = 1)
Angst, Bier, Boden, boes, Buch, dunkel, Dunkelkammer, Dunkelmann, Elefant, Farbe, gefaehrlich, haft, Halbdunkel, Helligkeitsgrad, Keller, Klarheit, leuchtet, Maedchen, Maus, Projektor, Schlaf, schlafen, Schwere, Sonne, Stein, Stille, Tanzstunde, tiefdunkel, unsicher, verbrechen, Verdunkelung, Vorsicht, Wald, Walddunkel, was, Wort

3. Musik

No.	Response	Total
1.	Toen(e)	31
2.	Note(n)	18
3.	Jazz	16
4.	Klang	11
5.	Klavier	11
6.	Instrument	10
7.	Box	9
8.	Kunst	9
9.	Truhe	9
10.	Krach	8
11.	Schrank	8
12.	Beethoven	7
13.	Bach	6
14.	Harmonie	6
15.	Mozart	6
16.	schoen	6
17.	Geige	5
18.	Konzert	5
19.	laut	5
20.	Schallplatte	5
21.	Schlager	5
22.	Stueck(e)	5
23.	Trompete	5
24.	Melodie	4
25.	Radio	4
26.	Dichtung	3
27.	Gesang	3
28.	Lied(er)	3
29.	Oper	3
30.	Orchester	3
31.	Sprache	3
32.	Symphonie	3
33.	Tanz	3
34.	Zimmer	3
35.	Freude	2
36.	Freund	2
37.	Kunde	2
38.	Literatur	2
39.	Musiktruhe	2
40.	Operette	2
41.	Physik	2
42.	Unterricht	2

43-116. (f = 1)
Ausgelassenheit, berauschend, Blatt, Chello, Chopin, exakt, Floete, Genie, Geschichte, Geschrei, Gitarre, Gruenwald, gut, harmonisch, Hausmusik, Haydn, Heft, Horn, Klassik, klassisch, klingt, Konzertmusik, Largo, Laerm, Lehre, leicht, leise, Licht, Malerei, Mathematik, melodisch, modern, Muse, musikalisch, Musikbox, Musiker, Musikinstrument, Musikstueck, Musikstunde, Mutter, Orgel, Professor, Rausch, Rhythmus, Ruhe, Rundfunk, Russisch, Schoenheit, schraeg, schraege, Musik, Schule, Seele, Serenade, singen, Sphaerenmusik, Spieler, Sport, Studium, Stuhl, Suite, Tafel, Takt, Tinte, trara, Turandot, Unterhaltung, Violine, volks, warm, weiches Gefuehl, Wissenschaft, wohlklingend, zeichnen
(Illegible)

4. Krankheit

No.	Response	Total
1.	Gesundheit	51
2.	Tod	20
3.	Bett	19
4.	Grippe	19
5.	Fieber	12
6.	gesund	11

4. Krankheit (contd)

No.	Response	Total
7.	Arzt	10
8.	Fall	9
9.	schlecht	9
10.	schlimm	8
11.	Krankenhaus	7
12.	Leid	6
13.	Masern	6
14.	Schmerz(en)	6
15.	uebel	6
16.	Erreger	4
17.	Keim(e)	4
18.	Krankheitsfall	4
19.	serreger	4
20.	sfall	4
21.	Elend	3
22.	Herd	3
23.	Krankheitserreger	3
24.	Krebs	3
25.	Medezin	3
26.	Scharlach	3
27.	schulfrei	3
28.	schwach	3
29.	schwer	3
30.	Zustand	3
31.	Aerger	2
32.	Blinddarm	2
33.	Genesung	2
34.	Kopfweh	2
35.	Krankheitskeim(e)	2
36.	Lepra	2
37.	No response	2
38.	Schwaeche	2
39.	sterben	2

40-103. (f = 1)
Alter, Anfall, Arznei, Bahre, Bangheit,
Bauchweh, Bescheinigung, boese, Diphterie,
Erholung, Erkaeltung, Erscheinung, Fisch,
Geduld, Gelbsucht, Gift, Gips, Halsweh, heiss,
Herz, Hindernis, hoffnungslos, Hunger, Infektion,
Krankenzimmer, Krankheitsherd, Krankheitszustand,
leicht, liegen, Magen, Meniskus, Mensch, Metzger,
Morbitaet, Mumps, Mutter, Nasenkrankheit, Not,
Ohrenleiden, Portes, Pruefung, Rest, Schlankheit,
schwaecht, Schwester, Seuche, siech, skeim,
skorbut, Staerke, Symptom, Tablette, Tbc,
toedliche Krankheit, Tuberkulose, Tuch, Typhus,
Uebelkeit, unangenehm, Unbehagen, Ursache, Vater,
Winter, Zerfall

5. Mann

No.	Response	Total
1.	Frau	171
2.	Weib	15
3.	stark	13
4.	bar	8
5.	barkeit	7
6.	Hut	5
7.	Kraeftig	5
8.	Mensch	5
9.	gross	4
10.	Kind(er)	4
11.	Kraft	4
12.	haft	3
13.	Hose	3
14.	Arbeit	2
15.	Bart	2
16.	Character	2
17.	hart	2
18.	Held	2
19.	Mannschaft	2
20.	schaft	2
21.	staerke	2
22.	tapferkeit	2

5. Mann (contd)

No.	Response	Total
23.	Vater	2

24-87. (f = 1)
Adam, Anzug, arbeiten, Athlet, Beruf, Boy, Brief,
dann, Dienstmann, dumm, Dunkelmann, edel, Eduard,
Ehe, Ehemann, eine Phrase, einfach, Filmstar,
fuer Afrika, Fuss, Fussball, Gegengeschlecht,
Geschlecht, Geschoepf, Gestalt, grosse Gestalt,
Haus, Heros, im Mond, kann, Kante, Kerl, korrekt,
lichkeit, man, mannbar, Mannbarkeit, Maennertum,
Mannesruhm, Mannhaftigkeit, Mann im Mond,
Maennlichkeit, Maus, Mut, Nikolaus, NR, Partner,
Person, Priester, Radio, Raucher, reich, Riese,
Saeugling, schoen, Schuster, See-, singt, tapfer,
Tat, Thomas, Wert, Wesen, (?)

6. Tief

No.	Response	Total
1.	hoch	158
2.	Meer	19
3.	dunkel	11
4.	Bau	8
5.	See	8
6.	Abgrund	7
7.	Druck	6
8.	Loch	6
9.	Brunnen	5
10.	Wasser	5
11.	Tiefgang	4
12.	bodenlos	3
13.	Tal	3
14.	Tiefsee	3
15.	Wetter	3
16.	abgrundig	2
17.	blau	2
18.	flach	2
19.	Gang	2
20.	Graben	2
21.	Grube	2
22.	Hand	2
23.	Hoehle	2
24.	Schacht	2
25.	Schlag	2
26.	schlecht	2
27.	Stand	2
28.	Tiefdruck	2
29.	weit	2

30-83. (f = 1)
bedeutend, Bruecke, das Hoechste, deep,
Druckgebiet, e, Ebbe, enbach, endlos, Fall,
fallen, 50 m, fragen, furchtbar, gross, Grund,
halbtief, heit, Hoelle, Kanal, Land, leer,
Luftdruck, Mann, mannstief, Mulde, oben,
oberflaechl, Ozean, Plateau, Raum, Regen,
Schiff, Schlaf, schleckt-Wetter, schrecklich,
schwarz, schwindelig, sinken, Sprungturm,
Stufe, stuerzen, Taucher, Tiefe, tiefschwarz,
Tinte, Torf, traurig, unendlich, unergruendlich,
unheimlich, unten, weit unten, Wetterkunde

7. Weich

No.	Response	Total
1.	hart	127
2.	Bett	16
3.	Butter	13
4.	sanft	10
5.	Kissen	9
6.	Tiel(e)	9
7.	zart	9

7. Weich (contd)

No.	Response	Total
8.	heit	7
9.	Ei	6
10.	mollig	6
11.	Feder(n)	4
12.	Kaese	4
13.	Tier(e)	4
14.	butterweich	3
15.	Eisen	3
16.	fest	3
17.	lichkeit	3
18.	warm	3
19.	Weichling	3
20.	Wolle	3
21.	duenn	2
22.	elastisch	2
23.	Gummi	2
24.	Pril	2
25.	Quelle	2
26.	samt	2
27.	Schlamm	2
28.	Schnecke	2
29.	schoen	2
30.	Teich	2
31.	Watte	2
32.	weichherzig	2

33-94. ($f = 1$)
angenehm, bequemlich, biegsam, Bild, Birne, Daunen, dicht, Druck, en, Fisch, Fleisch, fleischig, Frau, Gegenteil, glatt, Glycerin, haltlos, Holz, Koerper, krumm, labil, lich, liegen, matschig, Meer, Mut, nachgeben, nachgiebig, NR, Pfirisch, Pflaume, Plasma, Polster, Sand, satt, sauer, schmackhaft, schmierig, Schnaps, Schnee, schwach, Schwamm, schwammig, schwarz, sehr, Sessel, Teig, Ton, unangenehm, verweichlicht, wach, Wachs, Waesche, weiche, Weichheit, weichlich, Weichlichkeit, weichlicht, Weichteil, Weichtier, wollen, Zartuch

8. Essen

No.	Response	Total
1.	trinken	76
2.	Hunger	40
3.	gut	23
4.	Mahlzeit	10
5.	schlafen	9
6.	Speise	8
7.	Zeit	8
8.	Brot	7
9.	Teller	7
10.	Fleisch	6
11.	Mittagessen	5
12.	Nahrung	5
13.	Tisch	5
14.	Essenszeit	4
15.	fressen	4
16.	satt	4
17.	Suppe	4
18.	szeit	4
19.	holen	3
20.	Mittag	3
21.	warm	3
22.	angenehm	2
23.	Appetit	2
24.	dampft	2
25.	Essentraeger	2
26.	Geschmack	2
27.	heiss	2
28.	Kotelett	2
29.	Loeffel	2
30.	Mahl	2
31.	No response	2

8. Essen (contd)

No.	Response	Total

32-104. ($f = 1$)
Abendessen, bald, Besteck, Bestellung, bluntsen, braten, Durst, Familie, Farben, fassen, fein, Frass, Freizeit, Fruehstueck, Gabel, gerne, Geschirr, Huhn, hungern, hungrig, Kalorien, Karte, Kartoffeln, Klau, Kloesse, krank, Lieblingsspeise, Lust, Magen, marken, Mehl, Mensa, Mensch, Milch, Nachessen, Nachmittag, Nachspeise, notwendig, Notwendigkeit, Nudeln, Obst, pikant, prima, Pudding, Quark, reichlich, Restaurant, saufen, sausgabe, scharf, Schinken, Schmalz, schmeckt, Schuessel, See, smarke, Sosse, Speisen, Stadt, straeger, Taetigkeit, Tee, Topf, Torte, Traeger, Trank, uebersatt, vollbringen, Wasser, Weihnachtgans, Wein, Wirtschaft, Wurst

9. Berg

No.	Response	Total
1.	Tal	116
2.	hoch	29
3.	Gipfel	19
4.	Alpen	12
5.	Spitze	10
6.	steil	9
7.	Hoehe	6
8.	Bahn	5
9.	Huegel	5
10.	Schnee	4
11.	Steiger	4
12.	Wald	4
13.	Bau	3
14.	Ebene	3
15.	Fels(en)	3
16.	Ferien	3
17.	Gebirge	3
18.	Haus	3
19.	Kuppe	3
20.	Riese	3
21.	Bergsteiger	2
22.	Bergsturz	2
23.	Erhebung	2
24.	Mount Everest	2
	(Mount Everest: 1	
	Mt. Everest : 1)	
25.	schoen	2
26.	Spessart	2
27.	Steigung	2
28.	Stein	2
29.	zackig	2

30-95. ($f = 1$)
Ansteig, Ausblick, Aussicht, Bergbahn, Bergung, berghoch, Bergkuppe, Bergpredigt, Bergspitze, Bergsteigen, Bergwald, Bergwerk, Blume, Burg, Engleberg, Fluss, Freude, Fuss, Futschiama, Gefahr, Gestein, gruen, gruenten, Hindernis, Hochberg, Hoelle, Huette, ig, Insel, Kampf, Kitsch, klettern, Kreuz, Licht, luftig, Matterhorn, Muehe, Nulde, Radfahren, Radtour, ragen, Rebe, Scherge, Schlucht, See, Skifahren, Sport, Stadt, Steinburg, Sturz, Tal und Berg, tief, Topf, Tour, unbezwingbar, Urlaub, Venus, Wand, wandern, Watzman, Werk, Wiese, wuchtig, Zenzel, Zugspitze, (τό ὄρος - Gr. for 'the mountain')

10. Haus

No.	Response	Total
1.	Hof	47
2.	Dach	37
3.	Tuer(e)	30
4.	Wohnung	19
5.	Garten	15
6.	Huette	13
7.	Fenster	9
8.	Gebaeude	4
9.	gross	4
10.	Villa	4
11.	Giebel	3
12.	Heim	3
13.	Maus	3
14.	Stadt	3
15.	Stall	3
16.	Stein	3
17.	weiss	3
18.	Arzt	2
19.	Bau	2
20.	Einfamilienhaus	2
	(Einfamilienhaus: 1	
	Einfamilienh. : 1)	
21.	Elternhaus	2
22.	Frau	2
23.	halt	2
24.	Hausbau	2
25.	Haustuer	2
26.	Heimat	2
27.	hoch	2
28.	Keller	2
29.	klein	2
30.	Landhaus	2
31.	neu	2
32.	Schloss	2
33.	schoen	2
34.	wohnen	2
35.	Zelt	2
36.	Ziegel	2

37-125. (f = 1)
Architektur, Backsteinhaus, Ball, Bauer, Baum, bequem, Besitz, Besitzer, Bewohner, Blockhaus, breit, Burg, Dachboden, Dachrinne, Dacht, Daheim, Dom, eigen, Eigentum, Eingang, Einrichtung, Familie, Fassade, Friede, Geborgenheit, Geburtsh., Gehoeft, gemuetlich, Goldbach, grau, grosses Gebaeude, Hausdach, Hauseingang, Hausierer, Haustier, Hauswand, Herr, hinter, Hochhaus, Hoehle, house, Hund, Huettl, Innenraum, Kante, Keil, Kind, Klausner, krumm, Laus, Mahl, Mauer, Maeuschen, Meister, Mietskaserne, NR, Obdach, party, Portal, Putz, rot, Ruhe, Saal, schief, Schornstein, Schule, Schulhaus, Schuppen, Schuessel, Schutz, schwarz, Siedlung, Strassenbild, Stuhl, Tier, Tor, Treppe, u Hof, Unterkunft, Wand, warm, Wart, Wesen, Wiese, Wirtshaus, Wohnhaus, wohnlich, Wohnstaette, Wolkenkratzer, zu Hause

11. Schwarz

No.	Response	Total
1.	weiss	147
2.	dunkel	19
3.	Farbe	17
4.	hell	17
5.	Nacht	14
6.	Wald	6
7.	rot	5
8.	Tafel	5
9.	Pech	4
10.	gelb	3
11.	Name	3
12.	Neger	3
13.	Pfarrer	3

11. Schwarz (contd)

No.	Response	Total
14.	tief	3
15.	Trauer	3
16.	Brot	2
17.	Haar	2
18.	Mann	2
19.	Markt	2
20.	Schwarzfuss	2
21.	Schwarzkopf	2
22.	Schwarzseher	2
23.	Teufel	2
24.	Treffer	2
25.	vornehm	2

26-84. (f = 1)
Adler, Angst, Beere, Bild, blendet, bunt, CDU, CSU, farblos, finster, finsteres, Finsternis, Flagge, Fleck, Fuchs, gruen, heiss, Herr, Kater, katholisch, Katz, Kittel, Komposition, Kopf, Krankenhaus, Licht, Lichtwellen, Lieblingsfarbe, malen, Malerei, Mord, nachtschwarz, Pflanze, Plakat, Pulver, Punkt, Rock, Roehre, schlafen, Schlotfeger, Schmutz, Schuld, schwarzhaarig, Schwarzhaendler, Schwaerzlich, Schwarzpappel, Schwarztraum, Schwarzwald, Schwarzwuerfel, Schweiz, schw. Haare, Stoff, tiefschwarz, Tinte, Tusche, Unheil, unheimlich, wild, Zielscheibe

12. Hammelfleisch

No.	Response	Total
1.	essen	22
2.	Rindfleisch	22
3.	Braten	14
4.	schlecht	13
5.	fett	12
6.	Schweinefleisch	11
	(Schweinefleisch: 9	
	Schweinefl. : 1	
	Scheinefl. : 1)	
7.	Keule	9
8.	Kotelett	9
	(Hammelfleisch-	
	kotelett : 3	
	Kottelette: 1	
	Kottlets : 1	
	Kotelett : 4)	
9.	Schaf(e)	9
10.	zaeh	9
11.	gut	7
12.	Suppe	7
13.	Kalbfleisch	6
14.	Schinken	5
15.	Hammel	4
16.	Kuhfleisch	4
17.	Lamm	4
	(Lamm: 3	
	Lam : 1)	
18.	Tier	4
19.	No response	4
20.	England	3
21.	Hammelfleischsuppe	3
	(Hammelfleischsuppe: 2	
	Hammelfl.-Suppe : 1)	
22.	Mittagessen	3
23.	Nahrung	3
24.	nicht gut	3
25.	prima	3
26.	rot	3
27.	Schaffleisch	3
28.	schmeckt nicht	3
29.	Sosse	3
30.	Bohnen	2
31.	Butterdose	2
32.	ekel	2

12. Hammelfleisch (contd)

No.	Response	Total
33.	Geld	2
34.	Gemuese	2
35.	Goulasch	
	(Goulasch: 1	
	Gulasch : 1)	
36.	komisch	2
37.	Kraut	2
38.	Metzger	2
39.	Ochsenfleisch	2
40.	Reis	2
41.	saftig	2
42.	Schnitzel	2
43.	Schweinebraten	2
44.	stinkt	2
45.	Stueck	2
46.	Wolle	2

47-137. (f = 1)

Abendessen, Appetit, Arabien, beaf, Beafsteak, Berg, Bier, billig, Blockwurst, Bloedsinn, blutig, braun, brenzlig, Brot, Bruehe, Buechse, corned-beaf, engl: ham, dick, essbar, fein, Fettgeruch, Fleisch, Fleischart, Fleischer, furchtbar, Gaensebraten, gebraten, gekocht, Geschmack, Gestank, gesund, Graupensuppe, Hammelbeine, Hammelfleischbraten, Hammelfleisch-hauer, Hammelfleischrolladen, Hammelerde, Handschuh, H.-Braten, Hund, Hunger, idiotisch, Italien, Kalbfl., Kalbsfleisch, keinen Appetit, Kloesse, Knoedel, Koran, Kuh, Lebensmittel, mager, Mahl, Mahlzeit, Morokko, mutton, nein, nichts, Orient, Ostern, Rehbraten, Rehfleisch, Rind, roh, Salz, Samstag, sauer, Sauerkraut, saeuerlich, Schafstall, Schafzucht, schmackhaft, Schreiber, Schwein, sehr gut, selten, Semmel-teich, Speise, suess, uebel, uebler Geruch, ungeniessbar, unmoeglich, unschmeckhaft, weich, Weide, wohlschmeckend, Wurst, Ziegenfleisch, Zucker, 2.50 DM

13. Bequemlichkeit

No.	Response	Total
1.	Sessel	43
2.	Faulheit	29
3.	Sofa	23
4.	Ruhe	21
5.	faul	10
6.	Komfort	8
	(Komfort: 6	
	Comfort: 1)	
7.	gemuetlich	7
8.	Unbequemlichkeit	7
	(Unbequemlichkeit: 6	
	Unbequeml. : 1)	
9.	angenehm	6
10.	Luxus	6
11.	schoen	6
12.	gut	5
13.	Traegheit	5
14.	Arbeit	4
15.	Couch	4
16.	traeg(e)	4
17.	Behaglichkeit	3
18.	Bett	3
19.	Fleiss	3
20.	Gemuetlichkeit	3
21.	Haerte	3
22.	muede	3
23.	Muedigkeit	3
24.	unbequem	3
25.	behaglich	2
26.	Bequemlichkeitsfaktor	2
	(Bequemlichkeitsfaktor: 1	
	Bequemlichkeitfaktor : 1)	

13. Bequemlichkeit (contd)

No.	Response	Total
27.	Diwan	2
28.	Drang	2
29.	Ferien	2
30.	ja	2
31.	lahm	2
32.	Langsamkeit	2
33.	liebend	2
34.	Radio	2
35.	Sinn	2
36.	weich	2
37.	Wohnung	2
38.	Zigarette	2

39-128. (f = 1)

ahh, allgemein, Angst, Anstrengung, Arbeitsamkeit, aergerlich, Armut, auch gut, Ausgespanntheit, ausruhen, bequem, Bequemlichkeit, Bequemlichkeit-saeusserungen, Bequemlichkeitsdrang, Bequemlichkeitsgefuehl, Bequemlichkeitsgrad, Bequemlichkeitshalbe, Bequemlichkeitssinn, bloed, Buch, Clubsessel, comfortable, dumm, dusel, Eigenschaft, en, Ehrgeiz, erregt, faulenzen, faul liegen, fein, Fernseher, gefaehrlich, Genuss, Geste, Gipfel, Grad, gross, haben, Hagerkeit, hart, haesslich, Hastigkeit, herrlich, Horaz, Kommod, Konzentration, Krankheit, langsam, Langweile, Laschheit, lasten, Lehne, Lehnstuhl, leicht, Liegestuhl, modern, mollig, Muehe, Musse, Nuechternheit, Offenheit, Polster, Redlichkeit, ruhen, Salon, scheusslich, Schnelligkeit, Schlaraffenland, Schueler, schwach, schwache Wille, schwierig, selten, Sonntag, Sparta, Sport, Standpunkt, Strapaze, Stuhl, suche, teuer, Unannehmlichkeit, ungeniessbar, unmaennlich, Unruhe, Vorsicht, Waerme, Zimmer, Zivilisation, Zustand

14. Hand

No.	Response	Total
1.	Fuss	66
2.	Finger	56
3.	Arm	13
4.	Handschuh(e)	12
5.	Schuh(e)	11
6.	Tuch	10
7.	Flaeche	6
8.	Kuss	6
9.	Arbeit	5
10.	Ball	5
11.	Faust	4
12.	Fingernagel	4
13.	Glied	4
14.	Griff	4
15.	Herz	4
16.	Ring	4
17.	Tasche	4
18.	Druck	3
19.	Greifen	3
20.	Koerperteil	3
21.	lang	3
22.	Mensch	3
23.	Mund	3
24.	Schrift	3
25.	weich	3
26.	Gelenk	2
27.	Handflaeche	2
28.	Handtuch	2
29.	Hund	2
30.	rechte	2
31.	Schlag	2
32.	schoen	2
33.	Werkzeug	2
	(Werkzug: 1	
	Werzeug: 1)	

14. Hand (contd)

No.	Response	Total
34.	wichtig	2
35.	zart	2

36-104. (f = 1)
amputiert, arbeiten, Armband, Band,
Begruessungsmittel, beschuetzend, Besen,
Bewegung, breit, Bruderhand, Buch, Chirurg,
Daumen, fassen, feingegliedert, flach, Form,
fuehren, Fuehrung, fuellen, fuenf, geben,
Gespreiztfinger, Gruss, gruessen, gut,
Haendedruck, handgemein, Handtasche, handvoll,
hoch, Instrument, kalt, Klavierspiel, klein,
kommen mit!, Koerper, Kraft, leer, lieben,
Linie, Mann, Manus, Mappe, NR, notwendig, Ohr,
rucken, Schar, Schmerzen, schmieden, schmutzig,
schreiben, schwarz, Sclaff, stark, Teller, Tier,
Tisch, unentbehrlich, verbunden, Verkehrs-
polizist, verkrampft, Verletzung, voll, weiss,
Wunderwerk, Zweige, 5 finger

15. Kurz

No.	Response	Total
1.	lang	174
2.	Schrift	12
3.	schnell	9
4.	Weile	7
	(Weile: 3	
	Weil : 4)	
5.	klein	6
6.	Arbeit	5
7.	buendig	5
8.	gut	5
9.	Kurzschluss	5
10.	Waren	5
	(Waren: 3	
	Ware : 2)	
11.	dick	4
12.	Kurzchrift	3
13.	Kurzwaren	3
14.	Kurzweil	3
15.	Strecke	3
16.	Hose	2
17.	Nase	2
18.	Schlag	2
19.	Strich	2
20.	Zeit	2

21-92. (f = 1)
abgehackt, Angst, Antwort, atmen, Aufgabe,
Bast, behend, Blatt, Bleistift, Brief, Brille,
Buch, dumm, einfach, einswaengen, Elle, en,
entschlossen, Faden, Ferien, Fueller, ganz,
gesagt, Geschichte, Haar, Jugendvorname,
K-geschichte, kl. Mensch, kleiner Bleistift,
knapp, korken, kurz u. buendig, Kurzarbeit,
kurzsichtig, Kurzwort, Langenbezeichnung,
lineal, Mann, Metermass, nichtlang, n. gut,
NR, ploetzlich, Punkt, Rad, richtig, scharf,
Schluss, Schnelligkeit, Schrei, schroff,
Schurz, sichtig, Sichtigkeit, Spaziergang,
Sprung, Stab, Stange, Steno, Stenographie,
Stoppuhr, Strasse, stumpf, Stunde, Unterricht,
Vergnuegen, weiss, wenig, Wort, Wuerze,
(unintelligible), Zwerg

16. Obst

No.	Response	Total
1	Gemuese	58
2.	Apfel (Aepfel)	57
3.	Baum	16

16. Obst (contd)

No.	Response	Total
4.	Fruecht(e)	15
5.	Birne	13
6.	Banane	10
7.	Orange(n)	9
8.	essen	8
9.	suess	8
10.	Schale	6
11.	Suedfruechte	6
12.	gut	5
13.	Kirsche(n)	5
14.	Kuchen	5
15.	saftig	5
16.	Salat	5
17.	frisch	4
18.	Garten	4
19.	gesund	4
20.	Obstgarten	4
21.	Saft	4
22.	Sueden	3
23.	Teller	3
24.	Fleisch	2
25.	Geld	2
26.	Gesundheit	2
27.	gruen	2
28.	Herbst	2
29.	lecken	2
30.	Obstteller	2
31.	Pfirsich	2
32.	Pflaume(n)	2
33.	Sommer	2
34.	Speise	2
35.	Stand	2
36.	Tafel	2
37.	Wein	2

38-83. (f = 1)
Apfelbaum, Appetit, Erdbeere, Fallobst, Farben,
faules Obst, Fruechteschale, Fruehling-Sommer,
Geruch, Handel, Haendler, Jobst, kalt, Karren,
Kekse, Kernobst, Kiste, Korb, Land, Laden,
Mengen v. Fruechten, nahrhaft, Nahrung, Nuss,
Obsternte, Obstkuchen, Obstkueste, Obstladen,
Obstmarkt, Obstplatte, Obstsaft, Obststand,
Ost, Pomme, Preise, prima, prost, reif, rosig,
sauer, Stein, Tinte, Trauben, Tuete, Vegetarier,
Weintraube

17. Schmetterling

No.	Response	Total
1.	Falter	39
2.	bunt	19
3.	Vogel	17
4.	Bluete(n)	14
	(Bluete(n): 13	
	Bluehte : 1)	
5.	Insekt(en)	14
6.	flattern	13
7.	Tier	13
8.	Fliege	11
9.	Fluegel	11
10.	Blume	9
11.	fliegen	9
12.	Wiese(n)	9
13.	leicht	8
14.	Kohlweissling	7
15.	Nachtfalter	7
16.	Sommer	7
17.	Butterfly	6
18.	Pfauenauge	6
19.	Farbe(n)	5
20.	Fruehling	5
21.	Puppe	5
22.	Schwalbenschwanz	5
23.	gelb	4

17. Schmetterling (contd)

No.	Response	Total
24.	Raupe	4
25.	Biene	3
26.	Bluetler	3
27.	Larve	3
28.	Sammlung	3
29.	Schmetterlingsbluetler	3
30.	blau	2
31.	fangen	2
32.	Fuehler	2
33.	Maus	2
34.	s Fluegel	2
35.	Schmetterlingsfluegel	2
36.	schoen	2
37.	weiss	2
38.	Zitronenfalter	2
39.	(illegible)	2

40-88. ($\underline{f}$ = 1)
Admiral, Apollo, Art, blaue Luft, Blumenwiese,
Facettenaugen, Faenger, Farbenpracht,
Flatterer, flattert, Fledermaus, Fluegelschuppen,
Flugzeug, Gaukeler, gaukeln, gaukelnd,
Gliederfuessler, Japan, Kaefer, Kraut,
leichtbewegt, Lippenbluetler, Maikaefer, Messing,
Nachtigall, nett, niedlich, Puccini, rot, s Netz,
s Puppe, sanft, Schlag, Schmetterlingaehnlich,
Schmetterlingsart, Schmetterlingsnetz, Schwalbe,
Schwimmbad, Sonne, Spaziergang, Spiel, Tand,
Totenkopf, Trompete, unbestaendig, vertraut,
Wurm, zart, zerbrechlich

18. Glatt

No.	Response	Total
1.	Eis	131
2.	rauh	49
3.	Glatteis	12
4.	gefaehrlich	9
5.	eben	8
6.	Glas	8
7.	Spiegel	6
8.	weich	6
9.	Aal	5
10.	Strasse	5
11.	rutschen	4
12.	Eisbahn	3
13.	fallen	3
14.	rutschig	3
15.	ausrutschen	2
16.	Fall	2
17.	Flaeche	2
18.	glaenzend	2
19.	glitschig	2
20.	grob	2
21.	gruen	2
22.	kalt	2
23.	rasiert	2
	(rasiert: 1	
	rasier : 1)	
24.	rund	2
25.	Schlange	2
26.	stumpf	2
27.	Tisch	2

28-80. ($\underline{f}$ = 1)
Auto, bergig, blank, Bleistift, Brain, Blatt,
E Strasse, Ebene, Eisflaeche, Eislauf, Gefahr,
geschabt, Glattstrich, gleiten, hart, hell,
hinfallen, Hochglanzplatte, liege, matt,
Metall, nass, nicht, glatt, Papier, Parkett,
poliert Holz, Politur, rot, Rutschbahn,
rutscherig, Rutschgefahr, sauber, schief,
Schlittschuh, schluepfrig, schmierig, Schnee,
Schneematsch, schoen, schwer, schwierig,
Ski Piste, spiegelglatt, sproede, steil,
Stein, unbequem, Unfall, unrasiert, verknittert,

18. Glatt (contd)

No.	Response	Total

Vorsicht, Winter, zart

19. Kommandieren

No.	Response	Total
1.	befehlen	76
2.	gehorchen	34
	(gehorchen : 33	
	u. gehorchen: 1)	
3.	Militaer	28
4.	Befehl	19
5.	Soldat(en)	13
6.	General	11
	(General : 10	
	(Der) General: 1)	
7.	Feldwebel	10
8.	Barras	7
	(Barras: 6	
	Barass: 1)	
9.	08/15	7
10.	Spies	7
	(Spies : 2	
	Spiess: 5)	
11.	angeben	6
12.	Offizier	6
13.	Kommiss	5
14.	Kommando	4
15.	Oberst	3
16.	Unteroffizier	3
17.	Chef	2
18.	exezieren	2
19.	folgen	2
20.	Heer	2
21.	Kommandant	2
22.	Krieg	2
23.	Leutnant	2
24.	schreien	2

25-100. ($\underline{f}$ = 1)
ab, Angeber, Angeberei, anschreien, Armee,
auftragen, barsch, Bleistift, bruellen,
Bundeswehr, der, Diktatur, Drill, gehen,
gehorsam, halt!, hart, helfen, Herr,
herrnkommandieren, herrschsuechtig, herumhetzen,
hinlegen, Hitler, Holz, Imperator, Kaserne,
Kommandeur, kommandierender General, Kompanie,
koennen, kontrollieren, laut, Lehrer, Marine,
marschiere, marschieren, Mathematiklehrer,
Muesse, nicht ausfuehren, nicht gehorchen,
nieder, nix, da, NR, Ober...der, Oberbefehlshaber,
pfui, Polizist, Preusse, raten, raus, reden, Ruf,
rufen, schimpfen, Schleifer, Schreck, Schule,
Schwiegermutter, Seminar, sich k. lassen, Stadt,
Stimme, stramm stehen, Ton, Trill, Truppe, Tyrann,
ungerecht, ungeschickt, verletzen,
vorkommandieren, Wehrmacht, Wehrpflicht, Wut,
Zwang

20. Stuhl

No.	Response	Total
1.	Bein(e)	71
2.	Tisch	66
3.	Lehne	34
4.	Sessel	17
5.	Stuhlbein(e)	13
6.	sitzen	11
7.	bequem	8
8.	hart	8
9.	Sitzgelegenheit	8
10.	Kissen	7

20. Stuhl (contd)

No.	Response	Total
11.	setzen	7
12.	Sitz	6
13.	Hocker	5
14.	Moebel	5
15.	Bank	4
16.	Holz	4
17.	Stuhllehne	4
18.	unbequem	3
19.	Zimmer	3
20.	Bequemlichkeit	2
21.	Gang	2
22.	Pfuhl	2
23.	Schule	2
24.	Sitzflaeche	2
25.	Stuhlgang	2
26.	Wohnzimmer	2

27-59. (f = 1)
Bett, Buero, Einrichtung, eiserner Stuhl, elektrisch, Fenster, Fest, fuer, Gastwirtschaft, Geraete, Haus, Holzstuhl, Hose, klein, Kueche, Lehnstuhl, Loge, modern, muede, Muedigk., Nagel, Petticoat, Polster, Ruhepause, Schemel, Schraube, Schreiner, Sofa, Studium, Teller, Wand, Zimmerstuhl, 4 Beine

21. Suess

No.	Response	Total
1.	sauer	129
2.	Zucker	35
3.	Bonbon	15
4.	bitter	10
5.	Kirsche(n)	8
6.	Schokolade	7
7.	Waren	7
8.	Kuss	6
9.	Honig	5
10.	angenehm	4
11.	gut	4
12.	Maedchen	4
13.	Obst	4
14.	Geschmack	3
15.	Most	3
16.	Stoff	3
17.	Suessigkeit	3
18.	Birne	2
19.	fein	2
20.	Gebaeck	2
21.	herb	2
22.	Kind	2
23.	Kuchen	2
24.	Praline(n)	2
25.	prima	2
26.	Speise	2
27.	suessauer	2
28.	Suesswaren	2
29.	zuckersuess	2
30.	Zunge	2

31-85. (f = 1)
Ananas, anmutig, Apfel, Apfelsine, Banane, bringen, Elektrogeschaeft, essen, Feigen, fest, Gebirgslied, Genuss, gutschmeckend, Holz, Jacke, Jud, Kaffee, Kino, Kompott, koestlich, kuessen, Liebe, lieblich, Lippenstift, Muth, Nachspeise, naschen, nett, nicht, Nuss, NR, Paprika, Pudding, Reaktion, Schlagsahne, schmecken, Schweiss, suesser Kaefer, Suessholz, suesslich, Suesspeise, Suessstoff, Suesswasser, Tabak, Tuch, Wasser, weich, Wein, weiss, Wohlgeschmack, wuerzig, Zahnarzt, zart, Zungenspitze
(Illegible)

22. Pfeifen

No.	Response	Total
1.	singen	51
2.	schrill	18
3.	laut	15
4.	Toen(e)	8
5.	Kopf	6
6.	rufen	6
7.	zwitschern	6
8.	Hund	5
9.	Locomotive	5
10.	Pfeife	5
11.	Rauch	5
12.	rauchen	5
13.	schreien	5
14.	Vogel	5
15.	Zug	5
16.	Eisenbahn	4
17.	Floete(n)	4
18.	grell	4
19.	johlen	4
20.	lustig	4
21.	Mund	4
22.	Orgel	4
23.	Pfiff	4
24.	Schlager	4
25.	zischen	4
26.	blasen	3
27.	groehlen	3
28.	hoeren	3
29.	jodeln	3
30.	Laerm	3
31.	Lippen	3
32.	Pfeifenkopf	3
33.	Tabak	3
34.	Triller	3
35.	Bub	2
36.	Freund	2
37.	Junge(n)	2
38.	Kommando	2
39.	lachen	2
40.	laermen	2
41.	Lied	2
42.	Mann	2
43.	Ohr(en)	2
44.	Pfeiffenstiel	2
45.	Schiedsrichter	2
46.	schoen	2
47.	Signal(e)	2
48.	tanzen	2
49.	trillern	2

50-133. (f = 1)
Alarm, Angst, anstrengend, Arbeit, Deckel, drohnen, Erkennungspfiff, frech, Freudeausdruck, Froehlichk., Fussball, Gassenjunge, gedacht, gehorchen, geigen, Geraeusch, gespitzte Lippen, gruen, halbstark, Halbstarker, hameln, Hauptmann, Heim, horchen, husten, im, jaulen, kann ich nicht, Kasernenhof, klopfen, knallen, Konzert, Krach, kreischen, Kunstpfeifer, lange, Lausbuben, Lausejunge, Lautaeusserung, Lerche, Maedchen, Musik, NR, Orgelpfeife, Pfeifender, pfeifen mit den Fingern, Pfeifentabak, Pfeifendeckel, Pfeifenkonzert, Pfeifenspieler, Physik, quietschen, Raucher, rauchig, ringen, roh, Ruf, ruhig, Schaffner, schluchzen, schrecklich, Schule, schwitschern, Spatzen, Spaziergang, Spitz, Stiel, Stil, Stimme, Strasse, Strassenjunge, toenen, traellern, trillen, trompeten, Tuch, Unsinn, vergnuegt, vorpfeifen, Wellenlehre, Wind, wispern, Zaehne

23. Frau

No.	Response	Total
1.	Mann	131
2.	Mutter	18
3.	Kind(er)	16
4.	schoen	9
5.	Liebe	7
6.	Weib	7
7.	Maedchen	6
8.	Dame	5
9.	Haar(e)	5
10.	Hausfrau	5
11.	Rock	5
12.	Ehe	4
13.	Geschlecht	4
14.	Hoelle	4
15.	Kleid(er)	4
16.	Mensch	4
17.	Gattin	3
18.	Haus	3
19.	lichkeit	3
20.	enzimmer	2
21.	fraulich	2
22.	gut	2
23.	Hut	2
24.	Kueche	2
25.	lich	2
26.	Mode	2
27.	No response	2
28.	Schuerze	2
29.	Tanz	2
30.	tanzen	2
31.	zart	2
32.	Zimmer	2

33-94. (f = 1)
Adam, alt, anderes Geschlecht, anmuetig, Berlin, Bett, Charme, dick, Ebenmass, echt, elegant, enhaar, enkleid, Eva, Familie, Frauen, Frauenfussball, Frauengold, Frauenkrankheit, Frauenschuh, Frauentum, Fraeulein, Fraulichkeit, Geburt, Gelegenheit, gross, Guete, guetig, gutgekleidet, Haushalt, Heirat, Herr, huebsch, Ideale, jung, Knecht, Knoten, lieblich, liebreizend, Matrone, Milch, Monroe, Orna, Partner, Pfleger, Reiz, Sau, Schauspielerin, schlank, Schoenheit, Schwamm, Sex, Vamp, Venus, Vorsicht, warten, weibl. Wesen, weiblich, weich, (weich, mollig), Wein, zarte Gestalt

24. Kalt

No.	Response	Total
1.	warm	120
2.	Winter	46
3.	heiss	33
4.	Eis	24
5.	Frost	6
6.	Wasser	6
7.	frieren	5
8.	nass	4
9.	essen	3
10.	kuehl	3
11.	Speise	3
12.	Wetter	3
13.	abstossend	2
14.	Dusche	2
15.	eisig	2
16.	Kaelte (Kaelte: 1 e: 1)	2
17.	kaltstellen	2
18.	Kleidung	2
19.	Mantel	2
20.	Nordpol	2
21.	Schnee	2

24. Kalt (contd)

No.	Response	Total
22	unangenehm	2

23-77. (f = 1)
beissend, Bett, bitter, bitterkalt, Blut, Coca cola, dunkel, e Platte, Eisen, eisigkalt, eiskalt, Eisschrank, Farbe, Freude, frigide, frisch, Fuesse, Groenland, Handschuhe, hart, Heimat, Herz, ja, kalt, kaltbluetig, Kaltbluetigkeit, kalte Haende, kaltes Bueffet, Kaltheit, Kaltleim, kaltnass, Kaltspeise, Keller, Klasszimmer, Kreide, Kuehlschrank, langsam, lau, Luft, Mundstueck, Ofen, Pelz, schlecht, schnaeuzig, Schneemann, schrecklich, Schulzimmer, schuetteln, Spaziergang, Tod, ungemuetl., Wind, Wintermorgen, Zimmer, zittern

25. Langsam

No.	Response	Total
1.	schnell	146
2.	Schnecke	34
3.	traeg(e)	20
4.	keit	7
5.	lahm	7
6.	fahren	4
7.	bequem	3
8.	Langweile	3
9.	Langsamkeit	3
10.	muede	3
11.	Strassenbahn	3
12.	Auto	2
13.	bedaechtig	2
14.	behaebig	2
15.	denken	2
16.	eilig	2
17.	Fussgaenger	2
18.	gemuetlich,	2
19.	gut	2
20.	langsam fahren	2
21.	No response	2
22.	rasch	2
23.	Tempo	2
24.	zaeh	2
25.	Zug	2
26.	(illegible)	2

27-94. (f = 1)
Arbeiter, Aerger, Bahn, beharrlich, beim 100 m Lauf, Bein, Bummelbahn, doof, (drove) slowly, Eile, Eisenbahn, Ente, essen, Fahrt, Fahrung, Faulheit, fett, flink, Flugzeug, Fuhrwerk, Fussgeher, Gang, gehen, gemaechlich, geschwind, Handwagen, hastig, kurz, lange Leitung, laufen, Lehrer, Lloyd, Moped, neu, Onkel Otto, Pflechmatiker, phlegmatisch, Rad, Rennwagen, ruhig, schleichend, Schnecke, schneller, Schnellestempo, schrecklich, Schulaufgabe, Schule, schwelig, sicher, sprechen, still, Stoiker, Strasse, Stuhl, Stutz, Teich, Teig, Transuse, troedeln, Trottel, unbequem, unruhig, Verkehrsschild, Wabu, wachsen, Wasser, Zeit, Ziel

26. Wuenschen

No.	Response	Total
1.	Weihnachten	52
2.	Geschenk(e)	28
3.	wollen	19
4.	begehren	18
5.	hoffen	14
6.	bitten	10

26. Wuenschen (contd)

No.	Response	Total
7.	schenken	9
8.	verlangen	8
9.	erhalten	7
10.	Auto	6
11.	befehlen	6
12.	erfuellen	6
13.	Geld	6
14.	sehnen	6
15.	Wunsch	6
16.	Buech(er)	4
17.	fordern	4
18.	geben	4
19.	Glueck	4
20.	wuenschenswert	4
	(wuenschenswert: 2	
	wuenscheswert : 1	
	-swert : 1)	
21.	bekommen	3
22.	ersehnen	3
23.	Fest(e)	3
24.	Sehnsucht	3
25.	viel(e)	3
26.	Bitte	2
27.	erwarten	2
28.	fluchen	2
29.	Freude	2
30.	Gabe	2
31.	Geburtstag	2
32.	haben	2
33.	Haus	2
34.	koennen	2
35.	no response	2
36.	Traum	2
37.	verzichten	2
38.	Wuenschelrute	2
	(Wuenschelrute: 1	
	-lrute : 1)	
39.	wunschlos	2

40-105. (f = 1)
ablehnen, alles, angenehm, anspruchsvoll,
Ausdruck, Begehr, Begierde, beten, Christkind,
denken, der, entbehren, Erfolg, Erfuellung,
Erwartung, erwuenschen, Ferien, Fuehrerschein,
Gebet, gerne haben, Geschenke, Gier, Glueckwunsch,
gratulieren, Hoffnung, Hund, Hunger, Klugheit,
lassen, lieben, Liste, Lust, Maerchen, moechten,
Musik, nicht bekommen, Neuheit, noten, ohne,
reich, reisen, Roller, Ruhe, Rute, ruten,
Schenke, Schlaf, schlafen, singen, suchen,
Tonbandgeraet, Toto, traeumen, tuenchen,
tunschen, unerfuellbar, Unsinn, verabscheuen,
vergeblich, Verstellung, waehlen,
Weihnachtswuensche, Wert, Wunschkonzert,
Wunschliste, Wunschtraum, Zukunft

27. Fluss

No.	Response	Total
1.	Wasser	47
2.	Main	35
3.	Strom	34
4.	Bach	26
5.	Bett	14
6.	Ufer	11
7.	Rhein	10
8.	baden	9
9.	Lauf	9
10.	Meer	8
11.	tief	8
12.	See	7
13.	Tal	7
14.	Flussbett	6
15.	breit	5
16.	schwimmen	5

27. Fluss (contd)

No.	Response	Total
17.	Landschaft	4
18.	Schiff	4
19.	Boot	3
20.	Bruecke	3
21.	Bad	2
22.	Berg	2
23.	Donau	2
24.	fliessen	2
25.	Flussufer	2
26.	Frau	2
27.	Gewasser	2
28.	Kuss	2
29.	Mississippi	2
30.	rauschen	2
31.	Schwimm	2
32.	Teich	

33-84. (f = 1)
Amazonas, Bein, Biegung, Blatt, Dichtung, Don,
Faehre, Ferne, Fisch, flumen, Flusslauf,
Flussniederung, Frau v. Fluss, Gabelung,
Gebirge, Gebirgsfluss, Geographie, glaenzend,
glatt, Halt, Hund, Kahn, kalt, Landkarte, lang,
meine Heimat, Moldau-Thema, Namen, nass, Natur,
Neckar, Oder, paddeln, platschert, Redefluss,
reissend, river, Schifffahrt, Schiller,
Schlange, schmutzig, schnell, Strasse, Tech,
Tiber, traege, Traegstrom, Verkehr, Wake, Weg,
Welle, Wiese

28. Weiss

No.	Response	Total
1.	schwarz	129
2.	Schnee	35
3.	hell	26
4.	Farbe	11
5.	rot	10
6.	Wand	7
7.	blau	4
8.	dunkel	4
9.	Kleid	4
10.	Kohl	4
11.	schneeweiss	4
12.	grau	3
13.	schoen	3
14.	Waesche	3
15.	Dorn	2
16.	grell	2
17.	Kalk	2
18.	Licht	2
19.	Papier	2
20.	Reinheit	2
21.	sauber	2
22.	Suwa	2
23.	Unschuld	2
24.	Weisskraut	2
25.	Wurst	2

26-87. (f = 1)
Betttuch, Blume, Bluete, Boot, braun, Braut,
Brot, Deckfarbe, el, en, Engel, Freude,
Gegensatz, gelb, glanz, grob, heit, Helle,
Helligkeit, Hemd, Hochzeit, kahl, kalt, klar,
Kontrast, Krankenhaus, Kraut, Kreide, Lackfarbe,
Leinen, Leinwand, leuchtend, Lichtflut, Lilie,
ling, Maedchen, Maigloeckchen, Malerei, Mehl,
Melodie, Name, Papierblatt, Pfarrer, Reflexion,
rein, Russland, Schaum, Scheiss, Schlager,
schmutzig, Schulaufgabe, Schwan, Seele, stuhr,
Tanne, Tischtuch, Tuch, warm, Wein,
Weissnaeherin, Weisspapier, zart

29. Schoen

No.	Response	Total
1.	haesslich	71
2.	Maedchen	29
3.	schlecht	19
4.	Frau(en)	15
5.	gut	14
6.	heit	11
7.	Wetter	11
8.	herrlich	7
9.	huebsch	7
10.	Blume(n)	6
11.	Bild	5
12.	Kunst	5
13.	Natur	5
14.	angenehm	4
15.	Schoenheit	4
16.	unschoen	4
17.	bildschoen	3
18.	sauber	3
19.	aussehen	2
20.	bunt	2
21.	Film	2
22.	Freude	2
23.	glatt	2
24.	hell	2
25.	Kind	2
26.	klar	2
27.	Landschaft	2
28.	Musik	2
29.	reizend	2
30.	tanzen	2
31.	wunderbar	2

32-113. (f = 1)

Anmut, ansprechend, aestetisch, Ausdruck, Auto,
beautiful, bildhuebsch, blau, Bleistift, blond,
brav, Buch, Datum, dunkel, edel, Eisenbahn,
erhaben, Fehler, Ferien, Fest, Figur, Filmstar,
fliessende Formen, Flugzeug, freundlich,
garstig, Gegend, Gegenstand, Geld, Genuss,
Geschenk, Gesicht, grau, grausam, gustig, Haar,
Hand, Handschaft, Haus, heiss, heiter, hurtig,
ideal, kalt, Kindheit, Klasse, Komposition,
Konzert, Kunstwerk, Lollobrigida, Malerei,
Mallovia, modern, Mutter, nett, Park, Pferd,
Rahmen, rein, Rhoen, rot, scheusslich, -born,
schoenes Wetter, Schoenheitskonkurrenz, sehr,
sein, Sessel, Sommer, Standbild, Tanzabend,
Tanzstunde, tausendschoen, uebel, Wasser,
Weihnacht, weiss, wundervoll, Zimmer, zart,
(καλός)-Gr. for 'beautiful'

(Illegible)

30. Fenster

No.	Response	Total
1.	Glas	50
2.	Licht	27
3.	Tuer(e)	26
4.	Rahmen	23
5.	Kreuz	16
	(Kreuz: 15	
	Kreiz: 1)	
6.	Brett	12
7.	Scheibe	10
8.	Haus	8
9.	Laden	8
10.	Bank	7
11.	Vorhang	7
12.	Ausblick	6
13.	Oeffnung	6
14.	Fensterbrett	5
15.	gross	5
16.	offen	4
17.	Aussicht	3
18.	Fensterbank	3
19.	Fensterkreuz	3

30. Fenster (contd)

No.	Response	Total
20.	Fensterrahmen	3
21.	Fluegel	3
22.	Gardine(n)	3
23.	Hof	3
24.	hell	3
25.	kalt	3
26.	Lichteinlass	3
27.	Loch	3
28.	Strasse	3
29.	Blick(en)	2
30.	Fensterladen	2
31.	Scherben	2
32.	Sims	2
33.	Tor	2
34.	weit	2
35.	Window	2
36.	Zimmer	2
37.	zu	2

38-94. (f = 1)

Abend, aussen, bequem, blank, Blumen, breit,
Dunkelheit, Durchblick, durchsichtig, Eis,
entzwei, Fenstergitter, Fensteroeffnung,
Fensterputzer, Fenstersims, Ferne, Flaeche,
Freiheit, Freizeit, Frischluft, Gitter, Griff,
Helligkeit, Hochhaus, Hoehle, klar, Knopf,
Kuechenfenster, Landschaft, Leiter, Lichtquell,
Lichtzufuhr, Luft, Musik, Nische, No response,
oeffnen, Rechteck, Rumba, rund, schauern,
Schnee, Schulfenster, Spiegel, Stein, Stuhl,
Sturz, Tagleuchter, Umgebung, vereist, vier-
teilig, weiter Blick, Welt, Wetter, Wind,
Wohnung, Zug

31. Rauh

No.	Response	Total
1.	glatt	47
2.	reif	30
3.	zart	17
4.	rauhreif	16
5.	Winter	16
6.	hart	13
7.	weich	13
8.	Frost	5
9.	herzlich	5
10.	Rauheit	5
11.	Reibeisen	5
12.	roh	5
13.	Bart	4
14.	Bein	4
15.	Feile	4
16.	Gebirge	4
17.	grob	4
18.	Hut	4
19.	kalt	4
20.	sanft	4
21.	eben	3
22.	Eisen	3
23.	Haend(e)	3
24.	heit	3
25.	herrlich	3
26.	Klima	3
27.	Oberflaeche	3
28.	Sandpapier	3
29.	Wetter	3
30.	Wind	3
31.	abstossend	2
32.	bitter	2
33.	Buerste	2
34.	Flaeche	2
35.	Haut	2
36.	herb	2
37.	holprig	2
38.	Leder	2

31. Rauh (contd)

No.	Response	Total
39.	Lederhose	2
40.	mild	2
41.	Raspel	2
42.	Rauhbein	2
43.	Schale	2
44.	ungehobelt	2

45-108. (f = 1)
Apfel, Asphalt, Bau, Berg, beschwerlich, Beton, blau, Bohrer, borstig, edel, eisig, Erzgebirge, fein, Felsen, Felswand, furchtbar, Gegend, geschmeidig, Gestein, gut, Hand d. Mutter, heiss, Heizung, Herbst, holperig, Holz, Igel, Jugend, kaltes Wetter, (kantig, spitzig), Kerl, kratzig, Natur, Papier, Pullover, Physik, rauhbeinig, rauhes Klima, Rinde, rissig, ruppig, Sand, schlecht, Schmerz, schmiegsam, Schmirgel, Schmirgelpapier, Schnee, schroff, Schule, Splitt, Stimme, stoppelig, Strasse, unangenehm, uneben, warm (weich, glatt), Wesen, wild, Witterung, wogegen, Wolle, Zunge

32. Buerger

No.	Response	Total
1.	Staat	45
2.	Stadt	34
3.	Bauer	17
4.	Speissbuerger	16
	(Spiessbuerger: 15	
	Spiessbuerg. : 1)	
5.	Meister	15
6.	Mann	12
7.	Buergermeister	10
8.	Staedter	10
9.	Mensch	9
10.	Soldat	7
11.	Spiesser	6
12.	Mittelalter	5
13.	satt	5
14.	tum	5
15.	Buergerschaft	4
16.	Buergersteig	4
	(Buergersteig: 3	
	B.-steig : 1)	
17.	spiess	4
18.	Staatsbuerger	4
19.	Arbeiter	3
20.	bequem	3
21.	brav	3
22.	Gesetz	3
23.	No response	3
24.	Sklave	3
25.	altmodisch	2
26.	Buergerrecht	2
27.	dick	2
28.	Franz. Revolution	2
29.	gut	2
30.	Kunde	2
31.	Politik	2
32.	solid(e)	2
33.	spiessig	2
34.	Untertan	2
35.	Zivilist	2

36-114. (f = 1)
Adliger, Aristokrat, Athener, Beamter, behabig, bewahren, Bewohner, Bourgoisie, Braeu, Buergerin, Buergertum, Buergerverein, Buergerversammlung, Buergerwehr, civil, Demokrat, Despot, deutsch, dickbaeuchig, Dorf, dumm, einst und jetzt, Einwohner, Erwachsener, Familie, Fleiss, Frank-reich, Frauchen, frei, Fremder, Geaechteter, gediegen, Gemeinde, Gerichtigkeit, Geschichte, Grieche, Guter, Haus, Herrscher, ich, Kaufmann, Keller, Kleinstadt, Koenig, Lehrer, Mantel,

32. Buerger (contd)

No.	Response	Total

Marktplatz, Minister, noetig, Ordnung, Pfarrer, Pflicht, Polizei, Praesident, rasch, recht, Rodin, Roemer, Ruhe, schlecht, Sessel, Spital, Staats, Staatsmann, Stadtbewohner, Stadtrat, Stadttax, Stand, Steig, Steuerzahler, Teilhaber, Tisch, Vagabund, von Calais, Wahl, waehlen, wohlhabend, Wuerger, zivil

33. Fuss

No.	Response	Total
1.	Schuh(e)	41
2.	Hand	38
3.	Zeh(en)	33
4.	Bein	31
5.	Ball	25
6.	Gelenk	10
7.	Fussball	6
8.	gehen	6
9.	laufen	6
10.	Sohle	5
11.	Fusszehe	4
12.	Koerper	4
13.	Koerperteil	4
14.	Arm	3
15.	gross	3
16.	Knoechel	3
17.	Kopf	3
18.	Lauf	3
19.	Abstreifer	2
20.	Arzt	2
21.	Ballett	2
22.	Boden	2
23.	breit	2
24.	Ende	2
25.	Fussende	2
26.	Glied	2
27.	Huehnerauge	2
28.	Knie	2
29.	lahm	2
30.	Marsch	2
31.	Mensch	2
32.	Plattfuss	2
33.	schnell	2
34.	Strom	2
35.	(illegible)	2

36-104. (f = 1)
Anatomie, Angel, Auto, Bach, bequem, Bett, Bewegung, blaue Flechen, Einlage, F. Angel, Ferse, Frau, Fussbinde, Fuesse, Fussgelenk, Fusskrankheit, Fussstapfen, Gang, gaenger, Gehwerkzeug, Geruch, Gestalt, Gestank, Glieder, Gliedmassen, grosse Fuesse, Haar, Hinkfuss, kalt, kaput, Kaese, Knochen, krank, Krankheit, Kuss, lang, Latte, marschieren, Mass, Nagel, ohne Namen, Osthopaede, Pedal, per, Pflege, Prothese, Rhein, Riss, Sand, Schemel, Schifffahrt, schlank, Schmerz, Schutz, Schweiss, Ski, Sport, Stand, Stapfe, stehen, Strumpf, Treppe, Tritt, Verletzung, Verstauchung, warm, Weg, Wunde, zierlich

34. Spinne

No.	Response	Total
1.	Netz	111
2.	Tier(e)	31
3.	Bein(e)	12
4.	ekel	11
5.	haesslich	9

34. Spinne (contd)

No.	Response	Total
6.	Insekt	9
7.	Kreuzspinne	7
8.	Spinnennetz	7
	(Spinnennetz: 5	
	Spinnetz : 1	
	-nnetz : 1)	
9.	eklig	6
	(eklig : 5	
	eckelig: 1)	
10.	Spinnwebe(n)	6
	(Spinnwebe(n): 2	
	-nwebe(n) : 4)	
11.	Webe(n)	6
12.	Feind	5
13.	Fliege	4
14.	ekelhaft	3
15.	Kaefer	3
16.	Kreuz	3
17.	lange Beine	3
18.	rei	3
19.	scheusslich	3
20.	schrecklich	3
21.	Faden	2
22.	Gespenst	2
23.	Gewebe	2
24.	Gift	2
25.	giftig	2
26.	Krebs	2
	(Krebs: 1	
	Kebs : 1)	
27.	langbeinig	2
28.	Nest	2
29.	Rad	2
30.	unheimlich	2
31.	Untier	2
32.	Vogel	2
33.	Vogelspinne	2

34-93. ($f = 1$)
Aberglaube, Abscheu, abscheulich, am morgen, an der Wand, Angst, Biologie, Dunkelheit, duenn, Ekliches, Elektriker, feindlich, Film, Furcht, Fussball, Fuesse, Gefahr, gefaehrlich, Gliederfuessler, grausig, Haesslichkeit, Hummel, interessant, Kehrber, kitzelig, krabbeln, Kralle, Kreuzotter, Kriminalroman, lang, Minne, Otter, pfui, rauben, Raeuber, Sage, Schlange, Schnecke, Schreck, Schreckengespenst, spinnen, Spinngewebe, Spinnstube, Staubnetz, Stelzbeine, Stich, Strumpf, Tarantel, Tuer, unangenehmes Gefuehl, unangenhm, Ungetuem, Unglueck, Verirrung, Volk, Wanne, Wanze, Web, weiss, Wobie

35 Nadel

No.	Response	Total
1.	Spitz	56
2.	Faden	51
3.	Stich	41
4.	Oehr	36
	(Oehr: 34	
	Oer : 2)	
5.	Spitze	16
6.	naehen	14
7.	stechen	11
8.	Schmerz	8
9.	Zwirn	8
10.	Kopf	5
11.	Schere	5
12.	Nadeloehr	4
13.	Schneider	4
14.	Stecknadel	4
15.	Nadelspitze	3
16.	stecken	3

35. Nadel (contd)

No.	Response	Total
17.	Werkzeug	3
18.	Blut	2
19.	duenn	2
20.	Holz	2
21.	Instrument	2
22.	Kissen	2
23.	Nadelstich	2
24.	Nagel	2
25.	scharf	2
26.	spitzig	2
27.	Stich	2

28-66. ($f = 1$)
Anstecknadel, au, Baum, blank, Bluttropfen, Chirurg, Dorn, Fall, Fleiss, flicken, Garn, Geraet, glaenzend, glatt, Grossmutter, Guertel, Haar, Handarbeit, Loch, Mensch, Metall, Nadelloch, Naeherin, Naehinstrument, Naehkorb, Naehzeug, nicht, Pick, Punkt, Radel, Stab, Stahl, Steckbest, Stoff, stopfen, Strick, stricken, Wolle
(Illegible)

36. Rot

No.	Response	Total
1.	gruen	38
2.	Farbe	24
3.	blau	22
4.	gelb	19
5.	weiss	17
6.	schwarz	16
7.	Liebe	14
8.	Stier	10
9.	grell	9
10.	Blut	7
11.	Lippe(n)	6
12.	Tuch	5
13.	Spektrum	4
14.	Verkehrsampel	4
15.	warm	4
16.	braun	3
17.	Haare	3
18.	Kehlchen	3
	(Kehlchen: 2	
	Kelchen : 1)	
19.	leuchtend	3
20.	Stierkampf	3
21.	Ampel	2
22.	auffallend	2
23.	Fahne	2
24.	Feuer	2
25.	feurig	2
26.	Gefahr	2
27.	Glut	2
28.	halt	2
29.	Kaeppchen	2
30.	Kommunismus	2
31.	Lippenstift	2
32.	rosa	2
33.	rotbraun	2
34.	Rotlauf	2
35.	schoen	2
36.	Signal	2
37.	Torrero	2
38.	Wut	2

39-119. ($f = 1$)
Auerhahn, Auge, Bart, Blindheit, blond, Blume, Buch, Dach, dunkel, dunkelrot, erotisch, erregend, Faden, Fenster, feurrot, Flagge d. Kommunism, Frucht, Fuchs, gefaehrlich, Gegenfarbe, gluehen, hell, Hemd, henburg, Herr, Herz, Heuschreck, Hitze, infra, Kaiser, Kohl, Kommunist, kommunistisch, Kopftuch, KPD, Kraut, Lauf, leuchten, leuchtet, Licht,

36. Rot (contd)

No.	Response	Total

Maedchen, malen, Meer, Mohn, Mond, Mund, Nelke, Ohr, Partei, Parteifarbe, purpur, Reiz, Reklame, rosarot, rotaeugig, rotbackig, rotblind, Rothosen, Rotkaeppchen, Rotkraut, Rotwein, rouge, Russland, Schal, scharf, schreiend, schrill, Sonne, Sowjet, SPD, stechend, stop, Teufel, tot, UdSSR, verfuehrerisch, Verkehr, Wein, Weissgeld, weit
(Illegible)

37. Schlafen

No.	Response	Total
1.	Bett	57
2.	wachen	45
3.	gehen	18
4.	Ruhe	18
5.	muede	17
6.	traeumen	14
7.	Nacht	12
8.	ruhen	10
9.	essen	6
10.	schnarchen	6
11.	tief	6
12.	Traum	6
13.	ausruhen	5
14.	Erholung	5
15.	aufwachen	4
16.	bequem	3
17.	gaehnen	3
18.	schlafen gehen	3
19.	wach sein	3
20.	warm	3
21.	Zeit	3
22.	arbeiten	2
23.	gesund	2
24.	Gesundheit	2
25.	gut	2
26.	lang(e)	2
27.	ruhig	2
28.	Schlaf	2
29.	Schlafenszeit	2
30.	schoen	2
31.	still(e)	2
32.	trinken	2
33.	wach	2
34.	Wecker	2
35.	wunderbar	2
36.	Zustand	2

37-90. (f = 1)
Abend, ahh!, angenehm, ausgehen, aufstehen, Bequemlichkeit, doesen, Eisen, Eisenwagen, entspannen, Entspannung, erholen, erwachen, faulenzen, fein, fest, Freiheitsbeschaeftigung, gaffen, geschl. Augen, hart, herrlich, Kissen, lassen, leben, liegen, moeglichst lange, Muedigkeit, nervoes, niesen, noetig, notwendig, Notwendigkeit, NR, pennen, Polster, rauchen, Relaxation, sanft, Schlafanzug, Schlafkrankheit, Schlafwagen, schlecht, schlummern, selten, Sonntag, szeit, toesen, tot, Unruhe, wachend, wecken, weich, wohlig, Wurst

38. Zorn

No.	Response	Total
1.	Wut	98
2.	Ausbruch	18
3.	rot	15
4.	Hass	7

38. Zorn (contd)

No.	Response	Total
5.	unbeherrscht	6
6.	Lehrer	4
7.	rasen	4
8.	Roete	4
9.	Sanftmut	4
10.	Aerger	3
11.	entbrannt	3
12.	Erregung	3
13.	Gelassenheit	3
14.	heftig	3
15.	Milde	3
16.	sanft	3
17.	wild	3
18.	wuetend	3
19.	Zornausbruch	3
	(Zornausbruch : 2	
	Zornesausbruch: 1)	
20.	zornig	3
21.	abscheulich	2
22.	Ader	2
23.	beben	2
24.	Beherrschung	2
25.	boese	2
26.	Charakter	2
27.	Eigenschaft	2
28.	furchtbar	2
29.	gefaehrlich	2
30.	Gemuet	2
31.	Igel	2
32.	Jaehzorn	2
33.	Leidenschaft	2
34.	Ruhe	2
35.	schimpfen	2
36.	Schlag	2
37.	schlagen	2
38.	unangenehm	2
39.	Unbeherrschtheit	2
40.	Zornader	2
	(Zornader : 1	
	Zornesader: 1)	

41-138. (f = 1)
Anfall, Angst, Anspannung, aufgeregt, aufregen, Aufregung, Ausdruck des Temp., Beleidigung, Blut, boshaftig, bruellen, Chemielehrer, ekelhaft, Egoismus, Eifer, erbeben, Erregtheit, erroete, Falten, Fluch, fluchen, Freude, Fruechte, fuerchte, Fussball, Fussstampfen, Gefuehl, Gefuehlsaeusserung, Gemessenheit, gerecht, gereizt, Gereizth., Gesicht, Gott, grausam, Groll, Grund, gut, Guete, Gutmuetigkeit, heiss, Hilfe, hochfahren, Impuls, Ira, jaeh, jaehzornig, Klassleiter, K.O., Koleriker, Korn, Krach, Krebs, Kuehlung, lachen, laecherlich, laut, Liebe, Mann, Mann (bestimmter), Miserfolg, Mitleid, Neid, platzen, Pruegelei, Rache, rasend, Regung, sachte, schelten, schlecht, schlechte Note, schrecklich, Selbstbeherrschung, selten, Splitter, spruehend, Stier, Stirnader, Stoff, Streit, Tasse, Temperament, Tod, Truthahn, Uebermut, ueberschnappen, Unmass, Vater, verbrannt, Versoehnung, zahm, Zaehneknirschen, zart, zeigen, Zornickel, zorniger Mensch, zu meiden

39. Teppich

No.	Response	Total
1.	weich	46
2.	Boden	21
3.	Perser	18
4.	Klopfer	13
5.	Laeufer	12
6.	Fussboden	10

39. Teppich (contd)

No.	Response	Total
7.	Perserteppich (Perserteppich: 7 Perser- : 3)	10
8.	Zimmer	10
9.	Muster	8
10.	Persien	8
11.	leis(e)	6
12.	Orient	6
13.	Bodenbelag	5
14.	klopfen	5
15.	Teppichklopfer	5
16.	warm(e)	5
17.	bunt	4
18.	Wand	4
19.	bequem	3
20.	Decke	3
21.	fliegen	3
22.	Matte	3
23.	Vorleger	3
24.	Witz	3
25.	Wolle	3
26.	angenehm	2
27.	Belag	2
28.	Bett	2
29.	Faser	2
30.	Fransen	2
31.	klapfen	2
32.	lautlos	2
33.	linoleum	2
34.	Parkett	2
35.	Persianer	2
36.	Schmuck	2
37.	schoen	2
38.	Staubsauger	2
39.	Teppichmuster	2
40.	Teppichschoner	2
41.	vornehm	2
42.	Wohnung	2
43.	Wohnzimmer	2

44-121. (f = 1)
Ableger, Absatz, Anzug, Arbeit, artig, Asche,
Behaglichkeit, Bequemlichkeit, Bruecke, dick,
dunkel, Einrichtung, eppich, Farbe, farbiq,
Flaeche, Fleck, fliessen, Floh, Form, Gardine,
Garn, Garten, Geld, gemuetlich, gewebt, gross,
gruen, Handtuch, Haus, hinlegen, Hinterhof,
Karoteppich, karriert, Luxus, mollig, Moebel,
Nadel, neu, no response, Ordnung, Polster,
Quaste, Reichtum, Rolle, rot, sanft, schmutzig,
Schoner, Schonung, Sessel, Staub, Stille,
Stueck, Teppichbesen, Teppiche, Teppichhaendler,
Teppichrand, Tepichsaum, Teppichwitz, teuer,
Tintenfleck, Tisch, Tischtuch, Trissbodenbelag,
Tuch, unsere Wohnung, Unterlage, Vorlage,
Wandteppich, Waerme, Webekunst, Weberei,
Wohnungzierde, wollig, Zimmerruhe, zu Hause
(Illegible)

40. Maedchen

No.	Response	Total
1.	Junge	45
2.	Frau	18
3.	Knabe	18
4.	schoen	18
5.	huebsch	14
6.	jung	10
7.	tanzen	10
8.	Schule	8
9.	Haar(e)	6
10.	Liebe	6
11.	nett	6
12.	Name	5

40. Maedchen (contd)

No.	Response	Total
13.	Schoenheit	5
14.	Schwester	5
15.	Freundin	4
16.	Jungfrau	4
17.	Kind	4
18.	lieb	4
19.	Pferdeschwanz	4
20.	schlank	4
21.	blond	3
22.	Bub(e)	3
23.	Bursch(e)	3
24.	Kleid	3
25.	klein	3
26.	Tanzkurs	3
27.	Auge	2
28.	aussehen	2
29.	beachtenswert	2
30.	Bett	2
31.	Dienstmaedchen	2
32.	Frauelein	2
33.	Geschlecht	2
34.	gut	2
35.	Jugend	2
36.	Laendler	2
37.	Maedchenhandel(er)	2
38.	Mann	2
39.	Mensch	2
40.	No response	2
41.	Pensionat	2
42.	suess	2
43.	Tanzstunde	2

44-124. (f = 1)
Abstand, albern, angenehme Gesellschaft,
anmutig, Anne, Backfisch, Bad, breit, charmant,
du, elegant, faul, Flirt, Freizeit, freundlich,
Fruehling, fuer alles, Gans, Gegenstueck zu
Junge, Geld, gescheit, Geschenk, Gesicht,
Girl, Grazie, Handel, Heim, helfen, Helga, hell,
her, Herz, Hose, Huft, Hut, Idiosie, interessant,
junge Dame, Kaetchen, Kleidung, kuessen, lachen,
Lana, lang, leider, Liebchen, lieblich,
Maedchenbeine, maedchenhaft, Maedchenkammer,
Maedchenname, Mode, Moeglichkeit, M. Pensionat,
Musik, Mut, Mutter, Oper, Rebecca, Rock, rufen,
sanft, scheu, schick, schoenes Gesicht, Schuhe,
Schuerze, schutzbeduerftig, Sexappeal, Strasse,
Strumpf, Unschuld, Verfuehrer, Vergnuegen,
weibl. Wesen, weiblich, Zeitverschwendung,
Zerbrechliches!, Zimmer, Zoepfe, (ὀρος)-Gr. for
'mountain'

41. Hoch

No.	Response	Total
1.	tief	156
2.	Berg	16
3.	Turm	15
4.	Haus	12
5.	Bau	9
6.	Hochhaus	6
7.	niedrig	6
8.	Baum	5
9.	Zeit	5
10.	Druck	4
11.	Eifelturm	4
12.	Hochdruck	4
13.	weit	4
14.	Wolkenkratzer	4
15.	Luft	3
16.	Wetter	3
17.	Antenne	2
18.	Dom	2
19.	Gebaeude	2
20.	Gebirge	2

41. Hoch (contd)

No.	Response	Total
21.	gross	2
22.	Schornstein	2
23.	schwindelig	2
24.	Zugspitze	2

25-83. (f = 1)
abrupt, Alpen, Atmosphaere, Aussicht, Bahn, breit, Buch, Burg, Druckgebiet, Duesenjaeger, endlos, erhebend, Fernsehturm, Fest, flach, Flugzeug, gefaehrlich, Geist, gewaltig, gutes Wetter, hager, hell, herunterfallen, hinauf, Hoch- und Tiefbau, Hochalp, Hochebene, Hochgebirge, Hochwasser, Hochzeit, Hunde, Karriere, Kirche, Leiter, Luftdruck, maechtig, Mast, NR, Reck, relativ, riesig, Saeule, Schwindel, Sitz, Spannung, Sprung, Stange, steil, still, Tanne, turmhoch, unendlich, unheimlich, unsinnig, Wald, Wand, Wanderung, weittragend, wolkenlos

42. Arbeiten

No.	Response	Total
1.	faulenzen	30
2.	schlafen	26
3.	ruhen	18
4.	schaffen	16
5.	schwer	14
6.	Schule	13
7.	Muehe(n)	12
8.	ausruhen	8
9.	fleissig	6
10.	Geld	6
11.	faul	5
12.	muede	5
13.	no response	5
14.	essen	4
15.	Freude	4
16.	schnell	4
17.	Schweiss	4
18.	Anstrengung	3
19.	Arbeiter	3
20.	Bau	3
21.	Fleiss	3
22.	langsam	3
23.	Lohn	3
24.	schlecht	3
25.	Zeit	3
26.	anstrengend	2
27.	Beschaeftigung	2
28.	Fabrik	2
29.	graben	2
30.	hart	2
31.	lernen	2
32.	Muehsal	2
33.	nichts tun	2
34.	notwendig	2
35.	Pflicht	2
36.	Pickel	2
37.	Ruhe	2
38.	Schaufel	2
39.	schoen	2
40.	Schularbeit(en)	2
41.	Schulaufgabe(n)	2
42.	traeg(e)	2
43.	tun	2
44.	Werk	2

45-133. (f = 1)
(sich) abmuehen, anarbeiten, anstrengen, Arbeit, Arbeitenzeit, Arbeitsamt, Arbeitspferd, Aerger, arm, Ausgaben, ausspannen, Autobahn, Bauarbeit, befriedigend, Bequemlichkeit, bereiten, Beruf, beten, bewegen, Buecher, Buerger, Buero, Bursch, der, Dreck, dreschen, Einsatz, eisig, Erfolg, erringen, Eaulheit, fein, Ferien, Freund, gehen,

42. Arbeiten (contd)

No.	Response	Total

gern, gut, Hausarbeiten, Hausaufsatz, helfen, Koennen, Last, Lebenssinn, lesen, leider, leisten, mit Mass, muehsam, Musse, Notwendigkeit, notw. Uebel, Papier, plagen, (sich) plagen, prima, Produktion, Prolet, putzen, Qual, Russland, samt, schade, schaufeln, scheu, schuften, segen, Sprung, stramm, strebsam, Studium, stur, teilen, tief, Tisch, unangenehm, verbittertes Gesicht, verdienen, vergessen, Werkstatt, Werktag, Werkzeug, wichtig, Wirklichkeit, Wohltat, wollen, Work-camp, working, wuehlen, Zufriedenstellendes

43. Sauer

No.	Response	Total
1.	suess	129
2.	Essig	23
3.	Gurken	20
4.	Kraut	19
5.	bitter	15
6.	Salz	10
7.	Sauerkraut	10
8.	Kirsche(n)	6
9.	Teig	6
10.	Lehrer	5
11.	Zitrone	5
12.	herb	4
13.	Apfel	3
14.	essen	3
15.	Geschmack	3
16.	Sauerteig	3
17.	schlecht	3
18.	Wein	3
19.	Arbeit	2
20.	Milch	2
21.	Most	2
22.	Quitte	2
23.	salzig	2
24.	scharf	2
25.	Schule	2
26.	schweiss	2
27.	Speise	2
28.	unangenehm	2

29-69. (f = 1)
Abscheu, Abwehr, alt, Ampfer, Bauer, beissend, Braten, Brot, Bruch, Englisch, Gericht, guenstig, Hering, kalt, keit, klein, Kohl, Konrad, lieb, Mathematik, Medezin, Miene, Muedigkeit, Name, Not, NR, Obst, Pfarrer S., Professor, Reaktion, Sauerampfer, Sauerbruch, Saeure, Sauerklee, schade, schlafen, Schorsch, suesssauer, warm, widerlich, wildes Obst

44. Erde

No.	Response	Total
1.	Himmel	32
2.	Mond	26
3.	rund	16
4.	Kugel	13
5.	Acker	11
6.	Boden	11
7.	Wasser	10
8.	Ball	9
9.	Luft	8
10.	schwarz	8
11.	Meer	7
12.	Mutter	7
13.	Land	6

44. Erde (contd)

No.	Response	Total
14.	Sonne	6
15.	Welt	5
16.	braun	4
17.	Grab	4
18.	no response	4
19.	Weltall	4
20.	alt	3
21.	Garten	3
22.	Heimat	3
23.	kalt	3
24.	nass	3
25.	Planet	3
26.	Sand	3
27.	schmutzig	3
28.	Sputnik	3
29.	warm	3
30.	Antenne	2
31.	Brot	2
32.	Dreck	2
33.	Duft	2
34.	dumpf	2
35.	feucht	2
36.	fruchtbar	2
37.	Fruchtbarkeit	2
38.	Globus	2
39.	Gras	2
40.	Kosmos	2
41.	Mensch	2
42.	rot	2
43.	See	2
44.	Tal	2
45.	Ton	2

46-123. (f = 1)
Apfel, Aequator, Bahn, Bauer, beben, Beton, Bewegung, Brocken, duftig, Erdallen, Erdball, Erdbeben, Erdbewegung, erdhaft, Erdnuss, Erdschwere, Erdverhaften, Fall, Gebilde, Geologie, Gestalt, Graben, gross, grosse Flaeche, gruen, Grund, heiss, herb, Huegel, jung, kahm, klein, Lehm, Loes, Mars, Mondbahn, Mutter...., Naturstoff, neu, nmuehe, nreich, nrund, Pearl S. Buck, Pferde, Pflanze, Pol, Politik, Regen, Reichtum, reisen, religioes, rissig, Rond, rote Erde, Schatz, Schlamm, Schmuck, Schmutz, schoen, Sehnsucht, singen, Staub, Stein, Sterne, Teich, tief, Tier, trabant, trocken, Umfang, vergaenglich, Wachstum, weich, Weite, Weltkugel, Weltraum, Winter, (Γη - Gr. for 'Erde')

45. Sorge

No.	Response	Total
1.	Kummer	52
2.	Not	32
3.	Muehe	15
4.	Angst	14
5.	Leid	11
6.	Mutter	11
7.	Falte(n)	9
8.	Schule	9
9.	Freude	8
10.	Last	7
11.	Sorglosigkeit	7
12.	Arbeit	5
13.	Geld	5
14.	Kind(er)	5
15.	schwer	5
16.	sorglos	4
17.	Cura	3
18.	Eltern	3
19.	Frau	3
20.	Plage	3
21.	Qual	3

45. Sorge

No.	Response	Total
22.	Sorgen	3
23.	voll	3
24.	drueckend	2
25.	Familie	2
26.	frei	2
27.	Fuersorge	2
28.	Gram	2
29.	grau	2
30.	haben	2
31.	keine	2
32.	Krankheit	2
33.	reich	2
34.	sorgenfrei	2
35.	sorgenvoll	2

36-122. (f = 1)
Abhaermen, Abitur, Alltag, alte Frau, Alter, aengstlich, Aerger, arm, arme Frau, Armut, Ausgelassenheit, Beruf, beschwerlich, Bezahlung, bitter, Brot, Depression, Dichter, Drangsal, dunkel, fahlen, Fall, faul, Fleiss, Freiheit, Fuelle, Gedanken, Geldnot, Geliebte, gleich, griechisch, griesgraemig, gross, Haus, heiraten, heiss, Herz, Hilfe, immer, keine Sorge machen, klein, leben, Leichtsinn, Liebe, los, lustig, Macht, meine Mutter, Menschlichkeit, Mitsorge, Morgen, muede, Muehsal, Musse, Muessiggang, neu, nichts fuer mich, Noten, ohne Sorge, Personifikation d. S., Pflicht, Rolle, Ruhe, Runzel, Schlaf, schlecht, schwierig, Seele, Sorge tragen, Sorgender, Sorgenlast, sorgenlos, Sorgerecht, Sorgfalt, Stirne, tragen, ueber etwas, uberlegen, unangenehm, Unglueck, Unnuetz, Unruhe, Vaterland, vergessen, Vorsehung, Winter, Zukunft

46. Soldat

No.	Response	Total
1.	Kreig	53
2.	Militaer	17
3.	Bundeswehr	16
4.	Uniform	13
5.	Gewehr	12
6.	Buerger	10
7.	Zivilist	10
8.	Offizier	7
9.	stramm	7
10.	marschiersen	6
11.	Kaserne	5
12.	Mann	5
13.	Militaerist	5
14.	sein	5
15.	Armee	4
16.	kaempfen	3
17.	Schutz	3
18.	Soldatentum	3
19.	Tod	3
20.	Wehrmacht	3
21.	Wehrpflicht	3
22.	Arbeiter	2
23.	Drill	2
24.	Feld	2
25.	Haltung	2
26.	hart	2
27.	Heer	2
28.	Held	2
29.	Helm	2
30.	Kampf	2
31.	Kaempfer	2
32.	Kind	2
33.	Kommando	2
34.	Kommis	2
35.	Mensch	2
36.	nie	2

46. Soldat (contd)

No.	Response	Total
37.	Schuetzengraben	2
38.	Staat	2
39.	Stahlhelm	2
40.	tapfer	2
41.	Wehrdienst	2

42-139. (f = 1)
Ablehnung, Anzug, Arbeit, Arm, Barras, Bauer,
Befehl, Beruf, Beschuetzer d. Vat., Blei, Bonn,
Bruder, Bundesw., Deutscher, dienen, Eid, ekel,
enanzug, entum, eska, Fahne, Feldwebel, fest,
Freier, Freude, Fussoldat, Gefreiter, gemein,
G.I., Grab, Gras, guter, Hauptmann, Heimat,
heimatliebend, heute, Hitler, ja, Kanone,
Kleidung, Kneipe, kommandieren, Konrad, kraftvoll,
Krieger, leichtsinnig, Mann in Uniform,
Marinesoldat, Militaerdienstzeit, Militaerwesen,
Musik, Mut, niemals, noetig, notwendig, nuetzlich,
Opfer, Panzer, Parademarsch, Pflicht, pfui!'
Privatmann, Proletat, Rakete, Rekrut, Sadismus,
schlau, schnell, schneidig, schrecklich, Schuss,
Sold, Soldaten, Soldatenleben, Soldatenlied,
Soldatenmanier, Soldateska, Soldat sein, Soldier,
Soeldner, spielen, spiess, Sprache, stattlich,
toeten, Unteroffizier, Vater, Vaterland,
Verteidiger, Waffe, Wehrbeitrag, zackig, Zink,
Zinnsoldat, Zivil, Zivilperson, II. Weltkrieg,
III. Reich

47. Kohl

No.	Response	Total
1.	Gemuese	94
2.	essen	29
3.	Kraut	15
4.	Ruebe(n)	12
5.	gruen	9
6.	Kopf	9
7.	Garten	7
8.	Hase(n)	7
	(Hase(n): 6	
	Haase : 1)	
9.	Kohlkopf	7
10.	Salat	7
11.	Suppe	7
12.	Blumenkohl	6
13.	Rabi	5
14.	Raupe(n)	5
15.	Wirsing	5
	(Wirsing : 4	
	Wirsching: 1)	
16.	Pflanze	4
17.	Rabe(n)	4
18.	Weissling	4
	(Weissling: 3	
	Weisling : 1)	
19.	Blatt	3
20.	Quatsch	3
21.	Sauerkraut	3
22.	schlecht	3
	(schlecht: 2	
	schleht : 1)	
23.	weiss	3
24.	Abscheu	2
25.	Blume(n)	2
26.	Geruch	2
27.	Kohle	2
28.	Mist	2
29.	Mittagessen	2
30.	Obst	2
31.	riecht	2
32.	Rosenkohl	2
33.	Rotkohl	2
34.	Weisskohl	2
35.	wohl	2

36-91. (f = 1)
annehmbar, blau, Blaukraut, Bloedsinn, Dampf,

47. Kohl (contd)

No.	Response	Total

Dampfer, ekel, Endivien, erzaehlen, fett, Frass,
Gruenkohl, gut, Hackbau, hart, Haus, hohl, kalt,
Kartoffel, klein, Kohldampf, Kohlenpott,
Kohlpflanze, Kohlrabe, kohlweisslig,
Kohlweissling, Krampf, Krautkopf, Kuechengeruch,
Kugel, Lauch, Meise, Mensa, Mittagstisch,
Nahrungsm., NR, Polen, prima, Quark, roh, rot,
sauer, schmackhaft, schmeckt schlecht, schmeckt,
Schmetterling, Senf, Spinat, Spct,
Suppenschuessel, Unfug, Unsinn, verkohlen,
Winter, Wurst, Ziege

48. Hart

No.	Response	Total
1.	weich	136
2.	Stein	24
3.	Stahl	20
4.	Holz	15
5.	Eisen	11
6.	Arbeit	6
7.	fest	6
8.	Wachs	6
9.	Diamant	4
10.	Ei(er)	4
11.	Mann	4
12.	Wurst	4
13.	Nuss	3
14.	Schlag	3
15.	schwer	3
16.	arbeiten	2
17.	Bett	2
18.	Gummi	2
19.	hartherzig	2
20.	Herz	2
21.	Mut	2
22.	Schule	2
23.	streng	2
24.	Stuhl	2
25.	Widerstand	2

26-87. (f = 1)
abgehaertet, Angst, Apfel, Aufsatz, Bank,
beissen, bitter, Bleistift, Brett, Brot, derb,
dick, dumm, duenn, e, Eis, eisenhart, fair,
Faust, Feind, gefaehrlich, gefroren, Gegenstand,
geizig, gekocht, Gemse, glatt, grausam, grimmig,
harte Eier, harte Nuss, hartleibig, Hartwurst,
herb, herzig, kalt, kaempfen, knochenhart,
Kolik, Kopf, Laubgew., Lebkuchen, liegen, Muehe,
NR, rauh, Schaedel, scharf, Schmerz, Schulbank,
sein, smart, Soldat, steif, Steinboden,
steinhart, Stich, Weg, Welsch, Wesen, Winter
(Illegible)

49. Adler

No.	Response	Total
1.	Vogel	68
2.	fliegen	15
3.	Gebirge	13
4.	Auge(n)	12
5.	Raubvogel	11
6.	Geier	9
7.	Horst	9
8.	Falke	7
9.	hoch	7
10.	schwinge	7
11.	schwingen	7
12.	Lueft(e)	6
13.	Fluegel	5

49. Adler (contd)

No.	Response	Total
14.	Koenig	5
15.	majestaetisch	5
16.	Alpen	4
17.	Berge	4
18.	Fittich(e)	4
19.	Fliege	4
20.	Schnabel	4
21.	Wappe(n)	4
22.	Adlerauge(n)	3
23.	Flug	3
24.	Kraft	3
25.	stolz	3
26.	Aquilo	2
27.	erhaben	2
28.	Flieger	2
29.	fliegt	2
30.	frei	2
31.	gewaltig	2
32.	gross	2
33.	Himmel	2
34.	Kralle	2
35.	kuehn	2
36.	Maus	2
37.	Nase	2
38.	No response	2
39.	Raub	2
40.	schnell	2
41.	Spatz	2
42.	stark	2
43.	Steinadler	2
44.	Tier(e)	2

45-115. ($f = 1$)
Aar, Adlerflug, adlergleich, Adlerhorst, Adlernest, Adlerschwingen, ausgebreitete Fluegel, Auto, Bein, Deutschland, dumm, edel, Fels, Felsen, fern, Film, first, Fisch, (Fluegel, braun), Freiheit, gefaehrlich, Gefild, grausam, Grippe, Habicht, Hecht, Hehleraugen, Heimatfilm, heise, Henne, herrlich, hochfliegend, Hochflug, Hoehe, Holz, Kampf, Klaue, Kondor, kreischen, Lamm, Legion, Macht, Majestaet, Mut, Nachtigall, Nest, Pfau, rassig, raeuben, Raeuber, reid, ruhig, scharfe Augen, scharfes Auge, Schnelligkeit, Segelflug, segeln, sehen, Sehnsucht, Seltenheit, Stein, Sturzflug, Tapferkeit, Taube, Tierreich, Traeger, Traum, Vater, Wanderung, weit, wild

50. Magen

No.	Response	Total
1.	Darm	46
2.	Hunger	34
3.	essen	27
4.	Geschwuer	16
5.	Schmerz(en)	16
6.	Saeure	15
7.	Bauch	9
8.	leer	8
9.	Organ	7
10.	Verdauung	7
11.	Eingeweide	5
12.	knurren	5
13.	knurrt	5
14.	Verstimmung	5
15.	voll	4
16.	Leber	3
17.	Bauchweh	3
18.	Krampf	3
19.	Krankheit	3
20.	Krebs	3
21.	Speise	3
22.	verdauen	3
23.	Verdauungsorgen	3

50 Magen (contd)

No.	Response	Total
24.	Weh(e)	3
25.	Appetitt	2
26.	bitter	2
27.	brennen	2
28.	Galle	2
29.	Gastritis	2
30.	Koerper	2
31.	Koerperteil	2
32.	krank	2
33.	Magenbitter	2
34.	No response	2
35.	Saft	2
36.	Schlag	2
37.	schlecht	2
38.	Stomach	2
39.	verderben	2
40.	verdorben	2

41-101. ($f = 1$)
Ausgang, Balsam, Bauchhoehle, Bein, beruhige, Beschwerde, Blaehungen, Blinddarm, brummt, Chirurgie, doof, druecken, Epikureer, fein, Funktion, Geburtstagfeier, Gedaerm, Gefuehl, Gemuese, Gesundheit, Glein, gross, hungrig, Inhalt, inneres, Joghurt, kalt, Kuh, leiden, Luftballon, Lunge, Magendurchbruch, Magengeschwuer, magenkrank, Magenoperation, Magensaft, Magensaeure, Magenverstimmung, Mensch, Niere, noch gut, Partie, plump, rundlich, rund nicht gut, satt, Schlund, schwer, Sorge, Steine, Stimmung, Stomachus, Tiefe, Torte, tragen, Uebelkeit, verdaut, Verdauung, verstimmt, Vieh, Wand

51. Stiel

No.	Response	Total
1.	Besen	126
2.	stumpf	19
3.	Blume	13
4.	Stengel	12
5.	Besenstiel	9
6.	lang(e)	8
7.	Apfel	7
8.	Auge(n)	7
9.	Blatt	6
10.	Bluete	6
11.	Hacke	6
12.	Holz	6
13.	Schaufel	6
14.	Stange	6
15.	Frucht	4
16.	Hammer	4
17.	Lampe	4
18.	Pfanne	4
19.	Bleistift	3
20.	Griff(e)	3
21.	Loeffel	3
22.	Pflanze	3
23.	stechen	3
24.	Baum	2
25.	Feder	2
26.	kurz	2
27.	Pappen	2
28.	Pfeifenstiel	2
29.	Schaft	2
30.	Spaten	2
31.	Stab	2
32.	Stielbluete	2

33-77. ($f = 1$)
Axt, Beherrschung, Beil, bequem, Besen-A., Blumenstiel, breit, Buerste, damit, Eis, Faden, fassen, Fenster, Gattung, Gemuese, gerade, glatt, Grammatik, Griffel, Haelter, hart, heben, heilangen, Instrument, Kirsche, Kunde,

51. Stiel (contd)

No.	Response	Total
	(langer) Stock, Laterne, los, Nahrung, Pril, putzen, Rumpf, Schaufelstiel, Sichel, Stachel, Stamm, Stiefel, Stielanger, Stielende, Stift, Stock, wackelt, Werkzeug (Illegible)	

52. Lampe

No.	Response	Total
1.	Licht	117
2.	hell	43
3.	Schirm	29
4.	Birne	19
5.	Lampenschirm	12
6.	Tisch	11
7.	Beleuchtung	5
8.	leuchten	5
9.	Leuchter	5
10.	Hase	4
11.	Helligkeit	4
12.	Beleuchtungskoerper	3
13.	Lampenfieber	3
14.	lesen	3
15.	Schein	3
16.	Stehlampe	3
17.	dunkel	2
18.	gelb	2
19.	Glas	2
20.	Laterne	2
21.	modern	2

22-73. (f = 1)
Abend, angenehm, Antwort, anzuenden, Bergwerk, Bogen, brennt, Buch, Decke, Elektrizitaet, Fieber, Funkel, Gemuetlichkeit, Glanz, glueh, Gluehbirne, Grubenlampe, gutes Buch, heimlich, (hell, warm), Kerze, Kirche, Knopf, lampenfoermig, Lampenlicht, Leitung, leuchtend, moderne Kunst, Nachttisch, Ofen, Petroleumlampe, Rampe, Rampenlicht, rot, Russ, Schalter, Schlampe, schmal, Schreibtisch, Stall, Stander, Stille, Strahl, Strom, Stuhl, Taschenlampe, Teppich, Test, Tisch, Wachtisch, Zimmer, 220 V.

53. Traeumen

No.	Response	Total
1.	schlafen	67
2.	Schlaf	54
3.	wachen	30
4.	suess	16
5.	Nacht	15
6.	schoen	15
7.	Wuensch(e)	8
8.	schaeume	5
9.	angenehm	4
10.	Phantasie	4
11.	Angst	3
12.	Bett	3
13.	saeumen	3
14.	Traum	3
15.	Alptraum	2
16.	denken	2
17.	doesen	2
18.	Heimat	2
19.	lang	2
20.	Maerchen	2
21.	phantasieren	2
22.	Ruhe	2
23.	sanft	2
24.	schlecht	2

53. Traeumen (contd)

No.	Response	Total
25.	suessen	2
26.	Traumbild	2
27.	Traeumerei(en)	2
28.	wach sein	2
29.	wahr	2

30-100. (f = 1)
abwechselnd, Alp, Alpadler, Angsttraeumen, Annehmlichkeit, Aufgabe, baden im Sommer, Bild, Daeumchen, der, de See, Dummheit, duerfen, Erinnerung, erschuetternd, essen, Fantasie, fliegen, Freude, gebraucht, Gegenwirklichkeit, Geld, Gesicht, Glueck, Halt, herrl., Himmel, Ideale, Illusion, koennen, kurz, kuessen, leicht, lesen, Maedchen, muede, Naturerscheinung, nicht, notwendig, NR, prima, real, Romantik, ruh. schlafen, schweben, See, Sehnsucht, selig, Seligkeit, sinnen, sinnieren, Tanz, taeuschen, Tiefenpsychologie, Tilgung, Traumfrau, traumhaft, unangenehm, unruhiger Schlaf, Unsinn, vergessen, vertraeumen, vertraeumt, von Erlebnissen, Vorstellung, wach, was, weben weich, wunderbar, Zustand

54. Gelb

No.	Response	Total
1.	rot	40
2.	Farbe	34
3.	gruen	29
4.	blau	16
5.	Neid	11
6.	weiss	11
7.	schwarz	10
8.	orange	9
9.	grell	8
10.	hell	8
11.	Zitrone(n)	8
12.	Blume(n)	7
13.	sucht	7
14.	falsch	4
15.	Hass	4
16.	Schmetterling	4
17.	Sonne	4
18.	braun	3
19.	Chinese	3
20.	Gelbsucht	3
21.	grau	3
22.	hart	3
23.	Kleid	3
24.	Ei	2
25.	fahl	2
26.	Filter	2
27.	Gelbfieber	2
28.	Gift	2
29.	graesslich	2
30.	haesslich	2
31.	im	2
32.	lila	2
33.	neidisch	2
34.	Sommer	2
35.	unschoen	2
36.	Vorsicht	2
37.	Zitronenfalter	2

38-108. (f = 1)
Achtung, alte Jungfer, Ami-autoschild, Ampel, angenehm, Auto, Badehose, bescheiden, Birne, Blatt, Bluse, Bluete, Butter, China, Chin. Seide, Cowboyhemd, Dotter, Dottergelb, Eifersucht, Fahne, Falschheit, Fluegel, frieren, Gefahr, Gehirn, gelbe Gefahr, Gelbfieber, Gelbkreuz, gelblich, Gelbschnabel, Geschlecht, giftig, goldgelb, gut, Himmel, kalt, Kerze, Kissen, knallgelb, leuchtend, Licht, neutral, nicht immer angenehm, NR, ocker, Pflanze, Quarantaene,

54. Gelb (contd)

No.	Response	Total

Reiz, rosa, rose, rube, scheel, Scheinwerfer,
Schlamm, schmierig, schoen, schwach, Schwefel,
Sonneblume, Spektralfarben, suechtig, Tanzkleid,
typisch, unangenehm, unklar, Verkehr,
Verkehrslicht, Wachs, Wand, Wasserfarben, weich

55. Brot

No.	Response	Total
1.	essen	66
2.	Butter	28
3.	Laib	20
4.	Nahrung	19
5.	Hunger	17
6.	Getreide	7
7.	Baecker	6
8.	Leben	6
9.	Broetchen	5
10.	schwarz	5
11.	backen	4
12.	hart	4
13.	Krume	4
	(Krume : 3	
	Krumme: 1)	
14.	Messer	4
15.	Not	4
16.	Aufstrich	3
17.	braun	3
18.	Butterbrot	3
19.	Fleisch	3
20.	gut	3
21.	Kartoffel	3
22.	Kuchen	3
23.	Mehl	3
24.	Scheibe	3
25.	Schwarzbrot	3
26.	Teig	3
27.	Wasser	3
28.	Wein	3
29.	Weissbrot	3
30.	Abendessen	2
31.	Arbeit	2
32.	Brotkrume	2
33.	Gott	2
34.	herb	2
35.	Nahrungsmittel	2
36.	Pause	2
37.	Rund	2
38.	suess	2
39.	taeglich	2
40.	Wurst	2
41.	zu Hause	2

42-107. (f = 1)
angeschn. Brotlaib, barken, blau, Brot,
Brotkasten, Brotlaib, brotlos, Brotnot, Brot-
suppe, duftend, einkaufen, er, Ernaehrung,
essig, Esswaren, fein, fest, fett, frisch,
Fruehstueck, Geborgenheit, geht, gelb,
Gerechtigkeit, Geschmack, gib, grau, Kasten,
Knusprig, Korb, Korn, kraeftigt, Kruemel, Land,
Lebensmittel, Leib, Lohn, Marmelade, Milch,
Nahg., nis, Obst, Preis, Pumpernickel, Ration,
Reformhaus, Religion, Rinde, rot, Sakrament,
satt, sattessen, Schinken, Schnitte, Speise,
Stolle, Stueck, taeglich Brot, Tisch, trinken,
Vaterunser, weich, weit, Weizen, Zeit, Zucker

56. Gerechtigkeit

No.	Response	Total
1.	Gericht	39
2.	Ungerechtigkeit	31
3.	Richter	23
4.	Justiz	20
5.	Unrecht	15
6.	Recht	10
7.	Tugend	10
8.	Gesetz	8
9.	Gott	8
10.	gut	7
11.	Justitia	6
12.	Liebe	6
13.	Sinn	6
14.	Gerechtigkeitssinn	5
15.	Freiheit	4
16.	Staat	4
17.	Wahrheit	4
18.	Gerechtigkeitsgefuehl	3
19.	gibt es nicht	3
20.	Ideal	3
21.	notwendig	3
22.	selten	3
23.	Ernst	2
24.	Faulheit	2
25.	Friede	2
26.	Frieden	2
27.	Guete	2
28.	Irrtum	2
29.	Jurist	2
30.	Jus	2
31.	Milde	2
32.	richtig	2
33.	Schlechtigkeit	2
34.	schoen waer's	2
35.	Schule	2
36.	Strafe	2
37.	Strenge	2
38.	ungerecht	2

39-116. (f = 1)
alte, ansehen, Beamter, Charakter, Demokratie,
Edelmut, erfahren, erstrebenswert, falsch,
Falschheit, Fehler, Fimmel, fordern, Fortuna,
Frau, G.goettin, G.sinn, gebrechen, Gefuehl,
Geld, gerade, Gerechtigkeitsfuehler, hart,
Haerte, Heine, hoehere, im Handeln, jawohl,
Ju, Justitia Fiat, kalt, keine, Kraft, Lehrer,
lesen, Luege, Mangelnde, Mann, Menschlichkeit,
niemals, ohne, Ordnung, Pflicht, Plato, reich,
relativ, Religionsunterricht, richten rot,
Ruhe, Sanfmuetigkeit, Schoenes, Schoenheit,
Schwert, sehr wichtig, sittlich. Vorderung,
Sokrates, Solon, Sowjetzone, ssinn, stiel,
streben, suess, Trauer, uebel, ueben, ueberall,
Uneinigkeit, Universitaet, unmoeglich, Urteil,
Vergeltung, Waage, Wert, wertvoll, Willkuer,
wuenschenwert, Zeitung

57. Junge

No.	Response	Total
1.	Maedchen	119
2.	Knabe	14
3.	frech	11
4.	Mann	9
5.	Bub(e)	8
6.	Lausbub(e)	8
7.	Kind	6
8.	klein	6
9.	Streiche	6
10.	Alter	4
11.	Freund	4
12.	Halbstarker	4
13.	Jugend	4
14.	alt(e)	3

57. Junge (contd)

No.	Response	Total
15.	Boy	3
16.	Bursche	3
17.	Kamerad	3
18.	lustig	3
19.	Maedel	3
20.	Mensch	3
21.	Schueler	3
22.	Spiel	3
23.	stark	3
24.	blond	2
25.	Bruder	2
26.	frisch	2
27.	Geschlecht	2
28.	Hose	2
29.	Jungenstreich	2
30.	Junge	2
31.	Kindheit	2
32.	Rowdy	2
33.	sein	2
34.	wild	2
35.	no response	2

36-109. ($\underline{f}$ = 1)

Abenteuer, Aerger, Baby, Ball, Bengel, Bett, Bild, blau, brav, Dung, echt, Fahrrad, fluegger Junge, Frohsinn, Frau, Freiheit, Freude, freudig, Frosch, Geburt, gluckl. Zeit, goldig, Greis, Hans, hart sein, Hunger, ich, jung u alt, jungenhaft, junger Mann, Kindheit, kleiner Junge, kratzig, kriegen, Kueche, lachen, Lause, Lausjunge, leben, lebensfroh, lebhaft, lieber J., Luemmel, Lunge, lustig, maennl. Wesen, Menschen, muekisch, nett, nname, nstreich, pruegeln, Ranzen, raufen, ruhig, Schelm, schlank, schneidig, schnell, schoen, schoenste Zeit, Sohn, Stein, tachzig, Teenager, Tierchen, tollend, u Alter, Ulli, Union, unreif, Verwandter, Weibchen, Zukunft

58. Licht

No.	Response	Total
1.	dunkel	72
2.	hell	51
3.	Lampe	30
4.	Schatten	16
5.	Sonne	15
6.	Helligkeit	10
7.	Strahl(en)	8
8.	grell	7
9.	Leben	6
10.	Leuchter	5
11.	Tag	5
12.	Dunkelheit	4
13.	Elektrizitaet	3
14.	Finsternis	3
15.	Freude	3
16.	Schein	3
17.	blenden	2
18.	Erleuchtung	2
19.	Glanz	2
20.	Helle	2
21.	Kegel	2
22.	Kerze	2
23.	Leitung	2
24.	Lichtblick	2
25.	Lichtschacht	2
	(Lichtschacht: 1	
	Lich schacht: 1)	
26.	Luft	2
27.	Morgen	2
28.	Nacht	2
29.	Neon	2
30.	Strom	2
31.	Waerme	2

58. Licht (contd)

No.	Response	Total
32.	Weihnachten	2
33.	(illegible)	2

34-89. ($\underline{f}$ = 1)

anschalten, Augenfleck, aus, Batterie, Birne, blau, Blitz, braun, Buch, Daemmerlicht, Draht, Edison, empfinden, Erloesung, Fackellicht, Ficht, Flut, Foto, Geist, Geschwindigkeit, Gott, Hoffnung, kalt, Keller, Klarheit, Klueft, Kuegelchen, lesen, lichtleer, Lichtreflex, los, machen, Maschine, Neonroehre, nuetzlich, Physik, physik. Erscheinung, Quelle, Reflex, Schacht, schalten, Schalter, Scheinwerfer, Schmerzen, Schoepfung, spricht, Strasse, Strom, Tagenlicht, Tageslicht, Technik, Telephon, Wahrheit, warm, weis, zart

59. Gesundheit

No.	Response	Total
1.	Krankheit	112
2.	gut	22
3.	krank	11
4.	Glueck	9
5.	Freude	8
6.	Kraft	8
7.	Leben	8
8.	wohl	7
9.	Arzt	6
	(Arzt : 5	
	Artzt: 1)	
10.	Sport	6
11.	wertvoll	6
12.	Zustand	6
13.	schoen	5
14.	Gesundheitszustand	4
15.	Krankenhaus	4
	(Krankenhaus: 1	
	Krankenh. : 1	
	Krankh. : 2)	
16.	stark	4
17.	Bett	3
18.	notwendig	3
19.	Tod	3
20.	Wohlbefinden	3
21.	Amt	2
22.	Doktor	2
23.	Gesundheitsamt	2
24.	herrlich	2
25.	in Ordnung	2
26.	kraeftig	2
27.	niesen	2
28.	samt	2
29.	szustand	2
30.	Wohlstand	2

31-103. ($\underline{f}$ = 1)

alles, angenehm, Arbeit, Aerger, bei guter G- sein, Bier, Dank, Dankbarkeit, das beste Gut, Dienst, Eltern, erhoffen, Erscheinung, erwuenscht, fein, frisch, Frische, Froehlichkeit, Frohsinn, Gabe, Gehirnschaden, Genesung, Geschenk, Geschenk Gottes, geschmeidig, Gesundheitsstand, gluecklich, Gottes Gabe, Grippe, gruen, Gute, haben, hatschi, Hoffnung, immer, ja, jung, kernig, Kinder, knapp, Land, Lebensstandard, leider, lustig, Mensch, munter, normal, noetig, NR, positiv, prost, Reichtum, rot, rote Wangen, Rundheit, Schlaganfall, schonen, schwach, sehr gut, Seltenheit, sschwaeche, Staats G.dienst, streben, strotzend, teuer, u langes Leben, weich, wert, wie schoen, Wunsch, wuenschenswert, zu wuenschen
(Illegible)

60. Bibel

No.	Response	Total
1.	Buch	59
2.	Religion	32
3.	Gott	25
4.	Christus	11
5.	Gotteswort	8
6.	Wahrheit	8
7.	Wort(e)	8
8.	Jesus	7
9.	Kirche	7
10.	lesen	7
11.	Lesung	7
12.	Testament	7
13.	Uebersetzung	6
14.	Wort Gottes	6
15.	Buch der Buecher	5
	(Buch der Buecher: 4	
	Buch d. Buecher: 1)	
16.	Glaube	5
17.	Neues Testament	5
	(Neues Testament: 3	
	N. Testament : 1	
	N. T. : 1)	
18.	Altes Testament	4
	(Altes Testament: 3	
	A. T. : 1)	
19.	Schrift	4
20.	Spruch	4
21.	dick	3
22.	Katechismus	3
23.	Text	3
24.	Adam	2
25.	alt	2
26.	Bibelstelle	2
27.	Bibelwort	2
28.	Fibel	2
29.	fromm	2
30.	hebraeisch	2
31.	heilig	2
32.	hl. Buch	2
33.	Moses	2
34.	Offenbarung	2
35.	Pfarrer	2
36.	Protestanten	2
37.	schwarz	2
38.	Weisheit	2
39.	Zitat	2

40-104. (f = 1)
Album, altmodisch, Angriffe, Auslegung, Belesung, Bibelausspruch, Bibelforscher, Bibelforschung, bibelkundig, Bibelspruch, Christ, Christentum, chr. Gericht, das Buch, dickes Buch, ehrwuerdig, Erbauung, evangelisch, Evangelium, Exegese, fest, Gebetbuch, Gesangbuch, Geschichtswerk, gut, Handschriften, hat doch recht, heilige, Homer, im, im Anfang erscheint, interessantestes Buch, Isiaias, Jesaja, Kenntnis, Kreis, Kritik, Lexikon, Liebe, luegt, Luther, Marx, "Mein Kampf", Mist, Nippel, NR, Ordnung, Pergament, Prophet, richtig, Richtigkeit, Roman, sauer, sehr alt, Seite, stimmt, unwissenschaftlich, Urtext, u. Schrift, Vers, Versenkung, Wald, wuchtig, wunderbar, Zweifel

61. Gedaechtnis

No.	Response	Total
1.	Gehirn	26
2.	Erinnerung	24
3.	Verstand	19
4.	Schwund	18
5.	denken	13
6.	Stueze	13
7.	vergessen	13
8.	gut	12

61. Gedaechtnis (contd)

No.	Response	Total
9.	Schule(n)	11
10.	Schwaeche	11
11.	schlecht(es)	10
12.	schwach	10
13.	lernen	7
14.	Vergesslichkeit	6
15.	Gedanke(n)	4
16.	Hirn	4
17.	Kopf	4
18.	Andenken	3
19.	Gedaechtnisstuecke	3
20.	Gedaechtnisschwund	3
21.	schwind(et)(en)	3
22.	Sinn	3
23.	Vermaechtnis	3
24.	erinnern	2
25.	Erlebnis	2
26.	Gedaechtnisstuetze	2
27.	Gedicht	2
28.	Hilfe	2
29.	intelligent	2
30.	Kirche	2
31.	Luecke	2
32.	merken	2
33.	no response	2
34.	Schulung	2
35.	Schwachsinn	2
36.	Staerke(n)	2
37.	Wissen	2
38.	Woert(e)	2

39-116. (f = 1)
Abendmahl, Arbeit, Auffassungsgabe, Aufgabe, Beanspruchung, behalten, Behaelter, Bescheidheit, Besinnung, Bild, bitter, Denkkraft, Eingedenk, erfahren, etwas laenger wissen, Fassungskraft, fehlt, Feier, fein, Frage, gedacht, Gedaechtnishilfe, gedaechtnisschwach, geistige Arbeit, genau, Glaube, Grips, gute Anlage, gute Sache, gutes, halten, Hausaufgaben, heben, keins, Klage, klein, kraeftiges, lang, Lexikon, Licht, Macht, Memoriae, Mens, Mensch, Mnemotechnik, noch in Ordnung, Notiz, Phantasie, prima, Quatsch, Roboter, Roehr, schnell, schon wieder, sehr wichtig, sensibel, sicher, Sieb, Studium, Talent, ueberlegen, Uebung, Veranlagung, verschwommen, Vokabelheft, voll, wach, Welt, werken, wichtig, Wiese, Wille, wo?, Wunde, Wunschtraum, Zahl, Zerstreutheit, 3 x 3 = 9

62. Schaf

No.	Response	Total
1.	Wolle	47
2.	Tier(e)	28
3.	Herde	17
4.	dumm	15
5.	Ziege	13
6.	Hammel	10
7.	Laemm(er)	10
8.	Bock	9
9.	Weide	9
10.	Kopf	8
11.	Rind	8
12.	Traum	8
13.	Ochs(e)	7
14.	Stall	7
15.	Esel	6
16.	Schafskopf	5
17.	Dummheit	4
18.	Kalb	4
19.	Fell	3
20.	Hirte	3
21.	Pelz	3
22.	Ruhe	3

62. Schaf (contd)

No.	Response	Total
23.	Schafwolle	3
24.	skopf	3
25.	weiss	3
26.	Bett	2
27.	bloecken	2
	(bloecken: 1	
	bloeken : 1)	
28.	brav	2
29.	Hammelfleisch	2
30.	Idiot	2
31.	Kamel	2
32.	Kuh	2
33.	maeh	2
34.	muede	2
35.	Pferd(e)	2
36.	Reh	2
37.	Schaefer	2
38.	Schimpfwort	2
39.	Schlaf	2
40.	schwarz	2
41.	wachen	2
42.	weich	2
43.	Wiese	2
44.	Wolltier	2

45-101. (f = 1)
Bein, bloed, Bloeder, Bruder, doof, du-!, dummer
Mensch, Erholung, erquickend, Finger, Fleisch,
Gemaelde, Gerber, Geruch, gesund, Gesundheit,
guckt, Haus, Haustiere, Hund, hueten, Kleintier,
Krankheit, krumm, Mensch, mittelmaessig, Nacht,
persisches Schaf, Reizname, relig. Symbol,
Ross, ruhig, sanft, Saeugetier, Schaffell,
Schafherde, Schafschur, Schlafmittel, Schwein,
sfell, suchen, Susi, Symbol, Tag, Tierreich,
traeumen, Unschuld, Vieh, weiche Wolle, Widder,
Wirbeltier, Wolf, wollig, Wort, Wunsch,
Zufriedenheit, zweideutig

63. Bad

No.	Response	Total
1.	Wasser	56
2.	Wanne	22
3.	warm	18
4.	schwimmen	16
5.	Brause	10
6.	sauber	10
7.	Sommer	10
8.	Erfrischung	8
9.	heiss	8
10.	angenehm	7
11.	erfrischend	6
12.	Sauberkeit	6
13.	Zimmer	6
14.	Badewanne	5
15.	Badezimmer	4
16.	nass	4
17.	Seife	4
18.	waschen	4
19.	erfrischen	3
20.	Erholung	3
21.	Freude	3
22.	Frische	3
23.	Ofen	3
24.	Schwimmbad	3
25.	Sonne	3
26.	Tuch	3
27.	Anstalt	2
28.	Badeanstalt	2
	(Badeanstalt : 1	
	(Bad)eanstalt: 1)	
29.	Badehose	2
30.	baden	2
31.	Badewasser	2

63. Bad (contd)

No.	Response	Total
32.	Brueckenau	2
33.	Dampf	2
34.	ewasser	2
35.	frisch	2
36.	gekachelt	2
37.	Haus	2
38.	Kachel	2
39.	Kissingen	2
40.	Nacht	2
41.	nehmen	2
42.	Salz	2
43.	Sauna	2
44.	schoen	2
45.	Schwimmer	2
46.	Stadt	2

47-109. (f = 1)
Affe, angenehmes, auf der Tenne, Badeanzug,
Badeofen, Badesalz, Bad in Badewanne, Bad
Neustadt, Dusche, eanstalt, Einrichtung,
Entspannung, ewanne, ezimmer, Ferien, Freitag,
geniessen, Genuss, gesund, Gesundheit, gruenes
Wasser, Hand, Handtuch, Hechtsprung, Heilung,
Hitze, Hygiene, kalt, Kaelte, keines, Kirche,
Kohlgrub, Koenig, Kuehl, lau, Maedchen,
Nauheim, Ostsee, plaetschern, prickelnd, Rad,
Reichenhall, rein, Reinheit, reinigen,
Reinigung, Reise, Ruhe, Schlaf, Sonntag, Speiche,
Spiel, Tat, Toilette, Toelz, turnen, viel,
Wannenbad, Waschbecken, Waesche, Wohlbefinden,
wohlig, Wohltat

64. Haeuschen

No.	Response	Total
1.	Garten	56
2.	klein	33
3.	Huette	24
4.	Haus	14
5.	Dach	9
6.	Wohnung	8
7.	Heim	6
8.	Wald	6
9.	gemuetlich	5
10.	Hexe	5
11.	Maeuschen	5
12.	Villa	5
13.	Eigenheim	4
14.	Eigentum	4
15.	Familie	4
16.	Gartenhaeuschen	4
17.	Palast	4
18.	Gaeuschen	3
19.	Kamin	3
20.	nett	3
21.	niedlich	3
22.	schoen	3
23.	Wochenende	
	(Wochenende: 2	
	Wochende : 1)	
24.	wohnen	3
25.	alleine	2
26.	Bude	2
27.	Einfamilienhaus	2
	(Einfamilienhaus: 1	
	Einfamilienh. : 1)	
28.	Gaertchen	2
29.	Giebel	2
30.	haben	2
31.	Haensel u Gretel	2
32.	no response	2
33.	Schornstein	2
34.	Stall	2
35.	Wohnlichkeit	2
36.	Wolkenkratzer	2

64. Haeuschen (contd)

No.	Response	Total
37.	Wunsch	2
38.	Zelt	2
39-124.	(f = 1)	

Abort, angenehm, aermlich, aus dem, aus dem
Haeuschen geraten, aus Lebkuchen, Backsteinhaus,
Baracke, bauen, behaglich, bei sich sein,
Besitz, Bettchen, bewohnen, Blausaeure, bloed,
Dorf, Einsamkeit, Ersparnis, Familienleben,
Ferien, Forsthaus, Frieden, freundlich, Fuss,
Gartenlaube, Geborgenheit, Gefaengnis,
Gemuetlichkeit, Glueck, Goldbach, gross, gruen,
Haensel, Haeuslein, Haeuslichkeit, Heimat,
heimisch, Herd, Hexenhaeuschen, Hochhaus,
Hundehaeuschen, Kamel, Kammer, Kinderspielzeug,
Kleid, kleiner Mann, kleines, kleines Gebaeude,
Land, Landhaeuschen, Laube, Lebkuchen, Liebe,
Maedchen, Maerchen, Maus, mein, mit Garten,
Naeschen, Oberbayern, offen, Puppenkueche,
Rauch, rennen, Romantisch, schief, Schloss,
schlot, schmecken, Schmuck, Schutz, sparen,
Spielzeug, Tisch, Tuer, Unterkunft, Urlaub,
Vorgarten, Witwe, Wochenend H., Wohnheim,
wohnlich, Wohnraum, Zimmer Zufriedenheit

65. Schnell

No.	Response	Total
1.	langsam	115
2.	Auto	19
3.	Flugzeug(e)	12
4.	Laeufer	11
5.	Rakete(n)	8
6.	Zug	8
7.	Duesenjaeger	6
8.	eilig	5
9.	rasch	5
10.	Blitz	4
11.	Flink	4
12.	hurtig	4
13.	Lauf	4
14.	pfeilschnell	4
15.	Sputnik	4
16.	Dienst	3
17.	Duesenflugzeug	3
18.	Gazelle	3
19.	hell	3
20.	Wind	3
21.	D-zug	2
22.	gehen	2
23.	hastig	2
24.	igkeit	2
25.	Licht	2
26.	lahm	2
27.	laufen	2
28.	100m Lauf	2
29.	quick	2
30.	rennen	2
31.	Schnellboot	2
32.	Schnelligkeit	2
33.	Sport	2
34.	Sprinter	2
35.	Temp	2
36.	Wiesel	2
37-107.	(f = 1)	

Arbeiter, Aufzug, beinig, beseeligend,
blitzschnell, Boot, Depp, dumm, ehrgeizig, Eile,
einsam, elegant, essen, Fangio, feurig, fix,
froh, gefaehrlich, geschwind, Geschwindigkeit,
Hast, Hausaufgaben, Hirsch, Hitze, Hose, Jet,
kommen, Lichtgeschwindigk., Lise, lose, lustig,
Maus, Meister, Mercedes, muede, noch schneller,
Porsche, rasen, rasend, Reaktion, Rekord,
Rennauto, Rennfahrer, Rennwagen, Sage, sausend,
Schell, Schnecke, Schnelllaeufer, schnelllebig,

65. Schnell (contd)

No.	Response	Total

Schnellzug, schrecklich, Schrift, sehr,
Stenographie, Tod, toll, traege, Traum, turnen,
Verkehr, Verkehrsmittel, Vogel, Vorteil, Wagen,
Waschmittel, Weg, Wettrennen, wie, Windhund,
300 SL.

66. Blau

No.	Response	Total
1.	Himmel	82
2.	gruen	33
3.	gelb	30
4.	rot	20
5.	Farbe	18
6.	betrunken	15
7.	weiss	12
8.	Alkohol	6
9.	grau	6
10.	Auge	5
11.	Bier	5
12.	Meer	5
13.	schwarz	5
14.	hell	4
15.	schoen	4
16.	Zustand	4
17.	besoffen	3
18.	himmelblau	3
19.	Marine	3
20.	violett	3
21.	Wasser	3
22.	dunkel	2
23.	orange	2
24.	Schnaps	2
25.	Wein	2
26-79.	(f = 1)	

angenehm, Arbeitskittel, aeugig, Band, Bart,
Beere, beruhigend, blau, blaue, Jungs,
Blaufarben, blausauer, Blaustich, Blitz, B.M.W.,
braun, duester, e, Engel, Fastenzeit, Ferne,
Fr. Marc., Hai, Hund, indigo, introvertiert,
Kreuz, Kristall, leuchtend, Lieblingsfarbe,
Lippen, Mantel, Maske, Matrose, matt, mod. Bild,
Montag, Montagmorgen, neu, Pferde, Pracht,
Reklame, ruhig, sauft, See, sehen, silber,
strahlend, tief, Tinte, Treue, Veilchen, Wal,
weit
(Illegible)

67. Hungrig

No.	Response	Total
1.	durstig	64
2.	essen	47
3.	satt	35
	(satt: 34	
	sat : 1)	
4.	Brot	12
5.	Magen	11
6.	Durst	7
7.	Wolf	7
8.	Arm(e)(en)	5
9.	muede	5
10.	Not	5
11.	sein	5
12.	Bettler	3
13.	gesaettigt	3
14.	gierig	3
15.	Hungrigkeit	3
16.	Krieg	3
17.	(illegible)	3

67. Hungrig (contd)

No.	Response	Total
18.	elend	2
19.	gefraessig	2
20.	Hund	2
21.	Hunger	2
22.	kalt	2
23.	krank	2
24.	Kriegsgefangenschaft	2
25.	leer	2
26.	Magenknurren	2
27.	Mensch(en)	2
28.	Mittag(s)	2
29.	nein	2
30.	no response	2
31.	oft	2
32.	Pause	2
33.	schlecht	2
34.	Schule	2
35.	schwum(m)rig	2
36.	sehr	2
37.	Speise	2
38.	unangenehm	2

39-106. (f = 1)
abgemagert, aktiv, arme Leute, aufhoeren zu
lernen, Augen, Bibelwort, boese, China, Chinese,
einsam, er, erzaehlen, fasten, Fisch,
Fluechtling, Gefangener, gehen, heiss,
heisshungrig, hohl, Honig, Hungrigkeitsgefuehl,
immer, ja, Kinder, knurren, Kohldampf, Kottlett,
Kraehe, leerer Magen, Loeffel, Loewe, manchmal,
Maul, Mittagessen, Mund, nicht sonderlich,
Notzeit, nuechtern, plagend, Qual, qualend,
Rindvieh, schlimmer als Heimweh, Schmerz,
schnell, Schnitzel, schoenes Gefuehl,
Schulestunde, Schulzeit, Schwaeche, Schwarzbrot,
Semmel, Sportplatz, Steppenwolf, Tier,
todhungrig, traurig, Ungarn, ungehalten,
unschoen, Wanderung, Wille, Zeit, Zigarette,
Zustand, Zwang, 1945

68. Priester

No.	Response	Total
1.	Kirche	54
2.	Pfarrer	44
3.	schwarz	28
4.	Laie	20
5.	Religion	13
6.	Gott	12
7.	fromm	5
8.	Mensch	5
9.	Geistlicher	4
10.	heilig	4
11.	Opfer	4
12.	Amt	3
13.	Gewand	3
14.	Kaplan	3
15.	Pfaff(e)	3
16.	Schwester	3
17.	Seelsorger	3
18.	(illegible)	3
19.	Altar	2
20.	Diener Gottes	2
21.	edel	2
22.	Gebet	2
23.	katholik	2
24.	katholisch	2
25.	Kutte	2
26.	Messe	2
27.	Priestertand	2
28.	Sakrament(e)	2
29.	Schaff	2
30.	Seele	2
31.	Seminar	2
32.	Stellvertreter	2

68. Priester (contd)

No.	Response	Total
33.	Talar	2
34.	Weihe	2
35.	Zeremonie	2

36-118. (f = 1)
alter Mann, "amen", andaechtig, Arbeiter
Priester, Aufgabe, Beichte, Beruf, Bibel,
Bischof, Buch, Camillo, Christ, Christus,
Dummkopf, Ehrfurcht, ein Geheimnis, einsam,
Eli, feierlich, gediegen, Gefolgsmann Gottes,
geistl., Gerecht, Gesang, Gottes, Gottesdienst,
gut, guetig, Helfer, Herz, Hilfswerk, hl. Mann,
hl. Messe, Hoher, hoher Priester, ideal,
Idealist, jenseits, Kanzel, Kirche
Wuerdentraeger, Kloster, Kreuz, Kulte, Kuester,
Lahm, Lehrer, Liebe, liest er, Mann mit
ausgebreiteten Haenden, Messopfer, Milde, Mind-
zenty, Ministrant, Missionaer, Misthaufen,
notwendig, Ordenskleid, Ordenspriester, Pastor,
Pater, Pateres, Pope, predigen, Priesteramt,
Priestersonntag, Priestertum, Rede, Robe,
rufen, Schafskopf, Scola, Soutane, sterben,
still, Suender, Tam, Teufel, Tochter, Trost,
Vater, weihevoll, (werden, ja), Wuerde

69. Ozean

No.	Response	Total
1.	Meer	112
2.	Schiff(e)	34
3.	Wasser	34
4.	weit	22
5.	Dampfer	19
6.	Weite	14
7.	Riese	7
8.	tief	7
9.	blau	6
10.	See	5
11.	Ozeanreise	4
12.	Atlantik	3
13.	atlantischer	3
14.	Unendlichkeit	3
15.	Weltmeer(e)	3
16.	Amerika	2
17.	gross	2
18.	Ozeandaempfer	2
19.	riesig	2
20.	salzig	2
21.	Sturm	2
22.	Tiefe	2
23.	unendlich	2

24-62. (f = 1)
auf dem Ozean, beaengstigt, blauer, endlos,
Erdkunde, ertrinken, Ferien, Fluss, Fluten,
Freiheit, Groesse, gruen, hoch, hohe Wellen,
Horizont, Land, Lindbergh, nass, Orkan,
Pazifik, Reise, Salz, Schiffahrt, schwimmen,
Seegang, Sonne, stiller, U-boot, ueberqueren,
unendliche Wasserflaeche, unergruendlich,
unheimlich, (weite, dunkel), weite Flaeche,
weiter, weite Welt, Welt, Weltkarte, Wogen

70. Kopf

No.	Response	Total
1.	Haar(e)	41
2.	Fuess(e)	22
3.	Hals	16
4.	Haupt	13
5.	Auge(n)	10
6.	Mensch	10

70. Kopf (contd)

No.	Response	Total
7.	Koerperteil	9
8.	Gehirn	8
9.	rund	8
10.	Gesicht	7
11.	Haut	7
12.	Hut	7
13.	denken	6
14.	Geist	6
15.	Kragen	5
16.	Tuch	5
17.	hoch	4
18.	Koerper	4
19.	Rumpf	4
20.	dick	3
21.	gross	3
22.	Hand	3
23.	Hirn	3
24.	hohl	3
25.	kopflos	3
26.	los	3
27.	Topf	3
28.	Weh	3
29.	Bedeckung	2
30.	Beine	2
31.	Birne	2
32.	Friseur	2
33.	Gips	2
34.	Glatze	2
35.	kahl	2
36.	klein	2
37.	Kohl	2
38.	Kopfjaeger	2
39.	Kopfsalat	2
40.	Kopfschmerzen	2
41.	Nase	2
42.	oben	2
43.	Ohr	2
44.	Organ	2
45.	Schaedel	2
46.	Stirn	2

47-122. (f = 1)
ab, Affe, Arm, auch, aussehen, Ball, Band, Bauch,
bis Fuss, braun, Charakter, Decke, Depp, dumm,
Ende, Franz. Revolution, Gedanke, (Gesicht, Haar),
Glut, Haarschnitt, hart, Head, Hinterkopf,
hoechster Punkt, hohe Stirn, Holz, Horn, Hose,
im Kopf u. Kragen, intelligent, Jaeger, Kehl,
Keil, Klarheit, Klugheit, Kopfform, Kopfhaar,
Kopfhaut, Kopfhoerer, Kopflosigkeit, Kopfsprung,
Kraut, Krone, Kropf, langsam, Maus, Mittel,
Muetze, NR, Pferdeschwanz, Politik, Portraet,
Punkt, Putz, Rauch, Revolution, rot, Salat,
Schafskopf, Schmerzen, Schrift, schwarz, Sitz
der Sinnesorgane, Spitze, Teil, Tropf, Unfall,
Vernunft, Verstand, Wasser, Wasserkopf, Wehmut,
wo dann, Wuschel, "zweideutig" Gestalt
(Illegible)

71. Ofen

No.	Response	Total
1.	Waerme	57
2.	warm	52
3.	Rohr	33
4.	heiss	32
5.	Herd	24
6.	Feuer	16
7.	Hitze	13
8.	Bank	8
9.	Heizung	8
10.	Tuer(e)	8
11.	Kohle	5
12.	kalt	4
13.	Ofenrohr	4

71. Ofen (contd)

No.	Response	Total
14.	Holz	3
15.	Ofentuer(e)	3
16.	schwarz	3
17.	Zimmer	3
18.	glueht	2
19.	Glut	2
20.	heizen	2
21.	Heizkoerper	2
22.	Kachel	2
23.	Kamin	2
24.	Rauch	2
25.	Winter	2

26-64. (f = 1)
alt, anheizen, aus, Behaglichkeit, Brot, Dach,
Einrichtung, Eisen, Gas, gluehen, Glutwaerme,
Heim, Heizer, Heizofen, Heizoel, Heizsonne,
hoffen, Kalbel, Kanone, knistert, Lampe,
Moebelstueck, mollig, Muetze, Ofenbank,
Ofenschirm, roh, Roehre, rund, Russ, russig,
schwarzes Rohr, Schirm, Stang, Stelle, Sterne,
Wand, warme Stube, zu

72. Lang

No.	Response	Total
1.	kurz	146
2.	Stange	11
3.	Strasse	9
4.	Bein(e)	8
5.	duenn	6
6.	Weg(e)	5
7.	gross	4
8.	weit(e)	4
9.	duerr	3
10.	Mensch	3
11.	sam	3
12.	Stiel	3
13.	Strecke	3
14.	Zeit	3
15.	bang	2
16.	breit	2
17.	ellenlang	2
18.	Ende	2
19.	Haus	2
20.	Holz	2
21.	langsam	2
22.	Linie	2
23.	Ohr	2
24.	Schiene(n)	2
25.	schmall	2
26.	sehr	2
27.	Spielplatte	2
28.	Zug	2

29-120. (f = 1)
Aussicht, Autobahn, Band, Bank, Baum, best.
Freund, Bett, Bohnenstange, bunt, Daddylangbein,
Dauer, dick, endlos, ermuedend, Faden, Freude,
Fussball, Gasse, gehen, Giraffe, Groesse, Haar,
halblang, Halm, Hand, Hange, Hannes, Holzwagen,
Hopfenstange, Junge, Keil, Landschaft, Langbein,
langbeinig, Laenge, laenger, langer Mann,
Langhaus, Langkeit, Langlauf, langlebig, Langmut,
Langweile, langwierig, Latte, Lauf, leben, Mann,
Mass, Mauer, Meter, Metermass, Mitschueler,
muede, Musik, oval, Richtstange, samkeit,
Schiff, schlafen, schnell, Schnur, Schrank,
Schule, Schueler, Schulstunde, Schulzeit, Ski,
spinnbeinig, Stab, Stiehl, stielig, Stock,
Stunde, Tanzkurs, traege, u. breit,
unaufhoerlich, unendlich, unereichbar, Unterricht,
Venus, Verstand, Vorlesung, Wanderung,
Wasserleitung, Wellensender, Weltraum, Wurst,
Zaunlatte, 1000m
(Illegible)

73. Religion

No.	Response	Total
1.	Glaube(n)	41
2.	Gott	30
3.	Kirche	22
4.	katholisch	21
	(katholisch: 17	
	kath. : 4)	
5.	Pfarrer	11
6.	Bekenntnis	10
7.	Weltanschauung	9
8.	Bibel	8
9.	Priester	7
10.	Christentum	6
11.	Konfession	6
12.	Opium	5
13.	Himmel	4
14.	Schule	4
15.	Unterricht	4
16.	Buddhismus	3
17.	Christ(en)	3
18.	Gemeinschaft	3
19.	Geschichte	3
20.	Gottlosigkeit	3
21.	leben	3
22.	Religionsfreiheit	3
23.	Roem. Kath.	3
24.	Toleranz	3
25.	Wissenschaft	3
26.	Anschauung	2
27.	Buddha	2
28.	christlich	2
29.	Christus	2
30.	Gefuehl	2
31.	gut	2
32.	Katholik	2
33.	Lehre	2
34.	notwendig	2
35.	Privatsache	2
36.	Religionslehre	2
37.	religionslos	2
38.	religioes	2
39.	Sausuebung	2
40.	slehre	2
41.	viel(e)	2
42.	Welt	2
43.	wichtig	2

44-120. ($\underline{f}$ = 1)
Aegypten, Angehoeriger, Anlage im Z.,
Ansichtssache, anti, Atheismus, Atheist, Aufgabe,
bekennen, beten, Bindung, bitternotwendig, Buch,
Confession, Ehrfurcht u. Liebe in Gott,
Erloesung, evangelisch, Evangelium, fein,
Festigung, fromm, fuer den Menschen, fuer jeden,
Gewissen, gewissenhaft, glaeubig, goettlich,
Gottverbundenheit, Gottverhaeltnis, heilig,
hell, innerlich, Intoleranz, Islam, jedem seine,
Jesus, kalt, Katechismus, keine, Kinder, kopten,
Kult, lahm, Latein, Lebensinhalt, lesen, Licht,
Lohn, Macht, Mensch, Mittelpunkt, mohamedanisch,
Nahrung, NR, Ordnung, Plage, Pygmaeen,
Religionsort, Religionsphilos., Religion-
sverhaeltnis, Religionszugehoerigkeit, richtig,
Rom, Rueckbindung, Sacrament, Sekte, Tiefe,
Ueberzeugung, Uneinigkeit, Verfolgung, Wahrheit,
Warschau, was, Zimmer, Zugehoerigkeit, Zweifel,
(?)

74. Whisky

No.	Response	Total
1.	Schnaps	54
2.	Soda	34
3.	Alkohol	23
4.	Getraenk	16
5.	scharf	16

74. Whisky (contd)

No.	Response	Total
6.	Flasche	14
7.	Amerika	11
8.	Wein	10
9.	trinken	9
10.	Rausch	8
11.	gut	7
12.	Branntwein	6
	(Branntwein: 4	
	Brandwein : 2)	
13.	Gin	6
14.	betrunken	5
	(betrunken: 4	
	betranken: 1)	
15.	Durst	5
16.	Glas	5
17.	Rum	5
18.	Cowboy	4
19.	Bar	3
20.	Bier	3
21.	schlecht	3
22.	betrinken	2
23.	blau	2
24.	Brandy	2
25.	brennt	2
26.	Cherry	2
27.	England	2
28.	Likoer	2
29.	Trunkenheit	2
30.	warm	2
31.	Wasser	2
32.	Whiskyflasche	2
33.	Wodka	2

34-93. ($\underline{f}$ = 1)
Abend, abzulehnen, Angabe, beissen, Brand,
brennend, brenzlig, Cincano, ekelhaft,
geheimnisvoll, gelb, Geld, gluck-gluck, gutes
Getraenk, heiss, herb, jede Menge, kalt, klar,
Kognak, Lage, Lustigkeit, Mars, Neujahr, nicht
Durst, NR, O.K., O la la, Party, pfui, prost,
Russland, sauer, saufen, Saeufer, Schnapsflasche,
Schottisch, Schottland, schrecklich, Scotch,
Scotch Whisky, Sekt, Stimmung, suff, teuer,
Texas, Tisch, trink, Trinker, unangenehm,
unwichtig, Verkaeufer, Whisky dry, Whiskyfahne,
Whiskysoda, Whisper, Wildwest, Wiskey u. Soda,
Wodka-Fox, Wunsch

75. Kind

No.	Response	Total
1.	klein	41
2.	Mutter	32
3.	Baby	19
4.	Mann	15
5.	Erwachsener	14
6.	Kegel	11
7.	Eltern	10
8.	Junge	7
9.	Frau	5
10.	heit	5
11.	Kinderwagen	5
12.	Mensch	5
13.	Bub(e)	4
14.	Greis	4
15.	Knabe	4
16.	nett	4
17.	spielen	4
18.	Wiege	4
19.	dumm	3
20.	erwachsen	3
21.	Kindheit	3
22.	Kindlichkeit	3
23.	Maedchen	3
24.	Rind	3

75. Kind (contd)

No.	Response	Total
25.	Saeugling	3
26.	Ehe	2
27.	Erziehung	2
28.	Geschrei	2
29.	hilflos	2
30.	jung	2
31.	Schlaf	2
32.	Schwester	2
33.	sorglos	2
34.	Spiel	2
35.	Spielzeug	2
36.	Vater	2
37.	Windel	2

38-130. (f = 1)
alt, Alter, Angst, Anmut, arm, Aermchen,
Babysitter, Bad, Bambino, Band, Bettchen, boese,
brav, Bruder, Embryo, Entwicklungsstadium, Erde,
Erwachsenen, Familie, frech, Garten, geben,
Glueck, grosse Augen, gut, haben, herzlich,
ich, jammern, Jugend, junger Mensch, Katze,
Kindergarten, Kindhaftigkeit, Kindermaedchen,
Kinderspiel, Kinderstuebchen, Kinderstube,
Kinderzimmer, kindisch, kindlich, Kindskopf,
Kindsmutter, Kleinkind, Komma, Kopf, laecheln,
lallen, laut, lieb, Liebe, liebenswert, liebes,
Mam, Mama, Mammi, Mausl, Menschlein,
minderjaehrig, muede, Nichte, niedlich, Opa,
Pepon, rund, Rundkopf, russisch, Saeuglingsheim,
Schimmel, schoen, schreien, Schreihals, schreit,
skopf, spielend, staufe, taeppisch, tollpatschig,
traeumen, unbeholfen, Unbeholfenheit, unreif,
Unschuld, unverdorben, Unvernunft, Volksschule,
Weib, weint, Wind, Winzigkeit, (zartes, kleines),
Zutrauen, zu beschuetzen

76. Bitter

No.	Response	Total
1.	suess	85
2.	herb	33
3.	Mandel(n)	29
4.	sauer	27
5.	Galle	9
6.	Reis	8
7.	Geschmack	7
8.	kalt	5
9.	essen	4
10.	Essig	4
11.	Not	4
12.	Salz	4
13.	zart	4
14.	Bitterkeit	3
15.	no response	3
16.	salzig	3
17.	scharf	3
18.	angenehm	2
19.	Aroma	2
20.	Arznei	2
21.	Gebet	2
22.	keit	2
23.	Magen	2
24.	schlecht	2
25.	Tablett(en)	2
26.	unangenehm	2
27.	Zitrone	2
28.	Zunge	2
29.	(illegible)	2

30-101. (f = 1)
Abscheu, Adverb, Ammoniak, Armut, Arzt, Ausdauer,
"Becherbitter", beissend, Bettler, Bier, Birne,
bitter, Bitterheit, bitterlich, Bittermandel,
Bittersee, bittersuess, chem. Stoff, edel, ekel,
Enttaeuschung, Erfahrung, fiehentlich, fordern,
Fuerwort, gallenbitter, Gaumen, Gesichtszug,

76. Bitter (contd)

grau, hager, hallbitter, hart, heit, Honig,
Jupiter, Kummer, Lauge, Leben, los, Marmelade,
Medezin, Mund, Myrrhe, nicht angenehm, nis,
Nuss, Obst, Pech, Pferd, pfui, Pille, rauh,
Reaktion, Reisessig, Revers, Ritter, Ruestung,
schal, scheusslich, schlechte Nuss, schoen,
schrecklich, Schweiss, schwer, sehr, Sekt,
Speise, spucken, ungut, Whiskey, Zange, Zwiebel

77. Hammer

No.	Response	Total
1.	Amboss	33
2.	Nagel	33
	(Nagel: 32	
	Nage : 1)	
3.	Stiel	32
4.	Sichel	30
5.	Schlag	27
6.	Werkzeug	17
7.	Zange	14
8.	schwer	13
9.	hart	12
10.	Eisen	8
11.	Arbeit	7
12.	schlagen	7
13.	Meissel	5
14.	Schmied(e)	5
15.	und Sichel	5
	(und Sichel: 1	
	u. Sichel : 4)	
16.	Gewalt	4
17.	Hammerschlag	4
18.	fest	3
19.	Hammerstiel	3
20.	klopfen	3
21.	Kopf	3
22.	Beil	2
23.	Daumen	2
24.	Geraet	2
25.	Hammerwerk	2
26.	Holzhammer	2
27.	Keule	2
28.	schlaegt	2
29.	werfen	2
30.	Wucht	2

31-75. (f = 1)
Arbeiter, au!, auf den Kopf schlagen, Boss,
Cafe, Decke, Feder, fein, Finger, Glocke, Gummi,
Hammerlock, Hammerwerfer, Handwerk, Haus, Holz,
Instrument, kaputt, Kasten, knallen, Korb, Kraft,
laermen, Molotow, Niederlage, NR, russisches
Symbol, Saege, Schlaf, Schlagholz, Schlosser,
Schmerz, Schmidt, Schraube, Schreiner, Stahl,
Stuhl, stur, Tisch, UdSSR, Vorschlag, Wappen,
werken, wuchtig
(Illegible)

78. Durstig

No.	Response	Total
1.	hungrig	73
2.	Wasser	51
3.	Bier	39
4.	trinken	23
5.	Wueste	14
6.	Hitze	9
7.	trocken	9
8.	Sommer	6
9.	satt	5

85

78. Durstig (contd)

No.	Response	Total
10.	heiss	4
11.	Durst	3
12.	Durstigkeit	3
13.	Milch	3
14.	no response	3
15.	Saft	3
16.	sehr	3
17.	sein	3
18.	bitter	2
19.	Fluessigkeit	2
20.	Getraenk	2
21.	ja	2
22.	keit	2
23.	muede	2
24.	Selterwasser	2
25.	Sonne	2
26.	Tee	2
27.	Trank	2
28.	Wein	2
29.	Whiskey	2

30-82. (f = 1)
Anstrengung, aeusserst unangenehm, bierdurstig,
brennend, Coca Cola, e Blicke, Eigenschaft,
essen, Exupery, fleissig, gering, Glas, Haupt,
Heizung, Hof, Hunger, Kaffee, Kamel, Kehle,
keitsgefuehl, krank, kuehl, lechzen, Lecker,
manchmal, matt, Mattigk., Not, Oase, pfui,
qualvoll, Quelle, saftig, Sahara, schlecht,
schlimmes Uebel, Schnaps, schnell, schrecklich,
Schriftwort, Schwindling, Seele, Sehnsucht,
Sommertag, sucht, suffig, u. hungrig,
vertrocknet, volle Zuege, Wetter, Wirtschaft,
wurstig
(Illegible)

79. Stadt

No.	Response	Total
1.	Land	86
2.	Dorf	42
3.	Haus ('‥er)	19
4.	Wuerzburg	15
	(Wuerzburg: 14	
	W'burg : 1)	
5.	gross	10
6.	Mauer	7
7.	Aschaffenburg	6
8.	Strasse(n)	6
9.	Schweinfurt	5
10.	Staat	5
11.	Verkehr	5
12.	Buerger	4
13.	Grossstadt	4
14.	Rat	4
15.	Siedlung	4
16.	Augsburg	3
	(Augsburg: 2	
	A'burg : 1)	
17.	Gemeinschaft	3
18.	Kino	3
19.	Menschen	3
20.	Teil	3
21.	(illegible)	3
22.	Bad	2
23.	Betrieb	2
24.	Geschaeft(e)	2
25.	Haeusermeer	2
26.	Kreis	2
27.	Laerm	2
28.	Menschenmasse	2
29.	Rauch	2
30.	Stadtrat	2
31.	Tor	2
32.	viele Leute	2

79. Stadt (contd)

No.	Response	Total
33.	weit(e)	2

34-100. (f = 1)
abgeschlossen, Addis Abeba, Athen, aufgebaut,
Bahn, Beleuchtung, Berlin, Bewohner, Bild,
Bummel, Buergermeister, City, Danzig,
Einkaufzentrale, Einwohner, Fahrplan, Frankf.,
frei, Gebiet, Geborgenheit, Gehoeft, Gewirr,
Graben, Grenze, Haine, Hauptstadt, Haeusergewirr,
Industrie, Klarstadt, Kleinstadt, laut, London,
Luft, Maerchen, Marktplatz, Masse, Mittelalter,
Mittelpunkt, Muenchen, New York, Ordnung, Paris,
Plan, Politik, Promenade, Rad, Rathaus, rauchig,
reich, Rom, Schaufenster, Sicherheit, Stadtart,
Stadtluft, Stadtstaat, Stein, Steinbloecke,
Strassenbahn, Tuere, Tuerme, u. Land, viele
Haeuser, Viertel, Vorstadt, Wald, wohnen,
zuviel Laerm

80. Quadrat

No.	Response	Total
1.	Viereck	45
	(Viereck: 44	
	4 eck : 1)	
2.	Rechteck	43
3.	Kreis	32
4.	Mathematik	28
	(Mathematik: 22	
	Mathem. : 3	
	Mathemat. : 2	
	Math. : 1)	
5.	Flaeche	21
6.	Geometrie	18
7.	Dreieck	13
8.	Figur	12
9.	viereckig	8
	(viereckig: 7	
	4 eckig : 1)	
10.	Ecke(n)	6
11.	eckig	6
12.	geom. Figur	6
13.	Meter	6
14.	Raute	5
15.	Seite(n)	5
16.	kubik	4
17.	Diagonale(n)	3
18.	no response	3
19.	Quadratur	3
20.	rechnen	3
21.	Form	2
22.	Formel	2
23.	gleich	2
24.	gleichmaessig	2
25.	Kubus	2
26.	Pythagoras	2
27.	Rechnung	2
28.	rund	2
29.	vier	2
	(vier: 1	
	4 : 1)	
30.	Wuerfel	2

31-71. (f = 1)
ausgeglichen, Baharat, Ebene, Ebenheit,
ebenmaessig, Fuss, genau, gl. Seiten, harmonisch,
Hochzahl, Karree, Kasten, Kreissektor, Kugel,
Linie, Papier, Prof. Amtmann, Punkt, Quader,
Quadrat Gr.flaeche, quadratig, quadratisch,
Quadratseit, Quadratwurzel, rechteckig, regular,
Rhombus, rot, Schule, Stadtform, Strecke,
Symbol, Tor, vier Ecken, 4 gl. Linien, warm,
Winkel, worin, Zahl, Zeichnung, Zirkel

81. Butter

No.	Response	Total
1.	Brot	60
2.	weich	44
3.	Milch	32
4.	Margarine	27
5.	Kaese	20
6.	Fett(e)	16
7.	gelb	14
8.	Butterbrot	8
9.	Dose	6
10.	essen	6
11.	Honig	6
12.	Nahrung	5
13.	Salz	5
14.	Schmalz	5
15.	gut	4
16.	Kuh	4
17.	Marmelade	4
18.	ranzig	4
19.	Buttermilch	3
20.	Speise	3
21.	teuer	3
22.	Aufstrich	2
23.	Eier	2
24.	Geschmack	2
25.	Lebensmittel	2
26.	Mutter	2
27.	no response	2
28.	Sahne	2
29.	Saeure	2
30.	suess	2
31.	Wurst	2

32-63. (f = 1)
aber, Bauer, Berlin, Blume, Buttersaeure,
Daenemark, Dreieck, Ernaehrung, frisch, Gefaess,
Geruch, Gesund, Hunger, Kartoffeln, knapp,
Landwirtschaft, Milchprodukt, Nahrungsm.,
Ordnung, Papier, Quark, Sauce, Schinken,
schlecht, schmelzen, selten, streichen, u. Salz,
Wein, weiss, zerlaeuft, Zucker

82. Arzt

No.	Response	Total
1.	Krankheit	38
2.	Doktor	37
3.	krank	30
4.	Helfer	22
5.	Medizin	21
6.	Hilfe	15
7.	weisser Mantel	8
8.	Krankenhaus	7
	(Krankenhaus: 6	
	Krankh. : 1)	
9.	weiss	7
10.	Arznei	6
	(Arznei: 4	
	Arnei : 2)	
11.	Gesundheit	6
12.	Schwester	6
13.	Kranker	5
14.	Patient	4
15.	Praxis	4
16.	Beruf	3
17.	Besuch	3
18.	Chirurg	3
19.	gesund	3
20.	helfen	3
21.	Kittel	3
22.	Kosten	3
23.	Rechnung	3
24.	Schmerzen	3
25.	Zahnarzt	3
26.	Auto	2
27.	Brille	2

82. Arzt (contd)

No.	Response	Total
28.	Hebamme	2
29.	Heiler	2
30.	Krankenschwester	2
31.	Land	2
32.	Medikament(e)	2
33.	Mediziner	2
34.	Spritze	2
35.	Zahn	2

36-100. (f = 1)
Angina, Angst, Apotheker, Aerztin, Arztrechnung,
Arztwohnung, Behandlung, beruehmt, Brandt,
bunt, Dichter, Diener Menschen, Dr. Med., Duft,
Eier, Facharzt, Farce, fein, Frau, Geld, genau,
Gesuch, Grippe, gut, guetig, Haus, heilen,
heilig, Heilung, helfend, hilfreich, Karbol,
Kaufmann, Klient, Klinik, Krankenbesuch,
leben, machen, Mantel, Medicus, Mensch, Narkose,
Nasenarzt, Ohrenarzt, Pfarrer, prak. Arzt,
Praktis, Psychologe, Retter, Ruhe, Saege,
schlecht bezahlt, scheussliche Gestalt,
Sprechstunde, Stelle, Strich, Studium, Titel,
Unruhe, Untersuchung, Vater, weisser Mann, Witwe,
Wohltaeter
(Illegible)

83. Laut

No.	Response	Total
1.	leise	118
2.	Ton	25
3.	Laerm	13
4.	Radio	12
5.	Musik	6
6.	Schrei	6
7.	Kind(er)	5
8.	Krach	5
9.	Lautsprecher	5
10.	still	5
11.	Malerei	4
12.	Ohr(en)	4
13.	Staerke	4
14.	lautlos	3
15.	Schall	3
16.	schreien	3
17.	Schule	3
18.	Sprache	3
19.	unangenehm	3
20.	Vokal	3
21.	Buchstabe	2
22.	Flugzeug	2
23.	Geschrei	2
24.	hell	2
25.	Hupe	2
26.	los	2
27.	Moped	2
28.	no response	2
29.	schrill	2
30.	Silbe	2
31.	Sirene	2
32.	Stimme	2
33.	Strasse	2
34.	stumm	2
35.	Wort	2

36-103. (f = 1)
A, Alphabet, Arbeit, Ausdehnung, Aussprache,
baut, bellen, Bruelle im Haus, droehnen, dumpf,
Einsamkeit, Geige, gerade, Geraeusch, Gesang,
grell, gut, Hilfe, hoch, hohl, hupen, Klang,
klar, klein, Knall, Kuh, laute, Laute,
Lauterkeit, lautlich, Lautmalerei, Lautschrift,
Lautverschiebung, (leise, Ton), lieblich,
malend, Milch, Mitlaut, Motor, Motorrad, O,
Ohrenschmerz, Ott, Pfeife, Pfiff, Physik,
ploetzlich, Qual, ruttig, Satz, schallend,

83. Laut (contd)

No.	Response	Total

Schmerz, schmerzend, Schrift, schwer, Sprecher, stark, Stille, stoerend, Stoerung, taub, toenen, toenend, toent, Turnstunde, unnatuerlich, unverschaemt
(Illegible)

84. Dieb

No.	Response	Total
1.	stehlen	38
2.	Nacht	32
3.	Diebstahl	17
4.	Gefaengnis	13
5.	Polizei	13
6.	Stahl	12
7.	Verbrecher	11
8.	Einbruch	9
9.	Raeuber	8
10.	Gauner	7
11.	Einbrecher	6
12.	Geld	6
13.	Hehler	6
14.	heimlich	6
15.	Beute	5
16.	Moerder	5
17.	schlecht	5
18.	Strafe	5
19.	Fenster	4
20.	fur, furis	4
21.	Gericht	4
22.	gut	4
23.	Raub	4
24.	verbrechen	4
25.	Bank	3
26.	dunkel	3
27.	Lump(en)	3
28.	Angst	2
29.	Diebesbande	2
30.	Gangster	2
31.	gemein	2
32.	Gesetz	2
33.	klauen	2
34.	lieb	2
35.	Maske	2
36.	schleichen	2
37.	Schloss	2
38.	schnell	2
39.	unehrlich	2
40.	unrecht	2
41.	Vorsicht	2

42-107. (f = 1)
Bankraub, Bankraeuber, bestrafen, Betrug, Betrueger, bringen, Buerger, Diebe, Diebessohle, Diebin, ehrlich, Ehrlichkeit, ehrl. Mensch, Eigentum, Eindringe ins Haus, Fahrraddieb, faul, Film, Finger, flicken, Frechheit, freudig, Frevler, Fruehstueck, Furien, Furor, geht um, Gelegenheitsdieb, Gerechtigkeit, Gold, Halunke, haengen, Haus, Hexe, Hund, Juwelen, Langfinger, Larve, leise, Linie, listig, Material, Maus, Mensch, mutig, Nacht (dunkel), nehmen, Person, Pistole, Polizist, Richter, ruhig, schlechter M., schlechter Mensch, schleichend, Schluessel, Schmuck, Schuft, Stoss, Strassenecke, Strassen-raeuber, Taschendieb, uebel, Wut, Zeitung, 1945

85. Loewe

No.	Response	Total
1.	Tiger	35
2.	Wueste	31
3.	Tier	24
4.	bruellen	21
5.	Maehne	17
6.	Raubtier	15
7.	Kaefig	8
8.	Maus	7
9.	Koenig	6
10.	Kraft	6
11.	Zoo	6
12.	Gebruell	5
13.	Leo	5
14.	wild	5
15.	Gefahr	4
16.	Katze	4
17.	Loewenmut	4
18.	Majestaet	4
19.	Mut	4
20.	Afrika	3
21.	Elefant	3
22.	Loewenzahn	3
23.	maechtig	3
24.	Raub	3
25.	reissend	3
26.	Schwanz	3
27.	stark	3
28.	Steppe	3
29.	Bestie	2
30.	gelb	2
31.	Hase	2
32.	Herrscher	2
33.	Hoehle	2
34.	Hund	2
35.	Kralle(n)	2
36.	laut	2
37.	Loewin	2
38.	Moewe	2
39.	mutig	2
40.	Radio	2
41.	Urwald	2

42-108. (f = 1)
Ameisenloewe, Angst, Baer, Bayern, bayr. Wahrzeichen, Berber, bissig, Blut, bruellt wie ein L., dazu, Dompteur, erhalten, Esel, Film, fressen, Freude, garstig, Gestank, Gewalt, gewaltig, gross, Haar, Herr, herrlich, Herz, Horoskop, Hunger, hungrig, Igel, Jagd, Junge, Kind, knurren, Lion, Loewenanteil, Loewenbaendiger, Loewenburg, Loewenmaedchen, Loewenmaehne, Loewenmaul, Macht, Maul, Meister, Mensch, MetroGoldw. Mayer, Natur, nzahn, Ochse, Pferd, Prachttier, Pranke, rachen, Raeuber, Sahara, Saugetier, Schaf, schnell, Stein, tapfer, Tatze, Tor, Ungeheur, Untier, Wildnis, Zahn, Zirkus, zittern

86. Freude

No.	Response	Total
1.	Leid	46
2.	Trauer	32
3.	Lust	18
4.	lachen	15
5.	Glueck	10
6.	Schmerz	9
7.	Musik	8
8.	Weihnacht(en)	8
9.	Geschenk	6
10.	Vergnuegen	6
11.	Angst	5
12.	Aerger	5
13.	schoen	5
14.	froh	4

86. Freude (contd)

No.	Response	Total
15.	gross	4
16.	Geburtstag	3
17.	hell	3
18.	jauchzen	3
19.	Jubel	3
20.	Liebe	3
21.	singen	3
22.	Tanz	3
23.	Wonne	3
24.	angenehm	2
25.	Ferien	2
26.	Fest	2
27.	Freud	2
28.	Gaudi	2
29.	Goetterfunken	2
30.	gut	2
31.	lustig	2
32.	rein(e)	2
33.	Scherz	2
34.	Spass	2
35.	Traurigkeit	2
36.	Vorfreude	2
37.	(illegible)	2

38-135. (f = 1)
Arbeit, Ausbruch, Ausdruck, Ausgelassenheit,
Begeisterung, best. Freundin, Bewegung,
Christbaum, das Schoenste, edler Goetterfunken,
Eifer, empfinden, Erfolg, Erholung, Fasching,
fein, Festtag, Freudeausbruch, Freudenhaus,
Freudenreich, Freudenstadt, freudig, Freudigkeit,
freudlos, Freundin, froehlich, geben, Gedicht,
Gefuehl, Geld, Gemeinschaft, Gemuet, Genuss,
Gericht, gern, gluecklich, Greuel, gute Note,
haben, Hass, helle, hellrot, herrlich, Hobby,
innerlich, innig, Jammer, juchhei!, Konzert,
Laerm, laut, leben, Lebenaeusserungen, lebhaft,
Licht, Luftsprung, Maedchen, munter,
Naturerscheinung, Neuigkeit, ngeheul, Note,
NR, schaden, schenken, Schiller, Schillers
Glocke, schoener Goetterfunken, schoepfen,
Schrei, schwer, Schwermut, selten, sollt ihr
immer haben, Sonne, Spaziergang, Spiel, springen,
spruehend, Sprung, Stille, Stimmung, Taumel,
Test, Tod, Ton, Traene, traurig, Trost,
Ueberfreude, viel zu wenig, weinen, weiss nicht,
Wiedersehenfreude, Wohlsein, womit, zechen,
Zustand

87. Bett

No.	Response	Total
1.	Schlaf	54
2.	schlafen	45
3.	weich	32
4.	Ruhe	21
5.	warm	18
6.	Kissen	9
7.	Decke	8
8.	liegen	7
9.	Stuhl	7
10.	Tuch	7
11.	Lager	6
12.	muede	5
13.	schoen	5
14.	Bettstatt	4
15.	Betttuch	4
16.	Gestell	4
17.	Nacht	4
18.	weiss	4
19.	Bettvorleger	3
20.	Feder	3
21.	federn	3
22.	statt	3
23.	Tisch	3

87. Bett (contd)

No.	Response	Total
24.	Traum	2
25.	bequem	2
26.	Bettstelle	2
27.	hart	2
28.	Matraze	2
29.	ruhen	2
30.	Schlafzimmer	2
31.	Schwere	2
32.	Sofa	2
33.	Stelle	2

34-84. (f = 1)
Abend, angenehm, Angenehmes, ausruhen, Bein,
Bettchen, Bettlacken, bettlaegerig, Bettvorhang,
Blatt, Brett, Couch, Daune, dunkel, Ehe,
Entspannung, Flaumfeder, Frau, Fussboden,
Gegenstand, gut, herrlich, Himmelbett,
hineinlege, hueten, laben, Leid, Liebe, Maedchen,
Moebel, Molch, mollig, Muedigk., Nachttisch,
nett, Polster, Ruhebett, Schlafsack,
Schlafstaette, Schuh, sehr gut, sein, Sessel,
spiessig, tief, Tier, Umrandung, Vorleger, Wand,
Waerme, wohlig

88. Schwer

No.	Response	Total
1.	leicht	145
2.	Gewicht	23
3.	Last	12
4.	Blei	11
5.	drueckend	10
6.	Arbeit	8
7.	Eisen	8
8.	hart	7
9.	Stein	6
10.	Kraft	4
11.	Schwerkraft	4
12.	Arbeiter	3
13.	krank	3
14.	langsam	3
15.	Punkt	3
16.	Saeck(e)	3
17.	traege	3
18.	Aufgabe	2
19.	Druck	2
20.	Hammer	2
21.	lastend	2
22.	Mut	2
23.	Sorge(n)	2

24-86. (f = 1)
aechzen, Amboss, beladen, Beruf, breit, Buerde,
darum, dick, Eisenblock, Feder, federn, Fest,
Flucht, frueh, gebeugter Mensch, heavy, Hof,
Jammer, Klotz, Koffer, Kohle, Kost, leer,
Leiste, Lerch, Mehlsack, Metall, Meteorstein,
muede, Muehe, mutig, NR, Platin, Platon, Ramm,
Rucksack, Sackgetreide, Schiff, schlimm,
Schularbeit, Schulaufgaben, Schule, schwarz,
Schwerarbeiter, Schwerathlet, Schwere,
schwerhoerig, Schwerlaessigkeit, Schwermut,
schwerspaet, schwierig, Sprache, Stahl, Tonne,
Traeger, tragisch, traurig, u. leicht,
verwundet, Wasser, wiegend, zu ertragen
(Illegible)

89. Tabak

No.	Response	Total
1.	rauchen	71
2.	Pfeife	56
3.	Rauch	55
4.	Zigarette	28
5.	Zigarre	9
6.	Dose	8
7.	Nikotin	8
8.	braun	5
9.	Genuss	5
10.	Qualm	5
11.	Alkohol	3
12.	Genussmittel	3
13.	Geruch	3
14.	Rum	3
15.	schlecht	3
16.	stinkt	3
17.	Gift	2
18.	Kautabak	2
19.	Kraut	2
20.	Raucher	2
21.	Tabakdose (Tabakdose : 1 Tabaksdose: 1)	2
22.	Tabakrauch	2
23.	Virginia	2

24-72. (f = 1)
Amerika, amerikanisch, angenehme Beschaeftigung,
antiAlkoholiker, beissend, beisst, Beutel,
Dunst, d. Rauchen, drinnen, Faser, fein, gehasst,
gelbe Blaetter, Gemuetlichkeit, Gier, Gin, gut,
kauen, Knaster, Kohldampf, Krebs, Kummer, Laster,
List, Maenner, M.B., Milch, Naturerzeugnis,
nicht, NR, Pfeifenqualm, Plantage, qualmig, Reiz,
Rucksack, sauer, Schnaps, sgeruch, Sommer, Stank,
Tabakbeutel, Tabakbuechse, Tabakpfeife,
Tabakraucher, teuer, ungesund, Wirtshause, Wolke

90. Baby

No.	Response	Total
1.	Kind	66
2.	Sitter	23
3.	schreien	19
4.	klein(es)	18
5.	Mutter	18
6.	Windel(n)	14
7.	Waesche	12
8.	Kleinkind	11
9.	Wiege	11
10.	Saeugling	9
11.	Kinderwagen	7
12.	Babysitter	6
13.	Babywaesche	5
14.	niedlich	5
15.	Schrei	4
16.	Flasche	3
17.	Geburt	3
18.	Hose	3
19.	rosa	3
20.	Wagen	3
21.	Ehe	2
22.	Geschrei	2
23.	goldig	2
24.	hilflos	2
25.	kl. Kind	2
26.	Korb	2
27.	Liebe	2
28.	Maedchen	2
29.	Milch	2
30.	nett	2
31.	Schnuller	2
32.	schreit	2
33.	suess	2

34-95. (f = 1)

90. Baby (contd)

No.	Response	Total

aber, Amerika, amerikanisch, Anfang, Ausland,
Babyanstalt, Babykorb, Babywindeln, betreuen,
Bett, boese, Bruder, bruellt, Butter, drollig,
ehh, Ernaehrung, fein, Freude, freundlich,
Gesicht, Greis, Griessbrei, Hilflosigkeit, im
Steckkissen, ja, Jaeckchen, Junge, kann nicht
laufen, Kissen, Klapper, Kleidchen, Kleidung,
kleines Wesen, Kosewort, Krach, Laerm, leben,
Mady, Milchflasche, neu, Nichte, Pflege, quaeckt,
Riese, rosarot, schmutzig, Schreihals, seltsam,
singt, Spass, Strampelhoeschen, strampeln,
Strasse, Strickweste, suesses kleines,
unbeholfen, Unbeholfenheit, Unschuld, Wickel,
zart
(Illegible)

91. Mond

No.	Response	Total
1.	Stern(e)	46
2.	Sonne	39
3.	Nacht	30
4.	Sputnik	19
5.	Schein	17
6.	Sichel	13
7.	rund	11
8.	Rakete	9
9.	Gestirn	8
10.	Erde	6
11.	hell	6
12.	Luna	6
13.	Scheibe	6
14.	Licht	5
15.	Himmelskoerper	4
16.	kalt	4
17.	Krater	4
18.	rot	4
19.	Finsternis	3
20.	gelb	3
21.	romantisch	3
22.	Satellit (Satellit: 2 Satelit : 1)	3
23.	Vollmond	3
24.	Bahn	2
25.	bleich	2
26.	Gesicht	2
27.	Himmel	2
28.	Kalb	2
29.	Mondfahrt	2
30.	Mondschein	2
31.	no response	2
32.	Planet	2
33.	weiss	2

34-92. (f = 1)
Abend, abnehmen, All, Anziehung, beleuchten,
beruhig., Deutsch, dunkel, Einsamkeit,
Erdtrabant, Erhabenheit, Fahrt, Gasse,
geheimnisvoll, Glanz, Halb, Halbmond,
Heimlichkeit, helle Nacht, Kaelte, Landschaft,
Lehrer, Leuchte, leuchtet, lohnt, Luna rosa,
Mai, Mann, Mars, mod. Bild, Mondbahn,
Mondfinsternis, Mondgebirge, Mondhalb,
Mondhysteria, Mondkalb, Mondlicht, Mond-
scheinsonate, mondsuechtig, Romantik,
scheinsonate, schlagen, Serenade, silber,
silbern, Spaziergang, Stille, Strahl, suechtig,
Tannen, Trabant, Trabant der Erde, Utopie,
vollbringen, Welt, Weltall, Weltraum, Wicht
(Illegible)

92. Schere

No.	Response	Total
1.	schneiden	48
2.	scharf	31
3.	Messer	29
4.	Schneider	23
5.	Nadel	22
6.	Papier	17
7.	Faden	10
8.	Schnitt	10
9.	Spitz	9
10.	schneide	8
11.	Stoff	7
12.	Licht	6
13.	Scherenschnitt	6
14.	Werkzeug	6
15.	Haar(e)	4
16.	Instrument	4
17.	naehen	4
18.	Friseur	3
19.	Gabel	2
20.	Handwerkzeug	2
21.	Nagel	2
22.	no response	2
23.	Schaerfe	2
24.	Schlag	2
25.	Schleifer	2
26.	schneid	2
27.	Zange	2
28.	zwei	2
29.	zwicken	2

30-91. (f = 1)
abtrennen, Anzug, Arm, Blechschere, Blitz, Blut,
Calypso, damit, Fest, Fingernagel, Garn, Geraet,
Gesetz, glaenzend, glitzern, Haare schneiden,
Hand, Handarbeit, Hausfrau, Hebel, Hof, Judo,
klapp, klappern, klein, Klinge, knirscht, Krebs,
Maehre, Massband, nfernrolt, Physik, rachen,
rasieren, Ratsch, Riss, (scharf, Spitz), Schere-
klinge, Scherenberg, Scherenkopf, Scherenschlag,
Scherenspitze, schleifen, Schliff, Schnabel,
Schneiderschere, schneidet, Schnitter, Schnitzel,
Schnur, Schwere, Silber, Spiel, Spitze, spitzig,
stechen, sticht, Tag, Tuch, Weinstock, Zeuge,
Zwitter

93. Ruhig

No.	Response	Total
1.	laut	45
2.	still	29
3.	langsam	16
4.	aufgeregt	14
5.	Gelassenheit	12
6.	leise	11
7.	schlafen	11
8.	Nacht	9
9.	Schlaf	8
10.	See	7
11.	unruhig	7
12.	nervoes	6
13.	Ruhe	6
14.	sanft	6
15.	Blut	5
16.	schnell	5
17.	Wasser	5
18.	erregt	4
19.	Gemuet	4
20.	hastig	4
21.	besonnen	3
22.	Sonntag	3
23.	Waeld(er)	3
24.	angenehm	2
25.	Bett	2
26.	bewegt	2
27.	bleiben	2

93. Ruhig (contd)

No.	Response	Total
28.	gemessen	2
29.	Leid	2
30.	Meer	2
31.	no response	2
32.	schoen	2
33.	Schule	2
34.	sicher	2
35.	traurig	2
36.	Unterricht	2
37.	warm	2

38-117. (f = 1)
Abend, alt. Mann, Alter, atmen, ausgeglichen,
bedaechtig, Bewegung, Blick, brav, Buddha, eben,
Eigenschaft, einsam, Erholung, ernst, Examen,
fleissig, fliessend, Fluss, freundlich, Geduld,
gehen, gehetzt, gemuetlich, gereizt, gesammelt,
gesetzt, gestern, Gewissen, gleiten, gross, gut,
heiter, heute, ich, Jubel, Kirche, Land, Laerm,
laermend, lebendig, Lehrer, Main, Mensch,
Mittag, Mittelmeer, muede, Mund, Nachtruhe,
nachts, notwendig, Oma, Park, Pause, Philosoph,
Ruhestand, ruhig bleiben, ruhige Zeit, ruhiger
Mensch, ruhigfliessend, Ruhigkeit, Ruhigstellung,
sachl., Schild, schlummernd, Schulaufgaben,
Seele, sein, sitzen, Stein, Stellung, Stunde,
summen, "Tacitus", Tal, Unruhe, Wartezimmer,
zufrieden, Zustand
(Illegible)

94. Gruen

No.	Response	Total
1.	Wiese	49
2.	gelb	39
3.	rot	36
4.	Gras	29
	(Gras : 28	
	Grass: 1)	
5.	blau	19
6.	Farbe	19
7.	Wald	18
8.	weiss	9
9.	grau	6
10.	Rasen	6
11.	schwarz	6
12.	Fruehling	5
13.	hell	4
14.	Hoffnung	4
15.	Span	4
16.	Baum	3
17.	schoen	3
18.	Ampel	2
19.	Blatt	2
20.	falsch	2
21.	grasgruen	2
22.	Heide	2
23.	Kohl	2
24.	lila	2
25.	Natur	2
26.	Schnabel	2

27-80. (f = 1)
abfahren, angenehm, Angst, arbeiten, Beine,
berugigend, Berugigung, Blaetter, blaugruen,
braun, brunett, darin, erquickend, fahren,
Flaeche, frei, Frosch, frueh, Garten, Gemuese,
giftig, Glueck, Greenhorn, grell, Gruenanlage,
Gruenfarben, gruenlich, Gruenstueck, Gruenzeug,
haesslich, Jaeger, Krankheit, lebhaft, mild,
NR, orange, pflanzen, reif, rosa, Ruhe, rund,
satt, schreiend, Schweinfurt, Tafel,
Verkehrsampel, Verkehrslicht, verwirrend,
violett, warm, Weide, zart, zeichnen, Zeug

95. Salz

No.	Response	Total
1.	Zucker	54
2.	bitter	32
3.	sauer	25
4.	Meer	15
5.	salzig	13
6.	scharf	11
7.	Pfeffer	10
8.	Suppe	9
9.	Wasser	9
10.	Gewuerz(e)	8
11.	weiss	8
12.	Erde	7
13.	Kartoffel(n)	7
14.	Fass	6
15.	Saeure	6
16.	Brot	5
17.	essen	5
18.	Bergwerk	4
19.	Essig	4
20.	Honig	4
21.	NaCl	4
22.	suess	4
23.	Hering	3
24.	Salzwasser	3
25.	beissend	2
26.	Butter	2
27.	Gitter	2
28.	Kochsalz	2
29.	Koerner	2
30.	kornig	2
31.	Kristall(e)	2
32.	Napt	2
33.	Natrium	2
34.	Salzburg	2
35.	Salzfass	2
36.	Schmalz	2
37.	See	2
38.	Sol(e)	2
39.	Wuerze	2
40.	(illegible)	2

41-83. (f = 1)
arm, Bag, Band, Behaelter, Chemie, Dose, Eier, Eltern, Gestein, Gurke, Halogene, haltig, herb, ihr seid das Salz der Erde, im Essen, Koch, kochen, Kristallmasse, Kuchen, Lager, lange, los, Malz, Meerwasser, Mineral, oft noetig, Pech, Prise, Pulver, Reichenhall, Salz im Gefaess, Salzletten, Salz und Essig, schlecht, schmerzend, Stein, Tomate, totes Meer, Tuete, unangenehm, wichtig, wuerzend, Wueste

96. Strasse

No.	Response	Total
1.	Weg	49
2.	lang	30
3.	Gasse	24
4.	Auto(s)	23
5.	Pflaster	18
6.	Bahn	11
7.	Verkehr	11
8.	Strassenbahn	9
9.	Asphalt	5
10.	breit	5
11.	Gehsteig	5
12.	grau	5
13.	Haus	5
14.	Land	4
15.	Landstrasse	4
16.	Platz	4
17.	Stadt	4
18.	Autobahn	3
19.	Dorf	3
20.	Laerm	3

96. Strasse (contd)

No.	Response	Total
21.	nass	3
22.	Teer	3
23.	Baum	2
24.	eng	2
25.	fahren	2
26.	Ferne	2
27.	gehen	2
28.	gerade	2
29.	glatt	2
30.	Lampe	2
31.	laut	2
32.	Name	2
33.	nname	2
34.	Ziel	2

35-110. (f = 1)
Abenteuer, alte, Anzug, Band, Bau, Belebung, Biegung, breites Band, Broadway, Bummel, Chaussee, dunkel, eben, einsam, Fahrung, Fenster, Film "La Strada", Fuesse, Garten, goldig, Hals, Hauptstrasse, Hausnummer, Heimweg, hell, Kino, Kirch, Kurve, Landschaft, (lange, schwarze Teerdecke), lange Strasse, "La Strada", laufen, leer, Loch, Nacht, New York, NR, Nummer, ohne Namen, parallele, Pfad, Rand, Raserei, Rasse, Regen, Route, Schaufenster, schlecht, schmal, Schmutz, schwarz, Seitenstrasse, Spazieren, Staub, Stein, Strada, Strassenzug, Street, Strich, Tal, Tod, trocken, Trottoir, Vagabund, Verkehrsnot, Verkehrsweg, verlassen, via, Wanderer, wandern, Weihnachtsdunst, weit, weite, Winkel, Wohnung

97. Koenig

No.	Response	Total
1.	Kaiser	50
2.	Krone	29
3.	Herrscher	27
4.	Reich	17
5.	Bettler	9
6.	Koenigin	9
7.	Monarchie	8
8.	Rex	6
9.	Untertan	6
10.	England	5
11.	Herr	5
12.	herrschen	5
13.	maechtig	5
14.	Koenigtum	4
15.	Macht	4
16.	Maerchen	4
17.	Monarch	4
18.	Buerger	3
19.	Fuerst	3
20.	gross	3
21.	Koenigreich	3
22.	Palast	3
23.	Regent	3
24.	Schloss	3
25.	Thron	3
26.	ueberholt	3
27.	Bauer	2
28.	Dame	2
29.	Glanz	2
30.	Gold	2
31.	Hof	2
32.	Mantel	2
33.	Praesident	2
34.	Prinz	2
35.	regieren	2
36.	Regierung	2
37.	Republik	2
38.	vorbei	2
39.	(illegible)	2

97. Koenig (contd)

No.	Response	Total

40-120. ($f = 1$)
Adenauer, All, aus damit, Befehlshaber,
Beherrscher, Belsazer, bringen, Burg, Demokrat,
der See, edel, Elefant, Erhabenheit, es war
einmal, Frau, glaenzend, Gustav, gut, Haar,
Hand, hell, Herrschaft, Herzog, ich, Imperator,
Kaiserin, Kanzler, Karte, King, King Lear,
Kleinheit, komisch, Koenigsee, Koenigsmacht,
Koenigspurpur, Krieg, (Krone, Mantel),
laecherlich, Land, Lehar, Ludwig, Ludwig XIV,
Maharadscha, Mann, Maus, Mensch, Mittelalter,
Oedipus, Ornat, Philipp, Pracht, Purpur, Quatsch,
ramandern, Rasselband, Roi, schoen, See,
sgeschlecht, Sitz, Solomon, spalast, sthron,
Strasse, Stuart, Stuhl, szepter, Test, Thronsaal,
Titel, tot, Tradition, Tyrann, und ich,
Vergangenheit, Volk, war einmal, Wittelsbacher
Dynastie, Zahn, Zepter, zeremoniell

98. Kaese

No.	Response	Total
1.	Butter	50
2.	Brot	37
3.	Milch	27
4.	Geruch	17
5.	essen	14
6.	Gestank	12
7.	Loecher	11
8.	stinkt	10
9.	Nahrung	8
10.	stinken	7
11.	Schweiz	5
12.	Allgaeu	4
13.	Kuchen	4
14.	Limburg	4
15.	Speise	4
16.	Alpen	3
17.	Creme	3
18.	Duft	3
19.	Emmentaler	3
20.	guter	3
21.	Quark	3
22.	riechen	3
23.	Schweizer	3
24.	Schweizerkaese (Schweizerkaese: 2 Schweizerk. : 1)	3
25.	Alm	2
26.	Bahnhof	2
27.	Freitag	2
28.	Kaesebrot	2
29.	Kuh	2
30.	Limburger	2
31.	Marke	2
32.	Rahm	2
33.	sauer	2
34.	Schachtel	2
35.	scharf	2
36.	Schinken	2
37.	Sorte	2
38.	stinkig	2
39.	weich	2
40.	wurmig	2
41.	Wurst	2

42-97. ($f = 1$)
Abscheu, abscheulich, ach, Apetitt, Bier,
Brotaufstrich, Buttersaeure, darinnen, dunkel,
fliessend, Fromage, Gebirge, geht, gelb, gelb
Geruch, Gemuese, Genuss, Herbes, Holland,
Hunger, Italien, Kaeseart, Kaeseglocke,
Kaesemarke, Kaeserei, klein, leise, Maden, mmh!,
Molke, Mund, Nahrungsm., Nase, nicht, NR, Onkel,
"Orinkaesehoch", Parmesan, pfui, riecht,

98. Kaese (contd)

No.	Response	Total

Romadour, Rotwein, Salz, Schimmel, schlecht,
Schmarn, Schmierkaese, siehe Arbeit, silber,
Sinkig, Tilsiter, Tisch, Tranquillus,
Vegetarier, Wuerze, Zutat

99. Bluete

No.	Response	Total
1.	Blume	71
2.	weiss	21
3.	Fruehling	15
4.	Baeum(e)	13
5.	Frucht	13
6.	Blatt	10
7.	Duft	10
8.	Pflanze	10
9.	schoen	10
10.	Apfel	7
11.	Honig	7
12.	Rose	7
13.	Schoenheit	6
14.	Knospe	4
15.	Mai	4
16.	Stengel	4
17.	Stiel	4
18.	zart	4
19.	Zeit	4
20.	Apfelbluete	3
21.	Biene	3
22.	Bluetenstaub	3
23.	bunt	3
24.	Kirschenbluete	3
25.	nstaub	3
26.	rot	3
27.	Sommer	3
28.	duftig	2
29.	Entfaltung	2
30.	Farben	2
31.	Kelch	2
32.	Kirsche(n)	2
33.	Schmetterling	2
34.	Staub	2

35-103. ($f = 1$)
Alter, aufgeblueht, Biologie, blau, bluehen,
Bluetenblatt, Bluetenfabrika, Bluetenfuelle,
Bluetenhang, Bluetenreich, bluetenweiss,
Bluetezeit, Dolde, duften, duftet, edel, frueh,
Fruehjahr, Geborgenheit, gruen, hell, herrlich,
Hyazynte, in B. stehen, Insekten, Japan, Jugend,
Kranz, leben, Lese, leicht, leuchten(d), Licht,
Milch, nblatt, Obstbaum, offen, Ohr, Pracht,
reif, rein, riechen, rosa, rosaweiss, rosig,
Stamm, Stand, Staubkorn, stehen, Stempel, still,
Strauch, suess, Tulpe, Tuer, Tuete, unberuehrt,
weich, Weissblume, weisser Kelch, Welk, Wiese,
Wind, Wonne, Zartheit, Ziel, Zustand, (ἄνθος- Gr.
'anthos')
(Illegible)

100. Aengstlich

No.	Response	Total
1.	Kind(er)	24
2.	Furcht	21
3.	mutig	21
4.	furchtsam	18
5.	feig(e)	12
6.	Angst	11
7.	Hase	10
8.	ruhig	10

100. Aengstlich (contd)

No.	Response	Total
9.	zittern	10
10.	Maedchen	8
11.	Feigling	7
12.	tapfer	7
13.	keit	6
14.	zaghaft	5
15.	Mensch(en)	4
16.	Angsthase	3
17.	aergerlich	3
18.	forsch	3
19.	furchtlos	3
20.	Gefahr	3
21.	Hasenfuss	3
22.	klein	3
23.	nervoes	3
24.	sehen	3
25.	verzagt	3
26.	Aengstlichkeit	2
27.	aufgeregt	2
28.	Eigenschaft	2
29.	Film	2
30.	froh	2
31.	froehlich	2
32.	furchtbar	2
33.	Gewissen	2
34.	krank	2
35.	laecherlich	2
36.	Maus	2
37.	Nebel	2
38.	nein	2
39.	nie	2
40.	Reh	2
41.	schlecht	2
42.	schuechtern	2
43.	.Schulaufgabe	2
44.	sicher	2
45.	still	2
46.	Traum	2
47.	vorsichtig	2

48-130. ($\underline{f}$ = 1)
albern, anklammern, ae. sein, Atombombe, bange,
bange Augen, baenglich, Beklemnis, besonnen,
blass, bloed, Chaplin, dreist, dumm, dunkel,
eilig, einfaeltig, Erlebnis, frei, freudig,
freudlich, frisch, fuerchten, furchtvoll,
gefasst, Gefuehl, gelassen, Geld, Gemuet,
gesund, Herzklopfen, hinkender Mensch, Hose,
Hund, hurtig, ich, Junge, kaum, keck, komisch,
kraenklich, Krieg, Kummer, langsam, leben,
leider, Lohn der Angst, Mimose, Mutter, Nacht,
nachts, naseweis, Nonne, NR, ooh, Reck,
schrecken, Schule, schwach, schwermuetig, sehr,
selbstbewusst, selten, sorgenvoll, sorglos,
sorgsam, stark, stumpf, Sturz, Tadel, Tod, tot,
traurig, Unangst, unwillig, verachten, verhalten,
vier, warum denn, zart, zerwirrt, Zug, Zunge

CHAPTER 4

INTERNATIONAL KENT ROSANOFF WORD ASSOCIATION NORMS, EMPHASIZING THOSE OF FRENCH MALE AND FEMALE STUDENTS AND FRENCH WORKMEN[1,2]

Mark R. Rosenzweig
University of California, Berkeley, California

This paper has three principal aims: (*1*) To sketch briefly the history of use of the Kent-Rosanoff list of word association stimuli, stressing studies conducted recently outside the United States and translations to other languages; (*2*) to describe the two sets of French word association norms included in this volume and the conditions under which they were obtained; (*3*) to compare some of the main characteristics of the sets of Kent-Rosanoff norms among countries and across languages.

HISTORICAL REVIEW

Until recent years, use of the standardized list of word association stimuli of Kent and Rosanoff (1910) was confined to the United States. After the report of Kent and Rosanoff, Woodrow and Lowell (1916) used the same list of stimuli with children and published complete norms. O'Connor (1928) and Russell and Jenkins (1954) reported complete sets of responses for adult American subjects. The norms of Schellenberg (1930), although never published, have been used by many investigators. Other unpublished American normative studies include those of Meals, Herrick, and Merow (1948) and Keene (1951). Lists of primary responses[3] have been put out by Tresselt, Leeds, and Mayzner (1955). These normative compilations have provided important tools for the study of verbal behavior, and the repeated sampling during the course of the last half-century has suggested major shifts of associative behavior in the United States (Jenkins & Russell, 1960).

Because of the increasing importance of this area of psycholinguistic research, it seemed worthwhile to extend such studies to another language. Therefore, I devoted a sabbatical semester in 1955-1956 to obtaining word association norms of French students and doing related research. The primary responses to the translation of the Kent-Rosanoff list were published soon thereafter (Rosenzweig, 1957), but the complete norms appear here for

[1] This article remains largely as it was written in 1963. When publication of this book was delayed, it was not possible to keep the article up to date, but certain revisions were made in 1969.

[2] The French norms to be reported here were obtained during two sabbatical semester leaves from the University of California, 1955-1956 and 1960-1961. Both semesters were spent at the Sorbonne, thanks to the generous hospitality of Professor Paul Fraisse, Directeur du Laboratoire de Psychologie Expérimentale et Comparée. The second of these semesters was also aided by a Fulbright Research Fellowship and by a Social Science Research Council Faculty Research Fellowship.

[3] The primary associative response to a stimulus is the response occurring most frequently among the set of responses elicited by that stimulus. The secondary response is the next most frequent, and so on.

the first time. Meanwhile, Mario Levi informed me of his unpublished Master's thesis, done at the University of Chicago, which gives most of the primary responses of Italian subjects to a translation of the Kent-Rosanoff list (Levi, 1949). Then, in 1958, Russell and Meseck obtained responses of German students to a translation of the Kent-Rosanoff list and reported the primary responses (Russell & Meseck, 1959); the complete norms of that study also appear for the first time in this volume (pp. 53-94). The first normative studies done by European investigators in Europe using translations of the Kent-Rosanoff list appear to be those of Italian psychologists. In 1957, Banissoni and Nencini published a preliminary note on a group test of associations using this list (Banissoni & Nencini, 1957). Then, Chiari (1959) published a partial list of primary responses of 77 Italian subjects to the Kent-Rosanoff stimuli.

In 1960, I compared associative responses in English, French, German, and Italian in a paper delivered at the International Congress of Psychology (Rosenzweig, 1961, 1962). This talk put me in touch with Margaret Miller and Dr. Kenneth M. Miller, Australian students of verbal behavior living in England. The Millers had given tests of word association to Australian subjects. Dr. Miller then became interested in questions raised by the comparison of associations in the United States, France, Germany, and Italy, and in order to obtain further material for comparison, he set out in 1961 to obtain norms in England. We later compared the norms obtained in the United States, Australia, and England (Rosenzweig and Miller, 1966). The English and the Australian norms are both given in partial form in this volume (pp. 53-94); that is, for each stimulus, the five most frequent responses of Australian and of English subjects are tabulated.

During a second sabbatical semester in France, 1960-1961, I did further work on associations of French adults and children. This included obtaining word-association responses of French workmen, and these norms will be presented along with the responses of French students. Preparation of norms for students and workers permits comparison of responses of groups that differ in social and educational backgrounds while belonging to the same "language community."

In 1963, Lambert and Moore (1966) tested Montreal high school and college students from three linguistic groups—French-Canadian monolinguals, English-Canadian monolinguals, and English-French bilinguals. The bilinguals were given both the English and the French versions of the test, with a 3-week interval between the two.

The largest scale collection of norms in a language other than English was performed by Kurcz (1966). She tested 1000 Polish students.

COLLECTION OF FRENCH NORMS

The French Word Association Test

The first step in this study was to prepare a French translation of the test of Kent and Rosanoff (1910). Preparing such a translation is not a simple straightforward task, as can be seen from the fact that the independent Italian translations of Levi (1949) and Chiari (1959) differed in 28 of the 100 stimuli! The French translation of Lambert and Moore (1966) differed in eight cases from my 1955 translation. Furthermore, Kurcz (1966), in her Polish study, followed rather different principles of translation from those to be described here.

In making the French translation, one prepared by Professeur Paul Fraisse for use in class laboratories at the Sorbonne was of considerable help. In general, our translation aimed for exactness, while employing words of relatively high frequency of usage, since most of the English stimuli have moderately high frequencies of usage. In about 60 of the 100 cases, the translation seemed obvious. In certain other cases, problems that arose and the solutions reached should be mentioned. (In a few of these cases, consideration of the results suggested that the translation could be improved, and two changes were made in the 1960 study.)

(1) In a number of cases, the part of speech of the English stimulus is ambiguous. For example, *comfort, command, whistle, wish, sleep,* and *dream* may be nouns or verbs. Such ambiguity is rarely possible in French; therefore, either a noun or a verb had to be chosen as the stimulus. It had been shown that responses of adults tend to be of the same part of speech as the stimulus (Bourdon, 1895; Woodworth, 1938). Therefore, the Minnesota norms of Russell and Jenkins (1954) were inspected to determine whether most of the Ss had responded to the stimulus in question with nouns or verbs. In the case of *comfort,* for example, the responses were chiefly nouns, so an equivalent noun, *confort,* was used in French. Only *wish* was translated as a verb (*désirer*). The word *dream* allowed a translation that could be either a verb or a noun (*rêve*).

(2) In some cases, it was not clear which sense of an English word to translate. For example, *short* can be

applied to a person, in which case it is translated as *petit,* or to a distance, in which case it is translated as *court,* or to a period of time, in which case it is translated as *bref.* Inspection of the 1954 Minnesota norms showed that most of the responses to *short* were terms that apply to people; therefore the translation adopted was *petit.* (Another approach to the problem of selecting which meaning to translate is to use the semantic count, as suggested by Rosenzweig and McNeill, 1962.)

(*3*) In some cases, the French terms selected had other meanings which interfered with their intended use. For example, *doux* was chosen as the best translation for *sweet.* However, the primary response *dur* (*hard*) revealed that most *S*s took *doux* in its other sense of *soft.* Similarly, *ordre* was used to translate *command.* The most common response was *désordre* (*disorder*), indicating that the meaning taken by the *S*s was not the intended one.

(*4*) Two English stimuli are best translated by a phrase in French: *hungry* (*avoir faim*) and *thirsty* (*avoir soif*). Since it was desired that each stimulus be a single word, the nouns *faim* and *soif* were used.

(*5*) Because of cultural differences, we did not in two cases use a word that exists in both languages. *Whiskey* is considered in France to be a foreign drink characteristic of Anglo-Saxon countries; therefore, *cognac* was used as a French equivalent. The word *Bible* exists in French as well as in English, but in French it has a connotation of Old Testament as opposed to New Testament. The term *Évangile* (*Gospels*) is employed much more frequently, and so it was used as the translation of the English term *Bible.*

(*6*) The words *sheep* and *mutton* are both best translated by the word *mouton.* Rather than use *mouton* twice in the list, the word *agneau* (*lamb* in the sense of the live animal) was used the second time. It was not known which meaning of *mouton* would be understood by most of the subjects. The test response indicate that "*mouton*" was understood as the live animal. Since this is so, *mutton* might have been translated by the name of some popular cut of lamb, such as *gigot.*

The test list was mimeographed on two pages. It followed the form of the Minnesota test blank, except that no spaces for identification for the *S* were included. Opposite each stimulus word was a blank for the response. In the 1955 study, there was also a third page with 30 more words, chosen specifically to investigate effects of grammatical form on response; the responses to these 30 additional words will not be treated in this report.

Subjects and Procedures

Students—1955 study. The *S*s included students in psychology courses at the Sorbonne and students in their last year at two Paris lycées. The test was administered by the regular class professor, with one exception: In the class of Professeur Fraisse, Madame G. Oléron administered the test.[4] Table 1 shows the number of students in each group. The table includes only those *S*s whose native language was French and who gave a legible response to every stimulus; the protocols of other *S*s were not tabulated.[5,6]

TABLE 1 *Student Subjects Taking the French Word Association Test, Classified by Sex, Institution, and Date of Test*

Institution	Dates of tests	Number of subjects	
		Women	Men
Lycée La Fontaine	Nov. 16 & 23, 1955	59	—
Lycée Lakanal	Nov. 19, 1955	—	58
Sorbonne	Dec. 1, 1955	51	19
Sorbonne	Jan. 3, 1956	74	27
Total		184	104

In each case, the professor read the instructions aloud to the class and maintained order during the test. These were the instructions given:

Ceci est une étude sur le comportement verbal qu'on est en train de faire à la Sorbonne. Cette expérience est sur

[4]Thanks are due to Mademoiselle Sauvage who administered the tests at Lycée La Fontaine, to Monsieur Jacob who administered them at Lycée Lakanal, to Madame Oléron who gave the first set at the Sorbonne, and to Monsieur Durandin who gave the tests in several classes at the Sorbonne.

[5]Thanks are due to Mrs. Ginette Henkin for help in the tabulation of the responses of the French students.

[6]It should be noted that a national election was held in France in January 2, 1956. The election campaign may have increased the number of responses related to politics, although no such response shows up as strikingly in the French norms as the stimulus-response pair *whistle-stop* in the American norms collected during and shortly after the presidential campaign of 1952.

l'association libre. Veuillez laisser les feuilles comme elles vous sont présentées, en les laissant retournées. (The experimenter then passed out the sheets, face down.)

Lorsque je vous dirai de tourner les feuilles, vous trouverez une liste de 130 mots. Lisez le mot N⁰ 1, puis écrivez en face le premier mot qui vous vient à l'esprit. Puis, passez au mot N⁰ 2 et écrivez encore le premier mot qui vous vient à l'esprit, et ainsi de suite dans l'ordre de présentation.

Ne donnez qu'un seul mot pour chaque réponse.

Ne sautez aucun mot.

Travaillez rapidement jusqu'à la fin de la liste.

Écrivez chaque mot très lisiblement.

Lorsque vous aurez terminé, tournez vos feuilles et écrivez en haut sur la feuille blanche la lettre qui sera au tableau noir à ce moment-là. Puis laissez les feuilles retournées, et attendez jusqu'à ce que tout le monde ait terminé.

Avez-vous des questions? (If there were questions, the experimenter replied by rereading the appropriate part of the instructions. He did not give any examples of responses.)

Alors, attention. Commencez.

At the end of the test, the Ss were asked to write on the forms their name, age, sex, native language, and certain other information.

Workmen—1960 study. The Ss were workmen in the construction industry who were being given a battery of placement tests at the Centre de Sélection Psychotechnique du Ministère du Travail in Paris.[7] The testing took place during December, 1960 and January, 1961 (about the same season as the testing of the students 5 yr earlier).

The great majority of the Ss were in their late teens or early twenties, and they were thus comparable to the French student group in age. The educational achievement of the Ss was inspected at a later date, at which time the records of 94 of the 115 Ss were still available at the Center. Thirty Ss had not obtained the Certificat d'Études Primaires, which required passing an examination upon the completion of primary schooling at age 14. Forty-one had the certificate but had not completed further studies. Twenty-three had taken further education and, of these, three had earned the Baccalauréat.

The results include responses of only those Ss whose native language was French. While for the students there were only a few blanks or illegible responses and protocols containing such flaws were eliminated from the tabulation, such treatment would have considerably reduced the initially small number of workmen. Forty-four of the workmen had one or more illegible responses and three of these Ss plus eight others had one or more blanks. All their protocols were therefore included, with the exception of that of one S whose responses were nonsensical throughout. The occurrence of illegible responses or blanks is noted at the bottom of each set of norms.[8]

Modified instructions were considered advisable by the staff of the Center, based on their experience with Ss there. The instructions devised included a few examples of possible responses to a sample word which did not appear in the test. Although the differences in the instructions given to the students and those given to the workmen may have played an important role in determining the marked differences between the two sets of norms, this seems doubtful for reasons given in detail elsewhere (Rosenzweig, 1964, pp. 66-67). The complete instructions given to the workmen follow:

Je vais vous distribuer des cahiers. N'ouvrez pas le cahier avant que je vous le dise.

(The leaflets were distributed with an orange cover sheet on top.) Sur la feuille orange, en haut et à droite, écrivez votre nom, en lettres majuscules d'imprimerie, et votre prénom.

Au dessous, écrivez la date: Nous sommes le . . .

Lorsque je vous le dirai, vous tournerez la page. Vous trouverez une liste de 100 mots. Vous lirez le mot N⁰ 1, et vous écrirez en face le premier mot qui vous vient à l'esprit. Par exemple, si le premier mot écrit sur la liste était "chien," et si le premier mot qui vous vient alors à l'esprit est "aboie," ou "chat," ou "noir," ou tout autre mot, c'est "aboie" ou "chat," ou "noir," ou tout autre mot, que vous écrirez: la seule chose importante, c'est de toujours écrire le premier mot qui vous vient à l'esprit, quel que soit ce mot.

Vous ferez de même pour le mot N⁰ 2, puis le mot N⁰3, et ainsi de suite jusqu'à la fin.

Il ne faut qu'un seul mot pour chaque réponse, mais vous ne devez sauter aucune ligne: vous commencez au mot N⁰ 1, en haut du premier côté de la feuille, et vous allez, en suivant l'ordre des numéros, jusqu'au N⁰ 100, au bas du deuxième côté.

Lorsque vous aurez terminé, vous écrirez sur la couverture orange, sous la date, l'heure qui sera inscrite au tableau, et vous poserez la feuille au coin de votre table.

Restez silencieux, pour ne pas gêner vos camarades.

[7]The word association test was included in the testing procedure by the kind permission of the director of the Center, Monsieur Daniel Dupuis, and the administration of the test was supervised by Monsieur André Ourlin. The tests were given by Mademoiselle Helène Le Bourlais and Monsieur Gabriel Freneau, psychotechnicians at the Center. Thanks are due to all of these psychologists for their willing aid and cooperation in this study.

[8]Madame Paulette Véron accomplished the difficult task of deciphering and tabulating the workers' responses.

Et surtout, rappelez-vous bien, pour chaque mot de la liste, il faut écrire le premier mot qui vous vient à l'esprit, quel que soit ce mot.

After the group had completed the test, they were requested to write down their age, native language, and certain further information.

CHARACTERISTICS OF THE NORMS

Where characteristics of the French norms and comparisons among international norms have already been described in publications, these will only be summarized briefly here. Certain other features will be considered in greater detail.

Diversity of Responses

Frequencies of high-ranking responses. Inspection of the student norms soon made it apparent that French students diversify their responses more than do American students: While the three most popular responses, summed over items, accounted for 46% of all responses in the Kent-Rosanoff norms, they accounted for 59% in the Russell-Jenkins norms. In notable contrast, the three most popular responses per stimulus made up only 37% of the responses of the Parisian students (Rosenzweig, 1959). Later, it was shown that French, German, and Italian Ss have rather similar frequencies of primary responses and that the communality of responses among American Ss is almost twice as great (Rosenzweig, 1961).

Table 2 gives the relative frequencies of common responses for Ss from seven countries. (Data from Italian studies are not included because a complete list of even primary responses is not available.) Inspection of the table supports the following conclusions:

(1) During the last 50 years, there has been a tendency within the United States for the primary response to account for an increasing proportion of all responses, as Jenkins and Russell (1960) have pointed out.

(2) Currently, the primary responses in France, Germany, and Poland have much lower relative frequencies than those in the United States; the European values are, in fact, lower than even the American values of 1910.

(3) This difference is not best characterized as occurring between European and American norms but, rather, as occurring between norms of European languages and norms of the English language.

TABLE 2   *Measures of Communality of Response in Several Studies of Word Association Norms*

| Investigators | Dates of testing | N | Percentage of Ss giving responses of following ranks: | | | | Slope of rank-freq. functions |
			1	2	3	1+2+3	
A. English language							
1. United States[a]							
Kent & Rosanoff	1910	1000	26.0	12.2	7.7	45.9	−1.3
O'Connor	1925	1000	33.8	13.4	8.0	55.2	−1.3[b]
Schellenberg	1927	925	28.9	12.1	7.9	48.9	−1.2[b]
Keene	1933	500	35.7	12.5	7.8	56.0	−1.4[b]
Russell & Jenkins	1952-1953	1008	37.5	13.6	8.0	59.1	−1.4
2. Australia							
Miller	1957-1958	200	36.5	12.4	7.6	56.5	−1.5[b]
3. England							
Miller	1961-1962	400	31.2	11.3	7.0	49.5	−1.4[b]
4. Canada							
Lambert & Moore	1963	206	33.3	11.5	7.4	52.2	−1.3
B. Other languages							
1. French							
Rosenzweig	1955-1956	288	20.6	9.6	6.8	37.0	−1.0
Rosenzweig	1960-1961	115	16.7	9.6	7.0	33.3	−0.9
Lambert & Moore	1963	136	23.7	11.2	7.5	42.4	−1.0
2. German							
Russell & Meseck	1958	331	22.5	9.5	6.6	38.6	−1.1
3. Polish							
Kurcz	1965	1000	18.5	10.5	7.4	36.4	−1.0[b]

[a]Percentages for US studies are from Jenkins and Russell (1960, Table 4, p. 299). [b]Slope estimated from data for the first three ranks.

Rank-frequency functions. The difference between speakers of English and of Western European languages in the diversification of their responses is also brought out by the use of the rank-frequency function. Skinner (1937) used this function to demonstrate that responses are drawn from a pool of associations with great regularity and that Zipf's formulation appears to apply to this behavior. To prepare a frequency distribution of responses, Skinner took the mean frequency of all 100 primary responses in the Kent-Rosanoff norms as the frequency for rank 1, the mean frequency of all secondary responses as the frequency for rank 2, and so on. These values were then put on log-log axes. The curve is reproduced in Fig. 1. (Note that the form follows Skinner in having the ordinate represent percentage rather than frequency of responses. This has the advantage for us of allowing comparison to be made with another group having a different number of *S*s.) Skinner described the plot of the Kent-Rosanoff data as follows:

> The curve is approximately linear for the 100 responses most likely to occur . . . . The set of stimulus words used by Kent and Rosanoff evolved from 71 to 280 different responses, with a median of 145. The curve . . . breaks at about the point at which only one-half the stimulus words are still evoking responses. Had 2,000 or 3,000 subjects been studied, the linear part of the curve might have been extended further, since longer lists for each stimulus word would have been obtained (Skinner, 1937, p. 72).

The slope of the curve appears to be about −1.3, and this value has been entered in the right-hand column of Table 2.

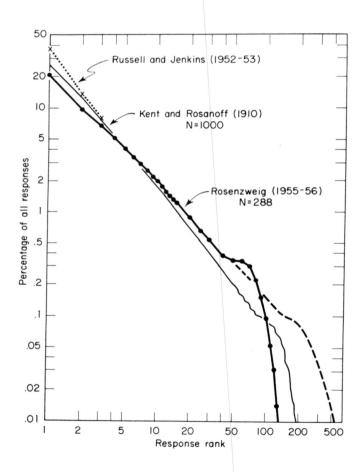

FIG. 1. Rank-frequency functions plotted on double logarithmic coordinates. The plot for the Kent-Rosanoff data is taken from Skinner (1937). The heavy curve represents the data of the French students, taken from the present norms. The dashed line to the lower right represents an extrapolation of the French data to a population of 1000 subjects, as described in the text. The dates are those of collection of responses, not those of publication.

Russell and Jenkins have not published a rank-frequency curve for their norms, but they report that the slope is −1.4. Figure 1 gives the first three points, based on their published data. The number of different responses per stimulus is about 90, as estimated from a sample of every tenth item. For the Australian data of Miller, the relative frequencies of the first three ranks were computed, and they are given in Table 2. Estimating by eye from these points, a rank-frequency slope of −1.5 is obtained. Similarly, a slope of −1.4 is estimated for the English data, using the first three ranks. The mean number of different responses per item in the English study is 86. The average slope for all of the English-language studies in Table 2 is −1.4 and only the study of Keene shows a slope as low as −1.2.

The curve for the French student norms has a slope of about −1.0, the theoretical value of Zipf. The French study included a smaller number of Ss than the American study, so the departure from linearity occurs higher on the curve. Russell (personal communication, 1963) calculated the values for the first 20 ranks in the German data; the slope is −1.1. The slope of the Polish data, estimated from the first three points, is about −1.0. Therefore, all three European studies show more gradual slopes than those for any of the English-speaking groups. The 288 French students had a mean of 89 different responses per stimulus. (The 331 German Ss give a mean of 100 different responses per stimulus.)

For both the studies of Kent and Rosanoff and of Rosenzweig, the average number of different responses per stimulus will be seen to correspond rather well to the response rank at which a curve breaks off into its steep final plunge. The dashed line at the lower right of the figure represents the French curve extrapolated to a sample of 1000 Ss, the number tested by Kent and Rosanoff and by Russell and Jenkins. The extrapolation indicates that 1000 French students would give about 250 different responses per stimulus, as compared with 145 in the Kent-Rosanoff norms and only 90 in the Russell-Jenkins data. Thus, the French student seems to be drawing more widely than the American from his pool of associations, and this in spite of the fact that the total French vocabulary is smaller than the total English vocabulary.

In this connection, it is interesting to note that the French workmen have a slightly shallower curve than the French students. The 115 workmen gave both a median and a mean of 51 different responses per stimulus. Because of the shallower slope, 1000 French workmen would be expected to give more different responses per item than 1000 French students.

Lambert and Moore concluded that in relative diversity of responses their "bilingual group presents different distributions when using the two languages, behaving like the English-Canadians when responding in French and more like the French-Canadians and French-French when responding in French" (Lambert & Moore, 1966, p. 315). Actually the bilingual group did not differ greatly according to the language they used, giving 44.8% high-ranking responses in English and 40.2% in French; in comparison, the English-Canadian monolinguals gave 52.2% and the French-Canadian monolinguals, 37.1%. Furthermore, the rank-frequency slopes of the bilinguals were −1.1 in both languages.

Jenkins and Russell (1960) have suggested increasing "test-wiseness" or "test-docility" to account for the greater communality existing in current American norms than in those of 1910. Perhaps the same hypothesis can be used to explain the greater communality among American than among French students and among students than among workers, since the first group in each pair would be expected to be the more "test-wise." The comparability of the Australian, English, and American norms introduces a note of caution, however, since it is not clear that students in all three countries are equally "test wise." Other reasons for doubting the value of this hypothesis have been given previously (Rosenzweig, 1964, p. 67).

Similarity of Content Among Studies

Similarity measured by identity of high-ranking responses. A simple and frequently used measure of similarity of responses among normative studies is to count the number of items for which the primary responses are identical. This method can even be used to compare norms in different languages, to the extent that confidence can be placed in the translation. Thus, Esper (1918), testing American students with 50 stimuli corresponding to those that others had used in Germany, reported that 35 of the 50 primary responses were equivalent for the two groups. Similarly, I reported (Rosenzweig, 1957) that the primary responses of French students agreed with those of the American students tested by Russell and Jenkins in 48 cases out of 99. (The base was 99 instead of 100 because of the the *sheep-mutton* problem mentioned above, p. 97.) Russell and Meseck (1959) reported 47 cases of agreement of primary responses between their German norms and the American ones. I later tabulated such agreements among English, French, German, and Italian norms (Rosenzweig, 1961, Table II, p. 349). Among these four languages, the greater the frequency with which a particular primary response was given within one language, the more likely was that response to agree in meaning with the primary responses to corresponding items in the other languages. This finding could not, however, be extended to relations between the Polish norms and those of the other four languages, according to Kurcz (1966). In contrast to the rather high numbers of agreements among student groups (including even groups who speak different languages), the responses of the French workmen agree with those of the French students in only 39 cases out of 98.

Lambert and Moore (1966) reported that their English-Canadian monolinguals showed 78% identity of primary responses with the American students of Russell and Jenkins. In contrast, their French-Canadian monolinguals showed only 44% identity of primaries with the 1957 French student norms.

Similarity measured by group overlap coefficients. For comparisons of normative studies made in the same language, a group overlap coefficient has been devised that takes all responses into account, instead of considering only those of high rank. This coefficient is similar in principle to the coefficients of "mutual frequency," "mutual relatedness," or "overlap" that have been used to quantify the commonness of associative responses made by the same group of Ss to different stimuli (Jenkins & Cofer, 1957; Bousfield, Whitmarsh, & Berkowitz, 1960; Deese, 1962). The group overlap coefficient, however, measures overlap of responses of two different groups to the same stimulus. The method of calculation of the coefficient is described and illustrated in Rosenzweig (1964). Since the coefficient is calculated in terms of proportions, the groups being compared do not have to be equal in number.

Group overlap coefficients were calculated in order to compare the French student and worker norms. The mean coefficient was 0.421. Group overlap coefficients between American student and worker[9] groups were found to be significantly higher than those between the French groups; the American mean was 0.521. When the responses of French male and female students were compared, the mean coefficient was 0.541. (The foregoing comparisons are given in greater detail in Rosenzweig, 1964.) The similarity was found to be even greater between English-speaking students among different countries: American-Australian, 0.608; American-English, 0.608, and Australian-English, 0.605 (Rosenzweig & Miller, 1966).

The French worker and student norms are thus seen to show relatively low overlap, as compared with other paired groups. This can probably be attributed to idiosyncratic features of the workers' responses, as will be brought out in the next section.

Lambert and Moore (1966) computed group overlap coefficients among the norms of their various Canadian groups and American students. Not surprisingly, the bilinguals showed greater overlap with monolingual French-Canadians when the bilinguals were tested in French than when tested in English (0.54 vs. 0.36); overlap of the bilinguals was not, however, much greater with the English-Canadian monolinguals in English than in French (0.45 vs. 0.40).

Form Classes of Responses

In an early French study on word associations (Bourdon, 1895), it was noted that the subjects tended to give responses that were of the same grammatical category as the stimuli. This has been verified many times since, with adult Ss who spoke other languages. The tendency to give a response of the same form class as the stimulus is, however, weak among young children, and it increases with age and education, as has been demonstrated with both American children (Ervin, 1957, 1961; Brown & Berko, 1960) and French children (Rosenzweig & Menahem, 1962).

A classification of the primary responses of French and American students and workers in terms of grammatical classes of stimuli and responses has been presented and analyzed in detail elsewhere (Rosenzweig, 1964). Here we need only note that agreement in part of speech between stimulus and primary response is high for American students (82 cases out of 100), for American workers (88/100), and for French students (87/100), but such agreement between stimulus and response is low for French workers (45/100). It is particularly in failing to give opposite or adjective-adjective responses that the French workmen deviate from the responses of the French students.

In giving responses that did not agree in form class with the stimuli, the French workmen resemble children. This suggested that formal education as well as age might be important in the development of what has heretofore been regarded as the typical adult form of response. However, a comparison between the least educated and the

[9]The data for American workers were obtained from a set of protocols very kindly furnished to me by Professor Margaret E. Tresselt.

most educated groups of workmen revealed essentially no difference between them either in form classes of responses or in percentage giving the same primary responses as the students. Perhaps social class, rather than educational level, is the important variable here. At any rate, it is clear that adult members of the same "language community" may differ significantly in associative responses.

Superordinate Responses

Jenkins and Russell (1960) have called attention to the striking decrease in the use of superordinate responses by American Ss since 1910—this decrease accompanying the increase in frequency of the primary responses. Using 39 superordinate responses identified by a panel of Ss they found that the use of these responses was only about half as frequent in 1952 as in 1910.

Similar analyses were made with the French norms and with responses of American workers. Two facts appear from these results: (1) In both the United States and France, superordinate responses of high rank are about twice as frequent among workers as among students. (2) Each French group gives only about half as many superordinates of high rank as the corresponding American group. If the decline in use of superordinate responses during the last 50 years in the United States merits our attention, then the relative rarity of superordinates in the French norms should not go unnoticed either. Lambert and Moore found that their French-Canadian students gave as high a proportion of superordinate responses as American or English-Canadian students. This " . . . eliminates the possibility that the French language limits superordinates in some way . . . ." (Lambert & Moore, 1966, p. 320).

Sex Differences in Associations?

Most studies with the Kent-Rosanoff list have pooled the responses of male and female Ss, it evidently having been assumed that there is no sex difference in word associations. It seems desirable to inquire whether this treatment is justified or whether there may, in fact, be significant differences in the associative habits of men and women.

Schellenberg (1930) found that women college students showed greater communality of response (i.e., gave their primary responses with significantly higher frequencies) than did the men students. Russell and Jenkins (1954, and this volume) did not tabulate their norms separately for the sexes. In an earlier report, however, they suggested that their finding of greater associative clustering in recall by women would be consistent with higher communality of response among the women (Jenkins & Russell, 1952). (We will see later that this conclusion is open to question.) Tresselt *et al.* (1955) have presented frequencies of primary responses for young adult men and women in the United States. Inspection of their table reveals only a slight tendency for the women to show a greater frequency of primary responses. In 53 out of the 100 cases, the women had the greater frequency; in two cases, the critical ratio of the difference found by Tresselt *et al.* was over 3.0 ($p < .001$). In five other cases, the proportion of Ss giving a popular (but not necessarily primary) response differed significantly between the sexes. Tresselt *et al.* conclude, " . . . the stimulus-words which elicit sex differences should be noted if communality is being utilized as a measure for random sampling of subjects" (p. 153). It would appear to be worthwhile, then, not to assume that men and women do not differ in their responses; rather, we will compare their responses in some detail.

The norms given in this volume for French students are presented separately for men and women, except that the responses that occurred only once are pooled. (The number of unique responses for each sex is shown.) As has been mentioned above, the group overlap coefficients for the men and women students had a mean of 0.541, and the primary responses of the men and women are the same in 75 out of the 100 cases. (This includes five cases where two responses were tied for primary position for one of the sexes.) In the study of Tresselt *et al.*, the primary responses of the men and women were the same in 82 of the 100 cases. (This includes four cases where two responses were tied for one sex.) Over the 100 items, the percentage of French women giving the primary response of their group was 20.7%, while the percentage of men giving their primary was 23.1%. For 34 items, there was a higher percentage of women giving their primary than of men giving their primary; for 65 items the men's percentage was the greater, and there was one tie. The proportion of cases for which the men showed greater consensus on the primary than did the women was significantly different from chance at better than the .01 level.

It should be noted that in the French study of association clustering in recall, the women showed somewhat more clusters in their responses than did the men (Rosenzweig, 1957). A similar finding had been reported for American Ss (Jenkins & Russell, 1952). Amount of clustering and frequency of the primary response have both been considered to be measures of the strength of associative bonds. When the results obtained from French men and French women are compared, however, the two measures point in opposite directions. The amount of clustering indicates that the women have stronger associations, but the relative frequencies of primary responses—the more direct measure—indicates that French men have stronger associations than the women. The failure of agreement between these two measures is embarrassing for current theory and cannot be reconciled on the basis of the existing data. Without analysis by sex of the Ss, this test of theory could not have been made.

Occurrences of differences in primary responses of men and women. The differences in primary responses between the two sexes occurred especially for items where the primary accounted for a relatively small proportion of the responses and was thus rather unstable. If we take the 25 primary responses with the highest frequencies among the French women, all 25 agree with the corresponding primary responses of the men; of the next 25, 23 agree; of the third set of 25 responses, 15 agree; of the 25 responses of lowest frequency among the women, only 12 agree with the primary responses of the men. When a similar analysis is made for the English data of Tresselt *et al.* (1955), the respective numbers of agreements are 25, 23, 21, and 13. Thus, the more frequent the primary response is in one sample, the more stable it is from sample to sample. (The somewhat greater agreement between the sexes in English than in French is consistent with the generally higher frequencies of primary responses in English as compared to French.)

It should not be concluded, however, that differences in primaries between the two sexes arise solely from statistical variability where no associative habit dominates the responses. Rather, analysis of the instances of disagreement reveals further regularity. We have mentioned above that responses that are the opposite of the stimuli are in many cases stable even across languages (Rosenzweig, 1961), and Carroll, Kjeldergaard, and Carton (1962) have demonstrated that responses to opposite-evoking stimuli account for much of the communality of responses to the Kent-Rosanoff list. Classification of opposites is not simple, especially as regards the distinction between opposite and coordinate relations; for example, Carroll *et al.* classify *man-woman* among their opposite stimulus-response pairs. We have therefore considered both opposite and coordinate responses. In Table 3 are listed all the 17 cases in which the primaries of the French men and women differed and in which one of the primaries was either an opposite or a coordinate response (or both). It will be seen that in the great majority of these cases, it is the primary response of the men that is the opposite or coordinate. Items 4, 6, and 86 are among the list of opposite-evoking stimuli of Carroll *et al.*, and in two of these three cases the men give an opposite primary response while the women do not, while for item 86 the situation is reversed. Furthermore, the majority of the primaries of the French men in Table 3 agree in meaning with the American norms. Thus, the failure of agreement between primaries of French men and women arises chiefly in cases in which the French women depart from the usual opposite or coordinate relationship; in three of the cases, in fact, their primary response is not even of the same part of speech as the stimulus. In this respect, as well as in the lesser frequencies of their primary responses, the French women differ more from English-speaking Ss than do the French men.

While there thus appear to be some systematic differences between the male and female French students in primary responses, it must be remembered that these appeared only when we set out specifically to analyze differences. For most of the items, the tendency to respond in terms of opposite or coordinate responses was strong enough to determine the primaries of both sexes. When a representative sample of items was taken, there was no significant difference in the percentage of all responses having the same grammatical class as the stimulus—in fact, the women gave 75% as against 68% for the men (Rosenzweig & Menahem, 1962). Similarly, although, as we have just seen, the men had a somewhat greater frequency of primary responses than the women, the rank-frequency data for the two sexes almost coincide on the log-log plot, and the slopes cannot be distinguished. Thus, the Kent-Rosanoff stimuli (whether in the original or in French translation) appear to elicit quite similar sets of responses from men and women. Systematic sex differences in the French student samples show up almost exclusively for items for which neither sex shows a primary response of high frequency.

SUMMARY

The Kent-Rosanoff list was translated into French and administered as a group test. Word association norms have been prepared for the following groups of Ss: (*1*) Students at the Sorbonne and Parisian lycées. The testing was done in 1955-1956, and separate norms were prepared for the two sexes (184 women and 104 men); (*2*) one

TABLE 3 *Examples of Differences in Primary Responses between French Women and Men Students*

Item	Stimulus	Women's Primary	Class[a]	Men's Primary	Class[a]
4	Maladie	Lit	–	Santé	O
6	Profond	Mer	A-N	Creux	O
9	Montagne	Neige	–	Plaine	O
17	Papillon	Aile	–	Fleur	C
27	Fleuve	Eau	S	Rivière	C, O (?)
30	Fenêtre	Rideau	–	Porte	C
33	Pied	Chaussure	–	Main	C, O (?)
37	Sommeil	Lit	–	Repos	C
50	Estomac	Digestion	–	Ventre	C
60	Evangile	Bible	C	Dieu	
62	Agneau	Doux	N-A	Brebis	C
64	Villa	Mer	–	Maison	C
70	Tête	Cheveux	–	Pied Veau[b]	C, O (?)
85	Lion	Crinière	–	Tigre	C
86	Joie	Tristesse	O	Bonheur	C
90	Bébé	Rose	N-A	Enfant	C
91	Lune	Nuit	–	Soleil Rousse[b]	C, O (?)

[a]A-N = adjective stimulus, noun respones; N-A = noun stimulus, adjective response; O = response is opposite of stimulus; C = response is coordinate with stimulus; S = response is the superordinate of the stimulus.

[b]Two responses were tied for primary position.

hundred fifteen workers in the construction industry, tested in 1960-1961.

Several characteristics of the French norms were pointed out. The present availability of Kent-Rosanoff norms gathered in several countries and in several languages has allowed investigators to make a number of comparisons and to test hypotheses about verbal habits:

(*1*) Subjects in France (as well as in Germany, Italy, and Poland) show a greater diversity of responses than do *S*s in the United States (or in Australia or England). This is demonstrated by the fact that only about one-fifth of the French students give the primary response (averaged over all 100 items), but almost two-fifths of American students give the primary response. It is also shown by the related fact that the rank-frequency plot has a slope of -1.0 for the data of French students and -0.9 for French workers, while it falls at a steeper slope for English-speaking *S*s (American, -1.4; Australian, -1.5; English, -1.4; Canadian, -1.3).

(*2*) The responses of French students are rather similar in content to those of American students, the primary responses being equivalent in meaning in 48 cases. The primary responses of German students agree with the French students' primaries in 45 cases, and with the American primaries in 48 cases. Polish primary responses show somewhat fewer agreements with those of English, French, or German, but in many cases in which the primaries were not equivalent, the secondary or tertiary responses did agree between Polish and the other languages. In contrast to the relatively high numbers of agreement among students who speak different West European languages, groups who speak the same language do not necessarily show greater or even equal numbers of agreements. This is demonstrated by the fact that the primary responses of the French workmen agree with those of the French students in only 39 cases.

(*3*) Within the same language, similarity between the responses of two groups of *S*s can be measured by the *group overlap coefficient*. The mean group overlap coefficient for responses of French workers and students is 0.421. This is significantly less than either the coefficient of overlap between American workers and students—0.521—or the overlap between male and female French students—0.541.

(*4*) It has previously been reported that most responses of adults agree in part of speech with the stimuli that evoked them. This can be tested more readily in French than in English, since there is less ambiguity about the grammatical classification of an isolated word in French than in English. With the French students, 87 primary responses agree in part of speech with their stimuli, but with the workers there are only 45 such agreements. Thus, the previous generalization requires restriction, since it does not apply well to responses of French workmen.

(5) Responses that are superordinates of the stimuli are less frequently given by French than by American Ss, and less frequently by students than by workers. French-Canadian students, however, gave as high a proportion of superordinate responses as did American or English-Canadian students.

(6) Separate tabulations of the responses of male and female students in France allowed comparisons to be made between them. The primary responses of the two groups are the same in 75 cases, and the group overlap coefficients average 0.541. Where primary responses of the men and women differ, there appear to be some systematic differences in response tendencies. Overall, however, the men and women students do not differ significantly in either the slope of their rank-frequency functions or the proportion of Ss giving responses of the same form class as the stimuli.

REFERENCES

Banissoni, P., & Nencini, R. (1961). Prime note sull'applicazione collettiva di un test di parole associate. *Atti dell' XI Congresso degli Psicologi Italiani.* Milan: Vita e Pensiero, 1957, p. 252. (Cited from Chiari, S., *Rivista di Psicologia,* 55, 143-155.)

Bourdon, B. (1895). Observations comparatives sur la reconnaissance, la discrimination et l'association. *Revue Philosophique de la France et de l'Étranger* 40, 153-185.

Bousfield, W. A., Whitmarsh, G. A., & Berkowitz, H. (1960). Partial response identities in associative clustering. *Journal of General Psychology,* 63, 233-238.

Brown, R., & Berko, J. (1960). Word association and the acquisition of grammar. *Child Development* 31, 1-14.

Carroll, J. B., Kjeldergaard, P. M., & Carton, A. S. (1962). Number of opposites vs. number of primaries as a response measure in free association tests. *Journal of Verbal Learning and Verbal Behavior* 1, 22-30.

Chiari, S. (1959). Associazioni di parole ed abitudini verbali. *Rivista di Psicologia* 53, 1-16.

Deese, J. (1962). On the structure of associative meaning. *Psychological Review,* 69, 161-175.

Ervin, S. M. (1957). Grammar and classification. *American Psychologist* 12, 370.

Ervin, S. M. (1961). Age changes in the determinants of word association. *American Journal of Psychology* 74, 361-372.

Esper, E. A. (1918). A contribution to the experimental study of analogy. *Psychological Review* 25, 468-487.

Jenkins, P. M., & Cofer, C. N. (1957). An exploratory study of discrete free associations to compound verbal stimuli. *Psychological Reports* 3, 599-602.

Jenkins, J. J., & Russell, W. A. (1952). Associative clustering during recall. *Journal of Abnormal and Social Psychology* 47, 818-821.

Jenkins, J. J., & Russell, W. A. (1960). Systematic changes in word association norms: 1910-1952. *Journal of Abnormal and Social Psychology* 60, 293-304.

Keene, C. M. (1951). Communality of response on a word-association test: A study of standardization procedures and an attempt to forecast moderate emotional maladjustment. Unpublished doctoral dissertation, Stanford University.

Kent, G. H., & Rosanoff, A. J. (1910). A study of association in insanity. I. Association in normal subjects. *American Journal of Insanity* 67, 37-96, 317-390.

Kurcz, I. (1966). Inter-language comparison of word-association responses. *International Journal of Psychology* 1, 151-161.

Lambert, W. E., & Moore, N. (1966). Word-association responses: Comparisons of American and French monolinguals with Canadian monolinguals and bilinguals. *Journal of Personality and Social Psychology* 3, 313-320.

Levi, M. (1949). An analysis of the influence of two different cultures on responses to the Rosanoff free association test. Unpublished Master's thesis, University of Chicago.

Meals, D. W., Herrick, C. J., & Merow, R. (1948). *Scoring sheet for reaction word experiment.* Pennsylvania (Mimeo.)

O'Connor, J. (1928). *Born that way.* Baltimore: Williams & Wilkins.

Rosenzweig, M. R. (1957). Études sur l'association des mots. *Année Psychologique* 57, 23-32.

Rosenzweig, M. R. (1959). Comparisons between French and English word association norms. *American Psychologist* 14, 363.

Rosenzweig, M. R. (1961). Comparison among word association responses in English, French, German, and Italian. *American Journal of Psychology* 74, 347-360.

Rosenzweig, M. R. (1962). Comparison among word association responses in English, French, German, and Italian. *Proceedings of the Sixteenth International Congress of Psychology, Bonn, 1960.* Amsterdam: North-Holland Publ., pp. 704-705.

Rosenzweig, M. R. (1964). Word associations of French workmen: Comparisons with associations of French students and American workmen and students. *Journal of Verbal Learning and Verbal Behavior* 3, 57-69.

Rosenzweig, M. R., & McNeill, D. (1962). Uses of the semantic count in experimental studies of verbal behavior. *American Journal of Psychology* 75, 492-495.

Rosenzweig, M. R., & Menahem, R. (1962). Age, sexe et niveau d'instruction comme facteurs déterminants dans les associations de mots. *Année Psychologique* 62, 45-61.

Rosenzweig, M. R., & Miller, K. M. (1966). Comparisons of word association responses obtained in the United States, Australia and England. *Journal of Verbal Learning and Verbal Behavior* 5, 35-41.

Russell, W. A., & Jenkins, J. J. (1954). The complete Minnesota norms for responses to 100 words from the Kent-Rosanoff word association test. Technical Report No. 11, University of Minnesota, ONR, Contract No. N8 onr-66216.

Russell, W. A., & Meseck, O. R. (1959). Der Einfluss der Assoziation auf des Erinnern von Worten in der Deutschen, Franzosischen, und Englischen Sprache. *Zeitschrift für Experimentalle und Angewandte Psychologie* **6**, 191-211.

Schellenberg, P. E. (1930). A group free-association test for college students. Unpublished doctoral dissertation, University of Minnesota.

Skinner, B. F. (1930). The distribution of Associated words. *Psychological Record* **1**, 71-76.

Tresselt, M. E., Leeds, D. S., & Mayzner, M. S. (1955). The Kent-Rosanoff word association: II. A comparison of sex differences in response frequencies. *Journal of Genetic Psychology* **87**, 149-153.

Woodrow, H., & Lowell F. (1916). Children's association frequency tables. *Psychological Monographs* **22** (5, Whole No. 97).

Woodworth, R. S. (1938). *Experimental psychology*. New York: Holt.

1. TABLE

Students						Workers		
No.	Response	Total	Female	Male		No.	Response	Total
1.	chaise	159	110	49		1.	ronde (rond)	27
2.	bois	18	11	7		2.	chaise (chaises)	19
3.	ronde (rond)	10	9	1		3.	bois	11
4.	pied	8	6	2		4.	manger	7
5.	nappe	5	4	1		5.	pied (pieds)	7
6.	meuble	4	3	1		6.	meuble	3
7.	repas	4	0	4		7.	verre	3
8.	verre	4	1	3		8.	assiette	2
9.	bureau	3	0	3		9.	carrée	2
10.	écrire	3	1	2		10.	couvert (couverte)	2
11.	maison	3	3	0		11.	nappe	2
12.	noire (noir)	3	1	2		12.	repas	2
13.	plume	3	2	1		13-40.	(f = 1)	28
14.	tabouret	3	1	2				
15.	banc	2	0	2				
16.	cahier	2	2	0				
17.	école	2	2	0				
18.	écriture	2	1	1				
19.	encrier	2	1	1				
20.	logarithme	2	0	2				
21.	manger	2	0	2				
22.	tapis	2	2	0				
23.	vase	2	2	0				
24-63.	(f = 1)	40	22	18				

Workers 13-40. (f = 1): banc, basse, bouge, cuisine, dessus, diné, école, encrier, fable, grince, hôtel, Jeannette, lit, musique, nourriture, de nuit, pliante, planche, propre, Pythagore, sale, sert, servie, siège, tablier, tréteau, vernis, viande

Students 24-63. (f = 1): acajou, aime, assiette, auteur, besoin, boire, bridge, chêne, chose, classe, cuisine, dessein, dur, encre, fauteuil, hier, instrument, jardin, lampe, lit, loi, Louis XVI, marbre, nombre, objet, pain, papier, planche, plancher, plate, plateau, salle à manger, silence, stylo, tablette, tablier, taire, tournante, verte, vin

2. SOMBRE

Students						Workers		
No.	Response	Total	Female	Male		No.	Response	Total
1.	clair (claire)	130	83	47		1.	noir (noire)	30
2.	nuit	39	27	12		2.	nuit	23
3.	noir (noire)	36	26	10		3.	clair (claire)	12
4.	obscur (obscure)	13	9	4		4.	gris	5
5.	ombre	6	3	3		5.	lumière	3
6.	ciel	5	5	0		6.	soleil	3
7.	triste	5	2	3		7.	esprit	2
8.	obscurité	4	1	3		8.	nuage	2
9.	arbre	3	3	0		9.	nuageux	2
10.	bois	3	1	2		10.	obscure	2
11.	lumière	3	1	2		11-41.	(f = 1)	31
12.	couleur	2	1	1				
13.	dark	2	1	1				
14.	forêt	2	2	0				
15.	gai	2	2	0				
16.	pièce	2	1	1				
17.	soleil	2	0	2				
18-46.	(f = 1)	29	16	13				

Workers 11-41. (f = 1): air, bateau, cave, ciel, coule, couleur, sans couleur, la classe, crépuscule, désespoir, dimanche, éclair, effrayant, épais, foncé, gaie, image, à jeun, jour, manteau, obscurité, ombre, pensée, pièce, rideau, rouge, ruelle, soir, tableau, triste, vent

Students 18-46. (f = 1): blanc, chasuble, clarté, classe, coin, crépuscule, désespoir, destinée, dimanche, éclairé, éteint, fade, foncé, fort, froid, lumineux, luminosité, manteau, neurasthénique, nuage, opaque, peur, plat, profond, robe, sinistre, soir, tunnel, vide

3. MUSIQUE

	Students					Workers	
No.	Response	Total	Female	Male	No.	Response	Total
1.	note (notes)	50	37	13	1.	douce	20
2.	piano	21	15	6	2.	classique	9
3.	chant	19	12	7	3.	note	9
4.	Bach	13	10	3	4.	chant	6
5.	Beethoven	12	6	6	5.	violon	6
6.	jazz	12	2	10	6.	jazz (de jazz)	5
7.	douce (doux)	10	6	4	7.	légère	3
8.	violon	9	7	2	8.	son	3
9.	harmonie	7	7	0	9.	agréable	2
10.	belle (beau)	6	6	0	10.	art (d'arts)	2
11.	Chopin	6	5	1	11.	danse	2
12.	mélodie	6	4	2	12.	gaie	2
13.	Mozart	6	3	3	13.	harmonieuse	2
14.	symphonie	6	2	4	14.	instrument	2
15.	son	5	4	1	15.	joie	2
16.	art	3	2	1	16.	orchestre	2
17.	chambre (de chambre)	3	1	2	17.	trompette	2
18.	classique	3	2	1	18-53.	(f = 1)	36
19.	concert	3	3	0			
20.	guitare	3	1	2			
21.	instrument	3	2	1			
22.	silence	3	0	3			
23.	solfège	3	1	2			
24.	air	2	1	1			
25.	bruit	2	1	1			
26.	Debussy	2	2	0			
27.	dessein	2	1	1			
28.	disque	2	2	0			
29.	douceur	2	2	0			
30.	harpe	2	1	1			
31.	joie	2	0	2			
32.	orchestre	2	2	0			
33.	papier	2	2	0			
34.	peinture	2	1	1			
35.	pick-up	2	1	1			
36.	poésie	2	2	0			
37.	portée	2	2	0			
38.	sonate	2	2	0			
39.	Wagner	2	1	1			
40-83.	(f = 1)	44	23	21			

Workers 18-53. (f = 1): accordéon, l'air, amusante, Bach, brillante, bruit, chausson, Chopin, clairon, clarinette, cri, danser, dessin, disque, enchantée, entraînante, fausse, frère, gamme, guitare, hall, harmonica, jouée, moderne, modulation, Mozart, pain, piano, Elvis Presley, recueil, romance, solfège, silence, sonore, symphonie, typique

Students 40-83. (f = 1): agréable, agrément, âme, amour, amusement, animal, Armstrong, beauté, cahier, clarinette, clé, danse, délassement, diaphone, do, dodécaphonique, durée, évasion, facile, fleur, frère, gaie, harmonica, instrumentale, joli, laid, lent, loisir, militaire, moeurs, morceau, musicien, nuit, orgue, plaisir, polyphonique, Ravel, Schubert, soir, sonore, symphonique, trompette, T. S. F., valse

4. MALADIE

	Students					Workers	
No.	Response	Total	Female	Male	No.	Response	Total
1.	lit	31	22	9	1.	grave	25
2.	santé	25	8	17	2.	contagieuse	10
3.	fièvre	15	15	0	3.	docteur	7
4.	mort	13	6	7	4.	hôpital	7
5.	médecin	12	7	5	5.	fièvre	5
6.	docteur	11	5	6	6.	rougeole	4
7.	grippe	9	4	5	7.	grippe	3
8.	rougeole	9	7	2	8.	santé	3
9.	grave	8	3	5	9.	bénigne	2
10.	tuberculose	8	6	2	10.	chien	2
11.	sommeil	6	4	2	11.	coeur	2
12.	contagieuse	5	3	2	12.	imaginaire	2
13.	souffrance	5	4	1	13.	malade	2
14.	cancer	4	4	0	14.	mortelle	2
15.	hôpital	4	2	2	15.	portant	2
16.	remède	4	3	1	16-50.	(f = 1)	35
17.	douleur	3	1	2			
18.	ennui	3	1	2			

Workers 16-50. (f = 1): alité, appendicite, casserole, cancer, cochon, curable, congestion,

4. MALADIE (contd)

Students

No.	Response	Total	Female	Male
19.	mal (maux)	3	3	0
20.	malaise	3	3	0
21.	terrible	3	2	1
22.	typhoïde	3	2	1
23.	choléra	2	1	1
24.	faiblesse	2	2	0
25.	guérison	2	2	0
26.	homme	2	2	0
27.	horrible	2	2	0
28.	laid (laide)	2	2	0
29.	médicament	2	2	0
30.	peste	2	1	1
31.	poumon (poumons)	2	0	2
32.	rhume	2	1	1
33.	scarlatine	2	2	0
34.	variole	2	0	2
35.	vieux (vieille)	2	2	0
36-110.	(f = 1)	75	50	25

air, alarmant, amère, angine, animal, aveugle, barbe,
bien-portant, blancheur, bleue, chagrin, chose,
chronique, cliché, coeur, contagion, crainte,
cutiréaction, défectueux, désagréable, enfant,
ennuyeux, état, faible, fané, feuille, folie,
grammaire, hypocondrie, incommodation, infection,
infirme, joie, laideur, longue, malade, malheur,
mauvais, mentale, microbe, morbide, mortelle, pâle,
pathologique, phtisie, piqûre, pitié, psychiâtrie,
psychose, pus, réflexion, rose, sain, Sainte Anne,
sang, sangsue, sciatique, scorbut, sécurité sociale,
sick, sinistre, soins, spirochettose, syphilis,
thermomètre, torture, toux, triste, typhus, ulcère,
varice, vérole, vert, viscère, vieillesse

Workers

No.	Response	Total

coqueluche, désespoir, état, fatigue,
du foie, incurable, infirme, infantile, infectieuse, lit, mauvaise,
médecin, médecine, mort, maudite,
mère, métro, mal, malheur, nerveux,
nature, plaindre, mauvaise santé,
soleil, sombre, souffrance, tête,
des yeux
(Illegible - 2)

5. HOMME

Students

No.	Response	Total	Female	Male
1.	femme	184	109	75
2.	grand	6	5	1
3.	être	6	3	3
4.	animal	5	4	1
5.	enfant	4	4	0
6.	mâle	3	2	1
7.	Adam	2	2	0
8.	amour	2	2	0
9.	barbe	2	1	1
10.	beau	2	2	0
11.	belle	2	1	1
12.	chapeau	2	2	0
13.	cheval	2	1	1
14.	espèce	2	2	0
15.	force	2	1	1
16.	intelligent	2	1	1
17.	Jean	2	1	1
18.	mari	2	2	0
19.	pantalon	2	2	0
20.	viril	2	1	1
21-72.	(f = 1)	52	36	16

anatomie, bébé, blanc, blond, bon, bruit, brun, carré,
célèbre, chauve, chien, complexité, costume, débile,
douleur, être humain, fort, froid, fromage, gai,
géant, homme, humanité, individu, intelligence, Jean-
Luc, méchant, mort, muscle, nègre, nez, noir, orgueil,
Paul, pensée, père, peuple, philosophie, plaisir,
poil, raisonnable, sérieux, solide, supérieur, tabac,
travail, type, vie, virilité, visage, vivant, voix

Workers

No.	Response	Total
1.	femme	32
2.	fort	16
3.	grand	9
4.	humain	4
5.	jeune	4
6.	travail	4
7.	blond	2
8.	brave	2
9.	enfant	2
10.	froid	2
11.	grenouille	2
12	intelligent	2
13.	viril	2
14-44.	(f = 1)	31

Adam, adulte, d'affaires, aisé,
athlète, beau, belliqueux, blanc,
bon, chaire, doux, effeminé, d'Etat,
force, habit, Hercule, inconnu, loi,
masculin, des neiges, pas, père,
pomme, robuste, des sciences, seul,
simple, songe, tranquille, végétal,
vieux
(Illegible - 1)

6. PROFOND

	Students					Workers	
No.	Response	Total	Female	Male	No.	Response	Total
1.	creux	31	13	18	1.	puits	15
2.	mer	27	16	11	2.	trou	11
3.	puits	27	20	7	3.	loin	9
4.	trou	17	10	7	4.	gouffre	6
5.	noir	14	13	1	5.	sommeil	6
6.	sombre	10	8	2	6.	abîme	5
7.	abîme	8	7	1	7.	noir	4
8.	eau (l'eau)	8	6	2	8.	silence	4
9.	rivière	8	4	4	9.	creux	3
10.	superficiel	8	4	4	10.	sentiment	3
11.	étroit	7	4	3	11.	vide	3
12.	silence	7	5	2	12.	bas	2
13.	gouffre	6	3	3	13.	couloir	2
14.	bas	5	4	1	14.	danger	2
15.	clair	5	2	3	15.	fossé	2
16.	obscur	5	2	3	16.	grand (très grand)	2
17.	haut	4	1	3	17.	haut	2
18.	large	4	2	2	18.	large	2
19.	grand	3	3	0	19.	long	2
20.	léger	3	2	1	20.	mer (la mer)	2
21.	précipice	3	3	0	21.	sombre	2
22.	ravin	3	2	1	22.	très	2
23.	vide	3	3	0	23-45.	(f = 1)	23
24.	adjectif	2	1	1			
25.	doux	2	0	2			
26.	dur	2	2	0			
27.	étang	2	2	0			
28.	long	2	2	0			
29.	net	2	2	0			
30.	océan	2	0	2			
31.	plat	2	2	0			
32.	vaste	2	2	0			
33-86.	(f = 1)	54	34	20			

Workers 23-45. (f = 1):
béant, dangereux, éloigné, émoi, fleuve, fond, sans fin, immense, incrusté, mètre, 8 mètres, mine, océan, oubli, pensée, plat, profondeur, ravin, rouge, soupir, sur, tournevis, travail
(Illegible - 1)

Students 33-86. (f = 1):
angoisse, bleu, bois, cave, caverne, ciel, coeur, creuser, danger, dangereux, élevé, épais, esprit, fleuve, fond, fossé, gris, infini, jaune, juste, lac, laid, loin, lumière, lumineux, maigre, mare, méchant, miroir, moi, néant, ouvert, petit, peu, peu profond, peur, plafond, plein, profond, recherche, Rorschach, salle, sérieux, sommeil, souffrance, sourd, sujet, surface, troublant, uni, vain, Valéry, vallée, volcan

7. MOU

	Students					Workers	
No.	Response	Total	Female	Male	No.	Response	Total
1.	dur (dure)	107	60	47	1.	dur (dure)	29
2.	flasque	13	10	3	2.	chat (de chat)	6
3.	chat	10	8	2	3.	molle	6
4.	fromage	10	6	4	4.	poumon	5
5.	beurre	9	7	2	5.	viande	5
6.	tendre	7	3	4	6.	beurre	4
7.	caramel	6	5	1	7.	caoutchouc	4
8.	éponge	6	4	2	8.	sable	4
9.	léger	6	4	2	9.	tendre	3
10.	mollusque	6	6	0	10.	contraire de dur	2
11.	chapeau	4	2	2	11.	éponge	2
12.	molle (mou)	4	3	1	12.	flasque	2
13.	pâte	4	3	1	13.	gomme	2
14.	sable	4	3	1	14.	liquide	2
15.	doux	3	3	0	15.	mastic	2
16.	épais	3	2	1	16	pâteux	2
17.	limace	3	2	1	17-50.	(f = 1)	34
18.	méduse	3	2	1			
19.	bouse	2	0	2			
20.	caoutchouc	2	2	0			
21.	coussin	2	0	2			
22.	doigt	2	2	0			
23.	élastique	2	1	1			
24.	foie	2	1	1			
25.	gras	2	2	0			

Workers 17-50. (f = 1):
argile, boeuf, calme, caramel, chair, clou, comme, déliquescent, détendu, écoeurant, enfance, enfant, enfoncer, l'été, extensible, extra, gras, indolent, invertébré, lâche, lent, limace, loin, malade, médiocre, mélasse, l'or, oreiller, de plaisir, ragoût, sans résistance, terrain,

7. MOU (contd)

Students					Workers		
No.	Response	Total	Female	Male	No.	Response	Total
26.	neige	2	2	0		vache, de veau	
27.	oreiller	2	2	0		(Illegible - 1)	
28.	vase	2	2	0			
29.	veau	2	1	1			
30-87.	(f = 1)	58	36	22			

adjectif, blanc, bleue, cervelle, cheval, chique,
chocolat, colle, compote, confiture, dégout,
désagréable, dilater, ferme, fluide, garçon, gâteau,
gelly, glaise, glue, gouache, graisse, homme, immobile,
inconsistant, indolence, lâche, langue, lent, liquide,
mastic, moëlle, moulin, mousse, muscle, néant, pain,
pieuvre, plastique, plat, plume, pouah, poumon, raide,
rond, roue, rude, sale, savon, sec, sol, solide, sot,
souple, stable, ver, viande, visqueux

8. MANGER

Students					Workers		
No.	Response	Total	Female	Male	No.	Response	Total
1.	boire	108	63	45	1.	boire	17
2.	dormir	26	21	5	2.	faim	12
3.	pain	25	19	6	3.	bien	10
4.	faim	16	10	6	4.	appétit	6
5.	table	7	6	1	5.	pain	6
6.	appétit	4	2	2	6.	dormir	5
7.	dîner	4	4	0	7.	poulet	4
8.	repas	4	2	2	8.	viande	4
9.	viande	4	2	2	9.	chaud	2
10.	assiette	3	2	1	10.	fruit	2
11.	déjeuner	3	1	2	11.	nourriture	2
12.	nourriture	3	3	0	12.	proprement	2
13.	vivre	3	2	1	13.	salade	2
14.	aliment	2	2	0	14-52.	(f = 1)	39
15.	bien	2	1	1			
16.	bois	2	0	2			
17.	courir	2	0	2			
18.	déguster	2	1	1			
19.	gâteau (gâteaux)	2	2	0			
20.	plat (plats)	2	2	0			
21.	saleté (saletés)	2	2	0			
22.	salle	2	1	1			
23-82.	(f = 1)	60	36	24			

aliments, appétissant, assiette,
auberge, avidement, bon, il y a bon,
bruit, casse-croûte, copieusement,
couvert, digérer, dîner, effectif,
à sa faim, froid, goinfre, goulûment,
indigestion, jeûner, lentement,
mâcher, midi, nourrir, comme un ogre,
peu, pommes, salé, sale, salle, sain,
sein, le soir, soupe, sucer, tomate,
victuailles, vie, vite
(Illegible - 2)

action, agréable, attendre, avaler, avoir faim, blanc,
bon, carotte, chaud, chou, comestible, confiture,
convenablement, côtelette, cuiller, digérer, dur,
durée, écrire, engouffrer, essen, faible, fourchette,
fruits, gaudé, geste, goûter, grandir, huîtres,
ingurgiter, inutile, jeûner, lentement, mâcher, mal,
manche, mets, midi, oeuf, ogre, papa, perdu, plaisir,
pomme, raisonnablement, réfectoire, riz, salade,
satisfaction, seul, soupe, sucer, tard, tartine,
verbe, vie, vin, vite, vitesse, voracité

9. MONTAGNE

Students					Workers		
No.	Response	Total	Female	Male	No.	Response	Total
1.	neige	38	28	10	1.	haut (haute)	22
2.	plaine	32	14	18	2.	neige	12
3.	mer	22	15	7	3.	mer	6
4.	Alpes (Alpe)	18	12	6	4.	plaine	4
5.	ski	18	14	4	5.	ski	4
6.	vallée	14	7	7	6.	Alpes	3
7.	hauteur	10	6	4	7.	blanche	3
8.	pic	10	6	4	8.	rocheuse	3
9.	haut (haute)	9	7	2	9.	air	2

9. MONTAGNE (contd)

Students					Workers		

No.	Response	Total	Female	Male		No.	Response	Total
10.	colline	8	4	4		10.	aride	2
11.	escalade	5	4	1		11.	hiver (d'hiver)	2
12.	blanc	4	3	1		12.	Mont-Blanc	2
13.	Mont-Blanc	4	1	3		13.	pierre	2
14.	sommet (sommets)	4	1	3		14.	sommet	2
15.	ciel	3	2	1		15.	vacances	2
16.	cîme	3	3	0		16-60.	(f = 1)	45
17.	mont	3	2	1				
18.	sapin	3	2	1				
19.	vert (verte)	3	3	0				
20.	air	2	1	1				
21.	ascension	2	1	1				
22.	beauté	2	1	1				
23.	belle (beau)	2	2	0				
24.	blancheur	2	2	0				
25.	bleu (bleue)	2	2	0				
26.	bois	2	2	0				
27.	chose	2	1	1				
28.	nuage	2	1	1				
29.	paysage	2	2	2				
30.	ravin	2	1	1				
31.	rivière	2	1	1				
32.	rocher	2	2	0				
33.	rocs	2	0	2				
34.	sport	2	2	0				
35.	vacances	2	2	0				
36-80.	(f = 1)	45	27	18				

Workers 16-60: agréable, air pur, altitude, avalanche, beauté, belle, blanc, chaînes, chapeau, chasse, élevée, énorme, environnante, Everest, falaise, de France, froid, grande, grimper, hauteur, immense, d'Italie, matière, métro, montagnard, monter, neigeuse, noire, plat, plateau, pointu, polaire, Pyrénées, rivière, rocailleuse, russe, Sainte-Geneviève, santé, sport d'hiver, Suisse, vache, vallée, vallon, verte

Students 36-80: abîme, abrupte, alpiniste, altitude, aride, boisée, chalet, Chamonix, chemin, choc, claire, contour, Crête, crevasse, dur, eau, élevée, énorme, escarpée, Everest, fleuve, forme, gabas, grandeur, grimper, hêtre, Himalaya, lac, liberté, lumière, massif, montée, partie, pâtre, pente, pointu, prairie, russe, silence, terre, toits, à vache, vache, val, versant

10. MAISON

Students					Workers		

No.	Response	Total	Female	Male		No.	Response	Total
1.	toit	43	32	11		1.	blanche	9
2.	foyer	19	11	8		2.	toit	8
3.	porte	12	6	6		3.	abri	5
4.	cheminée	11	10	1		4.	habitation	4
5.	famille	10	4	6		5.	villa	4
6.	jardin	10	8	2		6.	belle	3
7.	fenêtre (fenêtres)	9	8	1		7.	campagne	3
8.	campagne (de campagne)	7	3	4		8.	mur	3
9.	chambre	7	5	2		9.	rouge	3
10.	mur (murs)	7	3	4		10.	appartement	2
11.	abri	6	4	2		11.	brique	2
12.	chalet	4	3	1		12.	cabane	2
13.	fumée	4	4	0		13.	carrée	2
14.	basse	3	3	0		14.	chalet	2
15.	blanche	3	1	2		15.	chambre	2
16.	bois	3	1	2		16.	claire	2
17.	brique	3	1	2		17.	confortable	2
18.	chaleur	3	2	1		18.	famille	2
19.	château	3	1	2		19.	foyer	2
20.	confort	3	1	2		20.	jolie	2
21.	home	3	2	1		21.	neuve	2
22.	table	3	2	1		22.	repos (de repos)	2
23.	arbre	2	0	2		23.	tuile	2
24.	cabane	2	1	1		24-67.	(f = 1)	44
25.	case	2	1	1				
26.	chaud (chaude)	2	0	2				
27.	chaumière	2	2	0				
28.	chien	2	1	1				
29.	construction	2	1	1				
30.	cottage	2	2	0				
31.	demeure	2	1	1				
32.	fleur (fleurs)	2	2	0				

Workers 24-67: accueillante, aérer, agréable, Alfort, ardoise, base, basse, centre, chaleur, champêtre, château, chausson, confort, couche, ensoleillé, étage, feu, gens, grand, habitable, habiter, haute, humble, isolée, meublée, quatre murs, particulière, pavillon, petite,

10. MAISON (contd)

Students

No.	Response	Total	Female	Male
33.	feu	2	2	0
34.	habitat	2	0	2
35.	haute	2	2	0
36.	hôtel	2	0	2
37.	neuve	2	0	2
38.	pierre	2	1	1
39.	prairie	2	1	1
40.	rouge	2	2	0
41.	rustique	2	1	1
42.	sécurité	2	2	0
43.	vert	2	1	1
44.	volet	2	2	0
45-112.	(f = 1)	68	44	24

amour, appartement, atelier, âtre, balai, berger, bosse, bruit, chat, chez, cloître, close, confortable, dessin, douceur, douillet, doux, élevée, escalier, façade, faucille, ferme, forestière, froid, gaie, gourbi, gros, hutte, immeuble, intérieur, logis, ma maison, mas, mauvais, mère, moderne, nid, noire, objet, paix, palace, palais, parents, Paris, père, petite, plafond, plancher, propriété, reconstruction, repos, rideau, rue, silence, sol, solide, soumets, tapis, tuile, usine, vacances, vaste, vide, vie, villa, village, ville, volonté

Workers

No.	Response	Total

porte, préfabriquée, riche, rien, rurale, sale, solide, sombre, table, vieille, ville
(Illegible - 1)

11. NOIR

Students

No.	Response	Total	Female	Male
1.	blanc	116	73	43
2.	nuit	16	8	8
3.	rouge	15	9	6
4.	tableau	13	8	5
5.	sombre	12	8	4
6.	clair	9	8	1
7.	encre (d'encre)	8	4	4
8.	triste	7	5	2
9.	couleur	6	5	1
10.	deuil	6	5	1
11.	chat	4	2	2
12.	jaune	4	1	3
13.	obscur	4	2	2
14.	bleu	3	3	0
15.	nègre	3	2	1
16.	profond	3	3	0
17.	robe	3	3	0
18.	cirage	2	2	0
19.	enterrement	2	0	2
20.	foncé	2	1	1
21.	gris	2	2	0
22.	noir	2	0	2
23.	peur	2	1	1
24-67.	(f = 1)	44	29	15

affreux, animal, artichaut, beurre, cave, cheval, chien, ciel, corbeau, crâne, deep, diable, douleur, ébène, enfer, fond, de fumée, grand, jupe, loir, lumière, mauvais, obscurité, pancarte, peinture, philosophie, plat, pull-over, roman, rose, sale, Sénégal, tablier, ténèbres, tristesse, trou, tunnel, vase, vent, verre, vert, vide, vif, voir

Workers

No.	Response	Total
1.	blanc (et blanc)	24
2.	couleur	10
3.	chat	7
4.	sombre	7
5.	nuit	5
6.	bleu	4
7.	cirage	4
8.	deuil	4
9.	rouge	4
10.	triste	4
11.	tableau	3
12.	corbeau	2
13.	gris	2
14-48.	(f = 1)	35

brillant, cafard, chatte, clair, chien, charbon, comme, encre, Espagne, foncé, de fumée, funèbre, pompes funèbres, intentions, jais, jaune, jour, de loup, lumière, nègre, tête de nègre, obscur, opaque, peinture, peur, pot, réflexion, rocher, sale, suie, comme une taupe, taureau, ténèbre, vert, la voiture

12. MOUTON

Students

No.	Response	Total	Female	Male
1.	laine	72	47	25
2.	chèvre	27	14	13
3.	brebis	18	11	7
4.	animal	13	5	8
5.	vache	13	7	6
6.	berger (bergère)	12	8	4
7.	blanc	8	6	2
8.	prairie	7	4	3
9.	pré	7	7	0
10.	agneau (agnelle)	6	3	3
11.	doré	6	4	2
12.	frisé	6	6	0
13.	loup	5	3	2
14.	troupeau	5	2	3
15.	bête	4	4	0
16.	chien	4	4	0
17.	doux	4	2	2
18.	bélier	3	3	0
19.	côtelette	3	1	2
20.	duvernet	3	2	1
21.	herbe	3	3	0
22.	panurge	3	2	1
23.	patte (pattes)	3	1	2
24.	bêler	2	1	1
25.	boeuf	2	0	2
26.	bouc	2	1	1
27.	chat	2	1	1
28.	douceur	2	2	0
29-71.	(f = 1)	43	30	13

abeille, agile, Australie, beefsteak, bergerie, boucher, boucle, campagne, champ, chaume, cheval, cloche, corne, côte, grange, haricot, idiot, involontaire, marron, méchant, merinos, Mont Saint-Michel, montagne, moue, Noël, oie, d'or, ovin, pacage, pâture, pâturage, pied, porc, porte, ragoût, rond, sauce, saut, sauvage, touffu, troupe, vétérinaire, viande

12. AGNEAU

Workers

No.	Response	Total
1.	doux	16
2.	mouton	12
3.	brebis	10
4.	blanc	9
5.	bêle (bêler, bêlant)	8
6.	animal	7
7.	laine	6
8.	loup	4
9.	chèvre	3
10.	maigre	2
11.	tendre	2
12.	veau	2
13-45.	(f = 1)	33

âne, bande, bé, bêlement, berrichon, bible, boeuf, boucher, campagne, chien, chose, Christ, cochon, côtelette, craintif, dodu, douceur, épaule, gentil, gigot, gras, jeune, joli, manger, mignon, Pâques, pascal, pâturage, petit, pureté, sacrifice, tourterelle, trésor
(No response - 1)

13. CONFORT

Students

No.	Response	Total	Female	Male
1.	fauteuil (fauteuil en cuir)	54	36	18
2.	maison	27	19	8
3.	moderne	21	11	10
4.	agréable	9	7	2
5.	chaleur	9	6	3
6.	luxe	9	4	5
7.	bien-être	8	5	3
8.	chaud	8	8	0
9.	aise	6	2	4
10.	chauffage	5	5	0
11.	lit	5	2	3
12.	table	4	3	1
13.	tapis	4	4	0
14.	agrément	3	2	1
15.	aisance	3	1	2
16.	bien	3	2	1
17.	bourgeois	3	2	1
18.	chambre	3	2	1
19.	électricité	3	2	1
20.	inconfort	3	0	3
21.	misère	3	2	1
22.	radiateur	3	3	0
23.	appartement	2	1	1
24.	auto	2	0	2
25.	cuisine	2	2	0
26.	désagréable	2	2	0
27.	douillet	2	2	0
28.	dur (dure)	2	0	2

Workers

No.	Response	Total
1.	moderne	17
2.	fauteuil	15
3.	luxe	8
4.	bien	6
5.	agréable	5
6.	beau	3
7.	lit	3
8.	maison	3
9.	à l'aise	2
10.	chaleur	2
11.	home	2
12.	idéal	2
13.	ménager	2
14.	meuble (meubles)	2
15.	meublé	2
16.	richesse	2
17.	santé	2
18-54.	(f = 1)	37

abri, acceptable, aisance, apartement, bien-être, conformisme, confortable, dormir, douche, douillet, foyer, habitation, immense, immeuble, indispensable, intérieur, luxueux, mal, ménage, mi-temps, nécessité, pauvre, place, plaisir, poêle, possible, propre, renfort, repos, riche, sécurité, sensationnel, solide, stable, table, tous, tout

13. CONFORT (contd)

Students

No.	Response	Total	Female	Male
29.	foyer	2	2	0
30.	frigidaire	2	1	1
31.	home	2	1	1
32.	ménage	2	0	2
33.	musique	2	0	2
34.	pauvreté	2	2	0
35.	radio	2	1	1
36.	salle de bain	2	1	1
37.	voiture	2	1	1
38-99.	(f = 1)	62	40	22

actuel, les Anglais, américain, Amérique, argent,
baignoire, besoin, blanc, calme, canapé, chauffage
central, cheminée, chez soi, confortable, cosy,
dessert, détente, divan, épreuve, équilibre, fauteur,
formidable, gaieté, gêne, gros, homme d'affaires,
horreur, hôtel, hygiène, insalubrité, instabilité,
installation, intelligence, laine, logis, machine à
laver, mari, meuble, modernisme, moëlleux, mou,
parfait, pénible, pick-up, plaisir, pratique,
printanier, progrès, richesse, rideau, roquefort,
rouge, route, salle, salon, sécurité, siège,
télévision, train, U.S.A., velours, wagon-lit

14. MAIN

Students

No.	Response	Total	Female	Male
1.	pied (pieds)	71	45	26
2.	doigt (doigts)	60	39	21
3.	bras	20	11	9
4.	gant	14	8	6
5.	bague	9	9	0
6.	droite	7	3	4
7.	ongle	7	7	0
8.	longue	6	5	1
9.	travail	6	3	3
10.	sale	5	2	3
11.	pouce	4	1	3
12.	blanche	3	3	0
13.	crayon	3	1	2
14.	membre	3	1	2
15.	noir (noire)	3	1	2
16.	outil	3	2	1
17.	lignes	2	1	1
18.	pain	2	1	1
19.	paume	2	1	1
20.	petit	2	1	1
21-77.	(f = 1)	56	39	17

agile, agréable, alliance, amitié, bagne, bébé, belle,
caresse, cinq, Cocteau, corps, d'oeuvre, donner,
douce, Dürer, écrire, enfant, entière, expression,
faim, femme, fine, force, forte, froide, gauche,
habile, homme, instrument, jambe, jolie, manche,
manucure, manuel, maman, marbre, mariage, medium,
menuiserie, mise, objet, organe, ouvrir, penser,
phalange, piano, prendre, psychologie, Rodin, rose,
rue, saisir, toucher, tricot, vide, volonté

Workers

No.	Response	Total
1.	doigt (doigts, 5 doigts)	17
2.	pied	8
3.	d'oeuvre (oeuvre)	7
4.	sale	7
5.	droite	5
6.	travail	4
7.	blanche	3
8.	douce	3
9.	fort (forte)	3
10.	gant	3
11.	petit	3
12.	propre	3
13.	agile	2
14.	amitié	2
15.	bras	2
16.	dur	2
17.	fine	2
18.	gauche	2
19-55.	(f = 1)	37

anatomie, bague, caresse,
chirurgien, crayon, doué, écrire,
écrit, être, fragile, gain, gangs,
généreux, geste, grand, légère,
leste, lourde, 2 mains, maintient,
maître, manipuler, manucure, manuel,
membre, organe, partie, paume,
pogne, poigne, poignée,
recroqueviller, rouge, rugueux,
serrer, soignée, travailler

15. PETIT

Students

No.	Response	Total	Female	Male
1.	grand	134	81	53
2.	nain	31	20	11
3.	enfant	21	16	5

Workers

No.	Response	Total
1.	grand (et grand)	27
2.	nain	11
3.	enfant (enfants)	10

15. PETIT (contd)

Students

No.	Response	Total	Female	Male
4.	Poucet	12	7	5
5.	gros	6	5	1
6.	homme	4	3	1
7.	laid	4	4	0
8.	animal	3	3	0
9.	chat	3	2	1
10.	jeune	3	2	1
11.	mignon	3	2	1
12.	pied	3	3	0
13.	puce	3	3	0
14.	taille	3	2	1
15.	bébé	2	1	1
16.	court	2	1	1
17.	garçon	2	1	1
18.	gentil	2	1	1
19.	lit	2	2	0
20.	maigre	2	1	1
21.	microbe	2	0	2
22.	minuscule	2	2	0
23-61.	(f = 1)	39	22	17

adjectif, adorable, arbre, bas, berceau, Blanche-Neige,
caillou, calme, chaperon, charmant, chien, cousin,
drummling, épais, étroit, faible, fils, insignifiant,
joli, joyeux, long, lutin, main, malingre, matin,
minus, moi, oiseau, panier, papillon, quantité, réduit,
Roland, salon, soleil, souris, talon, temps, trapu

Workers

No.	Response	Total
4.	garçon	6
5.	chien	5
6.	gros	5
7.	Poucet	5
8.	pas grand	4
9.	mince	3
10.	minuscule	3
11.	homme	2
12.	lapin	2
13.	mignon	2
14.	oiseau	2
15-41.	(f = 1)	27

aiguille, aisé, animal, bas, chat,
cochon, complexe, court, cri, doigt,
handicapé, haut, jeune, main, microbe,
moustique, pain, poids, poussin,
rivière, taille, trapu, vertueux,
veste, vilain, village, volumineux,
(Illegible - 1)

16. FRUIT

Students

No.	Response	Total	Female	Male
1.	pomme (pommes)	62	47	15
2.	mûr	27	16	11
3.	orange	20	11	9
4.	poire	20	9	11
5.	pêche	14	10	4
6.	fleur (fleurs)	13	7	6
7.	arbre	10	6	4
8.	jus	8	6	2
9.	raisin	7	4	3
10.	vert	7	3	4
11.	été	5	3	2
12.	pépin (pépins)	5	3	2
13.	dessert	4	1	3
14.	manger	4	2	2
15.	soleil	4	3	1
16.	sucre	4	2	2
17.	défendu	3	1	2
18.	jardin	3	3	0
19.	légume	3	3	0
20.	rouge	3	2	1
21.	ver	3	3	0
22.	agréable	2	2	0
23.	amer	2	0	2
24.	ananas	2	1	1
25.	banane	2	1	1
26.	coupe	2	2	0
27.	feuille	2	1	1
28.	fraîcheur	2	2	0
29.	goût	2	2	0
30.	pamplemousse	2	2	0
31.	saveur	2	2	0
32-70.	(f = 1)	39	24	15

amande, baie, bon, branche, colimaçon, cerise, chaleur,
citron, comestible, compotier, confit, corbeille,
douceur, Eve, fondant, fraise, glacé, grain, graine,
grappe, grenade, hiver, jaune, juteux, mandarine,
mange, nourriture, oiseau, papillon, pelure, pommier,
rafraîchissant, rond, savoureux, sphère, soif, sucré,
véreux, verger

Workers

No.	Response	Total
1.	pomme (pommes)	18
2.	mûr (mûres, mûre)	16
3.	oranges	5
4.	arbres	4
5.	bon	4
6.	défendu	4
7.	poire	4
8.	banane	3
9.	juteux	3
10.	pêche	3
11.	saveur	3
12.	sucre	3
13.	vert	3
14.	amer	2
15.	doux	2
16.	été	2
17.	jus	2
18.	légume	2
19.	mer (de mer)	2
20.	raisin	2
21.	vitamine	2
22-47.	(f = 1)	26

aliment, Il y a bon, céréales,
cerise, cheveux, confit, croyance,
délicieux, frais, fraise, fromage,
fruité, fruitier, gâté, goût,
grappe, manger, melon, nature,
pulpe, saisons, santé, sauvage,
savoureux, soleil, succulent

17. PAPILLON

Students

No.	Response	Total	Female	Male
1.	fleur (fleurs)	30	17	13
2.	aile (ailes)	27	23	4
3.	couleur (couleurs)	23	17	6
4.	léger	18	16	2
5.	insecte	13	5	8
6.	oiseau	13	4	9
7.	chenille	11	5	6
8.	nuit (de nuit)	11	8	3
9.	bleu	9	7	2
10.	filet	8	5	3
11.	libellule	8	5	3
12.	vole	8	4	4
13.	légèreté	6	2	4
14.	blanc	5	1	4
15.	campagne	5	5	0
16.	été	5	3	2
17.	abeille	4	2	2
18.	mouche	4	1	3
19.	Brassens	3	1	2
20.	jaune	3	3	0
21.	noeud	3	1	2
22.	pré	3	3	0
23.	printemps	3	3	0
24.	rose	3	3	0
25.	beau	2	1	1
26.	beauté	2	0	2
27.	chasse	2	1	1
28.	chrysalide	2	1	1
29.	liberté	2	1	1
30.	maison	2	1	1
31.	vol	2	2	0
32.	volage	2	2	0
33.	voler	2	2	0
34-77.	(f = 1)	44	29	15

ailé, animal, avion, bariolé, bête à bon Dieu,
Binet-Simon, bombyx, chatoyant, des cieux, collection,
contravention, dialectique, diapré, doré, écumoire,
espace, fantaisie, fille, Fourier, guêpe, gris, haut,
jardin, joli, K.S., machaon, moustique, multicolore,
nature, nocturne, noir, orgueil, papille, papillonacées,
proie, robe, sciences, sphynx, soeur, soleil, solitude,
tache, vif, voleter

Workers

No.	Response	Total
1.	vole	12
2.	blanc	9
3.	de nuit (nuit)	9
4.	bleu	6
5.	rouge	6
6.	fleur (fleurs)	5
7.	léger	5
8.	été (l'été, d'été)	4
9.	vol	4
10.	oiseau (oiseaux)	3
11.	animal	2
12.	campagne	2
13.	champs (des champs)	2
14.	couleur (couleurs)	2
15.	insecte	2
16.	jaune	2
17.	libellule	2
18.	mouche	2
19-54.	(f = 1)	36

d'Afrique, aile, j'aime, beau,
beauté, bête, bois, chanson,
chenille, coccinelle, collection,
coloris, épuisette, évoluer, femme,
filet, folle, harmonie, instable,
jardin, jeune, loisir, moustique,
multicolor, nocturne, noir, papillon,
printemps, rue, silence, soie, soir,
soleil vélo, volage, voltige

18. LISSE

Students

No.	Response	Total	Female	Male
1.	rugueux	49	28	21
2.	doux	16	12	4
3.	dur	15	11	4
4.	plat	13	8	5
5.	table	12	10	2
6.	corde	11	5	6
7.	peau	10	5	5
8.	rude	9	5	4
9.	cheveux (cheveu)	8	7	1
10.	uni (unie)	6	4	2
11.	glissant	5	3	2
12.	mou (mol)	4	4	0
13.	poli (polie)	4	2	2
14.	agréable	3	2	1
15.	blanc	3	3	0
16.	brillant	3	1	2
17.	lac	3	1	2
18.	main	3	2	1
19	planche	3	1	2
20.	rêche	3	3	0
21.	soie	3	1	2
22.	bois	2	2	0
23.	caresser	2	2	0
24.	ébène	2	2	0

Workers

No.	Response	Total
1.	rugueux	13
2.	doux	10
3.	corde	7
4.	peau	5
5.	poli (polie)	5
6.	glissant (glissante)	4
7.	fleur	3
8.	glace	3
9.	table	3
10.	uni (unie)	3
11.	verni	3
12.	bois	2
13.	joli	2
14.	net	2
15.	pente	2
16.	plat	2
17.	rude	2
18-60.	(f = 1)	43

agréable, beau, beauté, blanc,
brillant, brille, Cadum, caressant,
chemise, ciment, cires, couleuvre,
crane, dur, l'eau, figure, fillette,
Formica, fragile, gant, glisse,
lasse, main, marbre, marche, métal,

18. LISSE (contd)

Students

No.	Response	Total	Female	Male
25.	epais	2	2	0
26.	feuille	2	1	1
27.	glace	2	1	1
28.	joue	2	1	1
29.	lys	2	2	0
30.	marbre	2	1	1
31.	métal	2	1	1
32.	miroir	2	2	0
33.	net	2	2	0
34.	plane	2	1	1
35.	plein	2	1	1
36.	rabot	2	2	0
37.	rond	2	2	0
38.	route	2	2	0
39.	satin	2	2	0
40.	toile cirée	2	2	0
41.	velours	2	2	0
42-103.	(f = 1)	62	33	29

abeille, abrupt, acier, adjectif, aigu, amarre, âpre,
aspérité, banane, bateau, bord, boule, calme, cerveau,
chat, chevelure, clair, classe, contraire, couleur,
douceur, durée, éclatant, facile, fade, feuille de
papier, fouillis, fourrure, glisse, glisser, gluant,
gras, gros, impeccable, lame de couteau, luisant,
matière, mer, montagne, mur, neige, nu, papier,
pâtisserie, pierre, plan, plan incliné, plancher,
pomme, puits, raboteux, râpeux, rouge, sable, savon,
solide, tableau, tendre, tissu, vallée, verre, vin

Workers

No.	Response	Total

mince, mou, de noms, papier, polir,
porte, rampe, râpe, rêche, rivière,
route, savon, soie, tapis, verre,
vert, voiture
(Illegible - 1)

19. ORDRE

Students

No.	Response	Total	Female	Male
1.	désordre	65	37	28
2.	rang	13	9	4
3.	chambre	8	8	0
4.	net	6	6	0
5.	ranger	6	5	1
6.	obéissance	5	2	3
7.	police	5	1	4
8.	soin	5	4	1
9.	discipline	4	3	1
10.	maison	4	4	0
11.	raison	4	1	3
12.	rangé	4	0	4
13.	armée	3	1	2
14.	bien	3	1	2
15.	logique	3	1	2
16.	mathématiques	3	1	2
17.	netteté	3	3	0
18.	numéro	3	2	1
19.	premier	3	3	0
20.	propreté	3	3	0
21.	rangement	3	3	0
22.	travail	3	1	2
23.	chef	2	2	0
24.	classe	2	1	1
25.	classement	2	1	1
26.	dur	2	1	1
27.	grandeur	2	2	0
28.	méthode	2	1	1
29.	méticuleux	2	1	1
30.	prêtre	2	1	1
31.	propre	2	2	0
32.	rangée	2	1	1
33.	refus	2	1	1
34.	règlement	2	1	1
35.	régulier	2	1	1
36.	religieux	2	2	0
37.	religion	2	1	1
38-126.	(f = 1)	99	66	33

Workers

No.	Response	Total
1.	désordre	12
2.	ranger (range, rangé)	8
3.	chef (du chef)	5
4.	propreté	5
5.	curé	4
6.	impératif	4
7.	armée	3
8.	bref	3
9.	commandement	3
10.	donné	3
11.	formel	3
12.	rang	3
13.	exécution	2
14.	du jour	2
15.	non	2
16.	obéir	2
17.	sévère	2
18.	strict	2
19-62.	(f = 1)	44

d'appel, banane, bien, bon, bureau,
bureaucratie, cahier, cinquième,
clair, classeur, colère, commander,
confort, contrainte, couvent, demande,
deuxième, discipline, droit, dur,
énergique, ennui, exécuter, famille,
flambeau, général, de grandeur, idiot,
loi, moine, numérique, obéissance,
obliger, ordure, oui, papier,
parfaite, police, propre, rangement,
règle, soldat, de se taire, tabouret
(Illegible - 3)

19. ORDRE (contd)

Students

No.	Response	Total	Female	Male

ami, appartement, autoritaire, beauté, Bergson, bon,
bref, brouillon, cadre, cahier, cahot, calme, casiers,
chaise, chiffre, choix, clair, clarté, classer,
classeur, clergé, colonel, contreordre, cosmique,
couvent, crayon, déduction, Descartes, désobéissant,
droit, drôle, emboîtement, énervant, ennui, ennuyeux,
entier, état, femme, Françoise, habitude, harmonie,
Hollande, idée, impératif, s'incliner, intérêt,
Légion d'Honneur, lent, ligne, luxe, Malte, manie,
ménage, mère, mesure, neuf, non-soumission, nouveau,
numération, numérique, obéir, odieuse, ordination,
ordure, oui, papier, parfait, partir, peigné,
pharmacie, pierre, planche, plat, point, public,
qualité, quelconque, rapport, régiment, règle, re-
marquable, rigide, routine, sagesse, salle, sec,
soldats, stand, strict, stylo, table, tableau,
taverne, température, tiroir, tohubohu, trois, un,
d'urgence

20. CHAISE

Students

No.	Response	Total	Female	Male
1.	table	66	38	28
2.	pied (pieds)	26	19	7
3.	paille	17	13	4
4.	asseoir (s'asseoir)	14	5	9
5.	assis	12	8	4
6.	banc	10	6	4
7.	barreau (barreaux)	10	9	1
8.	fauteuil	9	6	3
9.	meuble	9	6	3
10.	siège	9	5	4
11.	dossier	7	5	2
12.	bois (de bois)	6	6	0
13.	repos	6	3	3
14.	tabouret	6	4	2
15.	porteur (à porteur)	5	3	2
16.	bâton	4	3	1
17.	classe	3	2	1
18.	coussin	3	3	0
19.	Van Gogh (de Van Gogh)	3	2	1
20.	basse	2	1	1
21.	bras	2	2	0
22.	droite	2	0	2
23.	haute	2	2	0
24.	la	2	0	2
25.	objet	2	1	1
26-76.	(f = 1)	51	32	19

amphithéâtre, arbre, armoire, asseois, assise,
assistance, brun, bruyant, bureau, canapé, cannelage,
chaisière, Chesapeake, confort, cuisine, debout, Dieu,
dos, droit, dur, école, empaillée, d'enfants, fatigue,
de fer, ligne, longue, Luxembourg, malpropre,
mobilier, moi, Molière, mur, noire, osier, patte,
peinture, percée, prie-dieu, quatre, ronde, rouge,
roulon, salon, soir, sorcière, stable, tableau, tapis,
travailler, trouée, utile

Workers

No.	Response	Total
1.	table	13
2.	asseoir (s'asseoir)	10
3.	assis	10
4.	bois (en bois)	8
5.	longue	8
6.	tabouret	8
7.	fauteuil	6
8.	cassée (casser, cassé)	5
9.	banc	4
10.	basse	4
11.	porteur	4
12.	confortable	3
13.	éléctrique	3
14.	bancale	2
15.	confort	2
16.	repos (de repos)	2
17-39.	(f = 1)	23

anciennes, argent, assorties, barreau,
belle, dessus, dossier, dureté,
église, empaillée, fatigue, fatiguée,
isolée, jaune, mobiles, orientation,
de paille, pliante, porte, repas,
reposante, reposer, solide

21. DOUX

Students

No.	Response	Total	Female	Male
1.	dur (dure)	27	12	15
2.	mou (mol)	12	8	4
3.	agréable	11	10	1

Workers

No.	Response	Total
1.	agneau (agneaux)	12
2.	gentil (gentille)	7
3.	chat	5

21. DOUX (contd)

Students

No.	Response	Total	Female	Male
4.	duvet	11	7	4
5.	tendre	11	7	4
6.	fourrure	10	8	2
7.	chat	9	6	3
8.	amer	8	4	4
9.	lisse	8	5	3
10.	miel	8	4	4
11.	velours	8	6	2
12.	enfant	6	5	1
13.	moëlleux	6	5	1
14.	laine	5	3	2
15.	peau	5	1	4
16.	rude	5	3	2
17.	soie	5	4	1
18.	soyeux	5	4	1
19.	toucher (au toucher)	5	2	3
20.	bon	4	3	1
21.	caresse	4	3	1
22.	gentil	4	1	3
23.	sucré	4	3	1
24.	amour	3	2	1
25.	brutal	3	1	2
26.	calme	3	2	1
27.	douce	3	2	1
28.	douillet	3	2	1
29.	fort	3	2	1
30.	lit	3	3	0
31.	oreiller	3	2	1
32.	regard	3	1	2
33.	rugueux	3	2	1
34.	agneau	2	2	0
35.	climat	2	0	2
36.	édredon	2	2	0
37.	gentillesse	2	1	1
38.	léger	2	2	0
39.	mouton	2	1	1
40.	suave	2	1	1
41.	sucre	2	1	1
42-102.	(f = 1)	61	41	20

aide, aigre, air, ange, bébé, baiser, beau, bleu, bonbon, bonté, bras, câlin, caressant, chaud, clair, contact, coton, coussin, délicieux, doucement, douceur, faible, femme, fluet, fou, garçon, grossier, habile, jeune fille, joue, long, luisant, maigre, mauvais, méchant, mélancolie, mièvre, mignon, mousse, musique, oeil, patient, pêche, pétale, rat, rêche, satin, sévère, sirop, sombre, son, souffle, souple, sucrerie, sur, sweet, temps, tiède, timide, tissu, yeux

Workers

No.	Response	Total
4.	velours	5
5.	vin	4
6.	bon	3
7.	dur	3
8.	enfant	3
9.	fragile	3
10.	lisse	3
11.	tendre	3
12.	calme	2
13.	chaud	2
14.	douce	2
15.	léger	2
16.	main	2
17.	mouton	2
18.	soie	2
19.	soyeux	2
20-67.	(f = 1)	48

agréable, angora, baisers, billet, bise, câlin, cheveux, choux, coeur, colère, comme, coussin, docile, duvet, ferme, fille, front, garçon, gris, hiver, idée, maux, méchant, le miel, mignon, mou, murmure, musique, peau, pelage, plaisant, plat, poil, pusillamine, rêve, rosée, rude, savon, silence, solide, sourire, sucré, temps, toux, vieux, vent, violent, yeux

22. SIFFLET

Students

No.	Response	Total	Female	Male
1.	train	36	29	7
2.	agent (agent de police)	34	25	9
3.	strident	32	21	11
4.	bruit	30	19	11
5.	gare	13	9	4
6.	aigu	12	8	4
7.	chef de gare	11	3	8
8.	locomotive	11	5	6
9.	son (sons)	10	7	3
10.	roulette (à roulette)	9	3	6
11.	cri	7	4	3
12.	enfant (enfants)	4	4	0
13.	souffle	4	1	3
14.	désagréable	3	1	2
15.	dur (dure)	3	3	0
16.	bouche	2	1	1

Workers

No.	Response	Total
1.	agent (d'agent, agents, agent de police, l'agent)	13
2.	bruit	11
3.	strident	11
4.	train (de train)	10
5.	aigu	6
6.	locomotive	5
7.	arrêt	3
8.	gendarme	3
9.	à roulette (roulette)	3
10.	trompette	3
11.	arbitre (d'arbitre)	2
12.	bruyant	2
13.	chien	2
14.	fort	2
15.	long (longs)	2
16.	musique	2

22. SIFFLET (contd)

	Students			
No.	Response	Total	Female	Male
17.	bruyant	2	0	2
18.	chien	2	2	0
19.	école	2	2	0
20.	garçon	2	0	2
21.	musique	2	0	2
22.	ordre	2	1	1
23.	perçant	2	2	0
24.	tuitt (tutt)	2	0	2
25-75.	(f = 1)	51	32	19

appareil, appel, applaudissement, ballon, bille, bois, campagne, ceinturon, cheftain, chemin de fer, colonie, coup de, course, crayon, éclaireur, éclaireuse, flûte, football, fort, frère, gendarme, gosse, jeu, joie, jouet, juste, lugubre, mécontentement, noir, nuit, peur, pionne, pigeon, pipeau, police, policier, professeur, raide, rang, rauque, robinet, rossignol, siffle, sortie, souffler, soufflet, sport, stridence, théâtre, trompette, voix

	Workers	
No.	Response	Total
17.	rossignol	2
18-50.	(f = 1)	33

appel, appeler, bien, bouche, chante, chantier, cloche, coup, criard, dur, flic, flûte, gardien, guitare, inspiration, instituteur, jeux, klaxon, merle, oreille, peur, policier, puissant, rassemblement, rigoler, roule, siffle, sonner, souffle, tintamarre, trusquin, violent, vulgaire

23. FEMME

	Students			
No.	Response	Total	Female	Male
1.	homme	78	42	36
2.	enfant (enfants)	33	25	8
3.	mère	16	11	5
4.	beauté	9	3	6
5.	douceur	9	6	3
6.	cheveux (cheveu)	7	6	1
7.	amour	5	1	4
8.	beau (belle)	5	4	1
9.	blonde (blond)	5	4	1
10.	épouse	5	1	4
11.	fille	4	3	1
12.	élégance	3	3	0
13.	grande	3	2	1
14.	joli (jolie)	3	2	1
15.	laide (laid)	3	3	0
16.	robe	3	2	1
17.	silhouette	3	3	0
18.	tendresse	3	3	0
19.	chevelure	2	2	0
20.	clair	2	1	1
21.	élégante	2	1	1
22.	faible	2	1	1
23.	foyer	2	2	0
24.	grâce	2	0	2
25.	jeune fille	2	2	0
26.	jupe	2	2	0
27-101.	(f = 1)	75	49	26

adroite, aimable, arme, argent, assise, barbe, berceau, bonne, caramel, Catherine, cervelle, chaleur, chapeau, chatte, chienne, chignon, coeur, danse, danser, difficile, discrétion, doux, enceinte, endormie, être, Eve, faite, fard, féminin, fémininité, ferme, fesse, frère, frivolité, gaie, gamète, Giraud, humain, humanité, idéal, intérieur, Jeanne, légère, luxe, maman, mari, mariage, Marie, méchante, membre, menu, mesquine, mince, moi, molle, nu, obsession, peintre, personne, petit, pied, rose, sage, sale, sein, sexe, sirène, taille, tailleur, tranquilité, type, Vénus, violet, voiture, vraie

	Workers	
No.	Response	Total
1.	homme	22
2.	belle	16
3.	jolie	8
4.	ménage	7
5.	élégante	6
6.	enfant	6
7.	beauté	2
8.	doux (douce)	2
9.	féminin	2
10.	humain	2
11.	mariage	2
12-51.	(f = 1)	40

adulte, aimer, appeler, arbre, d'argent, blonde, Boudha, de chambre, cheveux, coléreuse, coquette, culotte, dame, enceinte, épouse, Eve, faible, famille, fatale, fièvre, folie, fragile, garçon, grande, grosse, indispensable, intelligente, d'intérieur, maman, mari, méchante, médecin, merveilleux, Paris, repos, respect, sexuel, sourire, tendre, union

24. FROID

	Students					Workers	
No.	Response	Total	Female	Male	No.	Response	Total
1.	chaud	96	56	40	1.	hiver (d'hiver, l'hiver)	22
2.	hiver (l'hiver)	42	29	13	2.	chaud (et chaud, chaude)	19
3.	glace (glace à manger)	28	18	10	3.	glace	8
4.	neige	19	15	4	4.	de canard (canard)	6
5.	vent	6	5	1	5.	sec	6
6.	frigidaire	5	4	1	6.	glacial (glaciale)	4
7.	sec	5	0	5	7.	dur	3
8.	chaleur	4	2	2	8.	glacé	3
9.	gelée	4	4	0	9.	rigoureux	3
10.	pôle (Pôle Nord)	4	3	1	10.	vif	3
11.	vif	4	3	1	11.	frigidaire	2
12.	blanc	3	3	0	12.	manteau (manteaux)	2
13.	désagréable	3	3	0	13.	neige	2
14.	frisson	3	2	1	14.	pôle (Pôle Nord)	2
15.	manteau	3	0	3	15.	tremble	2
16.	piquant	3	2	1	16-41.	(f = 1)	27
17.	canard (de canard)	2	1	1			
18.	feu	2	2	0			
19.	gel	2	0	2			
20.	glacial	2	1	1			
21-68.	(f = 1)	48	31	17			

abri, aride, beau, boisson, brumeux, cache-nez, il caille, chauffage, climat, désagréable, frileux, frisson, gel, givre, jeune fille, maudit, mordant, nature, noir, ouvrier, pénétrant, picotant, pôlaire, rude, sauter, soleil, temps
(Illegible - 1)

adjectif, bois, clair, clarté, contraction, déplaisir, douleur, doux, emmitoufler, engourdi, ennuyeux, esquimaux, faim, fer, fort, glacier, Grand Nord, grelotter, humide, inconfortable, laine, lézard, de loup, mal, maladie, mauvais, misère, montagne, nerf, le nord, noir, paulet, piquer, piqûre, pluie, radiateur, rigueur, rouge, rue, Russie, sensation, Sibérie, solitude, sombre, sports d'hiver, temps, tiède, voyage

25. LENT

	Students					Workers	
No.	Response	Total	Female	Male	No.	Response	Total
1.	rapide	73	39	34	1.	tortue	17
2.	escargot (l'escargot)	40	33	7	2.	doucement	10
3.	vite	28	13	15	3.	rapide	10
4.	tortue	22	16	6	4.	vite	10
5.	train	6	5	1	5.	escargot	9
6.	vif	6	4	2	6.	mou	8
7.	limace	4	3	1	7.	vif (vive)	3
8.	mou	4	1	3	8.	cheminement	2
9.	boeuf	3	2	1	9.	lente	2
10.	chenille	3	1	2	10.	limace	2
11.	écrire	3	2	1	11.	paresseux	2
12.	auto	2	1	1	12.	train	2
13.	autobus	2	2	0	13.	vitesse	2
14.	bête	2	0	2	14-46.	(f = 1)	33
15.	cerveau	2	1	1			
16.	énervant	2	2	0			
17.	énervement	2	1	1			
18.	locomotive	2	2	0			
19.	long	2	1	1			
20.	lourd	2	2	0			
21.	moi	2	0	2			
22.	paresse	2	1	1			
23.	peine	2	1	1			
24.	sûr	2	1	1			
25.	travail	2	1	1			
26-93.	(f = 1)	68	49	19			

l'âne, boiteux, bruit, calme, chant, cortège, couleuvre, cours, d'eau, à cuire, désagréable, dort, dur, éléphant, empoté, énervant, glacé, gros, horticulteur, limaçon, pénible, ralenti, retard, rouleau, souple, tango, comme tout, traîner, tranquille, va, vache, vieillard, pas vite, vivace
(No response - 1; Illegible - 2)

accéléré, agile, an, Arabe, bicyclette, brouette, calme, camion, chaland, char, chariot, charrette, chemin, cheval, coeur, court, diligence, doucement, douleur, doux, écriture, éléphant, ennuyeux, esprit, état, exacerbant, exaspérant, fainéant, fleuve, forme, foule, froid, geste, glissade, homme, idée, immobile, impatience, insuffisant, lentes, lenteur, marche, mouton, mouvement, nonchalant, parole, pas, pendule, piéton, prompt, racine, retard, retenue, salle, slow, soeur, sort, temps, terne, thème, traîner, traverser,

25. LENT (contd)

Students

No.	Response	Total	Female	Male

triste, un, vacances, valse, ver, voiture,

26. DÉSIRER

Students

No.	Response	Total	Female	Male
1.	vouloir	48	31	17
2.	aimer	28	16	12
3.	amour	18	7	11
4.	avoir	17	7	10
5.	ardemment	10	7	3
6.	attendre	8	6	2
7.	femme	7	2	5
8.	envier	5	3	2
9.	obtenir	5	3	2
10.	fort	4	1	3
11.	souhaiter	4	1	3
12.	vacances	4	2	2
13.	manger	3	2	1
14.	passion	3	2	1
15.	aspirer	2	2	0
16.	beaucoup	2	2	0
17.	besoin	2	2	0
18.	bonheur	2	2	0
19.	cadeau	2	1	1
20.	connaître	2	2	0
21.	envie	2	0	2
22.	fortement	2	2	0
23.	fruit (un fruit)	2	2	0
24.	joie	2	2	0
25.	non	2	2	0
26.	plaisir	2	1	1
27.	posséder	2	1	1
28.	recevoir	2	2	0
29.	réussir	2	0	2
30.	réussite	2	2	0
31.	rêve	2	2	0
32.	souhait	2	0	2
33.	vivement	2	2	0
34.	volonté	2	2	0
35-118.	(f = 1)	84	63	21

acheter, affectif, affecter, agir, agréable, apprécier,
ardent, argent, attente, avidité, belle, bête, bibelot,
boire, un bonbon, caprice, chagrin, chaise, chant,
chaussure, chercher, chien, chose, colère, convoitise,
corps, couleur, craindre, croire, cupide, cupidité,
demander, demeurer, désirée, détester, douleur,
espérer, étoile, être, faim, film, finir, force, fuir,
gâteau, gourmand, homme, lettre, maison, maman,
mariage, mourir, musique, Napoléon, Noël, ouvert,
passionément, péché, peine, perdre, ponédés, prendre,
quoi, raffoler, réaliser, refuser, rêver, richesse,
rien, rire, rivière, soupirer, survivre, tendre vers,
tension, tenter, tête, toute la tranquilité,
vaporisateur, je veux, vie, vivre, voilier

Workers

No.	Response	Total
1.	avoir	19
2.	vouloir	17
3.	femme	5
4.	aimer	4
5.	beaucoup	4
6.	envie	4
7.	une chose (chose)	3
8.	manger	3
9.	attendre	2
10.	auto	2
11.	cadeau (un cadeau)	2
12.	obtenir	2
13.	recevoir	2
14.	réussir	2
15.	tout	2
16.	voiture	2
17-55.	(f = 1)	39

adorable, aiguille, aller, amour,
appréhender, argent, aspirer, avion,
boire, le bon, bonheur, caprice,
chèrement, quelque chose, confort,
désert, désirer, désireux, dessin,
donner, dormir, envier, des fleurs,
fruit, futur, heureux, laissé,
un livre, depuis longtemps, Mai,
objet, obsession, pain, prendre,
près, travail, vivre, vivement, voir,
(Illegible - 1)

27. FLEUVE

Students

No.	Response	Total	Female	Male
1.	eau (eaux)	47	36	11
2.	rivière	40	19	21
3.	Seine (La Seine)	35	22	13
4.	profond	10	4	6
5.	mer	9	5	4
6.	rouge	6	4	2

27. RIVIÈRE

Workers

No.	Response	Total
1.	fleuve	17
2.	eau (eaux)	16
3.	coule	6
4.	limpide	6
5.	pêche	5
6.	claire (clair)	4

27. FLEUVE (contd)

Students

No.	Response	Total	Female	Male
7.	ruisseau	6	5	1
8.	Mississippi	5	3	2
9.	bleu	4	3	1
10.	calme	4	4	0
11.	film	4	3	1
12.	Gange	4	4	0
13.	Loire	4	4	0
14.	Renoir	4	2	2
15.	bateau	3	2	1
16.	jaune	3	2	1
17.	lac	3	2	1
18.	lit	3	2	1
19.	Nil (le Nil)	3	3	0
20.	noir	3	2	1
21.	Rhin	3	3	0
22.	vert	3	3	0
23.	barque	2	0	2
24.	berge	2	1	1
25.	cinéma	2	1	1
26.	coule	2	2	0
27	gris	2	2	0
28.	Inde	2	1	1
29.	large	2	1	1
30.	majesté	2	1	1
31.	plaine	2	1	1
32.	Pô	2	1	1
33.	remous	2	1	1
34.	le Rhône	2	0	2
35.	torrent	2	2	0
36-91.	(f = 1)	56	33	23

amazone, amour, arbre, bain, brillant, campagne, canot,
chose, couleur, cours, cours d'eau, crues, Danube,
descente, écoulement, élément, embouchure, estuaire,
étang, étincelant, Eure, fille, flou, gras, houleux,
immensité, impétueux, Indochine, inspiration, largeur,
lent, limon, lisse, méandre, nage, paisible, pays,
paysage, poisson, prairie, promenade, puissance,
puissant, rapide, rio, rives, sale, serpent, source,
temps, Tibre, tourbillons, tumultueux, vagues, vallée,
voyage

27. RIVIÈRE (contd)

Workers

No.	Response	Total
7.	poisson	4
8.	profond (profonde)	4
9.	bleu (bleue)	3
10.	lente	3
11.	torrent	3
12.	baignade	2
13.	calme	2
14.	en crue	2
15.	mer	2
16.	montagne	2
17.	sinueux	2
18.	vacances	2
19-47.	(f = 1)	29

amusement, argent, Armançon, bain,
banc, beau, champ, courant, cours
d'eau, eau coulant, gelée, grande,
jaune, joli, large, Loire, mystère,
nager, nez, pêcher, poésie, pont,
rapide, repos, sans retour,
ruisseau, Seine, tortueux, tumulteuse,
(Illegible - 1)

28. BLANC

Students

No.	Response	Total	Female	Male
1.	noir	94	54	40
2.	neige	59	39	20
3.	clair	7	3	4
4.	pureté	7	4	3
5.	linge	5	3	2
6.	pur	5	4	1
7.	bleu	4	3	1
8.	couleur	4	2	2
9.	drap	4	3	1
10.	oeuf	4	3	1
11.	bec	3	2	1
12.	immaculé (immaculée)	3	2	1
13.	jaune	3	3	0
14.	mariée	3	3	0
15.	papier	3	2	1
16.	propre	3	2	1
17.	robe	3	3	0
18.	rouge	3	1	2
19.	voile	3	3	0
20.	exposition de blanc	2	0	2
21.	lys	2	1	1
22.	néant	2	2	0
23.	nègre	2	2	0
24.	vert	2	2	0
25.	vide	2	2	0

Workers

No.	Response	Total
1.	neige (de neige, comme la neige)	31
2.	noir (noire)	19
3.	couleur	7
4.	propre	7
5.	bleu	4
6.	clair (claire)	4
7.	linge	4
8.	rouge	4
9.	papier	3
10-41.	(f = 1)	32

beau, bouche, chanson, chat, ciel,
coule, craie, draps, éclalant,
d'Espagne, frimas, immaculé, incolore,
joli, lait, maison, manteau,
de Meudon, mouton, oiseau, OMO,
ours, pâle, profond, pureté, réclame,
ruisseau, sale, tapis, vert, vin,
zinc

28. BLANC (contd)

Students

No.	Response	Total	Female	Male
26.	zinc (de zinc)	2	0	2
27-80.	(f = 1)	54	36	18

âme, ange, argent, bon, cheveux, ciel, clarté, colombe,
coton, craie, doux, droitesse, éblouissement, éclat,
enfant, ennui, d'Espagne, été, femme, fleur, froid,
fromage, innocent, jeu, laine, laiteux, lapin, lettre,
limpide, lumière, lune, mange, médecin, merle, mont,
mot, neigeux, nuage, peinture, persil, prisme, racisme,
riche, rose, saison, salle, seing, soleil, tache,
traine, tropical, tube, uni, vierge

29. BELLE

Students

No.	Response	Total	Female	Male
1.	femme	49	28	21
2.	bête (et la bête)	33	22	11
3.	laide (laid)	31	19	12
4.	jolie (joli)	21	10	11
5.	beau	17	12	5
6.	fille (jeune fille)	15	9	6
7.	nuit (de nuit)	12	8	4
8.	fleur (fleurs)	9	7	2
9.	au bois dormant (bois dormant)	6	6	0
10.	agréable	5	4	1
11.	cheveux	4	2	2
12.	statue	4	4	0
13.	bois (au bois)	3	1	2
14.	Cadix	3	1	2
15.	fée	3	3	0
16.	blonde	2	2	0
17.	étoile	2	2	0
18.	forêt	2	2	0
19.	mère	2	0	2
20.	poésie	2	2	0
21.	poupée	2	2	0
22.	pure	2	2	0
23-81.	(f = 1)	59	36	23

adjectif, affreux, Agnès, agrément, apaisement, aspect,
beauté, belles de nuit, bien, bijoux, bleu, cathédrale,
Catherine, charmante, charmeuse, chevelure, cloche,
coiffeur, conte, dame, damoiselle, danseuse, désir,
dormant, dormir, elle, enfant, esthétique, fleuve,
fontaine, froide, fourrure, gentille, Grèce, Hélène,
héroïne, inutilité, jour, ligne, lune, mer, merveilleux,
moi, neige, nue, orgueil, patiente, peinture, rare,
reine, rêve, rose, satisfaction, sexe, triste, unité,
Vénus, vilaine, Zelinde

29. BEAU

Workers

No.	Response	Total
1.	joli (jolie)	13
2.	laid (laide, et laid)	10
3.	soleil	9
4.	temps	8
5.	payasage	4
6.	admirable	2
7.	belle	2
8.	bien	2
9.	ciel	2
10.	dieu	2
11.	homme	2
12.	magnifique	2
13.	moche	2
14.	rêve	2
15.	spectacle	2
16.	vilain	2
17-65.	(f = 1)	49

agneau, ange, Apollon, arbre, art,
beauté, Brigitte, le cahier, charme,
château, chien, costume, désir,
désirable, Dieu antique, la femme,
fier, formidable, garçon, gracieux,
grand, jour, lisse, maison, malin,
manteau, mauvais, mauve, merveilleux,
midi, mirage, monteur, musique,
neige, net, pantalon, pays, pinson,
plaisir, pré, printemps, séduisant,
simple, splendide, tapis, teint,
village, visage, vue

30. FENÊTRE

Students

No.	Response	Total	Female	Male
1.	porte	35	14	21
2.	rideau (rideaux)	34	28	6
3.	ouverte	25	17	8
4.	carreau (carreaux)	22	11	11
5.	vitre (vitres)	19	14	5
6.	paysage	12	10	2
7.	cour (sur cour)	11	10	1
8.	maison	9	6	3
9.	ouverture	9	5	4
10.	jour (de jour)	7	4	3
11.	air	6	4	2
12.	ciel	5	3	2

Workers

No.	Response	Total
1.	ouverte (ouvert)	36
2.	carreaux (carreau)	14
3.	porte	9
4.	vitre (vitres)	6
5.	grande	4
6.	air	3
7.	baie	3
8.	ouverture	3
9.	rideaux (rideau)	3
10.	fermer (fermee)	2
11.	jour	2
12.	large	2

30. FENÊTRE (contd)

	Students					Workers	
No.	Response	Total	Female	Male	No.	Response	Total
13.	lumière	5	4	1	13.	voir	2
14.	soleil	5	3	2	14-38.	(f = 1)	25
15.	clarté	3	2	1			
16.	espace	3	2	1			
17.	espagnolette	3	2	1			
18.	jardin	3	3	0			
19.	liberté	3	2	1			
20.	arbre	2	0	2			
21.	château (de château)	2	1	1			
22.	croisée	2	1	1			
23.	haut (haute)	2	2	0			
24.	large	2	1	1			
25.	panorama	2	1	1			
26.	la rue	2	1	1			
27.	trou	2	2	0			
28.	volet (volets)	2	2	0			
29.	vue	2	1	1			
30-78.	(f = 1)	49	28	21			

Workers 14-38. (f = 1) 25:
arbre, balcon, blanc, cadre, cage, cassée, chambre, chêne, clarté, close, froid, jardin, laid, lucarne, lumière, luminosité, maison, paysage, regard, rue, tordu, vasistas, verre, vois, vu (Illegible - 1)

Students 30-78. (f = 1):
bois, Braque, carrés, chambranle, chassis, claire, classe, clos, cordon, croisillon, dehors, dortoir, éclairage, encadrement, espoir, étroite, facade, fermé, froid, givre, à guillotine, horizon, local, loquet, lucarne, lycée, nature, objet, ogivale, oiseaux, ovale, parc, passé, persienne, pièce, plaisir, regard, regarder, rêve, salle, store, transparence, transparent, veillée, vent, verre, vide, vision, vitrée

31. RUGUEUX

	Students					Workers	
No.	Response	Total	Female	Male	No.	Response	Total
1.	lisse	48	32	16	1.	dur (dure)	14
2.	bois	33	26	7	2.	lisse	7
3.	dur	25	17	8	3.	doux (douce)	6
4.	écorce	17	10	7	4.	arbre (l'arbre)	5
5.	doux	16	9	7	5.	bois	5
6.	désagréable	7	7	0	6.	lime	5
7.	pierre	7	4	3	7.	râpe	4
8.	âpre	6	2	4	8.	râpeux	3
9.	arbre (un arbre)	5	1	4	9.	rêche	3
10.	rude	5	3	2	10.	âpre	2
11.	table	5	2	3	11.	barbe	2
12.	main (mains)	4	3	1	12.	chêne	2
13.	mur	4	1	3	13.	désagréable	2
14.	poli	4	1	3	14.	écorce	2
15.	râpe	3	0	3	15.	toile emeri	2
16.	rêche	3	3	0	16.	hiver (l'hiver)	2
17.	rocher (rochers)	3	2	1	17.	langue	2
18.	sol	3	2	1	18.	pas lisse	2
19.	aspérité	2	1	1	19.	main	2
20.	cailloux	2	1	1	20.	rude	2
21.	chêne	2	2	0	21-59.	(f = 1)	39
22.	mal	2	2	0			
23.	mou	2	0	2			
24.	peau	2	2	0			
25.	sensation	2	1	1			
26.	serpent	2	2	0			
27-100.	(f = 1)	74	48	26			

Students 27-100. (f = 1):
accrocher, barbem, bâton, beau, brique, brosse, cancer, caractère, caresser, carton, chemin, ciment, comme, corde, couteau, crevasse, difficile, dossier, drap, épine, esthésiométrie, étagère, étoffe, fer, fin, fort, froid, granier, granit, gratture, gueux, irrégularité, laine, langue, langue de chat, lime, maris de paysan, mer, montagne, Montessori, motte, orange, papier, papier de verre, pardi, parquet, pierre ponce, plane, poil, poreux, professeur, rabot, raboteux, raide, râpeux, roche, rouge, "rough", rugosité, sable, sale, sanglier, solitude, sucre, tapis, tissu, toile, toile émeri, travail, tronc, tronc d'arbre, trous, uni, viril

Workers 21-59. (f = 1) 39:
accroche, acier, bien, bossu, brosse, cailloux, ciment, crocodile peau, croûte, froid, fromage, granit, guenille, hérisson, lumière, mal, manche, méchant, monstrueux, obséder, paillasson, peau, pierre, plat, poli, pouce, rabot, râpée, rugueux, sol, souple, tapis, taureau, tissus, comme tout, travail, tripe, vilain, visage
(Illegible - 2)

32. CITOYEN

Students					Workers		
No.	Response	Total	Female	Male	No.	Response	Total
1.	ville	20	13	7	1.	français (françaises)	25
2.	vote	20	16	4	2.	homme (hommes)	15
3.	citoyenne (citoyennes)	19	12	7	3.	citoyenne	6
4.	français	19	9	10	4.	libre	6
5.	homme	19	11	8	5.	patriote	5
6.	révolution	19	15	4	6.	bon	3
7.	patrie	18	12	6	7.	honnête	3
8.	république	15	10	5	8.	patrie	3
9.	état	12	4	8	9.	république	3
10.	cité	8	8	0	10.	combattant (combattants)	2
11.	élection (élections)	8	5	3	11.	nation	2
12.	pays	8	5	3	12.	personne	2
13.	nation	6	2	4	13.	révolution	2
14.	France	4	2	2	14.	soldat	2
15.	électeur	4	1	3	15-49.	($\underline{f}$ = 1)	35
16.	liberté	4	1	3			
17.	libre	4	3	1			
18.	démocratie	3	1	2			
19.	devoir	3	2	1			
20.	drapeau	3	3	0			
21.	femme	3	3	0			
22.	honnête	3	1	2			
23.	patriote	3	3	0			
24.	soldat	3	2	1			
25.	voter	3	3	0			
26.	camarade	2	1	1			
27.	Cicéron	2	2	0			
28.	civil	2	1	1			
29.	compatriote	2	1	1			
30.	déclaration	2	0	2			
31.	habitant	2	2	0			
32.	loi	2	2	0			
33.	Parisien	2	2	0			
34.	politique	2	1	1			
35.	Rome	2	2	0			
36-72.	($\underline{f}$ = 1)	37	23	14			

Workers 15-49 ($\underline{f}$ = 1): aimable, américain, ami, camarade, Citroën, civique, cocu, compatriote, complaisant, courageux, discours, droits, électeur, élection, énergique, faux, France, de Gaulle, gens, Guyemer, habitants, humain, liberté, maison, mauvais, monde, pauvre, peuple, pied, politique, révolutionnaire, société, tabouret, usine, votant
(Illegible - 1)

Students 36-72 ($\underline{f}$ = 1): acropole, anonyme, bon, bonnet, bourgeois, civisme, cocarde, communisme, communiste, contribuable, démocrate, droits, enfant, ennemi, Faure, fidèle, gens, hors-la-loi, illusion, Marsellaise, monde, moyen, nombre, nouveauté, ordre, oui, parfait, pauvre, républicain, règlement, Robespierre, romain, rouge, sang, société, urne, villageois

33. PIED

Students					Workers		
No.	Response	Total	Female	Male	No.	Response	Total
1.	chaussure	43	35	8	1.	chaussure (chaussures)	13
2.	main	35	19	16	2.	plat	12
3.	marche	18	10	8	3.	main	10
4.	jambe	17	8	9	4.	marche	8
5.	plat	15	10	5	5.	marcher	7
6.	soulier (souliers)	8	6	2	6.	jambe	4
7.	bot	7	6	1	7.	sales (sale)	4
8.	chaise	7	4	3	8.	bot	3
9.	orteil	7	6	1	9.	noir	3
10.	marcher	6	2	4	10.	nu (nus)	3
11.	membre	6	4	2	11.	orteil	3
12.	table (de table)	6	4	2	12.	soulier	3
13.	agile	5	2	3	13.	beau	2
14.	doigt (doigts)	5	2	3	14.	cor	2
15.	biche	4	3	1	15.	grand	2
16.	nu	4	4	0	16.	léger	2
17.	ongle	4	1	3	17.	propre	2
18.	bête	3	2	1	18.	à terre	2
19.	bras	3	3	0	19-47.	($\underline{f}$ = 1)	29
20.	football	3	0	3			
21.	porc	3	2	1			
22.	pouce	3	2	1			
23.	bas	2	2	0			

Workers 19-47 ($\underline{f}$ = 1): de biche, blessé, en bois, cabot, cheval, cochon, corps, derrière, droit, dur, enflé, ferme, football, fragile, gelé, genoux, loi, longueur,

33. PIED (contd)

Students

No.	Response	Total	Female	Male
24.	corps	2	2	0
25.	droit	2	1	1
26.	grue	2	1	1
27.	laid	2	2	0
28.	petit	2	2	0
29.	sol	2	2	0
30.	talon	2	1	1
31.	vache (de vache)	2	1	1
32.	veau	2	1	1
33-88.	(f = 1)	56	34	22

Achille, alouette, anatomie, argile, balle, bat, beau,
Berthe, blanc, cailloux, cassé, chamois, cheval,
clochard, coq, coulisse, courir, danse, debout, égalité,
enveloppe, épaule, extrémité, fin, fragile, gauche,
grand, instrument, Iseult, laideur, léger, levé, limacé,
locomotion, long, mal, médecin, mis à, mouvement, mur,
nez, nickelés, noir, organe, pas, poule, pourquoi, Rome,
rue, sable, sale, sécurité, selle, ski, sot, à terre

Workers

No.	Response	Total

marin, nez, d'oeuvre, palmé, palmes,
peau, petit, pierre, rond, de selle,
sensible
(Illegible - 1)

34. ARAIGNÉE

Students

No.	Response	Total	Female	Male
1.	toile (toile d'araignée)	107	67	40
2.	fil (fils)	12	5	7
3.	patte (pattes, 8 pattes)	12	9	3
4.	insecte	10	7	3
5.	noir (noire)	8	6	2
6.	soir (du soir)	8	4	4
7.	bête	7	4	3
8.	horreur	7	6	1
9.	plafond	7	6	1
10.	peur	5	5	0
11.	arachnide	4	0	4
12.	chagrin	4	3	1
13.	espoir	4	2	2
14.	grenier	4	3	1
15.	saleté	4	2	2
16.	velu (velue)	4	3	1
17.	laid	3	1	2
18.	mouche	3	3	0
19.	animal	2	1	1
20.	désagréable	2	2	0
21.	laideur	2	0	2
22.	matin	2	2	0
23.	mer (de mer)	2	2	0
24.	répugnant	2	0	2
25.	sale	2	1	1
26.	tisser	2	2	0
27-85.	(f = 1)	59	38	21

abeille, affreux, amusement, arabesque, arachnée,
aragne, araignée, arthropode, bestiole, bruit,
chenille, dégoût, épeuré, éponge, étoile, Fabre,
farce, fer, finesse, fourmi, frisson, gluant, grimpe,
haine, hideux, horrible, jambe, jardin, Kafka,
libellule, main, de malheur, mauvaise, méchanceté,
montre, moucheron, mouvement, mygale, patience, petite,
piquant, poils, propreté, puce, punaise, reptile,
répulsion, réseau, rond, sale bête, sauvage, sorcière,
sournois, spider, superstition, tissage, tordre,
tortue, visqueux

Workers

No.	Response	Total
1.	toile	24
2.	du soir (soir)	8
3.	insecte	5
4.	noir (noire)	5
5.	sale	5
6.	mouche	4
7.	bête	3
8.	grosse	3
9.	hideuse (hideux)	3
10.	laide (laid)	3
11.	papillon	3
12.	horreur	2
13.	de mer	2
14.	mygale	2
15.	pattes	2
16.	peur	2
17.	plafond	2
18-53.	(f = 1)	36

agressivité, aisance, animal, bru,
crabe, crasse, crochu, dédaigneux,
dégoût, dégoûtant, écraser, effroi,
enfermer, fourmi, fragile, gluante,
infecte, du matin, malheur,
mauvaise, piqûre, pressentiment,
punaise, répugnant, rouge, sale,
bête, scorpion, superstitieux,
tentacule, travail, tisse, velue,
vermine, vert, viande, vilaine
(No response - 1)

35. AIGUILLE

No.	Response	Total	Female	Male
Students				
1.	fil (de fil, fils)	72	47	25
2.	chas	17	9	8
3.	coudre	17	14	3
4.	piqûre	16	10	6
5.	pointu (pointue)	16	9	7
6.	couture	13	12	1
7.	piquer	12	10	2
8.	tricot	12	8	4
9.	piquant (piquante)	10	4	6
10.	pointe	6	2	4
11.	trou	6	5	1
12.	fine (fin)	5	4	1
13.	pique	4	2	2
14.	acier	3	3	0
15.	midi (du midi)	3	1	2
16.	pin	3	2	1
17.	tissu	3	3	0
18.	travail	3	3	0
19.	tricoter (à tricoter)	3	2	1
20.	anguille	2	1	1
21.	couteau	2	2	0
22.	douleur	2	0	2
23.	épingle	2	1	1
24.	long (longue)	2	0	2
25.	mal	2	2	0
26.	montagne	2	0	2
27.	montre	2	1	1
28.	sonde	2	1	1
29.	tirer	2	1	1
30-73.	(f = 1)	44	25	19

agilité, aiguë, appareil, arbre, bois, bras, broderie, ceinture, Cendrillon, châle, chat, chaussette, chausson, confort, à coudre, couturière, crayon, dé, eau, enfiler, fée, fer, file, filer, foin, gluant, grand-mère, laine, lin, mer, métier, minceur, nouille, pauvreté, percée, petite fille, pic, pieuvre, raccomoder, rail, robe, rocheuse, tailleur, verte

No.	Response	Total
Workers		
1.	fil	17
2.	pique (piqué, piquer)	16
3.	coudre (à coudre)	15
4.	pointue (pointu)	8
5.	fine (fin)	6
6.	foin	5
7.	piquante (piquant)	4
8.	tricoter (à tricoter)	3
9.	épingle	2
10.	pic	2
11.	piqûre	2
12.	tricot	2
13-45.	(f = 1)	33

aiguille, aiguisée, anguille, brillant, chaste, chat, couture, creuse, dent, émoussée, fer, file, gluante, invisible, laine, longue, machine à coudre, mince, montagne, petite-main, pin, pince, pointe, poison, rivière, roche, sifflet, table, tailleur, tordue, trou, tissu, vert

36. ROUGE

No.	Response	Total	Female	Male
Students				
1.	noir (noire, le noir)	51	32	19
2.	sang	44	29	15
3.	lèvre (à lèvre, rouge aux lèvres, rouge à lèvres)	25	17	8
4.	bleu	22	12	10
5.	vert	20	12	8
6.	couleur	10	3	7
7.	feu	7	3	4
8.	taureau	7	3	4
9.	Stendhal	6	3	3
10.	blanc	5	3	2
11.	drapeau	5	2	3
12.	vermeil	5	4	1
13.	vif	5	4	1
14.	communiste	3	1	2
15.	rose	3	2	1
16.	sombre	3	2	1
17.	ardent	2	2	0
18.	bonbon	2	0	2
19.	cerise	2	2	0
20.	coquelicot	2	2	0
21.	éclat	2	1	1
22.	gai (gaie)	2	2	0
23.	peinture	2	2	0
24.	robe	2	2	0
25.	signal	2	1	1
26.	vin	2	0	2
27.	violence	2	2	0

No.	Response	Total
Workers		
1.	sang (le sang, de sang)	29
2.	vif (vive)	11
3.	couleur	9
4.	noir (et noir)	6
5.	vert	6
6.	écarlate	4
7.	blanc	3
8.	bleu	3
9.	lèvres (lèvre)	3
10.	à lèvres (à lèvre)	2
11.	rose	2
12.	sombre	2
13.	tomate	2
14-46.	(f = 1)	33

beau, brûlure, cerise, chaperon, chaud, circulation, cirque, comme le ciel, coq, couchant, coucher de soleil, croix, danger, désir, écrevisse, feu, figure, fil, gris, jaune, manteau, ongle, pavillon, peinture, poisson, pomme, rideau, russe, soleil, taureau, tissu, trompette, vermillon

36. ROUGE (contd)

Students

No.	Response	Total	Female	Male
28-72.	(f = 1)	45	36	9

abat-jour, agressif, aigre, j'aime, aimer, arène, café, cahier, cape, circulation, corrida, criard, danger, écarlate, Espagne, étoffe, excitant, femme, flamboyant, folie, foulard, joie, Julien, jupe, lumière, lune, oiseau, ombre, passion, peau, plaie, pomme, Portugal, pourpre, rideau, soleil, soleil couchant, tableau, teint, toit, toréador, taureau, vermillon, violent, yeux

37. SOMMEIL

Students

No.	Response	Total	Female	Male
1.	lit	41	28	13
2.	repos	30	15	15
3.	dormir	28	16	12
4.	rêve (rêves)	27	19	8
5.	profond	18	15	3
6.	nuit (la nuit)	15	9	6
7.	veille	11	6	5
8.	fatigue	10	6	4
9.	léger	10	8	2
10.	cauchemar	4	3	1
11.	réveil	4	2	2
12.	dort	3	3	0
13.	douceur	3	2	1
14.	dur	3	2	1
15.	enfant	3	3	0
16.	éveil	3	1	2
17.	hypnose	3	3	0
18.	mouche (mouche tsé-tsé)	3	3	0
19.	oreiller	3	2	1
20.	plomb	3	1	2
21.	blanc	2	2	0
22.	calme	2	2	0
23.	chambre	2	2	0
24.	insomnie	2	0	2
25.	long	2	1	1
26.	lourd	2	1	1
27.	mort	2	1	1
28.	oubli	2	2	0
29.	rêver	2	2	0
30-74.	(f = 1)	45	24	21

allongé, apaisement, Bergson, bien-être, bienfaisant, bientôt, cachet, cure, délice, dodo, dormeur, dortoir, drôle, encre, s'endormir, ennui, état, évanouissement, Freud, hypothalamus, idéal, inconscience, inertie, lent, lever, Morphée, mourir, narcotique, néant, oui, paix, perdre, problème, rat, roux, sang, soir, solitude, somnanbule, soulagement, temps, tranquilité, tsé-tsé, vacances, yeux

Workers

No.	Response	Total
1.	dormir	21
2.	profond	19
3.	repos	12
4.	lourd	9
5.	léger	8
6.	lit	7
7.	dur	3
8.	fatigue	3
9.	de plomb	3
10.	rêve	3
11.	bienfaisant	2
12.	fatiguer (fatigué)	2
13.	lent	2
14.	nuit	2
15.	oreiller	2
16-32.	(f = 1)	17

bagne, baille, il y a bon, calme, chambre, désir, destin, dodo, douceur, douche, enfant, fin, long, pâle, rapide, réparateur, somme

38. COLÈRE

Students

No.	Response	Total	Female	Male
1.	rouge	40	29	11
2.	rage	11	8	3
3.	cri (cris)	10	5	5
4.	ire (ira)	9	4	5
5.	noir (noire)	9	8	1
6.	calme	7	4	3
7.	douceur	6	3	3
8.	enfant (enfants)	6	4	2
9.	fureur	5	2	3

Workers

No.	Response	Total
1.	noir (noire)	13
2.	froide (froid)	11
3.	méchant (méchante)	9
4.	forte	4
5.	ivre	4
6.	fâché	3
7.	folle (fou)	3
8.	mauvais (mauvaise)	3
9.	nerfs	3

38. COLÈRE (contd)

Students

No.	Response	Total	Female	Male
10.	folie	4	2	2
11.	méchanceté	4	2	2
12.	méchant	4	3	1
13.	raisin (raisins)	4	3	1
14.	terrible	4	3	1
15.	bruit	3	1	2
16.	dieu (dieux)	3	1	2
17.	geste (gestes)	3	2	1
18.	laideur	3	3	0
19.	mépris	3	3	0
20.	patience	3	1	2
21.	anxiété	2	1	1
22.	brutalité	2	0	2
23.	crise	2	2	0
24.	désagréable	2	2	0
25.	doux	2	2	0
26.	emportement	2	1	1
27.	folie	2	0	2
28.	fou	2	2	0
29.	furieux	2	0	2
30.	grimace	2	2	0
31.	haine	2	2	0
32.	homme	2	2	0
33.	horreur	2	2	0
34.	humeur	2	1	1
35.	irrascibilité	2	0	2
36.	ivre	2	1	1
37.	mauvaise	2	1	1
38.	peur	2	2	0
39.	pieds	2	2	0
40.	ridicule	2	1	1
41.	rougeur	2	2	0
42.	sentiment	2	2	0
43-145.	(f = 1)	103	63	40

adrénaline, agressivité, angoisse, argent, arrogant, aumonier, bête, bêtise, bizuth, caractère, casse, casser, chaleur, chaude, convulsé, coups, courroux, déformation, déréglement, désordre, diable, dispute, drift, éclatante, émotion, ennemi, épouvantable, état, excitation, fiancé, force, foudre, fracas, frapper du pied, froide, furie, gaieté, garçon, gentil, honte, impassibilité, impulsif, insupportable, intempestive, inutile, ire divine, irritation, irrité, jaune, jeunesse, joie, jour, laid, lait, liberté, mâchoires, maitrise, mal de tête, malade, maladie, oeil, orgeuil, parent, paresse, parole, passion, péché, père, peu, pire, pitié, poing, preste, à priori, puissance, raison, remords, risque, rongeur, sage, sagesse, sénile, sottise, stupide, subite, susceptible, sympathise, tampon, tapage, taper, tempérament, tempête, tête, tranquilité, trépigner, tristesse, vert, vibrer, vice, vif, violent, vivant, volonté

Workers

No.	Response	Total
10.	violent (violente)	3
11.	bagarre	2
12.	caractère	2
13.	enrager (enrage)	2
14.	grande	2
15.	de lion	2
16.	nerveux	2
17.	terrible	2
18.	violence	2
19-58.	(f = 1)	40

affaire, aigu, bêtise, bleu, brutale, calme, casser, chien, coléreux, coups, débris, déchainé, doux, dur, énervement, femme, fureur, furieuse, gâcher, gentil, impulsif, juron, maligne, manque de maitrise, monstrueuse, nuisible, passif, peuple, peur, pied, rouge, rougeur, seau d'eau, sévère, silence, stupide, subite, tendresse, tonnerre (Illegible - 3)

39. TAPIS

Students

No.	Response	Total	Female	Male
1.	moëlleux	31	24	7
2.	doux	27	18	9
3.	laine	22	18	4
4.	Orient (d'Orient)	15	12	3
5.	confort	12	8	4
6.	persan	11	4	7
7.	carpette	10	4	6
8.	Perse	9	5	4
9.	brosse	8	7	1
10.	douceur	8	5	3
11.	maison	6	5	1
12.	Maroc	6	4	2
13.	rouge	6	6	0
14.	sol	6	3	3

Workers

No.	Response	Total
1.	persan	15
2.	vert	9
3.	doux	7
4.	moëlleux	7
5.	d'Orient (Orient)	6
6.	rouge	4
7.	arabe	3
8.	sol	3
9.	chaud	2
10.	nappe	2
11.	pied	2
12.	salon	2
13.	tapisserie	2
14.	volant	2

39. TAPIS (contd)

Students

No.	Response	Total	Female	Male
15.	vert	6	4	2
16.	mou	5	1	4
17.	arabe	4	1	3
18.	épais	4	4	0
19.	parquet	4	3	1
20.	plancher	4	4	0
21.	chambre	3	3	0
22.	dessin	3	2	1
23.	salon	3	2	1
24.	turc	3	0	3
25.	calme	2	0	2
26.	couleur	2	2	0
27.	couverture	2	0	2
28.	dame (dames)	2	2	0
29.	fauteuil	2	2	0
30.	feutre	2	1	1
31.	flex	2	0	2
32.	frange (franges)	2	2	0
33.	gris	2	1	1
34.	laineux	2	1	1
35.	moquette	2	1	1
36.	mousse	2	2	0
37.	rideau	2	1	1
38.	rugueux	2	1	1
39-82.	(f = 1)	44	21	23

Afrique, Asie, Bagdad, blanc, chaleur, chaud, cheminee, coucher, décoration, descente de lit, divan, dormir, doucereux, feuille, fleurs, haut, lampe, lecture, luxe, mer, métier, meuble, les mille et une nuit, Mourzouk, nappe, objet, oriental, pantoufles, pétales, pied, poil, roulant, rustique, salle, Ségalot, souple, table, tapisserie, tenture, tigre, usé, vieilleries, volant, zéphyr

Workers

No.	Response	Total
15-63.	(f = 1)	49

A. F. N., aspirateur, battre, beau, brosse, bleu, carte, de chambre, chatoyant, chaussure, chemise, confort, couverture, décoration, drap, épais, escalier, essuyer, esthétique, fauve, feutre, gris, joli, de laine, pur laine, lino, de lit, dessous de lit, magnifique, marché, marcher, marches, marocain, mou, ours, Perse, plage, propre, repos, sale, silence, solide, splendide, table, tapisser, terre, par terre, toile, voile

40. FILLE

Students

No.	Response	Total	Female	Male
1.	garçon	100	71	29
2.	jolie	12	5	7
3.	enfant (enfants)	11	4	7
4.	jeune	10	7	3
5.	femme	8	6	2
6.	mère	8	5	3
7.	cheveu (cheveux)	7	6	1
8.	joie (de joie)	7	4	3
9.	natte (nattes)	6	5	1
10.	rue (des rues)	5	4	1
11.	blonde (blond)	4	3	1
12.	fils	4	1	3
13.	jeunesse	4	2	2
14.	prostituée (prostitué)	4	1	3
15.	soeur (ma soeur)	4	3	1
16.	danse	3	0	3
17.	fleur	3	1	2
18.	petite	3	3	0
19.	beauté	2	0	2
20.	belle	2	0	2
21.	bois	2	1	1
22.	cheveux de lin	2	0	2
23.	être	2	1	1
24.	femininité	2	2	0
25.	frère	2	2	0
26.	gaie	2	2	0
27.	publique	2	1	1
28.	putain	2	1	1
29.	robe	2	2	0
30.	ruban	2	2	0
31.	simple	2	2	0
32-90.	(f = 1)	59	37	22

affection, affreux, agitation, aimable, amie, amour,

Workers

No.	Response	Total
1.	garçon	15
2.	belle	10
3.	jeune	10
4.	enfant (enfants)	5
5.	jolie	5
6.	sage	5
7.	beauté	3
8.	bien	3
9.	amour	2
10.	calvaire (du calvaire)	2
11.	gentille	2
12.	laide	2
13.	soeur	2
14-60.	(f = 1)	47

aimable, aimante, amitié, basse, blonde, cheveux, démon, dévergondée, d'Eve, féminin, fillette, fils, forme, fortunée, frère, future-femme, pas, garçon, gars, gourde, homme, honnête, humaine, indiscrète, instruite, jouets, joyeux, jupe, légère, maniaque, manière, mère, mignonne, naïve, noir, de Paris, perdu, père petite, putain, robe, de roi, rue, sain, salle, seule, sexe, soirée
(Illegible - 2)

40. FILLE (contd)

Students

No.	Response	Total	Female	Male

bal, bijou, brun, camarade, cartable, chipie, compliqué,
coquette, coquetterie, courage, couture, démon, école,
encore, Eve, famille, fille, fille de joie, flanc,
foyer, fréquenter, gars, genres, gentille, gentillesse,
grande, jeux, jupe, longue, lycée, noeud, oui, parent,
perdue, père, prendre, du peuple, rien, rire, sage,
saine, sexe, solitude, sportive, tendresse, tête,
travailler, tresses, triste, trottoir, type, unique,
verte

41. HAUT

Students

No.	Response	Total	Female	Male
1.	bas	127	74	53
2.	montagne	16	12	4
3.	tour	10	7	3
4.	gratte-ciel	9	5	4
5.	maison	7	7	0
6.	sommet	7	6	1
7.	élevé	6	4	2
8.	grand	6	4	2
9.	plafond (de plafond)	6	4	2
10.	vent	6	4	2
11.	mur	5	3	2
12.	vertige	5	3	2
13.	arbre	3	2	1
14.	caisse	3	2	1
15.	chapeau	3	2	1
16.	cîme	3	2	1
17.	grandeur	3	2	1
18.	hurle vent	3	3	0
19.	Tour Eiffel	3	2	1
20.	armoire	2	2	0
21.	building	2	1	1
22.	ciel	2	2	0
23.	échelle	2	1	1
24.	homme	2	2	0
25.	loin	2	2	0
26.	long	2	1	1
27.	pavé	2	0	2
28.	pic	2	2	0
29-67.	(f = 1)	39	23	16

adjectif, en l'air, altitude, avion, but, cheminée,
clair, clocher, colis, colonne, le corps, court,
danger, dangereux, échafaudage, escalade, escalier,
de forme, fourneau, fragile, haut les mains, "Les
Hauts de Hurlevent", immeuble, inaccessible, mal,
mon travail, mont, Mont-Blanc, le nain, Nietzsche,
petit, placé, pointu, profond, rapport, taille,
talon, tomber, torsion

Workers

No.	Response	Total
1.	bas (basse)	30
2.	sommet	7
3.	grand	5
4.	montagne	5
5.	immeuble	4
6.	tour	4
7.	Tour Eiffel	4
8.	les mains	3
9.	mont	3
10.	petit	3
11.	toit (d'un toit)	3
12.	ciel	2
13.	échelle	2
14.	immense	2
15.	maison	2
16.	sapin	2
17-50.	(f = 1)	34

altitude, ardu, bâtiment, caisse,
clocher, colline, dangereux, élevé,
escabeau, l'étage, forme, girafe,
gratte-ciel, grue, inaccessible,
manège, de 3 mètres, Mont-Blanc,
monument, mur, nain, parasol,
perché, pied, physique, placer,
plafond, plateau, taille, talon,
tombe, tomber, vertiges, ville

42. TRAVAIL

Students

No.	Response	Total	Female	Male
1.	repos	20	11	9
2.	dur	18	11	7
3.	fatigue	17	10	7
4.	pénible	10	7	3
5.	labeur	9	6	3
6.	devoir (devoirs)	8	5	3
7.	santé	7	4	3
8.	loisir	6	3	3
9.	classe	5	3	2
10.	effort	5	3	2

Workers

No.	Response	Total
1.	dur	14
2.	santé	7
3.	facile	6
4.	fatiguant	4
5.	labeur	4
6.	repos	4
7.	ardu	3
8.	agréable	2
9.	argent	2
10.	assidue	2

42. TRAVAIL (contd)

	Students					Workers	
No.	Response	Total	Female	Male	No.	Response	Total
11.	acharné	4	2	2	11.	bon	2
12.	famille	4	1	3	12.	courage	2
13.	homme	4	3	1	13.	fainéant	2
14.	joie	4	3	1	14.	liberté	2
15.	lycée	4	3	1	15.	long	2
16.	manuel	4	3	1	16.	occupation	2
17.	paresse	4	2	2	17.	pénible	2
18.	patrie	4	2	2	18.	salaire	2
19.	peine	4	2	2	19.	soigné	2
20.	livre (livres)	3	3	0	20	travailleur	2
21.	occupation	3	1	2	21.	usine	2
22.	table	3	3	0	22.	vivre	2
23.	activité	2	1	1	23-64.	(f = 1)	42
24.	ardu	2	2	0			
25.	besogne	2	2	0			
26.	chain	2	2	0			
27.	courage	2	1	1			
28.	crayon	2	2	0			
29.	difficile	2	0	2			
30.	ennui	2	1	1			
31.	équilibre	2	2	0			
32.	étude (études)	2	2	0			
33.	gagner	2	1	1			
34.	horaire	2	1	1			
35.	humain	2	2	0			
36.	intérêt	2	2	0			
37.	liberté	2	2	0			
38.	ordre	2	1	1			
39.	ouvrier	2	1	1			
40.	plaisir	2	1	1			
41.	régulier	2	1	1			
42.	réussite	2	2	0			
43.	salaire	2	1	1			
44.	soigné	2	2	0			
45.	sueur	2	1	1			
46.	temps	2	2	0			
47.	vacances	2	1	1			
48.	vite	2	2	0			
49-134.	(f = 1)	86	55	31			

23-64. (f = 1) 42
acharné, amusant, atelier, bien, bois, boulot, brosser, chausson, chomage, condition, confortable, convenable, effort, embêtant, fatigue, force, forcé, fortune, homme, intellectuel, journalier, journée, lent, machine, manger, manuel, métier, minutieux, nonchalance, main d'oeuvre, outils, ouvrier, passe-temps, patrie, peine, rapide, remuer, rémunération, route, santé humaine, satisfaction, simple
(Illegible - 1)

49-134. (f = 1) 86 55 31
actif, agréable, algébrique, âme, ardeur, bien, bon, bureau, cahier, chaleur, conscience, cours, détente, difficultés, dissertation, école, écrire, élève, enchaînement, ennuyeux, fainéantisme, force, Friedmann, hauteur, 8 heures par jour, important, inconnu, intéressant, jour, laborieux, lassitude, lent, lenteur, loi, lumière, machine, main, manoeuvre, manucure, médecin, mérite, méthode, métier, mineur, ministre, musique, non, note, nuit, obligation, obligatoire, obsession, oisiveté, oeuvre, oubli, papier, passe-temps, patience, le père, plume, professeur, profitant, psychologie, puissance, rail, recherche, résistance, rêve, robuste, romain, sac, scolaire, sérieux, silence, sobre, soin, Sorbonne, stylo, succès, tâche, toujours, travailleur, triste, tristesse, veillée, vie

43. AIGRE

	Students					Workers	
No.	Response	Total	Female	Male	No.	Response	Total
1.	doux	86	51	35	1.	vinaigre	30
2.	vinaigre	54	35	19	2.	doux	17
3.	acide	18	14	4	3.	amer (amère, amers)	8
4.	vin	13	8	5	4.	vin	8
5.	amer (amère)	11	9	2	5.	citron	6
6.	lait	9	7	2	6.	acide	4
7.	fruit (fruit amer)	8	4	4	7.	mauvais	4
8.	sur (sure)	8	5	3	8.	sur	4
9.	citron	5	3	2	9.	fin	2
10.	goût	4	2	2	10.	goût	2
11.	pomme	4	1	3	11-39	(f = 1)	29
12.	sucré	4	2	2			

11-39 (f = 1) 29
bise, pas bon, breuvage, cerise,

43. AIGRE (contd)

	Students					Workers	
No.	Response	Total	Female	Male		No.	Response	Total

Students

No.	Response	Total	Female	Male
13.	vent	4	3	1
14.	aigu	3	3	0
15.	bise	3	2	1
16.	boisson	3	3	0
17.	âcre	2	1	1
18.	âpre	2	2	0
19.	cerise	2	2	0
20.	cidre	2	1	1
21.	déagréable	2	2	0
22.	dur	2	1	1
23.	groseille	2	2	0
24.	piquant	2	0	2
25.	soupe	2	2	0
26.	vieux	2	1	1
27-57.	(f = 1)	31	18	13

aigle, aigre-doux, aigrefin, aimable, aliment, artisan,
colère, dégoût, fin, fourré, froid, hiver, lait caillé,
mauvais, méchant, mégère, pamplemousse, pas mûr,
raisin, rance, répulsion, salé, saumâtre, sensation,
sirop, sourd, suave, sucre, thon, vieille fille, vif

Workers

No.	Response	Total

cidre, colère, crue, dégouté,
désagréable, détestable, dur, fou,
fruit, fruité, mauvais goût,
goût, inmangeable, langue, lait,
mécanique, méchanceté, méchant,
personne, pimenté, piquant, pluie,
sauce, soif, triste, vent
(No response - 1)

44. TERRE

Students

No.	Response	Total	Female	Male
1.	mer	31	18	13
2.	ciel	24	16	8
3.	ronde (rond)	21	16	5
4.	sol	10	5	5
5.	feu (de feu)	8	6	2
6.	lune	7	4	3
7.	paysan	7	4	3
8.	planète	7	7	0
9.	cuite	6	5	1
10.	ferme	5	4	1
11.	mappemonde	5	4	1
12.	dur (dure)	4	3	1
13.	hommes (des hommes)	4	2	2
14.	monde	4	1	3
15.	brun	3	2	1
16.	campagne	3	1	2
17.	champs	3	1	2
18.	culture (cultures)	3	2	1
19.	eau	3	1	2
20.	globe	3	1	2
21.	jardin	3	2	1
22.	labour	3	3	0
23.	neuve	3	2	1
24.	rouge	3	3	0
25.	Sienne (de Sienne)	3	1	2
26.	soleil (le soleil)	3	0	3
27.	air	2	1	1
28.	astre	2	1	1
29.	bas	2	1	1
30.	boue	2	1	1
31.	charme	2	1	1
32.	continent	2	1	1
33.	glaise	2	2	0
34.	humide	2	1	1
35.	inculte	2	2	0
36.	marron	2	2	0
37.	matière	2	1	1
38.	molle	2	1	1
39.	noir (noire)	2	2	0
40.	plein	2	2	0
41.	promise	2	1	1
42.	sable	2	2	0
43.	travail	2	2	0
44.	univers	2	1	1
45.	voyage	2	1	1
46-116.	(f = 1)	71	44	27

Workers

No.	Response	Total
1.	ciel	9
2.	ronde (rond)	9
3.	labour	5
4.	ferme	4
5.	monde	4
6.	basse	3
7.	cultivé (cultiver)	3
8.	de feu	3
9.	mer	3
10.	neuve	3
11.	planète	3
12.	sol	3
13.	champ (champs)	2
14.	dur (dure)	2
15.	fertile	2
16.	glaise	2
17.	grasse	2
18.	jardin	2
19.	humide	2
20.	molle	2
21.	paysan (paysans)	2
22.	promise	2
23-63.	(f = 1)	41

Adélie, air, arable, armée, astre,
belle, bonne, café, cailloux, cuite,
cultivable, découverte, eau, espace,
espoir, de France, froide, grande,
île, labourable, labourer, laboureur,
mère, métal, meuble, meule, mouillée,
notre, du pays, plantation, plante,
potier, récolte, sablonneuse, Sienne,
solitaire, stérile, terreur,
terreuse, Terre-Neuve, travaille
(Illegible - 2)

44. TERRE (contd)

Students

No.	Response	Total	Female	Male

Adélie, amour, basse, beauté, blé, bloc, bois, caillou,
cendre, cheval, colline, cosmos, courbature,
cultivateur, s'effrite, fertile, fleurs, froide,
fruits, Galilée, gazon, glèbe, grasse, humanité,
labouré, labourer, laboureur, lapin, lointaine, maçon,
main, maison, malléable, mère, montagne, motte, mousse,
le Nain, naturel, nourricière, nourriture, objet, ocre,
odeur, orange, orbite, pays, peine, plaine, poterie,
printemps, profondeur, Rhéa, richesse, rotondité,
rugueux, Sainte, sec, sphérique, tassé, terre, terreau,
terre-à-terre, Terre-Neuve, tombe, verre, vert, vie,
violente, visser, Zola

45. DIFFICULTÉ

Students

No.	Response	Total	Female	Male
1.	facilité (facilités)	37	17	20
2.	travail	27	17	10
3.	dur (dure)	13	9	4
4.	obstacle	12	9	3
5.	problème	12	9	3
6.	ennui (ennuis)	11	9	2
7.	courage	7	6	1
8.	effort (efforts)	7	4	3
9.	vaincre (à vaincre)	7	3	4
10.	facile	6	5	1
11.	ardu	5	2	3
12.	vie	5	3	2
13.	devoir	4	2	2
14.	mathématiques	4	2	2
15.	peine	4	3	1
16.	pénible	4	2	2
17.	surmonter	4	2	2
18.	vaincue (vaincues)	4	1	3
19.	difficile	3	2	1
20.	insurmontable	3	2	1
21.	tâche	3	3	0
22.	argent	2	1	1
23.	arrêt	2	1	1
24.	épreuve	2	2	0
25.	examen	2	1	1
26.	faculté	2	2	0
27.	montagne	2	2	0
28.	non	2	2	0
29.	résoudre	2	1	1
30.	souci (soucis)	2	2	0
31-118.	(f = 1)	88	59	29

abattre, aisance, aisé, amusement, âne, Anglais,
ascension, barrière, bonne, cahier, catastrophe, choix,
combat, complication, côté, croissante, danger,
désagréable, désagrément, désespoir, desordre, différence,
dureté, efficacité, embêtant, ennuyeux, entêtement,
enthousiasme, épine, équation, équilibre, erreur,
exploit, faite, fatigue, forêt de, fréquence, grande,
grosse, grossière, habitude, haut, idée, impasse,
impossibilité, inextricable, innombrable, insoluble,
intérêt, lassitude, légèreté, loisir, lutte, majeure,
mal, mal de tête, maths, métier, motrice, néant,
oeuvre, oui, pain, passagère, papier, pays, police,
pourquoi?, presse, prononciation, réelle, rencontrée,
réussir, réveil, rides, ronger, sans, sérénité, serrer
les dents, solution, soudaine, souffler, sourcils,
surmenage, test, vite, vivre, volonté

Workers

No.	Response	Total
1.	dur (dure)	10
2.	difficile	7
3.	ennui (ennuis, ennuie)	7
4.	facile	7
5.	grande (grand)	5
6.	argent (d'argent)	4
7.	souci (soucis)	4
8.	travail	4
9.	facilité (faciliter)	3
10.	apprendre (d'apprendre)	2
11.	grave	2
12.	surmonté (à surmonter)	2
13-69.	(f= 1)	57

acquise, aisance, assistance,
d'avoir, beaucoup, calcul, chance,
combattre, complication, compliqué,
diverse, écrire, embarras, embûche,
émulation, épreuve, examen, femme,
fertile, finance, assez fréquente,
impôts, incompréhension, insuffisance,
insurmontable, laborieux, majeure,
malade, marche, mauvaise, mentale,
moi, monstre, morale, né, sans nom,
obstacle, orientale, os, à passer,
patience, pécuniaire, pénible,
plaisir, problème, provisoire,
sensibilité, solitude, surmenage,
surmontable, train, tristesse, vie,
de la vie, victoire, vivre, d'y voir
(Illegible - 1)

46. SOLDAT

Students					Workers		
No.	Response	Total	Female	Male	No.	Response	Total
1.	guerre	59	32	27	1.	plomb (de plomb)	15
2.	plomb (de plomb)	32	18	14	2.	armée	13
3.	armée (l'armée)	26	18	8	3.	militaire	11
4.	uniforme	20	17	3	4.	courageux	5
5.	fusil	12	10	2	5.	fusil	4
6.	militaire	9	6	3	6.	brave	3
7.	homme	8	5	3	7.	guerre	3
8.	patrie	8	6	2	8.	quille (la quille)	3
9.	arme (armes)	7	7	0	9.	Algérie	2
10.	service (service militaire)	7	2	5	10.	caserne	2
11.	drapeau	5	3	2	11.	combattant	2
12.	bois	4	4	0	12.	jeune	2
13.	civil	4	0	4	13.	régiment	2
14.	courage	4	4	0	14-61.	(f = 1)	48
15.	kaki	4	3	1			
16.	caserne	3	3	0			
17.	général	3	0	3			
18.	inconnu	3	0	3			
19.	képi	3	3	0			
20.	baïonette	2	2	0			
21.	bleu	2	1	1			
22.	casque	2	1	1			
23.	citoyen	2	1	1			
24.	combat	2	1	1			
25.	français	2	1	1			
26.	héros	2	2	0			
27.	mort	2	2	0			
28.	troupe	2	2	0			
29-77.	(f = 1)	49	30	19			

14-61. (f = 1) 48: adj., agile, armé, armes, bagne, de bois, bon, camion, chef, citoyen, civil, 2ème classe, courage, défilé, déterminé, embêtant, fantassin, français, gradé, héros, indiscipliné, juste, libre, maréchal, mauvais, méritant, misère, moi, mort, non, parachutiste, paresseux, non patriotique, en patrouille, permission, perte, petit, prompt, aux rapports, soldes, solidarité, sport, tenu, troupe, troupier, uniforme, verte, vie

29-77. (f = 1) 49 30 19: absent, Algérie, américain, bataille, bataillon, bêtise, bientôt, calot, camaraderie, cantine, caporal, cavalier, chanson, chocolat, contrefort, courageux, ennui, fidèle, une fleur au chapeau, mon frère, front, guerrier, idiot, individu, infanterie, inutile, laid, maitresse, marche, marin, Marseillaise, mercenaire, Yves Montand, Napoléon, non, pays, paysan, rang, régiment revue, rouge, sabre, sciène, soldate, troufion, tué, tuer, tunique, Tunisie

47. CHOU

Students					Workers		
No.	Response	Total	Female	Male	No.	Response	Total
1.	fleur (chou-fleur, choux-fleurs)	88	48	40	1.	fleur (fleurs, en fleur)	37
2.	légume (légumes)	24	15	9	2.	Bruxelles (de Bruxelles)	8
3.	vert (vert tendre)	19	17	2	3.	légume (légumes)	8
4.	rave	17	8	9	4.	rouge	7
5.	jardin	9	8	1	5.	blanc	4
6.	rouge	9	8	1	6.	choux-fleurs	4
7.	carotte	8	6	2	7.	vert	4
8.	enfant	8	7	1	8.	à la crème (crème)	3
9.	Bruxelles	5	2	3	9.	salade	3
10.	champ (champs)	5	2	3	10.	chèvre	2
11.	crème	5	4	1	11.	chou (choux)	2
12.	salade	5	3	2	12-43.	(f = 1)	32
13.	chèvre	4	3	1			
14.	plante	4	2	2			
15.	pomme	4	3	1			
16.	potager	4	4	0			
17.	soupe	4	4	0			
18.	blanc	3	2	1			
19.	gâteau	3	3	0			
20.	navet	3	2	1			
21.	pou (poux)	3	3	0			
22.	repas	3	2	1			
23.	bébé	2	2	0			
24.	chenille	2	0	2			
25.	gras	2	0	2			
26.	mignon	2	1	1			

12-43. (f = 1) 32: aigre, amour, bon, carottes, champs, choucroûte, cuit, dîner, endives, enfant, farçis, la faim, ferme, feuille, une fille, Flandres, fourré, le garçon, hibou, jardin, malade, maraîcher, marmite, méchant, miel, navet, plante, pomme, pot-au-feu, rave, soupe, vin (Illegible - 1)

47. CHOU (contd)

Students

No.	Response	Total	Female	Male
27-69.	(f = 1)	43	25	18

agréable, agricole, aliment, amour, caillou, campagne, chasse, chou, choucroûte, chou rouge, Colette, culture, elle, farçi, garni, genou, gentil, grammaire, inabsorbable, infection, jardin-potager, laitue, lapin, limace, manger, maraîcher, marché, mauvais, mauvaise, odeur, naître, nourriture, odeur, personne, pommé, production, puits, rivière, rose, salé, saucisse, terre, vers, vin

48. DUR

Students

No.	Response	Total	Female	Male
1.	mou (mous)	82	47	35
2.	pierre	19	16	3
3.	fer (comme fer)	17	10	7
4.	doux	12	7	5
5.	bois	10	9	1
6.	acier	7	6	1
7.	sol	7	5	2
8.	cuire (à cuire)	5	1	4
9.	roc	5	3	2
10.	sec	5	3	2
11.	caillou (cailloux)	4	1	3
12.	difficile	4	3	1
13.	oeuf	4	1	3
14.	table	4	2	2
15.	tendre	4	3	1
16.	méchant	3	3	0
17.	amer	2	2	0
18.	aride	2	2	0
19.	banc	2	2	0
20.	couteau	2	1	1
21.	douleur	2	0	2
22.	facile	2	2	0
23.	ferme	2	2	0
24.	homme	2	0	2
25.	mal	2	2	0
26.	marbre	2	2	0
27.	oreille (oreilles)	2	2	0
28.	résistant	2	2	0
29.	rugueux	2	2	0
30.	vie	2	2	0
31-98.	(f = 1)	68	41	27

adjectif, affreux, aigle, alumine, âpre, bâton, blanc, blé, brutalité, caractère, carosserie, chemin, choc, ciment, col, combat, compact, dalle, désagréable, dureté, effort, ennuyeux, état, physique, fier, force, fort, friable, fuite, gangster, gentil, glace, gros, lame, léger, légion, lit, maître, malin, matière, métal, moi, mur, palper, pénible, pesant, plancher, plat, plomb, pointe, pointu, professeur, puissance, qualité, raide, résistance, réveil, rigide, rocher, rude, sain, sévère, solidé, solidité, têtu, le travail, travailler, verre, vif

Workers

No.	Response	Total
1.	mou	16
2.	fer (comme fer)	8
3.	acier	7
4.	pierre (la pierre)	6
5.	roc	6
6.	oeuf (oeufs)	5
7.	cailloux	4
8.	à cuire	4
9.	solide	4
10.	doux	3
11.	difficile	2
12.	glace	2
13.	roche	2
14.	souple	2
15-57.	(f = 1)	43

aimant, béton, bois, coriace, costaud, dédaigneux, Durandel, enfant, faible, faire, une femme, feuillade, fort, fortement, fragile, hiver, jeunesse, labeur, laborieux, léger, lutte, marbre, métal, nerveux, obscur, pain, pénible, plafond, plâtre, police, prison, regard, résistant, rocher, sec, semelle, silex, mi-temps, tendre, très, truand, vie, vif
(No response - 1)

49. AIGLE

Students

No.	Response	Total	Female	Male
1.	oiseau (l'oiseau)	46	29	17
2.	montagne	23	16	7
3.	nid	14	12	2
4.	Napoléon	12	9	3

Workers

No.	Response	Total
1.	oiseau (oiseaux, oiseau de proie)	17
2.	rapace	14
3.	noir	8
4.	montagne (montagnes)	7

49. AIGLE (contd)

No.	Response (Students)	Total	Female	Male
5.	rapace	12	4	8
6.	bec	9	6	3
7.	vautour	9	3	6
8.	noir	8	6	2
9.	proie	8	4	4
10.	hauteur	7	4	3
11.	vol	6	4	2
12.	aile (ailes)	5	4	1
13.	ciel	5	4	1
14.	serre	5	5	0
15.	blanc	4	2	2
16.	cîme	4	3	1
17.	roi	4	2	2
18.	aiglon	3	0	3
19.	haut	3	1	2
20.	majesté	3	0	3
21.	plume (plumes)	3	3	0
22.	royal	3	1	2
23.	altitude	2	0	2
24.	Asturies	2	1	1
25.	azur	2	1	1
26.	crochu	2	2	0
27.	emblème	2	0	2
28.	empire	2	2	0
29.	empereur	2	0	2
30.	faucon	2	1	1
31.	grandeur	2	2	0
32.	griffe	2	2	0
33.	meaux	2	2	0
34.	mont	2	2	0
35.	oeil	2	2	0
36.	orgueil	2	1	1
37.	plane	2	2	0
38.	planer	2	2	0
39.	rocher	2	2	0
40.	sommet	2	1	1
41-96.	(f = 1)	56	37	19

à deux têtes, aigre, aigrefin, air, Allemagne, des Alpes, altier, Ande, animal, arbre, beau, beauté, blanc, pignangue, casque, c'est un, condor, doux, élevé, élever, emporte, enfant, ensemble, espace, force, forêt, fort, géant, gloire, grand, héros, Hitler, impérial, Jupiter, liberté, magnifique, majestueux, mange, marine, moineau, mouton, neige, nuage, perçant, Phénix, pic, puissant, rapidité, regard, roitelet, royauté, soleil, son, survoler, tête, "vampire", voracité

No.	Response (Workers)	Total
5.	royal (royale)	7
6.	aiglon	4
7.	proie	4
8.	blanc	3
9.	épervier	3
10.	Napoléon	3
11.	vol (vole)	3
12.	aiguille	2
13.	fort	2
14.	méchant	2
15.	nid	2
16.	volet	2
17-48.	(f = 1)	32

air, altitude, beau, bec, chat, coquillage, cruel, à deux têtes, doux, faucon, géant, grand, gris, guettant sa proie, gueule, indien, mauvais, mésange, mont, oeil, pigeon, planer, plume, Pologne, roi, roux, royauté, serre, solitaire, sournois, splendeur, viande

50. ESTOMAC

No.	Response (Students)	Total	Female	Male
1.	digestion	25	20	5
2.	ventre	18	9	9
3.	faim	16	9	7
4.	intestin	15	7	8
5.	mal (maux)	14	10	4
6.	organe	14	7	7
7.	manger	12	2	10
8.	creux	7	6	1
9.	douleur	7	7	0
10.	crampe	6	6	0
11.	ulcère	6	4	2
12.	vide	6	4	2
13.	foie	5	3	2
14.	nourriture	5	2	3
15.	anatomie	4	3	1
16.	malade	4	3	1
17.	maladie	4	2	2
18.	poche	4	4	0
19.	repas	4	2	2

No.	Response (Workers)	Total
1.	faim	9
2.	fragile	8
3.	malade	7
4.	vide	6
5.	délicat	5
6.	foie	5
7.	ventre	5
8.	digestion	4
9.	corps	3
10.	mal (maux)	3
11.	alcool	2
12.	creux	2
13.	dilaté	2
14.	fatigué	2
15.	fer (du fer)	2
16.	garni (bien garni)	2
17.	intestin (d'intestins)	2
18.	maladie	2
19.	panse	2

50. ESTOMAC (contd)

Students

No.	Response	Total	Female	Male
20.	corps	3	2	1
21.	digérer	3	3	0
22.	indigestion	3	1	2
23.	rate	3	2	1
24.	tube digestif	3	2	1
25.	aigreur	2	0	2
26.	aliment (aliments)	2	2	0
27.	brulûre (brulûres)	2	1	1
28.	cancer	2	2	0
29.	digestif	2	1	1
30.	gésier	2	0	2
31.	membre (membres)	2	1	1
32.	panse	2	1	1
33.	plein	2	2	0
34.	sac	2	2	0
35.	sale	2	2	0
36.	sciences nat.	2	2	0
37.	tube	2	2	0
38.	vache	2	2	0
39.	viscère	2	2	0
40-106.	(f = 1)	67	42	25

acidité, acier, aérophagie, aigre, bile, bonbons, ceinture, chair, chaleur, charbon, coeur, coup, courage, crise, déjeuner, délicat, dilaté, dessin, embarras, Esope, essouflement, farci, de fer, fistule, fragile, fruit, gardénal, grêle, grenouille, gros, hamas, haricot, homme, inconnu, inconsistance, inintéressant, joie, La Fontaine, lourd, lourdeur, mal au coeur, médecin, morbide, muscles, muqueuse, noir, oesophage, pain, pancréas, paroi, peau, poulet, radio, rugueux, sciences, solide, souffrances, souple, suc, talon, trait, tranquille, trompette, tronc, tumeur, vésicule, vomissement

Workers

No.	Response	Total
20.	ulcère	2
21-58.	(f = 1)	38

absorber, appétit, blanc, boeuf, cancer, chaise, coeur, combat, corps humain, partie du corps, coups, crampe, crème, digère, douleur, douloureux, estomaqué, faible, grand, grognant, gros, léger, mange, mentor, mouton, d'oiseaux, organe, pierre, de plomb, rein, table, talon, tomate, vente, ventriloque, vin, vomissement (Illegible - 2)

51. TIGE

Students

No.	Response	Total	Female	Male
1.	fleur (fleurs)	100	74	26
2.	plante	32	20	12
3.	feuille	29	21	8
4.	vert (verte)	11	10	1
5.	arbre	7	4	3
6.	branche	6	3	3
7.	droit (droite)	5	1	4
8.	blé	4	2	2
9.	racine	4	1	3
10.	lion	3	2	1
11.	mince	3	2	1
12.	roseau (le roseau)	3	2	1
13.	souple	3	2	1
14.	finesse	2	1	1
15.	fragile	2	0	2
16.	grêle	2	2	0
17.	herbe	2	1	1
18.	lampe	2	0	2
19.	lisse	2	0	2
20.	souplesse	2	1	1
21.	tigre	2	1	1
22.	végétal	2	2	0
23-82.	(f = 1)	60	32	28

agressivité, allongé, animal, barre, Bengale, bête, bois, bon, bras, canine, chair, chat, cirque, croît, digitale, dureté, eau, élance, fauve, fer, férocité, fibre, fleuve, flexible, frêle, frise, girafe, grande, grimpante, gris, hampe, hampe florale, haute, liane, ligne, membre, noeud, organe, osier, palme, pituitaire, pointe, pousse, queue, raide, rampe, rigide, ronde, rose, rosier, saule, serpent, sève, support, svelte, tigelle, tordue, tronc, tulipe, verticale

Workers

No.	Response	Total
1.	fleur (fleurs)	17
2.	fer (de fer)	9
3.	longue (long)	9
4.	flexible	5
5.	verte (vert)	5
6.	mince	4
7.	plante	4
8.	arbre (d'arbre)	3
9.	fleurie (fleuri)	3
10.	rigide	3
11.	animal	2
12.	blé	2
13.	branche	2
14.	cigarette	2
15.	feuille	2
16.	fine	2
17.	noire (noir)	2
18.	royal	2
19.	souple	2
20-53.	(f = 1)	34

d'acier, barre, beau, bengale, bambou, bois, bourgeon, brousse, court, femme, féroce, filer, filetée, fougueux, grande, haute, d'herbe, Inde, jungle, lys, mécanique, outil, panthère, raide, rat, règle, roseaux, rouge, sauvage, souffle, tabac, table, tigre, tube (No response - 1)

52. LAMPE

Students

No.	Response	Total	Female	Male
1.	lumière (la lumière)	102	63	39
2.	chevet (de chevet)	25	16	9
3.	abat-jour	19	15	4
4.	pétrole	11	3	8
5.	ampoule	10	6	4
6.	huile	9	3	6
7.	clarté	6	3	3
8.	pied	6	4	2
9.	allumée	5	2	3
10.	éclairage	5	3	2
11.	éclaire	5	5	0
12.	claire (clair)	4	4	0
13.	douceur	4	3	1
14.	électrique	4	2	2
15.	verre	4	3	1
16.	électricité	3	0	3
17.	soir	3	3	0
18.	alcool	2	2	0
19.	chaleur	2	2	0
20.	chambre	2	2	0
21.	cul	2	1	1
22.	feu	2	1	1
23.	foyer	2	2	0
24.	intimité	2	2	0
25.	jaune	2	2	0
26.	lampadaire	2	0	2
27.	nuit	2	2	0
28.	obscurité	2	1	1
29.	soirée	2	1	1
30-68.	(f = 1)	39	28	11

allumer, appartement, bien, douce, duvet, éclat, éteinte, faible, file, lampiste, lumignon, maison, mineur, Musset, objet, opaline, pénombre, pigeon, professeur, raphie, réveil, réverbère, rosace, rouge, rousse, salle, salon, scintillante, soie, soleil, songe, table de chevet, de table, travail, vase, veillée, veilleuse, verte, vive

Workers

No.	Response	Total
1.	lumière	27
2.	chevet (de chevet, à chevet)	12
3.	pétrole (à petrole, de pétrole)	7
4.	éclair	6
5.	électrique	6
6.	souder (à souder)	6
7.	allumée (allumé)	4
8.	verte	4
9.	ampoule	3
10.	éclairage	3
11.	de poche (poche)	3
12.	éblouissante	2
13.	électricité	2
14.	éteinte	2
15.	forte	2
16.	pile	2
17-40.	(f = 1)	24

à arc, Aladin, alcool, abat-jour, basse, blanche, bleu, bleutée, chaumière, claire, cuiller, éclairée, feu, lampadaire, lumineux, Mazda, néon, petite, rouge, tamisé, témoin, tempête, veillée, 440 W

53. RÊVE

Students

No.	Response	Total	Female	Male
1.	sommeil	50	33	17
2.	bleu	19	13	6
3.	dormir	18	9	9
4.	nuit	17	12	5
5.	Freud	15	11	4
6.	cauchemar	14	9	5
7.	agréable	6	5	1
8.	douceur	6	4	2
9.	doux	6	4	2
10.	éveillé	5	2	3
11.	psychanalyse	5	5	0
12.	illusion	4	3	1
13.	imagination	4	3	1
14.	irréalité	4	2	2
15.	jeune fille (de jeune fille)	4	2	2
16.	lit	4	3	1
17.	songe	4	3	1
18.	bonheur	3	1	2
19.	désir	3	3	0
20.	évasion	3	2	1
21.	nuage	3	3	0
22.	réalité	3	2	1
23.	rose	3	2	1
24.	analyse	2	1	1
25.	de jeunesse	2	1	1
26.	joie	2	0	2

Workers

No.	Response	Total
1.	dormir	13
2.	cauchemar	8
3.	sommeil (sommeille)	8
4.	nuit (de nuit, la nuit)	7
5.	bleu (bleue)	6
6.	d'or	4
7.	songe	4
8.	doux	3
9.	d'enfant	3
10.	insomnie	3
11.	heureux	3
12.	beau	2
13.	joli (jolie)	2
14.	merveilleux	2
15.	réalité	2
16-59.	(f = 1)	44

si amer, d'amour, d'ange, anticipation, avenir, chimère, congé, dorme, évasion, femme, folie, hardi, histoire, horrible, idiot, illusion, inconscient, irréalisable, jeunesse, du jour, joyeux, léger, lit, magnifique, malaise, néant, noir, nuage, parle, penser, plaisir, plongée, profond, réalisable, réel, roi, rose, souvent, stupide, tigre,

53. RÊVE (contd)

Students

No.	Response	Total	Female	Male
27.	merveilleux	2	2	0
28.	or	2	0	2
29.	oubli	2	2	0
30.	poésie	2	1	1
31.	rêverie	2	2	0
32.	vague	2	2	0
33-99.	(f = 1)	67	37	30

abstrait, affreux, amie, d'amour, angoisse, Athalie, avenir, béatitude, beau, beauté, Bergson, blanc, blancheur, bon, bruit, charmant, en couleurs, couleuvre, délicat, délice, doré, drap, enfant, éveil, fatigue, fauteuil, féerie, fenêtre, flou, gaie, halo, illumination, image, incompréhensible, inconscient, irréel, joli, joyeux, léger, légèreté, lent, lenteur, livre, mélancolie, mirage, mort, obscène, obscurité, obscur, pensée, plaisir, printemps, poursuite, repos, réveil, seul, le soir, somnoler, sordide, surréalisme, tissu, un, Utopie, de valse, vie, vision, Zola

Workers

No.	Response	Total

trève, triste, de vacances, de valse
(No response - 1)

54. JAUNE

Students

No.	Response	Total	Female	Male
1.	vert	31	19	12
2.	citron	20	14	6
3.	serin	18	11	7
4.	or (d'or)	17	8	9
5.	bleu	14	8	6
6.	oeuf (d'oeuf)	14	9	5
7.	soleil	12	12	0
8.	rouge	11	6	5
9.	couleur	9	2	7
10.	noir	9	6	3
11.	cocu	7	1	6
12.	blanc	6	4	2
13.	canari	6	5	1
14.	chinois	6	3	3
15.	clair	6	1	5
16.	fleur	6	5	1
17.	bouton d'or	5	5	0
18.	poussin	5	3	2
19.	paille	4	2	2
20.	tournesol	4	3	1
21.	nain	3	2	1
22.	violet	3	3	0
23.	blé	2	1	1
24.	chambre	2	2	0
25.	clarté	2	1	1
26.	coucou	2	2	0
27.	fleuve	2	1	1
28.	jonquille	2	2	0
29.	mur	2	2	0
30.	orange	2	1	1
31.	papillon	2	2	0
32-85.	(f = 1)	54	38	16

aigre, anorak, ardent, banane, cahier, calme, canard, chenille, Chine, croisière, distinction, douceur, éclat, éclatant, épais, feuille, fidélité, gai, gaieté, grève, gréviste, gris, homme, i, Indochine, jalousie, joie, laid, lampe, lumière, lumineux, lune, lys, manteau, mari, Noirs, ocre, pâle, pin, pull-over, race, réveille, robe japonaise, sable, salon, souffre, sucre, syndicalisme, tapis, tricot, trompé, Van Gogh, vif, violent

Workers

No.	Response	Total
1.	citron	11
2.	couleur	11
3.	chinois	9
4.	oeuf (d'oeuf)	8
5.	pâle	7
6.	orange	6
7.	paille	6
8.	bleu (bleue)	5
9.	or (d'or)	5
10.	soleil	4
11.	vert	4
12.	rouge	3
13.	blanc	2
14.	canari	2
15.	feuille	2
16.	jaunisse	2
17.	serin	2
18-43.	(f = 1)	26

acajou, armoire, Asie, Chine, coeur, comme, corde, la craie, drapeau, éblouissant, épi, foie, forêt, gris, Japon, maladie, nain, noir, ocre, bouton d'or, pastel, peinture, printemps, safran, topaze, sauté

MARK R. ROSENZWEIG

55. PAIN

Students					Workers		
No.	Response	Total	Female	Male	No.	Response	Total
1.	vin (et vin)	30	18	12	1.	blanc	15
2.	blanc	19	13	6	2.	manger (mange, mangé)	14
3.	manger	19	12	7	3.	farine	9
4.	faim	16	11	5	4.	d'épice (épice)	6
5.	mie (de mie)	14	8	6	5.	bis	5
6.	dur	13	9	4	6.	dur	5
7.	nourriture	12	7	5	7.	frais	3
8.	sec	11	8	3	8.	nourriture	3
9.	bis	9	4	5	9.	seigle	3
10.	quotidien	8	5	3	10.	sec	3
11.	boulanger	7	4	3	11.	aliment	2
12.	beurre	6	5	1	12.	bon	2
13.	blé	5	4	1	13.	boulanger	2
14.	farine	5	4	1	14.	eau	2
15.	amour	4	1	3	15.	faim	2
16.	bon	4	3	1	16.	mou	2
17.	frais	4	1	3	17.	noir	2
18.	noir	4	2	2	18.	quotidien	2
19.	aliment	3	2	1	19.	symbole	2
20.	miche	3	2	1	20.	travail	2
21.	sel	3	2	1	21.	vin (et vin)	2
22.	viande	3	2	1	22-47.	(f = 1)	26
23.	boulangerie	2	1	1			
24.	brûlé	2	2	0			
25.	couteau	2	2	0			
26.	croissant	2	2	0			
27.	croûte	2	0	2			
28.	cuisine	2	2	0			
29.	épice (épices)	2	2	0			
30.	lait	2	2	0			
31.	main	2	1	1			
32.	pauvre	2	2	0			
33.	repas	2	2	0			
34.	sucre	2	1	1			
35.	table	2	2	0			
36.	travail	2	2	0			
37.	vie	2	2	0			
38-93.	(f = 1)	56	32	24			

Workers, No. 22-47:
beurre, bière, biscotte, blé, chasse, croustillant, cuit, doux, four, gâteau, goût, jeux, mie, miche, d'orge, planche, pom, rassis, repas, salé, santé, sucre, sylvestre, viande, vide, voir
(No response - 1)

Students, No. 38-93:
"...Amour et Fantaisie", "...Amour et Jalousie", appétit, beau, besoin, brioché, céleste, chaud, chocolat, Christ, cidre, corbeille, à couper, craque, déjeuner, Dieu, doré, drôle, eau, fantaisie, film, flûte, four, fromage, gâteau, gourmand, goûter, grillé, grossir, guerre, habitude, homme, justice, labeur, long, mâcher, miettes, moralité, nécessaire, nécessité, odeur, pain bis, pamplemousse, planche, prison, rassis, régime, repos, sandwich, saveur, seigle, sueur, tartine, tendre, trou, vivant

56. JUSTICE

Students					Workers		
No.	Response	Total	Female	Male	No.	Response	Total
1.	balance	24	16	8	1.	paix	16
2.	juge (juges)	24	15	9	2.	loi	9
3.	fait (est faite)	21	15	6	3.	faite (est faite)	8
4.	palais (Palais de Justice)	15	8	7	4.	juge	6
5.	égalité	12	4	8	5.	tribunal	5
6.	charité	11	4	7	6.	glaive	3
7.	loi (lois)	10	8	2	7.	raide	3
8.	tribunal	10	8	2	8.	égalité	2
9.	avocat	9	7	2	9.	homme (hommes)	2
10.	droit	9	5	4	10.	juste (justes)	2
11.	injustice	9	4	5	11.	loyal	2
12.	paix (de paix)	9	5	4	12.	palais	2
13.	liberté	4	3	1	13.	police	2
14.	Dieu	3	1	2	14.	procès	2
15.	faire	3	3	0	15-64.	(f = 1)	50
16.	mort (la mort)	3	1	2			

Workers, No. 15-64:
ânerie, avocat, balance, bandeau,

56. JUSTICE (contd)

Students

No.	Response	Total	Female	Male
17.	noire (noir)	3	3	0
18.	rare	3	1	2
19.	robe	3	3	0
20.	sociale	3	3	0
21.	coupable	2	1	1
22.	cour	2	2	0
23.	divine	2	0	2
24.	épée	2	1	1
25.	faux	2	2	0
26.	fête	2	1	1
27.	inégalité	2	0	2
28.	prison	2	1	1
29.	raide	2	1	1
30-111.	($\underline{f}$ = 1)	82	58	24

absente, accomplie, accusé, affection, aléa, amour,
amusant, arrangement, aveugle, barre de, barreau,
bâtiment, bien, blanc, boîteuse, bon, citoyen, Clermont,
colère, colonne, condamné, crime, crise, croche,
croyance, délit, déloyale, désir, devoir, dur, enfant,
équitable, équité, erreurs, fidélité, film, fou,
garçon, gendarme, glaive, huissier, idéal, idiot,
impartialité, impossibilité, incontrôlable, irréel,
juré, juste, lait, law, légalité, loyauté, magistrat,
maître, manches, Minerve, nécessité, non, normal,
oui, panem, patrie, pénale, perruque, peur, police,
pont, porte, problématique, procès, protection,
règle, rendre, rendue, rigueur, rouge, royale, société,
sommaire, vérité, vol

Workers

No.	Response	Total

bien, bonne, buffet, calomnie, crime,
difficile, divine, de Dieu, droit,
dur, égale, exemplaire, sera faite,
faux, flics, fraternelle, fraternité,
implacable, impartial, impitoyable,
infaisable, injuste, injustice,
justicier, légale, liberté, logique,
loyalisme, magistrat, mauvais,
à mort, parfaite, pointu, prime,
punir, raide, règlements, saucisse,
sévère, soi-même, société, tête,
utopie, vérité, voleur, voyou
(Illegible - 1)

57. GARÇON

Students

No.	Response	Total	Female	Male
1.	fille	117	68	49
2.	de café (café)	19	16	3
3.	enfant	12	8	4
4.	boucher	7	5	2
5.	école	4	3	1
6.	force	4	1	3
7.	d'honneur (honneur)	4	0	4
8.	jeune	4	2	2
9.	pantalon	4	4	0
10.	petit	4	4	0
11.	camarade	3	1	2
12.	coiffeur	3	1	2
13.	jeu	3	1	2
14.	bon	2	0	2
15.	course (courses)	2	1	1
16.	danse	2	2	0
17.	écolier	2	1	1
18.	fort	2	1	1
19.	frère	2	1	1
20.	grand	2	2	0
21.	homme	2	2	0
22.	jeunesse	2	0	2
23.	lycée	2	1	1
24.	mauvais	2	2	0
25.	rue (de la rue)	2	2	0
26.	silhouette	2	2	0
27.	turbulent	2	2	0
28-99.	($\underline{f}$ = 1)	72	51	21

adolescent, agressivité, ami, auto, autre côté, barbe,
bataille, blond, brouillon, bruit, brutal,
brutalité, casquette, cerceau, cheveux, cheveux en
brosse, clair, collégien, commis, cousin, courir,
culotte, culottes courtes, dur, ennui, franchise,
individu, innocent, insensible, intelligent,
intrépide, jambes, Jean-Claude, joie, jumeaux, laid,
liberté, lycéens, mâle, manqué, martial, méchant,
mignon, moi, moustache, neveu, noble, noeud, noir,
ouvreur, pistolet, Pull, restaurant, rien, rude,

Workers

No.	Response	Total
1.	fille (filles)	25
2.	de café (café)	6
3.	beau	4
4.	jeune	4
5.	sage	4
6.	course (de course)	3
7.	gentil	3
8.	intelligent	3
9.	méchant	3
10.	poli (polie, polis)	3
11.	boucher	2
12.	école	2
13.	enfant	2
14.	grand	2
15.	homme	2
16.	manqué	2
17.	masculin	2
18-59.	($\underline{f}$ = 1)	42

basket, bête, bien, bleu, blouson
noir, bon, boy, brun, bouton de
bureau, chambre, chemise, cinéma,
coiffeur, correct, culotte, docile,
dynamique, écolier, fils,
footballeur, force, fou, garçonnet,
honnête, humain, jeune homme,
jeunesse, joli, maçon, mâle, mur,
oeuf, petit, rageur, rapide, sale,
de salle, sympathique, terrible,
têtu
(Illegible - 1)

57. GARÇON (contd)

Students

No.	Response	Total	Female	Male

service, sexe, sifflet, solitude, sonore, sport, sympathie, sympathique, table, truand, turbulence, type, veau, vien, viril, vivacité

58. CLAIR

Students

No.	Response	Total	Female	Male
1.	obscur	88	53	35
2.	sombre	50	29	21
3.	lune (de lune)	23	18	5
4.	ciel (le ciel)	15	7	8
5.	matin	9	6	3
6.	eau	7	4	3
7.	jour (le jour)	6	5	1
8.	lumière	6	4	2
9.	lumineux	6	6	0
10.	yeux	6	5	1
11.	net (nette)	4	1	3
12.	soleil	4	4	0
13.	agréable	3	2	1
14.	foncé	3	2	1
15.	noir	3	2	1
16.	pur	3	1	2
17.	aube	2	2	0
18.	beau	2	1	1
19.	blanc	2	1	1
20.	chambre	2	2	0
21.	couleur	2	0	2
22.	gai (gaie)	2	2	0
23.	gaieté	2	1	1
24.	transparent	2	2	0
25-60.	(f = 1)	36	24	12

air, amour, bleu, bois, château, clair de lune, clair, comme de l'eau, diaphane, disque, espoir, fenêtre, jaune, jeune, joie, joyeux, léger, liberté, limpide, neige, nuit, ouverture, peinture, pièce, printemps, profond, propre, propreté, Rembrandt, rose, soeur, sourir, teint, teinte, tissu, triste

Workers

No.	Response	Total
1.	lune (de lune)	18
2.	sombre	12
3.	net (nette, et net)	11
4.	jour (le jour)	10
5.	matin	6
6.	eau	5
7.	lumière	5
8.	source	3
9.	agréable	2
10.	ciel	2
11.	eau de roche	2
12.	foncé	2
13.	gai	2
14.	obscur	2
15.	soleil	2
16.	transparent	2
17-44.	(f = 1)	28

aurore, bien, blanc, bleu, clair de lune, clairement, couleur, dévoiler, été, étoile, flou, fontaine, franchise, hiver, jeune, musique, noir, passant, précis, propre, tabouret, teint, temps, tendre, tissu, trouble, vieux, vif
(Illegible - 1)

59. SANTÉ

Students

No.	Response	Total	Female	Male
1.	maladie	53	31	22
2.	fragile	25	17	8
3.	bonne (bon)	16	13	3
4.	bonheur	15	10	5
5.	force	14	9	5
6.	hôpital	7	5	2
7.	joie	7	6	1
8.	beauté	6	3	3
9.	médecin	6	3	3
10.	bien-être	5	4	1
11.	délicate	5	2	3
12.	fer (de fer)	5	3	2
13.	malade	5	2	3
14.	sobriété	5	3	2
15.	docteur	4	2	2
16.	fragilité	4	2	2
17.	équilibre	3	3	0
18.	gaieté	3	3	0
19.	publique (public)	3	2	1
20.	solide	3	1	2
21.	sport	3	2	1
22.	travail	3	0	3

Workers

No.	Response	Total
1.	bonne	26
2.	de fer (fer)	10
3.	fragile	7
4.	sobriété	7
5.	délicate (délicat)	5
6.	force	5
7.	vie	4
8.	malade	3
9.	mauvaise	3
10.	prison	3
11.	bien	2
12.	corps	2
13.	indispensable	2
14.	maladie	2
15-46.	(f = 1)	32

bien-être, bien-portant, boisson, bonheur, campagne, chien, claire, courir, docteur, dur, écriture, fort, gaité, hésitation, hôpital, infirmière, irréprochable, jeunesse, joie, médiocre, merveilleux, morale, négligent, premier Janvier,

59. SANTÉ (contd)

Students

No.	Response	Total	Female	Male
23.	vigueur	3	3	0
24.	bien	2	0	2
25.	corps	2	1	1
26.	douleur	2	2	0
27.	état	2	1	1
28.	hygiène	2	0	2
29.	prison	2	1	1
30.	robuste	2	1	1
31.	rose	2	1	1
32	vacances	2	0	2
33-99.	(f = 1)	67	48	19

affable, affaiblie, agacement, agréable, bien-portant, bonté, calme, campagne, courage, désirable, désirer, Eisenhower, ennui, éternelle, fatigue, félicité, fermeté, fille, foie, forte, fraîcheur, funeste, guérison, haut, heureux, hydropisie, image, jeunesse, jeux, lit, maison, mauvaise, médicament, mens sana in corpore sano, mer, microbe, mort, nécessaire, non, pain, parfaite, pathologie, pleine, précaire, précieux, qualité, quiétude, rare, rendement, rire, rue, sain, salubre, sanatorium, service social, soin, souci, souhaits, sur terre, teint, tout, valide, vie, vigoureux, vivre, vitalité, voeux

Workers

No.	Response	Total

prospérité, puissante, robuste, rouge, trésor, vigueur, vigoureux, Vittel
(No response - 1; Illegible - 1)

60. ÉVANGILE

Students

No.	Response	Total	Female	Male
1.	Dieu	31	19	12
2.	Bible	30	26	4
3.	église	23	12	11
4.	Christ,(du Christ, le Christ)	21	10	11
5.	religion	16	10	6
6.	Jésus (Jésus-Christ)	13	8	5
7.	livre	12	9	3
8.	messe	11	6	5
9.	Saint Jean	10	7	3
10.	Saint Mathieu	8	4	4
11.	Saint	7	7	0
12.	parole	5	4	1
13.	prière	5	4	1
14.	vérité	5	2	3
15.	épîtres	4	0	4
16.	apôtre (apôtres)	3	2	1
17.	Saint Luc	3	2	1
18.	amour	2	2	0
19.	autel	2	2	0
20.	Coran (Koran)	2	1	1
21.	curé	2	2	0
22.	doctrine	2	2	0
23.	foi	2	2	0
24.	Jean	2	1	1
25.	Jéhovah	2	1	1
26.	Luc	2	1	1
27.	nouvel (nouvelle)	2	1	1
28.	prêtre	2	1	1
29.	quatre	2	0	2
30-86.	(f = 1)	57	36	21

Angleterre, automobile, béatitude, bonne nouvelle, bréviaire, caché, catholicisme, charité, Christianisme, clair, commandement, croyance, discuter, divin, dogme, évangélique, farde, histoire, idéal, judaïsme, juge de paix, lecture, loi, lointain, Marc, Mathieu, Messie, missel, mystification, nation, note, Palestine, pape, parabole, paradis, pasteur, piété, pitoyable, poissons, précepte, prison, protestant, rare, recueillement, respect, rêve, rien, sacré, sagesse, selon, sermon, soucis, stalles, symbole, triste, vie, vrai

Workers

No.	Response	Total
1.	église	13
2.	Bible	11
3.	messe	10
4.	saint (sainte)	8
5.	curé	7
6.	Dieu (Dieux)	6
7.	livre	3
8.	prière	3
9.	religion	3
10.	Saint Luc (selon St. Luc)	3
11.	bêtise	2
12.	catholique	2
13.	cloche	2
14.	de Jésus (Jésus-Christ)	2
15.	parole	2
16-47.	(f = 1)	33

année, bon, bouquin, catéchisme, chauffé, chrétien, Christ, croyance, dimanche, divin, écrit, évangéliste, grave, inconnu, juste, latin, légende, loi, mois, non, notre, opinion, parabole, prêché, profession, pur, pureté, quoi, Saint Pierre, de Saint Vincent de Paul, Seigneur, selon Saint Jean, vérité
(No response - 4; Illegible - 1)

61. MÉMOIRE

Students

No.	Response	Total	Female	Male
1.	souvenir (souvenirs)	50	29	21
2.	intelligence	19	10	9
3.	leçon	7	5	2
4.	livre	6	6	0
5.	oubli	6	1	5
6.	fidèle	5	3	2
7.	mot (mots)	5	3	2
8.	travail	5	2	3
9.	cerveau	4	3	1
10.	facilité	4	1	3
11.	habitude	4	1	3
12.	homme	4	2	2
13.	Bergson	3	2	1
14.	bonne	3	2	1
15.	chance	3	1	2
16.	courte	3	0	3
17.	faculté	3	2	1
18.	faible	3	2	1
19.	passé	3	2	1
20.	savoir	3	2	1
21.	trou	3	3	0
22.	visuelle	3	2	1
23.	affective	2	2	0
24.	amnésie	2	0	2
25.	d'un âne	2	2	0
26.	apprendre	2	2	0
27.	association	2	0	2
28.	Chateaubriand	2	1	1
29.	déficiente	2	1	1
30.	effort	2	2	0
31.	géographie	2	0	2
32.	histoire	2	2	0
33.	idée	2	1	1
34.	intellectuel (intellectuelle)	2	1	1
35.	maladie (maladies)	2	2	0
36.	mauvaise	2	1	1
37.	mort	2	1	1
38.	outre-tombe (d'outre-tombe)	2	1	1
39.	pensée	2	1	1
40.	psychologie	2	1	1
41.	rappeler	2	1	1
42.	santé	2	2	0
43.	test (tests)	2	1	1
44-140.	($\underline{f}$ = 1)	97	75	22

abstrait, absurde, analyse, ancien, d'ange, alphabet, appétit, apprentissage, atomisme, attention, aucune, bêtise, blanc, cervelle, cheval, par coeur, compliquée, conscience, couloir, cours, défaillance, défaut, défectueuse, différente, difficile, difficulté, distraction, document, durée, écrit, ennui, énorme, épreuve, esprit, étude, examen, fable, fatigue, foi, folie, force, fuite, de Gaulle, grenier, grimoire, gros livre, imagination, instinct, jeunesse, journal, lecture, lente, localisation, lyre, machine, de médecin, mémoire, mémorisation, mère, mnémonie, moyen, noms propres, pas, passable, pathologique, penser, peu, physique, philo, Piéron, poésie, poisson, précise, qualité, Rabelais, rappel, se rappeler, rapidité, récitation, réponse, réserve, rétention, T. Ribot, Ségur, sensibilité, Mme de Sévigné, simple, songe, sonnet, table de multiplacation, tombe, trace, trouver, utile, vacances, vacillantes, volonté

Workers

No.	Response	Total
1.	courte	16
2.	bonne	7
3.	livre	7
4.	souvenir	6
5.	d'éléphant (éléphant)	5
6.	cerveau	4
7.	tête	4
8.	longue	3
9.	esprit	3
10.	penser (pensé)	3
11.	clair (claire)	2
12.	difficile	2
13.	excellente	2
14.	d'homme	2
15.	intelligence	2
16.	infaillible	2
17.	rappelé (rappeler)	2
18-59.	($\underline{f}$ = 1)	42

absence, âge, d'un âne, aigu, belle, cervelle, chiffre, Churchill, clarté, compréhension, Daudet, défaillante, défunt, dur, école, écrivain, fatigue, forte, idée, il n'a pas, instruction, intelligent, moto, nécessaire, noir, d'or, oubli, pas, perdue, peu, rappel, se rappeler, retenir, rivière, singe, sur, théâtre, travaille, travaux, trou, d'un, volonté
(Illegible - 1)

62. MOUTON

	Students					Workers	
No.	Response	Total	Female	Male	No.	Response	Total
1.	brebis	31	15	16	1.	laine	15
2.	doux	25	20	5	2.	agneau	8
3.	loup	22	16	6	3.	blanc (blancs)	8
4.	mouton	22	15	7	4.	doux	8
5.	Pâques (Pâque, de Pâque)	15	9	6	5.	doré	6
6.	douceur	14	12	2	6.	frisé	6
7.	blanc	13	10	3	7.	bête	5
8.	Pascal	11	8	3	8.	animal (animaux)	4
9.	Dieu (de Dieu)	7	2	5	9.	brebis	4
10.	laine	6	4	2	10.	bêle	3
11.	bêlant	5	1	4	11.	loup	3
12.	animal	4	2	2	12.	Panurge	3
13.	bergerie (bergeries)	4	3	1	13.	berger	2
14.	lait (de lait)	4	1	3	14.	douceur	2
15.	bêlement	3	2	1	15.	Duvernet	2
16.	bêler	3	3	0	16.	méchoui	2
17.	prairie	3	3	0	17.	noir	2
18.	de Toscane (Toscane)	3	3	0	18.	pré	2
19.	bête	2	0	2	19.	troupeau	2
20.	bouc	2	0	2	20.	viande	2
21.	chèvre	2	2	0	21-44.	(f = 1)	24
22.	Christ	2	0	2			
23.	crèche	2	2	0			
24.	enfant	2	1	1			
25.	fable	2	2	0			
26.	frisé	2	2	0			
27.	gigot	2	2	0			
28.	Inde (Indes)	2	2	0			
29.	innocent	2	2	0			
30.	mère	2	0	2			
31.	mignon	2	0	2			
32.	paix	2	1	1			
33.	pasteur	2	0	2			
34.	pureté	2	2	0			
35.	viande	2	0	2			
36-93.	(f = 1)	58	37	21			

Workers 21-44. (f = 1):
bêlement, bétail, braie, Cantal, Causses, compté, docile, électricité, encre, Fernandel, gigot, gras, gros, guenon, herbe, lapin, manger, métro, moutonne, paisible, pelote de laine, tendre, vache, vieux
(No response - 1; Illegible - 1)

Students 36-93. (f = 1):
agnelet, agnelle, Algérie, attendrissement, autel, bélier, Bible, blancheur, boucles, broche, champ, chance, chevreau, cocarde, cornes, côte, craintif, croix, divin, eau, étable, faible, fête, fourrure, fragilité, gracieux, gris, herbe, Hostie, innocence, St. Jean-Baptiste, jeune, jeunesse, juif, langueur, mammifère, Mauriac, Mont St. Michel, mystique, ovin, parabole, petit, petit animal, pré, pur, religion, rivière, Ronsard, rôti, sacrifice, salade, sans tache, tendre, tendresse, troupeau, un, vache, Van Eyck, victime

63. BAIN

	Students					Workers	
No.	Response	Total	Female	Male	No.	Response	Total
1.	mer (de mer)	48	34	14	1.	douche	23
2.	eau	44	30	14	2.	chaud (chaude)	16
3.	chaud (trop chaud)	27	16	11	3.	mer (en mer, de mer)	11
4.	douche (douches)	22	8	14	4.	eau	5
5.	baignoire	18	13	5	5.	propreté	5
6.	froid	9	7	2	6.	propre	4
7.	agréable	8	4	4	7.	froid	3
8.	vapeur	8	5	3	8.	minuit (de minuit)	3
9.	chaleur	7	4	3	9.	vapeur (de vapeur)	3
10.	propreté	7	6	1	10.	laver (lavée)	2
11.	savon	6	3	3	11.	marié	2
12.	confort	4	4	0	12.	maure	2
13.	Marie	4	1	3	13.	piscine	2
14.	soleil	4	4	0	14.	santé	2
15.	turc	4	1	3	15.	savon	2
16.	détent	3	2	1	16.	de soleil (soleil)	2
17.	nage	3	1	2	17.	turc	2
18.	salle de bain	3	3	0	18-42.	(f = 1)	25

63. BAIN (contd)

Students

No.	Response	Total	Female	Male
19.	vacances	3	3	0
20.	délassement	2	0	2
21.	fraîcheur	2	2	0
22.	Méditerranée	2	2	0
23.	minuit (de minuit)	2	1	1
24.	piscine	2	0	2
25.	plage	2	1	1
26.	propre	2	2	0
27.	repos	2	1	1
28-67.	(f = 1)	40	26	14

Angleterre, bains de mer, béatitude, bien-être, bleu, bon, boue, calme, détendu, douceur, Espagne, frais, gonfler, d'huile, lavabo, maillot, marée, maritime, merveille, Meuse, monts, mou, mousse, mousseux, occupation, pieds, plongeon, rafraîchissement, rare, rivière, romain, salle, sandwich, sel, soif, soin, termes, tiède, ville, vrai

Workers

No.	Response	Total

Afrique, baignade, baignoire, bouche, boue, caleçon, de chaux, chose, détente, délassant, douceur, flasque, hygiène, loisir, maillot de bain, mouiller, nageur, pain, de pied, plage, relaxe, repos, rouge, sale, tiède
(Illegible - 1)

64. VILLA

Students

No.	Response	Total	Female	Male
1.	maison	41	20	21
2.	mer	33	24	9
3.	campagne (de campagne)	25	19	6
4.	vacances	18	14	4
5.	jardin	15	11	4
6.	confort	10	6	4
7.	été (d'été)	8	5	3
8.	soleil	6	6	0
9.	fleur (fleurs)	5	5	0
10.	plage	5	5	0
11.	Médicis	4	2	2
12.	repos	4	0	4
13.	romaine	4	2	2
14.	blanc (blanche)	3	3	0
15.	luxe	3	1	2
16.	rose (roses)	3	3	0
17.	banlieue	2	1	1
18.	belle	2	2	0
19.	Borghèse	2	1	1
20.	bourgeois	2	0	2
21.	bourgeoisie	2	1	1
22.	Cannes	2	2	0
23.	clair (claire)	2	2	0
24.	côte	2	2	0
25.	Côte d'Azur	2	2	0
26.	ensoleillée	2	2	0
27.	Italie	2	2	0
28.	lierre	2	1	1
29.	plaisir (de plaisir)	2	1	1
30.	Rome	2	2	0
31.	toit	2	2	0
32-102.	(f = 1)	71	35	36

affreux, agréable, Antibes, architecte, azur, barque, bateau, La Baule, beauté, bonheur, bord, bord de la mer, Capoue, chalet, chocolat, Cicéron, civilisé, confortable, coquette, cottage, demeure romaine, dunes, détente, espoir, d'Este, fenêtre, ferme, fortune, foyer, Franco, Gallo-Romaine, glycine, Goethe, habitation, immeuble, jolie, Juan-les-Pins, latin, lumière, lune, Marguerite, meublée, Midi, modeste, Nice, paisible, palais, Paris, plage, pelouse, petite, Pierre, pins, de plaisance, plane, propriété, riche, richesse, Romaine, des Roses, rouge, seule, somptueux, superbe, tante, taudis, tranquillité, Tusculanum, vert, vide, ville, villégiature

Workers

No.	Response	Total
1.	maison	19
2.	belle	5
3.	pavillon	5
4.	campagne	4
5.	coquette	3
6.	côte	3
7.	grande	3
8.	repos (de repos)	3
9.	vacances	3
10.	confort	2
11.	jolie	2
12.	maçon	2
13.	mer	2
14.	moderne	2
15.	propriété	2
16.	les roses (des roses)	2
17.	ville	2
18-67.	(f = 1)	50

abri, agréable, ancienne, ange, azur, blanche, chalet, château, chinoise, confortable, Côte d'Azur, dormir, Dufayel, ensoleillé, fortune, grandiose, habitation, hameau, honte, insalubre, jardin, Jeannette, luxe, Marquis, Médicis, au bord de la mer, neuve, opulence, paix, petite, provençale, en province, pur, rêve, mon rêve, riche, richesse, rouge, snob, du soleil, solide, somptueuse, sosie, sport, toit, tranquille, vaste, Vésinet, village, villégiature, à vendre

65. RAPIDE

	Students					Workers	
No.	Response	Total	Female	Male	No.	Response	Total
1.	train	101	74	27	1.	train	25
2.	lent	55	31	24	2.	vite	13
3.	avion	13	9	4	3.	éclair	9
4.	express	13	8	5	4.	avion	8
5.	éclair	12	10	2	5.	lent (lente)	8
6.	vite	9	3	6	6.	vitesse	5
7.	torrent	8	3	5	7.	express (l'express)	4
8.	vitesse	5	4	1	8.	vif	4
9.	Mistral	4	2	2	9.	voiture	4
10.	courant	3	3	0	10.	autos (automobile)	3
11.	flèche	3	0	3	11.	flèche	3
12.	fleuve	3	1	2	12.	course	2
13.	vif	3	2	1	13.	rivière	2
14.	auto	2	0	2	14.	torrent	2
15.	cheval	2	2	0	15-36.	(f = 1)	22
16.	chûte	2	2	0			
17.	Côte d'Azur	2	1	1			
18.	cours d'eau	2	1	1			
19.	course	2	2	0			
20.	ski	2	2	0			
21.	vent	2	2	0			
22.	voiture	2	1	1			
23-60.	(f = 1)	38	21	17			

Workers 15-36. (f = 1) 22:
abstrait, agile, agréable, aigle, construit, courant, court, descente, dur, dynamique, fragile, fusée, lentement, lièvre, Marseille, mécanique, net, P L M, précis, Rapide, svelte, vent
(No response - 1)

Students 23-60. (f = 1):
accéléré, Achille, adjectif, aigle, aigu, Amérique, amie, automobile, bateau, bicyclette, bleu, dégagement, dir, eau, écumeux, électrification, élevé, énervant, feu, léger, locomotive, mou, nerveux, oiseau, omnibus, Orient-Express, pipe, prompt, qualité, rivière, rochers, S.N.C.F., slow, sûr, Train-Bleu, vacances, Velox, vipère

66. BLEU

	Students					Workers	
No.	Response	Total	Female	Male	No.	Response	Total
1.	ciel	90	60	30	1.	ciel (le ciel, cieux, du ciel)	45
2.	mer (la mer)	42	27	15	2.	azur (d'azur)	9
3.	rouge	19	10	9	3.	mer	8
4.	vert	13	10	3	4.	blanc	6
5.	azur	10	6	4	5.	couleur	6
6.	blanc	10	7	3	6.	marine	3
7.	noir	7	3	4	7.	roi	3
8.	marine	6	6	0	8.	vert	3
9.	nuit	5	4	1	9.	rouge	2
10.	rose	5	4	1	10.	yeux	2
11.	couleur	4	0	4	11-38.	(f = 1)	28
12.	jaune	4	0	4			
13.	Auvergne	3	0	3			
14.	eau	3	2	1			
15.	de Prusse (Prusse)	3	3	0			
16.	roi	3	1	2			
17.	yeux	3	3	0			
18.	blanc-rouge	2	2	0			
19.	douceur	2	1	1			
20.	horizon	2	2	0			
21.	joie	2	2	0			
22.	lac	2	2	0			
23.	oiseau	2	1	1			
24.	outre-mer	2	0	2			
25.	pâle	2	1	1			
26.	route	2	2	0			
27.	train	2	1	1			
28-65.	(f = 1)	38	24	14			

Workers 11-38. (f = 1) 28:
beau, bistre, bland, blond, bleuet, bouche, clair, Côte d'Azur, Danube, digue, dindon, drapeau, foncé, jaune, marin, Méditerranée, nuance, nuit, outre-mer, pâle, pipe, reposant, rêve, saphir, table, temps, tendre, violet, voyant

Students 28-65. (f = 1):
beau, calme, chambre, doux, dur, émail, espoir, fleur, foncé, France, gris, joli, lune, marin, mauve, Méditerranée, midi, mouillée, nostalgie, papillon, Paris, pension, pétrole, pierre, pull-over, rapsodie, rivière, Route Bleue, soir, sombre, tapis, ton, torrent, uniforme, vêtement, violet, vitrail, Wallis

67. FAIM

Students					Workers		
No.	Response	Total	Female	Male	No.	Response	Total
1.	soif	66	39	27	1.	loup (de loup)	26
2.	pain	40	27	13	2.	plain (le plain)	15
3.	loup (de loup)	15	9	6	3.	manger (mangé)	12
4.	manger	15	8	7	4.	appétit	5
5.	estomac	12	10	2	5.	famine	5
6.	misère	10	6	4	6.	estomac	4
7.	pauvre	8	5	3	7.	soif	4
8.	appétit	6	3	3	8.	fin	3
9.	froid	6	4	2	9.	pauvreté	3
10.	affamé	4	4	0	10.	affamé	2
11.	guerre	4	4	0	11.	chien	2
12.	pauvreté	4	3	1	12.	guerre	2
13.	crampe	3	3	0	13.	misère	2
14.	désert	3	3	0	14.	nourriture	2
15.	famine	3	1	2	15.	pauvre	2
16.	mendiant	3	2	1	16-41.	(f = 1)	26
17.	nourriture	3	2	1	art, atroce, carreau, caserne,		
18.	repas	3	1	2	chaise, crever, dévorante, disette,		
19.	atroce	2	0	2	éprouvé, grande, heure, Inde,		
20.	Brésil	2	1	1	insatiable, pas manger, midi, d'ogre,		
21.	Chine	2	1	1	peuple, poulet, repas, rouge, sous-		
22.	désagréable	2	2	0	développé, terrible, toujours, triste,		
23.	dévorante	2	1	1	viande, vin		
24.	douleur	2	1	1			
25.	fin	2	0	2			
26.	Indes	2	1	1			
27.	mal	2	1	1			
28.	mort	2	2	0			
29.	ogre (d'ogre)	2	2	0			
30.	souffrance	2	1	1			
31-86.	(f = 1)	56	37	19			

abandonnés, alimentation, Asie, assiette, avidité,
beefsteak, besoin, biftek, bis, Chinois, chocolat,
colère, dégoût, déjeuner, dents, désir, dur, encore,
enfant, énorme, fatigue, fléau, frugal, fruits,
la grande faim, grève, Hindou, langue, légèreté,
maigre, malheur, malheureux, midi, misérable, monde,
mortelle, pauvre homme, pénible, plaisir, pleurs,
prolétariat, réalisme, réfectoire, satiété,
sensation, table, talon, tenace, terrible, tiraillement,
tous, tracas, tristesse, vagabond, ventre, vorace

68. PRÊTRE

Students					Workers		
No.	Response	Total	Female	Male	No.	Response	Total
1.	noir (noire)	37	25	12	1.	curé	19
2.	église	32	23	9	2.	église	18
3.	soutane	20	15	5	3.	catholique	4
4.	ouvrier	18	9	9	4.	messe	4
5.	curé	17	6	11	5.	saint	4
6.	messe	16	9	7	6.	noir	3
7.	religion	14	8	6	7.	abbé	2
8.	Dieu	7	2	5	8.	aumônier	2
9.	homme	6	3	3	9.	dévoué	2
10.	robe (robe noire)	6	6	0	10.	évangile	2
11.	pasteur	5	3	2	11.	moine (le moine)	2
12.	sacerdoce	5	4	1	12.	ouvrier	2
13.	ami	4	1	3	13.	prêcher (prêche)	2
14.	catholique	4	3	1	14.	religieux	2
15.	chasuble	4	3	1	15.	soutane	2
16.	abbé	3	3	0	16.	vocation	2
17.	Christ	3	2	1	17-56.	(f = 1)	40
18.	Communion	3	3	0	aimable, arrivés, bon Dieu, brigand,		
19.	ordre	2	2	0	calomnie, Charlemagne, chrétien,		
20.	autel	2	2	0	Christ, confession, couvent, curotin,		
21.	baptême	2	2	0	croyant, Dieu, écclésiastique, femme,		
22.	bonté	2	2	0	fonctionnaire, malade, mauvais,		
23.	bonze	2	1	1	mort, mourir, nom, office, Ordres,		
24.	clergé	2	2	0	paître, pape, papier, piété,		
25.	Corbeau	2	2	0	presbytère, rapide, réconfort,		

68. PRÊTRE (contd)

Students

No.	Response	Total	Female	Male
26.	foi	2	2	0
27.	hostie	2	2	0
28.	mission	2	1	1
29.	vicaire	2	0	2
30-90.	(f = 1)	61	38	23

agile, aide, amour, apôtre, archiduc, barette, bonne soeur, bure, charité, ciel, première Communion, confession, confier, croyance, dimanche, ecclésiastique, enterrement, envoyé, épiscopat, étrange, évangile, évêque, fidèle, un grand homme, grand prêtre, grandeur, idéal, individu, intermédiaire, inutile, Jean, Jésuite, journal, laïque, lassitude, livre, Maire, malade, mariage, Mexique, ministre, mort, mourir, mystère, office, officie, pardon, paroisse, pitié, prêtre-ouvrier, prière, réconfort, religieuse, religieux, résonner, sacré, saint, sermon, Supérieur, tonsure

Workers

No.	Response	Total

Religion, représentant, je ris, russe, sacerdoce, simulateur, toujours, tuyau vieux, la Vérité
(No response - 3)

69. OCÉAN

Students

No.	Response	Total	Female	Male
1.	mer	64	34	30
2.	Atlantique	22	11	11
3.	immensité	18	13	5
4.	eau (eaux)	16	10	6
5.	immense	15	8	7
6.	vague (vagues)	15	10	5
7.	bleu	14	9	5
8.	bateau (bateaux)	11	8	3
9.	infini	10	6	4
10.	Pacifique	6	3	3
11.	profond	6	3	3
12.	vacances	6	5	1
13.	vert	6	6	0
14.	vaste	5	2	3
15.	voyage	5	4	1
16.	étendue	4	2	2
17.	large	3	3	0
18.	glauque	2	1	1
19.	grand	2	1	1
20.	grandeur	2	2	0
21.	gris	2	2	0
22.	Indien	2	1	1
23.	lointain	2	2	0
24.	mère	2	1	1
25.	naufrage	2	1	1
26.	plage	2	2	0
27.	profondeur	2	1	1
28.	seul	2	2	0
29.	tempête	2	0	2
30-67.	(f = 1)	38	31	7

abîme, algue, Amérique, artiste, azur, bain, Bretagne, chose, cimetière, côte, départ, écume, éloignement, espace, flots, fond, glacial, gouffre, houle, île, Lautréamont, liberté, libre, mouvement, navire, néant, paquebot, plaine, perte, poisson, récif, rouge, Sud, terre, "Titanique", transatlantique, vent, vertige

Workers

No.	Response	Total
1.	mer	21
2.	Pacifique	13
3.	Atlantique	10
4.	Indien	9
5.	bleu (bleue)	8
6.	immense	6
7.	immensité	6
8.	vague	5
9.	grand	4
10.	large	3
11.	Arctique	2
12.	bateau	2
13.	glacial	2
14.	Océanie	2
15-35.	(f = 1)	21

baigner, Baltique, crayon, déchaîné, eau, glacé, grondant, inconnu, immergé, lointain, magnifique, marin, Mer Noire, naufrage, naviguer, Neptune, paquebot, rageur, tempête, tranquille, voyage
(Illegible - 1)

70 TÊTE

Students

No.	Response	Total	Female	Male
1.	cheveux (cheveu)	32	23	9
2.	veau (de veau)	24	14	10

Workers

No.	Response	Total
1.	dur (dure)	13
2.	veau (de veau)	8

70. TÊTE (contd)

	Students					Workers	
No.	Response	Total	Female	Male	No.	Response	Total
3.	pied (pieds)	16	6	10	3.	de mule (mule)	7
4.	corps	12	8	4	4.	cheveux (cheveu)	6
5.	Turc (de Turc)	12	6	6	5.	jambe (jambes, les jambes)	6
6.	yeux	11	10	1	6.	de Turc	4
7.	cerveau	10	6	4	7.	cerveau	3
8.	chef	9	6	3	8.	homme (d'homme, l'homme)	3
9.	intelligence	8	5	3	9.	linotte	3
10.	cou	7	3	4	10.	ronde	3
11.	ronde (rond)	6	6	0	11.	de bois	2
12.	chapeau	5	5	0	12.	chapeau	2
13.	homme	5	2	3	13.	folle	2
14.	oiseau	5	5	0	14.	intelligence	2
15.	visage	5	4	1	15.	penser (pense)	2
16.	crâne	4	3	1	16-63.	(f = 1)	48
17.	queue	4	1	3			
18.	esprit	3	2	1			
19.	membre (membres)	3	3	0			
20.	mort de mort)	3	3	0			
21.	sommet	3	1	2			
22.	bois	2	2	0			
23.	boule	2	2	0			
24.	bras	2	1	1			
25.	chauve	2	2	0			
26.	coupée	2	1	1			
27.	début	2	2	0			
28.	lard	2	0	2			
29.	mal	2	1	1			
30.	nu (nue)	2	1	1			
31.	organe	2	1	1			
32.	pensée	2	1	1			
33.	petite	2	2	0			
34.	réflexion	2	0	2			
35.	tronc	2	1	1			
36-108.	(f = 1)	73	44	29			

Workers 16-63:
en l'air, baissée, bêche, bleu, blonde, de boeuf, bras, brûlée, cervelle, chapître, chef, cheval, chevelue, chevelure, corps, cou, crâne, eau, échevelée, esprit, forte, grosse, haute, horrible, jaune, ligne, main, mal, migraine, motif, noble, un organe, d'or, pied, pioche, pleine, plomb, poitrine, poux, premier, queue, rien, sommet, tarte, tête, vilaine, yeux
(Illegible - 1)

Students 36-108:
agneau, aigle, ange, bateau, beauté, bec, bêche, blonde, boeuf, bonnet, bouclée, boucles, buste, capital, capitale, chemise, cheval, chevelure, de chien, coeur, compliquée, contre les murs, doute, dure, éclatement, élevé, à l'envers, épaule, épine, épingle, essentiel, femme, file, froide, forte, gullotine, haute, idée, important, large, de linotte, lion, lourde, moineau, mouton, mule, nègre, oeil, ombre, d'or, oreille, penser, personnage, personne, pleine, poisson, Ponce, rasée, Rodin, rondeur, sang-froid, seul, squelette, tatouage, tête à tête, tête d'or, tout, train, travail, troupeau, Valéry, vide

71. FOURNEAU

	Students					Workers	
No.	Response	Total	Female	Male	No.	Response	Total
1.	cuisine (de cuisine)	56	37	19	1.	chaud	15
2.	chaleur	27	16	11	2.	gaz (à gaz)	12
3.	poêle	27	12	15	3.	chaleur	8
4.	feu	26	16	10	4.	cuisine	8
5.	gaz (à gaz)	25	18	7	5.	feu (feux)	5
6.	noir	22	19	3	6.	rouge	5
7.	chaud	11	6	5	7.	charbon (à charbon)	4
8.	cuisinière (cuisinier)	10	6	4	8.	cuisinière (cuisinier)	4
9.	tuyau	9	6	3	9.	haut	4
10.	casserole	7	6	1	10.	poêle	4
11.	chauffage	4	1	3	11.	four	3
12.	haut	4	4	0	12.	noir	3
13.	rouge	4	4	0	13.	pain (à pain)	3
14.	brûler	3	2	1	14.	cheminée	2
15.	charbon	3	1	2	15.	charbon	2
16.	four	3	1	2	16.	cuire (à cuire)	2
17.	bois	2	1	1	17.	fonte	2

71. FOURNEAU (contd)

Students

No.	Response	Total	Female	Male
18.	chauffer	2	1	1
19.	flamme	2	2	0
20.	fournil	2	1	1
21.	pain	2	1	1
22-58.	(f = 1)	37	23	14

allumé, antiquité, appareil, bleu, bouilloire, braise,
brillant, brûlure, camp, canari, cendre, chaumière,
cheminée, chimie, choc, combustion, confort,
cuisson, dentellière, Eugénie, évier, fermée, fonte,
foyer, fumée, marmite, pétrole, pied, plat, poulet,
pruneau, rôti, suie, trou, veine, vieux, zébracier

Workers

No.	Response	Total
18.	fumant	2
19.	haut-fourneau (haut-fourneaux)	2
20.	sale	2
21-43.	(f = 1)	23

à alcool, blanc, braise, brûlant,
cageot, chapeau, chat, chauffage,
chauffer, éteint, four immense,
fourgon, fourmis, foyer, gloire,
graisseux, grand, gros feu, piano,
pipe, prêt, puissant, tuyau

72. LONG

Students

No.	Response	Total	Female	Male
1.	court	65	37	28
2.	large	34	20	14
3.	route	10	6	4
4.	chemin	9	5	4
5.	mince	9	8	1
6.	jour (jours)	8	5	3
7.	bâton	6	6	0
8.	grand	6	5	1
9.	pain	6	3	3
10.	maigre	5	4	1
11.	petit	5	2	3
12.	serpent	5	4	1
13.	étroit	4	0	4
14.	fil	4	3	1
15.	infini	4	4	0
16.	jambe	4	3	1
17.	nez	4	4	0
18.	courrier	3	0	3
19.	ligne	3	2	1
20.	règle	3	2	1
21.	tige	3	2	1
22.	arbre	2	2	0
23.	bras	2	2	0
24.	cheveux	2	2	0
25.	cou (cous)	2	1	1
26.	fatigue	2	2	0
27.	lent	2	2	0
28.	mètre	2	1	1
29.	rifle	2	0	2
30.	ruban	2	2	0
31.	train	2	1	1
32.	trajet	2	1	1
33.	ver	2	1	1
34-97.	(f = 1)	64	42	22

adjectif, allongé, asperge, attente, baguette, barbe,
bête, bois, bond, bref, Chine, corde, couloir, cour,
couteau, crayon, discours, Don Quichotte, ennui,
ennuyeux, espace, étang, étendu, fatiguant,
girafe, gouttière, haut, héron, l'hiver, horizon,
immense, immensité, indéfini, Island, jour sans pain,
jumeau, kilomètre, loin, longévité, longitudinal,
long way, main, mariage, Mississippi, moi, mur,
ovale, patiente, patte, pin, plaisir, pluie, pointe,
rail, rigide, rude, rue, scieur, temps, trait,
triste, turban, tuyau, vite

Workers

No.	Response	Total
1.	large (et large)	13
2.	court (courts, courte)	12
3.	chemin	8
4.	cheveux	5
5.	loin	5
6.	route	4
7.	fleuve	3
8.	grand	3
9.	jour	3
10.	mètre (le mètre)	3
11.	parcours	3
12.	longueur	2
13.	petit	2
14-61.	(f = 1)	48

allonge, allonger, attente, camion,
canon, cercueil, corde, cou, cours,
délais, dent, désir, ennuyé, énorme,
étendre, étendue, éternel, éternité,
fil, fil de fer, hiver, interminable,
Loire, maigre, métrage, de 7 mètres,
mince, Mississippi, moyen, pain,
pâturage, pipe-line, piste, planche,
plume, poil, rail, rectangulaire,
rifle, roue, temps, terrain, train,
trottoir, tunnel obscur, tuyau,
vie, voyage
(Illegible - 1)

73. RELIGION

Students

No.	Response	Total	Female	Male
1.	prêtre (prêtres)	24	14	10
2.	catholique	23	12	11
3.	église (l'Église)	23	18	5
4.	Dieu	16	9	7
5.	croyance	8	3	5
6.	athéisme	7	3	4
7.	chrétien (chrétienne)	5	4	1
8.	athée	4	1	3
9.	amour	4	3	1
10.	Christ	4	1	3
11.	foi	4	4	0
12.	protestant (protestante)	4	1	3
13.	sacré	4	4	0
14.	catéchisme	3	1	2
15.	culte	3	2	1
16.	curé	3	3	0
17.	évangile	3	3	0
18.	idéal	3	1	2
19.	messe	3	3	0
20.	mystère	3	2	1
21.	mystique	3	2	1
22.	piété	3	3	0
23.	vie	3	2	1
24.	abstrait	2	1	1
25.	Bouddhisme	2	1	1
26.	Bouddhiste	2	2	0
27.	catholicisme	2	1	1
28.	charité	2	2	0
29.	christianisme	2	2	0
30.	doctrine	2	2	0
31.	dogme	2	1	1
32.	guerre	2	0	2
33.	hindoue	2	1	1
34.	histoire	2	1	1
35.	lutte (luttes)	2	1	1
36.	noir (noire)	2	2	0
37.	opium	2	2	0
38.	othodoxe	2	1	1
39.	prière	2	1	1
40.	statue	2	2	0
41.	vérité	2	1	1
42-133.	(f = 1)	92	61	31

abstraction, anastrak, appui, ascétisme, baptême, bâtir, beau, beauté, bêtise, bien, bigot, blanc, bon, Bon Dieu, Bossuet, chaud, choix, communisme, couvent, croire, croix, dévotion, dévouement, différente, discipline, diversité, divinité, Eggu (professeur), ennui, épître, esprit, éthique, évêque, haut, homme, humilité, impiété, inutile, Islam, Israël, jaune, joie, juive, livre, Luther, magie, marxisme, métaphysique, moi, mormons, musulman, mythe, nature, naturelle, néant, nécessité, nombre, non, occidental, ordre, pape, pauvreté, Perses, poisson, poussière, pratiquant, principe, problème, pureté, religieux, relique, revue, rigolade, rigueur, rite, romaine, Rome, sagesse, secte, sérieux, schisme, solennel, spirituel, supériorité, superstition, sûreté, tradition, tranquilité, tristesse, universelle, ventre, Voltaire

Workers

No.	Response	Total
1.	catholique	36
2.	protestante (protestant)	9
3.	église	6
4.	chrétien (chrétienne)	5
5.	curé	4
6.	athée	3
7.	évangile	2
8.	foi	2
9.	païen (païenne)	2
10.	personnel	2
11.	politique	2
12.	prêtre	2
13-50.	(f = 1)	38

adéquate, apôtre, beauté, belle, bête, bonne, bouddhisme, bouddhiste, buffet, charité, cloître, conscience, couvent, croyance, croire, Dieu, dieux, différente, étoile, fanatique, française, glorieuse, idée, jeune, morale, mou, musulmane, nécessaire, nulle, pas, prière, pureté, race, relation, religieuse, rien, sacrée, sentiment
(No response - 2)

74. COGNAC

Students

No.	Response	Total	Female	Male
1.	alcool	37	23	14
2.	liqueur	23	18	5
3.	vin	17	11	6
4.	boisson	13	10	3
5.	eau-de-vie	13	9	4
6.	verre	12	11	1
7.	Armagnac	9	5	4
8.	bouteille	9	9	0

Workers

No.	Response	Total
1.	alcool	22
2.	fort	10
3.	Martell	9
4.	rhum	6
5.	boisson	5
6.	bon	4
7.	café	4
8.	liqueur	4

74. COGNAC (contd)

No.	Response (Students)	Total	Female	Male	No.	Response (Workers)	Total
9.	Martell	9	5	4	9.	vin	4
10.	chaleur	8	4	4	10.	ivresse	3
11.	Charentes (Charente)	8	6	2	11.	poison	3
12.	fort	7	4	3	12.	apértif	2
13.	boire	5	2	3	13.	Bisquit	2
14.	bon	5	2	3	14.	boire	2
15.	brandy	4	3	1	15.	bouteille	2
16.	brûlure	4	3	1	16.	eau-de-vie	2
17.	rhum	4	2	2	17-45.	(f = 1)	29
18.	whisky	4	0	4			
19.	étoile (étoiles)	3	1	2			
20.	fine	3	2	1			
21.	Hennessy	3	1	2			
22.	ivresse	3	2	1			
23.	jaune	3	3	0			
24.	affreux	2	2	0			
25.	chaud	2	2	0			
26.	couleur	2	1	1			
27.	digestif	2	2	0			
28.	trois étoiles	2	1	1			
29.	ivre	2	2	0			
30.	Jay	2	2	0			
31.	Normandie	2	2	0			
32.	publicité	2	1	1			
33.	sec	2	0	2			
34-95.	(f = 1)	62	33	29			

Workers 17-45. (f = 1) 29:
alcoolique, amer, Armagnac, il y a bon, brûlure, Charente, Cognac Jay, délice, délicieux, digestif, direction, dur, eau, gaie, goutte, indélébile, mort, Normandie, Pernod, picotant, rang, ravigotant, réconfort, saoul, sec, soif, sobriété, verre, whisky (Illegible - 2)

Students 34-95:
agréable, alcoolisme, Anglais, appéritif, argent, Bénédictine, bière, Bisquit, blond, bon repas, Bordeaux, brûlant, brûle, brun, bu, Calvados, champagne, cherry, cidre, dessert, estomac, folie, force, gin, huile, ignoble, ivrogne, jeune, joie, liquide, maladie, Marquet, mauvais, mauvaise odeur, miam-miam, naturel, oral, orangé, oubli, Perrier, piquant, porto, pousse-café, Prix Cognac Jay, raide, réconfortant, ridicule, roux, rue, sauterne, soif, une soirée, spirit, Suisse, tabac, tante, vacances, vieux, ville, velouté, violet, vodka

75. ENFANT

No.	Response (Students)	Total	Female	Male	No.	Response (Workers)	Total
1.	petit	34	23	11	1.	petit	9
2.	bébé	23	19	4	2.	sage	8
3.	mère	23	13	10	3.	terrible	7
4.	adulte	10	5	5	4.	gentil (gentille, gentils)	6
5.	douceur	5	5	0	5.	jeune	6
6.	jeu (jeux)	5	5	0	6.	gâté (gâte)	5
7.	jeunesse	5	4	1	7.	bébé	3
8.	joie	5	5	0	8.	homme	2
9.	sage	5	1	4	9.	jeunesse	2
10.	terrible	5	2	3	10.	jeux	2
11.	amour	4	2	2	11.	mignon	2
12.	blond	4	3	1	12.	naissance	2
13.	doux	4	4	0	13.	seul	2
14.	fille	4	3	1	14.	soigneux	2
15.	homme	4	1	3	15-71.	(f = 1)	57
16.	jeune	4	1	3			
17.	jouet (jouets)	4	3	1			
18.	parents (parent)	4	3	1			
19.	beau	3	3	0			
20.	beauté	3	2	1			
21.	gosse	3	1	2			
22.	maman	3	3	0			
23.	vieillard	3	2	1			
24.	aimer	2	2	0			
25.	berceau	2	1	1			
26.	boucle	2	2	0			
27.	choeur (de choeur)	2	1	1			
28.	école	2	2	0			

Workers 15-71. (f = 1) 57:
avenir, beaucoup, grand bébé, berceau, blond, bruit, cher, chétif, choux, crédule, criard, crier, délaissé, désir, douceur, doux, élevé, famille, fille, fort, fragile, gai, garçon, garçonnet, gentillesse, gosse, gracieux, humain, joie, joie immense, Jésus, impossible, insupportable, maigre, malheureux, marche, mariage, Marie, méchant, mère, môme, moyen, né, nom, père, personnage, prodigue, puérilité, pureté, roc, sale, souple, sourires,

75. ENFANT (contd)

Students

No.	Response	Total	Female	Male
29.	famille	2	1	1
30.	fils	2	0	2
31.	gamin	2	0	2
32.	garçon	2	0	2
33.	gâté	2	1	1
34.	gentil	2	1	1
35.	grec	2	0	2
36.	intérêt	2	2	0
37.	joli	2	1	1
38.	mignon	2	2	0
39.	nourrisson	2	1	1
40.	père	2	0	2
41.	tendresse	2	1	1
42.	turbulent	2	1	1
43-125.	($\underline{f}$ = 1)	83	55	28

adorable, agréable, amour paternel, Alain, ange,
de la balle, bêlant, bleu, brassière, calme, candeur,
chahut, charme, chéri, clarté, colonie, corps,
courir, début, délicat, délinquant, docile, enfantelet,
enfantin, faible, faiblesse, fatigue, fécondation,
femme, fillette, foyer, fragile, fragilité, frêle,
gaité, grand, grandir, grande personne, gras, grève,
Hervé, idiot, individu, ingénu, insupportable,
intéressant, intimité, joyeux, juneaux, laid, lange,
loup, lunette, malade, mâle, méchant, mes futurs
enfants, mon petit, mort, mystère, nain, naissance,
naturel, nourrice, pauvre, personne, plaisir,
pleurs, pouce, poupée, prairie, précoce, prodigue,
puéril, ras, rose, sale, sans, souhait, souvenir,
taire, tendre, visage

Workers

No.	Response	Total
	timide, trois, turbulent, vieux	

76. AMER

Students

No.	Response	Total	Female	Male
1.	doux (douce)	44	30	14
2.	citron	16	13	3
3.	aigre	13	9	4
4.	sucré	13	9	4
5.	acide	10	8	2
6.	riz	10	5	5
7.	fruit	8	4	4
8.	goût	8	8	0
9.	amande	7	3	4
10.	amertume	7	4	3
11.	fiel	7	3	4
12.	désagréable	6	5	1
13.	mauvais	6	4	2
14.	sûr	6	3	3
15.	âcre	5	4	1
16.	âpre	5	4	1
17.	mer	5	4	1
18.	pamplemousse	5	4	1
19.	Picon	5	3	2
20.	vinaigre	5	3	2
21.	bon	4	4	0
22.	dur	4	2	2
23.	bile	3	2	1
24.	endive	3	2	1
25.	orange	3	1	2
26.	salé	3	3	0
27.	Suze	3	1	2
28.	bitter	2	0	2
29.	bouche	2	2	0
30.	café	2	2	0
31.	chicorée	2	1	1
32.	dégout	2	0	2
33.	détestable	2	1	1
34.	médicament	2	2	0
35.	potion	2	2	0
36.	quinine	2	1	1

Workers

No.	Response	Total
1.	doux (douce)	11
2.	fiel	10
3.	aigre	8
4.	citron	8
5.	mauvais	6
6.	amande (amandes)	4
7.	acide	3
8.	pas bon	3
9.	sûr	3
10.	acre	2
11.	amertume	2
12.	désagréable	2
13.	endive	2
14.	fade	2
15.	goût	2
16.	orange	2
17.	pamplemousse	2
18.	vie	2
19.	vinaigre	2
20-55.	($\underline{f}$ = 1)	36

breuvage, catholique, chicotin,
coca, coing, cracher, dégout,
desséchant, dur, écoeurant, fleurs,
fruit, très mauvais goût, grimace,
il, le manger, médicament, mer,
piquant, pomme, pur, purge, raisin,
refus, sale, sauce, sel, situation,
soupe, suc, succulent, comme tout,
triste, victoire, vin, vomissement
(No response - 1; Illegible - 2)

76. AMER (contd)

Students

No.	Response	Total	Female	Male
37.	sel	2	1	1
38.	triste	2	0	2
39.	tristesse	2	1	1
40-89.	(f = 1)	50	26	24

affreux, aigrelet, aloès, amer, Amérique, Baudelaire,
bière, boire, boisson, commotion, déception, déplaisant,
désillusion, eau salée, écorce d'orange, faim, fier,
gentiane, grave, groseille, herbe, horreur, laid,
liqueur, mal, maladie, nuit, pain, peine, pépin,
piquant, pluie, pomme, profond, purge, râpe, Rimbaud,
Rubicond, saveur, sec, soif, souffrance, stupide,
sucre, temple, tendre, vie, vin, volonté, ysé

77. MARTEAU

Students

No.	Response	Total	Female	Male
1.	pilon	58	31	27
2.	clou (clous)	36	22	14
3.	enclume	33	24	9
4.	taper	16	15	1
5.	coup	15	10	5
6.	faucille	11	7	4
7.	outil	6	6	0
8.	bruit	5	3	2
9.	doigt (doigts)	5	3	2
10.	dur	5	4	1
11.	travail (le travail)	5	1	4
12.	frapper	3	2	1
13.	instrument	3	3	0
14.	lourd	3	2	1
15.	mal	3	2	1
16.	manche	3	2	1
17.	porte	3	2	1
18.	tenailles (tenaille)	3	1	2
19.	tête	3	3	0
20.	crime	2	2	0
21.	douleur	2	0	2
22.	fer	2	2	0
23.	force	2	0	2
24.	forge	2	2	0
25.	frappe	2	1	1
26.	idiot	2	1	1
27.	pince	2	0	2
28.	piqueur	2	0	2
29.	pneumatique	2	0	2
30.	pointe	2	2	0
31.	Russie	2	1	1
32-76.	(f = 1)	45	30	15

aiguille, appareil, blague, bois, bougie, bricolage,
bûcheron, carré, cave, charpentier, chaudronnier, choc,
cinglé, ciseau, cogner, coque, crâne, étau, étincelle,
famille, fou, frappé, Homécourt, léger, maillet,
marteau-pilon, métal, objet, pan, pile, piller,
planche, pointu, poisson, porc-épic, psychiâtre, quelque
chose assomant, réflexe, requin, scie, table, tape,
toc, toqué, vélo

Workers

No.	Response	Total
1.	pilon	13
2.	clou (clous)	8
3.	outil (outils)	8
4.	enclume	7
5.	lourd	6
6.	piqueur	5
7.	fer (de fer)	4
8.	bruit	3
9.	dur	3
10.	frappe	3
11.	mal	3
12.	pince (pinces)	3
13.	taper	3
14.	travail	3
15.	burin	2
16.	cogner (cogne)	2
17.	doigt	2
18.	gros	2
19.	menuisier	2
20-50.	(f = 1)	31

aïe! bricolage, de caoutchouc,
cassé, cognée, clouer coup, forge
forgeron, fort, fou, idiot,
instrument, jouir, justice, léger,
manche, mécanique, en mousse,
pansement, Pierre, pioche, plomb,
pneumatique, poinçon, pointe,
réflexe, scie, solide, tenaille, vif
(No response - 1; Illegible - 1)

78. SOIF

Students

No.	Response	Total	Female	Male
1.	faim	69	37	32
2.	eau	49	32	17
3.	désert (de désert)	30	21	9

Workers

No.	Response	Total
1.	désert	19
2.	boire (à boire, boit)	15
3.	eau (l'eau, d'eau, des eaux)	12

78. SOIF (contd)

Students

No.	Response	Total	Female	Male
4.	boire (à boire)	18	15	3
5.	vin	12	6	6
6.	verre	10	10	0
7.	boisson	7	3	4
8.	chaleur	6	3	3
9.	ardente	5	3	2
10.	Sahara	5	4	1
11.	sec	4	3	1
12.	désir	3	2	1
13.	étancher	3	2	1
14.	chameau	2	2	0
15.	citron	2	2	0
16.	Coca-Cola	2	1	1
17.	gorge	2	2	0
18.	inextinguible	2	1	1
19.	langue	2	1	1
20.	pénible	2	2	0
21.	poire	2	0	2
22.	sécheresse	2	2	0
23-71.	(f = 1)	49	30	19

aiguë, altéré, appel, arabe, aride, atroce, Bernstein, bière, boit, bon, bouche, bouteille, breuvage, cheval, citronnade, comédie, désaltérer, dur, été, fontaine, goûter, irrémédiable, ivre, jus, limonade, liquide, de loup, maladie, mer, mort, nécessité, orange, Périer, plaisir, raide, rassasié, salive, sed, sèche, sensation, souffrance, St. Exupéry, tenace, terrible, thé, de vie, vinaigre, Vittel, vive

Workers

No.	Response	Total
4.	faim (et faim)	10
5.	grande	3
6.	verre	3
7.	vin (de vin)	3
8.	aride	2
9.	atroce	2
10.	boisson	2
11.	chaud	2
12-49.	(f = 1)	38

Algérie, ardente, beaucoup, bière, boue, bouteille, brûlante, café, champagne, de courir, délire, dessert, détremper, enfer, envie, éponge, d'été, glouton, inaltérable, légère, lionne, de loup, manger, noir, pain, palais, palmier, poivre, Sahara, sèche, spongieuse, temps, tissu, travailler, trou, de voleur, whisky
(Illegible - 4)

79. VILLE

Students

No.	Response	Total	Female	Male
1.	Paris (de Paris)	51	32	19
2.	maison (maisons)	26	18	8
3.	cité	18	12	6
4.	campagne	17	13	4
5.	village	11	6	5
6.	bruit	10	7	3
7.	rue (rues)	10	8	2
8.	lumière (lumières)	9	6	3
9.	agglomération	6	4	2
10.	eau (d'eau, d'eaux)	6	3	3
11.	grande (grand)	6	5	1
12.	Claudel	5	2	3
13.	agitation	3	3	0
14.	capitale	3	1	2
15.	fumée (fumées)	3	3	0
16.	habitant	3	1	2
17.	toits	3	3	0
18.	usine	3	3	0
19.	cheminée (cheminées)	2	2	0
20.	enfant	2	2	0
21.	franche	2	0	2
22.	habitat	2	0	2
23.	hameau	2	1	1
24.	monument (monuments)	2	2	0
25.	morte	2	0	2
26.	noir	2	1	1
27.	pays	2	1	1
28.	peuple	2	0	2
29.	poussière	2	2	0
30.	Rome	2	1	1
31.	Sainte	2	0	2
32.	urbanisme	2	1	1
33.	villa	2	1	1
34-98.	(f = 1)	65	40	25

âcre, amas, auberge, automobile, beaucoup, Besançon, bleue, bruyant, Camus, carrée, carrefour, citadelle, citadin, citoyen, cohue, compliquée, costume, cour, désert, édifice, égiature, embouteillage, Europe, forte, fourmillement, foyer, France, gare, hiver, homme, immensité, immeuble, Lille, Lyon, merveille,

Workers

No.	Response	Total
1.	Paris	29
2.	grande (grand)	9
3.	village	5
4.	bruit	4
5.	maison	4
6.	de France	3
7.	lumière	3
8.	capitale	2
9.	cité	2
10.	eau	2
11.	endormie	2
12.	province	2
13-59.	(f = 1)	47

agglomération, agitée, d'Amiens, argent Auxerre, blanche, bled, Bordeaux, bruyante, Bugensais, campagne, carré, champignon, citadelle, château, cosaque, éternelle, étrangère, étroite, européen, fumée, gens entassés, granit, habitants, habitation, immense, importante, incendie, industrielle, lumière bruit, luxe, magnifique, moderne, monde, neuve, pays, petite, plaisir, population, region, ruer, sainte, sale, vaste, villa, villageois, Vitry
(Illegible - 1)

79. VILLE (contd)

Students

No.	Response	Total	Female	Male

métro, modernisme, môme, monde, muraille, nation, neuve,
nombre, ouverte, ouvrière, paix, passants, petite,
pittoresque, plaine, populace, province, rempart,
rouge, sale, sombre, tentacule, traffic, travail,
trépidant, triste, urbain, vilain, vitrage, voitures

80. CARRÉ

Students

No.	Response	Total	Female	Male
1.	rond	82	47	35
2.	rectangle	30	23	7
3.	géométrie	29	15	14
4.	cercle	12	6	6
5.	figure (figure géométrique)	9	9	0
6.	triangle	7	6	1
7.	foulard	6	5	1
8.	losange	6	6	0
9.	soie (de soie)	6	3	3
10.	côté	5	4	1
11.	cube	3	0	3
12.	fenêtre	3	1	2
13.	mouchoir	3	3	0
14.	noir	3	2	1
15.	angles	2	1	1
16.	as	2	1	1
17.	bridge	2	1	1
18.	carré	2	1	1
19.	choux	2	0	2
20.	diagonale (diagonales)	2	1	1
21.	jardin	2	2	0
22.	parfait	2	0	2
23.	quadrilatère	2	1	1
24.	surface	2	2	0
25.	tissu	2	2	0
26-87.	(f = 1)	62	42	20

ancien, angle droit, aporie, assurance, Barreau,
bateau, Binet, bizuth, blanc, boite, bureau, calcul,
carrelage, chambre, coin, cuisine, damier, Danton,
dé à jouer, défini, dessin, dessous-plat, droite,
dur, écharpe, est, fermé, forme, hanche, de
l'hypothénuse, jaune, jeu, ligne, lit, long, maison,
marelle, masculin, math, moi, net, ovale, papier,
partie, pelouse, pointu, quadrature, racine,
rectangulaire, régulier, rien, rigueur, rythme, salle,
soldats, soleil, solide, square, terrain, terre,
tête, tour

Workers

No.	Response	Total
1.	rond (ronde)	11
2.	rectangle	8
3.	surface	8
4.	d'as (as)	5
5.	table	4
6.	chambre	3
7.	côté	3
8.	de l'Est (Est)	3
9.	géométrie	3
10.	maison	3
11.	carrelage	2
12.	champs	2
13.	cube	2
14.	fromage	2
15.	jardin (du jardin)	2
16.	mouchoir	2
17.	parfait	2
18.	pierre (de pierre)	2
19.	racine	2
20.	terrain	2
21.	triangle	2
22-57.	(f = 1)	36

acueillant, boite, carreau, carrée,
chemin, choux, côtés égaux, cylindre,
écharpe, égaux, enfant, étoffe,
exact, figure, fleurs, grand, gris,
juste, à luzerne, magique,
mathématique, mauvais, 1 mètre carré,
mots croisés, noir, officier, point,
pointu, poker, pourtour, sauter, soie,
symétrie, de terre, ville, vitre
(Illegible - 5; No response - 1)

81. BEURRE

Students

No.	Response	Total	Female	Male
1.	mou	32	20	12
2.	jaune	28	21	7
3.	frais	22	10	12
4.	pain	22	17	5
5.	gras	17	12	5
6.	lait	17	12	5
7.	fromage	16	7	9
8.	rance	13	8	5
9.	tartine	13	11	2
10.	oeuf (oeufs)	5	4	1
11.	vache	5	2	3
12.	couteau	4	3	1
13.	cuisine	4	4	0

Workers

No.	Response	Total
1.	frais	18
2.	lait	13
3.	mou	13
4.	bon	5
5.	fromage	5
6.	Normandie	5
7.	noir	4
8.	aliment	3
9.	doux	3
10.	gras	3
11.	jaune	3
12.	salé (sales)	3
13.	tartine	3

81. BEURRE (contd)

Students

No.	Response	Total	Female	Male
14.	Normandie	4	3	1
15.	salé	4	3	1
16.	Charente (Charentes)	3	0	3
17.	ferme	3	2	1
18.	fondre	3	3	0
19.	fondu	3	2	1
20.	graisse	3	1	2
21.	margarine	3	1	2
22.	noir	3	2	1
23.	blanc	2	1	1
24.	canon	2	2	0
25.	denrée	2	1	1
26.	dur	2	2	0
27.	fil	2	1	1
28.	goûter	2	2	0
29.	manger	2	0	2
30.	matière (matière grasse)	2	0	2
31.	sel	2	1	1
32-74.	(f = 1)	43	26	17

aliment, bas-beurre, bon, café au lait, campagne, comestible, crème, crèmerie, déjeuner, dessin, douceur, écoeurement, épinard, étaler, faim, farine, fondant, frit, gant, gâteau, graine, grossir, guerre, Hollande, huile, laiterie, laitier, microbe, mollesse, motte, panier, papier, petit déjeuner, de Pierre Fontaine, prix, produit, protide, rouge, roux, sauce, tendre, toast, visqueux

Workers

No.	Response	Total
14.	vache	3
15.	Charente	2
16.	dur (dure)	2
17.	laitier	2
18.	manger	2
19.	rance	2
20-39.	(f = 1)	19

bois, de Bretagne, crème, croire, Danois, épicerie, faim, ferme, fondu, matières grasses, margarine, oeuf, pain, pasteurisé, petit, sauté, sel, suintant, viande
(Illegible - 2)

82. DOCTEUR

Students

No.	Response	Total	Female	Male
1.	maladie	62	40	22
2.	médecin	33	19	14
3.	malade	23	13	10
4.	médecine (en médecine)	15	9	6
5.	santé	9	6	3
6.	hôpital	7	5	2
7.	lunettes	6	4	2
8.	soin (soins)	6	5	1
9.	blanc	4	4	0
10.	lettres	4	2	2
11.	ami	3	3	0
12.	homme	3	2	1
13.	infirmier (infirmière)	3	2	1
14.	piqûre	3	3	0
15.	soigner	3	2	1
16.	bistouri	2	1	1
17.	confiance	2	2	0
18.	consciencieux	2	2	0
19.	guérir	2	1	1
20.	monsieur	2	1	1
21.	ordonnance	2	2	0
22.	père	2	2	0
23.	peur	2	1	1
24.	pharmacien	2	1	1
25.	remède	2	2	0
26.	sonnette	2	1	1
27.	toubib	2	1	1
28-107.	(f = 1)	80	48	32

allemand, amusant, apaisement, artiste, automobile, avenir, B.H., blouse, blouse blanche, bon, bonté, cabinet, campagne, chapeau, chauve, coeur, consultation, correpondant, croquemitaine, Cuche, D.F.M.P., dentiste, doctoresse, droit, drôle, écriture, enfant, entorse, épouvantail, équilibre, évêque, à éviter, Faust, grand, guimauve, guérison, guérisseur, hideux, horreur, hygiène, imposant, intelligent, jumeau, Kinsey, lasse, maison, maître, mal, malaise, mari, médicament, mépris, merci,

Workers

No.	Response	Total
1.	malade	16
2.	maladie	14
3.	médecin	7
4.	médecine (en médecine la médecine)	6
5.	soigne	6
6.	hôpital	3
7.	miracle	3
8.	toubib	3
9.	ausculter (ausculte)	2
10.	intelligent	2
11.	ès lettres	2
12.	Schweitzer	2
13-58.	(f = 1)	46

aimable, ami, blanc, bon, très bon, capable, charlatan, cher, consultation, corps humain, courageux, doux, droit, en droit, énergique, ennui, formidable, gentil, grand, guérir, incertitude, infirmier, instruit, laboratoire, mauvais, menteur, métier, nombre, oculiste, ordonnance, oreillons, en pharmacie, pharmacien, pic, piqûre, practicien, rapide, sec, sévère, simple, soigneur, soin, talentueux, traitaint, visite, des yeux
(Illegible - 2; No response - 1)

82. DOCTEUR (contd)

Students

No.	Response	Total	Female	Male

moustache, nombreux, papa, petite femme, peu-être,
pharmacie, photo, plaque, pressé, profession libérale,
psychiâtre, psychosomat, réconfortant, Roin, Sainte Anne,
salut, sauvage, ès sciences, Schlemmer, Schweitzer,
sévérité, spécialiste, sym., téléphone, trousse,
vétérinaire, voleur

83. BRUYANT

Students

No.	Response	Total	Female	Male
1.	enfant (enfants)	30	19	11
2.	calme	27	17	10
3.	rue (la rue)	25	18	7
4.	silencieux	17	7	10
5.	bruit	14	10	4
6.	ville (la ville)	12	8	4
7.	fatigue	8	5	3
8.	auto (autos)	7	7	0
9.	silence	7	4	3
10.	moteur	5	1	4
11.	chahut	4	3	1
12.	désagréable	4	2	2
13.	Paris	4	1	3
14.	trompette (trompettes)	4	4	0
15.	classe	3	2	1
16.	doux	3	2	1
17.	sourd	3	3	0
18.	sonore	3	2	1
19.	tapage	3	3	0
20.	tintamarre	3	1	2
21.	tranquille	3	2	1
22.	vacarme	3	2	1
23.	voiture (voitures)	3	1	2
24.	cour	2	1	1
25.	école	2	2	0
26.	fatiguant	2	2	0
27.	foule	2	0	2
28.	gai	2	1	1
29.	garçon	2	1	1
30.	jazz	2	0	2
31.	lent	2	1	1
32.	machine	2	2	0
33.	mal de tête	2	1	1
34.	sage	2	2	0
35.	turbulent	2	0	2
36-104.	(f = 1)	69	47	22

abusif, abrutissant, adjectif, affecté, affolé,
affreux, agaçant, agacement, agité, amer, amphi,
assomant, assourdissant, bavardage, calmé, canon,
chaos, clair, colère, collège, condamnable, compliqué,
corne, cours, crécelle, criard, crier, désagrément,
ennuyeux, épice, étonnant, ferraille, fière, fort, fou,
frères, galoches, garnement, ivre, jeu, jeune, klaxon,
lumière, mal aux oreilles, mer, métro, noir, odieux,
opaque, paix, pénible, phoner, porte, rauque,
réfectoire, remuant, salle, salsifis, sauvage, scie,
sifflet, soeur, son, strident, tête, tracas, train,
trop, vache

Workers

No.	Response	Total
1.	bruit (le bruit)	14
2.	enfant (enfants)	7
3.	train	4
4.	voiture (voitures)	4
5.	calme	3
6.	clair	3
7.	fort	3
8.	garçon	3
9.	rue	3
10.	agaçant	2
11.	auto (automobile)	2
12.	bruyère	2
13.	doux	2
14.	embêtant	2
15.	jeux	2
16.	machine	2
17.	marteau	2
18.	moto	2
19.	silencieux	2
20.	vacarme	2
21.	vitesse	2
22-64.	(f = 1)	43

absurde, faire du bruit, bruyante,
camion, catastrophe, cheval, chien,
la classe, cloches, circulation,
colère, danser, désagréable, écolier,
énervant, ennuyeux, exaspération,
fanfare, fatiguant, fauve, fête,
foudre, fragile, gai, gueulard,
hurlant, indiscipline, mauvais,
métro, noteur, musique, oreilles,
prêtre, silence, sourd, tambour,
tintamarre, tousser, tranquille,
travailler, troupeau, vif ville,
(Illegible - 4)

84. VOLEUR

Students

No.	Response	Total	Female	Male
1.	bicyclette (de bicyclette)	27	20	7
2.	gendarme	13	8	5
3.	prison	12	8	4
4.	bijou (de bijoux, bijoux)	10	9	1
5.	nuit	10	8	2
6.	argent	9	9	0
7.	enfant (enfants, d'enfants)	9	5	4
8.	volé	7	4	3
9.	bandit	6	4	2
10.	brigand	6	4	2
11.	honnête	6	3	3
12.	justice	5	3	2
13.	assassin	4	4	0
14.	casquette	4	4	0
15.	homme	4	3	1
16.	masque	4	1	3
17.	montre	4	1	3
18.	police	4	1	3
19.	à la tire (tire)	4	0	4
20.	cambrioleur	3	1	2
21.	gangster	3	2	1
22.	maison	3	2	1
23.	noir	3	3	0
24.	Bagdad	2	2	0
25.	butin	2	1	1
26.	cambriolage	2	1	1
27.	chemin (chemins)	2	0	2
28.	clé (clés)	2	2	0
29.	courir	2	1	1
30.	dérober	2	1	1
31.	escroc	2	1	1
32.	fenêtre	2	1	1
33.	filou	2	1	1
34.	habit (habits)	2	2	0
35.	larcin	2	1	1
36.	larron	2	1	1
37.	malhonnête	2	0	2
38.	obscurité	2	1	1
39.	pauvre	2	1	1
40.	pitié	2	1	1
41.	poursuite	2	0	2
42.	pris	2	2	0
43.	rapt	2	2	0
44.	silence	2	2	0
45.	tapinois	2	2	0
46.	voleuse	2	1	1
47-128.	(f = 1)	82	50	32

allumette, anxiété, attrapé, bagages, besoin, blond,
cache, chaîne, chanson, chiffons, corde, course,
criminel, déclassé, délinquante, délinquant,
déséquilibré, disparition, enfance, endives,
effroi, s'enfuit, flic, fripon, fugue, fuite,
de grand chemin, habile, Harpagon, honte, horrible,
idiot, incompréhensible, individu, ingrat, jaune,
juge, lampe, main, malin, masque, mauvais, méchant,
menottes, menteur, Mouloudji, naturel, néfaste,
objet, oiseaux, outil, paix, pas feutré, paysan,
pénible, peur, pince, pick pocket, probe, probité,
prophète, ramoneur, rapin, rat, rififi, roman,
roman récent, sac, sans lien, serrure, silencieux,
silhouette, société, soir, sombre, teint, tribunal,
valise, vice, vil, villa, Villon

Workers

No.	Response	Total
1.	prison	9
2.	bandit	7
3.	argent (d'argent)	6
4.	gendarme	5
5.	pie	5
6.	rapide	4
7.	arrêté (arrêtée)	3
8.	bijoux (de bijoux)	3
9.	justice	3
10.	pris	3
11.	police	3
12.	voler (volé)	3
13.	assassin	2
14.	bicyclette (de bicyclette)	2
15.	brigand	2
16.	gangster	2
17.	honnête	2
18.	malhonnête	2
19.	policier	2
20.	professionel	2
21.	voleuse	2
22-62.	(f = 1)	41

aguets, air, appât, attention, auto,
beaucoup, cambriolé, casseur,
délinquant, grand chemin, chevronné,
échoit, escroc, évadé, faux, filou,
gant, grand, habile, hors-la-loi,
juge, juste, malfaiteur, malin,
masque, mauvais, méfait, méchant,
métier, meurtre, noir, de pain,
tant pis, de pomme, puni, truand,
valise, visiteur, vole, voyous,
vomis
(Illegible - 2)

NORMS OF WORD ASSOCIATION

85. LION

Students

No.	Response	Total	Female	Male
1.	crinière	30	25	5
2.	tigre	30	16	14
3.	force	16	10	6
4.	lionne	13	7	6
5.	animal	10	8	2
6.	jungle	9	7	2
7.	zoo	9	4	5
8.	désert	8	6	2
9.	fauve	8	3	5
10.	roi	8	2	6
11.	Belfort (de Belfort)	7	4	3
12.	cage	6	6	0
13.	féroce	5	3	2
14.	forêt	5	5	0
15.	méchant	5	3	2
16.	noir	5	3	2
17.	or (d'or)	5	3	2
18.	rugissement	5	4	1
19.	bête	4	2	2
20.	griffe	4	3	1
21.	noblesse	3	2	1
22.	beauté	2	1	1
23.	blason	2	2	0
24.	chèvre	2	1	1
25.	chien	2	1	1
26.	cirque	2	1	1
27.	éléphant	2	2	0
28.	fort	2	0	2
29.	panthère	2	1	1
30.	puissance	2	1	1
31.	rat	2	1	1
32.	rouge	2	2	0
33.	statue	2	2	0
34.	terrible	2	1	1
35.	zodiaque	2	1	1
36-100.	($\underline{f}$ = 1)	65	41	24

Afrique, AOE, août, armes, Atlas, de l'Atlas, beau,
bête, féroce, brousse, brute, cactus, calme, car-
nivore, Cid, cirage constellation, couleur
courageux, crocodille, Denfert-Rochereau, dents,
dessin, Dieu, doux, effrayant, fable, férocité,
fierté, foire, fourrure, furieux, grand, grandeur,
homme, léopard, lionceau, louve, maigre, de Marly,
mari, métro, moucheron, Nicole, orgueil, pays chaud,
peur, queue, Richard, royal, rugir, rugit, rugissant,
sable, Sahara, sauvage, savane, seigneur, serpent,
souris, Tartarin, taureau, tignasse, vert, vorace,
zodiac

Workers

No.	Response	Total
1.	féroce	12
2.	lionne	8
3.	fauve	7
4.	animal (animaux)	6
5.	cage	5
6.	cirque	5
7.	roi	5
8.	rugit (rugir)	5
9.	méchant	4
10.	d'or	4
11.	Afrique (d'Afrique)	3
12.	crinière	3
13.	forêt	3
14.	sauvage	3
15.	rugissant	3
16.	Belfort	2
17.	force	2
18.	gros	2
19.	jungle	2
20.	tigre	2
21-49.	($\underline{f}$ = 1)	29

Afrique Noire, aigle, d'argent,
Atlas, bête, chair, chat, coureur,
courageux, couteau, enrage, fort,
fourmi, généreux, haine, grille,
Hercule, horoscope, intelligent,
liane, mauvais, des montagnes, noir,
rageur, sévère, superbe, vache,
viande, ville

86. JOIE

Students

No.	Response	Total	Female	Male
1.	tristesse	23	13	10
2.	bonheur	20	9	11
3.	rire (rires)	16	9	7
4.	vivre (de vivre)	14	10	4
5.	gaieté	11	7	4
6.	plaisir	9	4	5
7.	amour	8	4	4
8.	lumière	6	6	0
9.	soleil	5	5	0
10.	enfant (enfants)	4	3	1
11.	Noël	4	3	1
12.	peine	4	3	1
13.	pleur (pleurs)	4	2	2
14.	sourire	4	4	0
15.	vie	4	0	4
16.	beauté	3	3	0
17.	cri (cris)	3	2	1
18.	douleur	3	1	2

Workers

No.	Response	Total
1.	vivre (de vivre)	16
2.	heureux	10
3.	gaieté	6
4.	rire (de rire)	6
5.	content	5
6.	enfant (d'enfant)	5
7.	immense	5
8.	grande	3
9.	bonheur	2
10.	délire	2
11.	famille	2
12.	folle	2
13.	fête	2
14.	gai (gaie)	2
15.	musique	2
16.	offrir (d'offrir)	2
17.	plaisir	2
18.	profonde	2

86. JOIE (contd)

Students

No.	Response	Total	Female	Male
19.	heureux	3	2	1
20.	hymne	3	2	1
21.	ivresse	3	2	1
22.	malheur	3	2	1
23.	vacances	3	2	1
24.	agréable	2	1	1
25.	amertume	2	1	1
26.	Beethoven	2	1	1
27.	chagrin	2	2	0
28.	clarté	2	1	1
29.	colère	2	1	1
30.	douce (doux)	2	2	0
31.	douceur	2	2	0
32.	fête	2	2	0
33.	feu	2	1	1
34.	fille	2	1	1
35.	folie	2	1	1
36.	gai	2	1	1
37.	inconnue	2	2	0
38.	intense	2	2	0
39.	paix	2	1	1
40.	pure	2	2	0
41.	rare	2	2	0
42.	santé	2	1	1
43.	saut	2	2	0
44.	sereine	2	0	2
45.	triste	2	0	2
46-129.	(f = 1)	84	57	27

aiguë, allégresse, arbre, armer, beau, Bergson, Bible,
blé, bruyant, cadeau, caverne, chant, chrétien, clair,
coeur, de connaître, content, contentement, courir,
courte, danse, déborde, délice, délire, deuil,
difficile, dilater, divine, dos, douleureux, durée,
ébats, éclat, éclatement, élan, émotion, enfantine,
ennui, entière, espoir, exubérance, explosion, faiblesse,
famille, femme, foi, frustre, Gluck, hilare, humain,
illusion, insouciance, intérieure, larmes, liesse, mari,
la mer, merveille, merveilleux, musique, naissance,
océan, Pascal, pax, perspective, promenade, puissante,
pureté, rareté, réelle, retour, sauté, sauter, scoute,
sensation, sensible, ski, succès, symphonie,
9ième symphonie, théâtre, tranquille, travail, voyage

Workers

No.	Response	Total
19-57.	(f = 1)	39

d'aimer, argent, beaucoup, cadeau,
crayon, crie, débordante, délirante,
désir, dimanche, distraction, dur,
enfance, enfantine, épais, espoir,
fierté, fruit, inoubliable, jouir,
joyeux, mauvais, moto, naissance,
Noël, pauvre, peine, père, pleurer,
pureté, rare, saine, santé, soif,
triste, de tenir, tranquille,
tremblante, tristesse

87. LIT

Students

No.	Response	Total	Female	Male
1.	repos	37	24	13
2.	sommeil	32	19	13
3.	dormir	30	19	11
4.	drap (draps)	24	17	7
5.	cage	14	7	7
6.	chambre	11	7	4
7.	blanc	9	6	3
8.	doux	8	3	5
9.	coucher	5	3	2
10.	couverture (couvertures)	4	3	1
11.	enfant	4	3	1
12.	maladie	4	3	1
13.	bois	3	3	0
14.	chaise	3	1	2
15.	clos	3	2	1
16.	douillet	3	3	0
17.	fer	3	3	0
18.	malade	3	2	1
19.	nuit	3	2	1
20.	oreiller (oreillers)	3	2	1
21.	profond	3	3	0
22.	rêve	3	3	0
23.	table	3	1	2
24.	amour	2	1	1

Workers

No.	Response	Total
1.	dormir	29
2.	coucher (couche)	7
3.	douillet	7
4.	repos	7
5.	sommeil	7
6.	chaud	3
7.	drap	3
8.	doux	3
9.	dure	3
10.	moëlleux	3
11.	confortable	2
12.	covertures	2
13.	d'enfant	2
14.	literie	2
15.	table	2
16-45.	(f = 1)	30

amour, bayeau, bébé, blancheur, bon,
cage, chambre, couchette, défait,
dort, douceur, d'enfer, femme,
fenêtre, fer, grand, hôpital, jumeau,
lire, de malade, nuptial, passage,
petit, ressort, rivière, Seine, il
sommeille, sommier, souple, volupté
(Illegible - 2; No response - 1)

87. LIT (contd)

Students

No.	Response	Total	Female	Male
25.	bas	2	2	0
26.	chaleur	2	2	0
27.	ciel	2	1	1
28.	colonnes (a colonnes)	2	1	1
29.	détente	2	1	1
30.	douleur	2	1	1
31.	dur	2	0	2
32.	fatigue	2	0	2
33.	femme	2	0	2
34.	jumeau (jumeaux)	2	1	1
35.	moëlleux	2	2	0
36-84.	(f = 1)	49	33	16

agréable, allongé, armoire, avenir, baldaquin, barreau,
beauté, bien, bonheur, café, calme, camp, carpetté,
confort, couche, divan, dodo, doré, dort, douceur,
édredon, ennui, fauteuil, fille, gigogne, grand,
limon, au lit, literie, matelas, matin, meuble, moite,
mort, mou, nuptial, objet, plaisir, planche, plumes,
de plumes, rivière, A. Roussin, saut, soif, soir,
souffrance, superposé, triste

88. LOURD

Students

No.	Response	Total	Female	Male
1.	léger	69	36	33
2.	pesant	24	12	12
3.	poids	24	18	6
4.	sac (un sac)	19	16	3
5.	plomb	18	16	2
6.	fardeau	15	9	6
7.	camion	9	5	4
8.	pierre	8	7	1
9.	fatigue	5	3	2
10.	eau	4	2	2
11.	fatiguant	4	3	1
12.	marteau	4	2	2
13.	dur	3	1	2
14.	paquet	3	3	0
15.	pénible	3	2	1
16.	valise	3	1	2
17.	charge	2	1	1
18.	effort	2	0	2
19.	mal	2	2	0
20.	porter (à porter)	2	0	2
21.	responsabilité	2	2	0
22.	table	2	1	1
23.	temps	2	1	1
24.	tonne	2	2	0
25-81.	(f = 1)	57	39	18

acier, adjectif, animal, armoire, artillerie,
ascenseur, atmosphère, balance, caisse, chaîne,
charbon, chocolat, cil, court, danger, difficulté,
dos, doux, éléphant, esprit, estomac, étau,
exténuant, faute, fer, froid, haltère, indigeste,
kilog, lac, lent, lourdaud, massif, mou, muet,
noir, objet, orage, pain, pataud, pavé, paysan,
peine, pluie, plume, pomme de terre, porte-faix,
repas, richesse, sec, sombre, sommeil, son, sourd,
tournure, vie, vin

Workers

No.	Response	Total
1.	poids	19
2.	léger (et léger)	16
3.	fardeau (fardeaux)	10
4.	plomb	7
5.	camion	4
6.	pesant	4
7.	dur	3
8.	fatiguant	3
9.	gros	3
10.	sac	3
11.	énorme	2
12.	fer	2
13.	lourdaud	2
14.	pénible	2
15.	travail	2
16-48.	(f = 1)	33

ans, auto, bloc, la caisse, colère,
coustaud, courbature, enclume,
fatigue, force, fragile, franc,
haltère, idiot, impossible, 110
kilogs, lent, lourde, malin,
marteau, mercure, objet, pavé,
rugby, sable, sarment, solide,
temps, tonne, valise, vêtements,
vie, vieillard

89. TABAC

	Students			
No.	Response	Total	Female	Male
1.	fumée	73	52	21
2.	cigarette (cigarettes)	35	24	11
3.	pipe	34	21	13
4.	fumer	29	16	13
5.	blond	25	15	10
6.	fumeur	8	6	2
7.	odeur	6	5	1
8.	bureau	4	1	3
9.	nicotine	4	0	4
10.	Virginie	4	3	1
11.	cigare	3	2	1
12.	priser (à priser)	3	2	1
13.	bleu	2	1	1
14.	bon	2	0	2
15.	intoxication	2	2	0
16.	ivresse	2	2	0
17.	mauvais	2	2	0
18.	noir	2	2	0
19.	plaisir	2	1	1
20.	prise	2	1	1
21-64.	(f = 1)	44	26	18

agrément, alcool, allumette, amer, anglais, argent, Baudelaire, boite, brun, buée, Camafi, cancer, coin, défense, désagrément, drogue, épice, excitant, feuilles, fumé, fume-cigarettes, gris, hollandais, marron, mauvais odeur, poison, Polytechnique, pomme, pot, poumon, puant, puanteur, rêve, route, rude, tabac, tabatière, Thiers, trop, tue, valise, veuve, vice, vie

	Workers	
No.	Response	Total
1.	blond	20
2.	cigarette (cigarettes)	15
3.	fumer (fume)	15
4.	fumée	14
5.	pipe	6
6.	mauvais	3
7.	poison	3
8.	âcre	2
9.	blanc	2
10.	cigare (et cigare)	2
11.	fort	2
12.	fumeur	2
13.	gris	2
14.	Orient (d'Orient)	2
15-37.	(f = 1)	23

amer, américain, blague, café, cancer, défendu, désiré, doux, drogue, fin, Gauloises, Gitane, gentillesse, goût, infecte, maladie, moto, néfaste, nocif, plante, poivre, régie, rêve
(Illegible - 1; No response - 1)

90. BÉBÉ

	Students			
No.	Response	Total	Female	Male
1.	rose	25	16	9
2.	enfant	23	9	14
3.	berceau	18	13	5
4.	langes (lange)	18	15	3
5.	cris (cri)	15	9	6
6.	pleurs (pleur)	13	11	2
7.	biberon	7	3	4
8.	couches (couche)	6	3	3
9.	lait	6	4	2
10.	maman	6	4	2
11.	pleurer	6	4	2
12.	Cadum	5	1	4
13.	joie	5	2	3
14.	mignon	5	4	1
15.	nourrisson	4	3	1
16.	pleure	4	3	1
17.	douceur	3	3	0
18.	jeunesse	3	0	3
19.	joli	3	2	1
20.	joufflu	3	2	1
21.	mère	3	2	1
22.	petit	3	2	1
23.	sourire	3	3	0
24.	amour	2	2	0
25.	ange	2	1	1
26.	blanc	2	1	1
27.	blond	2	1	1
28.	charmant	2	1	1
29.	charme	2	2	0
30.	chou	2	2	0
31.	criard	2	0	2
32.	crier	2	0	2
33.	fragile	2	2	0
34.	jumeau (jumeaux)	2	2	0
35.	mou	2	2	0
36.	naissance	2	1	1
37.	petitesse	2	1	1

	Workers	
No.	Response	Total
1.	rose	10
2.	enfant	9
3.	beau	8
4.	mignon	7
5.	lange	4
6.	lune	4
7.	pleure	4
8.	berceau	3
9.	biberon	3
10.	landau	3
11.	bambin	2
12.	Cadum	2
13.	cris	2
14.	ennui	2
15.	gentil	2
16.	gracieux	2
17.	joli	2
18.	maternité	2
19.	petit	2
20.	pleurant	2
21.	pleurs	2
22.	sage	2
23-58.	(f = 1)	36

accouchement, amuser, bébé, bonne, charmant, Charrier, cher, cigarette, couche, criard, dort, famille, fille, fragile, fruit, gaieté, gosse, grand, gros, heureux, humain, joufflu, mère, môme, mouillé, naît, non, nourrissant, Ovomaltine, poupée, prime, pureté, rouspète, sain, souriant, vélo

90. BÉBÉ (contd)

Students

No.	Response	Total	Female	Male
38.	poupée	2	2	0
39.	rond	2	2	0
40.	tendre	2	2	0
41.	tendresse	2	2	0
42.	vagissement	2	1	1
43.	vie (vies)	2	1	1
44-104.	(f = 1)	61	38	23

adorable, allumette, aimé, aimer, animal, bain, beau, bercer, bonheur, bras, brailler, brun, bruyant, coucher, crie, délice, désagréable, dodo, dormir, dort, doux, éclat, femme, flasque, fragilité, François, gâté, gentillesse, homme, individu, innocence, insouciance, Jacques, jeune, layette, lit, lune, maillot, marmaille, mort, nouveau-né, occupation, parents, poids, porter, pouce, potelé, pourquoi, rire, sage, sein, sérieux, Sylvie, talc, tenir, téter, vagissant, velu, vieillard, voiture, yeux

91. LUNE

Students

No.	Response	Total	Female	Male
1.	soleil	32	17	15
2.	nuit	29	23	6
3.	miel (de miel)	20	9	11
4.	rousse	20	5	15
5.	clair (claire, clair de lune)	18	16	2
6.	ronde (rond)	17	14	3
7.	croissant	14	9	5
8.	ciel	13	9	4
9.	bleue (bleu)	9	8	1
10.	blanc (blanche)	7	4	3
11.	étoile (étoiles, les étoiles)	7	5	2
12.	pleine (pleine lune)	6	3	3
13.	clarté	5	5	0
14.	quartier	5	2	3
15.	astre (astres)	4	1	3
16.	jaune	4	3	1
17.	froid (froide)	3	1	2
18.	Musset	3	2	1
19.	rêve	3	3	0
20.	romantique	3	2	1
21.	brillant	2	2	0
22.	calme	2	0	2
23.	musique	2	2	0
24.	opale	2	2	0
25.	pâle	2	2	0
26.	pâleur	2	2	0
27.	soir	2	2	0
28.	taire	2	1	1
29.	vert (verte	2	1	1
30-77.	(f = 1)	48	29	19

ancien, argenté, beauté, belle, bêtise, bizarre, brume, chanson, chose, douceur, éclairer, éclipse, espérer, été, fou, froideur, fusée, impossible, La, luire, luit, lumière, lumière dans la nuit, lune, marée, matière, mélancolie, nuage, obsession, Pierrot, poésie, poète, promenade, pureté, quart, rayon, rêverie, rire, romantisme, rondeur, roseau, rouge, Sade, sereine, sourire, triste, tuer, vermifuge

Workers

No.	Response	Total
1.	de miel (miel)	23
2.	clair (claire)	12
3.	soleil	10
4.	nuit	7
5.	croissant	6
6.	rousse	5
7.	planète	4
8.	pleine	4
9.	ciel	3
10.	ronde (rond)	3
11.	soir	3
12.	astre	2
13.	fusée (fusées)	2
14.	loin	2
15.	satellite	2
16.	Spoutnik	2
17-38.	(f = 1)	24

artiste, belle, calme, éclair, éclairé, éloignée, émeraude, espace, étoile, frileux, globe, jaune, Jeanne, jolie, mousse, pâle, poupée, promenade, pur, quartier, Russie, rêver, terre, "tintavella"
(Illegible - 1)

92. CISEAUX

	Students					Workers	
No.	Response	Total	Female	Male	No.	Response	Total
1.	couper	64	40	24	1.	coupe (coupes)	15
2.	couture	24	22	2	2.	couper (à couper, coupé)	11
3.	tissus (tissu)	15	12	3	3.	tissus (tissu, à tissu)	10
4.	coupant	12	6	6	4.	coupant (coupants, coupante)	9
5.	aiguille (aiguilles)	11	8	3	5.	pointu (pointue, pointus)	8
6.	coupe (sa coupe)	11	8	3	6.	couture	7
7.	pointu (pointus)	10	9	1	7.	couturière	6
8.	couteau (couteaux)	7	3	4	8.	aiguisé (à aiguiser, aiguisés)	5
9.	fil	6	3	3	9.	couteaux (couteau)	5
10.	tenailles	6	4	2	10.	d'argent (argent)	4
11.	acier	5	2	3	11.	tailleur	3
12.	argent (d'argent)	5	3	2	12.	coiffeur	2
13.	couturier (couturière)	5	3	2	13.	fil	2
14.	dé (dés)	4	4	0	14.	taille	2
15.	froid (froids)	4	3	1	15.	tranchant	2
16.	papier	4	3	1	16-38.	(f = 1)	23
17.	tailleur	4	0	4			
18.	broder (à broder)	3	2	1			
19.	coudre	3	2	1			
20.	coupure	3	1	2			
21.	étoffe	3	2	1			
22.	trancher	3	1	2			
23.	aigu (aigus)	2	2	0			
24.	aiguisé (aiguisés)	2	1	1			
25.	bruit	2	2	0			
26.	coupent	2	1	1			
27.	croix	2	2	0			
28.	découpage	2	0	2			
29.	lame	2	1	1			
30.	outil	2	2	0			
31.	paire	2	2	0			
32.	pince	2	1	1			
33.	taille	2	1	1			
34.	toile	2	2	0			
35.	visse	2	1	1			
36-85.	(f = 1)	50	25	25			

Workers 16-38:
acier, aiguille, bistouri, de cableuse, canettes, cisaille, étoffe, eunuque, faucille, ferraille, fille, à froid, grand, habits, justice, mal, ongle, outil, petit, rasoir, toile, travailler, tremble (Illegible - 1)

Students 36-85:
affuté, amer, Anastasie, appareil, à bois, brillant, brillent, C. Dior, carrier, carte, cheveu, chirurgie, cicatrice, cisaille, coupé, courts, couturieux, cri-cri, déchirer, dentelles, draps, dureté, écorchure, effilé, enfants, fer, frêne, géographie, instrument, jeux, longs, métal, ongle, or, Paul, pluriel, point, pointe, Rabin, raccomodeuse, remouler, ronds, rouillé, rue, surréalisme, tailler, tisser, tranche, tranchant, veine

93. TRANQUILLE

	Students					Workers	
No.	Response	Total	Female	Male	No.	Response	Total
1.	calme (calmes)	55	39	16	1.	père	13
2.	père (le père)	25	14	11	2.	sage	11
3.	agité	12	3	9	3.	calme	10
4.	homme (l'homme)	12	8	4	4.	bruyant	4
5.	campagne	10	9	1	5.	paisible (et paisible)	4
6.	paix	8	4	4	6.	campagne	3
7.	paisible	8	5	3	7.	enfant	3
8.	repos	8	6	2	8.	heureux	3
9.	eau	7	6	1	9.	homme (l'homme)	3
10.	sage	6	4	2	10.	vie	3
11.	bruyant	5	4	1	11.	agneau (agneaux)	2
12.	vacances	5	2	3	12.	Baptiste (comme Baptiste)	2
13.	doux	4	2	2	13.	repos	2
14.	fauteuil	4	1	3	14.	satisfaisant	2
15.	lac	4	2	2	15-62.	(f = 1)	48
16.	lent	4	3	1			

Workers 15-62:
absolue, agité, ange, arabe, beau,

93. TRANQUILLE (contd)

	Students					Workers	
No.	Response	Total	Female	Male		No.	Response	Total

No.	Response	Total	Female	Male
17.	mer	4	4	0
18.	nuit	4	2	2
19.	quiétude	4	3	1
20.	coin	3	0	3
21.	dormir	3	1	2
22.	remuant	3	1	2
23.	assis	2	2	0
24.	Baptiste	2	1	1
25.	film	2	2	0
26.	jeu	2	2	0
27.	pré	2	2	0
28.	rivière	2	0	2
29.	silence	2	2	0
30.	soir	2	1	1
31.	solitude	2	2	0
32.	stable	2	1	1
33.	turbulent	2	1	1
34.	vert	2	1	1
35-100.	(f = 1)	66	44	22

adjectif, agréable, amitié, apaisant, apaisé, banlieue, boule, bruit, caressant, cependant, chaleur, chat, chausson, chien, cieux, clair, clairière, cô-Baptiste, crier, cris, enfant, ennuyeux, esprit, étang, fillette, flânerie, foyer, girafe, grand-papa, hamac, humain, indéfini, image, immobile, Kant, lit, lourd, mansuétude, mère, monotone, Orphéo, pas, paysage, Père tranquille, personnage, philosophie, placide, port, quiet, "quiet", religieux, reposé, rêve, sans bruit, satisfait, serein, silencieux, sobre, soirée, sommeil, tempérament, tourbillon, vie, vieux, vieillard, ville

Workers

No.	Response	Total

bien, boeuf, caractère, chaise, chat, décontracté, détente, docile, dormir, doux, eaux, embêtant, étonnant, film, gaieté, garçon, gentil, heure, joueur, joyeux, lac, lentement, lit, méchant, mer, la montagne, mouvementé, nuit, paix, pénard, personne, prairie, province, quiétude, reposant, rivière, ruisseau, solitude, songe, vacances, vieille, virilité, voleur
(Illegible - 1; No Response - 1)

94. VERT

	Students					Workers	

Students

No.	Response	Total	Female	Male
1.	pré (prés)	37	23	14
2.	feuille	20	15	5
3.	rouge	19	7	12
4.	arbre (arbres)	17	14	3
5.	prairie (prairies)	16	10	6
6.	herbe	15	13	2
7.	jaune	13	9	4
8.	gris (de gris)	10	5	5
9.	eau (d'eau)	9	8	1
10.	bleu	9	5	4
11.	campagne	8	6	2
12.	couleur	8	3	5
13.	pomme	8	7	1
14.	espérance	7	3	4
15.	forêt	5	4	1
16.	pâturage (pâturages)	4	2	2
17.	tapis	4	1	3
18.	bouteille	3	1	2
19.	chou (choux)	3	3	0
20.	feuillage	3	3	0
21.	galant	3	0	3
22.	mer	3	3	0
23.	paysage	3	3	0
24.	sombre	3	1	2
25.	calme	2	0	2
26.	champ	2	2	0
27.	espoir	2	1	1
28.	fleur (fleurs)	2	1	1
29.	fruit	2	1	1
30.	jade	2	2	0
31.	jardin	2	1	1
32.	nature	2	1	1
33.	noir	2	2	0
34.	pelouse	2	1	1
35.	printemps	2	2	0
36.	reposant	2	0	2

Workers

No.	Response	Total
1.	pré (prés, des prés)	18
2.	couleur	12
3.	jaune	7
4.	campagne	6
5.	prairie	5
6.	espérance	4
7.	feuille	4
8.	herbe (l'herbe)	4
9.	eau (d'eau)	3
10.	bleu	2
11.	clair	2
12.	épinard	2
13.	galant	2
14.	gris	2
15.	orange	2
16.	rouge	2
17.	tapis	2
18-50.	(f = 1)	33

blanc, boire, bureau, champ, champ de verdure, chemin, chou, émeraude, espoir, feuillage, forêt, gazon, il, de jade, jardin, lézard, montagne, nature, noir, nuance, opale, palme, patine, peinture, pendule, perroquet, de peur, pomme, printemps, tendre, la terre, voyant, wagon
(Illegible - 3)

94. VERT (contd)

Students

No.	Response	Total	Female	Male
37-70.	(f = 1)	34	21	13

Angleterre, angoisse, blanc, brun, clair, clarté, émeraude, été, fade, foulard, feu, feu rouge, gazon, glauque, huître, janus, jonquille, marron, paisible, paix, pâle, peur, pin, pleurer, repos, sapin, soleil, tendre, vallée, Van Gogh, végétal, vert, verdâtre, verdure

95. SEL

Students

No.	Response	Total	Female	Male
1.	mer	56	34	22
2.	poivre	47	33	14
3.	terre	21	10	11
4.	sucre	14	9	5
5.	marin	13	5	8
6.	marais	9	6	3
7.	salière	8	7	1
8.	fade	7	6	1
9.	de la terre	7	5	2
10.	eau	5	5	0
11.	cristaux	4	3	1
12.	cuisine	4	3	1
13.	gemme	4	0	4
14.	goût	4	3	1
15.	piquant	4	3	1
16.	salé	4	2	2
17.	amer	3	1	2
18.	blanc	3	0	3
19.	grains (grain)	3	2	1
20.	saveur	3	3	0
21.	aliment	2	1	1
22.	bon	2	2	0
23.	ClNa	2	0	2
24.	gris	2	1	1
25.	pain	2	2	0
26.	soif	2	2	0
27.	soupe	2	1	1
28.	vie	2	1	1
29-77.	(f = 1)	49	34	15

acide, âcre, aigre, arbre, argent, astuce, attique, baptême, beurre, Bible, boite, Bretagne, cérébos, chimie, condiment, crépitement, cristaux blancs, cruche, cuivre, désagréable, enfant, épice, feuille, fin, forêt, grimace, huître, langue, légume, limpide, mauvais, mince, nourriture, océan, orange, pâté, Petite Montagne, pleurer, poisson, pot, potage, riz amer, salade, salaison, Salzburg, sel de la terre, table, table servie, verser

Workers

No.	Response	Total
1.	mer (la mer, de mer)	30
2.	poivre	10
3.	fin	9
4.	aliment (aliments)	6
5.	marin	6
6.	salé	4
7.	sucre	4
8.	amer	3
9.	blanc	2
10.	mauvais	2
11.	salière	2
12.	sodium	2
13-46.	(f = 1)	34

âcre, albumine, assaisoné, de céleri, chimique, champagne, épice, fleur, fort, gemme, goût, gros, humide, marais, manger, mine, noir, orange, océan, pair, paquet, pique, riche, rose, sec, salaison, saline, sécheresse, soif, soude, soupe, symbole, table, vapeur, vie

96. RUE

Students

No.	Response	Total	Female	Male
1.	Rivoli (de Rivoli)	17	11	6
2.	maison (maisons)	13	11	2
3.	ville	13	8	5
4.	bruit	12	7	5
5.	étroite (étroit)	11	7	4
6.	avenue	10	5	5
7.	pavé (pavés)	10	8	2
8.	auto (autos)	9	7	2
9.	sombre	7	2	5
10.	trottoir	7	5	2
11.	voiture (voitures)	7	6	1

Workers

No.	Response	Total
1.	étroite (étroit)	10
2.	Rivoli (de Rivoli)	6
3.	large	5
4.	de Paris (Paris)	5
5.	boulevard	4
6.	déserte	4
7.	bruit	3
8.	bruyant	3
9.	cruelle	3
10.	gaité (de la Gaité)	3
11.	grande (grand)	3

96. RUE (contd)

	Students					Workers	

<table>
<tr><td colspan="5" align="center">Students</td><td></td><td colspan="3" align="center">Workers</td></tr>
<tr><td>No.</td><td>Response</td><td>Total</td><td>Female</td><td>Male</td><td>No.</td><td>Response</td><td>Total</td></tr>
<tr><td>12.</td><td>numéro</td><td>6</td><td>4</td><td>2</td><td>12.</td><td>sale</td><td>3</td></tr>
<tr><td>13.</td><td>boulevard</td><td>5</td><td>2</td><td>3</td><td>13.</td><td>animée</td><td>2</td></tr>
<tr><td>14.</td><td>bruyant (bruyante)</td><td>5</td><td>4</td><td>1</td><td>14.</td><td>avenue</td><td>2</td></tr>
<tr><td>15.</td><td>impasse</td><td>5</td><td>3</td><td>2</td><td>15.</td><td>noir (noire)</td><td>2</td></tr>
<tr><td>16.</td><td>circulation</td><td>4</td><td>3</td><td>1</td><td>16.</td><td>de la Paix (Paix)</td><td>2</td></tr>
<tr><td>17.</td><td>foule</td><td>4</td><td>4</td><td>0</td><td>17.</td><td>passage</td><td>2</td></tr>
<tr><td>18.</td><td>large</td><td>4</td><td>2</td><td>2</td><td>18.</td><td>petite</td><td>2</td></tr>
<tr><td>19.</td><td>noire</td><td>4</td><td>1</td><td>3</td><td>19.</td><td>soleil</td><td>2</td></tr>
<tr><td>20.</td><td>passant (les passants,
     passants)</td><td>4</td><td>2</td><td>2</td><td>20.</td><td>trottoir</td><td>2</td></tr>
<tr><td>21.</td><td>animation</td><td>3</td><td>2</td><td>1</td><td>21.</td><td>ville</td><td>2</td></tr>
<tr><td>22.</td><td>animé (animée)</td><td>3</td><td>2</td><td>1</td><td>22-64.</td><td>(f = 1)</td><td>43</td></tr>
<tr><td>23.</td><td>arbre (arbres)</td><td>3</td><td>3</td><td>0</td><td colspan="3">adresse, agglomération, animation,</td></tr>
<tr><td>24.</td><td>Lepic</td><td>3</td><td>1</td><td>2</td><td colspan="3">arrondissement, auto, autobus,</td></tr>
<tr><td>25.</td><td>passage</td><td>3</td><td>1</td><td>2</td><td colspan="3">Belleville bourg, des Boulets,</td></tr>
<tr><td>26.</td><td>route</td><td>3</td><td>0</td><td>3</td><td colspan="3">café, chaussée, chemin, circuler,</td></tr>
<tr><td>27.</td><td>ruelle</td><td>3</td><td>0</td><td>3</td><td colspan="3">courte, école, d'Emouette, endroits</td></tr>
<tr><td>28.</td><td>arrondissement</td><td>2</td><td>2</td><td>0</td><td colspan="3">entourés de maisons, d'enfer,</td></tr>
<tr><td>29.</td><td>artère</td><td>2</td><td>1</td><td>1</td><td colspan="3">habitation, isolée issue, Labiche,</td></tr>
<tr><td>30.</td><td>bec de gaz</td><td>2</td><td>1</td><td>1</td><td colspan="3">Lepic, sans loi, Longway, maison,</td></tr>
<tr><td>31.</td><td>Cardinet</td><td>2</td><td>2</td><td>0</td><td colspan="3">maman, Montreuil, nationale, numéros,</td></tr>
<tr><td>32.</td><td>cité</td><td>2</td><td>1</td><td>1</td><td colspan="3">passants, pittoresque, de la Prairie,</td></tr>
<tr><td>33.</td><td>droit (droite)</td><td>2</td><td>1</td><td>1</td><td colspan="3">promiscuité, quartier, Racine, route,</td></tr>
<tr><td>34.</td><td>gens</td><td>2</td><td>1</td><td>1</td><td colspan="3">Saint Martin, sombre, tranquille,</td></tr>
<tr><td>35.</td><td>gris</td><td>2</td><td>2</td><td>0</td><td colspan="3">petit village, Vitry, voitures</td></tr>
<tr><td>36.</td><td>Mazarine</td><td>2</td><td>0</td><td>2</td><td colspan="3">(Illegible - 2)</td></tr>
<tr><td>37.</td><td>Paix (de la Paix)</td><td>2</td><td>0</td><td>2</td><td></td><td></td><td></td></tr>
<tr><td>38.</td><td>Paris</td><td>2</td><td>0</td><td>2</td><td></td><td></td><td></td></tr>
<tr><td>39.</td><td>passage</td><td>2</td><td>0</td><td>2</td><td></td><td></td><td></td></tr>
<tr><td>40.</td><td>tranquille</td><td>2</td><td>1</td><td>1</td><td></td><td></td><td></td></tr>
<tr><td>41.</td><td>triste</td><td>2</td><td>1</td><td>1</td><td></td><td></td><td></td></tr>
<tr><td>42-124.</td><td>(f = 1)</td><td>84</td><td>60</td><td>24</td><td></td><td></td><td></td></tr>
</table>

Alésia, alignement, animal, animosité, asphalte,
d'Assas, autobus, automobile, Bâle, Blanche, calme,
camion, chaise, chanson, chat, chaussée, chemin,
chose, civilisation, coin, contact, corps, course,
Dickens, Dutourt, dynamomètre, embarras, encombrée,
encombrement, enfant, énumération, l'Est, Estrapade,
étouffant, fanaux, fenêtre, grande, habiter, home,
homme, issue, joie, sans joie, langueur, lieu, long,
longue, lumière, misère, mouvement, mouvementé,
sans nom, parallèle, clouté, passagère, Passy, personne,
petite, Pierre Cheist, place, plaque, population,
province, quartier, Quincanpoix, Royale, ma rue,
ruisseau, St. Jacques, Sal, Sceaux, sillon, soleil,
Solférino, sortie, Soufflot, street, tapage,
tramway, traverse, tristesse, via, villa, village,
volets

97. ROI

<table>
<tr><td colspan="5" align="center">Students</td><td></td><td colspan="3" align="center">Workers</td></tr>
<tr><td>No.</td><td>Response</td><td>Total</td><td>Female</td><td>Male</td><td>No.</td><td>Response</td><td>Total</td></tr>
<tr><td>1.</td><td>reine</td><td>64</td><td>43</td><td>21</td><td>1.</td><td>reine</td><td>14</td></tr>
<tr><td>2.</td><td>Mage (Mages)</td><td>35</td><td>22</td><td>13</td><td>2.</td><td>Mage (Mages)</td><td>12</td></tr>
<tr><td>3.</td><td>couronne</td><td>24</td><td>19</td><td>5</td><td>3.</td><td>soleil</td><td>11</td></tr>
<tr><td>4.</td><td>soleil</td><td>13</td><td>9</td><td>4</td><td>4.</td><td>chef</td><td>5</td></tr>
<tr><td>5.</td><td>Louis XIV</td><td>7</td><td>6</td><td>1</td><td>5.</td><td>couronne</td><td>5</td></tr>
<tr><td>6.</td><td>trône</td><td>7</td><td>5</td><td>2</td><td>6.</td><td>de France (France)</td><td>4</td></tr>
<tr><td>7.</td><td>Angleterre</td><td>6</td><td>4</td><td>2</td><td>7.</td><td>des Belges (belge)</td><td>3</td></tr>
<tr><td>8.</td><td>France</td><td>6</td><td>3</td><td>3</td><td>8.</td><td>fainéant</td><td>3</td></tr>
<tr><td>9.</td><td>lion</td><td>5</td><td>2</td><td>3</td><td>9.</td><td>Louis XIV</td><td>3</td></tr>
<tr><td>10.</td><td>royaume</td><td>5</td><td>3</td><td>2</td><td>10.</td><td>de Prusse (Prusse)</td><td>3</td></tr>
<tr><td>11.</td><td>monarque</td><td>4</td><td>1</td><td>3</td><td>11.</td><td>règne (régner)</td><td>3</td></tr>
<tr><td>12.</td><td>puissance</td><td>4</td><td>2</td><td>2</td><td>12.</td><td>Baudoin</td><td>2</td></tr>
<tr><td>13.</td><td>royauté</td><td>4</td><td>2</td><td>2</td><td>13.</td><td>Belgique</td><td>2</td></tr>
<tr><td>14.</td><td>carte (cartes)</td><td>3</td><td>3</td><td>0</td><td>14.</td><td>château</td><td>2</td></tr>
<tr><td>15.</td><td>grandeur</td><td>3</td><td>1</td><td>2</td><td>15.</td><td>lion</td><td>2</td></tr>
<tr><td>16.</td><td>histoire</td><td>3</td><td>1</td><td>2</td><td>16.</td><td>pouvoir</td><td>2</td></tr>
<tr><td>17.</td><td>monarchie</td><td>3</td><td>1</td><td>2</td><td>17-55.</td><td>(f = 1)</td><td>39</td></tr>
<tr><td>18.</td><td>pouvoir</td><td>3</td><td>1</td><td>2</td><td colspan="3">absolu, d'Angleterre, des animaux,</td></tr>
</table>

97. ROI (contd)

Students

No.	Response	Total	Female	Male
19.	apparat	2	0	2
20.	Cour	2	2	0
21.	éclat	2	1	1
22.	Louis	2	2	0
23.	peuple	2	1	1
24.	pourpre	2	2	0
25.	président	2	1	1
26.	prince	2	1	1
27.	république	2	2	0
28.	sceptre	2	2	0
29.	tête	2	1	1
30-97.	(f = 1)	68	42	26

abattre, absolutisme, s'amuse, antique, aristocratie, autorité, Babylone, beaux habits, des Belges, bleu, Bohème, boit, cercle, château, chef, chef d'état, de coeur, conte, Dagobert, dame, débonnaire, domine, empereur, enfant, état, étranger, fainéant, faste, fête, fève, fini, force, de France, galette, gouvernement actuel, Igor, 6 Janvier, Lear, Louis XVI, maître, majesté, majestueux, montagne, des Montagnes, neige, des Neiges, Pandore, pays, père, pion, régne, respect, régner, René, roitelet, roquet, royaliste, Salomon, sans tête, 17e siècle, sommeil, souverain, sujet, tambour, temps passé, triste, Versailles, d'Ys

Workers

No.	Response	Total

Auguste, avare, carreau, chaud, cour, dictature, dominer, drapeau, des fous, gouvernement, grand, grandeur, hauteur, Henri IV, heureux, histoire, lien, Louis, Louis Philippe, loyal, lys, magie, méchant, monarque, nuit, passé, péché, Président, et prince, respectable Royant, Saül, souverain, tout, usurper, vache

98. FROMAGE

Students

No.	Response	Total	Female	Male
1.	blanc	29	23	6
2.	gruyère (de gruyère)	28	14	14
3.	Camembert	25	17	8
4.	odeur	15	9	6
5.	lait	14	9	5
6.	beurre	13	7	6
7.	chèvre (de chèvre)	13	10	3
8.	dessert	12	7	5
9.	pain	10	8	2
10.	crème	7	5	2
11.	Hollande	6	4	2
12.	Brie (de Brie)	5	3	2
13.	mou	5	3	2
14.	Roquefort	5	2	3
15.	vache	5	4	1
16.	aliment	4	2	2
17.	faim	4	2	2
18.	fort	4	2	2
19.	rat	4	3	1
20.	vin	4	4	0
21.	bon	3	2	1
22.	manger	3	1	2
23.	rond	3	3	0
24.	souris	3	1	2
25.	trou (trous)	3	3	0
26.	coulant	2	0	2
27.	couteau	2	2	0
28.	fait	2	1	1
29.	goût	2	2	0
30.	gras	2	2	0
31.	laitage	2	0	2
32.	montagne	2	2	0
33.	sec	2	2	0
34.	sel	2	1	1
35.	tête	2	1	1
36.	vers	2	1	1
37-75.	(f = 1)	39	22	17

alpage, bleu, campagne, commerce, croûte, dégout, délice, étalage, étiquette, fable, ferment, fin, foire, La Fontaine, France, fruits, gastronomie, glacé, laiterie, marché, mauvais, médecine, mets,

Workers

No.	Response	Total
1.	Camembert	14
2.	bon	8
3.	blanc	6
4.	chèvre (de chèvre)	6
5.	frais	6
6.	lait	6
7.	pain	6
8.	beure	4
9.	dessert	4
10.	gruyère	4
11.	Hollande	4
12.	crème	3
13.	fort	3
14.	odeur	3
15.	Cantal	2
16.	fait	2
17.	puant	2
18.	Roquefort (de Roquefort)	2
19-45.	(f = 1)	27

aliment, aride, de campagne, casse-croûte, clair, cloche, coulant, très frais, goût, gras, laiterie, mangé, marche tout seul, mou, oeuf, plâtre, poil, Port Salut, pourri, repas, rouge, salé, sauté, sifflet, de tête, vache, vin
(Illegible - 3)

98. FROMAGE (contd)

Students

No.	Response	Total	Female	Male

Normandie, nourriture, odorant, oeufs, Pasteur, plat,
poire, Port Salut, pourriture, rance, repas, salé,
saloperie, Suisse, tartine, timbre

99. FLEUR

Students						Workers		
No.	Response	Total	Female	Male		No.	Response	Total
1.	rose	37	29	8		1.	rose	15
2.	beauté	15	6	9		2.	fanée (fané, faner)	9
3.	fruit	13	7	6		3.	joli (jolie)	6
4.	champs (des champs, champ)	10	7	3		4.	lys (de lys)	6
5.	couleur	10	7	3		5.	bleue (bleu)	4
6.	odeur	9	4	5		6.	jardin	4
7.	parfum	9	5	4		7.	parfum	4
8.	bleue (bleu)	8	6	2		8.	belle	3
9.	papillon	8	2	6		9.	champ	3
10.	rouge	8	7	1		10.	odeur	3
11.	fanée	7	5	2		11.	rouge	3
12.	jardin	7	5	2		12.	beauté	2
13.	lys (de lys)	6	2	4		13.	bouquet	2
14.	anémone	5	5	0		14.	jaune	2
15.	tige	5	3	2		15.	joie	2
16.	feuille	4	2	2		16.	marguerite	2
17.	joli (jolie)	4	4	0		17.	nature	2
18.	oeillet	4	2	2		18.	oeillet (oeillets)	2
19.	printemps	4	1	3		19.	printemps	2
20.	tulipe	4	3	1		20.	sentir	2
21.	coquelicot	3	2	1		21.	tulipe	2
22.	joie	3	3	0		22-55.	(f = 1)	34
23.	jaune	3	2	1				
24.	oranger	3	0	3				
25.	pétale (pétales)	3	1	2				
26.	prairie	3	2	1				
27.	violette	3	2	1				
28.	vase	3	3	0				
29.	belle	2	1	1				
30.	choux	2	0	2				
31.	eau	2	2	0				
32.	épanouie	2	1	1				
33.	été	2	2	0				
34.	lis	2	2	0				
35.	Lotus (de lotus)	2	1	1				
36.	marguerite	2	1	1				
37.	pots	2	0	2				
38.	pré (des prés)	2	1	1				
39.	rayé (rayée)	2	1	1				
40-104.	(f = 1)	65	45	20				

Students (40-104):
abeille, aimer, amusant, art, aubépine, azalée,
blancheur, blesser, bleuet, bouton d'or, buée,
calme, campagne, chrysanthème, Colin, dalhia,
délicatesse, effeuillée, églantine, enfant, envoi,
épis, femme, fête, fragile, fraîcheur, giroflée,
goût, Hollande, horticulture, insecte, iris,
jonquille, miel, mimosa, myosotis, nature, noyer,
odorant, oiseau, panier, pâquerette, parfumée,
paysage, de pêche, Petit Prince, peur, pissenlit,
pistil, plante, poésie, poirier, pois, poisson,
Provence, rhododendron, rideau, royale, sauvage, sent
bon, simplicité, symbole, tabac, vent, ville

Workers (22-55):
amer, d'artichaut, arbre, beau,
de belle couleur, bon, cadeau,
capucine, chambre, coupée, femme,
fine, fleuriste, gerbe, giroflée,
large, lilas, mur, Nice, d'oranger,
pêcher, pivoine, pense, possible,
rosé, sauvage, savon, sent bon,
soie, stupide, tige, vase, verte,
violette
(Illegible - 1)

MARK R. ROSENZWEIG

100. EFFRAYÉ

Students

No.	Response	Total	Female	Male
1.	peur	104	57	47
2.	apeuré	21	13	8
3.	enfant (l'enfant)	14	11	3
4.	calme	7	4	3
5.	peureux	6	4	2
6.	cheval (chevaux)	5	2	3
7.	affolé (affolée)	4	3	1
8.	crainte	4	3	1
9.	craintif	4	2	2
10.	oiseau	4	4	0
11.	chien	3	2	1
12.	fuite	3	3	0
13.	grimace	3	2	1
14.	horreur	3	1	2
15.	noir	3	3	0
16.	terreur	3	2	1
17.	tranquille	3	0	3
18.	angoissé	2	1	1
19.	biche	2	2	0
20.	bruit	2	2	0
21.	cri	2	2	0
22.	lapin	2	2	0
23.	pâle	2	2	0
24.	panique	2	1	1
25.	pleurer	2	2	0
26.	rassuré	2	2	0
27.	souris	2	1	1
28.	terrible	2	1	1
29.	terrifié	2	1	1
30.	yeux	2	1	1
31-98.	(f = 1)	68	47	21

accident, affolement, agneau, ahuri, aigle, alerte, amoureux, angoisse, attique, attitude, barrière, bruissement, bruyant, calmé, cause, cave, chat, comédie, consoler, courage, course, docile, doux, effacé, effaré, effarouché, épouvante, étonne, étonné, examen, fantôme, farouche, femme, film, frayeur, frisson, froid, fuir, hérissé, heureux, jeune, joyeux, larme, loup, maladif, malheureux, marteau, moi, moineau, nuit, obscurité, offusqué, orage, ours, par la vie, peu, pire, pitié, poule, rail, salir, secousse, seul, soir, sombre, sursaut, tremblant, tremblement

Workers

No.	Response	Total
1.	peur (de peur)	53
2.	effrayé	9
3.	apeurer (apeuré)	5
4.	peureux (peureuse)	5
5.	bruit	3
6.	loup (loups)	2
7.	lion (par le lion)	2
8.	sang-froid	2
9.	surprise	2
10-39.	(f = 1)	30

angoisser, bambin, biche, bois, d'un cauchemar, chat, cheval, chevreuil, chien, le diable, effarouché, faire, la peur, gouffre, inondation, loin, misère, monsieur, noir, oiseaux, panse, rassuré, réflexion, révolte, pour des riens, sang, soldat, solitude, souris, trahi, troublé
(Illegible - 2)

CHAPTER 5

FREE-ASSOCIATION RESPONSES TO THE PRIMARY RESPONSES AND OTHER RESPONSES SELECTED FROM THE PALERMO-JENKINS NORMS[1,2]

Geoffrey Keppel
University of California, Berkeley, California
and Bonnie Z. Strand
Georgetown University, Washington, D.C.

A useful supplement to free-association norms is the additional determination of associations to responses which were elicited on the original test. Not only would these supplemental norms increase the number of association hierarchies available to the investigator, but they would also provide information concerning the independent probabilities of chains of words. Examples of situations in which these latter probabilities have been of value are numerous. For instance, they allow the independent manipulation of associative directionality of pairs of words, e.g., A and B. That is, it becomes possible to choose word pairs on the basis of either the A-B or B-A associative strength. Storms (1958), for example, required unidirectional word pairs for his study of mediation via a "backward" word association. More generally, a listing of the associative probabilities of other words, given in response to B, would greatly increase the size of the pool of associative triads, i.e., A-B-C chains, which is available for the study of mediational phenomena. For example, Russell and Storms (1955) had to collect additional associative responses to study mediation in a four-stage chaining paradigm; Cramer (1967) was forced to combine several sets of unpublished norms in order to construct A-B-C chains in a comparison of transfer in the eight three-stage mediation paradigms.

The original norms can be used to discover A-B-C word chains or word pairs varying in degree of bidirectionality. However, such a procedure identifies only a limited number of usable word pairs or chains. Moreover, there is the possibility that the probability of any particular response may be increased through the exposure of that response before the association in question is taken. Such "priming" effects are known to occur (cf. Storms, 1958) and may result in a distortion of associative probabilities for certain of the word pairs on the association test. Thus, in view of the potential usefulness of the supplemental norms and the limited value of word chains derived from the original norms, it was decided to obtain association hierarchies for responses listed in the Palermo-Jenkins (1964) norms.

[1] The collection of these norms was facilitated by Grant MH-10249 from the National Institutes of Health. The data were analyzed and processed at the Institute of Human Learning which is supported by grants from the National Science Foundation and the National Institutes of Health.

[2] The authors wish to thank Vicky Campbell, Ed Eng, Sally Lorch, Marilyn Myers, and Judy Rupley for their help in preparing the norms for publication.

METHOD

Stimuli

A total of 234 words was selected from the Palermo-Jenkins (1964) norms for the association test. With one exception, the list included all of the primary responses of college students to the 200 words of the Palermo-Jenkins list. (The primary which was inadvertently omitted was *this*, the response to *that*.) In addition, a number of nonprimaries was chosen from the other strong responses to the stimulus words. These words were of at least 10% strength (100 occurrences in the 1000 *S*s), but they did not represent all such responses. One response which was neither a primary nor met the strength criterion appeared: *thing*, a response to *that*, of 3.5% strength. In what follows, reference to the Palermo-Jenkins norms and the present norms will be abbreviated PJ and KS, respectively. Table 1 presents the nonprimary responses which were used as stimuli, together with the appropriate PJ stimulus words. For convenience, stimuli which were selected because they were primary responses, but which were also strong nonprimaries for other stimuli, are listed in Table 1.

Procedure

The stimulus words were randomly ordered and typed on eight test pages, 29 or 30 words to a page, in a single, double-spaced column. A column of response blanks appeared to the right of each stimulus word. The order of the eight pages in the test booklets was randomized for each *S*. Instructions adapted from Palermo and Jenkins appeared on the cover of the test booklet. The *S*s were asked to go through the stimulus words in order and to write the first word they thought of for each of the stimulus words.

Subjects

The test was administered to 186 students of an introductory psychology course at the University of California, Berkeley, during a 50-min class session. Four *S*s were dropped from the analysis because they neglected to respond to one page of words. The final tabulations, then, were based upon a total of 182 *S*s, 99 females and 83 males.

RESULTS

Association Norms

The individual response hierarchies for each of the 234 KS stimulus words are listed alphabetically in the Appendix. To the right of each stimulus word, in parentheses, are given the PJ words for which the KS word was a primary or a strong nonprimary response. The first word listed is the PJ stimulus eliciting the KS word as a primary; the words following the semicolon are the PJ stimuli eliciting the KS words as a nonprimary response. In several cases, a given KS word is the primary response of several PJ stimuli. These words are included to the left of the semicolon. Finally, it should be noted that these listings represent only a small portion of relevant PJ stimuli. A complete enumeration of all PJ words eliciting any given KS stimulus as a response can be found in the response index of Palermo and Jenkins (1964, pp. 421-469).

Each hierarchy appears in the norms from strongest to weakest responses computed on the combined female and male totals. In order to facilitate comparisons with other norms, frequencies are listed as percentages. Responses of the same frequency rank appear alphabetically. Occurrences of illegible responses or omissions of responses are noted at the bottom of each hierarchy. Obvious misspellings were corrected by the scorers, but nonwords, multiple-word responses, and foreign words appear in the norms as given. Whenever both the singular and plural form of a word appeared as responses, combined percentages are given and the plural ending is indicated.

Comparisons with the Palermo-Jenkins Norms

Since the two norms are intended to be used in conjunction, it is of immediate interest to determine their comparability. A detailed comparison is possible since there is a considerable number (64) of duplications of specific word stimuli. A superficial perusal indicates relatively close agreement between the two norms in the particular high frequency responses elicited. There are some exceptions, however. For example, in both norms *chair* is the primary

TABLE 1 *Nonprimary Responses Used as Stimuli*

Palermo-Jenkins word	Response	Palermo-Jenkins word	Response
Afraid	Scared	Numbers	One
Am	Is	Ocean	Sea
An	Apple	Or	And
Appear	Disappear	Over	There
Baby	Boy	Playing	Fun
Bath	Water	Priest	Catholic
Beautiful	Girl, pretty	Red	Black
Bible	Book	Religion	Church
Bitter	Sour	River	Stream
Bread	Food	Running	Walking
Broader	Narrower	Scissors	Sharp
By	Now	See	Look
Cabbage	Food, vegetable	Sheep	Animal
Carpet	Floor, soft	Shoes	Socks
Chair	Sit	Short	Fat
Child	Mother	Sickness	Death, ill
Citizen	Person	Sit	Sat
Closer	Near	Sleep	Rest
Cold	Snow, warm	Smooth	Hard, soft
Come	Here	Soft	Pillow
Cottage	Lake	Soldier	Army, war
Dark	Night	Sour	Lemon
Deep	Dark, water	Speak	Spoke
Doctor	Sick	Spider	Bug, insect
Doors	Open	Square	Circle
Earth	Ground, round	Stand	Still
Easier	Hard	Stem	Leaf, plant
Eating	Drinking	Stomach	Ache
Farther	Nearer	Stove	Heat
Find	Lost	Sweet	Candy, sugar
Fingers	Toes	Take	It
Foot	Hand, leg, toe	That	Is, thing
Hand	Arm, finger	The	It
Hardly	Never	Then	There, when
Have	Had	There	Is
Health	Sick	They	We
However	Never	Thief	Robber
Hungry	Eat	Thirsty	Drink, dry
I	You	This	Is
Joy	Happiness, sorrow	Tobacco	Cigarette
Jump	Run	Us	Them, they
Justice	Judge, peace	Was	It
Lion	Animal	We	Are
Live	Life	Where	Here, when
Loud	Noise	Whiskey	Drunk
Moon	Night	White	Snow
Mountain	High	Why	Not, question
Music	Sound	Window	Door
Needle	Sharp	Wish	Want
Now	Never	With	Out

response to *table,* but while *table* is the primary response to *chair* in the PJ norms, *sit* is the primary in the KS norms. This discrepancy might be understood in terms of the priming process mentioned earlier. That is, the associative probability of any given response may be increased through its occurrence previously as a stimulus word. While any normative determination is subject to the effects of priming, strong biases for particular responses will occur only if the materials are presented in a constant order to all Ss.[3] This may be what happened in the case of the

[3]While the systematic influence of priming was greatly reduced in the KS norms, it was not completely eliminated, since the specific order of the words on each of the eight randomized stimulus sheets remained constant for all Ss.

primary response to *chair*. Specifically, Palermo and Jenkins used the same stimulus order in which *table* appeared in the first position and *chair* in the 20th position; in the present study the order of *table* and *chair* was varied.

In order to afford a more systematic comparison of the two norms and of the possibility of response priming, specific word pairs were chosen which were represented in the two norms and for which the response in question also occurred as a stimulus term in the PJ norms. (Three pairs were eliminated due to the possibility of priming in the KS determinations.) A total of 94 such pairs was identified. On the basis of the stimulus ordering reported by Palermo and Jenkins, these pairs were divided into those for which response priming could not have occurred, i.e., where the response occurred after the critical stimulus, and those for which priming may have occurred, i.e., where the response occurred before the critical stimulus. There were 64 pairs in the first category and 30 in the latter category.[4] The average associative strengths for the "nonprimed" associates were 18.5% and 16.4% for the PJ and KS norms, respectively, $p > .05$. This finding, then, indicates that the two norms are relatively comparable. The strengths for the "primed" associates were 30.6% and 22.2%, respectively, $F(1, 29) = 19.35, p < .01$. A comparison of the two sets of percentages shows that the interaction is significant, $F(1, 92) = 8.66, p < .01$, suggesting that a small priming effect (roughly 6%) may have been present in the PJ data. Thus, while these differences will probably not greatly influence the learning phenomena produced with these materials, they at least point up the sensitivity of the association procedure to temporary response sets produced as a consequence of the multiple-testing nature of the usual association test.

Bidirectionality of the Palermo-Jenkins Stimuli and Primaries

In this section and the one which follows, combinations of the PJ and KS norms are reported. Table 2 presents a listing of all PJ stimuli and primary responses in the first two columns.[5] In the next two columns the associative strengths of the A-B association (based upon PJ values) and the B-A association (based upon the KS norms) are given. Due to the inclusion in both norms of certain stimuli which also happened to be primaries, there is independent information concerning the directionality of 20 word pairs. These duplications have been noted in the third column by means of a number indicating the row in which the reverse of the word pair occurs. For example, the first word pair, *boy-girl*, indicates that the reverse order, *girl-boy*, appears in the third row. In practice, of course, an investigator may wish to average the two listings.

The word pairs are ordered in terms of degree of bidirectionality, i.e., the value of the lowest (A-B or B-A) percentage. As in the complete listing of the norms, singular and plural forms have been combined. The PJ words appear as in the original, with the primary listed as the stronger form, e.g., for *dogs*, *cats* was the primary, while for *citizen*, *man* was the primary. The B-A strengths also take into account both the singular and plural forms of the original stimulus word, e.g., for the pair *dogs-cats*, the strength of *cats-dog* is included in the indicated B-A strength. For ease of reference, the next column indicates whether the word pairs represent a bidirectional pair formed by primaries in both directions. Approximately 43% of the word pairs in Table 2 are of this nature. The second-to-last column provides a measure of mutual relatedness (MR), i.e., the degree to which the two elements of the word pair tend to elicit common associates. The actual measure used was a modification of the one reported by Marshall and Cofer (1963, pp. 410-413). Specifically, instead of a complete comparison of all responses in the two hierarchies, the comparison was limited to the ten most frequent responses, converted to percentages, given to each of the two separate stimuli, including the actual stimulus term (cf. Marshall & Cofer, 1963). The percentages reported in Table 2, then, indicate roughly the amount of associative communality present between the two elements of each word pair. The final column gives a ranking of associative strength in terms of the MR index.

[4] Three potentially primed responses were placed in the nonprime category. These were cases in which the priming stimulus occurred in the previous day's testing of these *S*s.

[5] It should be noted that Table 2 does not represent an exhaustive account of the bidirectionality of word pairs found in the two norms. The 201 entries given in Table 2 are limited to word pairs formed by PJ stimuli and their respective primary responses. Information concerning additional word pairs may be obtained from nonprimary stimuli which were included in the present norms. Determinations of A-B and B-A strengths for nonprimary stimuli included in the present norms may be obtained easily by consulting Table 1 and the relevant response hierarchies in the Appendix. Furthermore, there are a number of stimuli which happened to be used on one of the two norms and which would also provide estimates of the bidirectionality of nonprimaries. These word pairs can be found through a careful reading of the two sets of response hierarchies. No attempt was made to do this for the present report.

TABLE 2 *Bidirectionality and Relatedness of Palermo-Jenkins Stimuli and Primaries*

Palermo-Jenkins S (A)	Primary (B)	Strength[a] A → B (%)	Strength B → A (%)	Two-way primary?	MR index	Rank in MR
1. Boy	Girl	70.5 (3)	71.4	Yes	72.7	2
2. Dogs	Cats	82.6	64.2	Yes	74.5	1
3. Girl	Boy	59.8 (1)	70.8	Yes	68.4	3
4. High	Low	56.8	64.2	Yes	61.2	6
5. His	Hers	68.0	51.6	Yes	63.4	5
6. Me	You	62.4 (15)	51.1	Yes	60.3	9.5
7. Butter	Bread	57.5 (25)	48.9	Yes	54.8	16
8. Slow	Fast	63.4	47.8	Yes	58.6	12
9. King	Queen	65.3	47.2	Yes	59.4	11
10. Faster	Slower	49.4	46.7	Yes	53.6	19.5
11. He	She	61.2	46.7	Yes	60.8	7
12. Woman	Man	53.0 (29)	46.7	Yes	53.2	22.5
13. Needle	Thread	45.7	56.0	Yes	55.8	13.5
14. Here	There	66.9 (32)	45.6	Yes	64.4	4
15. You	Me	60.8 (6)	45.6	Yes	60.6	8
16. White	Black	50.0 (17)	44.5	Yes	49.4	29
17. Black	White	58.5 (16)	43.4	Yes	53.6	19.5
18. Chair	Table	42.8 (55)	45.6	Yes	46.6	34
19. On	Off	42.3	56.0	Yes	51.1	25
20. Hammer	Nail	49.5	41.7	Yes	50.4	27
21. Sell	Buy	56.5	41.7	Yes	55.2	15
22. Green	Grass	41.2	74.1	Yes	60.3	9.5
23. Short	Tall	41.1	46.7	Yes	47.3	31
24. Salt	Pepper	40.8	64.2	Yes	54.1	18
25. Bread	Butter	46.6 (7)	40.1	Yes	45.4	36
26. Buying	Selling	41.0	39.0	Yes	43.7	38
27. Younger	Older	52.5	39.0	Yes	50.6	26
28. In	Out	38.5	54.9	Yes	52.2	24
29. Man	Woman	67.1 (12)	38.4	Yes	55.8	13.5
30. Now	Then	37.8 (33)	51.6	Yes	49.8	28
31. Spider	Web	37.8	67.5	Yes	53.2	22.5
32. There	Here	36.8 (14)	66.1	Yes	54.6	17
33. Then	Now	36.0 (30)	37.3	Yes	40.6	48
34. Dark	Light	61.8 (42)	35.1	Yes	48.8	30
35. Cold	Hot	32.9	56.0	Yes	45.2	37
36. Sweet	Sour	35.4 (38)	32.9	Yes	36.4	62.5
37. This	That	44.4	32.9	Yes	46.8	33
38. Sour	Sweet	48.7 (36)	32.4	Yes	43.6	39
39. Him	Her	63.6	31.3	Yes	53.5	21
40. Over	Under	38.7	30.7	Yes	38.5	55
41. Soft	Hard	30.4 (44)	48.3	Yes	40.2	49.5
42. Light	Dark	48.8 (34)	30.2	Yes	41.8	45
43. They	Them	30.8	28.5	Yes	38.9	54
44. Hard	Soft	58.5 (41)	26.9	Yes	43.4	40
45. Thinner	Fatter	32.1	26.9	Yes	35.7	65
46. Live	Die	33.2	25.3	Yes	33.0	72
47. Blue	Sky	25.2	58.2	Yes	42.3	43
48. Closer	Nearer	24.7	28.0	Yes	41.7	46
49. Foot	Shoe	26.2 (76)	24.2	Yes	27.3	100
50. City	Town	23.2	30.7	Yes	33.2	71
51. Health	Sickness	23.0 (106)	43.9	Yes	37.1	60.5
52. House	Home	23.0	42.8	Yes	38.2	56
53. To	From	22.0 (72)	28.5	Yes	34.8	67
54. Lion	Tiger	21.6	22.0	Yes	30.0	86
55. Table	Chair	69.3 (18)	21.4	No	46.0	35
56. Sleep	Bed	21.3 (99)	35.1	Yes	31.7	76
57. See	Saw	21.1	22.0	Yes	23.4	120
58. Guns	Shoot	20.1	25.3	Yes	29.8	88.5

TABLE 2 (continued)

Palermo-Jenkins S (A)	Primary (B)	Strength[a] A → B (%)	Strength B → A (%)	Two-way primary?	MR index	Rank in MR
59. Always	Never	50.7	19.8	Yes	42.6	42
60. Rough	Smooth	30.4 (68)	19.8	No	29.4	91.5
61. Children	Kids	19.6	29.1	Yes	32.6	73
62. Why	Because	19.6	34.0	Yes	31.2	78.5
63. Hotter	Colder	49.0	19.2	Yes	37.1	60.5
64. Us	We	51.0	19.2	No	47.2	32
65. Find	Lose	19.0	21.4	Yes	25.8	104
66. We	They	35.5	18.1	No	43.2	41
67. With	Without	18.1	22.0	Yes	23.9	116.5
68. Smooth	Rough	24.3 (60)	17.6	Yes	26.9	101.5
69. Doctor	Nurse	17.3	30.7	Yes	31.8	75
70. Deep	Shallow	17.1	39.5	Yes	36.2	64
71. Become	Became	19.2	17.0	Yes	25.2	107
72. From	To	19.8 (53)	17.0	Yes	24.2	115
73. Sheep	Lamb[b]	21.2	17.0	Yes	28.0	98
74. Sheep	Wool[c]	18.7	17.0	Yes	21.4	129.5
75. Go	Come	16.5 (81)	25.8	Yes	28.1	97
76. Shoes	Feet	37.4 (49)	16.5	Yes	28.6	94.5
77. A	An	15.9 (98)	16.5	Yes	24.6	110.5
78. Stand	Sit	38.3	15.9	No	29.8	88.5
79. Square	Round	31.5	15.4	Yes	30.4	84
80. People	Crowd	15.0	35.7	Yes	29.4	91.5
81. Come	Go	35.5 (75)	13.7	No	29.9	87
82. Mountain	Hill	21.4	13.7	No	27.4	99
83. Get	Got	13.2	13.2	Yes	18.0	146.5
84. Long	Short	63.4	13.2	No	39.5	52
85. Cry	Baby	28.4 (86)	12.1	Yes	21.2	131
86. Baby	Cry	11.9 (85)	13.7	Yes	13.6	172
87. Cars	Trucks	11.6	34.0	Yes	28.6	94.5
88. Take	Give	11.6	43.4	Yes	31.2	78.5
89. Carpet	Rug	31.1	11.5	No	33.3	70
90. Speak	Talk	25.2	11.5	No	24.6	110.5
91. Am	I	24.2	11.0	No	19.5	140.5
92. I	Me	38.3	11.0	No	41.4	47
93. It	Is	36.3	11.0	No	32.0	74
94. Was	Is	24.8	11.0	No	30.6	83
95. Doors	Windows	39.7	10.4	Yes	31.6	77
96. Hungry	Food	41.3	10.4	No	35.2	66
97. Is	Are	10.3	14.8	No	17.6	152
98. An	A	18.5 (77)	9.9	No	22.0	126.5
99. Bed	Sleep	57.7 (56)	9.9	Yes	36.4	62.5
100. Child	Baby	17.3	9.9	No	24.8	108.5
101. Window	Glass	21.6	9.9	Yes	21.7	128
102. Head	Hair	19.4	9.3	Yes	15.2	161
103. Thief	Steal	26.4	9.3	No	23.2	121
104. Whistle	Train	10.6	9.3	No	11.3	179
105. Quietly	Softly	15.5	8.8	Yes	17.8	150
106. Sickness	Health	36.9 (51)	8.8	No	26.4	103
107. Where	There	20.5	8.8	No	30.2	85
108. Dream	Sleep	48.5	8.2	No	30.9	80
109. Afraid	Fear	27.8	7.7	Yes	24.5	112
110. Fingers	Hand	45.7	7.7	No	30.8	81.5
111. Ah	Oh	31.3	7.1	No	24.3	114
112. And	But	23.3 (122)	7.1	No	20.5	136
113. Butterfly	Moth	12.4	7.1	No	20.4	137
114. Cabbage	Lettuce	14.0	7.1	No	25.3	106
115. Lift	Carry	20.8	7.1	No	17.9	148
116. Or	Nor	19.1	7.1	No	17.8	150

TABLE 2 *(continued)*

Palermo-Jenkins S (A)	Primary (B)	Strength[a] A → B (%)	Strength B → A (%)	Two-way primary?	MR index	Rank in MR
117. Playing	Working	14.2	7.1	No	12.8	175.5
118. Command	Order	25.6	6.6	No	16.9	156
119. Fruit	Apple	45.4	6.6	No	34.6	68
120. Scissors	Cut	67.9	6.6	No	40.2	49.5
121. Street	Road[c]	11.8	6.0	No	15.6	160
122. But	And	10.0 (112)	5.5	No	16.6	157.5
123. However	But	16.5	5.5	No	18.4	144
124. Easier	Harder	41.9	4.9	No	29.6	90
125. Bitter	Sweet	54.4	4.4	No	38.0	57
126. By	Near	13.4	,4.4	No	12.8	175.5
127. Cheese	Mouse	14.0	4.4	No	10.6	184
128. Hand	Foot	23.5	4.4	No	16.3	159
129. Joy	Happy	26.0	4.4	No	18.6	143
130. Therefore	Because	20.3	4.4	No	18.0	146.5
131. Justice	Law	24.3	3.8	No	17.8	150
132. Beautiful	Ugly	16.9	3.3	No	18.8	142
133. Earth	Dirt	14.3	3.3	No	14.6	165.5
134. Only	One	35.9	3.3	No	20.7	134
135. Make	Do	9.3	2.7	No	9.2	190.5
136. Thirsty	Water	43.2	2.7	No	30.8	81.5
137. Kittens	Cats	72.3	,2.2	No	42.0	44
138. Loud	Soft	42.3	2.2	No	24.8	108.5
139. Music	Song	16.8	2.2	No	14.3	167
140. My	Mine	14.3	2.2	No	23.5	119
141. Of	Course	12.0	2.2	No	7.2	199
142. River	Water	28.6	2.2	No	18.2	145
143. Wish	Dream	15.0	2.2	No	8.8	192.5
144. Yellow	Color	9.2	2.2	No	21.4	129.5
145. Broader	Wider	23.2	1.6	No	24.4	113
146. For	What	14.8	1.6	No	12.6	177
147. Heavy	Light	42.2	1.6	No	23.9	116.5
148. How	Now	22.1	1.6	No	14.7	164
149. Lamp	Light	70.6	1.6	No	40.0	51
150. Priest	Church	22.5	1.6	No	17.2	154.5
151. Quiet	Loud	25.3	1.6	No	23.6	118
152. Red	White	16.3	1.6	No	17.3	153
153. Stem	Flower	39.8	1.6	No	22.4	123
154. Stove	Hot	22.6	1.6	No	13.7	171
155. What	Question	11.0	1.6	No	7.5	197
156. Blossom	Flowers	64.0	1.1	No	39.0	53
157. Moon	Star	23.9	1.1	No	22.0	126.5
158. Religion	God	23.8	1.1	No	17.2	154.5
159. Whiskey	Drink	32.8	1.1	No	25.5	105
160. As	Is	16.9	.5	No	14.6	165.5
161. Bible	God	31.6	.5	No	20.9	133
162. Carry	Hold	10.2	.5	No	13.0	174
163. Comfort	Soft	10.1	.5	No	9.9	188
164. Cottage	House	26.4	.5	No	20.0	138
165. Eagle	Bird	57.9	.5	No	37.3	59
166. Have	Not	15.3	.5	No	8.8	192.5
167. Jump	High	16.4	.5	No	11.2	180
168. Numbers	Letters	19.3	.5	No	10.3	185
169. Ocean	Water	36.2	.5	No	19.5	140.5
170. Oh	My	17.0	.5	No	10.2	186
171. So	What	28.6	.5	No	22.4	123
172. Stomach	Food	24.2	.5	No	21.0	132
173. Swift	Fast	45.2	.5	No	33.8	69
174. Although	Because	10.7	0	No	9.9	188

TABLE 2 *(continued)*

Palermo-Jenkins S (A)	Primary (B)	Strength[a] A → B (%)	Strength B → A (%)	Two-way primary?	MR index	Rank in MR
175. Anger	Mad	35.2	0	No	20.6	135
176. Appear	See	21.8	0	No	14.8	162.5
177. At	Home	18.4	0	No	11.6	178
178. Bath	Clean	35.4	0	No	22.4	123
179. Because	Of	16.3	0	No	9.9	188
180. Citizen	Man	15.6	0	No	8.4	194
181. Clearer	Foggy[d]	5.8	0	No	6.8	200
182. Clearer	Than[d]	5.8	0	No	3.5	201
183. Eating	Food	42.3	0	No	26.9	101.5
184. Farther	Away	19.0	0	No	13.8	170
185. Hardly	Ever	20.5	0	No	19.8	139
186. If	It	9.5	0	No	7.8	195
187. Memory	Mind	11.7	0	No	13.2	173
188. Mutton	Lamb	31.7	0	No	29.2	93
189. Quickly	Fast	41.6	0	No	28.4	96
190. Running	Fast	24.2	0	No	14.0	169
191. Salty	Sweet	10.7	0	No	11.0	181
192. Sit	Down	27.1	0	No	14.1	168
193. Slowly	Fast	34.7	0	No	22.2	125
194. Soldier	Man	18.1	0	No	10.7	183
195. Tell	Me	25.1	0	No	14.8	162.5
196. The	Boy	13.4	0	No	9.2	190.5
197. Tobacco	Smoke	48.2	0	No	37.5	58
198. Trouble	Bad	10.7	0	No	7.4	198
199. Very	Much	27.1	0	No	16.6	157.5
200. Who	Is	12.8	0	No	10.8	182
201. Working	Hard	14.6	0	No	7.7	196

[a]Numbers in parentheses indicate row of reverse word pairs. See text.
[b]Largest response with both singular and plural counted.
[c]Largest single response.
[d]One of a tied pair of primary responses.

Word Chains Constructed from Primary Responses on the Two Norms

A final abstraction of the two norms is a specification of triads of words, A, B, and C, which are interrelated in an associative chain. These chains are given in Table 3. The words listed in the first column (A) are PJ stimuli and those in the column labeled B are the primary responses given to A. The percentage associative strengths for these primaries are indicated in the column between A and B. Similarly, the primary response to B, as determined by the KS norms, is given in the column labeled C and the B-C strength between the B and C columns. Finally, the percentage A-C strengths, based upon the PJ norms, are presented in the last column of Table 3. (The A-B-C triads are ordered in terms of decreasing A-C strength.) There are of course, a large number of nonprimary responses to A (Table 1) which would allow a greater variation in A-B strength than represented in Table 3. Moreover, there are an even greater number of nonprimary C responses which were given to the 234 KS stimuli. Thus, the triads enumerated in Table 3 and those obtainable from the complete association norms listed in the Appendix greatly increase the number of A-B-C chains which are available to the investigator in the study of mediational phenomena.

TABLE 3 *Percentage Strengths for A-B-C Chains*

Palermo-Jenkins Word (A)	Strength A → B (%)	Primary (B)	Strength B → C (%)	Strongest response to primary (C)	Strength A → C (%)
Thirsty	43.2	Water	13.2	Drink	28.9
Mutton	31.7	Lamb	17.0	Sheep	28.8
I	38.3	Me	45.6	You	27.7
Tobacco	48.2	Smoke	28.5	Cigarette(s)	21.8

TABLE 3 *(continued)*

Palermo-Jenkins Word (A)	Strength A → B (%)	Primary (B)	Strength B → C (%)	Strongest response to primary (C)	Strength A → C (%)
Where	20.5	There	45.6	Here	18.7
My	14.3	Mine	49.4	Your(s)	18.6
Hungry	41.3	Food	33.5	Eat	17.4
Hardly	20.5	Ever	32.4	Never	16.1
Street	11.8	Road	8.2	Car(s)	15.8
Swift	45.2	Fast	47.8	Slow	15.5
Carpet	31.1	Rug	18.7	Floor	15.3
Bitter	54.4	Sweet	32.4	Sour	14.9
Beautiful	16.9	Ugly	20.9	Pretty	14.7
Red	16.3	White	43.4	Black	13.9
Broader	23.2	Wider	24.2	Narrower	13.1
Us	51.0	We	21.4	They	10.7
Eagle	57.9	Bird	24.7	Fly(ies)	9.5
Carry	10.2	Hold	26.4	On	9.4
Memory	11.7	Mind	18.7	Think	9.1
Quiet	25.3	Loud	28.0	Noise	8.7
Stomach	24.2	Food	33.5	Eat	8.6
Quickly	41.6	Fast	47.8	Slow	8.5
Cabbage	14.0	Lettuce	19.8	Green(s)	8.0
Cottage	26.4	House	40.1	Home	7.5
Butterfly	12.4	Moth	16.5	Fly(ies)	7.2
Yellow	9.2	Color	31.8	Red	6.9
Appear	21.8	See	21.4	Look	6.1
Rough	30.4	Smooth	22.0	Soft	5.6
Mountain	21.4	Hill	14.8	Climb	5.3
Was	24.8	Is	12.6	Not	4.9
We	35.5	They	22.5	Them	3.9
But	10.0	And	14.3	Then	3.8
Priest	22.5	Church	17.6	God[a]	3.7
Slowly	34.7	Fast	47.8	Slow	3.3
Salty	10.7	Sweet	32.4	Sour	2.9
Joy	26.0	Happy	28.0	Sad	2.8
Moon	23.9	Star	13.7	Bright	2.7
Music	16.8	Song	45.0	Sing	2.7
Playing	14.2	Working	36.8	Hard	2.7
Kittens	72.3	Cats	64.2	Dog(s)	2.6
Fruit	45.4	Apple	17.6	Tree	2.5
Am	24.4	I	38.4	Me	2.4
Therefore	20.3	Because	34.0	Why	2.4
At	18.4	Home	42.8	House	2.1
Lift	20.8	Carry	8.2	Load	2.0
Long	63.4	Short	31.8	Tall	1.9
Blossom	64.0	Flowers	14.3	Pretty	1.8
So	28.6	What	10.4	Why	1.8
Comfort	10.1	Soft	26.9	Hard	1.7
Tell	25.1	Me	45.6	You	1.7
Although	10.7	Because	34.0	Why	1.5
Cheese	14.0	Mouse	14.8	Rat	1.5
Dream	48.5	Sleep	9.9	Bed	1.5
For	14.8	What	10.4	Why	1.5
Bath	35.4	Clean	35.1	Dirty	1.4
Scissors	67.9	Cut	10.4	Knife	1.4
Farther	19.0	Away	19.8	Go(es)	1.3
However	16.5	But	7.7	Why	1.3
Thief	26.4	Steal	21.4	Take	1.3
Stem	39.8	Flower	6.6	Rose[a]	1.2
The	13.4	Boy	70.8	Girl	1.2

TABLE 3 *(continued)*

Palermo-Jenkins Word (A)	Strength A → B (%)	Primary (B)	Strength B → C (%)	Strongest response to primary (C)	Strength A → C (%)
Child	17.3	Baby	12.1	Cry	1.0
If	9.5	It	20.9	Is	.9
Or	19.1	Nor	41.7	Neither	.9
Earth	14.3	Dirt	11.5	Mud[a]	.8
Speak	25.2	Talk	12.1	Fast	.8
Whiskey	32.8	Drink	24.7	Water	.8
Easier	41.9	Harder	34.0	Softer	.7
Ah	31.3	Oh	22.0	My	.5
Fingers	45.7	Hand	28.6	Glove(s)	.5
Clearer	5.8	Foggy[a]	14.8	Day	.4
How	22.1	Now	37.3	Then	.4
Running	24.2	Fast	47.8	Slow	.4
By	13.4	Near	46.7	Far	.3
Heavy	42.2	Light	35.1	Dark	.3
Justice	24.3	Law	34.0	Order	.3
Lamp	70.6	Light	35.1	Dark	.3
As	16.9	Is	12.6	Not	.2
Clearer	5.8	Than[a]	9.9	Then	.2
Have	15.3	Not	9.3	No	.2
Loud	42.3	Soft	26.9	Hard	.2
Numbers	19.3	Letters	19.8	Write	.2
Sit	27.1	Down	41.7	Up	.2
What	11.0	Question	72.5	Answer	.2
Anger	35.2	Mad	19.2	Angry	.1
Eating	42.3	Food	33.5	Eat	.1
Is	10.3	Are	18.7	You	.1
It	36.3	Is	12.6	Not	.1
Only	35.9	One	57.1	Two	.1
Table	69.3	Chair	35.1	Sit	.1
Trouble	10.7	Bad	50.0	Good	.1
Wish	15.0	Dream	31.8	Sleep	.1
An	18.5	A	12.1	B	0
And	23.3	But	7.7	Why	0
Because	16.3	Of	10.4	Course	0
Bible	31.6	God	8.8	Heaven	0
Citizen	15.6	Man	46.7	Woman	0
Come	35.5	Go	18.1	Away	0
Command	25.6	Order	13.2	Law	0
Earth	14.3	Dirt	11.5	Clean[a]	0
Hand	23.5	Foot	16.5	Shoe	0
Jump	16.4	High	51.1	Low	0
Make	9.3	Do	22.0	Not	0
Ocean	36.2	Water	13.2	Drink	0
Of	12.0	Course	11.0	Psychology	0
Oh	17.0	My	28.6	Your(s)	0
Priest	22.5	Church	17.6	Steeple[a]	0
Religion	23.8	God	8.8	Heaven	0
River	28.6	Water	13.2	Drink	0
Sickness	36.9	Health	15.9	Wealth	0
Soldier	18.1	Man	46.7	Woman	0
Stand	38.3	Sit	47.2	Down	0
Stem	39.8	Flower	6.6	Pretty[a]	0
Stove	22.6	Hot	56.0	Cold	0
Very	27.1	Much	28.6	More	0
Whistle	10.6	Train	14.3	Track(s)	0
Who	12.8	Is	12.6	Not	0
Working	14.6	Hard	48.3	Soft	0

[a]One of a tied pair of primary responses.

REFERENCES

Cramer, P. (1967). Mediated transfer via natural language association. *Journal of Verbal Learning and Verbal Behavior* 6, 512-519.

Marshall, G. R., & Cofer, C. N. (1963). Associative indices as measures of word relatedness: a summary and comparison of ten methods. *Journal of Verbal Learning and Verbal Behavior* 1, 408-421.

Palermo, D. S., & Jenkins, J. J. (1964). *Word association norms: grade school through college.* Minneapolis: University of Minnesota Press.

Russell, W. A., & Storms, L. H. (1955). Implicit verbal chaining in paired-associate learning. *Journal of Experimental Psychology* 49, 287-293.

Storms, L. H. (1958). Apparent backward association: a situational effect. *Journal of Experimental Psychology* 55, 390-395.

A (An;)

No.	Response	F	M	Tot.	%
1.	b	12	10	22	12.1
2.	an	9	9	18	9.9
3.	one	7	5	12	6.6
4.	the	7	3	10	5.5
5.	apple	4	2	8	4.4
6.	thing	5	1	6	3.3
7.	dog	2	3	5	2.7
8.	boy	4	-	4	2.2
9.	house	3	1	4	2.2
10.	man(men)	3	1	4	2.2
11.	boat	2	1	3	1.6
12.	book	2	1	3	1.6
13.	girl	-	3	3	1.6
14.	grade	1	2	3	1.6
15.	it	1	2	3	1.6
16.	letter	2	1	3	1.6
17.	person	1	2	3	1.6
18.	shoe	2	1	3	1.6
19.	and	1	1	2	1.1
20.	article	1	1	2	1.1
21.	bed	-	2	2	1.1
22.	go	2	-	2	1.1
23.	nothing	1	1	2	1.1
24.	or	1	1	2	1.1
25.	pillow	2	-	2	1.1
26.	what	-	2	2	1.1

($\underline{f}$ = 1, .5%, $\underline{n}$ = 49)
a, acorn, a good grade, alphabet, Andrea, another, anticipation, bad, ball, B.C., "be", blank, day, e, element, 1st, fit, god, good, Hester, horse, I, lady, light, little, mother, nail, never, nut, of, one, painting, pen, pig, place, problem, silly, sleep, something, song, story, stutter, top, trunk, two, wall, window, woman, world

Ache (; Stomach)

No.	Response	F	M	Tot.	%
1.	pain	50	47	97	53.2
2.	head	8	5	13	7.1
3.	hurt	10	3	13	7.1
4.	back	7	3	10	5.5
5.	tooth	5	2	7	3.8
6.	sore	3	2	5	2.7
7.	foot(feet)	1	2	3	1.6
8.	bone(s)	1	1	2	1.1
9.	feel	1	1	2	1.1
10.	muscle	2	0	2	1.1
11.	stomach	0	2	2	1.1
12.	tummy	2	0	2	1.1

($\underline{f}$ = 1, .5%, $\underline{n}$ = 23)
acne, and pain, Apache, arm, aspirin, belly, bend, calf, calve, cry, ear, exercise, fitness, heart, hypochondriac, me, ouch, painful, sleep, soothe, soul, throat, toe
(Illegible - 1)

An (A;)

No.	Response	F	M	Tot.	%
1.	a	19	11	30	16.5
2.	apple	19	7	26	14.3
3.	other	6	7	13	7.1
4.	the	7	4	11	6.0
5.	and	7	2	9	4.9

An (A;) (contd)

No.	Response	F	M	Tot.	%
6.	another	3	5	8	4.4
7.	one	5	3	8	4.4
8.	animal	4	2	6	3.3
9.	ant	3	3	6	3.3
10.	it	1	3	4	2.2
11.	of	2	2	4	2.2
12.	answer	1	2	3	1.6
13.	elephant	3	0	3	1.6
14.	object	2	1	3	1.6
15.	vowel	2	1	3	1.6
16.	article	2	0	2	1.1
17.	history	1	1	2	1.1
18.	if	0	2	2	1.1
19.	or	1	1	2	1.1
20.	orange	2	0	2	1.1

($\underline{f}$ = 1, .5%, $\underline{n}$ = 35)
act, alligator, angel, Ann, Annapolis, arm, army, ass, body, cat, consonant, eagle, egg, embryo, error, hour, ideal, iota, is, item, nothing, oath, ogre, old, only, ostrich, over, owl, particle, something, synonym, this, what, year, you

And (But; Or)

No.	Response	F	M	Tot.	%
1.	then	15	11	26	14.3
2.	or	8	13	21	11.5
3.	now	9	9	18	9.9
4.	also	11	2	13	7.1
5.	but	7	3	10	5.5
6.	if	2	6	8	4.4
7.	so	5	2	7	3.8
8.	more	3	3	6	3.3
9.	the	5	0	5	2.7
10.	an	1	3	4	2.2
11.	me	3	1	4	2.2
12.	so forth	1	2	3	1.6
13.	too	2	1	3	1.6
14.	what	1	2	3	1.6
15.	you	1	2	3	1.6
16.	again	1	1	2	1.1
17.	always	0	2	2	1.1
18.	both	2	0	2	1.1
19.	he	0	2	2	1.1
20.	of	1	1	2	1.1
21.	therefore	1	1	2	1.1
22.	when	1	1	2	1.1
23.	with	1	1	2	1.1

($\underline{f}$ = 1, .5%, $\underline{n}$ = 32)
a, addition, Andy, choose, conjunction, continue, end, equation, et, finish, forever, I, it, love, never, not, nothing, our, over, play, sand, some, so on, they, this, though, thus, us, we, why, yes, yet

Animal (; Lion, Sheep)

No.	Response	F	M	Tot.	%
1.	dog	24	17	41	22.5
2.	vegetable	6	8	14	7.7
3.	cat	9	3	12	6.6
4.	man	3	5	8	4.4
5.	farm	2	5	7	3.8
6.	horse	5	2	7	3.8
7.	cow	3	2	5	2.7

Animal   (; Lion, Sheep) (contd)

No.	Response	F	M	Tot.	%
8.	cracker(s)	2	3	5	2.7
9.	bear	3	1	4	2.2
10.	beast	2	2	4	2.2
11.	bird	3	1	4	2.2
12.	fox	2	1	3	1.6
13.	fur	2	1	3	1.6
14.	plant	2	1	3	1.6
15.	forest	1	1	2	1.1
16.	life	0	2	2	1.1
17.	pet	2	0	2	1.1
18.	run	0	2	2	1.1
19.	sheep	2	0	2	1.1

(f = 1, .5%, n = 51)
angel, angry, bad, beaver, big, boy, brute,
butcher, care, clever, creature, cruel, dead,
death, deer, despise, dig, eats, elephant, fat,
father, Figi, food, frog, furry, goat, herd,
hunter, husbandry, instinct, kitten, lamb, like,
lion, mammal, moves, mule, owl, pig, puppy,
putrid, singers, skin, sound, swinging, tamer,
tiger, trees, turtle, you, zoo
(No response - 1)

Apple   (Fruit; An)

No.	Response	F	M	Tot.	%
1.	tree	16	16	32	17.6
2.	red	14	9	23	12.6
3.	pie	7	6	13	7.1
4.	fruit	7	5	12	6.6
5.	core	5	6	11	6.0
6.	pear	7	2	9	4.9
7.	eat	5	3	8	4.4
8.	cider	3	2	5	2.7
9.	green	4	1	5	2.7
10.	orange	4	1	5	2.7
11.	crunch	2	2	4	2.2
12.	seed(s)	1	3	4	2.2
13.	worm	2	1	3	1.6
14.	a	0	2	2	1.1
15.	Adam	1	1	2	1.1
16.	banana	1	1	2	1.1
17.	candy	2	0	2	1.1
18.	cart	0	2	2	1.1
19.	food	2	0	2	1.1
20.	grape	0	2	2	1.1
21.	juice	1	1	2	1.1
22.	lunch	2	0	2	1.1
23.	sauce	1	1	2	1.1
24.	sin	0	2	2	1.1

(f = 1, .5%, n = 26)
Adam & Eve, Adam's, an, apple tree, bite, cinnamon,
crispy, crunchy, day, delicious, eye, faith, grandfather, head, juicy, Newton, of my eye, orchard,
plum, polish, quarter, scrapple, sweet, tasty,
teacher, treat

Are   (Is; We)

No.	Response	F	M	Tot.	%
1.	you	19	15	34	18.7
2.	is	20	7	27	14.8
3.	they	10	7	17	9.3
4.	we	2	12	14	7.7
5.	there	7	2	9	4.9
6.	am	6	2	8	4.4
7.	not	2	6	8	4.4
8.	exist	4	3	7	3.8
9.	aren't	2	4	6	3.3
10.	were	4	2	6	3.3

Are   (Is; We) (contd)

No.	Response	F	M	Tot.	%
11.	here	2	3	5	2.7
12.	now	1	2	3	1.6
13.	be	2	0	2	1.1
14.	far	1	1	2	1.1
15.	good	0	2	2	1.1
16.	our	1	1	2	1.1
17.	yes	1	1	2	1.1

(f = 1, .5%, n = 28)
alive, both, existence, exists, expenisve, gold,
gone, has, have, imagine, many, me, might be,
mine, ore, plural, present, reality, some, sunt,
still, those, together, verb, was, what, will,
will be

Arm   (; Hand)

No.	Response	F	M	Tot.	%
1.	leg	44	32	76	41.7
2.	hand(s)	7	15	22	12.1
3.	chair	10	9	19	10.4
4.	band	8	3	11	6.0
5.	muscle	1	5	6	3.3
6.	long	3	2	5	2.7
7.	pit	2	1	3	1.6
8.	shoulder	1	2	3	1.6
9.	carry	2	0	2	1.1
10.	hammer	2	0	2	1.1
11.	law	0	2	2	1.1
12.	sleeve	2	0	2	1.1

(f = 1), .5%, n = 29)
appendage, armor, army, around, bend, between,
body, broken, cast, elbow, extend, fingers, fold,
good, held, hold, neck, phallus, rest, side,
skin, strap, strong, tan, thin, tired, warrior,
wrestle, wrist

Army   (; Soldier)

No.	Response	F	M	Tot.	%
1.	Navy	43	42	85	46.7
2.	man(men)	9	4	13	7.1
3.	soldier(s)	5	1	6	3.3
4.	uniform	4	2	6	3.3
5.	draft	0	5	5	2.7
6.	war	2	3	5	2.7
7.	bad	2	1	3	1.6
8.	no	0	3	3	1.6
9.	service(s)	1	2	3	1.6
10.	brown	2	0	2	1.1
11.	green	2	0	2	1.1
12.	march	1	1	2	1.1

(f = 1, .5%, n = 47)
abuse, Air Force, away, awful, band, barracks,
beans, boots, boy, brat, chair, cot, discipline,
enlist, fight, foot, game, G.I., gray, grip, gun,
Hitler, idiots, infantry, job, kill, Lieutenant,
meningitis, now, nurse, object, rats, rebels,
regiment, regimentation, ridiculous, salvation,
sergeant, silly, strong, tank, train, uniforms,
went, West Point, work, you

Away   (Farther;   )

No.	Response	F	M	Tot.	%
1.	go(es)	19	17	36	19.8
2.	far	17	13	30	16.5
3.	from	16	11	27	14.8
4.	gone	11	5	16	8.8
5.	here	1	7	8	4.4
6.	near	4	2	6	3.3
7.	home	0	5	5	2.7
8.	to	3	1	4	2.2
9.	sea	0	3	3	1.6
10.	with	2	1	3	1.6
11.	beyond	2	0	2	1.1
12.	close	1	1	2	1.1
13.	fly	0	2	2	1.1
14.	leave	1	1	2	1.1
15.	move	1	1	2	1.1
16.	now	2	0	2	1.1
17.	out	0	2	2	1.1
18.	toward	1	1	2	1.1

($\underline{f}$ = 1, .5%, $\underline{n}$ = 28)
abroad, alone, a path, away, banish, boy friend, come, distant, echo, forever, free, me, mountains, navy, New York, ocean, Paso Robles, return, roll, run, today, together, towards, travel, trip, vacation, we, yonder

Baby   (Child, Cry;   )

No.	Response	F	M	Tot.	%
1.	cry	11	11	22	12.1
2.	child(ren)	11	7	18	9.9
3.	girl	10	7	17	9.3
4.	boy	7	4	11	6.0
5.	cute	5	4	9	4.9
6.	mother	6	1	7	3.8
7.	small	2	5	7	3.8
8.	doll	3	2	5	2.7
9.	soft	5	0	5	2.7
10.	diaper(s)	2	2	4	2.2
11.	adult	1	2	3	1.6
12.	bottle	2	1	3	1.6
13.	helpless	2	1	3	1.6
14.	pink	3	0	3	1.6
15.	tiny	2	1	3	1.6
16.	young	2	1	3	1.6
17.	brother	1	1	2	1.1
18.	carriage	0	2	2	1.1
19.	chair	0	2	2	1.1
20.	infant	1	1	2	1.1
21.	kitten	1	1	2	1.1
22.	marriage	0	2	2	1.1
23.	milk	0	2	2	1.1
24.	sitter	1	1	2	1.1
25.	warm	2	0	2	1.1

($\underline{f}$ = 1, .5%, $\underline{n}$ = 40)
affectionate, atomic, baby, bale, beautiful, booties, born, car, cat, cherub, clean, cradle, cream, dog, family, fetus, food, happiness, job, laugh, love, lovable, man, married, mine, morning, new, nice, no, none, offspring, powder, rattle, red, shower, sit, trouble, want, wet, wife
(Illegible - 1)

Bad   (Trouble;   )

No.	Response	F	M	Tot.	%
1.	good	49	42	91	50.0
2.	girl	11	7	18	9.9
3.	boy	4	11	15	8.2
4.	evil	3	1	4	2.2
5.	mad	1	2	3	1.6

Bad   (Trouble;   ) (contd)

No.	Response	F	M	Tot.	%
6.	naughty	2	1	3	1.6
7.	people	2	1	3	1.6
8.	breath	2	0	2	1.1
9.	tries	0	2	2	1.1
10.	ugly	1	1	2	1.1
11.	wrong	2	0	2	1.1

($\underline{f}$ = 1, .5%, $\underline{n}$ = 36)
cheat, child, day, dog, dumb concept, faith, feel, filth, great, habit, hidden, horrible, nasty, nice, no, noisy, note, objectionable, ordinary, outlaw, poor, punish, rotten, rut, sad, seed, shock, sorrow, stuff, taste, value, vile, weather, westerns, wolf, woman
(Illegible - 1)

Became   (Become;   )

No.	Response	F	M	Tot.	%
1.	become	15	16	31	17.0
2.	was	12	13	25	13.7
3.	is	6	2	8	4.4
4.	ill	3	2	5	2.7
5.	what	2	3	5	2.7
6.	good	2	2	4	2.2
7.	bad	1	2	3	1.6
8.	becomes	2	1	3	1.6
9.	changed	2	1	3	1.6
10.	famous	2	1	3	1.6
11.	sick	1	2	3	1.6
12.	successful	3	0	3	1.6
13.	be	2	0	2	1.1
14.	because	1	1	2	1.1
15.	becoming	2	0	2	1.1
16.	began	2	0	2	1.1
17.	change	2	0	2	1.1
18.	did	1	1	2	1.1
19.	doctor	1	1	2	1.1
20.	future	2	0	2	1.1
21.	great	1	1	2	1.1
22.	man	1	1	2	1.1
23.	now	2	0	2	1.1
24.	old	2	0	2	1.1
25.	well	0	2	2	1.1

($\underline{f}$ = 1, .5%, $\underline{n}$ = 58)
about, acting, again, a man, angry, aroused, aware, begot, being, better, big, born, butt, clear, close, dame, dead, developed, ended, five, found, grow, had, honest, imagine, improved, innate, insane, Kafka, king, left, live, lot, mad, made, married, new, not, of, of age, other, passive, President, saw, social worker, sorry, strong, stupid, suck, them, today, turned, transformed, transition, weak, will, will be, worse
(Illegible - 2)

Because   (Although, Therefore, Why;   )

No.	Response	F	M	Tot.	%
1.	why	35	27	62	34.0
2.	of	9	8	17	9.3
3.	reason	9	6	15	8.2
4.	therefore	2	6	8	4.4
5.	if	3	3	6	3.3
6.	since	4	2	6	3.3
7.	for	3	2	5	2.7
8.	what	1	3	4	2.2
9.	you	3	1	4	2.2
10.	because	2	1	3	1.6
11.	just	1	2	3	1.6

Because (Although, Therefore, Why;) (contd)

No.	Response	F	M	Tot.	%
12.	they	2	1	3	1.6
13.	answer	0	2	2	1.1
14.	explain	1	1	2	1.1
15.	no	1	1	2	1.1
16.	now	1	1	2	1.1
17.	she	1	1	2	1.1
18.	then	1	1	2	1.1
19.	yes	1	1	2	1.1

($\underline{f}$ = 1, .5%, $\underline{n}$ = 32)
about, accordingly, always, any, believe, cause,
'cuz, due to, eat, excuse, for the reason, have,
he, him, hope, I, is, it, look, love, maybe,
necessary, no answer, question, remember, see,
sing, so, that, time, tired, when

Bed (Sleep;)

No.	Response	F	M	Tot.	%
1.	sleep	38	26	64	35.1
2.	soft	8	6	14	7.7
3.	sheet(s)	5	4	9	4.9
4.	pillow	4	3	7	3.8
5.	room	0	5	5	2.7
6.	sex	3	2	5	2.7
7.	good	2	1	3	1.6
8.	post(s)	2	1	3	1.6
9.	spread	3	0	3	1.6
10.	warm	3	0	3	1.6
11.	blanket(s)	0	2	2	1.1
12.	comfort	1	1	2	1.1
13.	cover(s)	1	1	2	1.1
14.	flower(s)	1	1	2	1.1
15.	in	2	0	2	1.1
16.	love	1	1	2	1.1
17.	red	1	1	2	1.1
18.	rest	2	0	2	1.1
19.	side	1	1	2	1.1
20.	spring(s)	1	1	2	1.1
21.	table	1	1	2	1.1
22.	time	1	1	2	1.1

($\underline{f}$ = 1, .5%, $\underline{n}$ = 42)
back, bad, bedded, big, bold, chair, comfortable,
common, cot, couch, cozy, dead, dream, feather,
fellow, girl, green, hard, kind, large, lay, lie,
long, lying, made, mate, mattress, messy, need,
nest, night, pleasure, relax, smooth, stand,
stead, story, stream, Ted, tree, water, wet

Bird (Eagle;)

No.	Response	F	M	Tot.	%
1.	fly(ies)	25	20	45	24.7
2.	sing(s)	14	7	21	11.5
3.	tree(s)	7	5	12	6.6
4.	wing(s)	6	3	9	4.9
5.	bath	5	3	8	4.4
6.	nest	5	2	7	3.8
7.	cage	0	4	4	2.2
8.	lady	3	1	4	2.2
9.	blue	3	0	3	1.6
10.	canary	0	3	3	1.6
11.	feather(s)	2	1	3	1.6
12.	free	2	1	3	1.6
13.	robin	3	0	3	1.6
14.	sky	1	2	3	1.6
15.	beak	1	1	2	1.1
16.	brain	1	1	2	1.1
17.	call	0	2	2	1.1
18.	cat	2	0	2	1.1
19.	dog	0	2	2	1.1

Bird (Eagle;) (contd)

No.	Response	F	M	Tot.	%
20.	flying	1	1	2	1.1
21.	plane	0	2	2	1.1
22.	see	1	1	2	1.1
23.	song	1	1	2	1.1
24.	swallow	1	1	2	1.1

($\underline{f}$ = 1, .5%, $\underline{n}$ = 34)
air, bee, birds, book, bush, carefree, chirp,
covered, cry, cuckoo, dead, digs, doll, duck,
eagle, flip, fly free, go, green, gun, high,
hum, lark, mammal, perky, prey, seed, shit,
sister, soft, stork, talk, tweet, twitter

Black (White; Red)

No.	Response	F	M	Tot.	%
1.	white	48	33	81	44.5
2.	dark	9	7	16	8.8
3.	night	4	4	8	4.4
4.	sheep	4	4	8	4.4
5.	cat	4	2	6	3.3
6.	horse	4	0	4	2.2
7.	coal	2	1	3	1.6
8.	house	2	1	3	1.6
9.	red	0	3	3	1.6
10.	velvet	1	2	3	1.6
11.	blue	0	2	2	1.1
12.	board	1	1	2	1.1
13.	color	1	1	2	1.1
14.	good	0	2	2	1.1
15.	like	0	2	2	1.1
16.	man	0	2	2	1.1
17.	Muslim	0	2	2	1.1
18.	Negro	1	1	2	1.1

($\underline{f}$ = 1, .5%, $\underline{n}$ = 31)
bad, bird, blacker, blank, book, brown, civil
rights, conglomeration, crepe, death, dress,
duer, flower, green, hair, jack, Joe, me, mist,
nothing, orange, problem, satin, see, separation,
sky, solemn, thing, vacant, widow, yellow

Book (; Bible)

No.	Response	F	M	Tot.	%
1.	read	29	23	52	28.5
2.	page(s)	8	5	13	7.1
3.	study	5	4	9	4.9
4.	cover	3	5	8	4.4
5.	worm	2	6	8	4.4
6.	store	6	1	7	3.8
7.	shelf	3	3	6	3.3
8.	learn	2	3	5	2.7
9.	mark	3	1	4	2.2
10.	paper	3	1	4	2.2
11.	binding	3	0	3	1.6
12.	case	2	1	3	1.6
13.	end	1	2	3	1.6
14.	candle	1	1	2	1.1
15.	knowledge	1	1	2	1.1
16.	look	1	1	2	1.1
17.	open	2	0	2	1.1
18.	pen	0	2	2	1.1
19.	rack	1	1	2	1.1
20.	table	1	1	2	1.1
21.	text	1	1	2	1.1

($\underline{f}$ = 1. .5%, $\underline{n}$ = 41)
bat, bell, bell and candle, Bible, bore, chair,
check, enjoy, fiction, good, Hesse, holder,
idea, interesting, keep, king, learning, lesson,
letters, library, long, magazine, marker, red
binding, report, Salinger, scholar, school,

Book   (; Bible) (contd)

No.	Response	F	M	Tot.	%

seclusion, song, stork, teacher, test, time, tin, title, tray, valuable, volume, words, write

Boy   (Girl, The; Baby)

No.	Response	F	M	Tot.	%
1.	girl	71	58	129	70.8
2.	man	3	2	5	2.7
3.	child	3	0	3	1.6
4.	him	2	1	3	1.6
5.	young	2	1	3	1.6
6.	friend	1	1	2	1.1
7.	lad	0	2	2	1.1
8.	male	2	0	2	1.1
9.	oh	0	2	2	1.1

($\underline{f}$ = 1, .5%, $\underline{n}$ = 31)
baby, barefoot, blonde, brother, date, effeminate, fraternity, friendly, good, he, hid, how, innocent, it, little, lonely, love, meets, mischief, naughty, ran, run, Scout, small, soon, sports, tall, that, when, whew!, youth

Bread   (Butter;   )

No.	Response	F	M	Tot.	%
1.	butter	46	43	89	48.9
2.	water	9	14	23	12.6
3.	wine	14	7	21	11.5
4.	white	10	1	11	6.0
5.	food	1	5	6	3.3
6.	eat	2	3	5	2.7

($\underline{f}$ = 1, .5%, $\underline{n}$ = 27)
bakery, beans, Bible, brown, cheese, corn, crumbs, dead, dry, French, fruit, hard, line, money, pan, Russia, rye, sandwich, soft, stale, staple, store, sweet, thread, toast, wheat, winner

Bug   (; Spider)

No.	Response	F	M	Tot.	%
1.	insect	17	21	39	20.9
2.	beetle	7	6	13	7.1
3.	spider	7	2	9	4.9
4.	Beatle	4	3	7	3.8
5.	fly	6	1	7	3.8
6.	bite	5	1	6	3.3
7.	crawl	4	2	6	3.3
8.	me	1	5	6	3.3
9.	rug	0	5	5	2.7
10.	small	2	3	5	2.7
11.	ugly	2	2	4	2.2
12.	black	3	0	3	1.6
13.	kill	2	1	3	1.6
14.	squash	1	2	3	1.6
15.	-aboo	1	1	2	1.1
16.	bed	2	0	2	1.1
17.	bother	0	2	2	1.1
18.	grasshopper	1	1	2	1.1
19.	mosquito	1	1	2	1.1
20.	moth	0	2	2	1.1
21.	plant	2	0	2	1.1

($\underline{f}$ = 1, .5%, $\underline{n}$ = 53)
annoy, annoying, ant, bad, bait, bee, Beetle-grimace, big, black widow, bomb, butterfly, cabana, cockroach, crawly, creep, creepy, dead, dig, eck, grass, gripe, hard, hate, hornet,

Bug   (; Spider) (contd)

No.	Response	F	M	Tot.	%

horrible, hurt, ick, juice, killer, lady, leave, lug, man, mice, night, off, out, Rogers, smashed, snail, snug, spiracle, squashed, squish, sting, tree, ugh, under, unpleasant, weapon, weird, wings, worm

But   (And, However;   )

No.	Response	F	M	Tot.	%
1.	why	8	6	14	7·7
2.	and	7	6	13	7.1
3.	no	6	5	11	6.0
4.	however	5	5	10	5.5
5.	not	5	5	10	5.5
6.	what	4	5	9	4.9
7.	then	2	4	6	3.3
8.	because	3	2	5	2.7
9.	if	2	3	5	2.7
10.	except	4	0	4	2.2
11.	for	2	2	4	2.2
12.	never	3	1	4	2.2
13.	now	3	1	4	2.2
14.	you	1	3	4	2.2
15.	ass	0	3	3	1.6
16.	excuse	3	0	3	1.6
17.	maybe	1	2	3	1.6
18.	or	3	0	3	1.6
19.	when	2	1	3	1.6
20.	cigarette	1	1	2	1.1
21.	conjunction	0	1	2	1.1
22.	could	1	2	2	1.1
23.	good	1	1	2	1.1
24.	me	1	1	2	1.1
25.	nevertheless	1	1	2	1.1
26.	nothing	1	1	2	1.1
27.	objection	2	1	2	1.1
28.	oh	1	0	2	1.1
29.	stop	2	1	2	1.1
30.	to	0	2	2	1.1
31.	wait	2	0	2	1.1
32.	yes	1	1	2	1.1

($\underline{f}$ = 1, .5%, $\underline{n}$ = 38)
a, above, also, although, anyway, ask, before, between, butt, butter, cigar, comma, confusion, delay, derriere, end, hesitate, how, I, in, insist, instead, interject, neat, neither, only, on the other hand, out, pause, question, some, still, -ter, tho, try, who, wrong, yet

Butter   (Bread;   )

No.	Response	F	M	Tot.	%
1.	bread	31	42	73	40.1
2.	milk	5	5	10	5.5
3.	yellow	7	3	10	5.5
4.	melt	7	2	9	4.9
5.	fat	4	4	8	4.4
6.	knife	2	5	7	3.8
7.	cream	4	1	5	2.7
8.	spread	4	1	5	2.7
9.	soft	3	1	4	2.2
10.	cow	3	0	3	1.6
11.	fattening	3	0	3	1.6
12.	greasy	3	0	3	1.6
13.	margarine	1	2	3	1.6
14.	salt	1	2	3	1.6
15.	better	0	2	2	1.1
16.	cheese	2	0	2	1.1
17.	churn	1	1	2	1.1
18.	jam	1	1	2	1.1

Butter   (Bread;   ) (contd)

No.	Response	F	M	Tot.	%
19.	oleomargarine	2	0	2	1.1
20.	rich	2	0	2	1.1

($\underline{f}$ = 1, .5%, $\underline{n}$ = 24)
butter, dairy, dish, eat, finger, fly, good,
malleable, mess, oil, oily, oleo, pancakes,
popovers, pudding, real, skidgrease, smooth,
sugar, syrup, table, toast, up, yellow rectangle

Buy   (Sell;   )

No.	Response	F	M	Tot.	%
1.	sell	39	37	76	41.7
2.	money	8	9	17	9.3
3.	clothes	5	2	7	3.8
4.	purchase	3	3	6	3.3
5.	book(s)	3	2	5	2.7
6.	things	4	1	5	2.7
7.	food	1	3	4	2.2
8.	goods	3	0	3	1.6
9.	apple(s)	1	1	2	1.1
10.	house	1	1	2	1.1
11.	me	0	2	2	1.1
12.	more	2	0	2	1.1
13.	nothing	2	0	2	1.1
14.	shop	2	0	2	1.1
15.	steal	1	1	2	1.1
16.	store	2	0	2	1.1
17.	what	0	2	2	1.1

($\underline{f}$ = 1, .5%, $\underline{n}$ = 41)
account book, away, bargain, barter, before, beg,
bonds, bought, can't, car, compare, comprar,
cost, counter, cry, dinner, everything, fun, gets,
give, groceries, hold, it, lone, lose, lots, new,
obtain, one, pay, ring, shopping, silverware,
sold, stockings, them, this, toy, try, why, word

Candy   (; Sweet)

No.	Response	F	M	Tot.	%
1.	sweet(s)	37	26	63	34.6
2.	cane	6	12	18	9.9
3.	apple(s)	5	7	12	6.6
4.	baby	3	5	8	4.4
5.	bar	3	4	7	3.8
6.	eat	4	3	7	3.8
7.	good	5	1	6	3.3
8.	store	4	2	6	3.3
9.	child	2	2	4	2.2
10.	gum	3	0	3	1.6
11.	red	1	2	3	1.6
12.	sticky	2	1	3	1.6
13.	sugar	0	3	3	1.6
14.	chocolate	1	1	2	1.1
15.	cotton	2	0	2	1.1
16.	fattening	2	0	2	1.1
17.	girl	0	2	2	1.1

($\underline{f}$ = 1, .5%, $\underline{n}$ = 31)
chewy, coke, dandy, dish, dog, egg, food, gooey,
handy, insipid, kiss, kisses, Mandy, mint, mouth,
name, no, Pandy, peanut brittle, peppermint,
please, pop, property, she, sick, sickening,
stick, stripper, taste, Terry Southern, toy

Carry   (Lift;   )

No.	Response	F	M	Tot.	%
1.	load	8	7	15	8.2
2.	on	7	7	14	7.7
3.	lift	9	5	13	7.1
4.	away	2	10	12	6.6
5.	hold	6	5	11	6.0
6.	books	6	3	9	4.9
7.	bring	6	3	9	4.9
8.	me	3	3	6	3.3
9.	take	3	3	6	3.3
10.	heavy	4	1	5	2.7
11.	off	1	3	4	2.2
12.	tote	3	1	4	2.2
13.	transport	0	4	4	2.2
14.	back	2	1	3	1.6
15.	bear	2	1	3	1.6
16.	burden	2	1	3	1.6
17.	drop	0	3	3	1.6
18.	baby	2	0	2	1.1
19.	groceries	1	1	2	1.1
20.	horse	1	1	2	1.1
21.	lug	1	1	2	1.1
22.	out	1	1	2	1.1
23.	over	1	1	2	1.1
24.	thing(s)	1	1	2	1.1
25.	water	2	0	2	1.1

($\underline{f}$ = 1, .5%, $\underline{n}$ = 42)
across, along, arm, backhoe, bag, bed, bread,
briefcase, Carey, cart, cash, cat, charge,
fetch, forward, grant, grudge, help, her, home,
keep, pail, pick, porter, pull, purse, responsibility, shouldered, slow, stone, tarry, threshold,
throw, tired, tow, travel, truck, walk, went,
with, wood, work

Catholic   (; Priest)

No.	Response	F	M	Tot.	%
1.	church	17	18	35	19.2
2.	Protestant	14	16	30	16.5
3.	priest	14	12	26	14.3
4.	religion	12	7	19	10.4
5.	Jew	4	1	5	2.7
6.	Jewish	3	1	4	2.2
7.	me	1	3	4	2.2
8.	God	1	2	3	1.6
9.	nun(s)	3	0	3	1.6
10.	universal	1	2	3	1.6
11.	all	1	1	2	1.1
12.	believe	2	0	2	1.1
13.	cross	2	0	2	1.1
14.	man	1	1	2	1.1
15.	order	2	0	2	1.1
16.	religious	0	2	2	1.1
17.	Roman	1	1	2	1.1

($\underline{f}$ = 1. .5%, $\underline{n}$ = 36)
archaic, Baptist, bigot, bishop, cathedral,
celibate, Christian, creep, dark, devout,
dictatorial, dorm, faith, false, girl, glamour,
good, hell, is, kids, mess, mother, narrow,
nonsense, nope, paradoxy, Pope, question, relic,
ritual, robe, rule, stilted, strictness, ugh,
very complicated

Cats   (Dogs, Kittens;   )

No.	Response	F	M	Tot.	%
1.	dog(s)	57	60	117	64.2
2.	mouse (mice)	4	5	9	4.9
3.	fur	3	2	5	2.7
4.	kittens	4	0	4	2.2

Cats (Dogs, Kittens;) (contd)

No.	Response	F	M	Tot.	%
5.	meow(s)	2	1	3	1.6
6.	pet(s)	1	2	3	1.6
7.	soft	2	1	3	1.6
8.	fight	1	1	2	1.1
9.	hate	2	0	2	1.1
10.	paw	0	2	2	1.1
11.	whiskers	2	0	2	1.1

($\underline{f}$ = 1, .5%, $\underline{n}$ = 29)
bats, black, boats, cool, covered, cry,
dots, eyes, feline, female, fire, fleas, flies,
Gussie, hay fever, independent, many, mine, sleek,
slink, sneaky, stinky, Sydney, tired, trouble,
twelve, wonderful, worthless
(No response - 1)

Chair (Table;)

No.	Response	F	M	Tot.	%
1.	sit	35	29	64	35.1
2.	table	24	15	39	21.4
3.	arm	4	2	6	3.3
4.	cushion	2	3	5	2.7
5.	seat	3	2	5	2.7
6.	bed	2	2	4	2.2
7.	pillow	2	2	4	2.2
8.	broken	2	1	3	1.6
9.	rest	1	2	3	1.6
10.	sofa	2	1	3	1.6
11.	soft	3	0	3	1.6
12.	stool	0	3	3	1.6
13.	wood	1	2	3	1.6
14.	comfort	2	0	2	1.1
15.	desk	1	1	2	1.1
16.	floor	1	1	2	1.1
17.	lair	1	1	2	1.1
18.	leg	2	0	2	1.1
19.	wooden	2	0	2	1.1

($\underline{f}$ = 1, .5%, $\underline{n}$ = 24)
back, big, brown, church, comfy, couch, craftman-
ship, divan, electric, fall, hair, hand, hard,
lift, men, organize, relax, rock, rocking, stove,
structured, sturdy, take, tire
(Illegible - 1)

Church (Priest; Religion)

No.	Response	F	M	Tot.	%
1.	God	20	12	32	17.6
2.	steeple	16	16	32	17.6
3.	religion	4	4	8	4.4
4.	go	4	2	6	3.3
5.	school	4	2	6	3.3
6.	Sunday	3	2	5	2.7
7.	pew	2	2	4	2.2
8.	temple	4	0	4	2.2
9.	priest	2	1	3	1.6
10.	state	2	1	3	1.6
11.	big	1	1	2	1.1
12.	building	2	0	2	1.1
13.	Catholic	1	1	2	1.1
14.	Christ	1	1	2	1.1
15.	no	0	2	2	1.1
16.	people	0	2	2	1.1
17.	pray	2	0	2	1.1
18.	quiet	2	0	2	1.1
19.	step(s)	1	1	2	1.1
20.	white	1	1	2	1.1
21.	worship	1	1	2	1.1

($\underline{f}$ = 1, .5%, $\underline{n}$ = 56)
advice, alienated, atheist, bell, Bible, bore,

Church (Priest; Religion) (contd)

No.	Response	F	M	Tot.	%

carrots, cathedral, Christmas, closed, congrega-
tional, crutch, cupola, divine, door, enemy,
fathers, goer, going, good, hallelujah, home,
house, hypocrisy, impressive, inspired, jail,
kill, meeting, men, monastery, money, mosque,
nonsense, nothing, novice, peace, Piedmont,
Pope, red, rewarding, ridiculous, rigid, serene,
sing, sleep, solemn, spire, status, street,
sunny, symbol, synagogue, Unitarian fellowship,
web, Wordsworth
(No response - 1)

Cigarette (; Tobacco)

No.	Response	F	M	Tot.	%
1.	smoke	48	40	88	48.3
2.	butt	8	4	12	6.6
3.	cancer	5	3	8	4.4
4.	light	5	2	7	3.8
5.	holder	3	3	6	3.3
6.	lighter	4	2	6	3.3
7.	cigar	2	3	5	2.7
8.	burn	1	3	4	2.2
9.	match(es)	1	3	4	2.2
10.	ash(es)	2	1	3	1.6
11.	bad	0	2	2	1.1
12.	case	0	2	2	1.1
13.	filter	0	2	2	1.1
14.	smells	2	0	2	1.1
15.	tobacco	1	1	2	1.1
16.	white	2	0	2	1.1

($\underline{f}$ = 1, .5%, $\underline{n}$ = 27)
ashtray, buds, burning, but, chic, cough, death,
fag, habit, ick, Kent, lit, machine, mouth, nervous, out, pleasure, relax, round, silly, sliver,
smoker, smoking, stamp, stink, ugh, warm

Circle (; Square)

No.	Response	F	M	Tot.	%
1.	round	39	13	52	28.5
2.	square	19	27	46	25.3
3.	around	7	6	13	7.1
4.	sphere	2	2	4	2.2
5.	friends	2	1	3	1.6
6.	line	1	2	3	1.6
7.	one	3	0	3	1.6
8.	ring	0	3	3	1.6
9.	ball	1	1	2	1.1
10.	circumference	1	1	2	1.1
11.	close	0	2	2	1.1
12.	dot	1	1	2	1.1
13.	geometry	1	1	2	1.1
14.	it	2	0	2	1.1
15.	theater	1	1	2	1.1
16.	wheel	0	2	2	1.1

($\underline{f}$ = 1, .5%, $\underline{n}$ = 39)
arts theater, box, center, chalk, charmed, circus,
closeness, compass, cross, cube, de Francois,
draw, enclosed, entire, game, mystic, number,
of friends, park, path, pencil, pi, pie, pin,
radial, radius, rectangle, ridiculous, Scotland,
sewing, sit, star, that, them, thin, this,
triangle, unity, Zeta Psi

Cut   (Scissors;   )

No.	Response	F	M	Tot.	%
1.	knife	9	10	19	10.4
2.	scissors	10	2	12	6.6
3.	hurt	5	6	11	6.0
4.	blood	7	3	10	5.5
5.	out	5	4	9	4.9
6.	finger	7	1	8	4.4
7.	tear	4	4	8	4.4
8.	bleed	3	4	7	3.8
9.	slice	4	3	7	3.9
10.	up	1	5	6	3.3
11.	paper	4	1	5	2.7
12.	down	2	2	4	2.2
13.	arm	1	2	3	1.6
14.	bread	1	2	3	1.6
15.	off	1	2	3	1.6
16.	saw	3	0	3	1.6
17.	across	2	0	2	1.1
18.	break	2	0	2	1.1
19.	deep	1	1	2	1.1
20.	glass	2	0	2	1.1
21.	grass	1	1	2	1.1
22.	hair	2	0	2	1.1
23.	hand	1	1	2	1.1
24.	it	0	2	2	1.1
25.	open	1	1	2	1.1
26.	pain	1	1	2	1.1
27.	razor	0	2	2	1.1
28.	run	1	1	2	1.1
29.	sever	0	2	2	1.1
30.	slash	1	1	2	1.1
31.	throat	2	0	2	1.1

($\underline{f}$ = 1, .5%, $\underline{n}$ = 34)
antiseptic, back, blend, blitz, buy, class, clean,
cutting, dig, dolls, edge, fix, fold, grow, heal,
her, in, it out, material, me, meat, red, ribbon,
rip, scar, sew, shape, sharp, short, some, stab,
thin, through, tree

Clean   (Bath;   )

No.	Response	F	M	Tot.	%
1.	dirty	32	32	64	35.1
2.	neat	5	2	7	3.8
3.	white	5	2	7	3.8
4.	clothes	4	2	6	3.3
5.	house	4	2	6	3.3
6.	nice	4	2	6	3.3
7.	soap	2	4	6	3.3
8.	good	3	2	5	2.7
9.	up	3	2	5	2.7
10.	Mr.	0	4	4	2.2
11.	clear	1	2	3	1.6
12.	cut	0	3	3	1.6
13.	shower	1	2	3	1.6
14.	wash	3	0	3	1.6
15.	bright	1	1	2	1.1
16.	room	1	1	2	1.1
17.	shine	1	1	2	1.1
18.	sterile	2	0	2	1.1
19.	teeth	1	1	2	1.1
20.	work	1	1	2	1.1

($\underline{f}$ = 1. .5%, $\underline{n}$ = 42)
air, careful, cold, diaper, dirt, dry, erotic,
expected, face, Ford, free, fresh, hair, healthy,
heart, impeccable, important, just, kitchen, man,
necessary, now, over, rug, rut, sanitary, scrub,
shining, silver, snow, sox, sparkle, sparkling,
spotless, stove, sweet, table, tidy, towel,
underwear, water, worker

Colder   (Hotter;   )

No.	Response	F	M	Tot.	%
1.	hotter	19	16	35	19.2
2.	warmer	18	15	33	18.1
3.	ice	11	7	18	9.9
4.	winter	6	3	9	4.9
5.	than	4	4	8	4.4
6.	snow	4	2	6	3.3
7.	hot	3	2	5	2.7
8.	warm	1	4	5	2.7
9.	freeze	2	2	4	2.2
10.	weather	2	2	4	2.2
11.	freezing	3	0	3	1.6
12.	coldest	1	1	2	1.1
13.	frigid	2	0	2	1.1
14.	icy	1	1	2	1.1
15.	shiver	1	1	2	1.1
16.	sweater	2	0	2	1.1
17.	water	1	1	2	1.1
18.	white	1	1	2	1.1

($\underline{f}$ = 1, .5%, $\underline{n}$ = 38)
ache, Alaska, Berkeley, blue, change, chill,
chilled, cleaner, clearer, coke, cool, crisp,
cuts, dampness, day, drier, feel, frozen,
glitter, hostile, hurt, mean, milk, O.K., pain,
pole (north), rain, refrigerator, see, soon,
temperature, uncomfortable, valuable, water,
wet, wind, window, windy

Color   (Yellow;   )

No.	Response	F	M	Tot.	%
1.	red	32	26	58	31.8
2.	blue	17	18	35	19.2
3.	green	9	5	14	7.7
4.	bright	7	5	12	6.6
5.	black	6	4	10	5.5
6.	blind	1	4	5	2.7
7.	white	1	3	4	2.2
8.	yellow	3	1	4	2.2
9.	brown	0	2	2	1.1
10.	crayons	2	0	2	1.1
11.	hair	2	0	2	1.1
12.	light	0	2	2	1.1
13.	rainbow	0	2	2	1.1

($\underline{f}$ = 1, .5%, $\underline{n}$ = 30)
blank, beauty, colorwheel, dark, exciting, fast,
gay, glass, hue, item, life, multiplicity, of,
orange, picture, pigment, pink, rose, run, scheme,
see, somber, subtle, T.V., unhappy, vibrant,
vivid, warm, wheel, why

Come   (Go;   )

No.	Response	F	M	Tot.	%
1.	go	30	17	47	25.8
2.	here	18	17	35	19.2
3.	on	4	7	11	6.0
4.	came	5	4	9	4.5
5.	now	4	4	8	4.4
6.	see	3	3	6	3.3
7.	in	1	4	5	2.7
8.	over	4	1	5	2.7
9.	to	2	3	5	2.7
10.	home	2	2	4	2.2
11.	again	1	2	3	1.6
12.	please	3	0	3	1.6
13.	along	2	0	2	1.1
14.	away	0	2	2	1.1
15.	back	1	1	2	1.1
16.	down	1	1	2	1.1
17.	walk	2	0	2	1.1
18.	went	1	1	2	1.1

Come (Go;) (contd)

No.	Response	F	M	Tot.	%
19.	where	1	1	2	1.1

($\underline{f}$ = 1, .5%, $\underline{n}$ = 27)
advance, approach, arrive, beckon, children, close, coming, command, enter, game, hither, later, live, lose, me, move, near, night, phase, place, quick, to me, true, up, with, wonder, you

Course (Of;)

No.	Response	F	M	Tot.	%
1.	psychology	14	6	20	11.0
2.	school	12	5	17	9.3
3.	class	10	4	14	7.7
4.	study(ies)	6	6	12	6.6
5.	grade(s)	4	5	9	4.9
6.	golf	5	2	7	3.8
7.	rough	2	5	7	3.8
8.	subject	4	3	7	3.8
9.	hard	3	3	6	3.3
10.	action	3	2	5	2.7
11.	of	1	3	4	2.2
12.	route	2	2	4	2.2
13.	intercourse	2	1	3	1.6
14.	lecture	1	2	3	1.6
15.	stream	2	1	3	1.6
16.	work	2	1	3	1.6
17.	answer	1	1	2	1.1
18.	boring	0	2	2	1.1
19.	coarse	0	2	2	1.1
20.	Psychology 1B	0	2	2	1.1
21.	river	2	0	2	1.1
22.	run	1	1	2	1.1
23.	smooth	2	0	2	1.1
24.	take	2	0	2	1.1
25.	this	1	1	2	1.1

($\underline{f}$ = 1, .5%, $\underline{n}$ = 39)
bind, change, confusion, direction, education, even, event, fine, flunk, French, fruitless, good, hair, harsh, history, inter-, Latin, learning, natural, obstacles, obvious, path, plan, professor, road, sandpaper, section, set, stream bed, test, time, trail, unit, vulgar, water, way, went, woman, worse
(Illegible - 1)

Crowd (People;)

No.	Response	F	M	Tot.	%
1.	people	40	25	65	35.7
2.	mob	12	10	22	12.1
3.	around	1	4	5	2.7
4.	group	2	3	5	2.7
5.	large	1	3	4	2.2
6.	push	2	2	4	2.2
7.	gather	2	1	3	1.6
8.	lonely	1	2	3	1.6
9.	many	0	3	3	1.6
10.	mass	2	1	3	1.6
11.	noise	2	1	3	1.6
12.	place	0	3	3	1.6
13.	room	1	2	3	1.6
14.	demonstration	1	1	2	1.1
15.	game(s)	0	2	2	1.1
16.	gathering	1	1	2	1.1
17.	lost	1	1	2	1.1
18.	noisy	1	1	2	1.1
19.	rally	2	0	2	1.1
20.	riot	2	0	2	1.1
21.	Sproul	1	1	2	1.1

($\underline{f}$ = 1, .5%, $\underline{n}$ = 40)
alone, attention, bad, big, boo, bunch, circle,

Crowd (People;) (contd)

close, crowded, crowds, demonstrate, demonstrators, dizzy, hear, heavy, here, in, interesting, loneliness, me, mess, milling, mouth, out, pandemonium, pleaser, Reisman, roar, scare, scared, shout, sole, stand, stomp, street, stuffy, together, up, warm, wild

Cry (Baby;)

No.	Response	F	M	Tot.	%
1.	baby	14	11	25	13.7
2.	tear(s)	17	6	23	12.6
3.	laugh	8	6	14	7.7
4.	sad	7	5	12	6.6
5.	out	3	7	10	5.5
6.	loud	4	3	7	3.8
7.	sob(s)	3	3	6	3.3
8.	weep	5	1	6	3.3
9.	child	1	2	3	1.6
10.	scream	1	2	3	1.6
11.	shout	2	1	3	1.6
12.	wail	2	1	3	1.6
13.	aloud	1	1	2	1.1
14.	feel	1	1	2	1.1
15.	happy	1	1	2	1.1
16.	hard	2	0	2	1.1
17.	help	1	1	2	1.1
18.	howl	1	1	2	1.1
19.	noise	0	2	2	1.1
20.	pain	0	2	2	1.1
21.	sigh	0	2	2	1.1
22.	sing	0	2	2	1.1
23.	sorror	0	2	2	1.1
24.	unhappy	1	1	2	1.1
25.	whine	0	2	2	1.1
26.	why	1	1	2	1.1
27.	yell	2	0	2	1.1

($\underline{f}$ = 1, .5%, $\underline{n}$ = 37)
a lot, asleep, bawl, behave, call, can't, complain, cried, die, eagle, emotional, freedom, grief, grimace, hurt, indecision, lamb, lie, lonely, loudly, love, moan, mourn, no, now, peace, said, screamed, shame, softly, sorry, squeal, twice, want, wept, whale, what about?

Dark (Light; Deep)

No.	Response	F	M	Tot.	%
1.	light	30	25	55	30.2
2.	night	15	8	23	12.6
3.	black	9	0	9	4.9
4.	shadow(s)	4	5	9	4.9
5.	bright	1	6	7	3.8
6.	room	4	3	7	3.8
7.	horse	0	3	3	1.6
8.	stairs	1	2	3	1.6
9.	Alvin	1	1	2	1.1
10.	brown	1	1	2	1.1
11.	cave	1	1	2	1.1
12.	closet	2	0	2	1.1
13.	dim	1	1	2	1.1
14.	low	2	0	2	1.1
15.	-ness	0	2	2	1.1
16.	scary	2	0	2	1.1
17.	silent	2	0	2	1.1
18.	white	1	1	2	1.1

($\underline{f}$ = 1, .5%, $\underline{n}$ = 46)
Al, alley, below, cloud, cold, colors, corner, dank, dark, darker, deep, down, eyebrows, eyes, fink, flowers, friendly, girl, gloom, green, hall,

Dark   (Light; Deep) (contd)

No.	Response	F	M	Tot.	%

isolation, lark, long, mind, mystery, narrow,
nice, nite, obscure, out, passage, peaceful,
river, shade, sin, skinned, sky, sleep, soft,
storm, there, valley, well, windows, womb

Death   (; Sickness)

No.	Response	F	M	Tot.	%
1.	life	28	21	49	26.9
2.	die	7	5	12	6.6
3.	end	4	5	9	4.9
4.	black	5	2	7	3.8
5.	dark	5	0	5	2.7
6.	grave	4	1	5	2.7
7.	sad	3	2	5	2.7
8.	bad	0	4	4	2.2
9.	gone	3	1	4	2.2
10.	coffin	0	3	3	1.6
11.	dead	2	1	3	1.6
12.	sorrow	1	2	3	1.6
13.	away	1	1	2	1.1
14.	birth	0	2	2	1.1
15.	come(s)	2	0	2	1.1
16.	dying	2	0	2	1.1
17.	fear	2	0	2	1.1
18.	inevitable	2	0	2	1.1
19.	mourn	1	1	2	1.1
20.	salesman	0	2	2	1.1
21.	skull	1	1	2	1.1

($\underline{f}$ = 1, .5%, $\underline{n}$ = 54)
alive, awful, clouds, dealing, earth, emptiness,
envious, escape, fantastic, fog, forever, freedom,
friendly, good, grief, grim, happens, health,
heaven, horrible, ill, infiltrates, J.F.K.,
Kennedy, live, lonesome, maybe, me, nice, no,
nothing, now, of a Salesman, out, pain, part,
peace, rate, rest, shadow, silent, someday,
sometime, still, tired, universe, unhappiness,
unpleasant, valley, walk, watch, will, wing, yes

Die   (Live;   )

No.	Response	F	M	Tot.	%
1.	live	24	22	46	25.3
2.	dead	8	11	19	10.4
3.	death	9	7	16	8.8
4.	end	6	4	10	5.5
5.	hard	3	3	6	3.3
6.	forever	3	1	4	2.2
7.	leave	3	0	3	1.6
8.	sad	1	2	3	1.6
9.	sleep	3	0	3	1.6
10.	birth	2	0	2	1.1
11.	dye	0	2	2	1.1
12.	fear	2	0	2	1.1
13.	grave	0	2	2	1.1
14.	old	0	2	2	1.1
15.	soon	2	0	2	1.1
16.	stop	1	1	2	1.1
17.	when	0	2	2	1.1
18.	young	2	0	2	1.1

($\underline{f}$ = 1, .5%, $\underline{n}$ = 53)
alive, awake, bliss, block, born, bury, bye,
cast, cease, coffin, cold, come, craps, depart,
depression, dice, down, else, empty, family, for,
gamble, gone, hurrah, ill, inconsequential, kill,
later, leap, life, living, loot, man, mob, must,
never, no, nothing, now, once, pass, peace, pity,
quiet, red, sadness, someday, sorrow, sterben,
then, well, white, yes

Dirt   (Earth;   )

No.	Response	F	M	Tot.	%
1.	clean	8	13	21	11.5
2.	mud	18	3	21	11.5
3.	brown	12	3	15	8.2
4.	ground	8	5	13	7.1
5.	filth	5	5	10	5.5
6.	dirty	3	4	7	3.8
7.	earth	3	3	6	3.3
8.	grime	1	5	6	3.3
9.	black	2	2	4	2.2
10.	dust	2	2	4	2.2
11.	floor	2	1	3	1.6
12.	grimy	3	0	3	1.6
13.	road	0	3	3	1.6
14.	wash	3	0	3	1.6
15.	dark	2	0	2	1.1
16.	grass	1	1	2	1.1
17.	house	0	2	2	1.1
18.	plant(s)	1	1	2	1.1
19.	sand	1	1	2	1.1
20.	shirt	1	1	2	1.1
21.	shoe(s)	1	1	2	1.1
22.	soil	1	1	2	1.1
23.	soot	0	2	2	1.1
24.	track	0	2	2	1.1

($\underline{f}$ = 1, .5%, $\underline{n}$ = 43)
bad, bath, bike, campus, children, cleanliness,
clod, clothes, country, decay, die, door, dusty,
eat, elbow, face, farm, feet, food, foul, grease,
gray, loader, lust, mess, must, pants, path,
poor, rubbish, shovel, shower, sickening, smut,
snow, soft, thick, throw, toes, toil, ugly,
worm, yes

Disappear   (; Appear)

No.	Response	F	M	Tot.	%
1.	appear	17	16	33	18.1
2.	vanish	16	10	26	14.3
3.	gone	11	4	15	8.2
4.	reappear	4	5	9	4.9
5.	go	4	4	8	4.4
6.	hide	4	2	6	3.3
7.	invisible	3	3	6	3.3
8.	ghost	2	3	5	2.7
9.	away	4	0	4	2.2
10.	magic	1	3	4	2.2
11.	see	2	2	4	2.2
12.	fog	2	1	3	1.6
13.	go away	2	1	3	1.6
14.	smoke	2	1	3	1.6
15.	dark	1	1	2	1.1
16.	fade	1	1	2	1.1
17.	find	0	2	2	1.1
18.	from	1	1	2	1.1
19.	mystery	1	1	2	1.1
20.	never	2	0	2	1.1
21.	now	0	2	2	1.1
22.	quickly	0	2	2	1.1
23.	remove	0	2	2	1.1

($\underline{f}$ = 1, .5%, $\underline{n}$ = 35)
air, amaze, cake, childhood, clue, come, completely, desire, die, discover, dissolve, down, drain,
dust, empty, escape, fire, flaunt, frog, ink,
light, lost, magician, man, mist, no, object,
occurrence, poof, runaway, safety pin, show,
why, wish I could, youth

Do   (Make;   )

No.	Response	F	M	Tot.	%
1.	not	24	16	40	22.0
2.	don't	17	16	33	18.1
3.	it	9	8	17	9.3
4.	you	5	4	9	4.9
5.	act	1	4	5	2.7
6.	make	2	3	5	2.7
7.	this	3	2	5	2.7
8.	work	4	0	4	2.2
9.	did	3	0	3	1.6
10.	something	2	1	3	1.6
11.	what	1	2	3	1.6
12.	yes	2	1	3	1.6
13.	accomplished	2	0	2	1.1
14.	believe	2	0	2	1.1
15.	die	0	2	2	1.1
16.	done	1	1	2	1.1
17.	nothing	2	0	2	1.1
18.	now	0	2	2	1.1
19.	we	1	1	2	1.1

($\underline{f}$ = 1, .5%, $\underline{n}$ = 37)
action, better, care, come, command, complete,
dew, does, do not, effect, exist, forget, good,
here, I, job, line, move, must, now, order,
perform, play, please, re-, see, sing, smile,
so, that, think, too, try, undo, when, will, write
(Illegible - 1)

Door   (; Window)

No.	Response	F	M	Tot.	%
1.	open(s)	22	11	33	18.1
2.	window	19	9	28	15.4
3.	knob	5	11	16	8.8
4.	shut	9	1	10	5.5
5.	close	5	4	9	4.9
6.	bell	2	6	8	4.4
7.	handle	2	6	8	4.4
8.	closed	3	3	6	3.3
9.	slam	3	3	6	3.3
10.	way	3	3	6	3.3
11.	jam	2	2	4	2.2
12.	opening	2	2	4	2.2
13.	room	2	2	4	2.2
14.	jamb	0	3	3	1.6
15.	frame	0	2	2	1.1
16.	green	1	1	2	1.1
17.	knock	2	0	2	1.1
18.	sill	1	1	2	1.1
19.	through	2	0	2	1.1

($\underline{f}$ = 1, .5%, $\underline{n}$ = 27)
bar, ceiling, draft, entrance, flag, floor, free,
gate, hall, hallway, hinge, hole, house, know,
label, latch, mahogany, mat, none, port, portal,
sex, square, stuck, swings, tür, wood

Down   (Sit;   )

No.	Response	F	M	Tot.	%
1.	up	45	31	76	41.7
2.	below	7	7	14	7.7
3.	fall	7	4	11	6.0
4.	under	2	7	9	4.9
5.	there	4	3	7	3.8
6.	ground	4	0	4	2.2
7.	stairs	1	3	4	2.2
8.	town	1	3	4	2.2
9.	hole	2	1	3	1.6
10.	low	2	1	3	1.6
11.	soft	0	3	3	1.6
12.	duck	2	0	2	1.1

Down   (Sit;   ) (contd)

No.	Response	F	M	Tot.	%
13.	earth	1	1	2	1.1
14.	in	1	1	2	1.1
15.	jump	1	1	2	1.1

($\underline{f}$ = 1, .5%, $\underline{n}$ = 36)
and out, around, beat, beside, bloody, blue,
cast, chimney, dark, dead, ditch, dive, downcast,
excitement, feathers, floor, grass, hell, here,
hill, hole, lawn, leaves, lie, no, out, over,
seagull, silky, steep, street, sun, sweep, to,
valley, wind

Dream   (Wish;   )

No.	Response	F	M	Tot.	%
1.	sleep	27	31	58	31.8
2.	night	7	3	10	5.5
3.	sweet	7	0	7	3.8
4.	nightmare	5	1	6	3.3
5.	Freud	3	2	5	2.7
6.	girl	1	4	5	2.7
7.	pleasant	4	1	5	2.7
8.	fantasy	3	1	4	2.2
9.	wish	4	0	4	2.2
10.	awake	2	1	3	1.6
11.	day	0	3	3	1.6
12.	nice	2	1	3	1.6
13.	peace	1	2	3	1.6
14.	bad	1	1	2	1.1
15.	good	2	0	2	1.1
16.	of	1	1	2	1.1
17.	state	1	1	2	1.1
18.	story	0	2	2	1.1
19.	world	0	2	2	1.1

($\underline{f}$ = 1, .5%, $\underline{n}$ = 52)
again, awaken, baby, beautiful, bed, blue, boy,
bright, can't, Chagal, color, creme, deep, demon,
dreamt, fog, fun, groggy, had, happy, hazy,
home, homesick, I, I don't dream, image, land,
like, love, lover, me, never, often, open,
peaceful, pillow, pretend, relax, reverie, sand,
see, strange, subconscious, surprise, think,
thought, time, uneasy, unreal, wake, wonder,
wonderful
(Illegible - 2)

Drink   (Whiskey; Thirsty)

No.	Response	F	M	Tot.	%
1.	water	26	19	45	24.7
2.	drunk	10	13	23	12.6
3.	beer	5	7	12	6.6
4.	drank	7	4	11	6.0
5.	thirsty	6	2	8	4.4
6.	wine	1	6	7	3.8
7.	thirst	2	4	6	3.3
8.	eat	2	3	5	2.7
9.	glass	2	3	5	2.7
10.	liquid(s)	2	3	5	2.7
11.	milk	2	3	5	2.7
12.	booze	1	1	2	1.1
13.	coffee	2	0	2	1.1
14.	cool	2	0	2	1.1
15.	guzzle	1	1	2	1.1
16.	hard	0	2	2	1.1
17.	liquor	2	0	2	1.1
18.	merry	1	1	2	1.1
19.	sip	1	1	2	1.1
20.	swallow	1	1	2	1.1
21.	taste	2	0	2	1.1
22.	up	1	1	2	1.1

Drink   (Whiskey; Thirsty) (contd)

No.	Response	F	M	Tot.	%
23.	whiskey	2	0	2	1.1

($\underline{f}$ = 1, .5%, $\underline{n}$ = 25)
beverage, champagne, cold, deep, detest, Diet-Rite, drive, father, fun, gone, happy, hot, it, pop, rum, Scotch, sink, sleep, sob, soda, soft, tea, throat, Tom Collins, well
(Illegible - 1)

Drinking   (; Eating)

No.	Response	F	M	Tot.	%
1.	water	21	12	33	18.1
2.	drunk	9	13	22	12.1
3.	beer	6	5	11	6.0
4.	eating	4	3	7	3.8
5.	fun	3	2	5	2.7
6.	smoking	2	3	5	2.7
7.	wine	3	2	5	2.7
8.	thirst	2	2	4	2.2
9.	thirsty	2	2	4	2.2
10.	liquid	3	0	3	1.6
11.	liquor	3	0	3	1.6
12.	party(ies)	2	1	3	1.6
13.	alcohol	0	2	2	1.1
14.	booze	1	1	2	1.1
15.	drink	0	2	2	1.1
16.	fountain	1	1	2	1.1
17.	glass	2	0	2	1.1
18.	good	1	1	2	1.1
19.	gourd	2	0	2	1.1
20.	guzzling	1	1	2	1.1
21.	hard	2	0	2	1.1
22.	laughing	1	1	2	1.1
23.	no	1	1	2	1.1
24.	rum	1	1	2	1.1
25.	sad	0	2	2	1.1
26.	singing	1	1	2	1.1

($\underline{f}$ = 1, .5%, $\underline{n}$ = 49)
bored, bourbon, champagne, club, coke, college, cups, disgusting, divine, eat, enjoyable, extent, father, full, fool, Gene, gin, habit, helps, horror, imbibing, lab, life, light, lots, me, much, nice, now, pleasant, quench, reveling, sang, Scotch, seeing, sick, sing, sleepy, soaking, sobbing, social, spilling, spitting, superfluous, swallow, uncontrolled, wet, whiskey, what

Drunk   (; Whiskey)

No.	Response	F	M	Tot.	%
1.	beer	6	8	14	7.7
2.	drink(s)	3	11	14	7.7
3.	sick	6	5	11	6.0
4.	wine	4	5	9	4.9
5.	drank	4	4	8	4.4
6.	liquor	5	3	8	4.4
7.	water	6	1	7	3.8
8.	sober	4	2	6	3.3
9.	happy	3	2	5	2.7
10.	alcohol	2	2	4	2.2
11.	no	3	0	3	1.6
12.	stagger	1	2	3	1.6
13.	booze	1	1	2	1.1
14.	bum	1	1	2	1.1
15.	fun	1	1	2	1.1
16.	gin	1	1	2	1.1
17.	gone	1	1	2	1.1
18.	good	2	0	2	1.1
19.	inebriated	2	0	2	1.1
20.	me	0	2	2	1.1

Drunk   (; Whiskey) (contd)

No.	Response	F	M	Tot.	%
21.	never	1	1	2	1.1
22.	sunk	0	2	2	1.1
23.	tipsy	0	2	2	1.1

($\underline{f}$ = 1, .5%, $\underline{n}$ = 67)
away, bombed, boys, champagne, crazy, darn, detest, drinking, driver, driving, ecstasy, Edward, father, feel, fool, Frank, gassed, gay, hangover, happiness, high, horrible, hung, hunk, interesting, intoxicated, laughter, love, man, mentally incoherent, milk, mother, much, night, obnoxious, often, out-of-it, party, picnic, pity, red, sad, Scotch, senseless, shit, silly, skunk, sleepy, smoke, soused, still, stoned, stumble, stupid, Susie, tramp, trouble, ugly, unfortunate, unhappy, uninhibited, vino, vodka, waver, whiskey, wobbly, yes
(Illegible - 1)

Dry   (; Thirsty)

No.	Response	F	M	Tot.	%
1.	wet	36	30	66	36.2
2.	clean	4	5	9	4.9
3.	clothes	6	1	7	3.8
4.	ice	2	4	6	3.3
5.	tear(s)	5	1	6	3.3
6.	up	2	4	6	3.3
7.	arid	2	3	5	2.7
8.	martini	1	3	4	2.2
9.	thirsty	2	2	4	2.2
10.	cold	2	1	3	1.6
11.	desert	1	2	3	1.6
12.	eye(s)	2	1	3	1.6
13.	hair	3	0	3	1.6
14.	mouth	3	0	3	1.6
15.	bone(s)	2	0	2	1.1
16.	cleaner	0	2	2	1.1
17.	hot	1	1	2	1.1
18.	it	1	1	2	1.1
19.	nose	2	0	2	1.1

($\underline{f}$ = 1, .5%, $\underline{n}$ = 44)
alone, bread, calf, chemistry, cleaning, cracked, dead, dishes, ears, eyed, feel, feet, gin, goods, hay, hurt, kill, me, nausea, off, often, out, parched, powder, rinse, rot, salt, sand, scaly, sec, sherry, still, sun, thirst, towel, tower, try, warm, water, well, wine, wipe, wit, yellow

Eat   (; Hungry)

No.	Response	F	M	Tot.	%
1.	drink	31	27	58	31.8
2.	food	27	28	55	30.2
3.	hungry	4	2	6	3.3
4.	well	2	2	4	2.2
5.	ate	1	2	3	1.6
6.	fat	1	2	3	1.6
7.	gorge	3	0	3	1.6
8.	ball	0	2	2	1.1
9.	foot	0	2	2	1.1
10.	lot(s)	2	0	2	1.1
11.	me	0	2	2	1.1
12.	meat	1	1	2	1.1
13.	mouth	2	0	2	1.1
14.	much	2	0	2	1.1

($\underline{f}$ = 1, .5% $\underline{n}$ = 36)
candy, cherries, consume, devour, digest, dinner, egg, famished, feast, full, get fat, guano, hamburger, heartily, heavily, hit, hunger, live, lunch, milk, more, munch, never, no, nothing, now,

Eat　　　　(　; Hungry) (contd)

No.	Response	F	M	Tot.	%

occupy, often, quick, sick, steak, swollen, table,
too much, weight, yummy

Ever　　　　(Hardly;　)

No.	Response	F	M	Tot.	%
1.	never	29	30	59	32.4
2.	always	19	9	28	15.4
3.	more	9	11	20	11.0
4.	forever	8	2	10	5.5
5.	after	2	2	4	2.2
6.	for	0	4	4	2.2
7.	lasting	0	4	4	2.2
8.	now	2	2	4	2.2
9.	done	2	0	2	1.1
10.	green	1	1	2	1.1
11.	perhaps	2	0	2	1.1
12.	present	1	1	2	1.1
13.	ready	0	2	2	1.1

($\underline{f}$ = 1, .5%, $\underline{n}$ = 39)
action, again, been, better, ending, eternal,
eternity, ever, gone, happy, heavens, hope,
infinity, Johnny, last, live, long, more shall be,
no, not, once, only, outer space, prove, shall,
since, skepticism, so, then, there, though, tree,
true, universe, wandering, was, wear, without,
wondering

Fast (Quickly, Running, Slow, Slowly, Swift;　　)

No.	Response	F	M	Tot.	%
1.	slow	47	40	87	47.8
2.	run	7	4	11	6.0
3.	quick	4	3	7	3.8
4.	speed	4	3	7	3.8
5.	car	3	3	6	3.3
6.	faster	4	1	5	2.7
7.	talk	3	2	5	2.7
8.	moving	1	3	4	2.2
9.	talker	2	1	3	1.6
10.	eat	1	1	2	1.1
11.	guy	2	0	2	1.1
12.	hungry	1	1	2	1.1
13.	move	1	1	2	1.1
14.	rapid	0	2	2	1.1
15.	still	1	1	2	1.1
16.	train	0	2	2	1.1

($\underline{f}$ = 1, .5%, $\underline{n}$ = 33)
acting, bread, breathless, change, die, do,
enthusiastic, food, game, gone, hard, head,
home, horse, Jones, last, meal, moon, not good,
now, pill, plane, purr, rat race, runner, speedy,
starve, straight, swift, then, walk, worker, zoom

Fat　　　　(　; Short)

No.	Response	F	M	Tot.	%
1.	thin	16	18	34	18.7
2.	skinny	12	13	25	13.7
3.	obese	3	4	7	3.8
4.	man	2	4	6	3.3
5.	pig	4	2	6	3.3
6.	blubber	3	2	5	2.7
7.	slim	2	3	5	2.7
8.	food(s)	3	1	4	2.2
9.	girl	1	3	4	2.2

Fat　　　　(　; Short) (contd)

No.	Response	F	M	Tot.	%
10.	ugly	3	1	4	2.2
11.	big	1	2	3	1.6
12.	heavy	1	2	3	1.6
13.	me	3	0	3	1.6
14.	rat	2	1	3	1.6
15.	short	1	2	3	1.6
16.	woman	1	2	3	1.6
17.	boy	0	2	2	1.1
18.	butter	0	2	2	1.1
19.	calories	2	0	2	1.1
20.	chubby	0	2	2	1.1
21.	grow	1	1	2	1.1
22.	lady	2	0	2	1.1
23.	lipid	2	0	2	1.1
24.	person	1	1	2	1.1
25.	plump	1	1	2	1.1
26.	round	1	1	2	1.1

($\underline{f}$ = 1, .5%, $\underline{n}$ = 44)
acid, adipose, banana, bony, cheeks, cheese-
burgers, cholesterol, diet, eat, fat, fatter,
flabby, frail, glob, globule, glycol, grease,
greasy, hard, heart attack, horse, huge, Italian,
jolly, lard, layers, lazy, lean, look, lot, lumps,
mama, not, one, overweight, people, protein,
protrude, pudgy, slob, slobby, soft, tissue,
yellow

Fatter　　　　(Thinner;　)

No.	Response	F	M	Tot.	%
1.	thinner	31	18	49	26.9
2.	skinnier	9	3	12	6.6
3.	eat	2	4	6	3.3
4.	slimmer	2	4	6	3.3
5.	diet	5	0	5	2.7
6.	food	4	1	5	2.7
7.	skinny	3	2	5	2.7
8.	thin	3	2	5	2.7
9.	wider	1	4	5	2.7
10.	slim	2	2	4	2.2
11.	bigger	1	2	3	1.6
12.	pig	1	2	3	1.6
13.	than	3	0	3	1.6
14.	big	0	2	2	1.1
15.	calories	2	0	2	1.1
16.	fattest	1	1	2	1.1
17.	heavy	1	1	2	1.1
18.	larger	0	2	2	1.1
19.	man	0	2	2	1.1
20.	me	2	0	2	1.1
21.	no	1	1	2	1.1
22.	obese	0	2	2	1.1
23.	plump	1	1	2	1.1
24.	round	2	0	2	1.1
25.	shorter	0	2	2	1.1
26.	stomach	0	2	2	1.1
27.	ugly	0	2	2	1.1
28.	wide	0	2	2	1.1

($\underline{f}$ = 1, .5%, $\underline{n}$ = 41)
belt, better, bloated, boy, bread & butter,
brother, burst, butter, cheeks, eater, filled,
gigantic, girl, grotesque, grow, guess so,
heart, lady, leaner, lethargic, lighter,
Metrecal, milk, more, mother, never, obeser,
people, problem, repugnant, sad, slender,
sloppy, sorry, stout, studying, stuff, uglier,
waist, women, worse

Fear (Afraid;)

No.	Response	F	M	Tot.	%
1.	afraid	9	5	14	7.7
2.	fright	9	4	13	7.1
3.	scared	7	4	11	6.0
4.	hate	4	6	10	5.5
5.	scare	4	2	6	3.3
6.	anger	2	3	5	2.7
7.	anxiety	4	1	5	2.7
8.	dark	5	0	5	2.7
9.	not	1	4	5	2.7
10.	bad	1	3	4	2.2
11.	courage	1	3	4	2.2
12.	trembling	1	3	4	2.2
13.	cry	2	1	3	1.6
14.	pain	2	1	3	1.6
15.	tremble	1	2	3	1.6
16.	unknown	3	0	3	1.6
17.	hide	2	0	2	1.1
18.	horror	2	0	2	1.1
19.	itself	0	2	2	1.1
20.	never	0	2	2	1.1
21.	run	0	2	2	1.1
22.	what	2	0	2	1.1

($\underline{f}$ = 1, .5%, $\underline{n}$ = 72)
about, animal, birds, black, brave, bugs, chill,
cliffs, closed, cold, comfort, composure, confidence, crowd, danger, dear, death, demonstrations,
dislike, dread, drive, elicit, emotion, evoked,
expression, fall, feeling, fire, foreign, frightened, frightening, from, -ful, God, grades, grief,
hair, hatred, havoc, height, help, here, hold,
hope, horrible, ignorance, laugh, love, man,
metus (L.), move, no, oppression, panic, parents,
rage, real, refuge, rules, scream, shake, shout,
smell, snake, some, sorrow, stricken, terror,
them, think, Tom, woman

Feet (Shoes;)

No.	Response	F	M	Tot.	%
1.	shoe(s)	14	16	30	16.5
2.	toe(s)	16	8	24	13.2
3.	walk	14	7	21	11.5
4.	hand(s)	7	4	11	6.0
5.	leg(s)	5	5	10	5.5
6.	foot	4	5	9	4.9
7.	cold	2	4	6	3.3
8.	hurt	5	1	6	3.3
9.	bare	3	0	3	1.6
10.	run	2	1	3	1.6
11.	stand	0	3	3	1.6
12.	tired	2	1	3	1.6
13.	ache	2	0	2	1.1
14.	flat	0	2	2	1.1
15.	large	1	1	2	1.1
16.	sore	1	1	2	1.1
17.	smell	0	2	2	1.1
18.	smelly	2	0	2	1.1
19.	two	2	0	2	1.1
20.	warm	0	2	2	1.1
21.	wet	2	0	2	1.1

($\underline{f}$ = 1, .5%, $\underline{n}$ = 35)
ankles, apart, arms, athlete, below, chair, dance,
difficult, dirty, felt, fought, go, grass, hot,
in, Indians, little, measurement, pink, place,
pretty, running, sandals, sat, small, spoiled,
sting, stink, stool, sweet, toenails, tracks,
tree, ugly, yards

Finger (; Hand)

No.	Response	F	M	Tot.	%
1.	hand	25	22	47	25.8
2.	nail	12	7	19	10.4
3.	point(s)	11	5	16	8.8
4.	ring	7	8	15	8.2
5.	cut	6	3	9	4.9
6.	toe	8	1	9	4.9
7.	tip(s)	3	4	7	3.8
8.	thumb	2	3	5	2.7
9.	digit	2	2	4	2.2
10.	long	4	0	4	2.2
11.	broken	0	3	3	1.6
12.	bowl	0	2	2	1.1
13.	foot	2	0	2	1.1
14.	move	2	0	2	1.1
15.	snap	0	2	2	1.1

($\underline{f}$ = 1, .5%, $\underline{n}$ = 36)
appendage, arm, bang, bend, bite, cry, dirty,
donut, five, fuck, gold, his, hurt, index, it,
lick, lickin', lift, linger, love, mingle,
moving, painting, phalanges, polish, sex,
short, sign, small, straight, stuck, tiny,
touch, victory, waggling, write

Floor (; Carpet)

No.	Response	F	M	Tot.	%
1.	wax	11	9	20	11.0
2.	wood	7	10	17	9.3
3.	ceiling	6	8	14	7.7
4.	ground	4	6	10	5.5
5.	rug	5	4	9	4.9
6.	board	2	4	6	3.3
7.	hard	3	3	6	3.3
8.	wall(s)	4	2	6	3.3
9.	clean	2	2	4	2.2
10.	dirty	4	0	4	2.2
11.	door	1	3	4	2.2
12.	polish	3	1	4	2.2
13.	tile(s)	3	1	4	2.2
14.	bottom	1	2	3	1.6
15.	dirt	1	2	3	1.6
16.	sit	2	1	3	1.6
17.	sweep	2	1	3	1.6
18.	chair	1	1	2	1.1
19.	fall	2	0	2	1.1
20.	first	1	1	2	1.1
21.	green	1	1	2	1.1
22.	mop	1	2	2	1.1
23.	scuff	1	1	2	1.1
24.	table	1	1	2	1.1
25.	walker	2	0	2	1.1
26.	waxed	2	0	2	1.1

($\underline{f}$ = 1, .5%, $\underline{n}$ = 44)
bare, below, beneath, broom, care, covering,
dance, dorm, foot, hall, hide, him, house,
Johnson's, kill, lie, linoleum, main, mat, plow,
polisher, roof, sand, scrub, shiny, show, sitting,
sleep, slip, solid, space, stand, still, store,
support, sweeper, third, 2, under, varnish, walk,
wash, wet, wooden

Flower (Stem;)

No.	Response	F	M	Tot.	%
1.	pretty	6	6	12	6.6
2.	rose	8	4	12	6.6
3.	pot	3	8	11	6.0
4.	petal(s)	5	5	10	5.5
5.	smell	5	5	10	5.5
6.	bloom	4	4	8	4.4

Flower (Stem;) (contd)

No.	Response	F	M	Tot.	%
7.	daisy	5	2	7	3.8
8.	sweet	3	3	6	3.3
9.	yellow	3	2	5	2.7
10.	beauty	1	3	4	2.2
11.	garden	4	0	4	2.2
12.	bird	2	1	3	1.6
13.	blossom	0	3	3	1.6
14.	bud	1	2	3	1.6
15.	color	1	2	3	1.6
16.	drum	2	1	3	1.6
17.	song	2	1	3	1.6
18.	stem	2	1	3	1.6
19.	beautiful	1	1	2	1.1
20.	bee	1	1	2	1.1
21.	bright	2	0	2	1.1
22.	delicate	1	1	2	1.1
23.	flour	0	2	2	1.1
24.	grass	1	1	2	1.1
25.	grow	1	1	2	1.1
26.	plant	1	1	2	1.1
27.	red	2	0	2	1.1
28.	seed	0	2	2	1.1
29.	show	1	1	2	1.1
30.	vase	0	2	2	1.1

($\underline{f}$ = 1, .5% $\underline{n}$ = 47)
again, arrangement, aster, basket, bed, box, bread, bush, cart, colorful, chrysanthemum, cut, daffodil, decoration, drum song, fade, farmer, fragile, fragrance, fragrant, gay, girl, green, happiness, insect, joy, lovely, meadow, mower, nature, nice, none, odor, purple, sale, sensuous, ship, shop, simplicity, spring, star, sunlight, tree, tulip, wave, wildwood, wonder
(Illegible - 1)

Flowers (Blossom;)

No.	Response	F	M	Tot.	%
1.	pretty	17	9	26	14.3
2.	smell	9	7	16	8.8
3.	pot(s)	3	10	13	7.1
4.	rose(s)	6	3	9	4.9
5.	color(s)	6	2	8	4.4
6.	trees	2	6	8	4.4
7.	bloom(s)	5	2	7	3.8
8.	yellow	4	3	7	3.8
9.	grow	2	4	6	3.3
10.	sweet	2	4	6	3.3
11.	garden	3	2	5	2.7
12.	petals	3	2	5	2.7
13.	beautiful	2	1	3	1.6
14.	red	3	0	3	1.6
15.	bed(s)	0	2	2	1.1
16.	blossom(s)	1	1	2	1.1
17.	daisies	1	1	2	1.1
18.	open(s)	2	0	2	1.1
19.	pink	0	2	2	1.1
20.	song(s)	1	1	2	1.1

($\underline{f}$ = 1, .5%, $\underline{n}$ = 46)
artificial, away, beauty, bees, birds, blooming, bouquet, bright, broken vase, bunch, candy, carnations, cool, country, cut, daffodils, dead, death, die, fields, gone, good, grass, green, happiness, hospital, lilacs, many, nature, nice, none, nothing, odor, pick, picked, plant, seeds, sickness, spring, stems, stream, Sue, sun, weeds, white, wildwood

Foggy (Clearer;)

No.	Response	F	M	Tot.	%
1.	day	13	14	27	14.8
2.	dew	10	12	22	12.1
3.	San Francisco	11	4	15	8.2
4.	cold	6	7	13	7.1
5.	cloudy	4	6	10	5.5
6.	clear	2	5	7	3.8
7.	London	3	3	6	3.3
8.	gray	4	1	5	2.7
9.	mist	2	3	5	2.7
10.	night	2	3	5	2.7
11.	wet	2	3	5	2.7
12.	Bay	3	1	4	2.2
13.	damp	4	0	4	2.2
14.	cloud(s)	1	2	3	1.6
15.	misty	2	1	3	1.6
16.	morning	1	2	3	1.6
17.	unclear	0	3	3	1.6
18.	weather	2	1	3	1.6
19.	beach	1	1	2	1.1
20.	city	2	0	2	1.1
21.	cool	1	1	2	1.1
22.	dim	1	1	2	1.1
23.	rainy	2	0	2	1.1
24.	sky	2	0	2	1.1
25.	smoke	2	0	2	1.1

($\underline{f}$ = 1, .5%, $\underline{n}$ = 24)
accident, Berkeley, bottom, bright, cat, colder, dank, dingy, dry, friendly, Frisco, hair, haze, hazy, isolation, midst, mysterious, ocean, smog, smoky, soupy, storm, sunny, thoughts
(Illegible - 1)

Food (Eating, Hungry, Stomach; Bread, Cabbage)

No.	Response	F	M	Tot.	%
1.	eat	35	26	61	33.5
2.	hungry	9	10	19	10.4
3.	good	10	1	11	6.0
4.	drink	3	6	9	4.9
5.	hunger	3	4	7	3.8
6.	cake	2	1	3	1.6
7.	health	2	1	3	1.6
8.	meal	1	2	3	1.6
9.	thought	0	3	3	1.6
10.	bread	0	2	2	1.1
11.	fun	0	2	2	1.1
12.	lunch	1	1	2	1.1
13.	meat	1	1	2	1.1
14.	milk	1	1	2	1.1
15.	plate	1	1	2	1.1
16.	steak	1	1	2	1.1

($\underline{f}$ = 1, .5%, $\underline{n}$ = 48)
appease, apple, baby, bacon, banana, bed, chew, chicken, Christmas, coloring, costs, cruel, custard, dessert, diet, dinner, dish, drug, empty, existence, fat, fork, full, get, ice cream, manger, mart, mood, mouth, nature, necessity, never, nourish, nourishment, pang, refrigerator, sex, shelter, shrimp, smell, stomach, store, sweet, taste, tea, warmth, was, water
(Illegible - 1)

Foot (Hand;)

No.	Response	F	M	Tot.	%
1.	shoe	13	17	30	16.5
2.	toe(s)	13	11	24	13.2
3.	ball	1	9	10	5.5
4.	feet	6	4	10	5.5
5.	leg	4	6	10	5.5

Foot   (Hand;   ) (contd)

No.	Response	F	M	Tot.	%
6.	hand	5	3	8	4.4
7.	step	4	4	8	4.4
8.	walk	3	2	5	2.7
9.	ankle	3	0	3	1.6
10.	kick	2	1	3	1.6
11.	small	2	1	3	1.6
12.	sore	2	1	3	1.6
13.	stool	1	2	3	1.6
14.	ache	1	1	2	1.1
15.	arm	2	0	2	1.1
16.	bare	1	1	2	1.1
17.	doctor	2	0	2	1.1
18.	door	1	1	2	1.1
19.	fall	2	0	2	1.1
20.	hold	1	1	2	1.1
21.	hurt	2	0	2	1.1
22.	rule	0	2	2	1.1
23.	smell	2	0	2	1.1

($\underline{f}$ = 1, .5%, $\underline{n}$ = 41)
Achilles, action, amoeba, arch, arched, bear, big, bloated, boil, boot, cold, corns, dirty, elbow, finger, floor, gear, green, gun, hard, head, heel, infection, itch, loose, move, nail, ped, pedal, pink, rest, root, sandal, shoo, ski, soft, stamp, stand, table, tired, wear
(Illegible - 1)

From   (To;   )

No.	Response	F	M	Tot.	%
1.	to	28	24	52	28.5
2.	here	13	7	20	11.0
3.	there	6	6	12	6.6
4.	where	8	4	12	6.6
5.	you	5	3	8	4.4
6.	away	2	4	6	3.3
7.	me	1	4	5	2.7
8.	now	2	3	5	2.7
9.	come	2	2	4	2.2
10.	go	2	1	3	1.6
11.	him	3	0	3	1.6
12.	it	2	1	3	1.6
13.	them	3	0	3	1.6
14.	by	1	1	2	1.1
15.	coming	2	0	2	1.1
16.	for	1	1	2	1.1
17.	home	1	1	2	1.1
18.	of	1	1	2	1.1
19.	the	0	2	2	1.1
20.	under	2	0	2	1.1
21.	whence	0	2	2	1.1

($\underline{f}$ = 1, .5%, $\underline{n}$ = 30)
about, add, address, always, at, bed, books, Brooklyn, de, elsewhere, Eric, Erich Fromm, foam, gift, give, hat, Illinois, is, letter, only, out, place, poor, ran, sender, take, to be, when, whom, whose

Fun   (; Playing)

No.	Response	F	M	Tot.	%
1.	game(s)	17	16	33	18.1
2.	happy	6	8	14	7.7
3.	frolic(s)	7	6	13	7.1
4.	laugh	9	2	11	6.0
5.	play	3	7	10	5.5
6.	house	4	4	8	4.4
7.	sun	3	3	6	3.3
8.	joy	4	0	4	2.2
9.	party	1	3	4	2.2

Fun   (; Playing) (contd)

No.	Response	F	M	Tot.	%
10.	run	3	1	4	2.2
11.	beach	1	2	3	1.6
12.	dance	1	2	3	1.6
13.	happiness	1	2	3	1.6
14.	laughter	1	2	3	1.6
15.	swimming	2	1	3	1.6
16.	yes	3	0	3	1.6
17.	date	2	0	2	1.1
18.	enjoyment	0	2	2	1.1
19.	excitement	1	1	2	1.1
20.	gay	2	0	2	1.1
21.	sadness	1	1	2	1.1
22.	time(s)	1	1	2	1.1

($\underline{f}$ = 1, .5%, $\underline{n}$ = 45)
archaic, bore, car, carefree, clothe, country, crazy, day, drinking, enjoy, fair, filled, find, fun, girls, good, gun, have, having, her, interesting, jokes, kicks, look, merry-go-round, Mike, money, park, people, picnic, pun, red, sad, Saturday, sex, silly, smash, Spain, spook, suds, sunshine, swim, today, trite, work

Girl   (Boy; Beautiful)

No.	Response	F	M	Tot.	%
1.	boy	76	54	130	71.4
2.	blonde	1	2	3	1.6
3.	cute	1	2	3	1.6
4.	friend	1	2	3	1.6
5.	me	3	0	3	1.6
6.	pretty	1	2	3	1.6
7.	young	1	2	3	1.6
8.	child	1	1	2	1.1
9.	female	1	1	2	1.1
10.	leg(s)	0	2	2	1.1
11.	pink	2	0	2	1.1
12.	sex	0	2	2	1.1

($\underline{f}$ = 1, .5%, $\underline{n}$ = 24)
affair, baby, bad, beautiful, beauty, brown, canister, curls, dress, face, figure, Friday, Gabrielle, I, male, man, mother, nice, sad, sister, such, talk, teeth, woman

Give   (Take;   )

No.	Response	F	M	Tot.	%
1.	take	43	36	79	43.4
2.	me	8	9	17	9.3
3.	gave	4	4	8	4.4
4.	receive	3	3	6	3.3
5.	donate	4	1	5	2.7
6.	now	1	4	5	2.7
7.	get	2	2	4	2.2
8.	love	3	1	4	2.2
9.	money	2	2	4	2.2
10.	share	1	3	4	2.2
11.	charity	2	1	3	1.6
12.	and take	1	1	2	1.1
13.	away	1	1	2	1.1
14.	back	2	0	2	1.1
15.	crusade	1	1	2	1.1
16.	gift	1	1	2	1.1
17.	up	2	0	2	1.1

($\underline{f}$ = 1, .5%, $\underline{n}$ = 31)
CARE, church, dimes, dog, donation, donor, extend food, generous, given, good, grab, hand, heart, help, her, in, it, more, offer, pillow, pleasure, possess, present, sacrifice, self, them, to, United Crusade, use, value

Glass (Window;)

No.	Response	F	M	Tot.	%
1.	window	6	12	18	9.9
2.	drink	11	5	16	8.8
3.	water	11	5	16	8.8
4.	clear	10	4	14	7.7
5.	break(s)	8	3	11	6.0
6.	broken	5	5	10	5.5
7.	cut	2	4	6	3.3
8.	door	2	3	5	2.7
9.	pane	5	0	5	2.7
10.	vase	3	1	4	2.2
11.	blower	2	1	3	1.6
12.	house	1	2	3	1.6
13.	jar	2	1	3	1.6
14.	milk	0	3	3	1.6
15.	mirror	0	3	3	1.6
16.	see	2	1	3	1.6
17.	beer	2	0	2	1.1
18.	bottle	1	1	2	1.1
19.	china	0	2	2	1.1
20.	clean	1	1	2	1.1
21.	drinking	0	2	2	1.1
22.	eye	2	0	2	1.1
23.	glasses	0	2	2	1.1
24.	green	1	1	2	1.1
25.	stained	1	1	2	1.1

($\underline{f}$ = 1, .5%, $\underline{n}$ = 41)
ass, beads, blow, blown, bottom, bowl, brittle,
cage, Carter, container, cover, crock, crystal,
cutter, goblet, home, ice, insight, jaw, lake,
lass, light, pack, pain, plate, pitcher, rod,
sharp, sheet, silver, smooth, splinter, stone,
through, through the looking glass, tube, wet,
windshield, wine, wool, work

Go (Come;)

No.	Response	F	M	Tot.	%
1.	away	23	10	33	18.1
2.	come	16	9	25	13.7
3.	stop	11	5	16	8.8
4.	ahead	7	7	14	7.7
5.	to	4	4	8	4.4
6.	home	5	2	7	3.8
7.	gone	3	2	5	2.7
8.	now	2	3	5	2.7
9.	run	2	3	5	2.7
10.	there	2	3	5	2.7
11.	leave	2	2	4	2.2
12.	went	3	1	4	2.2
13.	where	2	2	4	2.2
14.	get	1	2	3	1.6
15.	green	1	2	3	1.6
16.	on	0	3	3	1.6
17.	stay	2	1	3	1.6
18.	around	1	1	2	1.1
19.	back	0	2	2	1.1
20.	down	2	0	2	1.1
21.	far	1	1	2	1.1
22.	man(men)	2	0	2	1.1
23.	out	0	2	2	1.1
24.	start	1	1	2	1.1

($\underline{f}$ = 1, .5%, $\underline{n}$ = 20)
action, along, bed, command, fact, fast, further,
go, goal, merry-go-round, move, off, school,
screw, see, slow, speed, team, tell, throw
(No response - 1)

God (Bible, Religion;)

No.	Response	F	M	Tot.	%
1.	heaven	13	3	16	8.8
2.	damn	3	10	13	7.1
3.	almighty	5	4	9	4.9
4.	church	4	3	7	3.8
5.	good	3	2	5	2.7
6.	man	2	3	5	2.7
7.	love	3	1	4	2.2
8.	no	1	3	4	2.2
9.	belief	2	1	3	1.6
10.	Christ	1	2	3	1.6
11.	country	1	2	3	1.6
12.	father	2	1	3	1.6
13.	fearing	0	3	3	1.6
14.	is	1	2	3	1.6
15.	universe	2	1	3	1.6
16.	all	1	1	2	1.1
17.	faith	1	1	2	1.1
18.	fear	0	2	2	1.1
19.	He	1	1	2	1.1
20.	help	2	0	2	1.1
21.	holy	1	1	2	1.1
22.	Jesus	1	1	2	1.1
23.	mother	1	1	2	1.1
24.	my	2	0	2	1.1
25.	non-existent	1	1	2	1.1
26.	power	1	1	2	1.1
27.	question	1	1	2	1.1
28.	religion	1	1	2	1.1
29.	unknown	2	0	2	1.1
30.	up	2	0	2	1.1
31.	what	1	1	2	1.1
32.	who	1	1	2	1.1

($\underline{f}$ = 1, .5%, $\underline{n}$ = 63)
above, air, alone, angel, atheist, bad, believe,
Bible, bless, blessed, blue, closer, dammit,
death, devil, doubt, doubtful, earth, eternal,
fake, Fountainhead, friendly, ghost, gods, gone,
goodness, hate, hath, hell, hope, hypocrite,
image, indefinite, infinite, Jewish, king, large,
life, like, Lord, me, might, nil, none, not,
omnipotent, peace, perhaps, problem, ?, ridiculous, rod, saint, security, silly, sits, spirit,
supreme, where, white, whole, you, Zen
(No response - 1)

Got (Get;)

No.	Response	F	M	Tot.	%
1.	get(s)	15	9	24	13.2
2.	had	10	14	24	13.2
3.	have	8	7	15	8.2
4.	it	5	7	12	6.6
5.	received	4	1	5	2.7
6.	took	2	3	5	2.7
7.	up	3	1	4	2.2
8.	caught	2	1	3	1.6
9.	gave	2	1	3	1.6
10.	has	2	1	3	1.6
11.	home	3	0	3	1.6
12.	take	2	1	3	1.6
13.	German	1	1	2	1.1
14.	give	2	0	2	1.1
15.	go	0	2	2	1.1
16.	God	1	1	2	1.1
17.	good	1	1	2	1.1
18.	gotten	0	2	2	1.1
19.	hit	1	1	2	1.1
20.	into	1	1	2	1.1
21.	much	1	1	2	1.1
22.	nothing	1	1	2	1.1
23.	obtained	1	1	2	1.1
24.	out	1	1	2	1.1
25.	that	0	2	2	1.1
26.	to	1	1	2	1.1

Got (Get;) (contd)

No.	Response	F	M	Tot.	%

($\underline{f}$ = 1, .5%, $\underline{n}$ = 49)
back, bought, car, cold, did, forget, forgot,
found, gain, gift, girl, given, Gotham, gout,
grab, gut, hat, hold, horse, hunger, kept, lost,
lot, me, mine, money, more, news, no, nowhere,
obtain, off, one, owned, present, receive,
relieve, rendered, rewarded, sick, some, sought,
spanking, stuck, them, wanted, well, what, work
(Illegible - 1)

Grass (Green;)

No.	Response	F	M	Tot.	%
1.	green	79	56	135	74.1
2.	trees	1	5	6	3.3
3.	soft	4	0	4	2.2
4.	leaf(ves)	2	1	3	1.6
5.	ass	0	2	2	1.1
6.	blades	1	1	2	1.1
7.	lawn	0	2	2	1.1
8.	pot	1	1	2	1.1

($\underline{f}$ = 1, .5%, $\underline{n}$ = 25)
brown, carpet, crab, creeps, cut, damp, dewy,
field, freshness, greener, greenest, growing,
Gunther, hill, long, now, prickly, rass, rustle,
sit, sled, slob, tall, top, yes
(No response - 1)

Ground (; Earth)

No.	Response	F	M	Tot.	%
1.	hog	15	9	24	13.2
2.	dirt	15	8	23	12.6
3.	floor	15	8	23	12.6
4.	earth	6	6	12	6.6
5.	hard	4	5	9	4.9
6.	walk	4	3	7	3.8
7.	wet	4	3	7	3.8
8.	sky	4	1	5	2.7
9.	work	2	3	5	2.7
10.	cold	0	4	4	2.2
11.	brown	2	1	3	1.6
12.	foot(feet)	2	1	3	1.6
13.	rules	2	1	3	1.6
14.	air	0	2	2	1.1
15.	ball	2	0	2	1.1
16.	beef	0	2	2	1.1
17.	cover	0	2	2	1.1
18.	play	2	0	2	1.1
19.	round	1	1	2	1.1
20.	soil	1	1	2	1.1
21.	sound	0	2	2	1.1
22.	swell	0	2	2	1.1
23.	up	1	1	2	1.1

($\underline{f}$ = 1, .5%, $\underline{n}$ = 34)
basketball, block, breaking, broken, center,
chuck, coffee, cow, dead, down, electricity,
firm, gainer, grass, grounded, grow, hamburger,
high, hugger, lightning rod, meat, mud, protoplasm,
rocks, safe, sausage, sea, shit, sit, soft, solid,
tent, terrain, there

Had (; Have)

No.	Response	F	M	Tot.	%
1.	have	7	15	22	12.1
2.	lost	8	2	10	5.5
3.	did	6	3	9	4.9
4.	has	7	2	9	4.9
5.	been	4	4	8	4.4
6.	it	2	5	7	3.8
7.	gone	4	1	5	2.7
8.	not	1	4	5	2.7
9.	done	2	2	4	2.2
10.	enough	1	3	4	2.2
11.	hat	2	2	4	2.2
12.	once	2	2	4	2.2
13.	owned	2	2	4	2.2
14.	was	3	1	4	2.2
15.	bad	1	2	3	1.6
16.	fun	3	0	3	1.6
17.	hold	1	2	3	1.6
18.	money	1	2	3	1.6
19.	past	3	0	3	1.6
20.	taken	2	1	3	1.6
21.	want	3	0	3	1.6
22.	come	1	1	2	1.1
23.	get	1	1	2	1.1
24.	kept	2	0	2	1.1
25.	mine	2	0	2	1.1
26.	nothing	0	2	2	1.1
27.	possess	2	0	2	1.1

($\underline{f}$ = 1, .5%, $\underline{n}$ = 50)
ad, baby, before, belong, belonged, destroyed,
dog, each, everything, existed, friends, girl,
give, got, gun, hades, hadn't, hammer, head,
heard, him, his, horse, I, just, keep, lad,
name, needed, never, one, own, possessed, rich,
rug, sad, seen, some, spent, still, succeeded,
then, this, time, took, tree, verb, will, woman
yesterday

Hair (Head;)

No.	Response	F	M	Tot.	%
1.	head	7	10	17	9.3
2.	long	8	7	15	8.2
3.	blond	8	4	12	6.6
4.	brown	7	4	11	6.0
5.	comb	7	3	10	5.5
6.	black	4	4	8	4.4
7.	color	4	3	7	3.8
8.	brush	6	0	6	3.3
9.	cut	3	3	6	3.3
10.	oil	3	3	6	3.3
11.	clean	4	0	4	2.2
12.	dryer	1	2	3	1.6
13.	soft	0	3	3	1.6
14.	bristle	1	1	2	1.1
15.	chest	1	1	2	1.1
16.	curl(s)	2	0	2	1.1
17.	face	1	1	2	1.1
18.	messy	2	0	2	1.1
19.	net	2	0	2	1.1
20.	root(s)	1	1	2	1.1
21.	smooth	1	1	2	1.1
22.	thin	1	1	2	1.1
23.	wash	2	0	2	1.1

($\underline{f}$ = 1, .5%, $\underline{n}$ = 54)
bald, bear, boy, braids, breadth, car, chin,
cream, curly, dandruff, dark, do, dry, end, eyes,
fair, fine, fur, fussy, fuzzy, girl, grass,
grows, hairy, lock, long blond, man, mess, much,
Nair, neat, nose, on, piece, pretty, rare, read,
red, shampoo, shave, shine, shiny, spray,
straight, strand, strange, stringy, style,
swinging, thick, tortoise, tuft, wind, yellow

Hand (Fingers; Foot)

No.	Response	F	M	Tot.	%
1.	glove(s)	27	25	52	28.6
2.	finger(s)	9	11	20	11.0
3.	foot(feet)	10	7	17	9.3
4.	arm	6	5	11	6.0
5.	shake(s)	7	2	9	4.9
6.	hold	6	2	8	4.4
7.	ring	3	2	5	2.7
8.	ball	2	2	4	2.2
9.	warm	1	2	3	1.6
10.	clean	0	2	2	1.1
11.	in	1	1	2	1.1
12.	leg	1	1	2	1.1
13.	over	1	1	2	1.1
14.	saw	0	2	2	1.1
15.	wash	2	0	2	1.1
16.	work(s)	1	1	2	1.1
17.	write	0	2	2	1.1

(f = 1, .5%, n = 37)
Beatles, bone, broken, crayon, cuff, curve, face, fast, grasp, grenade, gun, heavy, help, hoof, hurt, itch, Jed, masculine, me, mouse, move, out, paint, palm, part, pen, person, sand, saw, second, signal, soft, some, strong, sweat, touch, warmth

Happiness (; Joy)

No.	Response	F	M	Tot.	%
1.	joy	18	13	31	17.0
2.	sadness	9	6	15	8.2
3.	smile	6	2	8	4.4
4.	puppy	6	1	7	3.8
5.	love	3	3	6	3.3
6.	good	3	2	5	2.7
7.	fun	2	2	4	2.2
8.	health	1	3	4	2.2
9.	warm	2	2	4	2.2
10.	gay	2	1	3	1.6
11.	glad	3	0	3	1.6
12.	me	1	2	3	1.6
13.	warmth	2	1	3	1.6
14.	bright	2	0	2	1.1
15.	content	1	1	2	1.1
16.	ecstasy	1	1	2	1.1
17.	free	1	1	2	1.1
18.	light	1	1	2	1.1
19.	never	0	2	2	1.1
20.	pain	1	1	2	1.1
21.	Peanuts	0	2	2	1.1
22.	pleasure	1	1	2	1.1
23.	sad	0	2	2	1.1
24.	sorrow	0	2	2	1.1

(f = 1, .5%, n = 64)
action, away, bliss, book, boyfriend, Charles, Charlie, Charlie Brown, cheer, child, clouds, contentment, darkness, delight, dog, elusive, ephemeral, family, feel, feeling, forever, friend, gaity, giggle, gladness, gloomy, God, golden, great, grief, happy, heaven, home, important, is, joyfulness, jubilant, laughter, life, loneliness, lucky, marriage, misery, nature, neurosis, peacefulness, Plato, puppy (warm), question, quiet, satisfaction, security, so, sometimes, spring, success, sun, thought, try, unhappy, Utopia, wealth, wish, yes

Happy (Joy;)

No.	Response	F	M	Tot.	%
1.	sad	27	24	51	28.0
2.	gay	7	2	9	4.9
3.	joy	2	6	8	4.4
4.	glad	6	1	7	3.8
5.	go lucky	4	3	7	3.8
6.	man	2	4	6	3.3
7.	smile	4	2	6	3.3
8.	day(s)	3	2	5	2.7
9.	laugh	2	2	4	2.2
10.	go	2	1	3	1.6
11.	me	2	1	3	1.6
12.	dog	0	2	2	1.1
13.	fun	1	1	2	1.1
14.	good	1	1	2	1.1
15.	jovial	2	0	2	1.1
16.	joyful	0	2	2	1.1
17.	joyous	1	1	2	1.1
18.	love	2	0	2	1.1
19.	no	2	0	2	1.1
20.	warm	1	1	2	1.1

(f = 1, .5%, n = 55)
angle, baby, birthday, blue, bright, carefree, cheerful, content, contented, ecstatic, excitement, fearful, feel, great, happy, here, hour, house, ignorant, is, Isles, laughter, light, loud, lucky, merry, mommy, mood, never, nice, not, not too, now, only, people, pleased, pleasure, road, Rockefeller, Rocky, satisfied, serene, ski, sometimes, song, soon, spirit, sports, sunshine, today, unhappy, vacation, Valentine's, very happy, wonderful

Hard (Soft, Working; Easier, Smooth)

No.	Response	F	M	Tot.	%
1.	soft	47	41	88	48.3
2.	rock	3	3	6	3.3
3.	cold	2	2	4	2.2
4.	difficult	3	1	4	2.2
5.	day	2	1	3	1.6
6.	easy	3	0	3	1.6
7.	steel	0	3	3	1.6
8.	wood	1	2	3	1.6
9.	bed	1	1	2	1.1
10.	bone	0	2	2	1.1
11.	cement	1	1	2	1.1
12.	floor	2	0	2	1.1
13.	ground	1	1	2	1.1
14.	hammer	0	2	2	1.1
15.	head	2	0	2	1.1
16.	nail(s)	1	1	2	1.1
17.	rough	2	0	2	1.1

(f = 1, .5%, n = 50)
apple, back, ball, biscuits, blow, bools, can, candy, chair, claw, core, cry, day's, day's night, decision, durable, egg, feel, fought, French bread, glass, good, happen, hitting, iron, knot, life, living, night, on, palate, red, road, Sam, seats, see, shale, shot put, show, smooth, soft-less, solid, table, task, test, tight, to, unyielding, way, work

Harder (Easier;)

No.	Response	F	M	Tot.	%
1.	softer	35	27	62	34.0
2.	than	10	6	16	8.8
3.	try	7	5	12	6.6
4.	easier	7	2	9	4.9
5.	work	3	3	6	3.3

Harder   (Easier;   ) (contd)

No.	Response	F	M	Tot.	%
6.	rock	2	3	5	2.7
7.	faster	3	1	4	2.2
8.	hit	3	1	4	2.2
9.	soft	2	2	4	2.2
10.	difficult	3	0	3	1.6
11.	steel	0	3	3	1.6
12.	test	2	1	3	1.6
13.	hammer	0	2	2	1.1
14.	hard	1	1	2	1.1
15.	more	2	0	2	1.1
16.	wood	2	0	2	1.1

(f = 1, .5%, n = 43)
always, bat, brick, brittle, chair, choking,
compare, day, denser, easy, fight, firmer, force,
get, glass, gone, hair, harder, hardest, hurt,
life, press, purer, push, realize, rough, rougher,
scared, sharper, slower, smoother, stiffer, strove,
sweat, task, teacher, tedious, then, tough,
water, way, wish, worse

Health   (Sickness;   )

No.	Response	F	M	Tot.	%
1.	wealth	15	14	29	15.9
2.	good	16	6	22	12.1
3.	sickness	8	8	16	8.8
4.	sick	5	4	9	4.9
5.	well	4	4	8	4.4
6.	happiness	2	4	6	3.3
7.	happy	4	1	5	2.7
8.	illness	1	3	4	2.2
9.	important	4	0	4	2.2
10.	life	1	3	4	2.2
11.	strong	3	1	4	2.2
12.	poor	2	1	3	1.6
13.	center	1	1	2	1.1
14.	clean	1	1	2	1.1
15.	department	0	2	2	1.1
16.	disease	2	0	2	1.1
17.	food	1	1	2	1.1
18.	gesundheit	1	1	2	1.1
19.	insurance	1	1	2	1.1
20.	me	0	2	2	1.1
21.	pills	2	0	2	1.1
22.	strength	0	2	2	1.1
23.	welfare	1	1	2	1.1
24.	wise	1	1	2	1.1

(f = 1, .5%, n = 44)
A.M.A., bad, cheerful, clinic, cold, death, doctor,
education, excellent, fair, fitness, forecast,
great, gym, have, hazard, home, hospital, hurt,
hygiene, ill, Kaiser, magazine, meals, medicine,
money, officer, pink, principle, public, resort,
regulations, safe, security, service, sports,
spry, straight, strange, valuable, vigor, Vitamin
C, well-being, yes

Heat   (; Stove)

No.	Response	F	M	Tot.	%
1.	hot	27	18	45	24.7
2.	cold	11	17	28	15.4
3.	warm	8	5	13	7.1
4.	sweat	5	7	12	6.6
5.	sun	7	1	8	4.4
6.	warmth	5	2	7	3.8
7.	fire	2	3	5	2.7
8.	food	1	2	3	1.6
9.	heater	0	3	3	1.6
10.	light	2	1	3	1.6

Heat   (; Stove) (contd)

No.	Response	F	M	Tot.	%
11.	beat	1	1	2	1.1
12.	day	0	2	2	1.1
13.	energy	2	0	2	1.1
14.	exhaustion	2	0	2	1.1
15.	stove	2	0	2	1.1
16.	wave	0	2	2	1.1
17.	weather	1	1	2	1.1

(f = 1, .5%, n = 41)
annoy, beach, beer, boil, bright, burnt, capacity,
desert, do, drink, eat, electric, endure, estrous,
fast, feel, fuel, furnace, good, happy, hard,
heart, hit, house, intense, it, lazy, meat,
miserable, on, oven, pad, perspire, rash, reaction, smoke, summer, thirsty, today, water,
window

Her   (Him; his)

No.	Response	F	M	Tot.	%
1.	him	35	22	57	31.3
2.	his	17	5	22	12.1
3.	she	12	8	20	11.0
4.	girl	2	6	8	4.4
5.	he	2	5	7	3.8
6.	me	1	3	4	2.2
7.	friend	2	1	3	1.6
8.	dress	1	1	2	1.1
9.	hand	2	0	2	1.1
10.	is	0	2	2	1.1
11.	it	0	2	2	1.1
12.	life	1	1	2	1.1
13.	love	0	2	2	1.1
14.	purse	1	1	2	1.1

(f = 1, .5%, n = 47)
answer, belong, bitch, body, breasts, clothes,
Denise, doll, eyes, face, feminine, Ferlinghetti,
friendly, give, green, hair, hers, intelligence,
island, lady, like, little, looks, man, mean,
nor, nose, only, other, own, pink, possess,
pretty, raincoat, room, sad, shoes, someone,
standing, that one there - not boy, their,
towels, we, when, with, word, yours

Here   (There; Come, Where)

No.	Response	F	M	Tot.	%
1.	there	67	58	125	66.1
2.	now	22	13	35	19.2
3.	are	2	2	4	2.2
4.	class	2	0	2	1.1
5.	place	1	1	2	1.1

(f = 1, .5%, n = 14)
ein, farm, hear, her, here, is, near, not,
position, rabbit, room, school, today, where

Hers   (His;   )

No.	Response	F	M	Tot.	%
1.	his	54	40	94	51.6
2.	mine	8	14	22	12.1
3.	their(s)	5	6	11	6.0
4.	yours	6	1	7	3.8
5.	towel	3	3	6	3.3
6.	is	3	2	5	2.7
7.	ours	2	2	4	2.2
8.	its	1	1	2	1.1

Hers   (His;) (contd)

No.	Response	F	M	Tot.	%
9.	my	1	1	2	1.1
10.	possession	2	0	2	1.1
11.	that	0	2	2	1.1
12.	there	1	1	2	1.1

(f = 1, .5%, n = 23)
alone, antelope, attached, beagle, bed, bra, dress, good, hair, him, individuality, lucky, me, now, others, own, room, there's, was, we, what, whose, world's

High   (Jump; Mountain)

No.	Response	F	M	Tot.	%
1.	low	54	39	93	51.1
2.	mountain(s)	8	6	14	7.7
3.	up	7	2	9	4.9
4.	sky	2	2	4	2.2
5.	tall	2	2	4	2.2
6.	building	1	2	3	1.6
7.	moon	2	1	3	1.6
8.	Sierra	2	1	3	1.6
9.	ball	0	2	2	1.1
10.	dry	1	1	2	1.1
11.	hill	1	1	2	1.1
12.	ladder	2	0	2	1.1
13.	mighty	0	2	2	1.1
14.	noon	0	2	2	1.1
15.	peak	1	1	2	1.1
16.	place	1	1	2	1.1
17.	wall	0	2	2	1.1

(f = 1, .5%, n = 31)
above, airplane, altitude, bridge, brow, ceiling, cliff, concentration, deck, deep, dizzy, fall, freedom, giddy, hot, jump, mark, oxygen, over, pressure, put, roof, slope, smashed, temperature, than, top, way, weak, wide, zorched

Hill   (Mountain;)

No.	Response	F	M	Tot.	%
1.	climb	13	14	27	14.8
2.	mountain	12	13	25	13.7
3.	dale	7	4	11	6.0
4.	steep	7	2	9	4.9
5.	valley	5	4	9	4.9
6.	high	7	1	8	4.4
7.	green	4	3	7	3.8
8.	top	2	4	6	3.3
9.	side	2	3	5	2.7
10.	tree(s)	4	1	5	2.7
11.	mound	2	2	4	2.2
12.	rise	4	0	4	2.2
13.	grass	3	0	3	1.6
14.	vale	1	2	3	1.6
15.	walk	3	0	3	1.6
16.	dorm	2	0	2	1.1
17.	house	1	1	2	1.1
18.	Jack	1	1	2	1.1
19.	rolling	2	0	2	1.1
20.	round	2	0	2	1.1

(f = 1, .5%, n = 43)
battle, beacon, brown, calm, cat, country, dell, dill, Easter, flower, fraternity, goal, ground, hall, hat, haunted, have to climb it, heap, home, Jack and Jill, lock, low, lump, meadow, Mike, mole hill, over, pasture, phallus, pill, riding, road, rock, roll, street, summer, sun, tall, tiresome, trudge, up, view, well

Hold   (Carry;)

No.	Response	F	M	Tot.	%
1.	on	23	25	48	26.4
2.	hand(s)	17	9	26	14.3
3.	tight	10	7	17	9.3
4.	grasp	5	5	10	5.5
5.	it	2	3	5	2.7
6.	drop	3	1	4	2.2
7.	out	1	3	4	2.2
8.	still	3	1	4	2.2
9.	have	0	3	3	1.6
10.	keep	2	1	3	1.6
11.	me	2	1	3	1.6
12.	release	1	2	3	1.6
13.	take	2	1	3	1.6
14.	up	3	0	3	1.6
15.	close	1	1	2	1.1
16.	fast	1	1	2	1.1
17.	grab	2	0	2	1.1
18.	hang	1	1	2	1.1
19.	head	1	1	2	1.1
20.	stop	1	1	2	1.1
21.	tightly	2	0	2	1.1
22.	touch	2	0	2	1.1

(f = 1, .5%, n = 30)
baby, book, carry, caught, cling, down, find, fold, football, force, girl, give, grip, hard, her, leave, lose, me tight, mouth, my, near, onto, possess, rope, stay, tear, there, this, to, wrestling

Home   (At, House;)

No.	Response	F	M	Tot.	%
1.	house	41	37	78	42.8
2.	family	6	3	9	4.9
3.	sweet	4	3	7	3.8
4.	place	2	3	5	2.7
5.	security	3	1	4	2.2
6.	fire(s)	2	1	3	1.6
7.	hill	1	2	3	1.6
8.	love	3	0	3	1.6
9.	parents	2	1	3	1.6
10.	warmth	2	1	3	1.6
11.	far	0	2	2	1.1
12.	happiness	0	2	2	1.1
13.	heart	2	0	2	1.1
14.	hearth	2	0	2	1.1
15.	is	0	2	2	1.1
16.	live	2	0	2	1.1
17.	mine	2	0	2	1.1
18.	nice	1	1	2	1.1
19.	range	1	1	2	1.1
20.	room	2	0	2	1.1
21.	town	1	1	2	1.1
22.	where	1	1	2	1.1

(f = 1, .5%, n = 40)
away, bad, body, brave, building, castle, comfort, coming, cozy, dog, door, friends, go, gone, good, hall, happy, here, is not a house, lawn, life, longing, made, mother, never, New York, roam, sadness, Sauger, secure, shit, sleep, soft, today, ugly, warm, why, wife, window, wonderful

Hot   (Cold, Stove;)

No.	Response	F	M	Tot.	%
1.	cold	50	52	102	56.0
2.	dog(s)	2	4	6	3.3
3.	water	2	4	6	3.3
4.	lunch	4	0	4	2.2
5.	sweat	3	1	4	2.2

Hot   (Cold, Stove;   ) (contd)

No.	Response	F	M	Tot.	%
6.	plate	2	1	3	1.6
7.	stove	2	1	3	1.6
8.	burn	2	0	2	1.1
9.	chocolate	1	1	2	1.1
10.	coffee	2	0	2	1.1
11.	fire	2	0	2	1.1
12.	touch	2	0	2	1.1
13.	warm	1	1	2	1.1

($\underline{f}$ = 1, .5%, $\underline{n}$ = 42)
acid, bath, beach, bed, bod!, damn, day, desert,
excited, feel, food, hotter, humid, hurt, iron,
light, like, milk, muggy, ouch, oven, pain, painful, pan, pancakes, peanuts, pepper, radiator,
rod, sand, sandwich, sex, shower, soup, spur,
stench, stuff, stuffy, summer, sweater, tea, today

Ill   (; Sickness)

No.	Response	F	M	Tot.	%
1.	sick	61	43	104	57.1
2.	well	3	10	13	7.1
3.	cold	1	4	5	2.7
4.	health	3	2	5	2.7
5.	bed	3	1	4	2.2
6.	healthy	1	3	4	2.2
7.	bad	2	1	3	1.6
8.	doctor	2	1	3	1.6
9.	come	2	0	2	1.1
10.	happy	1	1	2	1.1

($\underline{f}$ = 1, .5%, $\underline{n}$ = 37)
Alfred, aunt, back, brother, crummy, death,
depressed, dizzy, eagle, effect, fed, feel,
fume, George III, good, hill, hospital, humor,
hurt, Illinois, lay, leave, looking, nausea,
nauseous, ness, pain, pale, sill, sweet, thoughts,
tired, unhealthy, void, weak, wife, will

House   (Cottage;   )

No.	Response	F	M	Tot.	%
1.	home	41	32	73	40.1
2.	live	4	3	7	3.8
3.	big	3	2	5	2.7
4.	hill	4	1	5	2.7
5.	brick	1	2	3	1.6
6.	building	2	1	3	1.6
7.	door	2	1	3	1.6
8.	roof	2	1	3	1.6
9.	window(s)	2	1	3	1.6
10.	car	1	1	2	1.1
11.	dwelling	1	1	2	1.1
12.	family	1	1	2	1.1
13.	garden	1	1	2	1.1
14.	louse	1	1	2	1.1
15.	mine	1	1	2	1.1
16.	mouse	0	2	2	1.1
17.	white	1	1	2	1.1
18.	wood	2	0	2	1.1

($\underline{f}$ = 1, .5%, $\underline{n}$ = 58)
black, block, boat, boot, cabin, chair, children,
chimney, city, clean, cold, cottage, dark,
demolish, destroyed, dog, doll, father, fence,
fireplace, fly, fraternity, free, front-door,
green, haunt, haus (Ger.), haven, hell, his,
hold, horse, independent, jail, large, lived,
mansion, mother, Negro, old, place, protection,
Rising Sun, room, Rumford Act, safety, sell,
shelter, shingle, small, square, sun, this, toll,
trailer, Un-American, warm, why
(Illegible - 1)

Insect   (; Spider)

No.	Response	F	M	Tot.	%
1.	bug	43	26	69	37.9
2.	bite(s)	10	12	22	12.1
3.	fly	4	5	9	4.9
4.	bee	2	6	8	4.4
5.	worm(s)	4	4	8	4.4
6.	spider	6	1	7	3.8
7.	ant	4	2	6	3.3
8.	repellent	1	4	5	2.7
9.	small	5	0	5	2.7
10.	beetle	2	2	4	2.2
11.	grasshopper	3	1	4	2.2
12.	mosquito	2	1	3	1.6
13.	animal	0	2	2	1.1
14.	butterfly	1	1	2	1.1
15.	kill	1	1	2	1.1
16.	moth	1	1	2	1.1
17.	ugly	2	0	2	1.1

($\underline{f}$ = 1, .5%, $\underline{n}$ = 21)
arthropod, black widow, bomb, bumblebee, carni-
vore, caterpillar, cockroach, cute, floor, flower,
legs, mine, nuisance, order, pest, repulsive,
squash, squirm, tree, unpleasant, wasps
(Illegible - 1)

I   (Am;   )

No.	Response	F	M	Tot.	%
1.	me	38	32	70	38.4
2.	you	26	11	37	20.3
3.	am	10	10	20	11.0
4.	myself	4	3	7	3.8
5.	they	2	3	5	2.7
6.	ego	1	3	4	2.2
7.	self	1	3	4	2.2
8.	dream	1	2	3	1.6
9.	it	1	1	2	1.1
10.	think	0	2	2	1.1
11.	we	2	0	2	1.1
12.	will	0	2	2	1.1

($\underline{f}$ = 1, .5%, $\underline{n}$ = 24)
blonde, clothes, do, entity, eye, go, he, life,
like, love, man, numb, over, person, see, she,
sigh, that's me, the, want, whole, wish, work,
worry

Is   (As, It, Was, Who; Am, That, There, This)

No.	Response	F	M	Tot.	%
1.	not	12	11	23	12.6
2.	are	13	7	20	11.0
3.	it	6	14	20	11.0
4.	was	12	8	20	11.0
5.	isn't	9	8	17	9.3
6.	exist(s)	6	3	9	4.9
7.	am	2	4	6	3.3
8.	that	4	2	6	3.3
9.	here	1	3	4	2.2
10.	be	3	0	3	1.6
11.	he	1	2	3	1.6
12.	there	2	1	3	1.6
13.	and	1	1	2	1.1
14.	from	0	2	2	1.1
15.	going	1	1	2	1.1
16.	island	1	1	2	1.1
17.	now	1	1	2	1.1

($\underline{f}$ = 1, .5%, $\underline{n}$ = 38)
a, ain't, alive, all, always, as, at, back, come,
equals, gone, has, his, how, Isle, maybe, me,
near, nice, of, or, over, question, quis, school,
thine, to be, transitive, true, wasn't, well,

Is (As, It, Was, Who; Am, That, There, This)(contd)

No.	Response	F	M	Tot.	%

what, will, will be, wonderful, yes, yet, you

It   (If; Take, The, Was)

No.	Response	F	M	Tot.	%
1.	is	22	16	38	20.9
2.	that	16	10	26	14.3
3.	was	10	11	21	11.5
4.	thing	5	9	14	7.7
5.	they	6	1	7	3.8
6.	them	1	3	4	2.2
7.	it	0	3	3	1.6
8.	neuter	1	2	3	1.6
9.	seems	1	2	3	1.6
10.	this	1	2	3	1.6
11.	at	2	0	2	1.1
12.	him	1	1	2	1.1
13.	monster	2	0	2	1.1
14.	neutral	2	0	2	1.1
15.	sex	0	2	2	1.1
16.	the	2	0	2	1.1

($\underline{f}$ = 1, .5%, $\underline{n}$ = 48)
animal, anything, boy, can, does, dog, else, floor, general, grow, has, her, hit, homework, house, hurt, inanimate, last, mass, might, misfit, moves, movie, never, no, object, of, pit, problem, rain, runs, sentence, sexless, she, shit, should, smells, tag, talks, their, thou, unknown, us, water, will, word, would, you

Judge   (; Justice)

No.	Response	F	M	Tot.	%
1.	jury	10	14	24	13.2
2.	court	8	11	19	10.4
3.	law	14	4	18	9.9
4.	man	5	2	7	3.8
5.	not	2	5	7	3.8
6.	lawyer	4	1	5	2.7
7.	bench	2	2	4	2.2
8.	black	3	1	4	2.2
9.	wig	3	1	4	2.2
10.	budge	0	3	3	1.6
11.	decide	2	1	3	1.6
12.	gavel	2	1	3	1.6
13.	just	1	2	3	1.6
14.	me	2	1	3	1.6
15.	robe	2	1	3	1.6
16.	fair	1	1	2	1.1
17.	find	1	1	2	1.1
18.	justice	2	0	2	1.1
19.	opinion	2	0	2	1.1
20.	punish	0	2	2	1.1

($\underline{f}$ = 1, .5%, $\underline{n}$ = 62)
act, anxiety, authority, bar, be, beard, bigot, campus, condemn, crime, criminal, criterion, criticize, cry, decision, decree, educated, equity, fat, father, God, guilty, hard, harsh, him, honest, honesty, hurt, judged, judgment, learned, lucid, mayor, none, now, nudge, omniscient, persecute, pomposity, prejudice, punishment, rate, reform, respect, roommate, say, see, sentence, share, sober, sternness, study, supreme, them, think, ticket, trial, unjust, verdict, will, witness, Woody

Kids   (Children;   )

No.	Response	F	M	Tot.	%
1.	child(ren)	34	19	53	29.1
2.	play	6	9	15	8.2
3.	goats	6	5	11	6.0
4.	fun	4	3	7	3.8
5.	noise	4	3	7	3.8
6.	brats	1	4	5	2.7
7.	parents	3	2	5	2.7
8.	young	3	2	5	2.7
9.	cute	1	3	4	2.2
10.	love	1	3	4	2.2
11.	mother	4	0	4	2.2
12.	family	3	0	3	1.6
13.	many	3	0	3	1.6
14.	noisy	1	2	3	1.6
15.	boys	1	1	2	1.1
16.	little	0	2	2	1.1
17.	school	0	2	2	1.1
18.	yours	2	0	2	1.1

($\underline{f}$ = 1, .5%, $\underline{n}$ = 46)
adults, are, babies, boys & girls, candy, car, cats, coming, cry, dirty, dogs, have, home, hope, important, innocent, joy, lambs, lots, mine, mud, none, nose, nuisance, pregnant, problems, quiz, restless, run, say, scream, sisters, sneaky, song, stationwagon, tads, teases, their, there, today, too many, trouble, wife, yes, youth

Lake   (; Cottage)

No.	Response	F	M	Tot.	%
1.	water	16	13	29	15.9
2.	blue	10	5	15	8.2
3.	Tahoe	7	6	13	7.1
4.	pond	7	5	12	6.6
5.	river	7	4	11	6.0
6.	boat	4	4	8	4.4
7.	Mead	2	6	8	4.4
8.	stream	4	3	7	3.8
9.	tree(s)	3	2	5	2.7
10.	bed	3	1	4	2.2
11.	fish	0	4	4	2.2
12.	ocean	4	0	4	2.2
13.	cold	0	3	3	1.6
14.	swim	0	3	3	1.6
15.	beauty	1	1	2	1.1
16.	calm	2	0	2	1.1
17.	clear	1	1	2	1.1
18.	forest	1	1	2	1.1
19.	Michigan	2	0	2	1.1
20.	mountains	2	0	2	1.1
21.	shore	1	1	2	1.1
22.	swan	2	0	2	1.1

($\underline{f}$ = 1, .5%, $\underline{n}$ = 40)
Arrowhead, Berryessa, death, dog, dunk, emerald, front, fun, Geneva, George, Higgins, large, lazy, like, Loman, look, lost, Louise, Madden, mirror, place, quiet, round, sail, sailing, scene, sea, serenity, side, ski, skiing, sky, slake, smooth, swimming, Vista, wall, wet, wide, woods

Lamb   (Mutton; Sheep)

No.	Response	F	M	Tot.	%
1.	sheep	15	16	31	17.0
2.	wool	11	17	28	15.4
3.	chop(s)	13	10	23	12.6
4.	soft	11	2	13	7.1
5.	gentle	3	2	5	2.7
6.	leg	0	4	4	2.2

Lamb   (Mutton; Sheep) (contd)

No.	Response	F	M	Tot.	%
7.	God	3	1	4	2.2
8.	stew	3	1	4	2.2
9.	baa	1	2	3	1.6
10.	little	1	2	3	1.6
11.	meat	1	2	3	1.6
12.	slaughter	2	1	3	1.6
13.	baby	1	1	2	1.1
14.	cuddly	2	0	2	1.1
15.	deer	1	1	2	1.1
16.	dinner	1	1	2	1.1
17.	eat	1	1	2	1.1
18.	lion	1	1	2	1.1
19.	shoulder	1	1	2	1.1
20.	woolly	2	0	2	1.1

($\underline{f}$ = 1, .5%, $\underline{n}$ = 42)
beef, Biblic, bleat, blood, bone, calf, calm,
Christ, Christmas, cook, cow, cuddle, curry,
cute, docile, duck, Easter, enjoyment, ewe, eye,
food, frolic, garlic, kitten, leg of, limb,
lovable, meek, nice, nose, pastures, Pilaf, pity,
roast, rug, shank, skin, sucker, tame, tough,
theirs, white

Law   (Justice;   )

No.	Response	F	M	Tot.	%
1.	order	29	33	62	34.0
2.	judge	7	1	8	4.4
3.	justice	5	2	7	3.8
4.	lawyer	2	5	7	3.8
5.	police	5	1	6	3.3
6.	rule	3	3	6	3.3
7.	book(s)	1	4	5	2.7
8.	school	5	0	5	2.7
9.	enforcement	3	1	4	2.2
10.	obey	3	1	4	2.2
11.	officer	1	3	4	2.2
12.	abiding	2	0	2	1.1
13.	and order	1	1	2	1.1
14.	bad	1	1	2	1.1
15.	crime	0	2	2	1.1
16.	disobedience	1	1	2	1.1
17.	disorder	0	2	2	1.1
18.	just	0	2	2	1.1
19.	legal	0	2	2	1.1
20.	library	2	0	2	1.1

($\underline{f}$ = 1, .5%, $\underline{n}$ = 45)
abide, and, arm, attorney, black, break, cop,
court, enemy, enforce, enforcing, equal, ever
wrong, fair, force, Hammurabi's, idea, is, jail,
Jerry, judgment, land, legislature, liberty, loud,
man, mend, nature, necessary, peace, requires,
responsibility, restraint, security, sign, stable,
state, strength, strict, study, traffic, unjust,
unlawful, violation, who
(Illegible - 1)

Leaf   (; Stem)

No.	Response	F	M	Tot.	%
1.	tree	41	38	79	43.4
2.	green	28	9	37	20.3
3.	fall(s)	5	2	7	3.8
4.	autumn	4	1	5	2.7
5.	page	1	3	4	2.2
6.	branch	1	2	3	1.6
7.	maple	1	2	3	1.6
8.	brown	1	1	2	1.1
9.	Ericson	0	2	2	1.1
10.	fig	0	2	2	1.1

Leaf   (; Stem) (contd)

No.	Response	F	M	Tot.	%
11.	flower	1	1	2	1.1
12.	leaves	1	1	2	1.1
13.	twig	2	0	2	1.1

($\underline{f}$ = 1, .5%, $\underline{n}$ = 32)
ball, blade, book, bread, bush, chair, curl-green,
dead, divided, drop, edge, fallen, falling, fragile, frail, life, light, loaf, mold, mole, nut,
oak, path, plant, rain, shake, stem, straw,
sugar, tea, then, turn

Leg   (; Foot)

No.	Response	F	M	Tot.	%
1.	arm	24	13	37	20.3
2.	foot(feet)	15	11	26	14.3
3.	lamb	3	7	10	5.5
4.	muscle	1	8	9	4.9
5.	broken	5	2	7	3.8
6.	knee	4	2	6	3.3
7.	walk	4	2	6	3.3
8.	body	2	2	4	2.2
9.	girl	1	3	4	2.2
10.	hair	2	2	4	2.2
11.	long	4	0	4	2.2
12.	hurt	2	1	3	1.6
13.	limb	1	2	3	1.6
14.	shoe(s)	3	0	3	1.6
15.	toe	1	2	3	1.6
16.	big	1	1	2	1.1
17.	calf	2	0	2	1.1
18.	cast	1	1	2	1.1
19.	joint	1	1	2	1.1
20.	pants	1	1	2	1.1
21.	stand	1	1	2	1.1
22.	thigh	0	2	2	1.1

($\underline{f}$ = 1, .5%, $\underline{n}$ = 39)
aches, action, ankle, beauty, bend, bitchen, bite,
bone, calve, chair, crossed, door, down, extremity, feminine, flesh, go, hairy, horn, horny,
horse, hose, injury, loose, nice, peg, runs,
shape, sharp, smooth, sock, sore, splint, sting,
tibia, tired, white, woman, wooden

Lemon   (; Sour)

No.	Response	F	M	Tot.	%
1.	sour	29	29	48	26.4
2.	tree	17	20	37	20.3
3.	yellow	15	5	20	11.0
4.	lime	6	7	13	7.1
5.	juice	4	5	9	4.9
6.	bitter	3	5	8	4.4
7.	ade	3	2	5	2.7
8.	tea	3	1	4	2.2
9.	drink(s)	1	2	3	1.6
10.	peel	1	2	3	1.6
11.	acid	1	1	2	1.1
12.	drop	1	1	2	1.1
13.	green	2	0	2	1.1
14.	lemonade	2	0	2	1.1
15.	orange	1	1	2	1.1
16.	pie	2	0	2	1.1
17.	rind	1	1	2	1.1

($\underline{f}$ = 1, .5%, $\underline{n}$ = 18)
aide, apple, bush, car, delicious, demon, drift,
eat, fish, fruit, ice cream, Jack, John, Kool-Aid,
nice, squeeze, tangy, tart

Letters (Numbers;)

No.	Response	F	M	Tot.	%
1.	write	19	17	36	19.8
2.	mail(s)	10	4	14	7.7
3.	alphabet	5	5	10	5.5
4.	stamp(s)	5	4	9	4.9
5.	science(s)	4	3	7	3.8
6.	home	4	2	6	3.3
7.	love	4	2	6	3.3
8.	paper	3	3	6	3.3
9.	friend(s)	4	1	5	2.7
10.	writing	1	4	5	2.7
11.	editor	3	1	4	2.2
12.	envelope(s)	2	2	4	2.2
13.	ink	1	3	4	2.2
14.	send	2	2	4	2.2
15.	words	2	2	4	2.2
16.	and Science	2	1	3	1.6
17.	answers	2	0	2	1.1
18.	box	2	0	2	1.1
19.	correspondence	1	1	2	1.1

($\underline{f}$ = 1, .5%, $\underline{n}$ = 49)
a,b,c's, army, blue, book, boring, briefs, cards, desk, exciting, from, girl, graduate, green, happiness, head, ice box, indistinguishable, led, letter, lettuce, lost, many, messages, money, needed, none, numbers, pen, personal, pink, print, rare, receive, respond, Russian, scarlet, Screwtape, seldom, sent, stationery, status, steps, sword, syllables, symbols, to, writers, written, wrote

Lettuce (Cabbage;)

No.	Response	F	M	Tot.	%
1.	green(s)	24	12	36	19.8
2.	salad	14	14	28	15.4
3.	tomato(es)	12	12	24	13.2
4.	cabbage	5	8	13	7.1
5.	leaf(ves)	8	2	10	5.5
6.	rabbit	4	2	6	3.3
7.	vegetable	1	5	6	3.3
8.	head	4	1	5	2.7
9.	eat	1	3	4	2.2
10.	crisp	3	0	3	1.6
11.	food	1	2	3	1.6
12.	sandwich	1	2	3	1.6
13.	dressing	1	1	2	1.1
14.	carrot(s)	0	2	2	1.1
15.	petticoat	2	0	2	1.1

($\underline{f}$ = 1, .5%, $\underline{n}$ = 35)
behavior, boil, bug, celery, chew, clean, cold, come on, cool, crispy, crop, crunchy, cucumber, dead, die, fix, go, grass, green curly, heart, juicy, loose, mayonnaise, money, oil, plant, pray, regular, salt, slips, supper, swimming, thing, watery, yum

Life (; Live)

No.	Response	F	M	Tot.	%
1.	death	19	19	38	20.9
2.	magazine	12	11	23	12.6
3.	live	10	6	16	8.8
4.	long	8	5	13	7.1
5.	love	4	4	8	4.4
6.	good	3	4	7	3.8
7.	time	1	3	4	2.2
8.	great	1	2	3	1.6
9.	guard	1	2	3	1.6
10.	liberty	3	0	3	1.6
11.	living	2	1	3	1.6

Life (; Live) (contd)

No.	Response	F	M	Tot.	%
12.	lovely	2	1	3	1.6
13.	now	2	1	3	1.6
14.	science	2	1	3	1.6
15.	wonderful	3	0	3	1.6
16.	hard	1	1	2	1.1
17.	raft	0	2	2	1.1
18.	story	1	1	2	1.1

($\underline{f}$ = 1, .5%, $\underline{n}$ = 43)
action, beautiful, breath, crazy, darkness, dead, dear, dreary, enjoyable, entire, experience, facts, fast, full, generality, God, gone, grow, happiness, health, insurance, is, jacket, joy, line, lively, man, me, mix, mysterious, pleasure, sad, short, sick, spirit, stream, struggle, sun, trees, wonder, wow!, young, zing!

Light (Dark, Heavy, Lamp;)

No.	Response	F	M	Tot.	%
1.	dark	37	27	64	35.1
2.	bright	9	4	13	7.1
3.	bulb	5	8	13	7.1
4.	beam	3	8	11	6.0
5.	day	5	1	6	3.3
6.	sun	4	1	5	2.7
7.	heavy	2	1	3	1.6
8.	house	3	0	3	1.6
9.	lamp	2	1	3	1.6
10.	on	1	2	3	1.6
11.	see	3	0	3	1.6
12.	shine	2	1	3	1.6
13.	soft	1	2	3	1.6
14.	stream	1	2	3	1.6
15.	heat	2	0	2	1.1
16.	ray	0	2	2	1.1
17.	shade	2	0	2	1.1
18.	streaming	1	1	2	1.1
19.	street	2	0	2	1.1

($\underline{f}$ = 1, .5%, $\underline{n}$ = 36)
above, blazes, brown, candle, car, cigarette, clouds, concise, crack, damp, dawn, dim, dusk, enlightenment, foghorn, forest, fright, gay, God, nite, not, open, out, park, piazza, searchlight, shy, sight, skinned, star, sunshine, understand, unfriendly, warm, weight, window

Look (; See)

No.	Response	F	M	Tot.	%
1.	see	37	27	64	35.1
2.	out	10	12	22	12.1
3.	at	9	7	16	8.8
4.	there	3	3	6	3.3
5.	magazine	2	3	5	2.7
6.	listen	1	3	4	2.2
7.	up	1	3	4	2.2
8.	book	2	1	3	1.6
9.	door	1	2	3	1.6
10.	eyes	2	1	3	1.6
11.	where	2	1	3	1.6
12.	away	1	1	2	1.1
13.	back	2	0	2	1.1
14.	key	0	2	2	1.1
15.	saw	1	1	2	1.1
16.	sight	1	1	2	1.1

($\underline{f}$ = 1, .5%, $\underline{n}$ = 39)
always, around, below, blind, carefully, cook, don't, gare, glance, glare, glass, Guardi, handball, hard, here, life, like, list, looking, mirror, mountains, notice, open, over, point,

NORMS OF WORD ASSOCIATION

Look (; See) (contd)

No.	Response	F	M	Tot.	%

pretty, prohibit, quickly, search, she, sky, sly, stare, steady, strain, that, view, watch, world

Lose (Find;)

No.	Response	F	M	Tot.	%
1.	find	24	15	39	21.4
2.	win	12	8	20	11.0
3.	lost	9	6	15	8.2
4.	weight	10	3	13	7.1
5.	gain	5	6	11	6.0
6.	game	2	3	5	2.7
7.	money	0	5	5	2.7
8.	loose	0	4	4	2.2
9.	tight	2	2	4	2.2
10.	cry	2	1	3	1.6
11.	found	2	1	3	1.6
12.	gone	2	1	3	1.6
13.	forget	0	2	2	1.1
14.	friends	1	1	2	1.1
15.	key(s)	1	1	2	1.1
16.	noose	1	1	2	1.1
17.	ring	2	0	2	1.1

(f = 1, .5%, n = 47)
anxiety, bearing, cards, close, confidence, cost, dangling, despair, dice, dog, drop, ends, find, forever, fright, gamble, hanging, hard, head, it, keep, let, living, natcherally, never, nose, not have, nothing, oneself, place, sad, search, sentimental, shoe, sleep, stupid, thin, ties, train of thought, valuable, wallet, war, watch, way, winner, won, worry

Lost (Find;)

No.	Response	F	M	Tot.	%
1.	found	42	35	77	42.3
2.	gone	4	4	8	4.4
3.	dog	3	2	5	2.7
4.	find	1	3	4	2.2
5.	won	1	3	4	2.2
6.	article(s)	2	1	3	1.6
7.	forest	1	2	3	1.6
8.	in	1	2	3	1.6
9.	world	0	3	3	1.6
10.	forever	2	0	2	1.1
11.	horizon	1	1	2	1.1
12.	life	0	2	2	1.1
13.	now	2	0	2	1.1
14.	ring	1	1	2	1.1
15.	sad	2	0	2	1.1
16.	time	1	1	2	1.1
17.	wallet	1	1	2	1.1
18.	woods	0	2	2	1.1

(f = 1, .5%, n = 54)
abandoned, afraid, aimlessly, alone, away, bad, books, boy, cave, child, crying, curiosity, damn, dead, depress, desert, deserted, despair, dessert, disappeared, feel, fog, friend, frightened, gain, ghost, girl, hat, here, hope, idea, it, lake, lonely, looking, lose, mob, money, need, never, out, person, puppy, scared, seek, shears, soul, sweater, tear, together, tribes, unhappy, watch, weight

Loud (Quiet;)

No.	Response	F	M	Tot.	%
1.	noise	29	22	51	28.0
2.	soft	26	19	45	24.7
3.	voice	5	5	10	5.5
4.	noisy	3	4	7	3.8
5.	speaker	4	2	6	3.3
6.	talk	2	4	6	3.3
7.	clear	3	1	4	2.2
8.	mouth	2	2	4	2.2
9.	shout	3	1	4	2.2
10.	sound	1	3	4	2.2
11.	louder	2	1	3	1.6
12.	quiet	2	1	3	1.6
13.	sharp	0	3	3	1.6
14.	cry	1	1	2	1.1
15.	knock	0	2	2	1.1
16.	radio	1	1	2	1.1
17.	shriek	1	1	2	1.1
18.	unbearable	2	0	2	1.1

(f = 1, .5%, n = 22)
bang, bark, brawl, choir, colors, crass, enough, girls, hear, hi-fi, hurt, irrational, low, megaphone, music, painful, record, silent, speak, strong, television, yell

Low (High;)

No.	Response	F	M	Tot.	%
1.	high	65	52	117	64.2
2.	down	10	8	18	9.9
3.	below	1	1	2	1.1
4.	brow	1	1	2	1.1
5.	fat	0	2	2	1.1
6.	short	2	0	2	1.1
7.	table	0	2	2	1.1
8.	temperature	0	2	2	1.1
9.	under	1	1	2	1.1
10.	voice	2	0	2	1.1

(f = 1, .5%, n = 31)
average, bad, beam, behold, blow, blue, deep, degrading, depressed, depression, desk, grade, ground, hit, intelligence, ladder, loud, medium, melancholy, money, moral, morale, resistance, sad, score, spirits, sweet, tone, up, vulgar, woman

Mad (Anger;)

No.	Response	F	M	Tot.	%
1.	angry	19	16	35	19.2
2.	magazine	14	14	28	15.4
3.	crazy	9	4	13	7.1
4.	happy	5	6	11	6.0
5.	sad	6	3	9	4.9
6.	dog	3	5	8	4.4
7.	world	3	5	8	4.4
8.	insane	1	6	7	3.8
9.	bad	3	0	3	1.6
10.	A.E. Newman	1	1	2	1.1
11.	boy	1	1	2	1.1
12.	hate	1	1	2	1.1
13.	Hatter	2	0	2	1.1
14.	house	2	0	2	1.1
15.	hurt	2	0	2	1.1
16.	money	1	1	2	1.1
17.	sane	2	0	2	1.1

(f = 1, .5%, n = 44)
asylum, at, book, cap, comic, controlled, cross, cry, dope, fear, for it, frankness, free, furious, glad, inside, joy, lad, life, man, mental, morose, movie, murder, nice, people,

Mad (Anger;) (contd)

No.	Response	F	M	Tot.	%

Phil Silvers, rage, red, scramble, seldom, shout, sick, sorrow, strong, temper, touchy, tragic, ugly, very angry, wild, wrong, yes, zany

Man (Citizen, Soldier, Woman;)

No.	Response	F	M	Tot.	%
1.	woman(women)	43	42	85	46.7
2.	boy	3	1	4	2.2
3.	go(es)	2	2	4	2.2
4.	God	2	2	4	2.2
5.	good	2	2	4	2.2
6.	man(men)	3	1	4	2.2
7.	tall	4	0	4	2.2
8.	animal	1	2	3	1.6
9.	dog	2	1	3	1.6
10.	father	1	2	3	1.6
11.	girl	2	1	3	1.6
12.	strong	3	0	3	1.6
13.	big	2	0	2	1.1
14.	happy	1	1	2	1.1
15.	hat	0	2	2	1.1
16.	human	1	1	2	1.1
17.	male	1	1	2	1.1
18.	state	0	2	2	1.1

($\underline{f}$ = 1, .5%, $\underline{n}$ = 46)
about, alive, anthropology, ape, brave, briefcase, can, child, cool, dad, fat, fight, gone, hem, him, homo, hope, image, item, kind, lazy, love, lover, machine, mammal, mankind, mine, misunderstand, moon, must, no, none, old, origin, out, potential, power, provider, race, Ray, resourceful, supreme, universe, want, wife, young

Me (I, Tell, You;)

No.	Response	F	M	Tot.	%
1.	you	44	39	83	45.6
2.	I	11	9	20	11.0
3.	too	5	5	10	5.5
4.	they	5	2	7	3.8
5.	my	2	3	5	2.7
6.	girl	4	0	4	2.2
7.	myself	1	3	4	2.2
8.	he	1	2	3	1.6
9.	her	0	3	3	1.6
10.	mine	2	1	3	1.6
11.	them	2	1	3	1.6
12.	him	1	1	2	1.1
13.	individual	1	1	2	1.1
14.	me	2	0	2	1.1
15.	now	2	0	2	1.1
16.	self	1	1	2	1.1
17.	she	1	1	2	1.1

($\underline{f}$ = 1, .5%, $\underline{n}$ = 24)
a body, alone, am, ambitious, and, answer, bad, boy, feel, here, hot, hungry, it, Joan, pa, person, pronoun, see, short, standard, that, thee, try, who
(Illegible - 1)

Mind (Memory;)

No.	Response	F	M	Tot.	%
1.	think(s)	24	10	34	18.7
2.	brain	13	13	26	14.3
3.	matter	6	10	16	8.8
4.	body	4	9	13	7.1
5.	head	1	6	7	3.8
6.	care	2	2	4	2.2
7.	blank	1	2	3	1.6
8.	obey	3	0	3	1.6
9.	psyche	1	2	3	1.6
10.	self	1	2	3	1.6
11.	thought	2	1	3	1.6
12.	complex	1	1	2	1.1
13.	empty	1	1	2	1.1
14.	man	2	0	2	1.1
15.	soul	2	0	2	1.1
16.	wander(s)	0	2	2	1.1
17.	your(s)	1	1	2	1.1

($\underline{f}$ = 1, .5%, $\underline{n}$ = 55)
a blur, alert, amazing, arm, ask, attention, behave, bind, bother, business, clear, cries, dark, desire, don't, disobey, disturbed, ear, ego, Einstein, filled, fluid, God, good, if, intellect, intelligence, keen, knowledge, light, mad, me, mine, nowhere, of, psychological, psychology, quicksilver, reason, rules, runs, silence, slow, strive, strung, study, talk, thinking, tired, waste, with, wonder, work, working, you

Mine (My;)

No.	Response	F	M	Tot.	%
1.	your(s)	48	42	90	49.4
2.	his	4	3	7	3.8
3.	own	5	1	6	3.3
4.	hers	2	3	5	2.7
5.	theirs	4	1	5	2.7
6.	gold	4	0	4	2.2
7.	my	3	1	4	2.2
8.	ours	2	2	4	2.2
9.	me	2	1	3	1.6
10.	shaft	1	2	3	1.6
11.	book(s)	2	0	2	1.1
12.	dig	1	1	2	1.1
13.	mind	1	1	2	1.1
14.	no	2	0	2	1.1
15.	possession	2	0	2	1.1
16.	things	1	1	2	1.1

($\underline{f}$ = 1, .5%, $\underline{n}$ = 39)
and theirs, are, area, blow, car, cave, coal, deep, entrance, explosion, eyes, field, foot, forever, good, is, kind, land, love, memory, milk, no one's, O.K., personal, possess, pride, purse, reluctance, room, salt, share, sweeper, that, thine, this, was, what, wine, yes

Moth (Butterfly;)

No.	Response	F	M	Tot.	%
1.	fly(ies)	20	10	30	16.5
2.	ball(s)	10	10	20	11.0
3.	light	8	10	18	9.9
4.	bug	7	7	14	7.7
5.	butterfly	8	5	13	7.1
6.	insect	5	6	11	6.0
7.	mother	5	5	10	5.5
8.	flame	7	1	8	4.4
9.	hole(s)	5	2	7	3.8
10.	clothes	4	1	5	2.7
11.	wings	3	2	5	2.7

Moth   (Butterfly;   ) (contd)

No.	Response	F	M	Tot.	%
12.	flutter	1	3	4	2.2
13.	eaten	2	1	3	1.6
14.	candle	1	1	2	1.1
15.	cloth(s)	0	2	2	1.1
16.	eat	1	1	2	1.1
17.	lamp	1	1	2	1.1

(f = 1, .5%, n = 26)
antenna, bad, beauty, burnt, boy, caterpillar,
closet, cocoon, dart, dusty, flea, fuzz, hairy,
kill, lightbulb, monster, nerve, night, nuisance,
phantom, scream, spider, ugly, white, wool, worm

Mother   (; Child)

No.	Response	F	M	Tot.	%
1.	father	43	33	76	41.7
2.	child	8	3	11	6.0
3.	daughter	7	4	11	6.0
4.	love	4	4	8	4.4
5.	good	4	2	6	3.3
6.	home	1	3	4	2.2
7.	goose	0	3	3	1.6
8.	nice	2	1	3	1.6
9.	dad	1	1	2	1.1
10.	dear	1	1	2	1.1
11.	friend	1	1	2	1.1
12.	in-law	0	2	2	1.1
13.	kind	0	2	2	1.1
14.	mine	0	2	2	1.1
15.	mom	0	2	2	1.1
16.	understanding	1	1	2	1.1
17.	warmth	0	2	2	1.1
18.	woman	1	1	2	1.1

(f = 1, .5%, n = 39)
apple pie, baby, brother, care, children, dead,
Dorothy, elephant, fuck, hair, hate, helped,
hood, Hubbard, instinct, Kathleen, laugh, loving,
make, maternal, Mary (not Virgin Mary), moth,
New York, no, none, Oedipus, old, pearl, protect,
protection, rational, sad, there, universal-love/
particular person, warm, was, wonderful, write,
your
(No response - 1)

Mouse   (Cheese;   )

No.	Response	F	M	Tot.	%
1.	rat	16	11	27	14.8
2.	cat	12	9	21	11.5
3.	mice	7	5	12	6.6
4.	house	4	5	9	4.9
5.	trap	6	3	9	4.9
6.	roared	4	4	8	4.4
7.	cheese	5	3	8	4.4
8.	gray	5	2	7	3.8
9.	Mickey	4	3	7	3.8
10.	roar	3	3	6	3.3
11.	little	2	3	5	2.7
12.	man	2	3	5	2.7
13.	brown	2	1	3	1.6
14.	louse	1	2	3	1.6
15.	small	1	2	3	1.6
16.	caught	1	1	2	1.1
17.	cute	2	0	2	1.1
18.	fear	1	1	2	1.1
19.	hole	1	1	2	1.1
20.	home	1	1	2	1.1
21.	jump	1	1	2	1.1
22.	rodent	0	2	2	1.1
23.	run	0	2	2	1.1

Mouse   (Cheese;   ) (contd)

No.	Response	F	M	Tot.	%
24.	scared	1	1	2	1.1
25.	tiny	1	1	2	1.1

(f = 1, .5%, n = 29)
animal, always, cage, catch, cartoon, Disneyland,
fast, floor, funny, hate, inbred, it, moose,
mouth, my, no, on, Peter Sellers, pipsqueak,
pretensions, psychology, ran, soft, squeak,
squeal, tail, thing, tiger, twiskers

Much   (Very;   )

No.	Response	F	M	Tot.	%
1.	more	27	25	52	28.6
2.	many	13	7	20	11.0
3.	little	7	10	17	9.3
4.	better	5	7	12	6.6
5.	lot(s)	2	5	7	3.8
6.	few	1	5	6	3.3
7.	too	6	0	6	3.3
8.	a lot	4	1	5	2.7
9.	enough	1	2	3	1.6
10.	less	2	1	3	1.6
11.	lone	2	1	3	1.6
12.	money	1	2	3	1.6
13.	ado	1	1	2	1.1
14.	later	1	1	2	1.1
15.	too much	1	1	2	1.1

(f = 1, .5%, n = 39)
abundance, anger, bags, big, candy, crackers,
eat, eggs, enthusiasm, fan, faster, good, grapes,
grass, harder, hate, health, life, milk, mucho,
Munchnich, Munich, nearly, needed, nicer, nothing,
pilling, plenty, potatoes, reading, restraint,
rich, sair, some, tepid, the, to, warmth, what

My   (Oh;   )

No.	Response	F	M	Tot.	%
1.	your(s)	30	22	52	28.6
2.	mine	11	10	21	11.5
3.	own	6	4	10	11.0
4.	mother	6	3	9	4.9
5.	self	4	3	7	3.8
6.	goodness	4	1	5	2.7
7.	house	3	2	5	2.7
8.	me	2	3	5	2.7
9.	friend	1	3	4	2.2
10.	his	1	3	4	2.2
11.	home	2	1	3	1.6
12.	tooth	2	1	3	1.6
13.	book(s)	0	2	2	1.1
14.	brother	1	1	2	1.1
15.	dog(s)	0	2	2	1.1
16.	father	2	0	2	1.1
17.	love	1	1	2	1.1
18.	our(s)	2	0	2	1.1
19.	possession(s)	1	1	2	1.1
20.	their	1	1	2	1.1

(f = 1, .5%, n = 38)
blond, Bonnie, car, cat, dress, ego, feeling,
foot, God, hand, hope, horse, I, Lord, my, name,
not, nothing, oh!, oh my!, pen, person, property,
room, stomach, tale, test, they, thing, tie,
toothbrush, toy, wish, with, word, worth, you
you're

Nail   (Hammer;   )

No.	Response	F	M	Tot.	%
1.	hammer	38	38	76	41.7
2.	finger	11	5	16	8.8
3.	hit	3	6	9	4.9
4.	bite	3	2	5	2.7
5.	toe	5	0	5	2.7
6.	hard	3	1	4	2.2
7.	head	2	2	4	2.2
8.	polish	4	0	4	2.2
9.	sharp	3	1	4	2.2
10.	keg	1	2	3	1.6
11.	steel	0	3	3	1.6
12.	tack	2	1	3	1.6
13.	cross	1	1	2	1.1
14.	cut	1	1	2	1.1
15.	file	1	1	2	1.1
16.	hang	1	1	2	1.1
17.	pail	1	1	2	1.1
18.	thumb	1	1	2	1.1
19.	wall	1	1	2	1.1
20.	wood	1	1	2	1.1

($\underline{f}$ = 1, .5%, $\underline{n}$ = 29)
board, build, builder, carpenter, Christ, clean,
door, door jamb, galvanized, gray, grows, gum,
hand, happer, hold, long, mail, man, match, pain,
peg, root, rusty, scratch, stab, stiff, thin,
tooth, ugly

Narrower   (; Broader)

No.	Response	F	M	Tot.	%
1.	wider	24	12	36	19.8
2.	thin	8	10	18	9.9
3.	thinner	7	4	11	6.0
4.	road	4	4	8	4.4
5.	bridge	2	4	6	3.3
6.	tunnel	3	2	5	2.7
7.	shorter	2	2	4	2.2
8.	smaller	2	2	4	2.2
9.	than	3	1	4	2.2
10.	wide	1	3	4	2.2
11.	closer	1	2	3	1.6
12.	path	2	1	3	1.6
13.	small	2	1	3	1.6
14.	street	1	2	3	1.6
15.	tight	1	2	3	1.6
16.	alley	1	1	2	1.1
17.	close	1	1	2	1.1
18.	door	2	0	2	1.1
19.	longer	0	2	2	1.1
20.	margin	1	1	2	1.1
21.	passage	2	0	2	1.1
22.	slim	0	2	2	1.1
23.	slimmer	0	2	2	1.1
24.	straight	2	0	2	1.1
25.	strait	2	0	2	1.1
26.	thicker	0	2	2	1.1

($\underline{f}$ = 1, .5%, $\underline{n}$ = 45)
archway, bone, broad, broader, channel, crookeder,
dark, deeper, escape, fatter, hall, hallway, lane,
large, ledge, less, life, limits, long, mind,
narrow, narrowest, pass, passageway, perspective,
provincial, reason, room, skinnier, skinny, slit,
snake, sooner, space, steeper, stiller, straighter,
string, then, tighter, tiny, viewpoint, waist,
walls, way

Near   (By; Closer)

No.	Response	F	M	Tot.	%
1.	far	46	39	85	46.7
2.	close	20	15	35	19.2
3.	by	5	3	8	4.4
4.	here	3	2	5	2.7
5.	me	2	2	4	2.2
6.	nearer	1	3	4	2.2
7.	to	0	4	4	2.2
8.	you	3	1	4	2.2
9.	beer	2	0	2	1.1
10.	closer	1	1	2	1.1
11.	death	1	1	2	1.1

($\underline{f}$ = 1, .5%, $\underline{n}$ = 27)
air, at, beside, Christmas, dear, door, East,
hear, her, Hitler, home, house, human, intimate,
my God to Thee, never, next, school, sweat,
there, too, touching, to you, us, warn, warmth,
what

Nearer   (Closer; Farther)

No.	Response	F	M	Tot.	%
1.	closer	27	24	51	28.0
2.	farther	14	14	28	15.4
3.	far	11	5	16	8.8
4.	close	8	6	14	7.7
5.	than	5	5	10	5.5
6.	farer	7	1	8	4.4
7.	further	5	3	8	4.4
8.	to	4	3	7	3.8
9.	here	1	3	4	2.2
10.	come	2	0	2	1.1
11.	distance	1	1	2	1.1
12.	God	1	1	2	1.1
13.	me	1	1	2	1.1

($\underline{f}$ = 1, .5%, $\underline{n}$ = 28)
arrive, away, came, class, dear, happiness, home,
house, immediate, intense, kiss, mountain, move,
my, near, nearest, proximity, romance, sea, see,
shore, still, there, to thee, warm, warmer, yes,
you

Never   (Always; Hardly, However, Now)

No.	Response	F	M	Tot.	%
1.	always	20	16	36	19.8
2.	ever	20	12	32	17.6
3.	now	4	11	15	8.2
4.	again	5	7	12	6.6
5.	more	7	3	10	5.5
6.	no	7	2	9	4.9
7.	go	1	4	5	2.7
8.	do	2	2	4	2.2
9.	forever	3	1	4	2.2
10.	before	1	2	3	1.6
11.	mind	0	3	3	1.6
12.	never	0	3	3	1.6
13.	not	0	3	3	1.6
14.	sometimes	2	1	3	1.6
15.	eternity	2	0	2	1.1
16.	here	1	1	2	1.1
17.	impossible	1	1	2	1.1
18.	see	2	0	2	1.1
19.	then	0	2	2	1.1
20.	will	2	0	2	1.1

($\underline{f}$ = 1, .5%, $\underline{n}$ = 28)
be, can, cry, don't say, exist, infinity, kill,
land, lie, love, maybe, mother, neverland, nothing, on, only, perhaps, permanent, Peter Pan,
raven, reveal, seldom, stubborn, tall, unrealis-
tic, when, worry, yes

Night   (; Dark, Moon)

No.	Response	F	M	Tot.	%
1.	day	32	33	65	35.7
2.	dark	18	16	34	18.7
3.	cool	6	2	8	4.4
4.	sleep	4	3	7	3.8
5.	cold	3	3	6	3.3
6.	owl	4	2	6	3.3
7.	light(s)	2	3	5	2.7
8.	black	3	1	4	2.2
9.	darkness	3	1	4	2.2
10.	air	2	0	2	1.1
11.	gown	1	1	2	1.1
12.	iguana	2	0	2	1.1
13.	love	1	1	2	1.1
14.	stand	0	2	2	1.1
15.	stars	1	1	2	1.1
16.	time	0	2	2	1.1
17.	watch	0	2	2	1.1
18.	watchman	1	1	2	1.1

($\underline{f}$ = 1, .5%, $\underline{n}$ = 25)
clear, crisp, dull, exuberating, fall, friendly,
fun, heart, -ingale, life, long, -mare, moon,
peace, peaceful, plight, quiet, rest, see, shade,
sky, soft, stick, wool

Noise   (; Loud)

No.	Response	F	M	Tot.	%
1.	loud	38	29	67	36.8
2.	sound	5	8	13	7.1
3.	quiet	7	2	9	4.9
4.	hear	2	3	5	2.7
5.	racket	4	1	5	2.7
6.	bang	3	1	4	2.2
7.	boys	1	1	2	1.1
8.	city	1	1	2	1.1
9.	crowd	1	1	2	1.1
10.	disturb	0	2	2	1.1
11.	disturbance	1	1	2	1.1
12.	hurt	2	0	2	1.1
13.	kids	1	1	2	1.1
14.	maker	0	2	2	1.1
15.	music	2	0	2	1.1
16.	siren	0	2	2	1.1
17.	soft	2	0	2	1.1
18.	talk	0	2	2	1.1
19.	white	2	0	2	1.1

($\underline{f}$ = 1, .5%, $\underline{n}$ = 52)
aloud, apartment, bad, beatniks, bother, bothersome, box, cacophony, clatter, commotion,
concentration, din, discriminate, distracting,
dog, drilling, ear, explosion, fear, food, ghost,
hate, headache, heard, house, jeers, library,
lingo, makes, pad, pain, phone, radio, rancor,
rattle, ruckus, rustle, scrape, scream, shh,
shock, shout, shouting, silence, sleep, startle,
street, study, studying, toys, truck, Wagner
(Illegible - 1)

Nor   (Or;   )

No.	Response	F	M	Tot.	%
1.	neither	44	32	76	41.7
2.	not	11	6	17	9.3
3.	I	5	9	14	7.7
4.	or	8	5	13	7.1
5.	never	3	3	6	3.3
6.	this	3	0	3	1.6
7.	you	1	2	3	1.6
8.	bore	1	1	2	1.1
9.	either	1	1	2	1.1

Nor   (Or;   ) (contd)

No.	Response	F	M	Tot.	%
10.	if	0	2	2	1.1
11.	me	1	1	2	1.1
12.	no	0	2	2	1.1
13.	shall	1	1	2	1.1
14.	that	1	1	2	1.1
15.	them	1	1	2	1.1
16.	whore	0	2	2	1.1

($\underline{f}$ = 1, .5%, $\underline{n}$ = 32)
any, bad, before, California, denial, don't,
English, false, for, fun, he, him, home, including, Leif Ericson, more, Mrs, Carney, ni,
Norseman, Norwegian, nothing, now, other, the,
there, Thor, was, way, we, which, with, yet

Not   (Have; Why)

No.	Response	F	M	Tot.	%
1.	no	10	7	17	9.3
2.	now	9	7	16	8.8
3.	yes	5	8	13	7.1
4.	never	7	4	11	6.0
5.	here	4	6	10	5.5
6.	yet	5	5	10	5.5
7.	is	5	4	9	4.9
8.	nor	5	4	9	4.9
9.	good	4	1	5	2.7
10.	ever	4	0	4	2.2
11.	any	1	2	3	1.6
12.	do	1	2	3	1.6
13.	negative	2	1	3	1.6
14.	none	2	1	3	1.6
15.	so	3	0	3	1.6
16.	there	2	1	3	1.6
17.	but	1	1	2	1.1
18.	done	1	1	2	1.1
19.	forget	2	0	2	1.1
20.	knot	1	1	2	1.1
21.	me	1	1	2	1.1
22.	mine	1	1	2	1.1
23.	only	1	1	2	1.1

($\underline{f}$ = 1, .5%, $\underline{n}$ = 45)
again, allowed, am, at, aught, bad, better,
can't, don't, easy, else, enough, even, far,
forgot, got, green, have, hope, hopeless, I,
if, impossible, in, intelligent, living, lot,
maybe, negate, neither, nil, nothing, prohibit,
rope, shall, this, time, too, very, was, why,
will, without, you, yours
(No response - 1)

Now   (How, Then; By)

No.	Response	F	M	Tot.	%
1.	then	33	35	68	37.3
2.	never	10	7	17	9.3
3.	here	8	6	14	7.7
4.	immediately	7	1	8	4.4
5.	forever	6	1	7	3.8
6.	when	1	4	5	2.7
7.	is	2	2	4	2.2
8.	later	1	3	4	2.2
9.	now	1	2	3	1.6
10.	present	2	1	3	1.6
11.	do	2	0	2	1.1
12.	go	2	0	2	1.1
13.	is the time	2	0	2	1.1
14.	no	2	0	2	1.1
15.	right	0	2	2	1.1

($\underline{f}$ = 1, .5%, $\underline{n}$ = 38)
again, all, and, can, closer, come, come on,

Now — (How, Then; By) (contd)

No.	Response	F	M	Tot.	%

crow, fall, finish, freedom, he, hear, immediacy, isn't, live, moment, nothing, now, place, procedure, so, soon, sow, stop, sun, sweat, that, there, they, this time, time, today, urgent, we, what, world, yeah
(Illegible - 1)

Nurse — (Doctor;)

No.	Response	F	M	Tot.	%
1.	doctor	37	19	56	30.7
2.	white	19	7	26	14.7
3.	hospital	6	6	12	6.6
4.	sick	5	2	7	3.8
5.	care	1	4	5	2.7
6.	help	2	3	5	2.7
7.	baby	2	2	4	2.2
8.	cap	3	0	3	1.6
9.	girl	0	3	3	1.6
10.	maid	0	3	3	1.6
11.	medicine	3	0	3	1.6
12.	pretty	0	3	3	1.6
13.	uniform	1	2	3	1.6
14.	aid	2	0	2	1.1
15.	aide	1	1	2	1.1
16.	hat	2	0	2	1.1
17.	health	1	1	2	1.1
18.	patient	1	1	2	1.1
19.	wet	0	2	2	1.1

($\underline{f}$ = 1, .5%, $\underline{n}$ = 37)
bed, bottle, carry, Cora, cute, die, dispassionate, dress, Duckett, father, feed, fine, great, grouchy, heals, helper, helpful, hurt, kind, lady, mother, nice, no, packing, pin, registered, rub, safe, scalpel, sex, strong, tender, thermometer, unnecessary, woman, wound, yes

Of — (Because;)

No.	Response	F	M	Tot.	%
1.	course	5	14	19	10.4
2.	what	1	10	11	6.0
3.	from	5	4	9	4.9
4.	them	8	0	8	4.4
5.	thee	2	5	7	3.8
6.	to	6	1	7	3.8
7.	off	2	4	6	3.3
8.	it	4	1	5	2.7
9.	for	3	2	5	2.7
10.	mice	3	2	5	2.7
11.	the	5	0	5	2.7
12.	nothing	3	1	4	2.2
13.	this	2	2	4	2.2
14.	which	3	1	4	2.2
15.	on	2	1	3	1.6
16.	with	2	1	3	1.6
17.	about	2	0	2	1.1
18.	all	1	1	2	1.1
19.	de	2	0	2	1.1
20.	his	1	1	2	1.1
21.	if	2	0	2	1.1
22.	me	1	1	2	1.1
23.	mine	1	1	2	1.1
24.	no	2	0	2	1.1
25.	or	1	1	2	1.1
26.	preposition	1	1	2	1.1
27.	theirs	2	0	2	1.1
28.	you	1	1	2	1.1
29.	your(s)	1	1	2	1.1

Of — (Because;) (contd)

No.	Response	F	M	Tot.	%

($\underline{f}$ = 1, .5%, $\underline{n}$ = 51)
a, alone, and, any, at, beach, belong, Berkeley, binary, boys, by, Cal, done, have, her, house, importance, in, integrity, interest, its, liberty, life, look, love, man, more, much, my, necessity, not, now, oaf, officer, over, part, people, possess, possession, same, small, something, sorts, then, thee I sing, there, time, us, when, where, whom

Off — (On;)

No.	Response	F	M	Tot.	%
1.	on	55	47	102	56.0
2.	limits	5	3	8	4.4
3.	away	4	2	6	3.3
4.	it	1	3	4	2.2
5.	of	3	1	4	2.2
6.	out	3	1	4	2.2
7.	dark	1	1	2	1.1
8.	fall	0	2	2	1.1
9.	go	2	0	2	1.1
10.	light(s)	1	1	2	1.1
11.	shut	1	1	2	1.1
12.	switch	0	2	2	1.1
13.	take	1	1	2	1.1
14.	there	1	1	2	1.1
15.	to	1	1	2	1.1

($\underline{f}$ = 1, .5%, $\underline{n}$ = 36)
air, and, beam, beat, boole, Broadway, campus, clear, closed, clothes, coat, cough, down, drop, far, from, full, gone, hand, hat, lid, misplaced, now, road, rocker, stick, the, town, track, turn, up, when, with, world, wrong, yonder

Oh — (Ah;)

No.	Response	F	M	Tot.	%
1.	my	20	20	40	22.0
2.	no	23	16	39	21.4
3.	ah	6	7	13	7.1
4.	boy	3	3	6	3.3
5.	yes	4	2	6	3.3
6.	dear	5	0	5	2.7
7.	exclamation	4	1	5	2.7
8.	God	2	3	5	2.7
9.	surprise	4	1	5	2.7
10.	what	2	3	5	2.7
11.	yeah	2	3	5	2.7
12.	look	2	2	4	2.2
13.	well	1	3	4	2.2
14.	bad	1	1	2	1.1
15.	good	0	2	2	1.1
16.	me	0	2	2	1.1
17.	oh	1	1	2	1.1
18.	so	2	0	2	1.1
19.	why	1	1	2	1.1

($\underline{f}$ = 1, .5%, $\underline{n}$ = 27)
brother, die, excitement, exclaim, !, expression, freedom, goodness, ha, ho, how, I, la, lordy, non se l'orrio, now, O.K., Oklahoma, ouch, question, round, say, shit, shock, sorry, that, understand
(Illegible - 1)

Older   (Younger;   )

No.	Response	F	M	Tot.	%
1.	younger	39	32	71	39.0
2.	man	8	6	14	7.7
3.	people	6	3	9	4.9
4.	young	1	8	9	4.9
5.	sister	4	2	6	3.3
6.	brother	2	3	5	2.7
7.	person(s)	2	3	5	2.7
8.	wiser	2	3	5	2.7
9.	age	1	2	3	1.6
10.	newer	3	0	3	1.6
11.	parents	1	2	3	1.6
12.	than	2	1	3	1.6
13.	adult(s)	1	1	2	1.1
14.	aged	2	0	2	1.1
15.	beard	2	0	2	1.1
16.	grandfather	0	2	2	1.1
17.	mother	2	0	2	1.1
18.	sick	1	1	2	1.1

(f = 1, .5%, n = 34)
ancient, bolder, city, colder, dead, distant,
elders, euphemism, father, grandma, grandmother,
gray, grow, house, mature, me, monk, mossy,
oldest, ossification, respectable, senile, sicker,
sickly, sixty-four, slower, smolder, stick,
superiors, tale, time, wrinkle, wrinkled, years

One   (Only; Numbers)

No.	Response	F	M	Tot.	%
1.	two	52	52	104	57.1
2.	more	5	1	6	3.3
3.	only	5	1	6	3.3
4.	day	3	2	5	2.7
5.	many	3	2	5	2.7
6.	person	4	1	5	2.7
7.	is	3	1	4	2.2
8.	thing	2	2	4	2.2
9.	alone	3	0	3	1.6
10.	another	2	1	3	1.6
11.	love	3	0	3	1.6
12.	us	2	1	3	1.6
13.	individual	0	2	2	1.1
14.	number	2	0	2	1.1
15.	time	2	0	2	1.1
16.	unity	1	1	2	1.1

(f = 1, .5%, n = 23)
a, all, and, being, convex, done, end, few, five,
has, hour, in, life, man, me, must, no, no one,
single, solution, together, up, who

Open   (; Doors)

No.	Response	F	M	Tot.	%
1.	close	26	29	55	30.2
2.	door(s)	24	13	37	20.3
3.	shut	11	15	26	14.3
4.	closed	14	8	22	12.1
5.	up	4	5	9	4.9
6.	mouth	3	0	3	1.6
7.	book	1	1	2	1.1
8.	free	2	0	2	1.1
9.	letter	1	1	2	1.1
10.	this	0	2	2	1.1
11.	wide	1	1	2	1.1

(f = 1, .5%, n = 20)
air, always, box, car, end, enter, find, flash,
heart, hole, hurt, love, mouthed, now, oven,
sky, softly, spacious, the, trap

Order   (Command;   )

No.	Response	F	M	Tot.	%
1.	law	13	11	24	13.2
2.	command	9	3	12	6.6
3.	disorder	2	10	12	6.6
4.	chaos	5	4	9	4.9
5.	tell	4	2	6	3.3
6.	neat	3	2	5	2.7
7.	ask	3	1	4	2.2
8.	meal	3	1	4	2.2
9.	mess	1	2	3	1.6
10.	nun	3	0	3	1.6
11.	peace	0	3	3	1.6
12.	universe	2	1	3	1.6
13.	call	2	0	2	1.1
14.	class	2	0	2	1.1
15.	confusion	0	2	2	1.1
16.	demand	2	0	2	1.1
17.	genus	1	1	2	1.1
18.	menu	0	2	2	1.1
19.	number	0	2	2	1.1
20.	set	0	2	2	1.1
21.	unorder	1	1	2	1.1

(f = 1, .5%, n = 76)
acquire, action, agenda, answer, arrangement,
assembly, away, beauty, blank, bore, bother,
buy, calm, captain, catalog, category, Catholic,
cayase, closed, court, Dark Ages, disobey, dull,
eat, edict, fish, food, form, fraternal, gin,
go, help, him, imbed, it, kind, knight, mail,
Masonic, method, mind, more, not, obey, official,
of things, organization, organize, organized,
police, position, procedure, procession, public,
random, rank, rational, request, restaurant,
rhyme, room, row, rule, send, service, silence,
some, straight, superior, supplies, system,
take, waiter, words, wrong, yell

Out   (In; With)

No.	Response	F	M	Tot.	%
1.	in	60	40	100	54.9
2.	side	7	10	17	9.3
3.	door(s)	5	3	8	4.4
4.	away	4	3	7	3.8
5.	of	5	2	7	3.8
6.	there	2	4	6	3.3
7.	outside	2	2	4	2.2
8.	beyond	1	1	2	1.1
9.	free	1	1	2	1.1
10.	order	1	1	2	1.1
11.	outdoors	1	1	2	1.1

(f = 1, .5%, n = 25)
air, annihilate, back, classed, cold, desert,
done, enclosure, go, gone, hopeless, house, lout,
moded, now, put, reject, run, sight, strike,
through, unconscious, way, west, window

Peace   (; Justice)

No.	Response	F	M	Tot.	%
1.	war	32	33	65	35.7
2.	corps	11	7	18	9.9
3.	quiet	10	3	13	7.1
4.	dove(s)	6	1	7	3.8
5.	good	4	1	5	2.7
6.	earth	2	1	3	1.6
7.	piece	0	3	3	1.6
8.	warm	1	2	3	1.6
9.	always	0	2	2	1.1
10.	bomb	0	2	2	1.1
11.	core	0	2	2	1.1

Peace (; Justice) (contd)

No.	Response	F	M	Tot.	%
12.	love	0	2	2	1.1
13.	now	0	2	2	1.1

(f = 1, .5%, n = 55)
afternoon, be, beatnik, calm, Christmas, coexist-
ence, comfort, Communist, content, death, dream,
enjoyment, fear, free, freedom, God, goodwill,
greatest, happy, harmony, heaven, hope, it, it's
wonderful, joy, Kennedy, men, mind, mission,
necessary, offering, O.K., overt, prosperity,
questionable, relief, rest, serenity, shelter,
shield, smooth, soft, some, sought, treaty, U.N.,
universal, want, warless, what, white, wild,
world, wreath, yea

Pepper (Salt;)

No.	Response	F	M	Tot.	%
1.	salt	66	51	117	64.2
2.	hot	7	8	15	8.2
3.	tree	3	5	8	4.4
4.	black	4	3	7	3.8
5.	shaker	2	3	5	2.7
6.	sneeze	4	1	5	2.7
7.	corn	0	2	2	1.1
8.	green	0	2	2	1.1
9.	pot	2	0	2	1.1
10.	spice	1	1	2	1.1

(f = 1, .5%, n = 17)
accent, bite, Dr., dog, drink, fire, grows, Java,
meat, mottled, nickname, pepper tree, potato,
scatter, sour, sprinkle, tasty

Person (; Citizen)

No.	Response	F	M	Tot.	%
1.	people	17	18	35	19.2
2.	man	9	9	18	9.9
3.	me	11	1	12	6.6
4.	individual	6	2	8	4.4
5.	him	3	3	6	3.3
6.	human	2	4	6	3.3
7.	thing	2	3	5	2.7
8.	he	2	2	4	2.2
9.	boy	3	0	3	1.6
10.	girl	1	2	3	1.6
11.	lone	2	1	3	1.6
12.	one	3	0	3	1.6
13.	being	1	1	2	1.1
14.	clothes	0	2	2	1.1
15.	form	1	1	2	1.1
16.	good	2	0	2	1.1
17.	like	1	1	2	1.1
18.	live	1	1	2	1.1
19.	mother	1	1	2	1.1
20.	nice	0	2	2	1.1
21.	she	1	1	2	1.1
22.	them	2	0	2	1.1
23.	who	1	1	2	1.1
24.	you	1	1	2	1.1

(f = 1, .5%, n = 52)
affable, animal, beautiful, Betsy, bewildered,
Bill, church, conversation, crowd, different, 80,
empty, father, Fred, friend, girl friend, God,
gone, has, her, important, in, J.F.K., Kennedy,
listen, lonely, many, normal, object, one, parson,
Pearson, peer, personal, persons, real, saved,
self, single, sleeps, smile, Stan, Sue, talk,
talking, telephone, they, under, unique, us,
vegetable, what

Pillow (; Soft)

No.	Response	F	M	Tot.	%
1.	bed	17	20	37	20.3
2.	soft	19	13	32	17.6
3.	sleep	14	13	27	14.8
4.	head	8	5	13	7.1
5.	talk	8	5	13	7.1
6.	case	2	6	8	4.4
7.	feather(s)	3	2	5	2.7
8.	lie	3	2	5	2.7
9.	rest	2	2	4	2.2
10.	white	1	2	3	1.6
11.	comfort	1	1	2	1.1
12.	cushion	0	2	2	1.1
13.	fight	2	0	2	1.1
14.	sheet(s)	2	0	2	1.1
15.	sleepy	1	1	2	1.1

(f = 1, .5%, n = 25)
abstain, black, blanket, color, deep, die, flat,
fluffy, green, ground, mat, nice, plump, puff,
sack, set, softer, soft-head, softness, study,
throw, uncomfortable, union, unnecessary, yours

Plant (; Stem)

No.	Response	F	M	Tot.	%
1.	green	24	16	40	22.0
2.	grow	13	9	22	12.1
3.	tree	9	13	22	12.1
4.	flower(s)	10	1	11	6.0
5.	leaf(ves)	5	1	6	3.3
6.	animal	3	2	5	2.7
7.	garden	3	2	5	2.7
8.	life	2	3	5	2.7
9.	bush	1	2	3	1.6
10.	botany	2	1	3	1.6
11.	food	1	2	3	1.6
12.	seed(s)	1	2	3	1.6
13.	vegetable(s)	0	3	3	1.6
14.	water	1	2	3	1.6
15.	alive	2	0	2	1.1
16.	growth	1	1	2	1.1
17.	tall	2	0	2	1.1

(f = 1, .5%, n = 42)
ant, apple, begonia, big, box, bulb, cactus,
chlorophyll, clinical, cultivate, dig, dirt, eat,
eggplant, factory, fern, forest, free, fun, grass,
ground, heterogeneous, live, love, one, outdoors,
petunia, photosynthesis, plantation, plate, pot,
put, root, rubber, soil, sow, stem, struggles,
vest, violet, watch, Zoology 10

Pretty (; Beautiful)

No.	Response	F	M	Tot.	%
1.	girl	18	16	34	18.7
2.	ugly	17	9	26	14.3
3.	nice	8	9	17	9.3
4.	woman(women)	5	11	16	8.8
5.	cute	7	3	10	5.5
6.	good	4	4	8	4.4
7.	face	4	2	6	3.3
8.	beautiful	2	3	5	2.7
9.	hair	2	2	4	2.2
10.	lovely	4	0	4	2.2
11.	flower	2	1	3	1.6
12.	attractive	1	1	2	1.1
13.	feet	1	1	2	1.1
14.	lady	2	0	2	1.1
15.	soft	1	1	2	1.1

Pretty   (; Beautiful) (contd)

No.	Response	F	M	Tot.	%

(f = 1, .5%, n = 41)
aesthetic, beauty, car, clothes, cultivated, daughter, exquisite, eyes, fair, funny, gay, good looking, happy, have, healthy, interesting, legs, like, mad, marriage, mauve, me, mean, much, near, now, petty, pleasant, pleasing, Roy Orbison, see, sick, sincere, slow, smooth, sweet, twiddy, well, will, yellow, yes

Queen   (King;   )

No.	Response	F	M	Tot.	%
1.	king	49	37	86	47.2
2.	bee	6	12	18	9.9
3.	crown	6	6	12	6.6
4.	hearts	4	2	6	3.3
5.	Elizabeth	4	1	5	2.7
6.	England	4	1	5	2.7
7.	Mary	3	2	5	2.7
8.	spade(s)	2	2	4	2.2
9.	cards	0	3	3	1.6
10.	mother	1	2	3	1.6
11.	regal	2	1	3	1.6
12.	woman	1	2	3	1.6
13.	Ann	1	1	2	1.1
14.	ant	0	2	2	1.1
15.	rule	2	0	2	1.1
16	Victoria	1	1	2	1.1

(f = 1, .5%, n = 21)
bitch, castle, collar, dike, distinguished, elegant, gold, green, her, hop, lady, man, married, monarch, of, prince, riches, Shaw, sit, sovereignty, throne

Question   (What; Why)

No.	Response	F	M	Tot.	%
1.	answer	70	62	132	72.5
2.	ask	9	2	11	6.0
3.	mark	4	4	8	4.4
4.	why	4	0	4	2.2
5.	what	1	2	3	1.6
6.	test	0	2	2	1.1

(f = 1, .5%, n = 22)
air, -aire, an, demand, hand, him, insecurity, intelligent, interrogate, life, list, man, nervous, number, puzzlement, question mark, response, speak, teacher, this, unanswered, write

Rest   (; Sleep)

No.	Response	F	M	Tot.	%
1.	sleep(s)	38	31	69	37.9
2.	relax	12	4	16	8.8
3.	tired	5	4	9	4.9
4.	bed	3	4	7	3.8
5.	quiet	5	2	7	3.8
6.	room	1	5	6	3.3
7.	home	2	2	4	2.2
8.	nap	3	1	4	2.2
9.	peace	1	2	3	1.6
10.	afternoon	2	0	2	1.1
11.	assured	1	1	2	1.1
12.	a while	1	1	2	1.1
13.	care	0	2	2	1.1

Rest   (; Sleep) (contd)

No.	Response	F	M	Tot.	%
14.	couch	2	0	2	1.1
15.	ease	2	0	2	1.1
16.	lie	2	0	2	1.1
17.	now	1	1	2	1.1
18.	peaceful	1	1	2	1.1
19.	time	1	1	2	1.1
20.	vacation	1	1	2	1.1
21.	West	0	2	2	1.1

(f = 1, .5%, n = 33)
active, all, assure, desirable, die, eat, enjoy, feet, good, ill, in, later, lay, lazy, no, pause, period, quite, recline, remain, remainder, remaining, repose, reside, return, stop, sun, test, tomb, tranquil, well, wind, work

Road   (Street;   )

No.	Response	F	M	Tot.	%
1.	car	9	6	15	8.2
2.	street	5	6	11	6.0
3.	drive	2	6	8	4.4
4.	long	6	2	8	4.4
5.	travel	5	3	8	4.4
6.	way	5	3	8	4.4
7.	dirt	2	4	6	3.3
8.	hard	4	2	6	3.3
9.	bed	2	3	5	2.7
10.	side	5	0	5	2.7
11.	winding	3	2	5	2.7
12.	path	4	0	4	2.2
13.	bumpy	3	0	3	1.6
14.	highway	0	3	3	1.6
15.	home	2	1	3	1.6
16.	sign	2	1	3	1.6
17.	toad	1	2	3	1.6
18.	windy	2	1	3	1.6
19.	ahead	1	1	2	1.1
20.	country	0	2	2	1.1
21.	curvy	2	0	2	1.1
22.	down	1	1	2	1.1
23.	hog	1	1	2	1.1
24.	house	2	0	2	1.1
25.	narrow	1	1	2	1.1
26.	race	0	2	2	1.1
27.	ride	0	2	2	1.1
28.	run	1	1	2	1.1
29.	rut(s)	0	2	2	1.1
30.	stream	1	1	2	1.1
31.	turn	2	0	2	1.1
32.	walk	2	0	2	1.1
33.	work	0	2	2	1.1

(f = 1, .5%, n = 45)
adventure, apple, asphalt, avenue, backhoe, bend, below, black, block, branched, cobblestone, curves, driving, engineer, fixing, follow, go, high, intercourse, journey, low, map, open, pavement, pebbles, rail, rocky, runner, small, straight, take, tobacco, to where, track, tractor, trail, tree, twist, twisted, up, went, where, which, white, yellow

Robber   (; Thief)

No.	Response	F	M	Tot.	%
1.	thief	37	29	66	36.2
2.	baron	4	9	13	7.1
3.	steal(s)	9	3	12	6.6
4.	mask	3	5	8	4.4
5.	bank	2	4	6	3.3
6.	cop(s)	4	2	6	3.3

Robber   (; Thief) (contd)

No.	Response	F	M	Tot.	%
7.	bandit	1	4	5	2.7
8.	rubber	0	4	4	2.2
9.	burglar	3	0	3	1.6
10.	criminal	2	1	3	1.6
11.	crook	1	2	3	1.6
12.	band	1	1	2	1.1
13.	beggar	2	0	2	1.1
14.	jail	0	2	2	1.1
15.	jewels	1	1	2	1.1
16.	stealer	2	0	2	1.1

($\underline{f}$ = 1, .5%, $\underline{n}$ = 42)
arm, armed, bad, badman, barren, black, black mask, blindfold, book, brutalness, burglary, chase, crude, danger, desperate, dirty, disturbed, eye, felony, gets, handkerchief, house, jewelry, Los Angeles, lost, make, man, need, next door, night, not, police, robber, Robert, robs, run, safety, slop, sneak, theft, villain, you
(Illegible - 1)

Rough   (Smooth;   )

No.	Response	F	M	Tot.	%
1.	smooth	21	11	32	17.6
2.	tough	7	11	18	9.9
3.	ready	4	10	14	7.7
4.	rider(s)	5	7	12	6.6
5.	hard	8	2	10	5.5
6.	soft	5	3	8	4.4
7.	road	3	3	6	3.3
8.	going	3	1	4	2.2
9.	water(s)	1	3	4	2.2
10.	beard	2	1	3	1.6
11.	easy	2	1	3	1.6
12.	ride	1	2	3	1.6
13.	shod	1	2	3	1.6
14.	tumble	2	1	3	1.6
15.	bump(s)	2	0	2	1.1
16.	bumpy	2	0	2	1.1
17.	coarse	1	1	2	1.1
18.	ground	1	1	2	1.1
19.	harsh	1	1	2	1.1
20.	life	1	1	2	1.1
21.	scratchy	1	1	2	1.1
22.	sore	0	2	2	1.1
23.	weather	1	1	2	1.1

($\underline{f}$ = 1, .5%, $\underline{n}$ = 41)
bad, beauty, cement, cigarette, course, dirty, feel, fight, fighter, file, forest, friction, gang, golf, grate, hands, hew, hewn, hurt, leather, night, paper, rugged, sand, sandpaper, scrape, sharp, skin, splinter, start, steady, stimulus, stuff, surface, texture, tongue, uncut, up, waves, wood, wool

Round   (Square; Earth)

No.	Response	F	M	Tot.	%
1.	square	15	13	28	15.4
2.	circle	14	10	24	13.2
3.	ball	13	8	21	11.5
4.	table	3	8	11	6.0
5.	fat	6	3	9	4.9
6.	about	4	1	5	2.7
7.	hole	2	3	5	2.7
8.	rug	5	0	5	2.7
9.	smooth	2	3	5	2.7
10.	soft	4	1	5	2.7
11.	flat	2	2	4	2.2
12.	apple	0	3	3	1.6

Round   (Square; Earth) (contd)

No.	Response	F	M	Tot.	%
13.	house	1	2	3	1.6
14.	robin	2	1	3	1.6
15.	firm	1	1	2	1.1
16.	ground	0	2	2	1.1
17.	hat	1	1	2	1.1
18.	head	1	1	2	1.1
19.	hound	1	1	2	1.1
20.	ring	2	0	2	1.1
21.	short	1	1	2	1.1
22.	sphere	2	0	2	1.1

($\underline{f}$ = 1, .5%, $\underline{n}$ = 35)
around, baby, bally, body, bound, Cantor, circular, circumference, corner, curve, face, fall, frown, go, hamburger, handle, hill, hollow, merry go, moving, oblong, perfect, plump, round table, run, shoulders, sound, stomach, surround, tall, thin, top, turn, world, worthless

Rug   (Carpet;   )

No.	Response	F	M	Tot.	%
1.	floor	15	19	34	18.7
2.	carpet	15	6	21	11.5
3.	bug	5	7	12	6.6
4.	soft	4	5	9	4.9
5.	warm	3	3	6	3.3
6.	foot(feet)	3	1	4	2.2
7.	round	3	1	4	2.2
8.	bear	1	2	3	1.6
9.	dirty	0	3	3	1.6
10.	house	2	1	3	1.6
11.	orange	3	0	3	1.6
12.	slip	3	0	3	1.6
13.	throw	2	1	3	1.6
14.	walk	1	2	3	1.6
15.	wool	2	1	3	1.6
16.	braid	2	0	2	1.1
17.	braided	2	0	2	1.1
18.	dirt	1	1	2	1.1
19.	hearth	2	0	2	1.1
20.	hooked	2	0	2	1.1
21.	India	1	1	2	1.1
22.	lay	0	2	2	1.1
23.	oriental	1	1	2	1.1
24.	room	1	1	2	1.1
25.	sweep	0	2	2	1.1
26.	tack(s)	2	0	2	1.1
27.	thick	2	0	2	1.1
28.	tie	2	0	2	1.1

($\underline{f}$ = 1, .5%, $\underline{n}$ = 41)
bee, beige, brown, buy, chair, clean, cleaner, cover, dug, dust, fireplace, flees, fringe, jerk, lamb, lover, luxury, made, mat, moth, pelt, pug, pull, purple, rag, ragged, rats, shag, shampoo, shrug, sound, step, table, trip, vacuum, warmth, wash, weave, weaved, woven, wrap around
(Illegible - 1)

Run   (; Jump)

No.	Response	F	M	Tot.	%
1.	fast	31	17	48	26.4
2.	walk	12	16	28	15.4
3.	away	6	7	13	7.1
4.	skip	4	1	5	2.7
5.	fun	1	3	4	2.2
6.	hurry	3	1	4	2.2

Run   (; Jump) (contd)

No.	Response	F	M	Tot.	%
7.	jump	3	1	4	2.2
8.	legs	3	1	4	2.2
9.	down	2	1	3	1.6
10.	ran	2	1	3	1.6
11.	stop	0	3	3	1.6
12.	sweat	1	2	3	1.6
13.	around	1	1	2	1.1
14.	come	2	0	2	1.1
15.	hard	2	0	2	1.1
16.	leap	2	0	2	1.1
17.	out	0	2	2	1.1
18.	race	1	1	2	1.1
19.	sit	1	1	2	1.1

($\underline{f}$ = 1, .5%, $\underline{n}$ = 46)
after, ahead, along, blur, breathe, cat, chicken, dog, door, 880, exercise, fall, far, faster, feet, fever, field, fly, from, go, guide, home, long, looseness, move, off, out-of-doors, pant, play, rapid, rover, rum, running, scream, see, seek, shorts, slow, speed, sun, through, tiring, together, track, tremble, up

Sat   (; Sit)

No.	Response	F	M	Tot.	%
1.	sit	21	16	37	20.3
2.	down	23	13	36	19.8
3.	chair	16	8	24	13.2
4.	stood	5	8	13	7.1
5.	on	4	2	6	3.3
6.	Saturday	2	2	4	2.2
7.	seat	1	3	4	2.2
8.	there	1	2	3	1.6
9.	up	0	3	3	1.6
10.	beside	1	1	2	1.1
11.	in	1	1	2	1.1
12.	lay	1	1	2	1.1
13.	sitting	0	2	2	1.1
14.	squat	1	1	2	1.1
15.	stand	0	2	2	1.1
16.	still	2	0	2	1.1
17.	Sunday	1	1	2	1.1
18.	tired	1	1	2	1.1

($\underline{f}$ = 1, .5%, $\underline{n}$ = 33)
beach, before, behind, corner, cried, don't, fat, fell, find, free, hat, leave, nearer, over, plopped, quaintly, read, relax, relief, remained, sad, set, spat, squatted, stool, sun, table, thought, tuffet, upright, wait, wet, yesterday
(Illegible - 1)

Saw   (See;   )

No.	Response	F	M	Tot.	%
1.	see	25	15	40	22.0
2.	wood	20	14	34	18.7
3.	cut	5	7	12	6.6
4.	seen	7	5	12	6.6
5.	hammer	4	4	8	4.4
6.	her	2	6	8	4.4
7.	tooth(teeth)	1	5	6	3.3
8.	him	3	2	5	2.7
9.	looked	1	2	3	1.6
10.	tree(s)	2	1	3	1.6
11.	blade	1	1	2	1.1
12.	edge(s)	0	2	2	1.1
13.	heard	0	2	2	1.1
14.	rip	0	2	2	1.1
15.	sharp	0	2	2	1.1
16.	work	2	0	2	1.1

Saw   (See;   ) (contd)

No.	Response	F	M	Tot.	%

($\underline{f}$ = 1, .5%, $\underline{n}$ = 39)
buzz, conquered, detected, did, dust, energy, eye, far, file, his, half, hurt, I, it, ladder, lick, logs, look, lucky, lumber, mill, nail, needles, nothing, perceived, people, redwood, scene, seesaw, she, shovel, steel, stump, timber, toothed, vision, what, who, you

Scared   (; Afraid)

No.	Response	F	M	Tot.	%
1.	frightened	19	17	36	19.8
2.	afraid	18	9	27	14.8
3.	fear	9	7	16	8.8
4.	stiff	1	6	7	3.8
5.	fright	3	3	6	3.3
6.	run	3	2	5	2.7
7.	death	1	3	4	2.2
8.	running	3	1	4	2.2
9.	dark	2	1	3	1.6
10.	of	3	0	3	1.6
11.	scream	3	0	3	1.6
12.	alone	2	0	2	1.1
13.	heart	2	0	2	1.1
14.	holy	0	2	2	1.1
15.	me	2	0	2	1.1
16.	never	1	1	2	1.1
17.	no	1	1	2	1.1
18.	sacred	0	2	2	1.1

($\underline{f}$ = 1, .5%, $\underline{n}$ = 54)
angry, army, black, blank, blasphemy, blessed, boy, bugs, calm, chicken, cold, composed, cow, cry, disturbed, emotional, fearful, fight, final, for, frighten, ghost, go, green, hair, hatred, help, insecure, life, monster, nervous, night, not, nothing, now, people, person, police, red, religion, sacrament, saint, scarce, shake, shape, shook, sick, snake, sometimes, strangers, tremble, unknown, weak, witch

Sea   (; Ocean)

No.	Response	F	M	Tot.	%
1.	ocean	16	15	31	17.0
2.	water	10	6	16	8.8
3.	green	9	2	11	6.0
4.	salt	4	7	11	6.0
5.	blue	9	1	10	5.5
6.	shore	1	4	5	2.7
7.	sick	1	4	5	2.7
8.	wave(s)	4	1	5	2.7
9.	deep	1	3	4	2.2
10.	fish	2	2	4	2.2
11.	side	1	3	4	2.2
12.	foam	3	0	3	1.6
13.	weed	1	2	3	1.6
14.	breeze	1	1	2	1.1
15.	monster	2	0	2	1.1
16.	shell	0	2	2	1.1
17.	ship(s)	0	2	2	1.1
18.	swim	0	2	2	1.1
19.	urchin	0	2	2	1.1
20.	wolf	1	1	2	1.1

($\underline{f}$ = 1, .5%, $\underline{n}$ = 56)
Adriatic, anemone, around, bass, bay, beach, beautiful, beauty, big, big waves, boat, boot, calm, cold, danger, exciting, far, fever, freedom, friendly, fun, God, gray, immense, insecure, life, love, magazine, me, mer, mollusks, ocean and fish, powerful, red, restful, river, rocks, rough, run,

GEOFFREY KEPPEL AND BONNIE Z. STRAND

Sea (; Ocean) (contd)

No.	Response	F	M	Tot.	%

sailing, salt air, Sardinia, saw, scandal, scene, serpent, shine, song, turtle, unfathomable, wavy, wet, whale, wide, wind, worm

See (Appear;)

No.	Response	F	M	Tot.	%
1.	look	27	12	39	21.4
2.	saw	14	4	18	9.9
3.	hear	5	9	14	7.7
4.	me	3	7	10	5.5
5.	ocean	3	7	10	5.5
6.	eye(s)	6	3	9	4.9
7.	them	5	2	7	3.8
8.	blind	1	2	3	1.6
9.	her	0	3	3	1.6
10.	it	1	2	3	1.6
11.	watch	3	0	3	1.6
12.	what	2	1	3	1.6
13.	you	1	2	3	1.6
14.	blue	1	1	2	1.1
15.	candy(ies)	0	2	2	1.1
16.	feel	0	2	2	1.1
17.	him	1	1	2	1.1
18.	perceive	1	1	2	1.1
19.	see(s)	2	0	2	1.1
20.	shore	0	2	2	1.1
21.	sight	1	1	2	1.1
22.	view	2	0	2	1.1

($\underline{f}$ = 1, .5%, $\underline{n}$ = 39)
beauty, boat, bridge, circus, clearly, contacts, dear, distance, end, everything, fish, foam, Flip, freedom, grass, he, head, know, life, love, observe, picture, pry, realize, red, run, sea, season, stars, table, that, there, things, this, urchin, visability, water, wet, yes

Selling (Buying;)

No.	Response	F	M	Tot.	%
1.	buying	41	30	71	39.0
2.	buy	2	6	8	4.4
3.	book(s)	3	2	5	2.7
4.	sold	1	4	5	2.7
5.	goods	2	2	4	2.2
6.	salesman	2	2	4	2.2
7.	boat	3	0	3	1.6
8.	car(s)	0	3	3	1.6
9.	door	1	2	3	1.6
10.	giving	2	1	3	1.6
11.	man	2	1	3	1.6
12.	money	2	1	3	1.6
13.	business	2	0	2	1.1
14.	commercial	0	2	2	1.1
15.	magazines	2	0	2	1.1
16.	things	1	1	2	1.1
17.	ticket(s)	1	1	2	1.1
18.	wares	2	0	2	1.1

($\underline{f}$ = 1, .5%, $\underline{n}$ = 55)
advertisement, aggressive, barter, candy, cart, cheating, clothes, convincing, Dick, fast, fruit, getting rid of, habit, house, investing, it, jerk, job, line, loot, losing, market, meadows, merchant, mother, nefarious, no, oranges, pans, papayas, peddler, people, Peter Sellers, pitch, place, product, purchasing, rights, roof, sailboat, sailing, saleswoman, short, soap, spree, stocks, store, talk, them, toys, troublesome, typewriters, vending, vendor, well

Shallow (Deep;)

No.	Response	F	M	Tot.	%
1.	deep	35	37	72	39.5
2.	water	16	11	27	14.8
3.	pool	8	5	13	7.1
4.	pond	9	1	10	5.5
5.	lake	1	3	4	2.2
6.	stream	2	2	4	2.2
7.	well	2	2	4	2.2
8.	mind	2	1	3	1.6
9.	river	1	2	3	1.6
10.	thin	1	2	3	1.6
11.	wide	1	2	3	1.6
12.	low	1	1	2	1.1
13.	person	1	1	2	1.1
14.	shoal(s)	0	2	2	1.1
15.	wade	1	1	2	1.1

($\underline{f}$ = 1, .5%, $\underline{n}$ = 28)
bleak, cow, creek, depth, drown, dull, empty, feeling, grave, gulp, hole, hollow, ignorant, narrow, penetrating, pit, puddle, quick, sink, small, stupid, swift, swim, thinking, voice, walk, warm, weak

Sharp (; Needle, Scissors)

No.	Response	F	M	Tot.	%
1.	knife	18	18	36	19.8
2.	dull	4	11	15	8.2
3.	point	9	5	14	7.7
4.	blunt	4	5	9	4.9
5.	pointed	5	4	9	4.9
6.	cut	4	2	6	3.3
7.	nail	4	1	5	2.7
8.	pain	1	4	5	2.7
9.	soft	3	2	5	2.7
10.	hurt	4	0	4	2.2
11.	noise	3	1	4	2.2
12.	sound	3	1	4	2.2
13.	hard	3	0	3	1.6
14.	loud	1	2	3	1.6
15.	object	2	1	3	1.6
16.	pencil	1	2	3	1.6
17.	cheddar	1	1	2	1.1
18.	cheese	1	1	2	1.1
19.	edge	0	2	2	1.1
20.	keen	0	2	2	1.1
21.	needle	1	1	2	1.1
22.	ouch	1	1	2	1.1
23.	piercing	1	1	2	1.1
24.	pin	2	0	2	1.1
25.	razor	1	1	2	1.1
26.	stick	1	1	2	1.1
27.	tack	1	1	2	1.1

($\underline{f}$ = 1, .5%, $\underline{n}$ = 32)
acute, austere, bite, bitter, clear, corner, ears, feel, flat, glass, harsh, horse, jagged, music, narrow, neat, painful, pierce, pointy, puncture, round, slow, smart, smooth, strong, tasty, temper, thin, tone, tongue, touch, well

She (He;)

No.	Response	F	M	Tot.	%
1.	he	55	30	85	46.7
2.	her(s)	11	12	23	12.6
3.	girl	6	3	9	4.9
4.	is	2	4	6	3.3
5.	it	1	5	6	3.3
6.	they	3	2	5	2.7
7.	me	0	3	3	1.6
8.	woman	1	2	3	1.6

She (He;) (contd)

No.	Response	F	M	Tot.	%
9.	him	2	0	2	1.1
10.	looked	0	2	2	1.1
11.	looks	2	0	2	1.1
12.	loved	1	1	2	1.1
13.	we	0	2	2	1.1
14.	went	2	0	2	1.1

($\underline{f}$ = 1, .5%, $\underline{n}$ = 30)
aid, ate, beauty, bitch, body, book, clothes, cute, does, doesn't, eyes, fears, goat, has, instigator, Janis, legs, lives, Mary, nice, pretty, saw, shit, smiled, smiles, took, wed, will, won, you

Shoe (Foot;)

No.	Response	F	M	Tot.	%
1.	feet(foot)	23	21	44	24.2
2.	lace(s)	12	4	16	8.8
3.	horn	9	6	15	8.2
4.	tree	6	9	15	4.4
5.	shine	1	7	8	4.4
6.	sock(s)	5	3	8	3.8
7.	string	2	5	7	3.3
8.	wear	3	3	6	2.7
9.	brown	2	3	5	2.7
10.	fit(s)	5	0	5	2.2
11.	sole	2	2	4	2.2
12.	tie	4	0	4	2.2
13.	walk	3	1	4	2.2
14.	boot	1	2	3	1.6
15.	leather	1	2	3	1.6
16.	toe	0	3	3	1.6
17.	black	0	2	2	1.1
18.	sandal(s)	2	0	2	1.1
19.	size	0	2	2	1.1
20.	tight	0	2	2	1.1

($\underline{f}$ = 1, .5%, $\underline{n}$ = 24)
barefoot, box, cover, fifteen, heels, horse, loafers, noise, ouch, repair, ripped, salesman, shape, shoeless, shop, shorn, skinny, soft, sore, step, store, tan, tennis, tied

Shoot (Guns;)

No.	Response	F	M	Tot.	%
1.	gun(s)	24	22	46	25.3
2.	kill	18	14	32	17.6
3.	dead	5	4	9	4.9
4.	hit	2	4	6	3.3
5.	bang	3	2	5	2.7
6.	bullet(s)	2	3	5	2.7
7.	rifle	2	3	5	2.7
8.	aim	3	1	4	2.2
9.	hunt	1	3	4	2.2
10.	at	0	3	3	1.6
11.	deer	1	2	3	1.6
12.	die	2	1	3	1.6
13.	duck(s)	3	0	3	1.6
14.	him	1	2	3	1.6
15.	shot	1	2	3	1.6
16.	target	3	0	3	1.6
17.	arrow	2	0	2	1.1
18.	down	2	0	2	1.1
19.	fire	2	0	2	1.1
20.	it	1	1	2	1.1
21.	me	1	1	2	1.1

($\underline{f}$ = 1, .5%, $\underline{n}$ = 36)
animal, ball, bamboo, bear, Billy, bird, bow, buffalo, burn, buy, cat, dark, far, fast, fox, game, harm, heard, her, home, hunter, hurt, lion, loud, miss, murder, needle, never,

Shoot (Guns;) (contd)

No.	Response	F	M	Tot.	%

noise, orgasm, see, straight, star, trigger, up

Short (Long;)

No.	Response	F	M	Tot.	%
1.	tall	35	23	58	31.8
2.	fat	12	15	27	14.8
3.	long	11	13	24	13.2
4.	man	2	2	4	2.2
5.	me	3	1	4	2.2
6.	small	3	1	4	2.2
7.	stocky	2	2	4	2.2
8.	legs	2	1	3	1.6
9.	little	1	2	3	1.6
10.	thin	2	1	3	1.6
11.	cut	0	2	2	1.1
12.	skirt	2	0	2	1.1
13.	squat	0	2	2	1.1
14.	stout	0	2	2	1.1
15.	stuff	0	2	2	1.1

($\underline{f}$ = 1, .5%, $\underline{n}$ = 38)
age, big, boy, breath, cute, dumpy, end, girl, graph, green, hair, hand, heels, height, high, is, knobby, letter, midget, mother, not long, pants, person, pudgy, range, rib, shorts, sighted, sister, slow, sorrow, stubby, sweet, tiny, undershirt, used, walk, young

Sick (; Doctor, Health)

No.	Response	F	M	Tot.	%
1.	ill	18	18	36	19.8
2.	well	10	13	23	12.6
3.	bed	10	3	13	7.1
4.	bad	3	4	7	3.8
5.	hospital	3	3	6	3.3
6.	tired	3	3	6	3.3
7.	healthy	2	3	5	2.7
8.	health	2	2	4	2.2
9.	cold	1	2	3	1.6
10.	disease	1	1	2	1.1
11.	doctor	1	1	2	1.1
12.	dog	1	1	2	1.1
13.	green	1	1	2	1.1
14.	hurt	0	2	2	1.1
15.	nurse	2	0	2	1.1
16.	pain	1	1	2	1.1
17.	patient	1	1	2	1.1
18.	teeth	2	0	2	1.1
19.	unhappy	2	0	2	1.1
20.	white	1	1	2	1.1

($\underline{f}$ = 1, .5%, $\underline{n}$ = 57)
ailing, alone, apple, bet, better, bitter, boy, call, colitis, cough, Cowell, dark, dead, death, father, feeble, filth, girl, groove, hell, help, in bed, insane, leave, lovely, man, me, measles, mental, Mick, mother, nauseous, -ness, no, of, pale, pan, quick, sad, school, sea, shaky, sick, sicker, stake, stick, stomach, strong, sway, temperature, thermometer, throw up, unhealthy, vomit, weak, why, wife

Sickness (Health;)

No.	Response	F	M	Tot.	%
1.	health	39	41	80	43.9
2.	death	11	3	14	7.7
3.	illness	8	6	14	7.7
4.	ill	8	2	10	5.5
5.	bed	6	3	9	4.9
6.	disease	2	3	5	2.7
7.	sad	4	0	4	2.2
8.	sea	1	2	3	1.6
9.	vomit	1	2	3	1.6
10.	weak	3	0	3	1.6
11.	doctor	1	1	2	1.1
12.	fever	2	0	2	1.1
13.	well	0	2	2	1.1

($\underline{f}$ = 1, .5%, $\underline{n}$ = 30)
ache, age, asthma, awful, bad, cancer, child, cold, flu, grief, hard, help, hospital, injury, malady, malaria, man, measles, mental, misery, not me, plague, sadness, sin, stomach, tired, unfortunate, unhappiness, unnormal, yellow
(Illegible - 1)

Sit (Stand; Chair)

No.	Response	F	M	Tot.	%
1.	down	47	39	86	47.2
2.	stand	12	17	29	15.9
3.	chair	10	3	13	7.1
4.	in(s)	3	5	8	4.4
5.	sat	5	3	8	4.4
6.	relax	2	3	5	2.7
7.	still	4	0	4	2.2
8.	up	1	3	4	2.2
9.	lie	1	1	2	1.1
10.	seat	2	0	2	1.1

($\underline{f}$ = 1, .5%, $\underline{n}$ = 21)
behind, butt, class, couch, cross-legged, fat, Indian, lay, listen, mit, on, ouch, out, relief, rest, squat, straight, think, tired, together, wait

Sky (Blue;)

No.	Response	F	M	Tot.	%
1.	blue	64	42	106	58.2
2.	above	3	6	9	4.9
3.	high	1	6	7	3.8
4.	earth	3	2	5	2.7
5.	cloud(s)	1	4	5	2.7
6.	clear	2	2	4	2.2
7.	heaven(s)	4	0	4	2.2
8.	star(s)	1	3	4	2.2
9.	light	1	2	3	1.6
10.	ceiling	1	1	2	1.1
11.	cloudy	2	0	2	1.1
12.	fly	1	1	2	1.1
13.	sea	2	0	2	1.1

($\underline{f}$ = 1, .5%, $\underline{n}$ = 27)
all, beauty, below, black, endless, fall, falling, flying, fog, gray, hanging, infantile, lark, lie, limitless, moon, open, pie, plane, scraper, soar, sun, torn, universe, up, vast, white

Sleep (Bed, Dream;)

No.	Response	F	M	Tot.	%
1.	bed	7	11	18	9.9
2.	walk	6	11	17	9.3
3.	dream	9	6	15	8.2
4.	tired	8	4	12	6.6
5.	rest	7	3	10	5.5
6.	wake	5	3	8	4.4
7.	awake	3	3	6	3.3
8.	well	3	3	6	3.3
9.	good	2	2	4	2.2
10.	night	3	1	4	2.2
11.	sickness	1	3	4	2.2
12.	deep	0	3	3	1.6
13.	need	0	3	3	1.6
14.	now	1	2	3	1.6
15.	peace	2	1	3	1.6
16.	pillow	2	1	3	1.6
17.	snore	2	1	3	1.6
18.	sound	3	0	3	1.6
19.	soundly	3	0	3	1.6
20.	cold	0	2	2	1.1
21.	dark	1	1	2	1.1
22.	eat	2	0	2	1.1
23.	eyes	2	0	2	1.1
24.	quiet	2	0	2	1.1

($\underline{f}$ = 1, .5%, $\underline{n}$ = 43)
awaken, boy, close, dead, death, drift, drink, early, endless, enjoy, go, grateful, innocent, lie, little, long, morning, much, necessary, nice, nightgown, not, peaceful, placid, reap, relax, sick, sink, sleepwalk, slept, slumber, soon, talk, this morning, tight, time, tiredness, walker, wall, warm, warmth, wet, when
(Illegible - 1)

Slower (Faster;)

No.	Response	F	M	Tot.	%
1.	faster	45	40	85	46.7
2.	fast	1	6	7	3.8
3.	car	3	2	5	2.7
4.	than	3	2	5	2.7
5.	clean	2	2	4	2.2
6.	turtle	2	2	4	2.2
7.	walk	3	1	4	2.2
8.	water	4	0	4	2.2
9.	bath	3	0	3	1.6
10.	slow	2	1	3	1.6
11.	snail	2	1	3	1.6
12.	tortoise	1	2	3	1.6
13.	calm	2	0	2	1.1
14.	long	1	1	2	1.1
15.	molasses	1	1	2	1.1
16.	rain	2	0	2	1.1
17.	sluggish	1	1	2	1.1
18.	speed	1	1	2	1.1

($\underline{f}$ = 1, .5%, $\underline{n}$ = 40)
brakes, can't, cap, catch, cold, creep, down, dragging, driver, driving, dull, ease, easier, friction, gifts, haste, heavy, lead, less, morning, move, now, nude, pace, quick, quicker, quickly, red, rest, run, shower, slowest, still, student, stupid, surer, take, walking, weak, wet

Smoke (Tobacco;)

No.	Response	F	M	Tot.	%
1.	cigarette(s)	31	21	52	28.5
2.	fire	11	11	22	12.1
3.	cough	3	4	7	3.8
4.	bad	2	4	6	3.3

Smoke   (Tobacco;   ) (contd)

No.	Response	F	M	Tot.	%
5.	gray	6	0	6	3.3
6.	cancer	1	4	5	2.7
7.	cigar	0	4	4	2.2
8.	eyes	3	1	4	2.2
9.	inhale	1	2	3	1.6
10.	pipe	1	2	3	1.6
11.	ring(s)	3	0	3	1.6
12.	bed	1	1	2	1.1
13.	black	0	2	2	1.1
14.	chimney	1	1	2	1.1
15.	cloud	2	0	2	1.1
16.	curl	2	0	2	1.1
17.	fume(s)	1	1	2	1.1
18.	habit	1	1	2	1.1
19.	haze	0	2	2	1.1
20.	puff(s)	0	2	2	1.1
21.	screen	1	1	2	1.1
22.	smog	0	2	2	1.1
23.	soot	1	1	2	1.1
24.	tears	2	0	2	1.1

($\underline{f}$ = 1, .5%, $\underline{n}$ = 41)
air, acrid, barbecue, blow, blowing, bread,
ciggies, croak, curling, drink, dust, enough,
film, filter, freedom, grass, Half & Half,
house, irritate, malodorous, jumper, match,
mist, mouth, much, no, nothing, Platters, rise,
room, salmon, sand, see, shake, shop, sky,
smoke, stack, stink, white, yeah

Smooth   (Rough;   )

No.	Response	F	M	Tot.	%
1.	soft	24	16	40	22.0
2.	rough	22	14	36	19.8
3.	silk	4	7	11	6.0
4.	skin	3	6	9	4.9
5.	glass	4	1	5	2.7
6.	hard	2	2	4	2.2
7.	surface	2	2	4	2.2
8.	hair	1	2	3	1.6
9.	muscle	1	2	3	1.6
10.	Scotch	1	2	3	1.6
11.	sheet	1	2	3	1.6
12.	clear	2	0	2	1.1
13.	satin	2	0	2	1.1
14.	slick	0	2	2	1.1
15.	slippery	2	0	2	1.1
16.	water	2	0	2	1.1
17.	wrinkled	1	1	2	1.1

($\underline{f}$ = 1, .5%, $\underline{n}$ = 49)
body, breast, calm, cloth, cold, days, drink,
enamel, fair, fast, feel, feeling, finish, firm,
flow, going, good, jagged, legs, marble, move,
pillow, plane, rug, sailing, sea, shallow, shiny,
silky, sleek, slide, soothe, snow, stick, stone,
style, sure, sweet, talk, thin, touch, velvet,
velvety, warm, waves, wavy, which, whiskey, white

Snow   (; Cold, White)

No.	Response	F	M	Tot.	%
1.	white	43	32	75	41.2
2.	cold	8	8	16	8.8
3.	rain	2	6	8	4.4
4.	ski	4	4	8	4.4
5.	fall(s)	5	2	7	3.8
6.	ice	5	1	6	3.3
7.	mountain(s)	4	2	6	3.3
8.	ball(s)	2	3	5	2.7
9.	sleet	3	1	4	2.2

Snow   (; Cold, White) (contd)

No.	Response	F	M	Tot.	%
10.	plow	1	2	3	1.6
11.	fun	0	2	2	1.1
12.	queen	2	0	2	1.1
13.	slush	1	1	2	1.1
14.	soft	1	1	2	1.1

($\underline{f}$ = 1, .5%, $\underline{n}$ = 36)
abominable, black, bunny, Christmas, clean, coolness, crestline, crystal, damp, dirty, drift, falling, flake, fly, glisten, glitter, high, job,
light, lighting, man, me, melt, neige, New York,
rail, shoe, silence, sky, storm, swirl, under, wet,
whiteness, wind, wonderful

Socks   (; Shoes)

No.	Response	F	M	Tot.	%
1.	shoe(s)	48	47	95	52.2
2.	dirty	9	4	13	7.1
3.	hole(s)	5	4	9	4.9
4.	darn	7	0	7	3.8
5.	feet	2	5	7	3.8
6.	white	4	1	5	2.7
7.	black	0	3	3	1.6
8.	smell(s)	2	1	3	1.6
9.	wear	1	2	3	1.6
10.	gray	1	1	2	1.1
11.	knee	2	0	2	1.1
12.	knit	2	0	2	1.1
13.	mend	2	0	2	1.1
14.	sweat	0	2	2	1.1

($\underline{f}$ = 1, .5%, $\underline{n}$ = 26)
blocks, blue, bobby, box, Christmas, clothes,
enclose, garter, heels, holey, initiate, jock,
lax, match, roommate, sex, shirt, slacks, stink,
stockings, stripe, thin, underwear, warm, wet,
yarn
(Illegible - 1)

Soft   (Comfort, Hard, Loud; Carpet, Smooth)

No.	Response	F	M	Tot.	%
1.	hard	22	27	49	26.9
2.	pillow	4	6	10	5.5
3.	smooth	5	1	6	3.3
4.	sweet	5	0	5	2.7
5.	warm	4	1	5	2.7
6.	cotton	3	1	4	2.2
7.	loud	2	2	4	2.2
8.	gentle	1	2	3	1.6
9.	kitten	2	1	3	1.6
10.	shoe	3	0	3	1.6
11.	baby	1	1	2	1.1
12.	bed	1	1	2	1.1
13.	blanket	2	0	2	1.1
14.	breast	0	2	2	1.1
15.	chair	1	1	2	1.1
16.	down	0	2	2	1.1
17.	drink	1	1	2	1.1
18.	fat	1	1	2	1.1
19.	hair	1	1	2	1.1
20.	love	2	0	2	1.1
21.	music	2	0	2	1.1
22.	rug	1	1	2	1.1
23.	sharp	1	1	2	1.1
24.	skin	1	1	2	1.1
25.	swishy	2	0	2	1.1
26.	touch	1	1	2	1.1
27.	whisper	1	1	2	1.1
28.	words	2	0	2	1.1

Soft (Comfort, Hard, Loud; Carpet, Smooth) (contd)

No.	Response	F	M	Tot.	%

($\underline{f}$ = 1, .5%, $\underline{n}$ = 54)
act, animal, beautiful, body, breeze, carpet, cat, comfort, comfortable, couch, cuddly, desire, fall, feathers, feel, felt, flower, fluffy, fresh, fur, furry, fuzzy, girl, hand, harsh, hart, lame, lights, luscious, neat, nice, pink, pleasant, quiet, rough, round, shell, shit, silky, sleep, slow, snugly, soap, spongy, squishy, step, tender, texture, tissue, voice, weak, web, wet, wool

Softly (Quietly;)

No.	Response	F	M	Tot.	%
1.	quietly	11	5	16	8.8
2.	loudly	7	4	11	6.0
3.	walk	6	2	8	4.4
4.	gently	3	4	7	3.8
5.	lightly	3	4	7	3.8
6.	quiet	4	3	7	3.8
7.	tiptoe	4	3	7	3.8
8.	speak	3	3	6	3.3
9.	tread	2	4	6	3.3
10.	leave	2	3	5	2.7
11.	go	3	1	4	2.2
12.	hard	1	3	4	2.2
13.	breeze	1	2	3	1.6
14.	come	2	1	3	1.6
15.	creep	2	1	3	1.6
16.	hardly	1	2	3	1.6
17.	loud	1	2	3	1.6
18.	nice	2	1	3	1.6
19.	touch	3	0	3	1.6
20.	pad	2	0	2	1.1
21.	slipper(s)	1	1	2	1.1
22.	slowly	1	1	2	1.1
23.	smoothly	0	2	2	1.1
24.	sweet	0	2	2	1.1
25.	talk	1	1	2	1.1
26.	tender	2	0	2	1.1
27.	tenderly	1	1	2	1.1
28.	warm	1	1	2	1.1
29.	whisper	2	0	2	1.1

($\underline{f}$ = 1, .5%, $\underline{n}$ = 55)
beautiful, brush, call, calmly, caress, cat, cat's paws, close, cloud, creeping, dainty, distant, feet, foam, free, gentile, going, hair, harsh, hold, light, mellow, music, neatly, night, noise, noisily, padded, patter, pink, romantic, round, sang, shallow, shoeless, silently, sing, skin, sleep, snore, snow, soft, spoke, spoken, stealthy, step, stepping, stick, stroke, swaying, sweetly, tissue, wake

Song (Music;)

No.	Response	F	M	Tot.	%
1.	sing	43	39	82	45.0
2.	bird	4	11	15	8.2
3.	melody	3	2	5	2.7
4.	dance	4	0	4	2.2
5.	guitar	3	1	4	2.2
6.	music	1	3	4	2.2
7.	beauty	2	1	3	1.6
8.	book	0	3	3	1.6
9.	happy	1	2	3	1.6
10.	note(s)	1	2	3	1.6
11.	sheet	2	1	3	1.6
12.	chanson	1	1	2	1.1
13.	cheer	2	0	2	1.1
14.	pretty	2	0	2	1.1

Song (Music;) (contd)

No.	Response	F	M	Tot.	%
15.	singing	1	1	2	1.1
16.	sung	1	1	2	1.1
17.	sweet	1	1	2	1.1
18.	tune	2	0	2	1.1

($\underline{f}$ = 1, .5%, $\underline{n}$ = 39)
beautiful, bong, California, chant, child, clear, cry, end, fest, festive, for, free, fun, girl, glorious, Joan Baez, jolly, joy, Julie London, leader, like, lilt, lousy, lyric, mouth, night, off-key, of Roland, piano, practice, robin, Roland, sad, sang, singer, sky, title, voices, whistle

Sorrow (; Joy)

No.	Response	F	M	Tot.	%
1.	sad	18	17	35	19.2
2.	grief	20	5	25	13.7
3.	sadness	7	8	15	8.2
4.	happiness	4	7	11	6.0
5.	joy	7	1	8	4.4
6.	cry	4	3	7	3.8
7.	tear(s)	3	4	7	3.8
8.	death	3	2	5	2.7
9.	weep	2	3	5	2.7
10.	pain	2	2	4	2.2
11.	anger	0	2	2	1.1
12.	bad	2	0	2	1.1
13.	blue	1	1	2	1.1
14.	feel	1	1	2	1.1
15.	grieve	1	1	2	1.1
16.	misery	1	1	2	1.1
17.	song	1	1	2	1.1

($\underline{f}$ = 1, .5%, $\underline{n}$ = 46)
agony, always, anguish, apple, care, dark, depressed, despair, drowned, friendship, full, funeral, girl, gladness, glee, gloom, great, happy, hurt, impression, laughter, learn, leaving, loss, love, mandate, me, meaningful, mourn, mourning, much, no, not, pity, red, seldom, sometimes, sophistication, sorrowful, sorrowness, sparrow, sweet, unhappiness, waste, weakness, yes

Sound (; Music)

No.	Response	F	M	Tot.	%
1.	noise	31	18	49	26.9
2.	loud	17	13	30	16.5
3.	music	10	6	16	8.8
4.	hear	6	7	13	7.1
5.	ear(s)	2	3	5	2.7
6.	fury	2	2	4	2.2
7.	quiet	2	2	4	2.2
8.	off	0	3	3	1.6
9.	good	1	1	2	1.1
10.	happy	1	1	2	1.1
11.	hearing	1	1	2	1.1
12.	horn	1	1	2	1.1
13.	soft	2	0	2	1.1
14.	tone	0	2	2	1.1
15.	wave	1	1	2	1.1
16.	whisper	2	0	2	1.1

($\underline{f}$ = 1, .5%, $\underline{n}$ = 42)
across, advice, alarm, ball, bang, barren, bells, bird, blank, buzz, chirping, effects, gurgle, happiness, heard, high, laugh, less, light, megaphone, mound, mystifying, peaceful, plane, pretty, quality, record, riot, sad, safe, sense, sharp, sigh, silence, sonic, sweet, techniques, touch, trunk, unity, whistle, white

Sour (Sweet; Bitter)

No.	Response	F	M	Tot.	%
1.	sweet	37	23	60	32.9
2.	lemon(s)	16	8	24	13.2
3.	cream	14	8	22	12.1
4.	bitter	7	6	13	7.1
5.	dough	4	8	12	6.6
6.	milk	6	5	11	6.0
7.	grape(s)	4	5	9	4.9
8.	bread	2	2	4	2.2
9.	creme	2	1	3	1.6
10.	taste	0	3	3	1.6

($\underline{f}$ = 1, .5%, $\underline{n}$ = 21)
apple, bacteria, bad, contraction, fresh, fruit, grimace, horrible, mixer, mother, park, personality, pickle, pork, puss, salty, spoilt, sweat, vinegar, whiskey, yogurt

Star (Moon;) (contd)

No.	Response	F	M	Tot.	%
16.	beauty	2	0	2	1.1
17.	far	0	2	2	1.1
18.	galaxy	1	1	2	1.1
19.	high	2	0	2	1.1
20.	moon	0	2	2	1.1
21.	red	1	1	2	1.1
22.	sun	0	2	2	1.1
23.	white	2	0	2	1.1

($\underline{f}$ = 1, .5%, $\underline{n}$ = 35)
above, actor, astronomy, bar, brilliant, car, Christmas, comet, cross'd, evening, eyed, fall, fascinating, gazer, glimmer, good, hit, infinity, movie, myriads, Newman, planet, quasi-stellar, rhyme, Ringo, shiny, silent, silver, sky at night, spangled, stellar, twinkling, Walt Disney, wheel, wonder

Spoke (; Speak)

No.	Response	F	M	Tot.	%
1.	speak	18	10	28	15.4
2.	said	11	5	16	8.8
3.	talk	7	6	13	7.1
4.	word(s)	8	5	13	7.1
5.	talked	6	4	10	5.5
6.	spoken	4	3	7	3.8
7.	softly	4	2	6	3.3
8.	wheel	5	0	5	2.7
9.	together	2	2	4	2.2
10.	loud	1	2	3	1.6
11.	speech	0	3	3	1.6
12.	to	2	1	3	1.6
13.	bicycle	1	1	2	1.1
14.	heard	0	2	2	1.1
15.	here	0	2	2	1.1
16.	laughed	1	1	2	1.1
17.	listen	0	2	2	1.1
18.	of	1	1	2	1.1
19.	past	2	0	2	1.1
20.	say	0	2	2	1.1
21.	spake	2	0	2	1.1
22.	speaking	1	1	2	1.1
23.	spokesman	1	1	2	1.1

($\underline{f}$ = 1, .5%, $\underline{n}$ = 49)
aloud, already, answered, before, bike, clarity, class, eloquent, fast, French, God, harangue, harsh, he, hear, I, Indian, last, lecture, lecturer, loudly, me, meekly, message, more, movies, nicely, now, podium, preached, quiet, quietly, repeated, Rome, song, speaker, spoken to, then, this, tire, token, up, utter, uttered, voice, when, why, will, Zarathustra

Steal (Thief;)

No.	Response	F	M	Tot.	%
1.	take	25	14	39	21.4
2.	rob	12	6	18	9.9
3.	thief	8	9	17	9.3
4.	money	2	5	7	3.8
5.	bread	3	1	4	2.2
6.	food	1	3	4	2.2
7.	keep	1	3	4	2.2
8.	stole	3	1	4	2.2
9.	away	1	2	3	1.6
10.	bad	1	2	3	1.6
11.	from	3	0	3	1.6
12.	give	2	1	3	1.6
13.	never	2	1	3	1.6
14.	robber	1	2	3	1.6
15.	run	1	2	3	1.6
16.	theft	1	2	3	1.6
17.	bar	2	0	2	1.1
18.	base	2	0	2	1.1
19.	find	0	2	2	1.1
20.	hide	1	1	2	1.1
21.	mask	1	1	2	1.1
22.	shoes	2	0	2	1.1
23.	stolen	0	2	2	1.1

($\underline{f}$ = 1, .5%, $\underline{n}$ = 47)
all, applecart, bank, baseball, beg, borrow, buy, candy, car, cheap, cheat, coat, crime, dowager, fight, games, get, gone, goods, grab, gun, home, jewels, lift, Negro, no she didn't, nothing, potatoes, punish, purloin, quiet, quietly, rip, scheme, silver, something, steal, stealth, steel, swipe, thimble, things, throw, took, unfair, we'll, what

Star (Moon;)

No.	Response	F	M	Tot.	%
1.	bright	18	7	25	13.7
2.	sky	15	9	24	13.2
3.	light	6	13	19	10.4
4.	shine(s)	12	4	16	8.8
5.	twinkle	8	6	14	7.7
6.	shooting	4	1	5	2.7
7.	fish	0	4	4	2.2
8.	wish	4	0	4	2.2
9.	beautiful	2	1	3	1.6
10.	falling	2	1	3	1.6
11.	flower	1	2	3	1.6
12.	gaze	2	1	3	1.6
13.	heaven(s)	1	2	3	1.6
14.	night	1	2	3	1.6
15.	actress	0	2	2	1.1

Still (; Stand)

No.	Response	F	M	Tot.	%
1.	quiet	40	12	52	28.5
2.	night	10	5	15	8.2
3.	yet	6	9	15	8.2
4.	water	3	4	7	3.8
5.	now	3	3	6	3.3
6.	life	2	3	5	2.7
7.	is	4	0	4	2.2
8.	silent	1	3	4	2.2
9.	there	1	3	4	2.2
10.	moving	1	2	3	1.6
11.	another	1	1	2	1.1
12.	here	2	0	2	1.1
13.	placid	1	1	2	1.1
14.	small	2	0	2	1.1

Still (; Stand) (contd)

No.	Response	F	M	Tot.	%
15.	whiskey	1	1	2	1.1

(f = 1, .5%, n = 57)
active, again, alcohol, alive, alone, already, am, an, are, away, birth, booze, born, calm, cold, empty, even, evening, far, fast, forest, forever, hand, hard, hot, lake, liquor, moonshine, motion, mountain-meadow, mountains, move, -ness, never, no, noiseless, not, our, peace, quite, run, shiver, sit, slow, smooth, solitude, sorrow, stand, stay, stomp, then, trees, true, well, when, wine, yep

Stream (; River)

No.	Response	F	M	Tot.	%
1.	water	20	10	30	16.5
2.	river	18	10	28	15.4
3.	fish	5	9	14	7.7
4.	brook	7	5	12	6.6
5.	flow(s)	4	3	7	3.8
6.	consciousness	2	4	6	3.3
7.	creek	3	3	6	3.3
8.	lake	4	1	5	2.7
9.	run	4	1	5	2.7
10.	cool	2	2	4	2.2
11.	blue	2	1	3	1.6
12.	bubble	0	2	2	1.1
13.	fishing	1	1	2	1.1
14.	light	1	1	2	1.1
15.	mountain	1	1	2	1.1
16.	ripple(s)	2	0	2	1.1
17.	rocks	1	1	2	1.1
18.	shallow	0	2	2	1.1
19.	trickle(s)	0	2	2	1.1
20.	trout	1	1	2	1.1

(f = 1, .5%, n = 44)
beam, beautiful, big, bubbling, clean, clear, conscious, covered, creek bank, creme, cross, curve, dead, deep, down, engine, forest, front, glow, gurgle, life, line, love, music, Nevada Falls, pond, rapids, refreshing, running, seam, shallow, singing, slow, Strawberry, Strawberry Creek, swirling, thirst, thought, trees, trickling, walk, west, winding, winds

Sugar (; Sweet)

No.	Response	F	M	Tot.	%
1.	sweet	52	40	92	50.5
2.	cane	4	4	8	4.4
3.	spice	6	2	8	4.4
4.	coffee	4	3	7	3.8
5.	white	4	3	7	3.8
6.	honey	3	2	5	2.7
7.	salt	1	4	5	2.7
8.	tea	2	3	5	2.7
9.	candy	2	2	4	2.2
10.	lump(s)	1	3	4	2.2
11.	bowl	0	3	3	1.6
12.	cube	1	2	3	1.6
13.	loaf	1	2	3	1.6
14.	maple	0	3	3	1.6
15.	cake	2	0	2	1.1

(f = 1, .5%, n = 23)
beets, calories, can, Castro, cereal, cookies, cream, fattening, flies, formula, girl, glucose, gone, good, granulated, Kool-Aid, lumpy, polyhydroxyaldehyde, powder, sour, sticky, sweetness, taste

Sweet (Bitter, Salty, Sour;)

No.	Response	F	M	Tot.	%
1.	sour	29	30	59	32.4
2.	sugar	12	12	24	13.2
3.	candy	11	4	15	8.2
4.	bitter	5	3	8	4.4
5.	girl	1	5	6	3.3
6.	nice	2	2	4	2.2
7.	smell	1	3	4	2.2
8.	taste	3	1	4	2.2
9.	good	2	1	3	1.6
10.	honey	2	1	3	1.6
11.	kind	2	1	3	1.6
12.	sixteen(16)	3	0	3	1.6
13.	heat	1	1	2	1.1
14.	nothing	2	0	2	1.1
15.	pea(s)	2	0	2	1.1
16.	soft	2	0	2	1.1
17.	sticky	2	0	2	1.1

(f = 1, .5%, n = 36)
Adelaide, Adeline, angel, beet, bird, bread, breath, calorie, cookie, dessert, eat, flowers, gentle, grass, home, kid, lavender, law, loving, Mary, Maudlin, rolls, saccharine, smelling, smile, something, song, soul, Sue, sweat, talk, tasty, thing, tooth, woman, yes

Table (Chair;)

No.	Response	F	M	Tot.	%
1.	chair(s)	47	36	83	45.6
2.	leg(s)	9	7	16	8.8
3.	top	9	6	15	8.2
4.	cloth	4	9	13	7.1
5.	eat	2	2	4	2.2
6.	round	2	2	4	2.2
7.	food	0	3	3	1.6
8.	set	1	2	3	1.6
9.	floor	0	2	2	1.1
10.	manner(s)	1	1	2	1.1
11.	short	0	2	2	1.1
12.	study	2	0	2	1.1
13.	thing	2	0	2	1.1
14.	wood	2	0	2	1.1

(f = 1, .5%, n = 29)
bed, black, bowl, clothe, desk, formed, four legs, free, glass, hard, high, item, join, knife, knight, land, lamp, low, metric, oak, place, setting, shine, sitting, tennis, turn, tree, wax, weak

Talk (Speak;)

No.	Response	F	M	Tot.	%
1.	fast	14	8	22	12.1
2.	speak	12	9	21	11.5
3.	converse	3	5	8	4.4
4.	say	2	5	7	3.8
5.	walk	2	5	7	3.8
6.	mouth	4	2	6	3.3
7.	whisper	4	2	6	3.3
8.	listen	1	4	5	2.7
9.	loud	2	3	5	2.7
10.	about	3	1	4	2.2
11.	chatter	3	1	4	2.2
12.	babble	3	0	3	1.6
13.	chat	2	1	3	1.6
14.	people	2	1	3	1.6
15.	a lot	0	2	2	1.1
16.	communicate	2	0	2	1.1
17.	conversation	1	1	2	1.1
18.	gab	1	1	2	1.1

NORMS OF WORD ASSOCIATION

Talk   (Speak;   ) (contd)

No.	Response	F	M	Tot.	%
19.	laugh	1	1	2	1.1
20.	much	1	1	2	1.1
21.	noise	1	1	2	1.1
22.	nothing	2	0	2	1.1
23.	now	2	0	2	1.1
24.	slow	1	1	2	1.1
25.	speech	1	1	2	1.1
26.	to	1	1	2	1.1
27.	tongue	1	1	2	1.1

($\underline{f}$ = 1, .5%, $\underline{n}$ = 51)
aloud, always, baby, back, breathless, cheap,
company, continual, demonstration, discourse,
discuss, discussion, friends, garrulous, girl,
gossip, hear, jabber, learn, lecture, loquacious,
loudly, never, no, oh, old movies, over, parlor,
pillow, please, quickly, quiet, refreshing,
repeat, ridiculous, shape sounds, shout, sing,
small, soft, softly, steal, stop, stutter, tension,
tough, wildly, with, words, write, yak
(Illegible - 1)

Tall   (Short;   )

No.	Response	F	M	Tot.	%
1.	short	49	36	85	46.7
2.	thin	12	6	18	9.9
3.	man	7	4	11	6.0
4.	tree	4	1	5	2.7
5.	boy	1	3	4	2.2
6.	dark	3	1	4	2.2
7.	high	0	4	4	2.2
8.	small	1	3	4	2.2
9.	big	2	1	3	1.6
10.	me	1	2	3	1.6
11.	person	2	1	3	1.6
12.	skinny	0	3	3	1.6
13.	building	1	1	2	1.1
14.	slender	2	0	2	1.1

($\underline{f}$ = 1, .5%, $\underline{n}$ = 31)
blond, campanile, cool one, find, girl, grown,
guys, hat, height, imposing, Jack, law, lean,
legs, Lincoln, long, no, overbearing, rangy,
skyscraper, slim, statue, stilt, story, straight,
stranger, svelte, tail, taller, wall, wish

Than   (Clearer;   )

No.	Response	F	M	Tot.	%
1.	then	12	6	18	9.9
2.	more	8	6	14	7.7
3.	other(s)	8	5	13	7.1
4.	you	4	9	13	7.1
5.	that	5	7	12	6.6
6.	better	4	5	9	4.9
7.	this	4	4	8	4.4
8.	me	4	2	6	3.3
9.	now	1	5	6	3.3
10.	rather	3	2	5	2.7
11.	what	2	3	5	2.7
12.	ever	0	4	4	2.2
13.	or	4	0	4	2.2
14.	the	3	1	4	2.2
15.	comparison	3	0	3	1.6
16.	if	2	1	3	1.6
17.	though	1	2	3	1.6
18.	anything	1	1	2	1.1
19.	before	1	1	2	1.1
20.	besides	1	1	2	1.1
21.	bigger	2	0	2	1.1
22.	go	2	0	2	1.1

Than   (Clearer;   ) (contd)

No.	Response	F	M	Tot.	%
23.	her	1	1	2	1.1
24.	I	1	1	2	1.1
25.	it	1	1	2	1.1
26.	man	1	1	2	1.1
27.	tan	1	1	2	1.1
28.	those	1	1	2	1.1
29.	thou	1	1	2	1.1
30.	we	1	1	2	1.1

($\underline{f}$ = 1, .5%, $\underline{n}$ = 26)
Anne, as, but, conjunction, different, do, give,
greater, him, like, mother, noise, O.K., pan,
person, quam, sharper, since, small, taller,
therefore, they, tit tat, to, truck, van

That   (This;   )

No.	Response	F	M	Tot.	%
1.	this	36	24	60	32.9
2.	is	9	7	16	8.8
3.	there	9	5	14	7.7
4.	it	3	9	12	6.6
5.	thing	6	6	12	6.6
6.	which	6	0	6	3.3
7.	man	2	3	5	2.7
8.	was	1	4	5	2.7
9.	boy	2	1	3	1.6
10.	girl	1	2	3	1.6
11.	point	1	2	3	1.6
12.	they	3	0	3	1.6
13.	that	0	2	2	1.1
14.	the	2	0	2	1.1
15.	then	2	0	2	1.1
16.	what	0	2	2	1.1

($\underline{f}$ = 1, .5%, $\underline{n}$ = 32)
again, are, away, bastard, book, can, cat, creep,
contempt, day, desk, direction, dog, emphasize,
guts, house, if, isn't, mess, object, only,
person, place, plant, point, prejudice, something,
than, tree, unknown, way, we

Them   (They; Us)

No.	Response	F	M	Tot.	%
1.	they	29	23	52	28.5
2.	us	14	10	24	13.2
3.	those	3	10	13	7.1
4.	people	6	2	8	4.4
5.	their(s)	3	3	6	3.3
6.	we	3	3	5	3.3
7.	me	3	2	5	2.7
8.	there	2	3	5	2.7
9.	these	3	2	5	2.7
10.	are	3	0	3	1.6
11.	guys	2	1	3	1.6
12.	it	1	2	3	1.6
13.	others	2	1	3	1.6
14.	that	1	2	3	1.6
15.	away	2	0	2	1.1
16.	give	0	2	2	1.1
17.	group	1	1	2	1.1
18.	society	1	1	2	1.1
19.	too	0	2	2	1.1
20.	who	1	1	2	1.1

($\underline{f}$ = 1, .5%, $\underline{n}$ = 30)
above, again, alien, all, always, apes, apples,
boys, creatures, crowd, fear, gangsters, he,
house, indirect, love, monsters, motion picture,
observers, see, selves, separate, shot, stranger,
students, that has, them, then, the rest, towels
(Illegible - 1)

Then (Now;)

No.	Response	F	M	Tot.	%
1.	now	49	45	94	51.6
2.	when	10	7	17	9.3
3.	than	5	1	6	3.3
4.	there	5	1	6	3.3
5.	go	3	1	4	2.2
6.	he	0	4	4	2.2
7.	came	1	2	3	1.6
8.	here	2	1	3	1.6
9.	they	3	0	3	1.6
10.	what	0	3	3	1.6
11.	come(s)	1	1	2	1.1
12.	past	1	1	2	1.1
13.	story	1	1	2	1.1
14.	time	1	1	2	1.1
15.	we	2	0	2	1.1

($\underline{f}$ = 1, .5%, $\underline{n}$ = 28)
after, again, although, and, bad, before, but,
far, forever, good, how, if, it, later, mean,
next, of course, once, run, some, sometime,
stay, therefore, till, watch, while, yes,
yesterday
(Illegible - 1)

There (Here, Where; Over, Then)

No.	Response	F	M	Tot.	%
1.	here	47	36	83	45.6
2.	where	8	8	16	8.8
3.	are	9	3	12	6.6
4.	is	3	5	8	4.4
5.	now	3	4	7	3.8
6.	far	6	0	6	3.3
7.	over	2	4	6	3.3
8.	away	4	1	5	2.7
9.	place	1	4	5	2.7
10.	their	1	2	3	1.6
11.	fore	0	2	2	1.1
12.	go	1	1	2	1.1
13.	then	1	1	2	1.1
14.	was	1	1	2	1.1

($\underline{f}$ = 1, .5%, $\underline{n}$ = 22)
afar, after, and, arrive, be, beside, desirable,
existential, fact, far away, gone, mine, not here,
on, point, somewhere, there, this, tree, way,
we are, yonder
(Illegible - 1)

They (We; Us)

No.	Response	F	M	Tot.	%
1.	them	19	22	41	22.5
2.	we	19	14	33	18.1
3.	us	16	8	24	13.2
4.	are	7	8	15	8.2
5.	you	3	3	6	3.3
6.	other(s)	4	1	5	2.7
7.	people	2	2	4	2.2
8.	can	2	1	3	1.6
9.	come	1	2	3	1.6
10.	were	1	2	3	1.6
11.	who	1	2	3	1.6
12.	came	2	0	2	1.1
13.	friends	2	0	2	1.1
14.	go	2	0	2	1.1
15.	group	0	2	2	1.1
16.	he	1	1	2	1.1
17.	society	1	1	2	1.1
18.	their(s)	1	1	2	1.1
19.	unknown	1	1	2	1.1

They (We; Us) (contd)

($\underline{f}$ = 1, .5%, $\underline{n}$ = 26)
aren't, die, distant, Eleanor, feel, give, got,
had, impersonal, it, kids, left, never, old,
out, outside, paint, rats, rest, say, sing,
vague, want, weigh, went, will

Thing (; That)

No.	Response	F	M	Tot.	%
1.	it	17	16	33	18.1
2.	object	10	10	20	11.0
3.	that	2	4	6	3.3
4.	monster	3	2	5	2.7
5.	something	2	2	4	2.2
6.	this	2	2	4	2.2
7.	what	2	2	4	2.2
8.	amazing	1	2	3	1.6
9.	ball	2	1	3	1.6
10.	blob	3	0	3	1.6
11.	creature	1	2	3	1.6
12.	do	1	2	3	1.6
13.	there	1	2	3	1.6
14.	beast	1	1	2	1.1
15.	being	1	1	2	1.1
16.	car	1	1	2	1.1
17.	happen	1	1	2	1.1
18.	machine	0	2	2	1.1
19.	person	2	0	2	1.1
20.	think	2	0	2	1.1
21.	TV	0	2	2	1.1
22.	unknown	2	0	2	1.1
23.	which	2	0	2	1.1

($\underline{f}$ = 1, .5%, $\underline{n}$ = 67)
anything, appear, box, breast, bump, chair,
desired, desk, disaster, dog, done, event,
experience, feeling, find, girl, goat, hairy,
hand, happened, here, horror, horse, impossible,
insect, investigate, is, little, make, man,
mass, matter, metal, mountains, mouse, movie,
neuter, nondescript, paper, pen, picture, plan,
present, res, ring, road, rock, sex, southern,
spider, string, stuff, the, things, thought,
thug, tiger, to, touch, toy, tricycle, ugly,
vegetable, walks, weird, where, wing
(Illegible - 1)

Thread (Needle;)

No.	Response	F	M	Tot.	%
1.	needle	56	46	102	56.0
2.	bare	9	6	15	8.2
3.	sew	11	4	15	8.2
4.	string	5	2	7	3.8
5.	spool	3	3	6	3.3
6.	bed	2	1	3	1.6
7.	break	1	1	2	1.1
8.	cotton	0	2	2	1.1
9.	sewing	2	0	2	1.1
10.	silk	1	1	2	1.1
11.	silver	1	1	2	1.1
12.	thimble	1	1	2	1.1
13.	weave	0	2	2	1.1

($\underline{f}$ = 1, .5%, $\underline{n}$ = 18)
actual, blue, broke, carefully, cloth, dead,
frustration, knot, line, nettle, of gold, pull,
shirt, sow, thin, thought, thread roller, ties
(Illegible - 2)

Tiger   (Lion;   )

No.	Response	F	M	Tot.	%
1.	lion	25	15	40	22.0
2.	cat	10	12	22	12.1
3.	stripe(s)	14	8	22	12.1
4.	animal	6	7	13	7.1
5.	milk	5	0	5	2.7
6.	fierce	1	3	4	2.2
7.	jungle	2	2	4	2.2
8.	tank	1	2	3	1.6
9.	teeth	2	1	3	1.6
10.	yellow	2	1	3	1.6
11.	bright	1	1	2	1.1
12.	ferocious	1	1	2	1.1
13.	growl	2	0	2	1.1
14.	grr	2	0	2	1.1
15.	lily	1	1	2	1.1
16.	mouse	1	1	2	1.1
17.	tail	0	2	2	1.1

($\underline{f}$ = 1, .5%, $\underline{n}$ = 49)
angry, bay, beautiful, Black Sambo, burning,
butter, cage, claws, climb, dark, door, farm,
fear, football, forest, gas, graceful, gun,
hurt, India, interesting, jets, Jones, kill,
leopard, liar, lurks, march, Michigan, moth,
paper, paws, power, prowls, rag, Revlon, rough,
run, same, shark, spotted, striped, strong, tale,
toe, tomcat, tore, visual, war

To   (From;   )

No.	Response	F	M	Tot.	%
1.	from	18	13	31	17.0
2.	go	17	11	28	15.4
3.	be	3	9	12	6.6
4.	do	4	6	10	5.5
5.	you	5	4	9	4.9
6.	day	2	3	5	2.7
7.	at	3	1	4	2.2
8.	for	1	3	4	2.2
9.	the	4	0	4	2.2
10.	there	2	2	4	2.2
11.	away	3	0	3	1.6
12.	die	2	1	3	1.6
13.	toward(s)	0	3	3	1.6
14.	it	1	1	2	1.1
15.	live	1	1	2	1.1
16.	me	1	1	2	1.1
17.	much	2	0	2	1.1
18.	see	1	1	2	1.1
19.	them	2	0	2	1.1
20.	three	0	2	2	1.1
21.	together	0	2	2	1.1
22.	two	1	1	2	1.1
23.	whom	1	1	2	1.1

($\underline{f}$ = 1, .5%, $\underline{n}$ = 42)
about, act, address, adverb, and, approach, bad,
beach, bed, bring, by, distinction, feel, fly,
gift, give, have, heaven, help, him, home, in,
laugh, letter, louse, love, market, mother,
must, not, ocean, play, preposition, pro, school,
sentence, store, theater, threw, travel, west,
wife

Toe   (; Foot)

No.	Response	F	M	Tot.	%
1.	feet(foot)	34	25	60	32.9
2.	nail	22	15	37	20.3
3.	shoe	4	10	14	7.7
4.	heel	5	8	13	7.1
5.	big	5	1	6	3.3

Toe   (; Foot) (contd)

No.	Response	F	M	Tot.	%
6.	finger	3	1	4	2.2
7.	line	2	2	4	2.2
8.	hurts	2	1	3	1.6
9.	mark	0	3	3	1.6
10.	wiggle	2	1	3	1.6
11.	digit	1	1	2	1.1
12.	five	1	1	2	1.1
13.	hold	1	1	2	1.1
14.	in	1	1	2	1.1
15.	sandals	1	1	2	1.1
16.	stub	1	1	2	1.1
17.	toe nail	1	1	2	1.1
18.	ugly	2	0	2	1.1

($\underline{f}$ = 1, .5%, $\underline{n}$ = 20)
broken, corn, dancer, fat, food, footsie,
hangnail, hilarious, is, kick, knee, move,
out, point, pointed, polish, small, tip,
touch, wriggle

Toes   (; Fingers)

No.	Response	F	M	Tot.	%
1.	feet(foot)	41	31	72	39.5
2.	shoe(s)	8	10	18	9.9
3.	nail(s)	7	9	16	8.8
4.	fingers	6	3	9	4.9
5.	wiggle	7	1	8	4.4
6.	heel(s)	1	3	4	2.2
7.	feel	1	2	3	1.6
8.	sandals	1	2	3	1.6
9.	toenail(s)	1	2	3	1.6
10.	curled	2	0	2	1.1
11.	dirty	1	1	2	1.1
12.	five	2	0	2	1.1
13.	hurt	1	1	2	1.1
14.	pointed	0	2	2	1.1
15.	ten	1	1	2	1.1
16.	twinkle	1	1	2	1.1
17.	ugly	2	0	2	1.1

($\underline{f}$ = 1, .5%, $\underline{n}$ = 30)
arms, barefoot, before, big, count, cut, dance,
field, knees, knit, leg, leprosy, long, nose, on,
play, point, skim, small, smell, socks, sore,
stand, step on, tight, tip, tippy, two, wade, wet

Town   (City;   )

No.	Response	F	M	Tot.	%
1.	city	33	23	56	30.7
2.	country	10	7	17	9.3
3.	small	12	2	14	7.7
4.	house(s)	4	9	13	7.1
5.	village	6	4	10	5.5
6.	people	4	5	9	4.9
7.	hall	2	3	5	2.7
8.	crier	2	2	4	2.2
9.	home	1	3	4	2.2
10.	meeting	0	4	4	2.2
11.	building(s)	2	0	2	1.1
12.	down	1	1	2	1.1
13.	gown	1	1	2	1.1
14.	old-fashioned	1	1	2	1.1
15.	pity	1	1	2	1.1
16.	ship	0	2	2	1.1

($\underline{f}$ = 1, .5%, $\underline{n}$ = 34)
antiquated, bad, below, Berkeley, burg, Carmel,
crown, dies, fence, frontier, go, gone, group,
Gurneville, inn, leaves, limits, little, many,
metropolis, near, park, Puerto Vallarta, quaint,

Town   (City;   ) (contd)

No.	Response	F	M	Tot.	%

roofs, Ross, San Jose, store, strange, street, team, there, ville, water

Train   (Whistle;   )

No.	Response	F	M	Tot.	%
1.	track(s)	16	10	26	14.3
2.	whistle	12	5	17	9.3
3.	travel	5	5	10	5.5
4.	fast	5	3	8	4.4
5.	station	3	5	8	4.4
6.	car(s)	1	6	7	3.8
7.	go	3	3	6	3.3
8.	long	2	4	6	3.3
9.	caboose	3	2	5	2.7
10.	engine	1	4	5	2.7
11.	railroad	2	3	5	2.7
12.	bus	3	0	3	1.6
13.	choo-choo	3	0	3	1.6
14.	noise	2	1	3	1.6
15.	rail(s)	3	0	3	1.6
16.	robbery	1	2	3	1.6
17.	athlete(s)	1	1	2	1.1
18.	horn	2	0	2	1.1
19.	night	0	2	2	1.1
20.	run	2	0	2	1.1
21.	smoke	2	0	2	1.1
22.	stop	2	0	2	1.1
23.	thought(s)	2	0	2	1.1
24.	truck	0	2	2	1.1
25.	Zug	0	2	2	1.1

(f = 1, .5%, n = 46)
airplane, away, big, care, Chicago, chug, closed, coal, coming, compartment, dog, electric, fireman, freight, gone, il treno, James Bond, learn, leave, like, line, load, locomotive, metal, motion, move, N.Y., plane, power, ride, robber, seal, sit, slow, sooty, Spain, speed, sports, Stockton, Switzerland, toot-toot choo-choo, toy, trip, wagon, wheels, whiz

Trucks   (Cars;   )

No.	Response	F	M	Tot.	%
1.	car(s)	37	25	62	34.0
2.	big	7	4	11	6.0
3.	wheels	5	3	8	4.4
4.	driver(s)	2	4	6	3.3
5.	carry	1	4	5	2.7
6.	noise	5	0	5	2.7
7.	red	3	1	4	2.2
8.	tire(s)	2	2	4	2.2
9.	buses	0	3	3	1.6
10.	drive	0	3	3	1.6
11.	load	2	1	3	1.6
12.	trailer(s)	1	2	3	1.6
13.	trains	1	2	3	1.6
14.	go	2	0	2	1.1
15.	highway(s)	2	0	2	1.1
16.	huge	2	0	2	1.1
17.	large	1	1	2	1.1
18.	Mac	1	1	2	1.1
19.	roads	1	1	2	1.1
20.	rumble	2	0	2	1.1
21.	toys	2	0	2	1.1

(f = 1, .5%, n = 46)
automobiles, cafes, cats, cement, cranes, deliver, dray, driving, ducks, dump, dust, exhaust, fire, food, freeway, garbage, gone, haul, heavy, hills, international, kids, lights, lumber, Mack, motor,

Trucks   (Cars;   ) (contd)

No.	Response	F	M	Tot.	%

move, movement, noisy, pass, Pepsi, power, roar, Safeway, shipping, speed, stow, swim, tanks, teamsters, tracks, travel, vans, wages, wagons, work

Ugly   (Beautiful;   )

No.	Response	F	M	Tot.	%
1.	pretty	26	12	38	20.9
2.	man	6	8	14	7.7
3.	duckling	8	1	9	4.9
4.	beautiful	3	3	6	3.3
5.	homely	3	3	6	3.3
6.	duck	3	2	5	2.7
7.	sad	3	1	4	2.2
8.	thing	1	3	4	2.2
9.	awful	2	1	3	1.6
10.	face	1	2	3	1.6
11.	fat	1	2	3	1.6
12.	girl	1	2	3	1.6
13.	nice	2	1	3	1.6
14.	plain	1	2	3	1.6
15.	beast	2	0	2	1.1
16.	cute	1	1	2	1.1
17.	deformed	1	1	2	1.1
18.	horrible	1	1	2	1.1
19.	insect	2	0	2	1.1
20.	it	0	2	2	1.1
21.	me	1	1	2	1.1
22.	repulsive	2	0	2	1.1
23.	sin	1	1	2	1.1

(f = 1, .5%, n = 59)
American, as, bad, boy, clean, cool, creature, creep, cry, dangerous, dark, distasteful, duckling (sad), everyone, evil, fea, feo, few, fortune, Frankenstein, funny, gaunt, gorgeous, grotesque, healthy, horrid, ick, look, mangled, marred, misunderstood, monster, morose, mouse, muggy, murder, new, nose, personality, poverty, quick, regretful, rumor, scene, sisters, snake, still, such, Sumnor (Canterbury Tales), than, ugliness, unattractive, unpretty, woman, word, world, wound, yes, you
(Illegible - 1)

Under   (Over;   )

No.	Response	F	M	Tot.	%
1.	over	29	27	56	30.7
2.	below	10	6	16	8.8
3.	above	6	6	12	6.6
4.	neath	6	4	10	5.5
5.	down	6	1	7	3.8
6.	tree	4	3	7	3.8
7.	water	2	5	7	3.8
8.	beneath	2	3	5	2.7
9.	cover	2	3	5	2.7
10.	bed	1	3	4	2.2
11.	ground	2	2	4	2.2
12.	table	3	0	3	1.6
13.	up	3	0	3	1.6
14.	all	1	1	2	1.1
15.	around	1	1	2	1.1
16.	blanket	0	2	2	1.1
17.	bridge	2	0	2	1.1
18.	hill	2	0	2	1.1
19.	house	0	2	2	1.1

Under   (Over;   ) (contd)

No.	Response	F	M	Tot.	%

(f = 1, .5%, n = 31)
arm, belly, butt, covered, dark, deep, depression, dog, fail, fire, milkwood, near, nourished, on, pressure, rock, roof, scared, shadow, sheep, shelter, shirt, skin, sky, stove, there, the weather, top, 20, upon, wood

Vegetable   (; Cabbage)

No.	Response	F	M	Tot.	%
1.	carrot(s)	10	11	21	11.5
2.	eat	9	8	17	9.3
3.	fruit	4	8	12	6.6
4.	green	10	2	12	6.6
5.	garden	7	4	11	6.0
6.	pea(s)	4	6	10	5.5
7.	plant	2	6	8	4.4
8.	mineral	3	4	7	3.8
9.	food	2	4	6	3.3
10.	good	3	3	6	3.3
11.	animal	2	3	5	2.7
12.	tomato	5	0	5	2.7
13.	lettuce	3	0	3	1.6
14.	man	0	3	3	1.6
15.	beet(s)	0	2	2	1.1
16.	corn	2	0	2	1.1
17.	fat	2	0	2	1.1
18.	juice	2	0	2	1.1
19.	potato	1	1	2	1.1
20.	salad	1	1	2	1.1
21.	tree	0	2	2	1.1
22.	turnip	1	1	2	1.1

(f = 1, .5%, n = 40)
apple, artichokes, asparagus, brush, cabbage, celery, clean, cook, dinner, dislike, farm, flower, form, fresh, furgid, grandmother, grape, ground, grow, kitchen, lima beans, market, meat, no, nothing, oil, orange, people, poison, raw, root, sick, soup, spinach, squash, string beans, table, thing, yellow, zucchini

Walking   (; Running)

No.	Response	F	M	Tot.	%
1.	running	12	19	31	17.0
2.	talking	11	4	15	8.2
3.	fast	3	4	7	3.8
4.	stick	3	4	7	3.8
5.	legs	3	3	6	3.3
6.	slow	3	1	4	2.2
7.	slowly	2	2	4	2.2
8.	feet	2	1	3	1.6
9.	forest	1	2	3	1.6
10.	home	2	1	3	1.6
11.	path(s)	3	0	3	1.6
12.	run	0	3	3	1.6
13.	sleep	1	2	3	1.6
14.	sleeping	2	1	3	1.6
15.	standing	2	1	3	1.6
16.	through	2	1	3	1.6
17.	alone	1	1	2	1.1
18.	away	0	2	2	1.1
19.	distance	1	1	2	1.1
20.	down	0	2	2	1.1
21.	hike	2	0	2	1.1
22.	rain	1	1	2	1.1
23.	shoe(s)	0	2	2	1.1
24.	sidewalk	0	2	2	1.1
25.	sitting	2	0	2	1.1
26.	skipping	1	1	2	1.1

Walking   (; Running) (contd)

No.	Response	F	M	Tot.	%
27.	street	1	1	2	1.1
28.	talk	0	2	2	1.1

(f = 1, .5%, n = 57)
beach, breeze, cane, car, coming, country, dog, doll, dreaming, drink, dusk, field, freedom, garden, grass, hiking, hill, jumping, moonlight, mountains, move, nature, off, park, peace, pedestrian, poor, quickly, refreshing, relax, relaxing, ride, riding, road, sightseeing, sleepy, slush, softly, step, stopping, straight, stream, stride, stroll, strolling, to, together, toward, tour, trees, trip, trotting, unhappy, vigorous, walk, water, woods

Want   (; Wish)

No.	Response	F	M	Tot.	%
1.	need	18	20	38	20.9
2.	desire	21	11	32	17.6
3.	get	3	5	8	4.4
4.	wish	6	2	8	4.4
5.	give	3	2	5	2.7
6.	have	4	1	5	2.7
7.	nothing	5	0	5	2.7
8.	more	2	2	4	2.2
9.	take	1	3	4	2.2
10.	will	1	3	4	2.2
11.	ad	2	1	3	1.6
12.	love	2	1	3	1.6
13.	some	1	2	3	1.6
14.	something	0	3	3	1.6
15.	to	1	2	3	1.6
16.	another	2	0	2	1.1
17.	food	0	2	2	1.1
18.	her	0	2	2	1.1
19.	hunger	1	1	2	1.1
20.	like	1	1	2	1.1
21.	money	1	1	2	1.1
22.	success	0	2	2	1.1

(f = 1, .5%, n = 40)
apple, ask, badly, brains, crave, desperately, drink, easiness, enough, hate, haunt, haven't, help, hungry, hurt, it, keep, much, never, no, not, now, of, one, order, peace, poverty, purpose, rent, selfish, sleep, someone, the, thing, this, tree, wanting, wood, you, yours

War   (; Soldier)

No.	Response	F	M	Tot.	%
1.	peace	29	32	61	33.5
2.	fight	8	6	14	7.7
3.	bad	5	3	8	4.4
4.	death	5	3	8	4.4
5.	kill	2	4	6	3.3
6.	battle	3	1	4	2.2
7.	crime	3	1	4	2.2
8.	hate	3	1	4	2.2
9.	no	0	4	4	2.2
10.	blood	2	1	3	1.6
11.	hero	2	1	3	1.6
12.	shooting	2	1	3	1.6
13.	time	1	2	3	1.6
14.	bomb(s)	2	0	2	1.1
15.	famine	2	0	2	1.1
16.	horrid	2	0	2	1.1
17.	poverty	0	2	2	1.1
18.	Tolstoy	2	0	2	1.1
19.	Vietnam	1	1	2	1.1
20.	when	0	2	2	1.1

War   (; Soldier) (contd)

No.	Response	F	M	Tot.	%
21.	world	1	1	2	1.1

($\underline{f}$ = 1, .5%, $\underline{n}$ = 41)
air raid, appalling, arms, army, baby, brutal, chaos, clouds, club, destruction, die, disastrous, disgusting, disillusion, evil, fighting, for, Goldwater, green, head, help, hope, hope not, horror, hurt, Latin, Lord, mice, nerves, on, pestilence, poor, sad, scared, III, trouble, unreal, victory, violence, warrior, with

Warm   (; Cold)

No.	Response	F	M	Tot.	%
1.	cold	22	30	52	28.5
2.	soft	10	9	19	10.4
3.	hot	11	7	18	9.9
4.	cozy	6	0	6	3.3
5.	sun	4	2	6	3.3
6.	comfortable	4	0	4	2.2
7.	nice	3	1	4	2.2
8.	bed	0	3	3	1.6
9.	blanket	2	1	3	1.6
10.	cool	1	2	3	1.6
11.	fire	2	1	3	1.6
12.	heart	1	2	3	1.6
13.	weather	2	1	3	1.6
14.	close	2	0	2	1.1
15.	gentle	1	1	2	1.1
16.	good	1	1	2	1.1
17.	hand	2	0	2	1.1
18.	night	2	0	2	1.1
19.	puppy	1	1	2	1.1
20.	quilt	2	0	2	1.1

($\underline{f}$ = 1, .5%, $\underline{n}$ = 41)
affection, animal, baby, blooded, body, breast, candlelight, clothes, coat, comfort, cuddly, day, deep, dog, feel, happy, heat, home, house, indifferent, mellow, moist, near, personality, pleasant, quiet, room, safe, sands, scarf, secure, shine, springs, sweet, tingle, touch, up, water, wet, why, wipe

Water   (Ocean, River, Thirsty; Bath, Deep)

No.	Response	F	M	Tot.	%
1.	drink	14	10	24	13.2
2.	cold	9	7	16	8.8
3.	wet	6	8	14	7.7
4.	cool	5	4	9	4.9
5.	H$_2$O	5	3	8	4.4
6.	thirst	2	3	5	2.7
7.	thirsty	4	1	5	2.7
8.	clear	4	0	4	2.2
9.	faucet	1	3	4	2.2
10.	river	1	3	4	2.2
11.	swim	2	2	4	2.2
12.	deep	2	1	3	1.6
13.	dry	0	3	3	1.6
14.	glass	1	2	3	1.6
15.	soft	0	3	3	1.6
16.	well	2	1	3	1.6
17.	boy	1	1	2	1.1
18.	run(s)	2	0	2	1.1
19.	ski	1	1	2	1.1
20.	soap	0	2	2	1.1
21.	stream	1	1	2	1.1
22.	tap	2	0	2	1.1

($\underline{f}$ = 1, .5%, $\underline{n}$ = 58)
Berkeley, blue, boiling, box, bread, break, bridge, bucket, bug, can, closed, cooler, cup, desert,

Water   (Ocean, River, Thirsty; Bath, Deep) (contd)

down, drips, fall, fight, flood, fluid, food, free, gold, good, gutters, hard, heater, hill, hole, ice, irrigate, liquid, mystical, no, ocean, pail, pale, pellet, pool, refreshing, ripple, rushing, salt, sex, shed, sky, softly, sprayer, tank, tasty, tower, trickle, vapor, velvet, vitality, waiter, warm, wetness

We   (Us; They)

No.	Response	F	M	Tot.	%
1.	they	18	21	39	21.4
2.	us	22	13	35	19.2
3.	are	11	8	19	10.4
4.	you	8	4	12	6.6
5.	do	2	4	6	3.3
6.	together	6	0	6	3.3
7.	will	1	5	6	3.3
8.	want	1	4	5	2.7
9.	go	1	3	4	2.2
10.	have	1	3	4	2.2
11.	know	3	1	4	2.2
12.	them	1	3	4	2.2
13.	don't	2	1	3	1.6
14.	can	1	1	2	1.1
15.	me	0	2	2	1.1

($\underline{f}$ = 1, .5%, $\underline{n}$ = 31)
affirm, all, class, cry, did, eat, even, exclusive, family, friends, look, love, must, no, one, only, our, ourselves, parents, people, run, saw, shall, sow, the, them, think, undersigned, would, yep, you and I

Web   (Spider;   )

No.	Response	F	M	Tot.	%
1.	spider	69	54	123	67.5
2.	feet(foot)	6	8	14	7.7
3.	duck	3	2	5	2.7
4.	caught	3	1	4	2.2
5.	net	2	2	4	2.2
6.	life	1	2	3	1.6
7.	Charlotte	2	0	2	1.1
8.	cob	1	1	2	1.1
9.	nest	2	0	2	1.1

($\underline{f}$ = 1, .5%, $\underline{n}$ = 23)
around, cobweb, core, ebb, entanglement, footed, frog, line, neat, of rock, out, rock, silk, soft, spin, sticky, string, strong, tangle, tangled, trap, tree, Webb

What   (For, So;   )

No.	Response	F	M	Tot.	%
1.	why	11	8	19	10.4
2.	now	6	6	12	6.6
3.	question	7	5	12	6.6
4.	when	6	6	12	6.6
5.	where	5	5	10	5.5
6.	is	4	5	9	4.9
7.	that	5	4	9	4.9
8.	will	3	4	7	3.7
9.	not	4	2	6	3.3
10.	how	4	1	5	2.7
11.	if	2	3	5	2.7
12.	kind	4	1	5	2.7

What (For, So;) (contd)

No.	Response	F	M	Tot.	%
13.	this	1	4	5	2.7
14.	thing	3	1	4	2.2
15.	who	2	2	4	2.2
16.	for	2	1	3	1.6
17.	happen(s)	2	1	3	1.6
18.	next	1	2	3	1.6
19.	then	2	1	3	1.6
20.	want	1	2	3	1.6
21.	it	1	1	2	1.1
22.	?	1	1	2	1.1
23.	repeat	2	0	2	1.1
24.	the	1	1	2	1.1
25.	which	0	2	2	1.1

($\underline{f}$ = 1, .5%, $\underline{n}$ = 31)
adverb, are, ball, but, definition, did, do,
doing, ever, gold, good, God, happened, huh,
know, nerve, no, of it, or, puzzlement, Ray
Charles, said, say, slut, so, stupid, they,
time, to, too, was
(Illegible - 1; No response - 1)

When (; Then, Where)

No.	Response	F	M	Tot.	%
1.	now	36	28	64	35.1
2.	then	16	15	31	17.0
3.	where	10	15	25	13.7
4.	if	5	2	7	3.8
5.	never	3	3	6	3.3
6.	why	2	3	5	2.7
7.	ever	4	0	4	2.2
8.	question	3	1	4	2.2
9.	time	2	2	4	2.2
10.	I	1	2	3	1.6
11.	are	1	1	2	1.1
12.	do	1	1	2	1.1
13.	they	2	0	2	1.1
14.	will	1	1	2	1.1

($\underline{f}$ = 1, .5%, $\underline{n}$ = 20)
accident, always, cuando, growing, he, how, I
dunno, later, no, not, orange juice, say, song,
ten, there, though, was, what, whenever, you
(No response - 1)

White (Black, Red;)

No.	Response	F	M	Tot.	%
1.	black	43	36	79	43.4
2.	house	5	7	12	6.6
3.	bread	8	2	10	5.5
4.	snow	3	6	9	4.9
5.	clean	4	3	7	3.8
6.	dark	3	2	5	2.7
7.	pure	5	0	5	2.7
8.	mouse (mice)	2	2	4	2.2
9.	sheet	2	2	4	2.2
10.	blue	2	1	3	1.6
11.	red	1	2	3	1.6
12.	blank	2	0	2	1.1
13.	light	1	1	2	1.1
14.	nurse	2	0	2	1.1
15.	paper	1	1	2	1.1

($\underline{f}$ = 1, .5%, $\underline{n}$ = 33)
bright, brown, car, cold, collar, color, colorless,
drown, fish, flower, foam, frock, gloves, good,
kitten, man, milk, name, Negro, nothing, rat, rose,
Scotch, shirt, shoe, skin, slow, stuff, table,
uniform, wash, wheat, wine

Wider (Broader;)

No.	Response	F	M	Tot.	%
1.	narrower	23	21	44	24.2
2.	thinner	10	2	12	6.6
3.	than	4	7	11	6.0
4.	bigger	4	3	7	3.8
5.	road	5	2	7	3.8
6.	narrow	1	5	6	3.3
7.	open	2	3	5	2.7
8.	horizon	2	2	4	2.2
9.	longer	2	2	4	2.2
10.	river	2	2	4	2.2
11.	big	2	1	3	1.6
12.	broad	2	1	3	1.6
13.	broader	3	0	3	1.6
14.	larger	3	0	3	1.6
15.	path	3	0	3	1.6
16.	shorter	1	2	3	1.6
17.	smaller	2	1	3	1.6
18.	thin	0	3	3	1.6
19.	farther	2	0	2	1.1
20.	fatter	1	1	2	1.1
21.	higher	1	1	2	1.1
22.	love	1	1	2	1.1
23.	space	2	0	2	1.1
24.	stream	2	0	2	1.1
25.	view	2	0	2	1.1
26.	width	2	0	2	1.1
27.	windows	0	2	2	1.1
28.	world	0	2	2	1.1

($\underline{f}$ = 1, .5%, $\underline{n}$ = 34)
apart, bear, better, block, board, brighten,
easier, easy, essen, fat, field, free, grow,
hall, house, large, load, lower, measure,
Missouri, more, pavement, person, range, seat,
short, spacious, stiller, streets, tamer,
thicker, tree, way, wilder

Windows (Doors;)

No.	Response	F	M	Tot.	%
1.	door(s)	13	6	19	10.4
2.	light	10	8	18	9.9
3.	open	9	9	18	9.9
4.	glass	6	10	16	8.8
5.	shade(s)	4	6	10	5.5
6.	clean	3	3	6	3.3
7.	pane(s)	3	3	6	3.3
8.	see	3	3	6	3.3
9.	sill(s)	2	4	6	3.3
10.	air	3	2	5	2.7
11.	clear	4	1	5	2.7
12.	shut	3	1	4	2.2
13.	building	1	2	3	1.6
14.	closed	2	1	3	1.6
15.	dirty	3	0	3	1.6
16.	opening(s)	2	1	3	1.6
17.	shutters	2	1	3	1.6
18.	black	1	1	2	1.1
19.	curtain(s)	1	1	2	1.1
20.	high	2	0	2	1.1
21.	house	1	1	2	1.1
22.	square	2	0	2	1.1
23.	wide	1	1	2	1.1

($\underline{f}$ = 1, .5%, $\underline{n}$ = 34)
blinds, break, broken, close, cloudy, containment,
dark, down, frame, front, lite, look, many,
outdoors, outside, pains, radiator, reflection,
room, sash, scared, seal, shed, shrouded, sight,
sitter, stuck, sunset, tall, town, trees, view,
wash, wind
(Illegible - 2)

Without (With;)

No.	Response	F	M	Tot.	%
1.	with	23	17	40	22.0
2.	within	13	7	20	11.0
3.	money	3	3	6	3.3
4.	not	0	6	6	3.3
5.	you	5	1	6	3.3
6.	alone	5	0	5	2.7
7.	love	1	4	5	2.7
8.	none	4	1	5	2.7
9.	gone	4	0	4	2.2
10.	need	4	0	4	2.2
11.	have	3	0	3	1.6
12.	in	1	2	3	1.6
13.	lack	1	2	3	1.6
14.	lost	3	0	3	1.6
15.	any	2	0	2	1.1
16.	anything	1	1	2	1.1
17.	care	0	2	2	1.1
18.	deprived	1	1	2	1.1
19.	empty	1	1	2	1.1
20.	food	2	0	2	1.1
21.	home	0	2	2	1.1
22.	hope	1	1	2	1.1
23.	it	0	2	2	1.1
24.	me	2	0	2	1.1
25.	lacking	2	0	2	1.1
26.	nothing	1	1	2	1.1
27.	poverty	0	2	2	1.1
28.	sans	0	2	2	1.1
29.	sin	0	2	2	1.1

($\underline{f}$ = 1, .5%, $\underline{n}$ = 39)
absent, abundance, always, apart, askance, bereft,
boyfriend, cause, deprivation, deprive, despair,
fear, free, friends, hate, her, less, looking,
lose, missing, much, not have, ohne, only, pain,
paper, peace, people, poor, portfolio, sadness,
shelter, snake, spirit, swords, tears, unaided,
wanting, water

Woman (Man;)

No.	Response	F	M	Tot.	%
1.	man	43	27	70	38.4
2.	girl	7	9	16	8.8
3.	pretty	4	8	12	6.6
4.	mother	5	2	7	3.8
5.	sex	2	5	7	3.8
6.	love	1	4	5	2.7
7.	lady	4	0	4	2.2
8.	mature	3	1	4	2.2
9.	female	3	0	3	1.6
10.	me	3	0	3	1.6
11.	beauty	0	2	2	1.1
12.	body	1	1	2	1.1
13.	nice	1	1	2	1.1
14.	old	1	1	2	1.1

($\underline{f}$ = 1, .5%, $\underline{n}$ = 43)
beautiful, blonde, can, curve, delicate, Eve,
experience, face, fat, fears, fight, goes, good,
hair, hat, hate, heel, hit, hope, I, intellect,
interesting, life, loose, lover, lust, maybe,
mind, nude, O.K., one, person, purse, secure,
sexy, slender, stern, tree, wants, weak, wise,
wow, young

Wool (Sheep;)

No.	Response	F	M	Tot.	%
1.	sheep	16	15	31	17.0
2.	sweater	7	17	24	13.2
3.	warm	9	6	15	8.2
4.	lamb(s)	7	4	11	6.0
5.	cloth	4	5	9	4.9
6.	itch	1	6	7	3.8
7.	cotton	3	3	6	3.3
8.	skirt	5	1	6	3.3
9.	dress	5	0	5	2.7
10.	hot	2	2	4	2.2
11.	itchy	2	2	4	2.2
12.	scratchy	3	1	4	2.2
13.	yarn	3	1	4	2.2
14.	clothe(s)	3	0	3	1.6
15.	coat	2	1	3	1.6
16.	scratch	2	1	3	1.6
17.	blanket	2	0	2	1.1
18.	coarse	0	2	2	1.1
19.	fuzzy	2	0	2	1.1
20.	soft	1	1	2	1.1
21.	warmth	1	1	2	1.1
22.	winter	2	0	2	1.1

($\underline{f}$ = 1, .5%, $\underline{n}$ = 32)
blanked, clothing, color, cool, dark, darn, dog,
dye, fabric, fiber, fur, gather, gathering, heavy,
material, pajamas, prickly, protect, pull, scarf,
shears, shirt, slipper, socks, spin, suit, thick,
tickle, underwear, wear, white

Working (Playing;)

No.	Response	F	M	Tot.	%
1.	hard	32	35	67	36.8
2.	playing	9	4	13	7.1
3.	man(men)	4	4	8	4.4
4.	sweat	2	5	7	3.8
5.	labor	5	0	5	2.7
6.	money	4	1	5	2.7
7.	studying	3	1	4	2.2
8.	girl	1	2	3	1.6
9.	lazy	2	1	3	1.6
10.	loafing	0	3	3	1.6
11.	resting	0	3	3	1.6
12.	tired	2	1	3	1.6
13.	busy	2	0	2	1.1
14.	fun	1	1	2	1.1
15.	happy	1	1	2	1.1
16.	now	2	0	2	1.1
17.	play	1	1	2	1.1
18.	running	2	0	2	1.1
19.	school	2	0	2	1.1

($\underline{f}$ = 1, .5%, $\underline{n}$ = 44)
accomplishment, action, bad, because, being, blue,
Blue Cross, bore, carpentry, daily, day, field,
garden, hammering, hands, hot, hours, job, late,
mar, mother, on, party, pleasure, shirking, shop,
sitting, slave, slaving, sleeping, slow, strain,
summer, sweating, them, time, together, tough,
trouble, walking, well, willing, with, wood

You   (Me; I)

No.	Response	F	M	Tot.	%
1.	me	51	42	93	51.1
2.	are	12	5	17	9.3
3.	they	6	5	11	6.0
4.	can	1	3	4	2.2
5.	friend	3	1	4	2.2
6.	he	2	2	4	2.2
7.	I	3	1	4	2.2
8.	person	2	1	3	1.6
9.	him	1	1	2	1.1
10.	may	0	2	2	1.1
11.	too	0	2	2	1.1
12.	we	1	1	2	1.1

(f = 1, .5%, n = 34)
and, another, away, can't, come, economics, end,
fink, half, help, high, individual, is, lie,
Mike, must, other, people, questionable, see,
shoe, should, T.A. (Teaching Assistant), thee,
them, understand, unity, us, were, who, will,
young, you're, yours

CHAPTER 6

THE CALIFORNIA NORMS: ASSOCIATION AS A FUNCTION OF WORD FREQUENCY[1]

Leo Postman
University of California, Berkeley, California

This chapter presents norms of free association for samples of words varying widely in frequency of usage. Two sets of norms were obtained, one by the method of discrete association and the other by the method of continued association or production. In a test of discrete association, S responds to a stimulus with the first single word that comes to mind. The distribution of responses obtained from a group is often assumed to reflect the associative hierarchy as it exists for the individual S. In a test of continued association, S gives as many responses to a stimulus as he can within a specified period of time. The mean number of different responses per unit of time defines a measure of meaningfulness (m) of the stimulus word (Noble, 1952). In addition, the distribution of first responses to a stimulus generates an associative hierarchy comparable to that obtained from discrete associations. A comparison of the results obtained by the two methods is one of the questions of interest in the present study.

Word frequency is, of course, a major variable that is manipulated or must be controlled in most investigations using verbal materials. Information about the associative hierarchies and the meaningfulness of individual items is often valuable, if not essential, when the influence of word frequency on performance is considered. The analysis of the mechanisms responsible for the effects of frequency on associative learning and recall provides an obvious example. The present norms were intended primarily for use in the construction of experimental materials, and the selection of stimulus items was made with this purpose in mind. Since word length and part of speech are normally held constant in the investigation of other task variables, such as frequency, the stimuli were restricted to two-syllable nouns. With a view to permitting some control over formal interitem similarity in the construction of experimental materials, care was taken to draw the words in each sample from different parts of the alphabet.

The relations between stimulus frequency and selected characteristics of the response distributions were examined in a series of analyses to be reported below. Relevant earlier studies of the effects of stimulus frequency on free association were recently summarized by Cramer (1968, pp. 56-67) and will not be reviewed again here. Attention is called instead to some of the generalizations that were suggested by this survey of the available data. One conclusion of interest is that, in discrete association, increases in stimulus frequency are accompanied by a decrease in the heterogeneity of the responses, i.e., a decline in the number of different associations. There is at the same time an increase in the commonality of popular associations and, in particular, in the strength of the primary response. By contrast, the number of different responses given in continued association (m) increases as a function

[1] This research was facilitated by grants from the National Science Foundation and from the National Institute of Mental Health.

of stimulus frequency. The apparent contradiction between these findings—an increase in the number of different responses as a function of stimulus frequency in continued association and a decrease in discrete association—may be reasonably attributed to the difference between the two methods of testing. The total number of responses is fixed in discrete association but is allowed to vary in continued association. To account for the opposing trends, it is only necessary to make the following reasonable assumptions: (1) Both the number and the strength of associations increase with stimulus frequency; (2) a high level of absolute strength favors the occurrence of dominant responses in discrete association; and (3) continued association, by virtue of requiring a sequence of responses, will be sensitive to increases in the strength of multiple members of the hierarchy. These considerations point to the constraints that the method of testing imposes upon inferences about the distributions of associative strength. The juxtaposition of the two sets of norms obtained in the present study will serve to reinforce this conclusion.

METHOD

Stimulus Words

There were four samples of stimulus words consisting of 24 two-syllable nouns each. These samples were drawn from the following frequency intervals in the L count of Thorndike and Lorge (1944): 1-3, 10-33, 100-333, and 1000-3333. The successive intervals represent half-step increases on a logarithmic scale and cover a wide range of the domain of word frequency. The four frequency intervals in ascending order will be designated by the roman numerals I through IV. Table 1 lists all the words and their frequencies in the L count (T-L). It will be noted that the distribution of first letters is exactly the same in all four samples. In each case, six first letters are used once and nine first letters are used twice each.

TABLE 1 *Stimulus Words at Each Frequency Level*

No.	T-L range I, 1-3 Word	Frequency	T-L range II, 10-33 Word	Frequency	T-L range III, 100-333 Word	Frequency	T-L range IV, 1000-3333 Word	Frequency
1	Abbess	3	Arbor	29	Author	312	Answer	2132
2	Bramble	3	Basin	27	Belief	212	Building	1014
3	Buffoon	2	Burlap	18	Biscuit	132	Business	2850
4	Caucus	1	Carbon	26	Candle	148	Color	1541
5	Curfew	2	Cinder	15	Circus	110	Country	1714
6	Decoy	2	Discord	14	Device	151	Dinner	1266
7	Dotage	1	Dogma	12	Drama	151	Doctor	1631
8	Farthing	2	Fetish	13	Forest	209	Figure	1202
9	Gullet	2	Grocer	31	Glory	186	Garden	1036
10	Harem	2	Hermit	17	Highway	156	Husband	1788
11	Lorry	3	Lotion	30	Leather	171	Letter	1748
12	Mermaid	3	Magnate	15	Message	286	Moment	2396
13	Monsoon	2	Minstrel	20	Mortgage	195	Morning	2015
14	Oboe	1	Oatmeal	20	Oven	326	Office	1640
15	Oxide	1	Omen	11	Oyster	175	Order	1477
16	Pestle	3	Placard	27	Panic	147	Paper	1235
17	Prefix	2	Preview	27	Presence	277	Problem	1079
18	Ramrod	2	Relic	30	Region	149	Reason	1121
19	Sequel	3	Skillet	32	Sidewalk	123	Shoulder	1135
20	Stanza	3	Suffrage	24	Sofa	103	Story	1651
21	Tenure	3	Tempest	16	Tennis	215	Table	1325
22	Tortoise	2	Traitor	15	Tourist	116	Trouble	1180
23	Wampum	1	Wafer	16	Welfare	110	Window	1564
24	Wicket	3	Whisker	31	Wisdom	139	Woman	2431

Test of Discrete Association

In the administration of the test of discrete association, the procedure used by Russell and Jenkins (1954) was duplicated as closely as possible. The 96 stimulus words were numbered consecutively and listed on two pages, with a response blank next to each word. Two different random orders of presentation of the test words were used. The mean distance between the ordinal positions of the same words in the two forms of the test was 31.4 (*SD* = 23.7).

The most essential parts of the oral instructions, which were adopted from those of Russell and Jenkins, were as follows:

After each word write the first word that it makes you think of.

Start with the first word; look at it; write the word it makes you think of; then go on to the next word. Use only a single word for each response. Do not skip words. Give an association even if you are not sure about the meaning of a word. Work rapidly until you have finished all 96 words.

The test was administered to groups of *S*s during regular classroom periods.

Test of Continued Association

In the test of continued association or production, the procedure described by Noble (1952) was followed in most essential respects. The test booklet consisted of 96 pages, with one stimulus word per page. The stimulus word was printed 25 times along the left-hand side of the page, with a line after each repetition. The written instructions were identical with those used by Noble and included the following directions:

You will be given a *key* word and you are to write down as many *other* words which the key word brings to mind as you can. Be sure to think back to the *key* word after each word you write down because the test is to see how many other words the key word makes you think of. A good way to do this is to repeat each key word over and over to yourself as you write.

The words were presented in six different orders which were used equally often. The *S*s were allowed 50 sec to write down the responses to each stimulus. The test was again administered to groups of *S*s.

Subjects

All *S*s were undergraduate students at the University of California, Berkeley. The norms of discrete associations are based on the responses of 1000 *S*s who completed the test. Of these, 500 were enrolled in an English course for freshmen. This course is taken by students who fail to achieve a certain minimum score on an English placement test. The remaining 500 *S*s were advanced students who had either passed the course or had been exempted from it. These two groups are designated as the Low Language and High Language *S*s, respectively, in the tabulation of the responses. The total sample of *S*s included 522 men and 478 women.

The production test was administered to 96 *S*s, 29 men and 67 women. All but an occasional *S* were in the High Language category. Since neither the ability classification nor sex differences proved important in the analysis of discrete associations, these differences in the composition of the two samples were not considered critical.

RESULTS

Discrete Association

The tables of norms (pp. 260-320) list the responses in descending order of frequency for the total sample of 1000 *S*s. The frequencies of each response for the two ability groups and for men and women are also shown. It should be noted that the numbers of men and women in the sample were not equal (522 vs. 478), so that the entries are not directly comparable. A direct comparison would require conversion of the raw frequencies to percentages. No major differences between subgroups were in evidence, and the analyses of the results were restricted to the distributions for the total sample of 1000 *S*s.

Response heterogeneity. Since the responses are numbered consecutively in descending order of frequency, the total number of different responses given to a particular stimulus may be determined by reference to the appropriate table. The mean total numbers of different responses for the four frequency ranges were as follows, with the standard deviations given in parentheses: I, 201.0 (75.4); II, 191.6 (88.0); III, 142.0 (43.4); IV, 166.8 (53.8). The corresponding medians are 196.5, 150.0, 136.5, and 163.5. A Kruskal-Wallis analysis of variance shows the differences among the frequency ranges to be significant, $H = 10.94$, $p < .02$. The relation between stimulus frequency and response heterogeneity is curvilinear. As frequency increases, the number of different responses declines, but there is a reversal in the function at the highest frequency level. However, in spite of the reversal, the value for range IV remains substantially below that for range I. The presence of a curvilinear relation would not have been detected if the comparison had been restricted to two levels of frequency, as was done in previous studies (cf. Cramer, 1968, pp. 56-67). One plausible explanation of the observed trend would take its point of departure from the assumption that both the strength and the number of associations increase as a function of frequency. As has already been suggested, a high level of absolute strength would favor the occurrence of the dominant responses which lie well above the threshold of elicitation. The decline in response heterogeneity over the first three levels conforms to this expectation. At the highest frequency level, however, the increase in the number of potentially competing associations becomes sufficiently great to produce a reversal in the function. Thus, the relation between stimulus frequency and response heterogeneity appears to be determined jointly by changes in the strength and in the number of associations.

Rank-frequency functions. Table 2 shows the percentages of occurrence for the responses occupying the first five normative ranks. Median as well as mean percentages are presented. Attention is called, first of all, to the trend in the strength of the primary response. The percentage of occurrences of the primary association increases as a function of word frequency over the first three levels but shows a decline at the highest level. This reversal is more pronounced for the median than for the mean percentage values. The trend exactly complements that obtained for response heterogeneity. The inverse relation between the two sets of measures is not surprising, since the strength of the primary response is undoubtedly a major determinant of the degree of entropy in a distribution of associations. The changes as a function of word frequency in the measures of heterogeneity and in the strength of the primary responses may, therefore, be attributed to the same mechanisms.

The relation between stimulus frequency and response probability becomes less regular at the lower ranks, especially for the mean values. It is noteworthy, however, that there is continuing evidence of a reversal in the function at the highest level of stimulus frequency for the first four ranks. The suggested interpretation of the pattern of response probabilities receives independent support from the finding that Ss' ability to give consistent associations from one trial to the next is greater for stimuli of medium than of very low or very high frequency (Postman, 1964).

TABLE 2   *Rank-Frequency Functions at Each Frequency Level[a]*

| Frequency range | Rank | | | | | | | | | |
| | 1 | | 2 | | 3 | | 4 | | 5 | |
	Mean	Median	Mean	Median	Mean	Median	Mean	Median	Mean	Median
III	23.8	22.3	12.8	10.4	7.1	6.6	4.8	4.5	3.4	3.1
II	25.3	22.8	11.9	10.8	7.3	7.5	5.2	4.4	3.5	3.3
III	27.9	25.2	12.7	11.2	7.5	7.0	5.6	5.3	3.5	4.5
IV	26.5	18.8	10.7	10.2	6.3	5.8	5.1	5.0	4.0	3.7

[a]Entries are percentages of occurrence of responses.

Word frequency of responses. To the extent that free associates reflect a history of joint occurrence of the stimulus and the response in S's verbal environment, there should be a positive correlation between the frequencies of usage of the two terms. The expected correlation was obtained in the present data. Table 3 presents measures of the word frequency of the responses, based on the L count, for the first five normative ranks. The entries are the antilogs of the mean log frequencies of the responses at each rank. The word frequency of the primary response is clearly highest for range IV and lowest for range I, with ranges II and III yielding similar intermediate values. These differences are significant, $F(3, 92) = 2.74$, $p < .05$. The measures for the remaining ranks show some irregularities, but certain trends are nevertheless in evidence: (*1*) The stimulus and response frequencies continue to be positively correlated; (*2*) response frequency tends to decline as a function of normative rank; (*3*) relative to the stimulus array, the values for the responses show regression toward the mean of the frequency continuum. Thus, the frequencies of the responses are higher than those of the stimuli for ranges I-III but lower for range IV.

The positive correlation between stimulus and response frequencies is consistent with the assumption that the probability of the responses reflects prior co-occurrences in linguistic usage. The decline in response frequency as a function of normative rank indicates, however, that the position of an association in the hierarchy is determined by the sheer availability of the response as well. That is, the principle of "spew" (Underwood & Schulz, 1960) applies to the responses given on a test of free association.

TABLE 3   Word Frequency of Responses for Ranks 1-5
in Distributions of Discrete Associations[a]

Stimulus range	Rank				
	1	2	3	4	5
II	294	344	211	261	239
II	617	357	277	251	270
III	608	484	425	640	438
IV	1159	564	869	832	822

[a]Entries are antilogs of mean log frequencies.

Continued Association (Production Test)

Mean numbers of different responses. Table 4 shows for each stimulus the mean number of different responses per S (m). The relation between word frequency and m is positive. The average m values increase over the first three frequency ranges but show little change between the third and the fourth. The variabilities within the samples are comparable; the standard deviations of the m values are 1.28, 1.17, 1.50, and 1.14 for ranges I through IV, respectively.[2] It is apparent that there is some overlap among the distributions. However, the differences among the four groups of words are significant, $F(3, 92) = 16.05, p < .01$.

Hierarchies of initial responses. The first responses given by a group of Ss to a stimulus in the production test generate an associative hierarchy comparable to that obtained in discrete association. These tabulations may be found on pp. 249-259. The basic analyses carried out on the discrete associations were repeated for the initial responses on the production test.

(1) Number of different first responses. The numbers of different first responses to each stimulus are listed in Table 4. The average measures exhibit the same curvilinear trend as a function of word frequency as was observed for discrete associations—a decrease over the first three ranges followed by a reversal at the highest level of frequency. This trend, which is somewhat more regular for the medians than for the means, is less pronounced than in the previous analysis, and the differences among groups fail to reach statistical significance. Even though the very first responses on the production test are under consideration, there is less constraint on the choice of that response than in discrete association. Thus, S may review some of the possible responses before beginning to write them down, and the first one given may not necessarily be the first one that came to mind. In light of these considerations, the consistency of the trends in the two analyses is noteworthy.

(2) Rank-frequency functions. The mean and the median percentages of occurrence of the responses occupying the first five ranks of the distributions are shown in Table 5. For the primary responses, the mean percentages increase as a function of stimulus frequency, and there is no terminal reversal. However, as the discrepancies between the means and the medians indicate, the distributions for the three higher ranges were positively skewed; the medians fail to exhibit a systematic trend. For the remaining ranks, the difference between the two measures is small and, in spite of some irregularities, a curvilinear trend is in evidence. It is clear, however, that when Ss are set for multiple responding, the rank-frequency distributions are less sensitive to changes in stimulus frequency than under conditions of discrete association.

(3) Word frequency of responses. The relevant data are presented in Table 6. The antilogs of the mean log frequencies of the responses at each rank are shown as before. The values for the primary association again show a clear positive correlation between stimulus and response frequency. There is continuing evidence of this relation at the remaining ranks. In general, response frequency declines as a function of rank, although the presence of some

[2]The mean m values for men, in ascending order of stimulus frequency, were 7.72, 8.24, 9.39, and 9.58. For women, the corresponding values were 6.98, 7.99, 9.19, and 9.46. Thus, there is a difference in favor of the men which declines with word frequency. It will be recalled that the proportion of women Ss was higher for the test of continued association than for the test of discrete association. The sex differences in m values imply that there may be some bias in the comparison of the results obtained by the two methods. However, the assessment of relative trends as a function of word frequency should be influenced only minimally, if at all, by the presence of such a bias.

TABLE 4 *Summary of Results for Continued Association*

	Word	m	SE$_m$	No. diff. first Rs
	I. T-L Frequency Range 1-3			
1.	Abbess	4.60	.39	46
2.	Bramble	7.04	.38	39
3.	Buffoon	6.44	.41	42
4.	Caucus	7.50	.34	50
5.	Curfew	8.61	.33	47
6.	Decoy	7.58	.31	32
7.	Dotage	5.02	.37	56
8.	Farthing	6.36	.30	36
9.	Gullet	5.94	.33	40
10.	Harem	7.98	.33	26
11.	Lorry	5.90	.43	45
12.	Mermaid	10.01	.34	28
13.	Monsoon	8.57	.37	31
14.	Oboe	8.49	.30	28
15.	Oxide	7.61	.26	34
16.	Pestle	5.52	.37	40
17.	Prefix	7.38	.28	26
18.	Ramrod	6.74	.37	53
19.	Sequel	6.60	.31	49
20.	Stanza	8.34	.35	21
21.	Tenure	7.02	.32	47
22.	Tortoise	9.18	.34	14
23.	Wampum	7.69	.37	16
24.	Wicket	6.90	.35	37
	Mean	7.21		36.79
	Median	7.21		38.00
	II. T-L Frequency Range 10-33			
1.	Arbor	8.05	.39	38
2.	Basin	9.14	.34	35
3.	Burlap	8.38	.31	15
4.	Carbon	9.30	.31	23
5.	Cinder	9.62	.33	28
6.	Discord	6.94	.26	51
7.	Dogma	6.53	.29	53
8.	Fetish	5.68	.30	79
9.	Grocer	8.85	.33	36
10.	Hermit	8.50	.29	44
11.	Lotion	9.04	.32	31
12.	Magnate	6.88	.33	60
13.	Minstrel	9.07	.35	33
14.	Oatmeal	9.48	.32	30
15.	Omen	7.09	.29	43
16.	Placard	6.81	.36	48
17.	Preview	6.64	.30	34
18.	Relic	7.95	.35	23
19.	Skillet	10.22	.35	22
20.	Suffrage	7.71	.30	22
21.	Tempest	7.73	.33	27
22.	Traitor	7.47	.31	46
23.	Wafer	7.83	.33	35
24.	Whisker	8.64	.29	24
	Mean	8.06		36.67
	Median	8.00		34.50

TABLE 4 *(continued)*

	Word	m	SE$_m$	No. diff. first Rs
	III. T-L Frequency Range 100-333			
1.	Author	8.88	.32	21
2.	Belief	7.18	.29	42
3.	Biscuit	10.41	.37	42
4.	Candle	9.85	.32	23
5.	Circus	11.19	.46	23
6.	Device	6.86	.30	41
7.	Drama	9.90	.34	31
8.	Forest	11.29	.34	15
9.	Glory	7.72	.33	49
10.	Highway	10.77	.33	26
11.	Leather	10.14	.34	34
12.	Message	8.25	.34	42
13.	Mortgage	8.71	.32	23
14.	Oven	10.27	.31	23
15.	Oyster	10.31	.35	25
16.	Panic	8.47	.32	46
17.	Presence	6.23	.33	34
18.	Region	8.38	.38	33
19.	Sidewalk	9.92	.34	25
20.	Sofa	9.64	.35	24
21.	Tennis	12.35	.33	24
22.	Tourist	9.68	.33	50
23.	Welfare	7.69	.29	39
24.	Wisdom	7.88	.32	39
	Mean	9.25		32.25
	Median	9.66		32.00
	IV. T-L Frequency Range 1000-3333			
1.	Answer	8.35	.31	25
2.	Building	9.82	.34	47
3.	Business	9.45	.35	49
4.	Color	10.95	.38	30
5.	Country	10.66	.39	56
6.	Dinner	10.50	.38	27
7.	Doctor	10.04	.32	49
8.	Figure	9.05	.30	49
9.	Garden	11.97	.34	32
10.	Husband	8.80	.36	13
11.	Letter	9.95	.33	37
12.	Moment	7.41	.30	36
13.	Morning	10.30	.34	36
14.	Office	9.73	.32	44
15.	Order	8.34	.31	67
16.	Paper	10.81	.34	35
17.	Problem	8.70	.31	34
18.	Reason	7.16	.32	44
19.	Shoulder	9.48	.37	36
20.	Story	9.38	.34	30
21.	Table	10.57	.35	21
22.	Trouble	7.76	.30	57
23.	Window	9.86	.33	32
24.	Woman	8.90	.31	23
	Mean	9.50		37.88
	Median	9.60		36.00

deviant points must be noted. Finally, regression of the response values toward the mean of the frequency continuum is again apparent. For the most part, then, the trends observed for the responses in discrete association are confirmed.

TABLE 5   *Rank-Frequency Functions for First Responses in Production Tests*

| Frequency range | Rank | | | | | | | | | |
| | 1 | | 2 | | 3 | | 4 | | 5 | |
	Mean	Median	Mean	Median	Mean	Median	Mean	Median	Mean	Median
I	23.6	24.0	13.9	11.4	7.3	7.3	5.3	5.2	4.1	4.2
II	28.0	25.5	13.9	13.6	8.3	7.3	5.2	5.2	3.9	3.6
III	28.4	24.0	12.7	11.5	8.7	8.3	6.2	6.3	4.7	5.2
IV	30.1	26.0	10.2	9.4	6.4	6.3	5.0	5.2	3.8	4.2

Comparison of primary associations. In a large proportion of cases, the primary discrete association was also the most frequent first response on the test of production. The numbers of words (out of 24) in each frequency range to which the same primary response was given were as follows: I, 14; II, 14; III, 17; IV, 17. Within each range the percentages of occurrence of the shared primaries on the two tests are in close correspondence. The product-moment correlations are .79, .84, .95, and .88 for the four ranges, in ascending order of frequency.

TABLE 6   *Word Frequency of Responses for Ranks 1-5 in Distributions*
of First Responses in Production Test[a]

| Stimulus range | Rank | | | | |
	1	2	3	4	5
I	366	203	230	127	77
II	416	189	202	137	208
III	558	583	312	210	231
IV	975	460	533	1122	586

[a]Entries are antilogs of mean log frequencies.

Table 7 shows the mean percentages of occurrence of the shared primaries. The means for the responses that diverged in the two situations are presented as well. As was to be expected, the values are considerably higher when the primaries are the same than when they are different. The stronger an association, the more likely it is to be elicited consistently and regardless of variations in the conditions of testing. The probabilities of the shared primaries show a clear rise between the first and the second range and little systematic change thereafter. At the highest level of frequency, there is only a hint of a reversal for the test of discrete association and an increase for the test of continued association. By contrast, the means of the divergent associations first increase and then decrease. The reversal occurs between ranges II and III, i.e., at an earlier point on the frequency continuum than for the total samples of words.

TABLE 7   *Mean Percentages of Occurrence of Shared and Divergent*
Primary Responses in Tests of Discrete and Continued Association

| Frequency range | Discrete association | | Continued association | |
	Shared	Divergent	Shared	Divergent
I	27.0	18.4	28.0	17.5
II	32.0	20.9	35.0	21.2
III	32.4	17.2	33.1	17.0
IV	31.9	13.3	37.1	13.3

It is apparent that the divergent responses are largely responsible for the overall curvilinear relation between stimulus frequency and the percentage of occurrence of the primary association. Within a given frequency range, the divergent responses are lower in associative strength, and hence more vulnerable to competition, than the shared ones. It was suggested earlier that the relation between stimulus frequency and the probability of the primary response reflects changes in both associative strength and in the number of competing associations. The factor of associative growth is reflected directly in the trend for shared primaries which attain sufficiently high levels of absolute strength to ensure their dominance. The increases in competition assume a decisive influence in the case of the divergent associations which are at a lower absolute level of strength than the shared ones.

Overlap of discrete and continued associations. In the interpretation and application of norms of discrete association, it is commonly assumed that the distribution of responses obtained from a group reflects the hierarchies of the individual Ss. If this assumption is correct, the responses given to a stimulus in continued association should also be found in the normative distribution of discrete associations. Presumably, the continued responses provide direct information about the hierarchies of individual Ss that are believed to underlie the distributions of discrete responses.

In light of these considerations, the degree of overlap between the specific responses given on the two tests was determined. The responses given in continued association were classified into two categories: those that were present (P) and those that were absent (A) in the norms of discrete association. It should be noted that a much larger number of Ss was tested by the discrete than by the continued method. The reference norms were, therefore, sufficiently exhaustive to permit an accurate classification of the continued responses. The results show that the two categories of associations were almost equally probable. The mean percentages of A responses were 46.9, 44.1, 41.2, and 42.0 for ranges I-IV, respectively. The percentages show some decline as a function of stimulus frequency which may be attributed to the increasing strength of the domain of associations. The differences among the frequency ranges are significant, $F(3, 92) = 5.02, p < .01$. The finding that deserves major emphasis, however, is the high degree of divergence of the classes of discrete and continued associations. Undoubtedly, Ss' inevitable tendency to chain their associations on the production test is at least partly responsible for the lack of agreement between the two distributions of responses. However, the findings also serve to raise doubts about the basic assumption that a normative distribution of single responses permits a valid assessment of the associative hierarchies of individuals.

SUMMARY

Norms of free association were presented for samples of words varying widely in frequency of usage. One set of norms was obtained by the method of discrete association, and the other by the method of continued association or production. The relations between stimulus frequency and selected characteristics of the response distributions were examined. Under conditions of discrete association, the heterogeneity of responses first decreases and then increases as a function of stimulus frequency. A complementary trend shows an increase in the strength of the primary response followed by a terminal decline. These effects of stimulus frequency were interpreted as reflecting concurrent changes in the strength and the number of associations. The word frequency of the responses is positively correlated with that of the stimuli. This correlation points to joint occurrence in linguistic usage as a determinant of associative probability. The trends are similar, though less pronounced, for the distributions of first responses on the test of production. The mean number of different responses per stimulus (m) given on that test increases directly as a function of stimulus frequency. Finally, the specific responses given on the two tests show a high degree of divergence.

REFERENCES

Cramer, P. (1968). *Word association.* New York: Academic Press.

Noble, C. E. (1952). An analysis of meaning. *Psychological Review* 59, 421-430.

Postman, L. (1964). Acquisition and retention of consistent associative responses. *Journal of Experimental Psychology* 67, 183-190.

Russell, W. A., & Jenkins, J. J. (1954). The complete Minnesota norms for responses to 100 words from the Kent-Rosanoff word association test. Technical Report No. 11, University of Minnesota, Contract N8-onr-66216. Minneapolis, Minn.

Thorndike, E. L., & Lorge, I. (1944). *The teacher's word book of 30,000 words.* New York: Teachers College.

Underwood, B. J., & Schulz, R. W. (1960). *Meaningfulness and verbal learning.* Philadelphia: Lippincott.

I-1 Abbess

No.	Response	f
1.	abyss	8
2.	abbey	7
3.	church	4
4.	convent	3

5-14. ($\underline{f}$ = 2)
abbot, crevice, deep, fall, fat, hall, nothing, nun, sore, unknown
15-46. ($\underline{f}$ = 1)
abscess, amputation, award, Chaucer, chasm, Chinese, cross, dark, deep dark hole, depth, drop, Elizabeth, high point, incline, knowledge, lady, meaning, mountain, none, nunnery, old Roman Catholic church, opening, part, poll, protect, ravine, recede, recess, religion, truth, unknown word, women abbot
No Response: ($\underline{f}$ = 22)

I-2 Bramble

No.	Response	f
1.	bush(es)	26
2.	briar (brier) (s)	9
3.	thorn(s)	7
4.	ramble	6
5.	patch	3

6-11. ($\underline{f}$ = 2)
bramble, Brer Rabbit, gamble, scramble, thick, thicket
12-39. ($\underline{f}$ = 1)
bamboo, blackberry, branch, brush, careless, caught, dictionary, eyes, fumble, green, honey, ignorance, mish-mash, mix up, next word, noice, push, rattle, scratch, speck, stickers, sticky, tarn, tree, twig, unknown, weeds, woods
No Response: ($\underline{f}$ = 5)

I-3 Buffoon

No.	Response	f
1.	clown	26
2.	fool	9
3.	balloon	4

4-7. ($\underline{f}$ = 3)
animal, funny, idiot, laugh
8-10. ($\underline{f}$ = 2)
cause, joker, war
11-42. ($\underline{f}$ = 1)
actor, bassoon, big, bluff, boat, buffet, buffon skirt, court, dumbell, elephant, Falstaff, fat man, French, hole, horn, ignoramus, jocular, joke, jokester, jolly, Karamazov, lunch, opera, Pantaloon, pretend, question, raccoon, Roy, silly, stranger,

I-3 Buffoon (contd)

No.	Response	f

think, wind
No Response: ($\underline{f}$ = 7)

I-4 Caucus

No.	Response	f
1.	meeting	18
2.	politics	5
3.	body	4
4.	group	4
5.	senate	4

6-8. ($\underline{f}$ = 3)
congress, convention, party
9-15. ($\underline{f}$ = 2)
bone(s), census, election, government, loud, man(e), political
16-50. ($\underline{f}$ = 1)
add, Alice in W., assembly, burning, cabal, clique, committee, conversation, court, debate, desert, Faubus, gathering, kingfish, labor, Latin, mule, nothing, people, plenipotentiary, political convention, political party convention, president, questioners, quorum, rating, raucus, remains, smoke, social, talk, talking, vocabulary, vote, White House
No Response: ($\underline{f}$ = 3)

I-5 Curfew

No.	Response	f
1.	late	12
2.	time	12
3.	hour(s)	9
4.	law(s)	8

5-7. ($\underline{f}$ = 3)
bell, lockout, night
8-13. ($\underline{f}$ = 2)
children, deadline, 9 o'clock, police, teenagers, tolls
14-47. ($\underline{f}$ = 1)
army, be in, blackout, Campanile, cashew, climax, clock, cops, cover fire, dark, date, even, evening, hell, kids, knell, limit, 9 a.m., noise, 1:00, 1:00 a.m., perfume, restraint of young persons, rules, set time, shall not ring, shrill, street, 10 o'clock, 10 p.m., trouble, 12:00, 2:30, Women's Dormitory Association

I-6 Decoy

No.	Response	f
1.	duck(s)	46
2.	hunting	8
3.	trap	4

4-11. ($\underline{f}$ = 2)
deception, fake, false, fool, police, television, trick, wood duck
12-32. ($\underline{f}$ = 1)
ambush, army, bait, bullet, decoration, duck hunting, duck of wood, game, group, illusion, imitation, lure, navy, plant, spy, stage, subterfuge, trip, T.V. program, woman, wooden duck
No Response: ($\underline{f}$ = 1)

I-7 Dotage

No.	Response	f
1.	old	9
2.	old age	6
3.	love	4

4-7. ($\underline{f}$ = 3)
cottage, dote, doting, parent(s)
8-10. ($\underline{f}$ = 2)
attention, king, mother
11-56. ($\underline{f}$ = 1)
age, anecdotage, belief, child, delay, different, doctor, dot, doubt, dowager, dowry, drayage, elderly, fawn, fawning, fool, fondness, given, glory, grandmother, hanger-on, hen pecked, house, indulge, interest, line, measurement, not, nothing, owe, paints, pamper, paternal, precious, questioning, reward, senile, senility, servitude, simpering, sorry, spoiled, stage, typing, unknown
No Response: ($\underline{f}$ = 13)

I-8 Farthing

No.	Response	f
1.	money	28
2.	coin	7
3.	shilling	5
4.	bird	4
5.	England	4
6.	penny	4
7.	distance	3

8-11. ($\underline{f}$ = 2)
away, English, nothing, sou
12-36. ($\underline{f}$ = 1)
bettering, beyond, British, cent, chicken, colt, deep, distant, English denom. of $, faraway, frontier, gay, less, London, pence, pittance, poor, pound, reaching, sixpence, small coin, sparing, tuppence,

I-8 Farthing (contd)

No.	Response	f

worthless
No Response: (f = 8)

I-9 Gullet

No.	Response	f
1.	throat	23
2.	stomach	11
3.	chicken	8
4.	esophagus	4
5.	swallow	4
6.	mouth	3

7-9. (f = 2)
down, hole, nick
10-40. (f = 1)
anatomy, animal, biology, bird,
bullet, craw, crock, duck,
eating, fish, food, frog,
gizzard, glutton, guillet,
gulls, intestinal tract, knife,
medicine, opening, paramecium,
pelican, physiology, plate,
rhum, skillet, stab, trench,
trinket, unknown word, valley
No Response: (f = 6)

I-10 Harem

No.	Response	f
1.	woman(e)	28
2.	girls	19
3.	wife(ves)	7
4.	sultan	5
5.	Arab(s)	4
6.	Arabia	4

7-8. (f = 3)
East, shiek
9-11. (f = 2)
India, king, Persia
12-26. (f = 1)
Ali Baba, Arabian, dancer,
Engre, Far East, maharajah,
many Mohammedans, Negro,
oriental, plural wives, sex,
Siam, slaves, women (many)
No Response: (f = 2)

I-11 Lorry

No.	Response	f
1.	truck	12
2.	name	10
3.	boat(s)	5
4.	sorry	4

5-8. (f = 3)
cart, England, girl's name,
Peter
9-13. (f = 2)
bus, cab, girl, song, vehicle
14-45. (f = 1)
an English means of transportation, bank, Calhoun, carriage,
cole, dingy, English, gory,
hesitate, horse, Larry, lazy,
Linda, Lorraine Sassone, lorry,
machine, motor, nothing, person,

I-11 Lorry (contd)

No.	Response	f

rickshaw, river, sea, ship,
surrey, Tale of Two Cities,
tarry, test, van, wagon, war,
water, wonder
No Response: (f = 11)

I-12 Mermaid

No.	Response	f
1.	fish	24
2.	sea	19
3.	ocean	14
4.	woman(e)	6
5.	myth	4
6.	water	4

7-9. (f = 2)
beauty, merman, tavern
10-28. (f = 1)
Ann Blythe, coal, Disneyland,
fair, false, fanciful, feet
girl, half & half, half nude,
maid, mermaid, Mr. Peabody
order, sailor, scales, story,
swim, tail

I-13 Monsoon

No.	Response	f
1.	rain(s)	22
2.	storm	20
3.	wind(s)	13
4.	India	8
5.	typhoon	3

6-8. (f = 2)
climate, hurricane, weather
9-31. (f = 1)
boat, China, dark, disaster,
dock, doctor, English courses,
gale, Ghandi, Himalaya, Monday,
moon, mountains, orient, rainstorm, rainy, reverse, season,
ship, tornado, torrent, tropic,
water
No Response: (f = 1)

I-14 Oboe

No.	Response	f
1.	music	27
2.	instrument	22
3.	flute	7
4.	clarinet	5
5.	horn	5
6.	bassoon	3
7.	orchestra	3

8-10. (f = 2)
band, hobo, symphony
11-28. (f = 1)
abode, blank, deep, figure,
Japan, music instrument,
musical instrument, my poor
vocabulary, nothing, play,
player, questionable, stick,
strings, wind, wind instrument,
wit, woodwind

I-15 Oxide

No.	Response	f
1.	chemistry	23
2.	oxygen	13
3.	carbon	9
4.	iron	6
5.	rust	6
6.	zinc	4

7-8. (f = 3)
carbon dioxide, chemical
9-11. (f = 2)
air, hydrogen, ox hide
12-34. (f = 1)
acids, black, cantaloup,
compound, CO_2, copper, di-,
discoloring, element, ferrous,
gas, metal, mineral, ointment,
O_2, ox, oxygen(to do with),
paint, pent-, peroxide,
science, sodium, white

I-16 Pestle

No.	Response	f
1.	mortar	28
2.	flower	9
3.	pest(s)	5
4.	pedestal	3
5.	bother	2
6.	chemistry	2
7.	pistle	2

8-40. (f = 1)
annoyance, bad, beer, beetle,
bowl, brass, center of flower,
church, corn, dentist,
disease, don't know, famine,
high, highest, ignorance, jar,
medicine, pestish, pistil,
pistol, press, pretzel, rub,
silent, stand, step, stick,
stir, tire, tool, unknown,
westle
No Response: (f = 12)

I-17 Prefix

No.	Response	f
1.	before	35
2.	suffix	23
3.	word(s)	6
4.	beginning	5
5.	English	3

6-8. (f = 2)
first, language, syllable
9-26. (f = 1)
add, addition, advance, affix,
begin, book, dictionary,
grammar, grammar text, head,
part, peep, short, small
letters, spelling, sutter,
telephone number, to a word

I-18 Ramrod

No.	Response	f
1.	car(s)	10
2.	gun	7
3.	straight	7

I-18 Ramrod (contd)

No.	Response	f
4.	push	5
5.	steel	4
6.	pole	3
7.	stiff	3

8-12. (f = 2)
batter, cowboy('s), stick, straight as, western
13-53. (f = 1)
battering ram, bore, boss, break, cannon, car engine, car's part, chemistry, clean, coerce, Duane Eddy, foreman, iron, long, MacArthur, man, measure, metal, music, open, person, plunger, poke, posture, power, powerful, pushing, ram, rifle, Schabod, set, skinny, sphere, spoke, sports, stand, straight, television show, throat, tool, weapon, weed
No Response: (f = 6)

I-19 Sequel

No.	Response	f
1.	following	9
2.	story	7
3.	continuation	6
4.	next	6
5.	book	5

6-7. (f = 4)
follow, sequence
8-11. (f = 3)
addition, after, end, same
12-15. (f = 2)
analogous, continued, follow-up, novel
16-49. (f = 1)
aftermath, another, chapter, comes after, continuance, continue, continuing, counterpart, design, dislike, ending, equal, event, follower, heart, line, magazine, more, mystery, next part, next week, nothing, number, order, part, postlude, publisher, quite, rain, result, second, serial, time, unknown word
No Response: (f = 1)

I-20 Stanza

No.	Response	f
1.	music	19
2.	poem	14
3.	song	12
4.	line(s)	11
5.	verse	11
6.	phrase	7
7.	poetry	6

8-9. (f = 2)
paragraph, refrain
10-21. (f = 1)
bar, grand, hymn, Lanza, of course, part, prefix, score second, song part of a, Spencerian, word

I-21 Tenure

No.	Response	f
1.	office	14
2.	time	9
3.	teacher(s)	8
4.	teaching	6
5.	length	4

6-7. (f = 3)
hold, length of time
8-13. (f = 2)
holding, job(s), land, stay, tension, term
14-47. (f = 1)
administrative, bondage, could be, denture, duration, end, farm, hurt, insurance, iodine, last, length of stability, long, longevity, made, money, of office, old, period, position, president, retirement, school, security, seniority, strength, teeth, temporary, tenacity, term of office, three, three years, to lure, work
No Response: (f = 3)

I-22 Tortoise

No.	Response	f
1.	turtle	42
2.	shell	25
3.	hare	7
4.	animal(s)	6
5.	slow	5
6.	reptile	2

7-14. (f = 1)
bare, color, fish, koala bear, mortoise, ocean, smoke, soup
No Response: (f = 1)

I-23 Wampum

No.	Response	f
1.	Indian(s)	37
2.	money	36
3.	shell(s)	3
4.	trade	3
5.	beads	2
6.	teepee	2

7-16. (f = 1)
animal, barter, big chief, don't know, exchange, exotic, Indian money, N.Y., plum, wigwam
No Response: (f = 3)

I-24 Wicket

No.	Response	f
1.	basket	18
2.	croquet	14
3.	game	9
4.	cricket	6
5.	fence	5

6-11. (f = 2)
England, field(s), hoop, mallet, picket, wire

I-24 Wicket (contd)

12-37. (f = 1)
bad, ball, ball game, bank, bat, candle, catch, chain, chair, flashy, gate, goal, hammer, lawn, light, lighter, mean, pale, racket, sticky, stricken, tickets, unknown word, wacket, washed, wood
No Response: (f = 6)

II-1 Arbor

No.	Response	f
1.	tree(s)	22
2.	grape(s)	9
3.	rose(s)	7
4.	Ann	6
5.	garden	6

6-7. (f = 3)
harbor, vines
8-13. (f = 2)
Ann Arbor, drive, green, labor, shade, ship(s)
14-38. (f = 1)
Ann Arbor, Mich., Ann (Mich.), ant arbor, arbor, armor, boat, bored, bough, circle, day, flowers, gate, hard, lights, nights, of trees, overhead, plants, rose covered, trellis, tressle, vitae, vital, war, whale
No Response: (f = 3)

II-2 Basin

No.	Response	f
1.	wash	25
2.	sink	17
3.	bowl	7
4.	water	6
5.	bathroom	4
6.	river	4
7.	street	3

8-9. (f = 2)
big, pan
10-35. (f = 1)
area, big basin, big trees, cave, dam, disc, great basin, gully, houses, kitchen, metal, pink, plain, pot, ranges, round, soap, towel, trough, tub, valley, washing, wash hair, wash pan, water, lake, wild

II-3 Burlap

No.	Response	f
1.	sack(s)	44
2.	bag	34
3.	cloth	3
4.	material	3

II-3 Burlap (contd)

No.	Response	f

5-15. ($\underline{f}$ = 1)
bedspread, burlesque, burly,
costs, Paris, prison, rough,
sacking, slap, tent, thicket
No. Response: ($\underline{f}$ = 1)

II-4 Carbon

No.	Response	f
1.	paper	27
2.	copy	19
3.	dioxide	14
4.	black	9
5.	element	4

6-10. ($\underline{f}$ = 2)
chemistry, fire, gas,
tetrachloride, typewriter
11-23. ($\underline{f}$ = 1)
air, atom, coal, cycle, 14,
monoxide, oxygen, pardon,
Psych. 1A notes, ribbon,
secretary, three, typing

II-5 Cinder

No.	Response	f
1.	ash(es)	31
2.	fire	14
3.	eye	10
4.	Cinderella	5
5.	black	4
6.	path	4

7-12 ($\underline{f}$ = 2)
burn, chimney, Ella, smoke,
spark, track
13-28. ($\underline{f}$ = 1)
basement, Bible, block, cinder,
coal, cone, fireplace,
hot, match, organic, rock,
small, something you get in an
eye, soot, waste

II-6 Discord

No.	Response	f
1.	harmony	22
2.	disharmony	11
3.	fight	4
4.	music	3
5.	trouble	3
6.	unharmonic	3

7-11. ($\underline{f}$ = 2)
disagreement, disharmonious,
lack of harmony, strife, unhappy
12-51. ($\underline{f}$ = 1)
accord, against, agreement,
anger, awful, bad, chaos, dis-
connect, discuss, disdained,
displace, dissonance, distant,
harmonic, harsh, in, in in order,
incoherent, lack, mixed up,
modern, no harmony, noise, off
beat, off key, out of, out of
order, out of step, piano, play,
seeds, song, sound, struggle,
things, uneasy, unhappiness,

II-6 Discord (contd)

No.	Response	f

unity, unpleasant, upset

II-7 Dogma

No.	Response	f
1.	belief(s)	10
2.	doctrine	10
3.	church	7
4.	religion	6
5.	rule(s)	4

6-7. ($\underline{f}$ = 3)
dog, teaching(s)
8-14. ($\underline{f}$ = 2)
creed, dogmatic, edict, faith,
idea, strict, tradition
15-53. ($\underline{f}$ = 1)
attitude, bad, catholic,
Catholic Church, catholicism,
dictator, dilemma, dull,
European, experiment, fable,
Hitler, laws, mad, Marxianism,
mother, narrow-minded, play,
pressure, principle, propaganda,
puzzle, ritual, rut, same,
school, situation, statement,
stigma, straight-laced, strife,
stubborn, thoughts, tired,
truth, unsure, untruth,
unyielding, words

II-8 Fetish

No.	Response	f
1.	sex	3

2-11. ($\underline{f}$ = 2)
fish, fixation, habit, idiosyn-
crasy, particular, psychology,
religion, symbol, upset, women
12-79. ($\underline{f}$ = 1)
abnormal, accomplishment, after,
angry, attachment, belief,
bothersome, careful, child,
collector, complementary meeting
of, culture, deviant, dislike,
disturbed, fanatic, fashion,
feast, fethishism, foreign,
frantic, frill, fussy, hat,
holiday, idol, infantile,
language, law, little people,
magic, mania, mannerism, method,
nagging, nervous, opinion,
overboard, party, peculiarity,
perversion, perversity, petty,
phobia, pretend, primitive,
problem, psychiatry, term,
ritual, selfish, shibboleth,
shoe, sick, silly, simple,
skittish, squirm, sticky, strong
zeal, talisman, tradition, ugly,
unknown word, voodoo, weird,
whim, worry
No Response: ($\underline{f}$ = 5)

II-9 Grocer

No.	Response	f
1.	store	23
2.	food	18
3.	man	7
4.	grocery(ies)	5
5.	friendly	3
6.	market	3

7-13. ($\underline{f}$ = 2)
baker, businessman(e), clerk,
green, grocery store, merchant,
vegetables
14-36. ($\underline{f}$ = 1)
alpha beta, bill, buy, corner,
Daddy, entrepreneur, fat,
greengrocer, meat, miser,
money, nice man, oranges,
order, produce, public service,
sell, shelves, small man,
store owner, stove, supplies,
work

II-10 Hermit

No.	Response	f
1.	alone	20
2.	cave(s)	9
3.	man	9
4.	old	7
5.	recluse	7

6-10. ($\underline{f}$ = 2)
away, hills, hobo, isolated,
mountain(s)
11-44. ($\underline{f}$ = 1)
atheist, bearded, beatnik,
body, closed, closeness, crab,
creased, hermitage, holyman,
hovel, individualist,
J. Appleseed, Japan, Kermit,
lives alone, lonely, male,
money, monk, neurotic,
Nietzche, old man, person,
Peter, R. Walton, sick,
storybook, train, tramp, tree,
Winkle, woods

II-11 Lotion

No.	Response	f
1.	hand(s)	38
2.	cream	12
3.	hand lotion	4
4.	smooth	4
5.	suntan	4
6.	creamy	3
7.	soothing	3

8-11. ($\underline{f}$ = 2)
bottle, liquid, salve, soft
12-31. ($\underline{f}$ = 1)
chemicals, cosmetics, fad,
girl freshes, lotion, legs,
lubricant, make-up, motion,
ocean, pink, rub, silicare,
skin, soothing liquid,
sticky, sunburn, suntan lotion,
to apply, Winchell

II-12 Magnate

No.	Response	f
1.	magnet	6
2.	attract(s)	5
3.	chemistry	4
4.	steel	4

5-9. (f = 3)
big, business, man, money, tycoon

10-17. (f = 2)
attraction, electricity, iron, large, mental, oil, rich, stone

18-60. (f = 1)
authority, big business, big corporation leader, big man, bring forth, chemical, clinging, copper, court, district attorney, dominant, electro, executive, head, impressive, influential person, judge, lead, leader, lend, local, maggot, magnetic, magnetic poll, magnetism, magnify, metal, millionaire, mogul, movie, north, officer, official, polls, positive poll, railroad, ruler, science, shipping, social, sodium, spread out, unknown word
No Response: (f = 3)

II-13 Minstrel

No.	Response	f
1.	show	18
2.	song(s)	14
3.	music	12
4.	singer	11
5.	Negro	4
6.	wandering	3

7-12. (f = 2)
banjo, entertainer, man, mandolin, player, sing

13-33. (f = 1)
actor, Al Jolson, ancient, boy, cinder, court, entertain, gater, guitar, gypsies, knight, menstruation, middle ages, mikado, minister, musical, musician, showboats, singing, strolling, wanderer
No Response: (f = 1)

II-14 Oatmeal

No.	Response	f
1.	cereal	31
2.	breakfast	17
3.	mush	10
4.	cookie(s)	5
5.	food	5

6-8. (f = 2)
eat, oats, porridge

9-30. (f = 1)
bad, bowl, brown, children, corn, corn flakes, cream, don't like, goodies, lumps, manufacture, milk, morning, mushy, oatmeal, Quaker, salt, spinach, sugar, summer, terrible, ugh

II-15 Omen

No.	Response	f
1.	sign	22
2.	good	10
3.	evil	9
4.	bad	5
5.	portent	5
6.	ill	3

7-10. (f = 2)
amen, luck, superstition, warning

11-43. (f = 1)
Bible, blessing, Cassandra, charm, cracker, danger, deed dictionary, entrails, feeling, forbidding, foreboding, fortune, future, good luck, Greeks, harbinger, oman, ominous, praise, people, person, prayer, premonition, prophecy, religious, saying, sign-predictor, statement, token, trouble, witch, word
No Response: (f = 1)

II-16 Placard

No.	Response	f
1.	sign	23
2.	card	7
3.	poster	6
4.	placecard	5

5-9. (f = 2)
cardboard, name, placard, place, plaque

10-48. (f = 1)
adventure, advertising, advertisement, banquet, billboard, bridge, bulletin board, carry, dinner, don't understand, experiment, full, hand on the wall, information, letters, menu, note, object, order, Packard, paper, party, picture, play, playcard, post boards, posted, quarantine, school, shield, square, table, tablesetting, think, Toulouse Lautrec, unknown, warning, William, window
No Response: (f = 6)

II-17 Preview

No.	Response	f
1.	movie(s)	35
2.	before	12
3.	show	6
4.	review	3
5.	sneak	3

6-13. (f = 2)
attractions, coming, first, insight, look, motion pictures, see, theater

14-34. (f = 1)
beforehand synopsis, cinema, enjoyable, enlightenment, entice, film, first nights, future, hint, houses, idea, look ahead, look over, opening nite, over view, peek, picture, preview, proceed, see before,

II-17 Preview (contd)

No.	Response	f

showing

II-18 Relic

No.	Response	f
1.	old	51
2.	antique	14
3.	ancient	9
4.	bone	2
5.	holy	2

6-23. (f = 1)
aged, culture, dust, hang, helic, history, icon, left-over, momento, museum, painting, paleontology, past ages, precious, religious, remains, saints, word

II-19 Skillet

No.	Response	f
1.	pan	31
2.	frying pan	18
3.	fry	15
4.	cooking	4
5.	stove	4
6.	kitchen	3

7-11. (f = 2)
bacon, black, egg(s), fire, food

12-22. (f = 1)
B. B. Q., chicken, cook, electric, frying, griddle, mallet, oven, pot, skill, skillet

II-20 Suffrage

No.	Response	f
1.	woman(e) ('s)	46
2.	vote	17
3.	voting	11
4.	freedom	2
5.	release	2
6.	rights	2

7-22. (f = 1)
American, bad, emotional, equality, human, hurt, Negro, over 21, privilege, slaves, surface, Susan Anthony, tail, to suffer, woman's rights, woman's suffrage

II-21 Tempest

No.	Response	f
1.	storm	48
2.	Shakespeare	14
3.	teapot	6
4.	fury	2
5.	movie	2
6.	woman	2

II-21 Tempest (contd)

No.	Response	f
7-27.	(f = 1)	

battle, Calaban, element, evil,
fierce, fiery, frightening,
frigid, gust, play, rain, sex,
spoiled, stormy, temp, Tempest
Storm, tempestuous, trying,
turbulance, wanton, wind
No Response: (f = 1)

II-22 Traitor

No.	Response	f
1.	country	16
2.	Benedict Arnold	12
3.	spy	7
4.	enemy	5
5.	bad	4
6.	treason	3
7-14.	(f = 2)	

Arnold, betrayer, Burr, disloyal,
liar, man, patriot, turncoat
15-46. (f = 1)
Aaron Burr, apostate, betray,
betrayal, Brutus, buffoon,
cheater, cruel, depose, despise,
dishonest, distrust, espionage,
evil, flag, feel, German, hero,
killer, loser, mistake, mutiny,
revolution, savage, secret,
treachery, trait, unenlightened,
unpatriotic, villainous, war,
William

II-23 Wafer

No.	Response	f
1.	cookie(s)	24
2.	cracker	15
3.	thin	12
4.	communion	6
5.	candy	3
6.	food	3
7-9.	(f = 2)	

biscuit, mint(s), vanilla
10-35. (f = 1)
back, bread, Catholic religion,
chocolate, church, confession,
disc, dough, eat, eating, light,
loaf, looks, mouth, sign, slice,
small cracker, smell, sugar,
switch, tea, thin biscuit,
cookie, wafe, waffle, waif,
wine
No Response: (f = 1)

II-24 Whisker

No.	Response	f
1.	beard	30
2.	cat	10
3.	shave	10
4.	man	9
5.	hair	8
6.	face	5
7-8.	(f = 3)	

rough, whiskey

II-24 Whisker (contd)

No.	Response	f
9-10.	(f = 2)	

bristle, chin
11-24. (f = 1)
age, animal, beatnik, broom,
dad, hare, hillbilly, old man,
rabbit, razor, Santa Claus,
scratch, stiff, stubble

III-1 Author

No.	Response	f
1.	book(s)	56
2.	writer	11
3.	title	5
4-5.	(f = 3)	

story, write(s)
6-7. (f = 2)
novel, post
8-21. (f = 1)
Arthur, author, co-author,
copyright, critic, D. H.
Lawrence, editor, Hemingway,
idea, man, of a book, Suzuki,
Whitman, Yeats

III-2 Belief

No.	Response	f
1.	God	14
2.	religion	10
3.	faith	9
4.	idea	8
5.	believe	4
6-9.	(f = 3)	

creed, opinion, thought, truth
10-15. (f = 2)
conviction, disbelief, dogma,
religious, think, true
16-42. (f = 1)
action, apparent, child, church,
credulity, doctrine, fool, hope,
I, ideal, ideology, in religion,
love, misbelief, none, Plato,
prejudice, random, real,
reasonable, relief, saying,
strength, strong, understand,
unquestionable, view

III-3 Biscuit

No.	Response	f
1.	bread	10
2.	food	9
3.	eat	8
4.	honey	6
5.	dough	5
6-7.	(f = 4)	

butter, cookie
8-10. (f = 3)
dog, hot, oven
11-19. (f = 2)
bake, bakery, baking, bun, cake,
doughnut, flour, roll(s),
Sea Biscuit

III-3 Biscuit (contd)

No.	Response	f
20-42.	(f = 1)	

baked, baking pd., Balard,
basket, Betty Crocker,
breakfast, burnt, cracker,
crunch, gravy, hardtack, jam,
kitchen, maker, material,
meal, mix, mother's muffin,
ready mix, sea, triscuit,
yeast

III-4 Candle

No.	Response	f
1.	light	41
2.	flame	15
3.	stick	8
4.	wax	8
5-9.	(f = 2)	

candlestick, fire, holder,
lighter, power
10-23. (f = 1)
blow burns at both ends,
Christmas, dark, flicker,
glowing, handle, hold, Kim
Novak, romance, table, wick,
wish, yellow

III-5 Circus

No.	Response	f
1.	clown(s)	39
2.	animal(s)	11
3.	tent(s)	9
4.	elephant(s)	7
5.	fun	6
6.	horse(s)	4
7.	ring(s)	3
8.	performance	2
9-23.	(f = 1)	

Bailey, billboards, circle,
circus, dirty, dust, entertainment, frolic, maximus,
parade, peanuts, popcorn,
raise, Ringling Bros., zoo

III-6 Device

No.	Response	f
1.	method	15
2-3.	means, thing	8
4-5.	gadget, mechanism	6
6.	machine	5
7.	instrument	4
8-11	(f = 3)	

mechanical, trick, use, way
12-13. (f = 2)
tool, useful
14-41. (f = 1)
added, apparatus, artifact,
bomb, button, clever,
contraption, Dark (novel),
device, fix, help, invention,
lock, manipulate, motor, need,
object, practical, schema,
scheme, selling, small,

III-6 Device (contd)

No.	Response	f

system, technique, thing-a-magig, time saving, trial, vice

III-7 Drama

No.	Response	f
1.	play(s)	38
2.	art(s)	8
3-4.	stage, theater	7
5.	Shakespeare	6

6-9. (f = 2)
acting, course, Greek, story
10-31. (f = 1)
act, actors, actress, Al Johnson, critic, department, dept., emotional, England, entertainment, event, Ibsen, intense, La Serva Padrona, lectures, major, mask, music, show, student, tragedy, trauma

III-8 Forest

No.	Response	f
1.	tree(s)	67
2.	green	7
3.	fire	6
4.	wood(s)	5

5-15. (f = 1)
coniferous, dark, evil, Germany, hills, lake, lamb, light, sequoia, trees - pines, Tucker

III-9 Glory

No.	Response	f
1.	flag	21
2.	old	8
3.	fame	5
4.	hallelujah	4

5-6. (f = 3)
hero, war
7-15. (f = 2)
great, heaven, high, honor, hound, morning, Old Glory, victory, win
16-49. (f = 1)
America, army, be, brave, bright, concept, country, defeat, France, game, girl's name, God, goodness, gore, greatness, happy, heroism, joy, Masoko, "Mine eyes have seen the --" poems, power, praise, pride, respect, retribution, revolution, sex, song, stars & stripes, sun, triumph, trumpet, winner

III-10 Highway

No.	Response	f
1.	road	28
2.	car(s)	23
3.	patrol	7
4.	byway	6
5.	freeway	4

6-7. (f = 3)
street, traffic
8-10. (f = 2)
auto(s), pavement, travel
11-26. (f = 1)
accidents, careful, concrete, construction, control, crash, drive, highway patrol, robber, Salinas, sign, super, tire, U.S., U.S.A., white line

III-11 Leather

No.	Response	f
1.	shoe(s)	16
2.	purse(s)	9
3-4.	goods, saddle	6
5-7.	animal(s), cow, hide	5
8.	belt	4

9-13. (f = 3)
bag, boots, horse, strap, wallet
14-18. (f = 2)
brown, chair, hard, sandals, smell
19-34. (f = 1)
black, feather, furniture, gloves, jacket, material, rich, shoemaker, soap, soft, tan, tanner, tooling, wood, work

III-12 Message

No.	Response	f
1.	letter	12
2.	note	11
3.	telegram	9
4.	messenger	7
5.	send	5

6-7. (f = 4)
Garcia, telephone
8-9. (f = 3)
communication, news
10-14. (f = 2)
communicate, important, telegraph, tell, written
15-42. (f = 1)
baby, brief, call, christmas, electric, hear, insight, joyful, joyous, long, Mary, massage, mess, Morse code, paper, pigeon receive, relate, relax, revelation, song, speech, spy, stroke, talk, unit, words, yellow paper

III-13 Mortgage

No.	Response	f
1.	house	39
2.	home	15

III-13 Mortgage (contd)

No.	Response	f
3.	loan	11
4-5.	debt, money	6
6.	bank	2

7-23. (f - 1)
bill, borrow, burn, contract, farm, gauge, insurance, landlord, late, lose the house, man, on house, paid, pay, property, realtor, rent

III-14 Oven

No.	Response	f
1.	stove	25
2.	hot	19
3.	bake	17
4.	heat	7
5.	cook	6

6-9. (f = 2)
bread, cake, food, warm
10-23. (f = 1)
bakery, baking, black, cooking, eat, hearth, Jews, kitchen, loving, martgage, oven, pie, range, womb

III-15 Oyster

No.	Response	f
1.	shell(s)	19
2.	stew	16
3.	sea	10
4.	clam	8
5-6.	fish, pearl(s)	7
7-8.	eat, food	4
9.	bay	3

10-11. (f = 2)
bed, ocean
12-25. (f = 1)
animal, bar, Boston, cloister, eating, hungry, on the half shell, river, salt water, seafood, seashore, Shakespeare, sick, wharf

III-16 Panic

No.	Response	f
1.	fear	21
2-3.	fright, run	8
4-5.	frightened, scared	3

6-17. (f = 2)
afraid, button, excited, fire, horror, mad, raid, scare, scream stricken, television, terror
18-46. (f = 1)
accident, alarm, animals, confusion, corrupt, crowd, economic depression, exams, excitement, finals, flight, frenzy, frighten, frigid, help, lost, midterm, mob, nerves, Pan, god of nature, panic button, picnic, rage,

III-16 Panic (contd)

No.	Response	f

storm, sudden fear, trauma,
unpleasant, war, worry

III-17 Presence

No.	Response	f
1.	here	27
2.	absence	16
3.	present(s)	7
4.	being	6
5.	appearance	
6-7.	attendance, God	3
8-9.	existence, person	2

10-34. (f = 1)
accompany, before, close company,
enjoyment, feeling, here & now,
in the, king, mind, now,
occurrence, opposite absence,
party, past, people, quite,
school, seeing, spirit, stage,
strong, to be, together, with

III-18 Region

No.	Response	f
1.	area	38
2.	place	6
3-4.	country, section	5
5-6.	district, land	4
7-9.	geography, God, local	3
10.	religion	2

11-33. (f = 1)
amount of land, artic, Baptist,
Bay region, California, earth,
farm, geographical, globe,
horizontal, location, N.W.,
protestant, quarters, regent,
serious, Spain, staff, state,
teachings, trees, unexplored,
vicinity

III-19 Sidewalk

No.	Response	f
1-2.	cafe(s), street	20
3.	cement	15
4-5.	New York, walk	6
6.	pavement	5
7-8.	concrete, crack(s)	3
9.	city	2

10-25. (f = 1)
blacktop, curb, hot, jump,
marbles, Paris, people,
prostitute, shopwindows, steps,
Sunday, walking, walkway,
white, wooden, W.P.A.

III-20 Sofa

No.	Response	f
1.	couch	29
2.	chair	14
3.	bed	11
4.	soft	6
5.	living room	4
6-7.	chesterfield, davenport	3

8-15. (f = 2)
comfort, cushion, divan,
furniture, home, lounge, rest,
sit
16-24. (f = 1)
long, room, round, seat,
sectional, sex, soda, pillow
No Response: (f = 1)

III-21 Tennis

No.	Response	f
1.	ball(s)	26
2.	game	17
3.	racket(quet)	9
4.	court	7
5.	play	6
6-8.	match, player, sport	4
9.	net	3
10.	golf	2

11-24. (f = 1)
athletes, bat net, circus club,
club, exercise, lazy men, menace,
ran, score, shoe, tennis ball,
tournament, watch, wire

III-22 Tourist

No.	Response	f
1.	travel(s)	15
2.	traveler	8
3-6.	American, people, trade, trip	4
7.	guide	3

8-18. (f = 2)
car, country, Europe, Hawaii,
Italy, man, person, sightseeing, tourista, trap, vacation
19-50. (f = 1)
attraction, automobile, away
from home, camp, Carmel, city,
court, crowds, foreign,
gawking, grand, hat, lazy, Los
Angeles, loud, money, motel,
offense, out of state, Paris,
park, pay, see, shorts, short-
sleeved shirt, sights, sight-
seer, south, stranger,
vacationer, visit, visitor

III-23 Welfare

No.	Response	f
1.	social	19
2-3.	good state	9
4.	help	7
5-6.	agency, charity	5

III-23 Welfare (contd)

No.	Response	f
7.	poor	3

8-13. (f = 2)
aid, child, organization,
public, relief, society
14-39. (f = 1)
benevolence, board, capitalism,
city, civil, committee, dept.,
education, Evelyn, gift, good
of, harmony, helping, homes,
island, man, people, poverty,
social welfare, social work,
social worker, student, truck,
work, worker, W.P.A.
No Response: (f = 1)

III-24 Wisdom

No.	Response	f
1.	knowledge	20
2.	wise	16
3.	truth	7
4.	tooth(ee)	4

5-9. (f = 3)
age(s), God, intelligence,
philosophy, smart
10-13. (f = 2)
education, magazine, old, sage
14-39. (f = 1)
aged, ancient, awareness,
charity, courage, doctor,
experience, I.Q., intellect,
intelligent, joy, love, of
the old, owl, prophet,
religious, seer or sage,
smartness, Socrates, Solomon,
Sophocles, strength, stupid,
success, teachers, under-
standing

IV-1 Answer

No.	Response	f
1.	question	58
2.	reply	6
3.	yes	5
4.	right	3

5-7. (f = 2)
correct, response, retort
8-25. (f = 1)
ask, bell, correctly, dusty,
finals, knowledge, letter,
math, problem, quiz, quotient,
return, score, sheet, tell,
test, true, words

IV-2 Building

No.	Response	f
1.	house(s)	14
2.	tall	9
3.	construction	7

4-6. (f = 4)
office(s), school, stone
7-9. (f = 3)
cement, edifice, structure

IV-2 Building (contd)

No.	Response	f

10-16. (f = 2)
blocks, brick, fall, high, large, loan, material(s)
17-47. (f = 1)
apartment, architect, architecture, big, bridges, build, business, castle, city, code, contractor, Empire State, engineer, fire, functional, ground, larger, live, lot, man, new, skyscraper, steal, steeple, store, street, structural, tearing, this, tower, wooden

IV-3 Business

No.	Response	f
1.	man(e)	16
2.	work	9
3-4.	money, office	7
5.	store	4
6.	firm	3

7-13. (f = 2)
address, busy, deal, letter, machine(s), pleasure, secretary
14-49. (f = 1)
activity, administration, affair, aid, appointment, associates, bad, building, Bus.Ad., businessman, company, cycle, economic, establishment, executive, father, friend, grocery, head, house, investment, job, organization, owner, partner, phone, private, professional, recession, S.F.S.C., show, Silver's jewelry, suit, thriving, white collar

IV-4 Color

No.	Response	f
1.	red	29
2.	hue	9
3.	black	8
4.	white	7
5.	bright	6
6.	blue	4

7-8. (f = 3)
beauty, paint
9-13. (f = 2)
brightness, crayon, harmony, vivid, wheel
14-30. (f = 1)
art, blazen, book, car, combination, eye, gay, green, light, look, muller, Picasso, pigment, rain, sea, spectrum, translucent

IV-5 Country

No.	Response	f
1.	U.S.A.	9
2.	city	7
3.	U.S.	5

IV-5 Country (contd)

No.	Response	f

4-5. (f = 4)
United States, side
6-9. (f = 3)
farm, home, land, nation
10-17. (f = 2)
America, beautiful, country, hills, house, quiet, state, trees
18-56. (f = 1)
affrontery, American, area, Atherton, black, camp, England, farm land, farmer, farming, field, flag, foreign, garden, girl, green, hillside, inn, landscape, living, meadow, nature, of origin, open spaces, parson, path, pleasant scene, ranch, region, roads, scence, solitude, squire, terra, this, train, trip, uninhabited, warm

IV-6 Dinner

No.	Response	f
1.	food	36
2.	eat	15
3-4.	meal, supper	6
5.	table	5
6.	time	3

7-10. (f = 2)
bill, diner, good, lunch
11-27. (f= 1)
afternoon, banquet, breakfast, dejeuner, eight o'clock, evening, fancy, feast, five o'clock, guests, hour, mealtime, party, pleasant, roast, silverware, tie

IV-7 Doctor

No.	Response	f
1.	nurse	16
2.	medicine	13
3.	lawyer	6
4-5.	hospital, patient(s)	5
6.	M.D.	3

7-11. (f = 2)
dentist, good, illness, medical, white
12-49. (f = 1)
bill, bones, book, broken arm, chaos, Clark, clean, cure, Dave, Dr., Dr. Lum, Dr. Moose, grandfather, healer, healing, health, hill, in the house, Kildare, kindly, learned, life, Madison, man, Mayo, money, nice, office, pain, physician, profession, school, science, sick, teacher, white coat, work, Zhivago

IV-8 Figure

No.	Response	f
1.	shape	10
2.	eight	8
3-4.	number(s), woman(e)	6
5-7.	form, ground, model	4
8-11.	girl, math, skating, square	3
12-15.	art, body, drawing, face	2

16-49. (f = 1)
abstraction of reality, add, arithmetic, bust, calculate, curve, 8, father, feature, figure of speech, geometric, geometry, good, lady, lines, lumpy, nice, numeral, 1-10, out, photography, physique, sculpture, sex, shapely, skate, skater, statue, statute, swimming suit, symbol, vase, weight, youth

IV-9 Garden

No.	Response	f
1.	flower(s)	45
2-3.	green, hose	5
4-7.	Eden, grow, plant(s), vegetable(s)	3
8-11.	party, pretty, tool(s), trees	2

12-32. (f = 1)
Adam & Eve, beauty, begonia, district, food, formal, gate, ground, grove, hedge, home, house, jardinier, lovely, path, soil, tend, trellis, wall, weeds, yard

IV-10 Husband

No.	Response	f
1.	wife	76
2.	man	9

3-13. (f = 1)
Ed, family, future, good, male, manager, marriage, me, provider, rich, work

IV-11 Letter

No.	Response	f
1.	write	24
2.	mail	8
3.	writing	6
4.	stamp	5
5-7.	alphabet, paper, writer	4
8.	note	3

9-17. (f = 2)
boy(s), card, envelope, friend, head, love, name, read, word

IV-11 Letter (contd)

No.	Response	f

18-37. (f = 1)
allon, Bette Davis, better Betty, business, Cambridge, communication, epistle, excitement, good news, home, joy, later, letterhead, missive, open, opener, pen, post office, type

IV-12 Moment

No.	Response	f
1.	time	27
2.	second	13
3.	minute	10
4.	now	9
5.	instant	4

6-7. (f = 2)
hour, short
8-36. (f = 1)
area, climax, comment, distance, existence, fleeting, force, glory, importance, just, later, mathematics, one, opportune, panic, present, product, product corr., short time, statistic, statistical, stop, supreme, then, time limit, to moment, wait, watch, while

IV-13 Morning

No.	Response	f
1.	sun	11
2-3.	early, night	9
4.	evening	8
5-6.	day, good	5

7-9. (f = 4)
bright, noon, sunshine
10-11. (f = 3)
dawn, glory, star
12-17. (f = 2)
afternoon, awake, light, sleep, sunrise
18-36. (f = 1)
after, alarm, alarm clock, arise, as opposed to evening, awaken, blue, breakfast, Morgen, sky, song, Tannhauser, tide, time, up, wake, waking, work

IV-14 Office

No.	Response	f
1-2.	building, business	13
3.	work	6
4-5.	desk(s), secretary	5
6-7.	doctor, typewriter	4
8.	room	3

9-15. (f = 2)
boy, bureau, executive, hours, machine, manager, women

IV-14 Office (contd)

No.	Response	f

16-44. (f = 1)
boss, chairs, city, clerical work, door, equipment, father, head, home, inter, job, large, nurse, office boy, paper, person, personnel, place, plan, political, post, post office, principals, space, store, summer, telephone, type, workers

IV-15 Order

No.	Response	f
1.	command	9
2-3.	neat, rank	5

4-6. (f = 3)
blank, court, mail
7-13. (f = 2)
arrangement, chaos, form, neatness, rule(s), send, unity
14-67. (f = 1)
alignment, appearance, army, arrange, assign, bad, book, border, boss, call, cause, class, come, conform, count, demand, design, direct, disorder, doctor, file, goods, harmony, in, invoice, larder, line, list, logic, martinet, math, menu, numbers, numerical, obey, office, parliamentarian, pattern, peace, phylum, precise, quickly, random, reverse, Robert's Rules, sales, send for, sense, sequence, shout, straight, tell, to make an, unorganized

IV-16 Paper

No.	Response	f
1.	pencil	31
2.	pen	11
3.	write	9
4.	white	6

5-12. (f = 2)
book, clip, dolls, mate, pin(s), sheet, wood, writing
13-35. (f = 1)
blank, bound, Crown Zellerbach, drive, English, hews, lines, news, notes, N.Y. Times, papier, pater, pulp, read, sack, school, taper, test, thin, typewriter, useful, weight, yellow

IV-17 Problem

No.	Response	f
1.	math	14
2.	solve	14
3.	solution	9
4.	child	6
5.	answer	4
6.	solving	4
7.	trouble	4

IV-17 Problem (contd)

No.	Response	f

8-11. (f = 3)
arithmetic, difficult, mathematic(s), test
12-17. (f = 2)
puzzle, question, school, task, work, worry
18-34. (f = 1)
distress, effect, homework, many, master, matter, me, men, physics, problematic, psychology, set, solve, create, solved, solver, statistics, thought

IV-18 Reason

No.	Response	f
1.	why	16
2.	think	12
3.	logic	6
4.	cause	5
5.	answer(s)	4
6.	explanation	4
7.	mind	4

8-9. (f = 3)
rational, thought
10-13. (f = 2)
excuse, purpose, reasonable, rhyme
14-44. (f = 1)
act, arguments, attempt, behind, chain, doubt, enlightenment, guess, history exam, Homo sapien, idea, inquiry, intellect, Kant, logical, motivation, none, philosophy, problem, question, rationale, reason, Rousseau, sane, statement, study, suggestion, thinking, treason, valid, wrong

IV-19 Shoulder

No.	Response	f
1.	arm(s)	29
2.	body	11
3.	bone(s)	8
4.	cold	5
5.	road	4
6.	blade	3

7-12. (f = 2)
broad, elbow, neck, soft, soldier(s), strap
13-36. (f = 1)
anatomy, back, bursitis, clavicle, cry, dress, flesh, football, highway, hill, holster, jacket, knee, lamb, man, muscle, narrow, pads, person, smooth, sore, strength, strong, throw ball

IV-20 Story

No.	Response	f
1.	book(s)	44
2.	take	9
3.	child(ren)	4
4.	tell	4
5.	fable	3
6.	short	3
7.	teller	3

8-10. (f = 2)
life, novel, plot
11-30. (f = 1)
Aesop, anecdote, anxiety, author, bedtime, building, fourth, funny, language, love, my, narrator, newspaper, pictures, shot, story book, telling, told, unreal, western

IV-21 Table

No.	Response	f
1.	chair(s)	67
2.	top	4
3.	wood	4
4.	food	2
5.	furniture	2
6.	set	2

7-21. (f = 1)
chart, comfort, contents, cover, eat, hard, lamp, legs, mats, O'Brien, paper, silverware, tablecloth, tennis, vote

IV-22 Trouble

No.	Response	f
1.	problem(s)	13
2.	bad	11
3.	worry	7
4.	help	4
5.	difficulty	3

6-11. (f = 2)
double, fear, police, sorrow, toil, woe
12-57. (f = 1)
accident, agony, aid, anxiousness, anxiety, black, blues, bother, bubble, caused, chaos, children, clock, danger, dangerous, darkness, disaster, disharmony, disillusioned, distress, hardship, injuries, maker, mess, middle name, mischief, misdemeanor, misfortune, much, music man, nobody knows, painful, panic, person, Psychology 1A, punish, punishment, sadden, sadness, solution, sore, spot, strife, tedious, wake, woman

IV-23 Window

No.	Response	f
1.	glass	26
2.	pane	17
3.	view	5
4.	house(s)	4
5.	sill	4

6-9. (f = 3)
light, look, open, shade
10-14. (f = 2)
clean, clear, door, out, see
15-32. (f = 1)
air, bay, big, building, opening, people, picture, plane, sash, scene, scenery, seat, shop, sun, trees, wall, washer, widow

IV-24 Woman

No.	Response	f
1.	man	61
2.	female	8
3.	lady	3
4.	mother	3
5.	girl	2
6.	me	2

7-23. (f = 1)
adult girl, art, beautiful, career, dress, dumb, face, feminine, in opposition to man, kind, Marilyn Monroe, maturity, pretty, pretty girl, putty, sex, suffrage

LEO POSTMAN

I-1 Abbess

No.	Response	Total	High Lang.	Low Lang.	Male	Female
1.	hole	94	47	47	59	35
2.	abscess	46	19	27	24	22
3.	tooth(teeth)	38	17	21	17	21
4.	abbey(s)	37	24	13	17	20
5.	abyss	29	15	14	16	13
6.	address	29	9	20	19	10
7.	church	22	13	9	9	13
8.	deep	18	7	11	11	7
9.	nun	18	13	5	2	16
10.	canyon	17	13	4	11	6
11.	cliff	16	9	7	7	9
12.	crevice	16	11	5	10	6
13.	sore	16	9	7	6	10
14.	nothing	15	5	10	8	7
15.	abbot	11	3	8	5	6
16.	cave	11	4	7	5	6
17.	woman(e)	11	5	6	8	3
18.	pit	10	5	5	4	6
19.	absent	9	4	5	4	5
20.	best	9	4	5	7	2
21.	chasm	9	6	3	5	4
22.	infection	9	2	7	5	4
23.	crack	8	4	4	1	7
24.	depth	8	6	2	4	4
25.	fat	8	3	5	3	5
26.	monastery	8	6	2	4	4
27.	crevasse	7	3	4	4	3
28.	blank	5	3	2	2	3
29.	gap	5	2	3	1	4
30.	monk	5	3	2	4	1
31.	name	5	–	5	4	1
32.	access	4	3	1	2	2
33.	bless	4	2	2	3	1
34.	castle	4	2	2	2	2
35.	cavern	4	3	1	3	1
36.	cavity	4	2	2	2	2
37.	convent	4	3	1	–	4
38.	empty	4	3	1	2	2
39.	opening	4	3	1	2	2
40.	what	4	2	2	4	–
41.	abbé	3	2	1	2	1
42.	add	3	1	2	2	1
43.	bird	3	1	2	1	2
44.	building	3	–	3	–	3
45.	caress	3	2	1	1	2
46.	dark	3	–	3	2	1
47.	darkness	3	–	3	2	1
48.	decay	3	1	2	1	2
49.	ditch	3	1	2	2	1
50.	bump	3	–	3	2	1
51.	excess	3	2	1	2	1
52.	extra	3	1	2	2	1
53.	gorge	3	2	1	2	1
54.	gully	3	3	–	–	3
55.	mountain(s)	3	2	1	1	2
56.	priest	3	1	2	–	3
57.	wound	3	1	2	1	2
58.	abscissa	2	1	1	1	1
59.	absence	2	1	1	2	–
60.	actress	2	1	1	1	1
61.	animal	2	1	1	2	–
62.	bad	2	1	1	1	1
63.	better	2	1	1	2	–
64.	boil(s)	2	1	1	2	–
65.	bottom	2	1	1	–	2
66.	count	2	1	1	2	–
67.	dictionary	2	1	1	–	2
68.	disease	2	2	–	1	1
69.	dress	2	–	2	1	1
70.	fall	2	–	2	–	2
71.	forward	2	1	1	2	–
72.	good	2	–	2	2	–
73.	Greek	2	1	1	–	2
74.	house	2	1	1	1	1
75.	hurt	2	1	1	1	1
76.	ill	2	1	1	–	2

I-1 Abbess (contd)

No.	Response	Total	High Lang.	Low Lang.	Male	Female
77.	London	2	2	–	1	1
78.	lost	2	1	1	–	2
79.	machine	2	–	2	1	1
80.	man	2	1	1	2	–
81.	missing	2	–	2	1	1
82.	nothingness	2	–	2	1	1
83.	now	2	1	1	2	–
84.	nunnery	2	2	–	–	2
85.	obsess	2	1	1	1	1
86.	obsession	2	–	2	1	1
87.	odd	2	–	2	2	–
88.	pain	2	–	2	1	1
89.	person	2	1	1	1	1
90.	priestess	2	2	–	2	–
91.	pus	2	2	–	2	–
92.	puss	2	–	2	2	–
93.	queen	2	1	1	–	2
94.	religion	2	2	–	–	2
95.	sick	2	1	1	2	–
96.	sickness	2	1	1	2	–
97.	too much	2	1	1	1	1
98.	unknown	2	1	1	2	–
99.	valley	2	1	1	1	1
100.	whole	2	–	2	–	2

101-331. (f = 1)
able, abnormal, abreast, absorb, abuse, after, against, aid, alas, ancient, anger, ape, architecture, arithmetic, ascend, assess, aup, authority, bare, basin, beads, beast, before, beginning, behind, beside, bess, black, bliss, blister, boredom, break, bridge, buy, cabbage, cancer, canon, cathedral, catholic, Chaucer, chess, child, China, Chinese, cist, cleft, clift, cloister, cloth, confounding, cool, Costello, cover, cow, crag, crater, crypt, cultivate, cut or bruise, dead, death, deceive, deepness, deject, depress, desk, determine, dip, disgust, doctor, doctrine, don't know, down, duchess, effect, emptiness, face, falling, figures, finish, fish, fissure, flee, flood, fool, fortification, fountain, frank, friar, full, girl, give, glacier, goddess, grand, ground, growth, guess, habit, hand, harass, heal, hell, high, hill, hint, hit, hold, hollow, home, horse, huh, impossible, infected, inquiry, kiss, knowledge, labyrinth, lady, large, late, ledge, life, Lincoln, line, live, location, lock, loose, lore, lose, loss, lots, low, luck, manner, mantissa, mask, math, mesa, mess, messy, miss, mistake, mixed, mother (spiritual), music, nasty, near, never, night, nine, no, noble, notion, number, obesity, obtuse, old, overcome, paper, people, Peru, phone, place, plutonic, poison, possess, power, precipice, princess, prioress, problem, punish, ravine, recess, refrain, rock, role, room, rot, rotten, royalty, running, school, sea, sense, sequel, shelter, sink, skin, slave, so, sound, sow, stay, stick, stone, stop, straight, strange, structure, style, subtract, support, suppress, sweet, talk, tardy, tax, telephone, term, time, to bless, tower, tress, try, unkind, use, vacant, vocabulary, void, wall, wart, water, watercress, well, word, worse, wow, wrong
(No response - 42; Illegible - 5)

I-2 Bramble

No.	Response	Total	High Lang.	Low Lang.	Male	Female
1.	bush(es)	194	107	87	84	110
2.	ramble	93	39	54	56	37
3.	thorn(s)	66	41	25	39	27
4.	talk	41	14	27	13	28
5.	weed(s)	29	18	11	13	16
6.	brush	26	14	12	16	10
7.	thicket(s)	24	10	14	13	11
8.	patch	21	12	9	9	12
9.	scramble	21	9	12	17	4
10.	berry(ies)	18	11	7	6	12
11.	briar(s)	18	9	9	7	11
12.	sticker(s)	17	8	9	12	5
13.	mess	13	4	9	8	5
14.	stick	11	8	3	3	8
15.	amble	10	4	6	5	5
16.	scratch	10	8	2	1	9
17.	sharp	9	5	4	3	6
18.	hurt	8	4	4	1	7
19.	run	8	2	6	5	3
20.	Brer Rabbit	7	4	3	5	2
21.	rabbit(s)	7	3	4	4	3
22.	babble	6	3	3	5	1
23.	gamble	6	3	3	4	2
24.	on	6	3	3	4	2
25.	walk	6	1	5	4	2
26.	branch(es)	5	4	1	2	3
27.	confusion	5	5	-	3	2
28.	mumble	5	2	3	3	2
29.	rumble	5	2	3	4	1
30.	tree(s)	5	2	3	1	4
31.	wander	5	2	3	1	4
32.	blackberry(ies)	4	3	1	-	4
33.	deer	4	1	3	3	1
34.	go	4	1	3	2	2
35.	noise	4	2	2	3	1
36.	nothing	4	2	2	4	-
37.	rattle	4	1	3	4	-
38.	word(s)	4	3	1	2	2
39.	brouse	3	-	3	2	1
40.	burr	3	2	1	2	1
41.	confused	3	2	1	1	2
42.	eggs	3	2	1	2	1
43.	forest	3	2	1	1	2
44.	mixed	3	-	3	2	1
45.	plant	3	1	2	3	-
46.	prick	3	1	2	1	2
47.	song	3	-	3	2	1
48.	trouble	3	1	2	2	1
49.	wonder	3	1	2	2	1
50.	woods	3	3	-	2	1
51.	baby	2	1	1	2	-
52.	Bambi	2	1	1	1	1
53.	bamble	2	-	2	1	1
54.	bird	2	2	-	2	-
55.	briar patch	2	1	1	1	1
56.	brook	2	-	2	1	1
57.	bubble	2	-	2	2	-
58.	car	2	2	-	1	1
59.	fight	2	1	1	1	1
60.	game(s)	2	1	1	-	2
61.	girl	2	2	-	1	1
62.	house	2	1	1	2	-
63.	lamb	2	1	1	1	1
64.	mix	2	1	1	2	-
65.	mix-up	2	-	2	1	1
66.	move	2	-	2	-	2
67.	old	2	1	1	1	1
68.	pain	2	1	1	2	-
69.	play	2	-	2	2	-
70.	prickly	2	2	-	2	-
71.	roam	2	-	2	2	-
72.	rush	2	-	2	1	1
73.	scrabble	2	1	1	1	1
74.	shambles	2	-	2	2	-
75.	slow	2	-	2	2	-
76.	talkative	2	1	1	-	2

I-2 Bramble (contd)

No.	Response	Total	High Lang.	Low Lang.	Male	Female
77.	tangle	2	2	-	2	-
78.	thorny	2	2	-	1	1
79.	twig	2	-	2	1	1
80.	underbrush	2	1	1	2	-
81.	unknown	2	1	1	1	1
82.	walking	2	2	-	1	1
83.	what	2	2	-	2	-

84-229. (f = 1)
adobe, along, animal, argue, bad, barn, beau,
bee, biscuit, bit, blank, bottle, bramblett,
bread, breakfast, broom, brummel, bumpity along,
bunch, bushes (also hare), bust, chatter, child,
coast, communication, continue, country, crawl,
crowd, cut, dance, desert, designing, did,
dilly, discord, disturb, don't know, dumb,
emerald, ending, fall, fence, field, floundering,
flowing, funny, gallon, garble, go along, goat,
gossip, grass, gravel, hardly, hedge, hell,
hide, hike, huckleberries, hurry, idea, immature,
kids, leaf, legs, lengthy, loose, many, marble
mass, meaningless, mess up, messy, mistake,
mixed up, mixture, movements, mull, mutter,
name, none, nonsense, O.K., ouch, path, person,
press, prickles, questioned, Rabbit Hill,
rambling, raspberries, red, ride, road, rocks,
rose, rosebush, rove, rundown, run-together,
saunter, Scottish, scrambled, scratchy, scuffle,
seed, seeing, seen, shack, shriek, singing,
slowly, south, speech, spread, sticky, stiff,
studder, stumble, stutter, sweet, talking,
tangled, thick, thick bush, thin, thistles,
through, throw, time, torn, traffic, tumbleweed,
twisted, uneasiness, unsure, upset, Vermont,
vines, vociferous, water, why, wire, wreck
(No response - 15; Illegible - 4)

I-3 Buffoon

No.	Response	Total	High Lang.	Low Lang.	Male	Female
1.	clown	123	83	40	59	64
2.	fool	94	55	39	56	38
3.	balloon	63	26	37	27	36
4.	buffalo	45	15	30	20	25
5.	idiot	43	28	15	31	12
6.	animal	36	18	18	16	20
7.	wind	22	5	17	9	13
8.	baboon	18	8	10	13	5
9.	monkey	18	10	8	12	6
10.	instrument	14	4	10	8	6
11.	storm	14	8	6	6	8
12.	stupid	14	7	7	11	3
13.	typhoon	14	7	7	4	10
14.	big	12	9	3	3	9
15.	funny	12	6	6	5	7
16.	joker	12	9	3	6	6
17.	ape	9	4	5	3	6
18.	dope	9	4	5	8	1
19.	joke	9	6	3	6	3
20.	buffet	8	3	5	5	3
21.	goon	8	6	2	4	4
22.	music	8	2	6	2	6
23.	oaf	7	6	1	4	3
24.	buff	6	4	2	4	2
25.	dress	6	3	3	1	5
26.	dumb	6	1	5	4	2
27.	fat	6	4	2	2	4
28.	large	6	1	5	1	5
29.	nothing	6	-	6	3	3
30.	bassoon	5	2	3	3	2
31.	comic	5	3	2	3	2

I-3 Buffoon (contd)

			High	Low		
No.	Response	Total	Lang.	Lang.	Male	Female
32.	goof	5	2	3	5	-
33.	jerk	5	3	2	4	1
34.	loudmouth	5	2	3	3	2
35.	baffle	4	1	3	2	2
36.	bluffer	4	4	-	1	3
37.	food	4	-	4	3	1
38.	laugh	4	1	3	1	3
39.	mistake	4	2	2	2	2
40.	bluff	3	1	2	1	2
41.	braggart	3	1	2	2	1
42.	buffer	3	-	3	3	-
43.	crazy	3	1	2	2	1
44.	dinner	3	-	3	3	-
45.	dolt	3	3	-	3	-
46.	full	3	-	3	-	3
47.	gun	3	-	3	2	1
48.	loud	3	2	1	2	1
49.	nut	3	2	1	2	1
50.	pill(s)	3	1	2	1	2
51.	pirate	3	2	1	1	2
52.	racoon	3	2	1	2	1
53.	saloon	3	1	2	1	2
54.	table	3	-	3	2	1
55.	tycoon	3	-	3	1	2
56.	aspirin	2	-	2	2	-
57.	ass	2	-	2	2	-
58.	billow	2	1	1	-	2
59.	billowy	2	2	-	-	2
60.	blow	2	1	1	-	2
61.	blowhard	2	1	1	1	1
62.	blown	2	1	1	-	2
63.	bufferin	2	-	2	2	-
64.	foolish	2	2	-	1	1
65.	French	2	-	2	-	2
66.	hit	2	-	2	-	2
67.	jester	2	-	2	1	1
68.	laughter	2	2	-	1	1
69.	noise	2	1	1	1	1
70.	rain	2	-	2	1	1
71.	sail	2	-	2	-	2
72.	ship	2	2	-	-	2
73.	spoon	2	1	1	2	-
74.	tornado	2	2	-	1	1

75-270. (f = 1)
anchor, anima, anthropology, baffon, ball, band,
bang, bank, bar, base, bastard, beat, big blow,
big crash, Billy, blank, blast, block, blockade,
blow-up, boar, boaster, boffle, bommerang, bow,
brass, brat, bridge, broom, buff color, buffle,
buffon, bull, bullan, bus, bustle, cannon,
caucus, cigar, circle, circus, city, clear,
cloud, clumsy, coin, confuse, confused, crash,
cup, cyclone, dessert, dish, don't know, "dope",
Dostoevsky, drink, drunkard, duffo, dunce,
eating, elephant, England, error, explosion,
Falstaff, farce, fight, file, filler, fish,
flamboyant, flat, foreign, French scientist,
frills, fun, geography, Gilbert, goat, goofer,
goofy, gorilla, Groucho, gusty, hair, headache,
heavy, horn, ignorant, Italian comic opera,
jokester, kid, kidding, lagoon lead, light,
longshoreman, lost, lunch, luncheon, mad, man,
material, meal, meaning, mess, miss, monsoon,
muffin, mushroom, noon, obese, object, oboe,
odd, off, old man, open, outburst, pantaloons,
person, Phil, pie, plaire, plenty, polish,
pontoon, poor, pow, powder puff, prank, pretty,
puffy, question, quick, red, regiment, rich,
rock, rough, rub, rustle, sand, satire, saying,
science, screwball, scoundrel, sea, see,
Shakespeare, shoe, showoff, silly, silver,
skeleton, skirt, slip, slob, slop, snafoo, sore,
spinaker, spittoon, spoof, spook, stripped,
stuffed shirt, stump, stupe, stupidity, talker,
test, tide, to conceal, tramp, trick, trouble,
type, tyrant, ugh, war, warm, water, weapons,

I-3 Buffoon (contd)

weather, whale, what, windy, wipe, wise guy,
word, writing, yes, zoo
(No response -21; Illegible - 4)

I-4 Caucus

			High	Low		
No.	Response	Total	Lang.	Lang.	Male	Female
1.	meeting	156	86	70	89	67
2.	politics	63	41	22	29	34
3.	group	43	22	21	24	19
4.	talk	35	21	14	21	14
5.	convention(s)	29	17	12	21	8
6.	discussion	25	11	14	13	12
7.	body	24	10	14	14	10
8.	cactus	18	9	9	10	8
9.	government	18	8	10	7	11
10.	plant	17	7	10	8	9
11.	senate	17	9	8	3	14
12.	congress	15	10	5	9	6
13.	party	14	6	8	8	6
14.	vote	13	5	8	6	7
15.	white	13	10	3	8	5
16.	committee	12	4	8	3	9
17.	dead	12	2	10	5	7
18.	mountain(s)	12	10	2	9	3
19.	animal(s)	9	4	5	2	7
20.	gathering	9	4	5	5	4
21.	argument	8	6	2	5	3
22.	caucasian	8	5	3	4	4
23.	debate	8	3	5	6	2
24.	desert	8	2	6	5	3
25.	election(s)	8	5	3	2	6
26.	circus	7	3	4	2	5
27.	senator(s)	7	6	1	3	4
28.	man(e)	6	4	2	1	5
29.	math	6	1	5	2	4
30.	mess	6	3	3	1	5
31.	noise	6	4	2	1	5
32.	race	6	3	3	3	3
33.	Alice	5	4	1	3	2
34.	legislature	5	2	3	2	3
35.	nothing	5	1	4	2	3
36.	people	5	3	2	2	3
37.	session	5	1	4	4	1
38.	Democrat(s)	4	3	1	1	3
39.	forum	4	2	2	1	3
40.	skeleton	4	1	3	2	2
41.	speech	4	3	1	1	3
42.	abacus	3	3	-	2	1
43.	argue	3	1	2	1	2
44.	calculus	3	1	2	3	-
45.	careful	3	1	2	2	1
46.	conference	3	1	2	2	1
47.	confusion	3	1	2	1	2
48.	Faubus	3	-	3	3	-
49.	Greek	3	1	2	1	2
50.	hide	3	-	3	3	-
51.	loud	3	1	2	1	2
52.	low	3	-	3	3	-
53.	majority	3	2	1	3	-
54.	mix-up	3	2	1	3	-
55.	person	3	1	2	2	1
56.	plain	3	1	2	3	-
57.	political	3	3	-	3	-
58.	politician(s)	3	2	1	3	-
59.	quorum	3	2	1	1	2
60.	Republican(s)	3	3	-	1	2
61.	smoke	3	2	1	3	-
62.	trouble	3	1	2	2	1

I-4 Caucus (contd)   I-5 Curfew

No.	Response	Total	High Lang.	Low Lang.	Male	Female
63.	Alice in Wonderland	2	1	1	1	1
64.	assembly	2	2	-	1	1
65.	bones	2	-	2	1	1
66.	carcus	2	1	1	2	-
67.	cautious	2	-	2	-	2
68.	center	2	1	1	2	-
69.	chaos	2	1	1	-	2
70.	club	2	1	1	1	1
71.	count	2	1	1	1	1
72.	court	2	-	2	2	-
73.	death	2	-	2	1	1
74.	disc	2	1	1	1	1
75.	doctor	2	-	2	1	1
76.	fight	2	2	-	2	-
77.	flower	2	1	1	1	1
78.	funny	2	-	2	2	-
79.	gather	2	-	2	1	1
80.	hurt	2	-	2	1	1
81.	Indian(s)	2	1	1	-	2
82.	many	2	1	1	-	2
83.	meet	2	1	1	1	1
84.	name	2	1	1	2	-
85.	noisy	2	-	2	1	1
86.	opinion	2	1	1	1	1
87.	place	2	-	2	2	-
88.	political party	2	2	-	1	1
89.	raucous	2	1	1	-	2
90.	remain(s)	2	1	1	-	2
91.	riot	2	1	1	2	-
92.	rowdy	2	-	2	1	1
93.	secret	2	1	1	1	1
94.	sharp	2	1	1	1	1
95.	skin	2	1	1	-	2
96.	sticky	2	2	-	-	2
97.	stop	2	-	2	1	1
98.	talking	2	1	1	1	1
99.	thorn(s)	2	-	2	-	2
100.	tough	2	1	1	-	2
101.	upset	2	-	2	1	1
102.	whole	2	-	2	-	2

103-266. (f = 1)
ancestors, ask, ass, awful, back, bad, behind,
bird, black, blind, book, brains, burr, cache,
calccase, campaign, cancer, candidate, candy,
carrot, case, caterpillar, caucasus, cause,
censor, census, chalk, chemistry, Chinese,
church, city, civics, closed, clouds, coarse,
cocky, commotion, congressional, consensus,
conversation, core, corpse, council, country,
crowd, dead animal, delay, deep, democracy,
democratic, discuss, dog, eat, elephant, end,
event, evil, failure, fat, filibuster, fish,
flitty, fluster, focus, fool, four, fun, G.O.P.,
groom, help, history, hold, horse, instrument,
Jack, jack-ass, lady, Latin, learning,
legislation, lion, list, mad, malady, males,
match, mathematics, mean, meat, melon, middle,
moaning, mock, most, number, oh, pain, paky,
pancreas, parliamentary procedure,
pelican, petition, plank, plateau, pole,
pompous, population, power, prefix, president,
prickle, prickly, problem, prod, puzzled,
question, racket, racys, rear, region, representative, representative of, review, roar,
Roman, room, rostrum, rough, ruckus, sarcastic,
scavenger, sea, seat, seclusion, senatorial,
Shakespeare, small, smooth, snake, sore, speak,
spines, stal, stickers, storm, story, study,
survey, table, Texas, town, trees, try, uproar,
Venezuela, voting, what, White House, window,
wonder, wonderful, word, workshop, you
(No response - 11; Illegible - 3)

No.	Response	Total	High Lang.	Low Lang.	Male	Female
1.	time	210	95	115	96	114
2.	late	118	52	66	66	52
3.	hour(s)	78	44	34	40	38
4.	lockout	74	50	24	17	57
5.	night(s)	66	36	30	41	25
6.	law(s)	50	29	21	34	16
7.	police	39	21	18	30	9
8.	limit(s)	36	21	15	25	11
9.	ten(10:00)	31	11	20	16	15
10.	bell(s)	18	12	6	5	13
11.	restriction	17	9	8	11	6
12.	cop(s)	11	3	8	9	2
13.	two-thirty (2:30)	11	7	4	2	9
14.	deadline	9	4	5	4	5
15.	eleven(11:00)	9	3	6	4	5
16.	teenagers	8	5	3	4	4
17.	date(s)	7	2	5	3	4
18.	ten-thirty (10:30)	7	2	5	2	5
19.	bed	5	1	4	2	3
20.	dark	5	3	2	5	-
21.	girl(s)	5	1	4	5	-
22.	ten(10)o'clock	5	5	-	3	2
23.	clock	4	2	2	1	3
24.	end	4	1	3	3	1
25.	home	4	3	1	1	3
26.	midnight	4	3	1	3	1
27.	parents	4	-	4	2	2
28.	regulation(s)	4	2	2	-	4
29.	sleep	4	2	2	3	1
30.	trouble	4	-	4	3	1
31.	army	3	2	1	1	2
32.	bad	3	1	2	2	1
33.	children	3	3	-	3	-
34.	11 o'clock	3	3	-	1	2
35.	evening	3	1	2	-	3
36.	juvenile	3	1	2	2	1
37.	light(s)	3	-	3	-	3
38.	policeman(e)	3	1	2	1	2
39.	rule	3	1	2	-	3
40.	12:00	3	-	3	2	1
41.	after	2	-	2	2	-
42.	bedtime	2	1	1	1	1
43.	close	2	-	2	2	-
44.	curtail	2	1	1	1	1
45.	darkness	2	-	2	1	1
46.	fun	2	-	2	2	-
47.	late hours	2	1	1	2	-
48.	limitation	2	2	-	1	1
49.	9:00	2	-	2	1	1
50.	restraint	2	1	1	1	1
51.	stop	2	2	-	2	-
52.	street	2	1	1	1	1
53.	10:00 P.M.	2	2	-	2	-
54.	time limit	2	-	2	1	1
55.	whistle	2	-	2	-	2
56.	young	2	1	1	1	1

57-142. (f = 1)
age 16, awful, boys, bugle, campused, candle,
car, caught, corner, countryside, crew, crewcut,
curfew, curlew, curtex, curve, cut, cutout,
dawn, delinquency, delinquents, disobedience,
dog, drink, early hour, eat, 8, 8 o'clock,
eighteen, 11:00 P.M., fast goodnight kiss, fire,
forbidden, free, fun ruined, get in, good-night,
grandfather, hall, holding, hoodlums, jail,
juvenile home, kids, late night, light-out, mad,
minors, Nazis, none, occupation, of age, 1:00,
1 P.M., outside, people, probation, punishment,
restrain, restrict, ridiculous, right, ringing,
safety, Santa Rosa, sea, 7:30, signal, silence,
sorority, staying in, strict, shut-out,
subordinance, suppression, taps, teenage, teens,
tight, time element, time to get in, tired,

I-5 Curfew (contd)

			High	Low		
No.	Response	Total	Lang.	Lang.	Male	Female

ugh, under 18, youngsters, youth
(No response - 1)

I-6 Decoy

			High	Low		
No.	Response	Total	Lang.	Lang.	Male	Female
1.	duck(s)	494	267	227	272	222
2.	fake	42	23	19	26	16
3.	hunting	40	26	14	24	16
4.	false	25	10	15	14	11
5.	fool	24	10	14	19	5
6.	bird(s)	20	11	9	7	13
7.	trap	17	8	9	10	7
8.	trick	14	7	7	3	11
9.	television	11	3	8	7	4
10.	police	9	3	6	6	3
11.	deceive	8	4	4	2	6
12.	dummy	7	2	5	6	1
13.	hide	7	3	4	2	5
14.	substitute	7	3	4	2	5
15.	war	6	2	4	4	2
16.	unreal	5	2	3	-	5
17.	water	5	2	3	1	4
18.	avoid	4	1	3	1	3
19.	decorate	4	1	3	1	3
20.	detour	4	2	2	-	4
21.	football	4	-	4	3	1
22.	gun(s)	4	2	2	2	2
23.	hunt	4	2	2	4	-
24.	lure	4	3	1	4	-
25.	man	4	1	3	3	1
26.	person	4	2	2	2	2
27.	ambush	3	1	2	1	2
28.	away	3	-	3	1	2
29.	bait	3	1	2	2	1
30.	decay	3	2	1	-	3
31.	duck hunting	3	2	1	3	-
32.	hidden	3	1	2	2	1
33.	object	3	2	1	1	2
34.	shoot	3	-	3	2	1
35.	spy	3	1	2	1	2
36.	stooge	3	2	1	1	2
37.	wood	3	-	3	-	3
38.	army	2	1	1	1	1
39.	astray	2	-	2	1	1
40.	convoy	2	1	1	-	2
41.	danger	2	2	-	1	1
42.	deceit	2	1	1	1	1
43.	deception	2	2	-	2	-
44.	device	2	-	2	-	2
45.	distract	2	1	1	-	2
46.	duck hunt	2	2	-	2	-
47.	falsity	2	2	-	2	-
48.	fraud	2	2	-	-	2
49.	front	2	1	1	-	2
50.	girl	2	1	1	2	-
51.	imitation	2	-	2	2	-
52.	lead	2	1	1	1	1
53.	mistake	2	1	1	1	1
54.	navy	2	1	1	-	2
55.	phoney	2	-	2	1	1
56.	policewoman	2	1	1	-	2
57.	shooting	2	1	1	1	1
58.	smart	2	-	2	1	1
59.	sneak	2	2	-	1	1
60.	sucker	2	1	1	2	-
61.	target	2	1	1	1	1
62.	T.V. program	2	1	1	-	2

63-202. (f = 1)
abrustion, accomplice, aid, aim, alley, alloy,

I-6 Decoy (contd)

			High	Low		
No.	Response	Total	Lang.	Lang.	Male	Female

allure, alluring, allusive, animal, another,
assume, avert, away out, back, bad, bandits,
Bev Garland, blame, blind, boats, boy, boycott,
bullet, buoy, busy, camouflage, capture, car,
cheat, clever, comrade, cop, copy, cow, coy,
criminal, dangerous, deacons, deceiver, decor,
decoration, deviate, dice, dinner, distraction,
ditch, diversion, diversive, divert, dodge,
dupe, emblem, end, enemy, evade, extremity, fad,
fall-guy, feign, following, fooling, foolish,
game, go around, gone, helper, hideaway, hunter,
identify, illusion, imagine, impersonator,
innocent, instead, instrument, kids, labyrinth,
letter, look, maneuver, mean, metal, misguide,
model, money, movie, mystery, note, nothing,
not real, oboe, open, outlet, picture, pigeon,
play, plot, point, policeman, program, puzzle,
rabbit, rat, real, road, roadblock, run, running,
save, sea, secret, see, sent, setting, sham,
ship, sidetrack, sly, snare, some, something,
stooley, stool pigeon, stop, story, stunt, style,
time, to get rid of, trademark, trickery, truck,
turn, T.V. show, use, wait, warning, watch, woman

I-7 Dotage

			High	Low		
No.	Response	Total	Lang.	Lang.	Male	Female
1.	dot(s)	109	47	62	56	53
2.	old	63	25	38	32	31
3.	cottage	30	15	15	16	14
4.	mother(s)	26	16	10	8	18
5.	age	25	19	6	12	13
6.	parent(s)	20	14	6	3	17
7.	money	17	10	7	11	6
8.	dosage	16	5	11	8	8
9.	line(s)	16	3	13	6	10
10.	love	16	11	5	6	10
11.	nothing	16	3	13	4	12
12.	dote(s)	14	8	6	3	11
13.	spot(s)	14	4	9	11	3
14.	medicine	11	3	8	3	8
15.	point(s)	10	4	6	6	4
16.	old age	9	4	5	5	4
17.	period(s)	9	5	4	8	1
18.	slow	9	6	3	5	4
19.	affection	7	4	3	1	6
20.	amount	7	3	4	3	4
21.	attention	7	7	-	1	6
22.	carry	7	3	4	5	2
23.	dodge	7	5	2	4	3
24.	doting	7	2	5	1	6
25.	grandmother	7	6	1	2	5
26.	like	7	3	4	1	6
27.	spoiled	7	5	2	1	6
28.	care	6	3	3	3	3
29.	gift	6	6	-	1	5
30.	girl(s)	6	3	3	4	2
31.	give	6	1	5	2	4
32.	what	6	4	2	4	2
33.	aunt	5	4	1	-	5
34.	game	5	4	1	2	3
35.	house	5	1	4	3	2
36.	spoil	5	4	1	2	3
37.	time	5	4	1	2	3
38.	word	5	2	3	4	1
39.	devotion	4	3	1	3	1
40.	dose	4	-	4	2	2
41.	dotage	4	1	3	4	-
42.	doubt	4	1	3	2	2
43.	giving	4	4	-	1	3

I-7 Dotage (contd)

No.	Response	Total	High Lang.	Low Lang.	Male	Female
44.	help	4	3	1	3	1
45.	homage	4	4	–	4	–
46.	lazy	4	1	3	3	1
47.	loving	4	3	1	3	1
48.	mortgage	4	2	2	3	1
49.	boat(s)	3	–	3	2	1
50.	dog	3	2	1	2	1
51.	dotto	3	1	2	1	2
52.	dowry	3	2	1	1	2
53.	feeble	3	2	1	3	–
54.	fondness	3	2	1	1	2
55.	grandparent(s)	3	3	–	1	2
56.	mark	3	–	3	2	1
57.	note(s)	3	1	2	2	1
58.	peace	3	3	–	3	–
59.	pill(s)	3	–	3	3	–
60.	saying	3	2	1	2	1
61.	voltage	3	2	1	2	1
62.	adage	2	1	1	2	–
63.	add	2	2	–	–	2
64.	animal(s)	2	–	2	1	1
65.	blank	2	–	2	1	1
66.	cat	2	1	1	1	1
67.	dash	2	1	1	1	1
68.	daughter	2	–	2	1	1
69.	dictionary	2	1	1	1	1
70.	doctor	2	1	1	–	2
71.	donate	2	1	1	1	1
72.	dope	2	1	1	–	2
73.	dotting	2	–	2	1	1
74.	dough	2	1	1	1	1
75.	dull	2	–	2	1	1
76.	dumb	2	–	2	2	–
77.	fondle	2	1	1	1	1
78.	fool	2	1	1	–	2
79.	garage	2	1	1	1	1
80.	good	2	1	1	2	–
81.	greedy	2	–	2	–	2
82.	heritage	2	2	–	2	–
83.	hinder	2	1	1	1	1
84.	holes	2	–	2	2	–
85.	home	2	–	2	2	–
86.	leaning	2	1	1	–	2
87.	lineage	2	–	2	2	–
88.	man	2	1	1	1	1
89.	matron	2	2	–	1	1
90.	miss	2	–	2	1	1
91.	mother-in-law	2	1	1	2	–
92.	old woman	2	1	1	–	2
93.	paper	2	1	1	1	1
94.	part	2	1	1	1	1
95.	pay	2	1	1	–	2
96.	pigs	2	1	1	2	–
97.	plant(s)	2	–	2	2	–
98.	poor	2	1	1	2	–
99.	potage	2	1	1	1	1
100.	protectiveness	2	1	1	1	1
101.	puzzle	2	1	1	2	–
102.	question	2	1	1	1	1
103.	relatives	2	1	1	1	1
104.	sea	2	–	2	2	–
105.	senescence	2	2	–	–	2
106.	sleep	2	2	–	2	–
107.	spoiling	2	1	1	2	–
108.	storm	2	1	1	1	1
109.	think	2	–	2	2	–
110.	unknown	2	–	2	2	–
111.	weight	2	2	–	1	1
112.	wife	2	1	1	–	2

113-337. (f = 1)
abstract, acreage, act, addition, adore,
affectionate, allowance, amour, ancient, avoid,
barge, benevolent, bird, bloat, blue, boy,
bragging, car, cater, cereal, certain, child,
Christ, class, clear, cloth, cluster, complain,
compliment, concern, condone, count, cow,

I-7 Dotage (contd)

creaky, cut, date, Dave, debt, deciding,
discontent, dockage, docks, doddle, dodgers, doe,
doll, dolly, dolt, domination, domineer, dominos,
don't know, donut, doten, dotted, dotty, dowager,
dump, empty, English, escape, excess, expectation, extra, farthing, favor, favorite, feeling,
flitting, foliage, follow, fondling, food,
forage, frills, funny, gloating, grammar, graph,
grass, ham, hate, heavy, heiress, hovering,
hypochondriac, idiot, idol, idolatry, ill,
indulge, indulgence, influence, journey, kind,
kiss, knowledge, lady, laugh, leavings, letter,
liking, linger, lives, load, magnanimous, maid,
map, maternal, meanings, mess, mile, mileage,
miser, name, no, novel, number, old lady, old
maid, old man, oldster, overbearing, overdo,
overdose, overhearing, owing, own, package, pain,
partiality, paternal, patronization, payment,
peer, people, percentage, place, play, poison,
poker, polka, pontiac, port, portion, potatoe,
praise, punctuation, questionable, rain, ransom,
red, rely, relying, rubbish, ruffled, sabotage,
sad, same, scattered, school, scram, seat,
section, see, senile, senility, sense, serfdom,
series, share, shiftless, sickly, skipping,
slavish, slowness, small, small amount, some,
sorrowful, soup, sponsor, spotage, spotted,
spouse, static, stepmother, stick, stop, story,
stupid, stuttering, subservient, superfluous,
sweet, thinking, thought, Titania, torteridge,
tots, tottering, town, tree, trite, T.V., two,
type, vitamins, votage, vote, wage, wardrobe,
waste, watch, weather, while, white, widow,
wiser, woman, worry, worship, write, yea, young
(No response - 32; Illegible - 9)

I-8 Farthing

No.	Response	Total	High Lang.	Low Lang.	Male	Female
1.	money	333	187	146	183	150
2.	penny	56	34	22	25	31
3.	coin(s)	38	24	14	14	24
4.	away	30	14	16	13	17
5.	England	22	12	10	15	7
6.	distance	21	5	16	9	12
7.	farther	20	5	15	13	7
8.	going	19	4	15	9	10
9.	small	16	8	8	13	3
10.	shilling	15	12	3	8	7
11.	child(ren)	13	6	7	7	6
12.	far	13	9	4	5	8
13.	nothing	13	4	9	10	3
14.	English	11	4	7	4	7
15.	father	11	3	8	7	4
16.	near	10	5	5	4	6
17.	bird	9	4	5	4	5
18.	cent	9	4	5	6	3
19.	distant	9	5	4	4	5
20.	little	9	4	5	4	5
21.	young	8	4	4	1	7
22.	deer	7	3	4	5	2
23.	animal	6	5	1	2	4
24.	farming	6	2	4	4	2
25.	baby	5	1	4	2	3
26.	farm	5	3	2	3	2
27.	go	5	4	1	2	3
28.	pence	5	3	2	3	2
29.	sixpence	5	3	2	2	3
30.	British	4	2	2	4	–
31.	poor	4	2	2	1	3

I-8 Farthing (contd)

			High	Low		
No.	Response	Total	Lang.	Lang.	Male	Female
32.	pound	4	4	-	3	1
33.	dollar	3	3	-	2	1
34.	frothing	3	2	1	-	3
35.	further	3	-	3	-	3
36.	horse	3	1	2	2	1
37.	mile	3	-	3	1	2
38.	offspring	3	2	1	2	1
39.	parting	3	-	3	2	1
40.	sea	3	1	2	-	3
41.	son	3	3	-	-	3
42.	apart	2	-	2	-	2
43.	close	2	-	2	-	2
44.	coming	2	1	1	-	2
45.	deep	2	-	2	1	1
46.	farmer	2	1	1	1	1
47.	farting	2	1	1	2	-
48.	food	2	-	2	2	-
49.	horizon	2	-	2	1	1
50.	knowledge	2	1	1	1	1
51.	lamb	2	1	1	-	2
52.	leaving	2	-	2	1	1
53.	length	2	-	2	2	-
54.	long	2	2	-	2	-
55.	longing	2	1	1	1	1
56.	lost	2	-	2	-	2
57.	measure	2	1	1	-	2
58.	mother	2	1	1	1	1
59.	near thing	2	1	1	1	1
60.	nearing	2	-	2	-	2
61.	racing	2	1	1	1	1
62.	religion	2	2	-	2	-
63.	ship(s)	2	-	2	1	1
64.	silver	2	2	-	2	-
65.	thing	2	1	1	1	1
66.	two pence	2	2	-	-	2
67.	what	2	1	1	2	-
68.	word	2	1	1	2	-

69-225. (f = 1)
a stray, across, action, adding, advancing, alone,
Arnold Bennet, axe, bit, blank, boat, books,
Briton, broadening, bucket, building, bushel,
calf, calling, careless, carthing, cheap,
chilling, clearing, closer, closing, clothing,
courage, crying, cuddle, depth, device, Dickens,
disappearing, don't, don't know, duck, duel,
early, eating, education, educatory, ending,
extending, far away, farce, fat, fathom, fireplace, fishing, fleeing, foam, fool, foreign,
foundling, franc, friend, froth, furling, future,
gas, gathering, gone, gröscher, grow, half penny,
helpful, helpless, here, home, homeless, huh,
infant, inkling, kidding, know, last, leave,
literature, lonely, loud, love, mad, making out,
many, march, marching, meager, measurement,
mills, mothering, moving, Mr. Farthing, nautical,
nearer, new, nice, nickel, 1984, no, no good,
none, noud, 1, panting, part, pass, pecuniary,
penniless, people, person, pfenning, piece of gum,
planting, play, portion, possible, poverty,
proceeding, question, quid, ranch, ring, room,
run, rushing, science, Shakespeare, shortening,
sick, small coin, smallness, sole, soothing,
starving, stop, stretching, study, studying,
sum, tempting, that, throwing, tired, tooth, toy,
track, travel, traveling, trip, wander, water,
woods, worker, working, worth, writer
(No response - 16; Illegible - 5)

I-9 Gullet

			High	Low		
No.	Response	Total	Lang.	Lang.	Male	Female
1.	throat	180	99	81	90	90
2.	stomach	170	80	90	98	72
3.	chicken	74	36	38	36	38
4.	fish	63	33	30	33	30
5.	food	56	29	27	37	19
6.	bird	36	17	19	16	20
7.	mouth	23	12	11	12	11
8.	gully	17	11	6	8	9
9.	gut(s)	15	7	8	13	2
10.	esophagus	14	8	6	10	4
11.	eat	13	5	8	10	3
12.	swallow	13	6	7	8	5
13.	bullet	12	4	8	3	9
14.	gull(s)	10	4	6	6	4
15.	stream	10	5	5	1	9
16.	anatomy	7	5	2	5	2
17.	drink	7	4	3	3	4
18.	body	6	3	3	1	5
19.	gizzard	6	2	4	5	1
20.	pan	6	2	4	1	5
21.	skillet	6	4	2	3	3
22.	belly	5	5	-	5	-
23.	deep	5	-	5	-	5
24.	ditch	5	-	5	1	4
25.	full	5	2	3	2	3
26.	intestine(s)	5	2	3	3	2
27.	neck	5	2	3	3	2
28.	seagulls	5	5	-	3	2
29.	craw	4	4	-	3	1
30.	cup	4	1	3	2	2
31.	France	4	1	3	3	1
32.	glutton	4	2	2	3	1
33.	hole	4	2	2	1	3
34.	nothing	4	-	4	-	4
35.	organ	4	3	1	1	3
36.	biology	3	1	2	2	1
37.	foot	3	-	3	2	1
38.	French	3	2	1	2	1
39.	frog(s)	3	2	1	1	2
40.	gun	3	1	2	-	3
41.	inside	3	2	1	1	2
42.	knife	3	2	1	2	1
43.	man	3	2	1	3	-
44.	opening	3	1	2	2	1
45.	pig	3	-	3	1	2
46.	sea	3	1	2	2	1
47.	valley	3	3	-	-	3
48.	digestion	2	2	-	1	1
49.	fat	2	1	1	-	2
50.	galley	2	1	1	1	1
51.	glass	2	-	2	2	-
52.	guillotine	2	2	-	-	2
53.	gutter	2	-	2	1	1
54.	kill	2	-	2	1	1
55.	liver	2	2	-	2	-
56.	palate	2	1	1	2	-
57.	paramecium	2	2	-	2	-
58.	pelican	2	1	1	1	1
59.	person	2	-	2	1	1
60.	pipe	2	1	1	1	1
61.	tongue	2	-	2	1	1
62.	travel	2	1	1	2	-
63.	tube	2	2	-	2	-
64.	turkey	2	2	-	1	1
65.	water	2	-	2	-	2
66.	what	2	-	2	2	-

67-176. (f = 1)
alley, ally, ancient, animal, apple, axe, baby
seagull, bay, bed, beer, big, body organ, bottle,
bread, breath, buffoon, built, can, chew, cloth,
clothing, cobbler, complex, crop, dagger,
dictionary, dig, dog, duel, easily, eating,
empty, fastener, feast, feed, fire, friend,
fullet, gall, giblet, gillet, gills, goblet,
gorge, greed, green, gullible, Gulliver, gulp, H,
handy, hanging, hatch, head, heart, help, history,

I-9 Gullet (contd)

High Low

No.	Response	Total	Lang.	Lang.	Male	Female

hog, huh, ick, indentation, internal, lung,
mammals, meat, metal, open, passage, physical,
piece, pirate, place, pouch, poultry, presidents,
quail, question, rain, range, ravine, razor,
river, satisfaction, save, scope, selfish,
Shakespeare, shark, size, slit, slob, sloppiness,
soup bone, spontaneous, stew, stick, stingy,
story, stuff, sword, terrible, thorax, tomlet,
trough, war, waterway, western, whale, windpipe,
worm
(No response - 7; Illegible - 2)

I-10 Harem

High Low

No.	Response	Total	Lang.	Lang.	Male	Female
1.	woman(e)	340	185	155	193	147
2.	girl(s)	241	110	131	128	113
3.	wife(ves)	66	32	34	38	28
4.	Arabia	20	8	12	7	13
5.	sheik(s)	19	9	10	13	6
6.	sex	16	10	6	16	-
7.	sultan	16	10	6	8	8
8.	king(s)	15	8	7	2	13
9.	India	13	4	9	3	10
10.	group	12	5	7	6	6
11.	Arab(s)	10	5	5	2	8
12.	many	8	-	8	2	6
13.	Harlem	6	2	4	5	1
14.	veil(s)	6	6	-	1	5
15.	basketball	5	2	3	3	2
16.	lady(ies)	5	4	1	1	4
17.	man(e)	5	4	1	-	5
18.	Negro(es)	5	2	3	4	1
19.	scarem	5	4	1	4	1
20.	Egypt	4	-	4	1	3
21.	polygamy	4	3	1	2	2
22.	silk	4	2	2	1	3
23.	skirt	4	2	2	1	3
24.	color	3	1	2	2	1
25.	colored(s)	3	1	2	2	1
26.	dancer(s)	3	1	2	1	2
27.	female(s)	3	1	2	1	2
28.	fun	3	1	2	3	-
29.	New York	3	1	2	1	2
30.	orgy	3	3	-	3	-
31.	Arabian	2	1	1	-	2
32.	Asia	2	-	2	1	1
33.	dance	2	1	1	1	1
34.	East	2	-	2	1	1
35.	fat man	2	-	2	1	1
36.	hair	2	-	2	1	1
37.	harlot	2	2	-	2	-
38.	harm	2	2	-	1	1
39.	maharajah	2	2	-	-	2
40.	many wives	2	1	1	1	1
41.	marriage	2	1	1	-	2
42.	Middle-East	2	2	-	2	-
43.	orient	2	1	1	-	2
44.	people	2	1	1	-	2
45.	prince	2	-	2	1	1
46.	Saudia Arabia	2	2	-	1	1
47.	section	2	-	2	2	-
48.	shah	2	2	-	1	1
49.	tribe	2	2	-	-	2
50.	whore	2	2	-	2	-

51-157. (f = 1)
Africa, Alī Khan, Arabian Nights, Araby,
beautiful woman, bigamy, bigotry, blank, body,
boy, brood, calif, castle, chief, chiffon, clown,
concubine, confusion, Constantinople, convenience,

I-10 Harem (contd)

High Low

No.	Response	Total	Lang.	Lang.	Male	Female

crowded, dames, dark, Egyptian, excitement,
exotic, family, fine, fraternity, gaiety, girl
friend, girls - many, Globe Trotters, good,
Haji Baba, Harlem Globe Trotters, harmony, heaven,
hermit, hoax, home, illegal, Indian man, infidel-
ity, iron, Islam, Jim, least, legs, life, lots
of women, love, luxury, marry, masks, menagerie,
Mike, money, mormon, Morocco, Moslem, much, nice,
nocturne, noisy, out-dated, palace, pants,
paradise, perfidy, person, pillows, place,
pleasure, plurality, polygamist, potentate,
queen, question, rabbit, reaction, riches, risque,
rock & roll, scary, seals, several, Siam, skarem,
slaves, soft, song, stomachs, stripped, women,
sultry, Syria, tent, three, titles, turk, villain,
wealth, widows, wild, wind, wow, yes
(No response - 3)

I-11 Lorry

High Low

No.	Response	Total	Lang.	Lang.	Male	Female
1.	name	96	32	64	53	43
2.	truck	78	48	30	64	14
3.	girl(s)	66	33	33	35	31
4.	boat	51	27	24	28	23
5.	Larry	33	9	24	22	11
6.	England	28	15	13	12	16
7.	sorry	25	15	10	11	14
8.	car	23	14	9	16	7
9.	Peter	23	11	12	11	12
10.	carriage	18	12	6	11	7
11.	cart(s)	13	10	3	5	8
12.	worry	13	3	10	6	7
13.	glory	11	5	6	4	7
14.	money	10	5	5	5	5
15.	story(ies)	10	4	6	5	5
16.	cab(s)	9	5	4	6	3
17.	Laurie	9	6	3	2	7
18.	nothing	9	2	7	4	5
19.	wagon	9	4	5	6	3
20.	boy	8	1	7	5	3
21.	horse	8	6	2	4	4
22.	man	8	3	5	6	2
23.	ship(s)	8	3	5	5	3
24.	bus	7	4	3	5	2
25.	gory	7	3	4	4	3
26.	London	7	2	5	4	3
27.	taxi	7	3	4	6	1
28.	water	7	3	4	1	6
29.	dock	6	5	1	4	2
30.	lottery	6	3	3	3	3
31.	buggy	5	3	2	2	3
32.	ferry	5	3	2	2	3
33.	wait	5	3	2	1	4
34.	bay	4	3	1	1	3
35.	English	4	3	1	1	3
36.	lazy	4	1	3	2	2
37.	praise	4	3	1	2	2
38.	slow	4	-	4	1	3
39.	streetcar	4	-	4	1	3
40.	Tory	4	2	2	1	3
41.	transportation	4	3	1	3	1
42.	vehicle	4	2	2	-	4
43.	Annie	3	1	2	1	2
44.	bird	3	3	-	2	1
45.	game	3	3	-	1	2
46.	low	3	2	1	2	1
47.	Pier	3	2	1	1	2
48.	question	3	1	2	1	2
49.	rock	3	2	1	-	3

I-11 Lorry (contd)

No.	Response	Total	High Lang.	Low Lang.	Male	Female
50.	tarry	3	–	3	–	3
51.	tram	3	1	2	2	1
52.	travel	3	2	1	1	2
53.	what	3	1	2	1	2
54.	bridge	2	–	2	–	2
55.	British	2	–	2	2	–
56.	coach	2	2	–	1	1
57.	continuous	2	–	2	1	1
58.	Dale	2	1	1	1	1
59.	doctrine	2	2	–	2	–
60.	don't know	2	–	2	1	1
61.	dory	2	2	–	1	1
62.	dowry	2	1	1	–	2
63.	elevator	2	1	1	1	1
64.	funny	2	2	–	1	1
65.	girl's name	2	1	1	2	–
66.	green	2	–	2	2	–
67.	harbor	2	2	–	–	2
68.	Hardy	2	2	–	1	1
69.	Lorrie	2	1	1	2	–
70.	Nelson	2	–	2	–	2
71.	person	2	1	1	1	1
72.	place	2	2	–	1	1
73.	quarry	2	1	1	1	1
74.	ride	2	1	1	1	1
75.	sad	2	1	1	–	2
76.	salt	2	1	1	–	2
77.	sea	2	2	–	–	2
78.	song	2	2	–	1	1
79.	surrey	2	1	1	–	2
80.	Tale of Two Cities	2	1	1	1	1
81.	test	2	2	–	–	2
82.	torie	2	2	–	1	1
83.	tree(s)	2	1	1	–	2
84.	van	2	2	–	2	–
85.	wharf	2	–	2	–	2
86.	wonder	2	2	–	1	1

87-292. (f = 1)
abbey, alcove, Ann, anoire, anything, argue, attic, automobile, awake, awards, baby, bad, bard, be, bells, bet, bettle, Blackley, blank, blonde, blood, bo, board, boast, Bonnie, boring, bowery, Britian, Brother Larry, building, buoy, Calhoun, camberos, cap, carry, cart or carriage, cave, celery, cemetery, children, Chinese, chore, Clark, conveyance, cop, corry, country, court, cousin, cow, crevice, crown, Davies, deep, Dickens, done, door, dorry, doubt, driver, Dudley, farm, father (Larry), flurry, folk, forlorn, friend, fruit, gambling, gay, gooney, grass, Gruman, Guam, gully, hand cart, happy, hard, Hawaii, hayloft, help, high, hotel, how, hurry, ivy, Jane, jeep, jewelry, Jim Lawry, John, Johnson, joke, Karen, knoll, lace, lag, lagoon, lane, large, lark, late, later, leaf, Leary, Lee, lee, Levin, li, light, linger, loathe, lobby, lock, loiter, lonely, Lori, Lorie, Lorraine, lorry, lot, louse, love, meadow, meaning, meeting, milk, movie, Mr., Mrs. Meanings, neighbor, never, nice, noise, none, pen, Peter Lorre, pill, Piper, place to stay, plane, plays, poet, policeman, poor, porto, procrastinate, quay, questioning, quiet, railroad, ramble, remain, rest, restaurant, row, rowboat, sade, sadness, sang, Scotland, side, singing, smoky, snow, some, sorrow, speak, stable, star, street, stupid, swamp, swear, sweet, tast, tax, Terry, thing, tired, torro, tough, tower, trail, train, transport, trolling, unknown, valley, vocabulary, walk, wanger, waterfront, weary, webb, western, when, white, Whiteneck, Whitlock, who, why, wicked, win, work, yacht harbor
No response - 26; Illegible - 5)

I-12 Mermaid

No.	Response	Total	High Lang.	Low Lang.	Male	Female
1.	fish	297	153	144	143	154
2.	water	117	55	62	49	68
3.	sea(s)	110	60	50	41	69
4.	girl(s)	102	42	60	74	28
5.	woman(e)	61	28	33	49	12
6.	ocean	52	27	25	23	29
7.	swim	20	8	12	6	14
8.	tail	15	8	7	5	10
9.	beauty	14	7	7	8	6
10.	beautiful	13	4	9	9	4
11.	fin(s)	8	6	2	1	7
12.	merman(e)	8	7	1	4	4
13.	swimming	8	1	7	4	4
14.	green	7	4	3	1	6
15.	scale(s)	7	5	2	3	4
16.	sex	7	4	3	7	–
17.	fairy tale(s)	6	2	4	–	6
18.	sailor	6	2	4	4	2
19.	fish tail	5	4	1	4	1
20.	myth(s)	5	3	2	1	4
21.	pretty	5	2	3	4	1
22.	dream	4	3	1	4	–
23.	legend(s)	4	3	1	1	3
24.	man	4	2	2	3	1
25.	fable	3	2	1	2	1
26.	fantasy	3	2	1	–	3
27.	fish-woman(e)	3	1	2	2	1
28.	impossible	3	2	1	3	–
29.	Neptune	3	3	–	2	1
30.	body	2	1	1	1	1
31.	diver	2	1	1	2	–
32.	fake	2	1	1	2	–
33.	female fish	2	–	2	2	–
34.	fiction	2	1	1	2	–
35.	fisherman	2	–	2	1	1
36.	hair	2	–	2	1	1
37.	island	2	1	1	1	1
38.	lady	2	–	2	1	1
39.	Minnie	2	–	2	–	2
40.	nice	2	1	1	2	–
41.	sea woman	2	–	2	2	–
42.	seaweed	2	2	–	1	1
43.	siren	2	2	–	1	1
44.	skin diving	2	1	1	2	–
45.	wow	2	1	1	2	–

46-111. (f = 1)
babe, bass, beautiful fish, breasts, cool, desire, Esther Williams, fairy, fantastic, feet, female, fictitious, fish-girl, fishy, folk lore, gal, gills, gingerale, goodlooking fish, green lady, half fish, half woman; 1/2 fish, image, lagoon, love, Lorelei, lovely, maid, manmaid, mantee, me, mermaid, milk, mirage, Mr. Peabody, nude, nudity, paradise, phony, pretty girl, rising, rock, scaly, seahorse, sea-serpent, seashell, see, ship, silly, sink, skin, starfish, story, superstition, surf, swimmer, tale, tuna, tunafish, unique, unknown, wet, wicket, wife, woman and fish, yum
(No response - 1; Illegible - 1)

I-13 Monsoon

No.	Response	Total	High Lang.	Low Lang.	Male	Female
1.	wind(s)	222	118	104	107	115
2.	rain(s)	190	107	83	129	61
3.	storm(s)	154	82	72	107	47
4.	India	27	12	15	15	12
5.	moon	27	14	13	8	19
6.	weather	23	10	13	15	8
7.	typhoon	20	12	8	8	12

I-13 Monsoon (contd)

I-14 Oboe

No.	Response	Total	High Lang.	Low Lang.	Male	Female
8.	China	19	8	11	4	15
9.	water	10	5	5	5	5
10.	hurricane	9	5	4	7	2
11.	animal	8	3	5	1	7
12.	soon	8	1	7	3	5
13.	ship	7	2	5	2	5
14.	tornado	7	3	4	4	3
15.	island	6	2	4	–	6
16.	boat(s)	5	1	4	1	4
17.	climate	5	3	2	1	4
18.	nothing	5	1	4	1	4
19.	season	5	3	2	2	3
20.	bassoon	4	1	3	4	–
21.	country	4	2	2	–	4
22.	flood	4	3	1	3	1
23.	man(e)	4	1	3	2	2
24.	moron	4	1	3	1	3
25.	native(s)	4	1	3	1	3
26.	stone	4	1	3	–	4
27.	whiskey	4	1	3	3	1
28.	Asia	3	1	2	–	3
29.	desert	3	3	–	–	3
30.	light	3	–	3	1	2
31.	sand	3	–	3	–	3
32.	sea	3	–	3	2	1
33.	warm	3	2	1	1	2
34.	what	3	1	2	2	1
35.	bay	2	1	1	1	1
36.	beer	2	–	2	–	2
37.	Chinese	2	1	1	1	1
38.	geography	2	2	–	–	2
39.	goon	2	1	1	1	1
40.	Indian	2	1	1	–	2
41.	instrument	2	–	2	–	2
42.	mansion	2	1	1	1	1
43.	Monday	2	1	1	2	–
44.	monkey	2	2	–	1	1
45.	moonshine	2	1	1	1	1
46.	mushroom	2	2	–	1	1
47.	ocean	2	1	1	1	1
48.	Philippines	2	2	–	2	–
49.	rainy	2	1	1	2	–
50.	sun	2	1	1	1	1
51.	swamp	2	2	–	1	1
52.	tide	2	1	1	1	1
53.	time	2	–	2	1	1
54.	tropics	2	2	–	1	1
55.	weird	2	1	1	1	1

56-191. (f = 1)
alone, Annāpurna, ape, Arab, Arabic, army, baboon,
Babylon, bad, bad weather, bag, balmy, battle,
baysoon, big, book, boots, boulder, buffalo,
Burma, character, cocoon, coin, color, curtain,
deluge, destruction, distant, doctor, dragon,
dragoon, dreary, drink, duck, dusk, Egypt, Europe,
evening, flier, foreign, gale, gigantic, glass,
good, goose, gulf, Hawaii, honeymoon, horse, huge,
India rain, islands, Japan, Japenese, jungle,
lagoon, lake, large, large wind storm, late,
later, liquor, love, main, maroon, martyr, maw,
maybe, meaning, minister, money, mongoose,
monsieur, moor, mountain, **Mr.** Mooman, munsin,
name, Near East, noon, North Carolina, odd, one,
opal, orient, place, plane, plot, priest, racoon,
rage, rain(today), raining, rainstorm, rain-wind,
ran, religion, river, rock, rocket, sad, science
fiction, seasonal, see, shine, shiner, sky, so
soon, soup, sour, Southeast Asia, spoon, store,
summer, sunsoon, Syria, tank, temperature,
terrific, tidal wave, town, town-China, tycoon,
unjovial, vassal, violent, volcano, waves, wet,
wind and rain, windstorm, windy, wine, winter,
yellow, yoeman
(No response - 12)

No.	Response	Total	High Lang.	Low Lang.	Male	Female
1.	music	273	149	124	158	115
2.	instrument(s)	201	96	105	103	98
3.	flute	94	57	37	47	47
4.	horn	34	13	21	13	21
5.	orchestra	26	14	12	12	14
6.	clarinet	22	14	8	16	6
7.	band	11	6	5	5	6
8.	obey	11	1	10	3	8
9.	home	9	6	3	2	7
10.	violin	9	6	3	3	6
11.	play	8	3	5	2	6
12.	reed	8	5	3	6	2
13.	what	8	3	5	6	2
14.	abode	7	3	4	3	4
15.	bassoon	6	5	1	4	2
16.	house	6	4	2	1	5
17.	symphony	6	5	1	2	4
18.	'cello	5	4	1	2	3
19.	hobo	5	1	4	2	3
20.	black	4	1	3	2	2
21.	hoe	4	1	3	2	2
22.	musical	4	2	2	2	2
23.	musical instruments	4	3	1	–	4
24.	oboe	4	–	4	2	2
25.	pipe	4	2	2	3	1
26.	sound(s)	4	2	2	1	3
27.	woodwind	4	1	3	2	2
28.	bow	3	1	2	–	3
29.	concert(s)	3	1	2	1	2
30.	Indian	3	–	3	1	2
31.	musician	3	2	1	2	1
32.	odd	3	2	1	1	2
33.	ode	3	–	3	2	1
34.	question	3	–	3	2	1
35.	tramp	3	–	3	–	3
36.	bass	2	2	–	1	1
37.	blow	2	1	1	2	–
38.	bum	2	–	2	1	1
39.	clown	2	1	1	2	–
40.	doe	2	–	2	1	1
41.	duck	2	1	1	1	1
42.	hate	2	1	1	2	–
43.	hermit	2	1	1	1	1
44.	low	2	2	–	2	–
45.	man	2	–	2	1	1
46.	mother	2	1	1	–	2
47.	nothing	2	–	2	1	1
48.	obese	2	1	1	2	–
49.	piccolo	2	2	–	2	–
50.	round	2	1	1	1	1
51.	saxophone	2	1	1	2	–
52.	shoe	2	1	1	2	–
53.	snake	2	1	1	2	–
54.	song	2	1	1	1	1
55.	stone	2	2	–	2	–
56.	story	2	–	2	1	1
57.	trumpet	2	1	1	1	1
58.	tune	2	1	1	–	2
59.	warning	2	1	1	–	2

60-187. (f = 1)
abhor, abīde, adjective, arrive, arrow, art class,
bad, barb, Beethoven, Betty Beabody, bird, boat,
Bob Cooper, boy, bun, buoy, canal, Carol,
classical, creature, dance, Danny, death, dictionary, dictionary word, do, doorman, double reed,
drum, ear, elbow, England, faun, foot, for, fun,
game, garden, girl, go, Greek, gun, happy, harp,
honey, hot, hour, hut, idol, igloo, island,
Ivanhoe, Joe, Kobe, lake, land, light, line,
loathe, long, loss, loud, lousy, low-note, lump,
Marsha, me, mellow, mess, micro, Mitch Miller,
mole, Moses, mournful, music-sour, name, nice, no,
noise, note, Obadiah, obee, oblique, oblong,
oboed, O boy, omen, opera, performance, Peter,
place, player, pleasure, poem, poetry, raw, reedy,

I-14 Oboe (contd)

		High	Low		
No.	Response	Total	Lang.	Lang.	Male	Female

religion, rock & roll, Russell, see, sequel,
shell, short, silence, small clarinet, soft,
squeak, squeaking, stick, string, subtlety,
terrible, thin, thoughts, tight, time, toe,
train, trombone, tube, ugly, unknown, way, who,
wind, wind instruments, wood
(No response - 17; Illegible - 2)

I-15 Oxide

		High	Low		
No.	Response	Total	Lang.	Lang.	Male	Female
1.	chemistry	224	106	118	95	129
2.	oxygen	171	76	95	98	73
3.	carbon	117	70	47	42	75
4.	rust	51	27	24	40	11
5.	chemical(s)	50	25	25	26	24
6.	gas	38	20	18	12	26
7.	zinc	36	24	12	19	17
8.	air	35	13	22	12	23
9.	iron	31	17	14	23	8
10.	metal	17	10	7	12	5
11.	compound	12	5	7	11	1
12.	copper	12	2	10	8	4
13.	water	12	5	7	9	3
14.	chem.	8	4	4	5	3
15.	hydrogen	8	4	4	3	5
16.	peroxide	8	3	5	2	6
17.	white	8	5	3	5	3
18.	carbon dioxide	7	3	4	2	5
19.	lead	7	7	-	7	-
20.	powder	5	4	1	5	-
21.	burn	4	2	2	4	-
22.	CO_2	4	2	2	4	-
23.	ferrous	4	3	1	2	2
24.	science	4	1	3	1	3
25.	acid	3	1	2	1	2
26.	black	3	-	3	3	-
27.	bleach	3	1	2	1	2
28.	coating	3	2	1	3	-
29.	ferric	3	2	1	3	-
30.	heat	3	1	2	2	1
31.	hydroxide	3	2	1	1	2
32.	O_2	3	2	1	2	1
33.	ash	2	-	2	1	1
34.	burned	2	1	1	1	1
35.	burning	2	-	2	1	1
36.	color	2	-	2	2	-
37.	combination	2	1	1	1	1
38.	element	2	1	1	1	1
39.	fire	2	1	1	1	1
40.	magnesium	2	-	2	1	1
41.	metallic	2	2	-	2	-
42.	mineral	2	2	-	1	1
43.	oxen	2	1	1	1	1
44.	oxidation	2	2	-	2	-
45.	poison	2	1	1	1	1
46.	reaction	2	1	1	2	-
47.	red	2	1	1	1	1
48.	soap	2	2	-	1	1
49.	tarnish(es)	2	1	1	1	1

50-116. (f = 1)
barium, base, biology, breathing, burnt, carbide,
carbohydrate, carbon-di, carbonic, chemistry
table, Chem. 1^A, Chem. 1A & 1B, chloride,
chlorine, clean, corrode, CU_2O, detergent,
dioxide, dye, equation, fe, ferro, ferro-ferric
oxide, fumes, hair, hide, idle, important, ion,
iron rust, laboratory, mercuric, mercurochrome,
mercury, mixture of O_2, monoxide, nitrate,
nitrogen, odor, osmosis, O_3, ox, oxate, oxides,

I-15 Oxide (contd)

		High	Low		
No.	Response	Total	Lang.	Lang.	Male	Female

oxidizer, paint, PbO, physio, potassium, potassium
oxide, radical, residue, shoe polish, silver,
smog, smoke, sodium, solution, sox, strong,
subside, sulphur, tin, toxic, waste, yellow
(No response - 1; Illegible - 1)

I-16 Pestle

		High	Low		
No.	Response	Total	Lang.	Lang.	Male	Female
1.	mortar	194	110	84	125	69
2.	flower	79	39	40	45	34
3.	pest(s)	75	29	46	34	41
4.	chemistry	38	15	23	22	16
5.	pedestal	21	10	11	9	12
6.	pistol	20	12	8	10	10
7.	stand	20	11	9	12	8
8.	high	18	6	12	7	11
9.	gun	16	7	9	7	9
10.	bother	13	5	8	4	9
11.	stone	12	9	3	9	3
12.	bug(s)	10	2	8	3	7
13.	pester	9	4	4	3	6
14.	bowl	8	7	1	4	4
15.	disease	8	3	5	3	5
16.	nothing	8	2	6	2	6
17.	pestilence	8	5	3	5	3
18.	stool	8	6	2	4	4
19.	wrestle	8	5	3	4	4
20.	church	7	1	6	4	3
21.	hammer	7	5	2	3	4
22.	chair	6	3	3	2	4
23.	food	6	2	4	3	3
24.	grind	6	4	2	3	3
25.	nestle	6	3	3	4	2
26.	plague	6	4	2	1	5
27.	statue	6	1	5	3	3
28.	famine	5	3	2	4	1
29.	glass	5	4	1	4	1
30.	nuisance	5	3	2	-	5
31.	pistle	5	1	4	3	2
32.	animal	4	2	2	1	3
33.	blank	4	-	4	1	3
34.	corn	4	3	1	2	2
35.	drugs	4	2	2	3	1
36.	person	4	2	2	2	2
37.	pharmacy	4	1	3	2	2
38.	plant	4	3	1	2	2
39.	pretzel(s)	4	3	1	3	1
40.	stick	4	3	1	1	3
41.	thorn	4	2	2	2	2
42.	ant	3	2	1	1	2
43.	Indian(s)	3	1	2	2	1
44.	insect	3	2	1	-	3
45.	pesty	3	2	1	1	2
46.	petal	3	1	2	2	1
47.	rock	3	3	-	2	1
48.	stem	3	1	2	1	2
49.	step	3	2	1	2	1
50.	thistle	3	2	1	1	2
51.	what	3	2	1	2	1
52.	worry	3	1	2	1	2
53.	annoy	2	-	2	-	2
54.	annoying	2	1	1	2	-
55.	bad	2	1	1	2	-
56.	beer	2	1	1	1	1
57.	color	2	-	2	1	1
58.	cookie(s)	2	-	2	2	-
59.	cooking	2	1	1	-	2
60.	cup	2	2	-	1	1
61.	destroy	2	-	2	1	1

I-16 Pestle (contd)

No.	Response	Total	High Lang.	Low Lang.	Male	Female
62.	Elvis	2	1	1	2	-
63.	feet	2	1	1	-	2
64.	fool	2	-	2	1	1
65.	grinding	2	2	-	2	-
66.	grine	2	-	2	2	-
67.	masher	2	2	-	2	-
68.	medicine	2	1	1	-	2
69.	mortal	2	2	-	1	1
70.	nest	2	1	1	1	1
71.	object	2	1	1	1	1
72.	pedal	2	1	1	1	1
73.	peddle	2	1	1	1	1
74.	pink	2	-	2	1	1
75.	platform	2	1	1	-	2
76.	problem	2	1	1	-	2
77.	question	2	-	2	-	2
78.	rest	2	2	-	2	-
79.	rose	2	-	2	2	-
80.	seat	2	-	2	-	2
81.	shoot	2	-	2	1	1
82.	sick	2	1	1	2	-
83.	sister	2	2	-	1	1
84.	tall	2	-	2	2	-
85.	thing	2	1	1	-	2
86.	tool	2	1	1	2	-
87.	tower	2	1	1	1	1
88.	train	2	1	1	1	1
89.	trestle	2	-	2	-	2
90.	tube	2	-	2	2	-
91.	walk	2	1	1	1	1
92.	wonder	2	2	-	1	1

93-263. (f = 1)
above, always, ammunition, anger, art, awful,
beast, beater, beetle, board, boy, brew, bridge,
bud, bunch, bush, can, car, castle, chrome, cocoa,
column, conceited, cool, cowboy, crucible, crush,
deata, death, dirt, dish, disk, dog, don't know,
druggist, drugstore, elevated, elevation, Elvis
Presley, epidemic, epistle, evil, experiment,
father, fertilize, fireplace, friend, funny,
game, garden, glass rod, glen, go, god, golden,
grain, Greek, green, harm, heavy, hindering,
hostle, house, hustle, implement, ink, instrument,
irk, irritate, island, item, kids, kind, knot,
laboratory, ladder, lady, letter, level, limb,
little, locus, love, mantle, marriage, mechanical,
messel, mixer, motor, nag, name, on, one, pain,
part, paste, pastel, peanut, peat, peatstap,
pellet, penny, people, pepper, pesky, pestish,
pestle, piece, pill, pillar, pillow, pistil,
pitcher, plain, plaster, play, please, podium,
point, poor, post, pound, pounding, prestige,
prison, pulpit, pus, ramble, rat, reason, relic,
religion, religious, rod, shot, sickness, smell,
soft, sorry, speaker, speech, still, stima,
stoop, stop, store, strange, stump, sweater,
table, think, throne, time, token, top, tree,
trouble, try, turnstile, twisted, unusual, up,
utensil, vase, vessel, vocabulary, whistle, why,
wind, wood, worried
(No response - 29; Illegible - 4)

I-17 Prefix

No.	Response	Total	High Lang.	Low Lang.	Male	Female
1.	suffix	264	147	117	129	135
2.	before	260	114	146	141	119
3.	word(s)	105	57	48	50	55
4.	beginning	96	42	54	55	41
5.	first	34	13	21	20	14

I-17 Prefix (contd)

No.	Response	Total	High Lang.	Low Lang.	Male	Female
6.	English	23	9	14	10	13
7.	book(s)	18	9	9	9	9
8.	grammar	11	5	6	5	6
9.	begin	9	5	4	4	5
10.	letter(s)	8	5	3	3	5
11.	ending	7	3	4	3	4
12.	front	7	5	2	4	3
13.	spelling	5	1	4	2	3
14.	syllable(s)	5	1	4	1	4
15.	adjective	4	3	1	4	-
16.	end	4	4	-	2	2
17.	index	4	1	3	-	4
18.	pre	4	2	2	-	4
19.	preceding	4	3	1	4	-
20.	re	4	2	2	1	3
21.	start	4	3	1	3	1
22.	telephone	4	3	1	1	3
23.	number	3	2	1	1	2
24.	sub	3	3	-	1	2
25.	verb	3	1	2	1	2
26.	ad	2	-	2	-	2
27.	addition	2	1	1	1	1
28.	affix	2	1	1	2	-
29.	after	2	1	1	2	-
30.	ante	2	1	1	2	-
31.	ex	2	2	-	2	-
32.	in	2	2	-	1	1
33.	meaning	2	2	-	2	-
34.	name	2	2	-	1	1
35.	noun	2	2	-	1	1
36.	part	2	-	2	1	1
37.	precede	2	1	1	1	1
38.	reflex	2	1	1	1	1
39.	sentence	2	1	1	1	1
40.	stem	2	1	1	1	1
41.	Subject A *	2	-	2	2	-
42.	un	2	1	1	2	-

43-114. (f = 1)
add, additive, adverb, ahead, antifix, are,
beginning of, break, came before, change, comes
before, coming before, complex, con, dash, de,
definition, dictionary, dis, dis/appear, dog,
dry, en, first, word, fixe, for, forehand,
French, German, glass, head, im, in front of,
ing, interesting, into, library, locate, longer,
"me"tcalf, modify, mutilation, part of word,
preamble, prearrange, precedence, prediction,
preface, prefix, preplex, previous, pro,
pronominal prefix, rain, ramrod, reading, renew,
short, sink, stop, subject, surname, syllable
before, telephone number, the, three, verbal,
vowel, wood, working, wrench, (-mark)
(No response - 1)
* - (Introductory English course)

I-18 Ramrod

No.	Response	Total	High Lang.	Low Lang.	Male	Female
1.	gun(s)	258	130	128	187	71
2.	car	59	28	31	15	44
3.	song	59	15	44	27	32
4.	stick	45	23	22	12	33
5.	rifle	41	21	20	38	3
6.	rod	31	11	20	14	17
7.	straight	28	19	9	9	19
8.	stiff	21	15	6	8	13
9.	pole	18	8	10	6	12
10.	boss	11	4	7	10	1
11.	cowboy(s)	10	5	5	8	2
12.	canon(cannon)	9	3	6	9	-

I-18 Ramrod (contd)

No.	Response	Total	High Lang.	Low Lang.	Male	Female
13.	flower	9	7	2	2	7
14.	music	9	2	7	6	3
15.	push	9	5	4	7	2
16.	steel	9	4	5	5	4
17.	iron	8	7	1	1	7
18.	force	7	3	4	4	3
19.	bar	6	6	–	2	4
20.	foreman	6	3	3	5	1
21.	hot rod	6	1	5	2	4
22.	musket	6	5	1	6	–
23.	curtain	5	4	1	–	5
24.	instrument	5	4	1	1	4
25.	long	5	4	1	2	3
26.	piston	5	3	2	4	1
27.	poker	5	2	3	1	4
28.	record	5	3	2	2	3
29.	western(s)	5	2	3	4	1
30.	boat	4	3	1	–	4
31.	book	4	2	2	1	3
32.	fish	4	–	4	2	2
33.	fishing	4	3	1	1	3
34.	hard	4	2	2	2	2
35.	man	4	2	2	2	2
36.	name	4	1	3	–	4
37.	tool(s)	4	3	1	1	3
38.	T.V.	4	2	2	2	2
39.	weapon	4	2	2	1	3
40.	army	3	2	1	–	3
41.	board	3	2	1	–	3
42.	boy	3	–	3	1	2
43.	clean	3	1	2	3	–
44.	Duane Eddy	3	1	2	3	–
45.	engine	3	3	–	1	2
46.	lightening	3	1	2	–	3
47.	metal	3	–	3	–	3
48.	M-1	3	1	2	3	–
49.	pipe	3	2	1	1	2
50.	power	3	2	1	3	–
51.	rock & roll	3	1	2	2	1
52.	sheep	3	2	1	–	3
53.	staff	3	3	–	1	2
54.	strong	3	2	1	1	2
55.	train	3	1	2	2	1
56.	cartoon	2	1	1	–	2
57.	castle	2	1	1	2	–
58.	character	2	2	–	1	1
59.	cleaning	2	1	1	2	–
60.	fight	2	1	1	–	2
61.	fishing rod	2	–	2	2	–
62.	football	2	1	1	–	2
63.	forceful	2	1	1	2	–
64.	goldenrod	2	1	1	–	2
65.	hole	2	1	1	–	2
66.	machinery	2	2	–	2	–
67.	mechanics	2	1	1	–	2
68.	M-1 rifle	2	1	1	2	–
69.	movie	2	–	2	1	1
70.	painting	2	2	–	–	2
71.	pistol	2	1	1	1	1
72.	play	2	–	2	2	–
73.	pusher	2	1	1	2	–
74.	shaft	2	1	1	1	1
75.	skinny	2	1	1	–	2
76.	story	2	–	2	1	1
77.	thing	2	1	1	–	2
78.	tough	2	–	2	2	–
79.	wood(s)	2	–	2	1	1

80-231. (f = 1)
action, against, Amer. revolution, animal, any,
anywhere, article, auto, awful, backbone, bastion,
battlement, beat, bible, bicycle, bit, blunderbuss,
breakdown, bronze, bullet, bushrod, carburetor,
cattle, chaos, chisel, cleaner, club, comics,
confuse, construction, curtain rod, Dec. Art,
door, Doug, drive, driving, egghead, enter, evil,
excitement, explosion, farm, fire, fire iron,

I-18 Ramrod (contd)

fireplace, fishing pole, flint lock, fort,
Franklin (Ben), fright, frontier, fulcrum,
gangster, gear shift, get, goat, golden, goose,
gun cleaner, gung-ho, hasty, head, high school,
hit, horse, hurt, impact, Indian, intercourse,
iron bar, joke, large, leader, lieutenant, life
saver's pole, light, lightening rod, Lincoln,
line, long stick, loud mouth, machine, measure,
mechanical, medieval, middle, motor, muzzle,
nothing, object, oil, old, opposition, pen,
Penrod, pestle, physics, pile, pioneers, place,
plant, plunger, poke, police, politician,
popular, rabble rouser, railroad, ram, ramble,
rammer, rampage, Ramsey, Ramson, rock, rocket,
roughshod, running, ship, soldier, song title,
sound, stand, stave, stock, stone, straight as,
strict, strike, struggle, stuff, summer, talking,
teacher, television, topsy, tree, type, typsie,
unfairness, U.S. Cal. 30 M-1, utensil, Vikings,
violence, wand, war, welding, west, what,
Winchester, wind, woman
(No response - 11; Illegible - 1)

I-19 Sequel

No.	Response	Total	High Lang.	Low Lang.	Male	Female
1.	sequence	84	38	46	39	45
2.	following	65	33	32	24	41
3.	equal	60	28	32	35	25
4.	end	47	26	21	26	21
5.	follow(s)	45	27	18	19	26
6.	book(s)	43	28	15	13	30
7.	story	41	28	13	17	24
8.	next	30	10	20	9	21
9.	after	26	14	12	16	10
10.	same	24	10	14	14	10
11.	novel	21	18	3	7	14
12.	order	19	8	11	14	5
13.	time	18	7	11	8	10
14.	series	15	8	7	7	8
15.	event(s)	14	11	3	10	4
16.	ending	12	10	2	8	4
17.	movie	12	9	3	5	7
18.	continuation	10	3	7	2	8
19.	finish	10	6	4	7	3
20.	addition	9	4	5	4	5
21.	continue	9	4	5	–	9
22.	another	8	4	4	4	4
23.	noise	7	4	3	4	3
24.	serial	7	6	1	2	5
25.	again	6	5	1	2	4
26.	like	6	3	3	3	3
27.	number(s)	6	4	2	2	4
28.	squeal	6	–	6	5	1
29.	beginning	5	2	3	3	2
30.	continuance	5	2	3	3	2
31.	continued	5	3	2	1	4
32.	nothing	5	2	3	2	3
33.	sequel	5	1	4	4	1
34.	sequin(s)	5	2	3	1	4
35.	squirrel	5	2	3	2	3
36.	consequence	4	1	3	1	3
37.	happening(s)	4	2	2	3	1
38.	what	4	1	3	3	1
39.	yell	4	1	3	4	–
40.	cheat	3	–	3	3	–
41.	conclusion	3	2	1	1	2
42.	dress	3	2	1	2	1
43.	equivalent	3	3	–	3	–
44.	fight	3	–	3	1	2

I-19 Sequel (contd)

No.	Response	Total	High Lang.	Low Lang.	Male	Female
45.	in order	3	-	3	3	-
46.	kill	3	1	2	2	1
47.	list	3	2	1	1	2
48.	more	3	2	1	-	3
49.	parallel	3	3	-	2	1
50.	part	3	1	2	3	-
51.	quiet	3	-	3	3	-
52.	sea	3	-	3	1	2
53.	seagull	3	-	3	3	-
54.	second	3	1	2	2	1
55.	sentence	3	2	1	1	2
56.	similar	3	1	2	2	1
57.	storm	3	1	2	3	-
58.	succession	3	1	2	-	3
59.	town	3	1	2	3	-
60.	abbess	2	2	-	-	2
61.	analogy	2	-	2	2	-
62.	animal	2	-	2	2	-
63.	answer	2	1	1	1	1
64.	before	2	1	1	1	1
65.	bird(s)	2	-	2	1	1
66.	calm	2	-	2	1	1
67.	even	2	1	1	2	-
68.	follow up	2	-	2	1	1
69.	huh	2	-	2	2	-
70.	later	2	1	1	1	1
71.	mouse	2	-	2	2	-
72.	partner	2	2	-	2	-
73.	people	2	1	1	2	-
74.	picture	2	1	1	1	1
75.	pig	2	-	2	2	-
76.	play	2	2	-	2	-
77.	previous	2	-	2	-	2
78.	quail	2	-	2	1	1
79.	round	2	-	2	2	-
80.	screech	2	1	1	2	-
81.	sex	2	1	1	2	-
82.	soil	2	1	1	-	2
83.	together	2	-	2	1	1
84.	trees	2	1	1	1	1
85.	wind	2	1	1	1	1
86.	with	2	2	-	1	1
87.	woman	2	-	2	2	-

88-247. (f = 1)
act, action, afterglow, aftermath, afterwards,
anecdote, annals, arrangement, associated, author,
average, beg, black, blank, brakes, Calif., capit-
ulate, chapter, class, climax, close, colors,
come again, coming half, compare, concurrent,
connection(s), continuing, counterpart, decal,
definition, desk, dictionary, do, dog, duel,
duration, ed, elegy, enough, events order, final,
finis, first, fish, fool, fright, fur, future,
girls, give away, glisten, go, good, grey, group,
hand, happen, happiness, Heidi, helper, hold, in
sequence, instance, jewelry, joined, law, life,
line, literature, live, magazine, match, meeting,
mice, moon, mysterious, necklace, no, none, now,
nuts, open, opposite, peaceful, pen, penguin,
period, person, pinch, playwright, plural, poem,
port, preface, prelude, quell, rain, rat, red,
regal, ribbon, roses, row, same time, Santa Cruz,
saquel, satire, scream, screw, season, section,
segregated, segrin, sentiment, sequen, sequoia,
set, shiny, shriek, shrill, silent, similarity,
simile, sleepy, slow, soldier, song, space, speed,
spell, squall, square, squeek, squeeze, squelch,
stamp, stone, tale, talk, television, tense,
think, thought, tire, tolerance, Tues., twin, two,
uneven, uprising, use, violence, volume, water,
wave, week, went, word, work
(No response - 10; Illegible - 3)

I-20 Stanza

No.	Response	Total	High Lang.	Low Lang.	Male	Female
1.	music	282	132	150	135	147
2.	song(s)	195	97	98	109	86
3.	verse	92	48	44	54	38
4.	line(s)	87	42	45	41	46
5.	phrase	57	24	33	33	24
6.	poem(s)	53	52	1	20	33
7.	poet	32	1	31	17	15
8.	poetry	26	13	13	10	16
9.	paragraph	19	10	9	11	8
10.	bar(s)	10	6	4	6	4
11.	part	9	3	6	5	4
12.	sentence	9	4	5	3	6
13.	note(s)	7	3	4	3	4
14.	hymm	6	3	3	5	1
15.	sing	6	4	2	4	2
16.	chorus	5	3	2	4	1
17.	piano	5	2	3	3	2
18.	section	5	4	1	4	1
19.	group	4	2	2	3	1
20.	refrain	4	3	1	3	1
21.	singing	4	2	2	3	1
22.	first	3	-	3	2	1
23.	measure	3	1	2	-	3
24.	stand	3	1	2	3	-
25.	waltz	3	1	2	-	3
26.	band	2	-	2	1	1
27.	clause	2	1	1	1	1
28.	frame	2	2	-	2	-
29.	march	2	2	-	-	2
30.	read	2	-	2	-	2
31.	Souza	2	1	1	1	1
32.	Star Spangled Banner	2	1	1	1	1
33.	tune	2	1	1	-	2
34.	words	2	-	2	2	-

35-86. (f = 1)
bar-line, beginning, book, cadenza, chapter,
clef, eight bars, event, finale, five line staff,
flag, four lines, frightened, how, inning, last,
level, lightening, literature, long, lyrics,
Mario Lanza, melody, moment, movie, Mozart,
name, nat. anthem, national anthem, our flag,
paragraphy, passage, pause, posture, red, rhyme,
rote, Sanka, say, separation, situation, sonnet,
speech, staff, stance, Stanta Class, straight,
star, strength, study, syllable, Wordsworth
(Illegible - 1)

I-21 Tenure

No.	Response	Total	High Lang.	Low Lang.	Male	Female
1.	time	101	54	47	59	42
2.	office	72	44	28	44	28
3.	teacher(s)	57	34	23	23	34
4.	hold(s)	56	28	28	26	30
5.	length	23	15	8	11	12
6.	money	20	8	12	8	12
7.	tension	17	5	12	10	7
8.	term	17	8	9	13	4
9.	stay	16	14	2	12	4
10.	strength	15	10	5	8	7
11.	holding	14	7	7	8	6
12.	land	14	13	1	5	9
13.	tender	13	5	8	7	6
14.	end	12	5	7	5	7
15.	ten	12	4	8	8	4
16.	year(s)	12	5	7	8	4
17.	duration	10	9	1	7	3
18.	law	9	5	4	3	6
19.	manure	9	3	6	7	2

I-21 Tenure (contd)

No.	Response	Total	High Lang.	Low Lang.	Male	Female
20.	nothing	9	1	8	5	4
21.	security	9	5	4	4	5
22.	teaching	9	7	2	2	7
23.	lease	8	3	5	3	5
24.	soft	8	4	4	4	4
25.	texture	8	3	5	1	7
26.	hard	7	3	4	4	3
27.	job	7	7	–	4	3
28.	period	7	6	1	4	3
29.	demure	6	1	5	2	4
30.	lasting	6	5	1	3	3
31.	contract	5	4	1	4	1
32.	music	5	1	4	5	–
33.	school	5	3	2	2	3
34.	seniority	5	3	2	5	–
35.	temperature	5	–	5	2	3
36.	tennis	5	2	3	2	3
37.	act	4	3	1	1	3
38.	fear	4	1	3	1	3
39.	leave	4	2	2	2	2
40.	rent	4	4	–	1	3
41.	sound	4	3	1	2	2
42.	strong	4	4	–	1	3
43.	tight	4	1	3	2	2
44.	tremble	4	2	2	2	2
45.	what	4	1	3	4	–
46.	work	4	1	3	1	3
47.	base	3	–	3	2	1
48.	calm	3	1	2	2	1
49.	color	3	–	3	2	1
50.	high	3	1	2	1	2
51.	long	3	1	2	1	2
52.	old	3	1	2	–	3
53.	pay	3	1	2	2	1
54.	president	3	2	1	1	2
55.	singer	3	–	3	1	2
56.	slave	3	2	1	–	3
57.	teeth	3	–	3	1	2
58.	temper	3	1	2	2	1
59.	tense	3	–	3	1	2
60.	ten-year	3	–	3	3	–
61.	treasure	3	2	1	3	–
62.	voice	3	–	3	1	2
63.	age	2	–	2	2	–
64.	blank	2	1	1	1	1
65.	chemistry	2	1	1	–	2
66.	ease	2	1	1	–	2
67.	easy	2	–	2	1	1
68.	employment	2	2	–	–	2
69.	feel	2	1	1	1	1
70.	hot	2	–	2	2	–
71.	hurt	2	1	1	1	1
72.	iodine	2	1	1	–	2
73.	judge	2	1	1	1	1
74.	length of time	2	1	1	1	1
75.	life	2	1	1	1	1
76.	limited	2	–	2	1	1
77.	meeting	2	1	1	1	1
78.	mortgage	2	2	–	–	2
79.	physics	2	2	–	–	2
80.	plan	2	–	2	–	2
81.	professor	2	1	1	2	–
82.	quist	2	–	2	1	1
83.	reign	2	1	1	2	–
84.	right	2	2	–	2	–
85.	shy	2	1	1	1	1
86.	smooth	2	1	1	2	–
87.	story	2	2	–	–	2
88.	tax	2	2	–	1	1
89.	teach	2	1	1	1	1
90.	team	2	–	2	–	2
91.	tenant	2	2	–	–	2
92.	ten years	2	–	2	1	1
93.	tint	2	1	1	1	1
94.	tremor	2	–	2	2	–

I-21 Tenure (contd)

No.	Response	Total	High Lang.	Low Lang.	Male	Female
95.	unknown	2	1	1	1	1

96-300. (f = 1)
abatement, abscess, action, adrion, agenda, always, animal, annoy, anything, argument, ask, authority, bass, begin, bend, big word, bold, British, business, cancer, case, caste, check, come, court, dark, date, degree, dentist, denture, detain, dictator, dictionary, different, done, edione, education, educator, eleven, ending, endurance, existence, experience, expiration, extent, familiar, farm, father, fee, feelings, feudal, feudal system, field, find, fine, finish, forgot, free, French, funny, fuss, gesture, God, gold, government, grant, grasp, grass, great, guarantee, happening, hardship, have, heat, help, house, hotel, ink, insurance, joint, keep, know, lane, last, leniency, Lettie Jo (high school principal's daughter), lifetime, like, literature, loan, loin, lot, love, lovely, manly, mature, maybe, meaning, means, microoone, mood, more, mother, much, near, neat, not, noun, nuclear, number, object, obstruction, occupation, octopus, office act, of office, ownership, passes, payments, peaceful, people, perfume, physique, pleasure, position, presidency term, pressure, problem, professorship, program, question, rabbit, red, registration, remain, repeat, retaining, ridiculous, room, rot, rough, rumble, safety, science, sedate, seize, seven, shape, sharp, shot, sickness, silent, sing, snake, soap, song, sorrow, staid, standing, status, steel, sticky, stiff, strict, string, stupid, swave, Tampa, tape, tea, television, temp, temperament, tempest, temporary, tempt, tenable, tenacity, tendency, tendon, tenet, tent, tenth, tenture, tenure, termination, test, tightness, time limit, time of office, timid, treasurer, true, turmoil, turnover, type, unwelcome, vacation, vacuum, validity, vein, we, wire, woman, worker
(No response - 25; Illegible - 3)

I-22 Tortoise

No.	Response	Total	High Lang.	Low Lang.	Male	Female
1.	turtle	453	212	241	244	209
2.	shell(s)	167	112	55	60	107
3.	slow	83	38	45	55	28
4.	hare	65	37	28	38	27
5.	animal	42	15	27	20	22
6.	color	14	6	8	5	9
7.	green	10	6	4	4	6
8.	reptile(s)	9	2	7	8	1
9.	sea	9	3	6	7	2
10.	fish	8	5	3	3	5
11.	blue	7	3	4	3	4
12.	frog	7	3	4	4	3
13.	rabbit	7	2	5	5	2
14.	water	6	2	4	3	3
15.	hair	5	3	2	4	1
16.	snail	5	3	2	3	2
17.	old	4	1	3	2	2
18.	crawl	3	1	2	1	2
19.	desert	3	2	1	1	2
20.	ocean	3	–	3	2	1
21.	race	3	1	2	1	2
22.	soup	3	1	2	2	1
23.	stone	3	1	2	–	3
24.	turquoise	3	2	1	1	2
25.	age	2	2	–	1	1

I-22 Tortoise (contd)

No.	Response	Total	High Lang.	Low Lang.	Male	Female
26.	beach	2	2	–	2	–
27.	big	2	1	1	2	–
28.	cat	2	–	2	–	2
29.	shelled animal	2	2	–	1	1
30.	slowness	2	–	2	–	2
31.	swim	2	1	1	–	2
32.	torture	2	1	1	2	–

33-90. (f = 1)
amphibian, aqua, back, body, bones, bright, chest,
clown, comb, dessert, exercise, figure, flippers,
food, girl, glasses, good, ground, gullet,
happiness, hard, mammal, Mexican, Myrtle, nothing,
Peanut's pet turtle, pet, physiology, pig, pine,
poised, pond, reading, retraction, robin, rock,
room, rough, science, shy, silly, sister, snare,
stally, stork, stove, strick, tats, toad, torment,
tough, tropical island, turkey, twist, women,
wrinkled, wrong, zoo
(No response - 1; Illegible - 3)

I-23 Wampum

No.	Response	Total	High Lang.	Low Lang.	Male	Female
1.	money	490	246	244	308	182
2.	Indian(s)	318	155	163	130	188
3.	teepee	25	17	8	12	13
4.	bead(s)	19	14	5	6	13
5.	tent	10	4	6	3	7
6.	wigwam	7	4	3	1	6
7.	exchange	5	4	1	3	2
8.	trade	5	2	3	2	3
9.	weapon	5	2	3	1	4
10.	drum	4	1	3	–	4
11.	food	4	1	3	1	3
12.	animal	3	2	1	–	3
13.	barter	3	3	–	2	1
14.	Injun	3	3	–	2	1
15.	shells	3	1	2	2	1
16.	belt	2	–	2	2	–
17.	dollar	2	2	–	2	–
18.	dough	2	1	1	2	–
19.	fight	2	–	2	–	2
20.	Indian money	2	2	–	1	1
21.	noise	2	1	1	–	2
22.	want(s)	2	1	1	–	2

23-99. (f = 1)
beat 'um, beer, bird, blanket, candy, cash, cry,
dance, democratic, discussion, dope, Eskimo,
excitement, fun, game, gum, heat, Hell Week,
hit, house, huddle, hurt, idiot, Indiana, Indian
belt, Indian Village, liquor, many, meeting,
mixer, money (or Indian), need 'um, New Mexico,
night, none, nonsense, odd, pay, person, peyote,
place, plenty, psychology, pumpkin, red skin,
ridicule, rowdy, salt, scalp, seal, sea shells,
smoke, smooth, solution, spanking, Stanford,
stick, story, swamp, swat, talk, tobacco, treaty,
tree, tribe, trouble, ugh, ugly, vampire,
vitamin, vodka, wait, wamp, wander, war, weight,
welfare
(No response - 4; Illegible - 1)

I-24 Wicket

No.	Response	Total	High Lang.	Low Lang.	Male	Female
1.	basket(s)	239	115	124	97	142
2.	croquet	114	62	52	73	41
3.	fence	63	37	26	19	44
4.	game(s)	51	25	26	33	18
5.	chair	37	20	17	13	24
6.	bad	33	8	25	20	13
7.	cricket	32	19	13	25	7
8.	stick	26	19	7	10	16
9.	wicked	26	10	16	16	10
10.	wire	22	11	11	15	7
11.	candle	16	7	9	5	11
12.	sport(s)	16	8	8	13	3
13.	mean	15	5	10	7	8
14.	straw	15	6	9	3	12
15.	bale	13	1	12	6	7
16.	ball	10	10	–	6	4
17.	racket(quet)	10	3	7	7	3
18.	witch(es)	9	2	7	4	5
19.	cruel	8	4	4	7	1
20.	mallet	8	6	2	6	2
21.	tennis	8	2	6	6	2
22.	thicket	7	3	4	2	5
23.	clubs	6	3	3	4	2
24.	gate	6	3	3	1	5
25.	hoop(s)	6	4	2	6	–
26.	wood(s)	6	3	3	5	1
27.	bat	5	2	3	5	–
28.	English	5	3	2	4	1
29.	picket	5	2	3	1	4
30.	sticky	5	4	1	3	2
31.	ticket	5	4	1	2	3
32.	weave	5	3	2	5	–
33.	England	4	1	3	3	1
34.	lamp	4	2	2	3	1
35.	wicker	4	4	–	1	3
36.	baseball	3	2	1	3	–
37.	nothing	3	–	3	–	3
38.	basked	2	2	–	2	–
39.	boy	2	–	2	–	2
40.	bricket	2	–	2	2	–
41.	bush	2	–	2	1	1
42.	end	2	1	1	2	–
43.	forest	2	–	2	–	2
44.	goal	2	2	–	1	1
45.	golf	2	2	–	1	1
46.	grass	2	1	1	1	1
47.	hit	2	1	1	1	1
48.	la-crosse	2	1	1	2	–
49.	light	2	–	2	–	2
50.	mesh	2	1	1	1	1
51.	net	2	1	1	2	–
52.	reed(s)	2	2	–	1	1
53.	thick	2	1	1	2	–
54.	wick	2	2	–	2	–
55.	wish	2	1	1	–	2

56-153. (f = 1)
air-wick, arch, awful, backet, basket chair,
board, book, booth, British, broom, brush, cane,
cardboard, cat tails, Chip (a friend), cook, dark,
decoy, dense, equipment, evil, fibers, fireplace,
fish, flame, gadget, glass, good, green,
Halloween, hammer, happy, hard, hockey, hole,
interwoven, kind, lance, licket, lighter, loop,
made, marbles, match, metal, nice, nimble,
obstacle, odd, old, Oxford, paddle, pan, picket
fence, pole, polo, post, postal window, rabbit,
rickety, rod, rough, round, shrub, shrubbery, sin,
sinful, sinister, small, soccer, spike, steal,
sticket, stove wick, straw basket, stump, sun,
tangle, tensé, thing, thorns, ticket window,
tool, twig, ugly, vest, watch, weapon, weird,
weaving, weed, what, whisker, whoop, window,
wise, women, wrong
(No response - 14; Illegible - 2)

II-1 Arbor

No.	Response	Total	High Lang.	Low Lang.	Male	Female
1.	tree(s)	205	119	86	86	119
2.	harbor(our)	88	45	43	49	39
3.	grape(s)	87	51	36	47	40
4.	rose(s)	42	25	17	17	25
5.	Ann	37	21	16	27	10
6.	flower(s)	31	15	16	15	16
7.	vine(s)	28	19	9	15	13
8.	Michigan	27	12	15	25	2
9.	boat(s)	21	10	11	8	13
10.	arch	15	7	8	4	11
11.	garden	15	9	6	3	12
12.	ship(s)	12	5	7	6	6
13.	water	12	3	9	2	10
14.	Ann Arbor	11	6	5	9	2
15.	hate	10	6	4	3	7
16.	hide	10	2	8	5	5
17.	navy	10	4	6	10	–
18.	labor	8	3	5	3	5
19.	work	7	5	2	3	4
20.	green	6	2	4	1	5
21.	lights	6	2	4	4	2
22.	place	6	1	5	4	2
23.	town	6	3	3	5	1
24.	bay	5	4	1	4	1
25.	lattice	5	5	–	2	3
26.	love	5	2	3	4	1
27.	saw	5	3	2	5	–
28.	sea	5	1	4	3	2
29.	city	4	2	2	3	1
30.	cover	4	1	3	3	1
31.	day	4	1	3	2	2
32.	holiday	4	1	3	1	3
33.	joy	4	2	2	3	1
34.	keep	4	1	3	1	3
35.	leaves	4	2	2	–	4
36.	patio	4	1	3	2	2
37.	gateway	3	2	1	2	1
38.	help	3	–	3	1	2
39.	house	3	3	–	1	2
40.	over	3	–	3	3	–
41.	plants	3	1	2	2	1
42.	porch	3	2	1	3	–
43.	port	3	2	1	1	2
44.	protect	3	–	3	3	–
45.	shade	3	1	2	1	2
46.	amour	2	–	2	–	2
47.	Ann Arbor, Michigan	2	2	–	2	–
48.	arbor(s)	2	1	1	2	–
49.	awning	2	–	2	–	2
50.	branches	2	1	1	–	2
51.	bush(es)	2	1	1	1	1
52.	color	2	–	2	1	1
53.	cove	2	1	1	1	1
54.	covering	2	1	1	1	1
55.	dislike	2	1	1	2	–
56.	drill	2	–	2	2	–
57.	drive	2	2	–	1	1
58.	fence	2	1	1	1	1
59.	fruit	2	1	1	1	1
60.	gate	2	1	1	–	2
61.	grove	2	–	2	2	–
62.	hold	2	1	1	1	1
63.	inlet	2	1	1	1	1
64.	lone	2	–	2	2	–
65.	machine	2	1	1	2	–
66.	man	2	–	2	2	–
67.	ocean	2	1	1	1	1
68.	overhang	2	–	2	2	–
69.	passage	2	1	1	2	–
70.	press	2	–	2	2	–
71.	roof	2	–	2	1	1
72.	safety	2	2	–	1	1
73.	smell	2	1	1	1	1
74.	sheet	2	–	2	2	–
75.	trellis	2	1	1	2	–

II-1 Arbor (contd)

No.	Response	Total	High Lang.	Low Lang.	Male	Female

76-218. (f = 1)
abhor, abide, addition, against, anchor, ancient, angry, Annapolis, apple, arbitrate, arburtory, arc, archway, ardor, armed, armor, army, around, awl, backyard, boar, bold, book, booth, bough, bow, bridge, bright, brush, builder, change, China, church, cleave, cool, courteous, criminal, dark, door, dull, enclosed, end, energetic, field, forest, freedom, freeway, fresh, friends, furniture, gaiety, good, goodbye, grandma, grapevine, ham, hand, hedge, hid, hideaway, high, holder, hole, idem, know, lake, lilac, lover, love-seat, machinery, may, memorial, meat, Millinscatter, monastery, moonlight, motor, name, naval academy, navy academy, need, nest, New Hampshire, night, nine, no, oak, odor, opera, orchard, pay, peace, plank, planting, play, pleasant, ponder, pretty, quiet, quite, refuge, road, rod, room, rosebush, seat, see, shaded glen, shaft, Shakespeare, shame, shelter, state, stop, store, table, takeway, terrace, think, tie, tolerate, tools, top, trade, tressle, unnecessarily, vineyard, vita, vocabulary, wait, walk, want, war, warm, waterfront, water inlet, waves, wedding, wheel, windy, wisteria, word, wreath
(No response - 10; Illegible - 3)

II-2 Basin

No.	Response	Total	High Lang.	Low Lang.	Male	Female
1.	water	189	96	93	88	101
2.	sink	181	99	82	77	104
3.	bowl	145	73	72	82	63
4.	wash	144	67	77	69	75
5.	hole	23	14	9	16	7
6.	tub	22	14	8	11	11
7.	valley	20	5	15	16	4
8.	pan	13	8	5	7	6
9.	canyon	12	7	5	10	2
10.	big	11	3	8	7	4
11.	bottom	10	2	8	9	1
12.	bathroom	9	5	4	4	5
13.	soap	9	4	5	6	3
14.	washing	9	3	6	4	5
15.	deep	8	3	5	4	4
16.	river	8	4	4	6	2
17.	dish	7	2	5	5	2
18.	wash bowl	6	–	6	3	3
19.	mountain(s)	5	3	2	3	2
20.	toilet	5	2	3	2	3
21.	white	5	2	3	4	1
22.	bowel	4	2	2	1	3
23.	ditch	4	3	1	2	2
24.	land	4	3	1	–	4
25.	street	4	3	1	3	1
26.	bison	3	2	1	3	–
27.	depression	3	2	1	3	–
28.	desert	3	1	2	2	1
29.	flat	3	–	3	2	1
30.	lake	3	2	1	2	1
31.	pot	3	2	1	2	1
32.	wash basin	3	2	1	3	–
33.	wash cloth	3	–	3	–	3
34.	whole	3	2	1	–	3
35.	bath	2	1	1	–	2
36.	concave	2	1	1	1	1
37.	container	2	2	–	2	–
38.	enamel	2	1	1	–	2
39.	geography	2	–	2	–	2
40.	great	2	1	1	–	2

II-2 Basin (contd)

			High	Low		
No.	Response	Total	Lang.	Lang.	Male	Female
41.	hallow	2	2	-	1	1
42.	lowland	2	2	-	1	1
43.	park	2	2	-	1	1
44.	place	2	1	1	1	1
45.	plain(s)	2	1	1	1	1
46.	raisin	2	1	1	-	2
47.	towel	2	-	2	1	1

48-135. (f = 1)
agriculture, animal, arroyo, baby, baking, ball, bars, base, "(Basin) Street Blues", bay, bazoom, beer, big basin, bim, blues, boisa, bole, buffalo, cabin, cabinet, cannon, cavity, cellar, circular bowl, country, crater, crevice, curve, deer, desert depression, dirty, dry, dry land, ewer, face, faucet, forest, full, Grand Canyon, gulf, gully, hands, hasten, hollow, home, Jackson Lake, jungle, kitchen, lack, low, mason, mesa, Mexico, Mississippi, music, National Park, ox, pail, pan for washing, pit, pool, porcelain, porcelain bowl, ranch, rasin, receptacle, region, reservoir, resin, ridge, rock, rosin, sand, Santa Cruz, sick, snow, stream, terrain, Texas, top, trees, vase, wash basis, wash pail, washstand, western, Yellowstone, Yosemite
(Illegible - 2)

II-3 Burlap

			High	Low		
No.	Response	Total	Lang.	Lang.	Male	Female
1.	sack(s)	478	241	237	252	226
2.	bag(s)	235	124	111	128	107
3.	cloth(s)	36	19	17	28	8
4.	material	20	12	8	6	14
5.	rough	20	11	9	4	16
6.	potato(es)	14	7	7	8	6
7.	dress	9	4	5	3	6
8.	canvas	8	4	4	2	6
9.	gunny sack	8	4	4	5	3
10.	brown	5	2	3	-	5
11.	sac	5	-	5	3	2
12.	tree	5	2	3	3	2
13.	fabric	4	2	2	1	3
14.	fur	4	2	2	2	2
15.	burp	3	1	2	2	1
16.	chemise	3	2	1	3	-
17.	coarse	3	2	1	2	1
18.	cover	3	2	1	2	1
19.	flour	3	2	1	-	3
20.	initiation	3	3	-	3	-
21.	sack dress	3	1	2	2	1
22.	scratchy	3	3	-	-	3
23.	tent	3	3	-	2	1
24.	bad	2	1	1	1	1
25.	burl(s)	2	-	2	1	1
26.	cheap	2	1	1	1	1
27.	coat	2	-	2	-	2
28.	course	2	-	2	2	-
29.	curtain	2	1	1	1	1
30.	dog	2	1	1	2	-
31.	haircut	2	-	2	1	1
32.	horse	2	1	1	1	1
33.	leather	2	1	1	-	2
34.	loose	2	-	2	1	1
35.	potato sack	2	1	1	1	1
36.	race(s)	2	2	-	2	-
37.	rope	2	-	2	1	1
38.	rug	2	1	1	1	1
39.	saddle	2	1	1	-	2
40.	strap	2	1	1	1	1
41.	woven	2	1	1	2	-

II-3 Burlap (contd)

			High	Low		
No.	Response	Total	Lang.	Lang.	Male	Female

42-127. (f = 1)
adventure, Annie Oakley, army, barley, bird, bricks, buffoon, burlap, Burma, camp, chance, chickens, clothing, cork, costume, cotton, country, cross hatching, dirty, dusty, expensive, feed, feed sacks, fish, fishing, flower, fuzzy, girl, grain bag, gunny, hairy hard, hay, hoarse, house, India, instrument, invitation, itchy, laps, Latin banquet, mishap, muslin, old, over, overcap, picture, picture frame, plaster, purble, queen, rags, ranch, robe, rough weave, rushing, sacking, sag, sax, sentiment, sew, sheeting, shirt, skirt, smells, sock, soft, sport, stage props, stiff, suit, sweater, texture, thread, town, tramp, ugly, wall-covering, walls, water, weak, what, wicker basket, wool, work, wrap

II-4 Carbon

			High	Low		
No.	Response	Total	Lang.	Lang.	Male	Female
1.	paper	210	102	108	90	120
2.	black	134	62	72	78	56
3.	dioxide	94	60	34	45	49
4.	copy(ies)	93	60	33	33	60
5.	chemistry	69	24	45	35	34
6.	element	67	30	37	45	22
7.	coal	39	20	19	31	8
8.	monoxide	24	15	9	13	11
9.	atom	11	7	4	8	3
10.	diamond(s)	10	3	7	5	5
11.	oxygen	10	7	3	5	5
12.	tetrachloride	10	5	5	6	4
13.	charcoal	9	2	7	6	3
14.	oxide	8	4	4	7	1
15.	type	8	3	5	2	6
16.	C	7	3	4	5	2
17.	gas	7	6	1	2	5
18.	ink	7	1	6	1	6
19.	chemical	6	1	5	3	3
20.	CO_2	6	4	2	4	2
21.	fire	6	1	5	2	4
22.	hydrogen	6	3	3	4	2
23.	pencil	6	4	2	6	-
24.	typewriter	6	2	4	2	4
25.	typing	6	4	2	-	6
26.	chem.	5	1	4	4	1
27.	compound(s)	5	4	1	4	1
28.	organic	5	2	3	5	-
29.	coke	4	3	1	3	1
30.	soot	4	2	2	1	3
31.	ash(es)	3	2	1	2	1
32.	blue	3	-	3	-	3
33.	car	3	1	2	3	-
34.	chloride	3	1	2	2	1
35.	dirty	3	-	3	2	1
36.	fourteen	3	2	1	1	2
37.	rod	3	1	2	2	1
38.	wood	3	2	1	2	1
39.	air	2	2	-	1	1
40.	alcohol	2	1	1	1	1
41.	biology	2	1	1	-	2
42.	carbon dioxide	2	1	1	1	1
43.	carbon tetra-chloride	2	1	1	1	1
44.	engines	2	-	2	2	-
45.	funnies	2	1	1	-	2
46.	graphite	2	1	1	2	-
47.	gun	2	1	1	2	-
48.	lead	2	2	-	1	1
49.	life	2	1	1	1	1

II-4 Carbon (contd)

No.	Response	Total	High Lang.	Low Lang.	Male	Female
50.	molecule	2	1	1	1	1
51.	radioactive	2	1	1	1	1
52.	smoke	2	2	-	2	-
53.	water	2	-	2	-	2

54-116. (f = 1)
acid, arc, ate, battery, black mineral, blackness, blue-black, burned, burnt, carbon paper, Chem. 1A & 1B, comic, corner, cradle, crystal set, dark, dating, decay, deposits, desk, ditto, duplicator, duty, efficient, fireplace, funny, geology, hard, hard-black, hydrocarbon, inorganic, iron, isotope, lack, lamp, laughs, letter, living, machine, many, McDaniel, Mickey Mouse, mimeograph, mineral, moleculant, motor, none, organic chemistry, pegnoir, powder, rocks, science, silicon, sky, smut, sooty, sticky, substance, sugar, tet, twelve, two, white
(Illegible - 1)

II-5 Cinder

No.	Response	Total	High Lang.	Low Lang.	Male	Female
1.	ash(es)	242	126	116	107	135
2.	fire	172	85	87	84	88
3.	eye(s)	95	42	53	42	53
4.	coal(s)	55	31	24	33	22
5.	track(s)	53	23	30	52	1
6.	black	48	31	17	16	32
7.	burn	27	13	14	19	8
8.	fireplace	15	6	9	-	15
9.	hot	15	8	7	10	5
10.	soot	15	9	6	5	10
11.	wood	15	7	8	11	4
12.	Cinderella	14	8	6	2	12
13.	smoke	14	7	7	9	5
14.	apple(s)	13	3	10	3	10
15.	spark	11	8	3	8	3
16.	dust	10	5	5	4	6
17.	train	9	5	4	7	2
18.	charcoal	8	1	7	5	3
19.	carbon	7	5	2	6	1
20.	dirt	7	4	3	4	3
21.	cider	5	1	4	2	3
22.	cone	5	4	1	3	2
23.	path	5	4	1	3	2
24.	round	5	2	3	5	-
25.	block	4	1	3	3	1
26.	burning	4	1	3	4	-
27.	particle	4	3	1	2	2
28.	box	3	3	-	1	2
29.	chimney	3	1	2	1	2
30.	drink	3	1	2	2	1
31.	Ella	3	2	1	2	1
32.	hurt(s)	3	1	2	1	2
33.	railroad	3	2	1	3	-
34.	rock	3	1	2	3	-
35.	stone(s)	3	2	1	2	1
36.	tree	3	-	3	3	-
37.	burned	2	1	1	2	-
38.	burnt	2	2	-	2	-
39.	campfire	2	2	-	1	1
40.	Cindy	2	2	-	2	-
41.	coke	2	2	-	2	-
42.	dirty	2	1	1	1	1
43.	engine	2	1	1	2	-
44.	flame	2	1	1	1	1
45.	furnace	2	-	2	1	1
46.	story	2	1	1	1	1
47.	volcano	2	2	-	2	-

II-5 Cinder (contd)

No.	Response	Total	High Lang.	Low Lang.	Male	Female

48-119. (f = 1)
asphalt, binder, biting, bitter, black lava, brick, candy, chat, child, cremation, crumbly, cry, crystal, cup, darkness, death, dog, donuts, drive, driveway, fest, finger, flick, geometry, girl, gravel, hard, hearth, heat, incinerator, in my eye, kinder, light, lightness, liquid, locomotive, log, lot, money, moon, moonshine, Mt. Lassen, name, New York, oh, pie, pinder, pumpkin, road, roll, roof, sand, sender, shut, sliver, small, soldier, solid, splinter, sty, tear, tinder, tiny stone, tire, track field, truck, tube, warm, waste, wax, wet, yellow
(No response - 1; Illegible - 1)

II-6 Discord

No.	Response	Total	High Lang.	Low Lang.	Male	Female
1.	harmony	191	121	70	93	98
2.	music	63	31	32	34	29
3.	disharmony	26	19	7	17	9
4.	confusion	25	8	17	11	14
5.	noise	24	16	8	11	13
6.	unharmonious	21	10	11	8	13
7.	fight(s)	18	7	11	10	8
8.	argument	17	11	6	7	10
9.	chaos	16	5	11	9	7
10.	bad	15	7	8	12	3
11.	sound(s)	15	4	11	11	4
12.	wrong	15	9	6	6	9
13.	off	14	6	8	5	9
14.	trouble	13	7	6	5	8
15.	piano	12	6	6	4	8
16.	unhappy	12	7	5	2	10
17.	dissonance	11	9	2	4	7
18.	note(s)	11	5	6	4	7
19.	disagreement	10	6	4	5	5
20.	record(s)	10	3	7	6	4
21.	unhappiness	10	4	6	4	6
22.	cord(s)	9	2	7	4	5
23.	strife	9	3	6	3	6
24.	accord	8	3	5	5	3
25.	mess	8	2	6	5	3
26.	unrest	8	4	4	7	1
27.	concord	7	6	1	5	2
28.	discount	7	2	5	5	2
29.	argue	6	-	6	3	3
30.	disconnect	6	-	6	3	3
31.	disunity	6	2	4	2	4
32.	off key	6	4	2	2	4
33.	sour	6	3	3	3	3
34.	talk	6	2	4	4	2
35.	upset	6	2	4	3	3
36.	discontnet	5	3	2	4	1
37.	disorder	5	5	-	4	1
38.	cacophony	4	4	-	1	3
39.	clash	4	3	1	1	3
40.	disagree	4	2	2	1	3
41.	fighting	4	2	2	2	2
42.	quarrel	4	-	4	1	3
43.	sad	4	2	2	2	2
44.	unharmony	4	2	2	2	2
45.	unity	4	2	2	3	1
46.	unorganized	4	-	4	2	2
47.	apart	3	1	2	1	2
48.	awful	3	-	3	3	-
49.	break	3	2	1	1	2
50.	chord	3	3	-	1	2
51.	discard	3	-	3	2	1
52.	disregard	3	-	3	3	-

II-6 Discord (contd)

No.	Response	Total	High Lang.	Low Lang.	Male	Female
53.	dissension	3	3	–	3	–
54.	hard	3	2	1	2	1
55.	loud	3	3	–	–	3
56.	not even	3	3	–	2	1
57.	nothing	3	1	2	1	2
58.	throw away	3	–	3	2	1
59.	unharmonic	3	3	–	2	1
60.	unpleasant	3	2	1	2	1
61.	war	3	2	1	2	1
62.	against	2	–	2	2	–
63.	angry	2	1	1	1	1
64.	bedlam	2	2	–	–	2
65.	conflict	2	2	–	1	1
66.	confused	2	–	2	1	1
67.	conversation	2	2	–	1	1
68.	discordance	2	2	–	1	1
69.	disruption	2	2	–	1	1
70.	dissonant	2	2	–	–	2
71.	drop	2	–	2	1	1
72.	goddess	2	1	1	–	2
73.	good	2	1	1	2	–
74.	harp	2	1	1	2	–
75.	harsh	2	1	1	1	1
76.	key	2	–	2	1	1
77.	leave	2	–	2	1	1
78.	musical	2	2	–	1	1
79.	no harmony	2	1	1	2	–
80.	order	2	2	–	1	1
81.	out	2	2	–	1	1
82.	pain	2	1	1	2	–
83.	people	2	2	–	1	1
84.	rope	2	2	–	2	–
85.	say	2	2	–	1	1
86.	song	2	1	1	2	–
87.	talking	2	2	–	1	1
88.	throw	2	1	1	2	–
89.	unconnect	2	–	2	–	2
90.	union	2	2	–	1	1
91.	unison	2	1	1	1	1

92-287. (f = 1)
accordance, alarm clock, aloof, anger, away,
babbling, band, broken, cainpilmeli, Carol,
clashing, company, concordia, concurrment, confess,
connect, content, coordination, cordant, crumpled,
damn, dark, denounce, disagreeance, disagreeing,
disarranged, disconcern, disconnected, disconsert,
discontented, discontinue, discourse, disharmonious, disjunct, dislocate, dismiss, disorganiza-
tion, disorganized, displeasure, dispose, disturb,
disturbed, disunion, Dixie Land, drill, electricity, false, family, fates, feat, flat, folly,
fool, forget, friend(s), frustration, funny, give,
grief, grim, guitar, happiness, happy, harmonious,
harshness, heavenly, help, home, human, humiliation, hurts, incoherence, incord, incompatibility,
incorrect, insanity, jangled, jazz, judge, jumbled,
jump, June, lack, lack of harmony, leaving,
lecture, little, lose, maker, malfunction, melody,
messy, Miles Davis, minor, misfit, mislead,
mistake, mixed up, mixture, mix up, money,
mother-in-law, Near East, newspapers, no cord,
no good, no harmony (clash), noisy, nosey, not,
not aligned, not happy, not same, number, off
beat, off center, off tune, old, old clothes, on
cord, orchestra, ouch, out of order, out of tune,
pathos, progressive jazz, quieter, rambled, ravel,
reason, rechord, release, reverberation, rid,
riot, rough, ruffled, sadness, Schoenberg, screech,
sentence, separate, shout, silent, sing, singers,
sorrow, soundless, speak, spinal cord, squeaky,
stove, string, symphony, take apart, temper,
tension, terrible, think, thoughtless, throughout,
tune, tuning, ugliness, ugly, unattached, unaware,
unbelief, uncertain, unconnected, uncontent, undo,
uneasy, uneven, unfavorable, unharmonious
inharmony, unmusical, unpleasantness, unreasonable,

II-6 Discord (contd)

unsettled, unsound, unstable, untuneful, ununity,
unwanted, uproar, vibration, violin, vocal,
voice, what, wire, women, worry, yard, yelling
(No response - 5; Illegible - 1)

II-7 Dogma

No.	Response	Total	High Lang.	Low Lang.	Male	Female
1.	dog(s)	76	17	59	47	29
2.	church	52	34	18	25	27
3.	doctrine	47	33	14	20	27
4.	religion	36	24	12	20	16
5.	belief(s)	25	16	9	13	12
6.	problem(s)	20	12	8	11	9
7.	stigma	19	8	11	14	5
8.	law(s)	18	11	7	11	7
9.	dilemma	17	4	13	11	6
10.	rule(s)	17	14	3	4	13
11.	stubborn	17	10	7	7	10
12.	truth(s)	17	9	8	7	10
13.	cat(s)	15	5	10	9	6
14.	dogmatic	14	3	11	5	9
15.	idea(s)	14	8	6	7	7
16.	confusion	13	4	9	2	11
17.	faith	12	7	5	7	5
18.	puzzle	12	6	6	3	9
19.	catholic	11	6	5	6	5
20.	dictator	11	9	2	7	4
21.	ritual	8	5	3	3	5
22.	strict	8	3	5	2	6
23.	tired	8	3	5	5	3
24.	situation	7	3	4	4	3
25.	principle	6	4	2	4	2
26.	animal	5	1	4	2	3
27.	creed	5	4	1	3	2
28.	document	5	1	4	2	3
29.	fact(s)	5	4	1	3	2
30.	propaganda	5	3	2	2	3
31.	stale	5	3	2	3	2
32.	teaching(s)	5	3	2	4	1
33.	theory	5	3	2	1	4
34.	trouble	5	2	3	2	3
35.	lie(s)	4	3	1	2	2
36.	mess	4	1	3	1	3
37.	nothing	4	–	4	2	2
38.	opinion	4	1	3	3	1
39.	positive	4	1	3	2	2
40.	prejudice	4	1	3	2	2
41.	trite	4	2	2	2	2
42.	writing(s)	4	1	3	4	–
43.	catholicism	3	3	–	3	–
44.	catma	3	1	2	3	–
45.	conflict	3	3	–	2	1
46.	declaration	3	1	2	1	2
47.	habit	3	3	–	3	–
48.	hard	3	2	1	3	–
49.	Hitler	3	3	–	1	2
50.	mad	3	–	3	1	2
51.	paper(s)	3	3	–	–	3
52.	people	3	1	2	2	1
53.	plan	3	3	–	1	2
54.	play	3	1	2	1	2
55.	politics	3	1	2	1	2
56.	pope	3	1	2	1	2
57.	predicament	3	–	3	2	1
58.	rut	3	2	1	3	–
59.	sick	3	–	3	2	1
60.	strong	3	1	2	2	1
61.	tenet	3	3	–	–	3
62.	tree	3	–	3	1	2

II-7 Dogma (contd)

No.	Response	Total	High Lang.	Low Lang.	Male	Female
63.	true	3	1	2	1	2
64.	wood	3	2	1	2	1
65.	absolute	2	2	-	2	-
66.	attitude	2	2	-	1	-
67.	authority	2	2	-	1	1
68.	automatic	2	-	2	2	-
69.	axiom	2	2	-	2	-
70.	battle	2	-	2	1	1
71.	Bible	2	-	2	1	1
72.	bother	2	1	1	1	1
73.	chaos	2	1	1	-	2
74.	communism	2	1	1	1	1
75.	communist	2	1	1	2	-
76.	data	2	1	1	1	1
77.	drivel	2	1	1	-	2
78.	English	2	-	2	1	1
79.	enigma	2	-	2	2	-
80.	false	2	2	-	-	2
81.	fight	2	1	1	2	-
82.	flower	2	-	2	1	1
83.	God	2	1	1	-	2
84.	government	2	-	2	-	2
85.	ideal(s)	2	-	2	2	-
86.	letter	2	1	1	1	1
87.	literature	2	1	1	2	-
88.	man	2	1	1	1	1
89.	meaning	2	1	1	-	2
90.	morals	2	2	-	2	-
91.	mystery	2	1	1	-	2
92.	narrow	2	1	1	-	2
93.	persistence	2	1	1	2	-
94.	plight	2	2	-	2	-
95.	question	2	-	2	2	-
96.	routine	2	1	1	1	1
97.	ruling	2	1	1	1	1
98.	same	2	1	1	1	1
99.	saying	2	1	1	-	2
100.	slow	2	1	1	2	-
101.	state	2	1	1	2	-
102.	static	2	1	1	1	1
103.	stigmatic	2	-	2	2	-
104.	still	2	-	2	1	1
105.	stop	2	1	1	-	2
106.	stuck	2	2	-	2	-
107.	stupid	2	2	-	2	-
108.	time	2	1	1	1	1
109.	word	2	2	-	-	2

110-364. (f = 1)
A-bombs, accept, advertisement, against, allusion, ambition, anger, answer, anything, argument, army, article, atheist, away, back, bad, believe, below, biased, biasness, biogenetic laws, bigoted, block, bond, book, boredom, bound, Buddhism, bullheadedness, Caesar, canine, certain, certainty, certificate, changeable, characteristic, charter, China, Christian, Christianity, Christian-like, class, code, command, common belief, compact, complex, conformity, confused, confusing, continue, contract, conviction, criticize, cross, curtail, dad, danger, day, daze, defeat, degree, demanding, despot, dictatorial, dictionary, discord, disease, dispensationalism, dodge, dogma, dogmar, dogmatism, domineering, dormatory, drag, drama, dramatic, Eisenhower, emphatic, encyclical, episode, exaggerated, excessive, fame, fanatic, fate, fierce, finger, fixed procedure, forcing, fraternity, frustration, gear, Greeks, grind, guide, gullible, hackneyed, half, hazy, help, horse, ideology, idiot, ignorance, image, inflexible, injustice, inorder, intolerance, ism, issue, lady, language, Larry, Latin, laziness, lecture, lesson, Luther, manuscript, Marx, masonry, masons, matter, maze, mean, mechanical, medicine, meeting, monotonous, mores, mother dog, must, name, necessary, no religion, none, nonsense, not facts, obsession, overpowering, permanent, persistent,

II-7 Dogma (contd)

person, philosophy, pigheaded, place, platform, poem, poppycock, power, prejudiced, priest, profound, psychology, publication, puzzled, rainbow, rationalism, read, reason, rebellion, redundant, regret, religious, respect, repetition, repetitious, republican, right, rote, Russia, sad, scroll, sense, sheep, sigma, sign, skill, skillet, smell, somo, so true, Spanish Inquisition, speech, spirit, Sputnik, staid, stagnant, stagnation, Stalin, stand, standard, standstill, star, statement, steadfast, stern, stick, sticker, stiff, stifle, stillness, stimulus, stipulation, stoic, stopped, story, strength, stumped, stupidity, stupor, style, sure, swamp, system tag, tail, talk, teacher, teacherlike, theoretical, thing, think, thought, tiring, too much, tradition, trait, trash, treaty, type, tyranny, ultimatum, unacceptable, unchangeable, unchanged, uneasy, uneducated, unhappy, unquestioned, unreasonable, unstable, untrue, untruth, unusual, uselessnes verse, virgin, vocabulary, what, written, yes
(No response - 10; Illegible - 2)

II-8 Fetish

No.	Response	Total	High Lang.	Low Lang.	Male	Female
1.	fish	40	13	27	22	18
2.	particular	35	16	19	18	17
3.	charm	25	15	10	10	15
4.	silly	15	6	9	6	9
5.	small	12	7	5	6	6
6.	foot(ee)	11	3	8	6	5
7.	nervous	11	2	9	5	6
8.	idol	10	7	3	9	1
9.	squeamish	10	6	4	4	6
10.	fat	9	3	6	5	4
11.	fret	9	2	7	3	6
12.	bad	8	5	3	6	2
13.	fickle	8	3	5	5	3
14.	girl(s)	8	4	4	5	3
15.	hat	8	4	4	3	5
16.	nothing	8	1	7	2	6
17.	petty	8	4	4	4	4
18.	worry	8	4	4	2	6
19.	fiendish	7	1	6	1	6
20.	foolish	7	1	6	6	1
21.	selfish	7	2	5	1	6
22.	symbol(s)	7	5	2	6	1
23.	afraid	6	4	2	1	5
24.	baby	6	4	2	3	3
25.	ceremony	6	5	1	3	3
26.	fete	6	3	3	2	4
27.	habit	6	5	1	1	5
28.	odd	6	2	4	2	4
29.	squirmish	6	2	4	2	4
30.	childish	5	1	4	2	3
31.	fetus	5	3	2	4	1
32.	fiend	5	1	4	-	5
33.	food	5	3	2	3	2
34.	funny	5	1	4	2	3
35.	fussy	5	3	2	2	3
36.	problem	5	4	1	2	3
37.	quirk	5	3	2	2	3
38.	shy	5	3	2	4	1
39.	six	5	5	-	3	2
40.	tired	5	3	2	3	2
41.	wicked	5	3	2	1	4
42.	worried	5	2	3	2	3
43.	dance	4	1	3	3	1
44.	fanatic	4	2	2	1	3

II-8 Fetish (contd)   II-8 Fetish (contd)

No.	Response	Total	High Lang.	Low Lang.	Male	Female
45.	fancy	4	3	1	1	3
46.	feast	4	1	3	4	-
47.	finicky	4	3	1	3	1
48.	fretful	4	2	2	2	2
49.	mean	4	2	2	-	4
50.	party	4	3	1	-	4
51.	religion	4	2	2	-	4
52.	scared	4	3	1	3	1
53.	sly	4	3	1	2	2
54.	superstition	4	4	-	2	2
55.	superstitious	4	1	3	-	4
56.	upset	4	1	3	1	3
57.	weak	4	-	4	4	-
58.	woman(e)	4	2	2	2	2
59.	cat	3	2	1	2	1
60.	different	3	2	1	3	-
61.	evil	3	2	1	2	1
62.	fit	3	-	3	3	-
63.	gay	3	3	-	2	1
64.	get	3	2	1	1	2
65.	holiday	3	2	1	-	3
66.	hot	3	1	2	1	2
67.	hungry	3	3	-	1	2
68.	idiosyncrasy	3	2	1	2	1
69.	jumpy	3	1	2	1	2
70.	mad	3	2	1	1	2
71.	object	3	1	2	-	3
72.	obsession	3	2	1	3	-
73.	old	3	3	-	1	2
74.	peculiar	3	2	1	2	1
75.	picky	3	2	1	1	2
76.	relish	3	1	2	-	3
77.	ritual	3	2	1	2	1
78.	spoiled	3	1	2	2	1
79.	squirm	3	1	2	1	2
80.	squirmy	3	1	2	3	-
81.	strong	3	-	3	3	-
82.	thing	3	2	1	2	1
83.	tickle	3	-	3	1	2
84.	ticklish	3	1	2	1	2
85.	touchy	3	2	1	3	-
86.	ugly	3	1	2	1	2
87.	uneasy	3	-	3	1	2
88.	worship	3	2	1	2	1
89.	abnormal	2	1	1	1	1
90.	adjective	2	1	1	1	1
91.	amulet	2	2	-	1	1
92.	angry	2	-	2	1	1
93.	blank	2	2	-	1	1
94.	bosom	2	-	2	2	-
95.	bother	2	1	1	1	1
96.	bothered	2	1	1	1	1
97.	brave	2	-	2	1	1
98.	clean	2	1	1	1	1
99.	crazy	2	1	1	2	-
100.	custom	2	2	-	1	1
101.	difficult	2	-	2	1	1
102.	dislike	2	-	2	1	1
103.	doll	2	1	1	1	1
104.	eat	2	1	1	2	-
105.	fad	2	1	1	-	2
106.	fast	2	1	1	2	-
107.	feat	2	1	1	1	1
108.	feeling	2	1	1	-	2
109.	fight	2	-	2	2	-
110.	flighty	2	2	-	-	2
111.	flirty	2	1	1	-	2
112.	fun	2	1	1	2	-
113.	game	2	2	-	1	1
114.	gift	2	1	1	1	1
115.	hair	2	-	2	2	-
116.	happy	2	-	2	1	1
117.	hard	2	2	-	-	2
118.	idea	2	2	-	1	1
119.	like(s)	2	-	2	1	1
120.	mood	2	1	1	-	2

No.	Response	Total	High Lang.	Low Lang.	Male	Female
121.	mother	2	2	-	2	-
122.	no	2	2	-	2	-
123.	omen	2	2	-	2	-
124.	pamper	2	1	1	1	1
125.	person	2	2	-	1	1
126.	psychology	2	1	1	1	1
127.	queer	2	1	1	-	2
128.	restless	2	1	1	2	-
129.	ridiculous	2	1	1	2	-
130.	scare	2	1	1	2	-
131.	Scotch	2	2	-	2	-
132.	sex	2	2	-	2	-
133.	show	2	1	1	1	1
134.	sick	2	1	1	2	-
135.	sign	2	1	1	-	2
136.	skirmish	2	2	-	1	1
137.	stingy	2	2	-	2	-
138.	trouble	2	1	1	1	1
139.	troublesome	2	2	-	1	1
140.	unrestful	2	1	1	1	1
141.	voodoo	2	2	-	-	2
142.	wet	2	1	1	2	-
143.	whim	2	2	-	1	1
144.	witchdoctor	2	2	-	-	2
145.	worm(s)	2	2	-	1	1
146.	young	2	1	1	-	2

147-463.   (f = 1)

accomplish, accomplishing, affair, agnostic,
ambition, anatomy, ancient, annoy, annoyed, annoying, Arab, association, attitude, attraction,
away, awful, backdown, backward, bad luck, bag,
bat, belief, birth, blind, bonds, book, boring,
bossy, bothersome, bought, bound, bouquet, Brazil,
Buddha, bugaboo, cap, casts, catfish, catish,
catlike, celebrate, cell, chain, chance, character,
charming, childbirth, choosy, clothes, clover,
coin, complain, conformity, confused, coquettish,
cow, coy, crabby, crank, cranky, crazed, croquet,
cross, cult, cumbersome, dainty, dark, decay,
decorate, defete, delicate, design, desire, detail,
detain, deviation, die, disturbed, doctor, doubtful, door, doting, eccentric, enthusiasm, event,
exotic, faddish, failure, fair, false, fanciful,
febrile, fed, fed up, feeble, feed, feel, felt,
feigner, felish, feminine, fertility, fervent
desire, festival, fetch, fever, feverish, fez,
figgity, filling, fishy, fitting, fixation, flitty,
fluster, focus, fog, fond, foolhardy, foul, frenzy,
fretting, frightened, frigid, frill, frivolous,
fuss, fussy people, gala, garnish, gibberish,
giddy, girlish, glance, golf, gripe, guest, handi-
cap, hateful, heavy, help, Hitler, honor, horn,
horse, hunger, hurried, hurry, image, impatient,
India, Indian, infant, interest, Irish, issue,
jealous, Jewish, jittery, jungle, junk, lettuce,
literature, little, long, longing, lucky, madness,
man, mask, mason, meaning, mixed-up, monomaniac,
moody, most, moving, natives, neatness, never,
newborn, nice, nightgown, oddity, odor, old maid,
ordeal, ornery, outlandish, pat, peculiarity,
peculiar trait, peeve, perish, perversion, pervert,
petish, phallic, picking, pixie, plan, playful,
plaything, pomp, potty, prank, primitive, proud,
prudent, prudish, punish, puzzle, quaint, quarrel,
querulous, quite, quiver, rabbit, race, racket,
rash, ready, red, relic, repulsion, response,
rites, rod, roommate, rubbish, rule, rumor, sad,
sadist, sardines, sassy, scheme, Scottish, sea,
sensitive, sexy, sham, showy, sit, skiddish,
skiing, skimp, skimpy, skinny, slink, snake,
snobby, snubby, sore, splendor, spoil, squirming,
stale, stand, state, statues, stew, stick, sticker,
stink, stone, strength, strenuous, strive, stuck
up, stupid, sullen, Sweden, sweet, tact, tail,
talisman, task, tedious, temper, temperament,
tepid, terrible, test, tete, theory, think,

II-8 Fetish (contd)

		High	Low		
No.	Response	Total	Lang.	Lang. Male	Female

through, tied, time, timid, totem, toughy, trait, trickish, tricky, trinket, trivial, twitching, uncertain, unhappy, unliked, unreasonable, unsure, unusual, vocabulary, wanton, warm, waste, whimper, whirl, wiry, witch, witchcraft, womb, worn out, Yiddish
(No response - 27; Illegible - 8)

II-9 Grocer

			High	Low		
No.	Response	Total	Lang.	Lang.	Male	Female
1.	food(s)	388	182	206	194	194
2.	store	147	80	67	67	80
3.	man	60	27	33	28	32
4.	groceries	32	19	13	18	14
5.	market	27	15	12	10	17
6.	bill(s)	23	9	14	16	7
7.	sell(s)	19	7	12	13	6
8.	vegetable(s)	19	9	10	10	9
9.	seller	11	6	5	9	2
10.	bread	10	4	6	8	2
11.	apron	9	5	4	6	3
12.	clerk	9	2	7	7	2
13.	corner	8	7	1	5	3
14.	fruit	8	5	3	3	5
15.	meat	8	1	7	5	3
16.	money	8	4	4	5	3
17.	grocery	7	3	4	5	2
18.	apples	6	3	3	2	4
19.	buy	6	3	3	2	4
20.	green	6	5	1	3	3
21.	bag	5	4	1	2	3
22.	baker	5	2	3	3	2
23.	business	5	4	1	5	-
24.	businessman	5	3	2	3	2
25.	butcher	5	3	2	3	2
26.	can(s)	5	3	2	2	3
27.	friendly	5	2	3	-	5
28.	salesman	5	2	3	4	1
29.	box	3	1	2	1	2
30.	boy(s)	3	2	1	1	2
31.	buyer	3	-	3	2	1
32.	dad	3	1	2	1	2
33.	eat	3	2	1	2	1
34.	Italian	3	3	-	2	1
35.	lettuce	3	3	-	2	1
36.	merchant	3	3	-	3	-
37.	milk	3	2	1	2	1
38.	shop	3	2	1	2	1
39.	shopkeeper	3	3	-	2	1
40.	cashier	2	1	1	1	1
41.	friend	2	2	-	2	-
42.	goods	2	1	1	2	-
43.	Koplos Market	2	2	-	-	2
44.	oranges	2	2	-	1	1
45.	product(s)	2	1	1	1	1
46.	Safeway	2	-	2	1	1
47.	sales	2	2	-	2	-
48.	small	2	-	2	2	-
49.	strike	2	2	-	-	2
50.	supply(ies)	2	1	1	2	-
51.	worker	2	-	2	2	-

52-140. (f = 1)
bag of groceries, basket, Baywood store, beer, gib, Billy, candy, carrots, cash register, cat, celery, charge, checker, checkstand, client, commissary, corner grocer market, counter, crook, dark, dealer, dentist, dog, Dragomanovich, eating, economy, eggs, employer, fat man, food market, food store, foot, force, glasses, go,

II-9 Grocer (contd)

		High	Low		
No.	Response	Total	Lang.	Lang. Male	Female

grocery store, gross, grow, gum, happy, hard work, Homer Rickards, homey, housekeeper, husband, independent, jewels, Joe, labor, laborer, large, Laurnie, load, Louis, marketing, meatman, Monte Gardens, occupation, old, old man, Ossar, owner, pamphlet, paper bag, person, producer, proprietor, relic, retails, salami, servant, shopping, staple, storekeeper, story, supermarket, tailor, there, time, tin cans, tomatoes, trucks, uncle, unorganized, vender, warm, white, wholesale, work
(No response -1; Illegible - 2)

II-10 Hermit

			High	Low		
No.	Response	Total	Lang.	Lang.	Male	Female
1.	man(e)	145	75	70	81	64
2.	alone	129	67	62	55	74
3.	cave(s)	80	42	38	51	29
4.	beard	49	30	19	21	28
5.	recluse	39	24	15	18	21
6.	old	38	14	24	20	18
7.	lonely	37	13	24	16	21
8.	old man	30	15	15	13	17
9.	crab	23	13	10	12	11
10.	bum	19	7	12	12	7
11.	miser	19	11	8	11	8
12.	mountain(s)	18	10	8	8	10
13.	tramp	18	6	12	10	8
14.	loneliness	12	6	6	7	5
15.	introvert	11	4	7	7	4
16.	hobo	9	6	3	7	2
17.	lonesome	8	1	7	4	4
18.	secluded	8	7	1	3	5
19.	solitude	8	5	3	6	2
20.	seclusion	7	4	3	4	3
21.	isolation	6	2	4	3	3
22.	lazy	5	1	4	2	3
23.	bachelor	4	3	1	4	-
24.	cabin	4	3	1	3	1
25.	forest	4	2	2	1	3
26.	isolationist	4	3	1	2	2
27.	monk	4	-	4	1	3
28.	person	4	2	2	2	2
29.	Peter	4	1	3	3	1
30.	stupid	4	2	2	4	-
31.	Thoreau	4	2	2	2	2
32.	anti-social	3	2	1	2	1
33.	ascetic	3	-	3	2	1
34.	beggar	3	2	1	1	2
35.	dirty	3	2	1	1	2
36.	happy	3	2	1	2	1
37.	hide	3	3	-	1	2
38.	hill(s)	3	1	2	1	2
39.	idiot	3	-	3	3	-
40.	isolated	3	3	-	1	2
41.	lone	3	1	2	2	1
42.	poor	3	-	3	-	3
43.	woods	3	3	-	3	-
44.	beach	2	-	2	1	1
45.	beachcomber	2	-	2	1	1
46.	bearded man	2	2	-	1	1
47.	bug	2	-	2	1	1
48.	cage	2	1	1	-	2
49.	cave man	2	2	-	1	1
50.	clown	2	1	1	2	-
51.	desert	2	1	1	-	2
52.	eccentric	2	1	1	2	-
53.	esthetic	2	1	1	1	1
54.	extrovert	2	1	1	-	2
55.	fool	2	-	2	2	-

II-10 Hermit (contd)

No.	Response	Total	High Lang.	Low Lang.	Male	Female
56.	freedom	2	–	2	1	1
57.	Hermann	2	2	–	2	–
58.	hermitage	2	1	1	1	1
59.	hidden	2	1	1	–	2
60.	hut	2	–	2	–	2
61.	individualist	2	1	1	1	1
62.	isolate	2	–	2	–	2
63.	lonely person	2	1	1	–	2
64.	long beard	2	1	1	1	1
65.	me	2	2	–	1	1
66.	money	2	1	1	1	1
67.	nonconformist	2	1	1	1	1
68.	nut	2	–	2	1	1
69.	odd	2	1	1	1	1
70.	peace	2	–	2	1	1
71.	queer	2	1	1	2	–
72.	quiet	2	1	1	–	2
73.	ragged	2	1	1	1	1
74.	religion	2	1	1	1	1
75.	Rip Van Winkle	2	1	1	–	2
76.	seclude	2	2	–	1	1
77.	self	2	–	2	1	1
78.	short	2	–	2	2	–
79.	solitary	2	2	–	1	1
80.	Walden	2	2	–	1	1

81-213. (f = 1)
abnormal, age, aged, aloof, animal, apart, apple,
aunt, away, bawdy songs, beatnik, beer, Billy-
Goat Smith, bohemian, boo boo, boy, Buddhist,
bump, celibate, city, clam, cloistered, cookie,
crazy, dirt, dog, Dorman, dwarf, easy, Ezic,
fanatic, friar, friendly, frugal, fun, George,
German, glove, good, helmet, hermit, hideaway,
hold, hot, house, Humboldt, hunchback, inferiority,
island, Jose, Kermit, king, life, Lil' Abner,
little, live, loafer, lucky, man beard, man
(Thoreau), man with whiskers, medieval, Mike,
miner, misfit, mongrel, moron, Moses, moss hills,
mouse, nature, nonsense, non-socialist, nun, ogre,
old age, old extrovert, old man alone, outcast,
people-hate, persecuted, Peter the Hermit, Phil,
playboy, poor man, priest, prospector, prophet,
protection, rabbit, rags, rebel, rich, Robinson
Crusoe, rock, sad, sand, scavenger, sea, senior,
shack, sheep herder, shell, sheltered, sick person,
silent, slob, sloppy, snow - beard, solace, solo,
stay, stranger, tempest, thing, Tolstoy's story,
traveler, trees, ugly, uncle, unsociable, vagabond,
vagrant, wanderer, way, wealth, whisker, white,
wilderness, wisdom, wiser, witch, withdraw
(No response - 2; Illegible - 1)

II-11 Lotion

No.	Response	Total	High Lang.	Low Lang.	Male	Female
1.	hand(s)	308	150	158	136	172
2.	cream	197	96	101	103	94
3.	liquid	52	24	28	29	23
4.	skin	34	13	21	15	19
5.	smooth	25	16	9	5	20
6.	Jergens	18	11	7	6	12
7.	soft	18	14	4	5	13
8.	bottle	13	9	4	6	7
9.	smell	13	9	4	8	5
10.	cosmetic(s)	12	6	6	9	3
11.	motion	12	7	5	8	4
12.	creme	11	5	6	7	4
13.	hair	10	4	6	9	1
14.	oil	10	4	6	5	5
15.	soothing	9	5	4	2	7

II-11 Lotion (contd)

No.	Response	Total	High Lang.	Low Lang.	Male	Female
16.	tonic	9	2	7	8	1
17.	sooth(es)	8	4	4	5	3
18.	notion	7	4	3	5	2
19.	white	7	5	2	4	3
20.	hand cream	6	4	2	1	5
21.	sunburn	6	1	5	3	3
22.	Calamine	5	3	2	2	3
23.	face	5	1	4	3	2
24.	hand lotion	5	1	4	–	5
25.	shave	5	2	3	5	–
26.	suntan	5	2	3	3	2
27.	balm	4	4	–	3	1
28.	fluid	4	2	2	2	2
29.	mixture	4	1	3	3	1
30.	odor	4	1	3	4	–
31.	ointment	4	2	2	2	2
32.	perfume	4	–	4	3	1
33.	pink	4	2	2	1	3
34.	shaving	4	1	3	4	–
35.	sun	4	2	2	4	–
36.	water	4	–	4	4	–
37.	beauty	3	3	–	2	1
38.	creamy	3	2	1	1	2
39.	hand creme	3	2	1	3	–
40.	lanolin	3	1	2	3	–
41.	leg(s)	3	1	2	–	3
42.	location	3	1	2	1	2
43.	lotion	3	1	2	2	1
44.	medication	3	2	1	3	–
45.	oily	3	2	1	–	3
46.	place	3	3	–	3	–
47.	powder	3	–	3	3	–
48.	rub	3	1	2	3	–
49.	salve	3	3	–	2	1
50.	tan	3	–	3	1	2
51.	wet	3	–	3	–	3
52.	bath	2	1	1	–	2
53.	burn	2	2	–	2	–
54.	city	2	1	1	1	1
55.	cold	2	1	1	1	1
56.	cold cream	2	1	1	1	1
57.	cool	2	2	–	1	1
58.	London	2	2	–	1	1
59.	medicine	2	2	–	2	–
60.	smoothness	2	1	1	1	1
61.	soap	2	1	1	2	–
62.	solution	2	–	2	1	1
63.	sticky	2	1	1	–	2
64.	sum	2	–	2	1	1
65.	wash	2	–	2	2	–

66-138. (f = 1)
acnomel, alcohol, allergy, allotment, apply, aqua,
area, Avon, basin, Bay Rum Lotion, blue, bottle
of it, bread, care, Cashmere Bouquet, chapped,
China, cleanse, coat, complexion, cotton, crème,
dressing, face cream, feminine, first aid,
foolishness, girl, grease, hair oil, Johnson &
Johnson, lather, leaf, liquid(creamy), lode, lot,
make-up, Max-Factor, mild, milky, mix, moist,
moon, myrrh, palm, Palmolive, picture, Pond's
Lotion, portion, potun, protection, ?, rotation,
rubbing, Sea & Ski, shampoo, shaving lotion,
silicones, slimy, smelly, soft hands, spot,
stink, store, suntan lotion, suntanning, sweet,
talc, talcum, ticket, town, washing, women
(No response - 3; Illegible - 1)

II-12 Magnate

No.	Response	Total	High Lang.	Low Lang.	Male	Female
1.	iron	51	23	28	19	32
2.	magnet	44	17	27	24	20
3.	money	43	21	22	32	11
4.	attract(s)	41	24	17	22	19
5.	chemistry	33	14	19	10	23
6.	rich	33	20	13	23	10
7.	attraction	32	8	24	14	18
8.	steel	32	19	13	16	16
9.	metal(s)	30	14	16	10	20
10.	tycoon	27	20	7	19	8
11.	pull	25	6	19	8	17
12.	business	21	14	7	12	9
13.	large	20	7	13	9	11
14.	power	19	13	6	15	4
15.	magnesium	17	8	9	10	7
16.	judge	16	10	6	9	7
17.	ruler	15	8	7	9	6
18.	big	12	6	6	6	6
19.	draw	11	5	6	5	6
20.	physics	11	5	6	6	5
21.	man	10	10	–	5	5
22.	oil	10	6	4	7	3
23.	king	9	7	2	5	4
24.	millionaire	9	5	4	8	1
25.	wealth	9	7	2	5	4
26.	chemical	8	3	5	4	4
27.	electricity	8	3	5	8	–
28.	fly(ies)	8	3	5	5	3
29.	force	8	4	4	3	5
30.	great	8	3	5	5	3
31.	boss	7	5	2	5	2
32.	insect	7	4	3	1	6
33.	stick	7	3	4	2	5
34.	lead	6	2	4	2	4
35.	official	6	5	1	2	4
36.	potassium	6	5	1	3	3
37.	rock(s)	6	2	4	4	2
38.	worm(s)	6	3	3	3	3
39.	enlarge	5	1	4	3	2
40.	executive	5	3	2	3	2
41.	hold	5	3	2	2	3
42.	magistrate	5	1	4	2	3
43.	magnetic	5	3	2	1	4
44.	pin(s)	5	2	3	1	4
45.	science	5	4	1	2	3
46.	bug(s)	4	2	2	–	4
47.	horseshoe	4	3	1	1	3
48.	law	4	1	3	3	1
49.	leader	4	2	2	2	2
50.	manganese	4	1	3	2	2
51.	nothing	4	2	2	1	3
52.	pole(s)	4	2	2	4	–
53.	compass	3	3	–	1	2
54.	court	3	2	1	2	1
55.	maggot	3	1	2	2	1
56.	magna	3	1	2	2	1
57.	magnetize	3	2	1	2	1
58.	mineral	3	1	2	2	1
59.	North Pole	3	2	1	1	2
60.	rule(s)	3	2	1	1	2
61.	stagnate	3	1	2	2	1
62.	strong	3	–	3	–	3
63.	wealthy	3	2	1	3	–
64.	authority	2	2	–	1	1
65.	come	2	–	2	–	2
66.	copper	2	2	–	–	2
67.	document	2	2	–	1	1
68.	dog	2	1	1	1	1
69.	element	2	1	1	1	1
70.	finance	2	2	–	2	–
71.	financier	2	2	–	2	–
72.	head	2	2	–	1	1
73.	high	2	–	2	1	1
74.	huge	2	–	2	2	–
75.	important	2	1	1	2	–

II-12 Magnate (contd)

No.	Response	Total	High Lang.	Low Lang.	Male	Female
76.	judicial	2	1	1	–	2
77.	magnify	2	1	1	–	2
78.	magnitude	2	1	1	–	2
79.	nail	2	–	2	–	2
80.	north	2	1	1	1	1
81.	ore	2	–	2	2	–
82.	pick up	2	–	2	2	–
83.	red	2	2	–	1	1
84.	rich man	2	1	1	2	–
85.	sick	2	2	–	2	–
86.	silver	2	2	–	1	1
87.	throne	2	1	1	2	–
88.	together	2	–	2	–	2
89.	weight	2	1	1	1	1
90.	what	2	1	1	2	–

91–257. ($\underline{f}$ = 1)
accumulation, adhere, airplane, animal, ant, attach, awful, banker, baron, beech, beetle, bicarbonate, big boss, big shot, blue, book, boss-tycoon, bring, building, businessman, business wheel, buy, calcium, capitalist, Charlemagne, charta, charter, chief, cigar, cling, cognate, color, company, connection, contrast, crown, crystal, decide, declaration, diary, dictator, diplomat, dragnet, drawing, drawn, drawnness, draw together, duties, eat, electric, electric field, empty, encourage, enormous, enough, farce, field, filings, flux lines, free, Freud's theory, game, generous, geology, give, go, God, good, granite, grasp, gray, greatness, green, hairpin, hard, heavy, Henry Ford, Hugh, importance, impulse, industrialist, industry, investment, iron bar, iron piece, iron scraps, J. P. Rockefeller, justice, la authority, larger, Latin, lawyer, L.B. Mayer, leech, light, little, lines, magic, magician, Magna Carta, magnate, magnetic force, Magnin, Margie, master, mate, major, M.G., million, monopoly, monster, Morgan, mortgage, mosquito, nasty, nobel, object, order, orlon, paper, papyrus, penetrate, permanganate, person, physic, pig, pilgrims, plus, politics, poor, potentate, powerful, powerful man, principal, proclaim, pulling, question, rank, repulsion, richness, Rockefeller, royal, royalty, salt, size, society, solution, someone with money, stagnant, stall, steel bits, stone, store, straits, strength, strife, striking, stuck, success, suit, time, tool, true, typhoon, various, viceroy, white
(No response – 9; Illegible – 3)

II-13 Minstrel

No.	Response	Total	High Lang.	Low Lang.	Male	Female
1.	music	214	102	112	95	119
2.	show	100	52	48	48	52
3.	singer(s)	88	42	46	56	32
4.	song(s)	85	46	39	45	40
5.	Negro(es)	59	36	23	39	20
6.	man	49	21	28	22	27
7.	musician	43	17	26	23	20
8.	banjo	22	13	9	7	15
9.	sing	18	13	5	13	5
10.	guitar	15	10	5	7	8
11.	black	14	12	2	8	6
12.	colored	12	3	9	6	6
13.	wandering	11	7	4	7	4
14.	minister	10	3	7	4	6
15.	singing	10	5	5	8	2

II-13 Minstrel (contd)

No.	Response	Total	High Lang.	Low Lang.	Male	Female
16.	church	9	2	7	7	2
17.	clown	9	5	4	6	3
18.	lute	9	5	4	4	5
19.	player	9	6	3	4	5
20.	band	7	2	5	4	3
21.	funny	5	3	2	4	1
22.	play	5	3	2	4	1
23.	priest	5	1	4	1	4
24.	showman	5	3	2	4	1
25.	darky(ie)	4	4	-	3	1
26.	entertainment	4	4	-	1	3
27.	harp	4	2	2	1	3
28.	medieval	4	3	1	3	1
29.	vaudeville	4	3	1	2	2
30.	violin	4	2	2	3	1
31.	wanderer	4	1	3	4	-
32.	act(s)	3	-	3	2	1
33.	actor	3	2	1	2	1
34.	boy	3	3	-	2	1
35.	comedy	3	-	3	3	-
36.	instrument	3	1	2	1	2
37.	monkey	3	1	2	3	-
38.	musical	3	1	2	2	1
39.	person	3	-	3	3	-
40.	preacher	3	2	1	3	-
41.	traveler	3	-	3	2	1
42.	ballad	2	-	2	-	2
43.	castle	2	2	-	2	-
44.	circus	2	1	1	-	2
45.	dance	2	1	1	1	1
46.	dancer	2	1	1	-	2
47.	entertainer	2	1	1	1	1
48.	Europe	2	2	-	1	1
49.	hobo	2	2	-	2	-
50.	joker	2	-	2	1	1
51.	Jolson	2	2	-	2	-
52.	king	2	1	1	2	-
53.	laugh	2	-	2	2	-
54.	mandolin	2	2	-	1	1
55.	middle ages	2	2	-	1	1
56.	religion	2	1	1	1	1
57.	songster	2	1	1	2	-
58.	south	2	1	1	1	1
59.	travel	2	-	2	-	2
60.	traveling	2	-	2	-	2
61.	troubador	2	1	1	1	1
62.	vagabond	2	1	1	1	1
63.	wind	2	-	2	-	2

64-147. (f = 1)
Al Jolson, Allen-a-Dale, banjo player, bard,
black face, ceremony, clerical, color, colored
man, comedian, comic, cramp, cute, Danny Kaye,
dark, dirty, Dixie, Dixieland, dog, 18%, England,
Fay, flute, folk, fool, fun, grandpa, gypsy,
harmonica, hermit, jazz, jest, jester, joy,
lady, lazy, leader, long, louth, lyre, maker,
mammy, menstruate, minster, ministry, minor,
mister, money, music man, music show, music
wanderer, Negro, banjo, oboe, Odyssey, office,
old man, omen, orchestra, palace, people,
performer, poem, preaching, roam, Robinhood,
scop, servant, show business, show person,
slippers, songman, soup, speaker, strings,
strolling, strum, teacher, tin, variety, walk,
wander, wassail, women, worship
(No response - 1)

II-14 Oatmeal

No.	Response	Total	High Lang.	Low Lang.	Male	Female
1.	breakfast	246	105	141	121	125
2.	cereal	198	101	97	87	111
3.	food	139	55	84	96	43
4.	mush	129	84	45	63	66
5.	cookie(s)	41	24	17	20	21
6.	eat	28	13	15	18	10
7.	morning	11	3	8	6	5
8.	oats	11	4	7	10	1
9.	ugh	9	5	4	4	5
10.	grain	8	5	3	5	3
11.	wheat	7	4	3	1	6
12.	hot	6	4	2	3	3
13.	milk	6	3	3	4	2
14.	quaker(s)	6	5	1	2	4
15.	good	5	1	4	1	4
16.	mushy	5	3	2	2	3
17.	sugar	5	3	2	3	2
18.	flakes	4	2	2	-	4
19.	porridge	4	3	1	3	1
20.	terrible	4	2	2	4	-
21.	bowl	3	1	2	-	3
22.	bread	3	2	1	3	-
23.	cooked	3	2	1	3	-
24.	awful	2	-	2	1	1
25.	baby	2	-	2	1	1
26.	box	2	1	1	2	-
27.	cook	2	1	1	1	1
28.	cream	2	-	2	1	1
29.	dish	2	1	1	2	-
30.	dislike	2	1	1	-	2
31.	hate	2	2	-	1	1
32.	horse	2	2	-	1	1
33.	hungry	2	1	1	1	1
34.	lousy	2	1	1	2	-
35.	mess	2	1	1	-	2
36.	mother	2	2	-	1	1
37.	raisins	2	2	-	-	2
38.	soggy	2	-	2	-	2
39.	sticky	2	2	-	1	1
40.	thick	2	1	1	1	1
41.	warm	2	2	-	-	2
42.	yum	2	1	1	1	1

43-122. (f = 1)
allergic, baby food, bad, barf, basic, biscuit,
bland, boil, bowel, breakfast cereal, breakfast
food, breakfast meal, brown, butter, cakes,
camp, Cherrios, Co-op, corn, crackers, crap,
cream of wheat, crud, dry, eating, eggs, father,
filling, flat, food(breakfast), fraternity,
full, garbage, glue, granulated, grey, grind,
gut, health, healthful, hot cereal, ick,
indigestion, Kix, mills, monotone, muss, must,
nutritious, nourishment, oust, pablum, pancakes,
paste, play, pots, pudding, Roman, Saturday,
sawdust, school, sick, slime, slop, smell,
spoon, steck, sugar & cream, sweater, tan,
toast, traveling, ugly, water, wet, wheat germ,
while, worms, yetch, yummy
(Illegible - 1)

II-15 Omen

No.	Response	Total	High Lang.	Low Lang.	Male	Female
1.	sign(s)	196	114	82	105	91
2.	bad	96	51	45	56	40
3.	good	56	23	33	26	30
4.	evil	46	26	20	20	26
5.	amen	32	14	18	17	15
6.	warning	31	19	12	19	12
7.	luck	30	13	17	16	14

II-15 Omen (contd)

No.	Response	Total	High Lang.	Low Lang.	Male	Female
8.	superstition	22	10	12	9	13
9.	prayer	20	12	8	7	13
10.	saying	18	8	10	11	7
11.	deed	11	4	7	6	5
12.	prophecy	11	6	5	8	3
13.	foreboding	8	6	2	3	5
14.	man(e)	8	1	7	7	1
15.	end	7	1	6	2	5
16.	danger	6	2	4	2	4
17.	ill	6	3	3	4	2
18.	prediction	6	3	3	3	3
19.	witch(es)	6	5	1	2	4
20.	belief(s)	5	1	4	1	4
21.	Bible	5	1	4	2	3
22.	forewarning	5	2	3	2	3
23.	gift	5	1	4	1	4
24.	tale	5	3	2	-	5
25.	bad luck	4	1	3	1	3
26.	bird(s)	4	3	1	-	4
27.	Chinese	4	2	2	2	2
28.	fortune	4	1	3	3	1
29.	God	4	1	3	2	2
30.	god(s)	4	2	2	1	3
31.	good luck	4	1	3	2	2
32.	Greek(s)	4	1	3	1	3
33.	hex	4	2	2	2	2
34.	law	4	2	2	2	2
35.	meaning	4	2	2	2	2
36.	omelet	4	1	3	-	4
37.	ominous	4	4	-	2	2
38.	pray	4	1	3	4	-
39.	prophet	4	2	2	1	3
40.	token	4	3	1	4	-
41.	witchcraft	4	1	3	1	3
42.	word(s)	4	3	1	2	2
43.	black	3	2	1	3	-
44.	blessing	3	-	3	2	1
45.	charm	3	2	1	3	-
46.	country	3	-	3	3	-
47.	curse	3	2	1	1	2
48.	devil(s)	3	1	2	-	3
49.	dream	3	-	3	2	1
50.	fate	3	3	-	1	2
51.	future	3	-	3	2	1
52.	good sign	3	2	1	2	1
53.	idea	3	1	2	2	1
54.	Indian(s)	3	2	1	3	-
55.	message	3	-	3	2	1
56.	myth	3	1	2	3	-
57.	nonsense	3	1	2	2	1
58.	religion	3	3	-	1	2
59.	Shakespeare	3	2	1	2	1
60.	soothsayer	3	3	-	2	1
61.	story	3	3	-	1	2
62.	superstitious	3	1	2	3	-
63.	symbol	3	1	2	2	1
64.	taboo	3	2	1	1	2
65.	thought	3	2	1	1	2
66.	voodoo	3	3	-	2	1
67.	women	3	2	1	3	-
68.	book	2	1	1	1	1
69.	dark	2	1	1	-	2
70.	death	2	2	-	1	1
71.	fear	2	1	1	1	1
72.	final(s)	2	1	1	1	1
73.	food	2	-	2	-	2
74.	happening	2	1	1	-	2
75.	happiness	2	1	1	-	2
76.	mysterious	2	-	2	1	1
77.	news	2	2	-	1	1
78.	oath	2	2	-	-	2
79.	peace	2	1	1	-	2
80.	portent	2	2	-	-	2
81.	ritual	2	1	1	-	2
82.	signal	2	-	2	1	1
83.	sin	2	-	2	2	-

II-15 Omen (contd)

No.	Response	Total	High Lang.	Low Lang.	Male	Female
84.	song	2	1	1	2	-
85.	speech	2	1	1	2	-
86.	spell	2	1	1	1	1
87.	threat	2	1	1	1	1
88.	Viking(s)	2	-	2	1	1
89.	wiseman(e)	2	1	1	-	2
90.	wish	2	-	2	1	1

91-250. (f = 1)
above, Africa, agreement, albatross, alms, amulet, at last, axiom, bad deed, bad news, bad scene, benefit, black cat, black plague, boat, cabin, calm, cat, charge, church, clean, closing, cloudy, commoner, creed, cross, danger-sign, darkness, debt, demon, desert, dictionary, dire, dirt, doom, doubtful, dove, drug, eagle, eat, egg, elephants, fake, fantasy, fateful, feeling, forecast, forsee, foresight, foretelling, foretold, four-leaf clover, friend, garbage, goodness, good news, good or bad, Greece, guilt, gypsy, Hamlet, harbinger, hold, ill fall, indication, insight, jinx, Julius Caesar, legend, light, lightning, line, lucky, magic, manifest, maybe something good, money, monk, Moses, mystery, nature, necklace, necromancers, night, no, nomad, nothing, notice, nut, object, odd, ode, offering, oh, old, old men, om, Omar, omit, omnipotent, oracle, orgies, Oriental prophecy, out of order, owe, ox, pagan religion, pardon, parting, pass, people, perit, philosopher, phrase, pledge, poor, portend, portentous, precursor, predestination, premonition, prognostication, Prometheus, psychic, Romans, rule, sad, sadness, said, sailor, seagull, seer, semen, sentence, sermon, show, sigh, silence, silly, sorcery, speaking, spirit, statue, store, strong, swear, talisman, thing, tidings, trouble, truth, valuable, virtue, vision, vow, warn, wise, witchdoctor, worry, writing
(No response - 5; Illegible - 1)

II-16 Placard

No.	Response	Total	High Lang.	Low Lang.	Male	Female
1.	card(s)	158	69	89	80	78
2.	sign(s)	156	106	50	77	79
3.	name(s)	69	38	31	31	38
4.	poster	33	27	6	21	12
5.	board	31	15	16	15	16
6.	place	21	6	15	9	12
7.	paper	20	12	8	9	11
8.	bulletin	19	5	14	13	6
9.	placecard(s)	17	8	9	8	9
10.	dinner	15	4	11	8	7
11.	table	14	8	6	5	9
12.	billboard	13	7	6	5	8
13.	notice(s)	13	5	8	7	6
14.	cardboard	12	6	6	7	5
15.	word(s)	10	7	3	5	5
16.	pictures	9	6	3	4	5
17.	party(ies)	8	3	5	4	4
18.	plaque	7	2	5	4	3
19.	trophy	7	2	5	7	-
20.	advertisement	6	4	2	4	2
21.	game	6	2	4	4	2
22.	name card	6	3	3	4	2
23.	postcard	6	3	3	5	1
24.	white	6	3	3	2	4
25.	bulletin board	5	1	4	4	1
26.	play	5	3	2	3	2
27.	writing	5	3	2	1	4
28.	bridge	4	2	2	2	2

II-16 Placard (contd)

No.	Response	Total	High Lang.	Low Lang.	Male	Female
29.	letter(s)	4	3	1	4	-
30.	nothing	4	1	3	1	3
31.	plate	4	1	3	4	-
32.	school	4	1	3	2	2
33.	show	4	3	1	2	2
34.	wall	4	3	1	2	2
35.	bad	3	1	2	3	-
36.	banquet	3	2	1	1	2
37.	black	3	1	2	2	1
38.	book(s)	3	1	2	1	2
39.	football	3	3	-	3	-
40.	fun	3	-	3	1	2
41.	information	3	1	2	2	1
42.	language	3	2	1	2	1
43.	name tag	3	-	3	-	3
44.	note	3	1	2	1	2
45.	palace	3	-	3	2	1
46.	registration	3	1	2	3	-
47.	setting	3	1	2	3	-
48.	strike	3	2	1	3	-
49.	tag	3	2	1	1	2
50.	wood	3	2	1	-	3
51.	ace	2	1	1	-	2
52.	advertising	2	1	1	1	1
53.	award	2	1	1	1	1
54.	bus	2	2	-	-	2
55.	campaign	2	1	1	1	1
56.	car	2	1	1	2	-
57.	color	2	-	2	1	1
58.	convention	2	1	1	2	-
59.	discard	2	1	1	1	1
60.	doctor	2	2	-	-	2
61.	dull	2	-	2	1	1
62.	handbill	2	1	1	1	1
63.	here	2	1	1	1	1
64.	honor	2	1	1	-	2
65.	identification	2	1	1	2	-
66.	invitation	2	2	-	-	2
67.	marker	2	-	1	1	-
68.	music	2	1	1	1	1
69.	nameplate	2	1	1	1	1
70.	number	2	1	1	1	1
71.	peace	2	1	1	1	1
72.	poker	2	-	2	2	-
73.	post	2	2	-	1	1
74.	search	2	-	2	1	1
75.	seat	2	1	1	1	1
76.	see	2	-	2	1	1
77.	sit	2	1	1	1	1
78.	spelling	2	-	2	-	2
79.	sticker(s)	2	1	1	-	2
80.	stunt	2	2	-	2	-
81.	travel	2	1	1	2	-
82.	write	2	1	1	2	-

83-249. (f = 1)
ad, advertise, announce, announcement, anything,
are cards, arithmetic, armor, association,
Berkeley, birthday, blank, bombard, box, box
office, bright, business, call, caller, calm,
Carolee, cement, cheer, city, commercial, country,
crest, cue, cupboard, Dec. Art, decoration, desk,
dilly, diner, dining, directional, dish, display,
do, don't, door, drunk, dry, easy going, elf,
engraving, evil, experiment, face, famous, first,
flag, flash cards, folder, food, football game,
formal, frame, game football, gloomy, good, hard,
hell, help, herald, history, hot, hungry, hurt,
insignia, interesting, knight, lamp, large,
lazy, learn, lettering, license plate, look, man,
mat, metal, mood, movie, name-place, news, novelty,
object, parade, peaceful, pickard, pickets,
picture frame, placard, placed, placid, plain,
plastered, play card, playing card, plaza, pleasant, pleased, plockard, position, print, printing,
profession, profit, proverb, put, question, quiet,
rate, remove, restaurant, rooting section, rough,

II-16 Placard (contd)

sale, salesman, scene, seating, arrangement,
section, settled, shiffle, show card, sign
adverting, sign board, situation, skirt, slogan,
sluggish, smart, soft, Spanish, stamp, stand,
stately, statue, steel, store, story, strong,
sure, take, take care of, television, test,
Thanksgiving, thing, times, town, tray, trick,
T.V., U.C., uncertain, unknown, upper, villain,
vocabulary, what, wicket, window, work, written,
yellow
(No response - 16)

II-17 Preview

No.	Response	Total	High Lang.	Low Lang.	Male	Female
1.	movie(s)	312	170	142	157	155
2.	before	94	41	53	51	43
3.	show(s)	76	34	42	36	40
4.	sneak	61	32	29	31	30
5.	first	50	21	29	27	23
6.	see	36	18	18	19	17
7.	review	33	16	17	17	16
8.	picture(s)	25	15	10	12	13
9.	look	19	9	10	11	8
10.	beforehand	15	7	8	7	8
11.	play	15	9	6	11	4
12.	book	12	2	10	8	4
13.	peek	12	7	5	6	6
14.	beginning	11	4	7	8	3
15.	new	9	3	6	4	5
16.	glance	8	3	5	3	5
17.	glimpse	8	5	3	5	3
18.	coming	7	3	4	2	5
19.	introduction	7	1	6	6	1
20.	attraction	6	2	4	2	4
21.	insight	5	1	4	2	3
22.	interview	5	1	4	1	4
23.	showing	5	4	1	1	4
24.	ahead	4	2	2	3	1
25.	forecast	4	2	2	3	1
26.	magazine	4	2	2	2	2
27.	shorts	4	3	1	2	2
28.	start	4	2	2	4	-
29.	teaser	4	2	2	1	3
30.	parade	3	1	2	2	1
31.	people	3	1	2	1	2
32.	premiere	3	2	1	1	2
33.	see before	3	3	-	3	-
34.	theater(re)	3	1	2	-	3
35.	advance	2	2	-	-	2
36.	bad	2	1	1	-	2
37.	cinema	2	2	-	1	1
38.	coming attraction	2	1	1	-	2
39.	criticism	2	2	-	1	1
40.	excitement	2	2	-	1	1
41.	first showing	2	-	2	2	-
42.	foresight	2	2	-	1	1
43.	fun	2	2	-	1	1
44.	good	2	1	1	-	2
45.	lights	2	-	2	-	2
46.	look ahead	2	1	1	1	1
47.	motion picture	2	1	1	2	-
48.	newspaper	2	2	-	1	1
49.	read	2	-	2	1	1
50.	sight	2	-	2	1	1
51.	study	2	1	1	2	-
52.	surprise	2	1	1	1	1
53.	test	2	1	1	1	1
54.	writer	2	1	1	1	1

II-17 Preview (contd)

No.	Response	Total	High Lang.	Low Lang.	Male	Female

55-141. (f = 1)
act, actuality, after, anticipation, artist, author, awareness, blouse, blurb, broadcast, cartoon, chance, cinemascope, critic, curtain, delightful, early showing, end, entertainment, enticing, event, exciting, film, first glance at something, first look, foreglance, forelock, foresee, foreseeing, foretell, forthcoming, forward, furs, go over, glance at, guide, headstart, highlight, idea, in advance, inside story, interest, interesting, invention, judgement, look at before, looking, motion, move, mystery, news, newsreel, noise, notes, object, outline, paper, Paramount, picture of what is to come, precede, preface, prefix, prelock, preshow, pretext, reflection, scene, scoop, seeing, ships, show movies to come, sneak look, sneaky, society, soldiers, stage, summary, taste, tease, television, temptation, to implore, tonight, treat, vision, watch, words
(No response - 3)

II-18 Relic

No.	Response	Total	High Lang.	Low Lang.	Male	Female
1.	old	476	214	262	242	234
2.	antique(s)	117	76	41	66	51
3.	ancient	108	61	47	52	56
4.	saint	15	9	6	6	9
5.	Indian(s)	11	5	6	5	6
6.	religion	11	8	3	4	7
7.	fossil(s)	9	2	7	5	4
8.	past	9	6	3	5	4
9.	archeology	7	3	4	4	3
10.	bone(s)	7	4	3	1	6
11.	car	7	3	4	7	-
12.	age	5	4	1	4	1
13.	Egypt	5	2	3	3	2
14.	remain(s)	5	2	3	3	2
15.	statue	5	4	1	4	1
16.	anthropology	4	3	1	1	3
17.	artifact	4	4	-	4	-
18.	cherish	4	2	2	3	1
19.	object	4	2	2	2	2
20.	precious	4	4	-	1	3
21.	arrowhead	3	2	1	3	-
22.	church	3	1	2	1	2
23.	gun	3	1	2	3	-
24.	medal	3	3	-	-	3
25.	museum	3	1	2	3	-
26.	pyramid(s)	3	2	1	2	1
27.	ruin(s)	3	2	1	-	3
28.	sacred	3	1	2	1	2
29.	ship	3	2	1	2	1
30.	vase	3	2	1	2	1
31.	antiquity	2	2	-	2	-
32.	charm	2	1	1	2	-
33.	coin	2	1	1	2	-
34.	faith	2	-	2	2	-
35.	furniture	2	-	2	2	-
36.	good	2	-	2	1	1
37.	Greece	2	1	1	-	2
38.	history	2	2	-	1	1
39.	holy	2	2	-	-	2
40.	Incas	2	-	2	-	2
41.	mess	2	1	1	-	2
42.	piece	2	2	-	1	1
43.	relish	2	-	2	1	1
44.	souvenir	2	2	-	-	2
45.	stones	2	2	-	1	1
46.	time	2	-	2	-	2

II-18 Relic (contd)

No.	Response	Total	High Lang.	Low Lang.	Male	Female
47.	treasure	2	-	2	2	-
48.	wood	2	1	1	1	1

49-163. (f = 1)
ancestor, ancient statue, ancient thing, ancient times, anthro, antics, archaic, arrow, art, articles, ax, Aztecs, beautiful, beauty, before, body, bowl, broken, Catholic, cave, chair, Charlemagne, Christ, cloth, cobweb, columns, delicacy, digging, dish, England, enjoy, enjoyment, extra, favorite, funny, gems, God, god, gold, Grecian urn, ground, happy, heirloom, historic, historical, house, image, Indian arrowhead, interesting, item, jade, joke, keepsake, laugh, left, leftover, light, like, lines, long, Maya, memory, mend, mist, momento, Monroe, monument, new, odd, of, old buildings, old fashioned, old thing, omen, peace, pedestal, pen, picture, play, poem, pot, pottery, preciousness, prize, proof, rare, real, relevant, rely, remember, remembering, rememberance, reminder, remnant, replica, resemble, rest, scared, science, shoe, silver, something old, soup, sower, special, specimen, spice, stature, story, stunt, symbol, thing, tradition, woody, wreck
(No response - 2)

II-19 Skillet

No.	Response	Total	High Lang.	Low Lang.	Male	Female
1.	pan	440	216	224	220	220
2.	fry	75	36	39	47	28
3.	egg(s)	74	37	37	35	39
4.	frying pan	65	43	22	28	37
5.	food	47	18	29	31	16
6.	cook	35	20	15	19	16
7.	frying	32	17	15	16	16
8.	cooking	31	18	13	19	12
9.	stove	19	7	12	4	15
10.	bacon	18	7	11	8	10
11.	fish	16	8	8	11	5
12.	pot	14	8	6	7	7
13.	kitchen	12	8	4	4	8
14.	fire	10	5	5	5	5
15.	meat	9	1	8	7	2
16.	frypan	8	5	3	6	2
17.	hot	8	4	4	3	5
18.	grease	7	2	5	4	3
19.	pancake(s)	6	2	4	5	1
20.	iron	3	2	1	-	3
21.	kettle	3	2	1	3	-
22.	skill	3	3	-	3	-
23.	black	2	2	-	1	1
24.	eat	2	1	1	1	1
25.	hammer	2	2	-	1	1
26.	heavy	2	2	-	1	1
27.	oil	2	-	2	-	2
28.	oven	2	1	1	-	2
29.	potatoes	2	-	2	-	2
30.	smoke	2	1	1	2	-
31.	trout	2	2	-	1	1
32.	utensil	2	2	-	1	1
33.	woman(e)	2	1	1	2	-

34-75. (f = 1)
bad, bake, bat, black pan, burn, camping, chicken, chops, cuisine, culinary, dinner, electric, flat, fried chicken, fried egg, gillet, guillotine, gravy, hamburgers, handle, hashing, home, hot cakes, knife, ladle, metal, mother, outdoors, pan(frying), plate, play, sausage,

II-19 Skillet (contd)

No.	Response	Total	High Lang.	Low Lang.	Male	Female

sharp, ski, skillet, skittle, skull, spatula,
steak, tree, unclean, will
(Illegible - 1)

II-20 Suffrage

No.	Response	Total	High Lang.	Low Lang.	Male	Female
1.	woman(e)	349	174	175	192	157
2.	vote(s)	183	111	72	97	86
3.	voting	91	51	40	55	36
4.	right(s)	36	19	17	22	14
5.	suffer	33	11	22	18	15
6.	pain	31	18	13	17	14
7.	Negro(es)	26	14	12	16	10
8.	freedom	18	8	10	3	15
9.	slave(s)	13	3	10	4	9
10.	women's	12	4	8	5	7
11.	slavery	9	3	6	1	8
12.	poor	8	4	4	2	6
13.	hurt	7	3	4	2	5
14.	bondage	5	3	2	3	2
15.	equality	5	1	4	4	1
16.	help	5	1	4	3	2
17.	history	5	1	4	3	2
18.	surf	5	1	4	3	2
19.	bad	4	1	3	3	1
20.	children	4	2	2	1	3
21.	people	4	–	4	3	1
22.	trouble	4	1	3	3	1
23.	free	3	–	3	3	–
24.	law	3	1	2	1	2
25.	poverty	3	1	2	2	1
26.	punishment	3	–	3	2	1
27.	work	3	2	1	1	2
28.	abolition	2	2	–	1	1
29.	act	2	2	–	2	–
30.	burden	2	–	2	–	2
31.	election	2	1	1	–	2
32.	hardship	2	–	2	2	–
33.	harm	2	2	–	–	2
34.	Lincoln	2	2	–	1	1
35.	liquor	2	1	1	1	1
36.	privilege	2	1	1	1	1
37.	problem	2	1	1	1	1
38.	reform	2	1	1	–	2
39.	sad	2	1	1	–	2
40.	suffering	2	2	–	1	1
41.	war	2	–	2	1	1
42.	wound	2	–	2	2	–

43-138
agony, ail, alcohol, amendment, Anthony, Barton,
blood, camp, care, Carrie Nation, cause, chains,
China, Christ, church, constitution, crime, cross,
crusade, dry, early America, female, feudal,
fight, flags, good, government, gray women, home
for poor, honor, human, humanity, humble, hypochondriac, India, inspiration, integration,
intensely, know, liberty, low, manhood, martyrism,
masculinity, Mayflower, middle ages, misery, need,
1920, nothing, once, painful, parade, parents,
penitence, persecution, phooey, pity, politics,
prevail, rails, recognition, Russia, save, school,
segregation, silly, smart, sorrow, sorry, south,
strife, Susan Anthony, Switzerland, temperance,
terrible, thinking, tolerance, torture, treatment,
20th amendment, unfair, unhappiness, unhappy, unjust, voter, want, waterfront, weak, wealth,
whiskey, woman freedom suffrage, woman suffrage
leader, women voters, women's suffrage
(Illegible - 2)

II-21 Tempest

No.	Response	Total	High Lang.	Low Lang.	Male	Female
1.	storm(s)	529	297	232	305	224
2.	teapot	27	21	6	12	15
3.	Shakespeare	20	7	13	6	14
4.	wind	15	8	7	5	10
5.	woman(e)	15	5	10	9	6
6.	temper	12	3	9	5	7
7.	girl	10	5	5	8	2
8.	hot	10	5	5	6	4
9.	test tube	10	7	3	4	6
10.	bad	9	3	6	2	7
11.	fury	9	5	4	7	2
12.	wild	9	4	5	5	4
13.	trouble	7	1	6	3	4
14.	evil	6	2	4	1	5
15.	time	6	3	3	5	1
16.	tube	6	2	4	5	1
17.	calm	5	1	4	3	2
18.	devil	5	2	3	2	3
19.	temperation	5	4	1	2	3
20.	temptation	5	–	5	3	2
21.	wicked	5	–	5	2	3
22.	fugit	4	3	1	–	4
23.	mean	4	1	3	–	4
24.	mild	4	1	3	2	2
25.	siren	4	1	3	1	3
26.	stormy	4	3	1	1	3
27.	tempt	4	2	2	2	2
28.	weather	4	2	2	2	2
29.	alluring	3	1	2	1	2
30.	book	3	–	3	–	3
31.	burlesque	3	2	1	2	1
32.	gale	3	2	1	1	2
33.	hurricane	3	2	1	2	1
34.	man	3	–	3	1	2
35.	nothing	3	1	2	2	1
36.	play	3	1	2	2	1
37.	rain	3	3	–	1	2
38.	temperature	3	1	2	2	1
39.	temple	3	–	3	3	–
40.	tempter	3	3	–	–	3
41.	tempting	3	1	2	1	2
42.	tossed	3	2	1	1	2
43.	waves	3	1	2	2	1
44.	witch	3	1	2	2	1
45.	anger	2	2	–	1	1
46.	angry	2	–	2	1	1
47.	chaos	2	1	1	2	–
48.	cold	2	–	2	–	2
49.	Dan	2	–	2	2	–
50.	desire	2	–	2	1	1
51.	excitement	2	2	–	2	–
52.	fast	2	–	2	2	–
53.	female	2	1	1	–	2
54.	fun	2	1	1	1	1
55.	goddess	2	1	1	1	1
56.	hard	2	–	2	1	1
57.	high	2	1	1	–	2
58.	liquor	2	–	2	1	1
59.	lure	2	1	1	1	1
60.	rage	2	1	1	–	2
61.	sea	2	2	–	1	1
62.	sex	2	1	1	1	1
63.	sexy	2	2	–	2	–
64.	shrew	2	–	2	–	2
65.	tea	2	–	2	2	–
66.	tease	2	–	2	–	2
67.	teasing	2	1	1	1	1
68.	temperament	2	–	2	2	–
69.	trial	2	2	–	1	1
70.	troubled	2	1	1	–	2

71-210. (f = 1)
actress, allure, anti, bed, Bible, blow, brew,
broils, bug, buxom, child, church, clear, climax,
coming, conflict, cry, dame, dangerous, dare,
dark, disorder, Don, drinking, eat, emotion,
English, excited, experiments, femme fatal,

II-21 Tempest (contd)

		High	Low		
No.	Response	Total	Lang.	Lang.	Male	Female

fierce, fire, firey, foolish, forceful, friend, fugitive, God, good, grill, hat, heat, highest, horrible, hunt, hurry, Inca, intriguing, inviting, kill, kind, lake, land, leader, less, lie, like, lost, loud, lovely, luring, lust, luxury, Macbeth, mad, mice, mountain, movie, mythology, nice, nude, ocean, odd, pace, parody, passion, peace, place, poem, power, prophet, quarrel, raging, rampant, refuge, rising, rival, rough, rousing, Salome, school, ship, show, silly, sin, sinner, sister, sky, slow, soft, steady, stealthy, store, storm of bugs, storm on sea, story, strength, strict, stripper, sun, tall, tame, teacher, television, Tempest Storm, tempted, temptful, top, torment, torn, tough, troubador, turbulent, turmoil, type, unknown, vile, villain, violent, voice, volumptuous, war, warm, water, weird, wet, whirl, wind storm, windy, zeal
(No response - 7)

II-22 Traitor

No.	Response	High Total	Lang.	Low Lang.	Male	Female
1.	spy(ies)	87	47	40	49	38
2.	bad	80	40	40	38	42
3.	Arnold	54	33	21	39	15
4.	country	52	27	25	22	30
5.	enemy	50	24	26	24	26
6.	man	45	22	23	23	22
7.	treason	43	27	16	23	20
8.	B. (Benedict) Arnold*	39	15	24	24	15
9.	coward	24	12	12	16	8
10.	war	17	11	6	7	10
11.	evil	14	10	4	4	10
12.	communist(s)	13	4	9	4	9
13.	villian	13	10	3	6	7
14.	rat	12	4	8	9	3
15.	patriot	11	6	5	6	5
16.	thief	11	7	4	6	5
17.	Benedict	10	7	3	4	6
18.	Burr	10	6	4	6	4
19.	criminal	10	6	4	6	4
20.	death	8	4	4	5	3
21.	false	8	4	4	1	7
22.	rebel	8	2	6	5	3
23.	against	7	4	3	1	6
24.	hang	6	4	2	4	2
25.	hero	6	4	2	4	2
26.	A. (Aaron) Burr	6	4	2	2	4
27.	betray	5	2	3	3	2
28.	betrayer	5	3	2	-	5
29.	cheat	5	4	1	2	3
30.	crook	5	3	2	5	-
31.	disloyal	5	3	2	3	2
32.	flag	5	3	2	2	3
33.	convict	4	-	4	2	2
34.	deceiver	4	3	1	1	3
35.	gun	4	3	1	3	1
36.	Judas	4	3	1	-	4
37.	liar	4	2	2	2	2
38.	soldier	4	1	3	4	-
39.	unloyal	4	1	3	1	3
40.	wrong	4	3	1	1	3
41.	bad man	3	1	2	3	-
42.	deserter	3	2	1	1	2
43.	dictator	3	2	1	1	2
44.	dog	3	1	2	3	-
45.	exile	3	-	3	2	1

* - (Includes the response Ben. Arnold)

II-22 Traitor (contd)

No.	Response	High Total	Lang.	Low Lang.	Male	Female
46.	fool	3	-	3	2	1
47.	hanging	3	2	1	3	-
48.	hate	3	2	1	3	-
49.	history	3	-	3	2	1
50.	jail	3	2	1	1	2
51.	kill	3	1	2	3	-
52.	louse	3	2	1	1	2
53.	no good	3	1	2	2	1
54.	sabotage	3	1	2	2	1
55.	scoundrel	3	2	1	-	3
56.	Vic's	3	-	3	-	3
57.	America	2	1	1	-	2
58.	bad guy	2	1	1	1	1
59.	cause	2	2	-	-	2
60.	cheater	2	-	2	1	1
61.	citizen	2	1	1	-	2
62.	crime	2	2	-	-	2
63.	deceit	2	2	-	1	1
64.	die	2	1	1	2	-
65.	disgrace	2	1	1	2	-
66.	dislike	2	1	1	-	2
67.	espionage	2	-	2	1	1
68.	fiend	2	1	1	-	2
69.	France	2	-	3	-	2
70.	friend	2	2	-	2	-
71.	Hale	2	1	1	2	-
72.	heretic	2	1	1	-	2
73.	Hiss	2	1	1	2	-
74.	illegal	2	1	1	1	1
75.	loyal	2	1	1	1	1
76.	loyalist	2	-	2	-	2
77.	mean	2	-	2	-	2
78.	money	2	-	2	2	-
79.	offender	2	1	1	1	1
80.	Patrick Henry	2	1	1	1	1
81.	pirate(s)	2	1	1	-	2
82.	quisling	2	1	1	2	-
83.	robber	2	1	1	1	1
84.	Russia	2	-	2	-	2
85.	scum	2	2	-	2	-
86.	shot	2	1	1	1	1
87.	squealer	2	-	2	1	1
88.	Taylor	2	-	2	1	1
89.	trait	2	1	1	1	1
90.	traitress	2	-	2	-	2
91.	turncoat	2	-	2	2	-
92.	unfair	2	1	1	-	2
93.	unfaithful	2	1	1	-	2
94.	untrue	2	2	-	1	1
95.	unworthy	2	1	1	-	2
96.	U.S.	2	1	1	1	1
97.	Vic	2	2	-	2	-
98.	wicked	2	2	-	-	2

99-252. (f = 1)

agent, alien, American revolution, anger, army, assassin, bad stud, bag, bandit, banned, bear, beast, betrayal, betrayed, Bill, blood, Booth, born, brave, British, Brutus, Buhlig, bum, car, chains, cheap, chicken, Chinese, clay, collaborator, commie, compatriot, confused, conspirator, constitution, conviction, cunning, Dick, dirty, dishonest, dishonesty, disrespect, distrust, doctor, double-faced, Edward, enclosed, expel, faithful, farm, fear, fellow, flee, foreigner, forgive, fraud, gallows, Ganelon, gator, Germany, give-up, good, good person, government, guillotine, hanged, hatred, heather, heel, here, hills, hobo, horse, hostile, hypocrite, infamy, Jackson, Jap, John Booth, John Paul Jones, Korea, land, lie, mad, man B. Arnold, <u>Man Without A Country</u>, Marx, menace, misunderstand, Napoleon, nasty, nation, native, Nazi, Nolan, not, nothing, oppression, pain, Pat, patriotic, people, person, prison, prisoner, punishment, reason, red, relative, renegade, republic, respect, revenge, revolution, Robert E. Lee, rope, Russian, shame

II-22 Traitor (contd)

ship, shoot, skunk, slob, sneak, sneaky, Socrates, story, suitor, survivor, suspect, tailor, teller, terrible, thoughtful, trader, trap, travel, treachery, trickery, turn, two times, tyrant, unbeliever, unhappy, unjust, unknown, untrustful, untrustworthy, unwise, Urban VIII, victim, victor, victory, violence, you
(No response - 6; Illegible - 2)

II-23 Wafer

No.	Response	Total	High Lang.	Low Lang.	Male	Female
1.	cookie(s)	303	149	154	139	164
2.	cracker(s)	97	44	53	41	56
3.	thin	85	44	41	49	36
4.	food	73	32	41	44	29
5.	biscuit	49	29	20	21	28
6.	bread	32	20	12	23	9
7.	eat	30	12	18	13	17
8.	candy	23	12	11	12	11
9.	communion	21	13	8	9	12
10.	vanilla	19	13	6	9	10
11.	church	15	7	8	11	4
12.	waffle(s)	11	7	4	9	2
13.	small	10	3	7	3	7
14.	chocolate	7	4	3	3	4
15.	water	7	2	5	4	3
16.	drink	6	3	3	3	3
17.	ice cream	5	3	2	2	3
18.	pancake(s)	5	2	3	3	2
19.	sugar	5	2	3	4	1
20.	wine	5	3	2	2	3
21.	cool	4	-	4	1	3
22.	diet	4	3	1	-	4
23.	disc	4	3	1	4	-
24.	milk	4	2	2	2	2
25.	wet	4	2	2	4	-
26.	Host	3	1	2	3	-
27.	light	3	1	2	2	1
28.	mint	3	2	1	3	-
29.	poor	3	3	-	-	3
30.	round	3	1	2	1	2
31.	slice	3	-	3	3	-
32.	toast	3	2	1	3	-
33.	wanderer	3	2	1	1	2
34.	wave	3	-	3	2	1
35.	baby(ies)	2	-	2	1	1
36.	blue	2	-	2	1	1
37.	cold	2	1	1	2	-
38.	eating	2	2	-	2	-
39.	good	2	1	1	-	2
40.	hungry	2	-	2	1	1
41.	ice	2	2	-	-	2
42.	layer	2	-	2	2	-
43.	Mass	2	2	-	-	2
44.	nabisco	2	-	2	2	-
45.	orphan	2	1	1	1	1
46.	rye krisp	2	1	1	-	2
47.	sacrament	2	2	-	-	2
48.	salt	2	-	2	1	1
49.	sea	2	1	1	-	2
50.	square	2	1	1	1	1
51.	sweet	2	-	2	-	2
52.	table	2	1	1	1	1
53.	tramp	2	1	1	1	1
54.	wallet	2	1	1	2	-

55-154. (f = 1)
bar, bet, bisquick, boat, body, breakfast, brown, bun rabbit or biscuit, cake, calorie, Catholic, cheese, chew, cigarette, clear, confirmation,

II-23 Wafer (contd)

crisp, crumb, cup, dessert, do, drinking, dry, edible, England, Europe, fat, faucet, figure (human), fish, flake, flat, full, go, gone, hamburger, handle, H2O, holy, iron, lie, little, liquid, loaf, medicine, middle, missed, necco, nice, ocean, outstand, pail, paper, peppermint, pills, plate, pool, pound, reduce, release, religion, sailing, sandwich, sections, short, shredded, side, slim, snack, soft, solid, soup, stagger, still, stumble, substance, sugar wafers, swim, tablet, tale, tall, taste, tasty, tea, thin sheet, tongue, wafer, wait, wander, wanting, warf, waver, wax, wax paper, wayfarer, weaver, well, wheat, wheel, wiener
(No response - 4; Illegible - 1)

II-24 Whisker

No.	Response	Total	High Lang.	Low Lang.	Male	Female
1.	beard	245	131	114	133	112
2.	shave	165	79	86	119	46
3.	hair	101	51	50	59	42
4.	man(e)	51	26	25	10	41
5.	cat(s)	39	23	16	16	23
6.	face	38	16	22	22	16
7.	whiskey	28	13	15	19	9
8.	rough	27	11	16	7	20
9.	mustache	23	12	11	9	14
10.	razor	20	12	8	16	4
11.	chin	18	10	8	7	11
12.	broom	12	5	7	9	3
13.	Santa Claus	11	1	10	-	11
14.	shaving	11	4	7	8	3
15.	tickle	11	9	2	1	10
16.	dog	9	5	4	3	6
17.	brush	7	-	7	3	4
18.	old man	7	1	6	5	2
19.	scratch	7	7	-	2	5
20.	black	6	3	3	3	3
21.	drink	6	2	4	3	3
22.	sharp	6	2	4	2	4
23.	shaver	6	4	2	6	-
24.	bohemian	5	2	3	4	1
25.	drunk	5	3	2	4	1
26.	old	5	4	1	1	4
27.	scratchy	5	3	2	-	5
28.	stiff	5	5	-	1	4
29.	gray (grey)	4	2	2	1	3
30.	liquor	4	-	4	1	3
31.	boy(s)	3	2	1	-	3
32.	burn	3	1	2	1	2
33.	fuzzy	3	2	1	1	2
34.	white	3	2	1	1	2
35.	bristle(s)	2	2	-	-	2
36.	cheek	2	2	-	-	2
37.	fast	2	-	2	1	1
38.	growth	2	-	2	1	1
39.	itch	2	2	-	2	-
40.	nose	2	1	1	1	1
41.	Santa	2	2	-	-	2
42.	stick	2	1	1	2	-
43.	ticklish	2	1	1	-	2
44.	whiskers	2	-	2	-	2

45-120. (f = 1)
beatnik, beer, bend, bird, bitter, blade, boheim, booze, brisk, bristly, bush, bushy, cards, coarse, daddy, drunker, fair, friend, frisky, fun, fur, fuzz, grandfather, grandpa, grizzly, grow, hamster, hermit, hobo, horrible, hurt, indecision, jaw, Keith, Ken, loiter, male, manhood, man's,

II-24 Whisker (contd)

High Low

No.	Response	Total	Lang.	Lang.	Male	Female

mixer, mother, old crow, on cat, pain, pappy,
Pioneer Day, pop, professors, pull, puller, quick,
quiet, rabbit, rash, reeler, Rollectric, rub, rum,
seal, skin, small, soda, something to stay away
from, stickers, stickery, straight, straw, stubble,
sunburn, thick, tickly, tough, tusk, unshaven,
whiskering, yellow
(No response - 3; Illegible -2)

III-1 Author

High Low

No.	Response	Total	Lang.	Lang.	Male	Female
1.	book(s)	545	267	278	278	267
2.	writer(s)	193	91	102	109	84
3.	write	29	17	12	16	13
4.	man	27	12	15	17	10
5.	story	22	13	9	13	9
6.	Hemingway	12	7	5	6	6
7.	title	12	6	6	6	6
8.	novel	11	6	5	3	8
9.	poet	8	3	5	3	5
10.	writing	7	4	3	4	3
11.	person	6	3	3	1	5
12.	literature	4	2	2	2	2
13.	Poe	4	3	1	3	1
14.	Steinbeck	4	4	-	2	2
15.	Longfellow	3	3	-	1	2
16.	name	3	1	2	1	2
17.	work	3	2	1	1	2
18.	wrote	3	2	1	1	2
19.	creator	2	2	-	-	2
20.	critics	2	2	-	2	-
21.	Dickens	2	-	2	-	2
22.	famous	2	2	-	1	1
23.	Ferber	2	-	2	-	2
24.	Huxley	2	1	1	2	-
25.	originator(s)	2	1	1	2	-
26.	play	2	2	-	-	2
27	R. L. Stevenson	2	2	-	2	-
28.	Twain	2	1	1	1	1
29.	woman	2	-	2	2	-

30-111. (f = 1)
actress, Alcott, artist, authoress, beard,
Benedict, bookworm, Bruce Cotton, Buck Cassiren,
Chaucer, composer, Conrad, Costain, credit,
Dostoevsky, Douglas, Elliot, fame, goldbug,
grandparent, Gunther, Hawthorne, Heinlein, information, intelligent, Jackson, John, King,
lecturer, life, London, Mann, Mansfield, Maugham,
me, Miller, money, Mrs. Holtsmark, myself,
Nathaniel nom de plume, novelist, O'Henry,
O'Neill, origin, Orwell, Ovid, page, Paine, pen,
personage, pipe, pipe & suede jacket, plagiarism,
published, reading, savant, Scott, sell,
Shakespeare, Sinclair Lewis, sophistication,
spasm, speaker, Steinberg, Stevens, Stevenson,
Tale of Two Cities, text, thinker, thinking,
this, Thomas Mann, Thor, thought, typewriter,
view, Witcome, works, write book, written

III-2 Belief

High Low

No.	Response	Total	Lang.	Lang.	Male	Female
1.	religion	206	96	110	112	94
2.	God	94	43	51	43	51
3.	faith	76	39	37	35	41
4.	idea(s)	65	33	32	39	26
5.	thought(s)	39	17	22	20	19
6.	truth	38	20	18	15	23
7.	believe	23	6	17	16	7
8.	reason(s)	23	13	10	6	17
9.	think	23	12	11	10	13
10.	church	19	11	8	6	13
11.	know	19	9	10	6	13
12.	disbelief	17	8	9	14	3
13.	trust	16	6	10	8	8
14.	creed	15	10	5	8	7
15.	dogma	14	11	3	7	7
16.	ideal(s)	14	7	7	5	9
17.	true	13	5	8	8	5
18.	opinion	12	10	2	7	5
19.	conviction	10	7	3	8	2
20.	knowledge	10	7	3	5	5
21.	doctrine	9	4	5	4	5
22.	feeling(s)	9	3	6	5	4
23.	lie(s)	8	5	3	6	2
24.	right(s)	7	2	5	5	2
25.	strong	6	3	3	2	4
26.	wisdom	6	4	2	3	3
27.	Bible	5	1	4	3	2
28.	principle(s)	5	3	2	4	1
29.	false	4	2	2	3	1
30.	philosophy	4	1	3	-	4
31.	relief	4	1	3	1	3
32.	tenet	4	2	2	2	2
33.	understanding	4	3	1	-	4
34.	concept	3	3	-	1	2
35.	good	3	1	2	2	1
36.	hold	3	3	-	2	1
37.	hope	3	1	2	1	2
38.	I	3	1	2	1	2
39.	imagination	3	3	-	3	-
40.	life	3	-	3	1	2
41.	love	3	2	1	1	2
42.	none	3	3	-	3	-
43.	superstition	3	2	1	-	3
44.	tale	3	3	-	3	-
45.	theory	3	2	1	1	2
46.	tradition	3	1	2	2	1
47.	what	3	1	2	2	1
48.	belief	2	1	1	2	-
49.	Clifford	2	2	-	2	-
50.	custom	2	-	2	1	1
51.	desire(s)	2	-	2	1	1
52.	devotion	2	2	-	-	2
53.	ethics	2	2	-	1	1
54.	knowing	2	1	1	-	2
55.	moral(s)	2	1	1	1	1
56.	no	2	2	-	2	-
57.	non-belief	2	-	2	2	-
58.	nothing	2	-	2	-	2
59.	real	2	1	1	2	-
60.	realize	2	-	2	-	2
61.	religious	2	-	2	1	1
62.	understand	2	1	1	1	1
63.	way	2	-	2	-	2

64-165. (f = 1)
acquired, action, agnostic, agree, ascertation,
assailed, atheism, attitude, awful, bad, basic,
bias, blind, book, Buddha, catholic, Christian,
complicated, conception, concern, consistent,
create, credo, credulous, croyance, desk, dis-
believe, dismay, doubt, doubtful, encourage,
eyes, fact, fanatic, feel, fiction, fight,
follow, freedom, goal, great, happy, hearsay,
heathen, heritage, holy, ideology, idol, in,
individualism, ingrained, inhibition, interest,
intuitive, judgment, leaf, listen, lying, magic,
many, not, old, omen, people, person, ponder,

III-2 Belief (contd)

No.	Response	Total	High Lang.	Low Lang.	Male	Female

preach, preference, prejudice, pride, race,
radical, ready, reliance, religion, ridicule,
sacred, satisfaction, say, saying, school, search,
sincere, some, something, song, speech, stand,
standard, story, support, thinking, though,
transcendentalism, trouble, try, unbelief,
understandment, value, why, word, yes
(No response - 2; Illegible - 1)

III-3 Biscuit

No.	Response	Total	High Lang.	Low Lang.	Male	Female
1.	food	164	62	102	111	53
2.	dog(s)	104	67	37	49	55
3.	bread	98	46	52	42	56
4.	butter	74	46	28	30	44
5.	eat	71	36	35	39	32
6.	dough	63	38	25	37	26
7.	honey	29	15	14	10	19
8.	cookie	28	12	16	12	16
9.	hot	22	10	12	11	11
10.	roll(s)	20	7	13	11	9
11.	flour	18	8	10	5	13
12.	hard	17	9	8	11	6
13.	bun	13	7	6	6	7
14.	cake	13	5	8	8	5
15.	good	13	4	9	7	6
16.	breakfast	12	6	6	6	6
17.	muffin	12	9	3	4	8
18.	jam	11	6	5	3	8
19.	sea	11	7	4	9	2
20.	cracker(s)	10	2	8	4	6
21.	dinner	10	7	3	3	7
22.	brown	8	4	4	4	4
23.	cook	8	3	5	6	2
24.	horse	8	3	5	4	4
25.	Nabisco	8	4	4	5	3
26.	mix	7	5	2	4	3
27.	Bisquick	6	2	4	5	1
28.	eating	6	4	2	2	4
29.	oven	6	4	2	5	1
30.	tea	6	5	1	1	5
31.	bake	5	-	5	2	3
32.	gravy	5	2	3	3	2
33.	eater	4	2	2	3	1
34.	biscuit	3	2	1	2	1
35.	cooking	3	1	2	3	-
36.	cutter	3	3	-	3	-
37.	fluffy	3	2	1	-	3
38.	jelly	3	1	2	1	2
39.	baker	2	-	2	2	-
40.	Crocker	2	2	-	2	-
41.	crumb	2	2	-	-	2
42.	doe	2	2	-	2	-
43.	dry	2	2	-	-	2
44.	homemade	2	1	1	-	2
45.	hunger	2	1	1	-	2
46.	lunch	2	-	2	1	1
47.	pan	2	1	1	2	-
48.	round	2	1	1	-	2
49.	stale	2	-	2	-	2
50.	starch	2	-	2	1	1
51.	water	2	1	1	1	1

52-120. ($\underline{f}$ = 1)
bayer, Beatrice, Betty C., Betty Crocker, Betty
Crocker Bisquick, bicycle, blueberries, bog, box,
break, burnt, calories, candy, chew, chicken,
cinnamon, company, cornbread, crumpet, crunch,
cut, delicious, doughnut, eggs, England, English,
fattening, floury, foot, frozen, golden, great,

III-3 Biscuit (contd)

No.	Response	Total	High Lang.	Low Lang.	Male	Female

grocer, hardness, hardtack, home, laugh, meat,
melted butter, melting, milk, money, morning,
mother, national, N.B.C., Pillsbury, place,
powder, quick, racehorse, Rin-Tin-Tin, sawdough,
sell, Shredded Wheat, soft, steam, steel, Sunday,
Sunday breakfast, Sunshine, syrup, Texas, thin,
tisquit, wafer, warm, white, work

III-4 Candle

No.	Response	Total	High Lang.	Low Lang.	Male	Female
1.	light	435	210	225	230	205
2.	flame	115	65	50	63	52
3.	wax	115	56	59	58	57
4.	stick(s)	72	33	39	46	26
5.	fire	47	17	30	23	24
6.	wick	32	22	10	12	20
7.	burn(s)	24	15	9	10	14
8.	power	15	1	14	15	-
9.	holder	10	9	1	4	6
10.	Christmas	6	4	2	-	6
11.	church	6	2	4	3	3
12.	dark	4	1	3	2	2
13.	tallow	4	2	2	2	2
14.	birthday(s)	3	2	1	-	3
15.	blow	3	2	1	-	3
16.	burning	3	2	1	3	-
17.	flicker	3	3	-	1	2
18.	lit	3	1	2	1	2
19.	baby	2	1	1	-	2
20.	beeswax	2	2	-	-	2
21.	bell	2	2	-	1	1
22.	bright	2	2	-	1	1
23.	cake	2	-	2	1	1
24.	dinner	2	1	1	1	1
25.	evening	2	1	1	-	2
26.	glow	2	2	-	1	1
27.	hot	2	1	1	2	-
28.	lightning	2	1	1	1	1
29.	match	2	2	-	2	-
30.	night	2	-	2	1	1
31.	pinning	2	1	1	-	2
32.	religion	2	-	2	-	2
33.	snuffer	2	1	1	1	1
34.	soft	2	2	-	1	1
35.	table	2	1	1	-	2
36.	warm	2	2	-	-	2
37.	yellow	2	1	1	1	1

38-98. ($\underline{f}$ = 1)
abra, apple red, beautiful, big game week, book,
buggy, candle, candlestick, carbon, castle,
cavities, ceremony, chocolate, cozy, darkness,
ends, engagement, experiment, faith, flamer,
flax, foot, girl, glass, halo, handle, lavender,
Liberace, lighten, lights out, maker, mine,
minute, moonlight, moth, nightgown, no electricity, out, paper, paraffin, peace, photography,
piano, pledging, pretty, race, restaurant, Roman,
romance, Sabbath, steak, sweet, Texas, tradition,
wan, was, wedding, white, wicker, window, yellow
light
(Illegible - 1)

III-5 Circus

No.	Response	Total	High Lang.	Low Lang.	Male	Female
1.	clown(s)	357	194	163	185	172
2.	elephant(s)	102	51	51	47	55
3.	fun	102	46	56	51	51
4.	animal(s)	98	43	55	47	51
5.	tent(s)	48	27	21	29	19
6.	lion(s)	14	6	8	8	6
7.	ring(s)	14	10	4	8	6
8.	carnival	10	5	5	5	5
9.	horse(s)	10	3	7	3	7
10.	noise	8	3	5	3	5
11.	people	8	5	3	4	4
12.	show	8	2	6	4	4
13.	trapeze	8	4	4	3	5
14.	entertainment	7	4	3	6	1
15.	excitement	7	4	3	3	4
16.	funny	7	4	3	4	3
17.	act(s)	6	1	5	4	2
18.	laughter	6	4	2	3	3
19.	monkey(s)	6	3	3	5	1
20.	performer(s)	6	4	2	6	–
21.	boy	5	1	4	5	–
22.	time	5	3	2	4	1
23.	amusement	4	3	1	2	2
24.	crowd(s)	4	2	2	2	2
25.	gaiety	4	2	2	1	3
26.	gay	4	3	1	1	3
27.	parade	4	1	3	2	2
28.	round	4	3	1	3	1
29.	sawdust	4	3	1	2	2
30.	three-ring(s)	4	1	3	2	2
31.	tiger(s)	4	2	2	3	1
32.	circle	3	3	–	3	–
33.	color	3	2	1	2	1
34.	peanuts	3	1	2	–	3
35.	performance	3	2	1	2	1
36.	play	3	1	2	3	–
37.	red	3	2	1	1	2
38.	town	3	–	3	2	1
39.	dirt	2	–	2	–	2
40.	fair	2	–	2	1	1
41.	flags	2	–	2	1	1
42.	man	2	1	1	2	–
43.	maximus	2	1	1	1	1
44.	music	2	2	–	1	1
45.	player	2	–	2	–	2
46.	pony	2	1	1	1	1
47.	popcorn	2	–	2	1	1
48.	Ringling	2	1	1	1	1
49.	wagon	2	–	2	1	1

50-128. (f = 1)
acrobat, action, actor, arena, baby, Barnum, bear, bicycle, big, boring, bright, calliope, cat, child, children, circus, close, Clyde Beaty, colorful, comedy, confusion, conglomeration, Cow Palace, crazy, cry, dance, dancer, day, donkey, elephant riders, enjoyment, entertaining, farce, fea, fool, fun animals, garrets, gymnastics, gip, hay fever, house, idiot, jollity, junk, L.A., lady, laugh, lent, lights, lizards, loud, manager, many, merriment, mess, messy, midway, nothing, Oakland, party, perform, phoney, place, pleasure, ringmaster, Rome, seal, shallow, show business, shrine, sideshow, tightrope, Tim, tonite, top, trainer, travel, typewriter, weather

III-6 Device

No.	Response	Total	High Lang.	Low Lang.	Male	Female
1.	gadget	122	50	72	77	45
2.	machine	78	35	43	52	26
3.	tool	62	37	25	38	24
4.	method(s)	61	37	24	17	44
5.	mechanism(s)	60	36	24	25	35
6.	thing	55	28	27	26	29
7.	instrument	48	25	23	27	21
8.	way(s)	37	13	24	15	22
9.	gimmick	35	9	26	23	12
10.	mean(s)	32	19	13	16	16
11.	invention(s)	30	15	15	22	8
12.	scheme	28	14	14	9	19
13.	mechanical	19	10	9	11	8
14.	object	17	11	6	10	7
15.	trick	16	13	3	4	12
16.	mechanic(s)	12	4	8	4	8
17.	implement	11	5	6	7	4
18.	contraption	10	4	6	9	1
19.	vice	10	5	5	7	3
20.	work	10	6	4	2	8
21.	apparatus	9	6	3	2	7
22.	can opener	8	3	5	2	6
23.	advice	7	3	4	3	4
24.	article	6	5	1	2	4
25.	clever	6	4	2	4	2
26.	system	6	3	3	5	1
27.	use	6	4	2	2	4
28.	technique	5	1	4	–	5
29.	help	4	2	2	1	3
30.	lever	4	1	3	1	3
31.	aid	3	1	2	2	1
32.	car	3	1	2	3	–
33.	manner	3	2	1	–	3
34.	weapon	3	2	1	1	2
35.	action	2	1	1	1	1
36.	box	2	1	1	2	–
37.	business	2	1	1	1	1
38.	cheat	2	1	1	1	1
39.	dice	2	–	2	–	2
40.	divorce	2	1	1	1	1
41.	electrical	2	–	2	2	–
42.	equipment	2	–	2	1	1
43.	fix	2	–	2	2	–
44.	fixture	2	1	1	–	2
45.	gizmo	2	2	–	2	–
46.	good	2	1	1	2	–
47.	handy	2	1	1	–	2
48.	helper	2	2	–	–	2
49.	intricate	2	–	2	–	2
50.	inventor	2	1	1	2	–
51.	iron	2	–	2	–	2
52.	lock	2	2	–	1	1
53.	machinery	2	1	1	–	2
54.	physics	2	–	2	–	2
55.	plan	2	–	2	–	2
56.	screwdriver	2	1	1	1	1
57.	shop	2	1	1	2	–
58.	skillful	2	2	–	2	–
59.	toy	2	2	–	2	–
60.	tricky	2	2	–	1	1
61.	utensil	2	2	–	–	2
62.	wrench	2	1	1	2	–

63-174. (f = 1)
act, after, armour, assistance, atom, attachment, bent, bomb, book, brain, burglar, can, chair, cleverness, complex, complicated, complications, contraceptive, control, convenience, curiosity, deal, dentist, devil, devious, devise, Devon, disgust, dishwasher, drill, easy, electric, emblem, emery wheel, entertainment, facility, faucet, ferry, form, fraud, genius, girl, grease, grinder, hammer, handle, hardship, hole, hook, ice, idea, ingenuity, instruct, job, key, knife, language, lawyer, lice, lie, machiner, make, maker, means to acquiring something, menace, metal, motive, motor, move, musket, novice,

III-6 Device (contd)

No.	Response	Total	High Lang.	Low Lang.	Male	Female

office, opener, part, patent, pencil, pencil
sharpener, pin, play, pliers, practice, pressure,
project, pulley, rig, school, service, sharp,
shrewd, skill, skim, slide rule, sneak, sneaky,
something, suffice, switch, telegraph, telephone,
television, testing, think, though, thought,
torture, trickery, trinket, try, vehicle, watch,
wedding, wicked
(No response - 5; Illegible - 1)

III-7 Drama

No.	Response	Total	High Lang.	Low Lang.	Male	Female
1.	play(s)	450	225	225	238	212
2.	theatre(s)	71	34	37	27	44
3.	acting	68	29	39	31	37
4.	act	42	25	17	20	22
5.	actor(s)	34	15	19	18	16
6.	art	21	11	10	9	12
7.	stage	21	8	13	11	10
8.	show	17	8	9	10	7
9.	music	13	9	4	8	5
10.	Shakespeare	13	9	4	6	7
11.	tragedy	12	6	6	4	8
12.	movie(s)	9	8	1	4	5
13.	excitement	7	4	3	2	5
14.	Greek	7	2	5	5	2
15.	actress	6	1	5	6	-
16.	entertainment	6	2	4	4	2
17.	lecture	6	4	2	5	1
18.	critic	5	3	2	5	-
19.	opera	5	3	2	4	1
20.	suspense	5	5	-	3	2
21.	Hamlet	4	2	2	3	1
22.	speech	4	3	1	-	4
23.	story	4	2	2	2	2
24.	comedy	3	2	1	-	3
25.	dramatic(s)	3	2	1	1	2
26.	enjoyment	3	-	3	1	2
27.	exciting	3	1	2	-	3
28.	good	3	2	1	2	1
29.	picture	3	1	2	1	2
30.	pleasure	3	1	2	1	2
31.	production	3	2	1	2	1
32.	sad	3	2	1	1	2
33.	school	3	2	1	1	2
34.	Shaw	3	-	3	2	1
35.	action	2	2	-	2	-
36.	attention	2	2	-	1	1
37.	bad	2	1	1	1	1
38.	bore	2	1	1	2	-
39.	boring	2	1	1	2	-
40.	emotion	2	1	1	2	-
41.	funny	2	1	1	1	1
42.	Greek theater	2	-	2	1	1
43.	ham	2	1	1	2	-
44.	life	2	1	1	1	1
45.	literature	2	-	2	2	-
46.	mask(s)	2	1	1	1	1
47.	Medea	2	-	2	1	1
48.	melodrama	2	1	1	1	1
49.	mystery	2	1	1	1	1
50.	player(s)	2	2	-	2	-
51.	radio	2	2	-	1	1
52.	serious	2	1	1	1	1
53.	society	2	1	1	-	2
54.	student	2	-	2	2	-
55.	tears	2	1	1	1	1
56.	tension	2	2	-	2	-

III-7 Drama (contd)

No.	Response	Total	High Lang.	Low Lang.	Male	Female

57-149. (f = 1)
adventure, bald, beauty, boisterouseness, book,
card, Carol, chair, circus, class, classics,
climax, club, conflict, corn, costume, criticism,
dark, date, door, dream, dull, eat, emotional,
entertaining, fake, false, farce, father, film,
frightened, fun, geology, Greece, greet, harmony,
high school, horrible, horror, intellectual,
intense, interest, Janet Barnes, Juliet, Kathy,
laughter, lectures & music, lights, locus, lousy,
Macbeth, make-up, mispronunciation, movie stars,
murder, musical, nightmares, novel, nun, ocean,
opening, Othello, Pat, performance, phoney, pills,
playacting, playwright, pleasant, Rittinour,
scream, script, sequence, sex, sleep, soapbox,
sophisticated, South Pacific, stage play, state,
tale, teacher, tense, theme, tire, T.V., uninhibited, unreal, voice, watch, weight, woman, work

III-8 Forest

No.	Response	Total	High Lang.	Low Lang.	Male	Female
1.	tree(s)	718	362	356	370	348
2.	green	64	30	34	30	34
3.	wood(s)	39	19	20	22	17
4.	fire(s)	22	7	15	10	12
5.	dark	12	6	6	6	6
6.	beauty	11	4	7	5	6
7.	ranger	5	2	3	3	2
8.	beautiful	4	1	3	2	2
9.	camping	4	2	2	1	3
10.	jungle	4	2	2	1	3
11.	light	4	2	2	2	2
12.	mountain(s)	4	2	2	3	1
13.	nature	4	4	-	4	-
14.	pine(s)	4	3	1	3	1
15.	animals	3	-	3	1	2
16.	black	3	2	1	2	1
17.	cool	3	-	3	-	3
18.	darkness	3	3	-	2	1
19.	leaves	3	2	1	3	-
20.	redwood(s)	3	1	2	2	1
21.	deer	2	1	1	1	1
22.	dense	2	2	-	1	1
23.	forestry	2	1	1	2	-
24.	greenery	2	1	1	-	2
25.	hunt	2	1	1	2	-
26.	quiet	2	2	-	1	1
27.	Robinhood	2	2	-	-	2
28.	shady	2	2	-	-	2
29.	solitude	2	2	-	-	2

30-92. (f = 1)
air, birds, botany, calm, Camp Taylor, creeks,
deep, Derwald, desert, fir tree, flower, foliage,
forest, fox, fresh, fry, grass, greeness, green
trees, hills, knoll, landmark, lawn, life, lone,
love, loveliness, lumber, meadow, monkey, Mt.
Lemmon, outdoors, panoramic, peace, peaceful, pine
needles, pretty, primeval, raid, rain, rest, rich-
est, school, Schwavzwald, secluded, sequoia,
serenity, shrubbery, sierra, sky, smoke, stream,
summer, thick, timber, town, tuck, vacation,
valde, wet, wonderful, wooded, work
(No response - 1; Illegible - 1)

III-9 Glory

No.	Response	Total	High Lang.	Low Lang.	Male	Female
1.	flag(s)	132	72	60	73	59
2.	honor	76	35	41	39	37
3.	fame	55	24	31	28	27
4.	God	48	22	26	17	31
5.	victory	42	18	24	17	25
6.	praise	37	24	13	14	23
7.	hero	30	8	22	24	6
8.	war	28	16	12	19	9
9.	football	25	12	13	21	4
10.	hallelujah	20	13	7	11	9
11.	pride	19	12	7	13	6
12.	happiness	18	7	11	6	12
13.	good	17	9	8	10	7
14.	old	16	7	9	13	3
15.	light	14	7	7	6	8
16.	heaven	13	7	6	5	8
17.	happy	12	3	9	1	11
18.	be	11	6	5	6	5
19.	great	11	5	6	6	5
20.	power	8	4	4	6	2
21.	prestige	8	3	5	2	6
22.	army	7	5	2	6	1
23.	high	7	5	2	4	3
24.	hog	7	3	4	6	1
25.	morning	7	5	2	2	5
26.	hound	6	3	3	1	5
27.	patriotism	6	4	2	2	4
28.	song	6	1	5	2	4
29.	star(s)	6	2	4	4	2
30.	win	6	2	4	3	3
31.	battle	5	4	1	1	4
32.	blood	5	3	2	4	1
33.	courage	5	4	1	4	1
34.	joy	5	4	1	-	5
35.	peace	5	3	2	1	4
36.	proud	5	2	3	4	1
37.	valor	5	2	3	4	1
38.	country	4	1	3	3	1
39.	flower	4	-	4	1	3
40.	marine(s)	4	2	2	3	1
41.	splendor	4	2	2	3	1
42.	sun	4	3	1	2	2
43.	alleluia	3	1	2	2	1
44.	brave	3	2	1	3	-
45.	bravery	3	1	2	3	-
46.	death	3	1	2	2	1
47.	defeat	3	2	1	2	1
48.	ego	3	1	2	2	1
49.	famous	3	2	1	1	2
50.	forever	3	1	2	1	2
51.	gold	3	1	2	-	3
52.	gory	3	2	1	2	1
53.	guts	3	3	-	3	-
54.	soldier(s)	3	-	3	2	1
55.	work	3	2	1	2	1
56.	America	2	-	2	2	-
57.	angel	2	-	2	1	1
58.	beauty	2	1	1	-	2
59.	church	2	1	1	1	1
60.	conceit	2	2	-	1	1
61.	dishonor	2	-	2	1	1
62.	divine	2	-	2	-	2
63.	faith	2	1	1	1	1
64.	heroism	2	1	1	1	1
65.	horse	2	-	2	1	1
66.	laud	2	1	1	1	1
67.	man(e)	2	2	-	1	1
68.	nation	2	2	-	2	-
69.	parade	2	2	-	1	1
70.	path(s)	2	1	1	2	-
71.	patriotic	2	1	1	-	2
72.	red	2	1	1	1	1
73.	religion	2	2	-	1	1
74.	reward	2	1	1	-	2
75.	sad	2	1	1	1	1
76.	sadness	2	-	2	1	1

III-9 Glory (contd)

No.	Response	Total	High Lang.	Low Lang.	Male	Female
77.	triumph	2	-	2	-	2
78.	truth	2	1	1	1	1
79.	vain	2	1	1	-	2
80.	victorious	2	1	1	1	1
81.	winning	2	-	2	2	-
82.	wonder	2	2	-	-	2
83.	wonderful	2	-	2	-	2

84-232. ($\underline{f}$ = 1)
Abe Lincoln, acclaim, achievement, action, after achievement, American, American flag, Arizona, aromor, athletics, awe, badge, banners, basketball, beams, beautiful, best, Bible, big shot, blaze, bold, book, bound, boy, brass, braveness, bright, brightness, brilliance, bugles, Cal, California, celestial, Christmas, clouds, college, colorful, colors, complacency, conceited, constitution, cross, danger, deceit, desire, destitute, die, disgust, doctor, dogma, dust, esteem, eternity, falseness, far, father, fight, fighting, foreseeing, freedom, funk, future, games, general, girls, Gloria, glorify, glorious, glory-hound, goal, golden light, gospel, grandeur, grandness, Greece, halo, hate, haven, height, highest, history, homage, horray, idiot, kingdom, knowledge, Latin, lord, loud, lunacy, lure, lust, marine corps, medals, movies, Nero, nothing, nurse, old(flag), Old Glory, party, persecution, pink, poetry, pomp, popular, popularity, price, ra, radiant, raise, rays, rebel, recognition, renown, revelation, right, road, ruler, Russia, shame, shining, society, son, speech, spirits, splendid, sports, spotlight, state, story, success, sunset, supreme, sweat, task, top, trouble, United States, U.S., U.S.A., U.S. flag, war hero, white, win over, wisdom, won, yellow, yes
(No response - 1; Illegible - 2)

III-10 Highway

No.	Response	Total	High Lang.	Low Lang.	Male	Female
1.	road(s)	320	158	162	170	150
2.	car(s)	269	137	132	123	146
3.	street	40	17	23	24	16
4.	speed	32	19	13	15	17
5.	patrol	28	13	15	14	14
6.	freeway(s)	24	15	9	10	14
7.	travel	20	9	11	9	11
8.	traffic	15	5	10	8	7
9.	line(s)	12	8	4	6	6
10.	drive	11	4	7	7	4
11.	cop(s)	9	6	3	8	1
12.	fast	9	5	4	6	3
13.	pavement	9	6	3	3	6
14.	automobile	8	4	4	6	2
15.	101	8	1	7	6	2
16.	cement	7	2	5	5	2
17.	long	7	4	3	5	2
18.	police	7	3	4	2	5
19.	sign(s)	7	3	4	4	3
20.	white line	7	4	3	2	5
21.	accident(s)	6	3	3	2	4
22.	auto(s)	5	2	3	4	1
23.	99	5	4	1	3	2
24.	robber	5	4	1	2	3
25.	asphalt	4	3	1	3	1
26.	robbery	4	1	3	3	1
27.	straight	4	2	2	3	1
28.	concrete	3	2	1	2	1
29.	crash	3	-	3	1	2
30.	driving	3	1	2	1	2

III-10 Highway (contd)

No.	Response	Total	High Lang.	Low Lang.	Male	Female
31	home	3	1	2	1	2
32.	Los Angeles	3	2	1	1	2
33.	man(e)	3	1	2	3	–
34.	ride	3	3	–	1	2
35.	smooth	3	–	3	1	2
36.	transportation	3	3	–	3	–
37.	turnpike	3	2	1	2	1
38.	byway	2	–	2	2	–
39.	C.H.P.	2	1	1	2	–
40.	country	2	–	2	2	–
41.	death(s)	2	1	1	1	1
42.	endless	2	1	1	1	1
43.	gray	2	–	2	–	2
44.	highway man	2	2	–	1	1
45.	path	2	2	–	1	1
46.	patrolman	2	1	1	2	–
47.	ribbon	2	1	1	1	1
48.	route	2	2	–	–	2
49.	speeding	2	1	1	2	–
50.	super	2	2	–	2	–
51.	trip(s)	2	1	1	1	1
52.	299 W.	2	1	1	1	1

53-111. (f = 1)
air, airplane, bandit, beautiful, black, broad, Broderick Crawford, burro, busy, Camino, construction, curves, dirt road, drag, 81, engines, flat, 50, freedom, gravel, highlight, high-speeds, "Highwayman", highway patrol, job, lane, large, length, message, Mexico, night, noise, officer, open spaces, passageway, patrol car, paved road, plane, riding, shriek, 69, 66, slaughter, snake, speedway, state, stretch, telegraph, town, trail, train, traveling, trucks, two-lane, U.S. 299, valley, winding, work, wreck

III-11 Leather

No.	Response	Total	High Lang.	Low Lang.	Male	Female
1.	shoe(s)	145	66	79	79	66
2.	saddle(s)	85	41	44	45	40
3.	purse	73	36	37	5	68
4.	wallet(s)	60	33	27	37	23
5.	belt(s)	58	27	31	34	24
6.	strap	57	27	30	34	23
7.	cow(s)	38	12	26	27	11
8.	hide	37	23	14	17	20
9.	bag(s)	26	15	11	11	15
10.	horse(s)	26	13	13	15	11
11.	brown	21	16	5	7	14
12.	good(s)	19	8	11	8	11
13.	jacket	19	11	8	5	14
14.	tough	16	11	5	13	3
15.	coat	13	7	6	8	5
16.	smooth	13	7	6	4	9
17.	tan	13	7	6	7	6
18.	hard	12	10	2	8	4
19.	material	12	3	9	3	9
20.	upholstery	11	5	6	6	5
21.	boot(s)	9	4	5	5	4
22.	chair	9	3	6	5	4
23.	smell(s)	9	5	4	1	8
24.	soft	9	6	3	1	8
25.	pouch	8	4	4	7	1
26.	holster	7	5	2	7	–
27.	cowhide	6	4	2	5	1
28.	skin	6	4	2	4	2
29.	animal	5	2	3	4	1
30.	cattle	5	2	3	3	2
31.	neck	5	1	4	4	1
32.	rawhide	5	2	3	2	3

III-11 Leather

No.	Response	Total	High Lang.	Low Lang.	Male	Female
33.	suede	5	3	2	2	3
34.	harness	4	3	1	3	1
35.	strong	4	3	1	3	1
36.	thong	4	2	2	3	1
37.	case(s)	3	3	–	3	–
38.	cowboys	3	1	2	1	2
39.	gun	3	2	1	2	1
40.	red	3	1	2	–	3
41.	soap	3	2	1	3	–
42.	stiff	3	3	–	2	1
43.	stocking(s)	3	2	1	2	1
44.	tanning	3	2	1	3	–
45.	wool	3	3	–	2	1
46.	billfold	2	2	–	1	1
47.	book	2	2	–	1	1
48.	bridle	2	–	2	–	2
49.	buckle	2	1	1	2	–
50.	carved	2	1	1	1	1
51.	clothes	2	1	1	2	–
52.	clothing	2	1	1	2	–
53.	cover	2	1	1	1	1
54.	gloves	2	–	2	2	–
55.	nice	2	–	2	–	2
56.	paper	2	–	2	1	1
57.	sandals	2	–	2	1	1
58.	suitcase	2	1	1	1	1
59.	tools	2	–	2	–	2
60.	weather	2	1	1	1	1
61.	whip	2	1	1	2	–
62.	work	2	1	1	1	1

63-145. (f = 1)
artificial, baseball, basket, bather, binder, bootstrap, box, briefcase, brown smooth, bubble, calf, chamie, cloth, convertible, counch, covering, crafts, cure, Davy Crockett, dear, fake, fog, fur, genuine, gift, grain, grease, gunsling, handle, heather, hot, Indian, industry, lather, leathernecks, leather strap, luggage, metal, Mexico, mitt, moccasins, nap, odor, oil, plastic, pliable, protection, pungent, quality, raw, reddish, rifle, rough, rubber, sack, seatcovers, seats, shave, shine, shop, show, slide rule, sling, smelly, squeek, stamp, steer, stink, store, substance, sweat, tanned, thick, Tiajuana, tin, tooling, totes, trinket, wax, wealthy, whether, white, wood
(No response - 1; Illegible - 1)

III-12 Message

No.	Response	Total	High Lang.	Low Lang.	Male	Female
1.	note	186	93	93	83	103
2.	letter(s)	133	57	76	71	62
3.	telegram	42	25	17	27	15
4.	word(s)	42	28	14	24	18
5.	paper	31	13	18	12	19
6.	news	30	19	11	13	17
7.	code	22	15	7	13	9
8.	phone	20	8	12	3	17
9.	communication	18	13	5	12	6
10.	send	17	9	8	6	11
11.	telegraph	17	7	10	11	6
12.	answer	16	7	9	8	8
13.	messenger	14	7	7	7	7
14.	telephone	14	7	7	2	12
15.	writing	13	5	8	9	4
16.	secret	12	5	7	7	5
17.	thought	11	3	8	8	3
18.	speech	9	4	5	5	4
19.	unit(s)	9	6	3	6	3

III-12 Message (contd)

No.	Response	Total	High Lang.	Low Lang.	Male	Female
20.	information	8	4	4	6	2
21.	massage	7	6	1	4	3
22.	meaning	7	3	4	4	3
23.	pidgeon	7	3	4	2	5
24.	rub	7	3	4	4	3
25.	signal	7	1	6	4	3
26.	talk	7	6	1	6	1
27.	boy	6	3	3	2	4
28.	sign	6	3	3	4	2
29.	tell	6	4	2	4	2
30.	write	6	3	3	3	3
31.	call	5	1	4	3	2
32.	communicate	5	4	1	2	3
33.	good	5	3	2	2	3
34.	important	5	4	1	3	2
35.	runner	5	3	2	4	1
36.	sermon	5	3	2	2	3
37.	Garcia	4	3	1	3	1
38.	help	4	1	3	2	2
39.	listen	4	3	1	2	2
40.	radio	4	3	1	4	-
41.	read	4	1	3	3	1
42.	sent	4	1	3	1	3
43.	wire	4	-	4	1	3
44.	written	4	2	2	2	2
45.	announcement	3	3	-	1	2
46.	Bible	3	-	3	2	1
47.	cable	3	3	-	2	1
48.	gospel	3	1	2	3	-
49.	hear	3	2	1	-	3
50.	receive	3	3	-	2	1
51.	received	3	1	2	3	-
52.	relay	3	3	-	2	1
53.	report	3	3	-	2	1
54.	say	3	1	2	1	2
55.	sender	3	2	1	3	-
56.	short	3	2	1	1	2
57.	sore	3	1	2	3	-
58.	S.O.S.	3	2	1	3	-
59.	speak	3	1	2	2	1
60.	speaker	3	2	1	3	-
61.	truth	3	2	1	1	2
62.	bad	2	-	2	1	1
63.	bottle	2	2	-	-	2
64.	carrier	2	-	2	2	-
65.	data	2	1	1	1	1
66.	deliver	2	-	2	2	-
67.	friend(s)	2	-	2	-	2
68.	God	2	-	2	1	1
69.	hello	2	1	1	2	-
70.	love	2	1	1	1	1
71.	mail	2	2	-	1	1
72.	name	2	1	1	1	1
73.	notice	2	1	1	1	1
74.	preacher	2	-	2	-	2
75.	president	2	1	1	-	2
76.	relax	2	2	-	2	-
77.	saying	2	1	1	2	-
78.	see	2	-	2	1	1
79.	think	2	2	-	1	1
80.	urgent	2	-	2	1	1

81-194. (f = 1)
address, advice, announce, bad news, bird, book, bring, cablegram, called, caller, can, card, church, coach, confusion, contact, conversation, converse, convey, cool, correspondence, courier, crypt, dense, ditto, duty, ear, friendship, from, game, girlfriend, give, giver, gossip, graph, happy, Hermes, hope, idea, importance, inform, ink, inscription, king, language, late, Laverna, light, lines, listening, lost, maker, man, Mars, message, Messiah, minister, monk, Morse, none, notepad, omen, order, page, parents, particle, pen, phone call, plan, pleasant, point, pony express, postman, prayer, preach, pulpit, question, quick, relate, relief, religion, reply, rub-down,

III-12 Message (contd)

ruby, salvation, school, sending, shoulder, sidewalk, soothe, sound, speed, surprise, tale, teacher, teletype, teller, time, touch, traveler, tree, trouble, under, understanding, voice, vote, warning, Western Union, Western Union envelope, whisper, whom, wireless, yell, you
(No response - 2; Illegible - 3)

III-13 Mortgage

No.	Response	Total	High Lang.	Low Lang.	Male	Female
1.	house	328	165	163	163	165
2.	money	211	90	121	112	99
3.	debt(s)	66	36	30	45	21
4.	home	54	28	26	27	27
5.	loan(s)	40	19	21	24	16
6.	payment(s)	33	22	11	16	17
7.	rent	31	20	11	14	17
8.	pay	30	14	16	10	20
9.	owe	21	9	12	7	14
10.	bill(s)	19	8	11	7	12
11.	bank	12	6	6	6	6
12.	sell	10	5	5	6	4
13.	due	7	6	1	5	2
14.	trouble	6	3	3	4	2
15.	villain	6	3	3	3	3
16.	worry	6	3	3	3	3
17.	paper	5	3	2	2	3
18.	borrow	4	2	2	4	-
19.	lease	4	2	2	1	3
20.	poor	4	2	2	1	3
21.	sale	4	2	2	4	-
22.	deed	3	-	3	2	1
23.	land	3	2	1	1	2
24.	monopoly	3	1	2	2	1
25.	banker	2	2	-	2	-
26.	broke	2	1	1	1	1
27.	car	2	-	2	2	-
28.	cow	2	-	2	-	2
29.	finance	2	-	2	2	-
30.	insecurity	2	1	1	-	2
31.	last	2	2	-	1	1
32.	none	2	1	1	1	1
33.	note	2	-	2	2	-
34.	paid	2	1	1	2	-
35.	poverty	2	1	1	1	1
36.	problem(s)	2	1	1	-	2
37.	second	2	2	-	2	-

38-101. (f = 1)
advancement, anguish, bad, barn, body, Bus. Ad., buy, cash, certificate, cheese, church, complication, danger, dead, death, fear, foreclosure, fraternity, garage, gate, gauge, girlfriend, held, holder, in debt, indebtedness, insurance, I.O.U., lack, landlord, late, lawyer, lien, misery, money needed, more, morgue, mortar, mortgage, movies, never, ordered, owe money, owed, own, paper money, payable, payer, paying, property, reading, real estate, responsibility, rough, sad, school, Simon Legree, sold, struggle, suffer, tenant, tenting, threat, title

III-14 Oven

No.	Response	Total	High Lang.	Low Lang.	Male	Female
1.	hot	244	111	133	128	116
2.	stove	136	59	77	70	66
3.	heat	113	52	61	72	41
4.	bake	90	55	35	45	45
5.	food(s)	73	34	39	48	25
6.	cook	59	37	22	26	33
7.	cake(s)	48	25	23	17	31
8.	bread	41	24	17	20	21
9.	cooking	27	17	10	18	9
10.	pie	14	8	6	4	10
11.	roast(s)	14	7	7	10	4
12.	baking	13	6	7	5	8
13.	turkey	13	7	6	7	6
14.	door	12	9	3	6	6
15.	warm	9	4	5	4	5
16.	cookies	6	4	2	-	6
17.	biscuit(s)	4	1	3	2	2
18.	burn	4	1	3	-	4
19.	kitchen	4	3	1	2	2
20.	smell	4	4	-	1	3
21.	baked	3	1	2	2	1
22.	fire	3	-	3	1	2
23.	meat	3	2	1	2	1
24.	range	3	3	-	2	1
25.	black	2	2	-	2	-
26.	chicken	2	1	1	1	1
27.	dinner	2	1	1	1	1
28.	gas	2	2	-	2	-
29.	open	2	2	-	1	1
30.	pan(s)	2	-	2	1	1
31.	steak	2	-	2	2	-
32.	ware	2	1	1	2	-
33.	witch	2	-	2	-	2

34-74. (f = 1)
and, apple pie, aroma, bake bread, bakery, beef, box, brick, broil, broken, casserole, cleaner, cupcakes, dirty, dish, eat, electric, flame, furnace, future, gingerbread, ham, heater, home, icebox, master, odor, omen, own, retort, safety, security, shelf, sink, smoke, soldier, something hot, steamy, stoven, thermador, women
(Illegible - 1)

III-15 Oyster

No.	Response	Total	High Lang.	Low Lang.	Male	Female
1.	fish	152	68	84	59	93
2.	pearl(s)	151	83	68	72	79
3.	shell(s)	114	56	58	66	48
4.	clam(s)	89	54	35	41	48
5.	sea	72	27	45	41	31
6.	stew	71	36	35	41	30
7.	food	47	23	24	37	10
8.	eat(s)	27	9	18	17	10
9.	seafood	23	16	7	11	12
10.	ocean	22	13	9	13	9
11.	soup	16	6	10	7	9
12.	slimy	12	6	6	5	7
13.	crab	10	3	7	3	7
14.	water	10	1	9	4	6
15.	good	9	5	4	6	3
16.	shellfish	9	5	4	4	5
17.	ugh	9	6	3	4	5
18.	bed(s)	7	5	2	6	1
19.	bay	6	4	2	4	2
20.	slime	5	5	-	3	2
21.	abalone	4	1	3	3	1
22.	cracker	4	1	3	1	3
23.	fishing	4	2	2	4	-
24.	Hell Week	4	1	3	4	-
25.	lobster	4	2	2	4	-

III-15 Oyster (contd)

No.	Response	Total	High Lang.	Low Lang.	Male	Female
26.	mollusk	4	2	2	4	-
27.	taste	4	2	2	3	1
28.	animal	3	1	2	1	2
29.	dinner	3	2	1	2	1
30.	shrimp	3	1	2	2	1
31.	soft	3	1	2	1	2
32.	terrible	3	-	3	1	2
33.	bad	2	1	1	2	-
34.	bad taste	2	2	-	2	-
35.	disgusting	2	2	-	-	2
36.	dislike	2	2	-	-	2
37.	fisherman's warf	2	1	1	-	2
38.	fishy	2	1	1	-	2
39.	gray	2	-	2	-	2
40.	horrible	2	-	2	-	2
41.	seashore	2	2	-	2	-
42.	sick	2	-	2	1	1
43.	skindiving	2	1	1	2	-
44.	smell	2	1	1	1	1
45.	smoked	2	2	-	2	-

46-115. (f = 1)
anthropology, aphrodisiac, awful, beach, bi-sexual, bite, bivalve, blue, Boston, calm, can, caste, Christmas, claim, closed, dandruff, delicacy, delicious, eating, fish smell, Friday, glue, gritty, hate, indigestion, initiation, jelly, life, Louisiana, Maine, man, me, mess, molulicas, mussel, New England, no, oil, oogh, open, oven, pear, pig, pier, Piamo, "R", rat, red, restaurant, rotten, round, sand, seafish, sealife, seaside, sea water, size, slippery, snap, stewed, stubborn, summer, tasty, tight, ugly, Washington, white, Willapoint, world, zoology

III-16 Panic

No.	Response	Total	High Lang.	Low Lang.	Male	Female
1.	fear(s)	171	90	81	89	82
2.	fright	72	44	28	31	41
3.	run	55	21	34	36	19
4.	scared	50	18	32	18	32
5.	fire	47	25	22	22	25
6.	scare	29	17	12	9	20
7.	confusion	25	16	9	15	10
8.	terror	24	18	6	9	15
9.	button	23	12	11	17	6
10.	afraid	19	9	10	8	11
11.	help	19	7	12	13	6
12.	people	17	6	11	14	3
13.	stricken	16	4	12	7	9
14.	trouble	16	10	6	6	10
15.	mob	13	11	2	9	4
16.	chaos	12	5	7	3	9
17.	disaster	12	5	7	8	4
18.	scream	12	7	5	6	6
19.	calm	11	7	4	8	3
20.	hysteria	11	6	5	5	6
21.	hurry	10	6	4	8	2
22.	worry	10	6	4	3	7
23.	crowd	9	6	3	5	4
24.	frenzy	9	5	4	2	7
25.	frighten	8	3	5	3	5
26.	rush	8	4	4	5	3
27.	death	7	4	3	5	2
28.	depression	7	6	1	5	2
29.	frightened	7	3	4	5	2
30.	riot	7	4	3	4	3
31.	excite	6	2	4	4	2

III-16 Panic (contd)

No.	Response	Total	High Lang.	Low Lang.	Male	Female
32.	excitement	5	3	2	4	1
33.	finals	5	5	–	3	2
34.	nervous	5	2	3	2	3
35.	upset	5	1	4	2	3
36.	danger	4	2	2	1	3
37.	earthquake	4	1	3	1	3
38.	excited	4	–	4	–	4
39.	fast	4	1	3	1	3
40.	flee	4	2	2	2	2
41.	flood	4	1	3	2	2
42.	frustration	4	1	3	2	2
43.	mess	4	2	2	3	1
44.	noise	4	2	2	3	1
45.	pain	4	3	1	1	3
46.	picnic	4	2	2	2	2
47.	science fiction	4	–	4	2	2
48.	air raid	3	1	2	2	1
49.	control	3	1	2	1	2
50.	cry	3	2	1	3	–
51.	despair	3	3	–	–	3
52.	distress	3	2	1	1	2
53.	funny	3	1	2	1	2
54.	mass(es)	3	2	1	1	2
55.	1929	3	2	1	1	2
56.	test	3	1	2	2	1
57.	accident	2	1	1	2	–
58.	alarm	2	2	–	1	1
59.	anxiety	2	1	1	1	1
60.	crazy	2	–	2	2	–
61.	disorder	2	1	1	2	–
62.	freeze	2	1	1	1	1
63.	fun	2	–	2	2	–
64.	fury	2	1	1	–	2
65.	haste	2	1	1	1	1
66.	ignorance	2	2	–	1	1
67.	magazine	2	1	1	1	1
68.	plague	2	1	1	1	1
69.	raid	2	2	–	1	1
70.	rescue	2	–	2	–	2
71.	seize	2	1	1	2	–
72.	television	2	–	2	1	1
73.	T.V.	2	1	1	2	–
74.	war	2	–	2	–	2
75.	woman(e)	2	–	2	2	–

76-198. (f = 1)
action, all, anarchy, animal, atomic, atomic
warfare, awful, bad, bewildered, black, blanket,
blood, bomb, brakes, breathe, bridge, callous,
caution, city, clutch, commotion, complacent,
coolness, coward, crisis, dance, destruction,
die, disturb, disturbed, drowning, 1897, 1873,
1837, elevator, emergency, escape, everyone,
exams, flight, foolish, fools, frantic, frightening, fussy, Gargantua, gasp, ha ha, handy, heart,
helpless, hero, human, hurried, hustle, incoherent,
injury, insensibility, joke, keep cool, late,
leap, let go, lightening, loose reasoning, madness,
melee, mistake, motion, nervousness, now, outbreak,
pandamonium, peace, pressure, quickness, quiet,
rage, realization, red, relax, release, Rome,
running, running wild, save, scarce, school,
science fiction movie, seized, seizer, sharp,
shock, sick, silly, skirded, society, sociology,
stampede, stock, stupid, sudden, surprise, tension,
terrify, theater, theme, Titanic, trample, turmoil,
twitch, uncontrollable, uneasy, unrest, upheaval,
uproar, usually, view, water, what, wild, wreck,
yell
(No response - 1; Illegible - 1)

III-17 Presence

No.	Response	Total	High Lang.	Low Lang.	Male	Female
1.	here	319	131	188	167	152
2.	absence	181	105	76	82	99
3.	near	40	21	19	21	19
4.	being	34	22	12	23	11
5.	nearness	30	19	11	13	17
6.	there	23	10	13	9	14
7.	appearance	18	9	9	9	9
8.	God	15	10	5	8	7
9.	attendance	14	6	8	7	7
10.	absent	13	5	8	7	6
11.	person	10	7	3	6	4
12.	present	10	2	8	6	4
13.	people	9	3	6	3	6
14.	now	8	5	3	4	4
15.	feeling	6	4	2	4	2
16.	presents	6	4	2	3	3
17.	hear	5	2	3	2	3
18.	mind	5	2	3	2	3
19.	appear	4	3	1	3	1
20.	before	4	1	3	1	3
21.	close	4	2	2	2	2
22.	existence	4	1	3	2	2
23.	place	4	3	1	3	1
24.	room	4	1	3	3	1
25.	someone	4	–	4	1	3
26.	around	3	1	2	1	2
27.	attend	3	1	2	1	2
28.	class	3	3	–	2	1
29.	closeness	3	1	2	–	3
30.	divine	3	2	1	2	1
31.	felt	3	2	1	2	1
32.	love	3	2	1	–	3
33.	mine	3	2	1	3	–
34.	position	3	1	2	1	2
35.	real	3	1	2	1	2
36.	school	3	2	1	1	2
37.	sorority	3	1	2	–	3
38.	spirit	3	3	–	2	1
39.	to be	3	1	2	2	1
40.	with	3	2	1	2	1
41.	about	2	1	1	2	–
42.	alone	2	2	–	1	1
43.	attending	2	2	–	2	–
44.	aware	2	–	2	1	1
45.	boy(s)	2	1	1	–	2
46.	calm	2	1	1	2	–
47.	company	2	–	2	–	2
48.	first	2	1	1	1	1
49.	future	2	2	–	2	–
50.	gift(s)	2	–	2	2	–
51.	girl(s)	2	1	1	2	–
52.	living	2	–	2	1	1
53.	location	2	1	1	2	–
54.	nothing	2	–	2	1	1
55.	past	2	1	1	2	–
56.	presence	2	1	1	1	1
57.	proximity	2	1	1	2	–
58.	where	2	1	1	2	–

59-193. (f = 1)
ability, acquaintance, active, after, alertness,
among, ap, aroma, arrive, availability, awareness,
away, awful, be, beginning, Bill, bishop, bother,
car, catalyst, comfort, companion, completeness,
confidence, confusing, crowd, dance, date,
disappearance, do, door, eminence, enemy, entity,
essence, everybody, evident, evil, exit, face,
false, family, feel, following, force, fraternity,
ghost, give, go, gone, good, guest, happy, hard,
hate, hell, help, holiness, holy, human, I am
here, immaterial, in, initiation, introduction,
invitation, Ionce High, irritation, is, Italian,
know, known, life, line, live, Lyle, many people,
me, meeting, missing, occurance, of, of mind,
O.K., ominous, omni, omnipotent, omnipresence,
others, parents, party, passive, patience, peace,
personality, picky, poise, practice, pressure,

III-17 Presence (contd)

No.	Response	Total	High Lang.	Low Lang.	Male	Female

prestige, quest, reality, related, religion, removed, satisfying, seated, security, seeing, sense, show, sight, sixth sense, somebody, spook, stance, standing, state, stay, surround, surroundings, tangible, teacher, thing, think, thinking, thrill, together, unknown, vision, warmed, we, whereabouts, who, wonderful
(No response - 8; Illegible - 2)

III-18 Region

No.	Response	Total	High Lang.	Low Lang.	Male	Female
1.	area	402	214	188	195	207
2.	place	74	38	36	35	39
3.	section	46	17	29	19	27
4.	country	43	22	21	22	21
5.	land	36	16	20	17	19
6.	territory	24	6	18	11	13
7.	district	22	16	6	14	8
8.	mountain(s)	20	8	12	15	5
9.	map	13	7	6	6	7
10.	part	12	6	6	7	5
11.	religion	12	6	6	10	2
12.	location	9	5	4	3	6
13.	desert	8	2	6	1	7
14.	geography	8	6	2	4	4
15.	God	8	2	6	4	4
16.	forest(s)	7	5	2	6	1
17.	space	7	4	3	4	3
18.	state	7	4	3	3	4
19.	arctic	6	4	2	3	3
20.	California	6	1	5	2	4
21.	catholic	6	4	2	4	2
22.	climate	5	1	4	3	2
23.	legion	5	2	3	3	2
24.	Africa	4	-	4	2	2
25.	belief(s)	4	1	3	4	-
26.	church	4	2	2	1	3
27.	city	4	3	1	4	-
28.	faith	4	2	2	3	1
29.	hill(s)	4	1	3	3	1
30.	north	4	1	3	1	3
31.	park	4	2	2	4	-
32.	plain(s)	4	2	2	2	2
33.	trees	4	2	2	2	2
34.	U. S.	4	4	-	3	1
35.	weather	4	3	1	2	2
36.	Alaska	3	1	2	2	1
37.	Berkeley	3	1	2	2	1
38.	locality	3	2	1	2	1
39.	protestant	3	-	3	3	-
40.	south	3	1	2	2	1
41.	vicinity	3	1	2	1	2
42.	west	3	1	2	3	-
43.	western	3	3	-	-	3
44.	zone	3	1	2	2	1
45.	Arizona	2	1	1	1	1
46.	Bay Area	2	2	--	1	1
47.	board	2	1	1	1	1
48.	canyon	2	-	2	2	-
49.	cold	2	-	2	1	1
50.	division	2	1	1	2	-
51.	east	2	2	-	2	-
52.	football	2	-	2	2	-
53.	group	2	1	1	1	1
54.	home	2	-	2	1	1
55.	lake	2	1	1	1	1
56.	mountainous	2	2	-	-	2
57.	Oakland	2	-	2	1	1
58.	question	2	-	2	2	-

III-18 Region (contd)

No.	Response	Total	High Lang.	Low Lang.	Male	Female
59.	Tilden Park	2	2	-	2	-
60.	twelve	2	1	1	1	1
61.	unknown	2	1	1	2	-
62.	upper	2	-	2	2	-
63.	valley	2	2	-	1	1
64-163.	(f = 1)					

agriculture, America, American, arear, arid, atheist, auxiliary, bad, barren, bay, belt, big, body, boundary, central, Christ, conference, countryside, crew, Daughters of American Revolution, death, distance, error, farce, fog, foolish, foreign, foreign country, France, Fresno, geographic, geographical area, Girl Scouts, good, grass, Great Lakes, Greece, green, hate, heart, high, history, honor, hot, house, Jewish, jungle, life, local, locale, low, math, men, Mexico, Midwest, minister, nation, neighborhood, New York, nonsense, northern, of, ore, outpost, Placer, planning, plateau, port, priest, primitive, problem, province, rain, regal, rent, Rockies, rote, San Jose, San Miguel, scouts, sea, sector, Shasta, snow, Sunday, surface, tierra, tropic, unbeliever, unity, Vancouver, vast, view, warm, water, where, wilderness, wildlife, wooded hills, Yellowstone
(No response - 1)

III-19 Sidewalk

No.	Response	Total	High Lang.	Low Lang.	Male	Female
1.	street(s)	205	107	98	105	100
2.	cement	172	85	87	81	91
3.	walk	126	54	72	71	55
4.	cafe	52	35	17	27	25
5.	walking	50	21	29	29	21
6.	people	41	22	19	21	20
7.	concrete	36	23	13	28	8
8.	pavement	35	14	21	12	23
9.	crack(s)	25	16	9	10	15
10.	feet	17	7	10	9	8
11.	path	17	5	12	10	7
12.	curb	12	4	8	10	2
13.	New York	12	8	4	4	8
14.	city	10	8	2	6	4
15.	hot	8	1	7	5	3
16.	road	8	4	4	6	2
17.	gutter	7	3	4	5	2
18.	pedestrian(s)	7	4	3	5	2
19.	lines	6	2	4	2	4
20.	shoe(s)	5	3	2	4	1
21.	grass	4	2	2	2	2
22.	hard	4	2	2	1	3
23.	home(s)	4	2	2	3	1
24.	store(s)	4	1	3	3	1
25.	town	4	-	4	2	2
26.	walkway	4	2	2	1	3
27.	way	4	2	2	4	-
28.	building(s)	3	1	2	-	3
29.	fence	3	-	3	2	1
30.	grey	3	2	1	-	3
31.	lane	3	1	2	2	1
32.	run	3	3	-	1	2
33.	steps	3	1	2	-	3
34.	trees	3	1	2	-	3
35.	Berkeley	2	2	-	1	1
36.	dirty	2	-	2	1	1
37.	hill(s)	2	-	2	2	-
38.	none	2	-	2	1	1
39.	Paris	2	1	1	1	1
40.	parking meters	2	1	1	1	1

III-19 Sidewalk (contd)

No.	Response	Total	High Lang.	Low Lang.	Male	Female
41.	pathway	2	2	-	1	1
42.	roller skater	2	2	-	-	2
43.	school	2	-	2	-	2
44.	shopping	2	2	-	1	1
45.	straight	2	-	2	-	2
46.	stroll	2	1	1	2	-
47.	superintendent	2	2	-	2	-
48.	white	2	2	-	1	1

49-120. (f = 1)
aid, area, band, banquet, beach, bicycle, Biggs,
bike, board, boardwalk, bridge, broadwalk, campus,
cane, cars, children, clean, climb, College Ave.,
community, concrete squares, crowd, distance,
duty, east, egg, escalators, fair, footache,
ground, hopscotch, house, hulahoop, hurry, lampost,
letter, light, litter, man, meter, movement,
muddy, narrow, painter, paintings, papers, patio,
play, playland, plaza, rough, safe, sand, shops,
show, sidewalk, sideways, skate, slate, slug,
slippery, song, story, table, tired, trottoir,
urbanism, warm, wet, wide, wood, wooden

III-20 Sofa

No.	Response	Total	High Lang.	Low Lang.	Male	Female
1.	couch	259	135	124	145	114
2.	chair	179	88	91	86	93
3.	soft	90	52	38	42	48
4.	bed	68	36	32	43	25
5.	sit	61	29	32	25	36
6.	rest	31	7	24	21	10
7.	cushion(s)	28	15	13	13	15
8.	sleep	27	10	17	12	15
9.	comfort	19	8	11	10	9
10.	relax	15	5	10	10	5
11.	pillow(s)	12	8	4	5	7
12.	seat	12	6	6	5	7
13.	sitting	12	7	5	3	9
14.	divan	11	8	3	6	5
15.	davenport	10	6	4	8	2
16.	living room	10	6	4	2	8
17.	coach	9	5	4	-	9
18.	girl(s)	9	3	6	9	-
19.	chesterfield	8	4	4	4	4
20.	comfortable	8	6	2	3	5
21.	lounge	8	5	3	5	3
22.	love	8	4	4	6	2
23.	furniture	7	4	3	4	3
24.	lie	6	3	3	4	2
25.	sex	5	5	-	4	1
26.	lay	4	-	4	3	1
27.	relaxation	4	1	3	3	1
28.	room	4	1	3	-	4
29.	television	4	4	-	2	2
30.	home	3	2	1	3	-
31.	recline	3	-	3	2	1
32.	relaxing	3	1	2	2	1
33.	softness	3	2	1	-	3
34.	bench	2	2	-	1	1
35.	date(s)	2	1	1	-	2
36.	ease	2	-	2	1	1
37.	green	2	-	2	1	1
38.	house	2	1	1	1	1
39.	lazy	2	1	1	2	-
40.	necking	2	1	1	1	1
41.	people	2	1	1	1	1
42.	resting	2	1	1	1	1
43.	sleeping	2	-	2	1	1
44.	women	2	1	1	2	-

III-20 Sofa (contd)

No.	Response	Total	High Lang.	Low Lang.	Male	Female

45-82. (f = 1)
blue sofa, chaise, coffee table, couch or lying,
cozy, Danish, drapes, evening, fun, lamp, late,
long, lounge chair, lounging, lying, mantel,
maroon, mattress, nap, old, on, pig, red, resting
place, rug, seating, set, sink, sit down, sitting
down, soap, sofe, tired, to sit, two, warm,
water, wood

III-21 Tennis

No.	Response	Total	High Lang.	Low Lang.	Male	Female
1.	ball(s)	295	160	135	156	139
2.	game(s)	178	87	91	91	87
3.	racket(quet)	125	59	66	57	68
4.	sport(s)	78	36	42	43	35
5.	court(s)	44	25	19	23	21
6.	play	40	18	22	15	25
7.	fun	25	7	18	9	16
8.	golf	16	9	7	11	5
9.	shoe(s)	16	5	11	9	7
10.	player(s)	14	7	7	8	6
11.	anyone	10	8	2	7	3
12.	table	10	8	2	6	4
13.	hot	9	1	8	3	6
14.	net(s)	9	4	5	6	3
15.	exercise	8	4	4	4	4
16.	match	7	6	1	6	1
17.	white	6	4	2	4	2
18.	good	5	2	3	4	1
19.	playing	4	2	2	1	3
20.	athletics	3	3	-	1	2
21.	champion	3	3	-	2	1
22.	sun	3	1	2	1	2
23.	sweet	3	-	3	1	2
24.	team	3	1	2	3	-
25.	tennis ball(s)	3	2	1	2	1
26.	action	2	1	1	1	1
27.	P.E.	2	2	-	-	2
28.	ping pong	2	1	1	-	2
29.	shorts	2	1	1	2	-
30.	tired	2	1	1	1	1

31-103. (f = 1)
activity, Althea Gibson, athlete, Australia,
badminton, baseball, beat, bother, Carolee, champ,
club, college, cool, dad, Don, enjoyment, excitement, fan, fast, football, girls, Glen Ivy, glory,
goals, Gonzales, great, greatness, hobby, hold,
horn, Jack Kramer, jumping, June, lawn, Lew Hoad,
lithe, mad, old, Olmedo, open air, outdoors,
outside, pall, Pebble Beach, perspiration, Phys.
Ed., pleasure, Poncho G., Poncho Gonzales,
professional, race, rack, recreation, rich kids,
run, running, screens, skill, soccer, sound,
speed, sport-ball, star, summer, swimming, tennis
court, tournament, toward, ugly, vivacious, wall,
warm, work

III-22 Tourist

No.	Response	Total	High Lang.	Low Lang.	Male	Female
1.	travel	117	59	58	50	67
2.	traveler(s)	116	52	64	64	52
3.	car(s)	45	22	23	27	18
4.	vacation(s)	42	17	25	20	22
5.	visitor(s)	40	18	22	9	31
6.	camera(s)	33	25	8	17	16
7.	people	31	13	18	14	17
8.	money	25	12	13	19	6
9.	American(s)	23	17	6	16	7
10.	trade	18	10	8	11	7
11.	person	17	6	11	11	6
12.	Europe	16	8	8	4	12
13.	trip	15	7	8	6	9
14.	guide	13	4	9	7	6
15.	Mexico	12	6	6	8	4
16.	sightseer	12	4	8	7	5
17.	sight(s)	11	5	6	6	5
18.	stranger	11	5	6	5	6
19.	traveling	11	3	8	3	8
20.	country	10	8	2	4	6
21.	foreigner(s)	10	7	3	5	5
22.	motel	10	4	6	7	3
23.	see	10	4	6	5	5
24.	fun	9	–	9	3	6
25.	sightseeing	9	5	4	2	7
26.	man	8	3	5	5	3
27.	attraction(s)	7	3	4	5	2
28.	fool	7	6	1	5	2
29.	visit	7	4	3	2	5
30.	cabin	6	5	1	4	2
31.	rich	6	5	1	5	1
32.	San Francisco	6	1	5	5	1
33.	stupid	6	5	1	3	3
34.	beach(es)	5	1	4	3	2
35.	France	5	4	1	3	2
36.	Hawaii	4	3	1	2	2
37.	idiot	4	4	–	3	1
38.	look	4	1	3	3	1
39.	lost	4	2	2	1	3
40.	me	4	2	2	3	1
41.	strange	4	–	4	3	1
42.	sucker	4	3	1	4	–
43.	vacationer(s)	4	–	4	1	3
44.	wanderer	4	2	2	4	–
45.	baggage	3	2	1	1	2
46.	foreign	3	2	1	1	2
47.	glasses	3	–	3	2	1
48.	lodge	3	2	1	1	2
49.	Los Angeles	3	2	1	–	3
50.	luggage	3	3	–	1	2
51.	new	3	3	–	1	2
52.	passenger	3	2	1	2	1
53.	peasant	3	1	2	3	–
54.	resort	3	3	–	2	1
55.	sunglasses	3	1	2	2	1
56.	town	3	–	3	1	2
57.	trap	3	2	1	1	2
58.	woman	3	1	2	1	2
59.	amateur	2	1	1	–	2
60.	auto(s)	2	–	2	2	–
61.	boat	2	–	2	2	–
62.	bus	2	1	1	–	2
63.	dumb	2	1	1	2	–
64.	excitement	2	–	2	–	2
65.	family	2	1	1	–	2
66.	foreign country	2	1	1	2	–
67.	funny	2	1	1	2	–
68.	gullible	2	1	1	2	–
69.	happy	2	1	1	2	–
70.	inquisitive	2	1	1	1	1
71.	Italy	2	1	1	1	1
72.	journey	2	2	–	–	2
73.	lake	2	1	1	2	–
74.	looking	2	–	2	–	2
75.	motor	2	2	–	2	–
76.	native	2	1	1	–	2

No.	Response	Total	High Lang.	Low Lang.	Male	Female
77.	nut	2	1	1	2	–
78.	nuisance	2	1	1	1	1
79.	obnoxious	2	1	1	1	1
80.	parents	2	–	2	1	1
81.	Paris	2	1	1	–	2
82.	park(s)	2	1	1	2	–
83.	sightsee	2	2	–	2	–
84.	tour	2	–	2	1	1
85.	traffic	2	2	–	–	2
86.	train	2	2	–	–	2
87.	unfamiliar	2	–	2	1	1

88-221. ($\underline{f}$ = 1)
abroad, agency, alone, amazed people, Arab, away, Balboa, bear, beatnik, Belgium, boheme, bore, bothersome, buyer, cable car, cage, camp, canvas shoes, care, center, characters, class, clod, clown, club, clumsy, color, common, conformity, confusion, crabby, crowd, crowded, curiosity, dad, dislike, disliked, Don, dope, drive, drove, easterner, enjoyment, expensive, explorer, eyeballer, fake, fan, fat, forest, game, gape, gawking, gay, gimmick, gook, hate, haven, helpless, highway, hotel, house, house trailer, ick, inquisitiveness, interested, interesting, knowledge, Las Vegas, laugh, loafer, loud, maid, many, map, mob, motorist, mountain, New Mexico, noisy, North Beach, nosy, observing, odd, Okies, parrot, peering, person sightseeing, pest, places, plane, rates, review, riding, rubberneck, San Diego, Santa Barbara, sap, scenery, season, seer, settler, ship, showoff, sick, sissy, site-seeing, skylark, souvenir, Spain, spender, straw hat, student, suit, summer, sunburn, Tahoe, tourist, tourista, trailerhouse, travel agency, trouble, try, turn, typical, uncomfortable, vacationist, view, wandering, waste, white, wide-eyed, wife, Yellowstone
(No response - 1)

III-23 Welfare

No.	Response	Total	High Lang.	Low Lang.	Male	Female
1.	good	127	67	60	70	57
2.	help	108	39	69	54	54
3.	social	92	44	48	35	57
4.	poor	48	26	22	31	17
5.	child(ren)	46	24	22	28	18
6.	charity	38	18	20	14	24
7.	money	33	16	17	20	13
8.	health	31	15	16	17	14
9.	people	28	13	15	16	12
10.	care	27	14	13	9	18
11.	agency	21	12	9	8	13
12.	benefit(s)	17	10	7	9	8
13.	aid	16	13	3	6	10
14.	society	15	9	6	7	8
15.	state	14	12	2	11	3
16.	well-being	13	8	5	2	11
17.	safety	12	5	7	7	5
18.	worker	12	4	8	8	4
19.	board	11	11	–	4	7
20.	security	11	5	6	6	5
21.	happiness	9	4	5	4	5
22.	poverty	9	3	6	5	4
23.	needy	7	5	2	5	2
24.	service	7	6	1	2	5
25.	being	6	1	5	4	2
26.	Red Cross	6	2	4	3	3
27.	Salvation Army	6	3	3	3	3
28.	give	5	2	3	3	2

III-23 Welfare (contd) | III-24 Wisdom

No.	Response	Total	High Lang.	Low Lang.	Male	Female
29.	need(s)	5	1	4	2	3
30.	social worker	5	2	3	1	4
31.	community	4	1	3	1	3
32.	condition	4	2	2	1	3
33.	department	4	3	1	3	1
34.	fund(s)	4	1	3	3	1
35.	general	4	2	2	1	3
36.	good-will	4	2	2	2	2
37.	goodness	4	3	1	2	2
38.	woman(e)	4	2	2	2	2
39.	agent	3	2	1	3	–
40.	food	3	–	3	3	–
41.	organization	3	–	3	3	–
42.	orphan(s)	3	–	3	1	2
43.	problem	3	2	1	2	1
44.	relief	3	1	2	2	1
45.	status	3	2	1	3	–
46.	war	3	–	3	2	1
47.	well	3	2	1	3	–
48.	bum	2	1	1	2	–
49.	church	2	1	1	2	–
50.	city	2	2	–	1	1
51.	commission	2	2	–	–	2
52.	concern	2	–	2	–	2
53.	donation(s)	2	2	–	2	–
54.	family	2	–	2	1	1
55.	free	2	1	1	1	1
56.	happy	2	1	1	1	1
57.	helpfulness	2	1	1	–	2
58.	helping	2	1	1	1	1
59.	human(s)	2	2	–	–	2
60.	humanitarian	2	2	–	2	–
61.	humanity	2	1	1	–	2
62.	lady(ies)	2	2	–	2	–
63.	man	2	2	–	–	2
64.	nation	2	–	2	–	2
65.	office	2	1	1	1	1
66.	old	2	–	2	2	–
67.	old age	2	1	1	2	–
68.	peace	2	1	1	2	–
69.	public	2	–	2	1	1
70.	safe	2	2	–	1	1
71.	sick	2	1	1	–	2
72.	social security	2	1	1	1	1
73.	social work	2	2	–	1	1
74.	sociology	2	1	1	–	2
75.	student	2	1	1	1	1
76.	unfortunate(s)	2	–	2	1	1
77.	wealth	2	–	2	2	–
78.	well-off	2	1	1	2	–
79.	work	2	2	–	–	2

80-168. (f = 1)
advantage, affairs, Ann Ackerman, assistance,
A.S.U.C., bad, behavior, bureau, clerk, clothes,
committee, community service, cop, correction,
country, delinquency, disease, disgust, dispondent,
doctor, donate, Dorothea Dix, farewell, floods,
frame, giving, good of, goodbye, goods, government,
guidance, handicapped, handout, hell, helpful,
helplessness, home, hope, idiot, job, justice,
kids, kind, law, lazy, life, little child, me,
mine, mother, my, Negro, nurse, order, paper,
parents, philanthropy, plan, politics, poorness,
populace, position, pot, preamble, public service,
red, region, responsibility, rich, sad, sang,
sickness, social service sociologists, soup,
stability, survival, Sweden, taxes, turn out,
unhappy, union, U.S. aid, useless, volunteer,
waste, water, Y.M.C.A., your
(No response - 2; Illegible - 1)

No.	Response	Total	High Lang.	Low Lang.	Male	Female
1.	knowledge	303	180	123	155	148
2.	smart	93	38	55	57	36
3.	wise	80	33	47	35	45
4.	intelligence	57	34	23	30	27
5.	truth	53	32	21	31	22
6.	tooth(ee)	25	6	19	16	9
7.	brain(s)	24	6	18	16	8
8.	old	24	11	13	12	12
9.	thought(s)	21	12	9	11	10
10.	Socrates	16	11	5	7	9
11.	age	12	4	8	7	5
12.	learning	10	4	6	4	6
13.	books	9	7	2	7	2
14.	faith	8	6	2	5	3
15.	sage	8	4	4	2	6
16.	Plato	7	3	4	3	4
17.	Solomon	7	4	3	2	5
18.	virtue	7	1	6	1	6
19.	experience	6	2	4	3	3
20.	God	6	3	3	1	5
21.	man	6	4	2	5	1
22.	foolishness	5	2	3	3	2
23.	good	5	3	2	2	3
24.	power	5	2	3	3	2
25.	strength	5	3	2	1	4
26.	Aristotle	4	1	3	1	3
27.	beard	4	2	2	1	3
28.	education	4	1	3	1	3
29.	intelligent	4	1	3	3	1
30.	owl	4	1	3	2	2
31.	think	4	3	1	4	–
32.	Bible	3	2	1	2	1
33.	bright	3	2	1	2	1
34.	courage	3	2	1	1	2
35.	dumb	3	–	3	1	2
36.	ignorance	3	2	1	3	–
37.	intellect	3	2	1	1	2
38.	mind	3	–	3	–	3
39.	old man	3	2	1	2	1
40.	philosophy	3	1	2	1	2
41.	professor(s)	3	1	2	2	1
42.	prophet	3	1	2	1	2
43.	reason	3	3	–	3	–
44.	school	3	–	3	1	2
45.	stupidity	3	1	2	3	–
46.	ancient(s)	2	1	1	–	2
47.	brilliance	2	–	2	–	2
48.	brilliant	2	–	2	2	–
49.	college	2	–	2	2	–
50.	folly	2	2	–	2	–
51.	fool	2	1	1	1	1
52.	foolish	2	–	2	1	1
53.	grades	2	–	2	–	2
54.	health	2	1	1	2	–
55.	insight	2	1	1	2	–
56.	life	2	2	–	1	1
57.	pain	2	1	1	2	–
58.	pearls	2	1	1	–	2
59.	philosopher	2	1	1	–	2
60.	savant	2	2	–	–	2
61.	scholar	2	2	–	–	2
62.	sense	2	1	1	2	–
63.	smartness	2	1	1	2	–
64.	teacher(s)	2	2	–	1	1
65.	understanding	2	–	2	1	1
66.	wealth	2	–	2	2	–
67.	wise men	2	1	1	2	–
68.	wit	2	–	2	1	1
69.	youth	2	1	1	1	1

70-150. (f = 1)
acquired, age (old), advice, beauty, Buddha,
capacity, child, church, classics, common sense,
discrimination, Einstein, enhancement, enlightenment, father, fear of Lord, fine, freedom,
glasses, greatest, greatness, head, honor, ideas,
ideology, idiot, ignoramus, India, intellectual,

III-24 Wisdom (contd)

No.	Response	Total	High Lang.	Low Lang.	Male	Female

I.Q., joke, judgment, justice, keen, kindness,
king, know, knowledge lingers, knowlish, lack,
learned, light, like, magazine, Medusa, Milton,
money, moral, Moses, Mr. Lyman, none, oldness,
peace, people, philosophical, rat, reality,
sagacious, sagacity, Schweitzer, sharp, shrewdness,
skill, statues, stature, student, study, studying,
stupid, success, teach, thinking, time, uncle,
very wise, vision, where, wizard, woman, wonderful,
work
(No response - 1; Illegible - 2)

IV-1 Answer

No.	Response	Total	High Lang.	Low Lang.	Male	Female
1.	question(s)	550	255	295	278	272
2.	problem	47	18	29	25	22
3.	reply	46	26	20	26	20
4.	response	36	27	9	12	24
5.	right	22	8	14	11	11
6.	wrong	19	7	12	14	5
7.	yes	19	10	9	11	8
8.	respond	18	12	6	9	9
9.	solution	18	12	6	9	9
10.	correct	17	9	8	8	9
11.	ask	13	6	7	3	10
12.	test	10	5	5	6	4
13.	tell	9	5	4	6	3
14.	no	8	2	6	4	4
15.	book	6	4	2	5	1
16.	math	6	2	4	4	2
17.	talk	6	4	2	4	2
18.	answer	4	2	2	2	2
19.	me	4	3	1	2	2
20.	phone	4	3	1	4	-
21.	repeat	4	2	2	1	3
22.	say	4	3	1	2	2
23.	truth	4	2	2	2	2
24.	good	3	1	2	3	-
25.	knowledge	3	2	1	1	2
26.	now	3	1	2	1	2
27.	number	3	3	-	1	2
28.	retort	3	1	2	3	-
29.	speak	3	2	1	1	2
30.	word(s)	3	3	-	2	1
31.	conclusion	2	-	2	1	1
32.	finished	2	-	2	2	-
33.	mathematics	2	1	1	1	1
34.	quick	2	-	2	1	1
35.	quiz	2	2	-	2	-
36.	relief	2	2	-	2	-
37.	result	2	2	-	-	2
38.	solve	2	1	1	1	1
39.	solved	2	2	-	1	1
40.	study	2	2	-	1	1
41.	telephone	2	2	-	-	2
42.	think	2	2	-	-	2
43.	true	2	1	1	2	-
44.	what	2	1	1	1	1

45-121. (f = 1)
abstain, accumulate, analysis, ant, antwart, back,
big, brain, building, call, cancer, chemistry,
class, classroom, complex, contestant, cross,
don't, doubtful, final, finish, forgotten, girl,
give, happy, help, history test, homework, huh,
incorrect, inform, intelligence, know, letter,
lines, listen, logic, man, message, money, opinion,
pencil, Philip Wylie, please, puzzle, puzzled,
query, reason, reference, remark, responding, ring,

IV-1 Answer (contd)

No.	Response	Total	High Lang.	Low Lang.	Male	Female

sheet, song, spontaneous, state, studying, stupid,
success, table, talking, teacher, thing, thinking, thoughts, to, to tell, try, two-fourths,
voice, when, where, work, writing, yearling, yell,
young

IV-2 Building

No.	Response	Total	High Lang.	Low Lang.	Male	Female
1.	tall	95	51	44	51	44
2.	house(s)	93	38	55	59	34
3.	office(s)	54	35	19	24	30
4.	structure(s)	54	24	30	36	18
5.	construction	33	18	15	21	12
6.	school	31	12	19	12	19
7.	skyscraper(s)	30	20	10	15	15
8.	edifice	29	21	8	12	17
9.	high	26	16	10	11	15
10.	room(s)	26	9	17	10	16
11.	brick(s)	25	13	12	10	15
12.	large	22	9	13	9	13
13.	big	19	7	12	8	11
14.	stone(s)	18	9	9	9	9
15.	cement	17	10	7	9	8
16.	concrete	14	7	7	10	4
17.	city	11	4	7	6	5
18.	street	11	8	3	5	6
19.	architecture	10	5	5	5	5
20.	door	10	3	7	4	6
21.	window(s)	10	4	6	3	7
22.	height	9	5	4	5	4
23.	home(s)	9	4	5	3	6
24.	people	9	2	7	5	4
25.	place	8	2	6	5	3
26.	steel	8	7	1	6	2
27.	wood	8	5	3	5	3
28.	blocks	7	5	2	4	3
29.	elevator(s)	7	5	2	4	3
30.	floor(s)	7	4	3	2	5
31.	store	7	1	6	3	4
32.	material(s)	6	1	5	5	1
33.	shelter	6	3	3	2	4
34.	stairs	6	3	3	2	4
35.	work	6	2	4	5	1
36.	contractor	5	2	3	5	-
37.	empire	5	2	3	1	4
38.	glass	5	1	4	4	1
39.	architect	4	3	1	1	3
40.	build	4	2	2	4	-
41.	Dwinelle*	4	1	3	1	3
42.	L.S.B.**	4	1	3	1	3
43.	new	4	2	2	2	2
44.	apartment	3	1	2	2	1
45.	business	3	-	3	2	1
46.	code	3	3	-	3	-
47.	Empire State	3	1	2	1	2
48.	hall	3	2	1	-	3
49.	old	3	2	1	2	1
50.	progress	3	3	-	2	1
51.	tower	3	1	2	2	1
52.	administration	2	1	1	2	-
53.	box	2	1	1	2	-
54.	bread	2	1	1	2	-
55.	campus	2	1	1	-	2
56.	classes	2	1	1	1	1
57.	cold	2	2	-	-	2
58.	construct	2	2	-	-	2

* (Campus Bldg.)
** (Life Science Bldg.)

IV-2 Building (contd)

No.	Response	Total	High Lang.	Low Lang.	Male	Female
59.	downtown	2	2	-	1	1
60.	engineer	2	2	-	2	-
61.	engineering	2	-	2	2	-
62.	enter	2	1	1	1	1
63.	foundation	2	2	-	1	1
64.	frame	2	1	1	2	-
65.	granite	2	2	-	-	2
66.	grey	2	2	-	-	2
67.	ground(s)	2	2	-	2	-
68.	hotel	2	1	1	1	1
69.	housing	2	2	-	2	-
70.	huge	2	1	1	1	1
71.	immeuble	2	1	1	-	2
72.	job(s)	2	1	1	1	1
73.	Kaiser	2	-	2	1	1
74.	live	2	2	-	1	1
75.	lumber	2	1	1	1	1
76.	make	2	1	1	2	-
77.	modern	2	-	2	-	2
78.	site	2	-	2	-	2
79.	size	2	1	1	2	-
80.	stories	2	2	-	-	2
81.	up	2	2	-	1	1
82.	walls	2	1	1	-	2

83-218. (f = 1)
abode, Ad. Building, address, ads, aesthetics, alumni, always, American Trust, art, Bank of America, barn, bear, beauty, bid, blank, building, busy, Cal., campanile, candle, capitol, castle, cement structure, chair, Chem. Building, church, clothing, college, columns, confusion, constant, contract, construction, death, decor, design, destroying, device, element, empty, erect, erection, establishment, facade, fall down, father, food, fund, future, garage, great, here, high roof, hut, immense, Incas, inside, interesting, jump, knowledge, ladder, land, lawn, library, life, living, loan, lodge, machine, main, maintenance, majestic, making, massive, Matson, men, nail, New York, night, noise, noisy, number, obstruction, occupancy, paint, pavement, peace, permit, raise, rivet, road, roof, Russ, San Francisco, saw, scaffolds, Scott Co., shack, side, sidewalk, sight, sky, small, solid, song, spacious, square, stability, statue, steps, stolid, story, strength, strong, sturdy, suburb, tenement, terminal, theatre, tools, town, tree, trucks, 2, useless, view, well, Wheeler*, white, white structure, whole, workers, working, workmen, wow, zone
(No response - 1; Illegible - 1)
* (Campus Bldg.)

IV-3 Business (contd)

No.	Response	Total	High Lang.	Low Lang.	Male	Female
1.	money	139	69	70	103	36
2.	work	124	59	65	55	69
3.	man	75	40	35	34	41
4.	office(s)	64	35	29	25	39
5.	job	48	24	24	21	27
6.	occupation	35	18	17	17	18
7.	administration	20	8	12	12	8
8.	store	17	8	9	7	10
9.	pleasure	13	9	4	8	5
10.	enterprise	12	9	3	5	7
11.	letter	12	8	4	7	5
12.	affair(s)	11	7	4	7	4
13.	deal	10	6	4	3	7
14.	executive	9	4	5	6	3
15.	father	9	5	4	3	6

IV-3 Business (contd)

No.	Response	Total	High Lang.	Low Lang.	Male	Female
16.	good	9	5	4	6	3
17.	law(s)	9	3	6	3	6
18.	profession	9	6	3	3	6
19.	building(s)	8	2	6	3	5
20.	trade	7	3	4	2	5
21.	associate	6	5	1	3	3
22.	busy	6	2	4	1	5
23.	company	6	1	5	3	3
24.	industry	6	3	3	3	3
25.	success	6	1	5	4	2
26.	suit(s)	6	2	4	3	3
27.	big	5	5	-	4	1
28.	corporation	5	-	5	2	3
29.	firm	5	2	3	2	3
30.	machine	5	3	2	2	3
31.	manager	5	3	2	3	2
32.	paper(s)	5	1	4	2	3
33.	people	5	2	3	3	2
34.	place	5	2	3	3	2
35.	venture	5	4	1	3	2
36.	desk	4	3	1	-	4
37.	life	4	1	3	1	3
38.	partner	4	2	2	1	3
39.	play	4	3	1	2	2
40.	profit	4	3	1	2	2
41.	school	4	-	4	1	3
42.	boom	3	3	-	2	1
43.	car	3	1	2	2	1
44.	city	3	1	2	2	1
45.	dealing(s)	3	1	2	1	2
46.	dull	3	1	2	1	2
47.	duty	3	2	1	1	2
48.	economics	3	1	2	2	1
49.	education	3	-	3	-	3
50.	employment	3	2	1	2	1
51.	finance	3	3	-	1	2
52.	hard	3	3	-	1	2
53.	hour(s)	3	1	2	2	1
54.	interesting	3	2	1	1	2
55.	livelihood	3	1	2	2	1
56.	selling	3	1	2	2	1
57.	typewriter	3	1	2	-	3
58.	vocation	3	1	2	1	2
59.	women	3	2	1	1	2
60.	administer(ors)	2	-	2	1	1
61.	advertising	2	2	-	2	-
62.	agreement	2	-	2	1	1
63.	bad	2	2	-	1	1
64.	businessmen	2	-	2	-	2
65.	career	2	2	-	2	-
66.	concern	2	2	-	1	1
67.	construction	2	1	1	1	1
68.	depression	2	2	-	2	-
69.	establishment	2	2	-	2	-
70.	fast	2	1	1	1	1
71.	house	2	1	1	2	-
72.	insurance	2	-	2	-	2
73.	labor	2	1	1	1	1
74.	lawyer	2	2	-	-	2
75.	living	2	-	2	2	-
76.	men	2	-	2	-	2
77.	monkey	2	1	1	2	-
78.	none	2	2	-	1	1
79.	official	2	2	-	-	2
80.	operation	2	1	1	2	-
81.	order	2	1	1	-	2
82.	responsibility(ies)	2	1	1	1	1
83.	rich	2	-	2	2	-
84.	salesman	2	1	1	2	-
85.	shop	2	1	1	2	-
86.	time	2	1	1	1	1
87.	trouble	2	1	1	2	-
88.	typing	2	1	1	-	2
89.	world	2	1	1	-	2
90.	worry	2	1	1	2	-

IV-3 Business (contd)

		High	Low		
No.	Response	Total	Lang.	Lang.	Male Female

91-228. (f = 1)
accounting, action, address, advertise, advertisement, agent, appointment, associations, attire, bank, banking, bean, big business, booming, brief case, business, business ad., businessman, capitalism, capitalization, casket, cheat, chemist, cigar, Clif, collection, commendatory, commerce, commercial, competition, conferences, contract, contractor, crook, cutthroat, cycle, department, director, doctor, $, downtown, dress, drip dry, economy, effort, engineer, entrepreneur, estate, expenses, fail, failure, faith, falseness, financing, gamble, General Motors, glasses, graft, gray flannel, gray flannel suits, grocer, hatred, home, hurry, I.B.M., income, independent, industrial, keep out, later, leisure, life's work, lodge, major, management, managing, market, math, matter, maze, mean, meeting, meeting of men, mess, metropolis, mine, motel, newspaper, nosey, nothing, oil, opportunity, organization, outdoors, owner, parents, percentage, pharmacy, pressure, prim, product, promoter, proprietor, prosperity, ranching, real estate, recreation, regimentation, restaurant, safeway, sales, San Francisco, secretary, Shell Oil, shrewd, society, spats, stock, St. Oil Co., street, task, telephone, tension, traffic, transaction, trend, trip, type, useless, vacation, Wall St., Wally, warehouse, way, week magazine, white shirts, wise, working
(No response - 1)

IV-4 Color

		High	Low		
No.	Response	Total	Lang.	Lang.	Male	Female
---	---	---	---	---	---	---
1.	red	347	170	177	162	185
2.	blue	189	90	99	83	106
3.	black	68	25	43	45	23
4.	green	57	30	27	29	28
5.	white	33	20	13	24	9
6.	bright	27	16	11	11	16
7.	hue(s)	23	16	7	13	10
8.	rainbow	16	11	5	10	6
9.	yellow	12	9	3	7	5
10.	paint(s)	11	6	5	6	5
11.	light	10	5	5	6	4
12.	beauty	9	4	5	5	4
13.	blind	9	4	5	9	-
14.	pretty	9	3	6	1	8
15.	spectrum	8	4	4	8	-
16.	wheel	8	6	2	3	5
17.	gray(grey)	7	4	3	6	1
18.	pink	7	4	3	1	6
19.	eye(s)	6	1	5	3	3
20.	shade(s)	5	4	1	4	1
21.	brightness	4	1	3	1	3
22.	brown	4	3	1	1	3
23.	dye	4	-	4	2	2
24.	picture(s)	4	2	2	3	1
25.	vision	4	3	1	4	-
26.	art	3	-	3	2	1
27.	crayon(s)	3	2	1	3	-
28.	gold	3	-	3	-	3
29.	hair	3	2	1	1	2
30.	harmony	3	3	-	2	1
31.	race	3	-	3	3	-
32.	tint	3	2	1	1	2
33.	beautiful	2	-	2	1	1
34.	brilliance	2	1	1	2	-
35.	clothes	2	1	1	-	2
36.	lavender	2	-	2	-	2

IV-4 Color (contd)

		High	Low		
No.	Response	Total	Lang.	Lang.	Male	Female
---	---	---	---	---	---	---
37.	looks	2	1	1	2	-
38.	movies	2	1	1	2	-
39.	nature	2	1	1	1	1
40.	painting	2	-	2	1	1
41.	television	2	2	-	1	1
42.	texture	2	1	1	2	-
43.	tone	2	-	2	2	-
44.	vivid	2	2	-	2	-

45-117. (f = 1)
abstract, balance, blue, blue & gold, car, chromatic, cloth, code, color blind, cook, crayolas, dark, design, electromagnetic waves, enjoy, expression, face, film, flag, frequency, German, glory, good, guard, heliotrope, hill, history, jade, light rays, Little Rock, liveliness, mixture, multicolor, Negro, nothing, odd, orange, outdoors, pale, pallor, pastel, pattern, pen, perception, photography, plain, pleasant, property, psychology, purple, red & yellow, room, round, scheme, sensation, sense, sight, size, soft, stimulation, stimulus, thing, time, traitor, T.V., use, value, variety, various, view, void, warmth, wrong, yes
(No response - 1)

IV-5 Country

		High	Low		
No.	Response	Total	Lang.	Lang.	Male	Female
---	---	---	---	---	---	---
1.	farm(s)	68	34	34	43	25
2.	city(ies)	62	36	26	30	32
3.	America	49	21	28	22	27
4.	tree(s)	44	28	16	14	30
5.	land(s)	40	20	20	15	25
6.	U.S.	35	16	19	19	16
7.	nation	34	17	17	23	11
8.	hill(s)	33	14	19	22	11
9.	field(s)	29	17	12	11	18
10.	U.S.A.	23	14	9	13	10
11.	doctor(s)	22	12	10	11	11
12.	town(s)	21	9	12	6	15
13.	green	18	10	8	10	8
14.	home	18	8	10	12	6
15.	state	18	7	11	9	9
16.	United States	17	5	12	13	4
17.	air	16	8	8	5	11
18.	grass	14	6	8	6	8
19.	beauty	13	6	7	6	7
20.	club	13	10	3	11	2
21.	side	12	8	4	5	7
22.	cow(s)	11	6	5	5	6
23.	scenery	11	4	7	2	9
24.	house	10	6	4	7	3
25.	peace	10	7	3	5	5
26.	landscape	9	4	5	5	4
27.	place	9	3	6	6	3
28.	flag	8	6	2	6	2
29.	open	8	3	5	7	1
30.	people	7	2	5	7	-
31.	big	6	2	4	4	2
32.	space	6	4	2	3	3
33.	France	5	2	3	1	4
34.	free	5	2	3	4	1
35.	fun	5	2	3	2	3
36.	Germany	5	2	3	3	2
37.	girl(s)	5	3	2	5	-
38.	meadow(s)	5	4	1	3	2
39.	outdoors	5	2	3	3	2
40.	pretty	5	1	4	1	4
41.	road	5	3	2	1	4
42.	animals	4	-	4	1	3
43.	beautiful	4	2	2	1	3

IV-5 Country (contd)

No.	Response	Total	High Lang.	Low Lang.	Male	Female
44.	county	4	–	4	2	2
45.	fresh	4	1	3	2	2
46.	fresh air	4	3	1	–	4
47.	my	4	3	1	3	1
48.	patriot	4	3	1	2	2
49.	peaceful	4	2	2	2	2
50.	ranch	4	1	3	3	1
51.	rural	4	2	2	1	3
52.	citizen	3	3	–	2	1
53.	estate	3	2	1	2	1
54.	horses	3	–	3	–	3
55.	hunting	3	2	1	3	–
56.	man(e)	3	3	–	2	1
57.	mountain(s)	3	1	2	2	1
58.	nature	3	2	1	–	3
59.	pasture(s)	3	1	2	–	3
60.	store	3	1	2	2	1
61.	wonderful	3	–	3	–	3
62.	autumn	2	1	1	1	1
63.	boy	2	1	1	1	1
64.	China	2	–	2	1	1
65.	clean	2	1	1	–	2
66.	continent	2	1	1	–	2
67.	countryside	2	2	–	1	1
68.	earth	2	1	1	2	–
69.	fair	2	1	1	1	1
70.	farmland	2	–	2	1	1
71.	flat	2	1	1	1	1
72.	freedom	2	1	1	1	1
73.	garden	2	2	–	2	–
74.	God	2	2	–	2	–
75.	happy	2	–	2	–	2
76.	lake	2	1	1	1	1
77.	lane	2	1	1	1	1
78.	life	2	–	2	1	1
79.	live	2	1	1	1	1
80.	lonely	2	–	2	2	–
81.	map	2	2	–	1	1
82.	Mexico	2	1	1	2	–
83.	music	2	1	1	2	–
84.	nationality	2	1	1	1	1
85.	outside	2	2	–	1	1
86.	patriotism	2	2	–	1	1
87.	plains	2	1	1	–	2
88.	quiet	2	1	1	2	–
89.	relaxation	2	2	–	1	1
90.	Russia	2	1	1	2	–
91.	smell	2	1	1	1	1
92.	spacious	2	2	–	–	2
93.	Spain	2	–	2	1	1
94.	vacation	2	1	1	2	–
95.	valley	2	1	1	1	1
96.	village	2	2	–	1	1
97.	wide	2	–	2	1	1
98.	wind	2	1	1	2	–
99.	woods	2	–	2	2	–

100-209. (f = 1)
American, apart, army, barn, barren, belief, birth, camping, Canada, cattle, chicken, clerk, cousin, Cuba, death, democracry, dust, England, enjoyment, Europe, exercise, far, farmer, farmhome, farmhouse, fence, fish, forest, freshness, fruits, gentlemen, geography, glade, go, golf course, grandma, grandparents, great, Greece, healthy, heather, here, history, homeland, ione, larger, local, loud, love, loyalty, me, mine, My country 'tis of thee, name of, native, nice, Oklahoma, open space, organization, ours, out, pays, picnic, play, pleasant, politics, pride, problem, punishment, relax, relaxing, river, rolling land, room, rustic, rusticate, scene, scheme, seat, serenity, ship, Siam, sight, site, sleep, slum, solitude, South America, squire, story, suburb, sun, swamps, terrain, Texas, this, 'tis, travel, tweed, union,

IV-5 Country (contd)

united, unknown, vast, war, water, weeds, wheat, wilderness, yellow
(No response - 4; Illegible - 1)

IV-6 Dinner

No.	Response	Total	High Lang.	Low Lang.	Male	Female
1.	food	419	207	212	218	201
2.	eat	126	50	76	62	64
3.	supper	62	30	32	39	23
4.	lunch	61	33	28	32	29
5.	meal(s)	56	32	24	21	35
6.	table	23	14	9	10	13
7.	steak	20	7	13	14	6
8.	meat	14	8	6	3	11
9.	plate	14	12	2	9	5
10.	bell	13	7	6	5	8
11.	eating	12	8	4	5	7
12.	hungry	12	3	9	5	7
13.	evening	8	5	3	7	1
14.	breakfast	7	3	4	5	2
15.	time	6	–	6	3	3
16.	good	5	2	3	2	3
17.	hunger	5	4	1	3	2
18.	date	4	3	1	2	2
19.	dishes	4	1	3	–	4
20.	guest(s)	4	3	1	3	1
21.	home	4	3	1	3	1
22.	6:00(6 o'clock)	4	1	3	2	2
23.	ware	4	2	2	2	2
24.	dress	3	3	–	1	2
25.	engagement	3	2	1	1	2
26.	fork	3	2	1	–	3
27.	light(s)	3	1	2	3	–
28.	party	3	2	1	2	1
29.	turkey	3	1	2	2	1
30.	afternoon	2	–	2	2	–
31.	candlelight	2	2	–	–	2
32.	candles	2	1	1	–	2
33.	chicken	2	–	2	–	2
34.	eight	2	2	–	–	2
35.	family	2	2	–	1	1
36.	house	2	1	1	–	2
37.	jacket	2	–	2	1	1
38.	late	2	2	–	1	1
39.	pleasant	2	1	1	1	1
40.	relaxation	2	–	2	–	2

41-112. (f = 1)
bad, bat, beef, boarding house, cat, chair, club, conversation, cooking, dance, dancing, dark, delicious, dessert, dim, dime, dine, dining, drink, east, family in later afternoon, feast, feed, filet, fire, 5:30, fried chicken, fulfilment, full, garbage, great, greens, hamburger, happiness, hashers, hot, indigestion, Lantana, lighter, lots of food, man, meeting, menu, mittag, newspaper, night, noon, peas, people, person, potatoes, prepare, preparation, question, quiet, railroad, relax, restaurant, roast, show, silver, six, sleep, sterling, stomach, sup, tie, tooth, train, wife, wine, work
(No response - 1)

IV-7 Doctor

No.	Response	Total	High Lang.	Low Lang.	Male	Female
1.	medicine	187	97	90	79	108
2.	nurse(s)	177	76	101	90	87
3.	sick	47	18	29	20	27
4.	lawyer	43	24	19	25	18
5.	man	34	19	15	23	11
6.	help	30	13	17	16	14
7.	dentist	22	11	11	14	8
8.	white	22	8	14	7	15
9.	patient	19	10	9	9	10
10.	sickness	18	8	10	11	7
11.	physician	16	10	6	11	5
12.	pain	15	7	8	11	4
13.	health	13	6	7	5	8
14.	father	12	4	8	3	9
15.	illness	12	6	6	5	7
16.	shot(s)	11	5	6	5	6
17.	heal	10	7	3	5	5
18.	hospital	9	4	5	2	7
19.	money	9	–	9	8	1
20.	stethescope	9	7	2	5	4
21.	cure	8	6	2	5	3
22.	profession	8	4	4	4	4
23.	M.D.	7	5	2	5	2
24.	healer	6	4	2	1	5
25.	medic	6	3	3	4	2
26.	examination	5	1	4	2	3
27.	healing	5	2	3	3	2
28.	helper	5	4	1	4	1
29.	surgeon	5	4	1	3	2
30.	aid	4	3	1	2	2
31.	helpful	4	–	4	1	3
32.	ill	4	–	4	2	2
33.	medical	4	2	2	3	1
34.	office	4	2	2	2	2
35.	operation	4	3	1	–	4
36.	pills	4	3	1	1	3
37.	disease	3	1	2	2	1
38.	hurt	3	2	1	2	1
39.	me	3	1	2	2	1
40.	needle(s)	3	1	2	2	1
41.	quack	3	2	1	2	1
42.	school	3	2	1	2	1
43.	study	3	2	1	3	–
44.	surgery	3	–	3	1	2
45.	white coat	3	2	1	–	3
46.	Arzt	2	2	–	2	–
47.	bill	2	1	1	2	–
48.	care	2	1	1	–	2
49.	clean	2	1	1	–	2
50.	coat	2	1	1	2	–
51.	Cowell*	2	1	1	2	–
52.	curer	2	2	–	2	–
53.	death	2	1	1	1	1
54.	diagnosis	2	2	–	2	–
55.	education	2	1	1	1	1
56.	fee(s)	2	1	1	2	–
57.	friend	2	1	1	1	1
58.	glasses	2	1	1	1	1
59.	husband	2	–	2	–	2
60.	Jeckel	2	1	1	2	–
61.	kind	2	2	–	1	1
62.	knowledge	2	2	–	2	–
63.	Lindner	2	–	2	–	2
64.	operate	2	–	2	1	1
65.	person	2	2	–	–	2
66.	prestige	2	2	–	1	1
67.	rich	2	2	–	1	1
68.	smell	2	1	1	1	1
69.	tall	2	1	1	1	1
70.	trust	2	2	–	2	–
71.	wisdom	2	1	1	2	–
72.	witch	2	2	–	2	–

* (Campus Hospital)

IV-7 Doctor (contd)

73-192. (f = 1)
accident, Adams, Al, ambition, anticipation, assistance, bag, bandage, best, black case, blood, briefcase, brilliance, broken, brother, brown, career, careworn, case, check-up, cold, confidence, country, Cowell Hospital, curing, dad, daddy, Darryl, degrees, dentistry, dermatologist, Deter, doc, doctor, Dr. Anderson, Dr. Howard, duck, Epstren, exam, expensive, Faust, Finfield, fix, friendliness, good, goodness, great, green, hard worker, headband, healthy, helper to sick, help you, horrid, hospital-office, house, Howard, idiot, instruments, intelligence, intelligent, jerk, Kildare, knee, knife, law, learned, leather bag, man in a white gown, man in white, McMahan, medicine smell, men, mend, mercenary, misery, moneymaker, mud, nice, old, pediatrician, people, Ph.D., philosophy, phone, physical, poison oak, practitioner, professional, professor, protector, psychologist, relatives, reputation, respect, Rowe, Rowland, run, San Francisco, scalpel, Schwietzer, scissors, self-esteem, skill, smart, smile, Soderstrum, specialist, starch, struggle, student, suffering, sympathy, table, vaccine, watch, well, white uniform, wife, years
(No response - 1)

IV-8 Figure

No.	Response	Total	High Lang.	Low Lang.	Male	Female
1.	girl(s)	128	48	80	89	39
2.	number(s)	122	69	53	49	73
3.	woman(e)	99	56	43	81	18
4.	shape	80	30	50	31	49
5.	eight	47	23	24	28	19
6.	math	35	15	20	21	14
7.	statue	19	15	4	11	8
8.	good	17	8	9	9	8
9.	fat	16	7	9	1	15
10.	speech	15	8	7	10	5
11.	form	14	11	3	8	6
12.	person	14	7	7	3	11
13.	body	13	9	4	6	7
14.	slim	13	7	6	1	12
15.	face	10	9	1	5	5
16.	weight	10	3	7	1	9
17.	art	9	2	7	3	6
18.	curve(s)	8	3	5	4	4
19.	mathematics	8	2	6	2	6
20.	object	7	5	2	2	5
21.	sex	7	4	3	4	3
22.	skating	7	5	2	3	4
23.	beauty	6	1	5	3	3
24.	female	6	4	2	5	1
25.	ground	6	6	–	4	2
26.	nice	6	4	2	4	2
27.	problem(s)	6	2	4	2	4
28.	sculpture	6	3	3	2	4
29.	skate	6	6	–	3	3
30.	add	5	2	3	3	2
31.	diet	5	2	3	–	5
32.	line(s)	5	1	4	2	3
33.	money	5	5	–	4	1
34.	head	4	2	2	2	2
35.	legs	4	1	3	2	2
36.	letter	4	2	2	1	3
37.	model	4	2	2	2	2

IV-8 Figure (contd)

No.	Response	Total	High Lang.	Low Lang.	Male	Female
38.	one	4	3	1	3	1
39.	round	4	4	–	2	2
40.	size	4	1	3	1	3
41.	solve	4	3	1	1	3
42.	think	4	1	3	3	1
43.	wow	4	2	2	2	2
44.	write	4	1	3	1	3
45.	beautiful	3	1	2	2	1
46.	design	3	1	2	3	–
47.	drawing	3	3	–	1	2
48.	figurine	3	3	–	3	–
49.	geometry	3	1	2	2	1
50.	measurement(s)	3	2	1	3	–
51.	nine	3	1	2	2	1
52.	out	3	2	1	2	1
53.	pretty	3	1	2	1	2
54.	shadow	3	3	–	2	1
55.	symbol	3	1	2	2	1
56.	thin	3	1	2	–	3
57.	trim	3	1	2	–	3
58.	bad	2	–	2	–	2
59.	build	2	–	2	1	1
60.	calculate	2	1	1	1	1
61.	clothes	2	1	1	–	2
62.	cute	2	–	2	–	2
63.	girl friend	2	1	1	2	–
64.	glass	2	1	1	–	2
65.	lady	2	1	1	–	2
66.	man	2	1	1	1	1
67.	naked	2	–	2	1	1
68.	of speech	2	1	1	2	–
69.	painting	2	1	1	2	–
70.	perfect	2	1	1	1	1
71.	see	2	1	1	1	1
72.	sexy	2	2	–	1	1
73.	shapely	2	–	2	1	1
74.	silhouette	2	2	–	–	2
75.	small	2	2	–	–	2
76.	square	2	–	2	1	1
77.	straight	2	1	1	–	2
78.	tall	2	1	1	1	1
79.	three	2	–	2	1	1
80.	waist	2	–	2	–	2
81.	work	2	1	1	–	2

82-189. (f = 1)
algebra, analyze, animal, apply, arithmetic,
Bardot, bathing suit, batting, big, Brigette,
Brigette Bardot, built, caricature, chemistry,
circle, clay, computation, compute, corpse, dark,
data, digit, endeavor, Evie, example, exercise,
fatness, feed, feel, feminine, fig, fine, finesse,
food, frankly female, geometric, good & bad,
grace, hand, handsome, happenings, hateful, hert,
human, ice skater, idea, image, important, lade,
Laverna, Linda, little, long, lovely, male,
manikin, many, mark, meaning, mode, Monroe, motive,
mount, nice looking, no, numeral, of, outline,
overweight, paper, people, perfection, plastic,
plump, pole, politics, porcelain, profile, race,
reducing, representative, scale, serene, seven,
sharp, sketch, Slenderella, soft, spoon, stability,
stem, stop, study, swimsuit, symmetry, tabulate,
tape measure, Tempest Storm, terrible, thing, thumb,
tiny, vase, Venus de Milo, walk, watch it, whistle,
woman's.
(Illegible - 1)

IV-9 Garden

No.	Response	Total	High Lang.	Low Lang.	Male	Female
1.	flower(s)	592	299	293	270	322
2.	hose	42	25	17	25	17
3.	green	33	14	19	16	17
4.	plant(s)	33	12	21	22	11
5.	Eden	25	15	10	18	7
6.	vegetable(s)	19	11	8	17	2
7.	tool(s)	14	7	7	7	7
8.	rose(s)	13	9	4	4	9
9.	walk(s)	12	4	8	6	6
10.	dirt	11	4	7	6	5
11.	grow(s)	11	5	6	9	2
12.	work	11	8	3	8	3
13.	food	10	4	6	10	–
14.	beauty	7	2	5	4	3
15.	carrot(s)	7	2	5	7	–
16.	hoe	7	4	3	5	2
17.	house	7	5	2	4	3
18.	weed(s)	7	3	4	4	3
19.	grass	6	3	3	6	–
20.	trees	6	2	4	4	2
21.	yard	6	4	2	1	5
22.	beautiful	5	3	2	3	2
23.	pretty	5	2	3	2	3
24.	earth	4	1	3	2	2
25.	home	4	2	2	2	2
26.	water	4	1	3	1	3
27.	cool	3	1	2	1	2
28.	greens	3	1	2	–	3
29.	grove	3	2	1	1	2
30.	peas	3	2	1	2	1
31.	backyard	2	–	2	1	1
32.	bugs	2	–	2	2	–
33.	bushes	2	–	2	2	–
34.	colors	2	1	1	1	1
35.	Eve	2	–	2	1	1
36.	ground	2	–	2	1	1
37.	lawn	2	2	–	1	1
38.	plow	2	1	1	1	1
39.	snails	2	2	–	2	–
40.	soil	2	1	1	2	–
41.	spot	2	–	2	1	1
42.	tomato(es)	2	1	1	1	1

43-104. (f = 1)
beans, beets, bench, big, birds, blow, bowl,
camellias, carnations, colorful, corn, cultivated
earth, dark, dry, flagstone, fountain, fruit,
garden, gardener, gardening, gargle, greenery,
growing, how, imperial, Japan, Japanese, lawn
mower, lay, leaves, lettuce, lovely, Luxembourg,
mama, moist, moon, muffer, of Eden, outdoors,
outside, park, party, patch, path, patio, pest,
pleasure, poetry, rain, rake, relaxation, rocky,
romance, secret, slug, town, toy, trench, trowel,
verses, woman, wood
(No response - 1)

IV-10 Husband

No.	Response	Total	High Lang.	Low Lang.	Male	Female
1.	wife	731	376	355	391	340
2.	man	116	41	75	58	58
3.	love	21	10	11	2	19
4.	father	16	8	8	10	6
5.	marriage	15	8	7	10	5
6.	spouse	6	4	2	5	1
7.	fool	4	3	1	4	–
8.	home	3	1	2	1	2
9.	male	3	1	2	2	1
10.	mate	3	1	2	1	2
11.	me	3	2	1	3	–

IV-10 Husband (contd)

No.	Response	Total	High Lang.	Low Lang.	Male	Female
12.	strong	3	2	1	-	3
13.	children	2	2	-	-	2
14.	companion	2	2	-	1	1
15.	duty	2	-	2	-	2
16.	family	2	2	-	1	1
17.	ideal	2	1	1	-	2
18.	married	2	-	2	2	-
19.	money	2	1	1	2	-
20.	security	2	1	1	-	2
21.	work	2	-	2	1	1

22-79. (f = 1)
Alan, apron, back, band, Billy, brother, car,
caught, Chuck, chump, Clif, contentment, dad,
dead, dear, dilemma, doctor, Don, friend, fun,
gentle, get, golfer, handsome, happy, hermit,
Herr, house, Ken, kind, Louis, Lyle, married
man, mature, mine, mother, no, none, occupation,
pair, person, Peter, provider, Richard, Sam,
slippers, soon, suit & tie, support, supporter,
tall, thoughtful, Tom, twenty-five, ugly, why,
wish, woman

IV-11 Letter

No.	Response	Total	High Lang.	Low Lang.	Male	Female
1.	write	93	44	49	49	44
2.	envelope	71	36	35	41	30
3.	writing(s)	71	35	36	34	37
4.	stamp(s)	69	33	36	30	39
5.	paper	66	32	34	31	35
6.	mail	63	28	35	25	38
7.	word(s)	43	23	20	25	18
8.	pen	40	25	15	19	21
9.	opener	38	22	16	23	15
10.	news	32	19	13	17	15
11.	friend(s)	28	13	15	9	19
12.	alphabet	23	12	11	13	10
13.	home	16	6	10	6	10
14.	girl(s)	13	5	8	13	-
15.	name	12	1	11	8	4
16.	open	12	5	7	5	7
17.	A (a)	11	8	3	9	2
18.	love	11	6	5	5	6
19.	read	10	4	6	3	7
20.	correspondence	9	5	4	6	3
21.	message	9	6	3	4	5
22.	box	8	4	4	1	7
23.	communication	8	6	2	7	1
24.	head	8	6	2	5	3
25.	address	7	4	3	2	5
26.	card	7	4	3	3	4
27.	girl friend	7	3	4	7	-
28.	ink	7	4	3	3	4
29.	boyfriend	6	1	5	-	6
30.	note	6	4	2	3	3
31.	boy	5	1	4	-	5
32.	number	5	4	1	4	1
33.	book	4	2	2	3	1
34.	happiness	4	-	4	-	4
35.	latter	4	4	-	4	-
36.	mailbox	4	3	1	-	4
37.	parents	4	2	2	2	2
38.	reading	4	2	2	2	2
39.	receive	4	1	3	1	3
40.	symbol	4	4	-	-	4
41.	writer	4	2	2	2	2
42.	information	3	2	1	3	-
43.	knife	3	2	1	3	-
44.	letter opener	3	1	2	3	-
45.	pencil	3	3	-	3	-

IV-11 Letter (contd)

No.	Response	Total	High Lang.	Low Lang.	Male	Female
46.	science	3	1	2	1	2
47.	written	3	2	1	2	1
48.	black	2	2	-	2	-
49.	brief	2	2	-	2	-
50.	business	2	1	1	2	-
51.	capital	2	2	-	2	-
52.	carta	2	1	1	1	1
53.	epistle	2	-	2	1	1
54.	grade	2	2	-	2	-
55.	Greek	2	1	1	2	-
56.	mailman	2	1	1	2	-
57.	man	2	1	1	1	1
58.	mom	2	-	2	2	-
59.	person	2	-	2	1	1
60.	postman	2	2	-	2	-
61.	post office	2	2	-	1	1
62.	sports	2	-	2	2	-
63.	white	2	1	1	2	-

64-161. (f = 1)
abroad, alphabet soup, answer, anticipation,
application, arabic, Arlene, athletic, bed, Bob,
Carl, carrier, Chuck, closure, color, contents,
curiosity, David, Dear Abby, draft, editor,
enjoyment, F, figure, first, football, friendliness, fun, get, good, greetings, grey, happy,
hard, heart, hello, homework, hurry, ideas, J.,
James Woo, Jay, K, Kathy, language, Laverna,
lend, Leslie, lonely, long, lover, Mike, missile,
money, mother, my girl, no, numeral, office,
Ohio, one, opinion, page, papa, penny, people,
pleasure, post, postage, prison, procrastination,
reply, Richard, Roger, safety, Sandy, scaled,
send, short, signs, spell, spoon, stationery,
Susannah so fair, task, Ted, time, track,
trouble, uncle, uplift, vowel, wait, warmth,
Warren, Washington, Y, Z
(No response - 1; Illegible - 1)

IV-12 Moment

No.	Response	Total	High Lang.	Low Lang.	Male	Female
1.	time	255	123	132	136	119
2.	second(s)	166	74	92	81	85
3.	now	145	75	70	65	80
4.	minute	85	42	43	36	49
5.	instant	52	27	25	29	23
6.	hour	13	7	6	3	10
7.	inertia	13	10	3	13	-
8.	later	9	5	4	5	4
9.	physics	9	7	2	9	-
10.	wait	9	4	5	6	3
11.	force	8	7	1	8	-
12.	quick	8	3	5	1	7
13.	short	8	6	2	4	4
14.	present	6	5	1	2	4
15.	remember	6	1	5	4	2
16.	thought	6	1	5	2	4
17.	brief	4	4	-	1	3
18.	pause	4	2	2	1	3
19.	while	4	1	3	3	1
20.	bad	3	2	1	2	1
21.	clock	3	2	1	1	2
22.	decision	3	1	2	2	1
23.	hurry	3	1	2	2	1
24.	motion	3	1	2	1	2
25.	of inertia	3	3	-	2	1
26.	one	3	2	1	3	-
27.	period	3	3	-	3	-
28.	split	3	2	1	2	1
29.	action	2	1	1	2	-

IV-12 Moment (contd)

No.	Response	Total	High Lang.	Low Lang.	Male	Female
30.	after	2	1	1	2	-
31.	alone	2	-	2	1	1
32.	arm	2	1	1	2	-
33.	before	2	2	-	1	1
34.	bliss	2	2	-	1	1
35.	chance	2	2	-	-	2
36.	flash	2	2	-	-	2
37.	fleet	2	-	2	1	1
38.	fleeting	2	2	-	-	2
39.	great	2	2	-	-	2
40.	happiness	2	1	1	-	2
41.	how	2	-	2	2	-
42.	idea	2	-	2	1	1
43.	importance	2	2	-	1	1
44.	love	2	1	1	2	-
45.	musical	2	2	-	2	-
46.	next	2	1	1	1	1
47.	passing	2	1	1	1	1
48.	peace	2	1	1	1	1
49.	point	2	2	-	1	1
50.	precise	2	2	-	-	2
51.	short time	2	1	1	1	1
52.	silence	2	-	2	-	2
53.	silent	2	-	2	-	2
54.	soon	2	2	-	-	2
55.	space	2	2	-	1	1
56.	statue	2	-	2	1	1
57.	stop	2	1	1	1	1
58.	then	2	-	2	1	1

59-159. (f = 1)
anger, arrived, awful, Barbara, bat, blur, brief period, certain time, coming, dancing, date, dear, decisive, distance, duration, E.M. remember, engineering, eternity, event, every, fast, first, first moment, fore, girl, glance, glory, gone, happening, help, here, immediately, impulse, infinite, infinity, interval, it's gone, joy, joyful, just, kiss, know, levers, life, little, lost, lovely, madness, many, Mathus, Maureen, melt, memorable, memories, move, movement, music, musicale, of, old, once, opportune, peaceful, physic, please, pleasure, power, prayer, quickly, quickness, relax, relief, Rusel, sixty, sleep, small, sorrow, special, stay, still, stone, story, stupendous, sum, surprise, tense, test, thin, think, this, though, time-short, torque, trail, truth, unforgettable, waiting, walk, woman, wonder, wrong
(No response - 1; Illegible - 1)

IV-13 Morning

No.	Response	Total	High Lang.	Low Lang.	Male	Female
1.	night(nite)	170	82	88	80	90
2.	sun	140	69	71	71	69
3.	afternoon	59	32	27	32	27
4.	evening	57	33	24	24	33
5.	early	55	23	32	32	23
6.	noon	46	26	20	23	23
7.	sunrise	32	16	16	19	13
8.	day	25	14	11	9	16
9.	light	25	11	14	9	16
10.	sleep	22	8	14	13	9
11.	breakfast	18	9	9	12	6
12.	cold	17	7	10	12	5
13.	glory	16	8	8	10	6
14.	after	15	12	3	8	7
15.	dawn	15	10	5	11	4
16.	bright	14	6	8	7	7
17.	school	13	3	10	9	4

IV-13 Morning (contd)

No.	Response	Total	High Lang.	Low Lang.	Male	Female
18.	sunshine	12	7	5	8	4
19.	awake	11	4	7	6	5
20.	fresh	10	4	6	4	6
21.	tired	10	3	7	5	5
22.	cool	9	3	6	5	4
23.	bird(s)	8	3	5	6	2
24.	good	8	4	4	6	2
25.	star	8	6	2	5	3
26.	bed	7	3	4	1	6
27.	dew	7	1	6	3	4
28.	get up	6	3	3	-	6
29.	wake up	6	2	4	4	2
30.	a. m.	5	1	4	4	1
31.	awaken	5	4	1	1	4
32.	time	5	3	2	2	3
33.	arise	4	3	1	-	4
34.	fog	4	2	2	2	2
35.	mourning	4	2	2	4	-
36.	rise	4	3	1	3	1
37.	sleepy	4	1	3	3	1
38.	sunlight	4	3	1	3	1
39.	wake	4	2	2	3	1
40.	waking	4	1	3	1	3
41.	air	3	1	2	1	2
42.	beauty	3	2	1	-	3
43.	black	3	1	2	1	2
44.	daylight	3	3	-	2	1
45.	death	3	2	1	1	2
46.	eve	3	2	1	2	1
47.	hangover	3	2	1	3	-
48.	paper	3	2	1	2	1
49.	sad	3	3	-	1	2
50.	alarm	2	2	-	1	1
51.	alarm clock(s)	2	2	-	2	-
52.	awaking	2	2	-	1	1
53.	beautiful	2	-	2	1	1
54.	class(es)	2	1	1	1	1
55.	dove	2	-	2	-	2
56.	eggs	2	2	-	1	1
57.	flower	2	-	2	2	-
58.	freshness	2	1	1	1	1
59.	happiness	2	2	-	1	1
60.	new	2	2	-	-	2
61.	new day	2	1	1	2	-
62.	6:00(6 a.m.)	2	1	1	2	-
63.	twilight	2	1	1	-	2

64-119. (f = 1)
arising, awakening, begin, beginning, birth, blues, chilly, clear, clock, college, crispness, cry, crying, darkness, discomfort, docking, Electra, fear, fired, foggy, fortnight, getting up, grief, late, lavender, Marjorie, mood, moon, mornings, mourn, news, newspaper, now, pain, pink, rest, rising, sadness, shower, sickness, sight, sky, spring, suffering, sunny, sunny day, sunup, this, tomorrow, ugly, up, waken, waking up, window, work, yawning
(Illegible - 1)

IV-14 Office

No.	Response	Total	High Lang.	Low Lang.	Male	Female
1.	work	144	63	81	73	71
2.	desk	137	79	58	70	67
3.	room	93	44	49	54	39
4.	building(s)	88	38	50	41	47
5.	window(s)	78	48	30	36	42
6.	business	57	29	28	24	33
7.	hour(s)	40	11	29	22	18
8.	secretary	36	15	21	29	7

IV-14 Office (contd)   IV-15 Order

No.	Response	Total	High Lang.	Low Lang.	Male	Female
9.	door	20	10	10	11	9
10.	chair(s)	13	7	6	6	7
11.	man(e)	13	5	8	5	8
12.	place	13	6	7	7	6
13.	people	11	5	6	6	5
14.	job	10	7	3	6	4
15.	executive	9	7	2	6	3
16.	house	7	4	3	5	2
17.	doctor	6	4	2	2	4
18.	shop	6	5	1	4	2
19.	store	6	4	2	3	3
20.	boy	5	3	2	5	-
21.	busy	5	2	3	2	3
22.	clerk	5	1	4	5	-
23.	worker(s)	5	5	-	3	2
24.	bureau	4	4	-	-	4
25.	party	4	3	1	4	-
26.	typewriter	4	2	2	1	3
27.	boss	3	2	1	2	1
28.	father	3	2	1	1	2
29.	furniture	3	2	1	2	1
30.	girl	3	1	2	3	-
31.	headquarters	3	2	1	2	1
32.	law	3	2	1	2	1
33.	paper	3	2	1	3	-
34.	position	3	2	1	1	2
35.	president	3	-	3	1	2
36.	small	3	2	1	1	2
37.	big	2	2	-	-	2
38.	boredom	2	-	2	1	1
39.	box	2	1	1	1	1
40.	duty	2	2	-	1	1
41.	fear	2	-	2	-	2
42.	file(s)	2	1	1	1	1
43.	floor	2	1	1	-	2
44.	glass	2	1	1	-	2
45.	light	2	1	1	1	1
46.	machine(s)	2	1	1	-	2
47.	officer(s)	2	-	2	-	2
48.	principal	2	-	2	-	2
49.	school	2	-	2	1	1
50.	staff	2	2	-	2	-
51.	stuffy	2	2	-	-	2
52.	telephone	2	1	1	-	2
53.	type	2	-	2	-	2
54.	working	2	1	1	2	-

55-166. (f = 1)
Ad. Building, authority, bills, books, bore,
brass, businessman, car, city, class, clean,
clerical, closed, clutter, coffee, coffee break,
cold, counselor, counter, crew, crowdedness, dad,
dean, dean's, dentist, desk & file cabinet,
efficient, efficiency, employer, enclosure, enter,
factory, Franklin, Ft. Baker, glass door, government, green, hat, head, height, Hickok, high,
hold, holder, home, honor, ice, impersonal,
important, in, laboratory, letter, line, main
building, management, manager, Market St., mess,
name, newspaper, noisy, number, oak, off.,
office, official, old, open, organization, paper-
work, person, personnel, plant, plush, police,
politics, post office, power, practice, precision,
quiet, raise, registrar, reprimand, robust,
routine, rugs, sect'y, service, shelf, sister, sit,
site, space, Sproul Hall, stationery, stenographer,
student body, study, suit, talk, teacher, tension,
3307, tickets, town, typing, vineyard, who's,
women, workplace, workroom
(No response - 1; Illegible - 2)

No.	Response	Total	High Lang.	Low Lang.	Male	Female
1.	command	115	55	60	74	41
2.	disorder	33	17	16	18	15
3.	food	27	12	15	14	13
4.	rule(s)	27	19	8	13	14
5.	army	26	10	16	20	6
6.	chaos	26	15	11	12	14
7.	law	26	18	8	15	11
8.	neat	25	15	10	7	18
9.	rank(s)	20	16	4	14	6
10.	organization	18	12	6	5	13
11.	list	16	8	8	3	13
12.	neatness	15	7	8	2	13
13.	serene	15	15	-	9	6
14.	blank(s)	14	5	9	9	5
15.	menu	14	7	7	8	6
16.	line(s)	13	7	6	7	6
17.	peace	13	4	9	6	7
18.	confusion	12	3	9	8	4
19.	arrangement	11	5	6	9	2
20.	mess	11	6	5	5	6
21.	obey	11	5	6	4	7
22.	quiet	11	5	6	3	8
23.	sequence	11	-	11	7	4
24.	buy	10	4	6	4	6
25.	court	10	6	4	3	7
26.	demand	10	4	6	3	7
27.	number(s)	9	4	5	2	7
28.	class	8	3	5	1	7
29.	file(s)	8	3	5	2	6
30.	meal	6	4	2	4	2
31.	military	6	4	2	6	-
32.	discipline	5	1	4	4	1
33.	meeting	5	2	3	2	3
34.	restaurant	5	3	2	3	2
35.	right	5	5	-	4	1
36.	straight	5	3	2	2	3
37.	trouble	5	1	4	4	1
38.	want	5	3	2	4	1
39.	boss	4	3	1	1	3
40.	calm	4	2	2	3	1
41.	get	4	1	3	3	1
42.	justice	4	2	2	2	2
43.	logic	4	4	-	1	3
44.	money	4	2	2	3	1
45.	now	4	1	3	2	2
46.	order(s)	4	3	1	3	1
47.	paper	4	1	3	2	2
48.	R.O.T.C.	4	2	2	4	-
49.	sergeant	4	4	-	3	1
50.	system	4	1	3	3	1
51.	time	4	2	2	3	1
52.	way	4	3	1	-	4
53.	dinner	3	1	2	2	1
54.	first	3	1	2	2	1
55.	follow	3	2	1	2	1
56.	general	3	1	2	2	1
57.	government	3	3	-	1	2
58.	knight	3	3	-	3	-
59.	of	3	2	1	2	1
60.	organize	3	1	2	1	2
61.	receive	3	1	2	3	-
62.	room	3	-	3	-	3
63.	row	3	3	-	1	2
64.	school	3	2	1	1	2
65.	send	3	1	2	-	3
66.	sequel	3	1	2	1	2
67.	series	3	3	-	1	2
68.	silence	3	1	2	2	1
69.	waiter(s)	3	1	2	2	1
70.	waitress	3	2	1	-	3
71.	word(s)	3	2	1	1	2
72.	arrange	2	2	-	1	1
73.	ask	2	-	2	-	2
74.	beer	2	1	1	2	-
75.	bill	2	1	1	-	2
76.	call	2	2	-	1	1

IV-15 Order (contd)

No.	Response	Total	High Lang.	Low Lang.	Male	Female
77.	chronological	2	–	2	1	1
78.	clean	2	–	2	–	2
79.	column	2	1	1	1	1
80.	come	2	1	1	2	–
81.	fashion	2	1	1	1	1
82.	force	2	1	1	2	–
83.	group	2	–	2	1	1
84.	hamburger(s)	2	1	1	2	–
85.	invoice	2	2	–	1	1
86.	leader	2	2	–	2	–
87.	mail	2	–	2	1	1
88.	man	2	1	1	2	–
89.	method	2	1	1	2	–
90.	next	2	–	2	–	2
91.	obedience	2	–	2	1	1
92.	odor	2	2	–	2	–
93.	officer	2	2	–	1	1
94.	ordenes	2	–	2	1	1
95.	outline	2	–	2	1	1
96.	place	2	1	1	2	–
97.	police	2	2	–	2	–
98.	priest	2	1	1	1	1
99.	primate(s)	2	1	1	1	1
100.	rainbow	2	–	2	–	2
101.	reason	2	–	2	–	2
102.	regimentation	2	2	–	–	2
103.	religion	2	–	2	1	1
104.	request	2	–	2	1	1
105.	routine	2	–	2	1	1
106.	sect	2	–	2	–	2
107.	semblance	2	1	1	1	1
108.	sense	2	1	1	1	1
109.	side	2	1	1	–	2
110.	smell	2	1	1	–	2
111.	standard	2	–	2	1	1
112.	strict	2	–	2	–	2
113.	succession	2	–	2	1	1
114.	supply	2	1	1	–	2
115.	systematic	2	1	1	1	1
116.	tell	2	–	2	1	1
117.	universe	2	1	1	1	1

118-297. (f = 1)
active, adjust, alphabetically, anarchy, anthropology, armed services, around, arrow, article, ask for, authority, behavior, being, book, border, boredom, breakfast, brotherhood, business, buyer, Cal, can, cathos, caucus, character, characterized, chronology, clarify, clearness, clerk, community, complete, composition, congress, consistent, continuity, correct, country, coverage, day, decree, De Molay, direct, dissension, distinct, do, document, doing, drill, duties, duty, eat, Elks, essay, être, fad, family, final, fire, flank, following, form, fraternal, French-fries, gestapo, good, gravel, harmony, hashing, home, how, hurry, in, information, in line, instruction, it, judge, judiciary, jumble, king, loudness, mad, march, marching, masonic, math, mathematics, maticulate, mean, merchandise, more, mortar, mother, must, nature, never, new, not, one-two, orderliness, organized, out, out-of-order, over, pad, pain, parcel, parliament, passover, peaceful, pen, perfectionist, philosophy, phylum, pick, pie, placement, plan, play - Music Man, please, policy, power, precise, precision, preference, prescribe, president, procedure, procession, proper, punishment, quite, random, rebellion, receipt, recess, refrain, regime, regulation, religious, requisition, reserve, restriction, ring, Ruby, ruckus, ruler, run, sales, say, scouts, send for, sent, serve, sheet, sign, smoothness, social, soldier, spend, square, stop, stream, succeed, success, symbol, symmetry, take, teacher, terrible, to do, traffic, victors, weak, well-being, work, worries, yell, yelling
(No response - 2; Illegible - 1)

IV-16 Paper

No.	Response	Total	High Lang.	Low Lang.	Male	Female
1.	pencil	175	92	83	82	93
2.	pen	154	69	85	63	91
3.	write	92	46	46	56	36
4.	writing	46	19	27	20	26
5.	white	44	21	23	18	26
6.	news	39	20	19	24	15
7.	ink	32	22	10	16	16
8.	book(s)	29	15	14	18	11
9.	wood	25	10	15	15	10
10.	doll(s)	24	17	7	13	11
11.	clip	18	9	9	12	6
12.	newspaper	18	9	9	15	3
13.	work	15	4	11	10	5
14.	sheet(s)	14	5	9	3	11
15.	read	13	4	9	6	7
16.	boy	12	5	7	7	5
17.	school	10	5	5	2	8
18.	bag	9	6	3	5	4
19.	test(s)	9	4	5	6	3
20.	weight	9	6	3	7	2
21.	back	8	6	2	4	4
22.	homework	8	3	5	5	3
23.	money	8	4	4	6	2
24.	pulp	7	4	3	6	1
25.	word(s)	7	4	3	3	4
26.	flat	5	2	3	2	3
27.	letter	5	3	2	3	2
28.	papyrus	5	2	3	4	1
29.	tree	5	2	3	3	2
30.	paper	4	2	2	4	–
31.	smooth	4	3	1	2	2
32.	box	3	2	1	1	2
33.	cardboard	3	1	2	2	1
34.	draw	3	1	2	1	2
35.	material(s)	3	1	2	1	2
36.	notebook	3	–	3	3	–
37.	print	3	1	2	1	2
38.	route	3	2	1	1	2
39.	scissors	3	1	2	1	2
40.	thin	3	2	1	3	–
41.	black	2	–	2	2	–
42.	burn	2	2	–	2	–
43.	carbon	2	2	–	2	–
44.	card	2	–	2	1	1
45.	cloth	2	1	1	1	1
46.	English	2	1	1	–	2
47.	lined	2	–	2	2	–
48.	lines	2	–	2	–	2
49.	mache	2	1	1	1	1
50.	mill(s)	2	1	1	1	1
51.	pad(s)	2	2	–	1	1
52.	piece	2	1	1	–	2
53.	scroll	2	1	1	–	2
54.	story	2	1	1	2	–
55.	term	2	2	–	–	2
56.	text	2	–	2	2	–
57.	towel	2	1	1	1	1
58.	typewriter	2	1	1	1	1

59-141. (f = 1)
assignment, basket, bend, big, blank, blotter, brown, caper, cellulose, clean, clear, coarse, color, comics, company, composition, crackle, crayon, critical, cup, cutter, delivery, dog, draper, due, dwindle, exams, expense, fabric, factory, foil, gazette, glue, hanger, hard, home, information, knife, Los Angeles Times, machine, magazine, mate, moon, morning, multitude, napkin, new, newsprint, novel, office, onionskin, page, painting, paper money, pat, pepper, Pete, pin, poor, problems, quill, rags, rape, rat, reader, reading, report, sack, sand, sawmill, score, shut, slippery, stationery, tablet, texture, thesis, toy, wary, whiter, writing paper, yellow, Zellerbach
(No response - 1)

IV-17 Problem

No.	Response	Total	High Lang.	Low Lang.	Male	Female
1.	math	154	78	76	81	73
2.	trouble(s)	85	42	43	47	38
3.	solution	80	42	38	50	30
4.	answer(s)	74	34	40	43	31
5.	solve	57	32	25	32	25
6.	child	37	18	19	17	20
7.	difficulty(ies)	27	18	9	14	13
8.	worry(ies)	24	18	6	5	19
9.	mathematics	23	16	7	12	11
10.	work	22	11	11	14	8
11.	question	17	8	9	8	9
12.	school	17	7	10	9	8
13.	hard	16	5	11	10	6
14.	help	16	3	13	8	8
15.	think	15	4	11	9	6
16.	thought	14	4	10	8	6
17.	difficult	13	6	7	10	3
18.	puzzle	13	5	8	6	7
19.	solving	9	7	2	4	5
20.	task	9	7	2	4	5
21.	study	8	5	3	3	5
22.	thinking	8	4	4	4	4
23.	bad	7	4	3	3	4
24.	arithmetic	6	5	1	4	2
25.	number(s)	6	2	4	3	3
26.	test	6	5	1	4	2
27.	challenge	5	2	3	3	2
28.	dilemma	5	3	2	1	4
29.	people	5	1	4	2	3
30.	women	5	2	3	5	-
31.	homework	4	3	1	2	2
32.	psychology	4	3	1	2	2
33.	set	4	4	-	4	-
34.	confusion	3	1	2	2	1
35.	decision	3	2	1	2	1
36.	me	3	-	3	1	2
37.	obstacle	3	2	1	2	1
38.	physics	3	1	2	2	1
39.	schoolwork	3	3	-	2	1
40.	serious	3	2	1	3	-
41.	skill	3	1	2	1	2
42.	stuck	3	2	1	1	2
43.	time	3	1	2	3	-
44.	unhappiness	3	-	3	-	3
45.	unhappy	3	-	3	-	3
46.	add	2	-	2	-	2
47.	adolescent	2	2	-	-	2
48.	algebra	2	2	-	2	-
49.	big	2	1	1	1	1
50.	bother	2	-	2	-	2
51.	chemistry	2	1	1	1	1
52.	class	2	-	2	2	-
53.	delinquent	2	-	2	-	2
54.	device	2	1	1	-	2
55.	distress	2	2	-	-	2
56.	emotion	2	-	2	-	2
57.	frustration	2	1	1	-	2
58.	geometry	2	-	2	1	1
59.	girl	2	1	1	2	-
60.	how	2	-	2	1	1
61.	hurt	2	-	2	1	1
62.	issue	2	1	1	1	1
63.	love	2	1	1	-	2
64.	man(e)	2	-	2	-	2
65.	many	2	1	1	2	-
66.	money	2	1	1	2	-
67.	need	2	1	1	1	1
68.	sad	2	2	-	-	2
69.	sick	2	2	-	-	2
70.	sorrow	2	1	1	-	2
71.	taste	2	1	1	-	2
72.	teenage(ers)	2	1	1	-	2

73-187. ($\bar{f}$ = 1)
act, adolescence, advice, always, anthropology, anxiety, attack, black, block, Bob, books, boys, bridge, calculus, complex, complexity, concern,

IV-17 Problem (contd)

conclusion, confused, confusing, constant, courage, crazy, cry, debate, deep, delinquency, depression, discourage, discuss, disturbed, due, emotional, English, entanglement, everybody, example, fault, figure, fix, French, frightened, groups, guess, headache, idea, job, juvenile, kid, knot, life, logic, loneliness, Math 3-A, mean, mentality, mine, mirage, mistake, mixed up, mother, my, mystery, name-word, Nancy, nervousness, nuisance, obsession, own, pain, paper, perplexed, perplexing, perplexity, person, plenty, poor, priest, probe, problem, psychiatrist, punishment, puzzlement, puzzling, quarrel, race, radio, require solution, response, result, sadness, segregation, sex, sign, situation, solved, solver, statement, stomach, stop, strain, sweat, tackle, tail, talk, tough, turmoil, uneasy, unsolved, wanted, what, world, worried, wrong, yes

IV-18 Reason

No.	Response	Total	High Lang.	Low Lang.	Male	Female
1.	why	189	90	99	89	100
2.	answer	88	45	43	45	43
3.	logic	71	39	32	32	39
4.	thought	57	28	29	34	23
5.	think	39	20	19	20	19
6.	cause	37	20	17	18	19
7.	excuse	32	16	16	22	10
8.	problem(s)	24	10	14	16	8
9.	question	24	12	12	9	15
10.	idea(s)	18	9	9	8	10
11.	none	18	9	9	11	7
12.	right	18	10	8	7	11
13.	rhyme	17	11	6	10	7
14.	because	16	5	11	7	9
15.	good	13	7	6	9	4
16.	doubt	12	5	7	9	3
17.	for	12	7	5	5	7
18.	purpose	11	4	7	6	5
19.	action	8	4	4	5	3
20.	sense	8	5	3	3	5
21.	belief(s)	7	4	3	3	4
22.	explanation	7	2	5	1	6
23.	fact	7	2	5	4	3
24.	mind	7	5	2	2	5
25.	theory	7	-	7	3	4
26.	truth	7	3	4	4	3
27.	intelligence	6	3	3	5	1
28.	thinking	6	5	1	3	3
29.	explain	5	3	2	3	2
30.	philosophy	5	4	1	1	4
31.	rational	5	4	1	2	3
32.	bad	4	3	1	3	1
33.	knowledge	4	4	-	3	1
34.	math	4	2	2	2	2
35.	no	4	3	1	4	-
36.	proof	4	1	3	2	2
37.	understanding	4	1	3	2	2
38.	wisdom	4	3	1	1	3
39.	act	3	-	3	2	1
40.	argue	3	2	1	1	2
41.	argument	3	3	-	2	1
42.	geometry	3	1	2	-	3
43.	know	3	1	2	2	1
44.	life	3	2	1	2	1
45.	love	3	1	2	1	2
46.	motive	3	3	-	2	1
47.	order	3	2	1	-	3

IV-18 Reason (contd)

No.	Response	Total	High Lang.	Low Lang.	Male	Female
48.	rationalize	3	2	1	1	2
49.	rule	3	2	1	2	1
50.	though	3	1	2	3	–
51.	treason	3	1	2	3	–
52.	way	3	1	2	2	1
53.	wrong	3	1	2	3	–
54.	altitude	2	2	–	1	1
55.	doing	2	–	2	1	1
56.	evidence	2	2	–	–	2
57.	help(s)	2	1	1	1	1
58.	illogical	2	–	2	1	1
59.	intelligent	2	–	2	–	2
60.	judgment	2	1	1	2	–
61.	justification	2	2	–	2	–
62.	lie	2	1	1	2	–
63.	motivation	2	2	–	1	1
64.	need	2	1	1	2	–
65.	not	2	2	–	1	1
66.	reasonable	2	–	2	2	–
67.	season	2	2	–	2	–
68.	solve	2	2	–	1	1
69.	thing(s)	2	1	1	1	1
70.	understand	2	1	1	–	2
71.	what	2	–	2	1	1
72.	why for	2	–	2	1	1
73.	words	2	2	–	–	2

74-175. ($\underline{f}$ = 1)
able, age, analyze, aptitude, Aristotle, ask, attitude, been, book, brain, can, carefree, chemistry, cogitation, common, complex, concentration, conclusion, contrary, count, definition, dog, drink, duty, emotion, England, enlightenment, equals, fair, fast, for what, free-will, give, heart, hole, humans, ideal, ignorance, inductive, insanity, intellect, intent, intuition, is, just, law, live, living, madness, man, mathematic, method, mother, must, necessity, non-existent, note, nothing, notion, number, odd, opinion, people, Plato, poor, power, pride, private, quality, rationality, razor, reaction, real, realism, remain, renaissance, result, righteousness, same, sane, Sartre, science, senseless, strict, stupid, suggest, talk, teacher, tell, temper, time, trouble, true, uncertain, unreasonable, voice, validity, who, wits, wonder, work, yes
(No response - 4)

IV-19 Shoulder

No.	Response	Total	High Lang.	Low Lang.	Male	Female
1.	arm(s)	239	118	121	118	121
2.	body	88	38	50	41	47
3.	blade(s)	36	23	13	21	15
4.	bone(s)	34	15	19	11	23
5.	pad(s)	31	14	17	18	13
6.	soft	29	19	10	8	21
7.	broad	24	13	11	7	17
8.	strap(s)	23	11	12	10	13
9.	cry	21	13	8	5	16
10.	muscle	19	7	12	14	5
11.	neck	19	4	15	8	11
12.	sunburn	17	17	–	4	13
13.	head	16	11	5	4	12
14.	holster	16	9	7	14	2
15.	football	14	3	11	11	3
16.	gun	13	3	10	11	2
17.	man	13	6	7	8	5
18.	big	10	2	8	6	4
19.	back	9	5	4	7	2

IV-19 Shoulder (contd)

No.	Response	Total	High Lang.	Low Lang.	Male	Female
20.	sore	9	5	4	8	1
21.	strong	9	–	9	4	5
22.	road	8	3	5	6	2
23.	ache	7	1	6	4	3
24.	hurt(s)	7	3	4	6	1
25.	cold	6	3	3	5	1
26.	elbow	6	4	2	2	4
27.	hand	6	1	5	–	6
28.	lean	6	5	1	1	5
29.	strength	6	3	3	3	3
30.	white	6	5	1	1	5
31.	broken	5	3	2	2	3
32.	injury	5	1	4	5	–
33.	pain	5	2	3	1	4
34.	person	5	1	4	–	5
35.	rifle	5	2	3	5	–
36.	round	5	4	1	3	2
37.	block	4	2	2	4	–
38.	clavicle	4	3	1	4	–
39.	girl(s)	4	3	1	4	–
40.	meat	4	4	–	3	1
41.	purse	4	2	2	–	4
42.	skin	4	2	2	1	3
43.	bag	3	–	3	–	3
44.	beef	3	3	–	3	–
45.	boulder	3	3	–	2	1
46.	boy(s)	3	–	3	–	3
47.	carry	3	2	1	2	1
48.	dislocated	3	1	2	3	–
49.	hard	3	1	2	3	–
50.	large	3	1	2	1	2
51.	lift	3	1	2	2	1
52.	separation	3	1	2	3	–
53.	shirt	3	1	2	3	–
54.	soldier	3	–	3	2	1
55.	weight	3	3	–	2	1
56.	anatomy	2	1	1	1	1
57.	bare	2	2	–	2	–
58.	burden	2	2	–	1	1
59.	coat	2	–	2	2	–
60.	deltoid	2	–	2	2	–
61.	dress	2	1	1	–	2
62.	flesh	2	–	2	1	1
63.	high	2	–	2	1	1
64.	jacket	2	–	2	2	–
65.	joint	2	2	–	1	1
66.	knee	2	–	2	1	1
67.	lamb	2	1	1	2	–
68.	limb	2	1	1	1	1
69.	part of body	2	–	2	–	2
70.	rest	2	1	1	2	–
71.	rounded	2	–	2	1	1
72.	scapula	2	1	1	1	1
73.	sleeve	2	2	–	–	2
74.	smooth	2	1	1	1	1
75.	support	2	2	–	2	–
76.	weak	2	1	1	2	–
77.	weapon	2	1	1	2	–
78.	wheel	2	2	–	1	1
79.	wide	2	1	1	1	1
80.	wound	2	1	1	2	–

81-186. ($\underline{f}$ = 1)
accept, arch, arm-rifle type, army, athlete, Atlas, axe, bank, bent, black, brown, brush, bump, bumpy, burn, cane, car, chin, chip, comrade, collarbone, comfort, comforting, crew, curve, displaced, doctor, ear, edge, epaulet, espalier, fanny, figure, finger, fluff, girdle, gown, grey, hair, hairy, harness, height, help, highway, hit, hold, human, ice, injure, knapsack, leaning post, load, male, massage, me, message, M.I., misplaced, M-one, move, muscular, nudge, on, out, pack, part, part of person, patch, pectoral girdle, people, pin, posture, pull, push, right, roast, R.O.T.C., rub, shot put, should, shoulder, shoulder pad, shove, shudder, size, sleep, sling,

IV-19 Shoulder (contd)

No.	Response	Total	High Lang.	Low Lang.	Male	Female

sob, socket, square, strapless, suntan, sweater, take, tall, tan, tennis, tired, to bear, to lift, top, tote, warm, wear, woman, wrap
(No response - 3; Illegible - 1)

IV-20 Story

No.	Response	Total	High Lang.	Low Lang.	Male	Female
1.	book(s)	303	144	159	189	114
2.	tale(s)	173	96	77	81	92
3.	child(ren)	30	17	13	5	25
4.	read	28	14	14	15	13
5.	tell	27	13	14	13	14
6.	fairy tale(s)	20	10	10	5	15
7.	teller	19	8	11	12	7
8.	lie	17	6	11	12	5
9.	novel	16	7	9	8	8
10.	play	13	5	8	3	10
11.	fable(s)	10	7	3	2	8
12.	interesting	10	4	6	2	8
13.	long	10	6	4	4	6
14.	fairy(ies)	9	5	4	3	6
15.	fiction	9	4	5	2	7
16.	author	8	3	5	7	1
17.	listen	8	2	6	5	3
18.	short	8	5	3	6	2
19.	good	7	4	3	6	1
20.	interest	7	4	3	2	5
21.	reading	7	3	4	3	4
22.	told	7	6	1	2	5
23.	history	6	5	1	3	3
24.	plot	6	4	2	2	4
25.	telling	6	4	2	2	4
26.	building	5	3	2	4	1
27.	Cinderella	5	2	3	-	5
28.	time	5	1	4	4	1
29.	adventure	4	3	1	3	1
30.	entertainment	4	-	4	2	2
31.	fun	4	1	3	2	2
32.	picture(s)	4	2	2	1	3
33.	poem	4	3	1	3	1
34.	theme	4	1	3	2	2
35.	true	4	1	3	3	1
36.	bear(s)	3	2	1	1	2
37.	bedtime	3	1	2	-	3
38.	ending	3	1	2	1	2
39.	enjoyment	3	1	2	1	2
40.	glory	3	2	1	1	2
41.	house	3	3	-	3	-
42.	idea	3	1	2	3	-
43.	joke	3	2	1	3	-
44.	legend	3	-	3	2	1
45.	life	3	1	2	1	2
46.	magazine	3	2	1	1	2
47.	pleasure	3	2	1	1	2
48.	song	3	1	2	2	1
49.	words	3	2	1	2	1
50.	article	2	1	1	-	2
51.	childhood	2	1	1	1	1
52.	circus	2	1	1	-	2
53.	dirty	2	2	-	2	-
54.	doll	2	1	1	2	-
55.	end	2	2	-	1	1
56.	epic	2	1	1	2	-
57.	fantasy	2	1	1	1	1
58.	floor	2	-	2	-	2
59.	funny	2	2	-	1	1
60.	grandfather	2	1	1	1	1
61.	height	2	1	1	2	-
62.	hour	2	-	2	1	1

IV-20 Story (contd)

No.	Response	Total	High Lang.	Low Lang.	Male	Female
63.	message	2	1	1	1	1
64.	mother	2	1	1	2	-
65.	myth	2	2	-	2	-
66.	newspaper	2	1	1	2	-
67.	night	2	-	2	-	2
68.	old	2	2	-	1	1
69.	page(s)	2	1	1	2	-
70.	people	2	2	-	-	2
71.	relate	2	2	-	2	-
72.	relaxation	2	2	-	-	2
73.	romance	2	1	1	-	2
74.	story book	2	1	1	2	-
75.	write	2	-	2	1	1
76.	writer	2	1	1	2	-

77-171. ($\underline{f} = 1$) account, action, aid, anecdote, assignment, bad, balcony, bed, camp, composition, contents, cowboy, critique, describe, drama, dull, emotion, English, entertain, experience, fairy-teller, fall, false, falsehood, falsity, fireplace, fireside, fool, goal, grandma, Haiti, happy, histoire, humor, imagination, information, Jesus, journalism, kids, lesson, letter, liar, littleness, makeup, mine, mom, Monday night, Mother Hubbard, Mrs. Siffuast, mystery, narration, narrative, Peter Pan, Plato, pretend, princess, prose, radio, raconteur, relation, relaxing, remembering, rhyme, sad, school, Shirley Temple, snow job, Snow White, sound, South Pacific, Spanish, speak, story book dolls, stove, Susan, suspense, talk, talking, television, temper, theory, thought, The Possessed, toil, tory, to tell, train, traveler, truth, typewriter, universe, untold, value, verse, writings
(No response - 1; Illegible - 1)

IV-21 Table

No.	Response	Total	High Lang.	Low Lang.	Male	Female
1.	chair(s)	434	234	200	192	242
2.	food	73	34	39	47	26
3.	top	51	23	28	36	15
4.	cloth	40	21	19	20	20
5.	eat	39	17	22	21	18
6.	flat	29	18	11	18	11
7.	wood	25	6	19	15	10
8.	tennis	19	9	10	16	3
9.	leg(s)	18	9	9	10	8
10.	dinner	13	8	5	7	6
11.	set	12	5	7	6	6
12.	eating	11	7	4	7	4
13.	desk	10	2	8	7	3
14.	setting	10	5	5	1	9
15.	furniture	8	4	4	3	5
16.	round	8	2	6	4	4
17.	salt	8	4	4	6	2
18.	tablecloth	8	6	2	3	5
19.	plate(s)	6	1	5	2	4
20.	silverware	6	1	5	1	5
21.	dish(es)	5	-	5	1	4
22.	floor	5	1	4	2	3
23.	manner(s)	5	2	3	-	5
24.	ping-pong	5	3	2	4	1
25.	bench	4	-	4	2	2
26.	bread	4	2	2	4	-
27.	content(s)	4	1	3	3	1
28.	lamp	4	3	1	-	4
29.	mesa	4	2	2	3	1
30.	sit	4	2	2	2	2
31.	surface	4	2	2	3	1

IV-21 Table (contd)   IV-22 Trouble (contd)

No.	Response	Total	High Lang.	Low Lang.	Male	Female
32.	card(s)	3	2	-	3	-
33.	dining	3	-	3	-	3
34.	kitchen	3	1	2	1	2
35.	knife(ves)	3	1	2	2	1
36.	numbers	3	2	1	2	1
37.	people	3	-	3	1	2
38.	place	3	1	2	1	2
39.	room	3	1	2	3	-
40.	table	3	1	2	2	1
41.	breakfast	2	1	1	2	-
42.	brown	2	1	1	-	2
43.	cup	2	1	1	-	2
44.	fork	2	2	-	1	1
45.	graph	2	-	2	2	-
46.	hard	2	2	-	-	2
47.	lunch	2	2	-	2	-
48.	marble	2	2	-	-	2
49.	meal	2	1	1	-	2
50.	object	2	1	1	-	2
51.	spoon	2	2	-	2	-
52.	spread	2	2	-	2	-
53.	square	2	2	-	1	1
54.	support	2	2	-	2	-
55.	tisch	2	1	1	2	-
56.	wooden	2	1	1	1	1

57-118. (f = 1)
answers, board, bridge, butter, chemistry, clothing, covering, dine, dined, door, eat on, fable, four, games, house, logarithms, long, mahogony, mate, math, mathematics, menu, mountain, nothing, oak, on, onyx, paint, pen, pencil, pink, platter, play, put, rest, shoot, silver, sitting, smooth, solid, sound, stand, statistics, stool, sturdy, supper, sunlight, surface of table, tabloid, taboo, talk, things, time, tray, tür, type of, two, uncomfortable, waiter, water, wooden one, workplace
(No response - 2; Illegible - 1)

IV-22 Trouble

No.	Response	Total	High Lang.	Low Lang.	Male	Female
1.	problem(s)	132	64	68	52	80
2.	bad	110	51	59	62	48
3.	worry(ies)	57	39	18	25	32
4.	help	35	15	20	16	19
5.	police	22	11	11	17	5
6.	pain	21	15	6	7	14
7.	fight	18	6	12	13	5
8.	difficulty(ies)	17	15	2	7	10
9.	danger	15	9	6	8	7
10.	wrong	12	4	8	6	6
11.	boy(s)	11	-	11	3	8
12.	fear	11	5	6	4	7
13.	sorrow	10	6	4	2	8
14.	solution(s)	9	5	4	6	3
15.	delinquent(s)	8	4	4	2	6
16.	jail	8	2	6	7	1
17.	me	8	4	4	6	2
18.	bother	7	5	2	2	5
19.	time(s)	7	4	3	4	3
20.	confusion	6	2	4	2	4
21.	double	6	4	2	5	1
22.	evil	6	1	5	4	2
23.	maker	6	3	3	4	2
24.	school	6	4	2	4	2
25.	anxiety	5	3	2	2	3
26.	cause	5	3	2	2	3
27.	cop(s)	5	1	4	4	1
28.	crime	5	3	2	3	2

No.	Response	Total	High Lang.	Low Lang.	Male	Female
29.	girl(s)	5	4	1	4	1
30.	hard	5	3	2	1	4
31.	mess	5	1	4	4	1
32.	mischief	5	2	3	3	2
33.	peace	5	1	4	3	2
34.	people	5	-	5	3	2
35.	punishment	5	2	3	4	1
36.	River City	5	5	-	3	2
37.	unhappiness	5	3	2	1	4
38.	unhappy	5	2	3	2	3
39.	bubble	4	3	1	1	3
40.	chaos	4	2	2	3	1
41.	fun	4	1	3	4	-
42.	good	4	1	3	4	-
43.	happiness	4	3	1	2	2
44.	harm	4	2	2	-	4
45.	kids	4	1	3	1	3
46.	law	4	1	3	4	-
47.	man(e)	4	-	4	1	3
48.	sad	4	3	1	1	3
49.	scared	4	1	3	3	1
50.	strife	4	2	2	3	1
51.	woe(s)	4	1	3	3	1
52.	ahead	3	2	1	1	2
53.	black	3	1	2	1	2
54.	cry	3	2	1	2	1
55.	discord	3	2	1	3	-
56.	grades	3	2	1	3	-
57.	grief	3	2	1	3	-
58.	gun	3	1	2	2	1
59.	happy	3	1	2	1	2
60.	home	3	1	2	2	1
61.	misery	3	2	1	3	-
62.	question	3	1	2	1	2
63.	shooter	3	-	3	2	1
64.	sin	3	3	-	1	2
65.	song(s)	3	1	2	2	1
66.	sorry	3	3	-	2	1
67.	tension	3	1	2	2	1
68.	war	3	2	1	1	2
69.	with	3	2	1	2	1
70.	women	3	1	2	3	-
71.	world	3	1	2	2	1
72.	always	2	-	2	2	-
73.	anger	2	2	-	2	-
74.	area	2	-	2	2	-
75.	argument	2	2	-	1	1
76.	boil	2	2	-	2	-
77.	book	2	2	-	1	1
78.	cope	2	2	-	1	1
79.	delinquency	2	-	2	2	-
80.	Dennis	2	1	1	-	2
81.	difficult	2	1	1	1	1
82.	disaster	2	1	1	2	-
83.	disorder	2	2	-	1	1
84.	disturb(s)	2	2	-	-	2
85.	disturbance	2	2	-	2	-
86.	doubt	2	2	-	1	1
87.	ease	2	2	-	-	2
88.	Elvis	2	1	1	1	1
89.	engine	2	2	-	-	2
90.	fine	2	-	2	-	2
91.	fright	2	1	1	-	2
92.	Harry	2	1	1	1	1
93.	heartache	2	-	2	1	1
94.	hindrance	2	1	1	1	1
95.	hoodlums	2	1	1	1	1
96.	hurt	2	1	1	-	2
97.	issue	2	2	-	2	-
98.	lawlessness	2	2	-	1	1
99.	life	2	-	2	-	2
100.	misfortune	2	-	2	-	2
101.	mistake	2	-	2	1	1
102.	money	2	1	1	1	1
103.	music man	2	-	2	1	1
104.	noise	2	1	1	1	1

IV-22 Trouble (contd)

No.	Response	Total	High Lang.	Low Lang.	Male	Female
105.	predicament	2	1	1	2	-
106.	Presley	2	2	-	2	-
107.	sadness	2	2	-	-	2
108.	safe	2	-	2	-	2
109.	serious	2	1	1	1	1
110.	sex	2	1	1	-	2
111.	sick	2	1	1	-	2
112.	some	2	-	2	-	2
113.	spot	2	-	2	1	1
114.	tears	2	1	1	-	2
115.	think	2	-	2	2	-
116.	upset	2	2	-	-	2
117.	western(s)	2	-	2	2	-
118.	wife	2	1	1	2	-
119.	worried	2	-	2	1	1

120-290. (f = 1)
accident, action, adversity, again, agent, aid,
anguish, answer, anxious, argue, army, authority,
automobile accident, badness, bath tub, begin,
behavior, brother, bully, calm, car, care, carefree, caught, children, city, clouds, come,
communism, confused, consequences, content,
control, cowboy, crisis, curfew, dead, despair,
discernment, disobey, drinking, easy, Elvis
Presley, end, enemy, E.P., errors, everything,
feud, few, fighting, find, finish, fix, free, freedom, frequent, frustrated, frustration, fuss,
games, gray, grounded, hardship, harmony, headache,
hell, hole, homework, humiliation, in, indecision,
inevitable, irksome, itch, jeopardy, juvenile,
kindness, long, madness, make, marriage, math,
midterm, mind, miserable, mixer, motorcycle,
mountains, much, myself, need, no money, none,
nothing, officer, oh, omen, order, out, over,
parents, pena, perfect, persistent, person,
pestilence, physics, place, pleasure, pool, prison,
psychiatrist, punish, race, racial problem,
records, registration, relief, remedy, repair,
rescue, rest, riot, robbery, Russia, safety, scram,
self, sensible, shake, small, social, society,
S.O.S., south, spells, start, steal, storm, story,
struggle, suffering, sweat, teachers, teenagers,
terrible, test, theme, thinking, thought, tires,
toil, tomorrow, troops, trouble, turtle, unable,
unending, uneventful, us, virtue, vision, wall,
waste time, welcome, where, work, wrinkle,
wrong deed, you
(No response - 3)

IV-23 Window

No.	Response	Total	High Lang.	Low Lang.	Male	Female
1.	glass	252	129	123	166	86
2.	pane(s)	83	41	42	35	48
3.	door	82	47	35	45	37
4.	view	64	37	27	22	42
5.	open	35	18	17	15	20
6.	see	33	12	21	14	19
7.	air	32	11	21	15	17
8.	look	31	15	16	15	16
9.	shade	28	12	16	11	17
10.	house	27	11	16	14	13
11.	light	25	12	13	16	9
12.	curtain(s)	23	13	10	3	20
13.	clear	17	4	13	8	9
14.	sill	16	9	7	9	7
15.	sky	13	4	9	6	7
16.	opening	12	5	7	6	6
17.	office	11	6	5	9	2
18.	outside	11	6	5	3	8

IV-23 Window (contd)

No.	Response	Total	High Lang.	Low Lang.	Male	Female
19.	scene	8	4	4	3	5
20.	seeing	7	2	5	4	3
21.	clean	6	3	3	2	4
22.	ledge	6	5	1	2	4
23.	washer	6	4	2	3	3
24.	box	5	5	-	3	2
25.	pain	5	2	3	3	2
26.	scenery	5	2	3	2	3
27.	trees	5	3	2	3	2
28.	building	4	2	2	1	3
29.	dirty	4	3	1	2	2
30.	frame	4	2	2	2	2
31.	hole	4	3	1	1	3
32.	jump	4	2	2	2	2
33.	rain	4	3	1	2	2
34.	sash	4	1	3	3	1
35.	sight	4	2	2	2	2
36.	wash	4	1	3	3	1
37.	broken	3	1	2	3	-
38.	dirt	3	3	-	1	2
39.	room	3	3	-	-	3
40.	screen	3	3	-	1	2
41.	sun	3	1	2	2	1
42.	ticket(s)	3	1	2	1	2
43.	death	2	1	1	2	-
44.	fall	2	-	2	2	-
45.	fenetre	2	1	1	-	2
46.	fenster	2	2	-	2	-
47.	freedom	2	1	1	2	-
48.	lady	2	1	1	2	-
49.	landscape	2	1	1	1	1
50.	mirror	2	-	2	2	-
51.	mother	2	1	1	2	-
52.	out	2	1	1	-	2
53.	picture	2	1	1	-	2
54.	seat	2	-	2	1	1
55.	store	2	-	2	-	2
56.	street	2	-	2	1	1
57.	wall	2	1	1	-	2
58.	woman(e)	2	2	-	2	-

59-124. (f = 1)
apartment, barn, bay, black, blinds, book, break,
breath, cashier, casing, city, closed, cold,
cool, dept. store, display, doctor, edge, eye-
piece, face, fenestra, fenstern, figure, fresh
air, glass pane, green, horror, hours, high,
husband, jump out, life, look out, lucid, mountains, observe, outdoors, Payne, peep, peer,
people, plane, plate, rear, registration, see out,
see through, shadow, shape, shelf, shopper, show,
shut, shutter, square, sultry, sunlight, sunny,
transparency, transparent, vision, weather, wife,
window panes, wood, world

IV-24 Woman

No.	Response	Total	High Lang.	Low Lang.	Male	Female
1.	man(e)	448	229	219	189	259
2.	girl(s)	70	35	35	48	22
3.	female	54	27	27	30	24
4.	lady(ies)	37	16	21	13	24
5.	sex	31	20	11	29	2
6.	mother	29	16	13	12	17
7.	wife	20	11	9	15	5
8.	dress(es)	19	11	8	6	13
9.	pretty	19	11	8	9	10
10.	beauty	18	8	10	14	4
11.	love	18	10	8	12	6
12.	child(ren)	13	6	7	6	7
13.	woman(e)	11	4	7	8	3

IV-24 Woman (contd)

No.	Response	Total	High Lang.	Low Lang.	Male	Female
14.	clothes	10	3	7	2	8
15.	beautiful	9	1	8	7	2
16.	figure	8	6	2	5	3
17.	feminine	7	3	4	–	7
18.	fun	7	–	7	7	–
19.	me	7	5	2	1	6
20.	Eve	4	4	–	1	3
21.	old	4	–	4	2	2
22.	skirt(s)	4	1	3	2	2
23.	suffrage	4	2	2	3	1
24.	fat	3	1	2	1	2
25.	gentle	3	2	1	2	1
26.	house	3	1	2	–	3
27.	kind	3	1	2	3	–
28.	lovely	3	3	–	2	1
29.	person	3	1	2	2	1
30.	wow	3	1	2	3	–
31.	attractive	2	1	1	2	–
32.	body	2	1	1	2	–
33.	date(s)	2	–	2	2	–
34.	face	2	2	–	–	2
35.	femininity	2	1	1	–	2
36.	good	2	1	1	2	–
37.	hair	2	1	1	2	–
38.	hat(s)	2	–	2	1	1
39.	hater	2	1	1	1	1
40.	legs	2	–	2	2	–
41.	mate	2	–	2	1	1
42.	mom	2	1	1	1	1
43.	opposite	2	1	1	2	–
44.	Pat	2	–	2	2	–
45.	people	2	1	1	2	–
46.	shoes	2	1	1	–	2

47-141. ($\underline{f}$ = 1)
abrupt, Anne, art, attraction, badness, bar,
bathing suit, beads, big, black, blonde, breast,
Carolee, charm, chick, city, cloths, companion,
competition, confusion, crafty, Esta, fight,
fine, food, friend, garden, grace, graceful,
great, hate, her appearance, high heels, home,
housewife, husband, image, infant, in love,
intercourse, Isabel, Janet, Jayne Mansfield,
Jeanette, Laverna, lawyer, long hair, looks,
maid, many, marriage, money, motherhood, motherly,
Mrs., nice, oh boy, painting, Penny, personality,
pleasure, precious, pure, reproduction, rich,
romance, Roosevelt, Rozanne, sensible, sexy, she,
Signe, sister, skippy, sorority, Stinberg, stupid,
superior, sweater, talk, talkative, talking,
teachers, thin, time, uterus, Vickie, vote,
wanton, warm, weaker sex, womanhood, wonderful,
yes, young
(No response - 1)

CHAPTER 7

SINGLE-WORD FREE-ASSOCIATION NORMS FOR 328 RESPONSES FROM THE CONNECTICUT CULTURAL NORMS FOR VERBAL ITEMS IN CATEGORIES[1]

George R. Marshall
Sir George Williams University, Montreal, Canada
and Charles N. Cofer
Pennsylvania State University, University Park, Pennsylvania

In carrying out experiments on the role of the factor of categorization of words in clustering in free recall and comparing it to the associative relatedness of the words, we found it necessary to collect association norms for a variety of words contained in the Connecticut norms for responses to category names (Cohen, Bousfield, & Whitmarsh, 1957). These norms permitted us to construct pairs of words, categorized or not, with associative relatedness controlled in both directions. Available norms often would give associative distributions for one of the pair but not for the other.

We believe that these norms will have great value to investigators who require associative data for purposes of studying verbal concept formation and clustering in free recall. For such studies, it is often necessary to know not only the association response distribution for the concept or category term but also the distribution for the various instances of the category that are to be used.

Study of the data which are presented here has led us to the realization that there are all sorts of ways in which the associative relation between two or more words may be measured. We have identified in the literature, or developed ourselves, ten such indicies of associative relation. A description of these measures, their rationale and computation, and a consideration of their predictive utility may be found in Marshall and Cofer (1963).

METHOD

The single-response free word-association norms, reported in the Appendix to this chapter, were collected at Brooklyn College in the spring of 1961. The Ss were undergraduate introductory psychology students in the School of Liberal Arts and Sciences. The stimulus items used were selected from responses given to category titles (e.g., fruits, weapons, insects) in the "Cultural Norms for Verbal Items in 43 Categories" collected by Cohen *et al.* (1957).

The Ss in the Connecticut normative study were required to write the first four items they thought of as representative members of the specified class for each of the 43 categories or classes used. Therefore, the norms are multiple-response, controlled associations. The norms presented here are single-response free-association norms. Cohen *et al.* used 400 Ss and with four responses from each S, each category name has 1600 associative responses.

[1] The collection of these norms was carried out under contract NONR 285(47) between the Office of Naval Research and New York University during the spring of 1961. Reproduction in whole or in part is permitted for purposes of the United States Government.

TABLE 1 Stimulus Items Drawn from the Connecticut Norms[a]

I. Birds
1. Bluejay 3(160)
2. Canary 5(72)
3. Chicken 27(7)
4. Crow 6(70)
5. Dove 27(7)
6. Falcon 42(2)
7. Magpie 73(17)
8. Ostrich 35(54)
9. Owl 20(12)
10. Parrot 12(31)
11. Penguin 73(1)
12. Raven 24(9)
13. Robin 1(344)
14. Sparrow 2(190)
15. Stork 51(2)
16. Swallow 16(19)
17. Thrush 42(3)

II. Body parts
1. Ankle 46(2)
2. Arm 1(308)
3. Ear 10(27)
4. Elbow 46(2)
5. Foot 4(134)
6. Hand 5(132)
7. Head 3(220)
8. Hip 36.5(3)
9. Knee 30.5(4)
10. Leg 2(293)
11. Nose 5(32)
12. Rib 66(1)
13. Shoulder 21(8)
14. Stomach 17.5(13)
15. Toe 13(17)
16. Waist 46(2)

III. Clothes
1. Blouse 9(94)
2. Cloak 30.5(1)
3. Coat 5(128)
4. Dress 3(144)
5. Gown 26(2)
6. Hat 2(169)
7. Jacket 13(43)
8. Pants 4(130)
9. Scarf 23(5)
10. Shirt 1(203)
11. Slacks 19.5(10)
12. Suit 15(19)
13. Sweater 7(115)
14. Tie 11(60)
15. Trousers 14(35)
16. Vest 18(11)

IV. Countries
1. Arabia 61(1)
2. Chile 36.5(4)
3. Cuba 61(1)
4. Egypt 25.5(8)
5. England 3(214)
6. France 2(224)
7. Germany 4(134)
8. India 18.5(14)
9. Iran 61(1)
10. Korea 36.5(4)
11. Mexico 9(43)
12. Portugal 31.5(6)
13. Russia 5(111)
14. Spain 6(81)
15. Tibet 61(1)
16. Wales 45.5(2)

V. Drinks
1. Ale 10(27)
2. Beer 1(295)
3. Bourbon 9(54)
4. Brandy 11(23)
5. Champagne 12(14)
6. Cider 41.5(1)
7. Cognac 25.5(2)
8. Gin 3(214)
9. Rum 8(80)
10. Rye 7(108)
11. Scotch 6(127)
12. Vermouth 14(7)
13. Vodka 5(156)
14. Whiskey 2(228)
15. Wine 4(165)

VI. Earth formations
1. Beach 112(1)
2. Cliff 7(42)
3. Delta 112(1)
4. Dune 63(2)
5. Forest 112(1)
6. Harbor 112(1)
7. Island 35.5(5)
8. Lagoon 112(1)
9. Lake 6(72)
10. Mountain 1(307)
11. Ravine 30(6)
12. River 4(88)
13. Shore 63(2)
14. Stream 20.5(12)
15. Swamp 112(1)
16. Valley 3(167)

VII. Fish
1. Barracuda 44.5(3)
2. Carp 22(18)
3. Cod 6(91)
4. Fluke 35.5(6)
5. Herring 22(18)
6. Marlin 38.5(4)
7. Perch 3(101)
8. Pike 16(28)
9. Salmon 5(92)
10. Sardine 35.5(6)
11. Shark 10(59)
12. Snapper 44.5(3)
13. Sturgeon 44.5(3)
14. Trout 1(174)
15. Tuna 4(100)

VIII. Flowers
1. Aster 16(22)
2. Buttercup 27(8)
3. Daffodil 11(48)
4. Daisy 3.5(101)
5. Gardenia 9(51)
6. Lily 7(69)
7. Lilac 13(40)
8. Lotus 68(1)
9. Magnolia 68(1)
10. Marigold 21.5(14)
11. Orchid 5(89)
12. Pansy 8(59)
13. Poppy 23.5(12)
14. Rose 1(356)
15. Tulip 3.5(101)
16. Pony 47(1)

IX. Four-legged animals
1. Antelope 47(1)
2. Bear 5(66)
3. Beaver 32.5(2)
4. Buffalo 47(1)
5. Camel 47(1)
6. Cow 4(164)
7. Deer 7(47)
8. Dog 1(369)
9. Donkey 27.5(3)
10. Elk 47(1)
11. Fox 9.5(33)
12. Goat 14(22)
13. Horse 3(209)
14. Mule 20(7)
15. Pig 19(20)
16. Pony 47(1)
17. Zebra 27.5(3)

X. Fruits
1. Apple 1(373)
2. Apricot 11(12)
3. Banana 6(113)
4. Cantaloupe 27.5(1)
5. Date 20.5(2)
6. Fig 27.5(1)
7. Melon 27.5(1)
8. Nectarine 27.5(1)
9. Orange 3(228)
10. Peach 4(210)
11. Pear 2(294)
12. Pineapple 12(11)
13. Plum 5(12)
14. Prune 15(6)
15. Raisin 27.5(1)
16. Tangerine 15(6)

XI. House parts
1. Attic 15(23)
2. Balcony 82.5(1)
3. Beam 24(6)
4. Ceiling 8(50)
5. Chimney 10(36)
6. Door 3(202)
7. Floor 5(126)
8. Foyer 82.5(1)
9. Kitchen 82.5(1)
10. Lobby 52(2)
11. Lounge 50(2)
12. Patio 82.5(1)
13. Roof 1(242)
14. Stair 6(54)
15. Wall 4(156)
16. Window 2(220)

XII. Insects
1. Ant 2(228)
2. Bee 3(153)
3. Beetle 6(84)
4. Cricket 21.5(11)
5. Flea 10(37)
6. Gnat 16(20)
7. Hornet 17(17)
8. Locust 29(5)
9. Mantis 52(1)
10. Mosquito 4(150)
11. Roach 12(28)
12. Scorpion 52(1)
13. Spider 5(90)
14. Termite 20(12)
15. Tick 29(5)
16. Wasp 8(54)

XIII. Materials
1. Batiste 56(1)
2. Burlap 18(7)
3. Cashmere 26.5(4)
4. Chino 56(1)
5. Cotton 1(330)
6. Denim 26.5(4)
7. Felt 21.5(5)
8. Fur 56(1)
9. Hemp 56(1)
10. Jersey 56(1)
11. Lace 31(3)
12. Linen 6(108)
13. Poplin 56(1)
14. Silk 3(249)
15. Tweed 11(16)
16. Velvet 10(25)
17. Wool 2(270)

XIV. Metals
1. Aluminum 4(149)
2. Brass 9(72)
3. Bronze 11(29)
4. Copper 2(249)
5. Iron 1(29)
6. Lead 10(57)
7. Nickel 14(15)
8. Steel 3(186)
9. Tin 5(131)
10. Zinc 8(83)

XV. Musical instruments
1. Accordian 16(20)
2. Bass 15(24)
3. Bugle 20(12)
4. Clarinet 5.5(106)
5. Drums 4(145)
6. Flute 7(94)
7. Guitar 11(40)
8. Harmonica 26(5)
9. Harp 10(42)
10. Mandolin 33.5(2)
11. Piano 1(286)
12. Piccolo 24(8)
13. Trumpet 3(175)
14. Ukelele 44(1)
15. Violin 2(214)
16. Xylophone 28.5(3)
17. Zither 44(1)

XVI. Professions
1. Accountant 22(11)
2. Chemist 30.5(5)
3. Cook 161.5(1)
4. Dentist 4(74)
5. Detective 161.5(1)
6. Doctor 1(348)
7. Firemen 161.5(1)
8. Historian 63(3)
9. Jeweler 161.5(1)
10. Lawyer 2(182)
11. Mechanic 63(3)
12. Nurse 7(40)
13. Pilot 88.5(2)
14. Plumber 38.5(5)
15. Professor 3(97)
16. Teacher 5(62)

XVII. Seasonings
1. Chili 39(3)
2. Chives 75.5(1)
3. Cinnamon 6(62)
4. Cloves 8(42)
5. Garlic 5(70)
6. Ginger 27.5(6)
7. Mint 30(5)
8. Mustard 14(24)
9. Nutmeg 9(41)
10. Paprika 7(54)
11. Parsley 25(7)
12. Pepper 2(319)
13. Salt 1(342)
14. Sugar 4(90)
15. Syrup 75.5(1)
16. Vanilla 3(91)
17. Walnut 17(18)

XVIII. Trees
1. Birch 5(98)
2. Cedar 12(27)
3. Chestnut 11(29)
4. Cypress 26(6)
5. Dogwood 14(20)
6. Elm 3(200)
7. Maple 1(290)
8. Oak 2(288)
9. Pine 4(104)
10. Poplar 19.5(16)
11. Spruce 6(73)

XIX. Vegetables
1. Bean 4(118)
2. Beet 9(65)
3. Broccoli 15(26)
4. Cabbage 11(51)
5. Carrot 1(240)
6. Corn 6(112)
7. Cucumber 20(12)
8. Lettuce 7(93)
9. Mushroom 36(1)
10. Onion 17(17)
11. Parsnip 26(2)
12. Pea 2(199)
13. Potato 3(175)
14. Spinach 8(90)
15. Tomato 5(115)
16. Turnip 13(38)
17. Yam 36(1)

XX. Weapons
1. Bomb 8(51)
2. Boomerang 80(1)
3. Cannon 6(62)
4. Carbine 30(6)
5. Cudgel 80(1)
6. Dagger 18(14)
7. Gun 1(317)
8. Harpoon 49(2)
9. Hatchet 37(4)
10. Knife 2(306)
11. Lance 80(1)
12. Rifle 4(104)
13. Saber 42.5(3)
14. Sling 49(2)
15. Sword 3(111)
16. Tomahawk 80(1)

XXI. Weather
1. Drizzle 81(1)
2. Earthquake 22.5(9)
3. Fog 15(24)
4. Frost 55(2)
5. Hail 6(101)
6. Monsoon 43.5(3)
7. Rain 1(245)
8. Shower 81(1)
9. Sleet 5(116)
10. Snow 2(207)
11. Squall 55(2)
12. Storm 10(37)
13. Sunshine 17(16)
14. Thunder 13(29)
15. Tornado 4(118)
16. Typhoon 8(49)

[a]The number after a word is its rank as an associate to the category and the number in parentheses is its frequency of occurrence out of 1600 instances.

The stimulus items used in the present study are listed in Table 1, with the rank and frequency with which these responses were given to the category name in the Connecticut norms listed beside each word. Stimulus items were selected from only 21 of the 43 categories, and the number of stimuli from each category ranged from 10 to 18 words. The selection of stimuli was somewhat arbitrary, with the number of classes and stimuli limited by problems of tabulation and availability of Ss. However, we rejected stimuli which might be ambiguous, idiosyncratic, or judged relatively unfamiliar. For example, we did not use as stimuli such items as *22, teeth, foil,* given as *weapons* in the Connecticut norms.

The total number of stimulus words of 328 was broken down into three lists of equal length (110, 109, 109) and systematically randomized so that no two words from the same category were contiguous. Then these lists of words were presented to three different groups of Ss ($n = 100$ in each group) on mimeographed sheets, a word per line, with one single space provided for S's response to each stimulus item. A cover sheet, which prevented Ss from seeing the stimulus items, gave the following directions:

> This is an association test. On the following sheets you will see a list of over 100 words. Read each printed word and in the space beside it write the first word that it makes you think of: Start with the first word; look at it; write the word that it makes you think of; then go on to the next word. Give only one word for each printed word. Do not skip any words. Do not change a word after you have written it. Work rapidly until you have finished all the words. Wait for the signal to start. Are there any questions?

RESULTS

The frequency with which a word occurs as a response across the sample population of $n = 100$ determines the order of its listing in the norms. Thus, out of 100 Ss, 65 responded *bird* to the stimulus *bluejay* and this response, as the highest frequency response, is listed first in the associative responses to this stimulus.

The normative data are presented in the sequence shown in the list of stimulus items (see Table 1). Very minor errors in tabulation were not corrected, so that *n* varies from 99 to 102. It is believed that such minor errors will not affect the use of these norms and that, therefore, it is not worth the time and expense to correct them.

REFERENCES

Cohen, B. H., Bousfield, W. A., & Whitmarsh, G. A. (1957). Cultural norms for items in 43 categories. Technical Report No. 22, University of Connecticut, ONR Contract NONR-631(00).

Marshall, G. R., & Cofer, C. N. (1963). Associative indicies as measures of word relatedness: a summary and comparison of ten methods. *Journal of Verbal Learning and Verbal Behavior* 1, 408-421.

I-1 Bluejay (n = 100)

No.	Response	Total
1.	bird	65
2.	fly	3
3.	pretty	3
4.	robin	3
5.	blue	2
6.	colorful	2
7.	crow	2
8.	sing	2
9.	song	2

10-25. (f = 1)
beautiful, canary, corn, free, magpie, mean, noise, redbreast, sky, sparrow, spring, squawk, talk, team, treetop, warble

I-2 Canary (n = 100)

No.	Response	Total
1.	yellow	44
2.	bird	27
3.	sing	11
4.	song	5
5.	cat	3

6-15. (f = 1)
cage, chirp, fish, fly, pet, salmon, shrill, small, sweet, tweet

I-3 Chicken (n = 100)

No.	Response	Total
1.	food	9
2.	hen	8
3.	soup	8
4.	animal	6
5.	roast	6
6.	egg	4
7.	leg	4
8.	liver	4
9.	turkey	4
10.	wing	4
11.	bone(s)	3
12.	fat	3
13.	fowl	3
14.	Friday	3
15.	fried	3

16-43. (f = 1)
basket, bird, broth, cooked, coward, dinner, drumstick, eat, fence, fricasse, fruit, fry, girl, heart, house, ketchup, little, Margo, meat, pie, pot, poultry, pullet, Sabbath, salad, soft, whitemeat
(Illegible - 1)

I-4 Crow (n = 99)

No.	Response	Total
1.	bird	38
2.	black	25
3.	fly	3
4.	caw	2
5.	hawk	2
6.	noise	2

7-33. (f = 1)
animal, croak, cry, death, evil, feet, fish, fox, gloat, haul, head, Jim Crow, morning, night, pest, pie, scarecrow, seeds, sing, sleek, sparrow, straight, trees, voice, worm
(Illegible - 2)

I-5 Dove (n = 100)

No.	Response	Total
1.	bird	27
2.	peace	20
3.	white	15
4.	love	7
5.	fly	5
6.	beauty	4
7.	sweet	3
8.	coo	2
9.	gentle	2
10.	soap	2
11.	tail	2

12-22. (f = 1)
Eddie, lovers, pure, raven, sing, sky, swan, tonsils, tree, wings, yellow

I-6 Falcon (n = 100)

No.	Response	Total
1.	car	36
2.	bird	33
3.	eagle	3
4.	Ford	3

5-29. (f = 1)
beat, black, catch, clans, danger, dive, fleet, fly, funny, gang, hard, horror, monster, mystery, ocean, own, prey, quick, ride, sedan, slyness, sportscar, swift, tree
(Illegible - 1)

I-7 Magpie (n = 100)

No.	Response	Total
1.	bird	46
2.	crow	6
3.	mud	4
4.	talking	4
5.	apple	3
6.	chatterer	3
7.	pie	3
8.	black	2

I-7 Magpie (n = 100) (contd)

No.	Response	Total
9.	girl	2
10.	pumpkin	2

11-34. (f = 1)
animal, baby, brown, dessert, dirt, eat, elf, fairytale, fish, four, fry, haggard, homosexual, insect, jackdaw, king, music, nest, noise, sing, song, talks, ugly, voice, wing

I-8 Ostrich (n = 100)

No.	Response	Total
1.	feather(s)	29
2.	bird	17
3.	neck	10
4.	head	5
5.	hide	5
6.	long	5
7.	egg	3
8.	plume(s)	3
9.	animal	2
10.	hole	2
11.	sand	2

12-28. (f = 1)
big, buried, bury, cow, dumb, ground, headless, hidden, leg, nose, orange, reach, scared, skinny, snobbish, tall, white

I-9 Owl (n = 100)

No.	Response	Total
1.	bird	30
2.	eye(s)	18
3.	hoot	16
4.	who(o)	4
5.	wise	4
6.	night	3
7.	screech	3
8.	blind	2
9.	cigar	2
10.	hooting	2
11.	pussycat	2

12-25. (f = 1)
cat, chimney, dark, glasses, head, hog, howl, mammal, ooh, pirch, potato chips, reach, see, spy

I-10 Parrot (n = 100)

No.	Response	Total
1.	bird(s)	37
2.	talk(s)	20
3.	cracker	4
4.	parakeet	3
5.	beak	2
6.	mimmick	2
7.	noise	2
8.	repeat	2

I-10 Parrot (n = 100) (contd)

No.	Response	Total
9.	speak	2
10.	talking	2

11-34. (f = 1)
cage, canary, care, carrot,
chirp, colors, cookie, delicate,
dog, fever, green, jungle, life,
loud, mime, monkey, noisy,
Polly, repetition, singing,
south, squawk, stiff, voice

I-11 Penguin (n = 98)

No.	Response	Total
1.	bird	14
2.	cold	7
3.	tuxedo	7
4.	waddle	7
5.	Alaska	5
6.	book	4
7.	coat	4
8.	snow	4
9.	Arctic	3
10.	island	3
11.	suit	3
12.	Antarctic	2
13.	black	2
14.	cute	2
15.	fish	2
16.	fly	2
17.	ice	2
18.	north	2
19.	walk	2

20-40. (f = 1)
beak, black-white, cartoon, cool,
dove, duck, elephant, Eskimo,
flap, funny, go, Iceland, North
Pole, polar, seal, shirt,
stately, waiter, white, wings
(Illegible - 1)

I-12 Raven (n = 100)

No.	Response	Total
1.	bird	33
2.	black	29
3.	Poe (Edgar)	21

4-20. (f = 1)
B.V.D., crow, death, eat, fox,
free, haven, hawk, hell, hungry,
ominous, poem, quoth, red,
sadness, shiny
(Illegible - 1)

I-13 Robin (n = 100)

No.	Response	Total
1.	bird	54
2.	Hood	14
3.	red	9
4.	song	6
5.	nest	5
6.	redbreast	2
7.	sing	2
8.	spring	2

I-13 Robin (n = 100) (contd)

No.	Response	Total

9-14. (f = 1)
bluebird, boy, eggs, man,
singing, tweet

I-14 Sparrow (n = 100)

No.	Response	Total
1.	bird	66
2.	small	4
3.	chirp	3
4.	tree	3
5.	sing	2
6.	wing	2

7-26. (f = 1)
barrow, bread, breadcrumbs, cafe,
chicken, chirping, excrement,
flight, flimsy, fly, jump,
liberty, little, nest, protection,
robin, song, tiny, twitter,
victim

I-15 Stork (n = 101)

No.	Response	Total
1.	baby(babies)	44
2.	Club	13
3.	bird	11
4.	animal	5
5.	fly(flies)	5
6.	child(ren)	4
7.	beak	2

8-24. (f = 1)
bill, birth, bring, cane,
chimney, cork, girl, legs,
longlegs, neck, ostrich,
pigeon, ring, stands, Stork
Club, story, tall

I-16 Swallow (n = 101)

No.	Response	Total
1.	bird	34
2.	gulp	6
3.	eat	5
4.	chew	4
5.	choke	4
6.	digest	4
7.	drink	4
8.	food	4
9.	Capistrano	3
10.	seagull	3
11.	water	3
12.	deep	2
13.	tongue	2

14-37. (f = 1)
brook, call, cough, down, fish,
flew, fly, free, goose, hard,
mouth, music, saliva, sip, small,
soar, song, spring, stuck, sweep,
taste, throat
(Illegible - 2)

I-17 Thrush (n = 100)

No.	Response	Total
1.	bird	31
2.	push	8
3.	throw	5
4.	bush(es)	4
5.	brush	3
6.	cut	3
7.	beat	2
8.	hit	2
9.	move	2
10.	sing	2
11.	song	2

12-44. (f = 1)
castaway, close, fast, flower,
fly, force, forward, hunting,
hush, leap, mouth, music, open,
pine, robin, saw, snow, soiled,
spoil, stamp, suddenly, swab,
Tel Aviv, through, tongue,
toss, trash, warm, water, wave,
whip, wind, woods
(Illegible - 3)

II-1 Ankle (n = 99)

No.	Response	Total
1.	foot	23
2.	leg	16
3.	bone	13
4.	knee	12
5.	bracelet	9
6.	sock	4
7.	broken	2
8.	chain	2
9.	girl	2

10-25. (f = 1)
bandage, body, break, calf,
hump, lowliness, pain, pretty,
share, strap, swollen, thigh,
thin, toe, wide
(Illegible - 1)

II-2 Arm (n = 100)

No.	Response	Total
1.	leg	32
2.	hand	22
3.	armpit	4
4.	chair	3
5.	length	3
6.	long	3
7.	broken	2
8.	fingers	2
9.	sleeve	2
10.	sling	2

11-35. (f = 1)
amputee, bar, bleed, body,
bracelet, chain, dog, elbow,
foot, hair, hit, hold, hug,
human, joint, limb, muscle,
pyka (Russian), rest, shirt,
shoulder, sore, supply, swing
touch

II-3 Ear ($\underline{n}$ = 100)

No.	Response	Total
1.	hear	36
2.	lobe	15
3.	sound	6
4.	nose	5
5.	drum	4
6.	listen	4
7.	ring	4
8.	ache	3
9.	wax(y)	3
10.	bite	2
11.	eye	2
12.	head	2
13.	muff	2
14.	phone	2

15-24. ($\underline{f}$ = 1)
aid, Cochear, delicate, hurt, list, mark, noise, pinna, Sonotone, wash

II-4 Elbow ($\underline{n}$ = 100)

No.	Response	Total
1.	arm	27
2.	knee	17
3.	joint	10
4.	hand	7
5.	macaroni	6
6.	room	4
7.	bend	3
8.	bone	3
9.	point	3
10.	body	2
11.	poke	2

12-27. ($\underline{f}$ = 1)
agressive, finger, funny, grease, in, kick, lean, leg, limb, pointy, poking, push, rest, rush hour, sharp

II-5 Foot ($\underline{n}$ = 101)

No.	Response	Total
1.	toe(s)	32
2.	shoe(s)	26
3.	leg	6
4.	hand	4
5.	run	3
6.	bare	2
7.	feet	2
8.	walk	2
9.	walking	2

10-30. ($\underline{f}$ = 1)
ankle, arm, ball, body, corn, dance, end, hold, hot, hurt, kick, knee, moat, palm, person, right, socks, step, weary, would
(Illegible - 2)

II-6 Hand ($\underline{n}$ = 100)

No.	Response	Total
1.	finger(s)	20
2.	foot	14
3.	glove(s)	10
4.	arm	8
5.	hold	4

II-6 Hand ($\underline{n}$ = 100) (contd)

No.	Response	Total
6.	body	3
7.	leg	3
8.	shake	3
9.	nails	2
10.	thumb	2
11.	write	2
12.	writing	2

13-38. ($\underline{f}$ = 1)
apple, ball, band, bite, book, can, feet, fist, food, give, hand, homework, mantle, marriage, mat, mouth, movement, out, person, ring, strong, supplicate, toe, understanding, work
(Illegible - 2)

II-7 Head ($\underline{n}$ = 101)

No.	Response	Total
1.	hair	22
2.	body	7
3.	eye(s)	7
4.	face	6
5.	neck	5
6.	foot	4
7.	ache	3
8.	brain	3
9.	arm	2
10.	big	2
11.	feet	2
12.	hat	2
13.	mind	2
14.	shoulders	2
15.	think	2
16.	top	2

17-44. ($\underline{f}$ = 1)
bald, beautiful, chief, cold, dress, facial features, features, guillotine, high, hold, human, hunters, hurt, lights, line, man, officers, on, organ, pate, person, reason, roundback, scarf, shrunken, table, tail, tête

II-8 Hip ($\underline{n}$ = 100)

No.	Response	Total
1.	bone	21
2.	body	16
3.	thigh	9
4.	joint	8
5.	leg	6
6.	twist	4
7.	belt	2
8.	hep	2
9.	swing(er)	2

10-39. ($\underline{f}$ = 1)
anatomy, boy, broken, cat, curve, dig, doctor, femur, figure, flesh, foot, girl, hippopotamus, Hippothemus, hop, insurance, Jacob, limb, lip, Monroe, movement, nose, pelvis, person, shake, shoulder, side, snake, waste, wild

II-9 Knee ($\underline{n}$ = 100)

No.	Response	Total
1.	leg	36
2.	foot	28
3.	cap	10
4.	body	3
5.	bone	3
6.	joint	3
7.	elbow	2
8.	hand	2
9.	sock	2
10.	toe	2

11-19. ($\underline{f}$ = 1)
ankle, bend, bind, bruise, calf, hi, round, socks, walk

II-10 Leg ($\underline{n}$ = 100)

No.	Response	Total
1.	foot	19
2.	arm	18
3.	pants	6
4.	hair	5
5.	long	4
6.	broken	3
7.	toe	3
8.	ankle	2
9.	body	2
10.	dance	2
11.	girl	2
12.	run	2
13.	shoe	2
14.	swing	2
15.	walk	2
16.	wooden	2

17-40. ($\underline{f}$ = 1)
buttocks, chair, coat, fag, fall, Fatibia, food, fool, knee, lamb, length, limb, muscle, shade, sit, smooth, socks, stand, stiff, stocking, thin, trouser, turkey, work

II-11 Nose ($\underline{n}$ = 100)

No.	Response	Total
1.	face	29
2.	smell	14
3.	mouth	8
4.	eye(s)	6
5.	water	5
6.	long	4
7.	nostril	3
8.	breathe	2
9.	blow	2
10.	ear	2
11.	hook	2

12-34. ($\underline{f}$ = 1)
bleed, breath, cold, cone, dirty, feature, handkerchief, head, Naison, new, nipple, person, pimple, Pinnocchio, plastic surgery, plug, red, run, sneeze, snot, Solomon, spits, tree

II-12 Rib (n = 100)

No.	Response	Total
1.	bone	29
2.	steak	15
3.	body	14
4.	meat	8
5.	roast	5
6.	cage	4
7.	tickle	4
8.	chest	3
9.	side	3
10.	Adam	2
11.	broken	2

12-32. (f = 1)
back, blood, cog, disease, Eve, food, foot, funny, hard, human, joke, kid, loin, no, neckbones, part, pig, spare, support, trip, vertebrate

II-13 Shoulder (n = 100)

No.	Response	Total
1.	arm	32
2.	neck	9
3.	bone	6
4.	back	5
5.	blade	4
6.	broad	4
7.	lean	3
8.	soft	3
9.	body	2
10.	hurt	2
11.	pad	2
12.	straight	2

13-38. (f = 1)
big, Borden, boulder, branch, clam, clavicle, collar, embrace, hands, head, holster, hurts, lamb, man, movement, muscle, push, rest, road, sexy, shrug, skin, socket, strap, strong, touch

II-14 Stomach (n = 95)

No.	Response	Total
1.	organ	11
2.	ache	10
3.	intestine(s)	8
4.	eat	6
5.	food	6
6.	digestion	5
7.	hungry	4
8.	abdomen	2
9.	acid	2
10.	body	2
11.	esophagus	2
12.	hunger	2
13.	hurt	2
14.	ulcers	2
15.	upset	2

16-44. (f = 1)
break, churn, contracting, digest, digested, eating, enzymes, fat, fetal pig, full, gastric, gastric juice, gastrointeritis, girdle, it, juice, large, muscle, oval, pain, pancreas, pauch, pit, pump, sick, smell, stand, throat, tube

II-15 Toe (n = 100)

No.	Response	Total
1.	foot	37
2.	nail	21
3.	heel	5
4.	shoe	5
5.	stub	4
6.	finger	2
7.	five	2
8.	hold	2
9.	leg	2

10-29. (f = 1)
ballux, big, broken, corn, dance, digit, hit, hurt, ingrower, kick, knee, large, mark, show, step, stocking, sweaty, thumb, wiggle, wing

II-16 Waist (n = 100)

No.	Response	Total
1.	belt	17
2.	hips	14
3.	thin	9
4.	small	8
5.	coat	4
6.	girl	4
7.	narrow	4
8.	band	3
9.	line	3
10.	round	3
11.	size	3
12.	cinch	2
13.	dress	2
14.	head	2
15.	middle	2

16-35. (f = 1)
ankle, arms, bigger, blouse, busom, diet, fat, high, hold, inches, knee, measure, slim, spend, squeeze, strip, tight, wife, wrist
(Illegible - 1)

III-1 Blouse (n = 100)

No.	Response	Total
1.	shirt	19
2.	skirt	19
3.	girl	14
4.	sweater	6
5.	white	5
6.	button(s)	3
7.	open	3
8.	pretty	3
9.	wear	3
10.	bust	2

11-33. (f = 1)
blue, box, bulging, clean, clothing, color, delicate, feminine, fits, hand, iron, jersey, loose, louse, necklace, over, pants, print, scarf, shoulder, silk, soft, woman

III-2 Cloak (n = 99)

No.	Response	Total
1.	dagger	46
2.	coat	15
3.	black	7
4.	cape	6
5.	cover	6
6.	jacket	2
7.	villain	2
8.	wrap	2

9-21. (f = 1)
apparel, cloth, conceal, dark, dramatic, dress, hook, mantle, Raleigh, suit, sweep, tunic, velvet

III-3 Coat (n = 100)

No.	Response	Total
1.	hat	20
2.	warmth	17
3.	wear	10
4.	hanger	8
5.	jacket	7
6.	fur	5
7.	cold	3
8.	cover	3
9.	black	2
10.	clothing	2
11.	suit	2
12.	winter	2

13-31. (f = 1)
blue, boat, buttons, check, cloak, coat, dress, gloves, hook, houndstooth, protection, rack, red, sweater, tail, tee, war, wind, wool

III-4 Dress (n = 100)

No.	Response	Total
1.	gown	8
2.	shoe(s)	7
3.	skirt	7
4.	girl	6
5.	lace	6
6.	clothes	5
7.	clothing	5
8.	wear	5
9.	red	4
10.	wool	3
11.	blue	2
12.	garment	2
13.	nice	2
14.	pretty	2
15.	silk	2
16.	suit	2

17-48. (f = 1)
attire, belt, clear, cloth, coat, cotton, cute, date, don, flower, green, hat, length, modesty, monkey, naked, night, nylons, pants, party, print, satin, sheath, shroud, tight, up, wearing apparel, white, whole, woman, women, wrinkle

III-5 Gown (n = 100)

No.	Response	Total
1.	dress	46
2.	ball	10
3.	lace	5
4.	wedding	5
5.	cap	3
6.	long	3
7.	pretty	3

8-32. (f = 1)
ankler, ballroom, beautiful,
beauty, cloth, clothing, dance,
day, evening, fantasy, fun,
girl, glove, grown, marriage,
nice, party, prom, robe, shoes,
shroud, stockings, town, wear,
wearing apparel

III-6 Hat (n = 100)

No.	Response	Total
1.	head	38
2.	coat	11
3.	cap	5
4.	glove	5
5.	top	4
6.	brim	2
7.	cover(ing)	2
8.	ears	2
9.	hair	2
10.	lady	2
11.	man	2
12.	scarf	2
13.	suit	2

14-34. (f = 1)
apparel, army, bag, Barrett,
black, clothing, cold, Easter,
Easter bonnet, fatter, feathers,
felt, feminine, food, hat,
headcover, large, lost, shoes,
smell, sombrero

III-7 Jacket (n = 101)

No.	Response	Total
1.	coat	24
2.	warm	9
3.	clothing	5
4.	cold	5
5.	sweater	5
6.	poplin	4
7.	wear	4
8.	leather	3
9.	button(s)	2
10.	cover	2
11.	wearing apparel	2
12.	zipper	2

13-46. (f = 1)
also, autumn, beggarly, black,
boy, cloth, clothes, cupe,
dress, fit, funny, hat, hood,
jacket, lumber, mackinaw, man,
Open Road Club, pea, pocket,
short, ski, skirt, slug, sport,
spring, suede, suit, tie,
velvet, vest, winter, wool,
yellow

III-8 Pants (n = 99)

No.	Response	Total
1.	man	18
2.	shirt	12
3.	trousers	9
4.	legs	8
5.	suit	5
6.	boy	4
7.	slacks	4
8.	clothes	3
9.	belt	2
10.	breather	2
11.	cuffs	2
12.	jacket	2
13.	seats	2
14.	waist	2
15.	wear	2

16-37. (f = 1)
ants, blue, breath, brown, color,
covering, denim, dress, feet,
fight, fish, gasps, harp, ivy,
pair, rip, shorts, sit, tight,
tired, toreador, two

III-9 Scarf (n = 95)

No.	Response	Total
1.	neck	18
2.	head	12
3.	warmth	10
4.	kerchief	9
5.	wind	4
6.	cold	3
7.	silk	3
8.	cloth	2
9.	green	2
10.	girls	2
11.	red	2
12.	ribbon	2
13.	wool	2
14.	wrap	2

15-36. (f = 1)
accessory, bandana, chiffon,
clothing, coat, cover, female,
filmy, glove, Gypsy, hair, hat,
lace, murder, plaid, rope, shawl,
shoe, soft, tie, tight, white

III-10 Shirt (n = 101)

No.	Response	Total
1.	tie	23
2.	white	11
3.	sleeve(s)	7
4.	man	6
5.	pants	6
6.	tails	5
7.	wear	4
8.	blouse	3
9.	buttons	3
10.	clothes	3
11.	boy	2
12.	clean	2
13.	clothing	2
14.	color	2
15.	waist	2

16-35. (f = 1)
attire, blue, coat, collar, dress,
flirt, husband, iron, jersey,
neat, red, slacks, slove, sport,
stiff, straight, vest, warm,
wetness, wool

III-11 Slacks (n = 100)

No.	Response	Total
1.	pant(s)	44
2.	shirt(s)	6
3.	black	4
4.	clothes	3
5.	dress	3
6.	legs	3
7.	sweater	3
8.	tight	3
9.	boy	2
10.	shorts	2
11.	wear	2
12.	wool	2

13-35. (f = 1)
casual, children, clothing,
comfortable, don, fat, feet,
fix, flax, green, leisure,
man, mats, men, peg, pressed,
shoes, sneakers, torn,
trousers, warmth, women, worn

III-12 Suit (n = 100)

No.	Response	Total
1.	clothes	23
2.	coat	9
3.	dress	8
4.	jacket	8
5.	fits	6
6.	wear	5
7.	man	4
8.	pants	4
9.	clothing	3
10.	new	3
11.	trousers	2

12-36. (f = 1)
appropriate, armor, blue,
Brooks, case, cloth, collar,
elegant, hanger, leather, leg,
me, outfit, please, press,
sharp, slacks, sophistication,
Sue, tie, tweed, two-piece,
walking, woman, wool

III-13 Sweater (n = 101)

No.	Response	Total
1.	wool	16
2.	girl	13
3.	knit(ting)	12
4.	warmth	9
5.	skirt	7
6.	clothing	5
7.	wear	5
8.	blouse	3
9.	bust	3
10.	red	3
11.	soft	3
12.	breast	2
13.	jacket	2
14.	tight	2

15-30. (f = 1)
blue, body, cashmere, cloth,
coat, cold, dress, England,
fur, fur-blend, fuzzy, large,
pin, V-neck, wearing apparel,
winter

III-14   Tie   (n = 100)

No.	Response	Total
1.	shirt	22
2.	knot	15
3.	neck	12
4.	bow	4
5.	clip	4
6.	man	4
7.	untie	2
8.	up	2
9.	wear	2

10-42.   (f = 1)
accessory, all, bar, bind, bowtie, box, clasp, clothing, color, cravat, dress, fastener, fold, Gene's, gift, hate, high, hold, hurt, laces, neat, nice, night, nole, pin, sharp, shoe, slut, straight, string, thin, uncomfortable, wrapped

III-15   Trousers   (n = 100)

No.	Response	Total
1.	pants	57
2.	man	7
3.	slacks	6
4.	wear	4
5.	creased	2
6.	legs	2

7-28.   (f = 1)
belt, boss, boy, cuffs, Erp, farmers, fly, heavy. long, modesty, off, pair, pegged, penis, pockets, press, seat, shirt, shoes, suit, tailor, taper

III-16   Vest   (n = 99)

No.	Response	Total
1.	suit	11
2.	button(s)	9
3.	jacket	8
4.	pocket	8
5.	clothing	6
6.	shirt	6
7.	coat	4
8.	sweater	4
9.	tie	4
10.	wear	4
11.	clothes	3
12.	boy	2
13.	chain	2
14.	red	2

15-42.   (f = 1)
ballet, blouse, bowtie, brief, chest, cigars, color, courderoy, covering, English, executive, fink, fit, Ike, in, Ivy League, loud, satin, sharp, stiff, suave, violet, warmth, wearing apparel, weskit, yellow
(Illegible - 1)

IV-1   Arabia   (n = 100)

No.	Response	Total
1.	country	20
2.	Saudi	8
3.	Arabs	7
4.	camels	5
5.	desert	5
6.	night(s)	5
7.	sand	5
8.	Israel	3
9.	knight(s)	3
10.	Africa	2
11.	horse(s)	2
12.	Lawrence	2
13.	turban	2
14.	Turks	2

15-43.   (f = 1)
Arabian, bad, Bedwins, distant, dress, east, Egypt, Iran, Iraq, Lok, map, Moslems, mysterious, mystery, Nasser, notion, oil, perfume, shape, sheik, Siberia, silks, Syria, tents, trouble, U.A.R., Valentino, warm, wicket

IV-2   Chile   (n = 99)

No.	Response	Total
1.	country	14
2.	con carne	12
3.	sauce	12
4.	hot	8
5.	pepper	8
6.	South America	8
7.	Argentina	4
8.	saltpeter	3
9.	chilly	2
10.	cold	2
11.	mountains	2
12.	Spain	2
13.	warm	2

14-33.   (f = 1)
bay, beans, coffee, continent, deprived, drugway, earthquake, friend, hand, Mexico, missionary, nitrate, Peru, poor, revolution, sharp, small, taste, thin, tomato

IV-3   Cuba   (n = 101)

No.	Response	Total
1.	Castro	48
2.	country	10
3.	island	4
4.	sugar	3
5.	Fidel	2
6.	fighting	2
7.	Florida	2
8.	trouble	2

9-37.   (f = 1)
army fatigues, Batista, Batiste, beard, Carribbean, cigars, coast, death, disaster, fall, good, hot, Kennedy, motherland, nation, no, peasants, poor, Puerto Rico, rebellion, red, revolution, si, socialista, Spain, Spanish, U.S., warm

IV-4   Egypt   (n = 100)

No.	Response	Total
1.	country	19
2.	Nile	12
3.	land	6
4.	pyramid	6
5.	sphinx	6
6.	Arab(s)	4
7.	desert	4
8.	Israel	4
9.	Nasser	3
10.	pharoah	3
11.	ancient	2
12.	jewels	2
13.	mummy	2

14-40.   (f = 1)
antisemitism, Arabian, Athens, art, awful, bad, Cairo, Cleopatra, crypt, distant, exile, Egyptians, far, far away, gyp, hot, heat, Italy, Jordan, Middle East, North Africa, nation, sand, sun, Syria, trouble, war

IV-5   England   (n = 100)

No.	Response	Total
1.	country	17
2.	queen	17
3.	fog	6
4.	London	6
5.	land	4
6.	British	3
7.	Britain	3
8.	Ireland	3
9.	Europe	2
10.	France	2
11.	island	2
12.	isle	2
13.	king(s)	2
14.	rain	2
15.	Scotland	2

16-42.   (f = 1)
accent, alley, Churchill, cold, colony, continent, crown, democracy, Dover, empire, English, foggy, girls, John Bull, merry, moss, mother country, nation, navy, new, poetry, sea, socialist, Spain, stuffy, tea, wet

IV-6   France   (n = 100)

No.	Response	Total
1.	country	19
2.	Paris	18
3.	De Gaulle	10
4.	love	4
5.	England	3
6.	French	3
7.	sex	3
8.	beauty	2
9.	girls	2
10.	Italy	2
11.	Spain	2
12.	wine	2

IV-6   France   (n = 100)   (contd)

No.	Response	Total
13-42.	(f = 1)	

alas, ally, Bridgette Bardot,
Britain, Canada, Catholic, dance,
Europe, free, German, great,
green, land, language, man, map,
Mediterranean, Montand, nation,
Nuyen, oui, pig, romance, Sashe,
study, Sweden, travel, Tunis,
U.S.A., visit

IV-7   Germany   (n = 98)

No.	Response	Total
1.	country	24
2.	war	11
3.	Europe	5
4.	France	5
5.	Berlin	4
6.	Hitler	4
7.	Nazi	4
8.	hate	3
9.	land	3
10.	trouble	3
11.	Adenauer	2
12.	Austria	2
13.	blonde	2
14.	East	2
15.	England	2
16.	Germany	2
17.	people	2
18-35.	(f = 1)	

army, bad, conflict, Duetchland,
fight, five, Germans, gestapo,
Italy, large, machines, murder,
nation, Nordic, problem, Reich,
Rhine, ugh

IV-8   India   (n = 101)

No.	Response	Total
1.	country	24
2.	Nehru	14
3.	China	5
4.	elephant	4
5.	far	3
6.	Gandhi	2
7.	Indians	2
8.	Japan	2
9.	Pakistan	2
10.	sari	2
11.	spice(s)	2
12.	starvation	2
13.	warm	2
14-48.	(f = 1)	

Arab, Asia, British, Buddha,
Cornell, cover, cows, east,
foreign, Hindu, hot, hump,
hunger, houses, intrigue, kin,
nation, neutral, oboe, ocean,
odd, Orient, peace, poor,
poverty, red, romantic, Russia,
sex, state, strange, sun, Taj
Mahal, turban, tusk

IV-9   Iran   (n = 100)

No.	Response	Total
1.	country	27
2.	Iraq	19
3.	Egypt	5
4.	oil	5
5.	Shah	5
6.	Persia	3
7.	Turkey	3
8.	Arab(s)	2
9.	Asia	2
10.	desert	2
11.	Mideast	2
12.	trouble	2
13-35.	(f = 1)	

Bagdad, camel, doctor, east,
Far East, hot, iron, Israel,
Jordan, land, Moslem, nation,
princess, pearl, Russia, serfdom,
shiek, small, Syria, Tehran,
war, we
(Illegible - 1)

IV-10   Korea   (n = 101)

No.	Response	Total
1.	war	35
2.	country	17
3.	fight	9
4.	death	5
5.	fighting	4
6.	orphans	3
7.	army	2
8.	China	2
9.	Chinese	2
10.	Japan	2
11-30.	(f = 1)	

blood, Chinks, cold, communist,
division, famine, fiasco, Formosa,
Jap, kill, low, nation, now,
Orient, Pacific, rain, soldiers,
split, Truman, veteran

IV-11   Mexico   (n = 98)

No.	Response	Total
1.	Spain	14
2.	country	11
3.	city	9
4.	south	7
5.	bulls	3
6.	danger	3
7.	silver	3
8.	bolero	2
9.	bullfight	2
10.	excitement	2
11.	hot	2
12.	new	2
13.	siesta	2
14.	sombrero	2
15.	sunny	2
16.	warm	2
17-46.	(f = 1)	

bay, can't, color, dirty, disease,
dysenterry, Espana, exotic,
Fiesta, go, holiday, Indians,
lady, love, Oaxaco, peace, pot,
pueblar, revolution, salute,
Senorita, sleep, song, South
America, spice, splendor, Taman,
Texas, Tiajuana, vacation

IV-12   Portugal   (n = 100)

No.	Response	Total
1.	Spain	44
2.	country	25
3.	land	3
4.	Brazil	2
5.	Europe	2
6.	Lisbon	2
7.	place	2
8.	Spanish	2
9-26.	(f = 1)	

clean, colorful, dance,
dictator, drums, far, fishing,
Iberia, nation, pears, poetry,
South America, Spaniard, strip,
travel, Venice, visit, wine

IV-13   Russia   (n = 98)

No.	Response	Total
1.	country	28
2.	Communist	7
3.	red	7
4.	United States	6
	(U.S. 4; U.S.A. 1;	
	United States 2)	
5.	Khruschev	5
6.	communism	4
7.	Asia	3
8.	bad	2
9.	big	2
10.	mean	2
11.	peasant(s)	2
12.	snow	2
13.	Soviet	2
14.	U.S.S.R.	2
15-39.	(f = 1)	

adversary, bombs, China,
communistic, dark, death, dirt,
Europe, evil, freedom, Germany,
hammer and sickle, king, large,
nation, nyet, old, people,
samivar, Siberia, strange,
study, war, why

IV-14   Spain   (n = 100)

No.	Response	Total
1.	country	19
2.	bullfights	8
3.	France	7
4.	Franco	6
5.	Portugal	6
6.	rain	4
7.	sunny	4
8.	Europe	3
9.	guitar	3
10.	bolero	2
11.	Latin	2
12-47.	(f = 1)	

Barcelona, beach, bull,
costumes, dancing, dust,
England, Espanol, facist, far,
fire, flamenco, flowers,
foreign, gay, go, gondola,
green, Hemingway, Italy, Jack,
lace, Madrid, mantillas,
Morjorca, music, olives,
Picasso, red, romance, Rome,
skirt, Spanish, travel,
vermouth, war

IV-15 Tibet (n = 100)

No.	Response	Total
1.	country	23
2.	mountains	11
3.	China	7
4.	Lama	7
5.	India	5
6.	Asia	2
7.	east	2
8.	snow	2

9-49. (f = 1)
Africa, area, art, Ceylon,
Chinks, Cuba, Dali Lama,
darkskin, death, far, foreign,
high, Hilton, Himalayas,
horizons, hunger, Iraq, island,
king, Korea, land, large, Llosa,
Mongolians, nation, Nepal,
oriental, plain, remote, river,
Siberia, studying, suffering,
Taiwan, turban, unknown, vague,
visit, wilderness, yak, yama

IV-16 Wales (n = 99)

No.	Response	Total
1.	England	34
2.	Scotland	13
3.	country	11
4.	Prince	7
5.	Britain	4
6.	coal	2
7.	Duke	2
8.	Thomas	2
9.	whales	2

10-31. (f = 1)
accent, blow, Brittany,
Christman, cries, Dylan Thomas,
English, Europe, fish, hales,
Ireland, island, Lloyd, London,
mammals, mines, New Guinea,
ocean, place, Scot, Scotch,
tooth

V-1 Ale (n = 100)

No.	Response	Total
1.	beer	52
2.	drink	16
3.	ginger	8
4.	soda	3
5.	bitter	2

6-24. (f = 1)
Allice, Ballantine, brew, butter,
Canada, cold, dark, dizzy,
drinking, gin, herbs, hops,
liquor, pail, Pepsi Cola, sharp,
sour, whole, wine

V-2 Beer (n = 101)

No.	Response	Total
1.	drink	29
2.	pretzels	11
3.	foam	6
4.	ale	5
5.	bitter	4
6.	can	3

V-2 Beer (n = 101) (contd)

No.	Response	Total
7.	head	3
8.	cold	2
9.	mug	2
10.	smell	2
11.	stein	2

12-42. (f = 1)
band, barrel, baseball, belly,
birch, bottle, bubbles, cards,
cheer, draught, froth, gin, glass,
good, hair, keg, lousy, odor,
party, pizza, potato chips,
quench, Shlitz, slop, soap, sour,
stoned, taste, whiskey, wine,
yellow

V-3 Bourbon (n = 101)

No.	Response	Total
1.	drink	27
2.	whiskey	10
3.	liquor	7
4.	Scotch	7
5.	king	5
6.	bottle	3
7.	France	2
8.	ice	2
9.	Kentucky	2
10.	rocks	2
11.	rye	2
12.	soda	2
13.	straight	2
14.	water	2

15-40. (f = 1)
alcohol, aristocrat, bad, beer,
brandy, danger, double, drunk,
family, favorite, French, gin,
ginger, glass, highball, Louis,
New Orleans, on-the-rocks,
perfume, run, sick, smooth,
Southerner, tonic, wine, 428
East 98th Street

V-4 Brandy (n = 100)

No.	Response	Total
1.	drink	24
2.	wine	18
3.	liquor	12
4.	whiskey	8
5.	warm(th)	4
6.	beer	3
7.	sweet	3
8.	Cognac	2
9.	drunk	2
10.	hot	2

11-32. (f = 1)
alcohol, aroma, booze, cork,
dinner, dizzy, dog, gin, glass,
life, mix, Mo, Napoleon, pain,
sherry, sip, soothing, straight,
strong, tasty, terrible, vodka

V-5 Champagne (n = 100)

No.	Response	Total
1.	drink	20
2.	bubble(s)	16
3.	bubbly	10
4.	cocktail	7
5.	wine	4
6.	fun	3
7.	pink	3
8.	bottle	2
9.	drunk	2
10.	France	2
11.	good	2
12.	wedding	2

13-39. (f = 1)
affair, beige, Burgundy,
celebrate, cheer, chrystal,
coat tails, domestic, dry,
elegance, excercise, experience,
flow, gallery, happy, high,
hour, liquor, luxury, party,
rich, sauce, Alippwe, sparkle,
stakes, sweet, yellow

V-6 Cider (n = 100)

No.	Response	Total
1.	apple	46
2.	drink	24
3.	tree	9
4.	juice	3
5.	sour	2
6.	sweet	2

7-20. (f = 1)
acid, amber, bitter, drunk,
hard, high, oak, sap, seasoning,
song fest, sweet as apple,
tart, vinegar, wet

V-7 Cognac (n = 100)

No.	Response	Total
1.	drink	24
2.	liquor	24
3.	wine	18
4.	whiskey	8
5.	drunk	3
6.	brandy	2
7.	vodka	2
8.	warming	2

9-25. (f = 1)
alcohol, beer, Cognac, dizzy,
enemy, fine, France, heady,
ice, liquer, not, strong,
taste, together, tree, white
(Illegible - 1)

V-8 Gin (n = 101)

No.	Response	Total
1.	drink	30
2.	tonic	21
3.	rummy	8
4.	whiskey	7
5.	drunk	6
6.	liquor	5
7.	cards	3
8.	mill	3

V-8 Gin (n = 101) (contd)

No.	Response	Total
9.	rum	3
10.	vodka	3
11.	fizz	2

12-21. (f = 1)
alcohol, ale, bottle, drinking, good, highball, Rickey, soda, sour, strength

V-9 Rum (n = 100)

No.	Response	Total
1.	Coke	22
2.	drink	20
3.	whiskey	8
4.	sweet	4
5.	Jamaica	3
6.	beer	2
7.	bitter	2
8.	cane	2
9.	Puerto Rico	2
10.	rye	2
11.	Scotch	2

12-42. (f = 1)
ale, bad, bottle, brandy, cake, Calypso, candy, Carribean, cocoa, Coco Cola, Cuba, drunk, dum, eggnog, fruitcake, gum, hot, Ledum, liquor, molasses, odor, pirate, pot, pudding, rocks, soda, sour, stewed, sugar, tree
(Illegible - 1)

V-10 Rye (n = 98)

No.	Response	Total
1.	bread	43
2.	Scotch	10
3.	whiskey	10
4.	drink	8
5.	gingerale	7
6.	catcher	4
7.	liquor	2

8-21. (f = 1)
bad, Bourbon, crisp, gin, grain, pick-up, pumpernickle, rocks, sandwich, set-up, smells, soda, straight, wheat

V-11 Scotch (n = 101)

No.	Response	Total
1.	soda	22
2.	drink	21
3.	rye	11
4.	tape	9
5.	liquor	7
6.	whiskey	6
7.	Bourbon	3
8.	Irish	3
9.	alcohol	2
10.	drunk	2
11.	highball	2
12.	kilt	2
13.	plaid	2

V-11 Scotch (n = 101) (contd)

No.	Response	Total

14-22. (f = 1)
and soda, frugal, gin, Highlands, hop, man, on the rocks, sour, water

V-12 Vermouth (n = 100)

No.	Response	Total
1.	drink	30
2.	wine	18
3.	liquor	11
4.	gin	8
5.	sweet	5
6.	whiskey	5
7.	dry	3
8.	martini	3
9.	ale	2
10.	Scotch	2

11-23. (f = 1)
alcohol, bitter, Bourbon, cider, cocktail, flavor, glass, ook, sin, smooth, snow, vodka, warm

V-13 Vodka (n = 100)

No.	Response	Total
1.	drink	23
2.	Russia	10
3.	liquor	9
4.	wine	7
5.	drunk	6
6.	gin	6
7.	orange juice	6
8.	whiskey	4
9.	juice	3
10.	screw driver	3
11.	good	2
12.	orange	2

13-31. (f = 1)
alahot, alcohol, beer, bitter, Bloody Mary, Bob, Cognac, colorless, dizzy, gay, Jim, martini, potato, Russian, strong, water, wedding, white, yellow

V-14 Whiskey (n = 100)

No.	Response	Total
1.	drink	32
2.	sour	18
3.	drunk	9
4.	booze	3
5.	liquor	3
6.	rye	3
7.	Scotch	3
8.	beer	2
9.	drunkard	2
10.	gin	2
11.	proof	2
12.	sharp	2
13.	smell	2

14-30. (f = 1)
awful, bar, Barre, bottle, brand, bus, good, harsh, hot, J & B, rum, shot, sick, spirits, stimulant, vermouth, wow

V-15 Wine (n = 100)

No.	Response	Total
1.	drink	15
2.	red	15
3.	liquor	11
4.	grape(s)	8
5.	cellar	5
6.	drunk	5
7.	sweet	4
8.	whiskey	4
9.	dinner	2
10.	glass	2
11.	good	2

12-38. (f = 1)
bad, beer, beverage, bitter, Bourbon, Burgundy, chilled, Cognac, dine, dizzy, dry, fine, France, fruit, holiday, loses, love, mine, nice feeling, Passover, perfection, purple, sanctification, taste, white, women, yes

VI-1 Beach (n = 100)

No.	Response	Total
1.	sand	37
2.	swim	12
3.	shore	7
4.	comber	5
5.	sun	4
6.	sea	4
7.	water	4
8.	party	2
9.	people	2
10.	summer	2
11.	umbrella	2

12-30. (f = 1)
ball, bathe, bathing suit, bikini, boat, Dover, Florida, fun, head, island, nut, ocean, rest, rock, rod, space, tail, teach, waves

VI-2 Cliff (n = 99)

No.	Response	Total
1.	fall	17
2.	mountain	11
3.	hang	8
4.	high	8
5.	jump	7
6.	Dover	4
7.	drop	4
8.	dwelling	4
9.	edge	4
10.	danger	3
11.	hill	3
12.	steep	3
13.	Arquette	2
14.	over	2
15.	overhang	2
16.	top	2

17-31. (f = 1)
Arquet, dangerous, death, dine, drop off, Hagan, ledge, Livingston, precipice, rock, rugged, view, wall, white
(Illegible - 1)

VI-3   Delta   (n = 99)

No.	Response	Total
1.	Greek	11
2.	alpha	9
3.	phi	9
4.	rho	5
5.	river	5
6.	beta	3
7.	epsilon	3
8.	gamma	3
9.	letter	3
10.	sigma	3
11.	triangle	3
12.	airline	2
13.	lever	2
14.	math	2
15.	Mississippi	2
16.	plain	2
17.	plane	2

18-47. (f = 1)
airplane, calculus, change, D1, estuary, fertile, figs, forest, fraternity, inlet, jet, kappa, lamb, lambda, land, mesa, modulation, Nile, ocean, omega, pi, rays, ridge, sand, science, sea, sorority, tri, water, wing

VI-4   Dune   (n = 100)

No.	Response	Total
1.	sand	71
2.	hill	4
3.	desert	2
4.	Lorna	2
5.	soft	2

6-24. (f = 1)
animal, beach, blank, cone, dessert, done, down, dry, finish, food, fun, horse, moon, mound, oak, sandy, stretching, valley, wind

VI-5   Forest   (n = 100)

No.	Response	Total
1.	tree(s)	73
2.	green	7
3.	dark	3
4.	beautiful	2
5.	fire	2
6.	wood	2

7-17. (f = 1)
bewilderment, crowded, dense, fields, game animals, grove, jungle, light, lonely, primeval, wild

VI-6   Harbor   (n = 100)

No.	Response	Total
1.	boat(s)	36
2.	ship(s)	19
3.	dock	5
4.	Pearl	5
5.	water	5
6.	bay	4
7.	lights	4

VI-6   Harbor   (n = 100)   (contd)

No.	Response	Total
8.	port	4
9.	sea	4
10.	Belle	2
11.	inlet	2

12-22. (f = 1)
Anne, bell, Bock, Cape Cod, grudge, help, keep, pier, police, safe, sand

VI-7   Island   (n = 99)

No.	Response	Total
1.	water	24
2.	sea	9
3.	land	8
4.	alone	5
5.	Paradise	5
6.	Coney	4
7.	sun	4
8.	Hawaii	3
9.	peninsula	3
10.	Long	2
11.	Manhattan	2
12.	ocean	2
13.	sand	2
14.	tree	2

15-38. (f = 1)
camp, Carribean, deserted, desire, fish, floating, gold, Iceland, island, isle, isolation, Jamiaca, leisure, life, Long Island, love, peace, reef, sailor, secluded, small, trapped, treasure, tropical

VI-8   Lagoon   (n = 99)

No.	Response	Total
1.	water	17
2.	lake	5
3.	sleepy	5
4.	sea	4
5.	blue	3
6.	marsh	3
7.	blues	2
8.	calm	2
9.	cave	2
10.	dark	2
11.	jungle	2
12.	lazy	2
13.	mermaid	2
14.	river	2
15.	ship	2
16.	stream	2

17-59. (f = 1)
alone, angry, animal, arms, bay, black, civil, creek, dark waters, deep, dreamy, eerie, gloomy, goon, green, hidden, hollow, insects, island, J. Conrad, land, leaves, line, logs, mirky, monster, mud, ocean, peninsula, petting, poetry, pond, quiet, secret, serene, stale, swamp, swimming, underwater, valley, yell
(Illegible - 1)

VI-9   Lake   (n = 102)

No.	Response	Total
1.	water	20
2.	river	15
3.	swim	8
4.	Erie	7
5.	cool	4
6.	fishing	3
7.	bees	2
8.	boat	2
9.	canoe	2
10.	smooth	2
11.	Tahoe	2
12.	trees	2
13.	wet	2

14-41. (f = 1)
bay, bees, blue, calm, camp, country, drown, fish, George, house, lagoon, Lancelot, Lucerne, Mead, Michigan, ocean, placidness, resort, romantic, row, sail, sea, shore, shower, smooth, splash, Supluor, swim, trout, vacation, wide

VI-10   Mountain   (n = 100)

No.	Response	Total
1.	high	25
2.	hill(s)	12
3.	top	8
4.	snow	7
5.	Alps	5
6.	climb	4
7.	height	4
8.	peak	4
9.	range	3
10.	valley	3
11.	big	2
12.	climber	2
13.	loin	2
14.	stream	2
15.	tree(s)	2

16-30. (f = 1)
bear, breast, brook, cliff, crest, fountain, Himalayas, ice, joy, retreat, rocks, Sinai, slide, task, tunnel

VI-11   Ravine   (n = 102)

No.	Response	Total
1.	hole	10
2.	black	8
3.	bird	6
4.	deep	5
5.	gulley	5
6.	valley	5
7.	water	5
8.	ditch	3
9.	canyon	2
10.	cliff(s)	2
11.	drop	2
12.	gorge	2
13.	gulch	2
14.	hunger	2
15.	mountain	2
16.	Poe	2

VI-11 Ravine (n = 102) (contd)

No.	Response	Total

17-54. (f = 1)
ark, below, bramble, brush,
bushes, cave, cavern, chasm,
clearing, climbing, creep,
deadly, death, down, eat,
enclosure, fall, falling, far,
hard, head, house, hunger,
hungry, jail, large, luxurious,
marinb, no more, poor, roar,
rocks, steep, stream, trench,
vines, warm, west, western

VI-12 River (n = 102)

No.	Response	Total
1.	water	23
2.	flow	8
3.	stream	6
4.	Hudson	5
5.	bank	4
6.	run(s)	4
7.	boat	3
8.	deep	3
9.	swim	3
10.	wet	3
11.	cold	2
12.	flowing	2
13.	Jordan	2
14.	lake	2
15.	ocean	2
16.	red	2
17.	Styx	2

18-42. (f = 1)
canoeing, cross, current, dam,
Danube, dive, diver, down, dry,
ducks, flood, lazy, mouth, Nile,
old, outlet, Red River, road,
rove, sea, ships, swim, swine,
tributaries, winding, winds

VI-13 Shore (n = 101)

No.	Response	Total
1.	sea	32
2.	beach	17
3.	line	7
4.	sand	7
5.	water	7
6.	road	6
7.	ship	4
8.	waves	4
9.	ocean	3
10.	parkway	2
11.	side	2

12-21. (f = 1)
bay, boat, boy, coast, leave,
park, rocky, roof, swim, way

VI-14 Stream (n = 100)

No.	Response	Total
1.	river	20
2.	water	19
3.	flow	14
4.	brook	6
5.	cool	4

VI-14 Stream (n = 100) (contd)

No.	Response	Total
6.	fish	2
7.	fishing	2
8.	ripple	2
9.	salmon	2
10.	trickle	2
11.	waterfall	2

12-36. (f = 1)
boat, bubbling, calm,
consciousness, country scene,
erosion, fast, field, flee,
flood, flowing, harbor, life,
mountain, narrow, Never Sink,
ocean, pool, pour, reams,
running, runs, trees, wave

VI-16 Swamp (n = 100)

No.	Response	Total
1.	mud	20
2.	fox	6
3.	marsh	5
4.	wet	5
5.	bog	4
6.	water	4
7.	tree(s)	3
8.	desert	2
9.	ditch	2
10.	green	2
11.	jungle	2
12.	moss	2
13.	mush	2
14.	mushy	2
15.	sink	2

16-52. (f = 1)
alligator, bayou, black, brook,
bury, canoe, damp, dirt, dirty,
Everglades, Faulkner, fen, fish,
frog, gas, mosquito, mire, mist,
muck, murky, Okefonokee, pit,
quicksand, rat, reeds, region,
Rockerfeller, sand, soggy, soot,
south, stuck, sweep, upset,
valley, woods
(Illegible - 1)

VI-16 Valley (n = 100)

No.	Response	Total
1.	mountain(s)	13
2.	deep	11
3.	stream	10
4.	green	7
5.	low	7
6.	hill(s)	6
7.	death	3
8.	lily	3
9.	below	2
10.	dale	2
11.	depression	2
12.	forge	2
13.	grass	2
14.	land	2
15.	lovely	2
16.	meadow	2
17.	pleasant	2
18.	serene	2

19-38. (f = 1)
beautiful, bed, big, canyon,
cleft, country, desert, girl,
hobby, hole, lagoon, quiet,

VI-16 Valley (n = 100)(contd)

No.	Response	Total

river, slope, sun, sunset,
trees, walk, wet, women

VII-1 Barracuda (n = 100)

No.	Response	Total
1.	fish	62
2.	shark	9
3.	animal	6
4.	snake	5
5.	teeth	2

6-21. (f = 1)
chives, dangerous, dog, dope,
eel, food, maneating, Monroe,
museum, sharp, ship, spanish,
steak, swordfish, tree, wall

VII-2 Carp (n = 100)

No.	Response	Total
1.	fish	68
2.	harp	3
3.	smoked	2

4-30. (f = 1)
annoy, bones, canal, cavil,
cheap, chirp, complain, cringe,
critize, daddy, Daisy Meal,
expensive, food, good, it,
quarrel, sable, salmon, sharp,
shiny, slimy, smell, smoked,
sword, tasty, water, whitefish,
woman

VII-3 Cod (n = 100)

No.	Response	Total
1.	fish	72
2.	liver	6
3.	cape	4
4.	number	2

5-20. (f = 1)
alove, atheist, bones, chew,
cool, fillet, fishing, God,
hate, life, man, police,
religion, smell, water, where

VII-4 Fluke (n = 98)

No.	Response	Total
1.	fish	48
2.	music	9
3.	luck	3
4.	flounder	2
5.	flute	2
6.	instrument	2
7.	miss	2

8-35. (f = 1)
bad, bones, brown, different,
disease, error, failure, false,
fishing, foil, good, head, kite,
loose, mood, pie, play, rob, sea,
shrill, sneezing, spin, swim,

VII-4   Fluke   (n = 98)   (contd)

No.	Response	Total

tail, test, ugly, VD, white
(Illegible - 2)

VII-5   Herring   (n = 98)

No.	Response	Total
1.	fish	36
2.	salt(y)	8
3.	pickled	7
4.	smell	6
5.	bone	5
6.	red	5
7.	spicy	3
8-35.	(f = 1)	

bitter, breakfast, can, chopped,
creamed, delicious, distasteful,
dry, entree, Gleh, hors doevres,
mackerel, odor, onions, plate,
potatoes, Saturday, sauce, sea,
slimy, smoked, stink, Sunday,
terrible, thirst, unpleasant,
vinegar, wine sauce

VII-6   Marlin   (n = 100)

No.	Response	Total
1.	fish	52
2.	Brando	13
3.	bird	3
4.	magic	2
5.	magician	2
6.	man	2
7-32.	(f = 1)	

actor, au, Bill, boy, brand,
Dietrech, drama, fire, fishing,
garlic, good, Grace, gun,
hope, mar, Marilyn, name,
not clear, odd, picture, poetry,
rifle, scent, what, wood
(Illegible - 1)

VII-7   Perch   (n = 100)

No.	Response	Total
1.	bird	20
2.	fish	19
3.	sit	16
4.	tree	9
5.	branch	2
6.	rest	2
7.	seat	2
8.	stand	2
9.	stool	2
10.	twig	2
11-34.	(f = 1)	

atop, canary, climb, fall, fist,
fried, grey, high, limb, nest,
on, parakeet, prey, proud,
rail, rainbow, raven, roof,
roost, salmon, settle, sing,
stern, wood

VII-8   Pike   (n = 100)

No.	Response	Total
1.	fish	42
2.	peak(s)	32
3.	mountain	4
4.	fishing	2
5.	salmon	2
6.	whitefish	2
7-22.	(f = 1)	

bass, climb, dike, drive,
gefilte fish, high bar, hill,
Pike's Peak, pointy, rake, road,
sheet, spike, stick, tool, train

VII-9   Salmon   (n = 100)

No.	Response	Total
1.	fish	53
2.	upstream	5
3.	orange	4
4.	pink	4
5.	stream	4
6.	swim	3
7.	tuna	3
8.	jump	2
9.	sandwich	2
10.	swimming	2
11-28.	(f = 1)	

barracuda, can, canned, croquet,
downstream, eat, fishy, instinct,
migration, red, river, roe, run,
spawn, spawning, steak, tuna
fish, water

VII-10   Sardine   (n = 102)

No.	Response	Total
1.	fish	39
2.	can	24
3.	oil	5
4.	sandwich	5
5.	oily	3
6.	subway	3
7.	crowded	2
8.	good	2
9.	smell	2
10.	tight	2
11-24.	(f = 1)	

anchovy, bones, close, cramped,
crowd, horrible, onions, salmon,
salty, slimy, squashed, squeeze,
stuffed, tuna

VII-11   Shark   (n = 103)

No.	Response	Total
1.	fish	33
2.	danger	13
3.	bite	10
4.	teeth	8
5.	water	6
6.	whale	5
7.	ocean	3
8.	smell	3
9.	dangerous	2
10.	skin	2

VII-11   Shark   (n = 103)   (contd)

No.	Response	Total
11-27.	(f = 1)	

animal, bait, bark, big, blood,
dangerous, deadly, death, evil,
fishing, kill, Moby Dick, seal,
shark, sharp, ship, strength,
vicious

VII-12   Snapper   (n = 99)

No.	Response	Total
1.	fish	26
2.	turtle	18
3.	biter	9
4.	red	9
5.	dog	3
6.	dragon	3
7.	bug	2
8.	clam	2
9.	dapper	2
10-34.	(f = 1)	

bait, bite, bitter, blood,
bluefish, Chelydra, clip,
cookie, crab, crustcean,
doctor, enemy, frog, Guy, hurts,
Jacks, lively, run, sharp,
snip, tight, tin, whipper,
whipple, zipper

VII-13   Sturgeon   (n = 101)

No.	Response	Total
1.	fish	76
2.	lox	4
3.	doctor	3
4.	steak	2
5-20.	(f = 1)	

big, bird, cheese, cord, food,
knife, meat, roe, royalty,
stake, steelwool, stew, strange,
surgeon, tong, unknown

VII-14   Trout   (n = 100)

No.	Response	Total
1.	fish	68
2.	streams	8
3.	fishing	2
4.	food	2
5.	rainbow	2
6.	sea	2
7.	sport	2
8.	water	2
9-20.	(f = 1)	

bake, cat, cook, dish, fun,
good, hole, lake, run, smell,
swimming, yes

VII-15   Tuna   (n = 100)

No.	Response	Total
1.	fish	79
2.	salmon	3
3.	sandwich	3
4.	can	2
5.	greasy	2
6.	oil	2
7-15.	(f = 1)	

big, breakfast; Eca, fight, head, lunch, mayonnaise, migration, ordinary

VIII-1   Aster   (n = 95)

No.	Response	Total
1.	flower	46
2.	hotel	9
3.	star	5
4.	dog	3
5.	Lady	3
6.	theatre	3
7.	rich	2
8-31.	(f = 1)	

alder, behind, blooming, chocolate, color, daisy, fish, fruit, instrument, lily, Lord, pastor, pet, pet horse, place, red, rose, seed, senseless, shine, storm, tray, white, whot

VIII-2   Buttercup   (n = 100)

No.	Response	Total
1.	flower	29
2.	yellow	29
3.	sweet	8
4.	daisy	4
5.	bread	3
6.	H.M.S. Pinafore	3
7.	little	3
8.	chin	2
9.	popcorn	2
10-26.	(f = 1)	

butter, candy, child, cookie, countryside, cut, cute, girl, innocence, leaf, meadow, muffin, operetta, petite, poor, sline, white

VIII-3   Daffodil   (n = 99)

No.	Response	Total
1.	flower	40
2.	yellow	27
3.	pretty	4
4.	daisy	3
5.	cloud	2
6.	hill	2
7.	soft	2
8.	Wordsworth	2
9-25.	(f = 1)	

blow, breeze, common, corny, delicate, field, frail, garden, gentle, growing, love, pansy, poem, rain, spring, stem, sunflower

VIII-4   Daisy   (n = 100)

No.	Response	Total
1.	flower	55
2.	Mae	4
3.	May	4
4.	field(s)	3
5.	yellow	3
6.	girl	2
7.	love	2
8.	rose	2
9.	song	2
10.	spring	2
11.	sweet	2
12-30.	(f = 1)	

bud, built, chain, dog, eat, Fitzgerald, fresh, iris, maize, Miller, petal, plant, pollen, pretty, pull, push, smell, summer, wallflower

VIII-5   Gardenia   (n = 100)

No.	Response	Total
1.	flower	56
2.	smell	8
3.	garden	5
4.	rose	5
5.	white	5
6.	beauty	3
7.	love	2
8.	pengent	2
9.	sweet	2
10-21.	(f = 1)	

affection, bulb, corsage, dance, fragrant, grow, lapel, nostalgia, odious, pretty, prom, rotten

VIII-6   Lilac   (n = 101)

No.	Response	Total
1.	flower	30
2.	purple	12
3.	smell	12
4.	tree	6
5.	bush	5
6.	color	5
7.	sweet	4
8.	lavender	3
9.	violet	3
10.	daisy	2
11.	perfume	2
12-28.	(f = 1)	

aroma, beauty, bloom, blossom, cool, corsage, cosmetic, fragrance, fragrant, plum, pretty, roses, scent, spring, toilet water, transcend, valley

VIII-7   Lily   (n = 102)

No.	Response	Total
1.	flower	43
2.	pond	14
3.	white	14
4.	valley	5
5.	rose	3

VIII-7   Lily   (n = 102)   (contd)

No.	Response	Total
6-28.	(f = 1)	

beauty, death, Easter, flee, fresh, garden, gentle, Melly, mother, of the valley, of valley, orchid, plant, silly, smell, swamp, sweet, sweet scent, sweet smell, virgin, water, yellow
(Illegible - 1)

VIII-8   Lotus   (n = 99)

No.	Response	Total
1.	blossom	28
2.	eater	19
3.	flower	16
4.	leaf	3
5.	plant	3
6.	forget	2
7-34.	(f = 1)	

bad, beauty, bug, car, Chinese, death, devour, dope, exotic, green, insect, Japan, love, lovely, Maryuane, Odyssesy, oriental, Pearl Buck, petals, seed, seeken, sex, smell, sweep, Tennyson, tree, Ullysses, unusual

VIII-9   Magnolia   (n = 101)

No.	Response	Total
1.	flower	33
2.	blossoms	19
3.	tree	10
4.	south	8
5.	smell	7
6.	bush	3
7.	spring	2
8-26.	(f = 1)	

apple, boulevard, Chinese, Civil War, daisy, Family Show, NBC, 9-10 a.m., Faulkner, freshness, leaves, mongoloid, perfume, pink, scent, Sinatra, southern, sweet, The South, yellow
(Illegible - 1)

VIII-10   Marigold   (n = 100)

No.	Response	Total
1.	flower	51
2.	yellow	15
3.	gold	5
4.	name	3
5.	money	2
6.	orange	2
7.	pretty	2
8.	sweet	2
9-24.	(f = 1)	

beer, bright, colors, cousin, hayfever, leaf, none, plant, plant sale, rate, seed, shining, sing, spring, wonder, worm
(Illegible - 2)

VIII-11 Orchid (n = 100)

No.	Response	Total
1.	flower	49
2.	trees	11
3.	beauty	5
4.	apple	3
5.	beautiful	3
6.	field	3
7.	purple	3
8.	rose	3
9.	corsage	2
10.	fruit	2
11.	nice	2
12.	wedding	2

13-25. (f = 1)
dating, flee, flow, forest, green, happy, hide, lavender, life, preety, special, wine

VIII-12 Pansy (n = 100)

No.	Response	Total
1.	flower	45
2.	fairy	9
3.	daisy	6
4.	purple	4
5.	daffodil	2
6.	face	2
7.	fag	2

8-37. (f = 1)
boy, Brewer, Capote, cute, dance, effeminate, flimsey, girl, hello, innocence, love, men, music, name, pants, pick, play, pretty, sap, Sinatra, small, smell, smile, spring, sucker, tulip, violet, why, yellow, yokum

VIII-13 Poppy (n = 101)

No.	Response	Total
1.	seeds	55
2.	flower	22
3.	red	4
4.	opium	3
5.	garden	2

6-20. (f = 1)
black, donations, dope, Dorothy, eye, Faulkner, field, Flanders Field, peanuts, pep, rose, sailor, sleep, veteran, Veteran's Day

VIII-14 Rose (n = 100)

No.	Response	Total
1.	flower	40
2.	red	19
3.	petal	6
4.	smell	6
5.	bush	4
6.	colored	3
7.	sweet	3
8.	thorn	3
9.	tatoo	2
10.	tulip	2

VIII-14 Rose (n = 100) (contd)

No.	Response	Total
11-22.	(f = 1)	

beauty, child, cup, cushion, light pink, love, maize, Murphy, plant, wiolet, white, women

VIII-15 Tulip (n = 100)

No.	Response	Total
1.	flower	47
2.	Holland	10
3.	bulb	8
4.	rose	6
5.	petal	4
6.	Dutch	3
7.	yellow	3
8.	daisy	2

9-25. (f = 1)
bloom, blue, car, cute, garden, grace, history, kindergarten, lip, open, red, round, smile, stem, tulip, turnip, wax

IX-1 Antelope (n = 100)

No.	Response	Total
1.	deer	34
2.	animal	27
3.	horn(s)	4
4.	antlers	3
5.	cantelope	3
6.	elk	2
7.	reindeer	2
8.	tree	2

9-31. (f = 1)
beauty, bull, deed, ears, forest, giraffe, grace, graceful, hunter, hunting, kill, meat, melon, neck, pears, play, range, roam, run, running, skin, stag, ugly

IX-2 Bear (n = 98)

No.	Response	Total
1.	animal	20
2.	big	9
3.	fur	6
4.	hug	4
5.	trap	4
6.	forest	3
7.	brown	2
8.	cave	2
9.	cub	2
10.	grin	2
11.	honey	2
12.	rug	2
13.	tree	2
14.	wood(s)	2

15-51. (f = 1)
bare, Barney, bear, boar, cane, carry, cat, coat, cold, cut, danger, fear, fish, fox, fright, fuzzy, gruff, hunt, hunting, hybrinate, kill, large, lion, mountain, newborn, north, pinda, polar, snout, snow, tiger, toy, ursine, white, wine, zoo

IX-3 Beaver (n = 99)

No.	Response	Total
1.	dam	25
2.	fur	8
3.	animal	7
4.	coat	7
5.	busy	5
6.	eager	4
7.	hat	4
8.	build	3
9.	wood	3
10.	C.C.N.Y.	2
11.	hole	2
12.	tail	2
13.	teeth	2
14.	work	2

15-37. (f = 1)
bear, brook, champ, chew, cute, den, diligence, eat, forest, ham, heaver, hive, Leeta, log, muskrat, otter, pert, quick, skin, slap, type, warm, water

IX-4 Buffalo (n = 102)

No.	Response	Total
1.	animal	12
2.	Bill	11
3.	extinct	7
4.	nickel(s)	7
5.	bison	6
6.	Indian(s)	5
7.	city	4
8.	New York	4
9.	meat	3
10.	west	3
11.	antelope	2
12.	big	2
13.	deer	2
14.	large	2
15.	roam	2
16.	stampede	2

17-43. (f = 1)
Albany, antler, arrow, Bob, chips, college, filth, fool, Grover, gun, hairy, herd, horns, house, hunt, meet, mountains, Old West, ox, park, peak, plains, range, skin, University, wild, Wild Bill Hickok

IX-5 Camel (n = 99)

No.	Response	Total
1.	hump	25
2.	hair	15
3.	cigarette	13
4.	desert	8
5.	back	5
6.	coat	5
7.	Arab	4
8.	hide	3
9.	smoke	3
10.	water	2

11-25. (f = 1)
animal, Arabian, beige, big, boy, brown, brush, driver, eat, Egypt, flag, house, humy-water, oasis, The Orient, thirst

IX-6 Cow (n = 100)

No.	Response	Total
1.	milk	58
2.	animal	10
3.	moo	6
4.	bull	4
5.	horse	4
6.	bell	2
7.	dog	2
8.	food	2
9.	grass	2

10-19. (f = 1)
barn, bovine, calf, country,
Elsie, farm, Ilo, meat, pig,
utters

IX-7 Deer (n = 100)

No.	Response	Total
1.	animal	20
2.	antelope	16
3.	doe	7
4.	forest	7
5.	fawn	4
6.	graceful	3
7.	cow	2
8.	crossing	2
9.	hunting	2
10.	rain	2
11.	run(s)	2
12.	slayer	2
13.	smooth	2
14.	swift	2
15.	woods	2

16-40. (f = 1)
antlers, brown, catch, costly,
dear, female, fish, fleet, fox,
gentle, glen, gun, hunt, hunter,
love, lovely, meat, pretty,
reindeer, Rudolph, sleek, stag,
tenderness, tree, white

IX-8 Dog (n = 100)

No.	Response	Total
1.	cat	63
2.	bark	9
3.	animal	4
4.	bite	2
5.	bone	2

6-25. (f = 1)
bastard, Blacky, boxer, brave,
cocker spaniel, Cortt, cuddly,
Doberman pinscher, doe, domestic,
friend, furry, Kerry, legs, nose,
pet, poodle, Rover, spaniel,
trot

IX-9 Donkey (n = 101)

No.	Response	Total
1.	ass	31
2.	mule	16
3.	animal	14
4.	stubborn	7
5.	bray	3
6.	burro	3
7.	ride	3

IX-9 Donkey (n = 101) (contd)

No.	Response	Total
8.	serenade	3
9.	slow	3
10.	ears	2
11.	horse	2
12.	jackass	2
13.	kick	2
14.	riding	2

15-22. (f = 1)
carry, dumb, Eisenhower, goat,
Mexico, stubborness, stupid, yes

IX-10 Elk (n = 100)

No.	Response	Total
1.	deer	22
2.	animal	21
3.	tree	12
4.	moose	9
5.	antler(s)	3
6.	club	3
7.	fairy	3
8.	horn	3
9.	small	2

10-31. (f = 1)
antelope, bird, ears, elf, elk,
fairytale, fish, food, forest,
furniture, head, little, little-
man, lodge, pie, slap, sleek,
strength, tooth, white, wood
(Illegible - 1)

IX-11 Fox (n = 100)

No.	Response	Total
1.	sly	28
2.	animal	9
3.	red	7
4.	hunt	6
5.	wolf	5
6.	tail	4
7.	cat	3
8.	dog	3
9.	smart	3
10.	fur	2
11.	lair	2
12.	orange	2
13.	stole	2

14-37. (f = 1)
cagey, canary, chicken, clever,
collar, crow, fox, grapes, hound,
Ira, like, lion, lox, night, pox,
quick, rabbit, read, shrewd,
sneaky, sour grapes, syrup,
trot, typewriter

IX-12 Goat (n = 100)

No.	Response	Total
1.	milk	34
2.	animal	12
3.	beard	8
4.	Billy	3
5.	bleet	3
6.	horns	3
7.	mountain	3
8.	herd	2

IX-12 Goat (n = 100) (contd)

No.	Response	Total
9.	nanny	2
10.	old	2
11.	smell	2
12.	tee	2

13-36. (f = 1)
bell, boat, cheese, Dionipur,
dog, donkey, farm, funny,
garbage, goatee, hair, hill,
kick, lecherous, like, nose,
pig, sheep, skin, sound, stink,
stubborn, tin can, tragedy

IX-13 Horse (n = 100)

No.	Response	Total
1.	animal	21
2.	cow	9
3.	ride	9
4.	show	6
5.	dog	4
6.	mare	3
7.	rider	3
8.	riding	3
9.	saddle	3
10.	shoe	3
11.	pony	2
12.	race	2
13.	tail	2

14-43. (f = 1)
brown, buggy, cart, cat, colt,
cowboy, drawn, fall, fast,
flesh, gracefulness, heavy,
hoof, love, mane, neat,
palamino, pitch, racer, radish,
red, rid, rump, run, sex,
stable, stallion, sturrups,
sweet, Trigger

IX-14 Mule (n = 100)

No.	Response	Total
1.	stubborn	18
2.	donkey	14
3.	horse	14
4.	train	10
5.	animal	9
6.	ass	7
7.	dumb	3
8.	team	3
9.	kick	2
10.	slowness	2

11-28. (f = 1)
bugg, burro, comanchero, deer,
dirt, driver, dummy, jerk,
Jerusalem, mountains, pack,
packages, pork, ride, skinner,
stupid, tail, work

IX-15 Pig (n = 101)

No.	Response	Total
1.	fat	14
2.	animal	10
3.	sty	8
4.	dirt	7
5.	pork	7

IX-15   Pig   ($\underline{n}$ = 101) (contd)

No.	Response	Total
6.	hog	5
7.	pen	5
8.	dirty	4
9.	biology	3
10.	dissection	3
11.	fetal	3
12.	food	2
13.	slob	2
14.	sloppy	2

15-40.   ($\underline{f}$ = 1)
apple, cow, curly, dissect,
eater, feet, fetus, garbage,
hole, horse, house, latin,
market, nose, nursery, Orwell,
pea, pink, Piper Laurie, poke,
sloth, snort, snout, squeal,
ugly, wallow

IX-16   Pony   ($\underline{n}$ = 99)

No.	Response	Total
1.	horse	55
2.	ride	12
3.	express	7
4.	tail	4
5.	small	3
6.	colt	2
7.	cute	2
8.	Shetland	2

9-21.   ($\underline{f}$ = 1)
black, cart, dance, death, fun,
little, love, mane, mare,
Palisades, red, tiger, wagon

IX-17   Zebra   ($\underline{n}$ = 100)

No.	Response	Total
1.	stripe(s)	54
2.	horse	13
3.	animal	11
4.	striped	6
5.	Africa	3

6-18.   ($\underline{f}$ = 1)
bear, elephant, end, fast,
fight, giraffe, house, human,
lion, mule, spots, zebra, zoo

X-1   Apple   ($\underline{n}$ = 100)

No.	Response	Total
1.	red	23
2.	fruit	20
3.	cider	13
4.	pear	6
5.	tree	6
6.	eat	4
7.	core	3
8.	pie	3
9.	pit(s)	3
10.	hard	2
11.	sauce	2
12.	shiny	2

X-1   Apple   ($\underline{n}$ = 100) (contd)

No.	Response	Total
13-25.	($\underline{f}$ = 1)	

autumn, blossom, cherry, Eve,
food, golden, health, Jack,
juicy, many, sweet, worm
(Illegible - 1)

X-2   Apricot   ($\underline{n}$ = 101)

No.	Response	Total
1.	fruit	37
2.	juice	7
3.	orange	7
4.	peach	6
5.	good	4
6.	tree	4
7.	dried	3
8.	fig	3
9.	small	3
10.	food	2
11.	pit	2
12.	plum	2
13.	prune	2

14-32.   ($\underline{f}$ = 1)
brandy, can, color, cool, dried
out, eat, hairy, ice, lemon,
love, nectar, plant, round
smooth, stew, sweet, thick,
yellow, Yemen

X-3   Banana   ($\underline{n}$ = 100)

No.	Response	Total
1.	peel	20
2.	fruit	14
3.	yellow	11
4.	tree	10
5.	monkey	7
6.	split	5
7.	eat	4
8.	long	4
9.	slip	4
10.	boat	2
11.	sweet	2

12-28.   ($\underline{f}$ = 1)
bay, bunch, calories, cream,
drink, food, green leaves, hell,
ice cream, mushy, oil, penis,
phallous, spider, squash,
sugary, tropics

X-4   Cantaloupe   ($\underline{n}$ = 100)

No.	Response	Total
1.	fruit	40
2.	melon	18
3.	watermelon	5
4.	eat	4
5.	honeydew	3
6.	orange	3
7.	sweet	3
8.	antelope	2
9.	juicy	2
10.	plant	2
11.	spoon	2

X-4   Cantelope   ($\underline{n}$ = 100) (contd)

No.	Response	Total
12-27.	($\underline{f}$ = 1)	

animal, buns, deer, desert,
dessert, fish, food, pear,
ripe, running, sections, seed,
squash, summer, tasty,
vitamin C

X-5   Date   ($\underline{n}$ = 99)

No.	Response	Total
1.	fig	12
2.	girl(s)	11
3.	fruit	5
4.	boy	4
5.	night	4
6.	time	4
7.	fun	3
8.	sweet	3
9.	today	3
10.	eat	2
11.	food	2
12.	late	2
13.	love	2
14.	nut	2
15.	pit	2
16.	prom	2
17.	Saturday night	2
18.	with	2

19-51.   ($\underline{f}$ = 1)
apartment, appointment, ate,
Bob, book, calendar, due,
Emil, enjoy, evening, fate,
goodtime, guy, home, late,
marriage, Marty, North Pole,
November, now, oh, plum,
Saturday, September, show,
soon, take out, tree, year,
7/1/42, Nov. 30, Dec. 16, 1961

X-6   Fig   ($\underline{n}$ = 101)

No.	Response	Total
1.	Newton	21
2.	tree	21
3.	fruit	16
4.	date	14
5.	leaf	9
6.	seed	3
7.	sweet	3

8-21.   ($\underline{f}$ = 1)
Arab, bar, Bob, brown, figure,
food, good, juice, nut, olive,
plump, wasp, worms, you

X-7   Melon   ($\underline{n}$ = 100)

No.	Response	Total
1.	fruit	37
2.	cantelope	15
3.	eat	4
4.	round	4
5.	sweet	4
6.	watermelon	4
7.	ripe	3
8.	summer	3
9.	water	3

X-7 Melon (n = 100) (contd)

No.	Response	Total
10.	food	2
11.	honeydew	2
12-30.	(f = 1)	

candy, coater, delicious, fields, garden, good, green, head, juice, light, pantry, plant, seeds, "Smellon", soft, sour, sweetness, yellow (Illegible - 1)

X-8 Nectarine (n = 100)

No.	Response	Total
1.	fruit	50
2.	oranges	26
3.	juice	6
4.	peach	4
5.	sweet	4
6-15.	(f = 1)	

acid, apricot, cigarette, food, grape, green, shrink, sour, suck, yellow

X-9 Orange (n = 100)

No.	Response	Total
1.	fruit	26
2.	color	10
3.	juice	7
4.	peel	6
5.	orange	5
6.	red	4
7.	round	4
8.	drink	2
9.	eat	2
10.	light	2
11.	pit	2
12.	sour	2
13.	tangerine	2
14.	tree	2
15.	yellow	2
16-37.	(f = 1)	

ade, apple, aroma, bitter, black, bright, grape, green, hot, juicy, lemon, morning, nice, off yellow, pear, pink, squeeze, sun, Syracuse, tasty, temple, vitamin

X-10 Peach (n = 100)

No.	Response	Total
1.	fruit	25
2.	fuzz	13
3.	tree	10
4.	plum	8
5.	pear	6
6.	yellow	5
7.	eat	4
8.	fuzzy	4
9.	pit	4
10.	juicy	3
11.	summer	3
12.	soft	2

X-10 Peach (n = 100) (contd)

No.	Response	Total
13-25.	(f = 1)	

apricot, complexion, cream, Georgia, girls, piece, pink, ripe, round, shave, shaving, smooth, sun

X-11 Pear (n = 100)

No.	Response	Total
1.	fruit	42
2.	apple	14
3.	tree	7
4.	sweet	4
5.	eat	3
6.	food	3
7.	peach	3
8.	juicy	2
9.	plum	2
10.	shape	2
11.	shaped	2
12-27.	(f = 1)	

Bartlett, bear, delicious, desert, dignity, feather, funny, good, grape, look, nectar, oval, pair, ring, ship, yellow

X-12 Pineapple (n = 100)

No.	Response	Total
1.	fruit	26
2.	Hawaii	15
3.	juice	6
4.	food	5
5.	sweet	4
6.	yellow	4
7.	drink	3
8.	eat	3
9.	sour	3
10.	tart	3
11.	apple	2
12.	bitter	2
13.	sticky	2
14-35.	(f = 1)	

cheese cake, cherry, citrus fruit, dessert, eating, fillets, good, grape, grapefruit, grenade, hula dancer, island, kibbutz, leaves, pearl, plant, slices, sweetish, tangy, tree, turnover, water

X-13 Plum (n = 100)

No.	Response	Total
1.	fruit	25
2.	pudding	18
3.	tree	13
4.	purple	12
5.	color	3
6.	peach	3
7.	sweet	3
8.	beach	2
9.	black	2
10.	food	2
11.	pie	2
12.	red	2
13.	summer	2

X-13 Plum (n = 100) (contd)

No.	Response	Total
14-24.	(f = 1)	

blue, bruise, drum, juicy, Milt, oval, prunes, quench, ripe, sugar, trench

X-14 Prune (n = 99)

No.	Response	Total
1.	fruit	14
2.	juice	13
3.	plum	8
4.	dried	6
5.	raisin	6
6.	eat	5
7.	food	5
8.	block	3
9.	dry	3
10.	pit	2
11.	tree	2
12.	whip	2
13-43.	(f = 1)	

apricot, bathroom, bitter, black, bowel movement, brown, constipation, diarrehea, drink, fig, girl, go, grape, laxative, moon, old, pear, picture, prude, shrivled, soft, sour, stomach ache, strune, sweet, syrup, terrible, whither, wrinkled, yogurt

X-15 Raisin (n = 99)

No.	Response	Total
1.	grape(s)	18
2.	fruit	11
3.	cake(s)	10
4.	food	8
5.	sun	7
6.	bread	5
7.	sweet	5
8.	eat	3
9.	plum	3
10.	black	2
11.	candy	2
12.	nuts	2
13.	seed	2
14-34.	(f = 1)	

bran, brand, desert, dried, dry, flavor, graph, iron, Kugal, lowcalorie, nothing, peanuts, pear, play, protein, prune, reason, scrawny, small, sugar, wine

X-16 Tangerine (n = 101)

No.	Response	Total
1.	orange	51
2.	fruit	21
3.	eat	4
4.	peel	3
5.	color	2
6.	good	2
7.	pit(s)	2

X-16 Tangerine (n = 101) (contd)

No.	Response	Total

8-23. (f = 1)
apple, Basie, citrus, flower, juice, lemon, melon, peach, peeling, port, refresh, segments, slip, sour, sweet, vermillion

XI-1 Attic (n = 100)

No.	Response	Total
1.	house	13
2.	roof	8
3.	room	6
4.	basement	5
5.	cellar	5
6.	high	5
7.	storage	5
8.	top	5
9.	up	3
10.	apartment	2
11.	closed	2
12.	dirt	2
13.	dirty	2
14.	dust	2
15.	old	2
16.	toys	2

17-47. (f = 1)
above, alone, base, black, clothes, cold, congested, creeks, crowded, dampness, foyer, furniture, hall, hide, hot, jail, junk, locked up, musty, peak, Peloponeosus, picture, place, poet, rummage, shut, sleep, souvenier, stairs, studio, trunk

XI-2 Balcony (n = 98)

No.	Response	Total
1.	movies	9
2.	seat	9
3.	Romeo	8
4.	theatre	8
5.	Juliet	6
6.	stairs	4
7.	terrace	4
8.	high	3
9.	house	2
10.	love	2
11.	orchestra	2
12.	play	2
13.	rail	2
14.	roof	2
15.	top	2

16-50. (f = 1)
alcove, attic, attitude, beard, black, Broadway play, bugle, ceiling, curved, edge, elope, fall, fear, Genit, hub, ledge, opera, over, pier, porch, princess, raised, rest, scene, show, sing, smoke, spacious, stage, stays, tower, trellis, up, verranda, window

XI-3 Beam (n = 99)

No.	Response	Total
1.	light	48
2.	wood	6
3.	ceiling	4
4.	house	4
5.	roof	4
6.	bright	3
7.	ray	3
8.	stalk	3
9.	pole	2
10.	sun	2
11.	support	2

12-29. (f = 1)
beam, black, board, building, college, food, hand, lead, oh, panel, potato, rod, shine, steel, stick, structure, walking, wood red

XI-4 Ceiling (n = 100)

No.	Response	Total
1.	floor	22
2.	roof	18
3.	high	17
4.	top	10
5.	white	5
6.	height	4
7.	above	3
8.	fall	3
9.	wall	3
10.	up	2

11-23. (f = 1)
Celotex, dizzy, fad, house, lamp, light, over, overhead, paint, plaster, room, tall, wax

XI-5 Chimney (n = 101)

No.	Response	Total
1.	smoke	53
2.	sweep	10
3.	dirty	5
4.	soot	4
5.	fire	3
6.	Santa Claus	3
7.	black	2
8.	brick(s)	2
9.	house	2
10.	red	2
11.	sweeper	2

12-24. (f = 1)
coal, cut, dirt, fall, flue, pipe, Saint Nick, smell, stack, stoke, stone, structure, top

XI-6 Door (n = 100)

No.	Response	Total
1.	open	25
2.	knob	14
3.	house	7
4.	lock	6
5.	close	5
6.	entrance	4
7.	room	4
8.	window	4

XI-6 Door (n = 100) (contd)

No.	Response	Total
9.	handle	3
10.	closed	2
11.	latch	2
12.	out	2
13.	portal	2

14-33. (f = 1)
bell, class, doorknob, floor, foot, foyer, freedom, gate, go, hell, home, jamb, leave, mat, opening, porto, protection, stop, vestibule, wood

XI-7 Floor (n = 100)

No.	Response	Total
1.	wood	15
2.	ceiling	14
3.	walk	8
4.	board(s)	6
5.	ground	6
6.	wax	6
7.	bottom	3
8.	flat	3
9.	stand	3
10.	tile(s)	3
11.	carpet	2
12.	dance	2
13.	hard	2

14-41. (f = 1)
below, chair, clean, covering, dancing, deck, dirt, dirty, door, feet, kitchen, K.O., lay, linoleum, overwhelm, red, rug, sit, smooth, stamp, steps, street, sweeps, table, wall, wash, window, wipe

XI-8 Foyer (n = 101)

No.	Response	Total
1.	hall	27
2.	house	12
3.	room	10
4.	living room	6
5.	den	3
6.	kitchen	3
7.	small	3
8.	long	2
9.	rug	2
10.	table	2
11.	vestibule	2

12-40. (f = 1)
animal, anteroom, apartment, arch, attic, bury, closet, cold, crowded, dining room, door, entrance, fever, fireplace, gong, green, hallway, home, hotel, light, man, mirror, opening, parlor, skates, step, walk, wall, writer

XI-9 Kitchen (n = 100)

No.	Response	Total
1.	sink(s)	13
2.	food	12
3.	room	9
4.	stove	8
5.	cook	6
6.	house	5
7.	table	4
8.	white	4
9.	clean	3
10.	eat	3
11.	home	3
12.	apron	2
13.	dinette	2
14.	knife	2

15-37. (f = 1)
chair, cupboard, dining, door,
drudge, eating, floor, grandmother, linoleum, livingroom,
mother, pans, range, refrigerator, set, small, smell, soup,
spoon, stool, tools, topview,
work, yellow

XI-10 Lobby (n = 100)

No.	Response	Total
1.	hotel	19
2.	hall	14
3.	theater	7
4.	building	5
5.	congress	5
6.	people	4
7.	wait	4
8.	door	3
9.	foyer	3
10.	house	3
11.	politics	3
12.	room	3
13.	hobby	2

14-38. (f = 1)
carpeting, chair, doorman,
fight, interest group, lobbyist,
man, men, money, parlor, place,
politician, preasure, pursua-
sion, rug, senate, sitting,
stairs, store, sway, ugly,
U.N., vestibule, waiting, walker

XI-11 Lounge (n = 100)

No.	Response	Total
1.	rest	27
2.	chair	23
3.	couch	5
4.	sit	5
5.	room	4
6.	chaise	3
7.	relax	3
8.	social	3
9.	bed	2
10.	comfort	2
11.	sleep	2
12.	sofa	2

13-31. (f = 1)
cadet, cafeteria, cigarettes,
dance, easy, La Guardia,
lobby, loll, Lunh, mens room,
minor, modern, music, play,
recline, recreating, school,
smoke, Ura

XI-12 Patio (n = 99)

No.	Response	Total
1.	porch	31
2.	garden	8
3.	house	7
4.	veranda	5
5.	furniture	4
6.	terrace	4
7.	chair	3
8.	cool	2
9.	outdoors	2
10.	stones	2
11.	summer	2
12.	sun	2

13-40. (f = 1)
backyard, barn, champagne,
comfort, court, dress, exclusive,
food, fun, glass, Italy, light,
love, Madrid, outside, party,
peal, people, potato, relaxing,
room, seats, section, sit,
sunlight, sunshine, wealth

XI-13 Roof (n = 100)

No.	Response	Total
1.	top	30
2.	house	16
3.	high	5
4.	shingle	5
5.	protect	4
6.	cover	3
7.	rain	3
8.	tar	3
9.	tiles	3
10.	cat	2
11.	ceiling	2
12.	garden	2
13.	shelter	2
14.	thatched	2

15-32. (f = 1)
basement, black, blown, clothes-
line, danger, eave, fall, fix,
gutter, hot, man, over, Aky,
steep, sturdy, Techo, tin, wall

XI-14 Stair (n = 99)

No.	Response	Total
1.	case	19
2.	climb	16
3.	way	12
4.	steps	10
5.	fall	6
6.	well	5
7.	up	4
8.	walk	3
9.	down	2
10.	height	2
11.	winding	2

12-29. (f = 1)
ascend, balcony, carpet, chair,
ease, entrance, grandma, hair,
high, house, landing, paint,
slip, spiral, staircase, stoop,
tall, trip

XI-15 Wall (n = 100)

No.	Response	Total
1.	floor	13
2.	high	8
3.	picture	7
4.	ceiling	6
5.	block	4
6.	door	4
7.	paper	4
8.	house	3
9.	paint	3
10.	stop	3
11.	brick	2
12.	climb	2
13.	closed	2
14.	dark	2
15.	death	2
16.	hall	2
17.	solid	2
18.	stone	2
19.	street	2
20.	white	2

21-45. (f = 1)
barriers, blank, building, cell,
climbing, color, cracked,
enclosure, hard, Hersey, height,
loneliness, mall, over, paper,
plaster, prison, protection,
Satre, side, stony, strong,
tall, tree, where

XI-16 Window (n = 101)

No.	Response	Total
1.	pane(s)	41
2.	glass	11
3.	sill	10
4.	look	6
5.	open	6
6.	opening	3
7.	shade	3
8.	view	3
9.	bay	2
10.	door	2
11.	pain	2
12.	see	2

13-22. (f = 1)
blinds, box, clear, dirty,
frame, ledge, sex, sky,
transparent, tree

XII-1 Ant (n = 101)

No.	Response	Total
1.	hill	19
2.	bug	12
3.	insect	12
4.	crawl(s)	8
5.	small	8
6.	uncle	5
7.	eater	3
8.	anteater	2
9.	aunt	2
10.	bee	2
11.	hole	2
12.	tiny	2
13.	ugly	2
14.	work	2

15-34. (f = 1)
animal, beach, beetle, biology,
black, burrow, busy, crawling,
crush, dirty, dog, grasshopper,

XII-1   Ant   ($\underline{n}$ = 101)   (contd)

No.	Response	Total

insect-bug, love, mole hill, people, pest, picnic, red, termite

XII-2   Bee   ($\underline{n}$ = 100)

No.	Response	Total
1.	sting	29
2.	honey	23
3.	hive	10
4.	buzz	9
5.	insect	5
6.	bumble	3
7.	buzzy	2
8.	fly	2
9.	hum	2
10.	line	2
11.	spelling	2
12-22.	($\underline{f}$ = 1)	

beetle, bite, bog, bonnet, butter, deserted lot, drone, flower, sing, summer, work

XII-3   Beetle   ($\underline{n}$ = 100)

No.	Response	Total
1.	bug	50
2.	sting	10
3.	insect(s)	9
4.	black	3
5.	ant	2
6.	little	2
7-30.	($\underline{f}$ = 1)	

Bailey, bee, biology, bottle, buzzing, click, crawl, crawling, danger, dead, dirty, disgust, fetal, flee, fly, food, grass, horror, Japanese, lady bug, nusance, small, ugly, wasp

XII-4   Cricket   ($\underline{n}$ = 100)

No.	Response	Total
1.	noise	23
2.	game	14
3.	bug	11
4.	chirp	7
5.	bird	4
6.	baseball	3
7.	England	3
8.	sound	3
9.	bat	2
10.	chicken	2
11.	country	2
12.	insect	2
13.	night	2
14-35.	($\underline{f}$ = 1)	

animal, awake, ball, bee, Blake, bloke, chirping, crow, frog, grass, grasshopper, horse, match, play, playing, right-o, rub, rule, song, tweet, umbrella, wicket

XII-5   Flea   ($\underline{n}$ = 101)

No.	Response	Total
1.	fly	16
2.	dog	15
3.	circus	9
4.	insect	6
5.	itch	6
6.	bitten	5
7.	ant	4
8.	bug	4
9.	scratch	4
10.	small	4
11.	animal	3
12.	bite	3
13.	pest	2
14.	tick	2
15-32.	($\underline{f}$ = 1)	

big, blood, bothersome, bug, cat, cockaroach, disease, Ditto (my cat), Donne, filth, irritate, John Donne, lion, run, scratchy, speck, tiny, wiggly

XII-6   Gnat   ($\underline{n}$ = 100)

No.	Response	Total
1.	fly	20
2.	bite	18
3.	bug	14
4.	insect	11
5.	annoying	4
6.	sting	4
7.	hair	3
8.	flea	2
9.	mosquito	2
10.	Nathan	2
11.	pest	2
12-29.	($\underline{f}$ = 1)	

animal, bat, bud, cat, dark, flower, fly swatter, hurt, little, nuisance, pneumonia, rat, rock, sat, step, summer, tiny
(Illegible - 1)

XII-7   Hornet   ($\underline{n}$ = 101)

No.	Response	Total
1.	bee(s)	25
2.	sting	23
3.	nest	16
4.	wasp	6
5.	bug	5
6.	fly	4
7.	insect	4
8.	buzz	3
9.	hive	3
10.	hurt	2
11-20.	($\underline{f}$ = 1)	

annoying, beetle, bus, country, green, instrument, mad, net, sleep, trombone

XII-8   Locust   ($\underline{n}$ = 100)

No.	Response	Total
1.	bug	19
2.	insect	16
3.	plague	13
4.	grasshopper	3
5.	tree	3
6.	Bible	2
7.	blight	2
8.	famine	2
9.	fly	2
10.	pest	2
11.	valley	2
12-45.	($\underline{f}$ = 1)	

animal, ants, bees, black, caterpillar, crop, day of, destroy, devour, disease, disgust, disgusting, field, geometry, grass, ground, hardship, Israel, land, mass, Miss Omerod, much, pillage, plants, ply, rain-center, rampage, repulsive, scavenger, swarm, The Good Earth, ugly, wings
(Illegible - 1)

XII-9   Mantis   ($\underline{n}$ = 100)

No.	Response	Total
1.	praying	38
2.	preying	15
3.	insect	12
4.	bug	5
5.	cloak	3
6.	bird	2
7.	mantle	2
8.	uncertainty	2
9-29.	($\underline{f}$ = 1)	

away, bad, blank, clock, entres, fine, fly, flying, grasshopper, head, Mickey, missing, name, nants, pray, spindly, sweet, ugly, wierd, witches
(Illegible - 1)

XII-10   Mosquito   ($\underline{n}$ = 99)

No.	Response	Total
1.	bite	48
2.	fly	12
3.	sting	7
4.	bug	5
5.	insect	5
6.	blood	3
7.	buzz	3
8.	itch	2
9.	net	2
10.	summer	2
11-20.	($\underline{f}$ = 1)	

anapheles, annoy, annoying, flower, hurt, larvae, ouch, Panama, pest, Tulto

XII-11   Roach   (n = 100)

No.	Response	Total
1.	bug	25
2.	insect	14
3.	dirt	10
4.	cock	8
5.	crawl	4
6.	pest	4
7.	ants	3
8.	black	3
9.	cockroach	2
10.	Max	2
11.	mosquito	2
12.	rat	2
13.	ugly	2

14-32.   (f = 1)
animal, awful, beetle, bites, coach, disgusting, filth, fly, Hal, hot, John, kill, killer, maltz, palmetto bug, poach, powder, spray, ugh!

XII-12   Scorpion   (n = 101)

No.	Response	Total
1.	spider	17
2.	poison	11
3.	sting(s)	11
4.	snake	9
5.	deadly	7
6.	bugs	5
7.	insect	5
8.	danger	4
9.	fish	3
10.	constellation	2
11.	crawl	2

12-36.   (f = 1)
animal, arthroped, astrology, badman, bite, blood, Cancerian, dragon, eagle, evil, fear, fly, green, horror, legs, monster, needle, pain, red, sea, sore, star, terror, ugh, ugly

XII-13   Spider   (n = 101)

No.	Response	Total
1.	web	43
2.	crawl(s)	8
3.	black	7
4.	leg(s)	7
5.	insect	6
6.	ugly	4
7.	bug	3
8.	animal	2
9.	climb	2
10.	fly	2

11-27.   (f = 1)
black widow, crawling, crawly, disgust, eight, girl, hare, horrid, lace, Muffet, nest, prey, sneaky, terror, ugh, weave, widow

XII-14   Termite   (n = 101)

No.	Response	Total
1.	wood	28
2.	bug	21
3.	insect	11
4.	ant	5
5.	eat	5
6.	animal	3
7.	house	3
8.	pests	3
9.	chew	2
10.	dirt	2

11-27.   (f = 1)
annoyance, books, corrosion, crunch, decay, destroy, destructive, dirt, disgusting, exterminator, gnaw, holes, mischievous, parasite, rat, Reader's Digest, ugly, worm

XII-15   Tick   (n = 100)

No.	Response	Total
1.	tock	43
2.	clock	38
3.	bug	3
4.	watch	3
5.	insect	2
6.	noise	2

7-15.   (f = 1)
bite, Dick, fool, lack, lock, sound, time, ugly, work

XII-16   Wasp   (n = 100)

No.	Response	Total
1.	sting(s)	37
2.	bee	15
3.	bug	9
4.	fly	6
5.	insect	5
6.	bite	2
7.	hornet	2
8.	kill	2
9.	mosquito	2
10.	nest	2

11-28.   (f = 1)
beetle, black, coat, danger, evil, hasp, hit, hole, hurt, iron, little, moth, ouch, tiny, watch out for, went, wipe, yellow jacket

XIII-1   Batiste   (n = 102)

No.	Response	Total
1.	dictator	12
2.	Cuba	10
3.	material	10
4.	Castro	6
5.	cloth	5
6.	dress	4
7.	cotton	3
8.	lace	3
9.	man	3
10.	Vito	3
11.	Batista	2
12.	bread	2

XIII-1   Batiste   (n = 102) (contd)

No.	Response	Total
13.	person	2
14.	shirt	2

15-48.   (f = 1)
artist, bad, baptize, bat, brocade, color, cruel, current events, Folencigo, France, Jean, lousy, mean, painting, print, prison, rat, ruler, sewing, sheer, slow, soft, Spanish, strange, Trujillo, tyrant, veto, villain, Vito, wall, what?, white, yarn, Yugoslavia

XIII-2   Burlap   (n = 100)

No.	Response	Total
1.	bag	47
2.	sack	12
3.	material	6
4.	cloth	3
5.	covering	3
6.	rough	3
7.	coat	2
8.	fur	2
9.	harsh	2
10.	skin	2
11.	texture	2

12-27.   (f = 1)
burlesque, canvas, club, fiber, jacket, leather, potato, rock, should, skirt, snap, warm, wine, wood, wool
(Illegible - 1)

XIII-3   Cashmere   (n = 100)

No.	Response	Total
1.	sweater	69
2.	soft	11
3.	bouquet	4
4.	coat	3
5.	fur	3
6.	wool	3

7-13.   (f = 1)
cloth, kitten, rich, silky, soap, talc, vicuna

XIII-4   Chino   (n = 101)

No.	Response	Total
1.	pants	64
2.	material	5
3.	slacks	4
4.	cloth	2
5.	dishes	2

6-28.   (f = 1)
black, blue, boat, brown, casual, Chinese, cloth, clothing, country, Dino, dirty, dungaree, hat, Japan, little boy, old, Orient, plants, plate, rice, shiny, wool, work, yellow

XIII-5 Cotton (n = 100)

No.	Response	Total
1.	wool	10
2.	cloth	9
3.	shirt	8
4.	soft	7
5.	white	7
6.	dress	6
7.	gin	5
8.	material	5
9.	balls	4
10.	fabric	3
11.	south	3
12.	candy	2
13.	clothes	2
14.	ears	2
15.	linen	2
16.	plant	2

17-39. (f = 1)
blouse, bowe-wirle, calico,
clean, cool, crop, fields,
fluff, Fred, frock, iodine,
light, medicine, needle, pants,
pick, rayon, seed, shorts,
summer, swab, trees, warm

XIII-6 Denim (n = 100)

No.	Response	Total
1.	blue	29
2.	dungarees	17
3.	pants	15
4.	trouser	10
5.	cloth	4
6.	jeans	3
7.	slacks	3
8.	black	2
9.	material	2
10.	rough	2

11-23. (f = 1)
bad, baseball, cotton, cowboy,
heavy, house, jacket, jersey,
river, shorts, smooth, sturdy,
suit

XIII-7 Felt (n = 100)

No.	Response	Total
1.	hat	27
2.	material	14
3.	cloth	8
4.	touch(ed)	7
5.	soft	5
6.	smooth	4
7.	skirt	3
8.	wool	3
9.	cotton	2
10.	dress	2
11.	fur	2
12.	girl	2
13.	leather	2
14.	skin	2

15-31. (f = 1)
crepe, experienced, feel, fell,
good, hand, kindergarden, lining,
nice, nylon, rayon, salt, seen,
sensed, silk, squeeze, velvet

XIII-8 Fur (n = 100)

No.	Response	Total
1.	coat	26
2.	mink	14
3.	warm(th)	12
4.	soft	10
5.	animal	3
6.	expensive	3
7.	fox	3
8.	furry	2
9.	fuzzy	2
10.	piece	2
11.	smooth	2

12-33. (f = 1)
bear, chinchilla, elegance, flies,
fog, good, hairy, horse, jacket,
knit, leaf, mouton, music,
muskrat, pelt, rier, sable, sing,
skin, texture, true

XIII-9 Hemp (n = 100)

No.	Response	Total
1.	rope	33
2.	cord	5
3.	cloth	4
4.	plant	4
5.	linen	3
6.	material	3
7.	manilla	2
8.	sisal	2
9.	wool	2

10-51. (f = 1)
barley, cat, coal, course,
drink, drug, flax, flour, grass,
hamper, lotus, Mexico, noose,
orchard, paper, pot, prison,
robe, row, rye, sackcloth,
sail, sew, skip, skirt, smoke,
soft, string, sugar, tax,
thread, tide, tie, tobacco,
touch, tree, wear, weave, weed,
wheat, wood, Yucatan

XIII-10 Jersey (n = 101)

No.	Response	Total
1.	city	25
2.	state	14
3.	New	10
4.	cow	7
5.	material	7
6.	shirt	5
7.	eggs	4
8.	sweater	3
9.	blouse	2
10.	dress	2
11.	soft	2

12-31. (f = 1)
cloth, country Dix, fun, house,
itchy, knit, milk, Morristown,
New Jersey, nut, pigs, small,
sticky, sweated, tie, travel,
tubes, tunnel, warm

XIII-11 Lace (n = 100)

No.	Response	Total
1.	dresses	19
2.	shoe	6
3.	gown	5
4.	white	5
5.	tat	4
6.	cloth	3
7.	delicate	3
8.	Chantilly	2
9.	doily	2
10.	handkerchief	2
11.	ice	2
12.	material	2
13.	nightgown	2
14.	old	2
15.	pretty	2
16.	silk	2

17-50. (f = 1)
arsnic, beauty, blouse, crochet,
curtains, delicacy, design,
embroidery, face, felt,
feminine, fine, frill, fringe,
fur, hiking boot, intricate,
old fashioned, open network,
ornament, pink, play, poison,
Puerto Rico, purity, ruffles,
satin, sex, soft, string, swank,
tablecloth, trim, veil
(Illegible - 3)

XIII-12 Linen (n = 100)

No.	Response	Total
1.	sheet	11
2.	bed	10
3.	closet	10
4.	cloth	9
5.	white	8
6.	towel	5
7.	tablecloth	4
8.	clean	3
9.	flax	3
10.	Irish	3
11.	dress	2
12.	fine	2
13.	handkerchief	2
14.	napkin	2
15.	silk	2

16-39. (f = 1)
beauty, bedding, blouse,
captain, coat, cool, cotton,
course, fresh, lax, luxury,
material, nice, rayon, red,
shirt, shit, shower, sleep,
soft, strong, trousseau, trunk,
yard

XIII-13 Poplin (n = 100)

No.	Response	Total
1.	jacket	16
2.	material	11
3.	cloth	7
4.	trees	7
5.	flower	5
6.	coat	4
7.	seeds	4
8.	cotton	3
9.	dress	2
10.	wear	2

XIII-13 Poplin (n = 100) (contd)

No.	Response	Total

11-46. (f = 1)
bird, bread, bumpy, coarse,
corduroy, cry, dance, dictionary,
doubt, father, fruit, harsh, hat,
instrument, jasmin, jay,
nonsense syllable, old, plant,
polyester, pop, poppy, question
mark, rain, raincoat, red,
sailcloth, sew, sheet, shirt,
small, snap, spring, vest,
wood, Zenlaf
(Illegible - 3)

XIII-14 Silk (n = 100)

No.	Response	Total
1.	smooth	17
2.	soft	10
3.	stocking(s)	9
4.	dress	8
5.	satin	8
6.	worm	8
7.	cloth	4
8.	blouse	3
9.	cotton	3
10.	fine	3
11.	tie	3
12.	hat	2
13.	material	2
14.	rayon	2
15.	scarf	2

16-31. (f = 1)
beautiful, chiffon, China, cold,
feminine, fur, ivory, luxury,
milk, ribbon, scroll, silky,
skinny, skirt, thread, woman

XIII-15 Tweed (n = 99)

No.	Response	Total
1.	suit	33
2.	coat	13
3.	wool	5
4.	jacket	4
5.	material	4
6.	perfume	3
7.	colors	2
8.	pants	2
9.	skirt	2

10-41. (f = 1)
black and white, blue, boss,
brown, bush, checked, cloth,
English, enmeshed, fabric,
fall, fiber, grow, hiest, itch,
itchy, leaf, man, many, mixture,
neat, pattern, prickly, print,
solids, sportcoat, suits, tree,
twid, white, worster

XIII-16 Velvet (n = 101)

No.	Response	Total
1.	soft	36
2.	smooth	21
3.	blue	6
4.	dress	4

XIII-16 Velvet (n = 101) (contd)

No.	Response	Total
5.	material	4
6.	black	3
7.	cloth	2
8.	feel	2
9.	jacket	2
10.	national	2

11-29. (f = 1)
claw, coat, color, cotton,
courderoy, downy, felt, heavy,
pretty, purple, red, regal,
shirt, stiff, suade, suit,
svelt, sweater, torch

XIII-17 Wool (n = 101)

No.	Response	Total
1.	lamb(s)	19
2.	itch	8
3.	sheep	8
4.	warm	8
5.	cotton	7
6.	soft	6
7.	itchy	5
8.	sweater	4
9.	cloth	3
10.	material	3
11.	coat	2
12.	eyes	2
13.	heavy	2
14.	socks	2

15-36. (f = 1)
bunting, cashmere, clothes,
dress, fiber, fur, fuzz, iron,
jersey, knitting, leather, light,
over the eyes, piling, sheet,
skirt, slacks, song, suit,
winter, yarn
(Illegible - 1)

XIV-1 Aluminum (n = 100)

No.	Response	Total
1.	metal	17
2.	tin	12
3.	shiny	8
4.	foil	7
5.	silver	5
6.	pot(s)	4
7.	Alcoa	3
8.	bauxite	3
9.	iron	3
10.	steel	3
11.	windows	3

12-42. (f = 1)
alloy, awning, box, brass, can,
cars, cast, chest, copper,
element, forest, gold, grey,
hammerer, linoleum, material,
mine, modern, ore, pan, paper,
Reynolds, rust, rustproof,
salvaging, scratchy, shine,
shining, silvery, stormdoor,
sun, white

XIV-2 Brass (n = 99)

No.	Response	Total
1.	band	24
2.	knuckles	8
3.	shiny	8
4.	instrument	6
5.	gold	3
6.	pipe	3
7.	wind	3
8.	yellow	3
9.	hard	2
10.	loud	2
11.	metal	2
12.	nerve	2
13.	noisy	2
14.	rail	2

15-44. (f = 1)
ass, big shot, blong, bright,
buttons, candlesticks, copper,
drum, general, guts, horn,
iron, key, medal, nail, nut,
play, polish, ring, sax, shine,
slang, soldier, strangth,
sturdy, tack, trumpet, wood,
woodwind

XIV-3 Bronze (n = 101)

No.	Response	Total
1.	statue	22
2.	metal	15
3.	gold	12
4.	copper	7
5.	brown	5
6.	brass	3
7.	Age	2
8.	iron	2
9.	shiny	2
10.	silver	2
11.	tan	2

12-37. (f = 1)
antiques, bake, beauty, black,
color, earth, face, Greek,
hard, marble, Medieval history,
paint, plaque, sculpture,
shield, shine, shiney, silver,
slave, star, steel, stone,
suntan, tin, trim, tray, yellow

XIV-4 Copper (n = 100)

No.	Response	Total
1.	metal	15
2.	shiny	8
3.	brass	5
4.	pennies	5
5.	gold	4
6.	iron	4
7.	red	4
8.	tin	4
9.	Cu"	3
10.	head	3
11.	ore	3
12.	plate	3
13.	plating	3
14.	buttons	2
15.	mine	2
16.	policeman	2
17.	steel	2
18.	wire	2
19.	zinc	2

XIV-4 Copper ($\underline{n}$ = 100) (contd)

No.	Response	Total

20-43. ($\underline{f}$ = 1)
bass, bend, bronze, brown, chemistry, clad, coin, color, conductor, curb, dirty, electronics, heat, kettle, medallion, pot, rust, slop, snake, tarnish, teapot, toody, village, yellow

XIV-5 Iron ($\underline{n}$ = 99)

No.	Response	Total
1.	steel	19
2.	metal	11
3.	clothes	7
4.	hard	5
5.	ore	5
6.	press	5
7.	hot	4
8.	lead	4
9.	rusty	3
10.	brass	2
11.	fence	2
12.	fire	2
13.	steam	2
14.	strong	2
15.	tin	2

16-39. ($\underline{f}$ = 1)
bars, beard, black, board, clad, grey, hand, heavy, horse, industry, Iraq, like, lung, mine, nail, oxide, paints, plaid, ring, rust, sew, staircase, work, wrought

XIV-6 Lead ($\underline{n}$ = 100)

No.	Response	Total
1.	pencil	33
2.	follow	18
3.	metal	7
4.	heavy	4
5.	pipe	3
6.	bullet	2
7.	chemistry	2

8-38. ($\underline{f}$ = 1)
arm, ballet, band, bar, belly, black, bullet, conduct, conductor, copper, dominate, drive, dull, first, fishing, fool, house, led, out, rod, shield, shot, show, silver, sinker, steel, stray, take, walk, weight, win

XIV-7 Nickel ($\underline{n}$ = 100)

No.	Response	Total
1.	money	41
2.	dime	24
3.	coin	11
4.	penny	7
5.	element	2
6.	metal	2

XIV-7 Nickel ($\underline{n}$ = 100) (contd)

No.	Response	Total

7-19. ($\underline{f}$ = 1)
buff, cheap, circle, dollar, five, five cents, mineral, nickel, ore, pickle, rich, silver, valve

XIV-8 Steel ($\underline{n}$ = 101)

No.	Response	Total
1.	iron	26
2.	hard	12
3.	metal	7
4.	strong	6
5.	mill	6
6.	building	3
7.	girder(s)	3
8.	strength	3
9.	beams	2
10.	fire	2
11.	plate	2

12-40. ($\underline{f}$ = 1)
alloy, Bessemer, big, bomb, bridge, bright, broad, car, company, durable, hat, lumber, machinery, pipes, plumber, rich, rob, rod, rubber, sharp, shiny, steal, strings, stronger, sword, U.S., white, wool, wove

XIV-9 Tin ($\underline{n}$ = 101)

No.	Response	Total
1.	can	33
2.	metal	19
3.	iron	8
4.	pan	3
5.	thin	3
6.	box	2
7.	car	2
8.	copper	2
9.	soldier	2

10-35. ($\underline{f}$ = 1)
alloy, bang, cheap, Columbia, fin, horn, horse, light, mine, mineral, noise, pin, pipe, plate, pot, rave, rin, roof, rust, shaky, silver color, silvery, smith, soldier, sound, still, torn

XIV-10 Zin ($\underline{n}$ = 102)

No.	Response	Total
1.	metal	27
2.	copper	14
3.	ointment	11
4.	lead	7
5.	element	6
6.	oxide	6
7.	chemistry	4
8.	white	4
9.	gold	2

10-30. ($\underline{f}$ = 1)
alloy, antimony, battery, brass, chemical, formula, grey, hard, iron, leather, metal-alloy,

XIV-10 Zinc ($\underline{n}$ = 102)

No.	Response	Total

mine, nickel, ore, person, shiny, sulfide, tale, tin, Z, Zn"

XV-1 Accordian ($\underline{n}$ = 99)

No.	Response	Total
1.	music	21
2.	play	20
3.	instrument	9
4.	player	9
5.	piano	7
6.	squeeze	6
7.	wedding(s)	4
8.	file	2
9.	sound	2

10-28. ($\underline{f}$ = 1)
annoying, corny, dull, entertain, fag, folds, gay, gone, guitar, key, Marty, noise, plait, pleats, polka, pull, stretch, uncle, violinist

XV-2 Bass ($\underline{n}$ = 100)

No.	Response	Total
1.	fish	28
2.	low	14
3.	voice	8
4.	drum	6
5.	fiddle	4
6.	music	4
7.	treble	4
8.	bassoon	2
9.	deep	2
10.	instrument	2
11.	orchestra	2
12.	trout	2
13.	violin	2

14-33. ($\underline{f}$ = 1)
Bach, big, flounder, knob, loud, man, Mingus, player, rumble, shark, smelly, soprano, strumming, tender, trombone, tuba, viol, viola, yellow
(Illegible - 1)

XV-3 Bugle ($\underline{n}$ = 98)

No.	Response	Total
1.	blow	20
2.	horn	12
3.	taps	9
4.	army	8
5.	instrument	7
6.	call	6
7.	camp	4
8.	morning	4
9.	reville	4
10.	sound	3
11.	trumpet	3
12.	awaken	2
13.	loud	2
14.	music	2
15.	noise	2
16.	toot	2

XV-3 Bugle (n = 98) (contd)

No.	Response	Total
17.	war	2
18-25.	(f = 1)	

arms, band, flag, march, Phi Δ rise, shiny, sleep

XV-4 Clarinet (n = 100)

No.	Response	Total
1.	music	41
2.	instrument	26
3.	horn	8
4.	flute	2
5.	harmonica	2
6.	long	2
7.	saxaphone	2
8-24.	(f = 1)	

accordion, bass, Beethoven, blow, Goodman, hand, harsh, Jim, Mozart, musician, orchestra, piano, player, reed, songs, sword, whistle

XV-5 Drums (n = 101)

No.	Response	Total
1.	beat(s)	19
2.	noise	13
3.	music	9
4.	instrument(s)	6
5.	bang	5
6.	Mohawk	5
7.	boom	3
8.	Indian(s)	3
9.	Africa	2
10.	band	2
11.	jazz	2
12.	loud	2
13.	play	2
14.	rhythm	2
15.	sound	2
16.	sticks	2
17.	trumpet(s)	2
18-37.	(f = 1)	

beating, bongos, brother, bugle, congo, dances, doom, general, hear, hit, Olatunji, passion, pounds, primitive, raps, rich, roll, round, throb, thunder

XV-6 Flute (n = 100)

No.	Response	Total
1.	music	35
2.	instrument	13
3.	fish	5
4.	sound	3
5.	blowing	2
6.	high	2
7.	horn	2
8.	musician	2
9.	notes	2
10.	shrill	2
11.	sweet	2
12.	tweet	2

XV-6 Flute (n = 100) (contd)

No.	Response	Total
13-42.	(f = 1)	

band, bird, Britain, brut, cool, concerto, flounder, fluke, harp, loose, luck, melody, mouth, musical instrument, noise, orchestra, piper, pretty, silver, soft, soft music, song, squeek, tube, weary, whistle, white
(Illegible - 1)

XV-7 Guitar (n = 100)

No.	Response	Total
1.	music	20
2.	play	16
3.	folk song	7
4.	string(s)	7
5.	song	5
6.	strum	5
7.	banjo	4
8.	instrument	4
9.	pick	3
10.	sing	3
11.	Spanish	3
12.	ukelele	3
13.	folk	2
14.	player	2
15.	pleasant	2
16.	rock and roll	2
17-28.	(f = 1)	

band, camp, Chele, Chet Atkins, cowboy, dance, Elvis, Esteso, great, noise, pretty, west

XV-8 Harmonica (n = 101)

No.	Response	Total
1.	music	44
2.	instrument	23
3.	accordion	4
4.	tune	4
5.	organ	3
6.	piano	3
7.	song	3
8.	blow	2
9.	mouth	2
10-22.	(f = 1)	

clarinet, flute, melody, musica, noise, play, rod, sound, sweet, teeth, toot, unity, violin

XV-9 Harp (n = 101)

No.	Response	Total
1.	string(s)	17
2.	instrument	15
3.	music	14
4.	angel(s)	9
5.	play	7
6.	lyre	3
7.	melody	3
8.	piano	3
9.	violin	3
10.	heaven	2
11.	orchestra	2

XV-9 Harp (n = 101) (contd)

No.	Response	Total
12.	zither	2
13-33.	(f = 1)	

beautiful, bird, church music, cord, etherial, fingers, fish, flute, girl, Groucho, Harpo, harpsichord, Marks, Marx, mythology, on, orgasm, pluck, spring, stringed
(Illegible - 1)

XV-10 Mandolin (n = 101)

No.	Response	Total
1.	music	23
2.	guitar	12
3.	instrument	11
4.	play(s)	9
5.	banjo	8
6.	violin	8
7.	ukelele	4
8.	Italy	3
9.	lute	3
10.	piano	2
11.	romance	2
12.	string	2
13-25.	(f = 1)	

Bill Monroe, bone, dark, flute, fruit, Oriental, pick soft, song, string, strip, tinkle, twang, Venice

XV-11 Piano (n = 100)

No.	Response	Total
1.	play	25
2.	music	24
3.	instrument	9
4.	key(s)	8
5.	stool	3
6.	keyboard	2
7.	player	2
8.	tuner	2
9-34.	(f = 1)	

A. Rubenstein, Basie, bench, choir, concerto, dreamy, fingers, forte, ivory, Kup, large, leg, Liberace, Mozart, Phyllis, relaxation, Steinway, sound, talent, upright violin, wire, wood, xylophone
(Illegible - 1)

XV-12 Piccolo (n = 100)

No.	Response	Total
1.	music	32
2.	flute	21
3.	instrument	18
4.	sound	2
5.	sweet	2
6.	violin	2
7-29.	(f = 1)	

beets, bird, boy, canary, eye, fast, high, horn, long, man, mouth, musical instrument, nose, notes, orchestra,

XV-12 Piccolo (n = 100) (contd)

No.	Response	Total

pick grapes, Pinoccio, play, player, shoes, small, stick, strange

XV-13 Trumpet (n = 100)

No.	Response	Total
1.	blow	18
2.	horn	9
3.	music	8
4.	noise	8
5.	player	6
6.	instrument	5
7.	sound	5
8.	loud	4
9.	play	4
10.	blast	3
11.	saxophone	3
12.	angel	2
13.	blare	2
14.	brass	2
15.	bugle	2
16.	call	2

17-33. (f = 1)
bassoon, blues, clarion, concerto, cool, ear, Hicks, high, hot, jazz, Michael, Satchmo, sweet, trombone, tune, unblown, yell

XV-14 Ukelele (n = 100)

No.	Response	Total
1.	guitar	13
2.	play	12
3.	Hawaii	11
4.	banjo	10
5.	strum	10
6.	music	8
7.	Arthur Godfrey	6
8.	song	5
9.	string	4
10.	instrument	2
11.	mandolin	2

12-28. (f = 1)
cheerful, folks, Godfrey, harmonica, jazz, native, nice, pick, plunk, Roaring Twenties, Russia, sing, sound, trip, twang, Wheaton
(Illegible - 1)

XV-15 Violin (n = 100)

No.	Response	Total
1.	string	21
2.	play	20
3.	music	19
4.	instruments	5
5.	bow	4
6.	concerto	4
7.	concert	3
8.	bass	2
9.	fiddle	2
10.	mandolin	2
11.	piano	2

XV-15 Violin (n = 100) (contd)

No.	Response	Total
12.	sweet	2
13.	viola	2

14-25. (f = 1)
flute, Heifez, high pitch, lessons, moonlight, noise, orchestra, practice, soft, squeak, Statavarius, tender

XV-16 Xylophone (n = 100)

No.	Response	Total
1.	music	30
2.	instrument	27
3.	play	7
4.	piano	6
5.	noise	3
6.	jazz	2
7.	miramba	2
8.	silver	2
9.	trumpet	2
10.	vibes	2

11-27. (f = 1)
bank, bells, bones, bugle, chime, cool, enzyme, Hampton, hollow, jingle bells, microphone, musical, pronunciation, ringing, stand, sweet, violin

XV-17 Zither (n = 101)

No.	Response	Total
1.	instrument	19
2.	music	10
3.	wind	9
4.	flower	7
5.	play	4
6.	leather	3
7.	animal	2
8.	color	2
9.	whether	2
10.	zebra	2
11.	zither	2

12-50. (f = 1)
airplane, airy, angels, Apollo, blimp, block, breeze, cool, dither, ether, fern, flute, heath, heather, ink, jet, Lincoln, lousy, man, medieval, mogul, nebra, nether, nonsense syllable, piccolo, rubber, sea, soft, string, tie, ugly, victrola, weather, what, xylophone, Zenith, zephalyn, zing

XVI-1 Accountant (n = 99)

No.	Response	Total
1.	money	17
2.	figure	11
3.	number(s)	10
4.	C.P.A.	6
5.	lawyer	5
6.	math	5
7.	bore	4
8.	dull	3

XVI-1 Accountant (n = 99) (contd)

No.	Response	Total
9.	Marty	3
10.	add	2
11.	clerk	2
12.	man	2
13.	tax	2
14.	work	2

15-39. (f = 1)
arithmetic, blank, bookkeeper, books, boyfriend, busy, class, crook, desk, engineer, fag, farther, friend, invest, job, low, meticulous, Mr. Friedman, nasty, no., occupation, paper, pay, profession
(Illegible - 1)

XVI-2 Chemist (n = 100)

No.	Response	Total
1.	drug(s)	11
2.	chemical(s)	10
3.	doctor	8
4.	science	7
5.	chemistry	4
6.	experiments	4
7.	scientist	4
8.	biologist	3
9.	lab	3
10.	man	3
11.	money	3
12.	formula	2
13.	gold	2
14.	laboratory	2
15.	nut	2
16.	test tubes	2

17-46. (f = 1)
alcohol, apothecary, blast, bottles, burns, CO_2, disease, drink, element, engineer, experimenter, explosion, Fikers, Harry, Hord, ingeneur, jerk, knowledge, medicine, mixing, pharmacist, physicist, Ronald, search, smell, specialist, stupid, tobacco, tube, worker

XVI-3 Cook (n = 100)

No.	Response	Total
1.	food	45
2.	eat	8
3.	book	6
4.	chef	6
5.	bake	3
6.	burn	3
7.	kitchen	2
8.	me	2
9.	mother	2

10-32. (f = 1)
boil, broth, dinner, eggplants, fat, foot, gourme, grandma, hat, Julia, maid, man, meal, meat, mock, oven, prepare, rooster, servant, smoke, stew, supper, white hot

XVI-4 Dentist (n = 100)

No.	Response	Total
1.	teeth	41
2.	drill	17
3.	doctor	8
4.	cavities	6
5.	tooth	5
6.	pain	4
7.	hurt	3
8.	toothache	3

9-21. (f = 1)
ache, carie, detest, drillings,
fear, grind, hate, money,
Norman, Oh!!, scared, warm,
Z-z-z

XVI-5 Detective (n = 100)

No.	Response	Total
1.	police	13
2.	cop	10
3.	private eye	6
4.	crime	5
5.	story	5
6.	man	4
7.	spy	4
8.	sleuth	3
9.	Dick Tracy	2
10.	eye	2
11.	F.B.I.	2
12.	gun	2
13.	inspector	2
14.	investigator	2
15.	mystery	2
16.	policeman	2
17.	T.V.	2

18-49. (f = 1)
Agatha Christie, agent, badge,
book, brave, car, coat, cowboy,
delinquent, enforcement, fire,
fun, glasses, G-man, good,
Hawaiian Eye, hidden, Holmes,
Kingsley, liar, Mickey Spillane,
Mike Hammer, priers, private,
search, Sherlock Holmes, smart,
television, trench coat,
Untouchables, watch,
87th Precinct

XVI-6 Doctor (n = 100)

No.	Response	Total
1.	nurse	16
2.	medicine	12
3.	lawyer	7
4.	sick	6
5.	dentist	5
6.	white	5
7.	cure	3
8.	help	3
9.	healer	2
10.	hospital	2
11.	hurt	2
12.	ill	2
13.	M.D.	2
14.	patient	2
15.	physician	2
16.	protect	2
17.	satchel	2

XVI-6 Doctor (n = 100) (contd)

No.	Response	Total

18-42. (f = 1)
aid, bills, Casey, death, die,
Dolgin, Finkel, fix, heart,
Hertz, Indianchief, intern,
Kildare, Kramer, man, medic,
office, pain, PHD, pre-med,
psychologist, smart, Stan, wife,
Zhivago

XVI-7 Firemen (n = 100)

No.	Response	Total
1.	red	27
2.	fire	17
3.	policeman	10
4.	hat	4
5.	courage	3
6.	engine	3
7.	hose	3
8.	brave	2
9.	burn	2
10.	ladder	2
11.	protection	2
12.	save	2
13.	suspenders	2
14.	water	2

15-33. (f = 1)
cap, carry, chief, coat, danger,
dog, excitement, flame, fly,
gun, husky, Jones, ladybug, pole,
servant, siren, smoke, truck,
women

XVI-8 Historian (n = 100)

No.	Response	Total
1.	teacher	12
2.	scholar	9
3.	man	8
4.	Herodotus	7
5.	books	4
6.	history	4
7.	writer	4
8.	old	3
9.	Toynbee	3
10.	bore	2
11.	facts	2
12.	glasses	2
13.	knowledge	2

14-51. (f = 1)
artist, boring, bright, Brooklyn
College, brother-in-law, Cooper,
date, doctor, dry, educator,
factual, famous, fink, grammarian,
Greeks, Gunther, instructor,
Kant, liar, librarian, Lincoln,
map, musty, past, physicist,
psychologist, reader, recorder,
school, specialist, student,
stuffy, sylvan, textbook,
Thycidides, time, Wells, when

XVI-9 Jeweler (n = 100)

No.	Response	Total
1.	diamond(s)	35
2.	ring(s)	15
3.	watch(es)	11
4.	gem(s)	4
5.	jewelry	4
6.	money	4
7.	gold	3
8.	earring	2
9.	jewels	2
10.	man	2
11.	thief	2

12-27. (f = 1)
bracelet, coin, expensive,
furs, ice, I.D., lie, ocular,
parts, precision, rock, shine,
small eye, stiff, watchmaker,
wrist watch

XVI-10 Lawyer (n = 101)

No.	Response	Total
1.	doctor	28
2.	man	11
3.	court	7
4.	case(s)	4
5.	attorney	3
6.	judge	3
7.	briefcase	2
8.	father	2
9.	justice	2
10.	law	2
11.	Perry Mason	2
12.	profession	2
13.	professional	2
14.	suit	2

15-44. (f = 1)
advocate, ambulance, books,
boy, boyfriend, cake, constitution, counsel, crime, crook,
daddy, detective, Esq., fool,
friend, glasses, Indian,
investigator, joke, me,
shiester, shrewd, smart, speech,
sue, talk, time, verbal
(Illegible - 1)

XVI-11 Mechanic (n = 100)

No.	Response	Total
1.	car	36
2.	tool(s)	7
3.	machine	6
4.	worker	6
5.	auto	5
6.	grease	4
7.	man	4
8.	dirty	3
9.	work	3
10.	fixer	2
11.	grease monkey	2
12.	garage	2
13.	repairs	2

14-31. (f = 1)
automatic, automobile, classical, device, dirt, doctor,
engineer, experience, expert,
fix-it, greasy, hands, helper,
laborer, oily, science, slob,
system

XVI-12　Nurse　(n = 101)

No.	Response	Total
1.	doctor	28
2.	white	13
3.	help	5
4.	sick	5
5.	care	4
6.	good	3
7.	hospital	3
8.	mother	3
9.	cap	2
10.	comfort	2
11.	feed	2
12.	healer	2
13.	patient	2
14.	pretty	2

15-38.　(f = 1)
aid, blood, child, cure, feed, fix, friend, gentle, hat, health, ill, kind, me, medicine, nice, operation, Phillis, registered, save, sex, swell, treat, uniform, well, worse

XVI-13　Pilot　(n = 99)

No.	Response	Total
1.	plane	62
2.	fly	9
3.	ship	5
4.	airplane	2
5.	flier	2
6.	trip	2

7-23.　(f = 1)
airforce, betrayal, bombadeer, captain, crash, film, fish, flight, goggles, head, hemisphere, jet, light, navigator, sky, space, uniform

XVI-14　Plumber　(n = 101)

No.	Response	Total
1.	pipe(s)	24
2.	man	10
3.	fix	9
4.	faucet	5
5.	sink	5
6.	dirty	4
7.	leak(s)	4
8.	water	4
9.	plunger	3
10.	worker	3
11.	toilet	2

12-39.　(f = 1)
bathroom, bathyscaps, Bronsnick, builder, carpenter, Christ, coils, dad, dirt, drip, dumb, fixer, fixing, handyman, helper, iron, mess, money, occupation, pry, repairman, rich, superintendent, toilet bowls, uncle, work, wrench
(No response - 1)

XVI-15　Professor　(n = 101)

No.	Response	Total
1.	teacher	40
2.	man	8
3.	college	6
4.	school	6
5.	teach	5
6.	learned	4
7.	bad	2
8.	Schwartz	2

9-36.　(f = 1)
bald, beard, books, Brooklyn College, censored, class, classroom, doctor, dope, dream, English, erudite, fake, instructors, intelligent, K.L.R., knowledge, learn, leisure, professes, proud, slob, slow, smart, student, subject, university, Zuckerman

XVI-16　Teacher　(n = 101)

No.	Response	Total
1.	school	15
2.	student	9
3.	professor	8
4.	instructor	7
5.	man	5
6.	pupil	5
7.	pet	3
8.	desk	2
9.	fool	2
10.	smart	2

11-53.　(f = 1)
ask, blackboard, bored, boring, cap, class, course, Dewey, director, dull, education, educator, eh, father, friend, good, grades, guide, historian, history, inspiration, learn, lesson, mark, motivation, nasty, no, pedagogue, pencil, person, poor, prof, profession, respect, room, scholar, singer, stupid, taught, teaching, tyrant, writer, young

XVII-1　Chili　(n = 100)

No.	Response	Total
1.	hot	20
2.	food	10
3.	sauce	10
4.	country	9
5.	peppers	5
6.	South America	5
7.	spicy	5
8.	beans	4
9.	con carne	3
10.	Spain	3
11.	Argentina	2
12.	chile con carne	2
13.	cold	2
14.	Spanish	2
15.	soup	2
16.	spice	2

17-30.　(f = 1)
baby, boy, Brazil, brown, carni, Latin, Latin America, learn, Mexico, salad, somall, soul, state

XVII-2　Chives　(n = 100)

No.	Response	Total
1.	cheese	13
2.	food	10
3.	cream cheese	9
4.	hives	8
5.	olive(s)	7
6.	spice	7
7.	eat	4
8.	vegetable	3
9.	anchovies	2
10.	green	2
11.	onions	2
12.	pimentoes	2
13.	sound	2

14-40.　(f = 1)
archives, artichoke, bitter, bitters, car, cherries, chicken, clover, dictionary, disease, dislike, eggs, fruit, good, grapes, hand, knives, nuts, parsley, pickles, red, room, salad, sarcasm, sauce, seasoning, sour
(Illegible - 2)

XVII-3　Cinnamon　(n = 100)

No.	Response	Total
1.	spice	15
2.	toast	10
3.	brown	8
4.	cake	6
5.	flavor	5
6.	red	5
7.	bread	4
8.	raisin	3
9.	sugar	3
10.	sweet	3
11.	taste	3
12.	apple	2
13.	bitter	2
14.	bun(s)	2
15.	cookies	2
16.	seasoning	2
17.	smell	2
18.	spicy	2

19-39.　(f = 1)
apple pie, burn, cider, Coke, cottage cheese, dulcid, flavoring, fruit, hot, loaf, mice, nutmeg, pears, pepper, pie, pudding, rice pudding, roll, sharp, sprinkle, stick

XVII-4　Cloves　(n = 101)

No.	Response	Total
1.	spices	18
2.	hands	11
3.	flowers	9
4.	leaves	9
5.	garlic	5
6.	food	3
7.	grass	3
8.	green	3
9.	hot	3
10.	tree	3
11.	hat	2
12.	plants	2
13.	taste	2
14.	vegetable	2

XVII-4 Cloves (n = 101) (contd)

No.	Response	Total
15-40.	(f = 1)	

birds, brown, bud, bush, candle, chives, cold, dates, fingers, fruit, greens, ham, happy, herbs, lawn, leaf, meat, mint, olives, parsley, pastures, pickles, row, salt, scent, spinach

XVII-5 Garlic (n = 99)

No.	Response	Total
1.	smell	26
2.	bread	9
3.	spice	9
4.	bitter	8
5.	odor	5
6.	powder	5
7.	breath	3
8.	sharp	3
9.	stine(s)	3
10.	pepper	2
11.	salad	2
12.	salt	2
13.	steak	2
14.	tasty	2
15-32.	(f = 1)	

cooking, delicious, disagreeable, dry, flavor, fry, harsh, hot, Italian, meat, onion, pizza, repulsive, spaghetti, sprey, stale, thick, vampire

XVII-6 Ginger (n = 101)

No.	Response	Total
1.	ale	34
2.	bread	16
3.	spice(s)	16
4.	snap(s)	4
5.	drink	3
6.	Rogers	3
7.	spicy	3
8.	flavor	2
9.	peachy	2
10.	pepper	2
11.	sweet	2
12-25.	(f = 1)	

brown, cake, cinnamon, clove, cook, coral, food, girl's name, good, horse, liquor, mouth, peach, seasoning

XVII-7 Mint (n = 100)

No.	Response	Total
1.	candy	15
2.	green	14
3.	money	7
4.	sweet	7
5.	chocolate	6
6.	taste	5
7.	gold	4
8.	cool	3
9.	fresh	3
10.	julep	3

XVII-7 Mint (n = 100) (contd)

No.	Response	Total
11.	bitter	2
12.	coolness	2
13.	flavor	2
14.	flavored	2
15.	pepper	2
16-38.	(f = 1)	

cigarette, dislike, good, hard, hint, ice cream, jelly, lime, peppermint, pleasant, refresh, refreshing, scent, sensation, sharp, smell, sour, spearmint, spicy, sweet smell, tangy, tart, white

XVII-8 Mustard (n = 100)

No.	Response	Total
1.	frankfurter	15
2.	hot dog	13
3.	ketchup	12
4.	yellow	11
5.	seed	10
6.	salami	5
7.	plaster	4
8.	custard	3
9.	hot	3
10.	spice	3
11.	food	2
12.	green	2
13-29.	(f = 1)	

bread, brown, cake, condiment, corn, gas, gold, jar, odor, paste, pepper, pickle, plant, sauerkraut, sausage, sharp, spoon

XVII-9 Nutmeg (n = 100)

No.	Response	Total
1.	spice	22
2.	nut	8
3.	drink	6
4.	cake	5
5.	food	5
6.	egg-nog	4
7.	flavor	4
8.	seasoning	4
9.	candy	3
10.	fruit	3
11.	tree	3
12.	brown	2
13.	ginger	2
14.	pepper	2
15-41.	(f = 1)	

allspice, beer, cast, chipmunk, Christmas, cinnamon, coffee, Connecticut, cook, cooking, cork, cream, eggs, flower, foolish, garlic, herb, holly, honey, milk, New Years, nothing, oatmeal, peanut, princess, soda, thyme

XVII-10 Paprika (n = 100)

No.	Response	Total
1.	red	26
2.	spice	19
3.	seasoning	10
4.	bitter	5
5.	hot	4
6.	salt	4
7.	pepper	3
8.	spicy	3
9.	chickens	2
10.	food	2
11.	sharp	2
12-31.	(f = 1)	

allergy, apricot, baked fish, bird, childhood, cooking, drink, egg, gulash, like, meat, orange, potato, season, soup, spaish, steak, tangy, taste, turkey

XVII-11 Parsley (n = 100)

No.	Response	Total
1.	green	37
2.	salad	9
3.	eat	5
4.	lettuce	4
5.	potato	4
6.	vegetable	4
7.	season	3
8.	soup	3
9.	spice	3
10.	celery	2
11.	flakes	2
12.	garnish	2
13.	spinach	2
14-33.	(f = 1)	

beans, chicken soup, condiment, decoration, dill, dish, dry, food, fruit, leaves, lobster, nips, root, seed, snips, soap, sprig, taste, tease, turnip

XVII-12 Pepper (n = 100)

No.	Response	Total
1.	salt	46
2.	sneeze	10
3.	spice	6
4.	bitter	5
5.	hot	4
6.	sharp	4
7.	spicy	4
8.	black	3
9.	shaker	2
10.	steak	2
11-24.	(f = 1)	

bad odor, burning taste, cooking, Gomez, green, impudent, mint, onward, pickle, pungent, red, seasoning, sour, spot

XVII-13 Salt (n = 100)

No.	Response	Total
1.	pepper	32
2.	sugar	13
3.	taste	7

XVII-13 Salt (n = 100) (contd)

No.	Response	Total
4.	food	5
5.	spice	4
6.	bitter	3
7.	sea	3
8.	shaker	3
9.	sour	3
10.	bread	2
11.	chemical	2
12.	salt	2
13.	seasoning	2
14.	spicy	2
15.	sweet	2
16.	water	2

17-29. (f = 1)
cooking, eat, fault, Halite,
iodized, lake, malt, no, nuts,
ocean, sodium chloride,
tomatoes, white

XVII-14 Sugar (n = 100)

No.	Response	Total
1.	sweet	61
2.	cane	6
3.	tea	5
4.	coffee	4
5.	plum	3
6.	cubes	2
7.	spice	2

8-24. (f = 1)
beet, calories, candy,
carbohydrates, crop, day, fine,
free, granuals, honey, horse,
nice, saccarine, sucrose,
syrup, toothache, white

XVII-15 Syrup (n = 100)

No.	Response	Total
1.	maple	21
2.	sweet	21
3.	chocolate	13
4.	pancake	12
5.	sticky	5
6.	thick	5
7.	brown	2
8.	mustard	2
9.	toast	2
10.	tree	2

11-26. (f = 1)
cake, candy, cherry, Cokes,
corn, cream, drink, flavor,
good, gum, hot cakes, ketchup,
medicine, oak, ooze, slimey

XVII-16 Vanilla (n = 99)

No.	Response	Total
1.	chocolate	25
2.	ice cream	25
3.	flavor	10
4.	white	10
5.	sweet	5
6.	bean	3
7.	good	3
8.	cream	2

XVII-16 Vanilla (n = 99) (contd)

No.	Response	Total

9-25. (f = 1)
America, cake, candy, clean,
cooking, dripping, eat,
favorite, flavoring, malted,
pop, pudding, smell, snow,
soda, syrup

XVIII-1 Birch (n = 100)

No.	Response	Total
1.	tree	57
2.	Society	10
3.	John	8
4.	oak	3
5.	white	3
6.	wood	3

7-22. (f = 1)
bark, branch, Communists,
Conservatives, extreme, frost,
John Birch Society, leaf, log,
patriot, Rightist, rod, silver,
smoke wood, whip
(Illegible - 1)

XVIII-2 Cedar (n = 100)

No.	Response	Total
1.	tree	47
2.	wood	11
3.	chest	6
4.	oak	6
5.	closet	3
6.	grove	3
7.	Lebanon	3

8-28. (f = 1)
aroma, bench, brook, cedar chest,
cigar, color, eating, elm, food,
large, leaves, poplar, Rapids,
red, scent, seeds, smell, sweet,
table, tall, wive

XVIII-3 Chestnut (n = 100)

No.	Response	Total
1.	tree	34
2.	nut(s)	11
3.	brown	8
4.	squirrel	7
5.	winter	5
6.	food	4
7.	hot	3
8.	roast	3
9.	fire	2
10.	holiday	2
11.	roasting	2

12-30. (f = 1)
animal, apple, bake, burst,
chipmunk, Christmas, constipation,
edible, fruit, furniture, hard,
horse, peanut, potato, seed,
tired, turkey stuffing, warm,
wood

XVIII-4 Cypress (n = 101)

No.	Response	Total
1.	tree	41
2.	garden	18
3.	country	5
4.	island	5
5.	England	3
6.	cemetery	2
7.	Israel	2
8.	tall	2
9.	Van Gogh	2

10-30. (f = 1)
arbor, crave, Crete, dangling,
death, express, far, far away,
Florida, foreign, fruit,
goddess, green, grove, oak,
orange, place, swamp, war,
wood, youth

XVIII-5 Dogwood (n = 100)

No.	Response	Total
1.	tree	60
2.	flower	7
3.	furniture	2
4.	wood(s)	2

5-33. (f = 1)
bar, Blondie, burnt, cat,
character, clear, cow, damp,
dead, delicate, desk, door,
drift, forest, freedom, friend,
mahogony, patch, pine, plant,
redwood, ride, rough, sapwood,
saw, Sir, waterlogged, weed,
wetwood

XVIII-6 Elm (n = 98)

No.	Response	Total
1.	tree	79
2.	green	2
3.	maple	2

4-18. (f = 1)
bark, cool, disease, house,
leaf, movie, oak, park,
roominess, spreading, spring,
strength, towering, town, trep

XVIII-7 Maple (n = 100)

No.	Response	Total
1.	tree	58
2.	leaf	14
3.	syrup	10
4.	sugar	4
5.	wood	3
6.	oak	2

7-15. (f = 1)
cider, cone, forest, fruit,
furniture, green, gum, mut,
sweet

XVIII-8 Oak (n = 100)

No.	Response	Total
1.	tree	81
2.	wood	5
3.	acorn	2
4-15.	(f = 1)	

bark, gigantic, joke, large,
leaves, lone, poison-oak, red,
solid, strong, tall, teak

XVIII-9 Pine (n = 100)

No.	Response	Total
1.	tree	67
2.	needle	5
3.	cone	4
4.	scent	3
5.	smell	3
6.	cool	2
7.	forest	2
8.	wine	2
9-20.	(f = 1)	

box, brothers, camp, cheap,
coffin, evergreen, fragrance,
green, soothing, tall, waste,
worry

XVIII-10 Poplar (n = 100)

No.	Response	Total
1.	tree	60
2.	tall	7
3.	country	2
4.	elm	2
5.	famous	2
6.	happy	2
7.	known	2
8.	leaf	2
9.	seed	2
10-28.	(f = 1)	

band, bend, coat, cold, demand,
fad, fastest, friendly, greenery,
music, pine, polar, pop, popular,
race, rough, shake, soon, wood

XVIII-11 Spruce (n = 100)

No.	Response	Total
1.	tree	65
2.	up	2
3-35.	(f = 1)	

against, clean, comb, dark, dim,
eat, elm, fine, fir, forest,
fragrant, fresh, friend, good,
green, husband, juice, leaves,
like, man, maple, name, none,
pulp, sap, sharp, smell, spout,
spruce, street, tall, wood,
young

XVIII-12 Walnut (n = 99)

No.	Response	Total
1.	nut	26
2.	tree	11
3.	eat	8
4.	crack	7
5.	shell	6
6.	squirrel	5
7.	cake	3
8.	cashew	3
9.	good	3
10.	fruit	2
11.	ice cream	2
12.	nutcracker	2
13.	pecan	2
14.	sundae	2
15-31.	(f = 1)	

almond, bake, beer, chew,
cocoanut, color, figs,
furniture, hazel, oily, picture,
round, salad, seed, tabacco,
Thansgiving, Thoreau

XIX-1 Bean (n = 99)

No.	Response	Total
1.	soup	19
2.	sprout	12
3.	string	6
4.	lima	5
5.	Boston	3
6.	pea	3
7.	soy	3
8.	baked	2
9.	ball	2
10.	frankfurter	2
11.	plant	2
12.	pod	2
13.	stalk	2
14.	vegetable	2
15-48.	(f = 1)	

army, bacon, bag, bead, brain,
brown, can, carrot, dean, dozen,
food, green, growth, Jack,
kidney, lean, long, navy, pole,
pot, root, rye, school, seed,
shoo, shoot, skinny, small,
song, stroop, tall, tomato
sauce, tree, white

XIX-2 Beet (n = 100)

No.	Response	Total
1.	red	49
2.	vegetable	15
3.	soup	4
4.	sugar	4
5.	eat	3
6.	borscht	2
7.	carrot	2
8.	garden	2
9.	juice	2
10-26.	(f = 1)	

beetle, bleed, blood, camp, can,
flower, food, greens, hamburger,
lose, maroon, Nik, raw, reed,
rhythm, sour, tree

XIX-3 Broccoli (n = 100)

No.	Response	Total
1.	vegetable	26
2.	green	18
3.	spinach	15
4.	food	5
5.	ugh	4
6.	eat	3
7.	asparagus	2
8.	carrots	2
9.	lettuce	2
10.	sick	2
11.	spears	2
12-30.	(f = 1)	

Andy-Boy, cabbage, cauliflower,
cheese, diet, dinner, dish,
esparagus, good, health, ich,
leaf, mashed potatoes, plant,
spaghetti, sprouts, stench,
string bean, unfamiliar

XIX-4 Cabbage (n = 100)

No.	Response	Total
1.	soup	9
2.	green	7
3.	head	7
4.	leaf	7
5.	lettuce	7
6.	food	6
7.	corn beef	5
8.	stuffed	5
9.	vegetable	5
10.	rabbit	4
11.	smell	4
12.	eat	3
13.	meat	3
14.	patch	3
15.	cole slaw	2
16.	red	2
17.	sweet	2
18-36.	(f = 1)	

baby, cringed, garden, good,
grove, hash, king, odor,
pastrami, plant, salad, sister,
slaw, sourkraut, stew, taste-
less, tomato, tree, vinegar

XIX-5 Carrot (n = 99)

No.	Response	Total
1.	vegetable(s)	16
2.	rabbit	15
3.	orange	13
4.	peas	10
5.	eye(s)	7
6.	eat	6
7.	red	6
8.	top	5
9.	food	4
10.	celery	2
11.	root	2
12-25.	(f = 1)	

Bugs Bunny, crunch, crunchy,
hand, juice, new, parrot,
peal, pear, primary root, rat,
rouge, tomato

XIX-6 Corn (n = 100)

No.	Response	Total
1.	cob	20
2.	food	14
3.	field	8
4.	yellow	8
5.	kernel	5
6.	stalk	5
7.	vegetable	5
8.	peas	3
9.	pop	3
10.	wheat	3
11.	bread	2
12.	cook	2
13.	ear	2
14.	husk	2

15-32. (f = 1)
ball, brown, cream, dawn, endosperm, feet, foot, fruit, hunger, joke, leaves, oil, pad, potatoes, radish, seed, stoul, toe

XIX-7 Cucumber (n = 98)

No.	Response	Total
1.	pickle	21
2.	vegetable	19
3.	salad	14
4.	green	8
5.	food	6
6.	eat	5
7.	lettuce	4
8.	cold	2
9.	fruit	2
10.	plant	2
11.	tomato	2

12-26. (f = 1)
banana, coke, cool, cucumber, frankfurter, freshness, hard, peeling, radish, seeds, sweet, white
(Illegible - 1)

XIX-8 Lettuce (n = 101)

No.	Response	Total
1.	tomato(es)	27
2.	vegetable	13
3.	green	12
4.	leaf	5
5.	rabbit	5
6.	water	4
7.	money	3
8.	cool	2
9.	crisp	2
10.	eat	2
11.	head	2
12.	juicy	2
13.	salad	2

14-33. (f = 1)
broccoli, cabbage, carrot, crispy, cucumbers, eater, eggs, grass, juice, kale, loaf, patch, ruffage, russian dressing, salad dressing, spinach, string beans, tree, watery, wet

XIX-9 Mushroom (n = 100)

No.	Response	Total
1.	poison	21
2.	eat	10
3.	food	8
4.	vegetable	6
5.	cloud	5
6.	plant	5
7.	soup	4
8.	good	3
9.	toadstool	3
10.	barley	2
11.	forest	2
12.	grow	2
13.	sauce	2
14.	stool	2
15.	tree	2
16.	turnip	2

17-37. (f = 1)
beans, beet, black, bomb, cap, carrot, clover, cooked, dirt, fig, gravy, onions, saphophite, season, song, spore, squeeze, steak, tulip, umbrella, wild

XIX-10 Onion (n = 100)

No.	Response	Total
1.	tears	15
2.	smell	13
3.	cry	10
4.	bitter	5
5.	potato	5
6.	vegetable	5
7.	odor	4
8.	soup	4
9.	sharp	3
10.	stew	3
11.	eat	2
12.	taste	2
13.	together	2

14-40. (f = 1)
army, beet, bond, burn, button, club, confederacy, food, fried, intersection, label, leaves, meeting, out, pear, peel, pepper, plant, row, skin, south, soviet, strong, train, United States, watering eyes, white

XIX-11 Parsnip (n = 99)

No.	Response	Total
1.	vegetable	21
2.	green	6
3.	salad	6
4.	turnip	6
5.	food	5
6.	eat	4
7.	catnip	3
8.	celery	3
9.	parsley	3
10.	soup	3
11.	carrot	2
12.	cat	2
13.	leaf	2
14.	leaves	2
15.	poison	2

XIX-11 Parsnip (n = 99) (contd)

No.	Response	Total

16-42. (f = 1)
beet, bird, bleh, boody, broccoli, bum, cauliflower, cooking, diminutive, dog, leafy, mean, nose, nothing, pair, pear, Pickwick, Pierce, plant, preasure cooker, radish, restaurant, smart, spice, tomato, ugly, veg
(Illegible - 2)

XIX-12 Pea (n = 100)

No.	Response	Total
1.	pod	22
2.	green	20
3.	soup	9
4.	vegetable	8
5.	carrot(s)	5
6.	write	5
7.	ink	4
8.	pencil	3
9.	bean	2
10.	knife	2
11.	small	2

12-29. (f = 1)
garden, ich, inky, legume, mattress, Mendel, nib, pal, paper, poison, Primuss, princess, round, sea, smell, spaghetti, sweet, toilet

XIX-13 Potato (n = 99)

No.	Response	Total
1.	eye	8
2.	pancake(s)	7
3.	starch	6
4.	baked	5
5.	salad	5
6.	vegetable	5
7.	chips	4
8.	food	4
9.	mash	4
10.	yam	4
11.	fattening	3
12.	french fries	3
13.	peel	3
14.	bud	2
15.	dirt	2
16.	eat	2
17.	fried	2
18.	knish	2
19.	patch	2
20.	tuber	2

21-44. (f = 1)
beet, calories, carrot, field, filling, frig, ground, grow, head, iodine, latkes, macaroni, mark, pie, plant, potatoes, root, round, sack, soup, spud, tasty, tomato, white

XIX-14 Spinach (n = 100)

No.	Response	Total
1.	green(s)	32
2.	food	10
3.	vegetable	10
4.	potato(es)	6
5.	Popeye	4
6.	strength	4
7.	cream	3
8.	eat	3
9.	taste	3
10.	butter	2
11.	leaf	2
12.	strong	2

13-31. (f = 1)
bad, boul, carrot, delicious, dirt, good, grass, growth, hate, health, healthy, iron, leafy, mother, rich, seaweed, Spain, terrible taste, veg

XIX-15 Tomato (n = 100)

No.	Response	Total
1.	fruit	18
2.	vegetable	13
3.	red	12
4.	lettuce	11
5.	juice	5
6.	apple	3
7.	girl	3
8.	paste	3
9.	egg	2
10.	orange	2
11.	potato	2
12.	salad	2
13.	salt	2
14.	sauce	2
15.	soup	2

16-33. (f = 1)
cabbage, can, catsup, cucumber, food, garden, herring, juicy, ketchup, onion, peach, poison, plant, plump, rabbit, Russell, squeeze, surprise

XIX-17 Turnip (n = 100)

No.	Response	Total
1.	vegetable	22
2.	beet	5
3.	green(s)	5
4.	radish	5
5.	mushroom	4
6.	cabbage	3
7.	carrot	3
8.	eat	3
9.	fruit	3
10.	onion	3
11.	root	3
12.	bean	2
13.	bitter	2
14.	bland	2
15.	red	2
16.	tip	2

17-47. (f = 1)
apple, asparagus, awful, barley, cauliflower, disagreeable, disgusting, dogpatch, flower, food, hair, juice, ketchup, leaf, mush, necturin, nose, nothing, parsnip, pea, pie,

XIX-17 Turnip (n = 100) (contd)

No.	Response	Total

plant, plow, purple, seed, sharp, soup, sour, spinach, tobacco, white

XIX-18 Yam (n = 100)

No.	Response	Total
1.	potato	42
2.	sweet	11
3.	jam	5
4.	ham	4
5.	eat	3
6.	food	3
7.	orange	3
8.	Thanksgiving	3
9.	tree	3
10.	vegetable	3
11.	candy	2
12.	good	2

13-28. (f = 1)
bam, candied, cookies, corn, fig, fruit, gold, jaw, oak, pot, root, slap, sound, southern, tasty
(Illegible - 1)

XX-1 Bomb (n = 101)

No.	Response	Total
1.	death	9
2.	shelter	9
3.	war	9
4.	blast	8
5.	destruction	5
6.	noise	5
7.	explode	4
8.	explosion	4
9.	atom	3
10.	blow	3
11.	bang	2
12.	boom	2
13.	destroy	2
14.	drops	2
15.	ends	2
16.	fall	2
17.	hydrogen	2
18.	Russia	2
19.	shell	2

20-43. (f = 1)
A, A-bomb, atomic, attack, bay, country, disaster, final, fire, H, Hiroshima, hurt, Japs, kill, megaton, metal, mushroom, nihilistic, radiation, scare, site, smoke, terrible, weapon

XX-2 Boomerang (n = 101)

No.	Response	Total
1.	Australia	18
2.	return	12
3.	throw	7
4.	wood	4
5.	Aborigine(s)	3
6.	back	3
7.	Australian	2

XX-2 Boomerang (n = 101) (contd)

No.	Response	Total
8.	backfire	2
9.	come back	2
10.	fly	2
11.	hit	2
12.	horseshoe	2
13.	kangaroo	2
14.	stick	2
15.	toy	2
16.	weapon	2

17-49. (f = 1)
African, animal, arrow, backwards, boom, change, curved, De Castro sisters, explode, fall, firecracker, fireworks, fun, funny, game, gun, hurt, kickback, relay, ricochet, round, ruin, shot, smell, sound, stick, suicide, swing, tay, turn, upset, whoops, wrestling, zoom

XX-3 Cannon (n = 101)

No.	Response	Total
1.	ball	18
2.	gun	15
3.	fire	11
4.	towel	7
5.	shoot	6
6.	noise	5
7.	roar	5
8.	blast	3
9.	boom	3
10.	shot	3
11.	war	3
12.	bomb	2
13.	destruction	2
14.	law	2
15.	loud	2

16-29. (f = 1)
bang, Bilby, bursts, Des, fly, fodder, fort, hard, linen, Morgan, music, psychologist, smoke, sound

XX-4 Carbine (n = 100)

No.	Response	Total
1.	gun	22
2.	rifle	19
3.	car	7
4.	engine	7
5.	dioxide	5
6.	oil	4
7.	acid	3
8.	bullet	2
9.	gas	2
10.	ink	2
11.	machine	2
12.	monoxide	2

13-33. (f = 1)
auto, black, carbon, chemical, coal, CO_2, double, drugs, fluid, gabardine, hunt, odor, paper, pipe, shoot, water, weapon, white, wood, 30-30, 30 cal.
(Illegible - 2)

NORMS OF WORD ASSOCIATION

XX-5 Cudgel (n = 99)

No.	Response	Total
1.	hit	9
2.	beat	6
3.	hammer	6
4.	blow	5
5.	knife	4
6.	cuddle	3
7.	food	3
8.	squeeze	3
9.	bagle	2
10.	coax	2
11.	hug	2
12.	love	2
13.	move	2
14.	nudgel	2

15-60. ($\underline{f}$ = 1)
annoy, bag, bang, bat, bird,
blank, brain, cajole, cheap,
club, couch, cozy, dog, fondle,
force, friend, hold, home,
Jello, lox and cream cheese,
mangle, moment, nestle, nothing,
pudding, pull, push, rap,
Robin Hood, rod, roll, scarpel,
scythe, shake, shit, smudge,
stick, strike, stupid, sudjel,
tomb, understood, unknown,
what, wine, witch
(Illegible - 2)

XX-6 Dagger (n = 101)

No.	Response	Total
1.	knife	47
2.	stab	8
3.	sword	5
4.	blood	4
5.	kill	4
6.	death	3
7.	sharp	3
8.	blade	2
9.	danger	2
10.	stick	2

11-31. ($\underline{f}$ = 1)
baggage, bayonet, blond, book,
chest, cried, dagger, deep,
duel, evil, forest, gun,
killer, MacBeth, pulling, rag,
saber, soldier, spear, steel,
weapon

XX-7 Gun (n = 100)

No.	Response	Total
1.	shoot	25
2.	rifle	11
3.	shot(s)	10
4.	bullet(s)	9
5.	kill	6
6.	fire	3
7.	powder	3
8.	bang	2
9.	death	2
10.	pistol	2
11.	war	2
12.	weapon	2

13-35. ($\underline{f}$ = 1)
arms, army, barrel, blood,
boom, catch, danger, fight,
fun, Guam, harm, holster,
killing, knife, metal, noise,

XX-7 Gun ($\underline{n}$ = 100) (contd)

No.	Response	Total

power, revolver, skill, smoke,
sweet, tote, violence

XX-8 Harpoon (n = 100)

No.	Response	Total
1.	whale	27
2.	spear	18
3.	fish	8
4.	wind	5
5.	weapon	4
6.	death	2
7.	gun	2
8.	kill	2
9.	knife	2
10.	sharp	2
11.	sword	2
12.	throw	2

13-36. ($\underline{f}$ = 1)
Ahab, animal, blood, boo, cave,
dagger, disaster, ferry,
fisherman, fishing, fork, harp,
hit, hook, hunt, interesting,
rain, scene, ship, shoot,
skunk, stick, storm, water

XX-9 Hatchet (n = 100)

No.	Response	Total
1.	ax(e)	34
2.	knife	9
3.	tree	6
4.	hammer	5
5.	kill	5
6.	chop	4
7.	saw	4
8.	tool	4
9.	man	3
10.	weapon	3
11.	blade	2
12.	cut	2
13.	Lizzie Borden	2
14.	ratchet	2
15.	sharp	

16-28. ($\underline{f}$ = 1)
blood, burry, dead, fool,
handel, implement, Indian,
latch, murder, rifle, scalp,
Washington, week

XX-10 Knife ($\underline{n}$ = 101)

No.	Response	Total
1.	cut	25
2.	fork	22
3.	sharp	18
4.	stab	4
5.	blade	3
6.	kill	3
7.	bread	2
8.	spoon	2

9-30. ($\underline{f}$ = 1)
blood, blunt, bork, eat, edge,
evil, harm, hold, hurt, life,
mix, neck, note, point,
slaughter, slice, spear, steak,

XX-10 Knife ($\underline{n}$ = 101) (contd)

No.	Response	Total

stick, utensil, weapon, wife

XX-11 Lance (n = 101)

No.	Response	Total
1.	spear	19
2.	knight(s)	14
3.	sword	9
4.	cut	6
5.	weapon	4
6.	pierce	3
7.	sharp	3
8.	dance	2
9.	fight	2
10.	free	2
11.	knife	2
12.	throw	2
13.	thrust	2

14-43. ($\underline{f}$ = 1)
Arthur, blow, break, broken,
choke, dagger, dart, Don
Quijote, fighter, flag, foil,
hatchet, Ivanhoe, joust, King
Arthur, Lancelot, look, love,
needle, point, pointy, rope,
sharp, Sir, speers, stab,
sterling, string, tournament,
whip, wound

XX-12 Rifle (n = 100)

No.	Response	Total
1.	gun	35
2.	shoot	25
3.	shot	11
4.	range	4
5.	bullet	3
6.	fire	3
7.	hunting	2
8.	soldier	2
9.	target	2

10-22. ($\underline{f}$ = 1)
boy, butt, frontier, goat,
hand, kill, magnum, man,
pistol, slangs, sting,
trigger, weapon

XX-13 Saber (n = 101)

No.	Response	Total
1.	sword	34
2.	knife	25
3.	jet	8
4.	tooth	7
5.	dance	5
6.	know	3
7.	sharp	3
8.	fencing	2
9.	labor	2

10-21. ($\underline{f}$ = 1)
bear, cat, cut, epee, foil,
gun, mink, rapier, rat, rifle,
tiger, Turkish soldiers

XX-14 Sling (n = 100)

No.	Response	Total
1.	shot	40
2.	arm	28
3.	throw	5
4.	bandage	3
5.	cast	3
6.	hurt	2
7-25.	(f = 1)	

accident, arrow, break, broken, fling, help, hit, leather, ouch, pain, shoot, sick, slot, sting, stone, support, target, weapon, wound

XX-15 Sword (n = 101)

No.	Response	Total
1.	sharp	8
2.	fish	7
3.	knife	7
4.	duel	5
5.	fight	5
6.	knight	4
7.	lance	4
8.	weapon	4
9.	blade	3
10.	dagger	3
11.	fencing	3
12.	foil	3
13.	kill	3
14.	shield	3
15.	cut	2
16.	hero	2
17.	hurt	2
18.	sheath	2
19.	thrust	2
20-48.	(f = 1)	

aluminum foil, arrow, Arthur, blood, brave, buckler, chivallery, D'Artagon, death, die, draw, dual, epee, fencer, fighting, fire, gallantry, Hamlet, hit, holder, long, metal, pen, play, protection, scalpel, slice, spade, swallower

XX-16 Tomahawk (n = 100)

No.	Response	Total
1.	Indian	57
2.	hatchet	10
3.	scalp	7
4.	axe	4
5.	knife	3
6.	arrow	2
7.	chop	2
8.	kill	2
9.	weapon	2
10-20.	(f = 1)	

blade, cut, hammer, hurt, Mohawk, movie, rug, sharp, smash, Smith, throw

XXI-1 Drizzle (n = 100)

No.	Response	Total
1.	rain	66
2.	wet	4
3.	drop	3
4.	fog	3
5.	mist	3
6.	drip	2
7.	hail	2
8-24.	(f = 1)	

blue, cold, cold, dark, despair, drain, fast, frugle, headache, lightly, mice, nozzle, pour, snow, soft, unpleasant, water

XXI-2 Earthquake (n = 100)

No.	Response	Total
1.	shake	27
2.	disaster	7
3.	destruction	6
4.	San Francisco	6
5.	tremble	5
6.	death	4
7.	danger	3
8.	Calif.	2
9.	catastrophe	2
10.	crack	2
11.	rocky	2
12.	shock	2
13.	split	2
14-43.	(f = 1)	

bang, break, canyon, charge, crevice, eruption, fissure, Greece, hole, hurt, Lana, land, legs, Mexico, murmer, noise, people, roar, rumble, seismograph, shroow, sound, terror, thunder, tidal wave, tornado, trauma, tumble, violent, volcano

XXI-3 Fog (n = 100)

No.	Response	Total
1.	mist	15
2.	London	8
3.	misty	7
4.	rain	6
5.	cloud(s)	5
6.	dense	4
7.	smog	4
8.	damp	3
9.	grey	3
10.	thick	3
11.	weather	3
12.	danger	2
13.	haze	2
14.	horn	2
15.	night	2
16.	sight	2
17.	smoke	2
18.	stormy	2
19-43.	(f = 1)	

air, anger, bad weather, bank, black, blue, blurry, can't see, daze, deep, dew, dreary, England, heavy, leg, moodiness, morning, not clear, see, ship, sun, ugly, warts, west, wind

XXI-4 Frost (n = 100)

No.	Response	Total
1.	cold	45
2.	ice	11
3.	snow	6
4.	Robert	5
5.	bite	4
6.	Jack	4
7.	slow	4
8.	bitten	3
9.	winter	3
10.	chill	2
11.	white	2
12.	window(s)	2
13-21.	(f = 1)	

author, coldness, designs, heat, malted, nose, poem, tree, window pane

XXI-5 Hail (n = 99)

No.	Response	Total
1.	rain	10
2.	snow	8
3.	hello	7
4.	farewell	6
5.	Caesar	5
6.	Mary	5
7.	call	4
8.	Columbia	4
9.	greet	3
10.	hearty	3
11.	ice	3
12.	sleet	3
13.	storm	3
14.	salute	2
15.	slush	2
16.	stone	2
17-45.	(f = 1)	

ahoy, America, ave, bang, boils, cab, cleer, cold, cry, fail, hardy, happy, Hitler, joy, king, laud, lumps, regime, rock, ship, song, thin, to thee, tree, victory, wave, well, witches, World War II

XXI-6 Monsoon (n = 100)

No.	Response	Total
1.	wind	19
2.	rain	15
3.	storm	15
4.	typhoon	6
5.	season	5
6.	India	4
7.	blow	2
8.	hurricane	2
9.	Japan	2
10.	squall	2
11.	weather	2
12-37.	(f = 1)	

bad, chaos, China, climate, devastation, difficult, dove, earthquake, food, Good Earth, hot, love, rat, roof, smeller, South Seas, swamp, tide, trouble, valley, violence, water, wave, weird, wet, wicked

XXI-7 Rain (n = 100)

No.	Response	Total
1.	wet	25
2.	snow(s)	17
3.	water	11
4.	umbrella	5
5.	shine	4
6.	drop(s)	4
7.	fall	2
8.	hail	2
9.	storm	2
10.	weather	2

11-36. (f = 1)
April, bran, brown, cloud, deer, drought, falling, grey, growth, hat, liquid, pain, patter, precipitation, puddles, radiation, reading, silver, sleet, smell, soft, Spain, sun, time, walk, walking

XXI-8 Shower (n = 101)

No.	Response	Total
1.	water	18
2.	rain	16
3.	clean	12
4.	bath	7
5.	curtain(s)	6
6.	wet	4
7.	cleanliness	3
8.	April	2
9.	baby	2
10.	soap	2
11.	wash	2

12-38. (f = 1)
bestow, book, bridal, cap, closet, cool, dress, drops, engagement, flow, fresh, hat, in, needles, psycho, radiation, refresh, refreshing, rod, sing, snow, soft, stinging, sun, take, umbrella, youth

XXI-9 Sleet (n = 100)

No.	Response	Total
1.	snow	32
2.	rain	19
3.	hail	13
4.	cold	6
5.	slush	6
6.	slippery	4
7.	hard	2
8.	slip	2
9.	wet	2

10-23. (f = 1)
accident, boots, cool, hale, ice, mess, miserable, nasty, precipitation, sharp, sheet, sledding, weather, winter

XXI-10 Snow (n = 100)

No.	Response	Total
1.	white	43
2.	cold	13
3.	rain	9

XXI-10 Snow (n = 100) (contd)

No.	Response	Total
4.	ice	6
5.	wet	4
6.	winter	4
7.	melt	3
8.	clean	2

9-24. (f = 1)
ball, car, Christmas, crop, dirt, drift, flake, job, lovely, play, pretty, purity, shovel, slush, The Newmen, walking

XXI-11 Squall (n = 103)

No.	Response	Total
1.	storm	30
2.	wind	9
3.	rain	6
4.	animal	3
5.	bird	3
6.	dirt	3
7.	squalor	3
8.	boat	2
9.	fight	2
10.	fish	2
11.	noise	2
12.	squab	2
13.	squeal	2
14.	squell	2
15.	weather	2

16-43. (f = 1)
anger, big, blank, blow, cry, destruction, duck, eat, fire, food, fowl, loud, nothing, parents, pen, quail, raging, rat, sequel, snow, square, squeek, squemish, squirrel, stool, tempest, tumult, waves
(Illegible - 2)

XXI-12 Storm (n = 100)

No.	Response	Total
1.	rain	32
2.	wind	13
3.	lightning	5
4.	tempest	3
5.	thunder	3
6.	center	2
7.	cloud(s)	2
8.	weather	2
9.	window	2
10.	windy	2

11-44. (f = 1)
black, bleak, blow, cold, dead, destructive, disaster, evil, fear, fierce, fire, hail, horror, horse, howl, hurricane, island, loud, nasty, night, ominous, rage, scary, sea, sleet, storm trooper, tempestuous, tornado, torrent, tree, troop, volcano, wet, white

XXI-13 Sunshine (n = 100)

No.	Response	Total
1.	bright	18
2.	rain	9
3.	warm	8
4.	warmth	8
5.	light	5
6.	yellow	5
7.	day	3
8.	Florida	3
9.	tan	3
10.	beach	2
11.	brightness	2
12.	cookies	2
13.	hot	2
14.	nice	2
15.	state	2
16.	vitamin D	2

17-40. (f = 1)
cracker, daylight, daytime, flowers, good, happy, Nellie, pretty, ray, shy, smile, soft, sparkle, spring, sun, sunny, sunset, swimming, tanning, vitamin C, Vitamins, water, weather, white

XXI-14 Thunder (n = 100)

No.	Response	Total
1.	lightning	51
2.	rain	11
3.	storm	8
4.	noise	6
5.	loud	4
6.	dark	3
7.	fright	3

8-21. (f = 1)
blunder, bolt, boom, cloud, emotions, explosion, frightening, God, hail, look, shudder, snow, wonder, Zeus

XXI-15 Tornado (n = 100)

No.	Response	Total
1.	storm	23
2.	wind	20
3.	destruction	6
4.	hurricane	6
5.	wild	3
6.	windy	3
7.	bomb	2
8.	cyclone	2
9.	damage	2
10.	disaster	2
11.	fury	2
12.	rain	2
13.	tornado	2
14.	whirl	2

15-37. (f = 1)
black, bull, danger, death, Donna, graysmoke, horror, house, kill, monstrous, none, ruin, spiral, turmoil, twister, violence, weather, whirlpool, whirlwind, winds, Wizard of Oz, wreck, wreckage

XXI-16 Typhoon (n = 100)

No.	Response	Total
1.	storm	29
2.	wind	14
3.	hurricane	11
4.	rain	6
5.	destruction	3
6.	wave	3
7.	danger	2
8.	Gail	2
9.	money	2
10.	squall	2

11-36. (f = 1)
anger, big, black, blow,
Chinese, cloud, coward,
crooked, cyclone, disaster,
honey, Japan, Mary, millionaire,
mind, movie, power, rich, sea,
seller, ship, swine, Texas,
violence, water, whale

CHAPTER 8

A STUDY OF HOMOGRAPHS[1]

Phebe Cramer
University of California, Berkeley, California

One of the more confusing aspects of the English language results from the existence of words which look alike and/or sound alike, but have two (or more) distinctly different meanings. For example, the word *ball* may mean either a round or roundish thing, or it may mean a large formal party for dancing. As an isolated unit, the identical spelling and pronunciation of the word provides no clue as to which meaning is intended. Although our interpretation of the isolated unit may be influenced by the relative frequency with which the word is used to denote one, rather than the other, meaning, only the surrounding context makes clear which is the intended meaning.

Such words, which have the same (visual or sound) form, but more than one meaning, are called homonyms. If the two meanings of the word are represented by the same spelling, the word is a homograph. If the two meanings of the word are represented by the same pronunciation, the word is a homophone. A word may be both a homograph and a homophone, as in the example above of *ball*. Some words, however, are homographs but not homophones, as in *bass* (a low or deep sound) and *bass* (a fish). In this case, the different pronunciations provide the information as to which meaning is intended. On the other hand, some words may be homophones but not homographs, as in *red* (color) and *read* (past tense of the verb, to read). In this case, the different spellings provide the information as to which meaning is intended.

An interesting use of this characteristic of the language was made by Razran in his studies of semantic generalization (e.g., Razran, 1939). By choosing stimuli, such as *urn* and *style,* for conditioning, he was able to determine whether generalization was more likely to occur as a function of meaningful similarity between the conditioned stimuli (CSs) and generalization stimuli (GSs) (*vase, fashion*)—or whether generalization was more likely to be a function of physical (sound) similarity between the CSs and GSs (*earn, stile*). While the majority of findings of Razran and other investigators support the idea that generalization in adults is more likely to be determined by meaning than by sound, Luria and Vinogradova (1959) have shown that this relationship is reversed in individuals suffering from severe mental retardation, for whom phonic similarity is a more potent determinant of generalization than is meaning. Riess (1946) has reported this same finding for young children.

Because homonyms are so heavily dependent on context for their interpretation, they provide excellent material for studying the modification of verbal meaning as a function of experimental variations in context. As part of the

[1]This study was conducted at the Institute of Human Learning, which is supported by a grant from the National Institutes of Health.

author's interest in demonstrating that verbal meaning can be modified by associative priming, a group of homographs was selected to be used as stimulus words in a (primed) word association test. The experiment was successful in demonstrating that subjects could be primed to give alternatively, a response representing one or the other meaning of the homograph, depending on the type of priming (context) used (Cramer, 1968a). Prior to this experiment, however, it was necessary to determine just how often such alternative responses occurred in the absence of priming, i.e., in the normative situation. Since the standard word-association test lists (e.g., Palermo & Jenkins, 1964) include few homonyms, this question could not be answered from existing normative data. For this reason, a word-association test of 100 homographs was constructed for the purpose of determining the normative frequency of occurrence of responses representing alternative meanings of the stimulus words.

METHOD

Lists

The 100 homograph stimuli were chosen from *A Complete Dictionary of Synonyms and Antonyms* (Fallows, 1898), which provides a sizable collection of homographs and homophones. An attempt was made to select both mono- and disyllabic words, as well as words beginning with different letters of the alphabet. The stimulus words also were selected to represent differing degrees of frequency of usage in the language, as determined from Thorndike-Lorge (1944) ratings.

The 100 stimulus words and their Thorndike-Lorge (T-L) frequencies are given in the first two columns of Table 2. The two alternative meanings of each stimulus are given in Table 1. Additional meanings, where existent, are not listed.

Method

The test was administered in group form. A word association test booklet consisting of five pages, with 20 words per page, was prepared. The order of the words on any page was randomly determined. All possible combinations of the five pages were represented in the test booklets. A face sheet was attached to each booklet, asking for the age and sex of the subject, and providing standard instructions for a written word association test (see Palermo & Jenkins, 1964).

Subjects

The subjects were 109 students of elementary psychology at the University of California, Berkeley. They were tested during their regular class period.[2] Several additional test booklets were discarded for failure to follow instructions.

RESULTS

The responses from each booklet were tabulated and response distributions were drawn up. Subsequently, three independent judges rated all the responses to each stimulus with regard to whether they referred to meaning 1, meaning 2, or neither (see Table 1 for meaning 1 and meaning 2 definitions). The average interrater agreement over all 100 stimulus words for meaning 1 was $r_{33} = .95$. For meaning 2, $r_{33} = .94$ (cf. Guilford, 1954, pp. 395-397.)

The results derived from the normative data are presented in Table 2. For each stimulus, the primary response and its percentage frequency of occurrence, the number of different responses (D), and the mean number of responses referring to meaning 1 and to meaning 2, averaged over the three judges, is given. The "neither" category, not listed in Table 2 ("neither" = 109 minus meaning 1 minus meaning 2), is comprised of responses which refer to some additional meaning(s) of the stimulus, as well as to responses for which the meaning referent could not be determined. The data from Table 2 are summarized by T-L category in Table 3.

---

[2] I am thankful to Prof. Geoffrey Keppel for providing his class for this purpose.

TABLE 1 *Homographs: Meaning 1 and Meaning 2*

Ball
1. Anything round or roundish
2. A large formal party for dancing

Bass
1. Low or deep sound
2. Any of various spiny-finned fished, living in fresh water or in the ocean

Bat
1. Club used to hit the ball in baseball
2. A flying mammal with modified forelimbs which serve as wings

Beam
1. A large long piece of timber or metal
2. A ray of light

Bill
1. Account of money owed, as for work
2. Beak (part of a bird)

Bit
1. Part of a bridle that goes in a horse's mouth
2. A small piece; small amount

Boil
1. Bubble up and give off vapor
2. A painful red swelling on the skin, formed by pus

Bow
1. Bend the head or body in submission
2. Weapon for shooting arrows

Box
1. Container made of wood, metal, paper, etc.
2. Blow with the open hand

Calf
1. A young cow or bull
2. The thick fleshy part of the back of the leg below the knee

Cape
1. A sleeveless outer garment worn falling loosely from the shoulders
2. Point of land extending into the water

Carp
1. Find fault with
2. A freshwater fish that lives in ponds and slow streams

Case
1. Instance; example: a case of poor work
2. Covering

Club
1. A heavy stick
2. A group of people joined together for some special purpose

Compact
1. Closely joined
2. Agreement

Contract
1. Shrink
2. Agreement

Corn
1. A kind of grain that grows on large ears
2. A hardening of the skin, usually on a toe

Count
1. Name numbers in order
2. A European nobleman having a rank about the same as that of an English earl

Court
1. Court of law
2. Royal palace

Crank
1. Part of a handle of a machine connected at right angles to another part to transmit motion
2. Person with queer notions or habits

Date
1. Statement of time
2. The sweet fruit of a kind of palm tree

Drop
1. A small amount of liquid in a roundish shape
2. A sudden fall

Duck
1. A wild or tame swimming bird with a short neck, short legs, and webbed feet
2. Dip or plunge suddenly under water and out again

Entrance
1. Act of entering
2. Put into a trance

TABLE 1 (continued)

Excise
1. Tax on the manufacture, sale, or use of certain articles within a country
2. Cut out

Fair
1. Just; honest
2. Display of goods, products

Fawn
1. Deer less than a year old
2. Try to get favor or notice by slavish acts

Feet
1. Plural of foot: the part of the body that a person or animal stands on
2. Measure of length

File
1. Place for keeping papers in order
2. A steel tool with many small ridges used to smooth hard substances

Fine
1. Very good; excellent
2. Sum of money paid as a punishment

Fleet
1. Group of ships under one command
2. Swift, rapid

Flush
1. Blush; glow
2. Even; level

Foil
1. Turn aside or hinder
2. Metal beaten into a very thin sheet

Fuse
1. Part of a circuit that melts and breaks the connection when the current becomes dangerously strong
2. Melt; melt together

Grate
1. Framework of iron to hold a fire
2. Rub with a harsh sound

Grave
1. A hole dug in the ground where a dead body is to be buried
2. Earnest; thoughtful: grave words

Ground
1. Earth's surface; soil
2. Past tense and past participle of grind: wheat is ground to make flour

Hail
1. Greet; cheer
2. Frozen rain

Hard
1. Difficult
2. Not soft; not yielding to touch

Hide
1. Put or keep out of sight
2. Skin of an animal

Incense
1. Substance giving off a sweet smell when burned
2. Make very angry

Interest
1. A feeling of wanting to know, see, do, own, or share in
2. Money paid for the use of money

Intimate
1. Very familiar
2. Suggest indirectly

Iron
1. The commonest and most useful metal, from which tools, machinery, etc. are made
2. Tool for pressing clothes

Lap
1. The front part from the waist to the knees of a person sitting down
2. Lie together, one partly over or beside another: shingles on a roof lap

Lead
1. Show the way by going along with or in front of
2. A heavy, easily melted, bluish-gray metal, used to make pipe, etc.

Lean
1. Stand slanting, not upright; bend
2. With little or no fat

Like
1. Similar
2. Be pleased with

Limp
1. A lame step or walk
2. Lacking stiffness or firmness

March
1. Walk in time and with steps of the same length
2. The third month of the year, having 31 days

Maroon
1. Very dark brownish-red
2. Put (a person) ashore in a lonely place and leave him there

Mass
1. Lump: a mass of dough
2. Central service of worship in the Roman Catholic Church

Meal
1. Breakfast, lunch, dinner, supper, or tea
2. Ground grain; corn meal

Mean
1. Characterized by petty selfishness or malice: contemptibly disobliging or unkind (a surly man)
2. Low in quality or grade

Mine
1. Belonging to me: the book is mine
2. A large hole or space dug in the earth to get out something valuable

Mint
1. A sweet-smelling plant used for flavoring
2. Place where money is coined

Mole
1. A congenital spot of the skin, usually brown
2. A small animal that lives underground most of the time

Nag
1. Iritate or annoy
2. A horse, especially an inferior one

Net
1. An open fabric made of string, cord, thread, etc., as fish net, a tennis net, etc.
2. Remaining after deductions

Page
1. One side of a leaf or sheet of paper
2. A boy servant

Pass
1. Go by; move fast: pass another car on the road
2. Hand around

Pelt
1. Throw things at; attack
2. Skin, as of a fur-bearing animal before it is tanned

Perch
1. Bar, branch, or anything else on which a bird can come to rest
2. A small freshwater fish, used for food

Plant
1. A living thing that is not an animal; trees, shrubs, herbs, fungi, algae, etc., are plants
2. The buildings, machinery, etc., used in manufacturing some article

Plot
1. A secret plan
2. A small piece of ground

Port
1. Harbor; place where ships and boats can be sheltered from storms
2. A kind of wine

Pound
1. Measure of weight; 16 ounces
2. Hit or beat heavily again and again

Produce
1. Make, bring about; cause: hard work produces success
2. Yield: as in farm produce

Punch
1. Hit with the fist
2. A beverage: fruit punch

TABLE 1 (continued)

Pupil
1. A person who is learning in school or being taught by someone
2. The expanding and contracting opening in the iris of the eye

Race
1. Contest of speed, as in running, riding, etc.
2. A group of persons, animals, or plants connected by common descent or origin

Rake
1. Long-handled tool having a bar at one end with teeth in it, used for gathering together loose leaves, hay, straw, etc.
2. A dissolute person

Rash
1. Too hasty; reckless
2. A breaking out with many small red spots on the skin

Rear
1. The back part; back
2. Bring up, rear children

Refrain
1. Hold oneself back; refrain from crime
2. A phrase of verse repeated regularly in a song or poem

Refuse
1. Reject: refuse an offer
2. Rubbish

Rent
1. A regular payment for the use of property
2. A torn place

Rest
1. Sleep: have a good night's rest (recuperation)
2. What is left: those that are left

Sage
1. Wise: a sage adviser
2. A plant whose leaves are used in seasoning and in medicine

Scale
1. One of the thin, flat, hard plates forming the outer covering of some fishes, snakes, and lizards
2. A dish or pan of balance. Usually scales; an instrument for weighing

Second
1. Next after the first
2. 1/60 of a minute

Smack
1. Open (the lips) quickly as to make a sharp sound
2. Slap; crack (a whip, etc.)

Smelt
1. Melt (ore) in order to get the metal out of it
2. A small food fish with silvery scales

Sound
1. What can be heard: the sound of music
2. Free from injury, decay, or defect: sound fruit

Spray
1. Liquid going through the air in small drops
2. A small branch or piece of some plant with its leaves, flowers, or fruit

Spring
1. Leap; jump: spring into the air
2. Season after winter when plants begin to grow

State
1. Condition of a person or thing: in an excited state
2. A nation; one of several organized political groups of people that together form a nation: the US

Stern
1. Severe; strict: a stern master
2. The hind part of a ship or boat

Stick
1. Branch of a tree or shrub cut or broken off (walking stick, hockey stick, stick of chocolate)
2. Pierce with a pointed instrument; stab

Strand
1. Run aground; drive on the shore
2. One of the threads, strings, or wires that are twisted together to make a rope

TABLE 1 *(continued)*

Swallow
1. Take into the stomach through the throat: swallow food
2. A small, swift-flying bird with a deeply forked tail

Tap
1. Strike lightly
2. A stopper or plug to close a hole in a cask containing liquid

Taper
1. Make or become gradually smaller toward one end: a church spire tapers off to a point
2. Very slender candle

Temple
1. A building used for the service or worship of a god or gods
2. The flattened part of either side of the forehead

Tip
1. End; point: the tips of the fingers
2. A small present of money

Toll
1. Sound with single strokes slowly and regularly repeated
2. A tax or fee paid for some right or privilege

Top
1. The highest part: the top of a mountain, the top of one's voice
2. Toy that spins on a point

Wax
1. A yellowish substance made by bees for constructing their honeycomb
2. Increase

Well
1. All right: the job was well done (fully)
2. Hole dug or bored in the ground to get water, oil, gas, etc.

Will
1. The power of the mind to decide and do
2. A legal statement of a person's wishes about what shall be done with his property after he is dead

TABLE 2 *Homographs, Thorndike-Lorge Frequency, Primary Response and Percent Frequency, Number of Different Responses, and Mean Number of Responses Referring to Each Meaning*

Stimulus	T-L[a]	Primary R	% Frequency	D	$\bar{X}$ meaning 1 responses	$\bar{X}$ meaning 2 responses
Ball	AA	Bat	19.2	37	94.0	6.6
Bass	7	Fish	37.6	28	58.0	32.3
Bat	19	Man	49.5	30	22.0	21.0
Beam	42	Light	31.1	41	43.3	52.3
Bill	AA*	Money	24.7	38	84.3	13.0
Bit	AA	Horse	18.3	42	45.6	38.0
Boil	A	Water	27.5	34	88.6	11.0
Bow	A	Arrow	41.2	31	30.6	46.0
Box	AA*	Square	10.0	53	71.6	17.6
Calf	14	Cow	59.6	26	76.9	21.0
Cape	34	Cod	16.5	41	69.6	25.3
Carp	1	Fish	76.1	23	9.0	29.6
Case	AA*	History	13.7	56	73.3	14.6
Club	AA	Group	14.6	52	35.6	61.0
Compact	13	Small	21.1	33	63.0	4.6
Contract	A	Bridge	11.9	53	6.3	88.0
Corn	A	Cob	19.2	46	101.3	0.0
Count	AA	Numbers	63.3	27	98.0	7.3
Court	AA*	Law	15.5	41	73.3	14.6
Crank	8	Car	15.5	52	63.6	28.0
Date	AA	Girl	17.4	46	38.3	26.6
Drop	AA*	Fall	25.6	45	18.6	58.0
Duck	49	Bird	12.8	51	84.0	15.0
Entrance	A	Exit	49.5	19	87.3	1.0
Excise	2	Tax	70.6	25	78.0	8.3
Fair	AA	Unfair	8.2	35	42.6	15.3
Fawn	13	Deer	62.3	28	95.3	4.0
Feet	AA*	Shoes	22.0	42	91.3	6.3
File	43	Cabinet	22.9	50	63.3	23.0
Fine	AA*	Good	34.8	41	64.6	19.0

TABLE 2 (continued)

Stimulus	T-L[a]	Primary R	% Frequency	D	$\bar{X}$ meaning 1 responses	$\bar{X}$ meaning 2 responses
Fleet	A	Ship	52.2	25	78.3	20.6
Flush	23	Toilet	46.7	26	40.6	4.0
Foil	7	Aluminum	17.4	36	16.3	57.0
Fuse	7	Light	22.0	43	60.3	29.6
Grate	13	Cheese	12.8	56	47.3	16.0
Grave	A	Dead	18.3	40	84.3	19.7
Ground	AA	Hog	17.4	38	78.6	16.3
Hail	40	Rain	20.1	39	34.0	66.3
Hard	AA*	Soft	65.1	23	11.0	63.0
Hide	A	Seek	44.0	43	83.3	11.3
Incense	12	Smell	25.6	50	88.0	8.6
Interest	AA*	Money	13.7	61	68.3	31.6
Intimate	24	Close	27.5	36	35.0	4.0
Iron	AA	Steel	12.8	40	53.3	48.3
Lap	36	Sit	22.9	41	72.6	4.3
Lead	AA	Follow	32.1	34	47.0	51.0
Lean	A	Fat	17.4	41	28.3	60.0
Like	AA*	Love	33.9	27	14.6	75.6
Limp	15	Cripple	6.4	62	44.0	42.0
March	AA	Walk	11.9	54	64.0	37.6
Maroon	2	Red	21.1	36	64.6	28.6
Mass	A	Church	16.5	49	43.0	25.0
Meal	A	Food	31.1	24	86.6	9.3
Mean	AA*	Average	20.1	41	66.6	19.0
Mine	AA	Yours	48.6	29	64.0	37.6
Mint	13	Candy	22.0	30	77.3	25.6
Mole	14	Animal	11.0	42	31.3	63.0
Nag	5	Horse	23.8	34	70.0	27.3
Net	A	Fish	49.5	35	92.6	11.0
Page	AA	Book	33.0	26	85.3	20.6
Pass	AA*	Fail	11.9	51	57.3	14.3
Pelt	6	Fur	38.5	31	42.6	57.3
Perch	23	Sit	23.8	29	79.6	21.3
Plant	AA*	Green	18.3	37	97.0	2.6
Plot	36	Scheme	11.9	45	76.0	10.3
Port	A	Ship	18.3	35	76.0	13.6
Pound	AA	Weight	13.7	45	58.6	21.0
Produce	AA*	Vegetables	23.8	36	29.3	73.6
Punch	17	Hit	35.7	39	71.3	18.6
Pupil	A	Student	49.5	17	66.3	36.6
Race	AA	Run	17.4	45	75.0	24.6
Rake	13	Leaves	36.6	33	94.0	6.6
Rash	9	Red	11.0	48	43.0	55.6
Rear	A	End	33.0	22	95.3	1.0
Refrain	12	Stop	34.8	37	70.0	32.0
Refuse	AA	Deny	15.5	48	71.6	18.0
Rent	23	House	24.7	27	104.0	1.3
Rest	AA*	Sleep	31.1	40	91.6	6.3
Sage	15	Wise	27.5	34	47.3	50.3
Scale	A	Weight	27.5	30	11.0	77.0
Second	AA*	Minute	33.9	23	37.0	56.6
Smack	7	Kiss	31.1	27	59.6	42.6
Smelt	6	Fish	29.3	28	51.3	33.6
Sound	AA*	Noise	34.8	29	94.0	3.0
Spray	22	Can	19.2	39	98.3	4.0
Spring	AA	Fall	14.6	42	23.6	71.3
State	AA*	California	21.1	46	7.6	89.3
Stern	36	Strict	16.5	46	80.3	17.0

TABLE 2 *(continued)*

Stimulus	T-L[a]	Primary R	% Frequency	D	$\bar{X}$ meaning 1 responses	$\bar{X}$ meaning 2 responses
Stick	AA	Stone	10.0	48	53.6	18.3
Strand	12	Hair	41.2	31	21.0	81.6
Swallow	48	Bird	36.7	38	50.0	53.3
Tap	32	Water	25.6	28	65.3	37.0
Taper	12	Candle	26.6	47	55.0	31.0
Temple	A	Head	22.9	40	66.0	33.0
Tip	A	Waiter	26.6	36	38.0	54.0
Toll	10	Bridge	45.8	24	13.0	85.0
Top	AA	Bottom	57.7	28	54.6	21.3
Wax	28	Floor	28.4	29	94.6	5.3
Well	AA*	Water	25.6	29	28.6	68.3
Will	AA	Won't	9.1	53	57.0	38.0

[a]Words designated AA* are among the 500 most frequently occurring words.

DISCUSSION

While previous word association studies using nonhomograph stimuli have found a positive relationship between T-L frequency and strength of primary responses (cf. Cramer, 1968b), the present data suggest that this general finding does not apply to homograph stimuli. The trend, if any, is for less frequent stimuli to have slightly stronger responses and to elicit slightly fewer different responses. The data in Table 3 also indicate that, as homographs decrease in frequency over the first four Thorndike-Lorge categories, the difference between the number of responses referring to meaning 1 and to meaning 2 increases. For AA* homographs, the mean number of meaning 1 responses, averaged over the three raters, is 55.5; for meaning 2 responses, this value equals 35.6, for a difference of 19.9. For AA words, this difference is increased to 32.5; for A words, the difference is 35.8; and for 20-49/million, the difference is 50.6. In other words, when homographs are presented in isolation, i.e., without context, they are increasingly likely to be interpreted in terms of their more common meaning as a function of decreasing T-L frequency. Another way of stating this finding is to note that context becomes less important for interpreting which meaning of a homograph is intended as the frequency of usage of the homograph decreases.

It may be noted that the data for the least familiar homographs (1-19/million) do not fit the general pattern of increasing difference in meaning 1 versus meaning 2 responses. It might seem, therefore, that the interpretation of these homographs could be confusing in the absence of clarifying context. However, for this low frequency (1-19/million) category, the possible confusion appears to have been resolved grammatically. For 75.0% (21/28) of these homographs, the two alternative word meanings represent different parts of speech. The corresponding figure for AA* homographs is 36.8% (7/19); for AA = 52.6% (10/19); for A = 44.4% (8/18); and for 20-49 = 56.2% (9/16), indicating that the confusion between meanings for these latter homographs is less likely to be resolved by grammatical cues than in the case of the low familiar homographs.

TABLE 3 *Summary of Primary Response Strength, Number of Different Responses, and Number of Responses Referring to Meanings 1 and 2, by Thorndike-Lorge Category*

T-L Frequency	$\bar{X}$ strength of primary R	$\bar{X}$ no. Diff. Rs	$\bar{X}$ No. Rs for meaning 1	$\bar{X}$ No. Rs for meaning 2
AA* (n = 19)	25.2%	40.0	55.5	35.6
AA (n = 19)	22.4%	41.5	61.3	28.8
A (n = 18)	30.9%	34.6	64.6	28.8
20-49 (n = 16)	24.2%	37.9	72.1	21.5
1-19 (n = 28)	32.6%	36.2	54.9	38.4

These data suggest an interesting possibility for studying the longitudinal fate of homonyms. According to one linguistic theory (cf. Williams, 1944), the greater the conflict, or confusability, between the two meanings of a homonym, the greater the likelihood that one meaning will drop out of use in the language. The present data indicate that there is a difference among homonyms in the degree of meaning conflict, paralleling T-L frequency. According to the theory of homonymic conflict, those homonyms with the greatest meaning conflict, i.e., AA* words, should have this conflict resolved, over time, by a decrease in frequency of use of one of the meanings. Such a decrease should be reflected in word association data collected for these homographs at a subsequent point in time. Support for the theory of homonymic conflict would come from a finding that the frequency of meaning 2 responses has decreased for those homographs which currently show a large number of responses in both meaning categories.

The main utility of the homograph norms, however, is to provide a group of stimuli which allows two distinctly different interpretations and to indicate the most likely interpretation which occurs under standard word association test conditions. These data provide a baseline against which the effects of the experimental manipulation of context can be compared. They also provide information on a variety of other variables—such as primary response strength, heterogeneity of responses, number of responses representing each of the two alternative meanings, and familiarity—which may modify the importance of context for determining meaning.

REFERENCES

Cramer, P. (1968a). Mediated priming of polysemous stimuli. *Journal of Experimental Psychology* 78, 137-144.

Cramer, P. (1968b). Word association. New York: Academic Press.

Fallows, S. F. (1898). *A complete dictionary of synonyms and antonyms.* New York: Fleming H. Revell Co.

Guilford, J. P. (1954). *Psychometric methods.* New York: McGraw-Hill Co.

Luria, A. R., & Vinogradova, O. S. (1959). An objective investigation of the dynamics of semantic systems. *British Journal of Psychology* 50, 89-105.

Palermo, D. S. & Jenkins, J. J. (1964). *Word association norms.* Minneapolis: University of Minnesota Press.

Razran, G. (1939). A quantitative study of meaning by a conditioned salivary technique (semantic conditioning). *Science* 90, 89-90.

Reiss, B. F. (1946). Genetic changes in semantic conditioning. *Journal of Experimental Psychology* 36, 143-152.

Thorndike, E. L., & Lorge, I. (1944). *The teacher's book of 30,000 words.* New York: Bureau of Publications, Teacher's College, Columbia University.

Williams, E. R. (1944). *The conflict of homonyms in English.* New Haven: Yale University Press.

Ball

No.	Response	Total	%
1.	bat	21	19.2
2.	bounce	13	11.9
3.	round	10	10.9
4.	base	8	7.3
5.	game	6	5.5
6.	play	5	4.6
7.	hit	4	3.7
8.	dance	4	3.7
9.	throw	3	2.8
10.	boys	3	2.8
11.	red	2	1.8
12.	park	2	1.8
13.	player	2	1.8
14.	chain	2	1.8
15.	baseball	2	1.8

(f = 1, 0.9%, n = 22)
balloon, basket, beach, catch,
cut, doll, fence, fire, foot,
fork, fun, gown, hand, hoop,
kick, orbit, smash, soft,
sphere, stick, string, thunder

Bass

No.	Response	Total	%
1.	fish	41	37.6
2.	drum	12	11.0
3.	fiddle	11	10.1
4.	low	5	4.6
5.	treble	5	4.6
6.	guitar	4	3.7
7.	deep	4	3.7
8.	violin	3	2.8
9.	lake	2	1.8
10.	soprano	2	1.8
11.	horn	2	1.8
12.	instrument	2	1.8

(f = 1, 0.9%, n = 16)
bad, band, base, clarinet, cod,
compass, jazz, music, rod,
saxophone, sing, summer, tenor,
trombone, vile, voice

Bat

No.	Response	Total	%
1.	man	54	49.5
2.	ball	16	14.7
3.	fly	4	3.7
4.	cave	2	1.8
5.	mammal	2	1.8
6.	bird	2	1.8
7.	belfry	2	1.8
8.	animal	2	1.8
9.	wing	2	1.8
10.	batman	2	1.8
11.	ugly	2	1.8

(f = 1, 0.9%, n = 19)
base, baseball, blind, bug,
evening, eye, eyelash, glove,
handle, hat, hit, mad, rabies,
radar, rat, robin, spider,
wings, wood

Beam

No.	Response	Total	%
1.	light	34	31.1
2.	ceiling	14	12.8
3.	wood	9	8.2
4.	sun	6	5.5
5.	smile	3	2.8
6.	rafter	2	1.8
7.	mote	2	1.8
8.	high	2	1.8
9.	house	2	1.8
10.	shine	2	1.8
11.	pole	2	1.8
12.	lighthouse	2	1.8

(f = 1, 0.9%, n = 29)
bean, board, bridge, brightly,
building, construction, eaves,
girder, grin, headlight, hold,
I, laugh, look, on, pride,
radiator, rake, reach, ream,
red, redwood, rod, roof, steel,
support, sturdy, to, wooden

Bill

No.	Response	Total	%
1.	money	27	24.7
2.	pay	10	9.2
3.	check	10	9.2
4.	duck	7	6.4
5.	collector	5	4.6
6.	sale	5	4.6
7.	dollar	4	3.7
8.	fold	4	3.7
9.	bird	2	1.8
10.	debt	2	1.8
11.	tax	2	1.8
12.	rent	2	1.8
13.	owe	2	1.8
14.	green	2	1.8
15.	receipt	2	1.8

(f = 1, 0.9%, n = 23)
bead, beak, board, boy, buck,
charge, Congress, damn, deal,
due, gas, give, house, lading,
me, O'Fare, of rights, pill,
restaurant, sign, telephone,
waiter, 1st of month

Bit

No.	Response	Total	%
1.	horse(s)	21	19.3
2.	piece	18	16.5
3.	bite	8	7.3
4.	part	5	4.6
5.	dog	4	3.7
6.	little	4	3.7
7.	drill	4	3.7
8.	teeth	3	2.8
9.	small	3	2.8
10.	bridle	3	2.8
11.	paper	2	1.8
12.	snake	2	1.8
13.	ate	2	1.8
14.	tiny	2	1.8
15.	hard	2	1.8

Bit (contd)

No.	Response	Total	%

(f = 1, 0.9%, n = 26)
amount, art, brace, chew, eat,
harness, hit, honey, hurt, lip,
littler, metariff, mouth, nose,
nothing, of, off, O'Honey,
pierce, pit, portion, reins,
stallion, tear, tongue, tooth

Boil

No.	Response	Total	%
1.	water	30	27.5
2.	egg(s)	13	11.9
3.	cook	9	8.2
4.	hot	7	6.4
5.	bubble	7	6.4
6.	sore	4	3.7
7.	heat	3	2.8
8.	over	3	2.8
9.	burn	3	2.8
10.	pimple	2	1.8
11.	hurt	2	1.8
12.	foil	2	1.8
13.	potatoes	2	1.8
14.	oil	2	1.8

(f = 1, 0.9%, n = 20)
bake, broil, cauldron, cyst,
fester, fish, food, it, me,
milk, onion, out, point, pus,
roil, simmer, spaghetti, steam,
toil, vegetable

Bow

No.	Response	Total	%
1.	arrow	45	41.2
2.	curtsey	7	6.4
3.	tie	6	5.5
4.	ship	6	5.5
5.	bend	5	4.6
6.	ribbon	5	4.6
7.	down	5	4.6
8.	scrape	3	2.8
9.	stern	2	1.8
10.	boat	2	1.8
11.	gentleman	2	1.8
12.	head	2	1.8

(f = 1, 0.9%, n = 19)
admire, button, condescend,
hair, introduction, kneel, line,
low, no, now, out, port, rake,
sailing, servant, stage, string,
violin, wow

Box

No.	Response	Total	%
1.	square	11	10.0
2.	top	8	7.3
3.	fight	7	6.4
4.	container	6	5.5

Box (contd)

No.	Response	Total	%
5.	cardboard	5	4.6
6.	candy	5	4.6
7.	hit	4	3.7
8.	girl(s)	4	3.7
9.	carton	3	2.8
10.	glove	3	2.8
11.	lunch	2	1.8
12.	shoe	2	1.8
13.	cube	2	1.8
14.	fox	2	1.8
15.	jewelry	2	1.8
16.	round	2	1.8
17.	in	2	1.8
18.	hat	2	1.8
19.	case	2	1.8
20.	can	2	1.8
21.	present	2	1.8

($\underline{f}$ = 1, 0.9%, $\underline{n}$ = 29)
boy, brown, car, closed, cookie, corner, crate, car, fighter, groceries, hold, Jack, jar, little, mail, matches, office, open, package, plant, rebellion, sand, sandwich, sex, shape, small, spar, wood, wooden

Calf

No.	Response	Total	%
1.	cow	65	59.6
2.	leg	17	15.6
3.	young	3	2.8
4.	animal	2	1.8

($\underline{f}$ = 1, 0.9%, $\underline{n}$ = 22)
ankle, bearer, beef, California, cough, dog, eyes, farm, frog, heifer, horse, kid, knees, lamb, little, milk, mother, muscle, small, tamborine, thigh, weak

Cape

No.	Response	Total	%
1.	Cod	18	16.5
2.	batman	16	14.7
3.	coat	11	10.1
4.	cloak	7	6.4
5.	crusader	5	4.6
6.	bat	4	3.7
7.	Hope	4	3.7
8.	hood	4	3.7
9.	red	3	2.8
10.	Zorro	2	1.8
11.	Canaveral	2	1.8
12.	gown	2	1.8
13.	dagger	2	1.8
14.	hat	2	1.8

($\underline{f}$ = 1, 0.9%, $\underline{n}$ = 27)
bird, black, blue, buffalo, cap, carp, clothes, clothing, code, crown, Dracula, dress, fear, fisk, fly, hang, head, Horn, Kennedy, round, shawl, shoulders, stole, superman, swagger, villain, wool

Carp

No.	Response	Total	%
1.	fish	83	76.1
2.	nag	3	2.8
3.	harp	2	1.8
4.	rug	2	1.8

($\underline{f}$ = 1, 0.9%, $\underline{n}$ = 19)
bird, body, bricker, cap, complain, crap, end, fur, lake, mint, mother, red, river, smell, shallow, sound, what, wife, wrap

Case

No.	Response	Total	%
1.	history	15	13.7
2.	brief	9	8.2
3.	box	8	7.3
4.	lawyer	6	5.5
5.	book	6	5.5
6.	study	4	3.7
7.	suit	4	3.7
8.	court	3	2.8
9.	law	3	2.8
10.	file	2	1.8
11.	tractor	2	1.8
12.	valise	2	1.8
13.	trial	2	1.8

($\underline{f}$ = 1, 0.9%, $\underline{n}$ = 43)
Athena, attaché, attorney, bag, beer, bookcase, booze, bottles, cabinet, cans, coffin, compartment, container, criminal, fire, folio, food, ginger, glass, guitar, handle, hardened, hold, jewelry, knife, ligator, metal, oranges, point, purse, satchel, shell, show, stop, storage, suitcase, taste, trim, typewriter, violin, whiskey, wood, work

Club

No.	Response	Total	%
1.	group	16	14.6
2.	hit	14	12.8
3.	house	14	12.8
4.	organization	6	5.5
5.	join	4	3.7
6.	golf	3	2.8
7.	social	2	1.8
8.	foot	2	1.8
9.	sport	2	1.8
10.	beat	2	1.8
11.	gathering	2	1.8
12.	wood	2	1.8

($\underline{f}$ = 1, 0.9%, $\underline{n}$ = 40)
activity, bop, boys, card, cave, caveman, cliques, clover, crab, dance, date, duel, feet, fraternity, fun, head, hide, hike, interest, knife, meeting, men, news, night, park, pound, private, sandwich, scouts, shallow, sorority, spade, stick, stupid, union, unity, waste, weapon, whip, women

Compact

No.	Response	Total	%
1.	small	23	21.1
2.	car	20	18.3
3.	powder	13	11.9
4.	mirror	8	7.3
5.	make-up	6	5.5
6.	purse	4	3.7
7.	close	3	2.8
8.	girl	2	1.8
9.	vanity	2	1.8
10.	tight	2	1.8
11.	agreement	2	1.8
12.	comb	2	1.8
13.	neat	2	1.8

($\underline{f}$ = 1, 0.9%, $\underline{n}$ = 20)
bargain, case, concise, condense, cosmetics, deal, fast, gold, heavy, iron, kit, like, line, lipstick, Mayflower, precise, silver, strong, tide, tiny

Contract

No.	Response	Total	%
1.	bridge	13	11.9
2.	agreement	7	6.4
3.	paper	7	6.4
4.	law	6	5.5
5.	expand	5	4.6
6.	legal	5	4.6
7.	social	4	3.7
8.	bill	3	2.8
9.	sign	3	2.8
10.	break	3	2.8
11.	document	3	2.8
12.	binding	3	2.8
13.	agree	3	2.8
14.	deal	2	1.8
15.	obligation	2	1.8
16.	lease	2	1.8
17.	marriage	2	1.8

($\underline{f}$ = 1, 0.9%, $\underline{n}$ = 36)
bid, boy, broken, build, builder, buyer, car, catch, contact, covenant, cruel, engage, find, glass, government, hold, illness, job, lawyer, lens, libel, meeting, money, movie, muscle, mutual, obtain, pact, promise, remain, Sigma Pi, signature, too, work, yearly, yes

Corn

No.	Response	Total	%
1.	cob	21	19.2
2.	meal	9	8.2
3.	yellow	7	6.4
4.	ball	5	4.6
5.	bread	5	4.6
6.	ear	3	2.8
7.	grain	3	2.8
8.	maize	3	2.8
9.	wheat	3	2.8
10.	sweet	3	2.8
11.	plant	3	2.8
12.	flakes	3	2.8
13.	belt	3	2.8
14.	pone	2	1.8
15.	husk	2	1.8
16.	food	2	1.8

Corn (contd)

No.	Response	Total	%
17.	eat	2	1.8
18.	field	2	1.8

($\underline{f}$ = 1, 0.9%, $\underline{n}$ = 28)
acre, bet, boil, candy, carrot, crow, farm, flower, fritos, fritter, golden, green, horn, Indian, Iowa, kernel, Liberace, mash, midwest, nuts, oil, on cob, peas, pod, silk, smell, syrup, teeth

Count

No.	Response	Total	%
1.	numbers	69	63.3
2.	money	6	5.5
3.	one	5	4.6
4.	add	2	1.8
5.	Marco	2	1.8
6.	math	2	1.8
7.	enumerate	2	1.8
8.	down	2	1.8

($\underline{f}$ = 1, 0.9%, $\underline{n}$ = 19)
accountant, arithmetic, backwards, Basie, cards, countess, Dracula, duke, fingers, many, mount, royalty, run, sign, spell, tally, ten, up, well

Court

No.	Response	Total	%
1.	law	17	15.5
2.	judge	11	10.1
3.	room	10	9.2
4.	yard	7	6.4
5.	king	7	6.4
6.	jury	6	5.5
7.	tennis	6	5.5
8.	love	4	3.7
9.	justice	3	2.8
10.	girl(s)	3	2.8
11.	case	2	1.8
12.	martial	2	1.8
13.	boy	2	1.8
14.	marriage	2	1.8
15.	trial	2	1.8

($\underline{f}$ = 1, 0.9%, $\underline{n}$ = 25)
back, basketball, bench, box, building, count, Davis, divorce, fine, garden, high, him, house, jester, Louis XIV, mating, order, ship, short, solemn, Supreme, throne, traffic, win, woo

Crank

No.	Response	Total	%
1.	car	17	15.5
2.	turn	12	11.0
3.	case	9	8.2
4.	handle	7	6.4
5.	old	6	5.5
6.	engine	4	3.7
7.	nut	3	2.8

Crank (contd)

No.	Response	Total	%
8.	call	3	2.8
9.	fool	2	1.8
10.	spinster	2	1.8
11.	"pill"	2	1.8
12.	Ford	2	1.8

($\underline{f}$ = 1, 0.9%, $\underline{n}$ = 40)
auto, bent, bitch, codger, complaint, crackpot, cram, crowded, eccentric, fruit, full, funny, grind, grouch, gyrate, hag, idiot, joke, J.B.S., lady, letter, mean, Model A Ford, neck, old man, pin, rank, round, quack, shaft, shot, squeak, sore, tank, twin, twist, up, wind, witch, woman

Date

No.	Response	Total	%
1.	girl	19	17.4
2.	boy	10	9.2
3.	time	8	7.3
4.	today	6	5.5
5.	fun	5	4.6
6.	year	4	3.7
7.	fruit	4	3.7
8.	night	4	3.7
9.	month	3	2.8
10.	Saturday	3	2.8
11.	calendar	3	2.8
12.	march	2	1.8
13.	food	2	1.8
14.	book	2	1.8
15.	appointment	2	1.8
16.	fig 1	2	1.8

($\underline{f}$ = 1, 0.9%, $\underline{n}$ = 30)
address, birth, boyfriend, bread, call, car, companionship, dates, day, desert, double, eat, guy, him, January, late, love, make, me, name, now, nut, out, palm, raisin, sex, some, soon, steady, Terry

Drop

No.	Response	Total	%
1.	fall	28	25.6
2.	water	12	11.0
3.	rain	6	5.5
4.	ball	4	3.7
5.	in	4	3.7
6.	throw	3	2.8
7.	bucket	3	2.8
8.	down	3	2.8
9.	lose	3	2.8
10.	match	3	2.8
11.	kick	2	1.8
12.	dead	2	1.8
13.	pin	2	1.8
14.	out	2	1.8
15.	break	2	1.8

($\underline{f}$ = 1, 0.9%, $\underline{n}$ = 30)
airplane, book, bring, cake, chute, clumsy, cookies, dew, drip, earrings, eye, fetch, force, forever, forget, it, letter, low, medicine, ouch, parachute, pick,

Drop (contd)

No.	Response	Total	%

pour, release, rise, splat, stitch, stoop, stop, tear

Duck

No.	Response	Total	%
1.	bird	14	12.8
2.	pond	11	10.1
3.	goose	9	8.2
4.	bill	8	7.3
5.	water	6	5.5
6.	quack	5	4.6
7.	swim	3	2.8
8.	stoop	3	2.8
9.	dodge	2	1.8
10.	animal	2	1.8
11.	feet	2	1.8
12.	yellow	2	1.8
13.	blind	2	1.8
14.	hunt	2	1.8
15.	white	2	1.8

($\underline{f}$ = 1, 0.9%, $\underline{n}$ = 36)
aim, billed, billed platypus, call, chick, cringe, dance, dead, dip, dive, Donny, down, dug, face, fall, feathers, fowl, frog, fuzzy, geese, gizzard, hit, lame, low, mallard, out, paddle, pheasant, punch, rabbit, Ralph, roost, savory, throw, tuck, under

Entrance

No.	Response	Total	%
1.	exit	54	49.5
2.	door	28	25.7
3.	enter	5	4.6
4.	doorway	3	2.8
5.	hall	3	2.8
6.	opening	2	1.8
7.	open	2	1.8

($\underline{f}$ = 1, 0.9%, $\underline{n}$ = 12)
entry, exam, examination, front, gate, gateway, mystify, portal, portico, to, too, wide

Excise

No.	Response	Total	%
1.	tax	77	70.6
2.	cut	4	3.7
3.	extra	3	2.8
4.	health	2	1.8
5.	run	2	1.8
6.	precise	2	1.8

($\underline{f}$ = 1, 0.9%, $\underline{n}$ = 19)
body, concise, demonstrate, exert, extract, fight, healthy, it, jump, lesson, mix, mole, play, reduce, remove, surfing, tooth, weights, work

Fair

No.	Response	Total	%
1.	unfair	9	8.2
2.	good	8	7.3
3.	hair	8	7.3
4.	blonde	6	5.5
5.	light	5	4.6
6.	foul	5	4.6
7.	carnival	5	4.6
8.	deal	5	4.6
9.	cheat	4	3.7
10.	lady	2	1.8
11.	dark	2	1.8
12.	fun	2	1.8
13.	circus	2	1.8
14.	poor	2	1.8
15.	fine	2	1.8
16.	skin	2	1.8
17.	just	2	1.8

(f = 1, 0.9%, n = 38)
beautiful, bonny, booth, cheap, child, county, dirty, equal, even, game, go, grades, green, ground, honest, judge, justice, life, lovely, maid, maiden, medal, meddling, mild, move, not, ok, pale, passing, practices, pretty, severe, square, tent, ugly, unblemished, vanity, weather

Fawn

No.	Response	Total	%
1.	deer	68	62.3
2.	doe	13	11.9
3.	young	2	1.8
4.	woods	2	1.8

(f = 1, 0.9%, n = 24)
animal, antler, baby, bird, birth, dappled-Debussy "Faun", dear, degrading, fondle, grovel, handle, helpless, horse, lavish, lawn, obsequious, retreat, spawn, spots, timid, tired, venison, weak, yellow

Feet

No.	Response	Total	%
1.	shoe	24	22.0
2.	toes	15	13.8
3.	walk	10	9.2
4.	two	6	5.5
5.	hands	5	4.6
6.	legs	5	4.6
7.	foot	4	3.7
8.	arm(s)	4	3.7
9.	dance	2	1.8
10.	tired	2	1.8
11.	clay	2	1.8

(f = 1, 0.9%, n = 30)
ankle, body, bottom, club, corns, down, fast, feed, flat, ground, head, hurt, inches, iron, length, long, nail, pods, poem, rest, run, sandals, skin, sole, sore, steps, tower, walking, wax, webbed

File

No.	Response	Total	%
1.	cabinet	25	22.9
2.	nail	9	8.2
3.	papers	8	7.3
4.	card	6	5.5
5.	rank	3	2.8
6.	saw	3	2.8
7.	fingernail	3	2.8
8.	order	2	1.8
9.	cut	2	1.8
10.	drawer	2	1.8
11.	rasp	2	1.8
12.	iron	2	1.8
13.	secretary	2	1.8
14.	forget	2	1.8
15.	finger	2	1.8
16.	clerk	2	1.8

(f = 1, 0.9%, n = 34)
bastard, binder, box, cards, case, count, down, fill, index, keep, letters, line, list, lodge, metal, mild, office, plastic, purse, put, questions, report, safe, sheep, single, soldiers, sort, steel, suit, teeth, thin, through, tool, work

Fine

No.	Response	Total	%
1.	good	38	34.8
2.	pay	6	5.5
3.	coarse	5	4.6
4.	point	4	3.7
5.	print	4	3.7
6.	well	4	3.7
7.	money	3	2.8
8.	great	3	2.8
9.	small	3	2.8
10.	thin	2	1.8
11.	bad	2	1.8
12.	nice	2	1.8
13.	cop	2	1.8
14.	delicate	2	1.8
15.	narrow	2	1.8
16.	lovely	2	1.8

(f = 1, 0.9%, n = 25)
beautiful, bill, charge, course, dandy, day, dull, fine, finish, hair, move, pen, police, poor, quality, salt, sand, sandpaper, silk, silky, smooth, swell, tax, thick, $34

Fleet

No.	Response	Total	%
1.	ship	57	52.2
2.	fast	10	9.2
3.	Navy	8	7.3
4.	boat	5	4.6
5.	admiral	4	3.7
6.	foot	3	2.8
7.	swift	3	2.8
8.	feet	2	1.8

(f = 1, 0.9%, n = 17)
Army, faun, flip, Gulliver, harbor, humorous, instant, light, many, ocean, quick, run, sail, shine, sleet, street, swan

Flush

No.	Response	Total	%
1.	toilet	51	46.7
2.	red	16	14.7
3.	blush	13	11.9
4.	embarrass	3	2.8
5.	pink	3	2.8
6.	water	2	1.8
7.	flat	2	1.8

(f = 1, 0.9%, n = 19)
against, away, brush, calm, cards, down, even, fury, heated, hot, open, pale, plunger, rid, royal, rush, warm, wash, waste

Foil

No.	Response	Total	%
1.	aluminum	19	17.4
2.	sword	19	17.4
3.	tin	16	14.7
4.	fencing	8	7.3
5.	paper	5	4.6
6.	wrap	4	3.7
7.	sabre	3	2.8
8.	fence	3	2.8
9.	spoil	2	1.8
10.	villain	2	1.8
11.	silver	2	1.8
12.	stop	2	1.8
13.	foul	2	1.8

(f = 1, 0.9%, n = 22)
Alcoa, befuddle, double cross, épée, foil, fool, fumble, ha, hinder, lance, metal, oil, out, Reynolds, roast beef, robber, ruin, stunt, thwart, touche, weapon, wrapper

Fuse

No.	Response	Total	%
1.	light	24	22.0
2.	box	11	10.1
3.	melt	6	5.5
4.	electricity	5	4.6
5.	join	5	4.6
6.	together	5	4.6
7.	blow	4	3.7
8.	electric	3	2.8
9.	bomb	3	2.8
10.	unite	3	2.8
11.	bang	2	1.8
12.	ignite	2	1.8
13.	combine	2	1.8
14.	fission	2	1.8
15.	switch	2	1.8
16.	fire	2	1.8
17.	firecracker	2	1.8

(f = 1, 0.9%, n = 26)
bite, bond, breaker, burn, candle, confuse, connect, deny, diffuse, dynamite, electrical, explosion, explosive, force, heat, it, itch, lighter, link, lit, meet, one, plug, separate, TNT, watt

Grate

No.	Response	Total	%
1.	cheese	14	12.8
2.	iron	9	8.2
3.	fire	6	5.5
4.	carrot	5	4.6
5.	grill	4	3.7
6.	steel	4	3.7
7.	fireplace	4	3.7
8.	teeth	3	2.8
9.	sewer	3	2.8
10.	gate	3	2.8
11.	cover	2	1.8
12.	fence	2	1.8
13.	shred	2	1.8
14.	bars	2	1.8
15.	sound	2	1.8
16.	chop	2	1.8
17.	grind	2	1.8
18.	scrape	2	1.8

(f = 1, 0.9%, n = 38)
box, cellar, chess, cooking, draw, fear, fell, fish, front, furnace, grateful, great, grid, happy, hearth, horse, jar, light, meat, mesh, metal, mill, onions, orange, peel, physics, pick, pieces, prison, rasp, rub, sand, shock, sidewalk, skin, stove, street, window

Grave

No.	Response	Total	%
1.	dead	20	18.3
2.	death	13	11.9
3.	serious	10	9.2
4.	dig	8	7.3
5.	digger	7	6.4
6.	sad	5	4.6
7.	die	4	3.7
8.	stone	4	3.7
9.	yard	3	2.8
10.	cemetary	3	2.8
11.	bury	2	1.8
12.	dirt	2	1.8

(f = 1, 0.9%, n = 28)
affair, brave, brother, coffin, corpse, deep, ditch, dug, grass, grandmother, grey, grove, Hamlet, headstone, hole, home, ill, man, me, mound, severe, sick, side, situation, somber, stern, severe, tomb

Ground

No.	Response	Total	%
1.	hog	19	17.4
2.	dirt	18	16.5
3.	earth	16	14.7
4.	round	5	4.6
5.	floor	5	4.6
6.	low	3	2.8
7.	soil	3	2.8
8.	beef	3	2.8
9.	walk	2	1.8
10.	meat	2	1.8
11.	hard	2	1.8
12.	coffee	2	1.8
13.	sky	2	1.8
14.	work	2	1.8

Ground (contd)

No.	Response	Total	%
15.	hole	2	1.8

(f = 1, 0.9%, n = 23)
air, ball, basis, boat, crush, fine, firm, grass, grind, high, hills, level, mix, out, play, rocky, roof, swell, terra, trees, under, up, wet

Hail

No.	Response	Total	%
1.	rain	22	20.1
2.	snow	22	20.1
3.	stone	6	5.5
4.	call	5	4.6
5.	hearty	4	3.7
6.	storm	4	3.7
7.	sleet	4	3.7
8.	Caesar	3	2.8
9.	ice	2	1.8
10.	chief	2	1.8
11.	weather	2	1.8
12.	Columbia	2	1.8
13.	cheer	2	1.8
14.	queen	2	1.8
15.	greet	2	1.8
16.	hello	2	1.8

(f = 1, 0.9%, n = 23)
beauty, cold, dark, down, fire, friend, frost, greeting, hall, hard, hero, hi, king, mail, Mary, nail, sail, say, stop, to, well, worship, yell

Hard

No.	Response	Total	%
1.	soft	71	65.1
2.	easy	6	5.5
3.	hit	5	4.6
4.	rock	3	2.8
5.	difficult	3	2.8
6.	life	2	1.8
7.	ball	2	1.8
8.	steel	2	1.8

(f = 1, 0.9%, n = 15)
boys, brick, core, diamond, floor, heavy, homer, knock, lead, personality, rough, slab, stone, top, yellow

Hide

No.	Response	Total	%
1.	seek	48	44.0
2.	run	5	4.6
3.	find	4	3.7
4.	scared	3	2.8
5.	pelt	3	2.8
6.	cave	3	2.8
7.	skin	2	1.8
8.	afraid	2	1.8
9.	park	2	1.8
10.	leather	2	1.8
11.	out	2	1.8
12.	and seek	2	1.8

Hide (contd)

No.	Response	Total	%

(f = 1, 0.9%, n = 31)
animal, anxiety, behind, catch, club, conceal, disappear, discover, disguise, down, duck, eggs, fear, from, fun, fur, game, go, hidden, hide, horse, look, Nazi, now, open, peek, runaway, secret, seek, show

Incense

No.	Response	Total	%
1.	smell	28	25.6
2.	burn	9	8.2
3.	smoke	5	4.6
4.	burner	5	4.6
5.	church	4	3.7
6.	mad	3	2.8
7.	Japan	2	1.8
8.	perfume	2	1.8
9.	fire	2	1.8
10.	offering	2	1.8
11.	love	2	1.8
12.	fragrance	2	1.8
13.	Buddha	2	1.8
14.	license	2	1.8
15.	stink	2	1.8
16.	myrrh	2	1.8
17.	sweet	2	1.8

(f = 1, 0.9%, n = 33)
acrice, anger, beauty, bum, candle-altar, car, cedar, China, decrease, dense, dislike, enrage, flagrant, fragrance, incest, Irish, lamp, loose, lust, madden, mass, money, monk, nauseating, Oriental, powder, religion, scent, taboo, temple, worship, yogi

Interest

No.	Response	Total	%
1.	money	15	13.7
2.	hobby	9	8.2
3.	club	5	4.6
4.	percent	4	3.7
5.	like	3	2.8
6.	group	3	2.8
7.	bank	3	2.8
8.	rate	3	2.8
9.	desire	3	2.8
10.	sex	2	1.8
11.	activity	2	1.8
12.	nice	2	1.8
13.	book	2	1.8
14.	girl(s)	2	1.8
15.	apathy	2	1.8
16.	dull	2	1.8
17.	fun	2	1.8
18.	boring	2	1.8

(f = 1, 0.9%, n = 43)
anxious, art, awareness, bore, boredom, cars, conversation, dividend, doll, earnings, excite, excitement, fascinate, find, firm, football, good, hills, idea, in, intrigue, involvement, joy, lack, learn, lose, magazine, main, me, nine, paid, payment,

Interest (contd)

No.	Response	Total	%

people, read, savings, school, song, stimulate, strange, sucess, sum, think, women

Intimate

No.	Response	Total	%
1.	close	30	27.5
2.	love	19	17.4
3.	friend	12	11.0
4.	sex	4	3.7
5.	suggest	3	2.8
6.	relations	3	2.8
7.	warm	3	2.8
8.	friendly	3	2.8
9.	perfume	3	2.8
10.	personal	2	1.8
11.	relationship	2	1.8

($\underline{f}$ = 1, 0.9%, $\underline{n}$ = 25)
affair, bed, boy, desirable, dilatory, feel, friendship, girl, great, husband, involved, kiss, knowing, lotion, lover, man, marriage, mock, near, odor, pretend, relation, session, sincere, social

Iron

No.	Response	Total	%
1.	steel	14	12.8
2.	clothes	13	11.9
3.	board	10	9.2
4.	metal	7	6.4
5.	shirt	6	5.5
6.	ore	5	4.6
7.	press	5	4.6
8.	hot	4	3.7
9.	horse	4	3.7
10.	work	4	3.7
11.	filings	2	1.8
12.	bar	2	1.8
13.	gate	2	1.8
14.	lead	2	1.8
15.	flat	2	1.8
16.	hard	2	1.8
17.	blouse	2	1.8

($\underline{f}$ = 1, 0.9%, $\underline{n}$ = 23)
bag, bowl, fence, heavy, horseshoes, island, like, mask, mike, mill, mine, pad, pants, pig, railing, rock, rod, round, smelt, smelten, spike, stove, strong

Lap

No.	Response	Total	%
1.	sit	25	22.9
2.	dog	20	18.3
3.	legs	5	4.6
4.	lick	5	4.6
5.	tongue	3	2.8
6.	seat	3	2.8
7.	race	3	2.8
8.	track	3	2.8

Lap (contd)

No.	Response	Total	%
9.	knees	3	2.8
10.	soft	3	2.8
11.	cat	2	1.8
12.	rest	2	1.8
13.	run	2	1.8
14.	thigh	2	1.8
15.	head	2	1.8

($\underline{f}$ = 1, 0.9%, $\underline{n}$ = 26)
animal, chair, chew, child, drink, fast, fondle, front, genitals, girl, hers, ice cream, lay, love, luxury, milk, nap, overlap, pocket, robe, sensual, shirt, skirt, slurp, stomach, swim

Lead

No.	Response	Total	%
1.	follow	35	32.1
2.	pencil	17	15.6
3.	metal	9	8.2
4.	heavy	9	8.2
5.	gold	3	2.8
6.	weight	3	2.8
7.	iron	3	2.8
8.	on	2	1.8
9.	belly	2	1.8
10.	ball	2	1.8

($\underline{f}$ = 1, 0.9%, $\underline{n}$ = 24)
astray, away, balloon, bullet, dead, death, dog, feed, guide, hand, lead, led, like, pipe, plutonium, pull, rule, sheep, shield, silver, steel, take, water, wood

Lean

No.	Response	Total	%
1.	fat	19	17.4
2.	thin	12	11.0
3.	skinny	9	8.2
4.	meat	7	6.4
5.	tall	5	4.6
6.	slim	5	4.6
7.	to	3	2.8
8.	on	3	2.8
9.	over	3	2.8
10.	bacon	2	1.8
11.	tired	2	1.8
12.	weak	2	1.8
13.	man	2	1.8
14.	against	2	1.8
15.	hungry	2	1.8
16.	bend	2	1.8
17.	lie	2	1.8

($\underline{f}$ = 1, 0.9%, $\underline{n}$ = 27)
balance, bean, beefy, bent, building, depend, fall, forward, hard, hearty, horn, jolly green giant, lank, limber, me, mean, pencil, Pisa, post, push, rest, rich, roommate, Sheldon, shoulder, slender, yellow

Like

No.	Response	Total	%
1.	love	37	33.9
2.	dislike	21	19.3
3.	hate	10	9.2
4.	same	6	5.5
5.	as	4	3.7
6.	you	4	3.7
7.	friend	3	2.8
8.	me	3	2.8
9.	drink	2	1.8
10.	nice	2	1.8

($\underline{f}$ = 1, 0.9%, $\underline{n}$ = 17)
accept, admire, amiable, close, go, good, iron, kiss, might, not, nothing, people, prefer, self, similar, unlike, wow

Limp

No.	Response	Total	%
1.	cripple	7	6.4
2.	leg	7	6.4
3.	hurt	5	4.6
4.	soft	5	4.6
5.	rag	5	4.6
6.	walk	4	3.7
7.	weak	3	2.8
8.	crutch	3	2.8
9.	foot	3	2.8
10.	lame	3	2.8
11.	loose	3	2.8
12.	flaccid	2	1.8
13.	rigid	2	1.8
14.	body	2	1.8
15.	go	2	1.8
16.	soggy	2	1.8
17.	dead	2	1.8
18.	stiff	2	1.8
19.	lax	2	1.8
20.	fall	2	1.8
21.	protest	2	1.8

($\underline{f}$ = 1, 0.9%, $\underline{n}$ = 41)
ache, arm, away, back, bad, cane, collapse, demonstrate, die, disobedience-civil, frail, hand, hard, inactive, injury, jump, lank, lifeless, like, lima bean, limber, lisp, nodes, nonviolent, old, out, pain, ragdoll, relax, relaxed, sag, softly, sore, sprain, stick, straight, strong, tired, wimp

March

No.	Response	Total	%
1.	walk	13	11.9
2.	band	10	9.2
3.	soldiers	9	8.2
4.	parade	7	6.4
5.	army	6	5.5
6.	step	6	5.5
7.	April	4	3.7
8.	month	3	2.8
9.	time	2	1.8
10.	run	2	1.8
11.	toward	2	1.8
12.	feet	2	1.8
13.	in	2	1.8

March (contd)

No.	Response	Total	%
	($\underline{f}$ = 1, 0.9%, $\underline{n}$ = 41)		

along, attack, cadence, command, Berkeley, Birthday, boots, demonstrate, demonstration, dog, tall, fast, fifth, freedom, F.S.M., hare, Hitler, home, infantry, involved, jump, kites, left, line, marine, May, me, Oakland, one, onward, order, peace, ROTC, skip, through, tired, to, tramp, tune, VDC, wind

Maroon

No.	Response	Total	%
1.	red	23	21.1
2.	color	18	16.5
3.	island	14	12.8
4.	purple	13	11.9
5.	stranded	3	2.8
6.	gold	3	2.8
7.	ship	2	1.8
8.	white	2	1.8
9.	macaroon	2	1.8
10.	alone	2	1.8
11.	blue	2	1.8
	($\underline{f}$ = 1, 0.9%, $\underline{n}$ = 25)		

away, balloon, burgundy, cocoon, car, chain, cookie, dark, desert, fired, grease, grey, isolate, leave, lost, magenta, old, oleandor, platoon, rich, swamp, sweater, Tony, vibrant, viking

Mass

No.	Response	Total	%
1.	church	18	16.5
2.	weight	13	11.9
3.	people	10	9.2
4.	large	5	4.6
5.	physics	4	3.7
6.	Catholic	3	2.8
7.	energy	3	2.8
8.	force	3	2.8
9.	action	3	2.8
10.	matter	3	2.8
11.	grams	3	2.8
12.	group	3	2.8
13.	production	2	1.8
	($\underline{f}$ = 1, 0.9%, $\underline{n}$ = 36)		

acceleration, all, area, body, bulk, Cal, clift, crowd, culture, density, election, exodus, heavy, holy, hysteria, lump, magnitude, many, Mars, media, meeting, molecule, music, Newton, -ochist, of, peasants, priest, program, society, spinage, state, stupid, time, ton, velocity

Meal

No.	Response	Total	%
1.	food	34	31.1
2.	eat	22	20.2
3.	dinner	14	12.8
4.	corn	7	6.4
5.	ticket	6	5.5
6.	good	3	2.8
7.	steak	3	2.8
8.	breakfast	3	2.8
9.	time	2	1.8
	($\underline{f}$ = 1, 0.9%, $\underline{n}$ = 15)		

after, ate, chow, cook, deal, eel, golden, hungry, ice-cream, male, out, pin, quick, veal, worm

Mean

No.	Response	Total	%
1.	average	22	20.1
2.	cruel	18	16.5
3.	nasty	11	10.1
4.	angry	5	4.6
5.	nice	4	3.7
6.	kind	4	3.7
7.	ugly	3	2.8
8.	evil	3	2.8
9.	hard	3	2.8
10.	median	2	1.8
11.	happy	2	1.8
12.	old	2	1.8
13.	boy	2	1.8
	($\underline{f}$ = 1, 0.9%, $\underline{n}$ = 28)		

awful, crabby, cranky, cross, different, grouchy, gruff, harsh, hate, horrible, hurt, is, lean, man, middle, mode, Nick, poor, score, selfish, soup, statistics, stingy, to, unkind, violence, wicked, woman

Mine

No.	Response	Total	%
1.	yours	53	48.6
2.	gold	13	11.9
3.	coal	6	5.5
4.	me	3	2.8
5.	shaft	3	2.8
6.	ore	2	1.8
7.	hole	2	1.8
8.	field	2	1.8
9.	dig	2	1.8
10.	own	2	1.8
11.	his	2	1.8
12.	cave	2	1.8
13.	rock(s)	2	1.8
	($\underline{f}$ = 1, 0.9%, $\underline{n}$ = 15)		

children, destroy, Haiphong, Kampf, lawyer, mercury, mind, mineral, mountain, ours, possessive, sweeper, thine, war

Mint

No.	Response	Total	%
1.	candy	24	22.0
2.	money	17	15.6
3.	green	14	12.8
4.	julep	8	7.3
5.	coins	7	6.4
6.	cookie	5	4.6
7.	leaf	4	3.7
8.	chocolate	3	2.8
9.	eat	2	1.8
10.	leaves	2	1.8
11.	apear	2	1.8
12.	sweet	2	1.8
13.	good	2	1.8
	($\underline{f}$ = 1, 0.9%, $\underline{n}$ = 17)		

bitter, cool, creme, food, germ, herb, jelly, lean, lot, mine, patty, peppermint, sale, San Francisco, stick, tasty, wafer

Mole

No.	Response	Total	%
1.	animal	12	11.0
2.	hole	12	11.0
3.	face	10	9.2
4.	ground	9	8.2
5.	rodent	6	5.5
6.	rat	6	5.5
7.	wart	4	3.7
8.	mouse	3	2.8
9.	gopher	3	2.8
10.	brown	3	2.8
11.	hill	3	2.8
12.	black	3	2.8
13.	burrow	2	1.8
14.	pimple	2	1.8
15.	shrew	2	1.8
16.	skin	2	1.8
17.	dark	2	1.8
	($\underline{f}$ = 1, 0.9%, $\underline{n}$ = 25)		

beauty-spot, blemish, blind, bump, chair, chemistry, dairy, dig, dot, ear, earth, fungus, fur, ground hog, hair, lump, mall, mark, molecule, number, quantity, sole, spot, tunnel, weight

Nag

No.	Response	Total	%
1.	horse	26	23.8
2.	wife	17	15.6
3.	bitch	11	10.1
4.	hag	8	7.3
5.	mother	6	5.5
6.	woman	4	3.7
7.	bother	4	3.7
8.	scold	3	2.8
9.	shrew	3	2 8
10.	lag	2	1.8
11.	pester	2	1.8
	($\underline{f}$ = 1, 0.9%, $\underline{n}$ = 23)		

bag, bore, brag, "bug", cranky-, criticize, gossip, heckle, hen-peck, mare, me, mean, mother-in-law, no, old, patience, pencil, repeat, roommate, slim, tease, yell, whine

Net

No.	Response	Total	%
1.	fish	54	49.5
2.	tennis	6	5.5
3.	catch	5	4.6
4.	results	3	2.8
5.	profit	3	2.8
6.	butterfly	3	2.8
7.	volleyball	2	1.8
8.	rope	2	1.8
9.	fishing	2	1.8
10.	gain	2	1.8
11.	web	2	1.8
12.	ball	2	1.8

($\underline{f}$ = 1, 0.9%, $\underline{n}$ = 23)
count, fisherman, game, hair, hole, hold, income, lace, let, make, pet, plot, prong, ring, scoop, sieve, total, trap, twine, volly, wave, wet, whole

Page

No.	Response	Total	%
1.	book	36	33.0
2.	boy	14	12.8
3.	number	8	7.3
4.	paper	7	6.4
5.	turn	7	6.4
6.	call	5	4.6
7.	read	4	3.7
8.	leaf	4	3.7
9.	one	3	2.8
10.	torn	3	2.8
11.	two	2	1.8
12.	chapter	2	1.8

($\underline{f}$ = 1, 0.9%, $\underline{n}$ = 14)
blank, booklet, court, eleven, errand, hair, king, paragraph, print, reading, sheet, tear, this, white

Pass

No.	Response	Total	%
1.	fail	13	11.9
2.	go	10	9.2
3.	by	9	8.2
4.	football	5	4.6
5.	car	5	4.6
6.	word	5	4.6
7.	over	5	4.6
8.	mountain	4	3.7
9.	ticket	3	2.8
10.	out	3	2.8
11.	key	3	2.8
12.	check	2	1.8
13.	skip	2	1.8
14.	road	2	1.8
15.	walk	2	1.8

($\underline{f}$ = 1, 0.9%, $\underline{n}$ = 36)
along, around, away, ball, blank, book, butter, catch, class, course, Donner, exam, free, gate, give, grass, halt, hat, highway, ing, kiss, lane, leave, let, make, meet, move, offer, overtake, past, pull, run, test, through, under, valley

Pelt

No.	Response	Total	%
1.	fur	42	38.5
2.	beaver	10	9.2
3.	hit	10	9.2
4.	skin	5	4.6
5.	rain	4	3.7
6.	animal	3	2.8
7.	hide	3	2.8
8.	fox	3	2.8
9.	stone	3	2.8
10.	girl	2	1.8
11.	pill	2	1.8
12.	mink	2	1.8
13.	water	2	1.8

($\underline{f}$ = 1, 0.9%, $\underline{n}$ = 18)
Alaska, belt, chinchilla, coat, dog, felt, fish, food, pummel, rabbit, rail, rocks, snow, snowball, space, spelt, throw, woman

Perch

No.	Response	Total	%
1.	sit	26	23.8
2.	bird	22	20.2
3.	fish	21	19.3
4.	limb	4	3.7
5.	stand	3	2.8
6.	parrot	3	2.8
7.	on	3	2.8
8.	tree	3	2.8
9.	branch	3	2.8
10.	parakeet	2	1.8

($\underline{f}$ = 1, 0.9%, $\underline{n}$ = 19)
attack, bud, canary, climb, glower, high, lion, lofty, look, lost, nest, outlook, peek, perilous, place, position, up, upon, wave

Plant

No.	Response	Total	%
1.	green	20	18.3
2.	animal	15	13.8
3.	flower	12	11.0
4.	tree	11	10.1
5.	grow	7	6.4
6.	dig	4	3.7
7.	seed	3	2.8
8.	pot	2	1.8
9.	dirt	2	1.8
10.	leaf	2	1.8
11.	rose	2	1.8
12.	ground	2	1.8
13.	botany	2	1.8
14.	ivy	2	1.8

($\underline{f}$ = 1, 0.9%, $\underline{n}$ = 23)
Arthur, box, company, factory, fern, food, garden, greed, growing, growth, like, lily, oak, outside, paint, pumpkins, shrub, small, soil, sow, uproot, vine, worm

Plot

No.	Response	Total	%
1.	scheme	13	11.9
2.	plan	13	11.9
3.	story	11	10.1
4.	graph	8	7.3
5.	kill	6	5.5
6.	spy	4	3.7
7.	mystery	3	2.8
8.	grave	3	2.8
9.	crime	3	2.8
10.	ground	3	2.8
11.	novel	2	1.8
12.	sinister	2	1.8
13.	stage	2	1.8
14.	revenge	2	1.8
15.	intrigue	2	1.8
16.	land	2	1.8
17.	connive	2	1.8

($\underline{f}$ = 1, 0.9%, $\underline{n}$ = 28)
against, book, character, conspiracy, curve, danger, deception, design, drama, draw, game, garden, high, investigate, knot, lot, murder, paranoid, play, put, rage, rogue, sabotage, scene, slot, supense, theft, theme

Port

No.	Response	Total	%
1.	ship	20	18.3
2.	starboard	12	11.0
3.	call	10	9.2
4.	wine	9	8.2
5.	boats	7	6.4
6.	hole	7	6.4
7.	harbor	6	5.5
8.	sea	5	4.6
9.	left	2	1.8
10.	sail	2	1.8
11.	stern	2	1.8
12.	sherry	2	1.8
13.	right	2	1.8
14.	dock	2	1.8

($\underline{f}$ = 1, 0.9%, $\underline{n}$ = 21)
air, bay, bow, car, carry, commerce, drink, garage, gate, home, ocean, odd, of call, red, San Francisco, side, storm, track, water, wharf, whiskey

Pound

No.	Response	Total	%
1.	weight	15	13.7
2.	ounce	12	11.0
3.	hit	9	8.2
4.	cake	9	8.2
5.	dog	7	6.4
6.	candy	5	4.6
7.	shilling	4	3.7
8.	butter	3	2.8
9.	fat	2	1.8
10.	nail	2	1.8
11.	beat	2	1.8
12.	weigh	2	1.8
13.	meat	2	1.8
14.	money	2	1.8
15.	flesh	2	1.8
16.	English	2	1.8

Pound (contd)

No.	Response	Total	%

(f = 1, 0.9%, n = 29)
bang, cheese, coffee, dyne,
Ezra, food, foot, grown, hamburger, hammer, happy, inch,
klompjt, lake, lard, livre,
lugs, me, measure, mint, nails,
penny, potatoes, salt, slug,·
sound, spoiled, stake, ton

Produce

No.	Response	Total	%
1.	vegetables	26	23.8
2.	make	18	16.5
3.	market	7	6.4
4.	lettuce	6	5.5
5.	food	4	3.7
6.	eggs	4	3.7
7.	fruit	4	3.7
8.	goods	3	2.8
9.	grow	3	2.8
10.	reproduce	3	2.8
11.	meat	2	1.8
12.	farm	2	1.8
13.	product	2	1.8
14.	fish	2	1.8
15.	corn	2	1.8

(f = 1, 0.9%, n = 21)
apple, baby, cabbage, candy,
cause, crop, department, emit,
farmer, flesh, grain, green,
groceries, live, manufacture,
orange, poultry, reduce, sex,
wine, work

Punch

No.	Response	Total	%
1.	hit	39	35.7
2.	sock	10	9.2
3.	Judy	9	8.2
4.	bowl	5	4.6
5.	hurt	4	3.7
6.	drink	4	3.7
7.	alcohol	2	1.8
8.	cards	2	1.8
9.	bag	2	1.8
10.	nose	2	1.8
11.	poke	2	1.8

(f = 1, 0.9%, n = 28)
and Judy, ball, beat, boxing,
drunk, fruit, gin, gloves,
hard, Hawaiian, hide, holes, it,
juice, karate, line, me, midget,
munch, never, out, pinch,
smack, spike, stomach, strike,
tingly, you

Pupil

No.	Response	Total	%
1.	student	54	49.5
2.	eye	34	31.2
3.	school	4	3.7
4.	teacher	3	2.8
5.	iris	2	1.8

Pupil (contd)

No.	Response	Total	%

(f = 1, 0.9%, n = 12)
eyelid, fool, hat, it, kid,
learning, look, no, professor,
study, sweat, tired

Race

No.	Response	Total	%
1.	run	19	17.4
2.	horse	14	12.8
3.	people	6	5.5
4.	win	5	4.6
5.	fast	5	4.6
6.	track	4	3.7
7.	Negro	4	3.7
8.	car	4	3.7
9.	color	3	2.8
10.	riot	3	2.8
11.	foot	3	2.8
12.	speed	3	2.8
13.	rat	2	1.8
14.	space	2	1.8
15.	boats	2	1.8

(f = 1, 0.9%, n = 30)
anthropology, cars, Caucasian,
chase, Chinese, contest, creed
dash, differences, dog, finish,
first, gate, grate, hurry,
maze, minority, nation, national-
ity, none, pace, religion, right,
see, stop, strive, test,
track(sport), turtle, white

Rake

No.	Response	Total	%
1.	leaves	40	36.6
2.	hoe	21	19.3
3.	shovel	6	5.5
4.	lawn	4	3.7
5.	handle	4	3.7
6.	garden	3	2.8
7.	grass	3	2.8
8.	leave	2	1.8
9.	tool	2	1.8

(f = 1, 0.9%, n = 24)
broom, devil, dog, field, fork,
harlot, hose, in, low, manure,
mow, playboy, prongs, race,
ramble, rape, scratch, shallow,
snake, spendthrift, spread,
support, wake, work

Rash

No.	Response	Total	%
1.	red	12	11.0
2.	measles	7	6.4
3.	skin	6	5.5
4.	harsh	6	5.5
5.	hives	6	5.5
6.	judgment	6	5.5
7.	hasty	5	4.6
8.	quick	5	4.6
9.	itch	5	4.6
10.	bold	4	3.7

Rash (contd)

No.	Response	Total	%
11.	baby	3	2.8
12.	poison	2	1.8
13.	sudden	2	1.8
14.	allergy	2	1.8
15.	hard	2	1.8
16.	scar	2	1.8
17.	brash	2	1.8
18.	scratch	2	1.8

(f = 1, 0.9%, n = 30)
act, argue, bump, chickenpox,
diaper, fast, flu, foolhardy,
hurry, immature, impulsive,
irrational, irritate, me, mean,
medicine, mesh, oak, pimple,
poison oak, polish, raw, rush,
severe, smallpox, sore, statement, unthinking, unwary, wild

Rear

No.	Response	Total	%
1.	end	36	33.0
2.	front	20	18.3
3.	behind	14	12.8
4.	back	13	11.9
5.	horse	7	6.4
6.	car	2	1.8
7.	seat	2	1.8

(f = 1, 0.9%, n = 15)
admiral, after, ass, back porch,
badly, bottom, buck, bumper,
cheek, derriere, door, rear,
rise, side, view mirror

Refrain

No.	Response	Total	%
1.	stop	38	34.8
2.	song	14	12.8
3.	from	6	5.5
4.	music	5	4.6
5.	sing	4	3.7
6.	chorus	4	3.7
7.	keep	3	2.8
8.	refuse	2	1.8
9.	don't	2	1.8
10.	restraint	2	1.8
11.	tune	2	1.8
12.	stanza	2	1.8

(f = 1, 0.9%, n = 25)
abstain, cease, discipline, fain,
hesitate, indulge, inhibit,
laughter, lightly, never, no,
noise, prohibit, quit, resist,
restrain, sex, smoking, stay,
submissive, sustain, tan,
tolerate, verse, want

Refuse

No.	Response	Total	%
1.	deny	17	15.5
2.	garbage	14	12.8
3.	no	14	12.8
4.	accept	8	7.3
5.	stubborn	4	3.7

Refuse (contd)

No.	Response	Total	%
6.	won't	3	2.8
7.	waste	3	2.8
8.	ignore	2	1.8
9.	obey	2	1.8
10.	to	2	1.8
11.	demand	2	1.8
12.	negate	2	1.8
13.	reject	2	1.8

($\underline{f}$ = 1, 0.9%, $\underline{n}$ = 34)
acknowledge, adamant, ask, can,
child, combat, confuse, deduce,
desire, disagree, dislike, eat,
fuse, girl, invitation, not,
object, oppose, pay, permission,
push, rebuke, refuge, reply,
strong, stop, suffice, take,
toil, trash, turn, want, will,
words

Rent

No.	Response	Total	%
1.	house	27	24.7
2.	apartment	18	16.5
3.	money	13	11.9
4.	pay	11	10.1
5.	room	6	5.5
6.	lease	5	4.6
7.	high	4	3.7
8.	own	3	2.8
9.	sell	3	2.8
10.	buy	2	1.8

($\underline{f}$ = 1, 0.9%, $\underline{n}$ = 17)
base, bike, cabin, due, excise,
flat, hike, hill, home,
landlord, lend, low, monthly,
pad, sale, tax, tear

Rest

No.	Response	Total	%
1.	sleep	34	31.1
2.	relax	10	9.2
3.	room	8	7.3
4.	tired	7	6.4
5.	bed	5	4.6
6.	home	3	2.8
7.	ease	3	2.8
8.	nap	3	2.8
9.	stop	2	1.8
10.	nest	2	1.8
11.	remainder	2	1.8
12.	sit	2	1.8

($\underline{f}$ = 1, 0.9%, $\underline{n}$ = 28)
exercise, first, grass, hammock,
it, least, left, lest, lie,
many, now, other, pause, peace,
period, play, quiet, remain,
repose, respite, resting
potential, run, suffer, time,
too, weary, work

Sage

No.	Response	Total	%
1.	wise	30	27.5
2.	brush	27	24.8
3.	spice	7	6.4

Sage (contd)

No.	Response	Total	%
4.	bush	6	5.5
5.	prophet	4	3.7
6.	seasoning	3	2.8
7.	wisdom	3	2.8
8.	rage	2	1.8
9.	old	2	1.8

($\underline{f}$ = 1, 0.9%, $\underline{n}$ = 25)
Aristotle, bad, bearded, clover,
dressing, evangelist, fish,
flavor, girl, herb, honey, know,
liege, man, men, page, plant,
poem, president, purple, sea,
smart, story, turkey, twigs

Scale

No.	Response	Total	%
1.	weight	30	27.5
2.	weigh	24	22.0
3.	fish	10	9.2
4.	measure	6	5.5
5.	graph	4	3.7
6.	ruler	3	2.8
7.	pounds	3	2.8
8.	bathroom	2	1.8
9.	music	2	1.8

($\underline{f}$ = 1, 0.9%, $\underline{n}$ = 21)
down, grade, graduated, grating,
heavy, inches, librus, long,
mass, mountain, notes,
psychological, rating, register,
rocket, sing, slime, temperature,
tip, vector, wt.

Second

No.	Response	Total	%
1.	minute	37	33.9
2.	first	28	25.7
3.	time	12	11.0
4.	third	8	7.3
5.	1st	2	1.8
6.	hand	2	1.8
7.	hour	2	1.8
8.	fast	2	1.8
9.	later	2	1.8

($\underline{f}$ = 1, 0.9%, $\underline{n}$ = 14)
chance, dessert, fight, grade,
helping, moment, on the dot,
one, order, no, short, story,
thought, watch

Smack

No.	Response	Total	%
1.	kiss	34	31.1
2.	hit	29	26.6
3.	lips	13	11.9
4.	slap	3	2.8
5.	taste	2	1.8
6.	food	2	1.8
7.	lick	2	1.8
8.	cookie	2	1.8
9.	crackle	2	1.8
10.	dab	2	1.8
11.	hard	2	1.8

($\underline{f}$ = 1, 0.9%, $\underline{n}$ = 16)

Smack (contd)

No.	Response	Total	%

against, chomp, face, into, lip,
mug, out, ow, potato chip, pow,
quick, rough, sandwich, small,
softly, whop

Smelt

No.	Response	Total	%
1.	fish	32	29.3
2.	iron	28	25.7
3.	steel	5	4.6
4.	copper	3	2.8
5.	ore	3	2.8
6.	burn	3	2.8
7.	smell	3	2.8
8.	stink	2	1.8
9.	odor	2	1.8
10.	heat	2	1.8
11.	tar	2	1.8

($\underline{f}$ = 1, 0.9%, $\underline{n}$ = 17)
bad, black, fuse, gold, hurt,
it, lead, mold, nose, reel,
salmon, scent, snow, stunk,
tapeworm, when, whif

Sound

No.	Response	Total	%
1.	noise	38	34.8
2.	hear	14	12.8
3.	music	12	11.0
4.	fury	5	4.6
5.	loud	5	4.6
6.	horn	4	3.7
7.	bell	4	3.7
8.	waves	3	2.8
9.	ear	2	1.8
10.	silence	2	1.8
11.	hard	2	1.8

($\underline{f}$ = 1, 0.9%, $\underline{n}$ = 18)
car, doorbell, good, him, listen,
pang, pupil, round, school,
sight, smell, sonar, stereo,
strike, sweet, voice, water,
worries

Spray

No.	Response	Total	%
1.	can	21	19.2
2.	hair	14	12.8
3.	gun	12	11.0
4.	water	8	7.3
5.	paint	7	6.4
6.	ocean	4	3.7
7.	deodorant	4	3.7
8.	garden	4	3.7
9.	insect	2	1.8
10.	insecticide	2	1.8
11.	starch	2	1.8
12.	flowers	2	1.8

($\underline{f}$ = 1, 0.9%, $\underline{n}$ = 27)
air, button, color, cream, fog,
fumigate, gas, gay, grass, lay,
leaves, me, mist, mosquito,
perfume, salt, sea, sex, sprinkle,
spume, spy, stream, swoosh,
wash, weeds, wet, wine

Spring

No.	Response	Total	%
1.	fall	16	14.6
2.	summer	15	13.8
3.	water	9	8.2
4.	sprung	7	6.4
5.	flowers	6	5.5
6.	time	4	3.7
7.	jump	4	3.7
8.	board	3	2.8
9.	season	3	2.8
10.	fresh	3	2.8
11.	chicken	2	1.8
12.	trees	2	1.8
13.	song	2	1.8
14.	winter	2	1.8
15.	happy	2	1.8
16.	yellow	2	1.8
17.	spring	2	1.8

(f = 1, 0.9%, n = 25)
April, autumn, bed, blossoms,
bring, come, cool, dog, fling,
girl, hatch, later, mattress,
May, meadows, metal, plants,
rain, ring, steel, sun,
sunshine, up, well, wire

State

No.	Response	Total	%
1.	California	23	21.1
2.	government	12	11.0
3.	country	10	9.2
4.	union	8	7.3
5.	nation	4	3.7
6.	police	3	2.8
7.	capital	3	2.8
8.	city	2	1.8
9.	county	2	1.8
10.	united	2	1.8
11.	province	2	1.8
12.	condition	2	1.8
13.	say	2	1.8
14.	affairs	2	1.8

(f = 1, 0.9%, n = 32)
avenue, being, body, "Bundes",
capitol, civil, department,
event, expostulate, fair, hate,
house, idea, Indiana, local,
maid, Mass., mention, mind,
Minn., national, New York,
Ohio, out, pomp, property,
sentence, ship, statement,
tax, United States, universe

Stern

No.	Response	Total	%
1.	strict	18	16.5
2.	mean	8	7.3
3.	hard	7	6.4
4.	harsh	7	6.4
5.	angry	5	4.6
6.	hall	5	4.6
7.	bow	4	3.7
8.	severe	4	3.7
9.	boat	4	3.7
10.	cross	3	2.8
11.	fierce	3	2.8
12.	ship	2	1.8
13.	back	2	1.8
14.	end	2	1.8

Stern (contd)

No.	Response	Total	%
15.	forbidding	2	1.8
16.	somber	2	1.8
17.	serious	2	1.8

(f = 1, 0.9%, n = 29)
aft, austere, command, crappy,
cruel, easy, determined, drink,
face, father, frank, genetics,
grave, gray, grim, kind, lenient,
man, mother, Puritan, rear,
respected, rigid, side, steady,
strong, stupid, weak, woman

Stick

No.	Response	Total	%
1.	stone	11	10.0
2.	wood	10	9.2
3.	mud	9	8.2
4.	hit	8	7.3
5.	glue	6	5.5
6.	gum	6	5.5
7.	stuck	4	3.7
8.	twig	4	3.7
9.	pole	4	3.7
10.	club	3	2.8
11.	ball	2	1.8
12.	hurt	2	1.8
13.	branch	2	1.8
14.	rock	2	1.8
15.	pin	2	1.8
16.	big	2	1.8

(f = 1, 0.9%, n = 32)
around, baseball, bat, beat,
broom, candy, jab, limb,
lollipop, man, paddle, pear,
pierce, plunge, poke, rap, rod,
shift, shovel, smell, snake,
stab, steak, stick, stine,
sucker, to, tree, weapon,
wooden, yard, yellow

Strand

No.	Response	Total	%
1.	hair	45	41.2
2.	beach	10	9.2
3.	string	9	8.2
4.	thread	7	6.4
5.	island	4	3.7
6.	fiber	4	3.7
7.	piece	4	3.7
8.	pearls	3	2.8

(f = 1, 0.9%, n = 23)
abandoned, alone, Broadway, cord,
eyes, fray, golden, held, land,
leave, lock, race, river, rope,
sand, single, spaghetti, stand,
strange, theatre, thin, up, water

Swallow

No.	Response	Total	%
1.	bird	40	36.7
2.	gulp	8	7.3
3.	eat	7	6.4
4.	food	6	5.5

Swallow (contd)

No.	Response	Total	%
5.	drink	5	4.6
6.	throat	5	4.6
7.	Capistrano	3	2.8
8.	choke	3	2.8
9.	nest	2	1.8
10.	sparrow	2	1.8
11.	chew	2	1.8

(f = 1, 0.9%, n = 26)
bait, beer, chock, cough, digest,
dirt, dove, flight, fly, foot,
full, gurgle, hard, milk, mouth,
not, pill, pin, poison, soar,
sore, summer, tail, tongue,
water, whole

Tap

No.	Response	Total	%
1.	water	28	25.6
2.	beer	18	16.5
3.	hit	13	11.9
4.	dance	7	6.4
5.	knock	7	6.4
6.	rap	3	2.8
7.	touch	3	2.8
8.	door	2	1.8

(f = 1, 0.9%, n =]8)
away, blow, dancing, finger,
foot, hard, hole, knee, lightly,
on, once, pencil, pipe, punch,
room, shoulder, slight, springs,
stick, strike, syrup, table,
tape, tinker, toe, waterfaucet,
wire, wood

Taper

No.	Response	Total	%
1.	candle	29	26.6
2.	end	7	6.4
3.	cut	7	6.4
4.	off	6	5.5
5.	point	5	4.6
6.	narrow	5	4.6
7.	shirt	4	3.7
8.	slim	3	2.8
9.	pants	2	1.8
10.	slender	2	1.8
11.	cone	2	1.8
12.	thin	2	1.8

(f = 1, 0.9%, n = 35)
animal, beer, bench, close,
clothe, curtain, dancing
shadows, dress, drill, droop,
figure, fishline, handle, hit,
hog, hole, knocker, leg, length,
light, paper, pencil, phallic,
pig, plane, pointed, shorten,
slant, stick, tapir, tip,
topper, trim, widen, worm

Temple

No.	Response	Total	%
1.	head	25	22.9
2.	church	25	22.9
3.	worship	6	5.5
4.	God	5	4.6
5.	religion	4	3.7
6.	forehead	4	3.7
7.	Mormon	3	2.8
8.	Jew	2	1.8
9.	steeple	2	1.8
10.	gods	2	1.8
11.	shrine	2	1.8

($\underline{f}$ = 1, 0.9%, $\underline{n}$ = 29)
ball, bar, bell, brow, Buddha, Buddhist, cave, cheek, chew, columns, gray, hit, hypocrisy, house, Jewish, monk, Moslem, nice, pagoda, peak, prayer, priestess, round, school, Shirley, skull, sleep, synagogue, top

Tip

No.	Response	Total	%
1.	waiter	29	26.6
2.	end	11	10.1
3.	money	10	9.2
4.	top	10	9.2
5.	waitress	6	5.5
6.	off	4	3.7
7.	point	4	3.7
8.	hat	3	2.8
9.	restaurant	3	2.8
10.	over	2	1.8
11.	pen	2	1.8

($\underline{f}$ = 1, 0.9%, $\underline{n}$ = 25)
boat, bottle, cab, capsize, coin, cop, corn, edge, fall, give, head, helpful, horses, lead, nose, nothing, of toe, pay, pole, rich, scale, spill, tap, toe, 15 per cent

Toll

No.	Response	Total	%
1.	bridge	50	45.8
2.	gate	11	10.1
3.	bell	10	9.2
4.	money	7	6.4
5.	pay	7	6.4
6.	fee	4	3.7
7.	work	2	1.8
8.	plaza	2	1.8

($\underline{f}$ = 1, 0.9%, $\underline{n}$ = 16)
booth, call, charge, clock, cost, crossing, foil, house, knell, labor, lead, mole, payment, poll, price, sweat

Top

No.	Response	Total	%
1.	bottom	63	57.7
2.	spin	9	8.2
3.	hat	6	5.5
4.	tip	3	2.8
5.	high	2	1.8
6.	car	2	1.8
7.	spinning	2	1.8
8.	head	2	1.8

($\underline{f}$ = 1, 0.9%, $\underline{n}$ = 20)
convertible, down, drawer, executive, less, lid, mark, mountain, notch, of, pop, root, stairs, summit, table, that, tub, turning, vista, 1st

Wax

No.	Response	Total	%
1.	floor	31	28.4
2.	candle	17	15.6
3.	museum	9	8.2
4.	paper	9	8.2
5.	bee's	6	5.5
6.	wane	5	4.6
7.	ear	4	3.7
8.	skis	3	2.8
9.	car	3	2.8
10.	yellow	2	1.8
11.	shine	2	1.8
12.	dummy	2	1.8

($\underline{f}$ = 1, 0.9%, $\underline{n}$ = 17)
close, crew, doll, dummy, encaustic, free, grease, heat, max, old, shoe, slippery, slippy, sticky, tallow, teeth, work

Well

No.	Response	Total	%
1.	water	28	25.6
2.	deep	23	21.1
3.	good	16	14.7
4.	bucket	5	4.6
5.	hole	4	3.7
6.	done	4	3.7
7.	wishing	3	2.8
8.	dig	3	2.8
9.	sick	2	1.8
10.	up	2	1.8

($\underline{f}$ = 1, 0.9%, $\underline{n}$ = 19)
and good, bad, being, brick, dry, dug, enough, fall, healthy, hearty, ink, not, oil, poorly, sink, stop, tell, well, wish

Will

No.	Response	Total	%
1.	won't	10	9.1
2.	death	9	8.2
3.	not	8	7.3
4.	testament	8	7.3
5.	money	6	5.5
6.	mind	5	4.6
7.	want	5	4.6
8.	way	4	3.7
9.	desire	3	2.8
10.	strong	2	1.8
11.	shall	2	1.8
12.	free	2	1.8
13.	deed	2	1.8
14.	win	2	1.8
15.	die	2	1.8
16.	bequeath	2	1.8

($\underline{f}$ = 1, 0.9%, $\underline{n}$ = 37)
ace, allow, bold, cage, call, come, control, dead, destiny, do, document, future, give, govern, heart, hope, intent, last, lawyer, let, loose, may, mine, paper, power, predestination, steal, strength, testimony, unconscious, verb, voluntary, volition, weak, well, wheel, wish

CHAPTER 9

SUBSTITUTION, CONTEXT, AND ASSOCIATION[1]

Susan M. Ervin-Tripp
University of California, Berkeley, California

In the history of the word-association method, there has been little attention to the relation between associative structure and spoken discourse. The data reported in the norms for this chapter were collected with a specific theory in mind. Their peculiarities derive from this purpose. The theory, which is given fully in Ervin (1963) and McNeill (1963), basically assumed that associative relations arise either from co-occurrence in continuous speech, or from probabilities that one word will be substituted for another in the same frame. The predictions from these frequencies of substitution or succession then were corrected for the probabilities of occurrence of the individual words in isolation in speech, since the free-association task requires isolated one-word responses.

The theory was an attempt to subsume the grammatical and semantic constraints on contiguity and substitution under one operational test. The data listed in the tables are those which were necessary in order to test the notion that associative frequencies can be predicted from frequencies of cooccurrence or substitutability in continuous discourse. These include (*1*) associative responses in the usual sense, (*2*) frequencies with which words appeared near the stimulus word in sentences constructed by the *S*s, separately for antecedent and following context, and (*3*) the frequencies with which words were offered as possible substitutes for the stimulus words in the sentences collected to establish contextual frequencies. These four types of frequencies will be referred to as associations, precontext, postcontext, and substitutions.

The theory assumed that the fairly simple process involved in establishing associative frequencies would be well established by middle childhood, so there were no age constraints on data except that the same population had to be sampled for obtaining the predictive data for any given stimulus word. In fact, the same *S*s were used, which provides some special properties because of the possibility of memory of associative responses which were collected first (sentences followed, and substitutions were last). A fairly wide range of stimuli was desirable in both the sense of grammatical class and response commonality, in order to find what the limits of usefulness of the theory might be under various conditions. The usefulness of the data as norms is constrained by these peculiarities of the kinds of *S*s and materials used.

[1] The research was supported by grant M3772(A) of the National Institutes of Health. The aid of Jean Critchfield and Letizia Ciotti-Miller is gratefully acknowledged.

METHOD

Materials

Two sets of materials were collected from two different populations. The high-commonality list consisted of nouns, verbs, and adjectives known to have very high frequency primary associates: *boy, bread, hand, night, table, black, hot, long, slow, soft, come,* and *give.* Nine buffer words were interspersed to disrupt response sets. The same order was used for all *S*s. The grammatical list was grammatically heterogeneous and consisted of a range of words systematically sampling many grammatical classes, including question words, nouns, verbs (transitive and intransitive), adjectives, adverbs, pronouns, gerunds (verbs + "ing"), and various function words that do not normally occur in isolation, such as prepositions. The list was presented in constant order, with high-commonality buffer words between each pair of stimuli to prevent the tendency to string the stimulus words into sentences by inserting content-word associates. Thirty-eight of these key words were used in the analysis, all of high Thorndike-Lorge (1944) frequency.

Procedure

The grammatical list was presented as a list of words down the middle of a series of pages. A second page, placed over the first, was used for the writing of associative responses. Instructions were: "When you hear a word, it often makes you think of another word. *Foot* might make you think of *steps* or *walk* or *hand* or *in.* There is no right answer. We just want to know what other words these bring to mind. Write just one word in each space. Write as quickly as possible."

When the associations were completed, the students were asked to go back to the first booklet, and to write sentences containing the underlined words, one for each word, and if possible not to start the sentence with the key word. The buffer words were not underlined, so the students wrote sentences for every other word on the long list. These sentences were the source of the precontext and postcontext tallies.

Finally, after completion of all the sentences, the students were asked to write four words which could substitute for the key word in each sentence. Only the first word of the substitutions was tallied. Students spent three class periods, a week apart, on the task. Most students wrote the substitutions two weeks after they had written the associative responses. Since the associative responses were in a different booklet, they were working on the sentences and substitutions. Because of differences in speed and illegible responses, and because some sentences did not suggest substitutions, *N* was not the same for associations, sentences, and substitutions, and because the task was long, decreased in that order. Associations to homonyms like *hour* or *butt* instead of *our* and *but* were edited out as noisy to the predictive study.

The high-commonality list was much shorter—only 21 words in all. The students completed all the tasks within one class period, but because the associations were on a separate piece of paper which was immediately removed, they at least did not see, though they may have remembered, their associative responses while doing the other tasks. Ideally, both the stimulus words and the associations would have been absent during the substitution task. The order of tasks was the same for both groups of *S*s.

Subjects

The high-commonality list was used in one class hour with 102 men and 65 women who were college psychology students in a public city college. The grammatical list was used with 239 boys and 146 girls in a parochial high school in a suburb.

RESULTS

Analysis of Context Frequencies

The precontext counts and the postcontext counts had to be established in such a way as to closely represent the words most likely to occur as free associations. There was no pooling of responses different in tense or number, but words which appeared to be mere spelling variants were pooled. To find what to tally in the precontext, we examined whatever was to the left of the key word. If it was a function word, as defined below, we looked further left until we could locate a lexical word. For example, in "I like *coffee*," we would tally *like*, but in "I like my *coffee* hot" we would tally *like* and *hot*, rather than *my*. However, if the stimulus word was itself a function word, we tallied contextual words in the same class and linked by a coordinate conjunction. Thus, in the sentence "*We* and they are going" *and* would not be counted, but *they* would be counted. In this case, *they* would be tallied as in the postcontext of *we*. If there was no lexical word in the context, either a function word tally or a space was noted, to give a total of 100%. Thus, in the sentences "The *coffee* was black" and "*Coffee* is good," there would be precontext tallies of function word and space, respectively. There are listed in the Appendix tables and give an indication of words which lack contiguous associations because they tend to be used at the ends of sentences or to be preceded only by function words.

Omission of Function Words

Function words were omitted from the context count because the purpose was the prediction of associative responses. Because they are infrequent in isolation, function words are poor candidates as associative responses to content words. There are, in addition, other grounds for believing that function words are not processed by hearers or speakers in the same way as content words—the ability to use telegraphic style, the higher predictability of function words, their lower intensity and audibility.

Most of the words counted as function words fit the usual definitions—modifiers like *very, quite, rather;* auxiliary verbs like *has, can, should;* subordinate conjunctions like *so, if;* coordinate conjunctions like *and, or;* prepositions like *with, from, of;* nominative pronouns like *I, we, they;* copulas like *is, was, seems;* determiners like *the, a, my, our, their;* and *not*.

Certain classes of words that commonly are considered to be function words were not so treated because we had reason to believe they did not share the same pattern as the above list. They are words which do have some tendency to occur in isolation, which can answer questions, for example. These are objective pronouns such as *him, her, them, me, us,* and pronouns unmarked for case, like *this, those, some, it, you, mine,* and *ours*.

The resulting tallies of contextual dependencies are, for reasons of this grammatical editing, slightly different from other collocational studies. These differences will account for some differences in results.

Appendix Tables

The use of the Appendix tables can be illustrated with the stimulus word *swim*. There were 382 associative responses given to *swim*, which can be scanned in the fourth column, the primary being 104 *water*, and the secondary 36 *drown*. There were 379 sentences given. In these sentences, *swim* was the final word 208 times, and the initial word 26 times. A function word only preceded *swim* (e.g., *to swim*, or *I swim*) in 111 sentences. Substitutes for *swim* were given by 302 Ss. The primary was *run*, which was given 45 times. Examination of the row for *sink* will show how to read across for a given word. *Sink* was given 29 times as an associative response. When sentences were elicited, it preceded seven times (*sink or swim*) and followed twice. It replaced *swim* in the 302 sentences only once. In examining determinants of associative responses, one can look for instances of high frequency associative responses (like *water*) which lack frequencies in other columns, or vice versa. One might expect the first three columns to be relatively independent of one another.

DISCUSSION

Are the Contexts Like Natural Collocations?

The intent of the study was to use the eliciting of sentences as a short-cut to natural collocations, which consist in the study of contexts of words from natural language texts. The problem, of course, is that the elicitation conditions for these sentences were quite different from those for natural sentences in certain systematic ways.

Subjects' strategies of sentence production. Some simple sentences were used repeatedly, presumably because any stimulus word could easily be plugged in. This procedure appeared often in the content word study with the college students because the nouns and adjectives lent themselves to repeating sentence frames, e.g., "I like X." Such strategies would have two effects that would be different from those present in natural texts. They would artificially reduce the richness of context for given words and make contexts less constraining. They inflate the frequency of a few contextual forms. On the other side, inspection of concordances taken from conversations suggests that there is a good deal of repetition in conversation, so that there is artificial, if you like, inflation of very specialized sequences as second speakers repeat or quote first speakers. The effect, unless a sample is extremely large, is to produce sampling bias in these cases where some words have inflated frequencies. Here is an example. In a collocational study by John Sinclair at the University of Birmingham,[2] I have found on random pages quite a few instances of conversational follow-through on phrases which clearly affect the frequency of the contextual forms. Examples are these, in each case adjacent:

(1) "... we have a long history of white hair ...."
   "... You say you have a long history of white hair ...."
(2) "Of course, it was a long time ago ...."
   "You say it was a long time ago. Foiled again!"
(3) "The man who kicks is either ...."
   "... the other man who kicks is the ...."
   "... in relation to the man who kicks the ball ...."
   "... be standing behind the man who kicks it ...."

The effects of all of these strings is to alter the significant collocations. For example, in 91 occurrences of *man* in the above text of 135,000 spoken words, *kicks* appeared four times in the phrase "man who kicks" and yielded a significant score for collocational frequency overall and in postcontext. That is, there is a significantly greater tendency for "kicks" to occur if "man" is present. In other words, discourse regularities may tend to increase certain collocational occurrences both because of topic and because of phrase repetitions; in elicited sentences, biases towards phrase repetitions in the frames around the stimuli seem to exist. In both cases, a sample gives information that is slightly biased relative to a theoretically infinite natural text.

Did the Prior Associative Task Influence the Sentences?

One would have expected that the prior task would have increased the probability of high frequency associates being used in sentences. The best test of this hypothesis is the presence of paradigmatic items like opposites in sentences in cases where paradigmatic associations are known to be of high frequency.[3] The occurrence of such opposites or high-commonality substitute associates in the contexts was quite rare, though clearly it would have been possible to produce them. For example, *black-white, long-short, bread-butter, him-her,* and *hers-his* cooccurred in sentences in only 3-8% of the cases.

The only basis for judgments of the effects of the associative task that we can have is comparison with the Sinclair (1969) collocational study, which was obtained from a sample of 135,000 words of spoken English, from adults. We have drawn from this study those cases he has of paired opposites, since there were only two words that appeared in both studies. We can discuss, therefore, the similarity in profiles for the words used in both studies—*long* and *give*—and the evidence of similarity in context in the collocational study and in the elicited-sentence study for antonyms.

In the associative study, the chief precontext words for *long* were *it, how, its, road,* and *has.* In the collocational sequence in England, the most frequent precontext, excluding function words, were *how, it, its, have,* and *long.* In

[2] John Sinclair of the Department of English at the University of Birmingham very generously shared his collocational data for all antonyms in his corpus, including statistical analyses of significant collocates over chance expectations based on joint probabilities, as determined by his statistical collaborator, B. Daley. In discussing this material with reference to contexts, I have normally worked with the context directly rather than the significant collocates to make possible the comparison to my data.

[3] Terminology in this field has wavered. Saporta (1959), Jenkins (1954), and Deese (1962) used the term "paradigmatic" to refer to words identical in grammatical class, all others being "syntagmatic." Deese eliminated multiclass responses. Brown and Berko (1960) used the terms "homogeneous" and "heterogeneous" in approximately the same senses, adding a behavioral criterion in which the child used the response word in a sentence. Ervin (1961) used the term "syntagmatic" for all words differing in form class from the stimulus, and "paradigmatic" for words in the same form class judged unlikely to be contextual in child usage. Those homogeneous responses which judges considered could be contextual were omitted from the totals. Entwisle *et al.* (1964) employed both the homogeneous-heterogeneous distinction of Brown and Berko, and a new one. They used judges to define a "syntactic" response as any which could reasonably occur in the context of the stimulus word, the remainder being nonsyntactic. For this reason, their estimates of "syntactic" response frequencies were much lower than those to which they might be compared in the earlier studies. The two fundamental dimensions used in all of these studies are similarity vs. difference in grammatical class, and substitution vs. context in verbal history. The two dimensions have been distinguished in this article by the use of the terms paradigmatic syntagmatic for the first, and substitution context for the second.

the associative study, the postcontext leaders were *time, way, trip,* and *you.* In the English study, the most frequent forms following *long* (excluding *ago, enough,* and some syntactically omitted forms) were *way, time, you, play, long, while,* and *distance.* The similarities between these lists are apparent. In inspecting the collocational sequences, I found that discourse strings such as those indicated earlier occurred for several of these words, but that the most frequent forms, and those also found in the American adolescents were scattered through the text and were not topic limited.

One might judge from this comparison that the two methods yield quite similar results. The topics taken up by the two groups of speakers differed somewhat—California students talked more about driving, British university adults more about music and time—but the chief effect of the elicitation task appears to make the frequency gradients steeper and to narrow the contextual variety.

For *give,* the similarity is slightly less. The predominant precontext word for the Americans was *you,* with a scattering among other forms like *going, better,* and *all.* In the English collocational study, *you* also leads—but with 6% rather than 40% of the responses. The collocates preceding in both cases are largely nominative pronouns, and only the fact that *you* is unmarked allows it to enter the tally. In the postcontext, pronouns heavily dominate in both studies. In the American teenagers, *me* and *it* led, together accounting for a third of the replies. In the English study, *you* occurred 22%, with *them, it, him,* and *me* in descending frequency. The situation of discourse, by comparison with isolated sentence production, inflates the second person over the first, an understandable situational difference. The associative responses also yield *me* far more than *you.* We do not know whether this is because of the relative privacy of written responses or because of the peculiarities of teenagers. As in the case of *long,* the differences are partly semantic; structurally there were steeper frequency gradients.

Do Elicited Substitutions Match Similar Text Forms?

In the associative study, the possibility that associates can fit into the same contexts is assessed by asking Ss to make substitutions in contexts. When those substitutes are high frequency antonyms, one must assume that the contexts at least permit the replacement of antonyms. In the collocational study, there was a significance test for highly frequent cooccurrences. Significant collocates are those whose conditional frequency, given the occurrence of the key word, is higher than its general frequency in the total text at the .01 level. In other words, the significance estimate takes into account whether occurrences are correlated, not merely what the most frequent words are in the context.

The Sinclair (1969) study allows us to see if antonyms have similar significant collocates. This is a more sensitive test than mere similarity of context, since many different words in the same form class probably have similar contexts—for instance, verbs tend to be preceded by pronouns. On the whole, the answer is negative. Each of the antonyms had from 7 to 28 significant collocates, but most of these were unique to that word. The number of overlapping context words shared by the two antonyms in each pair ranged from 1 to 4, which is hardly impressive. Since we found a very substantial tendency to replace words with their opposites in the substitution task, we must infer that the presence of antonyms as associates made them available for use in the substitution task when the sentences permitted them, and made their frequency far higher than they would be in natural discourse.

The general conclusion we make then is that the elicited sentences may not give a particularly biased estimate of word contexts for the stimulus words, but that the substitution task (probably because it is relatively more artificial) elicits far more antonyms than one would expect on the basis of actual contextual similarities of antonyms.

Some Effects of the Grammatical Editing

The collocational study involved no editing and gives statistics on text frequencies regardless of the grammatical class of the forms. Because of the intent to predict associative frequency, words unlikely to appear as associates because of their form class, namely most function words, were edited out in the context count. The result is that the precontext and postcontext columns in the tables do not, in fact, show the adjacent word but the nearest content word in most cases. Thus, the tables are only useable in situations where this editing will not influence the results seriously.

There are a number of instances where this editing has apparently impaired even the relation to associates. For example, a common associate and a common postcontext word with *long* is *ago,* which was edited out of the context tally. Had the modifier been *very,* no problem would have existed, but modifiers which follow the head, such as *ago* and *enough,* are frequent associates. Indeed, we found bound morphemes occasionally as associates, suggesting that some people interpret the task not as giving a new independent word but as creating a new unit out of the stimulus word and something added.

Other examples where the associates clearly show contextual influence, but the editing destroyed the evidence in the contexts, are *because-of, has-not, here-is, it-is, it-was,* and *we-are.* No provision was made in our scoring for cases like *for-give* and *table-cloth,* in which the associate is used to form a larger unit.

Statistical Relation of Context, Substitutes, and Associations

The statistical relations among the four columns in the Appendix tables are discussed at length in Ervin (1963) and summarized in Tables 1-3. Table 1 shows that there is a considerable difference in the frequency of different grammatical classes in isolation, a factor that presumably alters the probability of words in these classes in the isolated response required in word association. Indeed, in connected discourse, content words comprise 56% of the text, whereas in single-word utterances in the same oral text, they comprised 98% of the total, exclusive of interjections. In connected discourse, nouns, verbs, indefinite pronouns, determiners, prepositions, auxiliaries, nominative pronouns, and copulas are most frequent, with adjectives and adverbs relatively infrequent. It can be seen in Table 1 that the associative probabilities of these different classes, as summarized from the response tables in the Appendix, are very different, depending on the type of stimulus word.

Because of their ambiguity, responses to question words and to objective and indefinite pronouns were not included in the associative probability count in Table 1. In the association tests, the percentages of content-word responses were 97% for content-word stimuli, 89% for question words, 85% for function words, and 69% for indefinite and objective pronouns, when paradigmatic responses (in the same form class as the stimulus word) were omitted.

TABLE 1   *Frequency of Grammatical Classes in Discourse and in Associations*

Response Class	Single-word Utterances	Associative probability[a]	
		Function word stimulus	Content word stimulus
Content words			
Question word	96	60	7
Noun	44	239	547
Adverb	27	72	50
Adjective	26	149	192
Verb	18	37	129
Indefinite pronoun	10	149	11
Proper Name	9	7	11
Number	8	13	–
Gerund or participle	2	3	11
Objective Pronoun	2	125	15
Function Words			
Modifier	2	–	4
Auxiliary Verb	1	7	1
Subordinate conjunction	1	11	–
Coordinate conjunction	–	11	–
Preposition	–	23	17
Nominative pronoun	–	24	2
Copulas	–	31	–
Determiner	–	18	1
not	–	17	1

[a]Frequencies per thousand responses excluding paradigmatic associations. For each class, averages were taken over words in remaining grammatical classes. Figures have been adjusted to base of 1000. Question words, and objective and indefinite pronouns, were excluded from the stimulus list.

The figures on Table 2 are obtained from a correlational study in which the associative frequency was to be predicted from the frequencies of words used in substitution and context. There is no appropriate statistical model for predictions in cases in which there is a logically necessary negative relation between determinants. Since it would be impossible for all determinant values to be high for a given item, the multiple correlation provides a very rough measure of success in prediction. The entries for the correlations are the frequencies in the Appendix tables treated as the scores of individuals. The individuals are the response words listed and the columns are the different tests. The beta weights for this multiple correlation are shown in Table 2, and they give a rough indication of the extent to which each of the variables is related to associative frequency.

TABLE 2 *Correlations with Associative Frequency*[a]

Stimulus word	N^c	Simple correlations			Beta coefficients[b]			Multiple R
		Substi-tution	Context		Substi-tution	Context		
			Pre	Post		Pre	Post	
And	259	.54	−.15	−.07	.54	−	−	.54
Because	151	.22	−.10	.14	.24	−	.17	.28
Black	144	.42	.24	.35	.44	.21	.29	.58
Boy	156	.64	−.12	−.03	.64	−	−	.64
Bread	167	.34	.09	.06	.40	.20	−	.40
Coffee	249	.14	.20	.43	.22	.21	.43	.51
Come	153	.43	−.20	.21	.46	−	.27	.51
Eat	247	.11	−.09	.19	.15	−	.22	.25
For	296	.28	−.00	.29	.33	−	.34	.44
From	228	.22	.14	.10	.26	.17	.17	.32
Game	322	.13	.35	.07	.16	.36	−	.39
Give	151	.23	−.13	.41	.32	−	.47	.52
Hand	194	.43	−.12	−.21	.43	−	−	.44
Has	221	.30	−.03	.07	.33	−	.14	.33
Hers	91	.72	.03	.24	.72	−	−	.72
Him	220	.42	−.12	.06	.42	−	−	.42
Hot	142	.36	.12	.07	.41	.20	−	.41
How	122	.43	−.19	.23	.41	−	.18	.47
If	162	.32	.05	.29	.33	−	.30	.45
It	229	.28	−.07	−.28	.28	−	−	.28
Long	174	.39	−.11	.17	.40	−	.18	.42
Meat	235	.18	.06	.05	.18	−	−	.18
My	237	.31	−.10	.04	.31	−	−	.31
Night	139	.40	.23	.19	.47	.22	.26	.54
Of	295	.42	.02	.13	.42	−	−	.42
Often	283	.50	−.24	−.25	.50	−	−	.50
Or	203	.42	−.16	−.11	.42	−	−	.42
Our	110	.55	−.12	−.07	.55	−	−	.55
Ours	202	.61	.02	.03	.61	−	−	.61
Quite	243	.30	−.17	.04	.30	−	−	.30
Reading	224	.10	−.08	.31	.15	−	.33	.35
Relax	245	.09	−.01	−.01	−	−	−	−
See	185	.02	.04	.12	−	−	−	−
Slow	167	.39	.02	.01	.39	−	−	.39
Soft	172	.31	.13	.25	.37	.22	.22	.45
Suddenly	239	.33	−.05	−.19	.33	−	−	.33
Swim	248	.08	−.10	.11	−	−	−	−
Table	186	.20	.05	.01	.20	−	−	.20
The	274	.26	.04	.08	.28	−	.12	.28
They	251	.39	−.00	−.13	.39	−	−	.39
Today	225	.61	−.16	.22	.59	−	.12	.62
Us	233	.42	−.19	−.18	.42	−	−	.42
Very	278	.27	−.25	.44	.29	−	.45	.53
Walk	245	.37	−.09	.01	.37	−	−	.37

TABLE 2 *(continued)*

Stimulus word	N^c	Simple correlations			Beta coefficients[b]			
		Substi-tution	Context		Substi-tution	Context		Multiple R
			Pre	Post		Pre	Post	
Washing	282	.27	−.11	.30	.29	−	.32	.41
We	171	.38	−.04	−.18	.38	−	−	.38
What	150	.48	.01	.17	.48	−	−	.48
Which	188	.46	.14	.10	.46	−	−	.46
Working	215	.03	−.18	.12	−	−	−	−
Write	274	.09	−.16	.07	−	−	−	−

[a]All variables were transformed to log $(x + 1)$. Because of the truncated distribution on all variables, the correlations must be considered crude estimates of relationship. The solution employed by Howes (1957) of extrapolating from a fractile is not possible for these data.

[b]Beta coefficients are given only for variables contributing a positive correlation to the multiple R, above the .05 level. Negatively related variables were edited out in the computer program.

[c]N is the number of different response words.

Words preceding the stimulus word were rarely frequent associates, as can be seen from the low precontext correlations and beta weights in Table 2 and by inspection of the Appendix tables. The negative correlations may arise from the predominance in precontexts of function words, like auxiliaries and nominative pronouns, which were infrequent associates. The only precontext that is a common associate is the adjective-noun, noun-adjective association. This is a case where English permits the adjective to follow the noun (e.g., "I like my coffee hot"), and indeed transformational grammar argues that the prenominal adjective is transformationally derived from a predicate adjective like "The coffee is hot."

There were four kinds of cases where postcontext significantly correlates with associative frequency, the noun-adjective, the instransitive verb and locative, the transitive verb and the object, and the preposition or the modifier (*very*) and its head. The Appendix tables clearly explicate the results in Table 2.

For all stimulus words except verbs and gerunds ("ing" verbs) there was a significant positive relation between association and substitution: i.e., use of semantically and grammatically paradigmatic words as associates. An effort to find out why some words elicited contextual associates and others substitutes was based on the assumption that contextual variety would favor paradigmatic associates. Table 3 includes three types of variables and their interrelations. The first is the steepness of the rank-frequency slope for substitution and context for a given stimulus word. This is assessed by the proportion giving the primary substitute, the primary and the secondary combined, and so on. This measure of variety or commonality is called the slope. The other two are measures of the tendency of the stimulus to elicit substitute or contextual associates. The first such measure is the simple correlation between associative frequency and substitution frequency, from column two of Table 2, and so on. When this correlation is high, many responses can be classed as substitutes. The third measure was obtained by examining the five most frequent associative responses for the stimulus. For each of these, it was possible from the Appendix tables to determine if the word occurred more often as a substitute or as a context. If the former, it was classed as a substitution-derived associate. These two measures of the tendency to elicit substitute or contextual associates are independent. If the most frequent associates are substitutions, the second measure will be high but not necessarily the first, which depends on the total list of associative responses.

The results indicate that where there is high commonality in substitutions, responses tend to be paradigmatic. Where there is a high primary in the precontext, or high commonality in the five most common postcontexts, the responses tend to be syntagmatic. An even better prediction of syntagmatic scores can be made (the multiple R) if a flat rank-frequency slope for substitutions occurs along with high commonality for contexts, or if both preceding and following contexts are considered at once. However one measures syntagmatic vs. paradigmatic response preferences, the importance of contextual variety stands out. Postcontext words show up more often than precontexts both as high commonality associates and as frequent associates across the whole associative response list. Indeed, precontexts seem to influence associative responses only if they also appear in postcontext lists, as in the case of adjective contexts for nouns.

TABLE 3 *Relation of Slope of Predictors to Correlation with Associative Frequency and to Number of Paradigmatic and Syntagmatic Associates*

Slope (% responses)	Correlation with assoc. freq. [a]			No. first 5 assoc.		
	Subst.	Pre	Post	Subst.[b]	Pre	Post
1st Subst.	.52	−.06	.14	.04	.12	.01
1st 2 Subst.	.66	−.13	−.21	.10	−.18	−.02
1st 5 Subst.	.74[c]	−.20	−.21	.16	−.20	.03
1st Pre	−.02	−.08	.41[c]	−.03	−.12	.18[c]
1st 2 Pre	−.02	−.01	.38	−.02	−.02	.14
1st 5 Pre	.07	.04	.30	.01	.01	.07
1st Post	−.12	−.01	.33	−.20	−.09	.42
1st 2 Post	−.11	−.04	.38	−.27	−.10	.50
1st 5 Post	−.11	−.08	.40[c]	−.33[c]	−.11	.58[c]
Multiple R	.74	−	.60	−.33	−	.63

[a]Simple correlations in Table 2 transformed to z.

[b]Those associative responses here called substitution associates were those among the five most frequent associates which had higher frequency as substitutes than in contexts.

[c]Simple correlations of variables contributing to the multiple correlation beyond the .05 level.

Influence of Grammatical Class

Inspection of Tables 1 and 2 and of the Appendix tables shows very clearly that grammatical classes differ greatly in their associative properties. The same predictive formula could not be used to relate the four columns in the Appendix tables, when the multiple correlations of Table 2 were computed.

There are two obvious differences between classes within the system employed here. One is that some classes are closed. Pronouns provide an example. The system of personal pronouns is a small highly structured set of few alternatives in contrast to the great variety possible for nouns. A consequence of these limitations is that the substitution and association slopes tend to be very steep. The steepest substitution slopes were those for *hers, ours, us,* and *we.* The associative slopes were also steep for these words.

A second difference lies in the type and variety of verbal contexts. It can be seen in Table 1 that nouns and adjectives were the most frequent associations for all stimuli. Words which occur before or after nouns and adjectives are therefore more likely, other things being equal, to elicit contextual responses.

A clear example is provided by the correlation of associative frequencies with preceding contexts in Table 2. For most classes, the primary antecedent in the Appendix tables is a verb or uninflected pronoun. Nouns are commonly preceded by nouns and adjectives as well as adverbs; adjectives by nouns. Thus for these classes, preceding context is a significant determinant; for the others, it is not.

Verbs were different from other classes in Table 2 in that for half of them there was no relation between either substitution or context and associative responses. More often than any other grammatical class, verbs commonly elicited words as associates which appeared only once or never on the other lists in the Appendix tables: (the numbers in parentheses indicate associative frequencies) *swim-water* (104), *walk-feet* (15), *relax-chair* (18), *eat-fat* (14), *see-blind* (29), *see-eye* (19), *write-paper* (25), *write-pen* (58), and *write-pencil* (23). The response *pen* or *pencil* proved to be correlated with the writing implement employed. It is possible that a sample of natural speech would show these responses to be more common than the experimentally produced sentences suggest. The very fact that these words were not employed for the sentences in the experiment, however, raises the question of the difference between the verbs and the other classes. Recent linguistic analyses (Fillmore, 1968) make the verb the center semantically of the sentence. It has also been argued that English verbs tend to include manner or locational information in the verb—e.g., *swim* means move oneself in water, *walk* means move oneself slowly with feet, so that in some sense both *water* and *feet* are contained in the verb. Another peculiarity of verbs is that the rank-frequency slope for substitution was flatter (for all but *come*) than for any words except *meat* and *bread*. The precontexts were largely pronouns, and hence relatively poor candidates for association. All of these features seem to bear on the relative unpredictability of association to verbs.

All of the adjectives employed as stimuli were high frequency words with common antonyms. For all, the correlation of substitution and association was about the same—between .37 and .44. Adjectives are commonly either preceded or followed by nouns—the best candidate for association. They may be adjacent to other adjectives. For both reasons, it would be expected that contextual associates might be common. This was indeed the case.

Although it is a common assumption that nouns usually follow adjectives in English, because of its constituent structure, this was not the case in the sentences produced here. If only primary contextual responses are considered, when nouns were the stimulus words for sentence construction, noun-adjective surpassed adjective-noun cases three to one, but with adjective stimuli, adjective-noun surpassed noun-adjective five to four.

Particular adjectives differed in the frequency with which nouns tended to precede or to follow. *Car, night,* and *cat* preceded *black* more often than they followed, *pillow* and *bed* more often preceded than followed *soft,* and *water* and *coffee* preceded *hot.* On the other hand, *long* more often was followed by the noun it modified. Another difference between adjectives was that some were more often adjacent to other adjectives. *Soft* was most often adjacent; 12% of the postcontexts were adjectives. For other words, the frequency was 5% or less. In Sinclair's (1969) text, *long* was followed by itself several times. The word *slow* is not included here as an adjective, since its contexts revealed it to be syntactically ambiguous—an adjective, verb, or adverb.

Personal pronouns and pronoun determiners represent the joint occurrence of a limited class size and a tight semantic system. Determiners tended to elicit as associates indefinite pronouns which could substitute for the determiner and noun—e.g., *my-mine, my-yours.* Nominative pronouns elicited objective pronouns as associates— *we-us.* In addition to these grammatical determinants, pronoun associates were structured by person, number, and sex, to correspond to the stimulus, e.g., *we-us, -they, -you.* To the extent that the association between personal pronouns occurred despite functional class, they represented unpredicted associations. Thus, the associate *we-us* or *my-mine* would be anticipated on the basis of neither substitution nor context. These changes of class most often represented a preference for context- rather than function-word responses. The most common associate to *my* is not *your* but *yours. Yours, ours,* and *theirs* were even offered as substitutes for *my* and *our,* suggesting both that it is hard to produce isolated determiners and that the tendency is to substitute for the larger noun phrase of which *my* and *our* are parts, as in the parallel construction *my book and ours.*

Coordinate conjunctions most often produced substitution associates; subordinate conjunctions also produced contextual associates. These differences were reflected in the slopes of the rank-frequency curves. The substitution slope was steeper and the postcontext slope shallower for the coordinate than for the subordinate conjunctions.

Contextual Associations

Correlations with context were variable. There were two obvious reasons: differences in the frequency of occurrence of the stimulus word in final or initial position in sentences, which limits the strength of contextual learning; and variations in the frequency of occurrence adjacent to words of low frequency in isolation. The words most commonly in final position (most often followed by "space") were *him, hers, ours, us,* and *hot.* For none of these was postcontext a determinant of associative strength.

Adjacent form class, as we have already indicated, is very important. Frequently, a common contextual verb or pronoun did not appear as an associate. In 25% of the sentences elicited by *quite,* it was preceded by *it,* but *it* was never given as an associate. *Eat* was followed by *it* more often than by *food,* but *food* was the primary associate. On the whole, nouns were preferred over pronouns, and verbs were infrequent as associates.[4]

Is contextual determination necessarily asymmetrical? From evidence in the Navaho language, where precontext associates were strong, we have argued elsewhere (Ervin & Landar, 1961) that the greater strength of postcontexts merely reflects English grammatical structure. The most common antecedent classes for all the stimuli except nouns and adjectives were verbs and pronouns, which have generally low probabilities as associates. The syntactic patterns of English generally place function words or modifiers before the head of a constituent. Thus, we have modifier-adverb, modifier-adjective, determiner-noun, auxiliary-verb, preposition-noun, question-word-sentence, conjunction-clause, and adjective-noun. Adjectives and adverbs have more flexibility of location, perhaps because of their status as content words. That is, adverbs both precede and follow verbs, and adjectives both precede and follow (in descriptive constructions) nouns.

[4] The low frequency of *it* in association illustrates the weakness of the estimation of frequencies in isolation by class, as shown in Table 1, rather than by word. Though *it* and *you* were both judged to be in the class of indefinite pronouns, *you* is more common that *it* both in single-word utterances and in associative responses.

This pervasive order may be described in many ways. It is reflected in the distribution of redundancy and information in the English sentence. It is not clear whether this property of English structure affects associations merely through the differentials in base associative probabilities for different classes, or whether it influences the set of subjects toward the task of association. At any rate, we cannot assume that this particular asymmetry is a general property in associative behavior.

Substitution Associations

The most common form of paradigmatic response is the antonym. Deese (1962) found a correlation of .89 between the Thorndike-Lorge frequency of an adjective and the frequency of antonym associates. Are antonym associations based on substitution, context, or both? For many stimuli, a word of very high frequency as a substitute also appeared on the context list, but not necessarily often. There were many antonym primaries that were rare or absent in contexts: *hot-cold, slow-fast, boy-girl, night-day, hand-foot,* and *soft-hard.* In 17 cases of antonym associative primaries, for all but one (*for-against*) the antonym was the primary substitute as well. Thus, it appears that in the majority of cases, substitution rather than context is significant in antonym associations.

The words which had both the lowest variety in substitutions and the highest correlations of substitution and association had two properties. One of these properties was a tightly structured semantic system. *Boy* is an example—presumably kin terms also would be. This system appears in the substitutes *girl, man, child,* and *male,* which reflect the sex-age dimensions signalled by the word. Adjectives were less systematic beyond the antonyms. Another property was a closed grammatical class. Instances included function words, question words, and pronouns. Because of the limited class size, the substitutions were highly concentrated. In such cases, the size of the relation between substitution and association depended on the base associative frequency of the class. Personal pronouns represented an intersection of these two properties and yielded the highest correlations of substitution and associative frequency.

We found that the number of common substitution associates was related to variety of content. When the strength of contextual determinants is spread out over a variety of possibilities, substitution responses become possible. This may be one reason why children and uneducated adults have fewer paradigmatic responses (Brown & Berko, 1960; Ervin, 1961; Rosenzweig, 1964; Rosenzweig & Menahem, 1962; Entwisle, Forsyth, & Muuss, 1964); contextual variety may be increased by education, and it may be related, as Bernstein's (1964) work suggests, to social class.

We have no evidence on contextual variety in the speech environment, or on skill in anticipation, which would permit testing of the various explanations for group or individual differences. Carroll (1962) has noted that there is a tendency to give contrastive responses which is independent of preferences for high-commonality responses, and there appear to be stable individual preferences for substitution or contextual associations in well-educated adults (Donner, 1964).

Additional Factors

In this analysis, we have sought to account for associative frequency on the basis of three factors alone. Inspection of the cases deviating markedly from prediction reveal some additional sources of variation in association. One of these, the difference in the response frequency of various grammatical classes, has already been considered.

While it is known that the influence of sound similarity on association decreases with age, there were clear indications that such similarities could enhance associative strength. There were several types in the data. One was declension: *give-gave, come-came, has-had, eat-ate, see-saw,* and *swim-swam.* Alliteration was common in high frequency associates: *him-her, for-from, hers-his, bread-butter, black-blue, coffee-cup, coffee-cream, it-is, long-length, my-me, what-why, which-what,* and *write-read.* Rhymes were *how-now, meat-eat, night-light, or-nor, walk-talk, which-witch, slow-go,* and *see-me.* In all of these cases, the predicted associative frequency was already high to begin with. In some cases, associative responses appeared neither as substitutes nor as contexts, so the sole basis for association was sound: *or-for, -are, -bore, -ore, -sore, -door, -oor, -oar, -our,* and *-whore.* Such cases appeared more often for the function words and for monosyllables. For the word *quite,* used correctly in sentences, the influence of *quiet* appeared in three of the four most frequent associations: *loud, very, quiet,* and *noisy.*

Summary of Results on Associative Genesis

We have discussed one use for the norms given here: the establishment of some estimates of previous verbal input as a basis for word association frequencies. We found some evidence that elicited sentences correspond roughly to natural sentences, at least that they are not heavily influenced by associative processes themselves. That would necessarily be the interpretation if elicited sentences contained many paradigmatic primary associates, but they do not. On the other hand, the method of eliciting substitutes does not appear to give as close a correspondence to replacement probabilities in natural discourse. In this case, the task seems to magnify the number of associative responses over what would appear in natural discourse, especially as judged from antonyms.

Associative response lists are heterogeneous in genesis, of course. Some come in part from sound correspondences, some apparently come from collocations in discourse. But where do antonyms and other high-commonality paradigmatic responses originate? This is not the place to develop a theory of such associations, but the recent developments in semantic theory (e.g., Katz & Fodor, 1963) and in studies of processing of sentences and of structures of lexical storage (e.g., Brown & McNeill, 1966; Deese, 1965) give some clues. Processing models imply that the lexicon has to be stored with minimal phonological identifying features, syntactic features (e.g., count noun), and contrastive or structurally organized semantic features (male, young) or other semantic relations to account for patterns of retrieval. The substitution tasks apparently obliges Ss to hunt for items most alike in syntactic and contrastive features. Since there is reason to believe that not all parts of the lexicon are structured in the same way—not all yield taxonomic contrastive hierarchies, for instance—it is likely that somewhat different developmental histories will be necessary in these cases (Kay, 1966). We can already see, from this study, that differences in grammatical form class have a major impact on associative structure, in large part due to collocational effects which are quite easily identified.

Other Uses for the Norms

Associative relations can be viewed as one way of assessing relations between words. Because of the ease of obtaining these performances, and because they have worked, psychologists have tended to lean heavily on measures of associative strength in studies employing words out of discourse context. The major point of this material is to indicate that the lexicon is structured in many ways, and that there are sentence-based devices for obtaining measures of relations between lexical items. Until we have better theories of processing of language, we have no reason to believe that a composite product such as an association is necessarily the best measure to use. We have evidence here that associative strength in fact is a very poor device for prediction of sequences in discourse, which is, after all, what we do with words most of the time. These norms provide three other sources of prediction of relations between words, which may be more appropriate for prediction of kinds of tasks in which there is verbal context than are associative norms. We can assume that as psychologists concern themselves increasingly with sentence processing, and with units of language larger than the word, they will find it increasingly desirable to know properties of words other than associative strength alone. These norms will provide aid for such studies.

REFERENCES

Bernstein, B. (1964). Elaborated and restricted codes: their social origins and some consequences. In J. J. Gumperz & D. Hymes (Ed.), The ethnography of communication. *American Anthropologist* 66, (No. 6, pt. 2), 55-69.

Brown, R. W., & Berko, J. (1960). Word association and the acquisition of grammar. *Child Development* 31, 1-14.

Brown, R. W., & McNeill, D. (1966). The tip of the tongue phenomenon. *Journal of Verbal Learning and Verbal Behavior* 5, 325-337.

Carroll, J. B., Kjeldergaard, P. M., & Carton, A. S. (1962). Number of opposites vs. number of primaries as a response measure in free association tests. *Journal of Verbal Learning and Verbal Behavior* 1, 22-30.

Deese, J. (1962). Form class and the determinants of association. *Journal of Verbal Learning and Verbal Behavior* 1, 79-84.

Deese, J. (1965). *The structure of associations in language and thought.* Baltimore: Johns Hopkins University Press.

Donner, R. A. (1964). Individual differences and paradigmatic word associations. Unpublished Ph.D. dissertation, University of California.

Entwisle, D. R., Forsyth, D. F., & Muuss, R. (1964). The syntactic-paradigmatic shift in children's word associations. *Journal of Verbal Learning and Verbal Behavior* 3, 19-29.

Ervin, S.M. (1961). Changes with age in the verbal determinants of word-association. *American Journal of Psychology* 74, 361-372.

Ervin, S. M. (1963). Correlates of associative frequency. *Journal of Verbal Learning and Verbal Behavior* 1, 422-431.

Ervin, S.M., & Landar, H. (1961). Navaho word-associations. *American Journal of Psychology* **76**, 49-57.

Fillmore, C. (1968). The case for case. In E. Bach & R. T. Harms (Eds.), *Universals in linguistic theory*. New York: Holt, Rinehart, & Winston, pp. 1-90.

Howes, D. (1957). On the relation between the probability of a word as an association and in general linguistic usage. *Journal of Abnormal and Social Psychology* **54**, 75-85.

Jenkins, J. J. (1954). In C. E. Osgood & T. A. Sebeok (Eds.), Psycholinguistics. *Supplement, Journal of Abnormal and Social Psychology* **52**, 114-116.

Katz, J. J., & Fodor, J. A. (1963). The structure of a semantic theory. *Language* **39**, 170-210.

Kay, P. (1966). Discussion of Colby's paper. *Current Anthropology* **7**, 20-23.

McNeill, D. (1963). The origin of associations within the same grammatical class. *Journal of Verbal Learning and Verbal Behavior* **2**, 250-262.

Rosenzweig, M. R. (1964). Word associations of French workmen: comparisons with associations of French students and American workmen and students. *Journal of Verbal Learning and Verbal Behavior* **3**, 57-69.

Rosenzweig, M. R., & Menahem, R. (1962). Age, sexe et niveau d'instruction comme facteurs determinants dans les associations de mots. *Année Psychologique* **62**, 45-61.

Saporta, S. (1959). In J. J. Jenkins (Ed.), *Associative processes in verbal behavior: a report of the Minnesota Conference*. Minneapolis: University of Minnesota, Department of Psychology.

Sinclair, John (1969). Personal communication.

Thorndike, E. L., & Lorge, I. (1944). *The teacher's word book of 30,000 words*. New York: Bureau of Publications, Teachers College, Columbia University.

1 And

No.	Response	Subst.	Pre	Post	Assoc.
1.	A	–	1	–	3
2.	add	–	–	–	1
3.	addition	–	–	–	2
4.	again	–	1	1	4
5.	all	–	–	2	1
6.	also	3	–	–	29
7.	am	–	–	–	1
8.	Andrew	–	–	–	1
9.	Ann	–	–	–	1
10.	another	–	–	–	3
11.	as well as	2	–	–	–
12.	atque	–	–	–	1
13.	away	–	–	–	1
14.	B	–	–	1	–
15.	babies	–	–	–	1
16.	bad	–	–	1	–
17.	ball	–	–	1	–
18.	band	–	–	–	1
19.	bat	–	1	–	–
20.	because	2	–	–	4
21.	beer	–	1	–	–
22.	before	1	–	–	–
23.	best	1	–	–	–
24.	big	–	2	–	–
25.	Bill	–	4	3	–
26.	blue	–	1	1	–
27.	Bob	–	1	–	–
28.	both	–	–	–	1
29.	boy	–	6	1	1
30.	boys	–	2	–	–
31.	busy	–	–	–	1
32.	but	51	–	–	37
33.	but not	3	–	–	–
34.	called	1	–	–	–
35.	came	–	5	1	–
36.	camping	–	–	1	–
37.	car	–	1	–	–
38.	cat	–	3	1	–
39.	cats	–	1	1	–
40.	chair	–	–	1	–
41.	cherish	–	–	1	–
42.	choked	–	–	1	–
43.	Chris	–	1	–	–
44.	cloth	–	1	–	–
45.	coffee	–	1	2	–
46.	come	–	9	–	–
47.	compound	–	–	–	1
48.	congratulated	–	–	1	–
49.	conjunction	–	–	1	8
50.	coordination	–	–	–	1
51.	cream	–	1	–	–
52.	creed	–	–	1	–
53.	Dan	–	–	–	1
54.	dance	–	–	2	–
55.	Dave	–	–	1	–
56.	Dick	–	1	1	–
57.	dig	1	–	–	–
58.	dog	–	2	5	1
59.	dogs	–	1	1	–
60.	Donna	–	1	–	–
61.	Dora	–	–	1	–
62.	eat	–	1	–	–
63.	eggs	–	–	1	–
64.	either	–	–	–	1
65.	El Cartis	–	–	1	–
66.	end	–	–	–	2
67.	England	–	1	–	–
68.	English	–	–	1	–
69.	et	–	–	–	3
70.	etch	–	–	–	1
71.	fashion	–	–	1	–
72.	fat	1	–	–	–
73.	father	–	–	3	–
74.	fine	–	1	–	–

1 And (contd)

No.	Response	Subst.	Pre	Post	Assoc.
75.	fly	–	–	1	–
76.	food	–	1	1	–
77.	foolish	–	–	1	–
78.	for	2	–	–	4
79.	foreve.	–	–	1	–
80.	forget	–	–	1	–
81.	France	–	–	1	–
82.	French	–	1	–	–
83.	from	1	–	–	–
84.	fruit	–	–	1	–
85.	Gert	–	1	–	–
86.	get	–	–	1	–
87.	get up	–	–	1	–
88.	girl	–	1	5	–
89.	girls	–	–	2	–
90.	go	–	2	5	3
91.	good	–	1	1	–
92.	grandpa	–	1	–	–
93.	green	1	–	–	–
94.	guess	–	–	–	1
95.	had	–	–	1	–
96.	ham	–	1	–	–
97.	hamburger	–	–	1	–
98.	hands	–	–	1	–
99.	happy	–	1	–	–
100.	hard	–	1	–	–
101.	Harry	–	–	1	–
102.	hat	–	1	1	–
103.	he	–	–	–	1
104.	her	–	–	4	1
105.	here	–	1	–	–
106.	hiking	–	1	–	–
107.	him	–	4	2	–
108.	Hinky	–	–	1	–
109.	his	–	1	–	–
110.	history	–	1	–	–
111.	hit	1	–	–	–
112.	horse	–	3	–	–
113.	hot dogs	–	–	1	–
114.	how	–	1	2	1
115.	I	–	–	–	2
116.	if	1	–	–	6
117.	include	–	–	–	1
118.	iron	–	1	–	–
119.	is	–	–	–	1
120.	it	–	–	–	2
121.	J	–	–	1	–
122.	Jack	–	3	1	–
123.	Jane	–	2	4	–
124.	Jeanie	–	–	1	–
125.	Jerry	–	–	1	–
126.	Jill	–	–	1	–
127.	Jim	–	2	4	–
128.	Jo	–	1	–	–
129.	Joan	–	2	1	–
130.	Joe	–	2	–	–
131.	John	–	6	–	–
132.	jump	–	1	1	–
133.	kill	–	–	1	–
134.	laughed	–	1	–	–
135.	learn	–	–	1	–
136.	left	–	1	3	–
137.	like	1	–	–	–
138.	live	–	–	1	–
139.	lives	–	1	–	–
140.	lookout	–	–	1	–
141.	love	–	2	–	–
142.	Marcia	–	–	1	–
143.	Mart	1	–	–	–
144.	Mary	–	2	2	–
145.	Maybe	1	–	–	–
146.	me	–	4	8	1
147.	meat	–	1	–	–
148.	Michael	–	1	–	–

1 And (contd)

No.	Response	Subst.	Pre	Post	Assoc.
149.	mine	–	–	1	–
150.	minus	1	–	–	–
151.	mom	–	1	–	–
152.	more	–	–	–	4
153.	more than one	–	–	–	1
154.	mother	–	4	–	–
155.	my	–	–	–	1
156.	Nancy	–	1	1	–
157.	needles	–	1	–	–
158.	nice	–	1	–	–
159.	Nina	–	–	1	–
160.	nor	3	–	–	–
161.	not	2	–	–	3
162.	not is	1	–	–	–
163.	now	1	–	2	5
164.	of	–	–	–	1
165.	of course	–	–	–	1
166.	on	–	–	–	2
167.	one	–	2	–	–
168.	or	59	–	–	34
169.	or milk	1	–	–	–
170.	orchestra	–	–	–	1
171.	other	–	–	–	1
172.	Peg	–	1	–	–
173.	pen	–	–	–	1
174.	pins	–	–	1	–
175.	plus	6	–	–	7
176.	potato chips	–	1	–	–
177.	preposition	–	–	–	1
178.	pretty	–	–	1	–
179.	rabbit	1	–	–	–
180.	race	–	1	–	–
181.	reason	–	1	–	1
182.	red	–	1	1	–
183.	returned	–	–	1	–
184.	ride	–	2	–	–
185.	Ron	–	–	1	–
186.	run	–	2	1	–
187.	Russ	–	1	–	–
188.	sad	–	–	1	–
189.	sand	–	–	–	1
190.	saw	–	–	1	–
191.	scarf	–	1	–	–
192.	score	–	2	–	–
193.	see	–	1	2	–
194.	series	–	–	–	1
195.	she	–	–	–	2
196.	Shirley	–	1	–	–
197.	shoes	–	–	1	–
198.	short	–	–	1	–
199.	show	–	1	–	–
200.	sick	–	2	–	–
201.	sing	–	1	–	–
202.	sister	–	1	–	–
203.	skip	–	–	1	–
204.	sleep	–	–	1	–
205.	sleet	–	–	1	–
206.	small	–	–	1	–
207.	so	2	2	2	9
208.	steel	–	–	1	–
209.	strike	–	1	–	–
210.	Sue	–	–	1	–
211.	Suzie	–	1	–	–
212.	swam	–	1	1	–
213.	tall	–	1	1	–
214.	tea	–	1	1	–
215.	tell	–	–	1	–
216.	terrible	–	1	–	–
217.	than	–	–	–	1
218.	that	–	–	6	–
219.	the	1	–	–	3
220.	them	–	1	1	2
221.	then	4	–	6	10
222.	there	–	–	–	1
223.	they	–	–	–	7
224.	this	–	6	–	2
225.	to	6	–	–	1
226.	together	–	1	–	1

1 And (contd)

No.	Response	Subst.	Pre	Post	Assoc.
227.	Tom	–	4	–	–
228.	too	–	–	–	1
229.	tree	–	–	–	1
230.	two	–	–	1	2
231.	Tyrone	–	1	–	–
232.	und	1	–	–	–
233.	unhappy	–	–	1	–
234.	us	–	1	–	–
235.	vase	–	1	–	–
236.	wake up	–	1	–	–
237.	walked	–	1	–	–
238.	war	–	–	1	–
239.	way	–	1	–	–
240.	we	–	–	–	1
241.	went	–	4	1	–
242.	what	–	–	3	6
243.	when	2	–	–	–
244.	where	–	–	1	–
245.	why	1	–	2	2
246.	will	1	–	–	–
247.	wine	–	–	1	–
248.	with	4	–	–	1
249.	write	–	1	–	–
250.	yes	1	–	–	–
251.	you	1	28	5	4
252.	young	–	1	–	–
253.	3	–	1	–	–
254.	4	–	–	1	–
255.	7	–	–	2	–
256.	8:00	–	1	–	–
257.	10	–	–	–	1

		Subst.	Pre	Post	Assoc.
Function Words		–	43	93	–
Space		–	24	–	–
N		174	265	265	261

2 Because

No.	Response	Subst.	Pre	Post	Assoc.
1.	about	1	–	–	–
2.	all	–	3	–	–
3.	all right	1	–	–	1
4.	also	–	–	–	2
5.	and	1	–	–	–
6.	answer	–	1	1	5
7.	as	3	–	–	–
8.	ate	–	1	–	–
9.	be	–	1	–	–
10.	became	–	–	–	2
11.	before	1	–	–	1
12.	began	–	–	–	1
13.	beside	–	–	–	1
14.	between	1	–	–	–
15.	boat	–	–	–	1
16.	but	1	–	–	1
17.	came	–	4	–	1
18.	cold	–	–	1	–
19.	come	–	3	–	–
20.	command	–	–	–	1
21.	cum	–	–	–	1
22.	dead	–	1	–	–
23.	denn	1	–	–	1
24.	did	–	–	–	1
25.	died	–	3	–	–
26.	don't know	–	–	–	1
27.	dumb	–	1	–	–
28.	early	–	1	–	–
29.	eat	–	1	–	–
30.	economic	–	–	1	–
31.	effect	1	–	–	–
32.	exclamation	–	–	–	1
33.	excuse	–	–	–	1
34.	excuses	–	–	–	6

397

2 Because (contd)

No.	Response	Subst.	Pre	Post	Assoc.
35.	fact	-	-	1	-
36.	failure	-	1	-	-
37.	fell	-	1	-	-
38.	flunked	-	1	-	-
39.	for	9	-	-	12
40.	forced	-	-	-	1
41.	Frankie Laine	-	-	-	1
42.	fun	-	-	-	1
43.	go	-	9	-	-
44.	going	-	1	-	-
45.	good	-	-	1	-
46.	hall	-	-	1	-
47.	happened	-	-	-	1
48.	hard	-	-	-	1
49.	he	-	-	-	4
50.	her	-	9	5	-
51.	here	-	3	-	-
52.	him	-	7	1	-
53.	his	-	-	1	-
54.	Hitler	-	-	1	-
55.	house	-	-	1	-
56.	how	1	-	-	2
57.	if	3	-	-	5
58.	I know	-	-	-	1
59.	I like you	-	-	-	1
60.	illness	-	-	1	-
61.	instead	-	-	-	1
62.	is no answer	-	-	-	1
63.	it	-	31	11	8
64.	it was	-	-	-	1
65.	just because	-	-	-	1
66.	left	-	1	-	-
67.	lost	-	1	-	-
68.	maybe	-	-	-	2
69.	me	-	-	2	-
70.	mine	-	1	-	-
71.	must	-	-	-	2
72.	naturally	1	-	-	-
73.	negoth	-	-	-	1
74.	nice	-	2	-	-
75.	no	1	-	-	1
76.	not	1	-	-	1
77.	not because	1	-	-	-
78.	now	2	1	-	1
79.	of	-	-	-	27
80.	of her	-	-	-	1
81.	of me	-	-	-	1
82.	of you	-	-	-	10
83.	on account of	4	-	-	1
84.	one	1	-	-	-
85.	only if	1	-	-	-
86.	or	-	-	-	1
87.	parce que	-	-	-	1
88.	party	-	1	-	-
89.	pitching	-	-	1	-
90.	position	-	-	-	1
91.	preposition	-	-	1	-
92.	problems	-	-	1	-
93.	porque	1	-	-	-
94.	quit	-	1	-	-
95.	quod	-	-	-	1
96.	rain	-	-	-	1
97.	ran	-	1	-	-
98.	reason	-	-	-	27
99.	right	-	-	-	1
100.	rue	-	-	-	1
101.	run	-	4	-	-
102.	said	-	1	-	-
103.	say	-	1	-	-
104.	school	-	1	-	1
105.	scold	-	-	-	1
106.	seminary	-	-	-	1
107.	sharp	-	-	-	1
108.	she	-	-	-	2
109.	sheet	-	-	-	1
110.	should of	-	-	-	1
111.	since	8	-	-	3
112.	so	1	-	-	-

2 Because (contd)

No.	Response	Subst.	Pre	Post	Assoc.
113.	something	-	-	-	1
114.	song	-	-	-	1
115.	sore	-	-	2	-
116.	so there!	-	-	-	1
117.	stopped	-	1	-	-
118.	stuff	-	-	1	-
119.	sure	-	-	-	1
120.	test	-	-	1	-
121.	that	-	6	1	1
122.	that's why	-	-	-	2
123.	them	-	-	1	-
124.	then	-	-	-	3
125.	therefore	-	-	-	4
126.	they	-	-	-	4
127.	they're	-	-	-	1
128.	this	-	5	-	-
129.	time	-	-	-	1
130.	to each's own	-	-	-	1
131.	tried	-	1	-	-
132.	trouble	-	-	-	1
133.	victimized	-	1	-	-
134.	want	-	1	-	-
135.	was	-	-	-	2
136.	we	-	-	-	5
137.	weak	-	1	-	-
138.	well	-	-	-	1
139.	went	-	6	-	-
140.	what	-	-	1	5
141.	when	8	-	-	2
142.	whence	-	-	-	1
143.	white	-	1	-	-
144.	who	-	-	-	2
145.	why	3	1	1	74
146.	won	-	1	-	-
147.	words	-	-	-	1
148.	wrong	-	1	-	-
149.	you	-	10	42	15
150.	your	-	-	-	1
151.	25	-	-	1	-

		Subst.	Pre	Post	Assoc.
Function Words		-	9	111	-
Space		-	55	5	-
N		57	199	199	295

3 Black

No.	Response	Subst.	Pre	Post	Assoc.
1.	a road	-	-	-	1
2.	associated	-	-	1	-
3.	automobile	-	1	1	-
4.	bad	-	-	-	1
5.	ball	-	-	1	-
6.	bark	-	-	-	1
7.	beautiful	1	-	1	-
8.	became	-	2	-	-
9.	big	2	-	-	-
10.	binder	-	1	-	-
11.	bird	-	1	-	-
12.	blackboard	-	-	-	1
13.	black	-	1	-	1
14.	block	-	-	-	1
15.	blouse	-	-	1	-
16.	blue	12	-	1	4
17.	board	-	-	-	1
18.	boat	-	1	-	-
19.	bounced	-	1	-	-
20.	bright	1	-	-	-
21.	brown	8	-	-	-
22.	car	-	17	7	2
23.	careful	-	1	-	-
24.	cat	-	9	6	3
25.	cat's	-	-	1	-

3 Black (contd)

No.	Response	Subst.	Pre	Post	Assoc.
26.	cats	-	-	2	-
27.	clean	1	-	-	-
28.	clear	1	-	-	-
29.	cloth	-	1	-	-
30.	clothes	-	-	2	-
31.	coal	-	-	-	2
32.	coat	-	1	1	-
33.	cold	3	1	1	-
34.	color	1	6	2	11
35.	colorer	-	-	-	1
36.	colors	-	-	1	-
37.	dark	17	-	1	9
38.	dark color	-	-	-	1
39.	dark in color	-	-	-	1
40.	darkness	2	-	-	1
41.	day	1	-	-	-
42.	death	-	-	-	2
43.	depression	-	-	-	1
44.	deteriorating	1	-	-	-
45.	dirty	-	1	-	1
46.	dismal	1	-	-	-
47.	dog	-	2	-	-
48.	door	-	-	1	-
49.	dress	-	3	5	2
50.	dull	1	-	-	-
51.	eight ball	-	-	-	1
52.	face	-	1	-	-
53.	frightened	1	-	-	-
54.	front	-	-	-	1
55.	good	3	-	-	-
56.	gray	6	-	1	-
57.	green	10	-	-	-
58.	ground	-	1	-	-
59.	habit	-	-	-	1
60.	hair	-	-	1	-
61.	hard	1	-	-	-
62.	has	-	1	-	-
63.	hat	-	-	1	-
64.	have	-	6	-	-
65.	heart	-	-	1	-
66.	hit	-	1	-	-
67.	hood	-	-	-	1
68.	horror	-	-	1	-
69.	horse	-	1	2	-
70.	I've	-	-	1	-
71.	ink	-	-	3	1
72.	it	-	9	-	-
73.	its	-	2	-	-
74.	jacket	-	-	1	-
75.	kitten	-	-	1	-
76.	knight	-	-	-	1
77.	lace	-	-	1	-
78.	like	-	5	-	-
79.	long	1	-	-	-
80.	made	-	1	-	-
81.	majestic	-	1	-	-
82.	man	-	1	-	1
83.	mark	-	-	1	-
84.	most	-	-	1	-
85.	mourning	-	-	-	1
86.	mystically	-	1	-	-
87.	new	1	4	-	-
88.	nice	1	-	-	-
89.	night	-	15	10	5
90.	nothing	1	-	-	-
91.	now	-	1	-	-
92.	old	2	-	-	-
93.	one	-	-	2	-
94.	opposite	-	3	3	-
95.	orange	1	-	-	-
96.	orchid	-	-	-	1
97.	other	1	-	-	-
98.	outlook	-	-	1	-
99.	paint	-	-	1	-
100.	paper	-	1	-	-
101.	pink	1	-	-	-
102.	pitch	-	1	-	-
103.	prefer	-	1	-	-

3 Black (contd)

No.	Response	Subst.	Pre	Post	Assoc.
104.	purse	-	-	1	-
105.	raven	-	-	1	-
106.	red	25	-	-	3
107.	room	-	1	-	-
108.	sharp	-	-	-	1
109.	sheep	-	-	1	1
110.	shiny	-	1	2	-
111.	shoes	-	1	4	-
112.	skirt	-	1	-	-
113.	sky	-	2	-	-
114.	sloe	-	-	-	1
115.	soft	1	-	-	-
116.	spade	-	1	-	-
117.	spot	-	-	1	-
118.	spots	-	-	1	-
119.	stallion	-	-	1	-
120.	starry	1	-	-	-
121.	stove	-	1	-	-
122.	suggestive	-	-	1	-
123.	suit	-	-	2	-
124.	sweater	-	2	-	-
125.	tail	-	-	1	-
126.	tan	1	-	-	-
127.	that's	-	1	-	-
128.	this	-	1	-	-
129.	tight	1	-	-	-
130.	tonight	-	-	1	-
131.	ugly	1	-	-	1
132.	unknown	1	-	-	-
133.	unusual	1	-	-	-
134.	uses	-	1	-	-
135.	velvet	-	-	1	1
136.	violets	-	1	-	-
137.	want	-	1	-	-
138.	warm	1	-	-	-
139.	wearing	-	1	-	-
140.	white	35	4	7	91
141.	wool	1	-	-	-
142.	wore	-	2	-	-
143.	yellow	2	-	-	1
144.	yellows	2	-	-	-

Function Words		-	23	1	-
Space		-	12	69	-
N		156	164	164	162

4 Boy

No.	Response	Subst.	Pre	Post	Assoc.
1.	adult	-	-	-	1
2.	all	-	1	-	-
3.	all right	-	-	1	-
4.	always	-	1	-	-
5.	around	-	-	1	-
6.	a small boy	-	-	-	1
7.	athletic	-	-	-	1
8.	baby	1	4	-	-
9.	ball	1	1	1	-
10.	bat	1	-	-	-
11.	began	-	-	1	-
12.	benevolent	-	-	-	1
13.	big	-	-	1	1
14.	bike	-	-	-	1
15.	born	-	-	1	-
16.	boys	1	-	-	-
17.	brain	1	-	-	-
18.	brilliant	-	1	-	-
19.	bring	-	1	-	-
20.	brother	-	-	1	1
21.	cake	1	-	-	-
22.	calf	1	-	-	-
23.	called	-	1	-	-
24.	came	-	-	1	-

4 Boy (contd)

No.	Response	Subst.	Pre	Post	Assoc.
25.	cat	1	–	–	–
26.	child	10	–	–	7
27.	class	–	–	3	–
28.	climbed	–	–	1	–
29.	considered	–	–	1	–
30.	cop	1	–	–	–
31.	cute	–	1	1	–
32.	daughter	1	–	–	–
33.	day	–	1	–	–
34.	doctor	1	–	–	–
35.	dog	4	–	1	2
36.	drink	–	–	1	–
37.	eats	–	–	1	–
38.	even	–	1	–	–
39.	fell	–	–	1	–
40.	first	–	1	–	–
41.	floor	1	–	–	–
42.	followed	–	–	1	–
43.	freckles	–	–	–	1
44.	friend	–	–	–	1
45.	Gary	–	1	–	–
46.	gender	–	1	–	–
47.	girl	80	1	2	117
48.	girls	2	1	–	–
49.	give	–	1	–	–
50.	go	–	–	1	–
51.	goes	–	–	1	–
52.	going	–	–	2	–
53.	good	–	5	5	–
54.	goof	–	–	–	1
55.	grew	–	–	1	–
56.	grown	–	–	1	–
57.	guy	1	–	–	–
58.	had	–	3	1	–
59.	hair	–	–	–	1
60.	handsome	–	1	1	–
61.	happily	–	–	1	–
62.	has	–	1	2	–
63.	head	–	–	–	1
64.	here	–	–	1	–
65.	he's	–	1	–	–
66.	hit	–	1	1	–
67.	home	–	–	1	–
68.	hurt	–	–	2	–
69.	husband	1	–	–	–
70.	I'm	–	1	–	–
71.	immature	–	–	1	–
72.	intelligent	–	2	2	–
73.	its	–	2	–	–
74.	jeans	–	–	–	1
75.	Jim	1	–	–	1
76.	John	–	1	–	–
77.	jumped	–	–	1	–
78.	kid	1	–	–	–
79.	know	–	1	–	–
80.	lad	2	–	–	–
81.	last	–	–	1	–
82.	late	–	–	2	–
83.	lazy	–	1	–	–
84.	Lee	–	1	–	–
85.	left	–	–	1	–
86.	liked	–	1	–	–
87.	likes	–	–	2	–
88.	little	–	5	–	–
89.	lonely	–	–	1	–
90.	look	–	1	–	–
91.	lost	–	–	4	–
92.	lounged	–	–	1	–
93.	love	–	1	–	–
94.	male	2	–	–	4
95.	males	–	–	–	1
96.	man	27	–	1	4
97.	Martin	–	1	–	–
98.	masculine	–	–	1	1
99.	me	–	–	–	2
100.	meet	–	1	–	–
101.	meets	–	–	1	–
102.	men	2	1	–	–

4 Boy (contd)

No.	Response	Subst.	Pre	Post	Assoc.
103.	mice	1	–	–	–
104.	nice	–	1	–	–
105.	only	–	1	–	–
106.	opposes	–	–	1	–
107.	pants	–	–	–	1
108.	prefer	–	1	–	–
109.	person	2	–	–	1
110.	plays	–	–	1	–
111.	precocious	–	2	–	–
112.	ran	–	–	6	–
113.	rare	–	–	1	–
114.	red	–	–	1	–
115.	rice	–	–	2	–
116.	riding	–	–	1	–
117.	rugged	–	–	1	–
118.	runs	–	–	1	–
119.	saw	–	2	2	–
120.	scout	–	–	1	–
121.	see	–	2	–	–
122.	sex	–	–	–	1
123.	shape	–	–	–	1
124.	shoe	–	–	–	1
125.	shy	–	–	–	1
126.	six	–	–	1	–
127.	small	–	2	1	1
128.	smart	–	1	2	–
129.	smile	–	–	–	1
130.	son	1	–	–	–
131.	soon	–	–	2	–
132.	spoil	–	–	1	–
133.	starting	–	1	1	–
134.	still	–	2	–	–
135.	street	–	–	2	–
136.	student	2	–	–	–
137.	take	–	1	–	–
138.	tall	–	2	5	1
139.	tallest	–	1	–	–
140.	team	–	–	1	–
141.	teeth	–	–	–	1
142.	ten	–	–	1	–
143.	Texas	–	–	1	–
144.	them	–	1	–	–
145.	there	–	–	1	–
146.	told	–	–	1	–
147.	Tom	–	–	–	1
148.	train	1	–	–	–
149.	two	–	–	1	–
150.	voice	1	–	–	–
151.	went	–	–	2	–
152.	who	–	1	–	–
153.	woman	1	–	–	–
154.	you	–	1	–	–
155.	young	–	–	2	1
156.	youngster	1	–	–	–

	Subst.	Pre	Post	Assoc.
Function Words	–	88	3	–
Space	–	1	55	–
N	155	162	162	164

5 Bread

No.	Response	Subst.	Pre	Post	Assoc.
1.	a loaf	–	–	–	1
2.	alone	–	–	4	–
3.	and butter	–	–	–	1
4.	apples	1	–	–	–
5.	ate	–	3	–	–
6.	automobile	1	–	–	–
7.	away	–	–	1	–
8.	bacon	1	–	–	–
9.	bad	1	–	–	–
10.	bake	–	2	–	1
11.	baked	–	2	–	–

5 Bread (contd)

5 Bread (contd)

No.	Response	Subst.	Pre	Post	Assoc.
12.	bakery	-	-	1	-
13.	baking	-	1	1	-
14.	beer	1	-	-	-
15.	best	-	1	2	-
16.	biscuits	6	-	-	-
17.	book	2	-	-	-
18.	bought	-	2	-	-
19.	box	-	-	1	-
20.	boy	1	-	-	-
21.	breakfast	1	1	1	-
22.	bring	-	1	-	-
23.	brown	2	2	-	1
24.	buns	1	-	-	-
25.	buttered	-	-	1	-
26.	butter	7	3	7	62
27.	buy	-	1	-	-
28.	cake	21	-	-	2
29.	candy	3	-	-	-
30.	cars	1	-	-	-
31.	cereal	3	-	-	-
32.	cheese	2	-	-	-
33.	child	1	-	-	-
34.	Christ	-	1	-	-
35.	clothes	6	-	-	-
36.	coffee	3	-	-	1
37.	complex	-	-	1	-
38.	consumed	-	-	1	-
39.	cookies	6	-	-	1
40.	cookie	1	-	-	-
41.	corn	1	-	-	-
42.	crumb	-	-	-	2
43.	crumbs	1	-	-	2
44.	crust	-	-	-	2
45.	dark	-	3	-	-
46.	day	1	-	-	-
47.	delicious	-	1	1	-
48.	diet	-	1	-	-
49.	dinner	-	-	1	-
50.	dog	1	-	-	-
51.	dough	1	-	-	3
52.	dry	-	-	1	-
53.	easy	-	-	1	-
54.	eat	-	8	-	13
55.	eatable	-	-	-	2
56.	evening	-	-	1	-
57.	explosives	1	-	-	-
58.	factory	-	1	-	-
59.	fast	-	-	1	-
60.	fed	-	1	-	-
61.	flour	-	-	-	4
62.	flower	1	-	-	-
63.	food	15	-	1	12
64.	forget	-	1	-	-
65.	French bread	-	-	-	1
66.	French	-	1	1	-
67.	fresh	-	2	4	-
68.	fruit	2	-	-	-
69.	garden	1	-	-	-
70.	garlic	1	-	-	-
71.	girls	1	-	-	-
72.	go	-	-	1	-
73.	goes	-	1	-	-
74.	good	-	1	11	-
75.	groceries	1	-	-	-
76.	had	-	3	-	-
77.	hard	-	1	-	-
78.	healthier	-	-	1	-
79.	home	-	2	1	-
80.	homemade	-	2	-	-
81.	honey	-	-	1	-
82.	hot	-	2	4	-
83.	hungry	-	-	-	1
84.	included	-	2	-	-
85.	intelligence	1	-	-	-
86.	jam	1	-	-	1
87.	knife	-	-	1	2
88.	life	-	-	2	1
89.	light	1	-	-	-
90.	like	-	5	-	-
91.	live	-	4	-	-
92.	loaf	-	7	-	1
93.	lots	-	1	-	-
94.	lunch	-	-	1	-
95.	lunches	-	-	1	-
96.	mainstay	-	-	1	-
97.	make	-	1	-	-
98.	makes	-	1	-	-
99.	making	-	2	-	-
100.	man	1	1	-	-
101.	Mary's	-	1	-	-
102.	meal	-	-	-	1
103.	meals	-	-	1	-
104.	meat	11	-	-	5
105.	milk	4	-	2	1
106.	moldy	-	-	1	-
107.	money	2	-	-	3
108.	music	1	-	-	-
109.	need	-	1	-	-
110.	nice	-	-	1	-
111.	now	-	-	1	-
112.	nut	-	1	-	-
113.	old	-	-	1	-
114.	out	-	2	-	-
115.	own	-	1	-	-
116.	paper	-	-	-	1
117.	pass	-	8	-	-
118.	pastry	1	-	-	-
119.	peanut butter	-	-	1	-
120.	people	1	-	-	-
121.	pie	2	-	-	-
122.	piece	-	1	-	-
123.	place	-	1	-	-
124.	pudding	1	-	-	-
125.	pumpernickle	-	-	-	1
126.	put	-	2	-	-
127.	rapidly	-	-	1	-
128.	rises	-	-	1	-
129.	roll	-	-	-	1
130.	rolls	2	-	-	-
131.	room	1	-	-	-
132.	rye	-	2	-	-
133.	sandwich	2	-	-	2
134.	serve	-	1	-	-
135.	shoe	1	-	-	-
136.	side	-	1	-	-
137.	smell	-	1	-	-
138.	smelled	-	-	1	-
139.	smells	-	-	1	-
140.	soft	-	-	1	-
141.	some	-	1	-	-
142.	soup	1	-	-	-
143.	sour	-	-	1	-
144.	spinach	1	-	-	-
145.	staff	-	-	1	-
146.	stale	-	-	10	-
147.	steak	2	-	-	-
148.	store	-	1	2	-
149.	table	1	1	2	-
150.	take	-	1	-	-
151.	tasty	-	1	-	-
152.	tea	1	-	-	-
153.	think	-	1	-	-
154.	toast	9	-	-	1
155.	toasted	-	-	1	-
156.	today	-	-	2	-
157.	tons	-	1	-	-
158.	want	-	1	-	-
159.	water	3	1	2	6
160.	went	-	1	-	-
161.	wheat	-	-	-	11
162.	whiskey	1	-	-	-
163.	white	-	5	-	7
164.	white bread	-	-	-	1
165.	wife	-	-	-	1
166.	wine	3	-	1	1
167.	wrapped	-	-	1	-

5 Bread (contd)

No.	Response	Subst.	Pre	Post	Assoc.
168.	yeast	-	-	-	2
	Function Words	-	47	4	-
	Space	-	5	67	-
	N	155	165	165	162

6 Coffee

No.	Response	Subst.	Pre	Post	Assoc.
1.	a lot	-	-	1	-
2.	addicted	-	1	-	-
3.	after	-	-	1	-
4.	Alka-Seltzer	1	-	-	-
5.	all	-	-	3	-
6.	almost	-	-	1	-
7.	am	-	1	-	-
8.	any	-	-	1	-
9.	apathetic	-	1	-	-
10.	ape	1	-	-	-
11.	apples	1	-	-	-
12.	aroma	-	-	-	3
13.	at all	-	-	1	-
14.	awful	-	-	1	-
15.	bacon	1	-	-	-
16.	bad	-	-	2	2
17.	bags	-	-	1	-
18.	banana	2	-	-	-
19.	base	1	-	-	-
20.	bath	1	-	-	-
21.	bean	-	-	1	11
22.	beanpole	-	-	-	1
23.	beans	-	-	1	9
24.	beatnik	-	-	-	1
25.	beer	15	-	-	-
26.	best	-	1	-	-
27.	beverage	-	-	-	1
28.	bitter	2	-	7	3
29.	black	-	8	28	38
30.	boating	1	-	-	-
31.	box	1	-	-	-
32.	boys	1	-	-	-
33.	Brazil	-	-	-	3
34.	bread	1	-	-	-
35.	breakfast	-	-	-	1
36.	break	1	-	8	3
37.	brown	-	-	-	3
38.	butter	1	-	-	-
39.	buy	-	1	-	-
40.	cafe	1	-	-	-
41.	caffeine	1	-	1	1
42.	cake	3	-	1	-
43.	can	-	-	-	1
44.	candy	2	-	-	-
45.	care for	-	1	-	-
46.	Carol	1	-	-	-
47.	cars	1	-	-	-
48.	cat	1	-	-	-
49.	cats	1	-	-	-
50.	cereal	1	-	-	-
51.	chocolate	1	-	-	-
52.	cigarette	-	-	1	1
53.	cigarettes	1	-	-	-
54.	clocks	1	-	-	-
55.	cloth	1	-	-	-
56.	clothes	2	-	-	-
57.	coat	1	-	-	1
58.	cocoa	2	-	-	-
59.	coffe break	-	-	-	1
60.	coke	4	-	-	-
61.	cold	-	-	1	1
62.	color	-	1	-	-
63.	colors	1	-	-	-
64.	contact	-	-	1	-
65.	cook	-	-	-	1
66.	Corvettes	1	-	-	-
67.	cotton	-	-	-	1
68.	cream	2	1	5	36
69.	cup	-	10	1	32
70.	cups	-	1	-	-
71.	dark	-	-	1	5
72.	Dave	-	1	-	-
73.	dear	-	-	1	-
74.	delicious	-	-	1	-
75.	diet	-	-	-	1
76.	dinner	-	-	2	-
77.	dirt	1	-	-	-
78.	dislike	-	7	-	1
79.	do	1	-	-	-
80.	dog	1	-	-	1
81.	donut	-	-	-	1
82.	drama	1	-	-	-
83.	drank	-	6	-	-
84.	dress	1	-	-	-
85.	drink	1	54	1	24
86.	drinking	-	1	-	-
87.	drinks	-	7	-	-
88.	eat	-	-	-	2
89.	eggs	1	-	-	-
90.	elephant	1	-	-	-
91.	enjoy	-	5	-	-
92.	espresso	-	-	-	1
93.	every	-	-	1	-
94.	evil	1	-	-	-
95.	fight	1	-	-	-
96.	fine	-	-	1	-
97.	fire	2	-	-	-
98.	fish	1	-	-	-
99.	flower	2	-	-	-
100.	Folgers	-	-	-	2
101.	food	5	-	-	2
102.	football	-	-	1	-
103.	fragrance	-	-	-	1
104.	fresh	-	1	-	-
105.	games	2	-	-	-
106.	gin	1	-	-	-
107.	girl	3	-	-	-
108.	girls	7	-	-	-
109.	go	-	-	1	-
110.	good	-	1	30	1
111.	grass	1	-	-	-
112.	green	-	-	1	-
113.	grind	-	1	-	2
114.	ground	-	-	-	4
115.	grown	-	-	2	-
116.	had	-	3	-	-
117.	hair	1	-	-	-
118.	hangovers	-	-	1	-
119.	has	-	1	1	-
120.	hate	-	18	-	-
121.	have	-	7	-	-
122.	heat	-	-	-	2
123.	high school life	1	-	-	-
124.	Hills Bros.	-	1	-	1
125.	him	2	-	-	-
126.	home	-	-	1	-
127.	hot	1	2	17	18
128.	hot chocolate	1	-	-	-
129.	house	-	-	1	-
130.	hunting	1	-	-	-
131.	ice	2	-	-	-
132.	ice water	1	-	-	-
133.	iced	-	-	-	1
134.	ink	1	-	-	-
135.	Irish	-	-	-	2
136.	Java	-	-	-	1
137.	jelly	1	-	-	-
138.	keeps	-	-	1	-
139.	kettle	-	-	-	1
140.	learning	1	-	-	-
141.	lemon	1	-	-	-
142.	like	-	101	-	-

6 Coffee (contd)

No.	Response	Subst.	Pre	Post	Assoc.
143.	liked	–	1	–	–
144.	likes	–	3	–	–
145.	liquids	2	–	–	1
146.	liquor	1	–	–	1
147.	love	–	1	–	–
148.	lovers	–	–	1	–
149.	make	–	3	–	–
150.	Maxwell	–	–	–	1
151.	men	1	–	–	–
152.	mild	–	–	1	–
153.	milk	52	–	1	16
154.	misers	1	–	–	–
155.	MJB	–	–	–	1
156.	morning	–	–	8	3
157.	much	–	–	2	–
158.	mud	1	–	–	1
159.	muscles	–	–	–	1
160.	mushrooms	1	–	–	–
161.	narcotics	1	–	–	–
162.	night	4	–	–	–
163.	nut	1	–	–	–
164.	often	–	–	1	–
165.	one	–	1	–	–
166.	orange	1	–	–	–
167.	paint	1	–	–	–
168.	pastime	–	–	1	–
169.	people	1	–	–	–
170.	persimmons	1	–	–	–
171.	pie	1	–	–	–
172.	pink dresses	1	–	–	–
173.	plant	–	–	1	–
174.	pleasing	–	–	1	–
175.	pleasure	–	–	–	1
176.	pot	–	–	1	5
177.	pound	–	–	1	–
178.	pulque	1	–	–	–
179.	quickly	–	–	1	–
180.	quiet	–	–	–	1
181.	rain	1	–	–	–
182.	raises	–	1	–	–
183.	rare	–	–	–	1
184.	ready	–	–	1	–
185.	real	–	1	–	–
186.	rich	–	–	–	1
187.	Ron	1	–	–	–
188.	royal	–	–	1	–
189.	said	–	–	1	–
190.	Sanka	–	1	–	3
191.	Sausalito	–	–	–	1
192.	school	3	–	–	–
193.	see	–	2	–	–
194.	seeds	–	–	–	1
195.	Seven Up	1	–	–	–
196.	shirt	–	–	1	–
197.	shoes	1	–	–	–
198.	skin	–	–	–	1
199.	sky	1	–	–	–
200.	sleep	–	–	–	2
201.	sleepless	–	–	1	–
202.	smell	–	2	–	4
203.	smells	–	1	2	2
204.	smog	1	–	–	–
205.	sober	–	–	–	1
206.	soda	1	–	–	–
207.	sometimes	–	–	2	–
208.	somewhere	–	–	1	–
209.	song	1	–	–	–
210.	soup	1	–	–	–
211.	spilled	–	1	–	–
212.	sports	1	–	–	–
213.	steam	–	–	–	2
214.	stimulation	1	–	–	1
215.	stimulating	–	–	1	1
216.	strong	–	1	2	1
217.	sugar	3	–	2	9
218.	sun	4	–	–	–
219.	sweet	1	–	–	2
220.	table	–	–	1	–

6 Coffee (contd)

No.	Response	Subst.	Pre	Post	Assoc.
221.	take	–	1	–	–
222.	tar	3	–	–	–
223.	taste	–	1	–	–
224.	tastes	–	–	2	–
225.	tea	128	–	4	88
226.	teachers	2	–	–	–
227.	television	–	–	–	2
228.	think	–	1	–	–
229.	toast	–	–	–	2
230.	tobacco	1	–	–	–
231.	toffee	–	–	–	2
232.	tomatoes	1	–	–	–
233.	trains	1	–	–	–
234.	tree	–	–	1	–
235.	ugh	–	–	–	1
236.	vodka	1	–	–	–
237.	waiter	–	–	–	1
238.	want	–	2	–	–
239.	warm	–	–	1	1
240.	warming	–	–	1	–
241.	water	7	–	–	1
242.	wheat	1	–	–	–
243.	where	–	1	–	–
244.	whiskey	4	–	–	–
245.	wine	1	–	–	–
246.	world	–	1	–	–
247.	worms	1	–	–	–
248.	you	5	–	–	–
249.	Yuban	–	–	1	–

	Subst.	Pre	Post	Assoc.
Function Words	–	24	–	–
Space	–	90	205	–
N	358	384	384	391

7 Come

No.	Response	Subst.	Pre	Post	Assoc.
1.	action	–	–	–	1
2.	advance	1	–	–	1
3.	age	–	–	1	–
4.	alone	–	–	1	–
5.	along	–	–	2	–
6.	also	–	–	1	–
7.	Ann	–	1	–	–
8.	approach	1	–	–	1
9.	are	1	–	–	–
10.	around	–	–	–	1
11.	arrive	4	–	–	1
12.	asked	–	1	–	–
13.	back	–	–	–	2
14.	be	2	–	–	–
15.	beach	–	–	1	–
16.	been	1	–	–	–
17.	believe	1	–	–	–
18.	bend	1	–	–	–
19.	Bill	–	1	–	–
20.	birds	–	1	–	–
21.	Bob	–	1	–	–
22.	boy	–	1	–	1
23.	call	–	–	1	–
24.	came	3	–	–	2
25.	car	–	–	–	1
26.	cat	–	1	–	–
27.	chair	–	–	1	–
28.	class	–	–	1	–
29.	corner	–	–	1	–
30.	crowd	–	1	–	–
31.	dance	2	–	1	–
32.	donate	1	–	–	–
33.	dread	1	–	–	–
34.	drive	1	–	–	–
35.	drop	1	–	–	–
36.	drop in	1	–	–	–

7   Come (contd)

No.	Response	Subst.	Pre	Post	Assoc.
37.	early	–	1	1	–
38.	easy	–	1	–	–
39.	eat	2	–	–	–
40.	enter	1	–	–	–
41.	fall	1	–	–	–
42.	far	–	–	1	–
43.	fight	1	–	–	–
44.	foreign	–	–	1	–
45.	foreword	–	–	–	1
46.	fun	–	–	–	1
47.	game	–	–	1	–
48.	get	2	–	–	1
49.	girls	–	1	–	–
50.	give	2	–	–	–
51.	go	76	–	3	102
52.	going	–	5	–	–
53.	gone	1	–	–	1
54.	had gone	1	–	–	–
55.	hears	1	–	–	–
56.	her	–	2	–	–
57.	here	–	–	10	15
58.	hills	–	–	1	–
59.	him	–	2	3	–
60.	home	–	–	10	8
61.	house	–	–	3	–
62.	how	–	1	–	–
63.	hurry	–	–	–	1
64.	immediately	–	–	–	1
65.	import	–	–	1	–
66.	in	–	–	–	1
67.	invited	–	1	–	–
68.	it	–	1	–	–
69.	itself	–	–	1	–
70.	Jane	–	1	–	–
71.	lady	–	1	–	–
72.	late	–	–	3	–
73.	later	–	–	2	–
74.	leave	4	–	–	1
75.	let	–	–	1	–
76.	library	–	–	1	–
77.	listen	1	–	–	–
78.	Mary	–	1	–	–
79.	me	–	–	26	1
80.	meeting	–	–	1	–
81.	morgue	–	–	1	–
82.	my direction	1	–	–	–
83.	never	–	1	–	–
84.	new	–	–	1	–
85.	night	–	1	–	–
86.	no	–	–	–	1
87.	now	1	–	1	–
88.	on	–	–	1	–
89.	opposite	–	1	–	–
90.	other	–	1	–	–
91.	over	–	–	11	–
92.	parents	–	–	1	–
93.	party	–	–	13	–
94.	pass	1	–	–	–
95.	Paul	–	1	–	–
96.	peace	–	1	–	–
97.	people	–	1	–	–
98.	pink	–	–	–	1
99.	play	1	–	–	–
100.	please	1	–	–	–
101.	proceed	1	–	–	–
102.	psychology	–	1	–	–
103.	quick	–	–	–	1
104.	realize	1	–	–	–
105.	return	4	–	–	–
106.	run	1	–	–	–
107.	said	–	3	–	–
108.	Sam	–	1	–	–
109.	school	–	–	5	–
110.	seasons	–	1	–	–
111.	see	1	–	3	1
112.	send	1	–	–	–
113.	shop	–	–	1	–
114.	sing	1	–	–	–

7   Come (contd)

No.	Response	Subst.	Pre	Post	Assoc.
115.	six	–	–	1	–
116.	sleep	1	–	–	–
117.	slow	–	1	–	–
118.	some	–	1	–	–
119.	soon	–	–	1	–
120.	speak	2	–	–	–
121.	start	1	–	–	–
122.	stay	5	–	–	1
123.	stay with	1	–	–	–
124.	stop	1	–	1	–
125.	sure	–	1	–	–
126.	talk	1	–	–	–
127.	teach	–	1	–	–
128.	team	–	1	–	–
129.	them	–	1	–	–
130.	to	–	–	–	1
131.	to go forth	–	–	–	1
132.	to me	–	–	–	2
133.	today	–	–	1	–
134.	told	–	1	–	–
135.	Tom	–	1	–	–
136.	tomorrow	–	–	1	–
137.	tonight	–	–	2	–
138.	too	–	–	2	–
139.	toward	–	–	–	1
140.	town	–	–	1	–
141.	travel	–	–	–	1
142.	us	–	2	4	–
143.	visit	–	–	1	–
144.	walk	2	–	–	1
145.	wanted	–	2	–	–
146.	wants	–	1	–	–
147.	wash	1	–	–	–
148.	went	–	–	–	1
149.	when	–	–	–	1
150.	whosoever	–	1	–	–
151.	with me	–	–	–	1
152.	world	–	–	1	–
153.	you	–	36	2	–

		Subst.	Pre	Post	Assoc.
Function Words		–	63	7	–
Space		–	13	23	–
N		145	167	166	160

8   Eat

No.	Response	Subst.	Pre	Post	Assoc.
1.	a lot	–	–	6	–
2.	absorb	1	–	–	–
3.	ahead	–	1	–	–
4.	all	–	–	12	–
5.	always	–	3	–	–
6.	and	–	–	–	1
7.	and run	–	–	–	1
8.	animals	–	1	–	–
9.	anymore	–	–	1	–
10.	anything	–	–	1	–
11.	apple	–	–	1	–
12.	apples	–	–	2	–
13.	ate	2	–	–	13
14.	aures	–	–	–	1
15.	banana	–	–	2	–
16.	barf	–	–	–	1
17.	be	–	–	1	–
18.	bears	–	–	1	–
19.	beat	2	–	–	1
20.	berries	–	–	1	–
21.	bite	1	–	–	1
22.	boys	–	1	–	–
23.	bread	–	–	1	–
24.	breakfast	–	–	9	–
25.	breathe	2	–	–	–
26.	burn	1	–	–	–

8 Eat (contd)

8 Eat (contd)

No.	Response	Subst.	Pre	Post	Assoc.	No.	Response	Subst.	Pre	Post	Assoc.
27.	cafeteria	–	–	–	1	105.	home	–	–	1	–
28.	cake	–	–	1	2	106.	horse	–	–	1	–
29.	calories	–	–	–	1	107.	hot dog	–	–	1	1
30.	came	–	1	–	–	108.	hunger	–	–	–	1
31.	candy	–	–	2	–	109.	hungry	–	1	–	5
32.	car	–	–	–	1	110.	ice cream	–	–	1	–
33.	carrot	–	–	–	1	111.	immediately	–	–	1	–
34.	cheese cake	–	–	–	1	112.	indigestion	–	–	–	1
35.	chew	4	–	–	1	113.	it	–	–	17	–
36.	chews	1	–	–	–	114.	Joan	–	1	–	–
37.	chicken	–	–	1	–	115.	Joe's	–	–	2	–
38.	chuck	–	–	1	–	116.	laugh	1	–	–	–
39.	claws	–	–	–	1	117.	learn	1	–	–	–
40.	cloud	–	–	1	–	118.	leave	2	–	–	–
41.	come	2	1	–	–	119.	lick	1	–	–	–
42.	consume	2	–	–	–	120.	light	–	–	–	1
43.	cook	6	–	–	1	121.	like	14	45	–	–
44.	cracker	–	–	1	–	122.	likes	–	5	–	–
45.	cream cheese	–	–	–	1	123.	little	–	–	2	1
46.	daisies	–	–	2	–	124.	live	1	1	2	–
47.	dance	3	–	–	–	125.	look	1	–	–	–
48.	delicious	–	–	–	1	126.	love	4	9	–	–
49.	devour	1	–	–	–	127.	loves	–	1	–	–
50.	diet	–	–	–	1	128.	lunch	–	–	6	3
51.	digest	2	–	–	–	129.	lunchtime	–	–	1	–
52.	dine	–	–	–	2	130.	make	3	–	–	–
53.	diner	–	–	–	1	131.	man	–	1	–	–
54.	dinner	–	–	10	5	132.	mashed potatoes	–	–	–	1
55.	dispose of	1	–	–	–	133.	me	–	–	2	–
56.	do	6	–	–	–	134.	meat	–	–	3	2
57.	dog	–	–	–	3	135.	melon	–	–	1	–
58.	don't	–	–	–	1	136.	melt	1	–	–	–
59.	doze	1	–	–	–	137.	milk	–	–	–	2
60.	dress	1	–	–	–	138.	monkeys	–	1	–	–
61.	drink	29	–	5	32	139.	moon	–	–	–	1
62.	drinks	1	–	–	–	140.	mother	–	–	1	–
63.	drive	1	–	–	–	141.	mouse	–	–	–	1
64.	eaten	–	–	–	2	142.	mouth	–	–	–	1
65.	eater	–	–	–	1	143.	much	–	–	9	–
66.	eating	–	–	1	1	144.	munch	–	–	–	1
67.	employ	1	–	–	–	145.	necessary	–	–	1	–
68.	enjoyment	–	–	–	2	146.	never	–	2	–	–
69.	enough	–	–	1	–	147.	not	1	–	–	–
70.	everyone	–	1	–	–	148.	nothing	–	2	1	–
71.	everything	–	–	1	–	149.	now	–	–	11	1
72.	fast	–	–	9	1	150.	nutrition	–	–	–	2
73.	fat	–	–	–	14	151.	often	–	3	1	–
74.	feast	1	–	–	–	152.	one	–	1	–	–
75.	feel	–	1	–	–	153.	oranges	–	–	1	–
76.	fight	1	–	–	–	154.	out	–	1	3	1
77.	first	–	–	1	–	155.	pea	–	–	–	1
78.	fish	–	–	2	2	156.	people	–	2	–	–
79.	fix	2	–	–	–	157.	pick	1	–	–	–
80.	food	–	1	14	152	158.	pie	–	–	1	1
81.	fork	–	–	1	2	159.	pizza	–	–	1	–
82.	fruit	–	–	1	–	160.	plate	–	–	–	1
83.	full	–	–	–	6	161.	play	13	–	–	–
84.	get	–	–	1	–	162.	please	–	5	–	–
85.	go	12	6	1	–	163.	pleasure	–	–	–	2
86.	go home	1	–	–	–	164.	popped	–	–	–	1
87.	gobble	2	–	–	–	165.	pork	–	1	–	–
88.	God	–	1	–	–	166.	potato chips	1	–	–	1
89.	going	–	6	–	–	167.	porridge	–	–	1	–
90.	good	–	3	5	5	168.	quickly	–	–	2	1
91.	grab	1	–	–	–	169.	rape	1	–	–	–
92.	great	–	–	1	–	170.	raw	–	–	–	1
93.	grow	1	–	1	–	171.	read	–	1	–	–
94.	hamburger	–	–	2	2	172.	ready	–	1	–	–
95.	hamburgers	–	–	1	1	173.	rice	–	1	–	–
96.	hardy	–	–	2	–	174.	ride	2	–	–	–
97.	hastily	–	–	1	–	175.	run	6	–	8	10
98.	hate	–	1	–	–	176.	sandwich	–	–	1	–
99.	have	2	1	–	–	177.	sat down	–	1	–	–
100.	hear	1	–	–	–	178.	seat	–	–	–	1
101.	here	–	–	2	–	179.	see	3	–	–	1
102.	hit	2	–	–	–	180.	serve	1	–	–	–
103.	Hitler	–	1	–	–	181.	shovel	1	–	–	–
104.	hobby	–	1	–	–	182.	sick	–	–	–	2

405

8 Eat (contd)

No.	Response	Subst.	Pre	Post	Assoc.
183.	sing	2	–	–	–
184.	sit	4	–	–	1
185.	sit down	–	1	–	–
186.	six	–	–	1	–
187.	sleep	23	2	–	29
188.	slow	–	–	1	–
189.	slower	–	–	1	–
190.	slowly	–	–	1	–
191.	smash	1	–	–	–
192.	smell	2	–	–	1
193.	smoke	1	–	–	–
194.	snails	–	–	1	–
195.	something	–	4	2	–
196.	son	–	–	1	–
197.	soon	–	–	2	–
198.	spice	–	–	–	1
199.	spinach	–	–	1	–
200.	stand	1	–	–	–
201.	start	1	–	–	–
202.	starve	–	–	–	2
203.	starved	–	–	–	7
204.	stay	1	–	–	–
205.	steak	–	–	2	3
206.	step on	1	–	–	–
207.	stink	1	–	–	–
208.	study	1	–	–	–
209.	stuff	1	–	–	1
210.	stuffed	–	–	–	2
211.	swallow	1	–	–	1
212.	swim	8	–	–	–
213.	take	3	–	–	–
214.	talk	8	–	1	2
215.	talks	2	–	–	–
216.	tell	1	–	–	–
217.	that	–	–	2	–
218.	think	2	–	–	–
219.	three	–	–	2	–
220.	threw	1	–	–	–
221.	throw	3	–	–	–
222.	time	–	3	–	–
223.	tonight	–	–	1	–
224.	touch	1	–	–	–
225.	try	–	1	–	–
226.	turkey	–	–	–	1
227.	up	–	–	–	1
228.	us	–	2	4	–
229.	vegetable	–	–	1	–
230.	vomit	–	–	–	1
231.	walk	5	–	–	–
232.	want	–	8	–	–
233.	want to be	1	–	–	–
234.	wanted	–	1	–	–
235.	wash	2	–	–	–
236.	watermelon	–	–	1	1
237.	weigh	–	–	–	1
238.	well	–	–	2	–
239.	well-balanced	–	–	1	–
240.	went	–	1	–	–
241.	what	–	–	–	1
242.	work	4	–	–	2
243.	yet	–	–	1	–
244.	you	–	39	2	–
245.	yummy	–	–	–	1
246.	Zip's	–	1	–	–
247.	$1.00	–	–	1	–
	Function Words	–	126	9	–
	Space	–	57	127	–
	N	238	361	361	376

9 For

No.	Response	Subst.	Pre	Post	Assoc.
1.	a while	–	–	1	–
2.	about	13	–	1	1
3.	after	2	–	–	3
4.	again	1	–	–	–
5.	against	9	–	–	40
6.	all	–	11	10	4
7.	always	–	1	–	1
8.	am	–	2	–	–
9.	and	1	–	–	1
10.	anything	–	3	–	–
11.	are	1	–	–	–
12.	arm	–	1	–	–
13.	around	1	–	–	–
14.	as	2	–	–	2
15.	ask	–	2	–	–
16.	asked	–	2	–	–
17.	at	6	–	–	1
18.	back of	1	–	–	–
19.	bad	–	–	1	–
20.	Barbara	–	–	1	–
21.	baseball	–	–	1	–
22.	be	–	–	–	1
23.	because	8	–	–	4
24.	because of	1	–	–	–
25.	beer	–	–	1	–
26.	before	1	–	–	1
27.	beside	2	–	–	–
28.	better	–	–	1	–
29.	between	1	–	–	–
30.	birthday	–	–	1	–
31.	black	–	1	–	–
32.	boat	–	2	1	–
33.	book	–	6	–	–
34.	boy	–	–	–	1
35.	bread	–	–	2	–
36.	bring	–	2	–	–
37.	broke	–	–	1	–
38.	but	1	–	–	1
39.	buy	–	1	–	–
40.	by	12	–	–	4
41.	by the	–	–	–	1
42.	by what	–	–	–	1
43.	cake	–	1	–	–
44.	call	–	2	–	–
45.	called	–	2	–	–
46.	came	–	2	–	–
47.	candy	–	1	–	–
48.	cheated	–	1	–	–
49.	chore	–	–	–	1
50.	Christmas	–	–	1	–
51.	city	–	1	–	–
52.	coat	–	1	–	–
53.	coke	–	–	1	–
54.	cold	–	–	1	–
55.	come	–	2	–	–
56.	coming	–	1	–	–
57.	conjunction	–	–	–	1
58.	core	1	–	–	–
59.	country	–	–	1	–
60.	cream	–	–	–	1
61.	cry	–	2	–	–
62.	day	–	–	1	–
63.	did	–	4	–	–
64.	dinner	–	–	2	–
65.	do	–	10	1	–
66.	dog	–	1	–	–
67.	doing	2	–	–	–
68.	doing there	1	–	–	–
69.	done	–	1	–	–
70.	door	–	–	–	1
71.	downtown	–	1	–	–
72.	dress	–	1	1	–
73.	during	1	–	–	–
74.	election	–	–	–	1
75.	even	–	–	–	1
76.	ever	–	–	1	2
77.	everybody	–	–	1	–
78.	everything	–	–	1	–

9 For (contd)

9 For (contd)

No.	Response	Subst.	Pre	Post	Assoc.	No.	Response	Subst.	Pre	Post	Assoc.
79.	example	–	–	1	–	157.	magnifier	–	–	1	–
80.	far	–	1	–	1	158.	man	1	–	–	–
81.	favorable	–	–	–	1	159.	Mary	–	–	1	–
82.	fight	–	–	–	1	160.	maybe	1	–	–	–
83.	fine	–	–	–	2	161.	me	–	1	34	16
84.	fit	–	–	–	1	162.	Mike	–	1	–	–
85.	five	1	–	–	5	163.	milk	–	–	1	–
86.	fool	–	–	–	2	164.	mom	–	–	1	1
87.	fore	1	–	–	1	165.	money	–	–	3	–
88.	fought	–	1	–	–	166.	more	–	–	–	3
89.	four	–	–	–	4	167.	my	–	–	5	–
90.	four and five	–	–	–	1	168.	next	–	–	1	1
91.	friend	–	–	1	–	169.	night	–	2	–	–
92.	from	12	–	–	7	170.	no one	–	–	1	–
93.	front	–	–	–	1	171.	nor	–	–	–	3
94.	fun	–	1	3	1	172.	not	7	–	–	1
95.	game	–	–	–	1	173.	nothing	–	1	1	–
96.	gave	–	1	–	–	174.	now	5	1	5	–
97.	get	–	–	–	1	175.	number	–	–	–	1
98.	gift	–	2	1	7	176.	of	1	–	–	3
99.	girl	1	–	2	–	177.	okay	–	1	–	–
100.	girls	–	–	1	–	178.	on	8	–	–	–
101.	give	–	–	–	17	179.	on account of	1	–	–	–
102.	give up	–	1	–	–	180.	once	–	2	–	–
103.	given by	1	–	–	–	181.	one	–	6	3	1
104.	giving	–	–	–	3	182.	only	1	1	–	–
105.	go	–	10	–	1	183.	or	1	–	–	8
106.	goes	–	1	–	–	184.	organization	–	–	1	–
107.	going	–	1	–	–	185.	package	–	1	–	–
108.	golf	–	–	–	2	186.	page	–	1	–	–
109.	gone	–	1	–	–	187.	paper	–	–	–	1
110.	good	–	3	2	1	188.	para	–	1	–	–
111.	goodness	–	–	1	–	189.	pay	–	1	–	–
112.	got	–	1	–	–	190.	people	–	–	2	–
113.	green	–	–	1	–	191.	person	–	–	–	1
114.	growth	–	–	1	–	192.	plus	1	–	–	–
115.	happiness	–	–	2	–	193.	por	–	–	–	1
116.	hard	–	1	–	–	194.	pray	–	1	–	–
117.	hat	–	1	–	–	195.	preposition	–	–	–	4
118.	he	–	–	–	2	196.	prepositions	–	–	–	1
119.	heaven's	–	–	1	–	197.	present	–	1	–	3
120.	help	–	–	–	2	198.	president	–	–	1	–
121.	her	–	–	17	7	199.	pro	1	–	–	–
122.	here	1	–	–	–	200.	punishment	–	1	–	–
123.	highest	–	–	1	–	201.	purpose	–	–	–	1
124.	him	1	2	39	17	202.	question	–	–	–	1
125.	his	–	–	2	1	203.	racing	1	–	–	–
126.	home	–	3	–	–	204.	ran	–	1	–	–
127.	how	1	–	–	2	205.	really	1	–	–	2
128.	I know	–	–	–	1	206.	reason	1	1	–	1
129.	if	1	–	–	4	207.	religion	–	–	1	–
130.	Ike	–	–	1	–	208.	ride	–	–	–	–
131.	I'm	–	2	–	–	209.	right	1	–	–	–
132.	in	1	–	–	–	210.	ring	–	1	–	–
133.	in place	–	–	–	1	211.	road	–	–	1	–
134.	in spite of	1	–	–	–	212.	romance	–	–	1	–
135.	intended	–	1	–	–	213.	runs	–	1	–	–
136.	is	6	–	–	–	214.	saved	–	1	–	–
137.	is it	2	–	–	–	215.	sell	–	1	–	–
138.	it	–	35	6	4	216.	sent	–	2	–	–
139.	it's	1	5	–	–	217.	service	–	–	–	1
140.	jerk	–	–	1	–	218.	shoot	–	1	–	1
141.	Joyce	–	–	1	–	219.	shore	–	–	–	1
142.	just	–	1	–	1	220.	show	–	–	2	–
143.	leaving	–	1	–	–	221.	so	–	–	–	2
144.	left	–	3	–	–	222.	some	–	–	1	–
145.	lense	–	1	–	–	223.	something	–	2	1	–
146.	life	–	1	–	–	224.	sore	–	–	–	1
147.	like	5	1	–	–	225.	sorrow	–	1	–	–
148.	likes	2	–	–	–	226.	sound	1	–	–	–
149.	lit	–	–	1	–	227.	Spanish	–	–	1	–
150.	live	–	2	–	–	228.	stand	–	1	–	–
151.	long	–	–	2	–	229.	stars	–	1	–	–
152.	look	–	1	–	–	230.	stayed	–	1	–	–
153.	looked	–	1	–	–	231.	stolen	–	–	1	–
154.	looking	1	1	–	–	232.	stop	–	1	–	–
155.	love	–	1	2	–	233.	store	–	6	–	–
156.	lunch	–	–	1	–	234.	student	–	–	1	–

9 For (contd)

No.	Response	Subst.	Pre	Post	Assoc.
235.	studying	–	–	1	–
236.	Sue	–	–	1	–
237.	sweet	–	–	–	1
238.	swimming	–	1	–	–
239.	tea	–	2	2	–
240.	test	–	2	–	–
241.	that	3	28	3	1
242.	the	–	–	–	1
243.	thee	–	–	1	–
244.	them	–	–	2	2
245.	then	–	–	–	1
246.	there	1	–	–	–
247.	thesis	–	1	–	–
248.	thing	7	–	–	–
249.	this	–	34	3	–
250.	through	2	–	–	1
251.	time	–	6	–	–
252.	to	40	–	–	32
253.	to get	2	–	–	–
254.	to give to	1	–	–	–
255.	to live	–	–	–	1
256.	to spend	1	–	–	–
257.	tolls	–	1	–	–
258.	Tom	–	–	1	–
259.	tonight	–	–	1	–
260.	too	1	–	–	2
261.	took	–	1	–	–
262.	toward	1	–	–	–
263.	towards	1	–	–	–
264.	try	1	–	–	–
265.	two	–	2	2	2
266.	us	–	–	5	4
267.	used	–	2	–	–
268.	usually	1	–	–	–
269.	vor	–	–	–	1
270.	vote	–	1	1	–
271.	wait	–	4	–	–
272.	walk	–	1	4	–
273.	want	–	1	–	–
274.	wants	–	–	1	–
275.	weather	–	–	1	–
276.	went	–	7	–	–
277.	what	–	34	9	37
278.	when	–	–	–	2
279.	where	–	–	–	1
280.	while	–	–	2	–
281.	white	–	–	1	–
282.	who	–	3	–	5
283.	whom	–	–	5	7
284.	why	3	–	–	3
285.	will	–	–	–	1
286.	with	31	–	–	9
287.	without	1	–	–	–
288.	wood	–	1	–	–
289.	word	–	–	–	1
290.	work	–	4	–	–
291.	worked	–	1	–	–
292.	yes	–	–	–	1
293.	you	–	2	61	26
294.	your	–	–	5	–
295.	zum Beispiel	1	–	–	–
296.	3	–	1	–	–
297.	4	–	–	–	3
298.	29¢	–	–	1	–
	Function Words	–	13	14	–
	Space	–	38	69	–
	N	238	391	391	379

10 From

No.	Response	Subst.	Pre	Post	Assoc.
1.	A	–	–	1	–
2.	about	5	–	–	–
3.	abroad	–	–	–	1
4.	Afghanistan	–	–	1	–
5.	Africa	–	–	1	–
6.	against	–	–	–	2
7.	age	–	–	–	1
8.	Alabama	–	–	1	–
9.	all	–	–	1	–
10.	among	1	–	–	–
11.	animal	–	–	1	–
12.	around	2	–	1	–
13.	arrived	–	1	–	–
14.	as	1	–	–	–
15.	asylum	–	–	1	–
16.	at	2	–	–	–
17.	away	–	3	–	6
18.	away from	1	–	–	–
19.	ball	–	1	–	–
20.	beginning	–	–	1	1
21.	behind	–	–	–	1
22.	below	1	–	–	–
23.	Belvedere	–	–	1	–
24.	better than	1	–	–	–
25.	big	–	–	1	–
26.	Bolivia	–	–	1	–
27.	bone	–	1	–	–
28.	book	–	2	–	–
29.	by	4	–	–	–
30.	by way of	1	–	–	–
31.	California	–	–	7	1
32.	called	–	1	–	–
33.	came	–	33	–	–
34.	car	–	–	–	2
35.	Carol	–	–	1	–
36.	China	–	–	1	–
37.	Christmas	–	–	–	2
38.	come	1	23	–	5
39.	comes	–	10	–	–
40.	coming	–	2	–	1
41.	Corky	–	1	–	–
42.	dance	–	1	–	–
43.	Dave	–	–	–	1
44.	dead	–	–	1	–
45.	depart	–	1	–	–
46.	depths	–	–	1	–
47.	Detroit	–	–	1	–
48.	die	–	–	–	1
49.	different	–	2	–	–
50.	direction	–	–	–	1
51.	dirty	–	1	–	–
52.	dumb	–	–	–	1
53.	earth	–	–	–	1
54.	England	–	–	1	–
55.	escape	–	1	–	–
56.	eternity	–	–	–	4
57.	Europe	–	–	–	1
58.	evil	–	1	–	–
59.	experiment	–	–	1	–
60.	Fairfax	–	–	–	1
61.	far	–	2	–	2
62.	fire	–	–	1	–
63.	five	–	–	1	–
64.	floor	–	–	2	–
65.	for	6	–	–	4
66.	forth	–	–	–	1
67.	fra	–	–	–	1
68.	France	–	–	2	–
69.	game	–	–	1	–
70.	get	–	–	–	1
71.	get up	–	1	–	–
72.	girl	–	–	–	1
73.	go	1	7	–	4
74.	going	1	1	–	5
75.	good	–	–	1	–
76.	got	–	1	–	–
77.	grape	–	–	1	–
78.	Hamlet	–	–	1	–

10 From (contd)

No.	Response	Subst.	Pre	Post	Assoc.
79.	head	–	–	1	–
80.	hear	–	1	–	–
81.	heaven	–	–	2	–
82.	Helen	–	–	1	–
83.	her	–	–	6	2
84.	here	–	1	44	14
85.	high school	–	–	1	–
86.	him	–	2	11	6
87.	his	–	–	1	–
88.	home	–	1	3	5
89.	house	–	–	1	2
90.	ice	–	–	1	–
91.	Idaho	–	–	1	–
92.	if	–	–	–	1
93.	in	6	–	–	–
94.	in place of	1	–	–	–
95.	Indiana	–	–	1	–
96.	Ireland	–	–	1	–
97.	it	–	21	2	2
98.	it's	1	–	–	–
99.	Italy	–	–	–	1
100.	Jane	–	–	2	–
101.	Japan	–	–	1	–
102.	Joan	–	–	–	1
103.	Johannesburg	–	–	1	–
104.	John	–	–	1	–
105.	Kansas	–	–	3	–
106.	lagoon	–	–	–	1
107.	last	–	–	1	–
108.	letter	–	6	–	3
109.	like	1	–	–	–
110.	little	–	–	1	–
111.	location	–	–	–	1
112.	Los Angeles	–	–	2	–
113.	low	–	–	1	–
114.	Lynn	–	–	1	–
115.	mail	–	–	–	2
116.	man	–	1	–	–
117.	Mars	–	–	9	1
118.	Maryel	–	–	1	–
119.	me	–	1	13	7
120.	Midwest	–	–	–	1
121.	miles	–	1	–	–
122.	Mill Valley	–	–	1	–
123.	Minnesota	–	–	1	–
124.	Missouri	–	–	1	–
125.	mom	–	–	–	1
126.	monster	–	–	1	–
127.	moon	–	–	1	–
128.	mud flats	–	–	1	–
129.	near	3	–	–	–
130.	New York	–	–	3	–
131.	now	1	–	10	5
132.	nowhere	–	–	1	1
133.	obtain	–	1	–	–
134.	of	3	–	–	8
135.	off	2	–	–	–
136.	Oklahoma	–	–	1	–
137.	old	–	–	1	–
138.	on	–	–	–	1
139.	one	–	–	2	1
140.	one day	–	–	–	1
141.	or	1	–	–	–
142.	orange	–	–	–	1
143.	other	–	–	1	–
144.	others	–	–	1	–
145.	our	–	–	–	1
146.	out	2	–	–	4
147.	outer	–	–	2	–
148.	out of	5	–	–	3
149.	people	–	–	–	1
150.	place	–	–	–	3
151.	play	–	1	–	–
152.	poor	–	–	1	–
153.	preposition	–	–	–	1
154.	proceed	–	–	–	1
155.	ran	–	2	–	–
156.	read	–	1	–	–

10 From (contd)

No.	Response	Subst.	Pre	Post	Assoc.
157.	received	–	2	–	–
158.	redwoods	–	–	1	–
159.	Reno	–	–	1	–
160.	return address	–	–	–	2
161.	Rick	–	–	1	–
162.	right	1	–	–	–
163.	room	–	–	3	–
164.	roses	–	1	–	–
165.	run	–	1	–	–
166.	San Francisco	–	1	1	–
167.	San Rafael	–	–	1	–
168.	saying	–	1	–	–
169.	school	–	–	2	1
170.	send	–	–	–	1
171.	sense	–	–	–	1
172.	sent	–	–	–	2
173.	side	–	–	1	–
174.	small	–	–	1	–
175.	some	–	–	–	1
176.	somewhere	–	–	–	1
177.	source	–	–	–	1
178.	south	–	–	1	–
179.	start	–	1	–	–
180.	St. Louis	–	–	–	1
181.	store	–	–	2	–
182.	stretched	–	1	–	–
183.	style	–	–	–	1
184.	swam	–	–	–	1
185.	sword	–	1	–	–
186.	table	–	–	1	–
187.	te	–	–	–	1
188.	tell	–	1	–	–
189.	Texas	–	–	7	–
190.	that	–	1	5	1
191.	the	–	–	–	1
192.	them	–	–	–	11
193.	then	–	–	1	1
194.	there	–	2	2	13
195.	these	–	–	–	1
196.	this	–	3	5	–
197.	three	–	–	1	–
198.	through	1	–	–	–
199.	time	–	–	1	–
200.	to	23	–	–	72
201.	Tom	–	–	1	–
202.	too	–	–	–	3
203.	top	–	–	2	–
204.	towards	–	–	–	1
205.	town	–	–	2	3
206.	train	–	–	–	1
207.	trip	–	1	–	1
208.	Uncle B.	–	–	1	–
209.	until	–	–	–	1
210.	us	–	–	–	3
211.	Venus	–	–	1	–
212.	Washington	–	–	1	–
213.	week	–	1	–	–
214.	went	–	7	–	2
215.	what	–	–	2	8
216.	whence	–	–	2	–
217.	where	–	–	7	29
218.	which	–	–	1	5
219.	who	–	1	–	6
220.	whom	–	–	2	6
221.	window	–	–	1	–
222.	with	2	–	–	1
223.	without	–	–	–	1
224.	wood	–	–	1	–
225.	written to	1	–	–	–
226.	you	–	1	1	9
227.	yours truly	–	–	–	1
228.	Zanzibar	–	–	1	–
	Function Words	–	28	3	–
	Space	–	67	13	2
	N	82	259	259	333

11 Game

No.	Response	Subst.	Pre	Post	Assoc.
1.	action	1	–	–	–
2.	activity	2	–	–	1
3.	affair	1	–	–	–
4.	against	–	–	1	–
5.	all	–	9	–	–
6.	an hour	1	–	–	–
7.	animal	–	–	–	1
8.	animals	–	1	–	1
9.	any	–	–	1	–
10.	appropriate	–	–	1	–
11.	at	–	–	–	1
12.	away	–	–	1	–
13.	bad	–	–	1	–
14.	ball	4	5	–	26
15.	ball games	–	–	–	1
16.	banquet	1	–	–	–
17.	baseball	3	10	1	17
18.	basketball	2	1	2	16
19.	battle	1	–	–	–
20.	bear	–	–	–	1
21.	big	–	5	–	1
22.	bird	–	–	–	3
23.	birds	–	1	1	–
24.	blast	1	–	1	–
25.	boat	2	–	–	–
26.	book	1	–	–	–
27.	boring	–	–	2	–
28.	bottle	1	–	–	–
29.	bout	1	–	–	–
30.	bowling	–	1	–	1
31.	boy	4	–	–	–
32.	buy	–	–	1	–
33.	called	–	–	3	–
34.	came	–	–	–	2
35.	canasta	–	–	2	–
36.	cancelled	–	–	2	–
37.	car	4	–	–	–
38.	Cardinal Puff	–	–	–	1
39.	cards	1	1	–	2
40.	catch	–	–	–	1
41.	Challenge	1	–	–	1
42.	chance	–	–	1	1
43.	checkers	–	1	–	–
44.	chess	–	–	–	1
45.	children	–	–	–	1
46.	chore	1	–	–	–
47.	church	1	–	–	–
48.	cinch	1	–	–	–
49.	circle	–	–	–	1
50.	class	2	–	–	–
51.	close	–	–	1	–
52.	clown	1	–	–	–
53.	come	–	2	–	–
54.	commission	–	–	1	–
55.	competitive	–	–	1	–
56.	competition	–	–	–	1
57.	contest	5	–	–	5
58.	correctly	–	–	1	–
59.	croquet	–	–	–	1
60.	culture	–	–	–	1
61.	dames	1	–	–	–
62.	dance	4	–	–	–
63.	darts	–	–	1	1
64.	date	1	–	–	–
65.	day	5	–	–	–
66.	days	1	–	–	–
67.	dead	1	–	–	–
68.	deer	1	–	–	1
69.	dice	–	–	–	1
70.	dirty	–	–	1	–
71.	distaste	–	–	–	1
72.	dive	1	–	–	–
73.	doctor	1	–	–	–
74.	dog	1	–	–	–
75.	doll	–	–	1	–
76.	domino	–	1	–	–
77.	drake	–	–	1	–
78.	drink	1	–	–	–

11 Game (contd)

No.	Response	Subst.	Pre	Post	Assoc.
79.	drums	1	–	–	–
80.	easy	–	–	1	–
81.	eat	–	1	–	1
82.	end	–	2	–	–
83.	endurance	–	–	–	1
84.	enjoyed	–	2	–	–
85.	enjoyable	–	1	1	–
86.	every	–	1	–	–
87.	excitement	–	2	5	–
88.	exciting	–	–	–	1
89.	faculty	–	1	–	–
90.	fair	–	1	–	1
91.	fairly	–	–	2	–
92.	fame	–	–	–	1
93.	farce	1	–	–	–
94.	fascinating	–	–	1	–
95.	fast	–	–	1	–
96.	favorite	–	3	–	–
97.	festival	1	–	–	–
98.	field	3	–	–	–
99.	fight	4	–	–	1
100.	find	–	1	–	–
101.	finished	–	–	1	–
102.	first	1	–	–	–
103.	fish	2	2	–	–
104.	fishing	1	–	–	–
105.	food	2	–	–	1
106.	football	2	17	–	35
107.	footsies	–	–	–	1
108.	Friday	–	–	1	–
109.	fun	1	4	14	45
110.	gambling	–	–	1	–
111.	giant	–	1	–	–
112.	girl	2	–	–	–
113.	girls	–	1	–	–
114.	go	–	6	–	–
115.	goes	–	–	1	–
116.	going	–	4	–	–
117.	golf	–	–	–	1
118.	good	1	11	6	1
119.	great	–	1	1	–
120.	grudge	1	–	–	1
121.	gun	1	–	–	–
122.	guns	1	–	–	–
123.	gym	–	–	1	–
124.	hand	1	–	–	–
125.	happy	2	–	–	–
126.	hard	–	–	1	–
127.	have	–	2	–	–
128.	hens	–	–	1	–
129.	here	–	–	1	–
130.	his	–	–	1	–
131.	hockey	–	1	–	1
132.	home	1	1	–	–
133.	hopscotch	–	2	–	–
134.	horn	3	–	–	–
135.	horses	4	–	1	–
136.	hot	–	–	1	–
137.	house	2	–	–	–
138.	how	–	1	–	–
139.	hunt	1	1	–	–
140.	hunting	1	–	1	–
141.	hunts	–	1	–	–
142.	hurt	–	–	–	2
143.	instrument	1	–	–	–
144.	it	–	5	–	–
145.	job	1	–	–	1
146.	join	–	1	–	–
147.	joke	–	–	–	1
148.	jumprope	1	–	–	–
149.	just	–	1	–	–
150.	kind	–	3	–	1
151.	kings	–	–	1	–
152.	knowing	1	–	–	–
153.	lame	1	–	–	1
154.	last	–	–	4	–
155.	lasted	–	–	1	–
156.	laws	–	–	1	–

11 Game (contd)

11 Game (contd)

No.	Response	Subst.	Pre	Post	Assoc.	No.	Response	Subst.	Pre	Post	Assoc.
157.	lazy	–	–	1	–	235.	Russian	–	–	1	–
158.	life	–	1	1	1	236.	same	–	–	–	1
159.	like	–	17	–	–	237.	sample	1	–	–	–
160.	liked	–	1	–	–	238.	sand	1	–	–	–
161.	likes	–	1	–	–	239.	saw	–	2	–	1
162.	lion	–	–	–	1	240.	school	–	–	–	1
163.	lost	–	4	1	1	241.	score	1	–	–	–
164.	lot	–	1	2	–	242.	screwy	–	1	–	–
165.	lots of them	–	–	–	1	243.	see	–	2	–	–
166.	love	–	2	1	4	244.	set	3	–	–	–
167.	made	–	1	–	–	245.	short	1	–	–	–
168.	make	–	1	–	–	246.	show	10	–	–	–
169.	man	3	–	–	1	247.	silly	–	1	–	–
170.	marbles	–	–	–	1	248.	ski	–	–	–	1
171.	match	2	–	–	–	249.	skill	–	–	1	–
172.	me	–	–	2	–	250.	softball	–	–	1	–
173.	meet	3	–	–	–	251.	some	–	2	–	–
174.	meeting	2	–	–	–	252.	soon	–	–	1	–
175.	method	1	–	–	–	253.	speech	2	–	–	–
176.	mom	1	–	–	–	254.	spent	–	–	–	1
177.	money	–	–	–	2	255.	spiel	–	–	–	1
178.	Monopoly	–	2	–	2	256.	sport	20	–	–	5
179.	movie	1	–	–	–	257.	sports	–	–	–	3
180.	movies	1	–	–	–	258.	spring	–	–	–	1
181.	name	1	3	–	2	259.	stadium	1	–	–	–
182.	needs	–	–	1	–	260.	start	–	1	1	–
183.	nice	–	1	–	–	261.	started	–	–	3	–
184.	noise	–	–	–	1	262.	still	–	1	–	–
185.	not	1	–	–	–	263.	store	2	–	–	–
186.	only	–	1	–	–	264.	story	2	–	–	–
187.	open	–	–	1	–	265.	stupid	–	–	1	–
188.	organ	1	–	–	–	266.	success	–	–	1	–
189.	out	–	1	–	–	267.	summer	–	–	–	1
190.	over	–	–	8	1	268.	swim	1	–	–	1
191.	park	3	–	–	1	269.	swim meet	1	–	–	–
192.	party	11	–	–	–	270.	swimming	–	–	–	3
193.	pastime	1	–	–	–	271.	tag	–	–	–	1
194.	people	2	–	–	–	272.	tame	–	–	–	1
195.	perennial	–	–	1	–	273.	taste	1	–	–	–
196.	piano	10	–	–	–	274.	tea	1	–	–	–
197.	picture	2	–	–	–	275.	team	2	–	–	–
198.	Ping-pong	–	–	–	4	276.	tennis	–	–	4	5
199.	place	2	–	–	–	277.	test	3	–	–	–
200.	plane	1	–	–	–	278.	tests	1	–	–	–
201.	play	11	47	1	94	279.	that	–	–	1	–
202.	played	–	9	5	2	280.	theater	1	–	–	–
203.	player	1	–	–	1	281.	their	–	1	1	–
204.	playing	–	3	–	–	282.	there	–	1	1	–
205.	playmate	–	–	–	1	283.	this	–	2	–	–
206.	plays	–	1	–	–	284.	Thursday	–	–	1	–
207.	pleasant	–	1	–	–	285.	time	1	1	2	3
208.	point	–	–	1	–	286.	today	–	–	6	–
209.	poker	–	1	1	–	287.	tomorrow	–	–	1	–
210.	pool	2	–	–	1	288.	tonight	–	–	3	–
211.	popular	–	1	–	–	289.	too	–	–	1	–
212.	pot	1	–	–	–	290.	took	–	1	–	–
213.	preserve	–	–	1	–	291.	tournament	2	–	–	1
214.	prize	1	–	–	–	292.	toy	2	–	–	2
215.	program	1	–	–	–	293.	track	–	–	–	1
216.	prohibit	–	1	–	–	294.	tree	1	–	–	–
217.	punishment	–	–	–	1	295.	trials	1	–	–	–
218.	put	–	1	–	–	296.	trick	2	–	–	–
219.	puzzle	–	–	–	2	297.	trophy	2	–	–	–
220.	puzzles	–	–	–	1	298.	truth	–	–	–	1
221.	quick	–	1	–	–	299.	tune	3	–	–	–
222.	quiz	–	–	–	2	300.	two	–	–	1	–
223.	race	5	–	–	–	301.	up	–	–	1	–
224.	races	1	–	–	–	302.	us	–	–	2	–
225.	racing	–	–	–	1	303.	violin	1	–	–	–
226.	radio	1	–	–	–	304.	volleyball	–	–	1	–
227.	ready	2	–	–	1	305.	walk	1	–	–	–
228.	record	1	–	–	–	306.	war	–	–	–	2
229.	requires	–	–	1	–	307.	well	–	–	4	–
230.	ride	1	–	–	–	308.	went	–	12	–	–
231.	right	–	–	1	–	309.	what	–	9	–	–
232.	rough	–	1	–	–	310.	where	–	–	–	1
233.	round	1	–	–	–	311.	why	–	–	–	1
234.	run	–	–	–	1	312.	wild	–	–	1	–

11 Game (contd)

No.	Response	Subst.	Pre	Post	Assoc.
313.	willing	1	–	–	1
314.	win	–	–	–	9
315.	winners	–	1	–	–
316.	winning	–	–	–	1
317.	won	–	12	3	4
318.	wonderful thing	1	–	–	–
319.	work	–	–	–	3
320.	world	2	–	–	–
321.	worth	–	–	2	–
322.	yellow ocher	–	–	–	1
323.	yesterday	–	–	2	–
324.	you	–	–	8	–
325.	your	1	–	–	–

Function Words		–	87	5	–
Space		–	6	193	–
N		259	365	365	380

12 Give

No.	Response	Subst.	Pre	Post	Assoc.
1.	accept	2	–	–	–
2.	administer	1	–	–	–
3.	all	–	3	1	–
4.	always	–	1	–	–
5.	and take	–	–	–	1
6.	asked	–	1	–	–
7.	assistance	–	–	1	–
8.	before	–	–	1	–
9.	best	–	1	–	–
10.	better	–	3	2	–
11.	big	–	1	–	–
12.	blood	–	–	–	1
13.	book	–	–	1	–
14.	boy	–	–	1	–
15.	break	1	–	–	–
16.	bring	4	–	–	–
17.	buy	2	–	–	–
18.	cancer	–	–	1	–
19.	care	–	–	1	2
20.	cause	–	–	1	–
21.	chance	1	–	–	–
22.	charities	–	–	1	–
23.	charity	1	–	6	2
24.	children	–	–	1	–
25.	collected	1	–	–	–
26.	come	1	–	–	–
27.	Community Chest	–	–	–	1
28.	contribution	3	–	–	2
29.	cough	1	–	–	–
30.	crusade	–	–	–	4
31.	crying	–	–	1	–
32.	dedicate	1	–	–	–
33.	donate	13	–	–	4
34.	donation	–	–	–	1
35.	everybody	–	1	–	–
36.	everyone	–	2	–	–
37.	exercise	1	–	–	–
38.	feel	1	–	–	–
39.	fight	1	–	–	–
40.	five	–	–	1	–
41.	fix	1	–	–	–
42.	free-hearted	–	–	–	1
43.	freely	–	–	–	1
44.	friendliness	–	1	–	–
45.	gave	5	–	–	7
46.	generous	–	1	–	1
47.	get	3	–	–	2
48.	given	–	–	–	1
49.	giving	–	–	–	1
50.	go	6	–	–	–
51.	going	–	4	–	–
52.	good	–	2	–	–

12 Give (contd)

No.	Response	Subst.	Pre	Post	Assoc.
53.	got	–	–	–	1
54.	grey	–	–	–	1
55.	guy	–	1	–	–
56.	hand	18	–	–	1
57.	handout	–	–	–	1
58.	have	1	2	–	–
59.	help	3	–	–	2
60.	her	–	–	2	–
61.	him	–	–	3	–
62.	hit	1	–	–	–
63.	ill	–	1	–	–
64.	in	–	–	–	1
65.	it	–	1	24	2
66.	it's	–	1	–	–
67.	Jim	–	1	–	–
68.	John	–	–	1	–
69.	keep	1	–	–	–
70.	land	3	–	–	–
71.	learn	–	1	–	–
72.	leave	2	–	–	–
73.	lend	3	–	–	–
74.	lie	1	–	–	–
75.	life	–	1	–	–
76.	like	–	2	–	–
77.	likes	–	1	–	–
78.	little	–	–	1	–
79.	live	1	–	–	–
80.	loan	1	–	–	–
81.	looks	1	–	–	–
82.	love	–	–	1	2
83.	mail	1	–	–	–
84.	make	3	–	–	–
85.	man	–	1	–	–
86.	Mary	–	1	–	–
87.	me	–	–	31	10
88.	money	–	–	4	4
89.	move	1	–	–	–
90.	now	–	–	–	2
91.	offer	3	–	–	–
92.	one	–	2	–	–
93.	opposite	–	1	–	–
94.	outstretched hands	–	–	–	1
95.	own	1	–	–	–
96.	pass	1	–	–	–
97.	pay	1	–	–	–
98.	pleasure	–	1	–	–
99.	pledge	1	–	–	–
100.	plenty	–	–	–	1
101.	present	1	–	–	–
102.	presents	–	–	1	–
103.	prize	–	–	1	–
104.	prove	1	–	–	–
105.	radiate	1	–	–	–
106.	ran	1	–	–	–
107.	read	–	1	–	–
108.	receive	1	–	7	10
109.	received	–	–	–	1
110.	reciprocate	–	–	–	1
111.	Red Cross	–	–	7	3
112.	relief	–	–	–	1
113.	return	2	–	–	–
114.	right	–	–	3	–
115.	sacrifice	1	–	–	–
116.	said	–	2	–	–
117.	say	1	–	–	–
118.	see	1	–	–	–
119.	sell	1	–	–	–
120.	send	5	–	–	–
121.	share	2	–	–	–
122.	she	–	–	–	1
123.	show	1	–	–	–
124.	so	–	–	1	–
125.	some	–	–	–	1
126.	speech	–	–	1	–
127.	take	24	–	5	72
128.	teacher	–	1	–	–
129.	tell	4	–	–	–
130.	test	–	–	1	–

12 Give (contd)

No.	Response	Subst.	Pre	Post	Assoc.
131.	that	–	–	1	–
132.	them	–	–	3	–
133.	this	–	–	1	–
134.	throw	3	–	–	–
135.	time	–	–	1	–
136.	to	–	–	–	1
137.	to them	–	–	–	1
138.	toy	–	–	1	–
139.	United Crusade	–	–	11	3
140.	up	–	–	1	–
141.	urged	–	1	–	–
142.	us	–	–	2	–
143.	U.S.	–	–	1	–
144.	want	–	1	–	1
145.	wants	1	–	–	–
146.	wonderful	–	1	1	–
147.	year	–	–	2	–
148.	yes	–	–	–	1
149.	you	–	30	7	1
150.	yourself	–	–	1	–

Function Words		–	71	2	–
Space		–	17	15	–
N		149	164	164	159

13 Hand

No.	Response	Subst.	Pre	Post	Assoc.
1.	a hand	–	–	–	1
2.	aches	–	–	1	–
3.	all	–	–	1	–
4.	anatomy	–	–	–	2
5.	arm	18	–	–	20
6.	arm in arm	1	–	–	–
7.	arm of the chair	1	–	–	–
8.	assists	–	–	1	–
9.	ball	–	1	–	–
10.	ban	1	–	–	–
11.	band	1	–	–	1
12.	bandaged	–	–	2	–
13.	bark	–	–	–	1
14.	beautiful	–	–	1	–
15.	big	–	2	2	–
16.	bigger	–	–	1	–
17.	black	–	1	–	–
18.	bleeding	–	–	1	–
19.	boat	1	–	–	–
20.	body	1	–	–	6
21.	book	2	1	–	–
22.	books	2	–	–	–
23.	boy's	–	4	–	–
24.	broke	–	2	–	–
25.	broken	–	–	3	–
26.	burned	–	2	1	–
27.	camera	1	–	–	–
28.	car	2	–	–	–
29.	card	1	–	–	1
30.	carried	–	–	1	–
31.	caught	–	1	–	–
32.	chair	1	–	–	–
33.	closed	–	1	–	–
34.	coat	1	–	–	–
35.	coin	–	1	–	–
36.	cold	–	1	4	–
37.	connect	–	1	–	–
38.	connected	–	–	1	–
39.	craft	–	–	–	1
40.	cut	–	4	1	–
41.	dark	–	–	1	–
42.	day	1	–	–	–
43.	deformed	–	–	1	–
44.	desk	1	–	–	–
45.	dirty	–	1	1	–

13 Hand (contd)

No.	Response	Subst.	Pre	Post	Assoc.
46.	dog	1	–	–	–
47.	dogs	–	1	–	–
48.	dollar	1	–	–	–
49.	door	–	–	1	–
50.	dry	–	–	1	–
51.	ear	1	–	–	–
52.	ears	2	–	–	–
53.	ego	1	–	–	–
54.	end	–	–	2	–
55.	everybody	–	1	–	–
56.	extended	–	1	–	–
57.	eye	2	–	–	1
58.	eyes	1	–	–	–
59.	face	1	–	–	2
60.	faster	–	–	1	–
61.	father's	–	1	–	–
62.	feel	–	–	1	–
63.	feet	3	–	–	2
64.	femur	1	–	–	–
65.	finger	5	–	–	14
66.	fingers	2	1	–	11
67.	five	–	–	1	–
68.	flat	–	–	–	1
69.	flesh	–	–	1	–
70.	flower	1	–	–	–
71.	foot	29	–	–	37
72.	gave	–	1	–	–
73.	girl	–	–	–	1
74.	give	5	–	–	1
75.	glove	2	–	–	7
76.	good	–	1	–	–
77.	grab	–	–	–	1
78.	grasp	–	–	–	1
79.	hair	1	–	–	–
80.	hand	–	–	1	–
81.	has	–	–	2	–
82.	hat	2	–	–	–
83.	have	–	1	–	–
84.	head	16	–	–	–
85.	heart	1	–	–	–
86.	held	–	1	–	–
87.	help	–	–	–	1
88.	helping	–	1	–	–
89.	her	–	1	–	–
90.	here	–	–	1	–
91.	high	–	1	–	–
92.	hold	–	7	–	1
93.	hot	–	–	1	–
94.	hurt	–	5	5	–
95.	hurts	–	–	2	–
96.	in hand	–	–	–	1
97.	injured	–	–	1	–
98.	it	–	1	–	–
99.	Judy's	–	1	–	–
100.	keys	–	1	–	–
101.	knight	1	–	–	–
102.	lap	1	–	–	–
103.	large	–	1	2	–
104.	leader	1	–	–	–
105.	left	–	2	–	1
106.	leg	5	–	–	3
107.	legs	1	–	–	–
108.	life	1	–	–	–
109.	long	–	–	1	–
110.	lotion	–	–	–	1
111.	man	–	–	1	–
112.	me	–	7	7	2
113.	mind	1	–	–	–
114.	mine	–	–	–	1
115.	mommy	–	–	1	–
116.	money	1	–	–	–
117.	mother	1	–	–	–
118.	motion	1	–	–	–
119.	mouth	2	–	–	1
120.	move	–	–	–	1
121.	moved	–	1	–	–
122.	music	–	–	–	2
123.	my	–	–	–	1

13 Hand (contd)

No.	Response	Subst.	Pre	Post	Assoc.
124.	nail	–	–	–	1
125.	nose	1	–	–	–
126.	note	1	–	–	–
127.	off	–	–	1	–
128.	organ	–	–	–	1
129.	over	–	–	–	1
130.	palm	–	–	–	1
131.	part	–	–	2	–
132.	part of the body	–	–	–	1
133.	pass	1	–	–	–
134.	pen	2	1	–	1
135.	people	1	–	–	–
136.	physical	–	–	1	1
137.	pink	–	–	–	1
138.	placed	–	1	–	–
139.	plate	1	–	–	–
140.	pocket	1	–	1	–
141.	potato	–	1	–	–
142.	pride	1	–	–	–
143.	proximal	–	1	–	–
144.	purse	1	–	–	–
145.	put	–	3	–	–
146.	quicker	–	–	6	–
147.	reach	–	–	–	1
148.	receive	–	–	–	1
149.	red	–	1	–	–
150.	right	–	2	–	–
151.	ring	–	–	–	3
152.	rocks	–	–	1	–
153.	saw	–	1	–	–
154.	scarf	1	–	–	–
155.	see	–	1	–	–
156.	shake	–	1	–	3
157.	shaking	–	–	1	–
158.	shook	–	3	–	–
159.	shoulder	–	–	–	1
160.	simple	–	–	1	–
161.	skin	1	–	–	1
162.	sky	–	–	–	1
163.	slave	1	–	–	–
164.	slender	–	1	–	–
165.	small	–	–	2	–
166.	some	–	–	–	1
167.	sore	–	1	1	–
168.	steady	–	–	1	–
169.	stem	1	–	–	–
170.	suitcase	1	–	–	–
171.	sweaty	–	–	1	–
172.	table	–	–	1	–
173.	take	–	2	–	–
174.	this	–	2	–	–
175.	throw	1	–	–	–
176.	tired	–	–	2	–
177.	touched	–	–	1	–
178.	tough	–	–	–	1
179.	towel	1	–	–	–
180.	two	–	2	–	–
181.	useful	–	–	1	–
182.	walked	–	1	–	–
183.	wallet	1	–	–	–
184.	warm	–	1	–	–
185.	wash	–	1	–	–
186.	watch	–	–	–	1
187.	word	1	–	–	–
188.	wrist	3	–	–	–
189.	writ	–	–	1	–
190.	write	–	–	1	–
191.	writing	–	–	–	4
192.	wrong	–	1	–	–
193.	yesterday	–	–	1	–
194.	you	–	3	–	–
	Function Words	–	65	6	–
	Space	–	2	69	–
	N	152	159	159	154

14 Has

No.	Response	Subst.	Pre	Post	Assoc.
1.	a lot	–	–	1	–
2.	always	–	2	–	–
3.	anyone	–	–	1	–
4.	apples	–	–	1	–
5.	as	–	–	–	3
6.	asked	–	1	–	–
7.	asthma	–	–	–	1
8.	baby	–	–	1	–
9.	bad	–	–	1	–
10.	ball	–	–	2	1
11.	basketball	–	–	1	–
12.	bass	–	–	–	1
13.	be	–	–	1	–
14.	beat	–	–	–	1
15.	been	–	–	30	62
16.	belongs	–	–	–	3
17.	best	–	–	1	–
18.	big	–	–	2	–
19.	Bill	–	2	–	–
20.	blue	–	–	1	–
21.	boat	–	–	3	1
22.	book	–	–	3	–
23.	bought	2	–	–	–
24.	brought	1	–	–	–
25.	brown	–	–	1	–
26.	brush	–	–	–	1
27.	Butch	–	1	–	1
28.	called	–	–	1	–
29.	can	1	1	–	1
30.	car	–	1	6	2
31.	cat	–	1	1	–
32.	caught	1	–	–	–
33.	charm	–	–	–	1
34.	clock	–	–	–	1
35.	coat	–	–	2	–
36.	cold	–	–	7	–
37.	colic	–	–	1	–
38.	come	–	–	6	5
39.	complex	–	–	1	–
40.	contains	2	–	–	1
41.	contracted	1	–	–	–
42.	crazy	–	–	–	1
43.	Dan	–	1	–	–
44.	day	–	1	–	–
45.	did	3	–	–	1
46.	died	–	–	1	–
47.	disappeared	–	–	1	–
48.	does	4	–	–	2
49.	doesn't	–	–	–	2
50.	dog	–	1	4	1
51.	done	–	–	2	1
52.	driver	–	–	1	–
53.	drives	2	–	–	–
54.	drum	–	–	1	–
55.	eaten	–	–	–	1
56.	enough	–	–	1	–
57.	everyone	–	–	1	–
58.	everything	–	–	4	2
59.	failure	–	–	–	1
60.	fallen	–	–	1	–
61.	father	–	1	–	–
62.	Father Burns	–	–	–	1
63.	finished	–	–	1	–
64.	five	–	–	1	–
65.	fleas	–	–	2	–
66.	flu	–	–	1	–
67.	food	–	–	1	–
68.	found	–	–	–	1
69.	four	–	–	1	–
70.	French	–	–	–	1
71.	fun	–	–	1	–
72.	funny	–	–	1	–
73.	get	–	–	–	1
74.	gets	–	–	1	–
75.	glass	–	–	1	–
76.	go	–	–	5	–
77.	gone	–	–	22	9
78.	good	–	–	6	–

14   Has (contd)

No.	Response	Subst.	Pre	Post	Assoc.
79.	goodies	–	–	–	1
80.	got	2	–	2	9
81.	green	–	–	1	–
82.	had	54	–	1	70
83.	hadn't	–	–	–	1
84.	hair	–	–	–	1
85.	happened	–	–	2	–
86.	has to	–	–	–	1
87.	has what?	–	–	–	1
88.	hasn't	8	–	–	17
89.	hat	–	–	1	–
90.	hates	2	–	–	–
91.	have	–	–	–	18
92.	he	–	–	–	2
93.	headache	–	–	1	–
94.	her	–	–	1	1
95.	high	–	–	1	–
96.	him	–	–	–	1
97.	his	–	–	1	9
98.	hobby	–	–	1	–
99.	hold	–	–	–	1
100.	horse	–	–	2	–
101.	hot	–	–	–	2
102.	house	–	1	–	–
103.	how	–	2	–	–
104.	how long	–	4	–	–
105.	invented	1	–	–	–
106.	is	8	–	–	4
107.	it	–	22	44	3
108.	jacket	–	–	1	–
109.	Jim	–	1	–	–
110.	John	–	2	1	–
111.	jumped	–	–	–	1
112.	keep	–	–	–	1
113.	killed	1	–	–	–
114.	knows	1	–	–	–
115.	leave	–	–	1	–
116.	left	1	–	1	–
117.	life	–	1	–	–
118.	likes	2	–	–	–
119.	lived	–	–	1	–
120.	lone	–	1	–	–
121.	long	–	6	4	–
122.	look	–	–	–	1
123.	lost	1	–	1	1
124.	love	–	–	1	–
125.	loves	2	–	–	–
126.	made	–	–	–	1
127.	makes	1	–	–	–
128.	Mary	–	2	–	–
129.	mass	–	–	–	2
130.	me	–	–	–	2
131.	measles	–	–	1	–
132.	mine	–	–	–	1
133.	money	–	–	1	2
134.	Mr. George	–	1	–	–
135.	much	–	–	–	1
136.	mumps	–	–	1	–
137.	must	–	–	–	1
138.	must go	1	–	–	–
139.	never	1	–	3	1
140.	new	–	–	5	–
141.	nice	–	–	4	–
142.	no one	–	–	1	–
143.	none	–	–	–	2
144.	not	–	–	–	16
145.	nothing	–	–	1	3
146.	now	–	1	–	2
147.	number	–	–	–	1
148.	one	–	1	6	1
149.	own	–	–	–	5
150.	owned	1	–	–	–
151.	owner	–	–	–	1
152.	ownership	–	–	–	1
153.	owns	5	–	–	4
154.	pan	–	–	–	1
155.	past	–	–	–	1
156.	pie	–	1	–	–

14   Has (contd)

No.	Response	Subst.	Pre	Post	Assoc.
157.	plague	–	–	1	–
158.	possess	–	–	–	5
159.	possesses	2	–	–	5
160.	possession	–	–	–	7
161.	possessions	–	–	–	1
162.	possessor	–	–	–	1
163.	pretty	–	–	1	–
164.	property	–	–	–	1
165.	purple	–	–	1	–
166.	qualifications	–	–	1	–
167.	rained	–	–	1	–
168.	read	1	–	–	–
169.	received	2	–	–	–
170.	red	–	1	–	–
171.	rich	–	–	–	1
172.	Ron	–	–	1	–
173.	said	1	–	–	–
174.	saw	1	–	–	–
175.	seen	–	–	–	1
176.	sense	–	–	1	–
177.	sent	–	–	1	–
178.	seven	–	–	1	–
179.	she	–	–	–	1
180.	ship	–	–	1	–
181.	shoes	–	–	1	–
182.	short	–	–	2	–
183.	sleep	–	–	–	1
184.	some	–	–	3	3
185.	someone	–	1	–	1
186.	Stude	–	–	1	–
187.	Susan	–	–	1	–
188.	swell	–	–	1	–
189.	tattoo	–	–	1	–
190.	the	–	–	–	1
191.	them	–	–	1	–
192.	this	–	–	5	1
193.	three	–	–	1	–
194.	tight	–	–	–	1
195.	time	–	–	–	1
196.	title	–	–	1	–
197.	to	–	–	–	2
198.	today	–	1	–	–
199.	took	4	–	–	–
200.	toothbrush	–	–	1	–
201.	tough	–	–	1	–
202.	toys	–	–	1	1
203.	two	–	–	2	–
204.	uses	1	–	–	–
205.	verb	–	–	–	2
206.	wants	5	–	–	1
207.	was	5	–	–	10
208.	weather	–	1	–	–
209.	what	–	6	1	11
210.	who	–	12	–	–
211.	why	–	1	–	–
212.	will	2	–	–	–
213.	will have	1	–	–	–
214.	with	–	–	–	1
215.	won	1	–	1	–
216.	wrecked	1	–	–	–
217.	you	–	1	1	1
218.	yours	–	–	–	1
219.	yoyo	–	–	1	–
220.	6	–	–	1	–
221.	52	–	–	1	–
	Function Words	–	191	66	–
	Space	–	63	4	–
	N	136	337	337	368

15 Him   15 Him (contd)

No.	Response	Subst.	Pre	Post	Assoc.	No.	Response	Subst.	Pre	Post	Assoc.
1.	a cat	2	-	-	-	79.	got	-	2	-	-
2.	a man	-	-	-	1	80.	grandfather	-	-	-	1
3.	accusative	-	-	1	-	81.	happy	-	-	1	-
4.	advantage	-	1	-	-	82.	hard	1	-	-	-
5.	all	-	1	-	-	83.	hate	-	17	-	-
6.	Allen	1	-	-	-	84.	have	-	1	-	-
7.	alone	-	-	-	1	85.	he	2	-	-	8
8.	apple	-	-	1	-	86.	hear	-	-	-	2
9.	arm	-	-	1	-	87.	help	-	1	-	-
10.	ask	-	1	-	-	88.	her	104	1	5	253
11.	asked	-	4	-	-	89.	here	1	-	2	1
12.	award	-	1	-	-	90.	hers	-	-	-	3
13.	ball	-	1	1	-	91.	herself	1	-	-	-
14.	bathrobe	-	-	-	1	92.	his	2	-	-	6
15.	beer	2	-	-	-	93.	hit	-	6	-	-
16.	before	-	-	1	-	94.	horses	1	-	-	-
17.	believe	-	1	-	-	95.	hour	-	-	1	-
18.	belonged	-	1	-	-	96.	hurt	-	1	-	-
19.	belongs	-	2	-	-	97.	hymn	-	-	-	1
20.	better	-	-	1	-	98.	I don't	-	-	-	1
21.	bib	-	-	-	1	99.	Ike	1	-	-	-
22.	bit	-	2	-	-	100.	informed	-	1	-	-
23.	bitter	-	-	-	1	101.	intelligent	-	-	1	-
24.	Bob	1	-	-	-	102.	it	22	8	-	4
25.	bone	-	-	1	-	103.	it's	-	1	-	-
26.	book	-	-	2	-	104.	Jim	4	-	-	-
27.	boy	-	-	-	32	105.	John	3	-	-	1
28.	boy friend	-	-	-	1	106.	Johnny	-	-	-	1
29.	Butch	1	-	-	-	107.	Judy	1	-	-	-
30.	call	-	2	-	-	108.	kind	-	1	-	-
31.	called	-	1	-	-	109.	know	-	8	-	-
32.	candy	1	-	-	-	110.	knows	-	1	-	-
33.	car	-	-	-	1	111.	lakes	1	-	-	-
34.	Charlie	-	-	-	1	112.	Latin class	-	-	-	1
35.	come	-	-	4	-	113.	left	-	1	1	-
36.	come back	-	-	1	-	114.	letter	-	1	-	-
37.	command	-	-	1	-	115.	like	-	88	-	1
38.	confess	-	-	1	-	116.	liked	-	2	-	-
39.	confident	-	-	-	1	117.	likes	-	12	-	-
40.	cool	-	-	-	1	118.	look	-	4	-	-
41.	corner	-	-	1	-	119.	lot	-	-	3	-
42.	cry	-	-	1	-	120.	love	-	19	-	1
43.	cute	-	-	-	1	121.	loves	-	3	-	-
44.	Dale	-	-	-	1	122.	made	-	1	-	-
45.	dance	-	-	1	-	123.	making	-	1	-	-
46.	Daniel	1	-	-	1	124.	male	-	-	-	2
47.	dead	-	-	1	-	125.	man	-	-	-	10
48.	detest	-	1	-	-	126.	matter	-	1	-	-
49.	did	-	-	3	-	127.	me	13	-	3	2
50.	dirty	-	-	1	-	128.	meet	-	1	-	-
51.	do	-	1	-	-	129.	mice	1	-	-	-
52.	dogs	2	-	-	-	130.	Mike	1	-	-	1
53.	dropped	-	1	-	-	131.	milk	1	-	-	-
54.	drunk	1	-	-	-	132.	mine	-	-	-	1
55.	eating	1	-	-	-	133.	money	1	-	-	-
56.	enjoy	-	1	-	-	134.	more	-	-	1	-
57.	Erick	1	-	-	-	135.	mother	1	-	-	-
58.	felt	-	1	-	-	136.	much	-	-	4	-
59.	fight	-	1	-	-	137.	muscles	-	-	-	1
60.	find	-	1	-	-	138.	my face	-	-	-	1
61.	fond	-	2	-	-	139.	name	-	-	1	-
62.	food	1	-	-	-	140.	Nancy	1	-	-	-
63.	found	-	1	-	-	141.	need	-	1	-	-
64.	four	-	-	1	-	142.	next	-	-	1	-
65.	friend	-	-	2	4	143.	nice	-	-	2	1
66.	fun	-	-	2	-	144.	now	-	-	1	-
67.	future	-	1	-	-	145.	O.K.	-	1	-	-
68.	game	-	-	1	-	146.	one	-	-	1	-
69.	gave	-	9	-	-	147.	only	-	-	1	-
70.	George	1	-	-	-	148.	person	-	-	-	1
71.	girls	1	-	-	-	149.	Phil	-	-	-	1
72.	give	-	7	-	-	150.	picture	-	1	-	-
73.	given	-	2	-	-	151.	pray	-	1	-	-
74.	go	1	8	2	-	152.	present	-	3	1	-
75.	God	-	-	-	1	153.	pronoun	-	-	-	1
76.	going	-	2	-	-	154.	Ralph	1	-	-	1
77.	going out	-	1	-	-	155.	Ray	-	-	-	1
78.	good	-	1	-	-	156.	rich	-	-	-	1

15 Him (contd)

No.	Response	Subst.	Pre	Post	Assoc.
157.	ride	–	–	1	–
158.	righter	–	–	–	1
159.	ring	–	–	1	–
160.	Ron	–	–	–	1
161.	Ronnie	1	–	–	–
162.	Rover	1	–	–	–
163.	run	–	–	1	–
164.	Russ	–	–	–	1
165.	said	–	1	–	–
166.	saw	–	18	–	–
167.	see	–	14	–	–
168.	seen	–	1	–	–
169.	sees	–	1	–	–
170.	sex	–	–	–	1
171.	shame	–	2	–	–
172.	she	1	–	–	9
173.	shot	–	1	–	–
174.	show	–	1	2	–
175.	speak	–	2	–	–
176.	stop	–	1	–	–
177.	Sue	1	–	–	–
178.	swim	–	–	–	1
179.	talk	–	4	–	–
180.	talked	–	1	–	–
181.	teacher	–	–	1	–
182.	tell	–	6	–	–
133.	that	1	8	2	1
184.	that boy	1	–	–	–
185.	the girl	1	–	–	–
186.	the man	3	–	–	–
187.	the stranger	1	–	–	–
188.	them	17	–	1	1
189.	there	–	–	2	–
190.	they	–	–	–	1
191.	things	–	1	–	–
192.	think	–	1	–	–
193.	this	1	2	–	–
194.	threw	–	2	–	–
195.	today	–	–	1	–
196.	told	–	7	–	–
197.	Tom	2	–	–	–
198.	too	–	–	1	–
199.	took	–	3	–	–
200.	town	1	–	–	–
201.	truth	–	–	1	–
202.	uptown	–	1	–	–
203.	us	6	–	–	–
204.	use	–	1	–	–
205.	Waldo	–	–	1	–
206.	want	–	1	–	–
207.	wanted	–	–	1	–
208.	well	–	–	1	–
209.	went	–	12	–	–
210.	what	–	2	2	–
211.	where	–	–	2	–
212.	who	–	–	–	1
213.	why	1	–	–	–
214.	wood	1	–	–	–
215.	worry	–	1	–	–
216.	wounds	1	–	–	–
217.	wrong	–	2	–	–
218.	yesterday	–	–	2	–
219.	you	18	–	–	2

Function Words		–	24	5	–
Space		–	5	288	–
N		241	376	376	380

16 Hot

No.	Response	Subst.	Pre	Post	Assoc.
1.	awfully	–	1	–	–
2.	bake	–	–	–	1
3.	bath	–	1	–	–
4.	bean	–	1	–	–
5.	beautiful	1	–	–	–
6.	became	–	1	–	–
7.	blue	1	–	–	–
8.	boiling	1	–	–	1
9.	bowl	–	1	–	–
10.	bread	–	–	–	4
11.	bright	1	–	–	–
12.	bun	–	–	–	1
13.	burn	–	–	–	5
14.	burner	–	1	–	–
15.	cakes	–	–	–	1
16.	Calif.	–	1	–	–
17.	car	–	4	–	2
18.	chocolate	–	–	–	1
19.	clean	1	–	–	–
20.	coal	–	1	–	–
21.	coffee	–	7	3	2
22.	cold	86	1	2	95
23.	Colorado River	–	–	1	–
24.	cool	5	–	–	–
25.	cusine	–	1	–	–
26.	day	–	2	11	–
27.	days	–	–	1	–
28.	degrees	–	–	–	1
29.	desert	–	1	–	–
30.	dinner	–	1	–	–
31.	dirty	1	–	–	–
32.	dog	–	–	2	4
33.	dogs	–	–	1	–
34.	drink	–	–	1	–
35.	drinks	–	1	–	–
36.	dry	3	–	–	–
37.	extremely	–	1	–	–
38.	fast	1	–	–	–
39.	faucet	–	1	–	–
40.	fire	–	5	–	5
41.	flame	–	1	1	–
42.	food	–	2	1	–
43.	foods	–	1	–	–
44.	forehead	–	1	–	–
45.	gay	1	–	–	–
46.	get	–	1	–	–
47.	girl	–	–	–	1
48.	gone	–	–	–	1
49.	good	3	–	–	–
50.	got	–	1	–	–
51.	handle	–	1	–	–
52.	have	–	1	–	–
53.	Hawaii	–	–	1	–
54.	head	–	–	–	1
55.	heat	1	–	–	2
56.	heated	1	–	–	–
57.	heater	–	–	–	1
58.	hell	–	–	1	–
59.	high	1	–	–	–
60.	hold	–	–	2	–
61.	how	–	2	–	–
62.	humid	3	–	–	1
63.	ice	1	–	–	–
64.	inside	–	2	1	–
65.	iron	–	2	1	1
66.	it	–	23	2	–
67.	it's	–	4	–	–
68.	labeled	–	1	–	–
69.	large	1	–	–	–
70.	like	–	5	–	–
71.	likes	–	1	–	–
72.	long	2	1	–	–
73.	love	–	1	–	–
74.	mad	1	–	–	–
75.	man	–	–	1	–
76.	meal	–	–	1	–
77.	milk	–	1	1	–
78.	miserable	–	1	–	–

16 Hot (contd)

No.	Response	Subst.	Pre	Post	Assoc.
79.	miserably	1	–	–	–
80.	molecules	–	–	–	1
81.	Monday	–	1	–	–
82.	months	–	1	–	–
83.	mush	–	–	1	–
84.	New Orleans	–	–	1	–
85.	nice	1	–	–	–
86.	night	–	–	1	–
87.	on	1	–	–	–
88.	one	–	1	–	–
89.	opposite	–	–	1	–
90.	ouch!	–	–	–	2
91.	oven	–	3	–	–
92.	pad	–	–	–	1
93.	pan	–	4	–	–
94.	pavement's	–	1	–	–
95.	plate	–	2	–	1
96.	pot	–	–	1	–
97.	potato	–	–	–	2
98.	prefer	–	1	–	–
99.	red	3	1	–	4
100.	right	1	–	1	–
101.	rod	–	–	–	2
102.	rough	1	–	–	–
103.	scalding	–	–	1	–
104.	snow	1	–	–	–
105.	so	–	1	–	–
106.	some	–	–	1	–
107.	something	–	1	–	–
108.	soup	–	4	1	–
109.	southern	–	–	1	–
110.	spice	1	–	–	–
111.	started	–	–	1	–
112.	state	–	–	1	–
113.	steam	–	–	–	2
114.	steaming	–	–	–	1
115.	stolen	1	–	–	1
116.	stone	–	–	–	1
117.	stove	–	13	1	7
118.	strong	1	–	–	–
119.	sultry	–	–	1	–
120.	summer	–	1	4	–
121.	sun	–	3	2	2
122.	swampy	1	–	–	–
123.	sweat	–	–	–	1
124.	sweet	1	–	–	–
125.	sweltering	1	–	–	–
126.	tea	–	–	1	–
127.	this	–	1	–	–
128.	today	–	2	2	–
129.	tonight	–	–	1	–
130.	touch	–	–	1	–
131.	touched	–	1	–	–
132.	uncomfortable	–	–	–	1
133.	uncomfortably	–	1	–	1
134.	use	–	1	–	–
135.	warm	20	–	–	1
136.	warmth	1	–	–	–
137.	water	–	15	3	2
138.	weather	–	4	1	–
139.	week end	–	–	1	–
140.	wet	1	–	–	–
141.	what	–	2	–	–
142.	yesterday	–	–	1	–
143.	29 palms	–	1	–	–
	Function Words	–	11	–	–
	Space	–	4	99	–
	N	153	165	165	164

17 How

No.	Response	Subst.	Pre	Post	Assoc.
1.	about	–	1	–	4
2.	about that	–	–	–	1
3.	again	–	–	–	1
4.	all	–	–	1	–
5.	am	–	–	–	1
6.	are	–	–	–	6
7.	ask	–	2	–	–
8.	asked	–	5	–	–
9.	beautiful	–	–	–	1
10.	because	–	–	–	3
11.	big	–	–	1	4
12.	blank	–	–	–	1
13.	book	–	–	1	–
14.	bow	1	–	–	–
15.	build	–	–	–	1
16.	can	–	–	–	2
17.	card	–	–	–	1
18.	choice	–	–	–	1
19.	climbing	–	–	–	1
20.	come	1	–	4	16
21.	como	1	–	–	–
22.	cow	–	–	–	3
23.	decide	–	1	–	–
24.	depends	–	1	–	–
25.	devil	–	–	–	1
26.	did	–	–	–	1
27.	directions	–	–	–	1
28.	do	–	–	14	4
29.	done	–	–	–	1
30.	earth	–	–	2	–
31.	easy	–	–	–	2
32.	ever	–	–	–	3
33.	explain	–	–	–	3
34.	expression	–	1	–	–
35.	family	–	–	1	–
36.	far	–	–	1	–
37.	fast	–	–	–	2
38.	find	–	–	–	1
39.	five	1	–	–	–
40.	found	–	1	–	–
41.	go	1	–	1	–
42.	grass	–	–	–	1
43.	hard	–	–	–	2
44.	hello	1	–	–	–
45.	her	–	1	–	–
46.	here	–	1	–	–
47.	high	–	–	–	1
48.	his	–	–	–	1
49.	hope	–	–	–	1
50.	Howdy Doody	–	–	–	1
51.	however	–	–	–	2
52.	idiot	–	–	–	1
53.	impossible	–	–	–	1
54.	incoherent	–	–	–	1
55.	Indian	–	–	–	4
56.	Indians	–	–	–	1
57.	is	–	–	–	1
58.	it	1	2	17	–
59.	kill	–	–	1	–
60.	know	–	18	–	2
61.	large	–	–	–	1
62.	learned	–	1	–	–
63.	long	–	–	3	3
64.	lovely	–	–	–	1
65.	make	–	–	–	1
66.	manner	–	–	–	1
67.	many	–	–	7	9
68.	many times	–	–	–	1
69.	me	–	4	–	–
70.	means	–	–	–	1
71.	method	–	–	–	1
72.	much	–	–	6	9
73.	mush	–	–	–	1
74.	nice	–	–	–	1
75.	not how	–	–	–	1
76.	not sure	–	–	–	1
77.	now	2	–	22	79
78.	often	–	–	2	1

17 How (contd)

No.	Response	Subst.	Pre	Post	Assoc.
79.	old	–	–	1	–
80.	plow	–	–	–	1
81.	possible	–	–	–	1
82.	problem	–	–	–	1
83.	puzzled	–	–	–	1
84.	question	–	–	1	18
85.	question mark	–	–	–	1
86.	right	1	–	–	–
87.	round	–	–	–	1
88.	said	–	–	1	–
89.	saw	–	1	–	–
90.	say	–	1	–	–
91.	see	1	2	–	–
92.	sew	–	–	–	1
93.	show	–	–	–	1
94.	that	2	1	5	–
95.	the	–	–	–	1
96.	the way	3	–	–	–
97.	theme	–	–	–	1
98.	then	–	–	1	2
99.	they	1	–	–	1
100.	this	1	5	3	1
101.	thus	–	–	–	1
102.	to	–	–	–	4
103.	told	–	1	–	–
104.	us	–	2	–	–
105.	was	–	–	–	1
106.	water	–	–	–	1
107.	way	–	–	–	4
108.	we	–	–	–	1
109.	went	–	1	–	–
110.	what	17	–	–	12
111.	what for	–	–	–	1
112.	when	14	3	–	12
113.	where	12	1	–	5
114.	which	–	–	–	2
115.	who	3	–	–	4
116.	whose	–	–	–	1
117.	why	30	–	1	50
118.	wonder	–	5	–	–
119.	world	–	–	1	–
120.	would	–	–	–	1
121.	wow	–	–	–	1
122.	you	–	–	104	–

Function Words		–	7	32	–
Space		–	181	16	–
N		94	250	250	331

18 Hers

No.	Response	Subst.	Pre	Post	Assoc.
1.	all	–	2	–	–
2.	ball	–	2	–	–
3.	bathroom	–	1	–	–
4.	bath towel	–	–	–	1
5.	bath towels	–	–	–	1
6.	beautiful	–	–	1	–
7.	best	–	–	2	–
8.	bigger	–	–	1	–
9.	blue	–	–	1	–
10.	Bob's	1	–	–	–
11.	book	–	8	–	–
12.	books	–	1	–	–
13.	boy	–	–	–	2
14.	bra	–	–	–	1
15.	car	–	2	–	1
16.	careful	–	–	–	1
17.	charm	–	–	1	–
18.	clothes	–	1	–	1
19.	coat	–	1	–	1
20.	dainty	–	–	–	1
21.	decide	–	–	1	–

18 Hers (contd)

No.	Response	Subst.	Pre	Post	Assoc.
22.	doll	–	–	–	1
23.	dress	–	3	–	2
24.	female	–	–	–	1
25.	fine	–	–	1	–
26.	gift	–	–	–	1
27.	girl	–	–	–	1
28.	girls	1	–	–	–
29.	goes	–	–	–	1
30.	gone	–	–	1	–
31.	good	–	–	1	–
32.	Grecian	–	–	1	–
33.	hair	–	–	–	1
34.	her	–	–	–	1
35.	herbs	–	–	–	1
36.	him	1	–	–	1
37.	his	50	6	3	114
38.	is	–	–	–	3
39.	it	–	42	1	–
40.	it's	–	–	–	1
41.	its	–	–	–	1
42.	Jane's	1	–	–	–
43.	jealous	–	–	–	1
44.	John's	1	–	–	–
45.	like	–	2	–	–
46.	liked	–	1	–	–
47.	likes	–	1	–	–
48.	lost	–	–	1	–
49.	love	–	–	–	1
50.	Mam's	–	–	–	1
51.	me	–	–	–	1
52.	mind	–	–	1	–
53.	mine	15	2	7	21
54.	money	–	–	–	1
55.	music	–	1	–	–
56.	my	–	–	–	1
57.	nice	–	–	1	–
58.	now	–	–	1	1
59.	nurse	–	1	–	–
60.	others	–	–	–	1
61.	ours	1	–	–	3
62.	own	–	–	–	1
63.	possession	–	–	–	2
64.	possessive	–	–	–	1
65.	pretty	–	–	1	–
66.	reality	–	–	1	–
67.	red	–	–	1	–
68.	right	–	–	1	–
69.	says	–	2	–	–
70.	share	–	–	–	2
71.	she	–	–	–	2
72.	sure	–	1	–	–
73.	table	–	–	1	–
74.	talent	–	–	–	1
75.	tender	–	–	–	1
76.	that	–	15	–	–
77.	theirs	8	–	–	4
78.	there	1	2	2	–
79.	this	1	13	–	–
80.	those	–	1	–	–
81.	toreadors	–	–	–	1
82.	tough	–	–	1	–
83.	towel	–	3	1	3
84.	towels	–	1	–	1
85.	wedding	–	–	–	1
86.	what	–	2	–	–
87.	why	–	–	–	1
88.	woman's	–	–	–	1
89.	wonderful	–	–	–	1
90.	wrong	–	–	1	–
91.	yours	2	–	4	8

Function Words		–	3	3	–
Space		–	22	99	–
N		83	142	142	203

19 If

No.	Response	Subst.	Pre	Post	Assoc.
1.	against	–	–	–	1
2.	all	–	1	–	1
3.	and	5	–	–	2
4.	any	–	–	2	16
5.	anyone	–	–	1	–
6.	anything	–	–	–	1
7.	as	1	–	–	2
8.	at	–	–	–	1
9.	at all	–	–	–	1
10.	awful	1	–	–	–
11.	because	3	–	–	5
12.	big	–	–	1	–
13.	big meaning	–	–	–	1
14.	big word	–	–	–	1
15.	book	–	–	–	1
16.	boy	–	–	–	1
17.	but	6	–	–	9
18.	cake	–	1	–	–
19.	Cal	–	–	–	1
20.	call	–	2	–	–
21.	can	1	–	–	–
22.	can't	–	–	–	1
23.	cats	–	–	–	1
24.	come	–	11	–	–
25.	conclusion	–	–	–	1
26.	condition	1	–	–	4
27.	conditional	–	–	–	1
28.	conjunction	–	–	–	3
29.	could	1	1	–	7
30.	cull	–	–	1	–
31.	dad	–	–	1	–
32.	definite	–	–	–	1
33.	die	–	3	–	–
34.	differ	–	–	–	1
35.	do	1	1	–	–
36.	doubt	–	–	–	1
37.	dream	–	–	–	1
38.	drive	–	1	–	–
39.	eat	–	1	–	–
40.	either	–	–	–	1
41.	even	–	–	–	1
42.	ever	–	–	–	1
43.	for	2	–	–	–
44.	future	–	–	–	1
45.	go	–	44	–	2
46.	going	–	1	–	–
47.	gum	–	–	–	1
48.	happy	–	–	1	–
49.	he	–	–	–	5
50.	her	–	2	–	–
51.	here	–	1	–	–
52.	him	–	1	–	–
53.	his	–	1	–	–
54.	how	1	–	–	1
55.	however	1	–	–	–
56.	I	–	–	–	2
57.	I may	–	–	–	1
58.	is	–	–	–	3
59.	it	–	13	23	10
60.	know	–	4	–	–
61.	leave	–	1	1	–
62.	left	–	1	–	–
63.	little	–	–	1	–
64.	long meaning	–	–	–	1
65.	look	–	1	–	–
66.	may	1	–	–	4
67.	maybe	6	1	–	50
68.	me	–	2	–	–
69.	meaning	–	–	–	1
70.	might	–	–	–	1
71.	mother	–	–	1	1
72.	neither	–	–	–	1
73.	never	–	–	–	1
74.	no	–	–	–	1
75.	not	1	–	–	20
76.	not sure	–	–	–	1
77.	nothing	1	–	–	1
78.	now	3	–	–	1

19 If (contd)

No.	Response	Subst.	Pre	Post	Assoc.
79.	O.K.	–	–	–	1
80.	oh	–	–	–	1
81.	om	–	–	–	1
82.	only	–	2	3	3
83.	or	–	–	–	12
84.	pen	–	–	–	1
85.	perhaps	–	–	–	1
86.	play	–	1	–	–
87.	please	–	–	–	2
88.	possibility	–	–	–	1
89.	possible	–	–	–	1
90.	prepositions	–	–	–	1
91.	probably	–	–	–	1
92.	proposition	–	–	–	1
93.	provided	1	–	–	–
94.	providing	1	–	–	–
95.	question	–	–	2	9
96.	questions	–	–	1	–
97.	Raphael	–	–	1	–
98.	result	–	–	–	1
99.	run	–	1	–	–
100.	sadness	–	–	–	1
101.	said	–	2	–	–
102.	school	–	–	–	1
103.	see	–	6	1	1
104.	seeing	1	–	–	–
105.	serve	–	–	–	1
106.	she	–	–	–	2
107.	ship	–	–	–	1
108.	should	1	–	–	1
109.	show	–	1	–	–
110.	si	1	–	–	1
111.	si si	–	–	–	1
112.	since	5	–	–	–
113.	skiing	1	–	–	–
114.	small	–	–	–	1
115.	so	2	–	1	13
116.	some	–	–	1	1
117.	something	–	–	–	1
118.	sometimes	–	–	–	1
119.	song	–	–	–	1
120.	soon	1	–	–	–
121.	sounds	–	1	–	–
122.	spells	–	1	–	–
123.	stay	–	2	–	–
124.	study	–	1	–	–
125.	subjunctive	–	–	–	4
126.	succeed	–	1	–	–
127.	supposing	1	–	–	2
128.	sure	1	–	–	1
129.	teacher	–	–	–	1
130.	that	2	2	–	3
131.	the	1	–	–	–
132.	the one	1	–	–	–
133.	them	–	–	–	2
134.	then	1	–	–	9
135.	there	–	–	–	1
136.	therefore	–	–	–	1
137.	these	–	–	–	1
138.	they	–	–	–	13
139.	tomorrow	–	–	1	–
140.	uncertainty	–	–	–	1
141.	unless	1	–	–	1
142.	walk	–	1	–	–
143.	was	–	–	–	2
144.	we	–	–	–	2
145.	were	–	–	–	2
146.	what	1	32	–	18
147.	what if	1	–	–	–
148.	when	42	–	2	16
149.	where	1	–	–	–
150.	whether	4	–	–	2
151.	which	–	–	–	1
152.	while	3	–	–	–
153.	why	6	–	–	8
154.	will	1	–	–	2
155.	wish	–	–	–	1
156.	wonder	–	4	–	–

19 If (contd)

No.	Response	Subst.	Pre	Post	Assoc.
157.	would	1	5	–	–
158.	yes	–	1	–	4
159.	yet	1	–	–	–
160.	you	–	9	146	17
161.	2	–	–	1	–
	Function Words	–	21	134	–
	Space	–	139	1	–
	N	118	328	328	359

20 It

No.	Response	Subst.	Pre	Post	Assoc.
1.	a cat	1	–	–	–
2.	a thing	–	–	–	1
3.	after	1	–	–	–
4.	after all	–	1	–	–
5.	all	1	–	4	–
6.	all right	–	–	1	–
7.	and	–	–	–	1
8.	ants	–	–	–	1
9.	anything	–	–	–	1
10.	appear	–	–	1	–
11.	ate	–	1	–	–
12.	baby	–	–	–	1
13.	back	–	–	1	–
14.	bad	–	–	2	–
15.	beautiful	–	–	1	–
16.	became	–	1	–	–
17.	before	–	–	1	–
18.	belongs	–	–	–	1
19.	big	–	–	3	1
20.	black	–	–	1	–
21.	blast	–	–	1	–
22.	blob	–	–	–	1
23.	book	–	–	–	1
24.	books	1	–	–	–
25.	came	–	2	1	5
26.	camera	–	–	–	1
27.	can	–	–	–	1
28.	candy	1	–	–	–
29.	car	–	–	–	1
30.	cat	–	–	–	1
31.	chase	–	3	–	–
32.	chased	–	1	1	–
33.	chasing	–	1	–	–
34.	cold	–	–	4	–
35.	come	–	–	2	–
36.	comes	–	–	–	1
37.	conspiracy	–	–	1	–
38.	cream	–	–	–	1
39.	cricket	–	–	1	–
40.	crocodile	–	1	–	–
41.	dark	–	–	2	–
42.	daylight	–	–	1	–
43.	dead	1	–	–	–
44.	dear	–	–	–	1
45.	death	–	–	1	–
46.	demonstrates	–	–	–	1
47.	did	–	3	–	–
48.	die	–	–	1	–
49.	do	–	10	–	–
50.	dog	–	–	–	5
51.	doing	–	–	1	–
52.	done	–	1	2	–
53.	double-header	–	–	1	–
54.	eat	–	–	–	1
55.	economical	–	–	1	–
56.	end	–	–	–	1
57.	everything	–	–	–	2
58.	far	–	–	2	–
59.	fear	–	–	–	1
60.	fella	–	–	–	1

20 It (contd)

No.	Response	Subst.	Pre	Post	Assoc.
61.	felt	–	1	–	–
62.	find	–	1	–	–
63.	fine	–	–	2	–
64.	finger	–	–	–	1
65.	fist	1	–	–	–
66.	flew	–	–	1	–
67.	food	–	–	–	1
68.	forget	–	–	1	–
69.	found	–	1	–	–
70.	fun	–	–	2	–
71.	gave	–	2	–	1
72.	get	–	1	–	–
73.	get away	–	–	1	–
74.	girl	–	–	–	1
75.	go	–	–	–	1
76.	goes	–	–	1	–
77.	going	–	1	–	–
78.	good	1	–	8	–
79.	half	–	–	1	–
80.	happen	–	–	–	2
81.	happened	–	–	2	–
82.	happens	–	–	2	–
83.	hard	–	–	1	–
84.	has	–	–	–	5
85.	have	–	1	–	–
86.	he	6	–	–	3
87.	hear	1	–	–	–
88.	her	5	–	2	–
89.	hers	–	–	2	2
90.	hide	–	1	–	–
91.	him	4	–	1	4
92.	hit	–	–	1	1
93.	hot	–	–	2	–
94.	how	–	1	–	–
95.	hurt	–	1	–	–
96.	hurts	–	–	2	1
97.	id	–	–	–	1
98.	I'm	1	–	–	–
99.	interested	–	–	1	–
100.	is	–	–	–	39
101.	it's	–	–	–	2
102.	its	–	–	–	2
103.	John	1	–	1	–
104.	kill	–	1	–	–
105.	knew	–	2	–	–
106.	know	–	2	–	–
107.	large	–	–	1	–
108.	late	–	–	3	–
109.	later	–	–	2	–
110.	let	–	1	–	–
111.	like	–	4	–	–
112.	likes	–	–	–	1
113.	lingers	–	–	1	–
114.	lit	–	–	–	1
115.	long	–	–	2	–
116.	look	–	2	–	–
117.	looks	–	–	1	–
118.	lost	–	–	1	–
119.	love	–	5	–	1
120.	lovely	–	–	–	1
121.	makes	–	–	1	1
122.	me	2	–	1	1
123.	mine	1	–	3	–
124.	M.I.T.	–	–	–	1
125.	Monday	1	–	–	–
126.	money	–	–	–	1
127.	monster	1	–	–	3
128.	moved	–	–	1	–
129.	moves	–	–	1	–
130.	movie	–	–	–	1
131.	much	–	–	1	–
132.	my	–	–	–	1
133.	neuter	–	–	–	6
134.	neutral	–	–	–	1
135.	nice	–	–	5	–
136.	night	1	–	–	–
137.	no	1	–	–	–
138.	nothing	–	–	–	2

20 It (contd)

No.	Response	Subst.	Pre	Post	Assoc.
139.	novel	−	−	−	1
140.	now	−	−	1	2
141.	object	−	−	−	2
142.	other	−	−	−	1
143.	our	−	−	1	−
144.	ours	−	−	1	2
145.	over	−	−	1	−
146.	pain	−	−	−	1
147.	pen	−	−	−	1
148.	pit	−	−	−	1
149.	pretty	−	−	2	−
150.	quick	−	−	1	−
151.	quickly	−	−	1	−
152.	rained	−	−	−	1
153.	raining	−	−	2	−
154.	right	−	−	1	−
155.	Rover	−	−	1	−
156.	run	−	1	−	−
157.	sad	−	1	1	−
158.	said	−	1	−	−
159.	same	−	−	1	−
160.	saw	−	2	−	−
161.	say	−	1	−	−
162.	see	−	5	−	−
163.	seems	−	−	−	2
164.	seen	−	1	−	−
165.	self	−	−	−	1
166.	sharp	−	−	1	−
167.	she	4	−	−	5
168.	shelf	−	−	1	−
169.	shines	−	−	−	1
170.	should	−	−	−	2
171.	sit	−	−	−	1
172.	so	−	−	−	1
173.	something	−	−	−	10
174.	stinks	−	−	1	−
175.	stop	−	1	−	−
176.	stranger	−	−	−	1
177.	stupid	−	−	2	−
178.	take	−	1	−	−
179.	take care	−	1	−	−
180.	taken	−	1	−	−
181.	tap game	−	−	−	1
182.	tastes	−	−	1	−
183.	teacher	−	−	−	1
184.	than	−	−	−	1
185.	that	16	2	1	33
186.	the	−	−	−	1
187.	the bone	1	−	−	−
188.	the cat	1	−	−	−
189.	the visit	1	−	−	−
190.	the work	1	−	−	−
191.	theirs	−	−	−	2
192.	them	10	−	−	9
193.	then	−	−	−	1
194.	there	1	2	1	3
195.	they	1	−	−	7
196.	thing	−	−	−	25
197.	this	4	5	−	1
198.	Thursday	−	−	1	−
199.	time	−	−	1	1
200.	to	−	−	−	1
201.	today	1	−	1	−
202.	took	−	2	−	−
203.	true	−	−	1	−
204.	two	−	−	1	−
205.	unknown	−	−	−	1
206.	up	−	−	−	1
207.	us	−	−	−	2
208.	use	−	2	−	−
209.	want	−	4	−	−
210.	was	−	−	−	28
211.	we	−	−	−	1
212.	went	−	−	−	2
213.	what	3	7	−	10
214.	where	−	1	−	−
215.	which	−	1	−	1
216.	white	−	−	1	−

20 It (contd)

No.	Response	Subst.	Pre	Post	Assoc.
217.	who	−	1	−	−
218.	whom	−	−	−	1
219.	why	1	−	1	−
220.	will	−	−	−	3
221.	wit	−	−	−	1
222.	wonderful	−	−	1	−
223.	word	−	1	−	1
224.	works	−	−	−	1
225.	you	1	−	2	7
226.	your	−	−	−	1
227.	yours	1	−	−	−
228.	3 o'clock	−	−	2	−
229.	4:15	−	−	1	−
	Function Words	−	16	16	−
	Space	−	100	65	−
	N	80	212	212	305

21 Long

No.	Response	Subst.	Pre	Post	Assoc.
1.	a long pier	−	−	−	1
2.	acquaintances	−	−	1	−
3.	adventurous	1	−	−	−
4.	ago	−	−	−	3
5.	bad	2	−	1	−
6.	banana	−	−	−	1
7.	barn	−	−	1	1
8.	big	1	−	−	2
9.	black	1	−	−	−
10.	board	−	−	3	−
11.	boat	−	1	−	−
12.	body	−	−	1	−
13.	boring	1	−	−	−
14.	broad	−	−	−	1
15.	car	−	−	2	−
16.	coat	−	1	−	−
17.	cold	2	−	−	−
18.	come	−	1	−	−
19.	complex	1	−	−	−
20.	concise	−	1	−	−
21.	course	−	−	1	−
22.	cow	−	−	−	1
23.	dachshund	−	1	−	−
24.	dark	−	−	1	−
25.	day	−	−	2	1
26.	distance	1	−	1	2
27.	distant	1	−	−	−
28.	dog	−	1	1	−
29.	down	−	1	−	−
30.	dress	−	2	−	−
31.	drive	−	−	1	−
32.	exciting	−	−	1	−
33.	extensive	1	−	−	−
34.	extreme	−	−	−	1
35.	far	2	−	−	−
36.	fast	2	−	−	−
37.	fat	2	−	−	−
38.	feet	−	1	−	−
39.	fingers	−	1	−	−
40.	foot	−	2	1	−
41.	forever	1	−	−	−
42.	funny	1	−	−	−
43.	gave	−	1	−	−
44.	get	−	−	1	−
45.	girl	−	1	−	−
46.	gone	−	−	1	1
47.	gong	−	−	−	1
48.	good	1	−	−	−
49.	gray	1	−	−	−
50.	had	−	1	−	−
51.	hair	−	4	3	1
52.	hairy	1	−	−	−

21 Long (contd)

No.	Response	Subst.	Pre	Post	Assoc.
53.	hands	–	1	–	–
54.	hard	2	–	–	–
55.	has	–	5	–	–
56.	have	–	1	–	–
57.	highway	–	–	1	–
58.	hikes	–	–	1	–
59.	him	–	1	–	–
60.	hot	1	1	–	–
61.	hot dog	–	–	1	–
62.	hot dogs	–	1	–	–
63.	house	–	1	1	–
64.	how	–	13	–	–
65.	it	–	29	2	–
66.	it's	–	10	–	–
67.	I've	–	–	1	–
68.	Jim	–	1	–	–
69.	John	–	–	–	1
70.	John Silver	–	–	–	1
71.	journey	–	–	1	–
72.	keep	–	1	–	–
73.	lake	–	2	–	–
74.	large	1	–	–	–
75.	late	2	–	–	–
76.	legs	–	1	1	–
77.	length	–	–	–	3
78.	lengthy	1	–	–	1
79.	letter	–	1	–	–
80.	life	–	1	–	–
81.	like	–	1	–	–
82.	line	–	1	2	1
83.	lingering	1	–	–	–
84.	little	1	–	–	–
85.	long	–	1	–	1
86.	low	–	–	2	–
87.	make	–	1	–	–
88.	mile	–	–	–	1
89.	miserably	–	1	–	–
90.	Mississippi	–	1	–	–
91.	monotonous	1	–	–	–
92.	much	1	–	–	–
93.	narrow	1	–	3	–
94.	new	1	–	–	–
95.	nice	3	–	–	–
96.	night	1	–	–	–
97.	nights	–	1	–	–
98.	noon	–	–	1	–
99.	now	1	–	1	–
100.	old	–	–	1	–
101.	opposite	–	1	–	–
102.	owned	–	1	–	–
103.	pass	–	–	2	–
104.	path	–	1	–	–
105.	pencil	–	2	–	–
106.	pencils	–	1	–	–
107.	pens	–	–	1	–
108.	period	–	1	–	–
109.	pier	–	–	–	1
110.	pole	–	–	2	1
111.	pretty	–	1	–	–
112.	rifle	–	–	–	2
113.	river	–	–	2	–
114.	road	–	6	3	1
115.	rod	–	–	–	1
116.	rope	–	2	–	–
117.	rough	1	–	–	–
118.	round	1	–	–	–
119.	route	–	1	–	–
120.	rugged	1	–	–	–
121.	ruler	–	–	1	–
122.	run	–	–	–	1
123.	school	–	–	–	1
124.	ship	–	–	–	1
125.	short	89	1	3	99
126.	shows	–	1	–	–
127.	skinny	–	–	–	1
128.	slender	–	–	–	3
129.	speech	–	1	1	–
130.	squat	1	–	–	–

21 Long (contd)

No.	Response	Subst.	Pre	Post	Assoc.
131.	statement	–	–	1	–
132.	stay	–	–	1	–
133.	stick	–	–	–	1
134.	story	–	1	–	–
135.	straight	1	–	1	1
136.	strange	1	–	–	–
137.	stretch	–	–	–	1
138.	stretched out	1	–	–	–
139.	string	–	–	–	1
140.	strips	–	–	1	–
141.	stubby	1	–	–	–
142.	sum	1	–	–	–
143.	table	–	3	–	1
144.	tail	–	–	2	1
145.	take	–	1	–	–
146.	takes	–	1	–	–
147.	tall	2	–	–	4
148.	tasting	1	–	–	–
149.	tedious	2	–	–	–
150.	terrible	1	–	–	–
151.	test	–	1	1	–
152.	that	–	2	–	–
153.	the	1	–	–	–
154.	they've	–	–	1	–
155.	thin	–	–	–	1
156.	this	–	2	–	–
157.	threw	–	2	–	–
158.	tight	–	–	–	1
159.	time	1	–	17	5
160.	Tipperary	–	–	1	–
161.	tiresome	1	–	–	–
162.	took	–	3	–	–
163.	track	–	1	–	–
164.	tracks	–	–	–	1
165.	train	–	3	1	1
166.	trip	–	1	6	–
167.	two	–	1	–	–
168.	waited	–	1	–	–
169.	walk	–	–	3	–
170.	way	–	–	15	–
171.	ways	–	–	1	–
172.	went	–	1	–	–
173.	wish	1	–	–	–
174.	you	–	1	5	–
	Function Words	–	20	0	–
	Space	–	3	51	–
	N	149	165	165	157

22 Meat

No.	Response	Subst.	Pre	Post	Assoc.
1.	a lot	–	1	–	–
2.	again	–	–	1	–
3.	age	–	1	–	–
4.	also	–	–	1	–
5.	animal	–	1	1	5
6.	animals	–	–	–	1
7.	ants	1	–	–	–
8.	anything	1	–	–	–
9.	ate	–	11	–	–
10.	awful	–	–	1	–
11.	axe	–	–	–	1
12.	bad	–	–	2	–
13.	ball	–	–	–	4
14.	balls	–	–	–	1
15.	bananas	1	–	–	–
16.	bean	1	–	–	–
17.	beat	–	1	–	2
18.	beaten	–	–	–	1
19.	beef	–	1	–	5
20.	best	–	–	1	–
21.	big	–	1	–	–

22 Meat (contd)

No.	Response	Subst.	Pre	Post	Assoc.
22.	biscuits	1	–	–	–
23.	blood	–	–	–	3
24.	bloody	–	–	1	–
25.	bone	–	–	–	1
26.	bread	4	–	1	4
27.	breakfast	–	–	1	–
28.	broiled	–	–	1	–
29.	brook	–	–	–	1
30.	burned	–	–	1	–
31.	butcher	–	–	–	4
32.	cake	4	–	–	1
33.	candy	4	–	–	–
34.	car	2	–	–	–
35.	carne	–	–	–	2
36.	carnivorous	–	–	–	1
37.	carrots	1	–	–	–
38.	cars	–	–	–	1
39.	cat	1	–	–	–
40.	cattle	–	–	–	1
41.	celery	1	–	–	–
42.	cheese	–	–	–	1
43.	chew	–	–	–	1
44.	chewy	–	–	1	–
45.	chicken	2	–	–	1
46.	chop	–	–	–	1
47.	chopper	–	–	–	1
48.	cleaner	–	–	–	2
49.	cleaver	–	–	–	1
50.	cold	–	–	1	1
51.	connect	–	–	–	1
52.	cook	1	–	–	–
53.	counter	–	–	1	–
54.	course	1	–	–	–
55.	cow	1	–	–	6
56.	cows	–	–	–	2
57.	crawling	–	–	1	–
58.	cut	–	1	–	–
59.	dark	–	–	1	–
60.	deer	1	1	–	2
61.	dinner	–	–	9	3
62.	dish of beef	–	–	–	1
63.	dislike	–	1	–	–
64.	dog	1	–	–	6
65.	dress	1	–	–	–
66.	drink	–	–	–	1
67.	dry	–	–	2	–
68.	duck	1	–	–	–
69.	eat	–	30	2	46
70.	eaten	–	–	1	–
71.	eater	–	–	1	1
72.	eating	–	–	1	–
73.	eats	–	2	–	1
74.	eggs	2	–	–	–
75.	everything	–	–	–	1
76.	except	–	–	1	–
77.	fat	1	–	–	–
78.	fats	–	–	–	1
79.	favorite	–	1	–	–
80.	feet	–	–	–	1
81.	fish	6	–	–	9
82.	fishing	1	–	–	–
83.	Fleisch	1	–	–	1
84.	flesh	2	–	–	–
85.	flowers	1	–	–	–
86.	food	15	–	1	54
87.	forgot	–	1	–	–
88.	freezer	–	–	1	1
89.	fresh	–	1	–	–
90.	Friday	–	–	10	1
91.	Fridays	–	–	1	1
92.	fried	–	–	–	1
93.	frozen	–	–	1	1
94.	fruit	2	–	–	–
95.	fry	–	1	–	–
96.	frying	–	–	–	1
97.	gas	1	–	–	–
98.	girl	1	–	1	6
99.	girls	2	–	–	1

22 Meat (contd)

No.	Response	Subst.	Pre	Post	Assoc.
100.	go	–	1	–	–
101.	good	1	4	28	7
102.	grill	–	–	1	–
103.	had	–	5	–	–
104.	ham	1	–	–	3
105.	hamburger	–	2	–	3
106.	hamburgers	–	1	–	1
107.	happy	–	–	1	–
108.	hatchet	–	–	–	1
109.	hate	–	1	–	1
110.	have	–	5	–	–
111.	healthy	–	–	1	–
112.	heat	–	–	–	1
113.	here	–	–	1	–
114.	high	–	–	1	–
115.	him	1	–	–	–
116.	horse	–	1	–	4
117.	horse meat	–	–	–	1
118.	horses	1	–	–	1
119.	hot dogs	–	–	–	1
120.	house	1	–	–	–
121.	hunger	–	–	–	2
122.	hungry	–	–	–	1
123.	inexpensive	–	–	1	–
124.	Joan	1	–	–	–
125.	juicing	–	1	–	–
126.	juicy	–	–	2	–
127.	kind	–	2	–	–
128.	lamb	2	–	1	–
129.	lamb chops	–	–	–	1
130.	last	–	–	1	–
131.	later	–	–	–	1
132.	leat	–	–	–	1
133.	light	–	–	–	1
134.	like	–	29	–	–
135.	lion	–	1	–	–
136.	living	–	–	1	–
137.	loaf	–	–	–	1
138.	locker	–	–	–	1
139.	love	1	3	–	–
140.	lunch	1	–	2	–
141.	M.R.	–	–	1	–
142.	main	–	–	1	–
143.	man	–	1	–	2
144.	market	–	–	4	4
145.	meatless	–	–	1	–
146.	meet	1	–	–	4
147.	melt	–	–	–	1
148.	met	–	–	–	2
149.	milk	1	–	–	1
150.	much	–	1	–	–
151.	neat	–	–	–	1
152.	necessary	–	–	1	–
153.	night	1	–	1	–
154.	nourishment	–	–	–	1
155.	often	–	–	1	–
156.	old	–	–	1	–
157.	only	–	–	1	–
158.	packages	–	–	1	–
159.	paper	–	–	–	1
160.	part	–	–	–	1
161.	peas	–	–	2	–
162.	people	2	–	–	–
163.	piece	–	2	–	1
164.	pig	1	–	–	–
165.	pork	–	–	–	1
166.	potato	–	–	1	5
167.	potatoes	3	–	–	2
168.	prepare	–	1	–	–
169.	prices	–	–	1	–
170.	prime	–	–	1	–
171.	prostitute	–	–	–	1
172.	protein	–	1	1	3
173.	rare	–	1	3	1
174.	rat	1	–	–	–
175.	raw	–	2	2	1
176.	red	–	–	–	9
177.	roasted	–	–	1	–

22 Meat (contd)

No.	Response	Subst.	Pre	Post	Assoc.
178.	rough	–	–	–	1
179.	salad	1	–	–	–
180.	sausage	–	–	–	1
181.	Sausalito	–	–	–	1
182.	see	–	1	–	–
183.	sheep	–	–	–	1
184.	sirloin	–	–	–	1
185.	smell	–	–	1	–
186.	smoke	1	–	–	–
187.	song	1	–	–	–
188.	sounds	–	1	–	–
189.	soup	1	–	–	1
190.	spinach	1	–	–	–
191.	spoiled	–	–	2	–
192.	staked	–	–	–	1
193.	stale	–	–	1	–
194.	steak	1	–	1	27
195.	steaks	–	–	–	1
196.	steer	–	–	–	2
197.	store	–	–	1	1
198.	stringy	–	–	–	1
199.	sun	1	–	–	–
200.	sweater	–	–	–	1
201.	sweet	–	–	1	–
202.	sweets	1	–	–	–
203.	table	–	–	1	–
204.	taste	–	–	–	1
205.	tastes	–	–	3	–
206.	tasty	–	–	1	–
207.	tea	1	–	–	–
208.	tender	–	–	3	2
209.	thank you	–	–	1	–
210.	that	1	2	–	–
211.	thaw	–	–	–	1
212.	think	–	1	–	–
213.	this	–	3	–	–
214.	time	–	–	1	–
215.	today	–	–	3	–
216.	tough	–	–	5	–
217.	turkey	1	–	–	–
218.	twice	–	–	1	–
219.	vegetable	–	–	–	1
220.	vegetables	2	–	–	3
221.	venison	–	–	–	1
222.	want	–	2	–	–
223.	weighs	–	1	–	–
224.	went	–	2	–	–
225.	what	–	1	–	–
226.	wheat	–	–	–	1
227.	where	–	2	–	–
228.	woman	–	–	–	1
229.	women	–	–	–	1
230.	word	–	1	–	–
231.	work	–	–	–	1
232.	worry	–	1	–	–
233.	wow	–	–	–	1
234.	yesterday	–	–	2	–
235.	you	–	–	2	–

Function Words		–	45	4	–
Space		–	41	76	–
N		99	225	225	327

23 My

No.	Response	Subst.	Pre	Post	Assoc.
1.	A	4	–	–	–
2.	a good	1	–	–	–
3.	all	–	1	–	–
4.	appendix	–	–	1	–
5.	baby	–	–	–	1
6.	back	–	–	2	–
7.	ball	–	–	2	–

23 My (contd)

No.	Response	Subst.	Pre	Post	Assoc.
8.	balloon	–	–	1	–
9.	baseball	–	–	2	–
10.	bed	–	–	–	3
11.	bedroom	–	–	1	–
12.	belonging to me	–	–	–	1
13.	belongs	–	–	–	1
14.	bike	–	–	1	–
15.	blood	–	–	1	–
16.	blue	–	–	–	1
17.	boat	–	–	–	1
18.	book	–	–	24	4
19.	books	–	–	1	–
20.	bought	–	1	–	–
21.	boy	2	–	–	1
22.	boy friend	–	–	3	–
23.	broke	–	2	–	–
24.	brother	–	–	12	1
25.	Bruckner	–	1	–	–
26.	cake	–	–	1	1
27.	called	–	1	–	–
28.	camera	–	–	1	–
29.	can	1	–	–	–
30.	car	–	1	12	9
31.	care	–	–	–	1
32.	cat	–	–	6	2
33.	chair	–	–	1	1
34.	chess	–	–	1	–
35.	clean	–	1	–	–
36.	clothes	–	–	1	1
37.	coat	–	–	5	1
38.	come	–	6	–	–
39.	cup	–	–	1	–
40.	dad	–	–	2	–
41.	dark	1	–	–	–
42.	darlings	–	–	1	–
43.	desk	–	–	1	–
44.	dinner	–	–	1	–
45.	dog	–	–	19	8
46.	dogs	–	–	1	–
47.	doll	–	–	1	–
48.	donkey	–	–	1	–
49.	Dor Allen	–	1	–	–
50.	dress	–	–	6	1
51.	ego	–	–	–	1
52.	egoism	–	–	–	1
53.	enjoyed	–	1	–	–
54.	etchings	–	–	1	–
55.	family	–	–	1	1
56.	father	–	–	5	1
57.	fault	–	–	1	–
58.	favorite	–	–	1	–
59.	feel	–	1	–	–
60.	feelings	–	–	1	–
61.	feet	–	–	–	1
62.	fell	–	1	–	–
63.	find	–	1	–	–
64.	finish	–	1	–	–
65.	food	–	–	1	–
66.	foot	–	–	3	1
67.	forgotten	–	1	–	–
68.	found	–	1	–	–
69.	friend	–	–	6	2
70.	friends	–	–	2	–
71.	girl	–	1	2	3
72.	girls	–	–	–	1
73.	glove	–	–	2	–
74.	go	–	1	–	–
75.	God	–	–	2	–
76.	going	–	1	–	–
77.	gold	–	–	1	–
78.	golf ball	–	–	1	–
79.	golly	1	–	–	–
80.	goodness	1	–	3	3
81.	grab	–	1	–	–
82.	grandmother	–	–	2	–
83.	gun	–	–	2	–
84.	hair	–	–	3	–
85.	hand	–	1	2	–

23 My (contd)

No.	Response	Subst.	Pre	Post	Assoc.
86.	has	–	1	–	–
87.	hat	–	–	5	3
88.	hate	–	1	–	–
89.	have	–	3	–	–
90.	head	–	–	1	1
91.	hearing	–	–	1	–
92.	heart	–	–	1	2
93.	heaven	–	–	–	1
94.	her	31	–	–	–
95.	hers	–	–	–	8
96.	hi	–	–	–	1
97.	him	–	1	–	2
98.	his	49	–	–	19
99.	hobby	–	–	1	–
100.	hold	–	1	–	–
101.	homework	–	–	1	–
102.	horse	–	–	3	–
103.	house	–	–	17	9
104.	how	–	1	1	–
105.	I	–	–	–	1
106.	idea	–	–	2	–
107.	income	–	–	1	–
108.	is	–	–	–	1
109.	it	–	21	–	–
110.	Jim's	1	–	–	–
111.	June's	1	–	–	–
112.	kill	–	1	–	–
113.	knife	–	–	1	–
114.	know	–	1	–	–
115.	last	–	–	1	–
116.	Latin	–	–	1	–
117.	leave	–	1	–	–
118.	leg	–	–	2	–
119.	life	–	–	2	1
120.	like	–	6	–	–
121.	look	–	1	–	–
122.	Lord	–	–	–	3
123.	lost	–	3	–	–
124.	love	–	3	5	3
125.	lover	–	–	1	–
126.	man	–	–	–	2
127.	manners	–	–	1	–
128.	Martian	–	–	1	–
129.	may	–	–	–	1
130.	me	–	7	–	18
131.	Min	–	–	–	1
132.	mine	1	–	–	46
133.	moon	–	–	1	–
134.	mother	–	–	24	2
135.	myself	–	–	–	2
136.	name	–	–	6	–
137.	new	–	–	1	–
138.	not really	–	–	–	1
139.	nothing	–	1	–	–
140.	now	–	1	–	–
141.	nut	–	–	–	1
142.	oh	3	–	–	2
143.	only	–	–	1	1
144.	our	8	–	–	3
145.	ours	–	–	–	10
146.	own	–	–	–	26
147.	pen	–	–	7	–
148.	pencil	–	–	5	–
149.	personal	–	–	–	1
150.	pie	–	–	–	1
151.	pipe	–	–	1	–
152.	pole	–	–	1	–
153.	poodle	–	–	–	1
154.	possess	–	–	–	1
155.	possession	–	–	–	8
156.	possessive	–	–	–	2
157.	problems	–	–	1	–
158.	property	–	–	1	–
159.	purse	–	–	3	–
160.	ran over	–	1	–	–
161.	reason	–	–	1	–
162.	record player	–	–	–	1
163.	records	–	–	1	–

23 My (contd)

No.	Response	Subst.	Pre	Post	Assoc.
164.	ride	–	–	1	–
165.	rifle	–	–	2	–
166.	ring	–	–	1	–
167.	rod	–	–	1	–
168.	Ron	–	–	1	–
169.	room	–	–	4	–
170.	said	–	–	1	–
171.	saw	–	2	–	–
172.	say	–	–	–	1
173.	scarf	–	–	1	–
174.	see	1	1	–	–
175.	self	–	–	–	10
176.	selfish	–	–	–	2
177.	shadow	–	–	1	–
178.	shoe	–	–	–	1
179.	sin	–	–	–	2
180.	sister	1	–	8	–
181.	skirt	–	–	1	1
182.	skis	–	–	1	–
183.	son	–	–	–	1
184.	soul	–	–	–	1
185.	speak	–	1	–	–
186.	stole	–	1	–	–
187.	stomach	–	–	2	–
188.	story	–	–	1	–
189.	strained	–	1	–	–
190.	suit	–	–	–	1
191.	sunny	–	–	1	–
192.	table	–	–	3	–
193.	take	–	1	–	–
194.	teddy bear	–	–	1	–
195.	that	1	30	–	–
196.	the	4	–	–	–
197.	their	3	–	–	2
198.	their gloves	1	–	–	–
199.	theirs	–	–	–	1
200.	them	–	–	–	1
201.	these	–	1	–	–
202.	they	–	–	–	1
203.	things	–	–	1	–
204.	this	1	25	1	–
205.	those	–	1	–	–
206.	tie	–	–	–	1
207.	time	–	–	1	–
208.	to	–	–	–	1
209.	today	–	1	–	–
210.	told	–	1	–	–
211.	took	–	5	–	–
212.	tooth	–	–	1	–
213.	touch	–	2	–	–
214.	toys	–	–	1	–
215.	true	–	–	1	–
216.	uncle	–	–	1	–
217.	understand	–	1	–	–
218.	usual	–	–	1	–
219.	vacation	–	–	1	–
220.	wagon	–	–	1	–
221.	wallet	–	–	1	–
222.	watch	–	1	1	–
223.	way	–	–	–	1
224.	we	–	–	–	1
225.	well	–	–	–	1
226.	what	–	–	8	1
227.	where	–	1	–	–
228.	wife	–	–	1	–
229.	will	–	–	1	–
230.	word	–	–	1	1
231.	work	–	–	1	–
232.	wow	1	–	–	–
233.	you	1	3	3	10
234.	your	50	–	–	36
235.	you're	–	–	–	1
236.	yours	1	–	–	48

		Subst.	Pre	Post	Assoc.
	Function Words	–	19	6	–
	Space	–	145	3	–
	N	170	325	325	367

426

24 Night

No.	Response	Subst.	Pre	Post	Assoc.
1.	air	–	–	1	1
2.	all	–	2	–	–
3.	and day	–	–	–	2
4.	arrived	–	–	1	–
5.	atmosphere	1	–	–	–
6.	automobile	1	–	–	–
7.	ball	1	–	–	–
8.	beautiful	–	2	1	–
9.	best	–	–	1	–
10.	bird	–	–	–	1
11.	black	1	1	4	8
12.	blackness	2	–	–	–
13.	blue-black	–	–	1	–
14.	boy	1	–	–	–
15.	car	1	–	–	–
16.	Christmas	–	–	2	–
17.	clear	–	–	3	–
18.	closet	1	–	–	–
19.	cloth	2	–	–	–
20.	cold	1	4	7	–
21.	color	3	–	–	–
22.	come	–	–	1	–
23.	comes	–	1	–	–
24.	cool	–	1	1	–
25.	crisp	–	1	–	1
26.	dark	4	11	18	28
27.	darkest	–	1	–	–
28.	darkness	6	–	–	4
29.	date	–	–	–	1
30.	dawn	2	–	–	1
31.	day	59	2	–	96
32.	daybreak	1	–	–	–
33.	different	–	–	1	–
34.	dim	–	–	1	–
35.	doing	–	1	–	–
36.	dress	1	–	–	–
37.	ends	–	1	–	–
38.	evening	10	–	–	–
39.	excitement	–	–	–	1
40.	exciting	–	–	1	–
41.	fall	–	–	1	–
42.	falls	–	–	2	–
43.	fell	–	–	1	–
44.	finally	–	–	1	–
45.	fly	–	–	–	1
46.	follows	–	3	1	–
47.	food	1	–	–	–
48.	Friday	–	3	–	–
49.	friend	–	–	1	–
50.	game	–	–	2	–
51.	gay	–	–	2	–
52.	go	–	2	–	–
53.	gone	1	–	–	–
54.	good	–	6	–	–
55.	good time	–	–	–	1
56.	gown	–	–	–	1
57.	gray	–	–	1	–
58.	hall	1	–	–	–
59.	has	–	–	1	–
60.	here	–	–	1	–
61.	hill	1	–	–	–
62.	home	2	4	–	–
63.	house	3	–	–	–
64.	in the morning	1	–	–	–
65.	inevitably	–	–	1	–
66.	it	–	4	1	–
67.	it's	–	1	–	–
68.	last	–	11	–	1
69.	late	1	2	–	–
70.	later	1	–	–	–
71.	leaves	1	–	–	–
72.	life	–	–	–	1
73.	light	–	–	–	3
74.	likes	–	1	–	–
75.	long	–	2	7	–
76.	longer	–	–	1	–
77.	midnight	2	–	–	–
78.	Monday	1	–	–	–

No.	Response	Subst.	Pre	Post	Assoc.
79.	moon	2	–	–	–
80.	morning	1	–	–	–
81.	mornings	1	–	–	–
82.	mud	1	–	–	–
83.	near	–	–	1	–
84.	new	1	–	–	–
85.	night	–	–	2	–
86.	nine	–	–	2	–
87.	October 4	6	–	–	–
88.	opposite	–	2	–	–
89.	out	–	2	–	–
90.	peace	–	–	–	1
91.	person	–	–	1	–
92.	prefer	–	1	–	–
93.	productive	–	–	1	–
94.	quiet	–	–	1	1
95.	remember	–	1	–	–
96.	roam	–	1	–	–
97.	room	2	–	–	–
98.	Saturday	–	1	–	–
99.	secrecy	–	–	1	–
100.	see	–	1	–	–
101.	seems	–	–	1	–
102.	shirt	1	–	–	–
103.	silent	–	–	1	–
104.	six	1	–	–	–
105.	sky	1	–	–	–
106.	soon	–	–	1	–
107.	sounds	–	–	1	–
108.	speech	–	1	–	–
109.	star	–	–	–	2
110.	star after star	1	–	–	–
111.	stars	–	–	3	2
112.	still	–	2	1	–
113.	storm	1	–	–	–
114.	stormy	–	1	–	–
115.	stove	1	–	–	–
116.	study	–	1	–	–
117.	summer	3	–	–	–
118.	Sunday	–	1	–	–
119.	sundown	1	–	–	–
120.	surely	–	–	1	–
121.	table	–	–	–	1
122.	tall	1	–	–	1
123.	ten	–	–	1	–
124.	this	–	1	–	–
125.	this evening	1	–	–	–
126.	time	2	–	1	1
127.	to day	2	–	–	–
128.	town	1	–	–	–
129.	train	–	1	1	2
130.	twilight	2	–	–	–
131.	warm	–	–	3	–
132.	water	2	–	–	–
133.	week	1	–	–	–
134.	window	1	–	–	–
135.	winter	1	–	–	–
136.	work	–	1	–	–
137.	year	2	–	1	–
138.	you	–	1	1	–
139.	8 o'clock	1	–	–	–

	Subst.	Pre	Post	Assoc.
Function Words	–	76	9	–
Space	–	4	64	–
N	155	166	166	163

427

No.	Response	Subst.	Pre	Post	Assoc.
1.	A	-	-	-	1
2.	about	17	-	-	3
3.	above	-	-	-	2
4.	age	-	-	1	-
5.	all	1	3	20	3
6.	America	-	-	2	-
7.	and	1	-	-	4
8.	another	-	-	1	1
9.	any	-	1	-	5
10.	anymore	-	-	1	-
11.	anything	-	1	1	-
12.	asked	-	1	-	-
13.	at	-	-	-	5
14.	aware	-	1	-	-
15.	backwards	-	1	-	-
16.	bank	-	1	-	-
17.	Bartletts	-	1	-	-
18.	be	-	2	-	-
19.	beat	-	-	-	1
20.	because	-	5	-	6
21.	belong	-	-	-	5
22.	belonging	-	-	-	1
23.	belongs	-	-	-	1
24.	belongs to	-	-	-	1
25.	best	-	6	-	-
26.	between	-	-	-	1
27.	Bill	-	-	1	-
28.	bird	-	-	1	-
29.	bit	-	1	-	-
30.	blackish	-	-	1	-
31.	blood	-	-	1	-
32.	blue	-	-	1	-
33.	boat	-	-	1	-
34.	book	-	2	-	-
35.	boss	-	1	-	-
36.	bottle	-	1	-	-
37.	bottom	-	1	-	-
38.	box	-	-	-	1
39.	boys	-	-	1	-
40.	Brown and Co.	-	-	1	-
41.	but	2	-	-	1
42.	by	3	-	-	2
43.	California	-	-	-	1
44.	car	-	-	-	1
45.	care	-	1	-	-
46.	Carl	-	-	1	-
47.	cat	-	-	-	1
48.	concepts	-	1	-	-
49.	congratulations	-	-	1	-
50.	connection	-	-	-	1
51.	contents	-	1	-	-
52.	cotton	-	-	1	-
53.	count	-	2	-	-
54.	course	3	-	33	14
55.	daughter	-	1	-	-
56.	day	-	1	1	-
57.	de	-	-	1	7
58.	deepest	-	1	-	-
59.	died	-	3	-	-
60.	dog	-	1	-	-
61.	doing	-	-	1	-
62.	dove	-	-	-	1
63.	dress	-	1	-	-
64.	drink	-	1	-	-
65.	drum major	-	-	1	-
66.	effect	-	-	1	-
67.	emancipation	-	-	1	-
68.	English	-	-	1	-
69.	explosion	-	-	1	-
70.	fables	-	-	1	-
71.	family	-	-	1	-
72.	father	-	1	-	-
73.	following	-	-	1	-
74.	food	-	-	2	-
75.	for	3	-	-	9
76.	freely	-	1	-	-
77.	friend	-	1	-	-
78.	from	6	-	-	10
79.	fruit	-	-	1	-
80.	game	-	-	1	-
81.	genitive	-	-	1	1
82.	George	-	-	1	-
83.	German	-	-	1	-
84.	girls	-	-	1	-
85.	glue	-	-	1	-
86.	God	-	-	2	-
87.	gold	-	-	1	-
88.	good	-	-	1	-
89.	gossip	-	-	1	-
90.	government	-	1	-	-
91.	great	-	-	1	-
92.	greatness	-	-	1	-
93.	guts	-	-	1	-
94.	half	-	1	-	-
95.	have	-	-	-	1
96.	he	-	-	-	1
97.	heard	-	2	-	-
98.	heart	-	1	1	-
99.	heat	-	1	-	-
100.	heaven	-	-	1	-
101.	hell	-	-	-	1
102.	her	-	-	4	1
103.	Hercules	-	-	1	-
104.	hills	-	-	1	-
105.	him	-	-	13	3
106.	himself	-	-	1	-
107.	his	-	-	-	4
108.	house	-	2	-	-
109.	if	-	-	-	9
110.	importance	-	-	1	-
111.	in	4	-	-	1
112.	Irish	-	-	1	-
113.	it	-	8	22	10
114.	itself	-	-	-	1
115.	Joseph	-	-	1	-
116.	Justine	-	-	1	-
117.	kind	-	1	-	-
118.	king	-	1	-	-
119.	knights	-	1	-	-
120.	know	-	4	-	-
121.	knows	-	1	-	-
122.	lazy	-	-	1	-
123.	letter	-	1	-	-
124.	liberty	-	-	1	1
125.	life	-	-	2	-
126.	like	-	-	-	1
127.	Lincoln	-	-	-	1
128.	loose	-	-	-	1
129.	lost	-	-	-	2
130.	lot	-	1	-	-
131.	louses	-	-	1	-
132.	love	-	4	2	4
133.	machine	-	1	-	-
134.	made	-	6	-	1
135.	man	-	3	-	1
136.	many	-	5	1	5
137.	Martian	-	-	1	-
138.	math	-	-	1	-
139.	matter	-	1	-	-
140.	me	1	1	3	3
141.	means	-	1	-	-
142.	meeting	-	-	1	-
143.	member	-	1	-	-
144.	men	-	-	1	2
145.	mice	-	-	4	-
146.	middle	-	1	-	-
147.	Mike	-	-	2	-
148.	mind	-	-	1	1
149.	mine	1	-	3	4
150.	Monte Cristo	-	-	1	-
151.	more	-	-	-	1
152.	most	-	1	-	-
153.	mother	-	1	-	-
154.	Mr. Brown	-	1	-	-
155.	muscles	-	-	1	-
156.	music	-	-	-	1

25 Of (contd)

No.	Response	Subst.	Pre	Post	Subst.
157.	my	–	–	–	3
158.	myself	–	–	–	1
159.	name	–	1	1	–
160.	nature	–	–	–	1
161.	nice	–	1	–	–
162.	night	–	–	–	2
163.	none	–	1	–	2
164.	not	1	–	–	1
165.	nothing	–	–	–	5
166.	noun	–	–	1	–
167.	now	–	–	–	3
168.	off	1	–	–	14
169.	office	–	–	1	–
170.	often	–	–	–	2
171.	old	–	–	1	–
172.	on	1	–	–	4
173.	one	–	9	–	1
174.	ones	–	–	1	–
175.	or	–	–	–	6
176.	our	–	–	–	2
177.	ours	–	–	–	1
178.	out	–	–	–	2
179.	ownership	2	–	–	1
180.	paper	–	–	1	–
181.	part	–	2	–	5
182.	peace	–	2	–	–
183.	pencil	–	1	–	–
184.	people	–	–	3	–
185.	pertaining	–	–	1	–
186.	plenty	–	1	–	–
187.	poison	–	–	1	–
188.	popcorn	–	–	–	1
189.	possessed	–	–	–	1
190.	possession	–	–	–	4
191.	possessive	–	–	–	1
192.	preposition	–	–	3	6
193.	prepositions	–	–	–	1
194.	queen	–	1	–	–
195.	queer	–	–	1	–
196.	ran out	–	1	–	–
197.	reading	–	1	–	–
198.	reform	–	–	1	–
199.	representative	–	1	–	–
200.	restless	–	–	1	–
201.	rock	–	1	–	–
202.	root	–	1	–	–
203.	round	–	–	1	–
204.	rules	–	1	–	–
205.	said	–	1	–	–
206.	same	–	1	–	1
207.	sentence	–	–	–	1
208.	sharp	–	–	–	1
209.	Sheba	–	–	1	–
210.	sick	–	–	1	–
211.	school	–	–	1	1
212.	so	–	–	–	1
213.	some	–	1	–	1
214.	someone	–	–	1	–
215.	something	–	–	–	1
216.	son	–	1	–	–
217.	song	–	1	–	–
218.	sort	–	1	–	–
219.	sorts	–	–	–	1
220.	source	–	–	–	1
221.	Spain	–	–	1	–
222.	Spanish	–	1	–	–
223.	statue	–	1	–	–
224.	steel	–	–	1	–
225.	stone	–	–	1	–
226.	store	–	–	–	1
227.	stories	–	–	1	–
228.	story	–	1	1	–
229.	strange	–	–	1	–
230.	strength	–	1	–	–
231.	strong	–	1	–	–
232.	sun	–	1	–	–
233.	sure	–	–	–	1
234.	suspicious	–	1	–	–

25 Of (contd)

No.	Response	Subst.	Pre	Post	Subst.
235.	table	–	1	–	–
236.	talked	–	1	–	–
237.	ten	–	–	1	–
238.	testing	–	–	1	–
239.	that	–	–	–	7
240.	that has	1	–	–	–
241.	that's	1	–	–	–
242.	the	–	–	–	5
243.	thee	–	–	1	–
244.	theirs	–	–	–	2
245.	them	–	–	10	10
246.	then	–	–	–	2
247.	there	–	–	–	1
248.	there's	–	–	–	1
249.	these	–	–	5	1
250.	they	–	–	–	2
251.	thing	–	–	–	1
252.	think	–	10	–	–
253.	thinking	–	2	–	–
254.	this	–	2	1	5
255.	those	–	–	3	–
256.	though	–	–	–	1
257.	thought	–	1	–	1
258.	time	–	–	–	1
259.	times	–	–	1	–
260.	tired	–	1	–	–
261.	to	3	–	–	10
262.	toe	–	–	–	1
263.	tone	–	–	–	1
264.	tribal	–	–	1	–
265.	Tuesday	–	–	1	–
266.	two	–	1	5	–
267.	type	–	1	–	1
268.	typewriter	–	–	–	1
269.	United States	–	1	–	–
270.	universe	–	–	1	–
271.	us	–	–	4	2
272.	valley	–	–	1	–
273.	wandering	–	–	1	–
274.	want	–	1	–	–
275.	way	–	2	–	–
276.	weak	–	–	–	1
277.	well	–	–	–	1
278.	what	4	20	9	27
279.	when	–	–	–	1
280.	where	–	–	–	1
281.	which	–	19	1	4
282.	who	–	–	–	2
283.	who has	1	–	–	–
284.	whom	–	–	3	3
285.	whose	–	–	–	2
286.	wine	–	–	1	–
287.	Wimpole St.	–	–	1	–
288.	with	3	–	–	6
289.	without	–	–	–	1
290.	wood	–	–	1	–
291.	words	–	–	–	1
292.	world	–	1	1	3
293.	you	–	1	17	3
294.	your	–	–	–	3
295.	yours	–	–	–	2
	Function Words	–	23	9	–
	Space	–	68	6	–
	N	60	288	288	347

26 Often

No.	Response	Subst.	Pre	Post	Assoc.
1.	a few	-	-	-	1
2.	a lot	-	-	-	3
3.	a lot of time	-	-	-	1
4.	after	-	-	1	-
5.	again	2	-	-	2
6.	all	-	-	-	1
7.	all day	1	-	-	-
8.	all the time	2	-	-	3
9.	all time	-	-	-	1
10.	alone	-	-	1	-
11.	always	20	-	-	11
12.	anytime	-	-	-	1
13.	attended	-	-	-	1
14.	baby	-	1	-	-
15.	ball	-	1	-	-
16.	ball game	-	1	-	-
17.	beat	-	-	1	-
18.	before	-	-	-	1
19.	boats	-	1	-	-
20.	books	-	1	-	-
21.	boredom	-	-	-	1
22.	breakfast	1	-	-	-
23.	by	1	-	-	-
24.	Cal Tjadar	-	-	-	1
25.	came	-	3	-	-
26.	capsized	-	-	1	-
27.	car	-	-	-	1
28.	carefully	1	-	-	-
29.	case	-	-	1	-
30.	change	-	-	-	1
31.	cheat	-	-	1	-
32.	chess	-	1	-	-
33.	close	-	-	-	1
34.	clothes	-	-	-	1
35.	coffee	-	1	-	-
36.	color	1	-	-	-
37.	come	-	7	3	1
38.	comes	-	4	2	-
39.	coming	-	-	-	1
40.	cotton	-	-	-	1
41.	crate	-	-	-	1
42.	cry	-	-	-	1
43.	daily	2	-	-	3
44.	date	-	-	-	1
45.	dates	-	1	-	-
46.	dear	-	-	1	-
47.	did	1	-	1	-
48.	didn't	1	-	-	-
49.	die	-	-	1	-
50.	do	4	2	8	-
51.	done	-	1	2	1
52.	don't	4	-	-	-
53.	dream	-	-	2	-
54.	drink	-	2	3	-
55.	drive	-	-	1	-
56.	drop	-	-	-	1
57.	early	1	-	-	-
58.	easily	1	-	-	-
59.	eat	-	4	5	1
60.	eats	-	1	-	-
61.	enough	-	-	-	2
62.	even	-	-	-	1
63.	every	2	-	-	1
64.	every day	2	-	-	-
65.	every time	-	-	-	1
66.	fast	3	-	-	3
67.	feel	-	-	1	-
68.	fell	-	-	1	-
69.	few	1	-	-	4
70.	fishing	-	1	-	1
71.	food	-	1	-	1
72.	forever	-	-	-	1
73.	forget	-	-	1	-
74.	forgotten	-	-	2	-
75.	frequent	1	-	-	14
76.	frequently	19	-	-	14
77.	fun	-	-	1	1
78.	games	-	2	-	-

26 Often (contd)

No.	Response	Subst.	Pre	Post	Assoc.
79.	get	-	-	2	-
80.	gift	-	-	-	1
81.	go	-	16	28	-
82.	goes	-	1	3	-
83.	golf	-	-	-	1
84.	gone	-	1	1	1
85.	good	2	-	-	-
86.	habits	-	-	-	1
87.	hair	-	1	-	-
88.	hallucinations	-	1	-	-
89.	happen	-	4	3	-
90.	happened	-	2	-	-
91.	happens	-	12	3	-
92.	happy	-	-	-	2
93.	hard	-	-	2	1
94.	hardly	1	-	-	-
95.	has	1	-	-	-
96.	have	-	-	2	-
97.	heard	-	-	1	-
98.	heartily	1	-	-	-
99.	heavy	-	-	1	-
100.	help	-	-	-	1
101.	hens	-	-	-	1
102.	her	-	7	1	-
103.	here	2	2	1	-
104.	hike	-	1	-	-
105.	him	-	9	2	-
106.	Historie	-	-	-	1
107.	home	-	-	1	-
108.	house	-	1	-	-
109.	how	-	-	-	1
110.	how far	-	-	-	1
111.	hungry	-	-	1	-
112.	hurry	-	-	-	1
113.	I hope	1	-	-	-
114.	it	-	25	3	-
115.	jump	-	1	-	1
116.	late	2	-	1	1
117.	lately	-	-	-	1
118.	lay	-	-	1	-
119.	least	-	-	-	1
120.	leave	-	1	1	-
121.	less	1	-	-	5
122.	lessons	-	-	-	1
123.	less often	-	-	-	1
124.	like	-	1	-	-
125.	like to	2	-	-	-
126.	little	1	-	-	-
127.	long	3	-	-	-
128.	lose	-	-	1	-
129.	lot	-	-	-	1
130.	lots	1	-	-	-
131.	love	-	-	-	1
132.	lugubrious	-	-	1	-
133.	many	1	-	-	16
134.	many times	5	-	-	-
135.	mass	-	-	-	1
136.	may	1	-	-	-
137.	me	-	5	-	1
138.	more	2	-	-	2
139.	more often	-	-	-	1
140.	much	12	-	1	4
141.	must	-	-	1	-
142.	near	1	-	-	2
143.	nearly	-	-	-	1
144.	need	-	-	1	-
145.	never	32	-	1	46
146.	new	-	-	-	1
147.	night	-	-	-	1
148.	none	-	-	-	1
149.	not	-	-	-	2
150.	not so often	-	-	-	1
151.	now	6	-	1	9
152.	occasionally	1	-	-	-
153.	occurring	-	-	-	1
154.	occurs	-	1	-	-
155.	of 5	-	-	-	1
156.	of 20	-	-	-	1

26 Often (contd)

No.	Response	Subst.	Pre	Post	Assoc.
157.	off	–	–	–	1
158.	oftener	1	–	–	–
159.	old	–	–	–	2
160.	once in a while	–	–	–	1
161.	people	–	3	1	–
162.	place	–	1	–	1
163.	play	–	–	–	1
164.	plays	–	–	1	–
165.	pretty	1	–	–	–
166.	pronunciation	–	–	–	1
167.	quick	–	–	–	1
168.	quickly	3	–	–	4
169.	quietly	1	–	–	–
170.	quite	–	–	–	2
171.	rains	–	1	2	–
172.	rare	–	–	–	2
173.	rarely	13	–	–	–
174.	read	–	3	3	–
175.	really	1	–	–	–
176.	reasonably	1	–	–	–
177.	recently	1	–	–	–
178.	recurring	–	–	–	1
179.	regular	–	–	–	2
180.	regularly	6	–	–	2
181.	relations	–	1	–	–
182.	repeat	–	–	–	1
183.	repeated	–	–	1	–
184.	ride	–	–	2	1
185.	right	–	–	1	–
186.	run	–	–	2	1
187.	runs	–	–	1	–
188.	sad	–	–	1	–
189.	said	–	–	1	–
190.	San Francisco	–	–	–	1
191.	say	–	1	–	–
192.	school	–	3	–	5
193.	see	–	–	8	–
194.	seems	–	–	–	1
195.	seen	–	1	1	–
196.	seldom	42	–	–	36
197.	sentence	–	1	–	–
198.	sex	–	–	–	1
199.	sharp	–	–	–	1
200.	short	–	–	–	1
201.	should	1	–	–	–
202.	show	–	3	4	–
203.	sick	–	1	–	–
204.	Sierra	–	–	1	–
205.	sit	–	–	2	–
206.	skate	–	1	–	–
207.	skiing	–	2	–	–
208.	skip	–	–	1	–
209.	sleep	–	2	–	–
210.	slight	–	–	–	2
211.	slow	1	–	–	1
212.	slowly	1	–	–	1
213.	smoke	–	–	1	–
214.	soft	1	–	–	–
215.	sometime	42	–	–	10
216.	soon	19	–	–	58
217.	sooner	–	–	–	2
218.	speak	–	1	1	–
219.	sporadically	1	–	–	–
220.	stopped	–	–	1	–
221.	store	–	1	1	–
222.	strangely	1	–	–	–
223.	stupid	–	–	–	2
224.	suddenly	2	–	–	1
225.	summer	–	–	1	–
226.	sweet	1	–	–	–
227.	swim	–	3	1	–
228.	swimming	–	2	–	–
229.	take	–	–	1	–
230.	talk	–	–	1	–
231.	talked	–	–	1	–
232.	tell	–	–	1	–
233.	ten	–	1	–	–
234.	ten by ten	–	–	–	1

26 Often (contd)

No.	Response	Subst.	Pre	Post	Assoc.
235.	tennis	–	1	–	–
236.	test	–	1	–	1
237.	tests	–	1	–	–
238.	that	1	1	1	–
239.	the	–	–	–	1
240.	them	–	1	–	–
241.	then	1	–	–	1
242.	there	2	7	2	–
243.	things	–	1	–	–
244.	think	–	–	2	–
245.	this	–	11	–	–
246.	thought	–	–	3	–
247.	three	–	–	–	1
248.	till	–	–	–	1
249.	time	–	–	–	3
250.	times	–	–	–	2
251.	tired	–	–	1	–
252.	today	2	–	–	–
253.	together	1	–	1	–
254.	told	–	–	2	–
255.	tomorrow	1	–	–	–
256.	too	1	–	–	–
257.	too often	1	–	–	–
258.	use	–	1	–	–
259.	usual	–	–	–	3
260.	usually	6	–	–	6
261.	very	3	–	–	2
262.	very much	–	–	–	1
263.	very often	1	–	–	–
264.	visit	–	1	–	–
265.	walk	–	2	4	1
266.	watch	–	–	–	1
267.	week ends	–	–	–	1
268.	well	5	–	–	–
269.	went	–	1	2	–
270.	when	1	–	1	1
271.	why	–	1	–	–
272.	will	1	–	–	–
273.	won	–	–	1	–
274.	wonder	–	–	2	–
275.	won't	1	–	–	–
276.	work	–	1	–	–
277.	worry	–	1	–	–
278.	worth while	1	–	–	–
279.	write	–	2	–	–
280.	wrong	–	–	1	–
281.	wrote	–	–	1	–
282.	Yeh!	–	–	–	1
283.	you	–	5	22	–

		Subst.	Pre	Post	Assoc.
Function Words		–	157	27	–
Space		–	22	156	–
N		320	378	378	381

27 Or

No.	Response	Subst.	Pre	Post	Assoc.
1.	about	1	–	–	–
2.	already	1	–	–	–
3.	also	–	–	–	1
4.	and	90	–	–	14
5.	another	–	–	–	1
6.	any	–	–	1	–
7.	apples	–	1	–	–
8.	are	–	–	–	3
9.	aut	–	–	–	1
10.	bacon	–	–	1	–
11.	bad	–	–	1	–
12.	Barbara	–	1	–	–
13.	because	2	–	–	–
14.	better	–	1	–	–
15.	Betty	–	–	1	–
16.	Bill	–	2	2	–

27 Or (contd)

No.	Response	Subst.	Pre	Post	Assoc.
17.	black	–	1	–	–
18.	boat	–	1	2	4
19.	Bob	–	1	3	–
20.	bore	–	–	–	2
21.	boy	–	1	–	–
22.	buggy	–	–	1	–
23.	but	3	–	–	15
24.	butterflies	–	1	–	–
25.	by	–	–	–	1
26.	by me	1	–	–	–
27.	cake	–	1	1	–
28.	call	–	1	–	–
29.	candy	–	2	–	–
30.	car	–	2	1	–
31.	Carol	–	1	1	–
32.	cat	–	–	1	1
33.	cats	–	2	–	–
34.	choice	–	–	–	4
35.	cigarettes	–	1	–	–
36.	clear	–	–	–	1
37.	coffee	–	3	1	–
38.	come	–	5	1	–
39.	conjunction	–	–	–	1
40.	conjunctions	–	–	–	1
41.	cookies	–	–	1	–
42.	correct	–	–	1	–
43.	cream	–	1	–	–
44.	cure	–	–	1	–
45.	dance	–	1	1	–
46.	decision	–	–	–	1
47.	die	–	–	2	–
48.	dive	–	1	1	–
49.	do	–	4	–	–
50.	dogs	–	–	2	–
51.	Don	–	–	1	–
52.	don't	2	1	–	–
53.	door	–	–	–	1
54.	drive	–	–	1	–
55.	eat	–	1	–	–
56.	eaten	–	–	1	–
57.	either	–	–	–	24
58.	else	–	–	–	12
59.	English	–	–	–	1
60.	for	–	–	–	7
61.	four	–	–	1	–
62.	Frank	–	1	–	–
63.	Fred	–	–	1	–
64.	from	–	–	–	1
65.	gardenias	–	–	1	–
66.	girl	–	–	1	–
67.	go	–	6	3	1
68.	goes	–	2	–	–
69.	gold	–	–	–	6
70.	good	–	2	–	–
71.	gum	–	–	1	–
72.	hate	–	–	1	–
73.	her	–	2	13	–
74.	here	–	3	1	–
75.	him	1	17	4	3
76.	his	–	–	2	–
77.	home	–	–	1	–
78.	hour	–	1	–	–
79.	house	–	2	–	–
80.	if	1	–	–	8
81.	instead of	1	–	–	–
82.	is	–	–	–	1
83.	it	–	3	3	2
84.	Jack	–	1	1	–
85.	Jane	–	3	–	–
86.	Jim	–	3	3	–
87.	Joe	–	3	1	–
88.	John	–	5	2	–
89.	July	–	–	1	–
90.	June	–	1	–	–
91.	kill	–	1	–	–
92.	last	–	1	–	–
93.	Lat.	–	–	1	–
94.	later	–	–	3	–

27 Or (contd)

No.	Response	Subst.	Pre	Post	Assoc.
95.	leave	–	1	1	–
96.	literature	–	1	–	–
97.	Lois	–	1	–	–
98.	loose	–	–	1	–
99.	Mary	–	1	3	–
100.	maybe	1	–	–	10
101.	me	–	14	11	3
102.	Mike	–	–	1	–
103.	milk	–	–	1	–
104.	mine	–	4	–	1
105.	more	–	–	–	5
106.	moths	–	–	1	–
107.	mouse	–	–	1	–
108.	neither	–	–	–	2
109.	never	1	–	1	2
110.	nor	10	–	–	42
111.	not	2	–	–	7
112.	now	–	4	–	1
113.	oar	–	–	–	1
114.	oars	–	–	–	1
115.	of	–	–	–	4
116.	on	–	–	–	1
117.	on the other hand	–	–	–	1
118.	one	–	8	–	2
119.	oor	–	–	–	1
120.	oranges	–	–	1	–
121.	ore	1	–	–	2
122.	other	–	–	8	5
123.	otherwise	–	–	–	1
124.	our	–	–	–	1
125.	over	–	–	–	1
126.	pay	–	–	1	–
127.	pepper	–	–	1	–
128.	put up	–	1	–	–
129.	question	–	–	–	1
130.	rat	–	1	–	–
131.	read	–	1	1	–
132.	receive	–	–	–	1
133.	right	–	2	–	–
134.	roses	–	1	–	–
135.	row	–	–	–	1
136.	run	–	1	1	–
137.	salt	–	1	–	–
138.	school	–	1	–	–
139.	she	–	–	–	1
140.	show	–	2	–	–
141.	shut up	–	–	1	–
142.	side	–	–	1	–
143.	sink	–	2	–	–
144.	sit	–	–	1	–
145.	soda	–	–	1	–
146.	something	–	–	–	1
147.	something else	–	–	–	1
148.	sooner	–	1	–	–
149.	sore	–	–	–	2
150.	speak	–	1	1	–
151.	stay	–	–	3	–
152.	steak	–	1	–	–
153.	stop	–	1	1	–
154.	sugar	–	–	2	–
155.	Susan	–	–	1	–
156.	swim	–	3	2	–
157.	tea	–	3	3	–
158.	tell	1	–	–	–
159.	test	–	1	–	–
160.	that	–	1	24	3
161.	them	–	1	–	1
162.	there	–	2	1	1
163.	they	–	–	–	1
164.	thin	–	1	–	–
165.	this	–	24	1	1
166.	Tim	–	–	1	–
167.	to	2	–	–	1
168.	tobacco	–	1	–	–
169.	today	–	1	–	–
170.	Tom	–	3	2	–
171.	tomorrow	–	–	1	–
172.	top	–	–	–	1

27 Or (contd)

No.	Response	Subst.	Pre	Post	Assoc.
173.	truck	–	–	1	–
174.	two	–	1	–	1
175.	two things	–	–	–	1
176.	until	1	–	–	–
177.	us	–	–	–	1
178.	walk	–	2	2	–
179.	was	1	–	–	–
180.	watch out	–	1	–	–
181.	water	–	1	–	–
182.	went	–	1	–	–
183.	what	–	1	4	11
184.	wheel	–	–	–	1
185.	when	1	–	2	2
186.	where	–	1	–	–
187.	white	–	–	1	–
188.	who	–	–	–	1
189.	whore	–	–	–	1
190.	why	–	–	–	2
191.	wine	–	–	1	–
192.	with	–	–	–	1
193.	without	1	–	–	–
194.	word	–	–	1	–
195.	work	–	–	–	1
196.	write	–	3	1	–
197.	wrong	–	–	2	–
198.	yes	–	1	–	–
199.	you	–	19	12	1
200.	your	–	–	–	1
201.	you're	–	–	–	1
202.	yours	–	–	3	–

Function Words	–	29	65	–
Space	–	6	0	–
N	125	252	252	255

28 Our

No.	Response	Subst.	Pre	Post	Assoc.
1.	again	–	–	–	1
2.	baby	–	–	1	1
3.	baggage	–	–	1	–
4.	bat	–	–	1	–
5.	bell	–	–	–	1
6.	best	–	–	1	–
7.	big	–	–	1	–
8.	bless	–	1	–	–
9.	blue	–	–	–	1
10.	boat	–	1	2	–
11.	book	–	1	5	2
12.	books	–	–	2	–
13.	boy	–	–	3	–
14.	brother	–	–	1	–
15.	car	–	–	14	–
16.	cat	–	–	5	–
17.	child	–	–	–	1
18.	church	–	–	1	–
19.	come	–	3	–	–
20.	country	–	–	1	–
21.	cup	–	–	1	–
22.	dad	–	–	1	–
23.	day	–	–	1	–
24.	dinner	–	–	1	–
25.	dog	–	1	11	–
26.	everyone	–	–	–	1
27.	faith	–	–	1	–
28.	family	–	–	–	1
29.	farm	–	–	1	–
30.	father	–	–	2	–
31.	friend	–	–	–	1
32.	game	–	–	–	1
33.	girl	–	–	–	1
34.	gold	–	–	1	–
35.	guest	–	–	1	–

28 Our (contd)

No.	Response	Subst.	Pre	Post	Assoc.
36.	happy	–	–	1	–
37.	health	–	–	1	–
38.	her	2	–	–	–
39.	hers	1	–	–	–
40.	him	–	1	–	–
41.	his	21	–	–	5
42.	his and mine	–	–	–	1
43.	home	–	–	10	5
44.	horse	–	–	1	2
45.	house	–	–	37	8
46.	household	–	–	1	–
47.	idea	–	–	1	–
48.	it	–	21	–	–
49.	land	–	–	–	1
50.	life	–	–	2	–
51.	like	–	4	–	–
52.	love	–	1	3	1
53.	man	–	–	1	–
54.	marks	–	1	–	–
55.	men	–	–	1	–
56.	might	–	–	–	1
57.	mine	1	–	–	7
58.	moment	–	–	1	–
59.	mommy	–	–	1	–
60.	mother	–	–	2	–
61.	my	5	–	–	2
62.	new	–	–	2	–
63.	one	1	–	–	–
64.	ours	–	–	–	3
65.	out	–	1	–	–
66.	own	–	–	–	1
67.	paper	–	–	1	–
68.	people's	1	–	–	–
69.	piteous	–	–	1	–
70.	plight	–	–	1	–
71.	possession	–	–	–	1
72.	possessive	–	–	1	1
73.	problem	–	–	1	–
74.	reason	–	–	1	–
75.	reclined	–	–	1	–
76.	red	–	–	1	–
77.	relationship	–	–	1	–
78.	sad	–	–	–	1
79.	say	–	1	–	–
80.	school	–	–	2	–
81.	state	–	–	1	–
82.	story	–	–	1	–
83.	table	–	–	1	–
84.	tent	–	1	–	–
85.	that	2	18	–	–
86.	the	1	–	–	–
87.	their	16	–	–	8
88.	theirs	3	–	–	4
89.	there	–	–	1	–
90.	this	–	20	–	–
91.	time	–	1	2	–
92.	told	–	1	–	–
93.	took	–	1	–	–
94.	town	–	–	1	–
95.	toy	–	–	1	–
96.	train	–	–	1	–
97.	trip	–	–	1	–
98.	turn	–	–	1	–
99.	us	1	–	–	4
100.	way	–	–	1	–
101.	we	–	–	–	1
102.	went	–	1	–	–
103.	where	–	1	–	–
104.	whose	–	–	–	1
105.	you	–	–	–	1
106.	your	12	–	–	13
107.	you're	–	–	–	1
108.	yours	1	2	–	9

Function Words	–	9	2	–
Space	–	65	7	–
N	68	157	157	94

29 Ours (contd)

No.	Response	Subst.	Pre	Post	Assoc.
1.	all	–	–	–	1
2.	an object	–	–	–	1
3.	and me	–	–	–	1
4.	baby	1	–	–	1
5.	bad	1	–	1	–
6.	ball	–	2	–	–
7.	basketball	–	–	–	1
8.	be	–	–	1	–
9.	bear	–	–	–	1
10.	beautiful	–	–	1	–
11.	become	–	1	–	–
12.	belong	–	–	–	1
13.	belongs to	–	–	–	1
14.	best	–	–	12	–
15.	better	–	1	11	–
16.	big	–	–	1	–
17.	bigger	–	–	1	–
18.	Bill's	1	–	–	–
19.	bird	–	1	–	–
20.	black	–	–	2	–
21.	blue	2	2	1	–
22.	boat	–	6	–	1
23.	book	–	9	–	–
24.	both	–	–	–	1
25.	both of us	–	–	–	1
26.	boy	–	–	1	–
27.	car	–	22	1	4
28.	cars	–	–	–	1
29.	cat	–	1	–	–
30.	child	–	1	–	–
31.	clothes	–	–	–	1
32.	collectively	–	–	1	–
33.	creamy	–	–	1	–
34.	cute	–	–	1	–
35.	day	–	–	1	–
36.	Dest	1	–	–	–
37.	did	–	–	1	–
38.	do	–	1	–	–
39.	dog	–	8	–	1
40.	Erik	1	–	–	–
41.	everybody	–	–	–	1
42.	everyone's	1	–	–	1
43.	everything	–	1	–	1
44.	family	–	–	–	3
45.	faster	–	–	1	–
46.	feel	–	1	–	–
47.	fell	–	–	1	–
48.	field	–	1	–	–
49.	finally	–	1	–	–
50.	fire	1	–	–	–
51.	first	–	–	1	–
52.	five	–	–	1	–
53.	forever	–	–	4	1
54.	friendliness	–	–	–	1
55.	friendship	–	–	1	1
56.	fulfilled	–	–	1	–
57.	fun	–	–	–	1
58.	gave	–	1	–	–
59.	gift	–	1	–	–
60.	God	–	1	–	–
61.	gone	1	–	1	–
62.	good	1	–	3	1
63.	greatest	–	–	1	–
64.	green	–	–	2	–
65.	Greg's	1	–	–	–
66.	group	–	–	–	1
67.	gun	–	1	–	–
68.	happiness	–	–	–	1
69.	happy	–	–	1	1
70.	have	–	2	1	–
71.	heavy	1	–	–	–
72.	here	–	–	3	–
73.	hers	18	–	–	3
74.	hill	–	1	–	–
75.	him	–	1	–	–
76.	his	48	1	2	7
77.	his too	–	–	–	1
78.	home	–	1	–	2

29 Ours (contd)

No.	Response	Subst.	Pre	Post	Assoc.
79.	horse	–	–	–	1
80.	hours	–	–	–	1
81.	house	–	13	1	5
82.	however	–	–	1	–
83.	Impala	–	–	–	1
84.	is	–	–	–	1
85.	it	7	85	1	–
86.	Johnny	–	–	–	1
87.	joining	–	–	–	1
88.	Joyce	–	–	1	–
89.	just	–	–	1	–
90.	keep	–	–	4	–
91.	know	–	–	1	–
92.	last	–	–	2	–
93.	life	–	–	1	–
94.	light	–	–	1	–
95.	like	–	4	–	–
96.	likes	–	1	–	–
97.	live	–	–	2	–
98.	lock	1	–	–	–
99.	look	–	1	–	–
100.	love	–	1	–	2
101.	main	–	–	1	–
102.	marked	–	1	–	–
103.	marriage	–	–	–	1
104.	me!	–	–	–	1
105.	mine	55	–	–	48
106.	minister	–	–	1	–
107.	moment	–	1	–	–
108.	mortgaged	1	–	–	–
109.	much	–	–	1	–
110.	my	–	–	–	1
111.	neither	–	–	–	1
112.	new golf clubs	–	–	–	1
113.	next	–	–	1	–
114.	nice	2	–	–	–
115.	nicer	–	–	1	–
116.	nicest	–	–	1	–
117.	noster	–	–	–	1
118.	not	1	–	–	1
119.	now	–	–	1	–
120.	object	–	–	–	2
121.	occur	–	–	1	–
122.	old	1	–	–	–
123.	one	–	–	2	2
124.	own	1	–	–	2
125.	ownership	–	–	–	3
126.	painted	–	–	1	–
127.	payed for	1	–	–	–
128.	peace	–	1	–	–
129.	peaceful	–	–	1	–
130.	people	–	–	–	2
131.	personal	–	–	–	1
132.	phone	–	1	–	–
133.	place	–	1	–	–
134.	play	–	–	1	–
135.	possession	–	–	–	7
136.	possessions	–	–	–	1
137.	possessive	–	–	1	–
138.	pretty	1	–	–	–
139.	private	–	–	–	1
140.	property	–	–	–	1
141.	put	–	1	–	–
142.	red	–	–	3	–
143.	relations	–	–	–	1
144.	Richmond	–	–	1	–
145.	right	–	–	2	–
146.	ring	–	–	–	1
147.	Ron's	–	–	–	1
148.	room	–	1	–	–
149.	same	–	–	1	–
150.	school	–	1	–	–
151.	seat	–	1	–	–
152.	separate	–	–	–	1
153.	sex	–	1	–	–
154.	share	–	–	–	2
155.	small	–	–	1	–
156.	smaller	–	–	1	–

29 Ours (contd)

No.	Response	Subst.	Pre	Post	Assoc.
157.	some	-	1	1	-
158.	stalled	1	-	-	-
159.	stole	-	1	-	-
160.	table	-	1	-	-
161.	take	-	-	1	-
162.	tall	-	-	1	-
163.	taste	-	-	1	-
164.	that	1	48	-	-
165.	the	-	-	-	1
166.	the car	1	-	-	-
167.	the Jones'	1	-	-	-
168.	thee	-	1	-	-
169.	their	1	-	-	4
170.	theirs	67	1	2	90
171.	them	2	-	-	1
172.	there	-	-	2	-
173.	there's	-	-	-	7
174.	these	-	2	-	-
175.	think	-	1	-	-
176.	this	1	38	-	-
177.	those	-	4	-	-
178.	today	-	-	1	-
179.	together	-	-	2	6
180.	tomorrow	-	-	1	-
181.	too	-	-	-	1
182.	took	-	1	-	-
183.	train	-	1	-	-
184.	true	1	-	2	-
185.	us	2	1	-	10
186.	use	-	-	1	-
187.	want	-	-	1	-
188.	wanted	-	1	-	-
189.	wants	-	1	-	-
190.	washing machine	-	1	-	-
191.	we	-	-	-	1
192.	wedding	-	-	-	1
193.	what	-	3	-	-
194.	where	-	1	-	-
195.	word	-	1	-	-
196.	worshipped	-	-	1	-
197.	worst	-	-	1	-
198.	yellow	-	-	2	-
199.	yes	-	-	-	1
200.	you	1	1	1	-
201.	your	1	-	-	2
202.	yours	90	3	13	111

Function Words		-	2	6	-
Space		-	80	238	-
N		320	379	379	377

30 Quite

No.	Response	Subst.	Pre	Post	Assoc.
1.	a good	1	-	-	-
2.	a little	1	-	-	-
3.	a lot	-	-	4	-
4.	a while	-	-	2	-
5.	absolutely	1	-	-	-
6.	accidental	-	-	1	-
7.	alike	-	-	-	1
8.	all	-	1	-	1
9.	all right	-	-	5	1
10.	almost	2	-	-	7
11.	always	2	-	-	1
12.	angry	-	-	1	-
13.	another	-	-	3	-
14.	astute	-	-	1	-
15.	awful	-	-	-	1
16.	awfully	3	-	-	-
17.	baby	-	-	-	1
18.	bad	-	-	2	1
19.	beautiful	-	-	1	-

30 Quite (contd)

No.	Response	Subst.	Pre	Post	Assoc.
20.	beauty	-	-	-	1
21.	bit	-	-	1	-
22.	boring	-	-	1	-
23.	boy	-	-	2	-
24.	bright	-	-	-	1
25.	British	-	-	-	1
26.	building	-	-	1	-
27.	calm	-	-	-	1
28.	capable	-	-	1	-
29.	certain	-	-	-	2
30.	certainly	1	-	-	-
31.	cheerful	-	-	-	1
32.	clear	1	-	1	1
33.	clever	-	-	-	1
34.	close	-	-	1	1
35.	coat	-	-	-	1
36.	cold	-	-	2	1
37.	contrary	-	-	-	3
38.	cranium	-	1	-	-
39.	cute	-	-	1	2
40.	day	-	1	2	-
41.	definitely	1	-	-	-
42.	difference	-	-	1	-
43.	different	-	-	1	-
44.	dirty	-	-	-	1
45.	do	-	1	-	-
46.	easy	-	-	2	1
47.	elite	-	-	-	1
48.	England	-	-	-	1
49.	English	-	-	-	1
50.	Englishman	-	-	-	1
51.	enjoyable	-	-	1	-
52.	enough	-	-	2	5
53.	essential	-	-	-	1
54.	everyone	-	1	-	-
55.	exact	-	-	-	1
56.	exactly	-	-	-	1
57.	excited	-	-	2	-
58.	experience	-	-	4	-
59.	extensive	-	-	-	1
60.	extraordinary	-	-	1	1
61.	extreme	1	-	-	3
62.	eye	-	-	-	1
63.	fact	-	-	1	-
64.	fast	-	-	1	-
65.	fat	1	-	1	1
66.	father	-	-	-	1
67.	feel	-	1	-	-
68.	felt	-	1	-	-
69.	few	-	-	1	3
70.	fight	-	-	-	1
71.	fine	-	-	-	1
72.	frank	-	-	-	1
73.	friendly	-	-	1	1
74.	full	-	-	-	1
75.	fun	-	-	2	-
76.	funny	-	-	1	-
77.	game	-	-	2	-
78.	girl	-	-	3	-
79.	girls	-	-	-	1
80.	go	-	1	-	1
81.	gone	-	-	-	1
82.	good	-	-	5	6
83.	handsome	-	-	1	-
84.	happy	-	-	5	2
85.	hard	-	-	1	4
86.	have	-	1	-	-
87.	heavy	-	-	-	1
88.	her	-	2	-	-
89.	here	-	-	3	-
90.	high-browed	-	-	-	1
91.	hilarious	-	-	1	-
92.	him	-	1	-	-
93.	home	-	-	-	1
94.	horrible	-	-	-	1
95.	how	-	-	-	1
96.	humid	-	-	1	-
97.	ill	-	-	1	-

30 Quite (contd)

No.	Response	Subst.	Pre	Post	Assoc.
98.	immediate	–	–	–	1
99.	impossible	–	–	1	–
100.	indeed	–	–	–	1
101.	interesting	–	–	2	–
102.	it	–	49	1	–
103.	job	–	–	1	–
104.	John	–	1	–	–
105.	joke	–	1	–	–
106.	Jones	–	–	1	–
107.	just	1	–	–	–
108.	kind	–	–	–	1
109.	lacking	–	–	–	1
110.	large	–	–	1	1
111.	late	–	–	1	–
112.	legal	–	–	1	–
113.	light	–	–	–	4
114.	like of noise	–	–	–	1
115.	little	–	–	–	3
116.	load	–	–	–	1
117.	lonely	–	–	1	–
118.	lonesome	–	–	–	1
119.	long	–	–	1	–
120.	looked	–	1	–	–
121.	loud	2	–	1	29
122.	lovable	–	–	1	–
123.	lovely	–	–	–	1
124.	machine	–	–	1	–
125.	mad	–	–	2	–
126.	man	–	–	2	–
127.	might	–	–	–	2
128.	mistake	–	–	–	1
129.	more	1	–	–	1
130.	morning	–	–	–	1
131.	mother	–	4	–	–
132.	much	–	–	–	2
133.	name	–	–	1	–
134.	near	–	–	–	1
135.	nearly	–	–	–	1
136.	neat	–	–	–	1
137.	necessary	–	–	1	–
138.	never	2	–	–	–
139.	nice	–	–	12	8
140.	night	–	–	–	1
141.	nix	1	–	–	–
142.	no	1	–	–	1
143.	noise	–	–	–	4
144.	noisy	–	–	–	11
145.	not	17	–	–	7
146.	now	1	–	1	5
147.	odd	–	–	1	–
148.	often	–	–	4	8
149.	old	–	–	5	5
150.	party	–	–	1	–
151.	patient	–	–	–	1
152.	peace	–	–	–	1
153.	peaceful	–	–	–	2
154.	peculiar	–	–	1	–
155.	perturbed	–	–	1	–
156.	pleasant	–	–	1	–
157.	please	–	1	–	1
158.	pleasing	–	–	1	–
159.	positively	1	–	–	–
160.	precise	–	–	–	1
161.	pretty	–	–	1	–
162.	prim	–	–	–	1
163.	quaint	–	–	–	2
164.	quick	–	–	–	1
165.	quiet	–	–	2	17
166.	quit	–	–	–	3
167.	quote	–	–	–	1
168.	rather	2	–	–	2
169.	ready	–	–	1	1
170.	real	1	–	–	–
171.	really	4	–	–	2
172.	relaxing	–	–	–	1
173.	restful	–	–	–	1
174.	right	1	–	8	8
175.	ripe	–	–	1	–

30 Quite (contd)

No.	Response	Subst.	Pre	Post	Assoc.
176.	rug	–	1	–	–
177.	sad	–	–	–	1
178.	safe	–	–	1	–
179.	satiated	–	–	1	–
180.	satisfactory	–	–	1	–
181.	school	–	1	–	1
182.	see	1	–	–	–
183.	seemingly	1	–	–	–
184.	seldom	–	–	–	1
185.	show	–	–	1	–
186.	sick	–	–	2	–
187.	silence	–	–	–	1
188.	silent	–	–	–	3
189.	simple	–	–	2	–
190.	sir	–	–	–	1
191.	situation	–	–	2	–
192.	slight	–	–	–	2
193.	slow	–	–	–	1
194.	small	–	–	3	8
195.	smart	–	–	1	1
196.	smile	–	–	1	–
197.	so	1	–	3	4
198.	some	–	–	–	1
199.	sometimes	–	1	–	–
200.	somewhat	–	–	–	1
201.	soon	–	–	1	4
202.	spell	–	–	1	–
203.	still	–	–	–	1
204.	stop	–	–	–	1
205.	story	–	–	1	–
206.	strong	–	–	–	1
207.	stupid	–	–	1	–
208.	sudden	–	–	1	–
209.	sunny	–	–	–	1
210.	sure	–	–	5	2
211.	surely	2	–	–	1
212.	surprised	–	–	2	–
213.	tame	–	–	1	–
214.	test	–	–	2	–
215.	that	–	12	–	–
216.	the thing	–	–	–	1
217.	there	–	–	–	1
218.	thing	–	–	2	1
219.	thirty	–	–	1	–
220.	this	–	11	–	–
221.	toy	–	–	1	–
222.	truck	–	–	1	–
223.	true	–	–	1	3
224.	ugly	–	–	1	–
225.	understand	–	–	1	–
226.	unexpected	–	–	1	–
227.	us	–	–	–	1
228.	very	28	–	–	22
229.	very much	–	–	–	2
230.	village	1	–	–	2
231.	warm	–	–	2	–
232.	weak	–	–	–	1
233.	weather	–	1	–	–
234.	well	–	–	18	8
235.	went	–	–	–	1
236.	what	1	–	–	2
237.	wins	–	1	–	–
238.	with	1	–	–	–
239.	wonderful	–	–	1	–
240.	work	–	–	–	1
241.	yes	–	–	–	2
242.	you	–	9	1	1
243.	young	–	–	–	2
	Function Words	–	74	–	–
	Space	–	27	4	–
	N	86	207	207	320

436

31 Reading

31 Reading (contd)

No.	Response	Subst.	Pre	Post	Assoc.
1.	ability	–	–	1	–
2.	again	–	–	–	1
3.	algebra	1	–	–	–
4.	all	–	–	3	–
5.	along	–	–	–	1
6.	aloud	–	–	1	–
7.	always	–	2	–	–
8.	arithmatic	–	–	2	1
9.	art	–	–	1	–
10.	awful	–	–	1	–
11.	back	–	–	–	1
12.	bad	–	–	1	1
13.	bed	–	–	–	1
14.	birds	–	–	2	–
15.	bleeding	–	–	–	1
16.	boating	1	–	–	–
17.	book	–	1	29	87
18.	books	–	–	10	31
19.	bore	–	–	1	–
20.	boredom	–	–	–	1
21.	bores	–	–	1	–
22.	boring	–	–	–	1
23.	borrowing	1	–	–	–
24.	boy	–	–	–	1
25.	brick	1	–	–	–
26.	Brönte	–	–	–	1
27.	burning	1	–	–	–
28.	buying	1	–	–	1
29.	calling	1	–	–	–
30.	caught	–	1	–	–
31.	chewing	1	–	–	–
32.	class	–	–	1	–
33.	contains	–	1	–	–
34.	cooking	1	–	–	–
35.	dancing	2	–	–	–
36.	dark	–	–	2	–
37.	destroying	1	–	–	–
38.	died	–	1	–	–
39.	difficult	–	–	–	1
40.	do	–	1	1	–
41.	doing	4	–	–	–
42.	done	–	–	1	–
43.	drinking	1	–	–	–
44.	easy	–	1	1	–
45.	eating	11	–	–	1
46.	education	–	–	–	1
47.	educational	–	–	2	–
48.	English	1	–	1	1
49.	enjoy	–	16	–	–
50.	enjoyable	–	–	1	–
51.	enjoyment	1	–	–	2
52.	essential	–	–	1	–
53.	eyes	–	–	–	2
54.	fast	–	–	3	1
55.	fasten	–	–	–	1
56.	favorite	–	–	2	–
57.	feeding	–	–	–	1
58.	find	–	2	–	–
59.	fine	–	–	1	–
60.	fun	–	–	28	1
61.	gain	–	–	1	–
62.	glasses	–	–	1	7
63.	go	–	1	–	–
64.	going	1	–	–	1
65.	gone	–	–	1	–
66.	good	1	4	12	2
67.	Greek	–	–	–	1
68.	habits	–	–	1	–
69.	hard	–	–	5	1
70.	hate	–	5	–	–
71.	hated	–	1	–	–
72.	have	–	1	–	–
73.	helpful	–	–	1	–
74.	her	1	2	–	–
75.	his	–	2	2	–
76.	hobby	–	1	–	–
77.	homework	–	–	–	1
78.	intellectual	–	–	–	1
79.	intellectuals	–	–	1	–
80.	interesting	–	–	3	2
81.	it	–	1	3	3
82.	"Yankee Priest"	–	–	1	–
83.	killing	1	–	–	–
84.	know	–	–	–	1
85.	knowledge	–	–	–	1
86.	lamp	–	–	1	–
87.	learn	–	–	–	2
88.	learning	3	–	–	3
89.	least	–	–	1	–
90.	leisure	–	–	–	1
91.	lesen	–	–	–	1
92.	Les Miserables	–	–	2	–
93.	lesson	–	–	–	1
94.	life	–	–	1	1
95.	light	–	–	–	3
96.	like	–	25	–	1
97.	likes	–	4	–	–
98.	limited	–	–	1	–
99.	listening	1	–	–	4
100.	literature	–	–	–	3
101.	living	–	–	1	–
102.	local	–	–	1	–
103.	long	–	–	1	1
104.	look	–	–	–	2
105.	looking	1	–	–	5
106.	looking at	1	–	–	–
107.	losing	–	–	–	1
108.	lot	–	3	–	–
109.	love	–	1	1	–
110.	lunch	1	–	–	–
111.	making	1	–	–	–
112.	material	–	–	2	3
113.	matter	–	–	–	1
114.	me	–	–	1	1
115.	means	–	–	1	–
116.	memorizing	–	–	–	1
117.	metallurgy	1	–	–	–
118.	Mickey Spillane	–	–	1	–
119.	much	–	1	1	1
120.	mystery	–	–	1	–
121.	new	–	–	1	–
122.	nice	1	–	1	–
123.	novel	–	–	1	2
124.	novels	–	–	1	–
125.	now	–	1	1	–
126.	one	–	–	2	–
127.	only	–	1	–	–
128.	"Peyton Place"	–	–	1	–
129.	paper	–	–	2	3
130.	pastime	–	1	–	–
131.	peacefully	–	–	1	–
132.	philosophy	–	–	–	1
133.	Playboy	–	–	1	–
134.	playing	3	–	–	–
135.	pleasant	–	–	1	–
136.	pleasurable	–	–	1	–
137.	pleasure	–	–	2	1
138.	poem	–	–	–	1
139.	poetry	–	–	1	–
140.	print	–	–	–	1
141.	printing	–	–	–	1
142.	quiet	–	–	–	1
143.	railroad	–	–	–	2
144.	Railroad Co.	–	–	1	–
145.	read	–	–	–	16
146.	red	–	–	–	2
147.	relaxation	–	–	–	1
148.	relaxes	–	–	–	1
149.	relaxing	–	–	1	1
150.	riding	1	–	–	–
151.	"Robe"	–	–	–	1
152.	room	–	–	2	1
153.	ruining	1	–	–	–
154.	running	5	–	–	–
155.	said	–	1	–	–
156.	sat	–	2	–	–

31 Reading (contd)

No.	Response	Subst.	Pre	Post	Assoc.
157.	saying	–	–	–	1
158.	school	2	–	2	3
159.	see	–	–	–	1
160.	seeing	1	–	–	6
161.	sending	1	–	–	–
162.	sewing	2	–	–	–
163.	sex	1	–	–	–
164.	shake	–	–	1	–
165.	Shakespeare	–	–	–	1
166.	showing	1	–	–	–
167.	silly	–	–	1	–
168.	singing	1	–	–	1
169.	sister	–	1	–	–
170.	sitting	1	–	–	–
171.	skimming	1	–	–	–
172.	skimming through	1	–	–	–
173.	skipping	1	–	–	–
174.	sleeping	7	–	–	–
175.	smart	–	–	1	–
176.	smelling	1	–	–	–
177.	source	–	1	–	–
178.	speaking	1	–	–	2
179.	spell	–	–	–	1
180.	spelling	3	–	–	–
181.	stand	–	1	–	–
182.	stimulates	–	–	1	–
183.	stock	–	1	–	–
184.	story	–	–	1	1
185.	strenuous	–	–	1	–
186.	study	–	–	–	3
187.	studying	5	–	–	3
188.	swimming	6	–	–	–
189.	talking	6	1	–	–
190.	tearing	2	–	–	–
191.	terrible	–	–	–	1
192.	test	–	–	1	1
193.	that	–	–	2	–
194.	"The Good Earth"	–	–	1	–
195.	think	–	2	–	–
196.	thinking	–	1	–	1
197.	this	–	2	8	3
198.	thought	–	–	–	1
199.	three	–	1	–	–
200.	through	–	1	–	–
201.	throwing	2	–	–	–
202.	time	–	1	–	–
203.	tired	1	–	–	4
204.	ton	–	2	–	–
205.	tried	–	1	–	–
206.	trouble	–	1	–	–
207.	understanding	1	–	–	–
208.	Union Pacific	1	–	–	–
209.	use	–	1	–	–
210.	waiting	–	–	–	1
211.	walking	7	–	–	–
212.	wasting	1	–	–	–
213.	watching	1	–	–	–
214.	what	–	1	–	–
215.	when	–	–	2	–
216.	who	–	1	–	–
217.	words	–	–	–	5
218.	work	1	–	–	2
219.	working	–	–	–	1
220.	write	–	–	–	4
221.	writing	26	1	9	79
222.	wrote	–	–	–	1
223.	yesterday	–	–	1	–
224.	you	–	7	1	–
225.	zigzag	–	–	1	–
		–			
Function Words		–	92	16	–
Space		–	94	80	–
N		139	298	298	362

32 Relax

No.	Response	Subst.	Pre	Post	Assoc.
1.	all	–	1	1	–
2.	at ease	–	–	–	1
3.	awhile	–	–	4	–
4.	back	–	–	–	2
5.	Bardot	–	–	–	1
6.	bath	–	–	–	1
7.	be	1	–	–	–
8.	be calm	1	–	–	–
9.	be happy	1	–	–	–
10.	be quiet	–	–	–	1
11.	beach	–	–	–	1
12.	bed	–	–	1	9
13.	before	–	–	1	–
14.	best	–	–	1	–
15.	bit	–	–	1	–
16.	bliss	–	–	–	1
17.	Bob	1	–	–	–
18.	bones	–	–	1	–
19.	breath	1	–	–	–
20.	Burgie	–	–	1	–
21.	busy	–	–	–	1
22.	California	–	–	1	–
23.	calm	–	–	–	3
24.	calm down	1	1	–	–
25.	came	–	1	–	–
26.	cat	–	–	–	1
27.	chair	–	–	–	18
28.	choir	–	1	–	–
29.	cigarette	–	–	–	1
30.	close	–	–	1	–
31.	collapse	1	–	1	1
32.	come	2	–	–	1
33.	come on	–	1	–	–
34.	comfort	–	–	–	2
35.	comfortable	–	–	3	2
36.	concentrate	–	–	–	1
37.	cool	–	–	–	2
38.	couch	–	–	–	4
39.	cry	1	–	–	–
40.	cushion	–	–	–	1
41.	cushions	–	–	–	1
42.	dance	2	–	–	–
43.	dear	–	–	1	–
44.	decline	–	–	–	1
45.	die	5	–	–	1
46.	do	1	1	–	–
47.	do it	2	–	–	–
48.	dream	–	–	–	1
49.	drink	2	–	–	1
50.	dull	–	–	–	1
51.	ease	–	–	–	4
52.	easily	–	–	1	–
53.	easy	–	2	1	14
54.	eat	13	–	–	2
55.	enjoy	–	–	15	8
56.	enjoyment	–	–	–	1
57.	ever	–	–	1	–
58.	exercise	–	–	–	1
59.	exercised	–	–	–	1
60.	exhausted	–	–	–	1
61.	Exlax	–	–	3	2
62.	facil	–	–	–	1
63.	fall apart	1	–	–	–
64.	fatigue	–	–	–	1
65.	fears	–	–	–	1
66.	feel	–	–	3	–
67.	find	–	–	1	–
68.	fine	–	–	–	1
69.	fingers	–	–	–	1
70.	fire	–	–	–	1
71.	fish	1	–	–	–
72.	flax	–	–	–	1
73.	frighten	1	–	–	–
74.	gentle	–	–	–	1
75.	get	–	–	1	–
76.	go	2	1	1	–
77.	good	–	2	1	2
78.	gracefully	–	–	1	–

No.	Response	Subst.	Pre	Post	Assoc.
79.	Greyhound	–	–	1	–
80.	grow	1	–	–	–
81.	happy	–	–	3	2
82.	hard	–	1	–	–
83.	have	–	–	5	–
84.	have fun	1	–	–	–
85.	her	–	2	–	–
86.	hit	–	–	–	1
87.	home	–	–	1	2
88.	hot	–	–	–	1
89.	it	–	–	6	–
90.	joy	–	–	–	1
91.	jump	2	–	–	–
92.	jumpy	–	–	–	1
93.	know	–	1	–	–
94.	later	–	–	1	–
95.	laugh	1	–	–	–
96.	laxed	–	–	–	1
97.	lay down	–	–	–	1
98.	lazy	–	–	–	3
99.	leave	1	–	2	–
100.	leisure	–	–	–	1
101.	let go	1	–	–	–
102.	let loose	–	–	–	1
103.	lie	1	–	–	2
104.	lie back	1	–	–	–
105.	lie down	–	3	1	–
106.	lied	–	–	–	1
107.	like	–	11	–	–
108.	limp	–	–	–	1
109.	live	1	–	6	–
110.	loaf	1	–	–	2
111.	long	–	–	1	–
112.	look	–	–	1	–
113.	lounge	–	–	–	1
114.	love	–	2	–	–
115.	lying down	–	–	–	1
116.	me	–	–	1	1
117.	means	–	–	1	–
118.	minute	–	–	3	–
119.	modern	–	–	–	1
120.	more	–	–	1	–
121.	move	–	–	–	1
122.	muscles	–	–	1	3
123.	music	–	–	–	1
124.	need	–	1	–	–
125.	needs	–	1	–	–
126.	nervous	–	–	–	6
127.	nice	–	1	–	2
128.	night	–	–	–	1
129.	not go	1	–	–	–
130.	not relaxed	–	–	–	1
131.	nothing	–	–	1	–
132.	now	–	–	10	6
133.	now and then	–	–	1	–
134.	often	–	–	4	–
135.	old	–	–	–	1
136.	one	–	1	–	–
137.	pain	–	–	–	1
138.	peaceful	–	–	–	1
139.	people	–	1	–	–
140.	period	–	–	1	–
141.	play	3	–	–	–
142.	pleasant	–	–	–	1
143.	please	–	14	3	1
144.	pleasure	–	–	–	1
145.	pray	1	–	–	–
146.	problem	–	1	–	–
147.	quiet	–	–	2	5
148.	quit	2	–	–	–
149.	ration	–	–	–	1
150.	read	2	–	–	1
151.	recline	–	–	–	7
152.	reflex	–	–	–	1
153.	refreshment	–	–	–	1
154.	relaxation	–	–	–	2
155.	rest	5	–	1	28
156.	resting	–	–	1	–

No.	Response	Subst.	Pre	Post	Assoc.
157.	run	1	–	–	1
158.	said	–	2	2	–
159.	sanguine	–	–	–	1
160.	school	–	–	2	1
161.	sea	–	–	1	–
162.	set	1	–	–	–
163.	settle	–	–	–	1
164.	shut up	2	–	–	–
165.	sigh	–	–	–	1
166.	sing	6	–	–	–
167.	sit	8	2	–	2
168.	sit back	–	2	–	–
169.	sit down	–	4	1	2
170.	skys	–	–	–	1
171.	sleep	17	3	2	57
172.	sleeping	2	–	–	–
173.	slow	–	–	–	1
174.	slow down	1	–	–	–
175.	slowly	–	–	1	–
176.	smile	1	–	–	–
177.	smoke	–	–	2	–
178.	soft	–	–	–	2
179.	sometimes	–	–	1	–
180.	son	–	–	1	–
181.	soon	–	–	2	–
182.	soothing	–	–	–	1
183.	sove	–	–	–	1
184.	speak	–	1	–	–
185.	stand	1	–	–	–
186.	sterns	–	–	1	–
187.	stop	1	–	–	–
188.	strain	–	–	–	1
189.	strained	–	–	–	1
190.	study	1	–	1	–
191.	suffocate	–	–	–	1
192.	summer	–	–	1	–
193.	summertime	–	1	–	–
194.	sun	–	–	1	1
195.	sweetie	–	–	1	–
196.	swim	7	–	–	2
197.	swoon	–	–	–	1
198.	take	–	–	5	–
199.	take it easy	–	–	–	1
200.	take off	–	1	–	–
201.	taking	–	–	1	–
202.	talk	2	–	–	–
203.	taught	–	–	–	1
204.	tax	–	–	–	1
205.	tense	–	1	–	26
206.	tension	–	–	–	7
207.	tensions	–	–	–	1
208.	that's for me	–	–	–	1
209.	then	–	–	–	1
210.	think	–	–	1	–
211.	this	–	–	3	–
212.	tight	–	–	–	2
213.	tighten	–	–	–	1
214.	time	–	3	–	–
215.	tire	–	–	–	1
216.	tired	–	–	1	9
217.	today	–	–	1	–
218.	together	–	–	1	–
219.	told	–	2	–	–
220.	Tom	–	1	–	–
221.	tomorrow	–	–	1	–
222.	tough	–	–	–	1
223.	tried	–	1	–	–
224.	try	–	9	–	2
225.	TV	–	–	–	1
226.	uncle	–	–	–	1
227.	uncomfortable	–	–	–	1
228.	unlax	–	–	–	1
229.	until	–	–	1	–
230.	us	–	4	–	–
231.	usually	–	1	–	–
232.	vacation	–	–	–	1
233.	walk	2	–	–	–
234.	want	–	4	–	–

32 Relax (contd)

No.	Response	Subst.	Pre	Post	Assoc.
235.	wanted	–	1	–	–
236.	warm	–	–	–	1
237.	went	–	1	–	–
238.	while	–	–	1	–
239.	wonderful	–	–	–	1
240.	work	4	–	–	6
241.	worry	–	–	–	2
242.	write	1	–	–	–
243.	yes	–	–	–	1
244.	you	–	20	17	1
245.	yourself	–	–	4	–

Function Words		–	58	19	–
Space		–	104	95	–
N		123	277	277	354

33 See

No.	Response	Subst.	Pre	Post	Assoc.
1.	all	–	–	1	1
2.	almost	–	1	–	–
3.	also	–	–	1	–
4.	animals	–	–	1	–
5.	answer	–	–	1	–
6.	anything	–	–	2	1
7.	ask	1	–	–	–
8.	bad	–	–	1	–
9.	ball	–	–	–	1
10.	beans	–	–	–	1
11.	beautiful	–	–	2	–
12.	before	–	–	1	–
13.	began	–	1	–	–
14.	believe	1	–	1	–
15.	bells	–	–	1	–
16.	better	–	–	1	–
17.	bird	–	–	2	–
18.	blend	–	–	–	2
19.	blind	–	–	–	29
20.	blinder	–	–	–	1
21.	boat	–	–	1	–
22.	boy	–	–	3	–
23.	bridle	–	1	–	–
24.	burn	1	–	–	–
25.	came	–	2	–	–
26.	candy	–	–	1	1
27.	car	–	–	1	1
28.	carrots	–	1	–	–
29.	cat	–	–	2	2
30.	catch	1	–	–	–
31.	children	–	–	1	–
32.	clearly	–	–	1	2
33.	clock	–	–	1	–
34.	color	–	–	–	2
35.	come	–	4	–	–
36.	contact lens	–	–	–	1
37.	cow	–	–	2	–
38.	crash	–	–	–	1
39.	dark	–	–	1	2
40.	days	–	1	–	–
41.	desire	–	–	1	–
42.	do	5	–	–	–
43.	dog	–	–	6	1
44.	dynamite	–	–	1	–
45.	eat	6	–	–	–
46.	elephant	–	–	1	–
47.	eye	–	–	–	11
48.	eyes	–	–	–	19
49.	far	–	–	1	1
50.	far away	–	–	–	1
51.	fee	–	–	–	1
52.	feel	3	–	–	–
53.	find	–	–	–	1
54.	flower	–	–	1	–

33 See (contd)

No.	Response	Subst.	Pre	Post	Assoc.
55.	flowers	–	–	1	–
56.	forever	–	–	–	1
57.	France	–	–	–	1
58.	girl	–	–	–	1
59.	glad	–	1	–	–
60.	glasses	–	–	–	3
61.	glee	–	–	–	1
62.	go	2	3	–	2
63.	going	–	1	–	–
64.	good	–	–	–	1
65.	hate	1	–	–	–
66.	he	–	–	–	1
67.	hear	12	–	–	16
68.	her	–	–	9	6
69.	here	–	–	–	2
70.	him	–	–	11	3
71.	horse	–	–	2	–
72.	house	–	–	2	1
73.	how	–	–	4	3
74.	hunt	1	–	–	–
75.	if	–	–	–	2
76.	it	–	1	12	5
77.	its	–	–	–	1
78.	Japan	–	–	1	–
79.	John	–	–	1	–
80.	kill	1	–	–	–
81.	kite	–	–	1	–
82.	know	3	–	–	1
83.	later	–	–	1	–
84.	learn	1	–	–	–
85.	leave	1	–	–	–
86.	light	–	–	–	6
87.	like	5	1	–	–
88.	look	2	2	–	39
89.	look at	4	–	–	–
90.	look for	1	–	–	1
91.	looks	–	–	–	1
92.	make	1	–	–	–
93.	man	–	–	2	–
94.	me	–	–	12	8
95.	meet	1	–	–	–
96.	men	–	1	–	–
97.	miss	1	–	–	–
98.	mountain	–	–	1	1
99.	mountains	–	–	–	1
100.	mouth	–	–	–	1
101.	mud	–	–	1	–
102.	nothing	–	–	1	1
103.	now	–	–	5	3
104.	ocean	–	–	1	1
105.	orange	–	–	1	–
106.	paper	–	–	1	–
107.	people	–	–	–	3
108.	perceive	2	–	–	1
109.	picture	–	–	1	1
110.	pope	–	–	–	1
111.	privilege	–	–	–	1
112.	race	–	–	1	–
113.	rainbow	–	–	1	–
114.	read	1	–	–	1
115.	rider	–	–	–	1
116.	road	–	–	1	–
117.	run	1	–	–	–
118.	said	–	–	1	–
119.	sailboat	–	–	–	1
120.	Sally	–	–	1	–
121.	sand	–	–	–	1
122.	saw	4	–	–	41
123.	saws	–	–	–	1
124.	scenery	–	–	–	1
125.	sea	–	–	1	6
126.	second	–	–	–	1
127.	seeing	–	–	–	2
128.	seen	–	–	–	3
129.	seesaw	–	–	1	–
130.	sehen	–	–	–	1
131.	ship	–	–	–	1
132.	show	1	–	1	2

33 See (contd)

No.	Response	Subst.	Pre	Post	Assoc.
133.	sight	1	-	-	6
134.	sign	-	-	-	1
135.	sky	-	-	-	1
136.	spell	1	-	-	-
137.	spy	1	-	-	-
138.	star	-	-	2	-
139.	steal	1	-	-	-
140.	straight	-	-	-	1
141.	sun	-	-	-	1
142.	sure	-	-	-	1
143.	swim	3	-	-	-
144.	talk	1	-	-	-
145.	talk to	1	-	-	-
146.	tea	-	-	-	1
147.	television	-	-	-	1
148.	tell	1	-	-	-
149.	that	-	-	3	1
150.	them	-	-	7	6
151.	things	-	-	-	1
152.	think	-	-	-	1
153.	this	-	-	1	-
154.	together	-	-	1	-
155.	Tommy	-	-	1	-
156.	top	-	-	1	-
157.	touch	1	-	-	-
158.	tree	-	-	1	-
159.	tried	-	1	-	-
160.	truck	-	-	-	1
161.	truth	-	-	1	-
162.	understand	3	-	-	-
163.	unperceive	-	-	-	1
164.	us	-	-	1	2
165.	video	-	-	-	1
166.	vido	-	-	-	1
167.	view	2	-	1	3
168.	vision	-	-	-	5
169.	visualize	-	-	-	1
170.	walk	3	-	-	-
171.	want	2	2	-	-
172.	wanted	-	1	-	-
173.	watch	2	-	1	1
174.	watched	1	-	-	-
175.	water	-	-	-	1
176.	well	-	-	3	-
177.	what	-	-	5	8
178.	where	-	-	-	1
179.	whiskey	-	-	1	-
180.	why	-	-	1	-
181.	window	-	-	-	1
182.	with	1	-	-	-
183.	without	-	-	1	-
184.	write	2	-	-	-
185.	you	-	38	36	3

Function Words		-	110	12	-
Space		-	53	27	-
N		91	226	226	318

34 Slow

No.	Response	Subst.	Pre	Post	Assoc.
1.	amble	-	-	-	1
2.	arriving	-	-	1	-
3.	auto	-	1	-	-
4.	backward	-	-	-	1
5.	barely	1	-	-	-
6.	beautiful	1	-	-	-
7.	bend	1	-	-	-
8.	Bill	-	1	-	-
9.	boat	-	-	1	-
10.	boy	-	5	1	-
11.	brake	1	-	-	-
12.	brother	-	1	-	-

34 Slow (contd)

No.	Response	Subst.	Pre	Post	Assoc.
13.	bus	-	2	-	1
14.	calm	1	-	-	-
15.	car	-	11	-	2
16.	careful	-	-	2	1
17.	carefully	2	-	-	-
18.	carelessly	1	-	-	-
19.	caution	-	-	-	1
20.	cautious	2	-	-	-
21.	cautiously	1	-	-	-
22.	children	-	-	1	1
23.	children crossing	-	-	-	1
24.	clock	-	2	-	-
25.	come	-	1	-	-
26.	crawl	-	-	-	1
27.	creep	-	-	-	1
28.	creepy	1	-	-	-
29.	crippled	1	-	-	-
30.	curve	1	-	-	-
31.	cute	1	-	-	-
32.	dangerous	-	-	1	-
33.	detour	-	-	1	-
34.	detriment	-	-	1	-
35.	dislike	-	1	-	-
36.	does	-	2	-	-
37.	donkey	-	-	-	1
38.	down	-	-	10	7
39.	drive	-	11	-	-
40.	drivers	-	-	1	-
41.	driving	-	2	-	1
42.	drove	-	1	-	-
43.	easy	3	-	1	-
44.	enough	-	-	2	-
45.	erratic	1	-	-	-
46.	erratically	1	-	-	-
47.	far	-	1	-	-
48.	fast	100	1	-	92
49.	faster	2	-	-	-
50.	fellow	-	1	-	-
51.	foot	-	-	1	-
52.	freeway	-	-	1	-
53.	getting	-	-	2	-
54.	girl	-	1	-	-
55.	go	3	25	-	2
56.	goes	-	1	-	-
57.	going	-	5	-	-
58.	good	1	-	-	-
59.	had	-	1	-	-
60.	has	-	1	-	-
61.	how	-	2	-	-
62.	hurry	1	-	-	-
63.	in	1	-	-	-
64.	indicated	-	1	-	-
65.	it	-	2	-	-
66.	Jim	-	1	-	-
67.	know	-	-	-	1
68.	lake	-	-	-	1
69.	landslide	-	1	-	-
70.	lazy	2	-	-	-
71.	learner	-	-	1	-
72.	learning	-	-	2	-
73.	lethargic	1	-	-	-
74.	lie	1	-	-	-
75.	loathing	1	-	-	-
76.	long	1	-	-	-
77.	man	-	1	-	-
78.	Mary	-	1	-	-
79.	me	-	-	1	-
80.	molasses	-	1	-	1
81.	move	-	-	-	1
82.	moves	-	3	-	-
83.	moving	-	-	3	-
84.	necessitated	-	1	-	-
85.	not fast	-	-	-	1
86.	pace	-	-	1	1
87.	past	-	-	1	-
88.	pokey	-	-	-	1
89.	process	-	-	1	-
90.	quick	1	-	-	1

34 Slow (contd)

No.	Response	Subst.	Pre	Post	Assoc.
91.	quickly	1	-	-	-
92.	quiet	1	-	-	-
93.	raft	-	-	1	-
94.	railroad tracks	-	-	1	-
95.	ran	-	3	-	-
96.	reactions	-	-	1	-
97.	read	-	2	-	-
98.	reader	-	-	3	-
99.	reads	-	1	-	-
100.	reasonable	1	-	-	-
101.	reduce speed	1	-	-	-
102.	reflexes	-	-	1	-
103.	retarded	1	-	-	-
104.	right	2	-	-	-
105.	rounding	-	-	1	-
106.	run	2	-	1	-
107.	runs	-	1	-	-
108.	sad	1	-	-	-
109.	safe	-	1	1	-
110.	safety	-	-	1	-
111.	said	-	1	-	-
112.	school	-	-	4	3
113.	seem	-	1	-	-
114.	sensible	1	-	-	-
115.	sharp	-	-	-	1
116.	sign	-	-	-	4
117.	slovenly	-	-	-	1
118.	slow	-	-	-	2
119.	slower	-	-	-	2
120.	slowly	2	-	-	-
121.	sluggish	-	-	-	1
122.	snail	-	-	-	2
123.	so	-	3	-	-
124.	sometimes	-	1	-	-
125.	speak	-	-	1	-
126.	speaker	-	-	1	-
127.	speed	1	-	1	2
128.	sports	-	-	1	-
129.	sticky	1	-	-	-
130.	stop	2	1	-	12
131.	stop sign	-	-	-	1
132.	stopping	-	-	-	1
133.	swiftly	1	-	-	-
134.	tall	-	1	-	-
135.	that	-	1	-	-
136.	there	1	-	-	-
137.	thinker	-	-	3	-
138.	thinking	-	1	1	-
139.	this	-	-	1	-
140.	time	-	-	1	-
141.	tired	1	-	-	-
142.	today	-	-	2	-
143.	town	-	-	1	-
144.	traffic	-	2	2	-
145.	train	-	-	1	-
146.	traveled	-	2	-	-
147.	try	-	1	-	-
148.	turning	-	-	1	-
149.	turtle	-	-	1	2
150.	twenty	-	-	1	-
151.	understand	-	-	1	-
152.	up	-	-	1	-
153.	us	-	1	-	-
154.	walk	-	4	-	1
155.	walked	-	1	-	-
156.	walker	-	-	-	1
157.	walking	-	3	-	-
158.	walks	-	1	-	-
159.	watch	-	1	-	-
160.	water	-	-	1	-
161.	went	-	5	-	-
162.	wit	-	-	1	-
163.	word	-	1	-	-
164.	work	-	-	2	-
165.	worker	-	-	1	-
166.	yellow	-	-	-	1

34 Slow (contd)

No.	Response	Subst.	Pre	Post	Assoc.
167.	you	-	5	1	-
	Function Words	-	27	6	-
	Space	-	3	82	-
	N	160	167	167	159

35 Soft

No.	Response	Subst.	Pre	Post	Assoc.
1.	a pillow	-	-	-	1
2.	amber	1	-	-	-
3.	angora	-	1	-	1
4.	answer	-	-	1	-
5.	babies	-	1	-	-
6.	baby	-	2	-	1
7.	ball	-	1	1	2
8.	beautiful	-	1	-	-
9.	became	-	1	-	-
10.	bed	1	14	5	5
11.	big	2	-	-	-
12.	black	1	-	-	-
13.	blanket	1	2	-	1
14.	blonde	-	-	1	-
15.	blue	1	-	2	-
16.	broken	1	-	-	-
17.	brown	2	-	-	-
18.	bunny	-	1	-	-
19.	butter	-	-	1	-
20.	calls	-	1	-	-
21.	callused	1	-	-	-
22.	cat	-	1	-	1
23.	cement	-	-	1	-
24.	chair	-	8	-	-
25.	chairs	-	2	-	-
26.	clean	1	-	2	-
27.	cloth	-	1	-	1
28.	coarse	2	-	-	-
29.	cold	2	-	-	-
30.	comfort	-	-	-	1
31.	comfortable	-	-	1	3
32.	comforting	1	-	-	-
33.	considerate	1	-	-	-
34.	cotton	-	1	-	6
35.	couples	-	-	1	-
36.	crabby	1	-	-	-
37.	cuddly	4	-	1	1
38.	cushion	-	-	-	1
39.	cute	1	-	-	-
40.	dark	1	-	1	-
41.	different	1	-	-	-
42.	dirty	2	-	-	-
43.	dog	-	-	1	-
44.	downy	1	-	-	-
45.	drink	-	1	2	1
46.	easy	-	-	-	1
47.	egg	-	-	1	-
48.	enough	-	-	2	-
49.	expensive	1	-	-	-
50.	eyes	-	-	1	-
51.	fat	-	-	-	1
52.	feathery	1	-	-	-
53.	felt	-	4	-	-
54.	firm	1	1	-	-
55.	fleece	-	-	1	-
56.	fluffy	2	-	-	3
57.	fruit	-	1	-	-
58.	funny	1	-	-	-
59.	fur	1	3	2	2
60.	furry	-	-	2	-
61.	fuzzy	3	-	-	1
62.	gentle	-	-	-	1
63.	girl	-	-	-	2
64.	God	1	-	-	-

35 Soft (contd)

No.	Response	Subst.	Pre	Post	Assoc.
65.	grain	-	1	-	-
66.	green	1	-	-	-
67.	ground	-	1	-	-
68.	had	-	1	-	-
69.	hair	-	6	-	3
70.	hand	-	-	1	1
71.	hands	-	4	2	-
72.	hard	55	-	2	76
73.	harsh	2	-	-	-
74.	has	-	4	-	-
75.	have	-	5	-	-
76.	heart	-	-	1	-
77.	heavy	-	-	-	1
78.	how	-	2	-	-
79.	hungry	1	-	-	-
80.	hurt	-	-	-	1
81.	inviting	1	-	-	-
82.	it	-	4	1	-
83.	kitten	-	4	-	1
84.	kittens	-	1	-	-
85.	Kleenex	-	-	-	2
86.	light	-	1	-	2
87.	like	-	2	-	-
88.	long	3	-	-	-
89.	look	-	-	1	-
90.	looks	-	1	-	-
91.	loud	4	-	-	4
92.	lovely	2	-	-	-
93.	material	-	2	-	-
94.	mattress	-	2	-	-
95.	melted	1	-	-	-
96.	mind	-	1	-	-
97.	moist	1	-	-	-
98.	molten	1	-	-	-
99.	mushy	1	-	-	-
100.	music	1	1	2	1
101.	nice	2	1	1	1
102.	night	-	1	-	-
103.	oily	1	-	-	-
104.	opposite	-	-	1	-
105.	opposition	-	2	-	-
106.	orange	-	-	1	-
107.	out	-	1	-	-
108.	peach	-	-	-	1
109.	person	-	-	1	-
110.	pillow	-	19	4	8
111.	pillows	-	1	-	-
112.	play	-	1	-	-
113.	pliable	1	-	-	-
114.	plushy	-	-	-	1
115.	poison	1	-	-	-
116.	prefer	-	1	-	-
117.	pretty	3	-	-	-
118.	pudding	-	1	-	-
119.	rabbit	-	2	-	1
120.	rare	-	-	1	-
121.	ripe	1	-	-	-
122.	rough	7	-	-	-
123.	round	1	-	-	-
124.	rubber	2	-	-	-
125.	seat	-	1	-	-
126.	seats	-	-	1	-
127.	sheets	-	-	1	-
128.	shoe	-	-	-	2
129.	shoulder	-	-	1	-
130.	shoulders	-	1	1	-
131.	silky	1	-	-	-
132.	skin	-	3	-	-
133.	slippery	1	-	-	-
134.	small	1	-	-	1
135.	smooth	3	-	-	4
136.	snow	-	1	-	1
137.	sofa	-	1	-	-
138.	soggy	1	-	-	-
139.	sometimes	-	1	-	-
140.	spoiled	1	-	-	-
141.	sponge	-	-	-	3
142.	spongy	1	-	-	-

35 Soft (contd)

No.	Response	Subst.	Pre	Post	Assoc.
143.	stiff	-	-	-	1
144.	strong	-	-	-	1
145.	sweater	-	4	1	-
146.	sweet	1	-	1	-
147.	take	-	-	-	1
148.	that	-	1	-	-
149.	that's	-	1	-	-
150.	theater	-	1	-	-
151.	things	-	-	1	-
152.	this	-	1	-	-
153.	throw	-	-	1	-
154.	tiny	1	-	-	-
155.	tissue	-	-	-	1
156.	touch	-	-	1	-
157.	toy	-	1	-	-
158.	turf	-	1	-	-
159.	types	-	1	-	-
160.	ugly	1	-	-	-
161.	underfoot	-	-	1	-
162.	velvety	1	-	-	-
163.	voice	-	-	1	-
164.	warm	5	-	5	4
165.	wearing	-	1	-	-
166.	what	-	1	-	-
167.	white	-	-	2	2
168.	wind	-	-	1	-
169.	woman	-	-	-	1
170.	wool	1	-	-	-
171.	yellow	-	-	1	-
172.	you	-	1	-	-
Function Words		-	19	2	-
Space		-	3	94	-
N		152	165	165	163

36 Suddenly

No.	Response	Subst.	Pre	Post	Assoc.
1.	abrupt	-	-	-	2
2.	abruptly	-	-	-	2
3.	accident	-	-	-	2
4.	actually	1	-	-	-
5.	after	1	-	-	1
6.	afterward	1	-	-	-
7.	alert	-	-	-	1
8.	all at once	1	-	-	3
9.	all of a sudden	1	-	-	-
10.	almost	2	-	-	-
11.	altogether	1	-	-	-
12.	always	1	-	-	1
13.	amazingly	1	-	-	-
14.	anything	-	1	-	-
15.	appeared	-	2	2	2
16.	arrived	-	2	-	-
17.	at once	2	-	-	2
18.	attack	-	-	-	1
19.	awfully	1	-	-	-
20.	bad	-	-	-	2
21.	ball	-	-	1	-
22.	bang	-	-	-	1
23.	bangs	-	-	-	1
24.	became	-	-	1	-
25.	before	1	-	-	1
26.	bell	-	-	2	-
27.	best	-	-	-	1
28.	bit	-	1	-	-
29.	blue	-	-	-	1
30.	boom	-	-	-	1
31.	broke out	-	-	1	-
32.	but	1	-	-	-
33.	called	-	-	1	-
34.	came	-	17	4	2
35.	car	-	2	2	-

36 Suddenly (contd)

No.	Response	Subst.	Pre	Post	Assoc.
36.	carefully	2	–	–	–
37.	cat	–	1	–	–
38.	caught	–	1	–	–
39.	change	–	–	–	1
40.	changed	–	–	1	–
41.	clash	–	–	1	–
42.	come	–	–	–	1
43.	crash	–	–	1	2
44.	crashes	–	–	–	1
45.	danger	–	–	–	1
46.	dark	–	–	1	–
47.	death	–	–	–	3
48.	delayed	–	–	–	1
49.	died	–	2	2	–
50.	disaster	–	–	–	2
51.	discovered	–	–	1	–
52.	dog	–	1	–	–
53.	done	–	–	–	1
54.	door	–	–	1	–
55.	dropped	–	–	2	–
56.	easily	–	–	–	1
57.	event	–	–	–	1
58.	everything	–	–	1	–
59.	excitement	–	–	–	1
60.	exciting	–	–	–	1
61.	explosion	–	–	1	–
62.	fainted	–	–	1	–
63.	fall	–	–	–	1
64.	fast	2	–	–	41
65.	fate	–	–	–	1
66.	fear	–	–	–	2
67.	fell	1	1	3	2
68.	felt	–	–	1	–
69.	fire	–	–	1	2
70.	flash	–	–	–	2
71.	for	–	–	–	1
72.	fright	–	–	–	2
73.	frightened	–	–	–	1
74.	funnily	–	–	–	1
75.	ghost	–	1	–	–
76.	go	–	1	–	–
77.	gone	–	–	1	3
78.	good	–	–	–	1
79.	gradually	1	–	–	1
80.	grasped	–	–	1	–
81.	great	–	–	1	1
82.	had	1	–	–	–
83.	happen	–	–	–	5
84.	happened	–	20	–	3
85.	happens	–	–	1	–
86.	hard	2	–	–	1
87.	hardly	–	–	–	1
88.	hasten	–	–	–	1
89.	have	–	–	1	–
90.	he	–	–	–	2
91.	heart	–	–	1	1
92.	help	–	–	–	1
93.	her	–	1	–	–
94.	hide	–	–	–	1
95.	his	–	–	2	–
96.	hit	–	–	–	1
97.	home	1	–	–	–
98.	how	–	–	–	1
99.	hurriedly	2	–	–	–
100.	hurry	–	–	–	1
101.	hurt	–	–	–	1
102.	I	–	–	–	1
103.	idea	–	–	1	–
104.	if	1	–	–	–
105.	immediately	4	–	–	4
106.	important	–	–	1	–
107.	infinity	–	–	1	–
108.	instantly	–	–	–	1
109.	interrupted	–	–	1	–
110.	it	–	5	44	1
111.	it became	1	–	–	–
112.	it's	1	–	–	–
113.	jump	–	–	–	3

36 Suddenly (contd)

No.	Response	Subst.	Pre	Post	Assoc.
114.	jumped	–	2	3	1
115.	just then	1	–	–	–
116.	killed	–	–	2	1
117.	kissed	–	–	1	–
118.	lapsed	–	–	–	1
119.	last	–	–	12	2
120.	last summer	–	–	–	2
121.	late	2	–	–	–
122.	lately	1	–	–	1
123.	later	–	–	–	1
124.	leaped out	–	–	1	–
125.	left	–	2	2	–
126.	light	–	–	7	1
127.	lightning	–	2	–	2
128.	lights	–	–	1	–
129.	long	–	–	–	1
130.	loud	–	–	1	–
131.	love	–	1	–	2
132.	me	–	3	–	–
133.	met	–	–	–	1
134.	Monday	1	–	–	–
135.	moods	–	1	–	–
136.	movie	–	–	–	1
137.	mow	–	–	–	1
138.	my heart	–	–	–	1
139.	mystery	–	–	–	1
140.	name	–	1	–	–
141.	never	2	–	–	2
142.	night	–	–	1	–
143.	noise	–	–	1	–
144.	noisy	–	–	–	1
145.	nothing	–	–	–	2
146.	now	2	–	–	34
147.	occasionally	1	–	–	1
148.	often	1	–	–	1
149.	open	–	1	–	1
150.	opened	–	1	–	–
151.	openly	–	–	–	1
152.	out	–	–	–	1
153.	plutselig	–	–	–	1
154.	pounced	–	–	1	–
155.	pronto!	–	–	–	1
156.	quick	1	–	–	22
157.	quickly	33	–	–	35
158.	quiet	–	–	–	2
159.	quietly	2	–	–	–
160.	quit	–	–	–	1
161.	radio	–	–	–	1
162.	rain	–	1	3	–
163.	rains	–	–	1	–
164.	raised	–	1	–	–
165.	ran	–	–	1	–
166.	rang	–	1	–	–
167.	rapidly	1	–	–	–
168.	realized	–	–	2	–
169.	record	–	–	–	1
170.	remembered	–	–	1	–
171.	right	1	–	–	1
172.	right away	1	–	–	1
173.	rocket	–	–	1	–
174.	roof	–	–	1	–
175.	rudely	1	–	–	–
176.	said	–	1	1	–
177.	screamed	–	1	1	–
178.	seldom	–	–	–	1
179.	shock	–	–	–	3
180.	short	1	–	–	–
181.	shorthand	–	–	–	1
182.	shortly	1	–	–	1
183.	shot	–	–	–	1
184.	sky	–	–	1	–
185.	slowly	13	–	–	17
186.	sometime	1	–	–	–
187.	soon	3	–	–	5
188.	sound	–	–	1	–
189.	spring	–	–	1	–
190.	stairs	–	–	1	–
191.	startle	–	–	–	1

36 Suddenly (contd)

No.	Response	Subst.	Pre	Post	Assoc.
192.	startled	–	–	–	3
193.	stop	–	2	–	5
194.	stopped	–	3	4	1
195.	storm	–	1	–	1
196.	strange	–	–	–	1
197.	struck	–	–	1	–
198.	stuck	–	1	–	–
199.	sudden	–	–	–	2
200.	summer	–	–	–	1
201.	sun	–	1	–	–
202.	surely	–	–	–	1
203.	surprise	–	–	–	8
204.	surprised	–	–	–	1
205.	surprisingly	1	–	–	–
206.	swiftly	1	–	–	–
207.	television	–	–	–	1
208.	terribly	1	–	–	–
209.	terror	–	–	–	1
210.	then	19	–	–	9
211.	there	–	–	–	3
212.	they	–	–	–	4
213.	this	–	–	–	1
214.	time	–	–	–	1
215.	to	–	–	–	1
216.	together	1	–	–	–
217.	took off	–	1	–	–
218.	town	–	–	–	1
219.	tragedy	–	–	–	1
220.	two	–	–	1	–
221.	unaware	–	–	–	1
222.	unexpected	–	–	–	1
223.	unexpectedly	–	–	–	5
224.	up	–	–	–	1
225.	urgent	–	–	–	1
226.	usually	–	–	–	1
227.	valley	–	–	4	1
228.	went	–	3	1	1
229.	when	7	–	–	3
230.	why	–	–	–	1
231.	wind	–	1	–	–
232.	woods	–	–	1	–
233.	world	–	–	2	–
234.	yell	–	–	–	1
235.	yesterday	3	–	1	–
236.	you	–	–	2	5
237.	500	–	–	1	–

Function Words		–	50	98	–
Space		–	175	61	1
N		137	314	314	365

37 Swim

No.	Response	Subst.	Pre	Post	Assoc.
1.	a while	–	–	1	–
2.	able	–	1	–	–
3.	across	–	–	6	–
4.	all	–	–	3	–
5.	always	–	2	–	–
6.	aquatic club	–	–	–	1
7.	arm	–	–	–	1
8.	ashore	–	–	1	–
9.	away	–	–	2	–
10.	back	–	–	1	–
11.	bad	–	–	1	–
12.	bank	–	–	1	–
13.	basketball	1	–	–	–
14.	bath	1	–	–	–
15.	bathe	2	–	–	1
16.	bathing suit	–	–	1	2
17.	baths	–	–	–	1
18.	bay	–	–	2	–
19.	be	1	–	–	–

37 Swim (contd)

No.	Response	Subst.	Pre	Post	Assoc.
20.	beach	–	–	–	1
21.	before	–	–	1	–
22.	better	–	–	2	–
23.	blue	–	–	–	1
24.	boat	–	–	–	1
25.	Bob	–	–	1	–
26.	bop	1	–	–	–
27.	bowl	1	–	–	–
28.	boy	–	1	1	–
29.	break	1	–	–	–
30.	breast stroke	1	–	–	–
31.	breathing	–	–	–	1
32.	bubbles	–	–	–	1
33.	butterfly	–	–	–	1
34.	call	1	–	–	–
35.	can't	–	–	–	1
36.	canal	–	–	1	–
37.	canoe	1	–	–	–
38.	champ	–	–	1	–
39.	channel	–	–	1	–
40.	children	–	1	–	–
41.	choke	–	–	–	1
42.	coach	1	–	–	–
43.	coffee grind	1	–	–	–
44.	cold	–	–	1	2
45.	come	4	1	–	–
46.	cook	1	–	–	–
47.	cool	–	–	1	4
48.	cooolness	–	–	–	1
49.	crawl	1	–	–	–
50.	dance	11	–	–	–
51.	date	2	–	–	–
52.	decided	–	1	–	–
53.	die	3	–	–	–
54.	dislike	–	1	–	–
55.	dive	11	–	–	19
56.	diver	–	–	–	1
57.	diving	–	–	–	1
58.	dog paddle	1	–	–	–
59.	drink	8	–	–	–
60.	drive	4	–	–	1
61.	drown	4	–	1	36
62.	drowned	–	–	–	4
63.	drowning	–	–	–	1
64.	drowns	–	–	–	1
65.	dry	–	–	–	1
66.	duck	1	–	–	–
67.	eat	18	–	–	–
68.	eating	1	–	–	–
69.	edge	1	–	–	–
70.	enjoy	–	1	–	–
71.	enjoyed	–	1	–	–
72.	evenings	–	–	1	–
73.	exercise	1	–	–	3
74.	far	–	–	2	–
75.	fast	–	–	11	6
76.	faster	–	–	2	–
77.	fastly	–	–	1	–
78.	feet	–	1	–	–
79.	fight	–	–	–	1
80.	fin	–	–	–	1
81.	fins	–	–	1	1
82.	first	–	–	1	–
83.	first aid	–	–	–	1
84.	fish	5	–	4	10
85.	fishes	–	1	–	–
86.	float	6	–	–	10
87.	fly	3	–	–	1
88.	fool	–	–	1	–
89.	fountains	1	–	–	–
90.	fun	–	–	4	6
91.	girls	–	1	–	–
92.	go	1	13	–	1
93.	go boating	2	–	–	–
94.	going	–	3	–	–
95.	golf	1	–	–	–
96.	good	–	1	6	–
97.	gray flannel	1	–	–	–

37 Swim (contd)

No.	Response	Subst.	Pre	Post	Assoc.
98.	great deal	-	-	1	-
99.	had	-	1	-	-
100.	hard	-	1	-	1
101.	hate	1	2	-	-
102.	have	-	1	-	-
103.	her	-	-	1	-
104.	here	-	-	2	-
105.	hike	6	-	-	2
106.	him	-	1	-	-
107.	his	-	-	1	-
108.	hot	-	-	2	-
109.	house	-	-	1	-
110.	hunt	3	-	-	-
111.	ice	-	-	-	1
112.	in	-	-	-	1
113.	irregularly	-	-	1	-
114.	is	1	-	-	-
115.	Joe	-	-	1	-
116.	jump	5	-	-	-
117.	Kerry	-	-	-	1
118.	kiss	3	-	-	-
119.	know	-	3	-	-
120.	knows	-	1	-	-
121.	lake	-	-	3	5
122.	last	-	-	1	-
123.	laugh	1	-	-	-
124.	learn	-	7	-	-
125.	learning	-	1	-	-
126.	life guard	-	-	-	1
127.	like	-	84	-	-
128.	likes	-	5	-	-
129.	long	-	-	1	-
130.	look	2	-	-	-
131.	lot	-	-	2	-
132.	love	2	15	-	-
133.	march	1	-	-	-
134.	Mayers	-	1	-	-
135.	me	-	-	2	1
136.	meet	-	-	5	-
137.	meter	-	-	1	-
138.	money	-	-	-	1
139.	moonlight	-	-	-	1
140.	morning	-	-	1	-
141.	move	-	1	-	1
142.	much	-	1	1	-
143.	near	-	-	1	-
144.	new	1	-	-	-
145.	nothing	-	1	-	-
146.	now	-	-	1	-
147.	ocean	-	-	1	-
148.	often	-	-	2	-
149.	other	-	-	1	-
150.	paddle	3	-	-	-
151.	paint	1	-	-	-
152.	pals	-	-	-	1
153.	Paul Daley's Swim School	-	-	-	1
154.	play	17	-	-	-
155.	play ball	1	-	-	-
156.	played	1	-	-	-
157.	pleasure	-	-	-	1
158.	plunge	2	-	-	-
159.	pool	-	-	5	15
160.	pools	-	-	-	1
161.	raft	-	-	1	-
162.	read	4	-	-	-
163.	refreshing	-	1	2	1
164.	relax	-	-	-	2
165.	relaxation	-	-	-	1
166.	relaxing	-	-	-	1
167.	rest	1	-	-	-
168.	ride	10	-	-	-
169.	rides	1	-	-	-
170.	right	1	-	-	-
171.	river	-	-	1	2
172.	row	1	-	-	2
173.	rowboat	-	-	1	-
174.	run	45	-	-	5

37 Swim (contd)

No.	Response	Subst.	Pre	Post	Assoc.
175.	runs	1	-	-	-
176.	sail	1	-	-	-
177.	Salt Lake	-	-	1	-
178.	sank	-	-	1	-
179.	sea	-	-	-	1
180.	seals	-	1	-	-
181.	see	1	-	-	-
182.	sew	2	-	-	-
183.	shark	-	-	-	1
184.	shore	-	-	2	-
185.	show off	1	-	-	-
186.	side	-	-	1	-
187.	sing	3	-	1	1
188.	sink	1	7	2	29
189.	sinking	-	-	-	1
190.	sit	1	-	-	-
191.	sits	1	-	-	-
192.	skate	2	-	-	-
193.	ski	3	-	-	1
194.	skin diving	-	-	-	1
195.	sleep	1	-	-	-
196.	slow	-	-	1	-
197.	slower	-	-	1	-
198.	smoke	1	-	-	-
199.	speak	2	-	-	-
200.	splash	-	-	1	4
201.	sport	-	-	-	3
202.	stay home	1	-	-	-
203.	stroke	1	-	1	2
204.	suit	-	-	1	8
205.	suites	-	-	-	1
206.	summer	-	-	4	3
207.	sun	-	-	-	2
208.	sunk	-	-	-	1
209.	survive	1	-	-	-
210.	swam	3	-	-	24
211.	swim suits	-	-	1	-
212.	swimming	-	-	1	1
213.	take	-	7	-	-
214.	talk	8	-	-	1
215.	Tam Pool	-	-	-	-
216.	tennis	1	-	-	-
217.	three	-	-	1	-
218.	tired	-	-	-	1
219.	today	-	-	7	-
220.	Tom	-	1	-	1
221.	took	-	1	-	-
222.	track	3	-	-	-
223.	tried	-	1	-	-
224.	tumble	1	-	-	-
225.	twice	-	-	1	-
226.	use	-	1	-	-
227.	wade	3	-	-	2
228.	wading	-	-	-	1
229.	walk	32	-	-	5
230.	walks	-	-	-	1
231.	wallow	1	-	-	-
232.	want	-	2	-	-
233.	wanted	-	1	-	-
234.	warm	-	1	1	-
235.	watched	-	1	-	-
236.	water	-	-	1	104
237.	water ski	-	-	1	-
238.	well	-	-	31	-
239.	went	-	2	-	-
240.	wet	-	-	-	4
241.	whales	-	1	-	-
242.	wide	-	-	1	-
243.	Wilson's	-	-	1	-
244.	win	-	-	-	1
245.	won	-	2	-	-
246.	work	-	-	-	-

37   Swim (contd)

No.	Response	Subst.	Pre	Post	Assoc.
247.	write	4	–	–	–
248.	you	–	38	1	–
249.	400 yd.	–	–	–	1
	Function Words	–	127	8	–
	Space	–	30	195	–
	N	302	379	379	382

38   Table

No.	Response	Subst.	Pre	Post	Assoc.
1.	a maple table	–	–	–	1
2.	antique	–	–	1	–
3.	apple	–	1	–	–
4.	aside	–	–	1	–
5.	ate	–	1	–	–
6.	basket	1	–	–	–
7.	beautiful	–	3	1	–
8.	bed	3	–	–	–
9.	bench	2	–	–	–
10.	Bible	–	–	–	1
11.	big	–	2	–	–
12.	bone	1	–	–	–
13.	book	2	2	–	1
14.	books	–	4	–	–
15.	booth	1	–	–	–
16.	box	1	–	–	–
17.	breakfast	–	–	–	1
18.	bridal	–	1	–	–
19.	broad	1	–	–	–
20.	broke	–	2	–	–
21.	broken	–	–	9	–
22.	brother	1	–	–	–
23.	brown	–	–	1	3
24.	buffet	3	–	–	–
25.	cake	1	–	–	–
26.	candles	–	1	–	–
27.	car	4	–	–	–
28.	card	–	1	–	–
29.	cart	1	–	–	–
30.	chair	33	3	1	70
31.	chairs	3	3	1	3
32.	Charlie	–	–	1	–
33.	cleared	–	–	1	–
34.	clock	5	–	–	–
35.	cloth	–	–	–	10
36.	coat	1	–	–	–
37.	convenient	–	–	1	–
38.	corner	–	–	1	–
39.	couch	2	–	–	–
40.	counter	3	–	–	–
41.	cover	–	1	–	–
42.	crawl	–	1	–	–
43.	cute	–	–	1	–
44.	date	1	–	–	–
45.	desk	13	–	–	7
46.	desks	–	1	–	–
47.	diner	1	–	–	–
48.	dinner	–	2	1	2
49.	dirty	–	–	1	–
50.	dish	–	–	–	1
51.	dishes	–	2	–	–
52.	dog	3	–	–	–
53.	doll	1	–	–	–
54.	door	1	–	–	–
55.	down	–	3	–	–
56.	dress	1	–	–	–
57.	eat	–	1	1	2
58.	elbows	–	1	–	–
59.	Ella	–	–	1	–
60.	feet	–	1	–	–
61.	fell	–	1	–	–
62.	fire	1	–	–	–

38   Table (contd)

No.	Response	Subst.	Pre	Post	Assoc.
63.	flat	–	–	1	4
64.	floor	6	–	1	–
65.	flowers	–	1	–	–
66.	food	1	3	–	9
67.	full	–	–	1	–
68.	furniture	1	–	–	–
69.	game	1	–	–	–
70.	garden	1	–	–	–
71.	get	–	1	–	–
72.	glass	–	–	–	1
73.	good	–	1	1	1
74.	greasy	–	–	1	–
75.	ground	2	–	–	–
76.	had	–	–	1	–
77.	handy	–	–	1	–
78.	hard	–	–	1	1
79.	has	–	–	6	–
80.	have	–	1	–	–
81.	help	–	–	–	1
82.	here	–	2	–	–
83.	high	–	1	1	–
84.	hill	1	–	–	–
85.	hold	–	–	1	–
86.	holds	–	–	1	–
87.	hour	–	–	1	–
88.	house	3	–	–	–
89.	it	–	3	–	–
90.	Jello	1	–	–	–
91.	kettle	1	–	–	–
92.	knives	1	–	–	–
93.	laden	–	–	1	–
94.	lamp	3	–	–	–
95.	large	–	–	2	–
96.	last	–	–	1	–
97.	lay	–	1	–	–
98.	leg	1	1	1	3
99.	legs	–	–	1	3
100.	level	–	–	1	1
101.	living room	1	–	–	–
102.	long	–	–	2	1
103.	look	–	1	–	–
104.	low	–	–	1	–
105.	made	–	2	2	–
106.	man	1	–	–	–
107.	many	–	1	–	–
108.	maple	–	–	–	1
109.	matching	–	–	1	–
110.	me	–	1	–	–
111.	meeting	1	–	–	–
112.	modern	–	–	1	–
113.	never	–	–	1	–
114.	new	–	2	–	–
115.	oak	–	1	–	–
116.	object	–	–	–	1
117.	okay	–	–	1	–
118.	old	–	2	–	–
119.	other	–	1	–	–
120.	over	–	1	–	–
121.	paint	1	1	–	–
122.	paper	–	–	–	1
123.	pen	–	1	–	–
124.	Ping-pong	–	–	–	1
125.	place	3	–	–	1
126.	placed	–	–	1	–
127.	platform	–	–	–	1
128.	prepared	–	–	1	–
129.	purchased	–	1	–	–
130.	push	–	1	–	–
131.	put	–	1	–	–
132.	quite	–	–	1	–
133.	radio	1	–	–	–
134.	right	–	–	1	–
135.	river	1	–	–	–
136.	room	2	1	1	–
137.	round	–	–	1	1
138.	rug	1	–	–	–
139.	salt	–	–	–	1
140.	sat	–	6	–	–

447

38   Table (contd)

No.	Response	Subst.	Pre	Post	Assoc.
141.	scene	1	–	–	–
142.	schedule	1	–	–	–
143.	seat	1	–	–	–
144.	set	–	17	5	–
145.	setting	1	–	–	1
146.	shelf	1	–	–	–
147.	shined	–	–	1	–
148.	shoe	–	–	1	–
149.	short	–	–	1	–
150.	sink	1	–	–	–
151.	sit	–	4	–	–
152.	small	–	–	3	–
153.	sofa	2	–	–	–
154.	soft	–	–	–	1
155.	solid	–	–	1	–
156.	soon	–	–	1	–
157.	spoon	1	–	–	–
158.	square	–	–	–	1
159.	stand	1	–	–	–
160.	stomach	1	–	–	–
161.	stood	–	1	–	–
162.	stove	3	–	2	–
163.	strong	–	–	2	–
164.	study	–	1	1	–
165.	support	–	–	–	1
166.	table	–	–	–	1
167.	table tennis	–	–	–	1
168.	tablecloth	–	–	–	2
169.	tall	–	–	–	1
170.	tangible	–	–	–	1
171.	that	–	1	–	–
172.	things	–	1	–	–
173.	this	–	1	–	–
174.	time	1	1	–	–
175.	top	–	–	–	10
176.	trays	1	–	–	–
177.	tree	1	–	–	–
178.	TV	2	–	–	–
179.	type	1	–	–	–
180.	well	–	–	1	–
181.	white	–	–	1	–
182.	wide	1	–	–	–
183.	window	1	–	–	–
184.	woman	1	–	–	–
185.	wood	–	–	–	7
186.	yesterday	–	–	1	–
					–
	Function Words	–	59	4	–
	Space	–	1	77	–
	N	149	164	164	162

39   The

No.	Response	Subst.	Pre	Post	Assoc.
1.	a	30	–	–	20
2.	a group called	1	–	–	–
3.	accident	–	–	1	–
4.	adjective	–	–	–	2
5.	adjectives	–	–	–	1
6.	afraid	–	1	–	–
7.	air	–	–	1	–
8.	all	1	–	–	2
9.	an	3	–	–	5
10.	and	–	–	–	12
11.	animal	–	–	–	1
12.	any	–	–	–	1
13.	apple	–	–	2	1
14.	arm	–	–	–	1
15.	article	–	1	–	16
16.	ask	–	1	–	–
17.	attribute	–	–	1	–
18.	back	–	2	3	–
19.	"Badders"	–	–	1	–

39   The (contd)

No.	Response	Subst.	Pre	Post	Assoc.
20.	bag	–	–	–	1
21.	ball	–	–	7	1
22.	banana	–	–	1	–
23.	barn	–	–	1	–
24.	basket	–	–	1	1
25.	bat	–	–	–	1
26.	beach	–	–	2	–
27.	bear	–	–	1	1
28.	bed	–	–	–	2
29.	beer	–	–	1	–
30.	beginning	–	–	1	1
31.	bell	–	–	2	1
32.	belong	–	1	–	–
33.	best	–	–	1	–
34.	big	–	–	4	–
35.	bird	–	–	1	–
36.	black	–	–	4	–
37.	blank	–	–	–	1
38.	blue	–	–	–	1
39.	boat	–	–	3	1
40.	book	–	1	12	7
41.	bottom	–	–	–	1
42.	bought	–	1	–	8
43.	boy	–	–	11	–
44.	boys	–	–	1	–
45.	bring	–	1	–	–
46.	broke	–	1	–	–
47.	buggy	–	–	1	–
48.	called	–	2	–	–
49.	came in	–	1	–	–
50.	car	–	–	13	7
51.	carrots	–	–	1	–
52.	cat	–	1	12	1
53.	chased	–	1	–	–
54.	closet	–	–	1	–
55.	coat	–	–	1	–
56.	coffee	–	–	1	–
57.	come	–	1	–	1
58.	conductor	–	–	1	–
59.	correct	–	–	1	–
60.	cow	–	–	2	2
61.	cup	–	–	–	1
62.	D	1	–	–	–
63.	dance	–	–	3	–
64.	darkness	–	–	1	–
65.	day	–	–	7	–
66.	deer	–	–	1	–
67.	desk	–	–	–	1
68.	dictionary	–	–	1	–
69.	dog	–	–	16	3
70.	don	–	–	–	1
71.	door	–	–	3	–
72.	duck	–	–	1	–
73.	el	–	–	–	1
74.	elephant	–	–	1	–
75.	end	–	–	4	18
76.	engine	–	–	1	–
77.	fat	–	–	–	1
78.	father	–	–	–	1
79.	find	–	1	–	–
80.	first	–	–	–	2
81.	fish	–	–	2	–
82.	five	1	–	–	–
83.	flew	–	1	–	–
84.	floor	–	–	1	–
85.	food	–	–	1	1
86.	football	–	–	1	–
87.	for the	1	–	–	–
88.	forget	–	1	–	–
89.	game	–	–	7	2
90.	gave	–	1	–	–
91.	girl	–	–	4	6
92.	girls	1	–	–	1
93.	glass	–	–	1	–
94.	go	–	4	–	–
95.	goat	–	–	1	–
96.	goes	–	1	–	–
97.	going	–	2	–	–

39 The (contd)   39 The (contd)

No.	Response	Subst.	Pre	Post	Assoc.		No.	Response	Subst.	Pre	Post	Assoc.
98.	goose	–	–	1	–		176.	right	–	–	2	–
99.	harpooned	–	1	–	–		177.	road	–	–	1	–
100.	hat	–	–	1	–		178.	rock	–	–	2	–
101.	hate	–	2	–	–		179.	rocket	–	–	–	1
102.	he	–	–	–	1		180.	room	–	–	1	–
103.	her	–	1	–	–		181.	run	–	1	–	–
104.	hi!	–	1	–	–		182.	rush	–	–	1	–
105.	hill	–	–	–	1		183.	same	–	–	1	–
106.	him	–	1	–	–		184.	sandpaper	–	–	–	1
107.	his	16	–	–	–		185.	saw	–	7	–	–
108.	hit	–	3	–	–		186.	schools	–	–	1	–
109.	hook	–	–	–	1		187.	sea	–	–	2	–
110.	hope	–	1	–	–		188.	secretary	–	–	1	–
111.	horse	–	1	5	2		189.	see	–	3	–	–
112.	house	–	–	7	10		190.	sentence	–	–	–	1
113.	if	–	–	–	2		191.	she	–	–	–	1
114.	in	–	–	–	1		192.	shot	–	1	–	–
115.	is	–	–	–	2		193.	show	–	–	6	–
116.	it	–	18	–	34		194.	simple	–	–	–	1
117.	its	1	–	–	–		195.	skinny	–	–	1	–
118.	jumped	–	2	–	–		196.	skins	–	–	1	–
119.	killed	–	1	–	–		197.	sky	–	–	1	–
120.	king	–	–	2	1		198.	slashes	–	–	–	1
121.	kitchen	–	–	1	–		199.	small	–	–	–	1
122.	knew	–	1	–	–		200.	society	–	–	1	–
123.	knock	–	1	–	–		201.	something	–	–	–	3
124.	la	–	–	–	1		202..	sound	–	–	–	1
125.	lamp	–	–	1	–		203.	special	–	–	–	1
126.	lazy	–	–	2	–		204.	spell	–	1	–	–
127.	le	–	–	–	1		205.	spirit	–	–	1	–
128.	leave	–	1	–	–		206.	star	–	–	–	1
129.	left	–	1	–	–		207.	start	–	1	–	–
130.	light	–	–	1	–		208.	stew	–	–	–	1
131.	lights	–	–	1	–		209.	stole	–	2	–	–
132.	like	–	2	–	–		210.	store	–	–	1	–
133.	likes	–	1	–	–		211.	story	–	–	1	–
134.	little	–	–	1	2		212.	strange	–	–	–	1
135.	living	–	–	1	–		213.	sun	–	–	1	1
136.	lonesome	–	–	1	–		214.	table	–	–	3	2
137.	look at	–	1	–	–		215.	talk	–	2	–	–
138.	lost	–	1	–	–		216.	tea	–	–	–	2
139.	main	–	–	–	1		217.	teacher	–	–	3	1
140.	major	–	–	1	–		218.	tell	–	1	–	–
141.	man	–	1	12	11		219.	test	–	–	2	–
142.	me	–	–	–	1		220.	that	17	6	–	10
143.	men	–	–	1	2		221.	the drag	–	–	–	1
144.	middle	–	–	1	–		222.	thee	–	–	–	5
145.	money	–	–	1	–		223.	their	3	–	–	1
146.	movie	–	–	2	–		224.	theirs	–	–	–	1
147.	muscle	–	–	–	1		225.	them	1	–	–	12
148.	my	13	–	–	–		226.	there	1	1	–	–
149.	name	–	–	–	1		227.	these	–	–	–	2
150.	night	–	–	2	–		228.	they	–	–	–	5
151.	nineteenth	–	–	1	–		229.	thing	–	–	2	8
152.	novel	–	–	1	–		230.	things	–	–	1	–
153.	of	–	–	–	1		231.	think	–	1	–	–
154.	oh	–	–	–	1		232.	this	8	6	–	7
155.	old	–	–	4	–		233.	tho	–	–	–	1
156.	one	3	–	3	9		234.	those	1	–	–	2
157.	ones	–	–	–	1		235.	thou	–	–	–	1
158.	only	–	1	1	–		236.	tie	–	–	–	2
159.	organization	–	–	–	1		237.	time	–	–	2	–
160.	other	–	–	2	–		238.	title	–	–	–	3
161.	our	6	–	–	–		239.	toe	–	–	–	1
162.	painting	–	–	1	–		240.	took	–	1	–	–
163.	particular	–	–	–	1		241.	tools	–	–	–	1
164.	pen	–	–	2	–		242.	town	–	–	1	–
165.	pencil	–	–	2	–		243.	track	–	–	1	–
166.	pens	–	–	1	–		244.	train	–	–	2	1
167.	people	–	–	–	1		245.	tree	–	–	1	1
168.	place	–	–	1	–		246.	trouble	–	–	1	–
169.	plan	–	–	1	–		247.	truth	–	–	1	–
170.	plane	–	–	1	–		248.	try	–	2	–	–
171.	poor	–	–	1	–		249.	use	–	1	–	–
172.	preposition	–	–	1	–		250.	wa wa wa	–	–	–	1
173.	prinicpal	–	–	1	1		251.	walked	–	1	–	–
174.	Quakers	–	–	–	1		252.	wall	–	–	–	1
175.	ridiculous	–	–	1	–		253.	want	–	1	–	–

39   The (contd)

No.	Response	Subst.	Pre	Post	Assoc.
254.	watch	–	–	–	1
255.	way	–	–	–	1
256.	weather	–	–	1	–
257.	went	–	5	–	–
258.	what	1	2	–	8
259.	wheat	–	–	–	1
260.	when	–	1	–	1
261.	where	–	1	–	–
262.	white	–	–	1	–
263.	who	–	–	–	1
264.	why	–	1	–	–
265.	wish	–	–	–	1
266.	wizard	–	–	1	–
267.	woman	–	–	–	1
268.	women	–	–	1	–
269.	word	–	1	1	3
270.	world	–	–	2	–
271.	wrong	–	–	2	–
272.	yes	–	–	–	1
273.	you	–	1	–	2
274.	20,0000	–	1	–	–

Function Words		–	11	–	–
Space		–	147	2	–
N		110	280	280	342

40   They

No.	Response	Subst.	Pre	Post	Assoc.
1.	a lot	–	–	–	1
2.	adults	1	–	–	–
3.	after	–	1	–	–
4.	against	–	1	2	–
5.	agrees	–	1	–	–
6.	Alice	1	–	–	–
7.	Alice and Jane	1	–	–	–
8.	alive	–	–	1	–
9.	all	1	1	2	2
10.	alone	–	–	1	–
11.	all right	–	–	1	–
12.	already	–	–	1	–
13.	always	–	–	5	–
14.	answered	–	1	–	–
15.	anyone	–	–	–	1
16.	apples	1	–	–	–
17.	are	–	–	–	4
18.	aren't	–	–	–	1
19.	arrive	–	–	1	–
20.	asked	–	1	2	–
21.	ate	–	–	1	–
22.	attended	–	–	1	–
23.	bad	–	–	3	–
24.	"band"	–	–	1	–
25.	baseball	2	–	–	4
26.	batty	–	–	1	–
27.	beaches	1	–	–	–
28.	beads	1	–	–	–
29.	beat	–	–	1	–
30.	belong	–	–	2	–
31.	better	–	2	–	–
32.	blasted	–	–	1	–
33.	books	1	–	–	–
34.	both	1	–	–	–
35.	bother	–	–	1	–
36.	boy	–	–	–	1
37.	boys	4	–	–	–
38.	brought	–	–	1	–
39.	buy	–	–	1	–
40.	came	–	–	18	–
41.	canasta	–	–	–	1
42.	candy is	1	–	–	–
43.	car	–	–	–	1
44.	children	1	–	–	1

40   They (contd)

No.	Response	Subst.	Pre	Post	Assoc.
45.	climbed	–	–	1	–
46.	cold	–	–	1	–
47.	come	–	–	17	1
48.	coming	–	–	12	–
49.	congress	1	–	–	–
50.	couple	–	–	–	3
51.	crazy	–	–	1	–
52.	criminals	–	–	1	–
53.	crowd	–	–	–	2
54.	cruelty	–	–	1	–
55.	crying	–	–	1	–
56.	cute	–	–	3	–
57.	dead	–	–	4	–
58.	did	–	–	4	2
59.	did it	–	–	–	1
60.	dislike	–	–	3	–
61.	do	–	–	4	–
62.	dogs	1	–	–	–
63.	doing	–	–	2	–
64.	each	1	–	–	–
65.	eat	–	–	3	–
66.	elope	–	–	1	–
67.	everyone	1	–	–	–
68.	fallen	–	–	1	–
69.	family	–	–	–	1
70.	fear	–	1	–	–
71.	feel	–	1	–	–
72.	felt	–	–	1	–
73.	for	–	1	–	–
74.	found	–	–	1	–
75.	friendly	–	–	1	–
76.	friends	1	–	3	4
77.	fun	1	–	3	8
78.	funny	–	–	2	–
79.	gang	–	–	–	2
80.	gave	–	–	1	–
81.	girl	–	–	–	1
82.	girls	1	1	–	3
83.	glad	–	1	–	–
84.	go	–	1	12	2
85.	going	–	–	15	–
86.	gone	–	–	1	–
87.	good	–	–	9	–
88.	got	–	–	2	–
89.	green	–	–	–	1
90.	group	–	–	1	15
91.	had	–	–	2	–
92.	happy	–	–	3	–
93.	hard	–	–	–	1
94.	hate	–	–	2	1
95.	hats	1	–	–	2
96.	have	–	–	2	2
97.	he	14	–	–	1
98.	he was	2	–	–	–
99.	he went	1	–	–	–
100.	hey!	–	–	–	1
101.	healthy	–	–	1	–
102.	help	–	–	1	–
103.	helped	–	–	–	2
104.	her	–	–	–	1
105.	herd	–	–	–	1
106.	here	–	–	22	–
107.	hers	1	–	–	–
108.	him	–	–	–	5
109.	his	–	–	–	1
110.	hit	–	–	1	–
111.	home	–	–	2	–
112.	hope	–	2	–	–
113.	hurt	–	–	–	1
114.	I	11	–	–	2
115.	I was	1	–	–	–
116.	inhibited	–	–	1	–
117.	is	–	2	–	–
118.	it	1	2	1	1
119.	it is	1	–	–	–
120.	Jerry	1	–	–	–
121.	Jim	1	–	–	–
122.	John and Mary	1	–	–	–

40 They (contd)

No.	Response	Subst.	Pre	Post	Assoc.
123.	Jones	1	–	–	–
124.	just	1	–	–	–
125.	kill	–	–	1	–
126.	kind	–	–	1	–
127.	knew	–	1	2	–
128.	know	–	1	6	–
129.	late	–	–	2	–
130.	laugh	–	–	1	–
131.	learn	–	–	2	–
132.	leave	–	–	1	–
133.	left	–	–	5	–
134.	like	–	–	14	–
135.	lion	–	–	–	1
136.	live	–	–	1	–
137.	look	–	–	1	–
138.	lousy	–	–	1	–
139.	love	–	–	4	–
140.	loved	–	–	1	–
141.	mad	–	–	1	–
142.	make	–	–	4	–
143.	man	–	–	–	1
144.	many	1	–	–	8
145.	may	–	–	–	1
146.	me	–	–	1	4
147.	men	4	–	–	–
148.	Mergatroid	1	–	–	–
149.	mixed up	–	–	1	–
150.	mom	–	1	–	–
151.	mother	1	–	–	–
152.	mountaineers	–	–	1	–
153.	my aunt	1	–	–	–
154.	neighbors	–	–	–	1
155.	nice	–	–	10	–
156.	no	1	–	–	–
157.	old	–	–	1	–
158.	ones	..	–	1	–
159.	only	–	–	1	–
160.	others	–	–	–	2
161.	ours	–	–	–	1
162.	parents	–	–	–	3
163.	party	–	–	–	1
164.	pencil	–	–	–	1
165.	people	4	–	–	38
166.	planning	–	–	1	–
167.	play	–	–	1	–
168.	played	–	–	1	–
169.	playing	–	–	1	–
170.	pleasant	–	–	1	–
171.	police	1	–	–	–
172.	pronoun	–	–	1	1
173.	quiet	–	–	1	–
174.	quit	–	–	1	–
175.	ran	–	–	4	–
176.	remember	–	1	–	–
177.	right	–	–	1	–
178.	run	–	–	1	–
179.	safe	–	–	1	–
180.	said	–	2	3	–
181.	saw	–	–	2	–
182.	say	–	1	2	–
183.	see	–	–	1	–
184.	seem	–	–	1	–
185.	Sharon	1	–	–	–
186.	shoot	–	1	1	–
187.	should	–	–	1	–
188.	sickening	–	–	1	–
189.	sing	–	1	1	–
190.	sisters	–	–	1	–
191.	society	–	–	–	1
192.	soft	–	–	1	–
193.	someone	1	–	–	–
194.	soon	–	1	–	–
195.	spoiled	–	–	1	–
196.	sport	14	–	–	3
197.	still	–	–	1	–
198.	stink	–	–	1	–
199.	stupid	–	–	1	–
200.	Suzie and Caroline	1	–	–	–

40 They (contd)

No.	Response	Subst.	Pre	Post	Assoc.
201.	tell	–	–	2	–
202.	that	1	–	–	–
203.	the ducks	1	–	–	–
204.	the group	1	–	–	–
205.	the people	1	–	–	–
206.	the soldiers	1	–	–	–
207.	their	–	–	–	4
208.	theirs	–	–	–	1
209.	them	13	1	1	148
210.	then	–	–	–	6
211.	there	–	–	5	–
212.	these	1	–	–	–
213.	they're	–	–	–	1
214.	think	–	2	1	–
215.	those	–	–	–	6
216.	those people	1	–	–	–
217.	thy	–	–	–	1
218.	to	1	–	–	–
219.	together	1	–	–	–
220.	tonight	–	–	1	–
221.	tried	–	–	1	–
222.	two	–	–	1	–
223.	until	–	–	–	1
224.	us	1	–	1	28
225.	used	–	–	1	–
226.	usually	–	1	–	–
227.	vigilantes	1	–	–	–
228.	want	–	–	9	–
229.	was	–	3	–	–
230.	we	78	–	–	32
231.	welcome	–	–	–	1
232.	well	–	–	1	–
233.	went	–	–	24	2
234.	were	–	–	–	2
235.	what	–	12	–	–
236.	what's	1	–	–	–
237.	when	–	13	–	–
238.	where	–	7	–	–
239.	who	6	9	–	7
240.	whom	–	–	–	1
241.	why	–	5	–	–
242.	will	–	–	1	–
243.	wish	–	3	–	–
244.	working	–	–	1	–
245.	wrong	–	–	1	–
246.	you	43	–	–	3
247.	yours	–	–	1	–

		Subst.	Pre	Post	Assoc.
Function Words		–	35	7	–
Space		–	265	27	–
N		245	386	386	393

41 Today

No.	Response	Subst.	Pre	Post	Assoc.
1.	"A"	–	1	–	–
2.	actions	–	–	–	1
3.	after	–	1	–	–
4.	Alaska	–	–	1	–
5.	always	1	1	1	–
6.	anyway	1	–	–	–
7.	anywhere	–	1	–	–
8.	arrived	–	1	–	–
9.	assignment	–	1	–	–
10.	ate	–	1	–	–
11.	bad	–	–	3	–
12.	basketball	–	1	–	–
13.	beautiful	–	–	6	–
14.	begin	–	1	–	–
15.	bell	–	–	–	1
16.	best	–	–	1	–
17.	birthday	–	2	–	–
18.	bore	–	–	1	–

41 Today (contd)

No.	Response	Subst.	Pre	Post	Assoc.
19.	brings	–	–	1	–
20.	busy	–	1	–	–
21.	called	–	1	–	–
22.	came	–	2	–	–
23.	car	–	–	1	1
24.	church	1	–	–	–
25.	circus	–	1	–	–
26.	cloudy	–	1	1	–
27.	cold	–	1	–	–
28.	come	–	1	1	–
29.	comes	–	1	2	–
30.	coming	–	1	–	–
31.	crazy	–	1	–	–
32.	D Day	–	–	1	–
33.	day	–	2	18	2
34.	do	–	2	–	–
35.	doing	–	1	–	–
36.	done	–	–	1	–
37.	dreary	–	–	–	1
38.	due	–	1	–	–
39.	during	–	1	–	–
40.	early	1	1	–	2
41.	eat	–	2	–	–
42.	elapse	–	–	1	–
43.	enough	–	1	–	–
44.	ever	1	–	–	–
45.	everyday	1	–	–	–
46.	fast	1	–	–	–
47.	figure	1	–	–	–
48.	final	–	–	1	–
49.	fishing	–	1	–	1
50.	forever	1	–	–	1
51.	fourth	–	–	1	–
52.	Friday	–	–	3	–
53.	fun	–	–	–	1
54.	future	–	–	–	3
55.	game	–	5	–	–
56.	game day	1	–	–	–
57.	get up	–	1	–	–
58.	go	–	14	3	1
59.	going	–	2	3	–
60.	golf	–	1	–	–
61.	gone	–	–	6	–
62.	good	–	–	4	–
63.	grub	–	–	–	1
64.	happen	–	2	–	–
65.	happened	–	1	–	–
66.	happening	–	1	–	–
67.	happens	–	1	–	–
68.	happy	–	–	–	3
69.	hard	–	–	1	–
70.	heavily	1	–	–	–
71.	her	–	2	–	–
72.	here	3	9	–	–
73.	him	–	1	–	–
74.	his	–	–	1	–
75.	hodie	–	–	–	1
76.	holiday	–	–	1	–
77.	home	–	2	–	–
78.	homework	–	–	–	1
79.	hot	–	4	3	1
80.	important	–	–	1	–
81.	is	–	–	–	1
82.	is ours	–	–	–	1
83.	it	4	12	1	–
84.	July 4	1	–	–	–
85.	June 24	1	–	–	–
86.	last	–	–	2	–
87.	later	–	–	–	1
88.	leave	–	–	1	–
89.	leaving	–	1	–	–
90.	life	–	–	1	–
91.	light	–	–	–	2
92.	like	–	2	–	–
93.	Lincoln's	–	–	1	–
94.	little	–	–	1	–
95.	live	–	3	–	–
96.	long	–	–	1	–

41 Today (contd)

No.	Response	Subst.	Pre	Post	Assoc.
97.	lousy	–	–	1	–
98.	love	–	–	–	1
99.	lovely	–	–	1	–
100.	lunch	–	–	–	1
101.	man	–	–	–	2
102.	Mar. 2	1	–	–	–
103.	March	–	–	1	1
104.	March 3, 1960	–	–	1	–
105.	Mary	1	–	–	–
106.	mass	–	1	–	–
107.	me	–	1	–	–
108.	meeting	–	2	–	–
109.	mine	1	–	–	–
110.	Monday	2	1	7	2
111.	more	–	–	–	1
112.	Morine	1	–	–	–
113.	morning	–	–	1	–
114.	mothers	–	–	–	1
115.	much	–	1	–	–
116.	nervous	–	1	–	–
117.	never	2	–	–	1
118.	newspaper	–	–	–	1
119.	nice	1	2	6	1
120.	night	1	–	–	1
121.	no!	–	–	–	1
122.	noon	–	–	1	–
123.	noontime	–	–	–	1
124.	now	35	–	–	53
125.	nowadays	1	–	–	–
126.	nude	1	–	–	–
127.	often	1	–	–	–
128.	one	–	1	1	–
129.	one in many	–	–	–	1
130.	opportunities	–	–	–	1
131.	opportunity	–	–	–	1
132.	other	–	–	–	1
133.	ours	–	–	2	–
134.	outside	–	1	–	–
135.	P.E.	–	–	–	1
136.	pick	–	1	–	–
137.	pictures	–	1	–	–
138.	planetarium	–	–	1	–
139.	planning	–	1	–	–
140.	play	–	1	–	–
141.	pleasant	–	–	1	–
142.	practice	1	–	–	–
143.	present	–	–	–	7
144.	present time	–	–	–	1
145.	pretty	–	–	1	–
146.	put	–	1	–	–
147.	rain	–	2	–	–
148.	rained	–	–	2	–
149.	raining	–	2	1	–
150.	ran	–	1	–	–
151.	Red Skelton	1	–	–	1
152.	right now	–	–	–	1
153.	rockets	–	–	–	1
154.	Russia	–	–	–	1
155.	said	–	1	–	–
156.	saw	–	1	–	–
157.	school	–	3	1	3
158.	seen	–	–	2	–
159.	show	–	1	–	–
160.	skirt	–	–	–	1
161.	sleep	–	–	–	1
162.	slow	–	–	–	1
163.	some	–	1	–	–
164.	some day	1	–	–	–
165.	sometime	–	1	–	–
166.	soon	1	–	–	–
167.	Span. 18A	–	1	–	–
168.	special	–	–	–	1
169.	spring	1	–	–	–
170.	stay	–	–	1	–
171.	study	–	1	–	–
172.	stupid	–	–	1	–
173.	suite	–	–	1	4
174.	sun	–	–	–	4

41 Today (contd)

No.	Response	Subst.	Pre	Post	Assoc.
175.	Sunday	1	–	1	–
176.	sunny	–	–	–	1
177.	sunshine	–	–	–	1
178.	swam	–	1	–	–
179.	swim	–	–	1	–
180.	T.V.	–	–	3	1
181.	taking	–	–	1	–
182.	tell	–	–	1	–
183.	terrible	–	–	1	–
184.	test	–	7	2	2
185.	that	–	2	–	–
186.	then	–	–	–	1
187.	thing	1	–	–	–
188.	think	–	2	–	–
189.	this	6	4	–	–
190.	this morning	1	–	–	–
191.	Thursday	–	–	19	4
192.	time	–	–	–	1
193.	tired	–	2	–	–
194.	today	–	–	1	–
195.	together	–	–	–	1
196.	tomorrow	79	2	18	162
197.	tonight	5	–	–	10
198.	took	–	–	1	–
199.	Tuesday	3	–	7	1
200.	understand	–	1	–	–
201.	us	–	1	–	–
202.	vacation	–	–	1	–
203.	war	–	–	1	–
204.	waste	–	1	–	–
205.	weather	–	1	–	–
206.	Wednesday	1	–	–	1
207.	went	–	2	1	–
208.	what	1	4	2	–
209.	when	1	1	–	1
210.	why	1	1	–	–
211.	why not?	–	–	–	1
212.	win	–	2	–	–
213.	windy	–	–	1	–
214.	wish	–	2	–	–
215.	wonderful	–	–	1	–
216.	work	–	2	–	3
217.	yes	1	1	–	–
218.	yesterday	40	–	4	66
219.	yesterday was	1	–	–	–
220.	you	–	1	1	–
221.	1 o'clock	–	–	1	–
222.	17	–	1	–	–
223.	3rd	–	–	2	–
224.	18th	–	–	1	–
225.	19th	–	–	2	–

Function Words		–	8	42	–
Space		–	181	133	–
N		215	359	359	378

42 Us

No.	Response	Subst.	Pre	Post	Assoc.
1.	advice	–	–	1	–
2.	all	–	4	–	4
3.	alone	–	–	2	–
4.	are	–	–	–	1
5.	army	–	–	–	1
6.	arrived	–	1	–	–
7.	ask	–	2	–	–
8.	asked	–	2	–	–
9.	attain	–	–	1	–
10.	back	–	–	1	–
11.	ball	–	1	–	–
12.	Barb	–	–	–	1
13.	beat	–	1	–	–
14.	belong	–	2	–	–

42 Us (contd)

No.	Response	Subst.	Pre	Post	Assoc.
15.	belonged	–	1	–	–
16.	belongs	–	7	–	–
17.	best	–	–	–	1
18.	better	–	1	1	–
19.	bird	–	–	1	–
20.	blamed	–	1	–	–
21.	Bonnie & I to	1	–	–	–
22.	both	–	1	–	3
23.	bother	–	1	–	–
24.	boys	1	–	1	1
25.	brother	–	–	–	1
26.	bus	–	–	–	3
27.	call	–	1	–	–
28.	called	–	2	–	–
29.	came	–	15	–	1
30.	came back	–	1	–	–
31.	car	–	1	–	–
32.	Casper	1	–	–	–
33.	Charlie and me	–	–	–	1
34.	children	1	–	–	–
35.	choose	–	1	–	–
36.	come	–	54	3	–
37.	comes	–	2	–	–
38.	coming	–	5	–	–
39.	cookies	–	–	–	1
40.	couple	–	–	–	2
41.	cut out	–	–	1	–
42.	dad	1	–	–	–
43.	danger	–	–	1	–
44.	Dave	–	–	–	1
45.	dear	–	–	1	–
46.	decide	–	–	1	–
47.	dinner	–	–	1	–
48.	do	–	2	3	–
49.	doing	–	–	1	–
50.	driving	–	2	–	1
51.	Eli	–	–	–	1
52.	everyone	–	–	–	1
53.	failed	–	–	1	–
54.	family	–	–	–	4
55.	find	–	1	–	–
56.	fire	–	–	–	1
57.	fix	–	–	1	–
58.	follow	–	1	–	–
59.	for	–	–	–	1
60.	forever	–	–	1	–
61.	forgive	–	1	–	–
62.	four	–	2	–	–
63.	friend	–	–	–	1
64.	friends	–	–	–	1
65.	fun	–	–	–	1
66.	fuss	–	–	–	1
67.	game	–	–	2	–
68.	gang	–	–	–	1
69.	gave	–	9	–	–
70.	get	–	3	–	–
71.	get away	–	1	–	–
72.	get out	–	–	1	–
73.	girl friend	–	–	–	1
74.	girls	2	–	–	2
75.	go	–	11	16	–
76.	going	–	5	3	–
77.	good	–	–	2	–
78.	group	–	–	–	6
79.	happen	–	1	–	–
80.	happy	–	1	–	1
81.	hates	–	3	–	–
82.	have	–	–	1	–
83.	heaven	–	–	–	1
84.	help	–	2	1	–
85.	helped	–	1	–	–
86.	her	14	–	–	–
87.	hers	1	–	–	–
88.	him	31	–	–	1
89.	hissing	1	–	–	–
90.	home	–	–	2	1
91.	house	–	1	–	–
92.	hurrah!	–	1	–	–

42   Us (contd)

No.	Response	Subst.	Pre	Post	Assoc.
93.	included	–	1	–	–
94.	it	3	32	2	–
95.	it's	–	4	–	–
96.	Jane	2	–	–	–
97.	Joe	1	–	–	–
98.	John	1	–	–	–
99.	join	–	1	1	–
100.	Joyce	1	–	–	–
101.	killed	–	1	–	–
102.	kiss	–	–	–	1
103.	know	–	1	–	–
104.	knows	–	1	–	–
105.	La Ravas Club	1	–	–	–
106.	leave	–	3	3	–
107.	leaving	–	–	1	–
108.	left	–	2	–	–
109.	lesson	–	–	1	–
110.	let	–	18	–	–
111.	like	–	11	–	–
112.	likes	–	6	–	–
113.	look	–	1	–	–
114.	look like	–	1	–	–
115.	love	–	1	–	1
116.	many	–	1	–	–
117.	marriage	–	–	–	1
118.	married	–	1	–	–
119.	marry	–	1	–	–
120.	matters	–	1	–	–
121.	me	102	–	–	7
122.	me and him	–	–	–	1
123.	mean	–	1	–	–
124.	means	–	1	–	–
125.	meet	–	1	–	–
126.	money	–	1	1	–
127.	mother	1	–	–	–
128.	MT & DC	–	–	–	1
129.	much	–	1	–	–
130.	nice	–	–	1	–
131.	none	–	1	–	–
132.	nosotros	1	–	–	1
133.	not	1	–	–	–
134.	one	–	1	–	–
135.	our	–	–	–	2
136.	ours	–	–	–	6
137.	ourselves	–	–	–	2
138.	over	–	–	–	1
139.	pair	–	–	1	–
140.	paper	–	–	1	–
141.	party	–	–	3	–
142.	Peg	–	–	–	1
143.	pen	–	–	–	1
144.	people	–	–	–	8
145.	play	1	–	2	–
146.	played	–	1	–	–
147.	please	–	–	–	1
148.	pleasing	–	1	–	–
149.	puc	–	–	–	1
150.	put	–	1	–	–
151.	Ralph	–	–	–	1
152.	related	–	1	–	–
153.	right	–	2	–	–
154.	run	–	–	1	–
155.	said	–	1	–	–
156.	same	–	1	–	–
157.	saw	–	5	–	–
158.	say	–	–	1	–
159.	school	1	–	1	–
160.	sea	–	–	1	–
161.	seashore	–	–	1	–
162.	see	–	4	–	1
163.	sent	–	1	–	–
164.	separate	–	1	–	–
165.	shot	–	1	–	–
166.	show	–	–	1	–
167.	sing	–	–	1	–
168.	snob	–	–	–	1
169.	something	–	–	2	–
170.	sometime	–	–	2	–

42   Us (contd)

No.	Response	Subst.	Pre	Post	Assoc.
171.	sounded	–	–	1	–
172.	spells	–	1	–	–
173.	still	–	–	1	–
174.	stop	–	1	–	–
175.	store	–	–	3	–
176.	strike	–	1	–	–
177.	stupid	–	–	1	–
178.	suddenly	–	–	1	–
179.	table	–	1	–	–
180.	take	–	6	2	–
181.	takes	–	1	–	–
182.	talk	–	4	–	–
183.	tell	–	12	–	–
184.	thank	–	1	–	–
185.	that	–	5	1	–
186.	the	1	–	–	–
187.	the class	1	–	–	–
188.	the gang	1	–	–	–
189.	their	–	–	–	1
190.	theirs	–	–	–	1
191.	them	72	–	–	50
192.	then	–	–	–	1
193.	they	–	–	–	36
194.	this	–	4	–	1
195.	three	–	1	1	–
196.	thus	–	–	–	2
197.	time	–	–	1	–
198.	together	1	–	–	19
199.	togetherness	–	–	–	1
200.	told	–	4	–	–
201.	tomorrow	–	–	1	–
202.	tonight	–	–	1	–
203.	too	–	–	–	1
204.	took	–	3	–	–
205.	town	1	–	–	–
206.	travel	–	1	–	–
207.	tread	–	1	–	–
208.	trip	–	–	1	–
209.	truth	–	–	1	–
210.	two	–	2	–	3
211.	two people	–	–	–	1
212.	U.S.S.R.	1	–	–	–
213.	visit	–	2	–	–
214.	wait	–	1	–	–
215.	walk	–	–	1	1
216.	want	–	2	–	–
217.	wants	–	2	–	–
218.	we	5	–	–	123
219.	went	–	6	1	–
220.	what	–	1	2	1
221.	when	–	–	1	–
222.	where	–	–	1	–
223.	which	–	1	–	–
224.	who's	–	1	–	–
225.	why	–	–	–	1
226.	work	–	1	1	–
227.	wrong	1	–	–	–
228.	yes	–	–	–	1
229.	you	20	4	2	40
230.	you and I	–	–	–	1
231.	you and me	–	–	–	2
232.	you – me	–	–	–	1
233.	your	–	–	–	1
	Function Words	–	16	11	–
	Space	–	5	247	–
	N	274	361	361	378

43 Very

No.	Response	Subst.	Pre	Post	Assoc.
1.	a lot	1	–	–	4
2.	adequate	–	–	1	–
3.	air	–	1	–	–
4.	all	–	–	–	1
5.	almost	3	–	–	1
6.	also	–	–	–	1
7.	always	5	–	–	1
8.	an extremely	1	–	–	–
9.	at all	1	–	–	–
10.	awful	1	–	–	2
11.	awfully	15	–	–	–
12.	bad	–	–	5	3
13.	beautiful	–	–	2	–
14.	berry	–	–	–	2
15.	berry-berry	–	1	–	–
16.	best	–	–	–	1
17.	bitter	1	–	–	–
18.	book	–	4	–	–
19.	boring	–	–	1	–
20.	boy	–	1	–	1
21.	bright	–	–	2	–
22.	brisky	–	–	1	–
23.	busy	–	–	1	–
24.	car	–	2	–	–
25.	certain	–	–	–	1
26.	clean	–	–	1	–
27.	close	–	–	1	–
28.	coal	–	1	–	–
29.	coffee	–	2	–	–
30.	cold	–	–	23	6
31.	colder	–	–	–	1
32.	color	–	1	–	–
33.	comfortable	–	–	2	–
34.	coming	–	1	–	–
35.	complete	–	–	–	1
36.	continually	–	–	1	–
37.	cool	–	–	–	2
38.	crazy	–	–	1	–
39.	cruel	–	–	1	1
40.	crying	1	–	–	–
41.	cute	–	–	3	–
42.	darkly	1	–	–	–
43.	darn	1	–	–	–
44.	date	1	–	–	–
45.	day	–	2	1	–
46.	different	–	–	–	2
47.	disgustingly	1	–	–	–
48.	doing	–	1	–	–
49.	dreadfully	1	–	–	–
50.	dress	–	1	–	–
51.	drunk	–	–	1	–
52.	dumb	–	–	1	–
53.	easily	–	–	1	–
54.	easy	–	–	1	2
55.	emphasis	–	–	–	1
56.	especially	1	–	–	–
57.	essential	–	–	1	–
58.	ever so	1	–	–	–
59.	every	–	–	–	2
60.	exceedingly	2	–	–	–
61.	exicted	–	–	1	–
62.	extreme	–	–	–	7
63.	extremely	27	–	–	9
64.	eyes	–	1	–	–
65.	fair	–	–	–	1
66.	fairly	4	–	–	–
67.	fascinating	–	–	1	–
68.	fast	–	–	5	1
69.	fat	–	–	1	1
70.	feels	–	1	–	–
71.	few	1	–	3	3
72.	fine	–	–	2	–
73.	football	–	1	–	–
74.	frightfully	1	–	–	–
75.	funny	–	–	2	2
76.	gets	–	1	–	–
77.	gloomy	–	–	1	–
78.	goes	–	1	–	–

No.	Response	Subst.	Pre	Post	Assoc.
79.	gold	–	–	–	1
80.	good	–	–	42	32
81.	gown	–	1	–	–
82.	great	1	–	–	–
83.	green	–	–	1	1
84.	grow	–	1	–	–
85.	hairy	–	–	–	3
86.	handsome	–	–	1	–
87.	happy	–	–	5	–
88.	hard	–	–	8	2
89.	hardly	1	–	–	2
90.	has	–	1	–	–
91.	hat	–	1	–	–
92.	haughty	–	–	1	–
93.	heavy	–	–	2	5
94.	hell	–	–	–	1
95.	her	–	5	–	–
96.	here	–	–	–	1
97.	high	–	–	1	–
98.	hike	–	1	–	–
99.	him	–	9	–	–
100.	hot	1	–	63	13
101.	hungry	–	–	1	–
102.	ice cream	–	1	–	–
103.	ill	–	–	3	–
104.	immaculately	1	–	–	–
105.	innocuous	–	–	1	–
106.	intelligent	–	–	1	–
107.	interesting	–	–	2	–
108.	ironically	1	–	–	–
109.	it	–	103	–	–
110.	Jerry	–	–	–	1
111.	Jim	–	1	–	–
112.	just so	–	–	–	1
113.	kind	–	–	1	1
114.	kind of	2	–	–	–
115.	late	–	–	1	–
116.	leaky	–	–	1	–
117.	leaving	–	1	–	–
118.	less	1	–	–	2
119.	life	–	2	–	–
120.	light	–	–	–	2
121.	like	–	–	–	2
122.	likely	–	–	1	–
123.	little	–	–	2	6
124.	long	–	1	–	–
125.	look	–	1	–	–
126.	loud	–	–	1	–
127.	love	–	1	–	1
128.	lovely	–	–	2	–
129.	low	–	–	1	–
130.	lucky	–	–	2	–
131.	mad	–	–	4	1
132.	makes	–	1	–	–
133.	many	1	–	3	8
134.	marry	–	–	–	1
135.	Mary	–	–	–	1
136.	me	–	3	–	–
137.	mean	–	–	1	–
138.	merry	–	–	–	5
139.	mighty	1	–	–	–
140.	minutely	1	–	–	–
141.	more	–	–	–	2
142.	most	5	–	–	2
143.	mother	–	1	–	–
144.	move	–	–	–	1
145.	much	4	–	34	85
146.	mucho	–	–	–	1
147.	natural	–	–	1	–
148.	never	1	–	–	5
149.	new	–	–	–	2
150.	next	–	–	–	1
151.	nice	4	–	26	17
152.	nicely	–	–	1	–
153.	night	–	1	–	–
154.	no	2	–	–	1
155.	not	54	–	–	8
156.	not much	–	–	–	1

43 Very (contd)

No.	Response	Subst.	Pre	Post	Assoc.
157.	not so	2	–	–	–
158.	not so much	1	–	–	–
159.	not very	1	–	–	–
160.	nothing	–	–	–	2
161.	often	1	1	4	9
162.	old	–	–	5	9
163.	only	2	–	–	–
164.	overdone	–	–	–	1
165.	pensive	–	–	1	–
166.	personal	–	–	–	1
167.	pie	–	1	–	–
168.	play	–	1	–	–
169.	pleasant	–	–	4	–
170.	precise	–	–	–	1
171.	pretty	7	–	9	1
172.	prove	–	1	–	–
173.	quiet	–	–	–	1
174.	quite	27	–	–	4
175.	raining	–	1	–	–
176.	rather	8	–	–	–
177.	real	7	–	–	2
178.	really	5	–	–	2
179.	repulsive	–	–	–	1
180.	rough	–	–	–	1
181.	run	–	–	–	1
182.	runs	–	2	–	–
183.	sad	–	–	2	–
184.	same	1	–	–	–
185.	scarce	–	–	–	1
186.	school	–	1	–	1
187.	seldom	1	–	–	2
188.	sensitive	–	–	1	–
189.	sets	–	1	–	–
190.	sheet	–	1	–	–
191.	shiny	–	–	1	–
192.	shouts	–	1	–	–
193.	show	–	2	–	–
194.	shy	–	–	1	–
195.	sick	–	–	5	–
196.	simple	–	–	2	–
197.	six	–	–	–	1
198.	ski	–	1	–	–
199.	skiing	–	1	–	–
200.	slightly	4	–	–	2
201.	slowly	–	–	1	–
202.	small	–	–	1	1
203.	smart	–	–	1	1
204.	so	12	–	–	–
205.	soft	–	–	1	–
206.	some	–	1	–	1
207.	sometime	1	–	–	–
208.	somewhat	1	–	–	1
209.	soon	–	–	4	4
210.	sorry	–	–	1	–
211.	still	–	–	1	–
212.	store	–	1	–	–
213.	strange	–	–	–	1
214.	strong	–	–	3	2
215.	such	–	–	–	1
216.	Sue	–	1	–	–
217.	sun	–	1	–	–
218.	sunny	–	–	1	–
219.	surely	–	–	–	1
220.	sweet	–	–	2	–
221.	swell	–	–	–	1
222.	swiftly	–	–	1	–
223.	swim	–	1	–	–
224.	talk	–	1	–	–
225.	talks	–	1	–	–
226.	taste	–	1	–	–
227.	tedious	1	–	–	–
228.	terribly	7	–	–	1
229.	test	–	1	–	–
230.	thank you	–	1	–	–
231.	thanks	–	1	–	–
232.	that	–	10	–	–
233.	that's	1	–	–	–
234.	these	–	1	–	–

No.	Response	Subst.	Pre	Post	Assoc.
235.	this	–	12	–	–
236.	thought	–	–	1	–
237.	tiger	–	1	–	–
238.	tired	–	–	9	4
239.	to the point	–	–	–	1
240.	today	–	3	–	–
241.	tomorrow	–	1	–	–
242.	too	21	–	–	2
243.	too many	–	–	–	1
244.	too much	–	–	–	2
245.	très	–	–	1	2
246.	true	–	–	–	1
247.	truly	–	–	–	2
248.	try	–	1	–	–
249.	tuna	–	1	–	–
250.	ugly	–	–	1	–
251.	uneven	–	–	–	1
252.	unhappy	–	–	1	–
253.	university	–	1	–	–
254.	unpleasant	–	–	1	–
255.	unusual	–	–	1	–
256.	us	–	–	–	1
257.	useful	–	–	2	–
258.	usually	1	–	–	–
259.	utmost	–	–	–	1
260.	vary	–	–	–	2
261.	veraction	–	–	–	1
262.	very, very	–	–	–	1
263.	warm	–	–	7	3
264.	water	–	2	–	–
265.	wearing	–	1	–	–
266.	weary	–	–	–	1
267.	weather	–	2	–	–
268.	well	–	–	8	4
269.	white	1	–	–	–
270.	windy	–	–	1	–
271.	wintery	–	–	1	–
272.	wonderful	–	–	1	–
273.	wonderful and	1	–	–	–
274.	word	–	1	–	–
275.	yes	–	–	–	1
276.	you	–	24	–	1
277.	young	–	–	2	2
278.	yours	–	–	–	1

		Subst.	Pre	Post	Assoc.
Function Words		–	99	5	–
Space		–	31	–	–
N		266	376	376	372

44 Walk

No.	Response	Subst.	Pre	Post	Assoc.
1.	a while	–	–	1	–
2.	ache	–	–	–	1
3.	across	–	–	1	–
4.	ahead	–	–	1	–
5.	all	–	–	3	–
6.	alone	–	–	7	–
7.	along	–	–	–	2
8.	ambulate	1	–	–	1
9.	around	–	–	–	1
10.	as we	–	–	–	1
11.	away	–	–	1	–
12.	awkwardly	–	–	1	–
13.	baby	–	–	1	–
14.	bath	1	–	–	–
15.	beach	–	–	1	–
16.	beat	–	–	1	–
17.	beer	1	–	–	–
18.	block	–	–	4	–
19.	boards	–	–	–	1
20.	boy	–	–	–	1
21.	can	–	5	–	–

44 Walk (contd)

No.	Response	Subst.	Pre	Post	Assoc.
22.	can't hear	1	–	–	–
23.	can't see	1	–	–	–
24.	car	–	1	–	–
25.	cat	1	–	1	–
26.	cement	–	–	–	1
27.	children	–	–	–	1
28.	class	–	–	1	–
29.	cold	–	–	–	1
30.	come	3	1	–	–
31.	concrete	–	–	–	1
32.	corner	–	–	1	–
33.	country	–	–	–	2
34.	crawl	1	–	–	1
35.	dance	1	–	–	–
36.	dark	–	–	–	1
37.	day	–	–	–	1
38.	die	1	–	–	–
39.	dislike	–	1	–	–
40.	dive	1	–	–	–
41.	do	1	–	–	–
42.	do physics	1	–	–	–
43.	dog	–	1	1	1
44.	dog trot	–	–	–	1
45.	downtown	–	–	2	–
46.	drink	4	–	–	–
47.	drive	16	–	–	1
48.	eat	3	–	–	–
49.	end	–	–	1	–
50.	enjoy	–	1	–	–
51.	every	–	–	3	–
52.	exercise	–	–	–	5
53.	far	–	–	1	1
54.	fast	–	1	15	6
55.	faster	–	–	7	–
56.	feet	–	–	–	15
57.	few	–	1	–	–
58.	find	–	1	–	–
59.	flowers	–	–	–	1
60.	fly	3	–	–	–
61.	foot	–	–	–	4
62.	forest	–	–	1	–
63.	friends	–	–	–	1
64.	fun	–	–	–	1
65.	funny	–	–	1	–
66.	game	–	–	1	–
67.	garden	–	–	1	–
68.	get	1	–	–	–
69.	girl	2	1	–	–
70.	go	8	13	–	4
71.	God	–	–	1	–
72.	good	–	–	1	–
73.	grass	–	–	1	–
74.	ground	–	–	–	1
75.	hall	–	–	–	1
76.	happily	–	–	–	1
77.	happiness	–	–	–	1
78.	hate	–	3	–	–
79.	here	–	–	2	–
80.	hike	4	–	–	7
81.	hiking	–	–	–	1
82.	hill	–	–	3	–
83.	hills	–	–	1	–
84.	him	–	2	2	–
85.	hitchhike	1	–	–	–
86.	home	–	–	30	5
87.	hoping	1	–	–	–
88.	house	–	–	1	–
89.	hunting	–	–	–	1
90.	hurry	1	–	–	1
91.	I like to	–	–	–	1
92.	in	–	–	–	2
93.	it	1	–	–	–
94.	Johnny	–	1	–	–
95.	journey	1	–	–	–
96.	jump	1	–	–	1
97.	kiss	1	–	–	–
98.	knock	–	–	–	1
99.	late	–	–	–	1

44 Walk (contd)

No.	Response	Subst.	Pre	Post	Assoc.
100.	learning	–	1	–	–
101.	leave	1	–	1	–
102.	legs	–	–	–	4
103.	lie	1	–	–	–
104.	lightly	–	–	–	1
105.	like	–	43	–	–
106.	little	–	1	2	–
107.	long	–	5	1	–
108.	lot	–	–	1	–
109.	love	–	6	–	–
110.	make friends	1	–	–	–
111.	me	–	–	28	–
112.	meeting	1	–	–	–
113.	mile	–	–	1	–
114.	mind	–	1	–	–
115.	mood	–	–	–	1
116.	moonlight	–	–	4	1
117.	moonlit	–	–	2	–
118.	more	–	–	1	–
119.	morning	–	–	1	–
120.	mountain	–	–	1	–
121.	move	–	–	–	4
122.	much	–	1	3	–
123.	nails	–	–	1	–
124.	never	–	3	1	–
125.	nice	–	1	–	–
126.	night	–	–	4	1
127.	nights	–	–	1	–
128.	now	–	1	4	–
129.	observe	1	–	–	–
130.	often	–	1	–	1
131.	over	–	–	–	1
132.	park	–	–	12	2
133.	path	1	–	1	2
134.	pavement	–	–	–	1
135.	pencil	1	–	–	–
136.	person	–	1	–	2
137.	place	–	–	–	1
138.	play	1	–	–	–
139.	play music	1	–	–	–
140.	please	–	2	–	–
141.	post	–	–	–	1
142.	powder	1	–	–	–
143.	promenade	1	–	–	–
144.	quickly	–	–	1	–
145.	quietly	–	–	1	–
146.	race	–	–	–	1
147.	rain	–	–	1	1
148.	ran	4	1	–	1
149.	rapidly	–	–	1	1
150.	read	4	–	–	–
151.	relaxing	–	1	–	–
152.	ride	40	–	–	8
153.	rides	1	–	–	–
154.	rifle	–	–	1	–
155.	road	–	–	1	3
156.	rode	1	–	–	–
157.	run	106	1	4	118
158.	running	2	–	–	1
159.	runs	–	–	–	1
160.	rush	–	–	–	1
161.	San Francisco	–	–	1	–
162.	sandwich	1	–	–	–
163.	school	–	–	17	–
164.	scouts	–	–	–	1
165.	see	2	–	–	–
166.	shade	–	–	–	1
167.	sheet	–	–	–	3
168.	shoe	–	–	–	1
169.	shoes	–	–	–	3
170.	short	–	–	1	–
171.	show	1	–	4	–
172.	sidewalk	–	–	1	5
173.	sing	3	–	–	–
174.	sister	–	1	–	–
175.	sit	3	–	–	2
176.	skip	6	–	–	2
177.	sleep	4	–	–	2

44 Walk (contd)

No.	Response	Subst.	Pre	Post	Assoc.
178.	slow	–	–	3	6
179.	slower	–	–	2	1
180.	slowly	–	1	9	–
181.	smell	1	–	–	–
182.	speak	1	–	–	1
183.	speaks	1	–	–	–
184.	speed	–	–	–	1
185.	stand	2	–	–	3
186.	station	–	–	1	–
187.	stay	1	–	–	–
188.	steel	–	–	–	1
189.	step	–	–	1	8
190.	steps	–	–	–	2
191.	stone	–	–	1	1
192.	stop	1	–	–	3
193.	store	–	–	5	–
194.	straight	–	–	3	4
195.	street	–	–	1	4
196.	streets	–	–	–	1
197.	stride	–	–	–	2
198.	stroll	19	–	–	7
199.	swiftly	–	–	1	–
200.	swim	11	–	–	2
201.	swing	1	–	–	–
202.	take	5	35	–	1
203.	taking	–	1	–	–
204.	talk	32	–	3	56
205.	talks	1	–	–	2
206.	then	–	–	1	–
207.	there	–	–	3	–
208.	think	4	–	–	1
209.	thinking	1	–	–	–
210.	third base	–	–	–	1
211.	three	–	–	1	–
212.	through	–	–	1	–
213.	tired	–	–	–	4
214.	today	–	–	2	–
215.	together	–	–	2	–
216.	took	–	12	–	–
217.	town	–	–	2	–
218.	track	1	–	–	1
219.	train	1	–	–	–
220.	trees	–	–	–	2
221.	trip	5	–	–	–
222.	triple	1	–	–	–
223.	trot	–	–	–	1
224.	trugged	1	–	–	–
225.	turn wolf	1	–	–	–
226.	upstairs	–	–	1	–
227.	walking	–	–	4	1
228.	want	–	4	–	–
229.	warm	–	–	1	–
230.	water	–	–	1	–
231.	way	–	–	–	1
232.	well	–	–	1	–
233.	went	–	8	–	–
234.	when	–	–	2	–
235.	where	–	–	1	–
236.	why	–	1	–	–
237.	window	–	–	1	–
238.	wine	–	–	–	1
239.	woods	–	–	3	1
240.	work	–	–	–	1
241.	write	2	–	–	–
242.	yes	–	–	–	1
243.	yesterday	–	–	1	–
244.	you	–	23	5	–
245.	2	–	–	1	–
Function Words		–	114	1	–
Space		–	79	112	–
N		345	382	382	382

45 Washing

No.	Response	Subst.	Pre	Post	Assoc.
1.	abhor	–	1	–	–
2.	acid	1	–	–	–
3.	action	–	–	1	–
4.	all	–	1	–	–
5.	always	–	4	–	–
6.	bad	1	–	–	–
7.	baking	2	–	–	–
8.	baseball	1	–	–	–
9.	bath	–	–	–	1
10.	bathing	–	–	–	1
11.	beating	1	–	–	–
12.	beats	–	–	1	–
13.	big	–	–	1	–
14.	blasted	1	–	–	–
15.	bleaching	1	–	–	–
16.	board	1	–	–	–
17.	bowling	1	–	–	–
18.	breaking	6	–	–	–
19.	broken	1	–	–	–
20.	brought	–	1	–	–
21.	brushing	1	–	–	–
22.	building	–	–	–	1
23.	burning	3	–	–	–
24.	car	3	–	18	2
25.	cars	–	–	1	–
26.	child	–	–	1	–
27.	clean	–	–	1	58
28.	cleaning	36	–	–	10
29.	cleanliness	1	–	–	–
30.	cleanse	–	–	–	1
31.	clear	–	–	–	1
32.	clearing	1	–	–	2
33.	cloth	1	–	–	–
34.	clothes	2	3	63	75
35.	clothesline	1	–	–	1
36.	combing	2	–	–	–
37.	comes	–	1	–	–
38.	coming	1	–	–	–
39.	cooking	10	–	–	1
40.	coughing	–	–	–	1
41.	cute	1	–	–	–
42.	cutting	2	–	–	–
43.	day	–	1	9	1
44.	desk	1	–	–	–
45.	destroying	1	–	–	–
46.	detest	–	1	–	–
47.	did	–	11	–	–
48.	difficult	–	–	1	–
49.	dinner	–	–	1	–
50.	dirt	1	–	–	6
51.	dirty	1	–	1	10
52.	dirtying	1	–	–	1
53.	dish	–	–	–	1
54.	dishes	7	–	33	18
55.	dislike	–	4	–	–
56.	displaying	1	–	–	–
57.	do	–	33	1	–
58.	does	–	14	–	–
59.	dog	–	–	3	–
60.	doing	6	2	–	–
61.	done	–	1	4	–
62.	dread	–	1	–	–
63.	dresses	–	–	1	–
64.	drinking	1	–	–	–
65.	driving	9	–	–	–
66.	dry	–	–	2	4
67.	dryer	–	–	–	1
68.	drying	39	–	–	61
69.	dusting	1	–	–	1
70.	dying	1	–	–	1
71.	eating	1	–	–	–
72.	enjoy	–	2	–	–
73.	essential	–	–	1	–
74.	every	–	–	2	–
75.	face	–	–	4	–
76.	family	–	–	1	–
77.	feeding	2	–	–	–
78.	feet	–	–	2	–

No.	Response	Subst.	Pre	Post	Assoc.
79.	finished	-	1	1	-
80.	fix	-	1	-	-
81.	fixing	1	-	-	-
82.	food	1	-	-	-
83.	fretting	1	-	-	-
84.	fruit	1	-	-	-
85.	fun	1	-	3	-
86.	get	-	1	-	-
87.	gets	-	-	1	-
88.	girl	-	1	-	-
89.	girls	1	-	-	-
90.	going	2	-	-	-
91.	golf balls	-	-	1	-
92.	gone	-	-	-	1
93.	good	-	-	4	1
94.	greasy	-	-	1	-
95.	hair	1	-	5	1
96.	hands	-	-	7	2
97.	hang	-	1	-	-
98.	hangs	-	-	1	-
99.	hard	-	-	3	2
100.	hate	-	18	-	-
101.	hates	-	5	-	-
102.	have	-	3	-	-
103.	health	-	-	-	1
104.	heavy	-	-	1	-
105.	hell	-	-	1	-
106.	her	-	4	3	-
107.	here	1	-	-	-
108.	him	-	1	-	-
109.	his	-	-	2	-
110.	hitting	1	-	-	-
111.	homes	-	-	1	-
112.	homework	3	-	-	-
113.	hour	-	1	-	-
114.	house	-	-	2	-
115.	house cleaning	1	-	-	-
116.	housework	2	-	-	-
117.	hurry	-	1	-	-
118.	if I can	2	-	-	1
119.	indicates	-	-	1	-
120.	iron	-	-	-	1
121.	ironing	37	-	3	14
122.	it	-	3	2	-
123.	job	-	1	-	-
124.	just	-	-	1	-
125.	keep	-	1	-	-
126.	keeping	1	-	-	-
127.	killing	1	-	-	-
128.	kitchens	1	-	-	-
129.	lady	-	-	-	1
130.	large	-	1	-	-
131.	later	-	-	1	-
132.	laundry	1	-	-	2
133.	letters	1	-	-	-
134.	like	-	23	-	-
135.	likes	-	3	-	-
136.	line	1	-	1	1
137.	looking at	1	-	-	-
138.	lot	-	3	-	-
139.	lousy	-	-	1	-
140.	loving	1	-	-	-
141.	lucky	-	-	-	1
142.	machine	1	-	22	13
143.	machines	-	-	-	1
144.	making	2	-	-	-
145.	me	1	-	1	-
146.	mending	4	-	-	-
147.	mom	-	2	-	1
148.	Monday	-	2	1	-
149.	mother	-	7	-	1
150.	mother's	-	1	-	-
151.	moving	1	-	-	-
152.	mowing	1	-	-	-
153.	mumbling	1	-	-	-
154.	myself	-	-	1	-
155.	necessary	-	-	2	-
156.	need	-	1	-	-
157.	needs	-	2	-	-
158.	new	1	-	-	-
159.	nice	-	-	-	1
160.	now	-	-	3	-
161.	old	-	-	-	2
162.	once	-	-	1	-
163.	out	-	-	1	-
164.	over	-	-	-	1
165.	own	-	1	-	-
166.	pain	-	-	1	-
167.	painting	2	-	-	-
168.	person	1	-	-	-
169.	pile	-	1	-	-
170.	plates	1	-	1	-
171.	Pocahontas	-	1	-	-
172.	polish	-	-	-	1
173.	polishing	2	-	-	-
174.	practicing	1	-	-	-
175.	praying	1	-	-	-
176.	preferred	-	1	-	-
177.	putting	1	-	-	-
178.	read	1	-	-	-
179.	reading	2	-	-	-
180.	ready	1	-	-	-
181.	received	-	1	-	-
182.	riding	2	-	-	-
183.	rinse	-	-	-	1
184.	rinsing	5	-	-	3
185.	ripping	2	-	-	-
186.	rubbing	1	-	-	-
187.	running	5	-	-	-
188.	sad	-	-	-	1
189.	sailing	1	-	-	-
190.	Saturdays	-	-	1	-
191.	scraping	1	-	-	-
192.	scrub	2	-	-	1
193.	scrub board	-	-	-	1
194.	scrubbing	1	-	-	1
195.	sewing	12	-	-	-
196.	shaving	1	-	-	-
197.	sheet	-	-	-	1
198.	shirt	-	-	4	-
199.	shirts	-	-	-	1
200.	shoes	-	-	1	-
201.	sign	1	-	-	-
202.	sink	1	-	-	-
203.	sleeping	1	-	-	-
204.	slow	-	-	1	-
205.	smells	-	-	1	-
206.	soak	-	-	-	1
207.	soap	-	-	-	14
208.	socks	-	-	1	1
209.	soda	-	-	2	1
210.	soft	1	-	-	-
211.	soiling	-	-	-	1
212.	some	-	-	1	-
213.	something	-	-	1	-
214.	soup	-	-	-	1
215.	spanking	1	-	-	-
216.	stacking	1	-	-	-
217.	started	-	1	-	-
218.	steak	1	-	-	-
219.	stop	-	1	-	-
220.	studies	1	-	-	-
221.	studying	1	-	-	-
222.	suds	-	-	-	1
223.	sudsing	1	-	-	-
224.	Sunday	-	-	1	-
225.	sweater	-	-	-	1
226.	sweeping	1	-	-	-
227.	swimming	2	-	-	1
228.	tail	1	-	-	-
229.	take	-	1	-	-
230.	takes	-	-	1	-
231.	talking	2	-	-	-
232.	tearing	2	-	-	-
233.	teeth	-	-	1	-
234.	tennis	1	-	-	-

45 Washing (contd)

No.	Response	Subst.	Pre	Post	Assoc.
235.	test	-	-	1	-
236.	them	1	-	1	-
237.	these	-	-	1	-
238.	things	-	-	1	-
239.	this	-	-	1	-
240.	Tide	-	-	-	1
241.	tired	-	-	-	1
242.	today	-	2	2	-
243.	tomorrow	-	-	2	-
244.	towel	-	-	-	2
245.	tub	-	-	1	1
246.	Tuesday	-	-	1	-
247.	underwear	-	-	1	-
248.	use	-	1	-	-
249.	used	-	1	-	-
250.	walking	2	-	-	-
251.	wash	-	-	-	1
252.	washing machine	-	-	-	3
253.	water	-	-	-	9
254.	waxing	3	-	-	-
255.	wear	-	-	-	1
256.	wearing	9	-	1	3
257.	weaving	-	-	-	1
258.	week's	-	-	1	-
259.	welding	1	-	-	-
260.	wet	-	-	-	2
261.	wetting	1	-	-	-
262.	what	-	-	1	-
263.	where	-	-	-	1
264.	while	-	1	-	-
265.	white	-	-	-	1
266.	whiteness	1	-	-	-
267.	whiter	-	-	-	1
268.	who	-	2	-	1
269.	whose	-	1	-	-
270.	will	-	-	-	1
271.	wiping	1	-	-	1
272.	wishing	-	-	-	1
273.	woman	-	2	1	-
274.	women	-	1	-	-
275.	work	4	-	-	6
276.	working	6	-	-	-
277.	wound	-	-	1	-
278.	wringing	1	-	-	2
279.	writing	1	-	-	-
280.	yesterday	-	-	1	-
281.	you	1	7	2	-

Function Words		-	137	10	-
Space		-	47	99	-
N		328	379	379	382

46 We

No.	Response	Subst.	Pre	Post	Assoc.
1.	accident	-	-	1	-
2.	all	-	-	4	2
3.	alone	-	-	1	-
4.	already	-	-	1	-
5.	always	-	-	1	-
6.	are	-	-	-	19
7.	argument	-	-	-	1
8.	art	-	-	-	1
9.	asked	-	1	-	-
10.	ate	-	-	5	-
11.	backwards	-	1	-	-
12.	bad	-	-	3	-
13.	belong	-	-	1	-
14.	best	-	-	1	-
15.	bet	-	1	-	-
16.	Betty	-	-	-	1
17.	books	1	-	-	-
18.	both	-	-	-	1

46 We (contd)

No.	Response	Subst.	Pre	Post	Assoc.
19.	boys	-	-	1	2
20.	brothers	-	-	2	-
21.	came	-	-	1	1
22.	can	-	-	-	1
23.	caught	-	-	2	-
24.	Chuck	-	-	-	1
25.	come	-	-	7	1
26.	coming	-	-	2	-
27.	communism	-	-	-	1
28.	correct	-	-	1	-
29.	Dan and I	-	-	-	1
30.	Daniel	-	-	1	-
31.	did	-	-	4	-
32.	do	-	-	5	-
33.	dog	-	-	-	1
34.	doing	-	-	1	-
35.	eat	-	-	-	1
36.	eating	-	-	1	-
37.	enjoyed	-	-	1	-
38.	family	-	-	-	3
39.	fat	-	-	4	-
40.	fine	-	-	1	-
41.	forward	-	1	-	-
42.	fought	-	-	1	-
43.	friends	-	-	-	1
44.	fun	-	-	1	-
45.	getting	-	-	1	-
46.	girl	-	-	-	1
47.	girls	-	-	-	1
48.	go	-	1	21	2
49.	going	-	-	24	-
50.	gone	-	-	2	-
51.	good	-	-	6	-
52.	grew	-	-	1	-
53.	group	-	-	1	3
54.	gun	-	-	-	1
55.	had	-	-	3	-
56.	happy	-	-	5	1
57.	hard	-	1	-	-
58.	hate	-	-	5	-
59.	have	-	-	1	2
60.	having	-	-	1	-
61.	heavy	-	-	1	-
62.	here	-	-	8	-
63.	him	-	-	-	1
64.	hold	-	-	-	1
65.	hope	-	1	-	-
66.	how	-	1	-	-
67.	human	-	-	1	-
68.	idiots	-	3	1	-
69.	it	-	3	-	-
70.	Jules	-	1	-	-
71.	juniors	-	-	1	-
72.	kill	-	-	1	-
73.	know	-	3	-	1
74.	Kris	-	-	-	1
75.	late	-	-	1	-
76.	leave	-	-	2	-
77.	leaving	-	-	1	-
78.	left	-	-	3	-
79.	like	-	1	16	-
80.	liked	-	-	1	-
81.	live	-	-	3	-
82.	love	-	1	6	2
83.	mad	-	-	1	-
84.	manage	-	-	1	-
85.	many	-	-	-	1
86.	march	-	-	1	-
87.	me	-	-	-	9
88.	me and you	-	-	-	1
89.	men	-	-	1	-
90.	mind	-	1	-	-
91.	must	-	-	-	1
92.	my	-	-	-	2
93.	nice	-	1	1	-
94.	nosotros	-	-	-	1
95.	now	-	-	-	1
96.	old	-	-	2	-

46 We (contd)   **47 What**

No.	Response	Subst.	Pre	Post	Assoc.
97.	one	-	-	1	1
98.	ones	-	-	1	-
99.	others	-	-	-	1
100.	our	-	-	-	2
101.	ours	-	-	-	1
102.	ourselves	-	-	-	1
103.	out	-	-	-	1
104.	people	1	-	1	5
105.	picnic	-	-	-	1
106.	plural	-	-	1	-
107.	radical	-	-	1	-
108.	ready	-	-	2	-
109.	ride	-	-	-	1
110.	run	-	-	1	-
111.	said	-	7	1	-
112.	saw	-	-	2	-
113.	say	-	1	-	-
114.	see	-	-	4	3
115.	shall	-	-	-	1
116.	sick	-	-	3	-
117.	sinned	-	-	1	-
118.	sit down	-	-	1	-
119.	six	-	-	-	1
120.	smart	-	-	2	-
121.	society	-	-	-	1
122.	sometimes	-	1	-	-
123.	sorry	-	-	1	-
124.	Spanish	-	1	-	-
125.	stay	-	-	-	1
126.	stayed	-	-	1	-
127.	stick	-	-	1	-
128.	student	1	-	-	-
129.	swimming	-	-	1	-
130.	take	-	-	1	-
131.	taking	-	-	1	-
132.	tam	-	-	-	1
133.	test	-	-	-	1
134.	than	-	-	-	1
135.	the gals	1	-	-	-
136.	the group	1	-	-	-
137.	them	-	-	-	18
138.	there	-	-	2	1
139.	they	59	-	-	73
140.	thin	-	-	1	-
141.	think	-	2	-	-
142.	those people	1	-	-	-
143.	together	-	1	2	10
144.	togetherness	-	-	-	1
145.	told	-	-	1	-
146.	translated	-	-	-	2
147.	two	-	-	1	-
148.	understand	-	-	1	-
149.	us	1	1	-	100
150.	use	-	-	-	1
151.	walking	-	-	1	-
152.	want	-	-	5	1
153.	went	-	1	19	3
154.	were	-	-	-	6
155.	what	-	4	-	-
156.	when	-	1	-	-
157.	where	-	7	-	-
158.	which	-	1	-	-
159.	who	-	1	-	2
160.	will	-	-	-	1
161.	win	-	-	2	-
162.	winning	-	-	1	-
163.	wish	-	1	-	-
164.	wrong	-	-	1	1
165.	year	-	-	-	1
166.	yes	-	-	-	1
167.	you	9	-	-	24
168.	young	-	-	1	-

		Subst.	Pre	Post	Assoc.
	Function Words	-	15	8	-
	Space	-	190	2	-
	N	75	254	254	341

No.	Response	Subst.	Pre	Post	Assoc.
1.	age	-	-	1	-
2.	also	-	-	-	1
3.	and	1	-	-	-
4.	answer	-	-	1	2
5.	anything	3	-	-	1
6.	are	-	-	-	1
7.	as	2	-	-	-
8.	asked	-	5	-	-
9.	assignment	-	-	1	-
10.	bad	1	-	-	-
11.	because	1	-	-	-
12.	bit	-	-	1	-
13.	blank	-	-	-	1
14.	bought	-	1	-	-
15.	boy	-	-	-	1
16.	came	-	-	1	-
17.	can	-	-	-	1
18.	car	-	-	-	4
19.	care	-	2	-	-
20.	cat	-	-	1	-
21.	coffee	1	-	-	-
22.	come	-	-	1	-
23.	crud	1	-	-	-
24.	date	-	-	2	-
25.	did	1	4	-	1
26.	do	-	2	2	4
27.	doing	-	1	-	-
28.	done	-	-	3	-
29.	dress	-	-	-	1
30.	eat	1	-	-	-
31.	English	-	-	-	1
32.	ever	-	-	-	1
33.	father	-	-	1	-
34.	fish	-	-	-	1
35.	following	-	-	1	-
36.	food	1	-	-	-
37.	for	-	-	-	3
38.	friend	-	-	-	1
39.	go	1	-	-	-
40.	going	-	1	-	-
41.	good	-	-	1	-
42.	guess	-	2	-	1
43.	gun	-	-	-	1
44.	happen	-	-	-	3
45.	happened	-	-	7	1
46.	Harry	1	-	-	-
47.	hat	1	-	-	1
48.	have	-	-	1	-
49.	hear	-	-	-	1
50.	hell	-	-	2	-
51.	hi	1	-	-	-
52.	him	1	1	-	1
53.	his	-	-	-	1
54.	how	46	-	-	24
55.	huh?	-	-	-	1
56.	ice	-	-	-	1
57.	if	-	-	-	1
58.	in	-	-	-	1
59.	it	4	1	33	1
60.	Jack	1	-	-	-
61.	Jane	1	-	-	-
62.	Judy	1	-	-	-
63.	kind	-	-	6	5
64.	knew	-	1	-	-
65.	know	-	27	-	-
66.	laugh	1	-	-	-
67.	left	-	-	1	-
68.	life	-	-	1	-
69.	like	1	3	-	-
70.	look	1	-	-	-
71.	Macy's	-	-	1	-
72.	made	-	-	1	-
73.	man	-	1	1	-
74.	matter	-	-	1	-
75.	me	1	4	-	-
76.	mine	-	-	1	-
77.	mom	1	-	-	-
78.	money	-	-	1	-

461

47 What (contd)

No.	Response	Subst.	Pre	Post	Assoc.
79.	mutt	-	-	-	1
80.	never	1	-	-	1
81.	new	-	-	9	2
82.	news	-	-	1	-
83.	next	-	-	-	1
84.	no	3	-	-	1
85.	not	-	-	-	6
86.	nothing	2	-	-	2
87.	now	3	-	2	10
88.	oh!	1	-	-	-
89.	old	-	-	-	1
90.	one	-	-	1	2
91.	paint	-	1	-	-
92.	pin	-	-	-	1
93.	pronoun	-	1	-	1
94.	puzzled	-	-	-	1
95.	que?	-	-	-	2
96.	quelle	-	-	-	1
97.	quest. mark	-	-	-	2
98.	question	-	-	3	71
99.	questioned	-	-	-	1
100.	questions	-	-	-	2
101.	rat	-	-	1	-
102.	reason	-	-	-	1
103.	repeat	-	-	-	3
104.	said	-	8	1	1
105.	say	-	4	-	1
106.	school	-	-	-	1
107.	show	-	-	1	-
108.	sirrah	1	-	-	-
109.	something	1	-	-	6
110.	stop	1	-	-	-
111.	stupid	-	-	1	-
112.	swimming	1	-	-	-
113.	talk	-	-	-	1
114.	that	24	4	36	41
115.	the	1	-	-	2
116.	the car	1	-	-	-
117.	thing	-	-	-	9
118.	think	-	-	-	1
119.	this	6	3	9	2
120.	thought	-	-	-	1
121.	time	-	-	11	2
122.	today	-	-	1	-
123.	town	-	-	2	-
124.	twelve	1	-	-	-
125.	uh!	-	-	-	1
126.	understand	-	2	-	1
127.	used	-	1	-	-
128.	was	-	-	-	2
129.	wet	1	-	-	-
130.	what?	-	-	-	1
131.	whatever	1	-	-	-
132.	when	5	-	-	18
133.	where	18	1	1	19
134.	which	20	-	-	4
135.	who	65	-	-	25
136.	whom	4	-	-	-
137.	whose	2	-	-	1
138.	why?	16	-	-	35
139.	why not	-	-	-	1
140.	wonder	-	1	-	-
141.	wood	-	-	-	1
142.	word	-	1	-	1
143.	words	-	-	-	1
144.	work	1	-	-	-
145.	world	-	-	1	-
146.	wrong	-	-	2	-
147.	yes	-	-	-	4
148.	you	1	3	138	2
	Function Words	-	9	57	-
	Space	-	285	28	
	N	257	380	380	374

48 Which

No	Response	Subst.	Pre	Post	Assoc.
1.	all	1	-	-	-
2.	also	-	-	-	1
3.	and	1	-	-	-
4.	answer	-	-	1	-
5.	any	1	-	-	1
6.	are	-	-	-	1
7.	asked	-	4	-	-
8.	ate	-	-	1	-
9.	ball	-	1	-	-
10.	batt	-	-	-	1
11.	because	-	-	-	1
12.	believe	-	-	1	-
13.	best	-	1	6	-
14.	better	-	-	8	-
15.	bigger	-	-	1	-
16.	bike	-	-	1	-
17.	birds	-	-	-	1
18.	bit	-	-	1	-
19.	bitch	-	-	-	2
20.	black	-	-	-	1
21.	boat	-	-	1	-
22.	book	-	-	1	-
23.	bottle	-	-	1	-
24.	boy	-	-	2	1
25.	broom	-	-	-	4
26.	brum	-	-	-	1
27.	buy	-	-	1	-
28.	came	-	-	1	-
29.	candle	-	-	1	-
30.	car	-	-	2	-
31.	cat	-	1	-	-
32.	choice	-	-	-	4
33.	choose	-	-	1	2
34.	chose	-	1	-	-
35.	closet	-	-	1	-
36.	come	2	-	-	1
37.	confuse	-	-	-	1
38.	correct	-	-	3	-
39.	course	1	-	-	-
40.	craft	-	-	-	1
41.	cua'l	-	-	-	1
42.	day	-	-	1	-
43.	decided	-	1	-	-
44.	decision	-	-	-	1
45.	decisions	-	-	-	1
46.	did	-	-	5	-
47.	ditch	-	-	-	1
48.	do	-	-	1	-
49.	dog	-	-	3	2
50.	each	-	-	-	1
51.	either	-	-	-	7
52.	elephant	-	-	1	-
53.	end	-	-	1	1
54.	English	-	-	-	2
55.	every	1	-	-	-
56.	family	-	-	1	-
57.	figure out	-	1	-	-
58.	five	1	-	-	-
59.	flowers	-	1	-	-
60.	for	-	-	-	1
61.	go	-	-	2	-
62.	going	-	-	1	-
63.	gone	-	-	1	-
64.	good	-	-	4	-
65.	green	-	-	-	1
66.	grow	-	-	1	-
67.	had	-	-	1	-
68.	hag	-	-	-	1
69.	halloween	-	-	-	1
70.	hand	-	-	-	1
71.	has	-	-	1	-
72.	hat	-	-	1	1
73.	have	-	-	1	-
74.	he is	-	-	-	1
75.	heel	-	-	1	-
76.	her	-	1	-	-
77.	here	-	-	2	-
78.	hers	-	-	1	-

No.	Response	Subst.	Pre	Post	Assoc.
79.	him	–	2	–	1
80.	his	1	–	–	–
81.	house	–	–	3	1
82.	how	1	–	–	2
83.	I	–	–	–	1
84.	is	–	–	–	3
85.	it	2	1	30	2
86.	Joe	–	1	–	–
87.	know	–	17	–	–
88.	learned	–	1	–	–
89.	like	–	2	1	1
90.	likes	–	–	1	–
91.	long	–	–	1	–
92.	man	–	–	1	1
93.	many	1	–	–	1
94.	me	–	1	–	–
95.	melts	–	–	1	–
96.	might	–	–	–	1
97.	mine	–	–	2	–
98.	mum	–	–	1	–
99.	music	–	1	–	–
100.	neither	1	–	–	–
101.	nice	1	–	–	–
102.	now	–	–	–	1
103.	of	–	–	–	1
104.	of two	–	–	–	2
105.	one	6	6	15	95
106.	ones	–	–	–	2
107.	only	2	–	–	–
108.	opposition	–	–	–	1
109.	other	–	–	–	1
110.	ours	–	–	3	–
111.	paper	1	–	–	–
112.	passionate	–	1	–	–
113.	pen	–	1	–	–
114.	people	–	–	–	1
115.	performed	–	–	1	–
116.	person	–	–	2	–
117.	pick	–	1	–	–
118.	pleased	–	–	1	–
119.	put down	–	–	1	–
120.	question	–	–	–	8
121.	questions	–	–	–	1
122.	race	–	–	1	–
123.	red	1	–	–	–
124.	right	–	–	7	–
125.	Ron	–	–	1	–
126.	room	–	–	1	–
127.	Salem	–	–	–	1
128.	same	–	1	–	–
129.	sand	–	1	–	1
130.	saw	–	1	–	–
131.	say	–	1	–	–
132.	school	–	–	–	1
133.	sentence	–	–	1	–
134.	short	–	–	–	1
135.	should	–	–	–	1
136.	stale	–	–	1	–
137.	strange	–	–	1	–
138.	sure	–	1	–	–
139.	switch	–	–	–	2
140.	take	–	1	–	–
141.	team	–	–	1	–
142.	that	25	7	8	27
143.	the	2	–	–	–
144.	theirs	–	–	–	1
145.	them	–	–	6	2
146.	then	–	–	–	1
147.	there	–	–	2	–
148.	these	–	–	2	–
149.	thing	–	–	–	3
150.	this	7	–	–	4
151.	those	–	–	–	1
152.	those there are	1	–	–	–
153.	time	–	1	–	1
154.	today	–	–	1	–
155.	true	–	–	1	–
156.	twins	–	–	1	–

No.	Response	Subst.	Pre	Post	Assoc.
157.	two	1	–	1	2
158.	ugly	1	–	–	–
159.	undecided	–	–	–	2
160.	us	–	–	19	–
161.	very	–	–	–	1
162.	was	–	–	–	5
163.	water	–	–	–	1
164.	way	–	1	16	11
165.	weather	–	–	–	1
166.	well	–	–	–	1
167.	what	34	–	–	56
168.	wheat	13	–	–	1
169.	when	–	–	–	4
170.	where	2	–	–	11
171.	whether	–	–	–	2
172.	which	–	1	4	–
173.	which one	–	–	–	2
174.	who	2	1	1	10
175.	whom	–	–	–	2
176.	whose	–	–	–	1
177.	why	3	–	–	1
178.	will	–	–	–	1
179.	witch	–	–	4	22
180.	witchery	1	–	–	–
181.	woman	–	–	–	1
182.	women	–	–	–	1
183.	word	–	–	–	1
184.	would	–	–	–	1
185.	you	–	–	78	–
186.	yours	–	–	10	–

		Subst.	Pre	Post	Assoc.
Function Words		–	4	50	–
Space		–	285	4	–
N		117	353	353	363

49 Working

No.	Response	Subst.	Pre	Post	Assoc.
1.	advancement	–	–	1	–
2.	all	–	–	3	–
3.	along	–	–	–	1
4.	always	–	–	–	1
5.	Arbeit	–	–	–	1
6.	around	–	–	–	2
7.	art	–	–	1	–
8.	bad	1	–	–	1
9.	barber	–	–	–	1
10.	belong	–	1	–	–
11.	boat	–	–	–	1
12.	body	–	–	1	–
13.	bore	–	–	1	–
14.	borrowing	1	–	–	–
15.	boy	–	1	1	–
16.	boys	–	1	–	–
17.	breathing	1	–	–	–
18.	bum	–	–	–	1
19.	business	–	–	–	1
20.	busy	1	–	–	2
21.	car	–	–	1	–
22.	cars	–	–	1	–
23.	caution	–	–	1	–
24.	city	–	–	1	–
25	conscientiously	–	–	–	1
26.	curse	–	–	1	–
27.	dad	–	1	–	–
28.	dancing	–	–	–	1
29.	day	–	–	1	2
30.	destroying	–	–	–	1
31.	difficult	–	–	1	–
32.	disgust	–	–	–	1
33.	dishes	–	–	–	1
34.	ditch digger	–	–	–	1
35.	doing	–	–	–	1

49 Working (contd)

No.	Response	Subst.	Pre	Post	Assoc.
36.	dreaming	1	–	–	–
37.	drinking	1	–	–	–
38.	drinks	–	1	–	–
39.	driving	–	–	–	1
40.	dying	1	–	–	–
41.	earning	–	–	–	2
42.	easy chair	–	–	–	1
43.	eating	4	–	–	–
44.	effort	–	–	–	1
45.	eight	–	–	–	1
46.	enjoy	–	4	–	–
47.	enjoyable	–	–	1	–
48.	exhaust	–	–	–	1
49.	fast	–	–	–	2
50.	feel	–	1	–	–
51.	fighting	3	–	–	–
52.	fine	–	–	1	–
53.	fishing	1	–	–	–
54.	flow	–	–	–	1
55.	flying	1	–	–	–
56.	for	–	–	–	1
57.	fun	–	–	10	3
58.	garden	–	–	1	–
59.	gardening	–	–	–	1
60.	gentle	1	–	–	–
61.	girls	1	–	–	–
62.	going	2	–	–	–
63.	good	–	–	5	–
64.	goofing off	1	–	–	–
65.	handsome	1	–	1	–
66.	hard	–	–	42	74
67.	hate	–	4	–	–
68.	here	–	–	2	–
69.	him	–	1	1	–
70.	himself	–	–	1	–
71.	home	–	–	1	–
72.	hour	–	–	–	1
73.	hours	–	–	–	2
74.	idle	–	–	–	1
75.	improving	–	–	–	1
76.	inspirational	–	–	1	–
77.	interesting	–	–	–	1
78.	it	–	4	1	–
79.	Jack	–	1	–	–
80.	jerking	–	–	–	1
81.	Joan	1	–	–	–
82.	job	–	–	1	7
83.	knew	–	1	–	–
84.	labor	–	–	1	6
85.	laborer	–	–	–	2
86.	laboring	1	–	–	–
87.	late	–	–	1	4
88.	lately	–	–	1	–
89.	laugh	–	–	–	1
90.	lazy	2	–	1	14
91.	learn	–	–	–	1
92.	leisure	–	–	–	1
93.	life	–	–	2	2
94.	like	–	11	–	–
95.	likes	–	1	–	–
96.	liking	1	–	–	–
97.	live	–	–	–	1
98.	living	–	–	–	4
99.	loaf	–	–	–	1
100.	loafing	1	–	–	13
101.	long	–	–	–	1
102.	love	–	1	–	–
103.	machine	–	–	1	–
104.	make	–	–	–	1
105.	making	–	–	–	1
106.	man	–	–	7	6
107.	men	–	4	2	3
108.	Mike	–	–	–	1
109.	mind	–	2	–	–
110.	modeling	–	–	–	1
111.	money	–	–	1	16
112.	motor	–	1	–	–
113.	mud	–	–	1	–

No.	Response	Subst.	Pre	Post	Assoc.
114.	nervous	–	–	–	1
115.	never	–	–	–	1
116.	nice	–	–	–	1
117.	no	–	–	–	1
118.	non-working	–	–	–	1
119.	not	1	–	–	1
120.	not for me	–	–	–	1
121.	nothing	–	–	–	1
122.	now	–	1	6	2
123.	office	–	–	–	1
124.	on	–	–	–	1
125.	once	–	–	1	–
126.	pain	–	–	1	–
127.	pays off	–	–	1	–
128.	pending	1	–	–	–
129.	people	–	–	1	1
130.	person	–	–	1	–
131.	perspiration	–	–	–	1
132.	place	–	–	–	1
133.	plane	–	–	1	–
134.	play	–	–	–	2
135.	playing	12	–	1	16
136.	pleasure	–	–	–	2
137.	plumbing	–	–	–	1
138.	practicing	–	–	–	1
139.	praying	1	–	–	–
140.	problem	–	–	1	–
141.	producing	–	–	5	–
142.	railroad	–	–	–	1
143.	reading	2	–	–	–
144.	relax	–	–	–	1
145.	relaxing	–	–	–	5
146.	release	–	–	–	1
147.	rest	–	–	–	4
148.	resting	–	–	–	1
149.	retired	–	–	–	1
150.	riding	2	–	–	1
151.	right	–	–	–	1
152.	running	6	–	1	–
153.	San Rafael	–	–	1	–
154.	school	4	–	–	2
155.	selling	1	–	–	–
156.	shop	–	–	–	1
157.	sitting	2	–	–	–
158.	slavery	–	–	–	1
159.	slaving	1	–	–	–
160.	sleeping	6	–	–	10
161.	slow	–	–	–	1
162.	smelling	1	–	–	–
163.	sometimes	–	–	1	–
164.	spelling	1	–	–	–
165.	start	–	1	–	–
166.	steady	–	–	–	1
167.	stick	–	–	–	1
168.	stop	–	1	–	–
169.	stopping	–	–	–	1
170.	store	–	–	1	–
171.	strenuous	–	–	–	1
172.	strike	–	–	–	1
173.	struggling	1	–	–	–
174.	study	1	–	–	–
175.	studying	–	–	1	–
176.	summer	–	–	1	–
177.	supplies	–	–	1	–
178.	survive	–	–	1	–
179.	sweat	–	–	–	3
180.	sweating	–	–	–	2
181.	swimming	4	–	–	–
182.	talking	3	–	–	–
183.	that	–	–	2	–
184.	then	–	–	1	–
185.	thinking	1	–	–	1
186.	this	–	–	2	–
187.	three	–	–	1	–
188.	time	–	–	–	1
189.	tired	–	–	–	6
190.	tires	–	–	1	–
191.	today	–	–	10	–

49 Working (contd)

No.	Response	Subst.	Pre	Post	Assoc.
192.	together	–	–	1	2
193.	tomorrow	–	–	3	–
194.	tonight	–	–	2	–
195.	too	–	–	–	1
196.	tough	–	–	1	–
197.	tree	–	–	–	1
198.	try	–	1	–	–
199.	trying	1	–	–	–
200.	unemployed	–	–	–	1
201.	useful	–	–	–	1
202.	walking	2	–	–	1
203.	Wednesday	–	–	1	–
204.	well	–	–	1	1
205.	when	–	–	–	1
206.	where	–	–	–	1
207.	who	–	1	–	–
208.	why	–	–	1	–
209.	with	–	–	–	1
210.	work	1	–	–	3
211.	worked	–	–	–	2
212.	writing	1	–	–	–
213.	yes	–	–	–	1
214.	you	–	14	2	–
215.	10	–	–	1	–
216.	$1.00	–	–	1	–

Function Words		–	92	–	–
Space		–	58	51	–
N		84	210	210	306

50 Write

No.	Response	Subst.	Pre	Post	Assoc.
1.	able	–	1	–	–
2.	all	–	2	–	–
3.	always	–	1	–	–
4.	am	2	–	–	–
5.	answer	1	–	–	–
6.	Arabic	–	–	1	–
7.	at all	–	–	1	–
8.	author	–	1	–	–
9.	autograph	1	–	–	–
10.	bad	–	–	3	1
11.	before	–	–	1	–
12.	better	–	–	1	–
13.	bite	1	–	–	–
14.	black	–	–	–	4
15.	blank	–	–	–	1
16.	Bob	–	–	1	–
17.	book	1	–	10	5
18.	books	–	–	–	3
19.	boring	–	–	1	–
20.	breathe	1	–	–	–
21.	bright	–	–	–	1
22.	bring	2	–	–	–
23.	burn	4	–	–	–
24.	buy	1	–	–	–
25.	call	3	–	–	–
26.	career	–	–	1	–
27.	cave man	–	–	–	1
28.	chalk	–	–	–	1
29.	class	–	1	–	–
30.	clear	–	–	–	2
31.	clearly	–	–	3	2
32.	clouds	–	–	–	1
33.	come	9	–	–	–
34.	communicate	–	–	–	1
35.	compose	5	–	–	–
36.	composition	–	–	4	2
37.	compositions	–	–	2	–
38.	construct	1	–	–	–
39.	cook	1	–	–	–
40.	correctly	–	–	1	–

50 Write (contd)

No.	Response	Subst.	Pre	Post	Assoc.
41.	correspond	1	–	–	–
42.	cramp	–	–	–	1
43.	creatively	–	–	1	–
44.	criticize	1	–	–	–
45.	curves	–	–	–	1
46.	dance	2	–	–	–
47.	dark	–	–	–	2
48.	dead	–	–	–	1
49.	define	1	–	–	–
50.	destroy	1	–	–	–
51.	Dick	–	–	1	–
52.	dictate	1	–	–	–
53.	dislike	–	1	–	–
54.	dislikes	–	1	–	–
55.	do	6	–	–	1
56.	do calculations	1	–	–	–
57.	dotted	–	–	1	–
58.	down	–	–	–	1
59.	draw	3	–	–	6
60.	dream	1	–	–	–
61.	dress	1	–	–	–
62.	drink	2	–	–	–
63.	drive	5	–	–	–
64.	easy	–	2	1	–
65.	eat	8	–	–	–
66.	edit	1	–	–	–
67.	English	–	–	1	6
68.	erase	–	–	–	2
69.	essay	–	–	1	2
70.	essays	–	–	1	–
71.	every	–	–	2	–
72.	fast	–	–	3	1
73.	faster	–	–	2	–
74.	feel	1	–	–	–
75.	fight	1	–	–	1
76.	finger	–	–	–	1
77.	fire	–	–	1	–
78.	fly	–	–	–	1
79.	forget	–	1	–	–
80.	forgot	–	1	–	–
81.	freely	–	–	–	1
82.	fun	–	–	1	–
83.	girl	–	1	–	–
84.	give	4	–	–	–
85.	go	4	–	–	–
86.	good	–	–	6	–
87.	great deal	–	–	1	–
88.	had	–	2	–	–
89.	hand	–	–	–	4
90.	hard	–	–	–	3
91.	hate	3	8	–	–
92.	have	–	2	–	–
93.	heat	–	–	–	1
94.	help	1	–	–	–
95.	her	–	1	4	–
96.	Herman	–	–	1	–
97.	him	–	–	6	–
98.	hit	2	–	–	–
99.	home	–	–	2	–
100.	how	–	1	–	–
101.	illegibly	–	–	–	1
102.	immediately	–	–	1	–
103.	ink	–	–	4	13
104.	inks	–	–	–	1
105.	iron	1	–	–	–
106.	it	–	–	1	–
107.	John	–	1	–	–
108.	kick	–	–	–	1
109.	kiss	1	–	–	–
110.	labor	–	–	1	–
111.	later	–	–	1	–
112.	laugh	1	–	–	–
113.	lead	–	–	–	1
114.	learn	1	2	–	–
115.	left	–	–	–	3
116.	legibly	–	–	–	1
117.	let	1	–	–	–
118.	letter	–	1	25	19

50 Write (contd)

No.	Response	Subst.	Pre	Post	Assoc.
119.	letters	–	–	17	3
120.	light	–	–	–	1
121.	like	1	49	–	–
122.	lilac	–	–	–	1
123.	line	–	–	–	1
124.	lines	–	–	–	1
125.	literature	–	–	–	3
126.	long	–	–	3	–
127.	look	1	–	–	–
128.	lots	–	–	1	–
129.	lousy	1	–	1	1
130.	love	2	1	1	–
131.	mail	4	–	–	1
132.	make	1	–	–	–
133.	many	–	–	4	–
134.	marry	1	–	–	–
135.	me	–	–	34	–
136.	might	–	–	–	1
137.	more	–	–	1	1
138.	move	1	–	–	–
139.	much	–	–	1	–
140.	name	–	–	1	1
141.	neatly	–	–	4	–
142.	necessary	–	1	–	–
143.	never	–	1	–	–
144.	next	–	–	1	–
145.	nice	–	–	1	–
146.	note	–	–	–	1
147.	novel	–	–	1	–
148.	now	–	–	3	1
149.	often	–	1	2	–
150.	ordeal	–	–	–	1
151.	out	–	–	–	1
152.	paint	3	–	–	–
153.	Papenhausen	–	1	–	–
154.	paper	–	–	1	25
155.	papers	–	–	1	–
156.	parents	–	–	–	1
157.	pen	–	–	2	58
158.	pencil	–	–	–	23
159.	pencils	–	–	–	1
160.	penmanship	–	–	–	1
161.	pens	–	–	–	1
162.	people	–	3	–	–
163.	place	1	–	–	–
164.	please	–	14	–	–
165.	poetry	–	–	2	1
166.	pole vault	1	–	–	–
167.	poorly	–	–	2	–
168.	print	12	–	–	27
169.	pseudo-Martian	–	–	1	–
170.	Ralph	–	–	–	1
171.	read	49	–	–	27
172.	reading	–	–	–	1
173.	reads	1	–	–	1
174.	really	–	1	–	–
175.	receive	4	–	–	–
176.	red	–	–	–	1
177.	relax	1	–	–	–
178.	remember	–	1	–	–
179.	ride	3	–	–	–
180.	right	–	–	1	–
181.	run	9	–	–	–
182.	Russ	–	–	1	–
183.	Saturday	–	–	1	–
184.	say	1	–	–	1
185.	school	–	–	1	2
186.	schreiben	–	–	–	2
187.	scratch	1	–	–	–
188.	scribble	3	–	–	9
189.	script	–	–	–	2
190.	see	9	–	–	2
191.	send	35	–	–	–
192.	sentence	–	–	7	1
193.	several	–	–	1	–
194.	sew	1	–	–	–
195.	sheet	–	–	–	1
196.	short story	–	–	1	–
197.	shorthand	–	–	–	1
198.	sing	9	–	–	1
199.	sit	1	–	–	–
200.	skate	1	–	–	–
201.	sleep	1	–	–	–
202.	sloppy	–	–	2	3
203.	slow	–	–	1	–
204.	slower	–	–	1	–
205.	smoke	1	–	–	–
206.	smooth	–	–	–	1
207.	softly	–	–	1	–
208.	something	–	–	1	1
209.	song	–	–	–	1
210.	songs	–	–	2	1
211.	soon	–	–	7	–
212.	soup	–	–	–	1
213.	Spanish	–	–	1	–
214.	speak	3	–	–	3
215.	speech	–	–	2	–
216.	spell	4	–	–	3
217.	spelling	–	–	–	1
218.	spit	1	–	–	–
219.	starting	–	1	–	–
220.	stop	2	–	–	–
221.	stories	–	–	4	1
222.	story	–	–	3	2
223.	study	1	–	–	–
224.	stuff	–	–	1	–
225.	stupid	–	–	–	1
226.	sugar	–	–	–	1
227.	swiftly	–	–	1	–
228.	swim	11	–	–	–
229.	swims	1	–	–	–
230.	talk	10	–	–	3
231.	talks	1	–	–	–
232.	tear	1	–	–	–
233.	telegraph	2	–	–	–
234.	tell	3	–	–	–
235.	tells	1	–	–	–
236.	that	–	–	2	–
237.	that is	1	–	–	–
238.	them	–	–	1	–
239.	theme	–	–	3	2
240.	themes	–	–	–	1
241.	these	–	–	1	–
242.	thesis	–	–	1	–
243.	think	–	1	–	3
244.	thinks	1	–	–	–
245.	this	–	–	2	–
246.	time	–	1	–	–
247.	tired	–	1	–	–
248.	today	–	–	1	–
249.	Tom	–	–	–	1
250.	tried	–	1	–	–
251.	type	4	–	–	3
252.	us	–	–	1	–
253.	used	–	2	–	–
254.	usually	–	1	–	–
255.	walk	5	–	–	1
256.	wall	–	–	1	–
257.	want	–	2	–	–
258.	weed	1	–	–	–
259.	well	–	–	21	–
260.	what	–	1	–	–
261.	when	–	–	1	–
262.	white	–	–	–	1
263.	win	1	–	–	–
264.	word	–	–	1	1
265.	words	–	–	2	5
266.	work	8	–	–	5
267.	writer	–	–	–	2
268.	written	–	–	–	2
269.	wrong	–	–	–	14

50   Write (contd)

No.	Response	Subst.	Pre	Post	Assoc.
270.	wrote	6	–	–	8
271.	you	–	28	5	–
272.	60	–	–	1	–
273.	200	–	–	1	–
274.	500	–	–	1	–
Function Words		–	157	7	–
Space		–	69	92	–
N		316	369	369	383